COMPUTER APPLICATIONS IN WATER RESOURCES

Proceedings of the Specialty Conference
sponsored by the
Water Resources Planning and Management Division
and the Buffalo Section
of the
American Society of Civil Engineers

Co-sponsored by the
Urban Water Resources Research Council, ASCE
The State University of New York at Buffalo
Buffalo District, U.S. Army Corps of Engineers
Technical Council on Computer Practices, ASCE

The Hyatt Regency
Buffalo, New York
June 10-12, 1985

Edited by Harry C. Torno

Published by the
American Society of Civil Engineers
345 East 47th Street
New York, New York 10017-2398

The Society is not responsible for any statements made or opinions expressed in its publications.

Copyright © 1985 by the American Society of Civil Engineers,
All Rights Reserved.
Library of Congress Catalog Card No.: 85-71267
ISBN 0-87262-467-6
Manufactured in the United States of America.

Program Organizing Committee

Richard M. Males, Chairman
Walter M. Grayman
William James

Local Arrangements Committee

Stanley J. Blas, Jr., Chairman

Maria Lehman	Dave Theilman
Angelo Coniglio	Tony Eberhardt
Dale Meredith	Michael Merritt
Tom Pieczynski	Ralph Rumer
Julian Snyder	Steve Yakisch

FOREWORD

The use of computers in all engineering disciplines has, in the past decade, increased to the point where virtually all engineers now use these powerful tools. This is especially true in the water resources field. In recognition of this fact, the Water Resources Planning and Management Division and the Buffalo Section, ASCE, assisted by the ASCE Urban Water Resources Research Council, The State University of New York at Buffalo, the Buffalo District, U.S. Army Corps of Engineers and ASCE Technical Council on Computer Practices, organized an ASCE Specialty Conference dedicated to the exchange of knowledge and experience in the applications of computer technology in all aspects of water resources. The Conference was held at The Hyatt Regency, Buffalo, New York, from June 10–12, 1985. The Technical Program Chairman was Richard M. Males, and the Local Arrangements Chairman was Stanley J. Blas, Jr.

The Conference format utilized concurrent sessions which included tutorials, technical paper presentations and general discussion. These Proceedings contain all papers presented at the Conference which were submitted to the Editor in time for their inclusion in this volume. The papers are in the order of their presentation at the Conference. Each of the papers has been accepted for publication by the Proceedings Editor. All papers are eligible for discussion in the Journal of the Water Resources Planning and Management Division, ASCE, and all papers are eligible for ASCE awards.

The Conference organizers extend their sincere appreciation to all authors and session chairmen for their contributions, and to everyone on the Local Arrangements Committee whose tireless efforts insured the success of the Conference.

CONTENTS

*Manuscript not available at time of printing.

*Manuscript not available at time of printing.

*Manuscript not available at time of printing.

*Manuscript not available at time of printing.

*Manuscript not available at time of printing.

*Manuscript not available at time of printing.

*Manuscript not available at time of printing.

*Manuscript not available at time of printing.

xiv

*Manuscript not available at time of printing.

*Manuscript not available at time of printing.

*Manuscript not available at time of printing.

*Manuscript not available at time of printing.

*Manuscript not available at time of printing.

COMPUTER IMPACTS ON WATER RESOURCES ENGINEERING

By Leo R. Beard[1], F. ASCE

Abstract: Computation capability has increased by a factor of one million over the past 30 years and has contributed greatly toward data management and the application of available technology to water problems. Although computers have extended technology in some areas, there is a critical need to overcome socio-political constraints that inhibit or prevent satisfactory solution to problems that are growing in extent and complexity.

For the past 30 years we have witnessed a phenomenal growth in computational capability and have made great progress in orienting analysis techniques and data management toward the most effective use of this expanding capability. As I review our progress to date, I see great strides in adapting and extending water resources technology to processing on the computer, but relatively slow progress toward fundamental break-throughs in engineering capability needed to respond to growing socio-economic problems. There are relatively few things we do today in water resources engineering that we could not do, although more slowly and less efficiently, 30 years ago.

In the area of flood control, the most common technology used in assessing flood frequency is that adopted by the U.S. Water Resources Council in 1976, which is not basically different from that used by the Corps of Engineers in 1952. The most commonly used rainfall-runoff technology is that contained in the HEC-1 computer model, which is based primarily on Corps of Engineers methods developed before 1950. The most commonly used technology for determining water-surface flood profiles is that contained in the HEC-2 computer model, which is based primarily on hydraulics technology developed before 1960.

In the area of water supply and storage-yield evaluations, the technology used in the 1950's is incorporated in computer programs such as HEC-3, which performs water and power system simulation analyses in seconds that took months in the days before computers.

In some areas, substantial progress has been made toward a far superior technological capability in the future. Applications of finite element analysis in groundwater and other studies, linear and dynamic programming in many modeling developments, and stochastic analysis in hydrologic models have

---

[1] Senior Staff Engineer, Espey, Huston & Associates; Professor of Civil Engineering, The University of Texas at Austin , Austin, TX

greatly extended the perceptions of water resources engineering. In essence, however, computer-associated mathematical developments have remarkably increased the scope, speed, accuracy and efficiency with which available technology can be applied, rather than created a fundamentally improved technology.

Let us look at a few examples of technological changes that are coming about and that typify technical prerequisites to attacking the broader engineering problems discussed later.

Perhaps the greatest need for technological break-through in water resources engineering lies in the area of stochastic hydrology. We need to extract maximum information from available data for use in assessing future potential. A great many stochastic analysis and generation models have been developed, but not a one that can predict multi-site sequences of potential future events that are more dependable as a design criteron than simply a recurrence of past events. Yet we are getting closer, and a break-through will depend on a few engineers and scientists who are mastering the very subtle complexities of statistical inference from data whose mathematical distributions are unknown. Without computers, such a break-through would be impossible. Because of computers, this field of research promises to resolve a fundamental impediment to the logical design of surface water supply systems and eventually flood control systems.

In fields where finite element analysis can be effectively applied, such as circulations in lakes, bays and estuaries, groundwater systems and even hydrometeorological systems, the computer can apply known physical principles to individual elements in order to solve large-scale problems that could not be feasibly solved without computers.

In the field of hydrologic engineering, in particular, we have been handicapped by our inability to measure the diversity of soils, vegetation and rainfall from point-to-point that so effectively impact our flood runoff and water supply. When we develop the capability of automatically sensing and entering millions of bits of data into a sophisticated mathematical model, we may be capable of a break-through in defining the intricate space-time variations of precipitation and accurately evaluating the resulting runoff.

To generalize, computers have been used to apply technology that has mostly been available, but to apply it for more rapid and less costly solutions and to problems that were mathematically intractable without high-speed computational devices. We are on the verge of greater things.

As computer users know, computation power in the best available systems has increased over the past 30 years by an order of magnitude every 5 years. This means that, in these 30 years, we have increased our capability and our efficiency by one million times. In the early days, many felt that the increasing efficiency of computers would simply put technicians out of work. As lower-level decision processes were increasingly relegated to the computer, lower-level professional engineers would be put out of work. This reaction was foolish, as we can all see now. Technicians are working with far more sophisticated technology than ever before, and young engineers are rising to successive levels of professional responsibility in a much shorter time than ever before.

Computers are freeing engineers from the computational details and, more important, from decision processes that can be reliably pre-programmed. Engineers are free to devote their attention to ever-higher-level decisions and, more important, to a broader decision framework. This applies all the way to the top of the engineering hierarchy, where top engineers now face problems of complex multidisciplinary scope that have never been solved in a scientific or engineering framework before. In his talk after the coffee break, I expect that Bill Johnson will cast some light on the more recent approaches to solving some of these problems.

However, in the context of solving the broader socio-economic problems, the engineering community in the United States has been handicapped by legal and political constriants and regulations that seriously constrict or actually preclude any reasonable, logical or scientific solution to broad social problems in water resources management. Some of these are worthy of discussion.

The U.S. Water Resources Council developed a concept of multi-objective management that precludes any rational decision process, because one cannot optimize more than one objective per problem. Not until relative values of different potential benefits can be established can this problem be solved scientifically.

The Water Resources Council also promulgated a discount rate on future project benefits that ignores inflation and consequently greatly devalues provisions for the future. For example, at a little over 7% discount rate, an acre-foot of water today is preferred to 1,000 acre-feet 100 years from now. Not until the government recognizes its role in preserving resources and a good life for future generations will this problem be solved.

In the Flood Insurance Act, the U.S. Congress has establishd the criterion of full allowable development above the 100-year flood level and almost no development at lower levels. This sets up a community for either freedom from flooding or a major disaster. With 15,000 communities subject to flooding, many from more than one source, the frequency of flooding in the "safe" area is 150 to 200 communities per year. Furthermore, the cost of flood insurance far exceeds the cost of flooding, or the program would not be viable.

The U.S. Congress passed the Endangered Species Act that so distorted social values as to preclude any scientific attempt at obtaining the best services and environment for society.

Concepts that are being promulgated of zero quality degradation in rivers and estuaries not only ignore the inevitable impact of a growing society, but, more importantly, effectively constrain any logical program for managing resources to produce the quality of life that society most needs and wants.

And finally, the concept of public participation, vital in many ways but carried to the extreme, is relegating to the layman decisions that can properly be made only by competent, informed, dedicated and experienced professionals. We sorely need a framework by which the public can establish a value system by which a professional can solve engineering problems without the myriads of arbitrary contraints that preclude a good general-welfare solution.

What I am saying, in essence, is that the civil engineering community has blithely accepted political decisions and strained itself to try to obtain solutions within the political and legal framework. Witness the millions of research dollars that have been spent on virtually futile multi-objected model designs and studies. Witness the acceptance of unreasonable discount rates in planning and designing for the future. Witness the resignation attitude of the civil engineering community toward public sentiment that loves lakes and hates dams. Witness the virtual abandonment of plans or concepts for inter-basin diversions and the inadequate demonstration in such plans that source areas would be fully protected. Witness the acceptance of flood insurance in lieu of the much more economical and socially acceptable program of flood control and flood proofing, including flood information and flood plain regulation.

There must be politically feasible, although admittedly difficult, alternatives. Civil engineers must work out solutions and transitions, and demonstrate to the public that they are politically and socially viable.

I have always felt, at least intuitively, that good technology will lead to good regulations. If political leaders and the people recognize that there is a firm answer to a specific problem within the framework of their value system, they will go along with it. If so, what does this portend for the future?

First, I would suggest that multi-disciplinary or interdisciplinary problems are, in fact, engineering problems in a broad sense. They require the application of scientific principles to the solution of problems for improving the general welfare through the provision of physical works and associated regulations. Engineers are the original environmentalists. Their mission is to adapt the environment to Society's needs and desires. They have been eminently successful at this, within the confines of political and institutional constraints.

We now need to broaden the traditional scope of civil engineering in several ways. We need to develop, through sociological studies, a value system whereby we can relate values of food, clothing, housing, security, happiness, freedom, dignity, fairness, beauty, environmental quality, ecological stability, and other societal values. We also need a logical framework by which we can relate future values to present worth. Surely water will be more valuable 100 years from now than today, rather than drastically less, as engineers have had to assume.

But how does all of this relate to the application of computers to water resources engineering? Progress in computer application to date has encompassed the scope of civil engineering to the extent that an engineer can formulate a much more sophisticated and dependable design today than 30 years ago, responding to specific objectives and constrained by rather rigid institutional, economic and social conditions. As Society recognizes the need for a considered set of present and future values, we will develop a value framework that reflects the wishes, desires and hopes of the people. As such a framework unfolds, the challenge to engineering technology will call for an increase of sophistication in our analyses commensurate to or exceeding the rate of increase of computer capability.

We will include in our construction consideration of the effects of noise, dust, erosion, changes in surrounding property values, etc. We will assess the impacts of energy uses on resource depletion as well as on air, land and water quality. We will evaluate logically the benefits of clean air, clean water, lake recreation, wild river preservation, fish and wildlife enhancement, and esthetics. Only by extending computer applications into the broad interdisciplinary areas not previously analysed in mathematical terms can we set up a technology that can lead to socio-political actions that best serve the public individually and collectively in a complex society.

To most, this may seem an idealistic dream and a political impossibility. It must not be. If civilization as we know it is to survive, we cannot continue to allow millions of acre-feet of water per year in excess of river, lake and estuary needs to waste into the ocean while near-by areas remain parched. We cannot continue a policy of flood insurance that subjects more than 100 communities per year to serious and often disastrous flooding in the areas designated to be safe from flooding. We cannot continue to prevent an arid region from using water falling as precipitation in its area simply because interests in downstream or remote regions have asserted a prior right to that water. We cannot continue to allow excessive river pollution by those who have established a right to pollute while, at the same time, requiring new sources to provide prohibitively expensive treatment or actually preclude new development. We cannot continue to deplete our ground water with the contention that it is far more valuable today than it will be in the future.

For the first time in the history of civilization, we have the computational capability to make civil engineering decisions in a scientific socio-economic framework. We have the computer technology. We do not have the framework. We do not want a Marxist-type solution to such a framework. We want one based on fairness to vested interests and on the fundamental desires of the people, individually and collectively, for necessities and luxuries and for security, happiness, freedom and dignity. Let us concentrate our efforts in water management toward this goal.

COMPUTERS IN A PLANNING CONTEXT: ANOTHER REALITY

William K. Johnson, M.ASCE[*]

Abstract. Over the past twenty years water resources planning has seen a great increase in the development of computer methods of analysis. This has transformed the way the hydrology, hydraulics, economics and facilities of water resource development are understood and analyzed. Because of this emphasis, the complex reality of planning itself has been neglected. Understanding this reality is essential, not only for the wise future development of water resources, but also for the wise and appropriate use of computer technology in planning.

Historical Roots

Over twenty years ago Arthur Maass, Director of the Harvard Water Program, introduced <u>Design</u> <u>of</u> <u>Water</u> <u>Resource</u> <u>Systems</u> with the statement,

"The purpose of this book is to improve the methodology of designing water-resource systems...Systematic research on the methodology of system design, such as underlies this book, has been neglected in spite of the marked growth during the last quarter-century of public interest in multiunit, multipurpose river development" (18).

A catalyzing agent in the effort to improve the methodology was the electronic digital computer. The computer not only reduced the time consuming and laborious engineering calculations of conventional methods, but allowed for consideration of many more design alternatives, introduced economic theories of optimal resource allocation, statistical theories of stochastic hydrology and decision-making under uncertainty (6). At the heart of this movement toward method, was the basic philosophy that,

"decision-making can be improved by reducing to formalized, quantitative form as many of the data and considerations of the problem as possible" (6).

To develop these quantitative methods for water resources planning, planning itself was characterized in a way which made it consistent with the methodology being developed.   Its human interaction, social context, comprehensive nature, and purpose were simplified. A different reality was conceived.

"...field level planning is concerned with formulating optimal programs, largely investment in nature, in a systems context, through

---

[*] Civil Engineer, The Hydrologic Engineering Center, Corps of Engineers 609 Second Street, Davis, CA 95616

use of principles of production and allocation economics and operations research. The problem is cast in terms of optimization: maximization of an objective function subject to constraints and to the production function." (14)

This perception of field level planning has guided the development of methodology, computer modeling and system analysis from its beginning to the present. An enormous amount of intellectual energy, research effort, and human and economic resources have gone into developing computer methods for water resources planning. This effort has made major improvements in the practitioner's ability to analyze, understand, and plan water resource systems. Perhaps, however, it is time to lessen the emphasis on computer methods and turn attention to the task of planning itself. Another reality. Such a redirection, building upon the advances in computer analysis, will require that the purpose of both water resource planning and computer technology be re-examined. It is the purpose of this paper to begin that effort, to provoke such thought.

Water Resources Planning

Water resources planning can be described by the words, principles and practice of the profession. Planning has a scope, richness and diversity unlike any other division of civil engineering. Planning of water resources in the United States, and in most countries of the world, has a history (21,29). It does not begin from nothing. Studies, investigations, and reports have gone on before (17). There are many reasons or purposes for water development: water supply, hydroelectric power, navigation, flood control, irrigation, water quality, and fishery and recreation (27,29). Whether planning for a single purpose or multiple purpose, multiple means are considered. Surface water storage and ground water withdrawal are traditional engineering approaches which will continue to be needed in the future (24). But planning, by its nature, must also consider alternatives such as water rights, regulation, land zoning, conservation, education and economic adjustments. Such diversity makes water planning interdisciplinary. The broad beneficial effects of water development are identified as economic development, environmental quality, social well-being and income redistribution (25,26). Data and information important in planning covers all areas of the social landscape: engineering, economic, legal, financial, institutional, environmental, political, social and public. Analysis in planning is not limited to hydrology, hydraulics and systems, but includes environmental analysis, institutional analysis and financial analysis. Water planning crosses institutional jurisdictions. Cooperation between public and private interests is essential. The context - the people, the institutions, the hydrology, the need - is unique for every study, whether a river basin or small community.

The principal purpose of water planning is to improve the quality of decisions for an industry, community, state or nation, to help them be better prepared for the future (5). Given the comprehensive nature of planning it is wisdom, not objective knowledge which is needed. It is synthesis, not analysis; unity, not division, which leads to quality decisions. Models, methods, computer technology and what they provide by way of understanding and knowledge are clearly necessary, but planning is not systems analysis.

Computer Technology

Computer technology as used here is intended to include the variety of analyses, methods, and models that are used in water resources and which rely upon a digital computer. Yet, computer technology is more than methods or models. It is a way of living, thinking, acting, relating (7,22,30). It is not a tool, it is not neutral. Choosing computer technology imposes its rules, conditions, organization, discipline and limited world view. It imposes a view that the world of water resources planning is a set of mathematically tractable problems awaiting solution. Through computer technology, the engineer can construct a reality, an artificial world of symbolism, which introduces into engineering work a quality of remoteness. Computer models and programs also introduce rationality, logic and efficiency. Paths are often signed the "one best way" (7,30). While the methods of computer technology require the discipline of logic and rationality, their use in water planning is often an act of faith.

The popular presence of computer technology in society can exert a signicant influence upon the way planning is done. Such influence comes in several ways. To begin, there is most certainly a cultural influence. This is a technological society; computer technology is deeply etched upon all that is done (7,30). It becomes an objective to incorporate computers into planning to the greatest extent possible. Not because they are needed, but because it is technically possible to do so. The desire to use a ground water model, for example, when there is neither data nor reason to do so.

A second influence is the consumptive nature of society: the desire to have the latest, fastest, largest, most versatile technology. Such a desire creates in turn a need to justify new uses, new applications. There is also the attraction of being able to create an artificial reality which can be used as a basis for inquiry, as a means of control, and as a source of certainty. Lastly, a not too trivial influence is the adoption of computer technology for personal recognition, status, reward and acceptance. Such a need can influence both the use and development of computer methods.

All of this is intended to suggest that there are a number of strong influences for the use of computer technology in water resources planning which are unrelated to what the technology might actually contribute, in a technical way, to the study. The question needs to be asked: Is the use of a particular computer model, method or technique being adopted because it will improve the quality of decisions or because it is popular, fashion forward, or personally gratifying?

Planning Practice

Reality, to those engaged in planning, is the concrete situation of which they are a part (3,4). The people, the hydrology, the institutions, the schedule, the funds, the regulations, all of these and more, make up the concrete situation. It is in specific, concrete situations, that planning is done. Every planning study, every episode in the life of the study is unique to some measure (3). To understand planning, to understand the decisions, to understand the presence or absence of some computer technology the reality of the concrete situation must be understood.

This reality, because of its complexity, is charged with ambiguity and uncertainty. The multiplicity of contexts and the different levels and manner of human interaction unique to each planning task, makes setting forth clear criteria difficult. Yet it is just these clear definitions of purpose which computer technology demands. The "one best way" of analysis gives way in practice to "do what you can."

Water planning in practice is a mix of two world views (4). One sees nature, and the natural processes related to water, as a puzzle to be solved. What is sought is to understand that phenomenon, represent it artificially with technology, and then use the representation to answer questions and provide information. The other view sees the contextual situation of water resource development and the task of making quality decisions about how to meet future needs. A radical shift is required to hold in tension both views. Our perception of the necessity and importance of computer analysis must be viewed differently.

Planning Theory

"A good theory is one that holds together long enough to get you to a better theory" (12). Water resources professionals have devoted little effort towards developing a theory of water planning in the past. The thought which has gone forth in this direction has been limited to the so-called "rational theory" (13,25). Under this theory, planning is described as: establishing goals and objectives, identifying alternatives, evaluating alternatives, and implementation. While simple and easy to conceptualize, these principles add little to an understanding of planning.

Developing a theory of planning can help practitioners think more deeply about the task of planning and improve it. To put the same another way: how much planning is needed, is there a way to reduce the costs of planning, to improve the quality, to make planning more responsive, to cut shelf-life? Like most theories, a theory of planning is a set of principles - hypothetical, conceptual and pragmatic - which form the general frame of reference for practice. Urban and regional planners have wrestled with this subject for sometime (5,8,9,13). There are many differences between water development and urban development, yet there is also much common ground and crossing lines of professional disciplines is necessary.

A better foundation, deeper theoretical and philosophical roots, holds the possibility of a clearer understanding of planning practice and the place of computer technology. Consider, for example, the role of information in planning (23). Information is a common thread which is woven into all aspects of water planning. Information links the individual with the institution, the planning with the decision maker, the technical with the social, the objectives with the evaluation. Information is a way for sharpening the purpose of planning and for achieving that purpose in an efficient manner. In many respects the study manager is a manager of information, yet planning is more than collecting and presenting information. And, lastly, applied to the topic at hand, computer technology stores, processes, analyzes and displays data and information. Information is just one dimension of planning which could deepen our understanding if it were developed in the context of a planning theory.

Planning Alternatives

Developing ways to meet present and future needs is at the heart of planning. If planning is to improve the quality of decisions, a broad range of alternative ways of meeting water needs must be explored. Formulating alternative plans is a creative exercise which is carried out in the context of a concrete situation. Formulation brings together the diversity of planning considerations and the means which are appropriate for the situation.

Historically, the water resource profession has progressed to an ever increasing number of alternative ways to plan and manage our nation's water resources. Forty years ago, Gilbert White suggested a broad range of alternatives for reducing the hazard of floods (28). Since that time the profession has progressed from knowing the names of these alternatives to welcoming their presence on the floodplain. Water supply planning now considers both the traditional water conservation through storage reservoirs and the more recent water conservation through reduced demand (16,24). Hydroelectric power planning has awakened to the potential of existing reservoir sites, small power developments and energy conservation.

In addition to these general trends, today there is consideration of public policies for land use based on water supply and policies for flood plain management. Legal aspects of wastewater applications, groundwater legal rights, Indian water rights and purchase of water rights are being addressed. The need is recognized for management of interstate aquifers, for reconciling regional and local water supply alternatives, for interbasin water transfers, for coordination of water quality and quantity. While there is continuing reliance upon groundwater withdrawal and reservoir storage, the potential for conjunctive use supply is considered. In formulating alternatives practitioners continue to be conscious of the importance of environmental and social goals.

Computer technology will always be an important aid in the process of plan formulation, often directing attention to specific alternatives. Yet, it cannot substitute for the creative process which must consider a much broader range of options. There is a need for the profession to devote greater effort to investigating alternative ways to meet water needs, to increase the effectiveness of policies and projects, and to understand better the creative process of plan formulation.

Planning Participants

The interpersonal relationships which characterize planning generally involve seven parties: client, management, study or project manager, technical staff, consultants, and public and private interests. Effective planning and appropriate use of computer technology often depends upon the nature and quality of the relationships which exist between these participants (22). Data collection for calibration and verification, often a costly task, must be paid for by the client, approved by management, and often receive the cooperation of public agencies and private organizations. Use of a particular model for analysis requires the allocation of study resources (funds, time, staff) by the study manager to the technical staff. More than one planning study has not used, or has misused, computer models because of a breakdown in these relationships.

The relationship between study manager, technical staff and consultant is of particular interest. Appropriate use of computer technology is achieved both in the counsel provided by the consultant as to which method of analysis should be used, and in the willingness of the consultant to adapt the selected technology to the concrete situation of the study. Wise counsel will consider the use of a full range of methods from simple to complex, from hand computations to computer models. Such counsel places the study and its needs above any desire to use the study to further a particular technology. This encourages a spirit of freedom and trust between those involved, and whatever method is chosen has a better chance of contributing meaningfully to the study.

Maintaining good working relationships between people is also important when planning is viewed not as a discrete, one time effort to produce a report, but as a continuous on-going process. In some studies the selection of a particular computer model is less important than its acceptance among potential users, for example, city, county, state agencies. Computer technology can be selected, scoped and applied in ways which provide useful information not only to the sponsoring agency, but to others, perhaps only indirectly involved in the study. It should be an objective of planning not only to improve the quality of decisions for the study, but also for others engaged in management of the water resources. This requires good relationships and appropriate technology.

Planning Analysis

An appropriate presence of computer analysis in planning requires that the practitioner's skills of critical thinking be sharpened, improved, and used (19). This is necessary not only to sort through the myths and fictions which influence our understanding of the value of the technology itself, but it is also necessary to properly place this technology in its appropriate role. Such thinking, while critical, should be constructive - uplifting, enhancing, seeking to find a better way, pointing to alternative paths. Consider, as an example of such thinking, the suggestion by Wolman that cost-benefit analysis is inappropriate for water supply in developing countries (31).

First to be considered, is the question of whether computer technology should be used at all. Both wisdom and courage are necessary to entertain, at the outset, the notion that computer analysis may not be appropriate in the concrete situation at hand. What information will be provided by the analysis? What data are required? What time and cost are involved? How will it be used? Are there alternative ways to obtain what is needed? These are questions which should be addressed when a study is begun.

It has been suggested that one benefit of an optimization model is that it allows consideration of a large number of alternative designs (6,11). In the world of mathematics and operations research, this is a valid problem. However, most often this is a mathematical reality, not a planning reality. One reason is that most planning situations have a history. Prior investigations and the experience of engineers who have worked on the watershed in prior years can narrow the design options. Legal and institutional constraints are another factor. The selection of an optimization model to screen 100,000 design variations is often less important than deciding how the floodplain should be managed.

Critical thinking is also needed in the calibration, verification and interpretation of computer models. Appropriate use implies correct use. This problem has been present for sometime, but it is even more urgent today. To calibrate carefully, verify or document either the application or development of a model is a tedious, time consuming task. It takes a great amount of professional discipline to do it well. In a culture noted for its impatience, the reality of careful, disciplined modeling is not easily realized.

Critical thinking regarding the use of the results of computer analyses needs to be carried out before the analyses are performed. Analyses should be shaped to the concrete situation of the planning effort. This is not an easy task because modeling efforts tend to take on a life of their own. Thought should be given to how the results will be used in the larger study.

Planning Research

The subject of water resources research has been addressed in the literature and at conferences over the past few years (2,10,15). Particular attention has been given to the federal role (10,15). The discussion in this paper, while focusing on the reality of water planning and its relationship to computer technology, suggests several areas of worthwhile research. These are: understanding the breath and interrelatedness of planning concrete situations; developing a theory of water planning; investigating alternative means to meet water needs; exploring the importance of interpersonal relationships; and examining the appropriateness of computer methods. Such a research agenda directs attention to the comprehensive nature of field level planning. As a consequence, the practitioner will be deeply involved. The concrete situation, the variety of considerations, the act of planning is what the practitioner knows best. In addition, such research will require the adaption of research methods of the social sciences (1,20).

Conclusions

It was mentioned in the beginning that the purpose of this paper is to provoke a re-examination of planning and computer technology in planning. Several specific topics are addressed and their importance discussed. Hopefully, this will lead to a lessening of emphasis in the analytical area and an increase in attention to field level planning. Such a shift is needed if planning is to serve to improve the quality of our decisions in the future.

Appendix. References

1. Babbie, Earl The Practice of Social Research, 3rd edition, Wadsworth Publishing Co, Belmont, California, 1983.

2. Beard, Leo R. "Effective Water Research Programs," Journal of the Water Resources Planning and Management Division, ASCE, Vol. 106, No. WR2, July 1980, pp. 409-412.

3. Bolan, Richard S. "The Practitioner as Theorist," Journal of the American Planning Association, Vol. 46, July 1980, pp. 261-274.

4. Bolan, Richard S. "The Promise and Perils of a Normative Theory of Planning ," in Evaluating Urban Planning Efforts, edited by Ian Masser, Gower Publishing Co., Great Britian, 1983.

5. deNeufville, Judith Innes "Planning Theory and Planning Theory and Practice: Bridging the Gap," Journal of Planning Education and Research, Summer 1983.

6. Dorfman, Robert "Formal Models in the Design of Water Resource Systems," Water Resources Research, Vol. 1, No. 3, 1965, pp. 329-336.

7. Ellul, Jacques The Technological Society, Alfred A. Knopf, New York, 1964.

8. Faludi, A. A Reader in Planning Theory, Pergamon Press, Oxford, 1973.

9. Freidman, John and Hudson Barclay, "Knowledge and Action: A Guide to Planning Theory," Journal of the American Institute of Planners, Vol. 40, January 1974, pp. 2-16.

10. Grigg, Neil S. "Management of US Water Research," Journal of the Water Resources Planning and Management Division, ASCE, Vol. 106, No. WR1, March 1980, pp. 143-158.

11. Hall, Warren A. and Dracup, John A. Water Resources Systems Engineering, McGraw-Hill, 1970.

12. Hebb, D.O. Psychology Today, November 1969. Quoted in reference 20, p. 54.

13. Hudson, Barclay M., "Comparison of Current Planning Theories: Counterparts and Contradictions," Journal of the American Institute of Planners, Vol. 45, October 1979.

14. Hufschmidt, Maynard F. "Field Level Planning of Water Resource Systems," Water Resources Research, Vol. 1, No. 2, 1965, pp. 147-163.

15. James, L. Douglas "Needed Federal Role in Water Research," ASCE Task Committee on Federal Participation in Water Resources Research, Water Resources Planning and Management Division, ASCE, 1983.

16. Johnson, William K. "Perspectives on Water Conservation," Journal of the Water Resources Planning and Management Division, ASCE, Vol. 107, No. WR1, March 1981, pp. 225-238.

17. Lee Wilson and Associates, Water Supplies for the Sante Fe Area, New Mexico: A Status Report, Sante Fe, NM, November 20, 1984.

18. Maass, Arthur, et al. Design of Water-Resource Systems: New Techniques for Relating Economic Objectives, Engineering Analysis, and Governmental Planning, Harvard University Press, 1962.

19. Majone, Giandomenico and Edward S. Quade, editors, Pitfalls of Analysis, International Institute for Applied Systems Analysis, John Wiley and Sons, 1980.

20. Mintzberg, Henry The Nature of Managerial Work, Harper and Row, New York, 1973.

21. Schad, Theordore M. "Water Resources Planning - Historical Development," Journal of the Water Resources Planning and Management Division, ASCE, Vol. 105, No. WR1, Proc. Paper 14410, March 1979, pp. 9-25.

22. Schon, Donald A. The Reflective Practitioner: How Professionals Think in Action, Basic Books Inc, 1983.

23. Skjei, Stephen S. Information for Collective Action, D.c. Heath, Toronto, 1973.

24. Texas Department of Water Resources, Water for Texas: A Comprehensive Plan for the Future, Austin, Texas, November 1984.

25. U.S. Water Resources Council, Principles and Standards for Planning Water and Related Land Resources, Federal Register, Monday, September 10, 1973, Part III.

26. U.S. Water Resources Council, Economic and Environmental Principles and Guidelines for Water and Realted Land Resources Implementation Studies, March 10, 1983.

27. "Water Policies for the Future," United States National Water Commission, United States Government Printing Office, Washington, D.C., June 14, 1973.

28. White, Gilbert F. Human Adjustments to Floods: A Geographical Approach to the Flood Problem in the United States, University of Chicago, Department of Geography, Research Paper No. 29, 1945.

29. White, Gilbert F. Strategies of American Water Management, The University of Michigan Press, 1969.

30. Winner, Langdon Autonomous Technology, The MIT Press, Cambridge, Massachusetts, 1977.

31. Wolman, Abel "Water Resources Management: International Challenge and Opportunities," Water Resources Bulletin, AWRA, Vol. 20, No. 5, October 1984, pp. 647-650.

Maximum Water Source Utilization Using Lotus 1-2-3

Harry L. Summitt, M. ASCE[1]
Thomas E. Raster[2]
Judd A. Ebersviller[3]

Abstract

This paper discusses the use of microcomputers to determine the optimum mix of sources for the Fargo-Moorhead area's water supply network. The area's major water source is the Red River of the North, which forms the border between Minnesota and North Dakota. It is supplemented by water from the Sheyenne River, a series of five surficial aquifers, and an in-stream reservoir. Water supply in the area is limited, and the need for accurate modeling to maximize its utilization efficiency continues to grow as demand increases. Earlier methods for predicting water supply and demand rates no longer reflected the situation's complexity. New procedures were needed to determine present and future levels of reservoir storage and groundwater development -- two factors that are crucial to the system's efficient operation.

In response, the mass supply and demand curves used in the past were modified with several new variables. Supply curves were redefined to account for treated storage, aquifer capabilities (including safe yield and short-term pumping rates), and existing reservoir capacities. Demand curves were also redefined to include peaking factors and fire demand, as well as evaporation and sedimentation, which are functions of reservoir size. The micro-based system was computerized on a spreadsheet format. It incorporates all the supply and demand curves and allows "what-if" queries to determine the effects of changes in supply or demand on water supply needs.

The paper outlines the development and use of the spreadsheet model to determine the best mix of water supply facilities and sources to meet projected demands of the Fargo-Moorhead urban area. It also examines the system's role in evaluating water conservation measures, and illustrates the advantages to be gained through conservation.

Introduction

Fargo, North Dakota and Moorhead, Minnesota are sister cities straddling the Red River of the North. The cities have at times been fierce rivals that frequently compete for commerce and industry in their efforts to grow. This rivalry is compounded by differing tax laws, water laws, and development incentives. Despite these individual and often opposing efforts, a common need exists for a concerted water resource strategy that acknowledges the fact of their shared supply. Regional cooperation is central to solving present and future water problems.

[1] Project Manager, E. A. Hickok and Associates, Inc., 545 Indian Mound, Wayzata, Minnesota 55391
[2] Manager of Urban Studies, St. Paul District Corps of Engineers, 1135 U.S. Post Office and Customs House, St. Paul, Minnesota 55101
[3] Hydrologist, E. A. Hickok and Associates, Inc.

16

These problems are closely related to the nature of the Red River of the North. The river is the major water source for a regional population that numbers more than 100,000; yet during low-flow periods this regional need cannot be met, and during droughts, the streamflow may dry up altogether. Late summer low-flows are often followed by heavy spring flooding. This seasonal dichotomy between water scarcity and destructive overabundance has plagued the region since its development.

Flood control is especially important for the region's future. Two natural factors combine to magnify the flooding: the river's northward drainage and the region's flat topography. As the Red River flows northward through the lake bed of extinct Lake Agassiz, ice blockages downstream in the north combine with snowmelt and spring rainfall in the south to create annual floods. The flatness of the region increases the area flooded; and since there are no valley walls to create reservoirs and no high ground to span with levees, flood control becomes very difficult.

The St. Paul District Corps of Engineers has undertaken the Fargo/Moorhead Urban Study to address these and other water and energy resource concerns. The study explores the issues of water supply and conservation, flood control, river bank instability, energy conservation, and water resources data management. The first of these studies, water supply and conservation, provides the basis for this paper.

Background

Water is supplied to the Fargo/Moorhead urban area from several sources, none of which is capable of meeting the demands by itself. Sources include the Red and Sheyenne Rivers, an in-stream reservoir on the Red River, and a series of small aquifers composed of glacial sand and gravel deposits. In addition, the Buffalo River, an off-stream reservoir and three other glacial aquifers could be developed if necessary.

Projected growth will increase municipal demand from approximately the 17 MGD average demand for the Fargo-Moorhead urban area today to over 26 MGD in year 2030, with short-term demands exceeding 56 MGD. Supplies for rural communities and agricultural operations must be drawn from the same sources, further increasing the pressure on these limited water resources. As a result, a regional approach was taken to address the water supply problems of the study area.

The Water Supply and Conservation study is aimed at providing a water supply system which will: 1) meet existing and projected needs 2) maximize use of limited resources, and 3) minimize cost. Initially this included assessing the capacity of existing facilities and available sources, assessing the costs of expanding facilities to utilize unused source capacity, and projecting demands throughout the 50-year study period.

Demands were compared with supplies by using a variation of the classical textbook mass curve analysis. In the textbook example, total supplies and demands (volume) are plotted against time. The supply curve is typically constructed from partial duration/low-flow stream analyses. The demand curve is a straight line through the origin with its slope equal to the average demand. The maximum vertical distance between the two curves represents the supply shortfall, and traditionally, the size of reservoir required. (See Figure 1.)

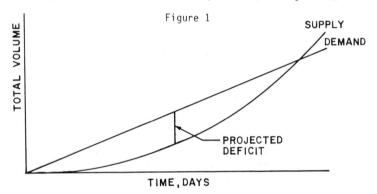

Figure 1

We built upon this textbook example in evaluating the Fargo/Moorhead water supply alternatives. Because of the large number of potential supplies (see Figure 2) as well as demands that will vary throughout the study period, numerous trials are required to determine the optimum mix of sources to satisfy demands at any point in time. Repetitive graphical analyses became much too cumbersome and time-consuming. To overcome these obstacles, a spreadsheet format was developed that allowed "what-if" trials with only a few keystrokes.

Spreadsheet Construction

A "curve" was developed for each of the supply and demand entries listed in Figure 2. Mass curves for the three rivers were constructed using partial duration analyses as mentioned above. More than 50 years of stream data were modeled with HEC-3 to simulate streamflows under future reservoir operating conditions, diversions, projected withdrawals and return flows. Using this modified streamflow data, low flows were evaluated for flow durations ranging from seven days to eight years. This provided the information necessary to construct mass curves for any recurrence interval from two to 200 years. A 50-year recurrence interval was selected for this study. Therefore, the 50-year seven-day low flow, 14-day low flow, 30-day low flow, etc., were used to compute total volumes for these durations. Plotting these values and drawing a curve through the points gives 50-year low-flow mass curves for each of the streams. The data for each stream was then input manually as a one line field in a spreadsheet program.

Figure 2

List of Potential and Existing Supplies and Demands

Supplies	Demands
Red River	Fargo
Sheyenne River	Moorhead
Buffalo River	West Fargo
In-Stream Storage	Dilworth
Off-Stream Storage	Fargo Fire Demand
Fargo Treated Storage	Moorhead Fire Demand
Moorhead Treated Storage	West Fargo Fire Demand
West Fargo Treated Storage	Dilworth Fire Demand
Dilworth Treated Storage	Red River Minimum Streamflow
Buffalo Aquifer	Sheyenne River Minimum Streamflow
West Fargo Aquifer	Buffalo River Minimum Streamflow
Moorhead Aquifer	Reservoir Sedimentation Allowance
Kragnes Aquifer	Reservoir Evaporation
Hickson Aquifer	Direct Rural, Industrial, Commercial
Page Aquifer	and Agricultural Demands
Sheyenne Delta Aquifer	

Aquifer mass curves were constructed using safe yield rates and pumping capacities. Safe yields of the various aquifers were obtained from previous studies, recharge estimates, or long-term groundwater level fluctuations in relation to long-term demands. Maximum withdrawals were limited to the aquifer safe yield over a one year period, but were allowed to be pumped at up to twice this rate for short periods of time to satisfy peak needs. Only the safe yield of each aquifer needed to be imputted: the mass supply at each time interval can be calculated by the computer. If pumping or piping limitations exist below safe yield limits, these constraints can also be included in the spreadsheet computations.

Storage, whether treated storage or raw water reservoirs, are included as a fixed volume supply (a horizontal straight line). Total supplies can then be determined as a composite of all the supply curves. Figure 3 illustrates a composite supply curve constructed from five supply sources.

Mass demand curves were created in much the same way. Average and maximum daily municipal demands were inputted for each of the four communities. The spreadsheet was designed to compute peaking factors for maximum day, maximum week, maximum month, etc., and then compute mass demands by using these peaking factors in conjunction with the average demands. The resulting demand curve is downwardly concave, maximizing demands at any point in time.

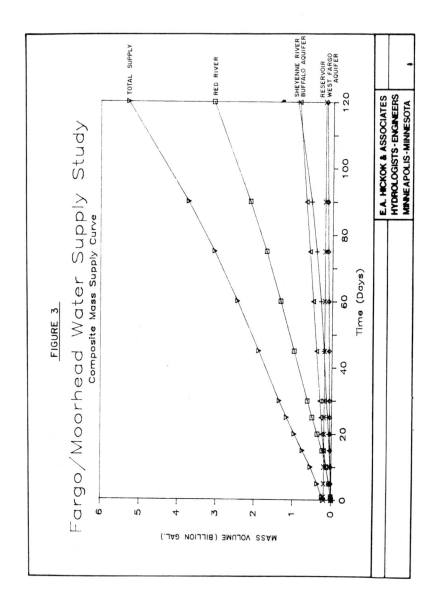

Fire flow demands were included as fixed volumes to be maintained at all times. The figure for each community was based on the deliverable water required by fire insurance guidelines, and an estimate of the frequency of fires for each community.

Other demands on each water source had to be included to assure the supplies were not overused. These demands included rural communities, private industries, private wells, livestock wells and agricultural users. These users withdraw from the same sources used by the Fargo/ Moorhead core communities, reducing the supplies available to these communities.

The remaining demand curves represent other water supplies that are unavailable for use. These include allowances for minimum reservoir pool levels, sedimentation, evaporation, and allowances for minimum streamflow releases. The sedimentation and minimum pool level allowance is a fixed volume based on the size of the reservoir. Evaporation allowances are computed with the spreadsheet for any given point in time by using reservoir size and average summertime evaporation rates. Minimum streamflows were assumed to be a fixed rate for each stream based on historical low-flow data and negotiations with natural resources and environmental groups. As with total supplies, total demands were determined as a composite of all demand curves -- each of which is one line item in the spreadsheet.

The spreadsheet was designed to sum all supplies and demands at each point in time and to find either the maximum shortage to be satisfied by increased storage, or the maximum shortage/day ratio to be satisfied by increased withdrawal pumping. The spreadsheet would compute either needed reservoir size (including allowances for minimum pool, sedimentation, and evaporation) or needed aquifer development (using rules for safe yield and maximum withdrawal rates). By assuming and fixing one of these, a combination of increased storage and groundwater supplies can be determined.

Spreadsheet Use

With all supply and demand curves loaded in the spreadsheet, looking at different alternatives was greatly simplified. Each urban core community could be evaluated individually, in combination with another community, or in a sub-regional system with all four communities. Alternative mixes of supply sources were evaluated to determine which mix best meets demands. Intermediate demands (say 1990, 2000, 2010, etc.) were run to determine phasing of construction. If implemented, conservation measures could alter projected demands. New demand figures reflecting this trend could be run to estimate reductions in facility development and overall costs.

The first spreadsheet iteration projected demands for the year 2030 and used existing supplies and facility capacities to determine ultimate needs. Figure 4 illustrates the total supplies and demands under this scenario and shows projected deficits. Figure 5 provides a closer look at the deficits. It shows a 140 million gallon shortfall over 20 days and a 300 million gallon shortfall over 60 days.

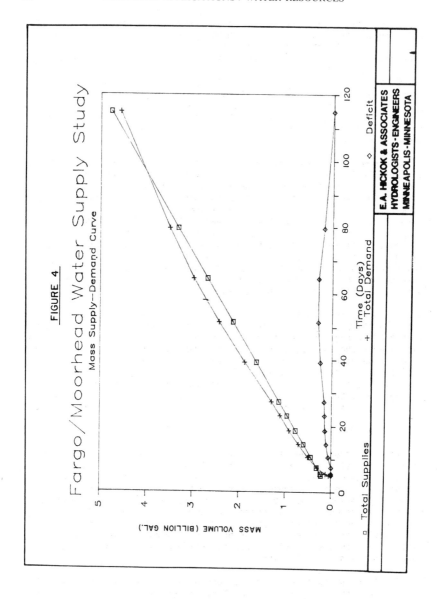

FIGURE 4

Fargo/Moorhead Water Supply Study
Mass Supply—Demand Curve

□ Total Supplies   + Total Demand   ◇ Deficit

E.A. HICKOK & ASSOCIATES
HYDROLOGISTS · ENGINEERS
MINNEAPOLIS · MINNESOTA

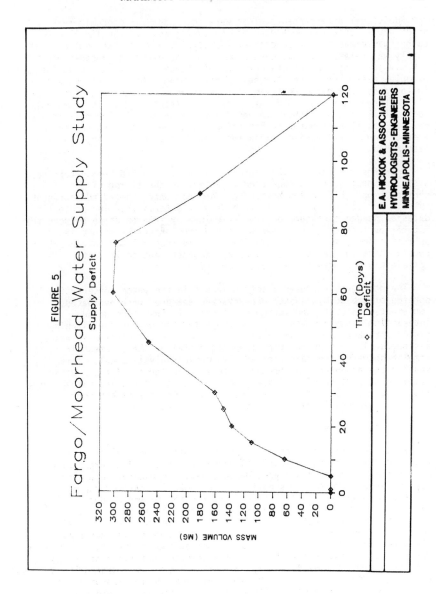

FIGURE 5

Fargo/Moorhead Water Supply Study

Additional or expanded sources were then added in economic rank order until projected demands could be satisfied. If the final added source was capable of producing excess supply, and its marginal cost of supply was relatively low, checks were made to determine whether previously justified expansions could be eliminated. In this study, for example, expansion of the Kragnes, Moorhead and Buffalo aquifers was followed by enlarging in-stream storage in economic ranking. Expansion of the three aquifers could not satisfy projected needs. The marginal cost of building a slightly larger dam would be relatively small if a new dam was already under construction, so a check was made to see whether any or all aquifer expansions could be eliminated in lieu of a larger dam.

Once the ultimate set of sources and facilities had been determined, a similar procedure was conducted to determine the timing of construction. With a few keystrokes, demands were changed to represent interim periods and the facility needs were determined. The projected dates of needed construction was determined by interpolating between the interim periods. The engineer was freed from extensive effort in selecting sources and sizing facilities, and thus allowed to concentrate on providing the set of facilities and sources that could most efficiently minimize present value costs.

The model again proved itself valuable in the water conservation portion of the study. Water conservation measures were evaluated. Implementation costs and estimates of effectiveness (including interaction between measures) were projected throughout the planning period for each measure and a rank order for cost effectiveness was assigned. These measures were then sequentially "implemented" in a simulation using the computerized mass curve analysis model. This enabled the engineers to more accurately determine the forgone water supply cost portion of the water conservation benefits, and perhaps more importantly illustrated to the local communities the effect they can have on water supply needs through conservation.

Project Conclusions

Study results show that the Fargo-Moorhead urban communities can best meet their needs by sharing limited resources. The computerized mass curve analysis showed groundwater, having downwardly concaved supply curves, and stream supplies, with upwardly concaved supply curves, are capable of complementing each other to smooth out fluctuations in supply. Stream-flows on average can supply urban core needs, but annual low-flow supplies will fall below total regional demands. Groundwater supplies can be pumped at rates in excess of safe yield for short periods to make up for streamflow shortages. By sharing resources, all communities have equal access to both types of sources. This eliminates the need for any community to be overly dependent on either streamflow or groundwater supplies, and enables economies of scale in water treatment facilities through expansion of one plant for surface water treatment and one plant for groundwater treatment.

The study presented a recommended plan for water supply system expansion and estimated the timing for needed construction. The recommended plan minimized present value costs (including operations and maintenance) within the constraints provided.

The computerized mass curve analysis was used in the final phase of the study to illustrate the effects of implementing a water conservation program. It showed the communities that through sharing limited resources and expanding existing wellfields in three aquifers, they can meet year 2030 demands without the need for a new low-head dam on the river while reducing the size of needed water and wastewater treatment facilities. The net savings to the communities is approximately $1.6 million dollars per year.

The computerized mass curve analysis model proved useful throughout the evaluation of alternatives, sizing and selection of sources, determination of facility construction timing, and the evaluation of conservation on water supply facilities.

PERSONAL COMPUTERS AND STORMWATER MANAGEMENT PROGRAMS

By Thomas N. Debo M. ASCE

ABSTRACT

Urban flooding and drainage problems are the result of
complex interactions between natural and man-made systems.
Comprehensive analysis of the hydrologic characteristics of
these problems often require the use of computer techniques
and models. Beginning in the early 1970's urban areas in
Georgia have been developing computer models and
integrating them into local stormwater management programs.
The development of hydrologic-hydraulic models in Georgia
is discussed and a recently developed model for use on
Apple and IBM personal computers is described.

INTRODUCTION

With the passage of the National Flood Insurance Act of
1968, communities desiring to qualify for federally
subsidized flood insurance are required to adopt land use
and control measures related to development within flood
plain areas. In compliance with this Act, many communities
have or are anticipating adopting drainage or flood plain
ordinances to control development within flood plain areas.
In addition, in recent years much attention has been
focused on the flooding problems of urbanized watersheds.
Politicians, administrators, planners, and engineers have
become aware of the tremendous economic damage potential
within urban flood plain areas. As a result some
communities have integrated their ordinances and
regulations with technical and engineering material and
developed comprehensive stormwater management programs to
deal with local flooding and drainage problems.

Associate Professor, Graduate City Planning Program,
College of Architecture, Georgia Institute of Technology,
Atlanta, Georgia, 30332.

Urban flooding and drainage problems are the result of complex interactions between natural and man-made systems. Comprehensive analysis of the hydrologic characteristics of these problems often require the use of computer techniques and models. Many such models have been developed and applied to urban flooding problems. Several communities in Georgia have developed hydrologic-hydraulic models as integral parts of their stormwater management program, while other communities are now in the process of developing such models. The development of local models in Georgia started in the early 1970's, before personal computers were available, and thus models were developed for use on large computer systems.

The purpose of this paper is to describe the development of the computer models in Georgia and the current use of personal computer models within stormwater management programs.

EARLY MODEL DEVELOPMENT

Like many urban areas, DeKalb County, Georgia in the early 1970's was experiencing the impact of urbanization on its drainage system. Each year thousands of drainage complaints were received by the drainage department, ranging from major flooding of houses and other structures to minor yard flooding. To deal with these problems the County developed a stormwater management program designed to alleviate existing problems and prevent new problems from being created. To assist in performing the hydrologic analysis and design of stormwater management facilites, the County contracted with the Georgia Institute of Technology to develop a computer model capable of simulating the flow of runoff through the different drainage systems throughout the County (Lumb and James, 1976). This simulaion model has and is being used for watershed planning, analysis and design of stormwater management facilities. The model is based on continuous simulation which provides continuous streamflow sequences covering a period of flows from a single drainage basin or a set of connected basins.

Because of the large data base necessary to use the simulation model, it must be run on a large computer system. Time and resources must also be allocated to the collection and input of large quantities of data. Experience has also shown that users of the model must be trained in hydrology and be familiar with using large computer programs. The simulation model has tremendous capabilities for analysis and design applications, but its use is limited to professionals qualified in the area of urban hydrology. Because of these limitations the model is not being widely used in DeKalb County and other cities and counties in the Atlanta Metropolitan Area (where DeKalb County is located) are not using the model.

COLUMBUS, GEORGIA MODEL

As a result of rapid development in Columbus, Georgia,
large volumes of surface runoff and erosion and sediment
problems prompted the Columbus Department of Community
Development to develop a stormwater management program for
the city (Debo and Ulrich, 1977). The Columbus Stormwater
Management Program was designed to develop criteria,
procedures and regulations to alleviate problems of
sediment, erosion and drainage, as well as protect
sensitive natural areas. One of the major elements of this
program was to take the computer model developed for DeKalb
County and make further developments for use in the
Columbus area. The model also went through a calibration
and verification process. One major change in the model
was the addition of an economic model to analyze the
economic benefits and costs associated with different
structural and   nonstructural flood mitigation measures
(Debo and Day, 1980).

After the urban flood simulation model was developed for
Columbus, it was applied to some test watersheds. The
model was then transfered to the Columbus Engineering
Department for future use. As often happens in local
government, after several years personnel changes in the
Engineering and Planning Departments resulted in a desire
to have some hydrology model which would be easier to apply
than the simulation model and not require the use of a
large computer system. In response to this desire, a
hydrologic model was designed for use on a Hewlett-Packard
41C programmable calculator. The calculator model is based
on the U. S. Department of Agriculture, Soil Conservation
Service (SCS) method for estimating volume and rate of
runoff in small watersheds (Kent, 1968). This method is
generally limited to drainage areas of 2,000 acres or less
and to watersheds that have average slopes of less than 30
percent. Given the storage limitations of the HP
calculator, the calculator model was strctured so that the
user inputs local data while the calculator proceeds
through the calculation of peak discharges and hydrograph
determination (Debo, 1984).

The programmable calculator model is presently being used
for hydrologic analysis, design of stormwater management
facilities and planning applications. The model is easier
an faster to use than manually applying the SCS method.
The model is also much easier to use than the computer
simulation model and does not require access to large
computer facilities, but it does not have the analysis
capabilities of the simulation model. The calculator model
is limited to estimating peak discharges and hydrographs
from uniformly developed watersheds.

INTRODUCTION OF PERSONAL COMPUTERS

Camden County is a small rural county in southeast Georgia frequented by many vacationers who enjoy the slow pace and unique environmental setting. Vast wetlands and swamps which dot the area are treasured places for both city and rural residents. Although this area is located less than an hour's drive from the large metropolitan area of Jacksonville, Florida, its slow growth and vast open areas have seen little change from one generation to the next. Several years ago the Federal Government decided to construct a naval submarine base in Camden County. As a result of this construction, specific areas of Camden County are quickly being developed for urban uses. This urbanization will have many effects on the character of the surrounding area.

Camden County has always had drainage problems. It is in the nature of its low, level coastal plain physiography. While in the past, under predominately rural uses, these difficulties could be ignored or at least tolerated, today they cannot. With the anticipated rapidly increasing urban land uses, poor drainage and flooding will become a pressing community problem. To cope with this problem a stormwater management program has been developed for this area (Debo, 1984). An integral part of this program was the development of a personal computer model for hydrologic and hydraulic evaluations. This model was designed for use on either an Apple IIe or IBM Personal Computer. The model is based on the Soil Conservation Service method for estimating volume and rate of runoff in small watersheds. Thus the model is very similar to the programmable calculator model although the personal computer model is easier to use, involves less input from the user, and was calibrated for use in the Camden County area (Debo, 1984)

HYDROS - ROUT MODEL

At the present time several urban areas in Georgia and the southeast are presently developing or anticipating the development of stormwater mangement programs. These programs will require hydrologic-hydraulic analysis techniques that should have the following characteristics:

* Designed to be used on personal computers.

* Have the capability of analyzing the hydrologic effects of urbanization.

* Capable of being calibrated and verified for local use.

* Include routing through channel and reservoir systems.

* Be easy to use for engineering personnel who are not familiar with using computers and developing computer programs.

* Not require extensive training in hydrology and hydraulics.

* Be nonpropriatory and relatively inexpensive to purchase.

In response to this need a personal computer program has been developed which is an extension of the model orginally developed for Camden County. The hydrology used in the model is based on the Soil Conservation Service Method which includes the standard Type II 24-hour curve, 24-hour curve developed by SCS for use in Florida, and a 72-hour curve developed for use in Florida. A routing model then uses the hydrographs generated by the SCS method and routes them through networks of channels and reservoirs, using an adaptation of a BASIC program developed by Richard J. Heggen (Heggen, 1983). The Muskingum method is used for routing through channels and a standard storage equation is used to route through reservoirs. Following is a flow chart of the model.

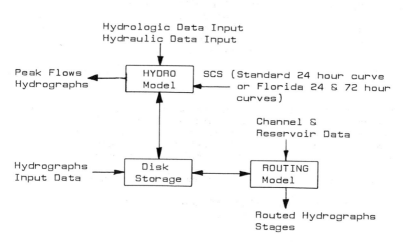

HYDROS MODEL

The HYDROS model is specifically designed to be "user friendly". The model is interactive and promps the user for the required input data. After the data are input to the model the user has the opportunity to change specific data blocks or individual data items. Thus it is easy to run the model several times while only changing specific data items. It is anticipated that this model will be used by personnel from city and county engineering departments in addition to local consultants. Although drainage and flood control problems are an important part of their work, these professionals also spend much of their time dealing with other engineering areas. Thus they may only use the model at infrequent intervals and would not want a model that required a lot of effort from the user.

Following is an example of a data input stream that would be required to run the model (underlined items are input by the user).

HYDROS MODEL - GEORGIA TECH, 1985

DESIGN STORM USED FOR THIS ALAYSIS IS THE 10 YEAR STORM.

****

INPUT THE FOLLOWING DATA FOR EACH SUB-WATERSHED

SUBWATERSHED NUMBER 1

AREA	400	ACRES
SLOPE	3	%
LENGTH	6200	FEET
% IMPERVIOUS	25	%
% CHANNELIZED	30	%
CURVE NUMBER	83	

SUBWATERSHED NUMBER 2

AREA	450	ACRES
SLOPE	4	%
LENGTH	7000	FEET
% IMPERVIOUS	30	%
% CHANNELIZED	25	%
CURVE NUMBER	86	

****

The model then calculates the peak discharge and hydrographs using the S.C.S. with the standard Type II curve or the special curves developed for the State of Florida. The user is then asked if he or she would like to

rout these hydrographs through a series of channels and
reservoirs. In the routing analysis the watershed is
divided into a series of members (channels and/or
reservoirs) for analysis. Following is an example data
stream that would be required to run the routing portion of
the model.

DO YOU WANT TO INPUT STORAGE IN CUBIC FEET OR ACRE FEET?
AF

DO YOU WANT TO USE A DATA SET ALREADY STORED IN A FILE? N
(The model allows the user to store data streams on files
for later use so these data do not have to be input each
time the model is used.)

ENTER TOTAL NUMBER OF MEMBERS IN THE ANALYSIS   4

ENTER NUMBER OF RESERVORIS   1

ENTER NUMBER OF TIME PERIODS FOR ROUTING   50

ENTER TIME STEP FOR ROUTING (HOURS)   .196

ENTER MEMBER NUMBER, X AND K FOR EACH CHANNEL
(X and K are Muskingum storage constants.)

1, .15, 1.5
2, .20, .95
3, .12, 1.25

ENTER RESERVOIR NUMBER AND NUMBER OF RATING CURVE VALUES

4, 5

ENTER STAGE, DISCHARGE, AND STORAGE FOR THE RESERVOIR

0, 0, 0
2, 300, 4
4, 700, 10
8, 1000, 25

ENTER MEMBERS FLOWING INTO MEMBER 2

0

ENTER MEMBERS FLOWING INTO MEMBER 3

1, 2

ENTER MEMBERS FLOWING INTO MEMBER 4

3
****

The routing model then routes the inflow hydrographs through the channel and reservoir system and prints out the time, inflow hydrograph, and outflow hydrograph for each member and the volume and stage for all reservoirs. The model then allows the user to change any of the input data items and run the model again.

CLOSING COMMENT

City and county governments in Georagia have been developing and using hydrologic-hydraulic computer models since the early 1970's. These models have ranged from simple hydrologic models on programmable calculators to state of the art models on large computer systems. Today the availability and use of personal computers is encouraging the development of models that can be used on these systems. Local governments and many consultants have a need for such models for the analysis and design of stormwater management facilities. The HYDROS model described in this paper is one such model which will be added to the other models that are now available to communities in Georgia and the southeast.

APPENDIX I. - REFERENCES

Debo T.N. "Drainage Planning in Camden County, Georgia", Public Works, 1984.

Debo, T.N. and G.N. Day "Economic Model for Urban Watesheds", Journal of the Hydraulics Division, ASCE 106, No. HY 4, 1980.

Debo, T.N. and B.O. Ulrich "Storm Water Management Program is Model for Others", Public Works, Volume 3, 1977.

Haggen, R.J. "Flood Routing on a Small Computer", Civil Engineering, ASCE, March 1983.

Kent, K.M. "A Method for Estimating Volume and Rate of Runoff in Small Watersheds", U. S. Department of Agriculture, Soil Conservation Service, SCS-TP-149, 1968.

Lumb, A.M. and L.D. James "Runoff Files for Flood Hydrograph Simulation", Journal of the Hydraulics Division, ASCE, 102, No. HY 10, 1976.

Micro Use in Water Management in the Brazos Basin

Sheryl L. Franklin

The Brazos River Authority, an agency of the State of Texas created to conserve and develop the surface waters of the 42,000 square mile (110,000 km) Brazos River Basin, is in the midst of a long term project to effectively integrate the use of microcomputers into the daily operation of water supply operations and reservoir control. The project consists of three major phases: automated data collection, data management and data analysis, performed to the greatest extent possible on its sixteen bit microcomputers using commercially available software. Applications programs are being developed to permit operation by personnel with little or no computer knowledge.

Introduction: The Basin and The Brazos River Authority

The Brazos Basin contains 42,000 square miles (110,000 km^2) and runs NW-SE across the central part of Texas as depicted in Figure 1. Although the basin is not heavily urbanized at present - the 1980 population was 1.53 million - Dallas, Fort Worth, Austin and Houston, with a combined 1980 population in excess of 3.13 million, lie within 30 miles (50 km) of the basin divide. The overall economy of the basin is based principally on agriculture, agribusiness, manufacturing and mineral production and processing. Principal crops include cotton, sorghums, vegetables, soybeans, peanuts and rice. Manufacturing activities include processing of oilseed, manufacture of earth-moving and farm equipment, mobile homes, glass products, tires, furniture, clothing and rocket fuel. Mineral activities include oil, gas, stone, cement, sand, gravel, clay, salt and sulphur production. In 1980, municipalities used 290 thousand acre-feet (360 x 10^6 m^3) of water (58% from surface supplies) manufacturing used 209.5 thousand acre-feet (260 x 10^6 m^3) of water (95% from surface supplies), and irrigation of 2.6 million acres (1 x 10^6 ha) used 3.4 million acre-feet (4 x 10 m) of water (124 thousand acre feet (150 x 10^6m^3) from surface supplies).

The Brazos River Authority (The "Authority") was created in 1929 to conserve and develop the surface waters of the basin. As such, it was one of the first agencies in the country to have jurisdiction over an entire river basin. Today the Authority has water resource management responsibility in twelve major reservoirs in the Brazos Basin containing conservation storage in excess of 2,100,000 acre-feet (2.5 x 10^9m^3). Figure 2 is a schematic representation of the

Water Resources Planner, Brazos River Authority, 4400 Cobbs Drive, Waco, Texas 76710.

basin reservoir system. Nine of these reservoirs have flood control
and two produce hydropower in addition to their water supply
purposes. Engineering studies are nearly complete on the feasibility
of developing two additional reservoirs and retrofitting hydropower
to an existing reservoir. Nine of the twelve reservoirs are operated
by the Fort Worth District of the U.S. Army Corps of Engineers with
water supply releases and withdrawals controlled by the Authority.
In addition to its three reservoirs, the Authority owns and operates
an integrated 200 mile (320 km) canal system in the Houston-Galveston
Gulf Coast area to convey water primarily for irrigation (rice), industrial (oil refining) and municipal (water supply) uses. Additional Authority activities include the operation of three regional
sewage treatment plants, water quality studies and water supply development studies for areas throughout the Brazos Basin.

The Project

     In order to more effectively manage its surface water supplies
in the basin, the Authority is in the midst of a project to integrate
microcomputers into the daily operations of water supply operations
and reservoir control. The goals of the project are two-fold: (1)
to develop programs on a microcomputer to obtain and reproduce in a
useful form the mass of data necessary to represent the daily status
of the Brazos Basin and (2) to use this data as input to develop a
daily simulation model to more effectively utilize and conserve this
water.   The programs are designed to be run in a network environment

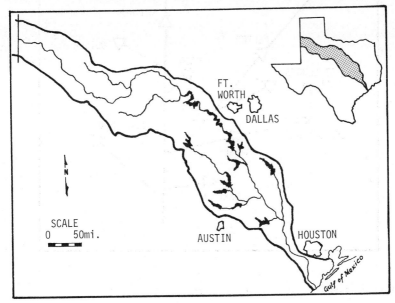

Figure 1 The Brazos River Basin
(1 mi = 1.61 km)

by operations or management staff with little or no computer experience from a terminal or micro on their desk. The project is being developed in three phases: in Phase I access of and successful file transfers between the federal (Corps of Engineers (COE) and U. S. Geological Survey (USGS)) and state (Texas Natural Resources Information System) agency computers are to be completed; in Phase II a database management program is to be written so that both the in-house and remote data files can be read, the data manipulated and daily reports of the river and reservoir status produced; and in Phase III simulation models will be developed to help manage the waters more efficiently.

A commercial software program is used to communicate between the dissimilar micros, minis and mainframes accessed. Programs have been developed which permit the operator to access the appropriate

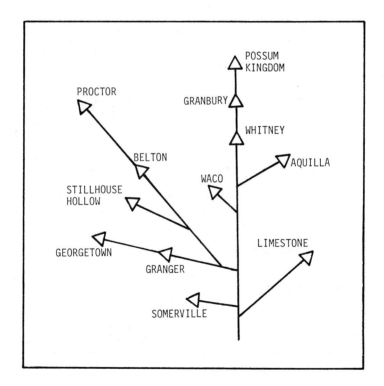

Figure 2   Schematic of the Brazos River Basin

computer and retrieve the data by answering simple yes or no questions; no knowledge of the host computer's operating system is necessary. A second, commercially-available database software package is
being used to design the databases, manipulate the data and produce
the reports. These programs are operated through a series of menus,
again requiring little computer knowledge on the part of the operator. The simulation models are being developed in-house using our
micros and communications programs to access a remote mainframe.
Once the simulation models have completed the testing phase, they
will be revised to run the mini, if possible.

Data Collection: Interagency Computer Links

    Hardware. The Authority owns two sixteen bit IBM compatible
micros, an Eagle 1600 and an AT&T PC6300, both with 256K memory and
dual floppy disk drives. Purchase of a minicomputer to increase
storage and run the simulation models is planned for next fiscal year
(starting September 1985). The Authority's computers are connected,
via a modem over computer grade telephone lines, with four other computers, in Austin or Fort Worth for data collection. In order to
reduce long distance telephone charges the Authority has obtained
foreign exchange line, which provide a local Fort Worth (or Austin)
lines at our Waco office.

    Real Time Data. Data concerning the stage of 24 streamgages
are collected daily during normal operations and as frequently as
hourly during flood events. Many of these stations are currently,
and by the time of publication all are scheduled to be, serviced by
data collection platforms (DCP) which transmit the data to a satellite. The Authority retrieves this data from a satellite downlink
connected to the COE computer in Fort Worth or the USGS Texas District Office computer in Austin.

    Daily summaries concerning the status of the nine federal reser-
voirs are retrieved daily from the COE computer. These summaries include information such as actual releases made, amount of evaporative
loss and reservoir elevation. There is still daily verbal communication between the agencies regarding requested water supply releases
from conservation storage, summaries of the Authority's reservoir operation and similar business. During COE flood operations regular
verbal communication regarding releases is maintained. The Authority
only controls flood operations on its three reservoirs.

    Historical Data. The Texas Natural Resources Information System
(TNRIS), located in Austin, is a major repository of historical data.
Data which the Authority uses includes historical hydrologic data,
water quality data, population projections, water rights and historical usage. In addition, the Texas Department of Water Resources
(TDWR) has many computer programs which are available to the Authority, such as reservoir operations, firm yield, and economic analysis.

    Communications   Software. A   commercially   available com-
munications package for 16 bit microcomputers is used to establish

communication between the Authority micros and the mainframes and
minis of other agencies. Two types of files may be run in this application environment; communications files to set the communications
parameters such as parity, number of data bits and stop bits as well
as auto dialing the phone number; and "program" files which can be
used to automate the session with the host computer. Program files
issue preprogrammed commands to the host computer and thereby eliminate the need for the Authority's micro operator to know or understand
the operating system of the host. These files are most useful for
repetitive sessions, such retrieving streamflow data every morning,
where little flexibility is needed and the session may proceed
through answering simple questions such as "For which day of the week
do you desire date?" and "Are you ready to log off?". The program
language is a pseudo-English language easily learned by one familiar
with programming. A semi-skilled operator is necessary for those
situations which require more interaction between host and operator.

Turning Data Into Information

    Once the raw data is accessed and stored on a floppy disk, it
must be processed to convert it to a more usable form. Since the
Authority uses data for many different purposes, many different applications programs, are used. A spreadsheet program is used for
budgeting and planning projections. BASIC programs are used for simple data manipulation and to convert data files into the format
needed to enter them into the database management files. A database
program is used to store, retrieve and manipulate the mass of daily
data used for operations. A companion paper, "DBase III, Micros and
Water Resource Management", describes in greater detail the database
programs. The rest of this section will merely outline the types of
work performed by the programs.

    One of the main purposes of the database program is to aid in
the determination of the daily basin status. As such, information of
importance includes the daily amount of water stored in the reservoirs, the flow rates in the rivers at various points, the amount of
water requested for diversions and relevant climatic conditions.
Since the Authority sells water, accounting must be kept of total
contracted water and total amount released to that contract for each
of the contracts. Annual water reports, showing monthly water use
are required by TDWR for the purposes of administrating water rights.
In addition, the Authority, in some cases, is not the most senior
water right holder in the basin and must generate complex reports
apportioning releases to dedicated contract releases, flow pass
through, flood releases and spills.

    The database management programs are divided into database
files, which store data, and programs to manipulate the data. Most
programs perform relatively simple data manipulation since much of
the operation is in the general form of a water balance. Early in
the design of the database programs it was decided to represent the
more complex and frequently changing relationships, such as river
stage-discharge, reservoir elevation-capacity and elevation-area, in

array rather than equation form. This required developing a methodology to manipulate database files in a matrix-type array foreign to
the database concept. This methodology is described in the companion
paper mentioned previously.

The database programs can be initiated from a menu environment
permitting operation by personnel unfamiliar with either the programs
or computers. The most common information requested concerning the
system has menu options to permit automatic issue of the reports.
Less common, though still somewhat frequent, reports can be created
by a series of menus walking the operator through the report generating sequence by selected questions. A fairly knowledgable operator
is still required for more unusual reports.

Analysis and Evaluation of Information

The ultimate goal of the computer project is the more efficient
use and conservation of the surface waters of the basin. On a daily
operating basis this means being able to evaluate the effects of specific release policies. In a basin as large and complex as the
Brazos, simulation models provide the best means of obtaining this
information.

Three types of simulation models are planned. Monthly models
will be used for in-house evaluation of operating rules, preliminary
yield studies to evaluate the effects of additional construction,
water quality determinations and to develop target levels for lake
surface elevations to approximate optimal operating levels to be used
in daily simulation models. These models are to be used primarily as
a means to evaluate operating rules. A second model will simulate
daily unregulated river flows to enable the Authority to better evaluate channel losses and travel times for the basin. The final model
will simulate the daily operation of the reservoirs.

These three models will work together to permit an early recognition of potential floods, the development of a flood disaster mitigation release policy, the development of a drought mitigation release policy, an "optimal" normal operation policy and help determine
the effects of retrofitting hydropower.

The long range goals of the project is to be able to determine
the short-term risk associated with a given selected release pattern
to meet a demand. Using stochastic hydrology, multiple sequences of
potential daily flow will be routed through the system and the final
state of the system at some short-term horizon (2 to 4 weeks) determined. When evaluated in a system operations mode such information
can provide notification of potential shortages in time to instigate
conservation measures or it may indicate the advisability of additional releases to lower lake levels in anticipation of heavy inflows.

Conclusions:

The Brazos River Authority is actively engaged in a project to integrate the use of microcomputers into the daily operations of water supply operations and reservoir control. The project was developed to retrieve, manipulate and store the data necessary to effectively manage the waters of the Brazos Basin. Commercially available software has been used, with applications programs written in-house for the specific needs of the Authority. Minimal computer literacy is necessary to obtain the most commonly requested information.

dBase III is a trademark of Ashton-Tate.

Use of Spreadsheets in Stormwater Modeling

Dr. Ronald L. Rossmiller, M ASCE*

Abstract

The use of microcomputers is becoming more and more prevalent in both large and small design offices as their first cost continues to decrease, as their capabilities continue to increase, and as software becomes more available. One particular type of software, spreadsheets, has the potential to have a large impact on rural and urban stormwater modeling. The reasons for this are discussed and examples are used to illustrate a few of the simpler types of stormwater problems which can be modeled using spreadsheets.

Introduction

Many small civil engineering firms, cities, and counties have acquired microcomputers in the last few years. Many types of work that they do do not require sophisticated software packages. Many of their tasks can be accomplished with the use of spreadsheets that they can develop themselves.

There are also many small civil engineering firms, cities, and counties just acquiring their first microcomputers. They may have little, if any, expertise in their use, no expertise in programming, and little confidence in applying available software. Spreadsheets are a non-threatening way to become acquainted with their new machines and to develop their own simple application packages without having to learn a programming language.

They can develop several simple spreadsheets that model both rural and urban stormwater problems and as their confidence grows, develop more complex spreadsheets in stormwater modeling and other areas as well. They might then be encouraged to buy some other software packages that fit their needs and are able to handle more complex situations. However, until that time, many of the design needs of a small firm and local levels of government can be done using spreadsheets. The reasons for this are discussed below.

Reasons for Using Spreadsheets

The knowledge of how to develop a spreadsheet can be acquired much more quickly than that needed to model the same process by writing a computer program. This is important to novice users because they can be successful the first day they use their new computers. By learning

*Associate Professor, Department of Civil Engineering, 351 Town Engineering Building, Iowa State University, Ames, Iowa 50011.

a few basics about spreadsheets, they can develop a simple spreadsheet
and be looking at formatted output the first day.

A spreadsheet consists of a matrix of rows and columns. Each cell
within the grid is designated by a row and column number (R10C4). Each
can be filled with a heading, number, equation, and/or logical expression. References to other cells allow previously determined variables
to be used in another equation. For example, several land uses might
have been combined to determine an average runoff coefficient in one
part of a spreadsheet which is then stored in R10C4. R10C5 might contain an equation for rainfall intensity. The drainage area might be
input to R10C6. The equation in R10C7 would reference the previous
three columns in the same row to determine the peak flow rate.

A computer program is essentially a black box. If someone other
than the developer of the program runs it, the user has no real feeling
for how the program modeled the process. On the other hand, a spreadsheet allows the user to see the flow of the process from beginning to
end. This gives the user more confidence in the spreadsheet and the
results obtained from it. In addition, a spreadsheet aids in the
understanding of the process being modeled because (1) it is developed
in the same manner that the problem is solved using manual methods;
(2) the user can see the relationship between the various portions of
the process; and (3) the filling in of the numbers in the cells is
sometimes slow enough that the user can follow the solution process on
the screen.

A spreadsheet facilitates asking "what if" questions. By changing
a single input, the effects of this change can be quickly seen. In
addition, its effect on each part of the process is displayed, thus
giving the user a better understanding of how the process works and the
sensitivity of the process to various changes. For instance, how much
shallower will the water be in an open channel for the design flow rate
if the roughness coefficient in Manning's equation is reduced from
0.030 to 0.015? Is this decrease in depth worth the additional cost of
the lining? Will the decrease in depth reduce the required right-of-
way width? Another "what if" question is how much deeper will the
water be in a detention pond if the size of the outlet storm sewer is
decreased one, two, or three sizes? Is the decrease in the cost of the
storm sewer offset by increased costs of whatever kind for the detention basin?

The form of spreadsheets is such that the output is ready for
inclusion in a report. By doing some planning at the beginning, the
developer of the spreadsheet can break the entire spreadsheet into
convenient pieces such that each piece is a page in a report with
suitable margins.

Examples of Spreadsheets

The results of designing for stormwater control in rural and
urban areas are usually structures such as culverts, storm sewers, and/
or detention basins. This requires the estimation of rainfall, the
runoff from this rainfall event as a peak flow rate or hydrograph, the
routing of the hydrograph, the sizing of conveyance and/or detention

structures, and the cost of the system.

Table 1 is the spreadsheet for the development of the working curve for reservoir routing. This curve integrates a depth-storage relation and a depth-outflow relation and is used in conjunction with an inflow hydrograph in a routing procedure to define the outflow hydrograph from a detention basin. The storage volume in column 2 and the outflow rate in column 3 could be the results of calculations made in another portion of the total spreadsheet.

Tables 2, 3, and 4 comprise a much more complex spreadsheet. Many communities across the United States have passed ordinances which require that peak flow rates after development has occurred should be no more than they were prior to development. This spreadsheet estimates the volume of temporary storage required to reduce the after-development rate to the pre-development rate and is based on the Soil Conservation Service (SCS) Technical Release Number 55 (TR-55) methodology (1).

Normally in Table 2, the precipitation would be the same for both the existing and developed conditions and the SCS curve numbers would be different for these two conditions. However, in this case the curve number is for the developed condition and the rainfall amounts represent the 5-year and 100-year, 24-hour amounts, respectively. These rainfall amounts were used because the outflow from the detention pond is limited by the capacity of the downstream channel which is about the 5-year event. The drainage area and precipitation amounts are input items. The curve number could have been calculated in another part of the spreadsheet.

The flow paths are used to estimate a time of concentration for the watershed using Fig. 3-1 in TR-55 (1). The length and slope of each flow path are inputs and are obtained from watershed maps. The "number" is obtained from Table 3 according to the type of flow path and is used in an equation, based on Fig. 3-1 in TR-55 (1), which yields the velocity of flow.

In Table 4, the runoff volume and time of concentration are calculated from equations contained in TR-55 (1). The unit peak flow rate is determined using the time of concentration in an equation which is based on Fig. 5-2 in TR-55 (1). The peak flow rate in cubic feet per second (cfs) is obtained by multiplying the unit peak flow rate by the drainage area and the runoff volume. The release rate is an input which in this case is the peak flow from the 5-year event.

The storage needed is based on the use of either Fig. 7-1 or Fig. 7-2 in TR-55 (1). The type of outlet and release rate in cubic feet per second per square mile (CSM) are used to determine whether Fig. 7-1 or Fig. 7-2 should be utilized. This decision, Fig. 7-1, and Fig. 7-2 are contained in the following equation that is located in the cell which displays the needed storage of 16.9 acre feet (20.8 km^3).

Table 1.—Working Curve for Reservoir Routing

DELTA T =   0.1

ELEVATION FT.	STORAGE AC. FT.	OUTFLOW CFS	2S/DELT + O CFS
178	0.00	0.0	0
179	0.01	10.0	12
180	0.12	26.0	55
181	0.50	48.0	169
182	1.30	68.0	383
183	2.49	86.0	690
184	4.06	100.0	1084
185	6.06	115.0	1584
186	8.34	128.0	2150
187	10.75	140.0	2746
188	13.33	240.0	3471
189	16.12	260.0	4167
190	19.10	280.0	4910

Table 2.—Input Data for Detention Basin Sizing

	WATERSHED CONDITION	
ITEM	EXISTING	DEVELOPED
DRAINAGE AREA SQ. MI.	0.23	0.23
PRECIPITATION, IN. 100-YR, 24-HR	4.00	6.50
CURVE NUMBER	90	90
FLOW PATH		
1. NUMBER	3.07	3.07
LENGTH, FT.	800	800
SLOPE, PERCENT	1.80	1.80
VELOCITY, FPS	0.95	0.95
2. NUMBER	6.96	6.96
LENGTH, FT.	2800	2800
SLOPE, PERCENT	1.30	1.30
VELOCITY, FPS	1.73	1.73
3. NUMBER	1.00	1.00
LENGTH, FT.	0	0
SLOPE, PERCENT	1.00	1.00
VELOCITY, FPS	0.25	0.25
4. NUMBER	1.00	1.00
LENGTH, FT.	0	0
SLOPE, PERCENT	1.00	1.00
VELOCITY, FPS	0.25	0.25

Table 3.—"Number" for Velocity Equation

NUMBER	DESCRIPTION
1.00	FOREST W/ HEAVY GROUND LITTER AND MEADOW
1.97	FALLOW OR MINIMUM TILL CULTIVATION
3.07	SHORT GRASS PASTURE AND LAWN
4.44	NEARLY BARE GROUND
6.96	GRASSED WATERWAY
9.36	PAVED AREA (SHEET FLOW) AND SHALLOW GUTTER FLOW

Table 4.—Estimating Detention Basin Storage Volume Required

| ITEM | WATERSHED CONDITION | |
	EXISTING	DEVELOPED
PRECIPITATION, IN. 100-YR, 24-HR	4.00	6.50
RUNOFF VOLUME, IN. 100-YR, 24-HR	2.92	5.33
TIME OF CONCENTRATION HR.	0.68	0.68
UNIT PEAK FLOW RATE CSM/IN.	420	420
PEAK FLOW RATE, CFS (Qin)	282	516
TYPE OF OUTLET WEIR = 1, PIPE = 2	2	
RELEASE RATE, CFS (Qout) , CSM	280 1217	
(Qout/Qin)	0.54	
STORAGE NEEDED AC. FT.	16.9	

Table 5.——Project Cost Sheet

ITEM	UNITS	AMOUNT	UNIT PRICE	TOTAL
12" RCP	lin. ft.	600	$15.00	$9000.00
18" RCP	lin. ft.	100	$18.00	$1800.00
24" RCP	lin. ft.	200	$23.00	$4600.00
30" RCP	lin. ft.	100	$30.00	$3000.00
36" RCP	lin. ft.	100	$40.00	$4000.00
42" RCP	lin. ft.	200	$50.00	$10000.00
48" RCP	lin. ft.	200	$66.00	$13200.00
MANHOLE	each	12	$1200.00	$14400.00
CATCH BASIN – TYPE 1	each	6	$1400.00	$8400.00
CATCH BASIN – TYPE 2	each	10	$1900.00	$19000.00
TOTAL				$87400.00

=IF(OR(AND(R[-8]C=1,R[-4]C<=150),AND(R[-8]C=2,R[-4]C<=300)),170.7*
R[-23]C[-5]*(R[-20]C[+1])^(0.83*(R[-4]C^0.13)/(R[-4]C)^0.49,(IF(
R[-2]C<=0.35,15.2*R[-20]C[+1]*R[-23]C[-5]/(R[-2]C)^0.323,7.52*
R[-20]C[+1]*R[-23]C[-5]/(R[-2]C)^0.993)))

Table 5 is an example of another simple, but useful, spreadsheet.
Every project requires a cost estimate. Each type of project includes
bid items which are similar from one project to the next. Individual
spreadsheets can be set up for each type of project with the item,
units, and unit price columns filled in. As updated cost information
is received, the unit price column for that item can be changed. Initially, the amount column can have zeros in each row. As the numbers
for a project are entered into the amount column, the total column for
each item and the grand total for the project are automatically filled
in because of the equations previously placed in the total column. The
equation for the total cost of each item is "=RC[-2]*RC[-1]". The
equation for the total project cost is "=Sum(R[-20]C:R[-2]C)". A
printout of this spreadsheet is ready for inclusion in the project file
and/or report.

These few examples are just a small sample of the many types of
stormwater related problems which can be modeled using spreadsheets.
Some of these others include peak flow rate determination using various
methods, normal and critical depth calculations, water surface profiles
in prismatic channels, culvert performance curves, pipe culvert design,
box culvert design, tapered inlet culvert design, inflow hydrograph
determination using various methods, reservoir routing, channel routing
using various methods, depth of flow in streets of various cross
sections, percent of flow captured by storm sewer inlets, connector
pipe design, and storm sewer design.

Summary

Microcomputers can be found in more and more design offices in
both the private and public sectors. This is because their price
continues to decrease as their capabilities and software availability
continue to increase. One type of software, spreadsheets, has the
potential to have a large impact on rural and urban stormwater modeling.
This is especially true for those small firms and agencies with little
or no experience with microcomputers. The reasons for this include the
level of knowledge needed to develop a spreadsheet, confidence in the
results obtained because of the manner in which spreadsheets are developed, the ease with which "what if" questions can be answered, and the
fact that printed output is ready for inclusion in a report. A few
examples of the types of stormwater related problems that can be addressed using spreadsheets were discussed. These are only the tip of
the iceberg in terms of the many problems that can be solved using
spreadsheets.

Appendix

1. "Urban Hydrology for Small Watersheds," Technical Release No. 55,
   Soil Conservation Service, 1975.

GEOGRAPHIC AND SPATIAL DATA MANAGEMENT AND MODELING

By Walter M. Grayman,[1] M. ASCE

ABSTRACT: A geographic information system is a computer based
technology for storing and using spatial data. Many alternative
methodologies exist for managing the three general types of spatial
data: areal data, terrain data, and network data. The primary uses for
spatial data, mapping and modeling, have been applied extensively in
the area of water resources.

INTRODUCTION

In most areas of analysis and modeling in the field of water
resources, the data and processes contain a geographic component. In
other words, in addition to the concepts of what and how much a piece
of data represents, the "where" of the data is important. Information
with a geographic component is referred to as "spatial" data and
computer based systems that have been developed for managing spatial
data are referred to as "geographic information systems" (GIS).

MODELING VS. MAPPING

The use of spatial data management within civil engineering
applications in general, and water resources planning and management in
particularly, has been predominantly in the arenas of modeling and
mapping. Though these two areas frequently are addressed together and
in fact are commonly present in many studies, the demands of these two
areas in terms of spatial data handling are quite different.

In the mapping area, the primary objective is to capture spatial
data from source mappage and to utilize the computer and a graphics
display mechanism to manipulate this data and to produce maps. The
level of detail that is required generally relates to the final use and
scale of the maps to be produced. Computer aided drafting is
frequently used for mapping, but is not usually considered to be
spatial data management.

In modeling, it is generally required to know the location of a
particular piece of information, and in addition, to know the
geographic relationship of that piece of information to other pieces of
information. For example, in the area of hydrologic modeling, it is
not sufficient to know what is happening to a drop of water at a
particular point; one must also know what is in the vicinity of that
point so that the transport of that drop may be predicted. The
mechanism for relating the spatial interrelationships is referred to as
the topological structure of the data base.

W.M. Grayman Consulting Engineer, Cincinnati, OH 45229

SPATIAL CONCEPTS

In its most basic form, all spatial data may be represented by a
point, line, or area; in advanced cases, a three dimensional solid
object may be used. Examples of these basic forms in the area of water
resources include the following:

* points - well locations, stream sampling points
* lines - streams, sewers, water pipes
* areas - drainage basins, political jurisdictions
* three dimensional objects - subsurface geologic structures

In geographic information systems it is common to group these
basic elements into higher order application oriented systems. Three
major groupings are areal data systems, terrain data systems, and
network data systems.

Areal data includes political and most physical data found on
thematic maps or captured through remote sensing techniques. Terrain
data refers to topographic information describing the land surfaces.
The third category, network data systems, includes information on
natural or man made systems such as rivers, pipe networks and roads.

REPRESENTATION OF AREAL INFORMATION

The representation, use and mapping of areal data has been the
primary application of geographic information and mapping systems for
the past two decades. In most cases, the base source mappage is a map
of an area depicting the geographic entities (physical or political)
and the boundaries between these entities. In recent years, products
derived by remote sensing have become another popular source of areal
data.

A common method of capturing and storing areal information is the
digitization and representation of the boundaries. Most mapping
systems, which require high quality representation of boundaries, use
methods which are generically referred to as polygon methods with a
polygon being defined as the area bounded by a complete boundary. In
pure mapping systems, the boundaries need only be a series of chains
(piece-wise linear collection of connected points) which when plotted
result in a holistic map. The World Data Bank (3) developed by the CIA
and frequently used for plotting world physical and political
boundaries is an example of such a polygon mapping system. In those
cases where some form of manipulation or analysis is required, a
topological structure is needed. Typically, a topologically structured
polygon system is constructed using a combination of nodes at the
junction of two boundaries, segments or chains defined as the
boundaries between two nodes, and polygons which may be defined by the
series of segments which together form the polygon boundary.
Frequently, a degree of redundancy is included by identifying the
polygons on each side of each segment. Such redundancy serves as a
check of the integrity of the representation and improves efficiency in
many analysis and mapping functions. The complete topological

representation of an area using a polygon system is illustrated in Figure 1.

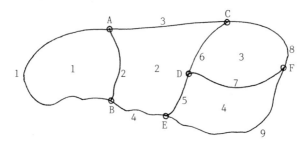

CHAIN DESCRIPTION:

CHAIN NO.	START NODE	END NODE	LEFT POLYGON	RIGHT POLYGON
1	B	A	–	1
2	A	B	2	1
3	A	C	–	2
4	B	E	2	–
5	D	E	4	2
6	D	C	2	3
7	F	D	4	3
8	C	F	–	3
9	F	E	–	4

POLYGON DESCRIPTION:

POLYGON NO.	CHAINS (IN CLOCKWISE ORDER)				
1	1	2			
2	3	6	5	4	2
3	8	7	6		
4	7	9	5		

Figure 1   Example Topologic Representation by a Polygon System

USGS has digitized major political and physical boundaries and features from 1:2,000,000 scale maps and these are available in a topologically structured form (5). The same agency is also currently preparing such digital data bases (known as digital line graphs or DLG) from smaller scale maps.

Though excellent for high quality representation of boundaries, polygon systems have limited capabilities in most analysis and modeling applications. Several other mechanisms for storing data in a form more compatible with analysis and modeling have evolved. These methods are illustrated in Figure 2 and described below.

The regular grid method, shown in Figure 2-b is the most commonly used method for storing and using spatial data. In fact, many GIS take advantage of the superior data capture capability of a polygon system and the better analysis capabilities of the regular grid through

a) Polygon Representation

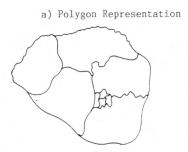

b) Regular Grid

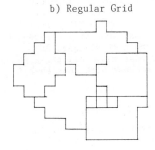

c) Quadtree

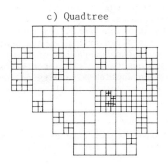

d) Run Length Encoding

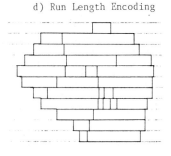

e) Triangulated Irregular Network

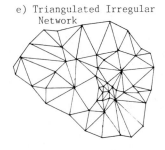

Figure 2   Alternative Methods for Representing Areal Data

a polygon-to-grid process which converts polygon data to a grid format. In use of a regular grid, an important decision concerns the selection of the grid size. If a grid is too gross, then boundaries may not be adequately represented. Smaller grids result in a much larger amount of data which must be stored and manipulated.

During the past decade, much attention has been spent on designing methods that have the superior data manipulation capabilities of a regular grid system but allow areas to be represented at different scales based on the degree of detail present. These systems are referred to generically as variable resolution methods. The three most common variable resolution methodologies are the quadtrees, run length encoding, and the triangulated irregular network (TIN). These methods are illustrated in Figure 2-c, d, and e.

In the quadtree methodology, a regular grid is placed over an area. For those parts where more detail is required, a grid box may be divided into four smaller grids, and this process replicated until the required amount of detail is achieved. In the run length encoding process, a regular set of rows are defined and within each row, the points at which boundaries occur are marked. In the TIN structure, irregular sized triangles are designed so that some triangle boundaries represent the boundaries of the base map and all triangles are homogeneous to the characteristics of the base map. All three methods have been applied with varying levels of success with none emerging as a clear cut answer to all problems.

DIGITAL TERRAIN MODELS

A particular type of area data that is present in many applications is terrain data. A geographic information system component designed specifically for use in storing and manipulating terrain data is referred to as a digital terrain model (DTM) or a digital elevation model (DEM). Several structures, akin to the structures described for areal information, have been used for terrain information. These methods include regular grids, irregular points, triangulated irregular networks, and contour representation.

The use of a regular grid has the same benefits that are present in representing other areal data: ease of storage and use. However, limitations include the large amount of work required to manually convert a map into a regular grid and the variable resolution problem. Additionally, many applications require a continuous surface representation which requires further conversion of a regular grid. USGS distributes regular gridded digital elevation models based on the 1:250,000 scale maps of the U.S.(9). Some smaller scale maps are also being produced by USGS in the same format. A data set of irregularly spaced points of elevation (with the points selected to represent key topographic features) is easier to create but suffers from the same deficiency in not providing a continuous surface. Digitization of contour lines, with either manual or automatic digitizing, is another procedure which requires further surface definition. A frequently used method is the creation of a triangulated irregular network from a data base of irregularly spaced points using a mathematical technique called

Delaunay triangulation (2). This effectively creates a continuous surface representation which may be used for mapping or analysis. This irregular grid may also be sampled at regular intervals to create a regular grid.

The representation of topography continues to be a developing field with improvements in capturing, storing and displaying terrain information occurring.

NETWORK INFORMATION

Another class of spatial data is information related to networks. This category of information is quite prevalent in the area of water resources including stream networks and pipe networks.

Networks are composed of a group of segments generally referred to as links, chains, reaches, segments, etc. In most network representations, a link node approach is used as illustrated in Figure 3-a.

a) Elements of a Link-Node System

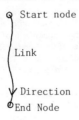

Start node

Link

Direction
End Node

b) Tree Structure   c) Looping Structure

Figure 3   Network Representation

A link is a section which may be either a straight line,

piecewise-linear, or a curve defined by a start node and an end node. Topological data structuresare common, in which the links used by each node and/or the links adjacent to each link are known. A network may be either directed or non-directed. In a directed network, each link has a direction and the end nodes may be referred to as the upstream or start node and the downstream or end node. Stream networks and sewer networks are examples of directed networks. Non-directed networks have no innate direction. Water distribution systems and road networks may be treated as directed or non-directed networks.

Networks may be further defined by their branching characteristics. Most stream networks are defined as tree structured networks as illustrated in Figure 3-b. In a tree structured network, links are directed and their is no more than one outlet link from a node and no loops exist. In a looping network (Figure 3-c), neither restriction is necessary. Road networks and water distribution systems are examples of looping networks. Because of the various restrictions, storage and handling of tree structures is easier.

APPLICATIONS IN WATER RESOURCES

The concepts of geographic information systems and related mapping and modeling have been applied quite widely in the area of water resources planning and management. Many examples of such applications are described in the Proceedings of the ASCE Conference "The Planning and Engineering Interface with a Modernized Land Data System" (8) and the ASAE "Hydrologic Transport Modeling Symposium" (1).

During the mid-1970's, GIS technology was used quite widely as part of regional water quality management (section 303 and 208 of Public Law 92-500) for suitability analysis, mapping, and hydrologic and non-point source modeling. Similarly, many states set up state-wide geographic data bases to assist in their programs. Federal agencies that have developed GIS technologies in the area of water resources include the Hydrologic Engineering Center with their HEC-SAM system (4) for flood plain analysis, EPA with its Reach File (6) for storing and using stream-related data, and the Fish and Wildlife Service's MOSS (7) for environmental impact analysis. Within the past few years a trend has existed to move some of these technologies to smaller computers so that they are available to local agencies and private consulting engineers.

CONCLUSIONS

The field of geographic data handling, mapping, and modeling has been an evolving field for the past two decades and one that continues to develop. The geographic information system has proven to be a potentially valuable organizing concept for spatial data in the field of water resources and an effective method of parameterizing and utilizing models requiring spatial data.

APPENDIX I.-REFERENCES

1. American Society of Agricultural Engineers, "Hydrologic Transport Modeling Symposium", Proceedings ASAE, St. Joseph, Mich., 1979

2. Boots, B.N., "Delaunay Triangles: An Alternative Approach to Point Pattern Analysis",Proc. Assoc. of Amer. Geog.,Pages 26-29, 1974

3. Central Intelligence Agency, "CAM-Cartographic Automatic Mapping Program Documentation", CIA, Washington, D.C.,1977

4. Davis, D.W.,"Flood Mitigation Planning Using HEC-SAM", U.S. Army Corps of Engineers, Hydrologic Engineering Center Tech. Rep. No. 73, Davis, CA,1980

5. Domaratz, M.A., et al,"Digital Line Graphs for 1:2,000,000 Scale Maps", USGS Circular 895-D, Reston, VA,1983

6. Horn, C.R. and W.M. Grayman, "National and Local Modeling of Water Quality Using the EPA Reach File and Related Data",presented at the June 10-12,1985 ASCE Specialty Conference on Computer Applications in Water Resources, held at Buffalo, N.Y.

7. Lee, J.E., Editor, "MOSS User´s Manual", Fish and Wildlife Service, Washington, DC, 1983

8. Marks, G.W., Editor, "The Planning and Engineering Interface with a Modernized Land Data System", Conference Proceedings, ASCE, New York, NY, 1980

9. USGS, "Digital Terrain Tapes User Guide", U.S. Dept. of the Interior, Washington, DC,1979

A Micro-Computer GIS for
Water Resources Planning

Richard H. Berich,* P.E., A.M. ASCE

ABSTRACT: Recent developments in micro-computers have enabled
water resources engineers to utilize advanced computer methods and
interactive color graphics for the analysis and planning of water
resources projects. A micro-computer based Geographic Information
System (GIS) offers even small consulting firms and government
agencies an affordable and powerful tool for analysis of both
geographic and demographic data as well as computation of hydrologic parameters for watershed modeling. Some of the specific
features of the micro-computer GIS include:

1)   Polygon, line, and point digitizing, raster (grid cell)
      conversion, and color display.

2)   Interactive color screen updating.

3)   Statistics, overlay, combination, and distance analyses.

4)   Computation of the Soil Conservation Service (SCS) runoff
      curve numbers and lag times and Snyder's lag coefficient.

5)   Presentation quality color slides, including titles, pie
      charts, and three-dimensional displays.

6)   Mouse-driven menu and file management.

7)   Dot matrix printer output of graphic images and scaled
      plotter maps.

8)   Incorporation of LANDSAT and external digital data into
      GIS.

Several applications of the GIS are examined including watershed
hydrologic modeling and interfacing with the SCS TR-20, and Corps
of Engineers (COE) HEC-1 hydrology models, water supply reservoir
site selection, and ground water resource analysis.

* Associate, Purdum and Jeschke, Consulting Engineers, 1029 North
Calvert Street, Baltimore, MD 21202.

INTRODUCTION

Planners and engineers recognize the need for the accurate transfer of data between analysts. They also recognize that the maintenance and updating of a data base is also important for its efficient reuse on various projects. It is this reuse of the data base that often justifies the substantial investment in its creation. Unfortunately, many water resources projects involve creation of map data that is not easily updatable or reusable for other applications. Maps are limited by a fixed scale and the inability to create overlays of more than a few variables. The accuracy of the analysis of map data is limited by manual measurement methods which are subject to random errors. A microcomputer based Geographic Information System (GIS) offers a practical solution to these problems.

A GIS is a digital cartographic data system used for the creation, analysis, updating, and transfer of map data. GIS computer systems are not new. Some, such as SYMAP and IMGRID were developed in the late 1960's and early 1970's at Harvard University and are widely used by planning agencies and academic institutions. These systems and many later generations of similar systems such as GRID by Environmental Systems Research Institute (ESRI) require either main frame or minicomputer capabilities. This has meant a substantial investment in hardware for the user. The dramatic improvements in the storage, computing capabilities, and interactive color graphics of microcomputers in the last three years, however, has made the GIS available to a much broader range of potential users both in the public and private sectors. Many planners and engineers who will comprise this new user group are not familiar with the concepts and capabilities of GIS. This paper will define several of the basic functions common in many GIS's, discuss some of the particular features of a current microcomputer based GIS, and describe several applications in the field of water resources planning.

THE BASICS

Geographic Information Systems store and analyze digital map data in raster form. A raster was originally defined as the area on which a video picture is displayed; however, when used with reference to a GIS file system, the term is synonymous with grid cells. Generally, the raster data is stored in individual files for each variable type. These may be raster files of soil types, land cover classifications, zoning, drainage areas, population density, or any other map data. The primary functions within the GIS involve the creation of raster files, the statistical analysis of the variables within one or more raster file, and the display of raster file maps on a color monitor, dot matrix printer, or plotting devise.

The method of entering data into the GIS varies and will be the major factor in determining the cost of data base creation. The basic forms of data entry into a GIS include:

1)   Individual cell encoding
2)   Table digitizing

3) Video digitizing
4) Remote sensing imagery

Early GIS programs required the user to manually encode variables for each grid cell through standard 80-column entry forms and punched data cards.

An improvement over individual cell encoding is achieved through the use of a digitizer. A digitizer is a table or board with an internal grid that converts the location of a pointer (cursor) into computer-readable coordinates. Polygon digitizing significantly reduces the time required for data entry as compared to manual encoding. The vertices of data polygons are entered by the digitizer which are in turn converted to grid cell (raster) files by the computer. Another advantage of polygon digitizing is that the user can select alternate cell sizes for later analyses. Since the original data is stored in polygon form, it may be converted to raster files of any size grid cell.

Improvements in color separation and filtering have recently enabled GIS digital raster data to be entered through the use of a video camera (1). Color coded maps are scanned by a video camera and the data converted to raster files. This process further reduces the time for data entry as well as the opportunity for human error.

The last form of data entry into a GIS is through the use of remote sensing imagery such as LANDSAT, aerial photography or laser imagery. LANDSAT data has been shown to be well suited for water resources applications involving identification of watershed land cover related parameters by Ragan and Jackson (2) and the Corps of Engineers (3). Like LANDSAT, aerial photography and laser imagery are also suited for large volume data base creation.

Once a raster data base is created, the GIS calculates statistics for each of the variables within the file. Several files can be analyzed simultaneously to produce pair-wise combinations, multiple overlays, and a number of other useful statistics. The GIS analysis may be used for a wide range of planning projects limited only by the availability and accuracy of the original map data. The original raster data as well as analysis results are generally displayed on a color video monitor while hard copies are produced on a dot matrix printer or pen plotter.

An important feature of most GIS's is their file updating capability. Maintenance of the data file is important for its reuse on later projects. Updating is accomplished by redigitizing map changes which change the original polygons or by direct editing of the raster files using the color monitor.

A MICRO-COMPUTER-BASED GIS

The IRIS GIS produced by Aeronca Electronics, Inc. of Charlotte, North Carolina is a current micro-computer based GIS. The hardware configuration consists of an IBM PC, or compatible, with hard disk or an IBM XT with a high resolution RGB color monitor, monochrome text monitor, digitizer, dot matrix graphics printer, and mouse controller.

The system, which sells for less than $20,000, is suitable for pro-
duction applications and utilizes mouse-driven menu, interactive color
graphics. The following is a brief description of some of the primary
functions.

1) Polygon, line, and point digitizing, raster (grid cell)
   conversion, and color display.

   The entry of map data into polygon files is accomplished using
   polygon, line, or point digitizing. For each of these
   methods, coordinates are stored by variable code number. An
   example would be a file of soil types converted to integer
   code where each code number represents a particular soil. The
   polygon files are then converted to grid cells of a user
   defined size and stored in raster files for each variable
   type. Typical water resources projects might involve creation
   of watershed subbasin code files, land cover files, hydrologic
   soil files, and slope category files. The final raster files
   are displayed on the color monitor at several user selected
   magnifications or to a specified scale on the graphics printer
   or plotter.

2) Interactive color screen updating.

   Updates or changes can be made to the raster files by digitizing new polygons or using the mouse to make changes on the
   color screen display. The mouse updating is similar to the
   digitizer entry with choices of polygon, line, or point updating. Grid cell row and column number, screen coordinates,
   and data base coordinates (UTM, state, or local coordinates)
   are displayed at all positions of the mouse cursor. All
   changes are subsequently added to the original raster file.

3) Statistics, overlay, combination, indexing, and distance
   analyses.

   Statistics are calculated for each raster file and printed in
   report format on an 8-1/2" x 11" sheet. Summary information
   includes the name of the file, number of rows and columns of
   the raster file, the coordinate of the upper left cell in the
   raster file, the dimensions of the cell and its area, the code
   numbers and names of all the variables in the file along with
   the total number of cells, area, and percent of total for each
   variable type.

   Two or more raster files can be overlaid to create a separate
   raster file with combinations of values from the original
   files. An example of the overlay feature would be an identification of what existing land use is found in one particular
   zoning classification. This analysis would overlay the
   existing land use raster file with the zoning raster file.
   Another application may be to identify the percentages of each
   soil type for existing croplands.

Pair-wise combinations of variables can be analyzed using two files. For this analysis the GIS identifies where combinations of variables from two raster files coexist. An example is a land use change analysis for LANDSAT classifications of 1974 and 1984 for a particular jurisdiction. Both raster files have the same land use codes, values 1 through 8. The GIS creates a matrix of possible combinations as shown in Figure 1. The analysis results in creation of a raster file with values from 1 to 64. Each value represents the location where pair-wise combinations exist between both the 1974 and 1984 raster files. For instance, a final value of 9 indicates a grid cell that has a land cover value of 1 in 1974 and 2 in 1984. If value 1 represents agricultural land and value 2 represents low density residential land; the cell, therefore, has changed from agricultural to low density residential in the period between 1974 and 1984. It may be seen that the values on the diagonal (1, 10, 19, 28, 37, 46, 55, and 64) indicate a no change condition between the two land cover files.

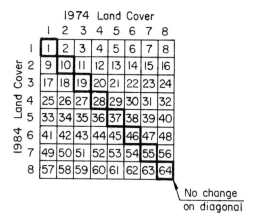

Figure 1.   Land Cover Change Analysis

The GIS can be used for suitability analyses using a procedure called indexing. Indexing involves the analysis of several raster files simultaneously to select and rank suitability based on a predetermined weighting. The weighting is in the following form:

$$I = C_1 V_1 + C_2 V_2 + C_3 V_3 + \ldots C_n V_n$$

in which I = index value
C_x = weighting coefficient
V_x = variable codes in separate data (raster) files

The variables in each file are recoded based on levels of desirability. An example may be soil erodibility with soil value 1 representing the most erodible soil and value 5 representing the least erodible soil. The weighting coefficients are selected by the user and represent the relative importance of each variable in the analysis. The resulting index value I is calculated for each cell and a new raster file map is created depicting the variation in suitability for the project area.

The GIS can create a raster file of distances from any cell value. The distance is measured in cell units. Figure 2 shows a search from value 7 in 3 cell units. Cells numbered 7 are the original value. Cells numbered 1 are within one cell distance from the value 7, cells numbered 2 are within two cells of the value 7, and so forth. The value 7 in this example may represent a stream, roadway, or other linear value. The search function is not limited, however, to linear variables. It may also be used to analyze noise levels from an airport, proximity to reservoirs, or distance from a particular zoning type.

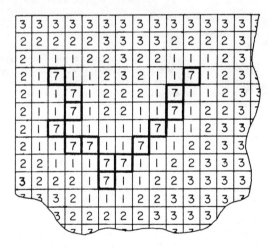

Figure 2. Distance Search

4)   Computation of the Soil Conservation Service (SCS) runoff curve numbers and lag times and the Snyder's lag coefficient.

The GIS provides an automated calculation for SCS runoff curve numbers which are widely used for hydrologic modeling of watersheds using the SCS TR-20 (5) and the Corps of Engineers HEC-1 (4) computer models. The runoff curve number calculation requires a land use raster file or zoning file, an SCS hydrologic soil group raster file, and a raster file of watershed subbasins. A summary report is printed that includes the area and percentage of land use and hydrologic soil types for each subbasin. The weighted curve number is calculated for each subbasin as well as the SCS lag time if average subbasin slopes are provided.

5)   Presentation quality color slides, including titles, pie charts, and three dimensional displays.

A 35 mm camera set on a tripod approximately six to ten feet from the color monitor will take excellent quality color slides and prints. The GIS mouse-driven menu and keyboard will allow the user to write text labels using several fonts to the graphic screen as well as construct color pie charts automatically proportioned to the percentage of each value in the raster file.

An additional feature using the color graphics monitor is the three-dimensional display of raster data. The file can be portrayed with user defined horizontal rotation, vertical angle, and height separation between file values. All graphic displays can be stored separately for future recall or copying.

6)   Mouse-driven menu and file management.

The IRIS GIS software is modular and runs within a main menu program on the monochrome monitor. The user simply points to a function and, using the buttons on the mouse, either executes the selected function or asks for help menus which describe that particular function. The raster file names are listed in a main library or multiple libraries of the user's choice. This will allow each project to have separate file libraries and provide rapid access to all data.

7)   Dot matrix printer output of graphic images and statistical data.

A dot matrix printer or color ink jet printer is used to create gray tone or color pictures of the graphics screen display. In addition to making hard copies of the graphics screen, two methods are available for producing maps at a scale determined by the user. The first uses the dot matrix printer in grey tones. A raster file of any size is printed in slices beginning at the upper left corner of the raster file. If the raster file is too large to fit on the paper another slice is made beginning where the first slice ended. The process continues until the file is completed. The slices may be attached to give a scaled map.

The second method of mapping is produced by a plotter. Raster files are plotted at a scale selected by the user.

8) Incorporation of LANDSAT and external digital data into the
    GIS.

    Many existing digital data bases can be utilized by IRIS GIS.
    The U.S. Geological Survey provides LANDSAT satellite imagery
    (6) and digital terrain data (7). The Soil Conservation
    Service provides digital soil data in some areas. Many local
    planning agencies also maintain digital data bases that may be
    useful for a variety of water resources projects. It is often
    necessary to reformat the data so that it is readable by the
    GIS software and the IBM PC/XT. The cost of reformatting
    data, however, is a small fraction of the cost of its
    re-creation.

EXAMPLE APPLICATIONS

1) Watershed Hydrologic Modeling

    The development of a rainfall-runoff hydrologic model such as
    SCS TR-20 or COE HEC-1 for watersheds over 2,000 acres has
    been a labor intensive task. It is not uncommon for 50 to 70
    percent of the project budget to be expended on the hydrologic
    modeling. This is especially true if the subbasins are
    numerous and multiple land use periods must be considered.

    For this example project the GIS is used to create raster
    files for all of the land surface characteristics including
    subbasins, existing land use, and zoning. The cost of LANDSAT
    land cover classifications as an alternative to digitizing
    existing land use maps should also be evaluated. The SCS soil
    types may be first classified into hydrologic soil groups and
    then digitized, or the actual soil types may be digitized
    directly. Digitizing the actual soil type requires more
    effort, but the data base is more useful for other
    applications. The actual soil classes, if digitized, may be
    recorded into separate files of SCS slopes and hydrologic soil
    groups.

    The SCS runoff curve numbers for existing and future land uses
    are calculated by the GIS using both existing land use and
    zoning raster files. The slope file may be used to compute
    SCS basin lag to estimate times of concentration. Subbasin
    areas, runoff curve numbers, and times of concentration are
    all input directly into either TR-20 or HEC-1.

2) Water Supply Reservoir Site Selection

    Potential reservoir sites for an expansion of the water supply
    for a county are to be identified. The site selection
    criteria have been determined to be the following:

    1) V_1 = Value of land

    2) V_2 = Disruption of wetland habitat

3) V_3 = Within 1,000 feet of a stream with a minimum drainage area of one square mile

4) V_4 = Land slope

5) V_5 = Soil permeability

6) V_6 = Distance from industrial zoned land

7) V_7 = Distance from major existing water transmission mains

The data base creation for this project includes the following tasks: recoding an existing zoning data base created for a watershed study to land cost values, digitizing and searching from streams with drainage areas greater than one square mile, and digitizing and searching from major water transmission mains. The remaining variables are derived from previous watershed projects which include existing land use files for wetlands, a recoded soil file for slopes and permeability, and a zoning file.

The analysis is performed using the indexing procedure to locate potential sites based on the following weighting:

$$I = (4*V_1)+(1*V_2)+(10*V_3)+(2*V_4)+(1*V_5)+(2*V_6)+(4*V_7)$$

When all variables are assigned values in ascending order of desirability the index value I represents the relative suitability of possible locations. A raster file is constructed by the GIS that has values of I. Potential reservoir sites are selected from locations having high index values.

3) Ground Water Resource Analyses

In order to plan future municipal water and sewerage facilities, planners intend to identify potential residential growth areas overlying soils that are unsuitable for septic systems or inadequate aquifers. It has been determined that future growth will likely occur within three miles of four major regional highways. The data files required are:

a)   Existing land use file taken from a previous study.

b)   Soil file taken from a previous study and recoded to suitability for septic systems.

c)   Zoning file from a previous study.

d)   Digitized U.S.G.S. groundwater availability maps.

e)   Digitized major regional highways and a search to identify areas within three miles.

The zoning file (#1) and existing land files (#2) are first overlain to identify undeveloped residential land (#1/2). Then this file (#1/2) is overlaid on the highway file (#3) to identify all undeveloped residential land lying within three miles of the major highways (#3/2/1). The specific areas that are unsuitable for septic system are found by overlaying this resulting file (#3/2/1) on the soil septic system suitability file. The specific areas that are unsuitable for individual well supply are identified by overlaying this same file (#3/2/1) and the U.S.G.S. groundwater availability maps. Both final maps (raster files) identify the most likely areas for future municipal utility systems.

SUMMARY

The development of low cost micro-computer based Geographic Information Systems such as IRIS GIS has made available a powerful planning and analysis tool for a broad spectrum of governmental agencies and private consulting firms. The micro-computer GIS takes advantage of recent developments in high resolution color graphics, digitized polygon data entry, and interactive menus for file creation, updating, and analysis. The GIS will justify the creation of data bases that can be shared by planners and engineers and reused on many varied projects. The results will be major cost savings, improved clarity of data transfer, and greater accuracy.

REFERENCES

1. Godfrey, K.A., Jr., "Rationalizing Land Records, Mapping, Planning," Civil Engineering, ASCE, Vol. 55, No. 2, p. 54, February 1985.

2. Ragan, Robert M., and Jackson, Thomas J., "Runoff Synthesis Using LANDSAT and SCS Model," Journal of the Hydraulics Division, ASCE, Vol. 106, No. HY5, Proc. Paper 15387, pp. 667-678, May, 1980.

3. U.S. Army Corps of Engineers, The Hydrologic Engineering Center, Davis, CA, Determination of Land Use from LANDSAT Imagery: Applications to Hydrologic Modeling, Research Note No. 7, November 1979.

4. U.S. Army Corps of Engineers, The Hydrologic Engineers Center (HEC), Water Resources Support Center, Davis, CA, HEC-1 Flood Hydrograph Package, 1981.

5. U.S. Department of Agriculture, Soil Conservation Service, Computer Program for Project Formulation Hydrology, Technical Release No. 20 (TR-20), May 1965.

6. U.S. Geological Survey, EROS Data Center, Sioux Falls, SD 57198.

7. U.S. Geological Survey, National Cartographic Mapping Center, 507 National Center, Reston, VA 22092.

Water Resources Applications of OCAP--Ohio's CNRIS

Robert L. Vertrees

Abstract

The Ohio Capability Analysis Program (OCAP) is a computer-based natural resources information system (CNRIS) operated since 1973 by the Ohio Department of Natural Resources (ODNR). The legislatively created purposes of OCAP are: ". . . to produce a natural resource inventory of Ohio and to provide technical resource information to people at the local level who make land use decisions" (4). By January, 1985 OCAP data bases for capability analysis purposes had been established for 33 of Ohio's 88 counties. These data bases typically include information about soils, groundwater availability, flood prone areas, geologic conditions, land use/land cover, and boundaries of natural and historical areas and governmental units.

The three basic purposes of this paper are: (1) to classify applications of OCAP to water and related land resources planning and management, (2) to briefly describe how these applications have used OCAP data bases and software programs, and, most importantly, (3) to document the importance of classifying users and applications of state-operated CNRIS in the light of today's fiscal restraints. The major conclusions are: (1) that in today's fiscal setting there are definite practical reasons for and benefits to be gained from scientifically classifying users and applications of governmentally operated CNRIS, and (2) that insofar as state-operated CNRIS are concerned these benefits have yet to be gained because little has been done to classify their users and applications and to share such information among states.

Introduction to CNRIS

The development and application of CNRIS represents a major innovation in natural resources planning and management that has taken place since the mid-1960s. CNRIS are used to organize, analyze, and display quantitative geographically referenced information about the natural resource base and human uses of and impacts upon that base. These systems have been initiated in many countries by governmental agencies, planning organizations, universities, and private research, consulting, or land management companies (2,3,7,8,12,13). CNRIS allow previously developed methods of natural resources planning, research, field

*Asst. Professor, School of Natural Resources, The Ohio State University, Columbus, Ohio 43210.
Salaries and research support provided by State and Federal Funds appropriated to the Ohio Agricultural Research and Development Center at The Ohio State University. OARDC Journal Article No. 47-85.

management, policy administration, or policy analysis to be accomplished much faster. New methods can be explored and, when found to be feasible, developed and implemented (7,14).

By 1980, approximately thirty state governments had either explored the possibilities of initiating a CNRIS or had begun to operate one. The systems of five of these states, including the first begun in 1966 by New York, had gone out of existence by 1980 because of lack of state funding or renewal of enabling legislation. In 1981, nineteen states operated a CNRIS or had one under development. Among the sixteen states with operational systems, Ohio is one of several that stresses the role of the systems in providing data services to governmental agencies or units (2,8). Among these states, Ohio appears to place the greatest emphasis upon providing services to local units of government and local planning organizations (8,12).

Introduction to OCAP and
Its Fiscal Situation

In keeping with the purpose of serving local decision-makers, ODNR shares the costs of establishing OCAP data bases and of producing OCAP outputs with local governments or planning organizations. A cost-sharing cooperative agreement is entered to establish data bases and to provide outputs to the units or organizations (4). Data included in the original data bases established for these initial users are available (with a few exceptions) for use by subsequent users of the original data bases. Subsequent users of OCAP include state and federal agencies, university researchers, private consultants, private land-owners, and others. They pay the full cost of OCAP services. By being able to make use of original data bases, OCAP costs are held down for subsequent users because the creation of data bases usually is the most costly of OCAP services. Subsequent users can have supplemental data bases created for their own particular purposes (14,15).

Since the creation of OCAP in 1973, appropriated state general revenue funds have been the primary source of support for the acquisition of OCAP hardware and specialized equipment, for the development of software, for the payment of staff salaries and wages, and for office operations. Appropriated funds have also been used to pay the state's share of the costs of developing original data bases and of providing outputs under cooperative agreements with counties, other local governments, and planning organizations. In recent years, these state appropriations have been reduced, and personnel ceilings have been established. (The information now being given about OCAP's fiscal situation was obtained from interviews with OCAP administrators.)

Categorical federal planning grants authorized by Section 701 of the Housing Act of 1954, as amended, were used by local governments and regional planning organizations to pay their share of the costs of developing original data bases and obtaining outputs under the cooperative agreements. After termination of these grants in the early 1980s, most of the locally borne share of the costs of developing full-scale data bases for capability analysis purposes has come from county general revenue funds. (One county's share came from a community development block grant.) Compared to the years when "701" grants were

available, fewer full-scale capability analysis projects are now underway at any given time.

Whereas fewer cooperative-agreement cost-sharing projects have been
initiated in recent years, two other types of users and applications
have been on the increase. The auditors of several counties have used
discretionary or "earmarked" funds at their disposal for the purpose of
appraising property values to pay for the entire costs of using OCAP in
assessing the current agricultural use value of farmland. Also, a
greater share of OCAP applications is now represented by subsequent
users of original data bases. The user charges paid by subsequent users
recover the full costs of using OCAP. These users apply OCAP in a variety of ways including, but not limited to, capability analysis projects.

In sum, OCAP's fiscal environment can be characterized as including:
(1) the termination of categorical federal planning grants, (2) some
reduction in state appropriations necessitated by factors such as inflation, the need to increase state outlays for unemployment compensation
and other social service programs because of relatively high unemployment rates, and the reluctance of voters to support tax increases, and
(3) the need to find alternative sources of revenue such as through
increased reliance upon user charges. This fiscal environment is not
unique to OCAP or to other governmentally operated CNRIS. Rather, it
characterizes the general situation that has faced governments and governmental programs at all levels (10,16).

Reasons for Classifying
Users and Applications

In the light of the foregoing, two reasons stand out for classifying CNRIS users and applications:

1. Such classifications are needed to evaluate how different types
of users who apply CNRIS in various ways respond to alternative revenue
mechanisms, such as user charges. These mechanisms should be judged
according to their legal, administrative, elasticity, stability, and
neutrality implications (16).

2. Faced with today's fiscal restraints, administrators of CNRIS
must know types of users and applications in order to fully and effectively document CNRIS benefits. Lawmakers and other decision-makers
require and expect such information from CNRIS administrators and from
CNRIS users.

Other reasons can be gleaned from the literature about CNRIS design
and operation (2,3,7,12,13). The ideal system shown on Figure 1 is
based upon this literature and upon the author's experience in using
OCAP. The system is driven jointly by opportunities to improve management of land and water resources and the applications by users who know
about those opportunities. Research must be conducted to identify such
opportunities and how they can be met through new applications. Other
research is needed to survey CNRIS users to determine their needs for
specific data and outputs that require specialized data processing
procedures and equipment.

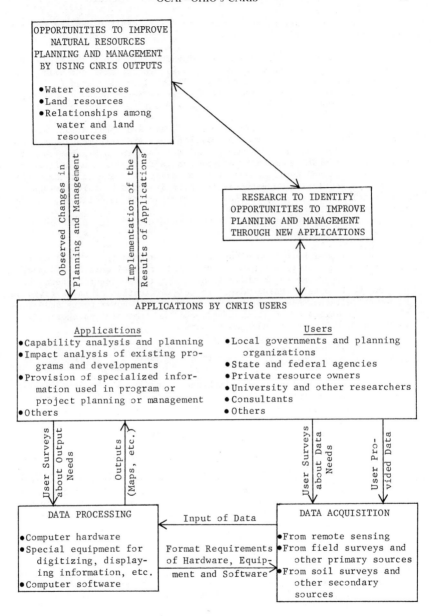

Figure 1. Flowchart of Ideal Relationships among Components
and Users of a Computer-Based Natural Resources
Information System (CNRIS)

A third and a fourth reason for classifying CNRIS users and applications can be identified from Figure 1:

3. By classifying users and by informing them about the types of applications made by others, formerly developed applications will be put to more use and ideas for new applications will be generated (7,14). Thus, system benefits will increase and can be documented as more opportunities are met to improve resource management.

4. Well designed classifications of users and applications are vital to structuring the types of user surveys and research about opportunities to improve resource management referred to on Figure 1. Along this line, it must be emphasized that unstructured lists of different types of users and applications or a few examples drawn at random from the entire population do not comprise well designed classifications. The principles of scientific classification should be followed, such as those given by Hempel (6).

Classifications of Users

Users of OCAP have been classified above according to: (1) whether they are initial users who have established original data bases under cost-sharing agreements, or (2) whether they are subsequent users who pay the full costs of using OCAP. The classification of users given on Figure 1 reflects this same breakdown. The local governments and planning organizations are initial users, and the remaining categories represent most types of subsequent users.

OCAP Outputs, Data Bases, and
Relevant Software Programs

OCAP outputs include: (1) black-and-white or colored computer maps, together with information given in a legend, and (2) tabular summaries or cross-summaries of data. The legend of maps includes a table of the number of cells and acres as well as the per cent of the entire map included in each of the designated map categories (4).

A classification of OCAP applications is provided on Table 1. It is important to note that these are virtually all applications to water and related land resources. Applications to land resources with no direct relationship to water resources are not included. "Not having a direct relationship to water resources" usually means that an application did not involve use of any of the information in an OCAP data base that applies to water resources.

The full implications of the types of applications shown on Table 1 can be realized by reviewing the range of information included in a typical original data base created for a full-scale capability analysis project by an initial user. Detailed soils information is usually the most comprehensive information included therein. The external attribute file that pertains to different soil mapping units contains soil limitation ratings applicable to: susceptibility to flooding, drainage, depth to seasonal water table, permeability, available water capacity, potential frost action, shrink-swell potential, erosion factors "K" and "T", erosion potential, corrosion potential for steel and concrete, depth to bedrock, per cent of slope, stoniness and rockiness, texture, horizon depths, two engineering texture classes, agricultural capability classes, and limitations for different land uses. Many of these ratings apply to water resources in their close relationship with soil resources and their uses.

Other information typically incorporated in these original data bases includes information about groundwater availability; flood prone areas; bedrock geology, depth to bedrock, and glacial or surficial geology; and various boundaries, including boundaries of local governmental units and zoning districts, boundaries of natural, historical, or archaeological areas, and boundaries of census tracts, traffic zones, watersheds, and areas served by various public services and utilities including water supply and wastewater treatment utilities. The information in these data bases about groundwater availability, flood prone areas, and boundaries of watersheds and water-related utility service areas joins the aforementioned information about soils as being most associated with water resources.

Approximately twenty software programs have been written for OCAP. Eleven perform operations on data bases, and are mainly of interest to OCAP personnel. OCAP users need to know the basic functions of most of the other programs. However, for the purpose of understanding Table 1, only three programs need to be considered that directly apply to the type of output received (as compared to the boundaries, scales, or other features of outputs).

The OGRE program is used to develop tabular summaries and cross-summaries of information and data printed without an accompanying computer map. The name "OGRE" represents the frustration of the programmer who wrote it (4). The various types of OCAP maps result from using either the MAP or the SEARCH programs.

The MAP program is flexible and complex. It includes nine electives or options, and is used in conjunction with several other programs that establish map boundaries, scales, and other features. The electives that apply to different types of capability analyses are applicable to understanding Table 1.

The simplist method of capability analysis involves the mapping of soil limitation ratings associated with different soil mapping units. These ratings come directly from the external attribute file for soils.

The second method makes use of the overlay elective. The computer "overlays" or combines information about any two mapping units in order to depict all possible combinations of category levels for the two mapping units.

The most complex method of capability analysis involves development of a mathematical model to rate the capability of the resource base of a designated area to support a particular land use. The land use is the dependent variable, and independent variables providing information about different mapping units are incorporated into the model. A numerical weight is assigned to each independent variable to indicate how it contributes to the capability to support the land use being rated.

Table 1.   Classification of Applications of OCAP to Water and Related
            Land Resources Planning and Management

I. Capability Analysis. Applications involving analysis of the capa-
    bility of the resource base to support various uses.

    A. Identification of areas with potential for residential, com-
        mercial, industrial, or other types of development. (Many
        users.)
        1. Areas served by public water and sewer utilities.
        2. Areas not served by public water and sewer utilities.
            a. Suitability for septic tank absorption fields.
            b. Groundwater yields.

    B. Identification of sites for the construction or upgrading
        of wastewater treatment plants and of the environmental
        impacts upon surrounding areas. (Miami Valley Region report.)

    C. Identification of areas suited for the on-land treatment and
        disposal of sewage sludge from wastewater treatment plants.
        (Ashland County report, Delaware County report, and other
        reports.)

    D. Identification of areas suited for sanitary landfills with
        the least potential for flooding and polluting groundwater.
        (Clark County report, Franklin County report, and other
        reports.)

    E. Planning of land uses in areas affected by the development,
        use, and/or protection of nearby surface waters.
        1. Corridors along streams. (Big Darby Creek report.)
        2. Lands near reservoirs. (Alum Creek Reservoir report.)
        3. Lake Erie coastal area. (Lake Erie Coastal Area report.)

II. Ex Post and Counterfactual Impact Analysis. An application by
    the author involving: (1) the ex post analysis of effects upon
    land use of existing water and sewer lines extended into a
    rapidly suburbanizing area, and (2) the counterfactual analysis
    of effects upon land use in the same area that might have result-
    ed if the water and sewer lines had been restricted to phased
    zones contiguous to the previously urbanized area. (See refer-
    ences 14 and 15.)

III. Program and Project Planning and Management. Applications involv-
     ing the provision of specialized types of resource information
     used in the planning and management of public programs or pro-
     jects.

     A. The provision of data to identify areas with different soil
         loss potential and different amounts of existing soil loss;
         information is used when planning multi-county nonpoint water
         pollution control strategies. (Northeast Ohio Areawide
         Coordinating Agency report and Miami Valley Region report,
         which only pertains to soil loss potential; also some county
         reports.)

Table 1. Continued

B. Estimation of the effects upon soil loss potential of alternative tillage systems and of stripping construction sites bare of vegetation. (Delaware County report; numerous other county reports also include the analysis of tillage systems.)

C. Estimation of the special property tax assessments to levy upon landowners within different drainage areas in order to pay off county drainage ditch projects. (Wyandot County.)

D. Estimation of the total area drained upstream from old bridges to be totally replaced; information is used when determining the structure size and total costs of new replacement bridges. (Clinton County.)

E. The provision of drainage-area, soils, and land-use data in four selected urban watersheds and the comparison of OCAP-provided data with planimetered data; comparisons were made to demonstrate the feasibility of using OCAP data in urban hydrologic watershed models. (See reference 9.)

The resultant computer map depicts locations of lands with different levels of limitations for the rated land use.

The SEARCH program allows boundaries on a map to be depicted at increasing distances for a single cell, a group of cells, or a line of cells. The locations of various map categories within each range of distances are indicated by different symbols and/or by a color scheme.

Before turning to a further explanation of Table 1, it needs to be said that two of the applications--the author's research (Category II) and the tax assessments (Category III.C)--involved the digitizing of property ownership boundaries into OCAP data bases. Furthermore, the author's research involved editing the land use/land cover information in an original data base to provide information about land use/land cover under pre-development and current conditions. The author's research also involved editing the soils base map to provide information about soils that were built upon or otherwise changed from their natural condition at the time when the detailed soil survey was conducted.

Classification of Applications

The three broad categories in the classification scheme are mutually exclusive and allow for the unique placement of all known applications of OCAP to water and related land resources planning and management. The first two categories are related by the concept of time.

Capability analysis is used when planning ahead for the use of resources. In effect, this is done by predicting the impacts that alternative land uses will have upon the resource base. It results in the selection of those uses that will minimize future impacts because the selected uses are best suited to the limitations of the particular resources. Each of the categories under Category I involved application of one or more of the capability analysis electives summarized above. Furthermore, Category I.B involved use of the SEARCH program.

Category II, the author's use of OCAP (14,15), involved looking back upon the land-use impacts of selected public programs and developments in a rapidly suburbanizing area. This research was inspired by previous ex post or "after-the-fact" analyses in the field of water resources economics (5) and by previous counterfactual analyses in the field of coastal zone planning and management (1). OCAP outputs were used to look back upon the amount and locations of open rural lands and of important farmlands that were actually developed upon under existing conditions. These conditions included construction of a major highway interchange several miles outside of a town and the outward extension of a sewer line and a water line to the interchange area. OCAP outputs were also used to look back in a counterfactual manner upon the amount and locations of open rural lands and of important farmlands that might have been developed upon if alternative policies and developments had been followed. The alternatives would have been designed to guide the location of population growth and of commercial activity to phased zones contiguous to the town. This research involved all three types of capability analysis electives and use of the SEARCH program and OGRE program.

Each category of applications classified within Category III involved the application of OCAP data bases to provide specialized types of information used when planning, administering, and/or managing water and land resources programs or projects. The descriptions of these categories on Table 1, when read in the light of what is said above, are meant to be self explanatory.

Conclusions

The scientific classification of users and applications of CNRIS operated by governmental agencies might be vital to the long-term fiscal and political viability of the systems. This paper has been focused upon state-operated CNRIS. Those state-operated CNRIS, such as OCAP, that serve local governments, planning organizations, and other users that cannot afford to operate their own CNRIS fulfil particularly important functions in natural resources planning and management. Without them, such users might not have access to any other CNRIS.

In the mid-1970s, the Council of State Governments sponsored much research about state natural resources data needs and information systems. See, for instance, references 3 and 11. It was then recommended that states share information about their experiences in designing, initiating, and applying CNRIS and other data management systems. Insofar as CNRIS are concerned, one must conclude that these recommendations have not been carried out. This paper was written to demonstrate how the users and applications of a state-operated CNRIS can be classified and to document practical reasons for doing so. One way of moving toward achievement of the aforementioned recommendation would be to classify the users and applications of other state-operated CNRIS and to establish a network for sharing such information among states.

Appendix.--References

1. Baer, W. C., and Fleming, S.M., "Counterfactual Analysis: An Analytical Tool for Planners," American Institute of Planners Journal, Vol. 42, No. 3, July, 1976, pp. 243-252.
2. Cornwell, S. B., "History and Status of State Natural Resources Systems," Report prepared for the Urban and Regional Information Systems Association, Chicago, Ill., 1981.
3. Council of State Governments, "Environmental Resource Data: Intergovernmental Management Dimensions," the Council, Lexington, Ky., 1978.
4. Gordon, G., "User's Guide to the Ohio Capability Analysis Program," Ohio Department of Natural Resources, Division of Water, Resource Analysis Section, Columbus, Dec., 1978.
5. Haveman, R. H., The Economic Performance of Public Investments: An Ex Post Evaluation of Water Resources Investments, The Johns Hopkins Press for Resources for the Future, Inc., Baltimore, Md., 1972.
6. Hempel, C. G., "Fundamentals of Taxonomy," Scientific Explanation, C. G. Hempel, ed., The Free Press, New York, N.Y., 1965, pp. 137-154.
7. McRae, S., and Shelton, R., "Resource Inventory and Information Systems for Land Use Planning," Guiding Land Use Decisions, D. W. Countryman and D. M. Sofranko, eds., Johns Hopkins University Press, Baltimore, Md., pp. 50-104.
8. Mead, D. A., "Statewide Natural-Resource Information Systems--A Status Report," Journal of Forestry, Vol. 79, No. 6, June, 1981, pp. 369-372.
9. Morris, J. R., "Hydrologic Parameters: Use of Existing Digitized Information," FPPU Report #1-82, Ohio Department of Natural Resources, Division of Water, Flood Plain Planning Unit, June, 1982.
10. Pechman, J. A., Federal Tax Policy, 4th ed., The Brookings Institution, Washington, D.C., 1983.
11. Schneider, W. J., Jr., "State Information Needs for Resource Management," Council of State Governments, Lexington, Ky., 1979.
12. Schneider, D. M., and Amanullah, S., "Computer-Assisted Land Resources Planning," Report No. 339, Planning Advisory Service, American Planning Association, Chicago, Ill., Jan., 1979.
13. Tschanz, J. F., and Kennedy, A. S., "Natural Resource Management Information Systems: A Guide to Design," Argonne National Laboratory, Energy and Environmental Systems Division, Argonne, Ill., July, 1975.
14. Vertrees, R. L., "Using the Ohio Capability Analysis Program (OCAP) to Depict Land-Use Impacts of Public Programs," Technical Papers, 1984 ACSM-ASP Fall Convention, American Society of Photogrammetry and American Congress on Surveying and Mapping, Falls Church, Va., 1984, pp. 345-356.
15. Vertrees, R. L., "Fuller Use of the Ohio Capability Analysis Program," Ohio Report, Vol. 70, No. 1, Jan.-Feb., 1985, The Ohio State University, Ohio Agricultural Research and Development Center, pp. 12-15.
16. Walzer, N., and Chicoine, D. L., eds., Financing State and Local Government in the 1980s: Issues and Trends, Oelgeschlager, Gunn & Hain, Publishers, Inc., Cambridge, Mass., 1981.

Geographic Information Systems:
A Planning Tool
Jim Riley[1] and Lynn J. Bernhard[2]

ABSTRACT

Geographic Information Systems provide an opportunity for water resource planners to examine potential impacts of proposed plans early in the study process. Conflicts can be identified for further study by using a GIS to display and collate information. A GIS has been developed for the Wasatch Front Total Water Management Study in Utah using an existing data base, remote sensing imagery, commercially available geographic data, and unique field gathered data.

Introduction

How many times would planners have benefited from having quick access to reliable, relevant planning data presented in map form during the planning process? Traditional hand drawn thematic maps are costly to prepare. Generally thematic maps are limited to important phases of the planning process because of preparation time and cost. Changes are difficult since the original must be modified by a draftsman or cartographer. Maps prepared in one scale are seldom presented at other scales since the process is complex and error prone. Adding overlays to the original map is easy, but the bulk of overlay media soon negates the overall quality of the map itself. A computer based geographic information system (GIS) provides a reasonable solution to the problem of preparing germane thematic maps early in the planning process.

The State of Utah Division of Water Resources and the U.S. Bureau of Reclamation have recently initiated a joint water management study for the locally-termed "Wasatch Front" area of Utah. The area extends approximately 200 miles along the base of the Wasatch Mountains from the Bear River Basin in north-central Utah, near the Utah, Idaho, and Wyoming borders to the Sevier River Basin in south-central Utah. Within this long, narrow strip of fertile but dry land resides approximately 80 percent of Utah's population.

In some areas of the Wasatch Front, presently developed supplies and planned water developments will be fully developed shortly after the turn of the century. The primary purpose of the Wasatch Front Total Water Management Study is to evaluate the presently developed and

---

[1]M. ASCE, Planning Team Leader, Bureau of Reclamation, P.O. Box 1338, Provo, Utah 84603

[2]M. ASCE, Chief, Engineering Branch, Bureau of Reclamation, P.O. Box 1338, Provo, Utah 84603

potential water supplies along the Wasatch Front in order to achieve
better water management and utilization of the resource.

Along the Wasatch Front, water development is a sensitive topic for
discussion. Due to the diverse interests of people, a water management
study can mean a variety of things. To some it may mean development,
while to others it is interpreted as conservation. Water projects
which are oriented toward stimulating the economy of a region are
presently experiencing difficulties. Whereas some people view additional storage reservoirs and transbasin diversions as the answer to
meeting future water needs, others counter with the argument that
conservation and water reuse should be the focus of attention.

Early discussions with special interest groups concerning the Wasatch
Front Total Water Management Study has rekindled the recreational and
environmental issues relating to instream flow. Many heated debates
stem from the fact that instream flow is not recognized as a beneficial
use. Special interest groups are frustrated that recreation opportunities and environmental issues appear to be an after-thought in
water development projects. In future water planning, they would like
to see recreational and environmental issues placed on parity with
economic development of a region.

A difficult aspect of this particular water management study and of
water resource planning in general, is the task of identifying pertinent resources and usages and defining the relative importance of
each. Data representing these resources and usages are dispersed among
Federal, state, local agencies, universities, and special interest
groups. No coordinated resource data base exists for the entire
Wasatch Front. However, through the use of a geographic information
system, this dispersed data may be integrated into a usable planning
tool.

To aid the water resource planner in the 1980's, and those of us
involved in the Wasatch Front Study in particular, a greater emphasis
will be placed on computer systems to store data for quick and easy
retrieval. Expanded use of computers will permit the following:

- A great many more alternatives or scenarios may be analyzed.

- Impact analyses may be completed quickly.

- More precise technical information may be entered into the planning
process.

- Information may be accessed quickly and displaced in an array of
formats.

- Desired relationships may be graphically displayed.

- Previous studies may be accessed.

- Development of a valid large-scale data base may be facilitated.

- Data becomes available at low cost.

- Interaction between agencies is promoted because of the need or a cooperative effort to develop the data base.

- The planner is able to build his own data base using fragmented bits of information.

- An accurate bibliography may be maintained.

- The analysis of alternatives that resurface several years in the future is facilitated.

- The planner is able to respond more quickly to "what if" questions.

For example, as a part of the Wasatch Front Total Water Management Study, data concerning stream fisheries, elk habitat, mule deer range, and other wildlife concerns is being obtained from Fish and Wildlife agencies. This information has been stored in the computer according to selected boundaries--in our case counties and the State of Utah. Next, the various counties and river basins are depicted graphically to show the effect on wildlife or habitat. These effects can then be scaled to determine impacts which receive consideration during the planning process. To illustrate, the following scenario is presented: An agency is to build a reservoir on a stream. The reservoir site is also an important elk wintering range and the stream is recognized as a fishery of significant value. The reservoir will provide a much-needed surface water recreation area including a flat water fishery.

Due to the varied interests that exist in today's society, the water resource planner needs to be able to answer questions quickly. How much elk habitat will be lost? How many miles of fishery will be lost? What class fishery is it? Using a geographic information system (GIS) the planner could quickly find the answers. Data stored in the GIS data base would be accessed and compared with the proposed reservoir site. Areas of intersections between the competing activities would then be calculated.

Many calculations and data projects would be possible to meet the needs of various planners and analysts. Linear features such as roads, canals, or pipelines could be studied using a "buffer" zone. Potential conflicts or impacts would be determined without extensive field survey. Untenable or environmentally unacceptable schemes could be identified early in the planning cycle. Limited staff time and money could then be directed towards alternatives that   meet political, environmental, and economic criteria.

The data in the GIS must be entered and manipulated before it can be effectively used. The data base preparation is costly. The true worth and economy of using a geographic information system comes when it is used for analysis and results are obtained in hours or days rather than weeks or months. Multiple alternatives can be examined in much shorter time than by using manual methods.

Data bases prepared for studies of the Central Utah Project, Bonneville Unit are being used in the Wasatch Front Total Water Management Study. Stream and fishery data acquired in the Jordan River Basin of central Utah are being used for planning analysis in conjunction with new data obtained specifically for the Wasatch Front study.

Incremental costs for future studies are reduced because the data bases can be enlarged rather than created anew. Digital data from other sources is available for large areas. Digital base cartography from the United States Geological Survey's National Cartographic Information Center (NCIC) has lowered the cost of obtaining both topographic and manmade features for the study area. NCIC has prepared high quality digital terrain models of most of the United States. Digital line graphs of cultural features and hydrography are published in increasing numbers. Remote sensing data can be integrated into the GIS data base. Much valuable information can be derived from satellite imagery and correlated with prior field data to derive previously unavailable analyses.

Water resource planners now have another tool available to them. Geographic Information Systems provide a method where large amounts of seemingly unrelated data can be compared and analyzed without extensive manual file data gathering. Data obtained from previous studies can be reused because now planners are able to manipulate it with computer speed. Human and fiscal resources can be directed towards activities which offer viable study options. The GIS literally opens a window to planners so that they may examine the opportunities for and impacts of water resource development.

STORAGE PROJECTION FOR RESERVOIR SYSTEMS

By Samuel K. Vaugh,[1] A.M. ASCE and David R. Maidment,[2] M. ASCE

ABSTRACT

Two methods are studied for determining the probability distribution of future levels of storage in a reservoir system: transient analysis and Gould's probability matrix method. In transient analysis, historical monthly inflow and net evaporation sequences of 1 to 5 years length are routed through the reservoir system with fixed initial storage, monthly demand pattern, and operating policy to determine the probability distribution of storage in annual time increments for each reservoir and for the total system. In Gould's method, the annual flows are assumed independent and the steady-state probability distribution of storage is found using the same hydrologic data, demand pattern, and operating policy.

These procedures are applied to the six-reservoir Highland Lakes System on the Lower Colorado River, Texas. Autocorrelation of annual inflows is insignificant at the 95% confidence level. For the conditions examined, variance of the probability distribution of storage is a maximum one year into the projection and diminishes thereafter as the results of the transient analysis converge toward their steady-state values. The time reliability of supply of the specified annual demand is evaluated as a function of initial storage.

INTRODUCTION

As surface water demands upon existing storage reservoirs and reservoir systems continue to grow, it is becoming increasingly important for water supply agencies to quantify the possible effects of various withdrawal rates on future storage and to evaluate the reliability that their system can meet future demands. Thus, the prime motivation of this study is the need to provide water supply agencies dependent upon surface water impoundments with an accurate means of investigating some of the ramifications of increasing (or decreasing) supply contracts and modifying system operation policies.

A computer model called PROSTOR (PROjection of STOrage) capable of projecting the probability distribution of reservoir storage for annual time increments into the future has been developed. PROSTOR

---

[1]Grad. Research Asst., Dept. of Civ. Engrg., The Univ. of Texas at Austin, Austin, Texas 78712.

[2]Asst. Prof., Dept. of Civ. Engrg., The Univ. of Texas at Austin, Austin, Texas 78712.

also provides an estimate of the time reliability of the system. In
this case, time reliability is a percentage computed by dividing the
number of months in which demands are met without drawing the storage
below the selected failure level by the total number of months in the
data set. Storage projections are computed for fixed initial
storages, operation policies, water demands, physical system
characteristics, and historical sequences of inflow and net water
surface evaporation.

PROJECTION METHODOLOGY

The program code for PROSTOR uses two projection methods:
transient analysis and Gould's probability matrix method.

(1) Transient Analysis

The computational procedure employed for transient analysis
begins with fixed initial storages in each reservoir and basically
routes historical sequences of hydrologic data through the system.
Given initial storage conditions, system operation rules, monthly
distributions of annual water demands, and a selected forecast period,
a set of possible future storages are computed using a monthly
operation simulation procedure based simply on the principle of
conservation of mass. The monthly mass balancing procedure which
begins at the most upstream reservoir and proceeds downstream may be
expressed as follows:

$$Z_t = Z_{t-1} + I_t - E_t - R_t - S_t$$

where: Z_t = end of month storage
        Z_{t-1} = beginning of month storage
        I_t = inflow during month t
        E_t = net evaporation during month t
        R_t = required release during month t
        S_t = spill during month t

The required release R_t is actually the sum of the products of each
annual demand times its monthly demand fraction times the portion of
the monthly demand to be supplied by the particular reservoir plus any
upstream releases during the current month. The net evaporation
volume E_t is the product of the net water surface evaporation in feet
and the beginning of month water surface area in acres. In the
application of the mass balancing algorithm, it is assumed that the
end of month storage volume in a reservoir may not be less than the
dead storage and that seepage into and leakage from the reservoirs are
negligible. Once the entire system has been operated for the current
month, simulation for the second month begins at the most upstream
reservoir.

The iterative procedure described above is continued until the
end of the specified projection period is reached. At this point, the
ending reservoir and system storages are tabulated, the storage in
each reservoir is reassigned its initial value, and monthly simulation
through the forecast period is performed beginning with the first
month of the second year of historic data. Use of this procedure
inherently assumes that each sequence drawn from the historic data set

is equally likely to occur during the selected projection period. If the projection period is greater than one year, it is assumed that the annual demands on the system as well as their monthly distribution are unchanged. It is also assumed that the use of overlapping hydrologic data sequences in the sequential routing procedure for multi-year projections has no significant effect on the projected probability distribution of storage. Preliminary tests have shown that no significant difference exists between the expected values of system storage computed using overlapping and non-overlapping data sequences for projection periods of 2 and 3 years. Throughout the iterative mass balancing procedure, a so-called "Envelope of Uncertainty" is also tabulated which represents the lowest and highest storages attained in each future month based on the given initial conditions.

Once simulation using each of the available years of historic data has been completed, the set (sample) of projected reservoir and system storages is complete and a probability distribution is fitted to the sample. Note that the number of values in the sample will be equal to the number of years of historic data minus the length of the forecast period plus one. This number is further reduced by one if the specified starting month is not January.

The probability distribution selected to be fitted to the sample of projected storage values is the 3 Parameter Gamma or Pearson Type 3 distribution. This distribution was selected because of its flexibility of functional shape as defined by three parameters and its general applicability in hydrologic frequency analysis. The probability density function for this distribution is presented below (2):

$$p(x) = \frac{1}{\alpha \Gamma(\beta)} \left\{ \frac{x-\gamma}{\alpha} \right\}^{\beta-1} e^{-\left\{ \frac{x-\gamma}{\alpha} \right\}}$$

where: $\beta = (2/C_s)^2$ = shape parameter

$\alpha = S_x/(\beta)^{.5}$ = scale parameter

$\gamma = x - S_x(\beta)^{.5}$ = location parameter

Γ = Gamma function

The determination of each of the above Pearson Type 3 distribution parameters β, α, and γ is based on the sample mean, x, standard deviation, S_x, and coefficient of skewness, C_s. The sample mean is equivalent to the expected value of storage at the end of the forecast period. Using the computed parameter estimates, the cumulative probability up to the top of each storage zone is evaluated and the transition probability associated with each zone is then be computed.

The Chi-Squared Test (1) is employed to test the hypothesis that the distribution fits the sample observations. This is a parametric test which compares the observed number with the expected number (based on the assumed distribution) of observations in a set of class intervals.

Output from the execution of PROSTOR in the transient projection mode is a tabular summary of results both for each major reservoir and the entire system including the following: 1) A listing of the percentage of active storage, actual storage volume, exceedance probability, and transition probability associated with each percentage zone, 2) A listing of the observed and expected number of observations in each zone and the related chi-squared increment, 3) The sample statistics and parameter estimates obtained by the Method of Moments, and 4) A plot of probability of exceedance versus active storage percentage.

(2) Gould's Probability Matrix Method

The probability matrix method developed by B.W. Gould (3) is essentially a modification of the Moran model (3). Advantages of the Gould method over the Moran model include the ability to account for seasonally varying water demands, defined system operation policies, and serial correlation of monthly streamflow volumes. The key assumption inherent in the application of the Gould method is that annual inflow sequences affecting the system are independent or, in effect, serial correlation of annual inflows is equal to zero. Perhaps the best means of understanding the mechanics of this method is to briefly detail its computational procedure.

The active storage volume of each reservoir and the entire system is divided into a number of zones of equal volume. The number of zones (K) required to adequately define the storage-probability relation is determined on the basis of the computed coefficient of variation of the annual inflows. For the Highland Lakes System, it was decided that twelve state zones would formulate the best model. Storage volumes less than or equal to the dead storage and storage volumes greater than or equal to the conservation storage are defined to be in Zone 1 and Zone 12, respectively. Thus, Zones 2 through 11 represent the active storage volume in 10% increments.

The continuity or mass balance equation as presented in the previous section is applied on a monthly basis beginning in any selected month. For each of the 12 starting zones, each of the N years of hydrologic data is considered independently. For each starting zone k and year n, the ending zone (or storage volume one year later) is determined by the repetitive application of the monthly mass balance equation and a tally sheet or matrix is thereby generated. After all routings have been performed, the number of elements in the tally sheet should be N x K (N years of hydrologic data times K zones) with subtotals of N in each column. By then dividing each element by N, a transition matrix is formed which expresses the probability of ending a year in each particular zone given the starting zone for that year.

The transition matrix is subsequently powered up (iteratively multiplied by itself) until the steady-state matrix is determined. When the steady-state condition has been achieved, each column in the matrix will be identical and express the long-term probability of storage being located in any particular zone at the beginning of the selected starting month. Another method of evaluating the steady-state probability distribution which is also based on the same general assumptions has been employed to facilitate comparison with storage projections computed using the methodology described in the previous section. By simply multiplying the transition matrix by a vector expressing the probable distribution of storage in a particular month, a vector expressing the probable distribution of storage one year later is obtained. If the transition matrix is then multiplied by this second vector, the probable distribution of storage two years later is obtained. Continuing this process which will be referred to as the n-step transition matrix procedure, the computed state vector soon approaches the steady-state condition.

Throughout the repetitive application of the continuity equation, an additional tally sheet or vector is accumulated in which the number of months of reservoir or system failure is tabulated for each starting zone. A failure is defined to have occurred when water demands in a particular month cannot be supplied without forcing the ending storage below the defined failure storage volume. In order to compute the probability of failure associated with each starting zone, each value in the vector is divided by the total number of months considered by the routing (12 x N). The time reliability associated with each zone is then computed as one minus the probability of failure.

Output from the execution of PROSTOR in the steady-state analysis mode includes: 1) The ending storage tabulation for each starting zone which ultimately defines the transition matrix, 2) A table summarizing the steady-state probability of occupying any storage zone and the probability of failure associated with each starting zone, and 3) A plot of time reliability versus active storage percentage.

APPLICATION TO THE HIGHLAND LAKES SYSTEM

The Highland Lakes System is located on the Colorado River west of the City of Austin in Central Texas and is owned and operated by the Lower Colorado River Authority (LCRA). The Highland Lakes System is comprised of six reservoirs in series beginning upstream with Buchanan and proceeding downstream through Inks, Lyndon B. Johnson (LBJ), Marble Falls, Travis, and Lake Austin. Only two of these lakes, Buchanan and Travis, are actually depleted on a regular basis to meet downstream water and local power demands whereas the other four essentially maintain a constant storage level. The combined conservation storage pools of Lakes Travis and Buchanan represent approximately 92% of the total system storage.

The most significant use of water supplied by the LCRA is the irrigation of rice fields by four large irrigation companies located near the Gulf Coast which amounts to about 520,000 acre-ft (6.396 X 10^8 m^3) per year. Annual municipal water demands of 90,000 acre-ft (1.107 X 10^8 m^3) for the City of Austin represent the second largest component of the use of Highland Lake System storage. Make-up water averaging 20,000 acre-ft (0.246 X 10^8 m^3) per year for the cooling pond at a power generation facility located near La Grange is also purchased as needed from the LCRA. The relative magnitudes of each of these demand components are 83% irrigation, 14% municipal, and 3% for cooling pond make-up. The monthly distribution of total annual demands was computed for each of the six major entities as the long-term average monthly percentage of total annual use.

Physical characteristics of the Highland Lakes System are the elevation-storage-surface area relationship and the conservation and dead storage volumes for each of the reservoirs. These were obtained from tables compiled by the LCRA.

Since only Lakes Travis and Buchanan are allowed storage fluctuation, the operating rules governing the monthly fulfillment of downstream demands were defined as follows:

Lake Travis Active Storage Percentage	Lake Buchanan Release
Greater than 72.0 %	0% of demand
Less than 72.0 % and greater than 58.8 %	35% of demand
Less than 58.8 %	90% of demand

Monthly net water surface evaporation data sets were obtained from the Texas Department of Water Resources (TDWR). The TDWR net evaporation data is available for the period 1940-81 and is computed for each "quadrant" within the state bounded by one degree meridians of longitude and parallels of latitude. In order to compute the net evaporation values applicable to each particular reservoir, the quadrant values were adjusted by an inverse distance ratio computed from the centroid of the reservoir to the center of the two nearest quadrants.

Within the period of available historical streamflow data (1940-82), a trend was noted in the time series of gaged streamflows in the Colorado River upstream of the Highland Lakes. This trend was apparently the result of extensive upstream reservoir implementation between the mid-forties and mid-sixties. It was felt that recorded inflows prior to 1966 did not reflect current hydrologic conditions in the Upper Colorado River Basin; therefore, inflows which have been adjusted by the TDWR to account for the effects of upstream reservoir development have been adopted for the 1941-65 period (4). Monthly reservoir inflows for the period 1966-81 were. calculated for each reservoir by a mass balancing procedure which essentially back-calculates inflow based on "known" beginning and ending storage, net evaporation, and upstream and downstream releases. Historical storage and release records were obtained from the LCRA Hydro Operations annual summary tables. As a result of employing this type of procedure, a small percentage of the computed inflows were negative. Negative inflow values were typically caused by under-estimation of evaporative losses during hot, dry months or incorrect estimation of upstream and downstream spills and releases during high flow periods. In order to conserve mass in the derivation of monthly reservoir inflow volumes, all computed negative flow values were set to zero and subtracted from the following month.

To justify the assumption that annual streamflows entering the Highland Lakes System are independent and identically distributed (iid), two tests each were performed on the time series of combined annual gaged streamflows entering the system and combined reservoir inflows determined as per the previous paragraph. The first set of combined flows was obtained from USGS records and it represents the monthly sum of gaged flows from the Colorado River at Red Bluff, the Llano River at Llano, and the Pedernales River at Johnson City for the period 1940-82 (5).

First, a Turning Points Test (6) was performed on the annual combined flow series (January - December) using the hypothesis that the values were random. The computed values for the z statistic for the combined gaged streamflows and the combined reservoir inflows were 0.123 and 0.126, respectively. Neither of these values exceeds the 95% confidence test statistic of 1.96. Hence, the conclusion is that we cannot reject that each of the combined annual flow series are random. Secondly, the lag-one serial correlation coefficient, r_1, was computed for the two annual sequences considering annual periods beginning in each of the twelve possible starting months. The results of these computations are presented in Table 1. Assuming that the combined flows are normally distributed, the confidence limits on r_1 may be evaluated as follows (1):

$$l = \text{lower bound} = (-1-z_{95\%}(n-2)^{.5})/(n-1) = -0.331$$
$$u = \text{upper bound} = (-1+z_{95\%}(n-2)^{.5})/(n-1) = 0.281$$

As is apparent in Table 1, none of the r_1 values of either of the combined data sets lie outside of these bounds. The maximum computed value of r_1, 0.142, indicates that only about 2% of the information contained in the following years flow is a result of the current years flow on the average. Therefore, we may conclude that the hypothesis that $r_1 = 0$ cannot be rejected at the 95% confidence level.

Table 1. - Serial correlation of annual flows calculated from different starting months of the year.

Combined Reservoir Inflows (1980 Conditions)

Jan	Feb	Mar	Apr	May	Jun	Jul	Aug	Sep	Oct	Nov	Dec
.107	.142	.068	-.006	.029	-.074	-.142	-.112	-.043	.017	.051	.069

Combined Gaged Streamflows

Jan	Feb	Mar	Apr	May	Jun	Jul	Aug	Sep	Oct	Nov	Dec
.010	.010	-.026	-.068	.006	-.031	-.112	-.095	-.016	.062	.010	-.004

PRESENTATION AND EVALUATION OF RESULTS

In order to test the storage projection model developed in the performance of this project, it was decided that reservoir and system storage projections for periods of one through five years in length should be made. These projections used the annual hydrologic data sets and demand distributions discussed in the previous section with January being the starting month from which projections began. January is the month of greatest significance for storage forecasting purposes in the Highland Lakes System because the LCRA annual water supply contracts with the major irrigation companies are negotiated during this month.

The initial percentages of active storage for each reservoir used in this analysis were:

Buchanan	Inks	LBJ	Marble Falls	Travis	Austin
44.59	100.00	100.00	100.00	32.54	100.00

These storages were chosen to approximate the pool levels that could be expected following a drought year. The defined "failure" storage for Lakes Buchanan and Travis was chosen arbitrarily as 225,000 acre-ft (2.767×10^8 m^3) and 400,000 acre-ft (4.920×10^8 m^3), respectively, and the selected "failure" storage for the system was 664,480 acre-ft (8.173×10^8 m^3).

A graphical presentation of the probability distributions of storage for projections of one, two, three, four, and five year length may be seen in Figure 1. This figure includes both projections generated by the model developed herein and the n-step transition matrix procedure as well as the envelope of uncertainty. In addition, Table 2 lends numerical values to some specific points of interest

shown in Figure 1. Employing the tabular output directly generated by
PROSTOR (on which Figure 1 and Table 2 are based), a reservoir system
operation agency such as the LCRA can scientifically evaluate the
possible effects of agreeing to supply a certain volume of water in
the coming years.

Table 2. - Tabular summary of Figure 1.

Projection Length (yrs)	Expected % Act. Storage	PROSTOR Coeff. of Variation	% Range of Envel. of Uncer.	n-Step Procedure Expected % Act. Storage
0	42.30	0.00	0.00	45.00
1	62.18	0.35	76.35	70.56
2	72.08	0.29	71.77	80.79
3	76.36	0.24	66.04	83.32
4	79.60	0.22	66.13	84.14
5	80.12	0.20	66.17	84.51

Several items of interest observed upon review of Figure 1 and
Table 2 are discussed below.
1) First of all, it is quite apparent that the expected percentage of
active storage increases and the variance about this expected
percentage decreases with increasing projection length. This pattern
of convergence is simply the result of the state of the system
becoming less and less dependent on the initial conditions and
approaching the steady-state for the particular starting month. It
should be noted that the storage projections generated by PROSTOR
converge after about five years to a steady-state condition that is
somewhat different than that computed by Gould's method.   This
discrepancy is partially explained by the fact that interyear serial
correlation in multi-year storage projections is accounted for in
PROSTOR by using annual hydrologic data sequences in historical order

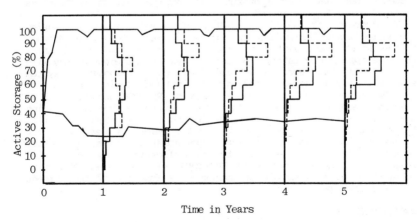

Figure 1. - Probability Distributions of Projected System Storage
with Envelope of Uncertainty: Transient Analysis = solid line,
Gould's Method = dashed line.

while Gould's method assumes that all years of data are mutually independent.

2) A brief investigation of the apparent effect of interyear serial correlation on multi-year storage projections was prompted by the discrepancy mentioned above. In an effort to emulate the assumption of mutually independent annual data sequences used in Gould's method, the 41 historical annual flows were randomly scrambled to obtain nine reordered annual data sets. Two and three year projections of system storage were then performed by transient analysis using each of the nine data sets. The mean of the nine expected active storage

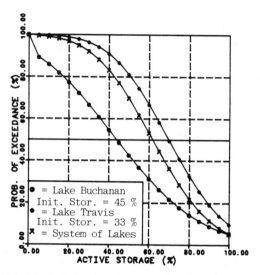

Figure 2. – Probability of Exceedance versus Active Storage Percentage, Annual Demand = 630,000 acre-ft (7.749 X 10^8 m^3), Starting Month = January.

percentages for the two and three year projection periods was 72.75% and 78.10%, respectively. These expected values are greater than those computed by transient analysis using the actual historical data sequence, but they do not approximate the expected storage percentages obtained using Gould's method.

3) The decreasing range of the envelope of uncertainty with increasing projection length emphasizes the approach of projected system storage to the steady-state condition after about three years. In addition, the envelope of uncertainty provides the system management agency with a measure of the "worst case" and "best case" response of system storage to a given demand based on historical hydrologic inputs.

Two other useful graphical outputs of PROSTOR are included as Figures 2 and 3. Figure 2 illustrates the probability of exceeding any percentage of active storage at the end of the projection period for each primary storage reservoir and the system as a whole subject to specified initial conditions, operation policies, and water demands. Figure 3 is generated by the application of Gould's Method (also coded as an option in PROSTOR) and expresses the time reliability of a reservoir or system as a function of the current active storage percentage.

CONCLUSIONS

In this paper, the theoretical basis of the developed computer model (PROSTOR) has been briefly detailed and an application of the model to the Highland Lakes System located on the Lower Colorado River has been presented. The results of this application indicate that the model is capable of providing acceptable projections of the probability distribution of storage in future years and estimates of system reliability subject to specified initial storage conditions, operation policies, and expected water demands.

Comparison of storage projections using transient analysis and Gould's method indicate that autocorrelation of annual inflow sequences may have a noticeable effect of the probability distribution of future storage even though the autocorrelation is statistically insignificant at the 95% confidence level. The envelope of uncertainty indicates that projected system storage approaches the steady-state condition approximately three years into the future for this application.

APPENDIX 1. - REFERENCES

1. Haan, C.T., "Statistical Methods in Hydrology," Iowa State University Press, Ames, Iowa, 1977.
2. Kite, G.W., "Frequency and Risk Analysis in Hydrology," Water Resources Publications, Fort Collins, Colorado, 1977.
3. McMahon, T.A., Mein, R.G., "Reservoir Capacity and Yield," Developments in Water Science, Vol. 9, Elsevier Scientific Publishing Company, Amsterdam, The Netherlands, 1978.
4. Texas Department of Water Resources, "Present and Future Surface Water Availability in the Colorado River Basin, Texas," LP-60, Austin, Texas, 1978.
5. Texas Department of Water Resources, "Streamflow and Reservoir-Content Records in Texas," Report 244, Austin, Texas, 1980.
6. Yevjevich, V., "Stochastic Processes in Hydrology," Water Resources Publications, Fort Collins, Colorado, 1972.

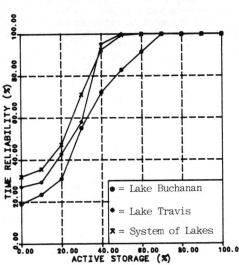

Figure 3. - Time Reliability versus Active Storage Percentage, Annual Demand = 630,000 acre-ft (7.749 X 10^8 m^3), Starting Month = January.

Design and Operating Rules for Reservoir Storage to Offset Future Consumptive Use

by Stuart S. Schwartz[1], and Daniel P. Sheer[2]

ABSTRACT

Anticipated consumptive users of the Potomac River could increase the risk of failure of the existing water supply system. To offset these consumptive impacts, future consumptive users will be required to supply make-up storage. Multiple objective system analysis is employed to size storage and determine operating rules so as to maintain water supply reliability.

Critical period analysis is used to determine the required volume of make-up storage to offset additional consumptive withdrawals. Operating rules for the entire system are characterized in terms of changes in pumping costs, environmental flow-by, drawdown patterns in existing reservoirs, and the required volume of make-up storage. Multi-objective analysis of system outputs identifies non-inferior operating rules. Using critical reservoir levels as a surrogate for system reliability, the trade-off between make-up volume and reliability is made explicit. This allows the simultaneous identification of the required storage volume, the operating rule for this make-up storage, and the rules to operate the entire system. Making the operating rules an explicit part of design, ensures that the reservoir can be operated for its intended purpose.

Sizing the make-up reservoir with this variation of critical period analysis incorporates existing skill in forecasting both streamflow and demand, with the hydrologic variation of the critical period. Instead of a single value of storage, a table of values is produced, depending on consumptive withdrawal as well as travel time and forecast error.

Introduction

The Washington Metropolitan Area (WMA) relies largely on the Potomac River for water supply. After many years of study, a coordinated regional operating plan was adopted by the water supply utilities serving the WMA, in order to significantly improve the system yield through largely non-structural means. Users of additional consumptive withdrawals, such as thermal electric power plants, will be required to supply sufficient reservoir storage to make-up for

---

[1,2] respectively, Water Resources Analyst, Director ICPRB Cooperative Water Supply Operations on the Potomac River (CO-OP)
Interstate Commission on the Potomac River Basin, Rockville, Maryland, 20852

their extractions during critical periods. This work describes a
method for determining the required volume of this make-up storage.

Water Supply for the Washington Metropolitan Area

The Washington Metropolitan Area (WMA) includes the District of
Columbia and the surrounding suburbs of Maryland and Virginia. Three
water supply utilities serve the WMA. The Washington Aqueduct
Division (WAD) of the U.S. Army Corps of Engineers serves the
District of Columbia, drawing all of its supply from two raw water
intakes on the Potomac River. The Washington Suburban Sanitary
Commission (WSSC) serves the Maryland suburbs drawing raw water from
both the Potomac River, and two local reservoirs on the Patuxent
River Basin. The Fairfax County Water Authority (FCWA) serves the
Virginia suburbs using an impoundment on the Occoquan River, as well
as a raw water intake on the Potomac. In addition, Bloomington and
Savage reservoirs, located five days travel time from the WMA,
provide an additional source of water supply storage.

In addition to meeting WMA demands, two environmental flowby
requirements further constrain operations. A minimum flowby
requirement of 100 MGD into the Potomac estuary has been adopted, as
well as a flowby target of 300 MGD between the two WAD Potomac
intakes located at Great Falls and Little Falls on the Potomac. The
intake at Great Falls is gravity driven, while extractions from the
Little Falls intake, incur a significant pumping cost. One way to
meet the flowby requirement at Great Falls is to release more water
from upstream reservoir storage. Alternatively, WAD withdrawals can
be shifted to the downstream intake at Little Falls. An interesting
tradeoff exists between the drawdown of upstream storage, and
additional pumping costs at Littel Falls.

The provision of a reliable water supply for the WMA has a long and
fascinating history. Sheer (3) provides a relatively recent view of
this problem. Recent modeling efforts concerned with this problem,
have led to a cooperative operating plan for the WMA system. Palmer
et al.(1,2) used an optimization approach to determine the system
yield for the multireservoir WMA system. The substantial gains to be
realized from joint operation, were dramatically demonstrated, and
the operational philosophy for the system was changed in a
fundamental way. Palmer et al. (2) also developed an interactive
simulation model which proved instrumental in implementing the
cooperative agreements, required to realize the gains that were
earlier shown to be feasible. A further refinement of this model was
adopted by the U.S. Army Corps of Engineers, and became a basic
analytical tool for the long-range phase of the Corps' MWA Water
Supply Study. Development of a daily operation simulation model
(DOPSIM), built upon the structure and insights drawn from these
previous modeling efforts. The work reported herein represents a
modification of this daily operating model, to address the planning
and reservoir sizing problem associated with future consumptive use.

Consumptive Use

The WMA utilities have adopted joint operating procedures to exploit
the water supply potential available on the Potomac. Recognizing the
potential impacts of an additional consumptive withdrawal, a decision
was made to require a consumptive user to provide make-up storage to
offset withdrawals during critical periods.

A common approach for sizing a make-up reservoir is to identify the
duration (in days) of a critical period based on historical flows,
and require a volume equal to the product of this critical period and
the consumptive withdrawal. An unanswered question is how to operate
this volume on a daily basis. When make-up reservoirs are located
several days travel time from a critical reach, releases must be
based on imperfect forecasts of flow and demand. Under these
conditions the effect of forecast uncertainty is to increase the
required storage volume. Make-up storage volumes must be determined
at the same time that realistic operating rules are identified, to
ensure that the proposed storage volumes can be operated to fulfill
design goals.

In low flow periods the impact of an additional consumptive
withdrawal could be felt in a number of ways. Such a withdrawal
could require larger upstream releases to allow flowby targets and
demands to be satisfied. Operations could also be changed to
satisfy more of the WMA demands from local water supply storage.
Either of these operational adjustments would incrementally deplete
reservoir storage, implicitly reducing the reliability of the WMA
water supply system. For some conditions, when the only impact of a
consumptive withdrawal is to degrade the 300 MGD flowby requirement
between Great Falls and Little Falls, the consumptive withdrawal may
be compensated for by shifting WAD water supply withdrawals to the
downstream intake at Little Falls. Although reservoir storage may
not be effected under these conditions, the additional pumping cost
is clearly an incremental impact of consumptive use. The allocation
of these consumptive impacts will be determined by the operational
responses adopted by the WMA.

Operating rules will determine both the required volume of make-up
storage, as well as the allocation of the impacts of consumptive use,
for the WMA system. The substantial gains that have been realized
through joint operation of the WMA water supply system, indicated the
value of determining operating rules for the system (including a
consumptive use), and the resulting required volume of make-up
storage, simultaneously.

Using the current operating rules as a guide, a diffeence rule for
the make-up storage was proposed which was entirely analogous to the
rule used to determine upstream releases. The release from the
make-up storage is based on the difference between the forecasts of
Potomac flow and WMA demands, on the day the augmenting release will
arrive. In this way forecast skill for flow and demand is
incorporated in daily operating decisions. This difference accounts

for any upstream release which will arrive on the same day. The difference is adjusted to account for the anticipated release from local storage, and a safety factor.

The operating rules for the new reservoir, as well as the existing storage volumes can be varied parametrically, shifting the allocation of demand between upstream, downstream, and make-up storage. Each parameterization of the rules for the new system could be described in terms of required volume of make-up storage and relative changes in 1) upstream storage, 2) downstream storage, 3) pumping costs, and 4) environmental flowby, compared to operation of the unmodified system. There is a clear conflict between the required volume of make-up storage, and drawdown of the water supply reservoirs. Conflicting goals also arise in allocating the impacts within the WMA. The choice of operating rules is clearly a multiobjective problem.

The volume of new augmenting storage and incremental Little Falls pumping were compared to upstream and downstream storage deviations to evaluate alternate operating rules. Multiple-objective analysis was used to identify a set of non-inferior operating rules. An operating rule is considered non-inferior if the only way in which one desirable system ouput can be increased is by reducing another. Many non-inferior operating rules can be eliminated from further consideration by inspection. For example, rules which produce deficits in both downstream and upstream storage fail to mitigate the impacts of consumptive use and are rejected. Any rule in which downstream storage is decreased more than upstream storage is raised, is unacceptable due to the higher relative value of downstream storage. Similar considerations allowed the choice of operating rule to be restricted to alternatives in which there was no net change in upstream storage. With this reduced set of non-inferior operating rules, the tradeoff between the change in downstream storage and the required volume of make-up storage was used to choose an operating rule.

The required volume of make-up storage was chosen to leave the total downstream storage volume unchanged (just under 3 billion gallons, in the example shown in Figure 1). This is the minimum volume of storage that can be jointly operated with the rest of the WMA system, to offset the major impacts of an additional consumptive withdrawal.

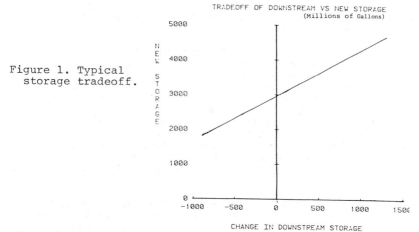

Figure 1. Typical
storage tradeoff.

Conclusion

Critical period anaysis has been used to determine operating rules
for a consumptive make-up reservoir, operated jointly with the WMA
water supply system. Identification of operating rules using
critical period hydrology, determines the required volume of storage.
Incremental changes in reservoir drawdown at the trough of the
critical period are used as measures of reliability for the water
supply system. In this way the minimum storage volume required to
offset the impacts of an aditional consumptive withdrawal are
determined, along with realistic operating rules.

Forecasts of demand and streamflow are used to determine daily
release volumes. As forecast error increases upstream, so does the
required storage volume for a given consumptive use. Instead of a
single value of required storage, a table of values is produced in
which make-up storage volume depends on both the size of the
consumptive withdrawal, and the location of the make-up reservoir,
expressed as travel time to the WMA.

Appendix- References

Palmer, R.N., Wright, J.R. Smith, J.A.,Cohon,J.L.,and ReVelle, C.S.,
"Policy Analysis of Reservoir Operation in the Potomac RiverBasin",
University of Maryland Water Resources Research Center Technical
Report No. 59 1979

Palmer, R.N., Smith, J.A., Cohon, J.L., and ReVelle, C.S., "Reservoir
Management in Potomac River Basin" ASCE Journal of the Water
Resources Planning and Management Division Vol. 108 No. WR1 1982
pp.47-66
Sheer, D.P. "Assured Water Supply for the Washington Metropolitan
Area" Interstate Commission on the Potomac River Basin Technical
Report 1982

Stochastic Modeling of Mean Areal Precipitation for
Generating Synthetic Streamflows

by Stuart S. Schwartz[1], James A. Smith[2], and Kathleen Hogan[3]

ABSTRACT

Statistical precipitation models used as input to conceptual
hydrologic models, offer an alternative mechanism for simulating
streamflow. In sparsely gauged catchments, or areas where gauging
has been discontinued, precipitation simulation can extend short or
incomplete gauge records.

Twenty years of mean areal precipitation data for 6 hour intervals
are analyzed, and a stochastic model of mean areal precipitation is
constructed for the North Branch, Potomac River. Simulated mean
areal precipitation is used as input to the Sacramento Soil Moisture
Accounting model to simulate streamflows. Statistics for simulated
streamflow and streamflow produced using historical precipitation are
compared to asses the representativeness of simulated precipitation.
Streamflow persistence is inferred to depend jointly on persistence
in precipitation sequences, and the influence of basin wide
conditions as represented by conceptual soil moisture storages.

Introduction

Experience with a drought management system for the Potomac River
Basin (Smith et al. (2)), has indicated the value of integrating
precipitation data with a conceptual hydrologic model to better
understand streamflow characteristics. Using historical
precipitation, with conceptual soil moisture storages that are
updated using current meteorological conditions, conditional
forecasts of low summer streamflow can be made throughout the spring
and early summer to anticipate extreme low flows in the late summer
and early fall. As an example, despite unusually dry weather in the
summer of 1983, the probability of low streamflow was confidently and
correctly forecast to be so low as to pose no threat to water supply
operation. Despite the lowest July-September rainfall total for the
past 30 years, no supplemental water supply releases were required.

This study concentrates on the North Branch of the Potomac River
Basin, a 230 square mile catchment, located in the Appalachian
Plateau province of the Central Appalachians. Bloomington Reservoir,
located on the North Branch, provides supplemental water supply

----

[1,2]respectively, Water Resource Analyst, Hydrologist Interstate
Commission on the Potomac River Basin, Rockville, Maryland 20852
[3] Department of Geography and Environmental Engineering, The Johns
Hopkins University, Baltimore, Maryland 21218

storage for the Washington D.C. Metropolitan Area as well as water
quality, recreation, and flood control benefits for the reaches
immediately downstream. Incorporating our understanding of
persistence of hydrologic time-series, into reservoir operations
offers a non-structural means to expand the range of achievalble
benefits. Using conceptual soil moisture storages, the value and
feasibility of extended water quality operations may be anticipated,
in advance of critical low flow conditions. Decomposition of high
flow events into the separable components of soil moisture and
precipitation may enhance the identification of flood risks.

As a first step toward incorporating basin wide hydrologic conditions
in water quality and flood control operation, this study uses a
conceptual soil moisture model to examine the interaction between
precipitation and soil moisture in producing streamflow. To this end
historical mean areal precipitation (MAP) at 6 hour intervals for the
month of March was routed through the Sacramento Soil Moisture
Accounting Model to produce historically derived runoff depths over
the entire North Branch Basin. For comparison, synthetic
precipitation was simulated using a first-order Markov chain and used
to produce simulated runoff using identical initial soil moisture
conditions. To evaluate the relative importance of persistence in
precipitation, a second model of MAP was developed. This second
model reproduced precipitation depths in the same frequency as the
historical data, in a completely random order. Each simulated MAP
sequence from this model could be viewed as a random sample taken
from the multinomial distribution in which the probabilities of
success corresponded to the observed frequency of occurrence of MAP
in each depth class. This model is referred to herein as the
multinomial precipitation generator. Imbedded in these streamflows
are errors in estimation of MAP, as well as the calibration and model
errors of the Sacramento model·.

Description of Precipitation

Mean areal precipitation at 6 hour intervals for the month of March
is used as input to the Sacramento model and this is the
meteorological variable for which statistical models are developed.
Summary statistics for historical MAP show a seasonal pattern of
storm occurrence and storm depths. As indicated in Figure 1a, the

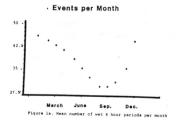

. **Events per Month**

Figure 1a. Mean number of wet 6 hour periods per month

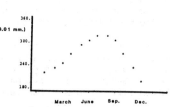

Mean Depth per Event

Figure 1c. Mean depth of precipitation per 6 hour wet period

Monthly Mean Areal Precipitation

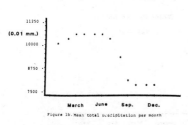

Figure 1b. Mean total precipitation per month

occurrence of 6 hour periods with non-zero MAP is highest in the winter and early spring, and lowest in August and September. In contrast to the frequency of wet events, the average depth per wet event (Figure 1c) is highest in the summer and early fall, and lowest in winter reflecting the seasonal change in storm patterns. Total precipitation depth in any month is clearly the product of number of events and the depth per event. The seasonal decrease in frequency of events, with a parallel increase in mean depths results in monthly precipitation totals achieving their maximum value in the spring (Figure 1b).

Markov Model of MAP

Since Gabriel and Neumann (1) demonstrated the fit of a Markov chain to daily rainfall occurrence, a number of workers have explored the first order Markov process as a model of persistent precipitation sequences with considerable, though not unequivocal success. Treating wet and dry periods as distinct states, 20 years of MAP were used to estimate monthly transition probabilities for a first order Markov chain. The sequences of wet and dry runs were tabulated, and tested against the geometric distribution parameterized with the estimated transition probabilities. Despite the visible scatter indicated in Figures 2a and 2b, the null hypothesis of a geometric distribution of runs lengths could not be rejected at the 0.005 percent significance level using the chi-square statistic.

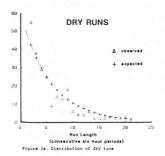

Figure 2a. Distribution of dry runs

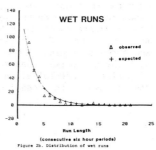

Figure 2b. Distribution of wet runs

The monthly transition probabilities also provided additional insight into the seasonal characteristics of precipitation on the North Branch. The "wet-wet" transition probability (Figure 2a) is highest in winter and early spring, declining steadily to a seasonal minimum in mid summer. The probability of a "dry-wet" transition (the initiation of a storm event) is highest in early fall, and lowest in

March (Figure 2b). Combining this description of precipitation occurrence with mean monthly depths per event, gives a more complete

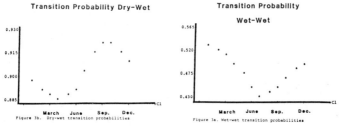

Figure 3b. Dry-wet transition probabilities

Figure 3a. Wet-wet transition probabilities

picture of the seasonal change in precipitation patterns. Spring precipitation tends to occur as extended sequences of moderate depth events. The presence of frozen ground, and snowmelt in the North Branch, with relatively longlasting precipitation events, is typically the cause of spring floods on the North Branch.

In summer and late fall the probability of initiation of a storm event is highest. The relatively low number of events during this time of the year indicates that precipitation in late summer and fall tends to be sporadic, consisting of relatively large magnitude, isolated events. Fall precipitation commonly results from airmass thunderstorms, with intense, localized cells of storm activity. The largest events in the historical record occurring in the fall, result from the passage of tropical cyclones over the basin.

A first order Markov chain was adopted as a simple model of March precipitation for the North Branch. Based on the historical distribution of MAP depths, 45 depth intervals were identified, and transition probabilities for a 45 state Markov chain were estimated. Using a pseudo-random number generator, the 45 state transition matrix was used to generate Markov sequences of synthetic March MAP. The historical frequencies of March MAP depths were similarly used to generate multinomial MAP. Cumulative density functions for the resulting sequences of synthetic MAP presented in Figure 4 show good agreement with the historical density of precipitation depths. Both sequences of synthetic precipitation were applied to the Sacramento Model to generate synthetic streamflow. These were compared to

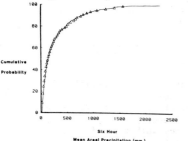

Six Hour
Mean Areal Precipitation (mm.)
Figure 4. Cumulative density function for 6 hour MAP depths
solid line- historical; triangle- Markov

streamflow using historical MAP and identical initial soil moisture conditions. Comparing the Markov chain model to the multinomial derived streamflows also provided a way to gauge the importance of persistence in precipitation, on streamflow.

The Sacramento Soil Moisture Accounting Model

The Sacramento model provides a conceptual accounting of the precipitation input to a drainage basin. The model represents the storage and movement of water beneath the surface, the transmission of groundwater to stream channels, and the evaporation and transpiration of water from the soil and stream channel. Soil moisture is represented in the model by several storage zones. Outflow components from the various conceptual soil moisture storage zones can be interpreted as baseflow, interflow, and overland flow.

The Sacramento model, used in conjunction with the Extended Streamflow Prediction procedure of the National Weather Service River Forecast System, has been shown to be particularly well suited for representing streamflow characteristics in the Potomac River Basin (Smith et al. {2}). The formulation of the model does introduce error into the derived streamflow sequences. While comparison of streamflows produced with alternate representations of MAP is internally consistent, comparisons to actual streamflows must be made with caution. For this reason, the scope of this analysis is restricted to streamflows derived using the Sacramento model.

Comparison of Derived Streamflows

Comparing streamflows derived from historical, Markov, and multinomial sequences of MAP, indicates persistent temporal characteristics of precipitation in streamflow. The CDF in figure 5 shows the close similarity between the distribution of streamflow depth generated from historical MAP, and the Markov model. While the agreement of flow frequencies was good, the Markov derived streamflow tended to under-represent intermediate flows in the 5-10 mm. range (Figure 6). In the Markov MAPs, precipitation occurrences greater than 10 mm. tended to occur in clusters. In the estimated transition probability matrix, several of the states corresponding to depths over 10. mm., only had non-zero transition probabilities to other intense rainfall states. This is attributable to the small number of large precipitation events in the historical record for March. Nonetheless, this suggests that the meteorological conditions producing infrequent intense storm events in March, need to be modeled as a separate, distinct process. The multinomial

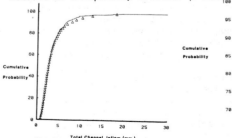

Figure 5. Cumulative density function for derived streamflow solid line- historical; triangle- Markov

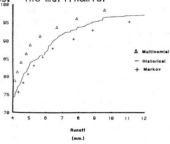

Figure 6. Cumulative density function for derived streamflow

precipitation sequences produced streamflows in which low flow events
(1-3 mm.) were under-represented. This can be attributed to the low
frequency of extended dry periods in the random precipitaion
sequences. Similarly, intermediate depth events (5-10 mm.) were
over-represented (Figure 6). In the multinomial precipitation
sequences, long runs of successive wet periods are uncommon, as are
higher flow depths. The lack of persistence in the multinomial
precipitation is clearly reflected in the frequency distribution of
derived streamflow.

To explore the temporal structure of derived streamflow,
autocorrelation functions and partial autocorrelation functions for
the three classes of derived streamflow were examined. The
autocorrelation and partial autocorrelation functions for streamflow,
show a striking similarity, despite the significant differences built
into the precipitation models. The value of the lag 1
autocorrelation coefficient is approximately the same for all three
of the derived streamflow sequences. Since the multinomial
precipitation is uncorrelated, the high value of the lag one
autocorrelation coefficient, suggests the dominant role of temporal
structure of the Sacramento model.

For a pure autoregressive process, an exponential decay of the
autocorrelation function would be expected. Autocorrelations
decrease uniformly with lag for historically derived streamflow, but
remain significantly different from zero beyond lag 10. One
explanation for this is the routing component of the Sacramento
model. The timing of instaneous runoff in the Sacramento model is
modified with a unit hydrograph to account for the temporal lag in
runoff contribution from subareas in the basin. For the North
Branch, the unit hydrograph distributes the runoff from a single
period over ten consecutive periods. The presence of significant
autocorrelation beyond lag ten strongly suggests model imposed
structure. This inference is again reinforced by the persistence of
significant autocorrelations in streamflow derived from multinomial
precipitation.

Discussion

The relative roles of precipitation and soil moisture in determining
streamflow characteristics can be identified. The consequences of
persistence in precipitation appear to be more prominent in
determining overall runoff volumes, and longer term flow frequency.
Without extended wet and dry periods, the natural variation in
streamflow is reduced, irrespective of soil moisture conditions.

The temporal relationship of successive streamflow values appears to
be significantly affected by the storage and movement of groundwater,
as represented by the Sacramento model. Soil moisture storage
appears to play a more significant role in the "memory" of March
streamflow, while persistence in precipitation seems to have a more
direct bearing on the magnitude and frequency of more extreme events.
This can be contrasted with summer and fall streamflow. During low

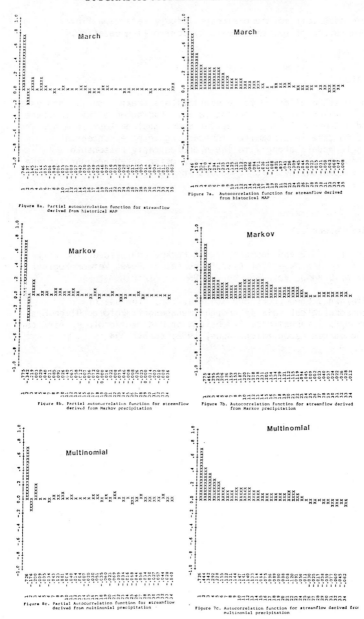

Figure 8a. Partial autocorrelation function for streamflow derived from historical MAP

Figure 7a. Autocorrelation function for streamflow derived from historical MAP

Figure 8b. Partial autocorrelation function for streamflow derived from Markov precipitation

Figure 7b. Autocorrelation function for streamflow derived from Markov precipitation

Figure 8c. Partial Autocorrelation function for streamflow derived from multinomial precipitation

Figure 7c. Autocorrelation function for streamflow derived from multinomial precipitation

Figure 8. Partial auto-
correlation functions

Figure 7. Auto correlation
functions

flow periods, soil moisture storage largely determines the
characteristics of extreme events by controlling baseflow.

Conclusion

Caution must be attached to generalizations drawn from the analysis
of one month of the year, on one basin. Furthermore the structure
imposed and error introduced by the model must be kept in mind. The
success to date in streamflow forecasting using a conceptual
hydrologic model, along with the hydrologically reasonable
relationships which can be reproduced, offer encouragement for the
use of conceptual hydrologic models in the operation of water
resource systems

Appendix-References

1. Gabriel, K.R., and Neumann,J., "A Markov chain model for daily
rainfall occurrence at Tel Aviv," Journal of Royal Meteorological
Society of London, Vol. 88, pp. 90-95

2. Smith,J.A., Sheer,D.P. and Schaake,J.C., "The use of
hydrometeorological data in drought management: Potomac River Basin
case study", International Symposioum on Hydrometeorology, American
Water Resources Association, June, 1982, pp.347-354

STOCHASTIC SIMULATION OF STREAMFLOWS

By Edmond D. H. Cheng,[1] M.ASCE

ABSTRACT: In order to provide a better method of
generating synthetic streamflow data, a stochastic model
of simulating long-term streamflows is developed.
Basically, this method uses historical streamflow data
to establish Markov transition probabilities at an intended
project site. These probabilities will be the guide for
producing synthesized streamflows for a desired period.
Applications of the model are illustrated.

INTRODUCTION

There are numerous models for use in generating synthetic data
(4,5,6,7,8,9). In water resources engineering, the linear autoregressive models were considered by far the most popular methods for
generating long-term streamflow records for planning and management
purposes (4,5). In these approaches, the serial correlation coefficients of historical flows are the key elements in the recursive simulation formula. However, these serial correlation coefficients have
to exceed the conventionally acceptable minimum values for meeting the
required statistical significance. Unfortunately, in many cases, not
all the serial correlation coefficients can meet this condition. As a
consequence, the simulated streamflows would be less desirable. To
improve this situation, a stochastic computer simulation model for
generating synthetic streamflow records is thus being developed.
Basically, this method uses historical streamflow data to establish
Markov transition probabilities at an intended project site. These
probabilities will be the guide for producing synthesized streamflows
for a desired period.

Illustration of this stochastic computer model, as well as
comparisons to the linear autoregressive model, at some streams in
Hawaii are demonstrated and reported herein.

SIMULATION MODEL

Many meteorological phenomena that are considered random in their
occurrences exhibit various degrees of periodicity and persistence.

---

[1]Associate Professor, Dept. of Civil Engineering, University of Hawaii
at Manoa, Honolulu, Hawaii 96822.

In regard to periodicity, the streamflows generally change with respect to time but largely recur from season to season or year to year. Persistence in flow patterns generally can also be observed. For instance, the magnitude of streamflow at any given hour is dependent on that of the previous hour or hours. These two fundamental characteristics of streamflows, fiz., persistence and periodicity, formed the basis of the stochastic simulation model.

After establishing the existence of persistence (Markov's property test, explained in a later section), the basic simulation strategy adopted in this paper is aimed at the phenomenon of seasonal periodicity of flow patterns. In this study, for a given season, streamflows are simulated on a monthly basis. Two major assumptions are made: (1) the correlation between two adjacent hourly wind speeds depends only on the time interval between them, and (2) the degree of expected persistence between successive streamflow records does not depend on the level of their magnitudes.

Three basic elements in the first order Markov chain model are: (1) state of streamflows (2) streamflow distribution functions, and (3) transition probability matrices.

State of Streamflows.—In the simulation process for a given wind site, the first step is to divide the entire range of observed streamflows into a finite number of states. This task is performed with reference to the probability histogram derived from the observed data for that project site. In principle, the stage divisions should be determined according to the shape of the probability histogram; therefore, state intervals will result in various non-equal sub-ranges of streamflows.

Distribution Functions.—The second basic element in the model involves the streamflow distribution functions, viz., the probability density functions (PDF) and the cumulative distribution functions (CDF) of streamflows in various states. In this study, three types of PDF are utilized to fit a streamflow histogram, viz., uniform, linear, and exponential functions. If relative uniform streamflows were observed within a state or states, constant values were assigned to that state or states. Likewise, if linear streamflow variations were observed in a state, a linear PDF would be assinged to that state. The exponential PDF is exclusively reserved for the last state in order to take care of extreme events.

Transition Probability Matrices.—In transition probability, p_{ij} is defined as the probability of a streamflow in state j which will occur in the next month, given that a streamflow in state i has occurred in this month.

For a stream of m finite states, p_{ij} is actually a conditional transition probability of streamflow Q_τ going from state i at month τ to streamflow $Q_{\tau+1}$ of state j at month $\tau+1$ or

$$p_{ij} = p(Q_{\tau+1}=j \mid Q_\tau=i) \quad \dots\dots\dots\dots\dots\dots\dots\dots\dots\dots\dots \quad (1)$$

With m states determined, an m x m transition probability matrix PM, can be determined as

$$PM = [p_{ij}] \quad \text{for } i,j = 1,2,\ldots,m \quad \ldots\ldots\ldots\ldots \quad (2)$$

in which, p_{ij} have the following properties:

$$\sum_{j=1}^{m} p_{ij} = 1, \quad \text{for } i = 1,2,\ldots,m, \quad \ldots\ldots\ldots\ldots \quad (3)$$

and

$$p_{ij} \geq 0, \quad \text{for all } i \text{ and } j. \quad \ldots\ldots\ldots\ldots \quad (4)$$

In the process of determining a transition probability matrix, first, an m x m tally matrix, TM, is computed from historical records as

$$TM = [f_{ij}], \quad \text{for } i,j = 1,2,\ldots,m \quad \ldots\ldots\ldots\ldots \quad (5)$$

where f_{ij} = the number of transitions of Q_τ going from state i at month τ to $Q_{\tau+1}$ of state j at the next month within a time period under consideration. Then the transition probability, p_{ij} can be estimated from the tally matrix as follows:

$$p_{ij} = f_{ij} / \sum_{j=1}^{m} f_{ij} \quad \ldots\ldots\ldots\ldots \quad (6)$$

for $i,j = 1,2,\ldots m$.

In this study, the variation of mean monthly streamflows is accounted for by grouping consecutive months with similar streamflows trends into a number of seasons for a year. If the number of seasons for a year is S, then a typical tally matrix for a given season s can be expressed as

$$TM(s) = [f_{ij}^s]. \quad \ldots\ldots\ldots\ldots \quad (7)$$

Therefore, by means of Eq. (6), the transition probability matrix will be

$$PM(s) = [p_{ij}^s] \quad \ldots\ldots\ldots\ldots \quad (8)$$

where $s = 1,2,\ldots,S$.

STREAMFLOW GENERATION

The key elements of generating streamflow data points at a given project site are briefly described as follows:

1. Determine the state of the succeeding month's streamflow: For any given streamflow in state i of this current month

(with specified season s), the succeeding month's streamflow
state interval "k" can be determined by the following
condition:

$$\sum_{j=1}^{k-1} p_{ij}^s \leq SR1 < \sum_{j=1}^{k} p_{ij}^s$$

where SR1 is a generated pseudo random number, which varies
uniformly from 0 to 1.

2. Determine the value of the succeeding month's streamflow $\bar{Q}_k$:
   With the state k determined in Step 1, the simulated $\bar{Q}_k$ for the
   succeeding month can be obtained from the following condition:

$$\frac{\int_{Q_k}^{\bar{Q}_k} f_k(Q)\,dQ}{\int_{Q_k}^{Q_{k+1}} f_k(Q)\,dQ} = \frac{\overline{d_1 d_2}}{\overline{d_3 d_4}} = SR2$$

where $\overline{d_1 d_2}$ and $\overline{d_3 d_4}$ are defined in Fig. 1, and

$f_k(Q)$ = PDF of the historical monthly streamflow in state
k;

Q_k = lower limit of the historical monthly streamflow
in state k;

$\dot{Q}_{k+1}$ = upper limit of the historical monthly streamflow
in state k;

SR2 = a generated pseudo random number varying uniformly
from 0 to 1.

3. Repeat Steps 1 and 2 until the desired length of simulation is
   attained.

In Steps 1 and 2, SR1 and SR2 are generated by calling the pseudo
random number generator GGUBS twice (3).

MARKOV PROPERTY AND STATIONARITY TESTS

In order to substantiate the major assumptions made earlier, a
test must be performed of the Markov property, i.e., the existence of
dependency between two adjacent monthly streamflows. This simulation
technique is only applicable to stationary time series; the intended
simulation model is a stationary first order Markov chain. Consequently, a test of stationarity of the historical streamflow time
series is necessary prior to the acceptance of the simulated results.
Anderson and Goodman's method (1) was used in performing these tests.

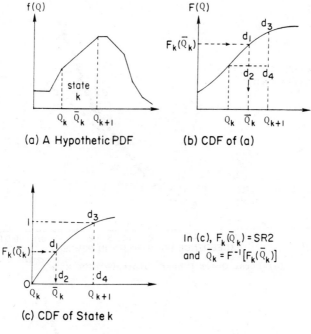

(a) A Hypothetic PDF

(b) CDF of (a)

(c) CDF of State k

In (c), $F_k(\bar{Q}_k) = SR2$
and $\bar{Q}_k = F^{-1}[F_k(\bar{Q}_k)]$

FIG. 1.-Hypothetic PDF and CFS of Hourly
Wind Speeds

APPLICATIONS

Based on the described method, a simulation computer code was
developed and utilized for generating monthly streamflow data at
Kalihi Stream on the island of Oahu and at Kohala Ditch on the island
of Hawaii (Big Island). In the process of simulation, at Kalihi
Stream, six state intervals and two seasons--dry and wet (November-May)
were considered. These decisions were made on the basis of 67 years of
historical streamflow records available at Kalihi Stream gaging station.
Similarly, on the basis of 33 years of historical data, seven state
intervals and two seasons--dry and wet (March-August) were adopted at
Kohala Ditch. It may be worthy to note that the definition of wet
seasons are almost opposite at the two stations considered. Both tests
of Markov property and stationarity of the historical records at the
two stream gaging stations were passed. One hundred years of monthly
streamflow records each were thus simulated for Kalihi Stream and
Kohala Ditch.

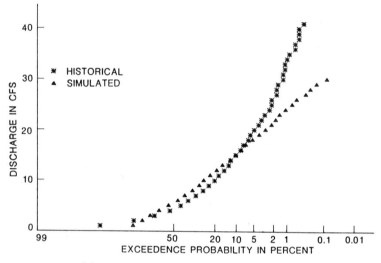

(a) First Order Linear Autoregressive Model

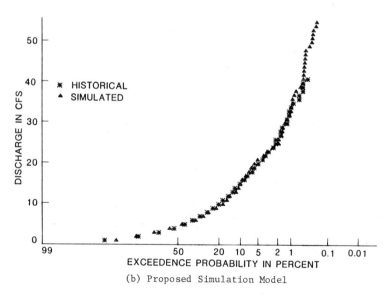

(b) Proposed Simulation Model

FIG. 2.-Duration Curves of Historical and Simulated Monthly
Streamflows at Kalihi Stream

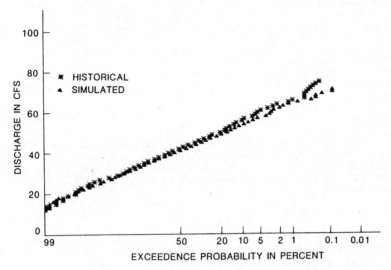

(a) First Order Linear Autoregressive Model

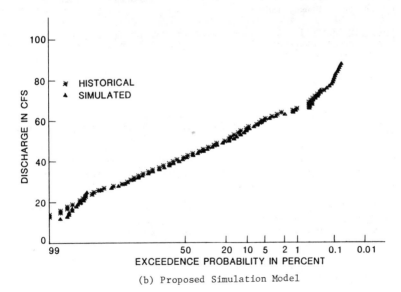

(b) Proposed Simulation Model

FIG. 3.-Duration Curves of Historical and Simulated Monthly
Streamflows at Kohala Ditch

Historical and synthesized (by means of first order linear auto-regressive model) streamflow records (2) were plotted in Figs. 2(a) and 3(a) for Kalihi Stream and Kohala Ditch, respectively. Similar plots for data generated from the proposed simulation model were also presented in Figs. 2(b) and 3(b). As clearly indicated in Fig. 2, in comparison with the historical records, the data synthesized by the first order linear autoregressive model is less desirable than those realized from Fig. 3 although a much better performance of the first order linear autoregressive model is observed at Kohala Ditch than at Kalihi Stream.

CONCLUSIONS

The characteristics of historical monthly streamflows at both Kalihi Stream and Kohala Ditch were adequately represented by those data generated from the proposed stochastic computer. These preliminary results imply that the proposed method may be superior to the popular linear autoregressive model.

APPENDIX I.—REFERENCES

1. Anderson, T. W., and Goodman, L. A., "Statistical Inference about Markov Chains," Annals of Mathematical Statistics, Vol. 28, 1957, pp. 89-110.

2. Baba, C., "Streamflow Generation Using the Markov Models," Unpublished Report, Department of Civil Engineering, University of Hawaii at Manoa, 1984.

3. Computer Subroutine Libraries in Mathematics and Statistics, International Mathematical and Statistical Libraries, Inc., Houston, Texas, 1979.

4. Fiering, M. B., Streamflow Synthesis, Harvard University Press, Cambridge, Massachusetts, 1967.

5. Fiering, M. B., and Jackson, B. B., Synthetic Streamflows, Water Resources Monograph 1, American Geophysical Union, Washington, D.C., 1971.

6. Matalas, N. C., and Jacobs, B., A Correlation Procedure for Augmenting Hydrologic Data, U.S. Geological Survey Professional Paper434-E, Washington, D.C., 1964.

7. Mejia, J. M., Rodriguez-Iturbe, I., and Dawdy, D. R., "Streamflow Simulation, 2, the Broken Line Process as a Potential Model for Hydrologic Simulation," Water Resources Research, Vol. 8, No. 4, 1972, pp. 931-941.

8. Scheidegger, A. E., "Stochastic Models in Hydrology," Water Resources Research, Vol. 6, No. 3, 1970, pp. 750-755.

9. Yakowitz, S. J., "A Nonparametric Markov Model for Daily River Flow," Water Resources Research, Vol. 15, No. 5, 1979, pp. 1035-1043.

APPLICATIONS OF SPREADSHEETS IN WATER RESOURCES

Thomas K. Jewell,* M. ASCE

Abstract

This paper will describe two applications of the spreadsheet MULTIPLAN (1) to water resources problems. Applications will include statistical analysis of water resources
data and design of a stormwater detention pond using dynamic
reservoir routing. Spreadsheets will be developed for each
application. The ease of performing sensitivity analyses
and analyzing alternative solutions through recalculation
of the spreadsheet, will be demonstrated for the applications. Generalization of the spreadsheet models to form
templates for the entry and solution of similar problems
will be discussed.

Introduction

Spreadsheets are powerful applications oriented
programs that can be effective tools in water resources
analysis and design. Spreadsheets, because of their rapid
recalculation capabilities, make it practical to examine
many alternatives. Users are also able to customize their
output for particular cases, while maintaining a flexible
spreadsheet structure that will accept input for a whole
category of problems. However, as with any other type of
analysis tool, spreadsheets have their limitations and rules
of usage that must be understood if they are to be used
effectively. One of the advantages of spreadsheets is that
they make computer analysis, and development of analysis
tools, available to users who have not had the time or
inclination to learn a computer programming language.

Statistical Analysis

Spreadsheets are ideal tools for assisting with the
analysis of problems that can be arrayed in a tabular
format. Finding the best fit straight line through a set of
data points using regression analysis is one such problem.

The equations given below produce the best fit straight
line by minimizing the sum of the squared deviations between
the data points and the regression line. In these, and
subsequent equations, summations are from 1 to n. To save

*Associate Professor, Dept. of Civil Engineering, Union
College, Schenectady, New York 12308

space, the following convention will be used for all sums:

$$\Sigma X = \sum_{i=1}^{n} X_i$$

The general regression equation is $Y = aX + b$, in which a and b are parameters estimated by the regression procedure, X is the independent variable, and Y is the estimated value of the dependent variable. Parameters a and b can be estimated by:

$$\overline{X} = \Sigma X/n \qquad \overline{Y} = \Sigma Y/n$$

$$a = (\Sigma XY - \overline{Y}\Sigma X)/(\Sigma X^2 - \overline{X}\Sigma X) \qquad b = \overline{Y} - a\overline{X}$$

$$\left. \right\} \quad (1)$$

One measure of the goodness of fit of the regression line is the correlation coefficient, which is found by the equation:

$$r = a[(\Sigma X^2 - n\overline{X}^2)/(\Sigma Y^2 - n\overline{Y}^2)]^{0.5} \qquad (2)$$

Examination of the above equations shows that all of the necessary sums can easily be calculated if the data is set up in a tabular format. Five columns are required, one each for the X and Y data values, one each for the X^2 and Y^2 calculated values, and one for the XY data value cross-products. Each column can be used to find the required summations. Other statistics in the spreadsheet also use the five key summations.

Spreadsheet.--Table 1 shows the spreadsheet for the linear regression. Note that row and column numbers have been added for reference purposes. Normally these would not be included in a printout for a report.

Columns two through six and rows five through eighteen of the spreadsheet contain the basic data for a problem in which it is desired to investigate the relationship between dissolved oxygen [mg/l] (Y) and flowrate [cfs] (X) for a small stream using ten data points. The designations of data and units have intentionally been left general so that once the spreadsheet is developed, it can easily be transformed into a template that can be used for other problems.

Before starting to develop the spreadsheet, it is essential to have a thorough knowledge of the theory and solution techniques to be used. It is also important to plan the layout of the spreadsheet output. The spreadsheet should be as compact as possible; and whenever feasible, it is best to place the output portion of the spreadsheet in the first seven columns. This is the number of columns normally printed out on a page. Intermediate calculations that do not need to be printed out can be accomplished in columns to the right of seven.

The block of cells in columns two through six that contains the raw and calculated data forms the heart of the

Table 1.--Linear Regression Spreadsheet

	1	2	3	4	5	6	7
1		REGRESSION ANALYSIS AND RELATED STATISTICS					
2	--						
3	n =	10		Degrees of Freedom =		8	
4							
5		X	Y	X^2	Y^2	XY	SSD Yest
6		--------	--------	--------	--------	--------	--------
7		6	7.9	36	62.41	47.4	2.9741058
8		10.5	10.2	110.25	104.04	107.1	0.0734393
9		19.4	13.4	376.36	179.56	259.96	8.2304441
10		10.9	9.4	118.81	88.36	102.46	0.3092081
11		1.1	9.7	1.21	94.09	10.67	0.1656048
12		13.6	12.9	184.96	166.41	175.44	7.6246066
13		3.7	8.9	13.69	79.21	32.93	0.3237099
14		67	12.9	4489	166.41	864.3	0.7249867
15		1	9	1	81	9	0.0819614
16		8.9	7.5	79.21	56.25	66.75	5.3859111
17		--------	--------	--------	--------	--------	--------
18	SUMS	142.1	101.8	5410.49	1077.74	1676.01	25.893978
19							
20	--						

```
21 Basic Statistics
22       Mean values
23            X(bar) =      14.21  Y(bar) =      10.18
24       Estimate of population standard deviation
25            S(X) = 19.411477    S(Y) = 2.1451755
26       Coefficient of variation
27            V(X) = 1.3660434    V(Y) = 0.2107245
28 -----------------------------------------------------------------
29 Regression   Y = aX + b
30                  a = 0.0676541      b = 9.2186348
31       Correlation
32            r =      0.612     r^2 =     0.375
33       Estimated value of Y for specified x
34            For X =       15       Y = 10.233447
35 -----------------------------------------------------------------
36 Confidence Interval Testing
37            Confidence interval = estimated value + or - t*s
38            t is from Student's t table for proper DF and alpha
39            s is the estimated standard deviation for the
40                 parameter or independent variable value
41       Estimated Standard Deviation for Slope of Regression Line
42            S(a) =  0.030894
43       For alpha =        0.05  and DF =        8      t =    2.306
44            you are        95 percent sure that the slope lies
45            between 0.1388958   and     -0.003588
46       Estimated Standard Deviation for Estimated Value of Y
47            S(Yest) = 1.8870659
48       For alpha =        0.05  and DF =        8      t =    2.306
49            you are        95 percent sure that the value of Y lies
50            between 14.585021   and     5.8818729
51 -----------------------------------------------------------------
52 Standard Error of Estimate
53            S(Y,X) = 1.7990962
54 =================================================================
```

spreadsheet, and should be developed first. The data in column seven can be ignored at this time, because it was added later to assist in calculating the standard error of estimate. It will be described at the appropriate time. After the headings have been entered, the first X and Y values can be entered in cells R7C2 and R7C3. Formulas to calculate the X^2, Y^2, and XY values for this row of data can be entered in cells R7C4, R7C5, and R7C6, respectively. Relative cell references should be used to facilitate rapid

development of the table, and transformation of the finished
spreadsheet to a template. For example, the XY value should
be calculated by the formula RC[-4]*RC[-3], which multiplies
the value in the same row, but four cells to the left, by
the value in the same row, but three cells to the left.
Similarly, the formula RC[-2]^2 will calculate the square of
each data value.

Rather than typing the three formulas for each row of
the table, the COPY command can be used to enter all of the
formulas in one operation. Move the cursor to cell R7C4,
which shows the value 36 on the screen.   Type   C, and the
COPY menu will appear. Type D for DOWN, 9 for the number of
cells (there are a total of 10 data values), and R7C4:R7C6
for the field. After entering these values and pressing
RETURN, the three formulas will be copied into the corresponding cells in rows eight through sixteen. Since relative
cell references were used in the original row, the cell
references for each new row will relate to that row. Now
the X and Y values for each row can be entered. As this is
accomplished, the calculated values will be generated.
MULTIPLAN provides the option of delaying calculation until
all data values are entered.

After building the five column table, the sums can be
calculated by using the SUM function of Multiplan.   For
example, SUM(R7:16C2) entered in cell R18C2 would sum the X
values and display the sum in that cell. If the table is
later expanded or shrunk, the row reference in the SUM
function will automatically be adjusted.   This allows the
development of a template spreadsheet that can be expanded
to fit any desired problem.

Formulas for some of the other key calculations will
now be discussed. The formula for calculating the slope of
the regression line, a, is contained in cell R30C3. It is:

        (R18C6-R23C5*R18C2)/(R18C4-R23C3*R18C2)   (3)

The values that these cell references refer to can be
ascertained from examining Table 1. It can be seen that
they correspond to the elements of the equation for a in
Equations 1.   The formula for calculating the correlation
coefficient is contained in cell R32C3, and is:

        R[-2]C*SQRT(R30C9/R31C9)   (4)

The R[-2]C refers to the value for a in cell R30C3. SQRT( )
is the internal square root function of MULTIPLAN. The cell
references within the parens, R30C9 AND R31C9, refer to
cells that contain formulas for finding

$$\Sigma X^2 - n\overline{X}^2 \text{ and } \Sigma Y^2 - n\overline{Y}^2$$

respectively.   These formulas are placed in separate cells

because they are used again in other statistical
calculations.

Column 7 can now be examined. The standard error of
estimate is the last statistic included in the spreadsheet.
It requires the calculation of the sum of the squared
differences between each measured Y value, and the estimated
Y value from the regression equation for the same value of
X. This data is most conveniently included as another
column in the tabular format. Each cell of this column
contains the formula:

(R30C3*RC[-5] + R30C5 - RC[-4])^2

The first two elements of this formula compute the estimated
Y value for the given X, and the last element is the
measured Y value. Note that the formula refers to cells
that are farther down, and to the left, in the spreadsheet.
The calculation sequence of the spreadsheet will
automatically adjust for this.

Verification and Use of the Spreadsheet.—When developing
the spreadsheet, it is essential to have some calculated
data to check the spreadsheet against. Once the spreadsheet
is completed, and is giving correct answers, it can be used
for further analysis, or used to develop a template for
other problems. Further analysis for a statistics spreadsheet such as the above would generally involve some sort of
sensitivity analysis. Further analysis for design purposes
will be described for the second spreadsheet in this paper.

Sensitivity analysis for this spreadsheet could involve
determining how much the regression equation and associated
statistics would change if suspected outlying or erroneous
data were removed. How much would any changes in the
existing data change the output? Or, how much would
additional data change the results, or the inferences from
the results?

Template.—After saving the finished spreadsheet on a
diskette, a template can be formed in the following manner.
Start by deleting all but two rows of the table. Then enter
zero for the X and Y values of the remaining two rows.
Blank out the value of n in cell R3C2. Note that several
formulas later on use this value of n, so error messages may
appear in these cells. These error messages will disappear
when data is reentered. Values for X in R34C3, alpha in
R43C3 and R48C3, and t in R43C7 and R48C7 should also be
blanked out. The template can be saved for future use.

When using the template for new problems, enter the
number of data values, n, the X value for which Y will be
predicted, and the alpha and t values for statistics as
desired. The t value (for the problem degrees of freedom
and the selected alpha) has to be looked up in standard

statistical tables and entered in the appropriate cell.
Finally, the table can be expanded to hold the desired
number of data values. Use the INSERT ROW command to enter
n-2 blank rows between the two data entry rows of the
template. Move the cursor to R7C4 and COPY DOWN the
formulas in cells R7C4:R7C7 for n-2 cells. This will
propagate the formulas in columns 4 through 7 for the new
table. You may want to turn off recalculation when
expanding the table. Finally, enter the X an Y values for
each data value, and accomplish recalculation.

Reservoir Routing

     A spreadsheet for designing a stormwater detention pond
will now be presented. Inflow to the detention pond will be
an unsteady flow hydrograph generated by a computer simulation or by design specifications. Design variables are the
geometry of the basin and the type and size of outlet
structure. Design specifications may limit the depth of
water in the detention basin, or put a maximum limit on the
outflow. A common method for routing an unsteady flow
hydrograph through a reservoir is the Storage-Indication
Working Curve Method. Outflow is assumed to be a function
of the water surface elevation in the reservoir. Relationships have to be known for the elevation vs. outflow, and
for the elevation vs. volume in storage. Knowing these two
functions, the curve 2S/t + O vs. O can be determined. In
this expression, S is the volume in storage, t is the time
step length used for the routing simulation, and O is the
outflow rate. The complete inflow hydrograph, as well as
the initial outflow, must be known. Using continuity,
2S/t + O for a time step can be determined by:

$$(2*S/t + O)_i = I_{i-1} + I_i + (2*S/t + O)_{i-1} - 2*O_{i-1} \qquad (5)$$

The 2S/t + O value can be used to find O for a time step by
applying the iteration option of MULTIPLAN.

Development of Spreadsheet.--Table 2 shows the output
portion of the spreadsheet. The first two sections of the
spreadsheet establish the geometry of the basin and the
parameters for the outlet structure. Any changes in the
values for these design dimensions and parameters will be
propagated throughout the spreadsheet. The inflow
hydrograph is contained in the first column of the
spreadsheet table. Note that the first row contains all
zeros. This is because the basin is assumed to be initially
dry. If the basin was not initially dry, the first line
could be modified to account for this.

     Examination of a row of the table is the best way to
see what the solution method is accomplishing. After that,
some of the fine points will be discussed. A typical row of
the solution table contains the five columns shown in Table
2, plus three auxiliary rows off to the right that contain

Table 2.--Reservoir Routing Spreadsheet

```
         1        2         3        4         5        6
 1 RESERVOIR ROUTING
 2
 3 STORAGE DATA
 4      Rectangular Basin with sloping sides
 5           First Bottom Dimension   175      feet
 6          Second Bottom Dimension   175      feet
 7                       Side Slope   2        horz/vert
 8
 9 OUTLET DATA
10      Standard Short Tube
11           Discharge Coefficient   0.82
12              Orifice Diameter     3        feet
13
14 ROUTING TABLE          Time Step Length (t)   900      seconds
15
16    Inflow    2S/t+O     Depth    Storage    Outflow
17    (cfs)     (cfs)      (feet)   (cubic ft) (cfs)
18    ------    -------    ------   ---------- ------
19    0         0          0        0          0
20    2         2.00       0.00     49.00      1.86
21    39        39.28      0.24     7414.52    22.81
22    129       161.65     1.49     47203.26   56.75
23    168       345.16     3.50     116159.95  87.00
24    108       447.16     4.60     156360.82  99.69
25    60        415.79     4.26     143903.68  96.00
26    21        304.80     3.06     100555.61  81.35
27    5         168.09     1.56     49506.65   58.07
28    0         56.96      0.40     12383.91   29.43
29    0         0.00       0.00     0.00       0.00
30    0         0.00       0.00     0.00       0.00
31    --------                                 --------
32    532     <== TOTAL IN      TOTAL OUT ==>  532.95
33                          CONVERGENCE CHECK  TRUE
34                          PERCENT ERROR      0.18%
35 NOTE: 1 ft = 0.305 m, 1 cu ft = 0.028 m^3.
```

interim values for the solution procedure. The formula in each column will be presented and discussed, with inter-action among columns highlighted. The formula of column 2 contains the cell references necessary to compute 2S/t + O for the time step. It also contains a logical statement to prevent 2S/t + O from taking on negative values. The formula is:

$$\text{IF(R[-1]C[-1]+RC[-1]+R[-1]C-R[-1]C+3]*2<0,0,}$$
$$\text{R[-1]C[-1]+RC[-1]+R[-1]C-2*R[-1]C[+3])} \qquad (6)$$

The IF statement in MULTIPLAN has the form IF(Logical Statement,True,False). If the logical statement is true, then the value or formula between the two commas is used. If it is false, the value or formula after the second comma is used. The first part of Equation 6 specifies that if the 2S/t + O of Equation 5 is negative, then 2S/t + O is set equal to zero. Otherwise, 2S/t + O is calculated as per Equation 5. Note that in Equation 6, R[-1] refers to time step i-1, and R refers to time step i. Column 3 contains the depth within the basin, which is used as the adjustment variable in this solution procedure. However, prior to discussing this column, it is important first to define the

three auxiliary columns to the right of the output table.
Column 8 contains the formula:

$$RC[-6]-(2*RC[-4]/t+RC[-3])\qquad(7)$$

which is the difference between the previous and present
estimates of 2S/t + O in the iterative process. One new
feature illustrated here is the naming of cells for future
reference. In this case, the cell containing the time step
length has been assigned the name t. Use of the name in the
formula will cause the value from the named cell to be used
in the calculation. This option is useful if the value in a
particular cell is to be used several times in formulas.
Column 9 contains the formula:

$$IF(RC[-6]<0,0,RC[-6])\qquad(8)$$

which is a storage location for the previous value of the
depth. Column 10 contains the formula:

$$IF(ABS(RC[-2])<0.1,0.001,0.01)\qquad(9)$$

which sets the factor to be used in calculating the depth
correction to be applied. If the absolute value of the
difference in 2S/t + O values is greater than or equal to
0.1, then the larger factor is used to speed convergence.
Once the difference is less that 0.1, the smaller factor is
used to increase accuracy. Depending on the magnitude of
the data values of a particular problem, these factors could
be adjusted to improve convergence or accuracy. Now column
3, which contains the formula:

$$IF(OR(ABS(RC[+5])<=0.01,RC<0),RC[+6],RC+RC[+7]*RC[+5])\quad(10)$$

can be examined. The OR construct specifies that if any of
the logical statements in the list within parens (two
statements in this case) are true, then the value or formula
between the commas (RC[+6] for this formula) is used.
Otherwise, the last one is used. For this problem, if the
difference in 2S/t + O values (stored in column 8) is less
than 0.01, there is no need to keep iterating for this time
step; the depth is as accurate as it needs to be, so the old
depth (stored in column 9) is used. Also, if the new depth
should be negative, the depth is set to the old depth.
Otherwise, the new depth is calculated by adding the product
of the 2S/t + O difference and the applicable factor from
column 10 to the present depth. Circular references are
involved here because the formula in column 3 is dependent
on columns 8, 9, and 10, which are in turn dependent on
column 3. Therefore, a single pass will not satisfy all of
the formulas, and iteration is necessary.

The formula in column 4 is straightforward. It is the
geometric expression that evaluates the volume in storage as
a function of the depth determined in column 3. The cells

containing the first bottom dimension, second bottom
dimension, and side slope, are referenced by the names B1,
B2, and SS respectively. The formula

    ((B1+2*SS*RC[-1])*(B2+2*SS*RC[-1])+B1*B2)/2*RC[-1]

calculates the volume in storage for a rectangular basin
with sloping sides. If a different geometrical shape is
desired, the formula would have to be modified. Column 5
contains the formula for calculating the outflow as a
function of the depth found in column 2. The formula is:

    IF(RC[-2]<=0,RC[-4]/2,ORIF*SQRT(RC[-2])))

The formula ORIF*SQRT(RC[-2]) is the orifice formula for
computing outflow. ORIF is the name referring to the cell
where the orifice coefficient, orifice area and the square
root of 2*g were multiplied together. The IF protects
against the chance that the depth is negative, which can
happen occassionally during the initial stages of iteration.
The way out of this is to set the outflow to one-half of the
inflow for the time step iteration. This provides a new
place from which to continue iterations.

    The iteration option is specified through the OPTIONS
portion of the MULTIPLAN menu. This has to be specified
before any recalculation is undertaken. Another block
within the OPTIONS menu calls for specifying COMPLETION TEST
AT:. If nothing is specified here, MULTIPLAN continues
iteration until the maximum change in any cell between
iterations is 0.001. However, the user has the option of
specifying a completion test, which has been done for this
spreadsheet. The cell to the right of the label
"CONVERGENCE CHECK" has been designated as the completion
test, and contains the formula

    AND(ABS(R[-1]C-RC[+3])<1,SUM(R[-12]C[+5]:R[-3]C[+5])
              <=0.001*COUNT(R[-12]C[+5]:R[-3]C[+5]))

which actually provides two convergence criteria. The
AND function requires that they both be true. The first is
that the difference between the sum of outflows from one
iteration to the next is less than 1.0. Cell R[-1]C
contains the sum of outflows for the present iteration, and
cell RC[+3] contains the sum of outflows for the previous
iteration. The second requires that all correction
sensitivity factors in column 10 be 0.001. This guards
against the chance that the sums of outflows might be
approximately equal before sufficient iterations have been
performed on all rows of the table. The COUNT function
computes the number of cells that contain numerical values
within the specified list.

    Also included is a calculation of the percent error
between total inflow and total outflow. If the percent

error is unacceptable, then changes in convergence criteria or correction sensitivity may be in order.

Iteration can be terminated during execution by pressing the CANCEL key. This is useful if the solutions start to oscillate without apparent convergence. Oscillations occurred for some hydrograph – basin size combinations for the spreadsheet illustrated here. The simple modification of dividing the depth corrections by two solved the convergence problem.

Use of the Spreadsheet.--Use of the spreadsheet as a design tool requires achieving an initial converged solution, checking the design criteria, changing design variable values if necessary, recalculating, and repeating until all design specifications are met. For example, the design for the basin depicted in Table 2 specified that the depth of water in the basin could not exceed five feet, and the maximum outflow could not exceed 100 cfs. The orifice was sized so that at a depth of five feet the outflow would be approximately 100 cfs. The dimensions of the basin were adjusted several times to produce the final output shown in Table 2. Additional analyses could be performed by super-imposing the new hydrograph over the old one, and continuing with the iterations, or the spreadsheet could be zeroed out and used as a template as described in the first example.

As can be seen, this type of spreadsheet is not something someone can pick up and use without any knowledge of MULTIPLAN. It also requires that the user have a good understanding of the calculation process for reservoir routing. This is, in effect, an advantage of this approach over standard computer packages that allow the user to get "answers" without understanding what the program is doing, or not doing, to produce them. In most cases, MULTIPLAN also has the advantage of overall speed. The calculation phase is slower than it would be for a high level language applications package, but the interactive stage of analyzing results and making modifications to the spreadsheet data is greatly facilitated.

Conclusions

MULTIPLAN is an efficient and valuable tool for accomplishing water resources design and analysis work. Learning to use it effectively is much easier than learning a high level language, and it has the advantage of not hiding the calculation process.

Appendix I.--References

1. Microsoft MULTIPLAN(tm) Electronic Worksheet, Version 1.2, Microsoft Corporation, 1984.

MICROCOMPUTER ANALYSIS OF HARBOR WIND DRIFT

Carl R. Johnson,[*] M. ASCE

Abstract

A microcomputer with general-purpose spreadsheet software was used to analyze wind drift on the water surface of Quincy Bay in Boston Harbor. Wind drift is the movement of the surface layer of a water body caused by the shearing force of the wind. The objective of the analysis was to determine the frequency with which wind drift would tend to transport wastewater effluents from off-shore outfalls towards the shoreline of Quincy Bay. The analysis was performed as part of a study conducted under contract with the Massachusetts Department of Environmental Quality Engineering, Division of Water Pollution Control. The method of analysis is described, and the use of spreadsheet software as an engineering tool is evaluated.

Study Area

The study area, Quincy Bay, is located in the southwest portion of Boston Harbor, and it is an area designated for swimming, recreational boating, and shellfish harvesting. The Bay, shown in Figure 1, has a surface area of about 15 sq km (6 sq miles) and a volume of about 73 million cubic meters (2.6 billion cubic feet) at mean high tide. The mean tidal range is 2.9 meters (9.4 feet). At the seaward boundary of the bay, there are four wastewater treatment plant outfalls and one major combined sewer overflow outfall. The total hydraulic design capacity of the outfalls is about 450 mgd. Effluent from these outfalls can occasionally be transported by both the wind and the tide toward the shoreline of Quincy Bay. The remaining discussion deals primarily with analysis of the wind-induced component of effluent transport. The Coriolis effect was considered to be small in relation to the wind and tide forces, and was not included explicitly in the analysis.

Wind Drift

Wind blowing across the surface of a water body causes a shearing action that moves the surface layer of the water. The movement in the surface layer is known as "wind drift".

---

[*] Environmental Engineer, Camp Dresser & McKee Inc., 1 Center Plaza, Boston, Massachusetts   02108

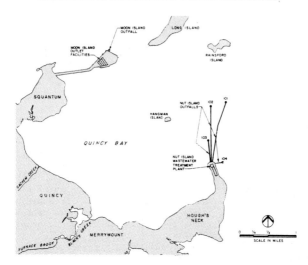

FIG. 1. Study Area

Wind drift is a significant force in moving the water surface in a
small bay which is subjected primarily to the forces of tide and
wind. The depth to which wind drift affects the water surface
depends on the wind speed and duration. The longer the wind blows
in one direction, the deeper is the layer of water subject to wind
drift. In a bay where there are twice-daily tide reversals, the
duration of interest for analyzing wind drift is 6 hours. This is
so because the movement of the tide typically overwhelms the
movement caused by wind drift. In a 6-hour period, wind drift will
generally affect the top 0.6- to 1-meter layer of water (2- to
3-foot). About 3 percent of the wind speed can be expected to be
imparted to this layer.

Wind Drift Excursions

    Both the distance and direction of effluent movements were
important in this analyis. Hereinafter, the term "wind drift
excursion" is used to mean the distance and direction that an
effluent plume is transported by wind drift.

    The analysis of wind drift was motivated by the question: under
what conditions can the tides and wind move the effluent plumes from
the wastewater outfalls and combined sewer overflow into Quincy Bay?
In this problem, the locations of the pollution sources are fixed by
the locations of the outfalls. Sensitive receptor areas -- beaches
and shellfish harvesting areas -- were identified, and these also

have fixed locations. In general, the outfalls are about 3.2 km (2 miles) and 30 to 60 degrees northeast from the receptor areas. Therefore, the analysis proceeded by determining the statistical frequency in which wind drift excursions of 3.2 km occur in the northeast to southwest direction.

Wind Data

The wind data for the analysis included 15-year average wind roses for each month, and one year of 3-hour wind observations. The 15-year wind roses covered the period 1950 to 1964. The 3-hour observations covered the calendar year 1983 and included time of observation, wind speed, and direction.

While is it possible to acquire a data tape with many years of wind data, such an approach was beyond the scope of this study. Further, before initiating such a larger-scale analysis implied by the use of many years of data on a tape, the microcomputer was chosen to conduct a prototype analysis for a more extensive data set that could be analyzed later on a larger computer.

Computer Tools

The selection of the computer tools was governed by the format of the available wind data, the need to develop wind statistics, and the need to graphically present results. The analysis was performed using a 16-bit 256K RAM microcomputer and general-purpose spreadsheet software with the capability to graph results, query the data, and perform calculations on the data file. The spreadsheet was used first as a means to store the 1983 wind data. The one year of 3-hour wind observations were entered by keyboard onto a diskette, and keyboard entry required about 45 minutes to enter each month of data. Next, the 1983 data were analyzed to determine if they were typical of long-term wind records; following that step, statistics for wind drift excursions were developed. These steps are described below, and Table 1 summarizes the use of the spreadsheet software as the engineering tool for executing these steps.

Generating Wind Roses

Because the detailed analysis of wind excursions was to be performed on one year of data for 1983, it was necessary to determine if the 1983 data were statistically representative of long-term conditions. In order to make this determination, monthly wind roses for 1983 were developed to compare to the 15-year average wind roses.

TABLE 1. USE OF THE SPREADSHEET SOFTWARE
IN THE WIND DRIFT ANALYSIS

Application	Spreadsheet Operations
Create a file with 2,920 3-hour observations of speed and direction	Establish a separate spreadsheet file for each month. Each file has three columns of data:

	Hour Speed Direction
	The hour column shows consecutive 3-hour intervals from the first to the last day of the month.
Generate monthly wind roses	Extract wind observations from the file based on 16 direction criteria, such as: 0 to 2, 3 to 4, 5 to 7, 8 to 9, etc., up to 35 to 36. Copy extracted records to another area of the spreadsheet for counting numbers of observations for each direction, and determining percentages for plotting each wind rose.
Generate wind drift profiles	Calculate a new spreadsheet column: "Drift", being the product of speed, duration, and cosine of wind direction with respect to designated direction. Multiply by "-1" to obtain direction toward which wind blows.
	Use graphing function of spreadsheet software to plot "Hour" column versus "Drift" column. See. Fig. 4.
Generate exceedance curves	Extract wind observations from the file based on Drift criteria: <4000, <3000, <2000, etc. Copy these observations to a new area of the spreadsheet for counting and determining percentages by month for plotting exceedance curves.

The 15-year average wind roses had been constructed using 16
compass points. In order to generate wind roses for 1983 with the
microcomputer, the same 16 compass points were used. The directions
of the wind in the 1983 data file consisted of degrees from true
north recorded in tens of degrees. Thus, North is 0, East is 9,
South is 18, and West is 27. A calm condition is assigned the
direction 36. The data file was queried to extract for each month
the 3-hour events that fell in the 16 respective sectors of the
compass. The wind roses were then computed by dividing the number
of extracted observations by the total number of observations for
each month.

The 1983 wind roses were superimposed on the 15-year wind roses
to show the correspondence in the wind data. Figure 2 shows a
typical comparison of the 1983 and 15-year wind roses. The use of
the general purpose spreadsheet software provided a means to quickly
demonstrate the correspondence between the single year of data and
the long-term record. As an engineering tool, it fulfilled the need
to confirm -- early in the analysis -- that the one year of data was
statistically representative of long-term conditions, and that
further detailed evaluation of the 1983 data was justified.

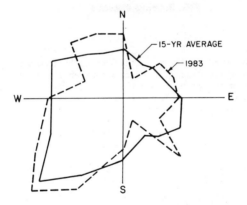

FIG. 2. Wind Roses for August

Vector Analysis

The next step was to analyze the wind data to determine the
frequency of winds in the direction northeast to southwest. This
step proceeded by computing vector components for each 3-hour wind
observation. Two vector components were defined: one parallel to,
and the other perpendicular to, the northeast-southwest direction
that was of interest. Figure 3 shows the way the vector components
were defined. The formula shown in Figure 3 was used to calculate
the wind drift excursion during each 3-hour observation. It was
assumed that the 3-hourly observations of velocity were indicative
of average velocities during the 3-hour period.

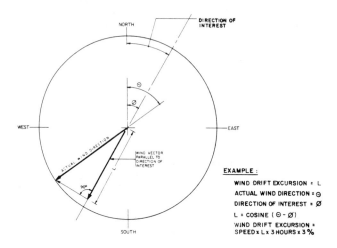

FIG. 3. Wind Vectors

Generating Profiles of Wind Drift Excursion

Each month of wind data was characterized by the method shown in Figure 3, then plotted as wind drift profiles shown in Figure 4. Two profiles were made for each month: one for the direction 30-degrees northeast, and one for the direction 60-degrees northeast. These directions spanned the compass arc defined by the major outfall locations and the shoreline receptor areas. Also, the use of the two directions added an ability to note the sensitivity of the analysis with respect to designated direction.

The wind drift profiles shown on Figure 4 show the distance that wind could transport the water surface layer in the absence of tide for each 3-hour interval of the month. Distances on the positive side of the ordinate represent excursions to the southwest (from the outfalls to the shoreline areas). Distances on the negative side of the ordinate represent excursions to the northeast (from the outfalls to the seaward, away from the shoreline areas).

Comparison of the wind drift profiles for the 30-degree and 60-degree direction shows that there are some wind events that produce a southwest excursion with respect to the 30-degree direction, while producing a northeast excursion with respect to the 60-degree direction. These events generally represent winds from the northwest between the compass points 300 degrees to 330 degrees where the cosine function changes from positive to negative with respect to the 30-degree and 60-degree directions.

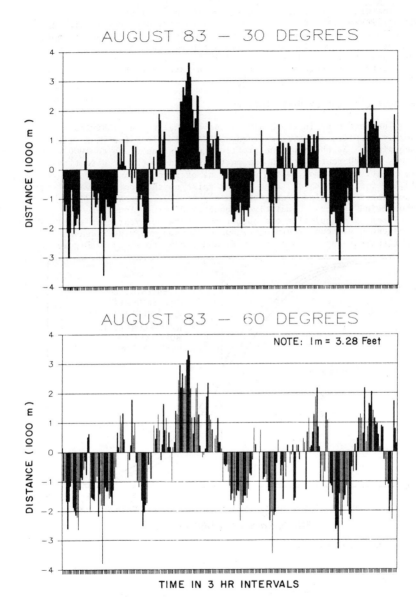

FIG. 4. Wind Drift Profiles

The wind drift profiles shown in Figure 4 illustrate the
variability of wind drift tendencies over time, and they provide a
means to compare seasonal differences in wind patterns that are not
obvious from inspection of wind roses alone. However, the profiles
are sensitive to the direction established for defining the vector
components, and there are limitations in interpreting the profiles.

Developing Frequency Distributions

The next step in the analysis was to analyze the individual
monthly profiles to develop frequency distributions for wind drift
excursions. As shown by the profiles, excursions of up to 1000
meters (3,280 feet) in both the northeast and southwest directions
are relatively common, while excursions of greater than 4000 meters
(13,100 feet) are rare. Each 3-hour spike on the profiles was
interpreted as a wind event, and in a year there are about 2,920
3-hour wind events. Cumulative frequency distributions were
developed by calculating the number of events per year that equalled
or exceeded various excursions. Summer season and winter season
distributions were also calculated, and these are shown on Figure 5.

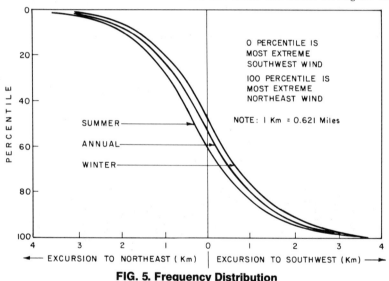

FIG. 5. Frequency Distribution

Use of the Frequency Distributions

The frequency distributions for wind excursions were used in
conjunction with tide frequencies to make predictions of effluent
movements in Quincy Bay. A 16-day field program of drogue tracking
provided empirical data for effluent movements under various wind
and tide conditions monitored on the water. The frequency distributions for wind and tide were then used with the drogue tracking

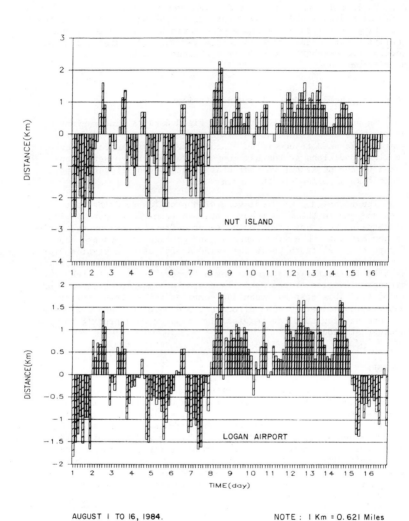

AUGUST I TO 16, 1984.   NOTE : I Km = 0.621 Miles

FIG. 6. Comparison of Wind Profiles

data to estimate the number of days per year that wastewater
effluent plumes could be moved into different points in Quincy Bay.
A multi-year record of coliform observations at the beaches and
shellfish harvesting areas in Quincy Bay was correlated with weather
records and discharge records from the outfalls to verify the
predictions made in this study.

Comparing the Records of Two Wind Stations

As part of the drogue tracking field work, a wind monitoring
station was established at Nut Island at Quincy Bay. This wind
station was used to determine if there were appreciable differences
in wind conditions at the bay compared to the wind observations
taken by the permanent weather station at Boston's Logan Airport,
about 8 km (5 miles) to the north.

The technique for displaying wind profiles described above was
used to compare the wind record obtained from the temporary wind
station in the study area to the records from the permanent station
at the airport. The wind observations of each station are shown on
Figure 6. The figure shows the "wind drift" at each station over a
16-day time period. The amplitude of the profile at the Nut Island
station is greater than at the Logan Airport station, because the
greater elevation of the Nut Island station made for greater wind
velocity. This display technique combines the factors of wind
observation interval, wind direction, and velocity into a profile
for one station that can be visually compared to a profile for
another station.

Summary

This study of wastewater effluent movements in a bay used a
combination of empirical drogue tracking data and a history of wind
records to analyze the frequency of effluent transport into the bay.
The microcomputer and spreadsheet software used in the study allowed
the development of a technique for analyzing and displaying wind
drift forces in the bay, and for comparing the results of different
wind monitoring records. The analytical procedures developed in
this study can be applied to a long-term record of wind data read
from a tape on a minicomputer. The microcomputer acted as a testing
ground, prior to investing the greater effort in a larger scale
analysis with many years of data.

Evaluation of Pretreatment and Sludge Disposal Plans

Deborah Thurston, Judy Kildow, John Busch[*]

A spreadsheet model is developed to assist municipal managers in evaluating industrial wastewater pretreatment plans and sludge disposal criteria. A case study is presented.

Introduction

To manage its wastewater treatment and sludge disposal operations, a municipality must develop pretreatment requirements for its contributing industries. Pretreatment standards were intended to control three impacts of industrial waste discharge to municipal systems; passing of untreated pollutants through the treatment process resulting in failure to meet effluent discharge standards or water quality standards, inhibition of the treatment process itself, and contamination of sludge. The first two impacts are relatively easy to assess, while the third is not. Yet, industrial wastewater influent to municipality owned wastewater treatment systems can contaminate municipal sludge to the point that it is difficult and costly to dispose of.

Objective

The objective of this model is to provide municipal system managers with an organized, comprehensive decision making decisions for evaluating the cost and feasibility of alternative industrial pretreatment requirements concurrently with alternative sludge disposal criteria. By analyzing the sludge contamination problem from the point of contaminant creation to the point of sludge disposal, rather than assuming a given level of contamination is unavoidable and accepting the costs of the available disposal options, it is hoped that a less expensive set of pretreatment/sludge disposal systems can be arrived at.

Methodology

We are using an IBM personal computer with Lotus 123 spreadsheet software. At this point, the model is limited to two industrial categories, eight companies, and six heavy metal contaminants.

The user can vary several parameters to "play" with alternative scenarios and determine the resulting distribution of pretreatment and sludge disposal costs between various industries and the municipality. Thus, it is possible to incorporate non-quantifiable political and environmental issues in a more concrete way than simply labelling an alternative "infeasible". The model makes it possible to quantify the cost of avoiding political or environmental harm by providing estimates

*This work was funded by the U.S. Environmental Protection Agency, Massachusetts Institute of Technology, Cambridge, MA, 02139, USA

of the cost difference between the least cost option and the most politically or environmentally acceptable alternative. Thus, the model can be used to analyze, select, and explain the basis for alternative programs.

Use of the Model for Analysis of Policy Alternatives

Generally, four parameters can be varied. These are industrial "pretreatment" technologies (including process and operational changes such as recycling and re-use), distribution of pretreatment requirements among industries (uniform vs. non-uniform standards), sludge disposal options, and sludge disposal criteria. Any one or combination of these parameters can be easily varied so that the user can determine "what if" a policy were implemented. A great number of scenarios can be quickly evaluated and compared.

The following alternatives are likely to be of greatest interest to municipal managers:

1. Requiring uniform industry compliance with various categorical pretreatment standards, including Best Available Treatment (BAT) and Best Practicable Treatment (BPT).

2. Pretreatment requirements necessary to insure that a specific municipal sludge disposal alternative is environmentally acceptable. Low-cost sludge disposal options which are made infeasible because of sludge contamination are easily identified.

3. Pretreatment requirements which minimize total cost by requiring higher levels of treatment for those industries whose unit removal costs are low, and less stringent requirements of industries whose unit removal costs are high.

4. The change in industry and municipal cost as a result of increasing or decreasing the stringency of sludge disposal criteria, for either uniform or non-uniform pretreatment requirements.

Model Structure Inputs consist of:

1) Publicly owned treatment works (POTW) characteristics

    Size in Millions of gallons per day (mgd)
    Amount of sludge currently generated
    Influent wastewater characteristics for chosen contaminants
    Removal efficiencies for chosen contaminants

2) POTW and Industry sludge disposal options and costs, up to 12 options

3) Industry inventory, up to 8 companies

    Industry Type
    Size in thousands of gallons of wastewater generated per day
    Volume of sludge currently generated
    Percent solids of sludge currently generated

Wastewater effluent characteristics
Removal efficiencies currently being achieved
Pretreatment alternatives available, removal efficiencies,
    sludge generation and capital, operating & maintenance costs
Selection of one pretreatment option for each industry for
    analysis

4. Sludge disposal criteria for each disposal option and for each
    contaminant

        For POTW sludge
        For Industry sludge

Model Structure OUTPUT consists of:

1) Composition of POTW and industrial sludge for each contaminant.

2) Total annual cost of pretreatment system.

3) Volume of sludge production for POTW and for each industry.

4) Sludge composition and removal rates at the POTW and at each
    industry for each contaminant.

5) Feasibility of each sludge disposal option for each industry and
    for POTW, with an indication of which contaminant(s) are
    exceeding the criteria.

6) Tabulation of sludge disposal costs for each feasible disposal
    option for POTW and each industry.

7) Selection of lowest cost feasible sludge disposal option for
    industry and POTW.

8) Tabulation of pretreatment costs and lowest cost sludge disposal
    option for each industry and POTW, also summarized in a TOTAL
    figure for the lowest cost achievable given a set of sludge
    disposal criteria and pretreatment requirements.

CASE STUDY

    The POTW serves a large coastal metropolitan area including
eight industries. Total wastewater flow is 50 million gallons per day
(MGD), with industrial wastewater accounting for approximately 10% of
the flow quantity. The municipal and industrial flow quantities and
strengths represent the typical situation of industrial flow accounting
for a relatively low percentage of wastewater flow quantity but a
relatively large percentage of wastewater pollutant loading. Therefore,
it is assumed that pretreatment of industrial wastewater will not
decrease POTW treatment costs nor will it significantly change the POTW
sludge production volume significantly.

    Five electroplaters and three tanneries were selected for analysis,
since they are a major source for the contaminants of concern. A
range of flow volumes and waste strength was selected from data in the
EPA Development Documents for Effluent Limitations Guidelines for these
two industries. Data was selected to represent normally expected

```
===========================================================
```

WASTE DEFINITION - LOCAL COMPANIES

```
===========================================================
```

		Waste Rmvl (mg/l)	Eff (%)	Sludge (ppm wet)	Effluent (mg/l)
	BOD	600	0%	–	600
	TSS	600	0%	0.00	600
Heavy Metals -----					
	Cadmium	0.03	0%	0.00	0.03
	Chromium	25.00	0%	0.00	25.00
	Copper	8.44	0%	0.00	8.44
	Lead	0.17	0%	0.00	0.17
	Mercury	0.00	0%	0.00	0.00
	Zinc	6.58	0%	0.00	6.58

Table 2 Example of Input Data for Local Industry

```
===========================================================
```

LOCAL SLUDGE DISPOSAL STANDARDS

```
===========================================================
```

Option 1 - Landfilling (dewatered sludge)
Option 2 - Landfilling (liquid sludge)
Option 3 - Land Application (non-food chain crops)
Option 4 - Land Application (food chain crops)
Option 5 - Land Application (compost)
Option 6 - Ocean Dumping (20 mile, tanker)
Option 7 - Ocean Dumping (60 mile, tanker)
Option 8 - Ocean Dumping (250 mile, barge)
Option 9 - Ocean Outfall
Option 10 - Incineration (fluidized bed)
Option 11 - Incineration (multiple hearth)
Option 12 - Hazardous Waste (secure landfill)

SLUDGE DISPOSAL STANDARDS

--- ALLOWABLE LIMITS -----

	UNITS	<---- Disposal Option Number ---->			
		1	2	3	4
Cadmium	ppm	100.0	500.0	1.0	0.1
Chromium	ppm	1000.0	3000.0	250.0	0.1
Copper	ppm	5000.0	10000.0	100.0	0.1
Lead	ppm	1000.0	2000.0	10.0	0.1
Mercury	ppm	15.0	20.0	3.0	0.1
Zinc	ppm	10000.0	20000.0	500.0	3.0

Table 3 Example of Input Sludge Disposal Criteria

```
:==================================================================
```

```
        COMPANY NUMBER:          7

               <---- Disposal Option Number ---->
          1    2    3    4    5    6    7    8    9    10   11   12
```

	1	2	3	4	5	6	7	8	9	10	11	12
Cadmium	1	1	1	1	1	1	1	1	1	1	1	1
Chromium	NA	1	NA	NA	NA	NA	1	1	NA	NA	NA	1
Copper	1	1	1	NA	NA	1	1	1	1	1	1	1
Lead	1	1	1	NA	NA	1	1	1	1	1	1	1
Mercury	1	1	1	1	1	1	1	1	1	1	1	1
Zinc	1	1	1	NA	1	1	1	1	1	1	1	1
VIABILITY	NA	1	NA	NA	NA	NA	1	1	NA	NA	NA	1

```
==================================================================
```

Table 4   Example of Output Sludge Disposal Option Feasibility for
Company Number 7

```
==================================================================
                                                              !
        SUMMARY OF PRETREATMENT/DISPOSAL COSTS
                                                              !
==================================================================
```

mpany Number	Pretreatment (k$/yr)	#	Sludge Disposal (k$/yr)	#	TOTAL (k$/yr)
1	$384.80	4	$29.32	7	$414.12
2	$79.51	1	$0.25	6	$79.77
3	$0.00	0	$0.00	0	$0.00
4	$573.97	4	$48.96	8	$622.93
5	$440.31	2	$4.90	8	$445.21
6	$604.75	3	$9.48	8	$614.24
7	$306.05	2	$3.91	7	$309.96
8	$29.40	1	$1.03	7	$30.44
POTW			$919.01	6	$919.01

```
==================================================================
```

| TOTALS | $1,479 | | $1,002 | | $2,481 |

```
==================================================================
```

Table 5   Example of Output Tabulation of Pretreatment Costs and
Lowest Cost Sludge Disposal Option for POTW and Each Industry

ranges. In order to more accurately reflect reality, waste strength
for larger dischargers was selected more toward median values, while
smaller dischargers were assigned lower or higher values. Three
alternative sets of sludge disposal criteria have been developed.

1. Set criteria at uniform existing levels of sludge contamination
    for all disposal alternatives. This would allow the use of all
    disposal options for the existing level of sludge quality, but
    would not allow increases in sludge contamination.

2. Set criteria at varying levels for the different disposal options.
    Strict, or only low levels of contamination would be allowed for
    disposal options which pose a greater potential threat to human
    health and the environment, such as application to food-chain
    crops. Less stringent, or higher, levels would be allowed for
    disposal options which do not pose a great threat, such as disposal
    in sealed containers in a specially designed "secured" landfill
    such as those for hazardous waste.

3. Set criteria at very stringent levels, varying with different
    disposal options. The ranking of disposal options in order of level
    of threat is the same as for the previous set of disposal criteria,
    but levels are set much lower.

    The three alternative pretreatment programs are:

1. No pretreatment required.

2. Uniform standard categorical pretreatment requirements for all
    industries. This appears to be equitable in that all industrial
    dischargers must conform to the same standards established by EPA.

3. Varying levels of pretreatment required of industries, based on the
    unit cost of pollutant removal. Industries with low treatment cost
    per unit of pollutant removed will be required to achieve greater
    levels of treatment.

    The pretreatment options used for electroplaters are Option 1,
precipitation and sedimentation (BAT, BPT); Option 2, same as Option 1
plus multi-media filtration; Option 3, same as Option 1 plus in-plant
controls for cadmium, such as evaporative recovery, ion exchange or
recovery rinses; and Option 4, which incorporates the concept of
"pollution prevention pays" by making process or operational changes
to decrease the amount of waste metal generated. Methods include
separating and recycling cooling water, employing countercurrent
rinses, substituting less harmful chemical for more toxic ones, mobile
tanks for concentrated acid collection, trapped rinses and sale of
by-product phosphoric acid, and oil skimmers.

    For tanneries, Option 1 is equalization, primary coagulation-
sedimentation, and extended aeration activated sludge (BAT, BPT);
Option 2, same as Option 1 plus in-plant controls to reduce wastewater
volume such as stream segregation, segregated stream pretreatment,
activated carbon addition; and Option 3, same as Option 2 plus
multimedia filtration.

RESULTS AND CONCLUSIONS

A summary table of results from the three pretreatment requirement scenarios and the three sets of sludge disposal criteria is
presented on the following page. Industry, POTW and total costs are
presented for each of the nine alternatives. Industry cost is composed
of both treatment and sludge disposal cost, while POTW cost is for
sludge disposal only.

1. For each of the three sets of sludge disposal criteria, the pre-
    treatment program resulting in the lowest total cost is "no pre-
    treatment required". Sludge disposal cost increases to the POTW
    as a result of sludge contamination ($715,000) are less than the
    cost of industrial pretreatment ($4,855,000 and $1,860,000), which
    would be required to avoid these costs to the municipality.

2. Non-uniform pretreatment requirements based on cost efficiency
    of contaminant removal for each industry are more expensive in
    total than no pretreatment requirements but less expensive than
    uniform pretreatment requirements. In each case, non-uniform
    pretreatment requirements which take advantage of the greater
    removal efficiencies of dischargers with lower unit removal costs
    result in total costs of approximately half that of uniform
    pretreatment requirements to meet the same sludge disposal criteria.

3. Uniform, categorical standard requirements represent the most
    costly method of meeting any of the three sets of sludge disposal
    criteria.

4. For each of the three sets of pretreatment requirements, the cost
    to the POTW of sludge disposal increases as sludge disposal
    criteria become more stringent. When no pretreatment is required,
    the cost to the municipality nearly doubles, increasing from
    $919,000 to $1,787,000. When either uniform or varied pretreatment
    is required, cost to the municipality increases by only 10% when
    stringent sludge disposal criteria are imposed. This finding
    vividly illustrates the reason for developing this model, that
    POTW's are incurring costs because of insufficient industrial
    wastewater pretreatment. The model can be used as a tool to
    quantify and assign those costs. The results can be used to devise
    an equitable cost distribution system.

5. The lowest total cost options are no pretreatment and sludge
    criteria set at either uniform existing contamination
    levels or varied levels to reflect a median range of contaminate
    levels found in sludge. As expected, POTW costs do not decrease
    for these two sets of sludge disposal criteria as a result of
    imposing pretreatment requirements, since the existing POTW meets
    the sludge criteria for the lowest cost option already, with no
    pretreatment.

6   The lowest cost POTW sludge disposal option feasible is always
    a form of ocean disposal. If disposal criteria for this option
    were more stringent, we could see greater increases in POTW sludge
    disposal costs as a result of sludge contamination.

7. More stringent sludge disposal criteria would tend to make total costs of pretreatment options which include both pretreatment and sludge disposal costs, particularly the non-uniform option, less than the total cost of no pretreatment.

Pretreatment Requirements*	Sludge Disposal Criteria		
	Uniform, Set at Existing Contamination Levels	Varied According to Disposal Option, Median Range	Varied According to Disposal Option, Strict Range
	Cost in $1000	Cost in $1000	Cost in $1000
0, or No Pretreatment	0 industry	0 industry	0 industry
	919 POTW	919 POTW	1,787 POTW
	919 total	919 total	1,787 total
1, or Uniform Categorical Standards	4,856 industry	4,538 industry	4,855 industry
	919 POTW	919 POTW	1,072 POTW
	5,775 total	5,457 total	5,927 total
Non-Uniform Requirements	1,861 industry	1,562 industry	1,860 industry
	919 POTW	919 POTW	1,072 POTW
	2,780 total	2,481 total	2,932 total

Table 1 Summary of Results of Case Study: Three Pretreatment Alternatives and Three Sets of Sludge Disposal Criteria

References

Booz-Allen & Hamilton, Inc., "An Overview of the Containments of Concern in the Disposal and Utilization of Municipal Sewage Sludge", Environmental Protection Agency, Sludge Task Force, April 1983, Washington, D.C.

EG&G Environmental Consultants, An Assessment of Costs for Ocean Disposal of Wastes by Barge, Waltham, MA, 1983.

JRB Associates, "Description of the EPA Computer Program/Model for Developing Local Limits," Permits Division, U.S. Environmental Protection Agency, November 1983, Washington, DC.

Metcalf & Eddy, Inc., Wastewater Engineering Treatment Disposal Reuse, McGraw-Hill Book Company, Second Edition.

Partington, B., Kohl, J., and Dorn, E., "Making Pollution Prevention Pay in the Electroplating and Metal-Finishing Industries," Workshop Summary, Water Resources Research Institute.

Putnam, Hayes & Bartlett, Inc., Impact of Pretreatment Guidelines on Waste Disposal, March 16, 1984.

SCS Engineers, "Cost Estimating Manual for Municipal Wastewater Sludge Transport, Storage, and Disposal," Final Report, U.S. Environmental Protection Agency, December 1983, Long Beach, CA.

Schatzow, S., Gorsuch, A., Eidsness, F., Denit, J., and Anderson, D., "Development Document for Effluent Limitations Guidelines New Source Performance Standards and Pretreatment Standards for the Leather Tanning and Finishing Point Source Category," Effluent Guidelines Division Office of Water, U.S. Environmental Protection Agency, November 1982, Washington, D.C.

Schatzow, S., Ruckelshaus, W., Denit, J., Stigall, E., and Kinch, R., "Development Document for Effluent Limitations Guidelines New Source Performance Standards for the Metal Finishing Point Source Category", Effluent Guidelines Division Office of Water Regulations and Standards, U.S. Environmental Protection Agency, June 1983, Washington, D.C.

Wastewater Treatment Plant Design, by A Joint Committee of the Water Pollution Control Federation and the American Society of Civil Engineers, Lancaster Press, Inc., Lancaster, PA, 1977.

MATHEMATICAL MODELING OF GROUND WATER FLOW

Christopher G. Uchrin[1], M. ASCE

ABSTRACT

Knowledge of ground water flow patterns is essential not only for assessment of the safe yield of the system for water supply purposes but also for modeling the transport and fate of contaminants which may have been introduced to an aquifer system. The theoretical basis for ground water flow models is rooted in fluid mechanics and hydraulics. Analytical solutions for certain special case ground water flow situations are part of the classical literature in the field (2,3,13,14,15). The advent of high speed digital computation has spawned a new era in ground water flow modeling such that solutions to previously unsolvable modeling equations can now be approximated by numerical techniques. A new body of "classical literature" is evolving (5,6) focusing on numerical methods.

Many numerical algorithms for ground water flow models have been published and are available in computer software packages. It is the job of the ground water specialist to select an appropriate model for the system at hand, based on the geophysical characteristics of the aquifer system, and data availability. This paper will examine the theoretical principles of ground water models with attention to the applicability of the models to real world systems. Representative numerical algorithms will be discussed as well as available analytical solutions.

Fundamental Laws

Ground water flow, more generally flow through porous media, is governed by two basic laws of fluid mechanics involving mass and energy balances coupled to a relationship between flow and energy dissipation. The continuity equation derives from a mass balance and is expressed as:

$$Q = AU = A_p U_p \quad \dots\dots\dots\dots\dots\dots\dots\dots\dots\dots\dots\dots\dots\dots\dots (1)$$

where Q is ground water flow $[L^3/T]$; A is total cross sectional area $[L^2]$; U is the superficial (Darcy) velocity $[L/T]$; A_p is the pore area $[L^2]$; and U_p is the pore velocity $[L/T]$. An analog to pipe flow can be

[1]Assistant Professor, Department of Environmental Science, Cook College, New Jersey Agricultural Experiment Station, Rutgers University, New Brunswick, NJ 08903.

drawn by considering the porous medium as a series of interconnected little pipes through which the water flows. The area and volume available for flow are therefore the void area and void volume, respectively. These are related by the porosity, n, which is defined:

$$n = \frac{\text{void volume}}{\text{total volume}} \cong \frac{A_p}{A} \quad \dots\dots\dots\dots\dots\dots\dots\dots\dots\dots\dots\dots\dots\dots(2)$$

The energy balance is the well known Bernoulli Equation with a significant difference. The kinetic energy term ($U_p^2/2g$, where g is the gravitational constant) can be neglected in ground water applications since velocities are generally small, such that:

$$H = \frac{p}{\rho g} + z \quad \dots\dots\dots\dots\dots\dots\dots\dots\dots\dots\dots\dots\dots\dots\dots\dots\dots\dots(3)$$

where H is the total energy head of the system [L]; p is the pressure [F/L^2]; ρ is the fluid density [M/L^3]; and z is the elevation of the system with respect to an arbitrary datum (often mean sea level–MSL). Further analogs can be drawn to classical fluid mechanics: confined aquifer systems can be considered analogous to pressure flow in pipes whereas unconfined aquifer systems can be considered analogous to open channel flow. Equation 3 is graphically displayed in Figure 1 as applies to both systems. It should be noted that the low velocities associated with ground water flow together with small "pipe diameters," d, results in small Reynolds Numbers ($Nr = U_p d/\nu$, where ν is the

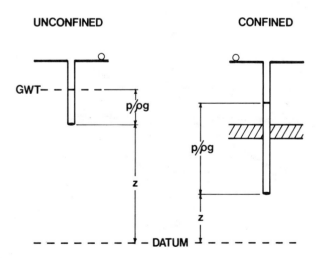

Figure 1. Total Head Schematic for Aquifer Systems.

kinematic viscosity of water) so that ground water flow is nearly always laminar (Nr < 1) whereas surface water flow tends to be turbulent.

Darcy's Law relates energy dissipation to flow and is expressed in one dimension, x, as:

$$U = -K \; \frac{dH}{dx} \quad \dotfill (4)$$

where K is the hydraulic conductivity [L/T]. Darcy's Law applies and can be expressed in three dimensions (x,y,z) as:

$$\vec{U} = -\underline{K} \; \nabla \cdot H \quad \dotfill (5)$$

where $\vec{U}$ is a three dimensional velocity vector, equal to u,v,w in x,y,z directions, respectively, and $\underline{K}$ is the hydraulic conductivity tensor, equal to K_x, K_y, K_z in the subscripted directions.

The Ground Water Diffusion Equation

Figure 2 displays an infinitesimal element at a position x,y,z in a saturated porous medium. A mass balance equation can be written about this element as:

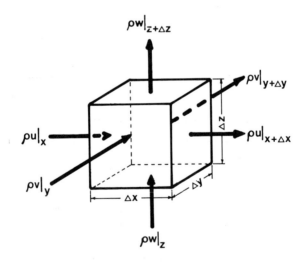

Figure 2.   Infinitesimal Aquifer Element.

$$\rho u|_x \Delta y \Delta z + \rho v|_y \Delta x \Delta z + \rho w|_z \Delta x \Delta y - \rho u|_{x+\Delta x} \Delta y \Delta z$$

$$- \rho v|_{y+\Delta y} \Delta x \Delta z - \rho w|_{z+\Delta z} \Delta x \Delta y = \frac{\rho S_s \Delta x \Delta y \Delta z}{\Delta t}[H|_{t+\Delta t} - H|_t] \quad \cdots\cdots\cdots (6)$$

where S_s is the specific storage $[L^{-1}]$, defined as the volume of water that a unit volume of aquifer releases from storage under a unit decline in hydraulic head (FC). Dividing by Δx, Δy, Δz, taking the limit as Δx, Δy, Δz, Δt approach zero and differentiating the resultant products obtains:

$$u\frac{\delta\rho}{\delta x} + v\frac{\delta\rho}{\delta y} + w\frac{\delta\rho}{\delta z} + \rho\frac{\delta u}{\delta x} + \rho\frac{\delta v}{\delta y} + \rho\frac{\delta w}{\delta z} = -\rho S_s\frac{\delta H}{\delta t} \quad \cdots\cdots\cdots\cdots (7)$$

Since the compressibility of water is small, changes in density can be considered negligable. Making this assumption and substituting Darcy's Law (Eqn. 5) obtains:

$$\frac{\delta}{\delta x}K_x\frac{\delta H}{\delta x} + \frac{\delta}{\delta y}K_y\frac{\delta H}{\delta y} + \frac{\delta}{\delta z}K_z\frac{\delta H}{\delta z} = S_s\frac{\delta H}{\delta t} \quad \cdots\cdots\cdots\cdots (8)$$

which is commonly called the ground water diffusion equation. It applies for both confined or unconfined aquifer systems.

Two Dimensional Systems

Many ground water systems can be modeled as two dimensional systems if ground water flow is predominantly in the horizontal directions. This greatly simplifies the ground water diffusion equation for both confined and unconfined systems. Both are discussed in the following sections.

Confined Systems. The ground water diffusion equation can be integrated over depth, z, between the interval [0,b] where b is the thickness of the aquifer. Further defining the transmissivity, T, as the product of the thickness, b, and the hydraulic conductivity, K, and substituting obtains:

$$\frac{\delta}{\delta x}(T_x\frac{\delta H}{\delta x}) + \frac{\delta}{\delta y}(T_y\frac{\delta H}{\delta y}) + = S_s b\frac{\delta H}{\delta t} \quad \cdots\cdots\cdots\cdots\cdots (9)$$

Unconfined Systems. These are more difficult than confined systems since the upper boundary is not necessarily static but may be moving as a function of time. If the assumption is made that H is constant over depth or flow is predominantly horizontal, then z is eliminated as a space variable. This is commonly referred to as "Dupuit's Assumption." Figure 3 displays a schematic of an infinitesimal element from such a system. A mass balance can be formulated about the system as:

$$\rho u \Delta y H \big|_x - \rho u \Delta y H \big|_{x+\Delta x} + \rho v \Delta x H \big|_y - \rho v \Delta x H \big|_{y+\Delta y} = \frac{S_y \Delta x \Delta y}{\Delta t} [H \big|_{t+\Delta t} - H \big|_t] \quad \ldots (10)$$

where S_y is the specific yield of the aquifer, defined as the volume of water that an unconfined aquifer releases from storage per unit surface area of aquifer per unit decline in the water table (4). Considering compressibility to be negligable and taking the limits as the finite differences approach zero obtains:

$$-\frac{\delta Hu}{\delta x} - \frac{\delta Hv}{\delta y} = S_y \frac{\delta H}{\delta t} \quad \ldots (11)$$

Substituting Darcy's law and rearranging yields:

$$\frac{\delta}{\delta x} K_x \frac{\delta H^2}{\delta x} + \frac{\delta}{\delta y} K_y \frac{\delta H^2}{\delta y} = 2 S_y \frac{\delta H}{\delta t} \quad \ldots (12)$$

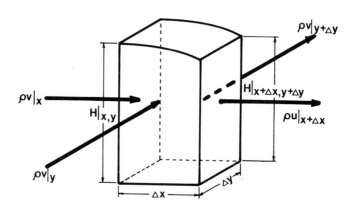

Figure 3.   Unconfined Aquifer Infinitesimal Element Schematic.

Simplifying Assumptions and Analytical Solutions

Often simplifying assumptions can be employed such that analytical solutions can be obtained for Equations 8, 9, and 12, in addition to assuming horizontal ground water movement. Among the most common are the assumptions that the medium is homogeneous (K_x and K_y are constant) and that the medium is isotropic ($K_x = K_y = K$). Cylindrical coordinates can then be applied such that:

$$x^2 + y^2 = r^2 \dotfill (12)$$

The ground water diffusion equation for confined aquifer systems the can be written:

$$\frac{\delta^2 H}{\delta r^2} + \frac{1}{r}\frac{\delta H}{\delta r} = \frac{S}{T}\frac{\delta H}{\delta t} \dotfill (13)$$

where S is the storage coefficient, equal to the product of the specific storage, S_s, and the aquifer thickness, b. For boundary conditions involving a discharge, Q, at the center, $r = 0$, and $H = H_o$ as r approaches infinity, and an initial condition of $H = H_o$, the solution to Equation 13 was given by Theis (13,14) as:

$$H(r,t) = H_o - \frac{Q}{4\pi T}[W(u)] \dotfill (14)$$

where $W(u)$ is the so-called "well function," tabulated in textbooks (2,4,15), and u is a grouping given by:

$$u = r^2 S/4Tt \dotfill (15)$$

Unsaturated Flow Modeling

Many pollutants enter ground water aquifers by first passing through the unsaturated zone. Examples include sanitary and industrial landfill leachates, septic tank effluents, spray irrigation of treated sewage, seepage from industrial wastewater lagoons and runoff retention basins, radioactive leakage from disposal sites, and infiltration of fertilizers and pesticides. Since by definition, the porous medium is not saturated, modifications to the parameters and equations used to describe saturated ground water flow must be made. The previously defined hydraulic conductivity is now defined as the "unsaturated hydraulic conductivity," $K(\theta)$, which is, as indicated, a function of the moisture content, θ. Total head has, in effect, no meaning, so a new variable, the total potential, or suction head, ψ, is used. The total potential includes suction or tension pressure effects. It is measured in the field and in the lab by a "tensiometer." Relationships between hydraulic conductivity and moisture content and suction head and moisture content are shown in Figure 4.

The continuity equation for one dimensional (vertical) unsaturated flow can be given as:

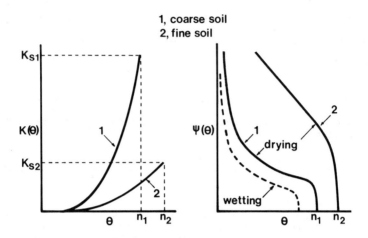

Figure 4. Unsaturated Hydraulic Conductivity, Suction Head, Moisture Content Relationships.

$$\frac{\delta \Theta}{\delta t} = - \frac{\delta q_z}{\delta z} \pm Q(z,t,\Theta) \quad \dots\dots\dots\dots\dots\dots\dots\dots\dots\dots\dots\dots (16)$$

where q_z is the vertical volumetric water flux $[L^3/L^2-T]$ and Q is a volumetric source (+) or sink (−) function $[L^3/L^2-T]$. Schwartzendruber (12) using Darcy's Law has shown that the volumetric flow rate is a fuction of the moisture content such that:

$$q_z = - D_z(\Theta) \frac{\delta \Theta}{\delta z} + K_z(\Theta) \quad \dots\dots\dots\dots\dots\dots\dots\dots\dots\dots\dots\dots (17)$$

where D_z is the vertical soil-water diffusivity $[L^2/T]$, given as:

$$D_z = K_z(\Theta) \frac{\delta \psi}{\delta \Theta} \quad \dots\dots\dots\dots\dots\dots\dots\dots\dots\dots\dots\dots\dots (18)$$

Substitution into Equation 16 yields the so-called "Richards Equation:"

$$\frac{\delta \Theta}{\delta t} = \frac{\delta}{\delta z} [D_z(\Theta) \frac{\delta \Theta}{\delta z}] - \frac{\delta}{\delta z} [K_z(\Theta)] - Q(z,t,\Theta) \quad \dots\dots\dots\dots (19)$$

Important assumptions implicit in the above derivation include no hysteresis effects in wetting and drying (shown in Figure 4), air compressibility is negligible and air pressure is atmospheric. Moisture content is the field variable which must be modeled. In some instances, it may be advisable to use a model based on the suction head which can be formulated:

$$\frac{\delta}{\delta z} \left[K(\psi) \frac{\delta}{\delta z} (\psi - z) \right] = C(\psi) \frac{\delta \psi}{\delta t} \quad \ldots\ldots\ldots\ldots\ldots\ldots\ldots\ldots(20)$$

where C is the specific water capacity, equal to $\delta\theta/\delta\psi$, and the suction head and unsaturated hydraulic conductivity are considered to be single valued functions of the moisture content (7). The Richards Equation can also be expanded to two or three dimensions, if necessary, by adding terms for horizontal fluxes to the continuity equation.

Unsaturated Flow Boundary Conditions

Both Dirichlet (constant value) and Neumann (constant flux) type boundary conditions can apply. For instance, the ground water table can be used as a vertical boundary at which, $\theta=n$. This boundary condition could also apply in a horizontal dimension at a water body. The Neumann boundary condition is usually used to describe the surface condition in the vertical direction and is formulated in one dimension as:

$$-D_z(\theta) \frac{\delta\theta}{\delta t} + K_z(\theta) = f(t); \quad @ \ z = 0 \quad \ldots\ldots\ldots\ldots\ldots\ldots(21)$$

where f(t) is a flux function accounting for the net infiltration after rainfall, evaporation, and irrigation (if appropriate). This function will be positive immediately after rainfall and could possibly equal zero should the previously unsaturated zone reach total saturation, in which case all the water would be transported away as runoff. This condition could therefore also be used to describe impervious layers, either above or below the surface. A negative flux would describe an evaporative condition.

Numerical/Computer Solutions to Ground Water Flow Problems

Some ground water flow and ground water solute transport problems can be solved using analytical methods if certain assumptions are made. Some of these solutions and the necessary assumptions are discussed herein. In many cases, however, these assumptions may require an over-simplification of the problem. A numerical solution is thus required.

A comprehensive presentation and review of the available methods for solving ground water flow problems is beyond the scope of this paper. A good primer has been prepared by Mercer and Faust (8). A brief description of the most common techniques follows.

Finite Difference. These systems literally break up the system to be modeled into grids, in which the spatial differentials, dx, dy, dz, are replaced by finite differences x, y, z. There are several ways in which the grids can be configured and difference equations formulated. Generally speaking, the finer the grids, the more accurate the approximations. Finer grids, however, require that more computation is required and also increases the opportunity for round-off errors to dominate. The advantages of finite difference methods include an easily understood theoretical basis, and easy data input. Disadvantages involve the possibility of high numerical dispersion, which could translate into low accuracy, and the need for regular grids which makes it difficult to model system with irregular geometries. Chu and Willis (1) recently modeled an unconfined system using an explicit finite difference technique. Hunt (5) is a good reference text for this method.

Finite Element. These systems divide a region into a series of subregions, or elements, whose shapes are determined by a set of points called nodes. Triangular elements can be used thus allowing for significant flexibility which is one of the primary advantages of this method. An integral approach is then used to approximate the differential equations. Huyakorn and Pinder (6) describe two methods for accomplishing this: the variational approach and the weighted residual approach (Galerkin). The dependent variables are then approximated in terms of interpolation, or basis, functions. An integral relationship must then be expressed for each element as a function of all the nodes of an element. The values of the integrals are then calculated for each element and combined together with the appropriate boundary conditions to yield a series of time dependent linear first-order differential equations. These are generally solved by a finite difference technique. Other advantages to this method, in addition to its ability to handle irregular geometries, include high accuracy. The principal disadvantage is the advanced mathematical basis which is not necessarily intuitive. As a result, this technique can be difficult to program and difficult to modify for data input conditions. Pinder has extensively used this technique for both flow and transport problems (6,9,10,11). Huyakorn and Pinder (6) is an excellent reference text for this method.

Summary

The complexities of ground water flow modeling revolve about the proper definition of the system and application of appropriate modeling equations and boundary conditions. The assumption making process is critical; while certain assumptions may greatly simplify a problem, they may render the answers meaningless due to oversimplification. This paper reviewed the basic theory behind ground water flow modeling with a focus on application to real systems.

Acknowledgements

This work was supported in part by the New Jersey Agricultural Experiment Station, Publication No. D-07525-1-85.

References

1. Chu, W.S., and R. Willis, "An Explicit Finite Difference Model for Unconfined Aquifers," Ground Water, Vol. 22, No. 6, 1984, pp. 728-734.

2. Davis, S.N., and R.J.M. DeWiest, Hydrogeology, John Wiley & Sons, New York, NY, 1966, 463.

3. DeWiest, R.J.M., Flow Through Porous Media, Academic Press, Inc., New York, NY, 1969, 530 pp.

4. Freeze, R.A., and J.A. Cherry, Groundwater, Prentice-Hall, Inc., Englewood Cliffs, NJ, 1979, 604 pp.

5. Hunt, B., Mathematical Analysis of Groundwater Resources, Butterworth & Co., London, U.K., 1983, 271 pp.

6. Huyakorn, P.S., and G.F. Pinder, Computational Methods in Subsurface Flow, Academic Press, New York, NY, 1983, 473 pp.

7. Khaleel, R., and T.-C. Yeh, "A Galerkin Finite-Element Program for Simulating Unsaturated Flow in Porous Media," Ground Water, Vo. 23, No. 1, 1985, pp. 90-96.

8. Mercer, J.W., and C.R. Faust, Ground-Water Modeling, National Water Well Association, 1981, 60 pp.

9. Pinder, G.F., "A Galerkin-Finite Element Simulation of Groundwater Contamination on Long Island, New York," Water Resources Research, Vol. 9, No. 6, 1973, pp. 1657-1669.

10. Pinder, G.F., and E. O. Frind, "Application of Galerkin's Procedure toAquifer Analysis," Water Resources Research, Vol. 8, No. 1, 1972, pp. 108-120.

11. Pinder, G.F., E.O. Frind, and S.S. Papadopulos, "Functional Coefficients in the Analysis of Groundwater Flow," Water Resources Research, Vol. 9, No. 1, pp. 222-226.

12. Schwartzendruber, "The Flow of Water in Unsaturated Soils," Chapter 6 in Flow Through Porous Media, Academic Press, New York, 1969, pp. 215-292.

13. Theis, C.V., "The Relation Between the Lowering of the Piezometric Surface and the Rate and Duration of Discharge of a Well Using Ground Water Storage," Trans. Am. Geophys. Union, Vol. 16, 1935, pp. 519-524.

14. Theis, C.V., "The Significance and Nature of the Cone of Depression in Groundwater Bodies," Econ. Geol., Vol. 33, 1938, pp. 889-920.

15. Todd, D.K., Groundwater Hydrology, 2nd ed., John Wiley & Sons, New York, NY, 1980, 535 pp.

SIMULATION OF GROUNDWATER FLOWS
IN LEAKY MULTI-LAYERED AQUIFER

Sam S. Y. Wang[1], M. ASCE, G. B. Chatterji[2] and T. Y. Su[3]

A newly developed computational methodology for simulating the groundwater flows in multi-layered aquifer is presented. The model is based on the finite element method following the Galerkin's approach. It can correctly describe the basic physical characteristics of the aquifer as well as adequately predict the trend of groundwater flows under realistic external influences. It can be widely applied to steady or transient, confined, phreatic, leaky, or non-leaky aquifers with single or multiple layered structure.

Introduction

With the rapid advancement of digital computer's capability and numerical solution methodology, the computational modeling and simulation of both physical phenomena and engineering systems have become not only viable and verifiable but also cost-effective research and engineering tools. They can be used in conjunction with the physical and other mathematical modeling methods to enhance the understanding of complex groundwater flows more effectively and efficiently. This paper is to present a newly developed computational model to simulate the characteristics of some general and realistic aquifers.

For brevity, only a minimum number of references are cited. A more comprehensive literature review is given by Chatterji (1). For realistic aquifers of highly irregular configuration, the models based on the finite difference method were found inconvenient, so that finite element and boundary element (or integral) methods were adopted. Zeinkiewicz (11) applied the finite element method in modeling subsurface hydrology in 1967. It was verified by Javandel/Witherspoon (5) when they studied a transient two-dimensional flow in a multi-layer aquifer in 1968-69. Zeinkiewicz/Parekh (12), Pinder/Frind (6), Huang/Sommerfeld (3), and Huang/Wu (4) utilized the Galerkin finite element method to investigate aquifer hydraulics of a variety of configurations well as conditions. Pinder and Gray's book on Finite Element Simulation in Surface and Subsurface Hydrology (7) provides

(1) Professor of Mechanical Engineering and Director of the Center for Computational Hydroscience and Engineering (CCHE), The University of Mississippi, University, MS 38677
(2) Formerly Research Assistant of CCHE
(3) Assistant Professor of Computer Science and Research Assistant Professor of CCHE

perhaps as another comprehensive coverage of the state of the art in the field at the time of its publication in 1977. More recently, Wang, et. al. (8,9) developed a depth-averaged finite element model and applied it to study the steady and transient flows in leaky and non-leaky aquifers.Their results are physically sound. This model was, later, modified for multiple-layered leaky aquifers with non-uniform physical parameters and irregular geometric configurations (10). It was used to determine the hydrological impact on aquifers due to surface mining operations. This paper is to present the most important information about the development and results of this latest finite element model for simulating the aquifer characteristics.

Mathematical Model Development

The three-dimensional groundwater flow in a general non-homogeneous, anisotropic, and leaky aquifer is governed by the following equation:

$$\frac{\partial}{\partial x} \left(K_x \frac{\partial \phi}{\partial x}\right) + \frac{\partial}{\partial y} \left(K_y \frac{\partial \phi}{\partial y}\right) + \frac{\partial}{\partial z} \left(K_z \frac{\partial \phi}{\partial z}\right) + Q = S_O \frac{\partial \phi}{\partial t} \tag{1}$$

where: K - Hydraulic conductivity
Q - Volumetric flux into the aquifer from point or distributed sources/sinks
S_O - Mediums storativity
x,y,z - Principal directions of the hydraulic conductivity tensor
ϕ - Piezometric head

In order to develop a cost-effective computational simulations model capable of performing both short- and especially long-term response estimates, the depth-averaged approach is adopted. This approximation is justifiable, if the aquifer is thin in the vertical direction compared to the horizontal dimensions and the magnitude of velocity components in the horizontal direction is much greater than that in the vertical direction. The coordinate system used for the depth averaged model is shown in Fig. 1.

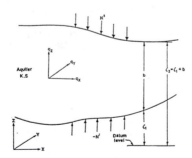

Fig. 1 Averaging the Flow in an Aquifer.

The resulting depth-averaged model for the systems uppermost unconfined aquifer is governed by:

$$\frac{\partial}{\partial X}(K_X(h-\eta)\frac{\partial h}{\partial X}) + \frac{\partial}{\partial Y}(K_Y(h-\eta)\frac{\partial h}{\partial Y}) + \bar{Q} + \frac{K_2'}{b_2}(h_b - h) = n_e\frac{\partial h}{\partial t} \qquad (2)$$

where: b_2 - Thickness of the semi-pervious layer below the aquifer
  h - Depth averaged piezometric head
  h_b - Depth averaged piezometric head in the aquifer below the considered aquifer .
  K - Hydraulic conductivity
  K_2' - Equivalent hydraulic conductivity of the semi-pervious layer below the aquifer considered
  n_e - Effective porosity
  Q - Vertical flux into the aquifer from point or distribute sources/sinks
  η - Bottom elevation

The equation for a general confined aquifer within the multi-layer system (shown in Figure 2) can also be developed in similar fashion.

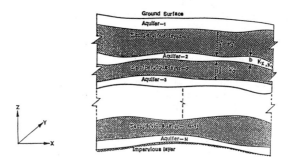

Fig. 2 Example of a Multi-Layer Aquifer

The boundary and initial conditions used in this model are chosen from the following basic cases depending on the need of a particular situation studied.

$$h = h_o(x,y,t_o) \quad \text{at } t = t_o \qquad (4)$$

$$h = h_1(x,y,t) \quad \text{on } \zeta_1 \qquad (5)$$

$$-(K_X(h-\eta)\frac{\partial h}{\partial X}n_X + K_Y(h-\eta)\frac{\partial h}{\partial Y}n_Y) = Q_s \text{ on } \zeta_2 \qquad (6)$$

$$-(K_X(h-\eta)\frac{\partial h}{\partial X}n_X + K(h-\eta)\frac{\partial h}{\partial Y}n_Y) = \frac{K''W''}{B''}(h_3 - h) \text{ on } \zeta_3 \qquad (7)$$

$$\bar{\phi} = \bar{\phi}_o(x,y,t_o) \quad \text{at } t = t_o \qquad (8)$$

$$\bar{\phi} = \bar{\phi}_1(x,y,t) \quad \text{on } \zeta_1 \qquad (9)$$

$$-(K_X b \frac{\partial \bar{\phi}}{\partial X} n_X + K_Y b \frac{\partial \bar{\phi}}{\partial Y} n_Y) = Q_S \text{ on } \zeta_2 \qquad (10)$$

$$-(K_X b \frac{\partial \bar{\phi}}{\partial X} n_X + K_Y b \frac{\partial \bar{\phi}}{\partial Y} n_Y) = \frac{K''W''}{B''} (\bar{\phi}_3 - \bar{\phi}) \text{ on } \zeta_3 \qquad (11)$$

where: B'' – Effective depth in the direction of the leaky inflow
$\quad\quad\quad K''$ – Equivalent hydrauic conductivity of a leaky zone on ζ_3
$\quad\quad\quad n_X, n_Y$ – Components of the inward pointing normal n on the boundary
$\quad\quad\quad \bar{h}_O,$ _ – Depth averaged piezometric head at time $t = t_O$
$\quad\quad\quad h_1, \bar{\phi}_1$ – Known depth averaged piezometric head on $_1$ boundary at all times
$\quad\quad\quad \bar{h}_3, \bar{\phi}_3$ – Known head outside the aquifer
$\quad\quad\quad Q_S$ – Inflow per unit length on the ζ_2 boundary
$\quad\quad\quad W''$ – Width perpendicular to inflow

Other quantities have been previously defined.

Finite Element Model

Due to the irregular geometric configuration of the realistic aquifer, the finite element model was applied to simulate the groundwater flows. A typical finite element mesh and boundary conditions are shown in Figures 3.

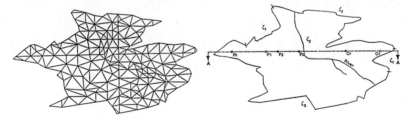

Fig. 3   Finite Element Mesh and Boundary Conditions of a Typical Aquifer

Within each triangular element, the linear interpolation function was used. Applying the Galerkin's method of weighted residual and after assemblying the local finite element equations, the followng set of global equations were obtained. For an unconfirmed aquifer, it is:

$$M\dot{\phi} + K\phi = f \quad \text{or} \quad m_{ij}\dot{\phi}_j + K_{ij}\phi_j = f_i \qquad (12)$$

where: $m_{ij} = \int_\Omega \overset{*}{S} N_i N_j \, d\Omega$

$$k_{ij} = \int_\Omega (K_X b \overset{*}{} \frac{\partial N_i}{\partial X} \frac{\partial N_j}{\partial X} + K_Y b \overset{*}{} \frac{\partial N_i}{\partial Y} \frac{\partial N_j}{\partial Y} + (-\frac{2}{h}) \frac{K'_2}{b''_2} N_i N_j) \, d\Omega$$

$$+ \int_{\zeta_3} (-\frac{2}{h}) \frac{K''W''}{B''} N_i^* N_j^* d\zeta_3$$

$$f_i = \int_{\zeta_2} N_i^* 2Q_s d\zeta_2 + \int_{\zeta_3} N_i^* 2 \frac{K''W''}{B''} h_3 d\zeta_3$$

$$+ \int_\Omega N_i (2\bar{Q} + 2 \frac{K_2'}{b_2'} h_b) d\Omega$$

$$s^* = \frac{n_e}{h}$$

$$b^* = 1 - \frac{n}{h}$$

$$\phi = h^2$$

And, for a confined aquifer, a similar equation is obtained

$$M\dot{\bar{\phi}} + K\bar{\phi} = f \tag{13}$$

where:

$$m_{ij} = \int_\Omega S N_i N_j d\Omega$$

$$k_{ij} = \int_\Omega (K_x b \frac{\partial N_i}{\partial X} \frac{\partial N_j}{\partial X} + K_y b \frac{\partial N_i}{\partial Y} \frac{\partial N_j}{\partial Y} + (\frac{K_1'}{b_1'} + \frac{K_2'}{b_2'}) N_i N_j) d\Omega$$

$$+ \int_{\zeta_3} \frac{K''W''}{B''} N_i^* N_j^* d\zeta_3$$

$$f_i = \int_{\zeta_2} N_i^* Q_s d\zeta_2 + \int_{\zeta_3} N_i^* \frac{K''W''}{B''} \phi_3 d\zeta_3$$

$$+ \int_\Omega N_i (\bar{Q} + \frac{K_1'}{b_1'}\phi_a + \frac{K_2'}{b_2'}\phi_b) d\Omega$$

Here, M and K represent matrices and the quantities $\bar{\phi}$, $\dot{\bar{\phi}}$ and f represent vectors. The interpolation and weighting functions along the boundaries are represented by N^*. The matrix k_{ij} and vector f_i may be modified by setting

$$\frac{K_2'}{b_2'} = 0$$

for the last aquifer of the multi-layered system. If the first layer of the system is confined, then

$$\frac{K_1'}{b_1'} = 0$$

is substituted into (13) to obtain the matrix equations.

Boundary conditions should be, first, discretized, if needed, and then, imposed into the set of global finite element equations. The formulation of the finite element model was, thus, completed.

Model Verification

In order to insure that the finite element model simulates the correct physical phenomena, it has been thoroughly tested using a large number of fundamental cases including some one- and two-dimensional cases with analytical solutions available. Due to the limited length of this paper, only the results of a few typical tests together with their verifications by either analytic solutions or physical data are given below:

  i) The influence on a confined aquifer by leakage from an adjacent aquifer under steady state condition is shown in Figure 4.

 ii) Drain of a phreatic aquifer from both ends was also simulated, as shown in Figure 5. The upper or free surfaces of the groundwater mound is seen decaying with time asymptotically to zero as time goes on, which is in agreement with the exact solution obtained by Glover (16).

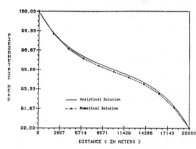

Fig. 4 Solutions of Confined   Fig. 5 Decay of Groundwater Mound
        Aquifer with Leakage   with Time

A two-dimensional arbitrarily, configurated, multiple-layered, leaky aquifer (see Figures 2 and 3) was chosen for testing under a variety of conditions.

  i) Effects of a river, as either a source or a sink in different seasons, on a single layer aquifer were studied. Reasonable results were obtained. (see Figures 6 and 7.)

 ii) The steady state piezometric head distributions in both leaky and nonleaky double-layer aquifers were numerically obtained for prescribed potential and flux boundary conditions on ζ_1 and ζ_2 respectively (see Figure 8).   Results are presented in Figure 9.

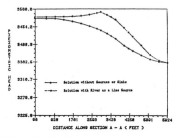

Fig. 6   Influence Due to River   Fig. 7   Influence Due to River
         in Wet Season   in Dry Season

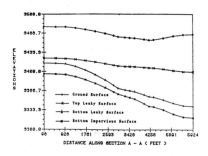

Fig. 8   Sectional Geology of the Multi-Layer Aquifer

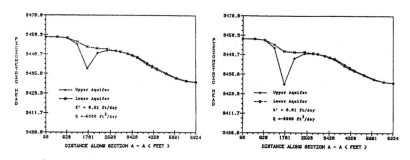

Fig. 9   Influence of Pumping in a Double Layer Leaky Aquifer

One example of verification with field data is given below.   Good

agreement between numerical prediction and field data collected at a
surface mining site near Decker, Montana has been obtained as shown in
Figure 10, below:

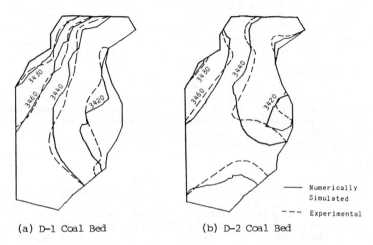

(a) D-1 Coal Bed   (b) D-2 Coal Bed

Fig. 10 Comparison between Computational Model and Field Data at
         Decker Mine in Montana.

Conclusions and Discussion

     Compuational models of both single and multi-layer aquifers have
been developed. They can be utilized to similate water flow through
confined, unconfined, and leaky confined aquifers with complex
geohydrology and highly irregular geometric configurations. They have
a variety of applications including the evaluation of responses to
leakage, pumping withdrawal of water from and recharge to an aquifer
involved as well as the assessment of both short- and long-term effects
of surface mining and excavation on or around an aquifer in terms of
water supply and quality.

     Computer experiments of aquifer characteristics, both steady and
transient conditions, were performed using the computer code developed.
One sees clearly that not only all basic physical principles of
groundwater flow are correctly represented but also the trend of
asymptotically approaching to the steady state solution of a transient
model is also obtained in one-dimensional as well as axisymmetric
cases.   The responses to withdrawal, recharge, and leakage of the
aquifer are also physically reasonable.

     The depth-integrated computational model has been found capable of
producing numerical simulation with adequate accuracy for "thin" aquifers, that is the vertical dimension of the aquifer is much small than
horizontal ones. The advantage of adopting this approximation is the
fact that it represents a tremendous savings in computing cost
especially for the long-term response simulation.

To further demonstrate the capabilities of the computer model in practical engineering application, the assessment of hydrological effects due to surface mining have been carried out. The results in terms of piezometric head distribution and velocity vector field for the cases of during a surface mining operation and after reclamation are given. The required pumping rate to keep the mining site dry during operation can also be estimated using the computational model. Good agreement between the computational model prediction and field data collection near Decker Mine in Montana has been obtained.

Acknowledgement

This work is a result of research sponsored in part by the Mississippi Mineral Resources Institute, under Grant #MMRI 84-25 Task B, and The University of Mississippi. Some computational methodology developed from a Grant #NASIAA-D-00050 from The Mississippi-Alabama Sea Grant Consortium was utilized.

References

(1)   Chatterji, G. B.,(1984), "Computer Simulation of Hydrological Effect of Surface Mining, M. Sc. Thesis, submitted to The University of Mississippi, December, 1984.

(2)   Glover, R. E., (1974), "Transient Ground Water Hydraulics," Department of Civil Engineering, Colorado State University, Fort Collins, Colorado.

(3)   Huang, Y. H. and Sonnefeld, S. I., (1974), "Analysis of Unsteady Flow toward an Artesian Well by Three Dimensional Finite Elements," Water Resources Research, Vol. 10, No. 3, pp. 591-596.

(4)   Huang, Y. H. and Wu, S. J., (1975), "Simulation of Confined Aquifers by Three-Dimensional Finite Elements," Proc., AICA Int'l Symp. on Computer Methods for Partial Differential Equations, Leigh University, pp. 251-258.

(5)   Javandel, I., and Witherspoon, P. A., (1969), "A Method of Analyzing Transient Fluid Flow in Multilayered Aquifers," Water Resuorces Research, Vol. 5, No. 4, pp. 856-869.

(6)   Pinder, G. F. and Frind, E. O., (1972), "Application of Galerkin's Procedure to Aquifer Analysis", Water Resources Research, 8(1), 108-120.

(7)   Pinder, G. F. and Gray, W. G., (1977), Finite Element Simulation in Surface and Subsurface Hydrology, Academic Press, NY.

(8)   Wang, S. Y. (1983) Studies on Hydrologic Impact of Surface Mining of Lignite by Computer Modeling, Technical Rept. CCHE-83-1, Submitted to Mississippi Mineral Resources Inst. published by Ctr. for Computational Hydroscience and Eng'g, The University of Mississippi.

(9)   Wang, S. Y. and Chatterji, G. B., (1984), "A Finite Element Model for Simulating Groundwater Flow in a Multi-Layer Aquifer," 48th Annual Meeting, Mississippi Acadamy of Sciences, Biloxi, Mississippi.

(10)   Wang, S. Y. and Chatterji, G. B. (1984) Development and Verification of Computer Models for Simulating Aquifer Character- istics and Responses. Technical Rept. CCHE-84-3, in preparation by Ctr. for Computational Hydroscience and Eng'g, The University of Mississippi.

(11) Zienkiewicz, O. C. and Cheung, Y. K., (1967), "The Finite Element Method in Structural and Continium Mechanics," McGraw-Hill Book Co., New York, Chap. 10, pp. 148-169.
(12) Zienkiewicz, O. C. and Pareth, C. J., (1970), "Transient Field Problems: Two-Dimensional and Three-Dimensional Analysis by Isoparametric Finite Elements," Int. J. Numer. Meth. Eng., 2, 61-71.

Analysis of Unsaturated Flow
Beneath a Landfill

Vedat Batu, M. ASCE; Jimmy Ho; and Joseph G. Yeasted, M. ASCE*

Using the linearized theory of flow in unsaturated porous media,
a mathematical model was developed to study the distribution and
extent of unsaturated flow from a source of infiltration at the soil
surface. Analytical solutions are provided for infiltration beneath
an idealized landfill, and the results are analyzed to determine the
limits of the unsaturated flow domain and the fraction of the total
infiltrating flow that passes beyond the vertical projection of the
landfill. The results indicate that the flow dispersion caused by
capillary effects in the unsaturated zone can be significant. The
model can be used to quantitatively assess the potential significance
of unsaturated flow distribution when applying and interpreting the
results of saturated flow models.

Introduction

Most groundwater contaminant transport models in use today are
applicable only to the saturated flow zone. As depicted in Fig. 1.a,
these models assume that any leachate infiltrating from a landfill
would move through the unsaturated zone unaltered in the vertical
direction until the uppermost aquifer is reached. That is, the
streamlines in the unsaturated zone are assumed to be vertical and to
be located only within the vertical projection of the landfill. The
primary reason for these simplifying assumptions is that saturated
flow theory cannot account for the more complex dynamics of flow in
the unsaturated zone caused, for example, by gravitational and
capillary forces, and evapotranspiration.

Fig. 1.b provides a more realistic depiction of flow in the
unsaturated zone. The streamlines in this case are convex and extend
for some distance beyond the vertical projection of the landfill. The
actual shape and lateral extent of the unsaturated flow domain is
dependent on many factors, including the soil characteristics in the
unsaturated zone (e.g., hydraulic conductivity, capillary forces) and
the boundary conditions (e.g., infiltration and evapotranspiration
patterns). The potential importance of unsaturated flow effects on
the amount and extent of contaminant migration is illustrated in
Figs. 1.a and 1.b. With the exception of localized hydrodynamic
dispersion, no migration of contaminants upgradient of point A would
be predicted by saturated flow models. It is likely that the results
of such models would not predict contamination of the nearby potable
water supply well. On the other hand, the unsaturated flow yield is

*Groundwater Hydrologist, Engineer, and Manager, respectively,
NUS Corporation, Park West Two, Cliff Mine Road, Pittsburgh, PA 15275

not directly influenced by the piezometric gradient of the underlying aquifer, and upgradient movement could occur before intercepting the saturated zone. The streamlines in the unsaturated zone could extend to a point of interception either with the well itself (point B) or with the saturated zone within the radius of influence of the well (point C). In either case, contamination of the well would occur even though saturated flow models would not predict its occurrence.

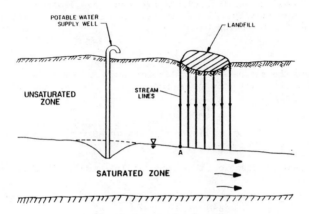

Fig. 1.a   Streamlines in Unsaturated Zone Assumed
            by the Saturated Flow Models

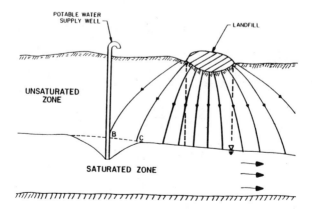

Fig. 1.b   Streamlines in Unsaturated Zone Based
            on Actual Field Conditions

In this paper, the linearized theory of flow in unsaturated porous media is used to develop a mathematical model of unsaturated flow beneath a landfill. Analytical solutions are provided for an idealized landfill subject to infiltration, and the results are analyzed to determine the limits of the unsaturated flow domain and the fraction of the total infiltrating flow that passes beyond the vertical projection of the landfill.

Mathematical Formulation of Unsaturated Flow Beneath a Landfill

For flows in unsaturated, homogeneous, and isotropic soils, the hydraulic conductivity (K) can be related to the soil water pressure head (h) by the following (6):

$$K(h) = K_s \exp(\alpha h) \qquad (1)$$

where K_s is the saturated hydraulic conductivity and α is an empirical coefficient characteristic of a given soil. The corresponding matric flux potential (Θ) is

$$\Theta = \int_{-\infty}^{h} K(h)dh = \frac{K_s}{\alpha}\exp(\alpha h) = \frac{K(h)}{\alpha} \qquad (2)$$

The differential equation that governs the matric flux potential is linear (7):

$$\frac{\partial^2 \Theta}{\partial x^2} + \frac{\partial^2 \Theta}{\partial y^2} + \frac{\partial^2 \Theta}{\partial z^2} = \alpha \frac{\partial \Theta}{\partial z} \qquad (3)$$

with the z-axis positive downwards. Raats (8) showed that for plane flow the stream function ψ satisfies the two-dimensional form of Eq. 3:

$$\frac{\partial^2 \psi}{\partial x^2} + \frac{\partial^2 \psi}{\partial z^2} = \alpha \frac{\partial \psi}{\partial z} \qquad (4)$$

In accordance with these differential relationships, the horizontal flux component (u), vertical flux component (v), and hydraulic head (H) are given by the following:

$$u = -\frac{\partial \Theta}{\partial x} = -\frac{\partial \psi}{\partial z} \qquad (5)$$

$$v = \alpha\Theta - \frac{\partial \Theta}{\partial z} = \frac{\partial \psi}{\partial x} \qquad (6)$$

$$H = \frac{1}{\alpha} \ln(\frac{\alpha\Theta}{K_s}) - z \qquad (7)$$

Flow analysis based on Eqs. 1-7 is called "quasilinear" because, although Eqs. 3 and 4 are linear, the analysis embodies with reasonable accuracy the strongly nonlinear decrease of K as h decreases through negative values.

In order to achieve an analytical solution of this "quasilinear" mathematical model for unsaturated flow beneath a landfill, the following simplifying assumptions are made (Fig. 2):

1. The landfill is of constant width (2L) in the x-z plane;
2. The landfill is infinitely long perpendicular to the x-z plane;
3. The water table (i.e., the saturated zone) is located at an infinite depth below the soil surface;
4. There is a constant and uniform infiltration rate (v_1) entering the unsaturated zone at the base of the landfill;
5. The soil in the unsaturated zone is homogeneous and isotropic;
6. There is a single-valued function relating the unsaturated hydraulic conductivity and the soil water pressure head given by Eq. 1 (i.e., hysteresis effects are neglected);
7. The flow is steady.

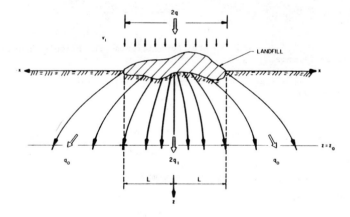

Fig. 2   Schematic Description of the Unsaturated Flow
Beneath an Idealized Landfill

The general solutions to Eqs. 1-7 for these idealized landfill conditions have been developed by Batu (2,3). The stream function (ψ) is given by:

$$\psi(x,z) = v_1 \int\limits_{0}^{\infty} f(\lambda)\sin(\lambda x)d\lambda \qquad (8)$$

where

$$f(\lambda) = \frac{2}{\pi\lambda^2} \exp(mz)\sin(\lambda L) \qquad (9)$$

$$m = \frac{\alpha}{2} - (\lambda^2 + \frac{\alpha^2}{4})^{1/2} \tag{10}$$

Using the method of Filon, Batu (3) performed a numerical integration of Eq. 8 to obtain:

$$\psi(x,z) = \frac{\beta \xi v_1 L}{2\pi} - \frac{v_1 x G_{2N}}{\pi \xi N^2} \sin(\frac{2N\xi L}{x})[\eta\cos(2N\xi) + \beta\sin(2N\xi)]$$

$$+ \frac{\beta v_1 x}{2\pi \xi} \sum_{n=1}^{N} \frac{G_{2n}}{n^2} \sin(\frac{2n\xi L}{x})\sin(2n\xi) \tag{11}$$

$$+ \frac{2\gamma v_1 x}{\pi \xi} \sum_{n=1}^{N} \frac{G_{2n-1}}{(2n-1)^2} \sin[(2n-1)\frac{\xi L}{x}]\sin[(2n-1)\xi]$$

where

$$G_{2N} = \exp\{\frac{\alpha z}{2} - [(\frac{2N\xi z}{x})^2 + \frac{\alpha^2 z^2}{4}]^{1/2}\} \tag{12}$$

$$G_{2n} = \exp\{\frac{\alpha z}{2} - [(\frac{2n\xi z}{x})^2 + \frac{\alpha^2 z^2}{4}]^{1/2}\} \tag{13}$$

$$G_{2n-1} = \exp\{\frac{\alpha z}{2} - \{[\frac{(2n-1)\xi z}{x}]^2 + \frac{\alpha^2 z^2}{4}\}^{1/2}\} \tag{14}$$

in which ξ, η, β, and γ are coefficients in Filon's numerical integration formula.

The corresponding solution for the matric flux potential was obtained as (2)

$$\Theta = v_1 \int_0^{\infty} g(\lambda)\cos(\lambda x)d\lambda \tag{15}$$

where

$$g(\lambda) = \frac{2}{\pi \lambda r(\lambda)} \exp(mz)\sin(\lambda L) \tag{16}$$

in which

$$r(\lambda) = \frac{\alpha}{2} + (\lambda^2 + \frac{\alpha^2}{4})^{1/2} \tag{17}$$

The method of Filon was also similarly applied to Eq. 15.

Application to an Idealized Landfill

Fig. 2 provides a schematic of unsaturated flow beneath a landfill for the idealized conditions previously discussed. The total flow infiltrating through a landfill of width 2L is given by 2q, so that:

$$q = Lv_1 \tag{18}$$

where the uniform infiltration rate v_1 can range from zero up to the value of the saturated hydraulic conductivity of the underlying soil (K_s). At any depth, $z = z_0$, the flow that passes within the vertical projection of the landfill is designated as $2q_I$, while the total flow that occurs outside of the vertical projection is given by $2q_0$. By symmetry, a flow of q_0 will occur on each side of the vertical projection. The continuity of flow requires that

$$q = q_I + q_0 \tag{19}$$

It is known that the difference between the values of two adjacent streamlines gives the flow rate through the streamtube formed by those streamlines. The components of flow in the unsaturated zone at any depth z_0 can, therefore, be computed as:

$$q_I = \sum_{i=1}^{n} (\psi_i - \psi_{i-1})_{z=z_0} = \sum_{i=1}^{n} (\Delta\psi_i)_{z=z_0} \tag{20}$$

$$q_0 = \sum_{i=n+1}^{p} (\psi_i - \psi_{i-1})_{z=z_0} = \sum_{i=n+1}^{p} (\Delta\psi_i)_{z=z_0} \tag{21}$$

where ψ_0 is the streamline at $x = 0$, ψ_n is the streamline at $x = L$, and ψ_p is the streamline at the outer limit of the flow domain. Once the values of the streamlines are obtained from the numerically integrated form (Eq. 11), Eqs. 20 and 21 can be used to compute the fractions of flow that occur within and outside of the vertical projection of the landfill.

The mathematical model developed in this paper was applied to two different soil types in order to analyze the behavior, extent, and distribution of unsaturated flow beneath a landfill. The soils, Chino Clay and Yolo Light Clay have been thoroughly researched and their hydraulic parameters are well documented (4,5). For Chino Clay, K_s = 197.856 x 10^{-4} m/day and α = 0.0685/m; for Yolo Light Clay, K_s = 80.61 x 10^{-4} m/day and α = 3.67/m. Values of α typically range from 0.01/m to 20/m (4,5), so the two soils under study are representative of widely-varying conditions.

For purposes of this study, the input infiltration rates (v_1, Fig. 2) were set equal to the saturated hydraulic conductivities (K_s), or 197.856 x 10^{-4} m^3/day/m^2 for Chino Clay and 80.61 x 10^{-4} m^3/day/m^2 for Yolo Light Clay. For an assumed landfill width of 200 m, the total infiltration rates (2 q) are 3.9571 m^3/day/m for Chino Clay and 1.512 m^3/day/m for Yolo Light Clay.

The coefficients in Filon's numerical integration formulas for the stream function and the matric flux potential were selected from the table given by Abramowitz and Stegun (1). These include: ξ = 0.05; η = 0.00000555; β = 0.66699976; and γ = 1.33300003. A value of N of at least 1500 was found to be necessary to achieve numerical convergence. A principal reason for the slow convergence was that the assumed 200 m width of the landfill caused the coordinates of the flow domain to be relatively large. The stream function given by Eq. 11

was found to converge much faster than the matric flux potential due to the presence of the squared terms n^2 and $(2n-1)^2$ in the denominators of Eq. 11.

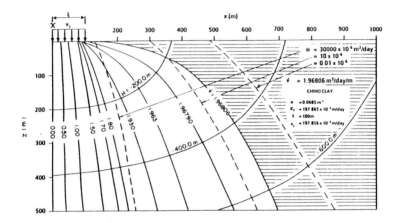

Fig. 3 Flow Net in the Unsaturated Flow Field
for Chino Clay

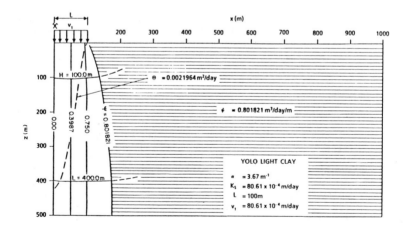

Fig. 4 Flow Net in the Unsaturated Flow Field
for Yolo Light Clay

Discussion of Results

The flow nets in the unsaturated flow field beneath the idealized landfill are presented for Chino Clay and Yolo Light Clay in Figs. 3 and 4, respectively. Because of the symmetry about the z-axis, only the right hand side of each flow field is presented. As would be expected, the streamlines and equipotential lines are orthogonal. At any depth z, the numerical values of the streamlines are observed to increase with increasing x until an approximately constant streamline value is reached (ψ = 1.96806 m^3/day/m for Chino Clay and ψ = 0.801821 m^3/day/m for Yolo Light Clay, as depicted by the shaded areas in Figs. 3 and 4). Since the flow between streamlines is equal to the difference in streamline values, the shaded areas represent zones of zero flow. The flow domain for each case is represented, therefore, by the unshaded areas.

The lateral extent of the flow domain is observed to increase with increasing depth, and to be much larger for Chino Clay than for Yolo Light Clay. The latter can be interpreted as being caused by more effective capillary forces for the Chino Clay, as represented by its lower α value. The effective flow domain for the Chino Clay is shown to extend over a distance several times greater than the width of the landfill. This illustrates that the direct use of saturated flow models, which ignore flow dispersion in the unsaturated zone under the assumption of vertical streamlines, could potentially result in serious misinterpretations if a soil such as Chino Clay is present. On the other hand, the assumption of unaltered vertical flow through the unsaturated zone would be appropriate for Yolo Light Clay.

Table 1 summarizes the results of the unsaturated flow model immediately beneath the landfill (z = 0m). In particular, the component of flow that occurs within the vertical projection of the landfill (q_I) is computed using Eq. 20. Since no flow dispersion would be expected to occur at the ground surface, the computed value of q_I should be equal to the total infiltration rate q, or 1.97856 m^3/day/m for Chino Clay and 0.806 m^3/day/m for Yolo Light Clay. The values of q_I in Table 1 indicate that over 99 percent of the infiltrating flow is accounted for by the model for each soil. It is also of interest that the amount of flow passing through each 10-meter increment along the x-axis should be uniform and should equal the total infiltration over a 10-meter incremental distance (0.197856 m^3/day/m for Chino Clay and 0.0806 m^3/day/m for Yolo Light Clay). The values of $\Delta\psi_i$ in Table 1 show that this condition is excellently reproduced by the model with the exception of a slight underestimation between x = 0m and x = 10m.

The dispersion of flow in the unsaturated zone as one proceeds vertically downward from the ground surface is illustrated in Figs. 5.a and 5.b for a depth of 100m. The plotted values of $\Delta\psi$ give the flow rate at 10-meter increments along the x-axis. As discussed previously, unsaturated flow in Chino Clay exhibits a considerably higher degree of dispersion than is the case for Yolo Light Clay. The values of the flow components q_I and q_O, were computed using Eqs. 20 and 21, and it is observed for Chino Clay that more than 20 percent of the total infiltration occurs beyond the vertical projection of the

landfill at a depth of 100m below the bottom of the landfill. For
Yolo Light Clay, only about 3 percent of the flow has crossed the
vertical boundary of the landfill. It is also noteworthy that greater
than 99 percent of the total infiltration is again accounted for by
the model results.

i	x_i (m)	Chino Clay ψ_i (m^3/day/m)	Chino Clay $\Delta\psi_i$ (m^3/day/m)	Yolo Light Clay ψ_i (m^3/day/m)	Yolo Light Clay $\Delta\psi_i$ (m^3/day/m)
0	0	0	–	0	–
1	10	0.187354	0.187354	0.076331	0.076331
2	20	0.385210	0.197856	0.156942	0.080611
3	30	0.583062	0.197852	0.237551	0.080609
4	40	0.780915	0.197853	0.318160	0.080609
5	50	0.978770	0.197855	0.398769	0.080609
6	60	1.176630	0.197860	0.479380	0.080611
7	70	1.374540	0.197910	0.559994	0.080614
8	80	1.572330	0.197790	0.640597	0.080603
9	90	1.770030	0.197700	0.721229	0.080632
10	100	1.963870	0.193840	0.800795	0.079566
$q_I = \sum_{1}^{10} \Delta\psi_i$			1.963870		0.800795

Table 1

Results of the Unsaturated Flow Values at z = 0m

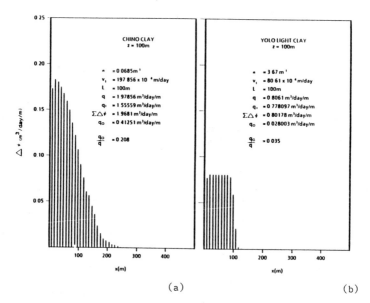

(a)   (b)

Fig. 5   Results of the Unsaturated Flow Model
at z = 100m

A similar analysis of model results was completed for other depths, and the results are summarized in Fig. 6. As indicated, the percentage of flow that occurs outside of the vertical projection of the landfill continues to increase with increasing depth, exceeding 45 percent at a depth of 500m for Chino Clay. The extent of the flow domain also continues to increase with depth, reaching a distance of over 500m for the landfill at a depth of 500m (refer to Fig. 3).

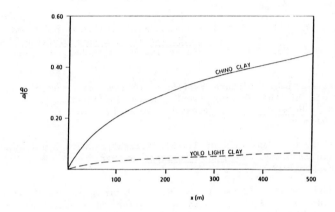

Fig. 6 Degree of Flow Dispersion at Various
Depths Below a Landfill

Summary and Conclusions

Using the linearized theory of flow in unsaturated porous media, a mathematical model was developed to study the distribution and extent of unsaturated flow from a source of infiltration at the soil surface. The numerical results showed that, depending on soil conditions, flow in the unsaturated zone can extend to distances several times the width of the landfill before reaching the saturated zone. In addition, the quantity of flow that could occur beyond the vertical projection of the landfill was also found to be a significant portion of the total infiltration. These results indicate the potential significance of flow dispersion in the unsaturated zone, and the serious consequences that could occur if such effects are not considered in the interpretation of results from saturated flow models. While simplifying assumptions are necessary for the application of the numerical model due to constraints on obtaining analytical solutions, the model can serve as a quantitative tool to assess the potential significance of unsaturated flow phenomena when applying saturated flow models at a particular site.

Appendix - References

(1) Abramowitz, M, and Stegun, I. A., "Handbook of Mathematical Functions with Formulas, Graphs, and Mathematical Tables," National Bureau of Standards, United States Government Printing Office, Washington, D.C., 1964.

(2) Batu, V., "Steady Infiltration From Single and Periodic Strip Sources," Soil Science Society of America Journal, Vol. 42, July-August, 1978, pp. 544-549.

(3) Batu, V., "Flow Net for Unsaturated Infiltration From Strip Source," Journal of the Irrigation and Drainage Division, ASCE, Vol. 105, No. IR3, Proc. Paper 14822, September 1979, pp. 233-245.

(4) Braester, C., "Moisture Variation at the Soil Surface and the Advance of the Wetting Front During Infiltration at Constant Flux," Water Resources Research, Vol. 9, No. 3, June 1973, pp. 687-694.

(5) Bresler, E., "Analysis of Trickle Irrigation with Application to Design Problems," Irrigation Science by Springer-Verlag, Vol. 1, 1978, pp. 3-17.

(6) Gardner, W. R., "Some Steady-State Solutions of the Unsaturated Moisture Flow Equation with Application to Evaporation from a Water Table," Soil Science, Vol. 85, April 1958, pp. 228-232.

(7) Philip, J. R., "Steady Infiltration From Buried Point Sources and Spherical Cavities," Water Resources Research, Vol. 4, October 1968, pp. 1039-1047.

(8) Raats, P.A.C., "Steady Infiltration From Line Sources and Furrows," Soil Science Society of America Proceedings, Vol. 34, September-October 1970, pp. 709-714.

Groundwater Models:
Converting Research Developments
into Practical Applications

Peter F. Andersen[*]
Associate Member, ASCE

Abstract

With the recent advent of numerical groundwater models to solve
real world water supply and contamination problems, various types of
codes have made their way from the research arena into the hands of
practicing professionals. With this transfer, there is sometimes a
polarization between code developers and code appliers. The code
developer, who is usually most interested in state-of-the-art, correct,
and cost-effective numerical and physical formulations, does not
consider the added effort of making a code user-friendly to be worthwhile. The code applier, on the other hand, is more concerned that the
code can be used without thorough knowledge of the mathematical formulation and inner workings of the programs. As a result of this
disparity, many practicing professionals have lost confidence in these
models as a tool for the solution of real world problems.

One method of bridging the gap between code developer and code
applier is through separate user-friendly computer programs called
preprocessors that prepare data before execution of the main program.
They can greatly facilitate data entry because the user is prompted
only for data required in the particular simulation. The time-
consuming and error-prone procedure of placing data in the correct
columns on the correct card images is eliminated because the preprocessor automatically formats the data file. It can also check data
for reasonableness and alert the user to potential problems.

Preprocessors are also invaluable for training seminars on usage
of a particular model. This has been demonstrated at groundwater
modeling short courses taught at Holcomb Research Institute and several
Water Management Districts in Florida.

Some of the most widely used computer codes now have preprocessors
available. These include the USGS (United States Geological Survey)
two-dimensional groundwater flow code, the new modular USGS three-
dimensional flow code, and a proprietary variable density saltwater
intrusion code.

[*]Civil Engineer, GeoTrans, Inc., 209 Elden Street, Suite 301, Herndon,
Virginia 22070.

Introduction

Groundwater has become a major national issue of the 1980's. What was once "out of sight, out of mind" may still be hidden from our view, but it now occupies the minds of others than the scientists, engineers, and well drillers who dealt with it in the past. As the need to assess and analyze groundwater systems increases, the methods of analysis become more varied and complex. Numerical groundwater modeling is one of the tools that can help us not only to understand groundwater systems, but also to effectively solve our problems.

Numerical modeling of groundwater is a relatively new field which was not pursued extensively until the mid-1960's (1). During the subsequent fifteen years, much progress was made in computer code development: describing the physics of flow, transport, deformation, or geochemistry, formulating mathematical methods for solving the equations developed, and programming the computer to carry out these computations. This effort had many fronts. As a result, more than 600 models, with varying degrees of complexity and diverse purposes, exist today.

Many of these codes were developed in the academic area with the expressed purpose of analyzing a specific physical phenomenon or solving a particular mathematical equation; little emphasis was placed on general applicability. As availability of groundwater models became known, various types of codes made their way from the research arena into the hands of practicing professionals. With this transfer, a polarization between code developer and code applier sometimes becomes evident. The code developer, who is usually most interested in state-of-the-art, correct, and cost effective numerical and physical formulations, does not consider worthwhile the effort required to make a code user-friendly or even understandable to others. The code applier, on the other hand, is more concerned that the code can be used without thorough knowledge of the mathematical formulation of the physical problem or the programming involved in solving it. As a result of this disparity, many practicing professionals have lost confidence in these models' ability to solve real world problems.

Characteristics of Usable Codes

There are several characteristics of groundwater models which increase usability. These include availability of model code, documentation, test and field validation, support/ maintenance, and user-friendliness (5). Most models developed by federal or state agencies, or by universities through funds from those agencies, are considered to be in the public domain and, thus, fully available. On the other hand, models developed by private industry, research institutions, and certain universities are usually proprietary, and are available only by purchasing, leasing, or using on a royalty basis (5).

Adequate documentation of a computer code includes code listing, user's manual, mathematical description of the model, sample problems and results, computer system requirements, validation and verification results, and code structure description. For most computer models, documentation is lacking in various degrees (1,2,5). Related to documentation is the support and maintenance of the code. A supported model is one for which assistance can be received if problems occur in implementation or execution. A maintained model is one that is updated when bugs or errors in the coding are discovered; other users are made aware of these changes.

In order for users to have confidence in the results of a numerical model it should be verified and field validated. Verification is the assurance that a computer code correctly performs the operations specified in a numerical model; validation is the assurance that a model as embodied in a computer code is a correct representation of the process or system for which it is intended (4). These elements of usability are all important, but are not the focus of this paper. They are discussed in detail by van der Heijde (5), Mercer and Faust (3), and Silling, (5).

The last element of code usability, user-friendliness, is the one with which this paper is concerned. Models that are easy to set up and run, and from which results are easily interpreted, are called user-friendly. These programs usually will detect input errors and alert the user before the run "bombs" or spends excessive CPU time to obtain worthless results. User-friendliness sometimes also implies the automation of tasks which would otherwise be quite tedious. One method of making models more user-friendly is through separate data entry and manipulation systems called preprocessors.

Using Preprocessors to Increase User-Friendliness

A preprocessor is an interactive, user-friendly computer program which prepares data for a model prior to execution of the model. It should be emphasized that the preprocessor is a "front-end" to a model, but not simply a version of a model with interactive capacities. Separate sessions for data preparation and model execution are possible. Advantages of separate programs are: (a) the data creation phase need not be repeated each run, (b) the data creation and model execution modes need not be performed immediately in sequence or by the same person, (c) execution of the model can still be performed in batch mode, and (d) the original source code for the model does not need to be modified.

Preprocessors usually have two separate modes: one for creating a new data set and another for modifying an existing data set. The creation mode formats and places data in the correct sequence for the particular problem defined by the modeler. The modification mode is used to focus on a particular piece of data, change it, reformat it, and prompt for any additional data required as a result of modification. This is useful for sensitivity analyses where certain parameters are independently changed for each run to assess their particular impact on the simulation. The time-consuming and error-prone procedure of placing data in the correct columns on the correct card images is eliminated because the modeler simply responds to questions displayed on the screen of the terminal. The preprocessor develops and formats the data file as required by the model without necessity for the modeler to work directly with the data file.

A preprocessor can also greatly facilitate data entry because it "asks for" only data required for a particular simulation. The modeler need not be confused by extensive model input instructions when only portions relevant to the specific application are needed. With the trend toward complex, highly generalized models to solve for a variety of groundwater flow or transport conditions, this is a very desirable feature. Data entry for heterogeneous array data is also eased by algorithms which have been included for zonation or repetition of parameters. Preprocessors can check data both for type (integer, real, characters) and reasonableness, and alert the user to potential problems. For example, if a porosity of 1.2 is entered, the program would either disallow this entry and request re-entry or print an error warning.

Code efficiency is another important consideration in groundwater modeling, particularly for large, three-dimensional applications. Efficiency is usually a measure of the amount of computer time required to achieve a solution. From a business standpoint, however, measures of efficiency must include both computer time and man-time required for data preparation. A numerical scheme may be extremely efficient, but the time saved there could be lost in excessive man-time required to prepare and debug data sets.

These features make preprocessors highly useful and desirable to all levels of professionals. Consulting firms and industry find them valuable because they virtually eliminate errors and thus conserve in-house data preparation time. Data preparation and set-up tasks can be more easily delegated to lower level staff. Preprocessors are useful for litigation purposes because model runs can be made readily during meetings or hearings without consulting a user's manual. Groundwater modeling short courses benefit because the time used in data set-up and debugging is greatly diminished. In teaching groundwater modeling at Holcomb Research Institute and several Water Management Districts in Florida, it became apparent that either students must use preprocessors to set-up data decks, or else data decks must be provided. Otherwise, much time is devoted to editor use and FORTRAN formatting rather than modeling and code usage. A HELP module has been installed in some short course preprocessors which can be accessed when the user needs a more comprehensive explanation of a parameter.

The one disadvantage of this tool is a potentially dangerous one: it could promote model misapplication to an even greater extent. Data entry and manipulation programs simplify the steps involved in modeling, but do not replace a strong background in hydrology and knowledge of the assumptions inherent in mathematical modeling. The ease with which a preprocessor can be used may encourage the worst abuse of computer models--accepting the results whether or not they make hydrologic sense.

Clearly, with proper knowledge and use, preprocessors are an invaluable asset in numerical groundwater modeling. Although the other characteristics--availability, documentation, support and maintenance, and testing and field validation--are also essential to facilitating

the transition from research developments to practical tools, preprocessors are a major step in making models user-friendly. Just as
user-friendly computer programs have been endorsed by business and
various specialized fields, preprocessors for groundwater models should
soon be widely available and utilized in the groundwater field.

Some of the most widely used computer codes now have preprocessors
available. These include the USGS two-dimensional groundwater flow
code, the new modular USGS three-dimensional flow code, and a proprietary variable density saltwater intrusion code.

Appendix 1. References

1. Bachmat, Y., Bredehoeft, J., Andrews, B., et al., Groundwater
    Management: The Use of Numerical Models, Water Resources
    Monograph, 5, American Geophysical Union, Washington, D.C., 1980.

2. Mercer, J.W., and Faust, C.R., Ground-Water Modeling, National
    Water Well Association, Worthington, OH, 1981.

3. Prickett, T.A., "Ground-water computer models: State of the Art,"
    Ground Water, Vol. 17, No. 2, March-April, 1979, pp 167-173.

4. Silling, S.A., "Final Technical Position on Documentation of
    Computer Codes for High-Level Waste Management," Report No.
    NUREG-0856, U.S. Nuclear Regulatory Commission, Division of Waste
    Management, June 1983.

5. van der Heijde, P.K.M., "Availability and Applicability of
    Numerical Models for Ground Water Resources Management,"
    Proceedings of the Practical Applications of Ground Water Models,
    National Water Well Association, Worthington, OH, August 1984.

SOFTWARE AUTHORING FOR THE REST OF US

John B. Bontje[1] and Barry J. Adams[2], M.ASCE

ABSTRACT

Computer modeling has assumed a steadily increasing role in the practice of hydrology over the past decade. The relatively sudden availability of low cost, moderately powerful personal computers has created an opportunity for hydrologic modelers to instruct a much greater number of engineers in the concepts and implementation of computational hydrology. The extent to which this opportunity will be used to improve hydrologic analysis carried out in the field will be determined by the ease with which these models can be applied and their results interpreted.

Extensive use of high resolution graphics, form-oriented full screen data entry, and contextual help messages have proven to be an effective means of structuring the dialogue between the user and the computer. The high cost of programming such an interface for individual applications has restricted the majority of potential water resources software authors from fully employing the communicative powers of the personal computer. The purpose of this paper is to outline a software authoring approach that can help alleviate this software development bottleneck.

----

[1]M.A.Sc. Candidate, Dept. of Civil Eng., University of Toronto, Toronto, Canada, M5S 1A4.

[2]Associate Professor, Dept. of Civil Eng., University of Toronto, Toronto, Canada, M5S 1A4.

INTRODUCTION

The rapid market acceptance of a few very well known, user programmable, business software products that fully exploit the potential of
the personal computer to change the manner in which data is generated
and manipulated has created the first mass market for computer software. In parallel, the standardization of a few operating systems and
hardware interfacing standards has also created a mass market for
microcomputer hardware accessories such as high capacity hard disks and
high resolution colour graphics video devices.

Mass market economies have sufficiently lowered the cost of computer hardware to again stimulate the growth of a large market for software products. Demand for software has served to highlight the fact
that the economies of software production have not changed significantly. Intense competition in the software marketplace has quickly led
users to consider as essential the following software package attributes:

   i) menu or form-oriented program control and data entry,
  ii) on-line, contextual help screens,
 iii) integrated graphics for the generation, review, and
     management of both input and output data, and
  iv) well-written instruction manuals.

These prerequisites have made the process of writing software for this
medium far more expensive than it was previously (see figure 1).

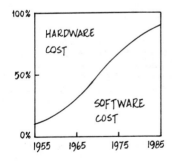

Figure 1. Distribution of hardware and software cost over time.
(After Horowitz et al, 1985)

Engineers writing and supporting hydrologic analyisis software for the personal computer medium have had difficulty incorporating these features into their products. Three reasons are advanced for this problem. First, the traditional process of algorithm development does not seem to recognize the impact that personal computers will have on the audience for such research. Many more solution algorithms - some posssibly relying on visual feedback and correction from a user - can be explored when the widespread availability of machines using modern user interfaces is assumed. Second, most hydrologic software users are resigned to running such programs in batch mode. These users will become more critical of the limitations of batch processing after the novelty of running them on desktop microcomputers dissipates   . Lastly, many engineer/software authors are not yet aware of the tools that exist to ease the very high cost of programming a modern user interface. This discussion   focuses on the third constraint.

DEFINING A SOFTWARE AUTHORING SYSTEM

Software authoring is a term used to describe the process of designing, testing, and implementing a software package that uses the appropriate combination of:

i) high speed calculation of application-specific algorithms, and
ii) elegant and clear data entry and results evaluation schemes.

Software authoring also implies that the author's primary goal is to communicate the application of an algorithm in every day practice, and not to become an expert in the architecture of the computer hardware and operating systems that are used to support this medium.

Most modern software packages are composed almost entirely of code supporting category ii) above, testifying to the difficulty of building a modern user interface. Graphics, text screen, and database subroutines are the three major components of interface programming. The fact that this generalization of program tasks can be made supports the premise that reusable program modules, each designed to perform no more than one of these three program functions, could be assembled and used in a highly cost-effective manner for the purpose of software authoring. Such a collection of software functions used in this manner is termed an authoring system.

It is not sufficient to claim that any collection of such functions can support software authoring as defined above. Each of the graphics, text screen, and database functions should possess the attributes of flexibility and simplicity of use so that they may be quickly reconfigured to service a wide range of software authoring subjects.

Designing a user interface is an iterative procedure. It is almost axiomatic that the initial data entry and graphics formats proposed by a software author will be rejected or at least modified by a representative set of program users. Designing a user interface that conforms to the way users think about their work will allow a more comfortable and sophisticated employment of the authored program by a wider audience. A software authoring system should allow the prototyping of an animated interface for both the author and the user to employ as a functioning prototype during the user interface specification discussions. The author is thus much less reluctant to modify the interface because of the relatively small amount of work required , while the user feels much more effective and valued as the results of these sessions are quickly incorporated into the prototype.

Requiring a software author to systematize and code these basic authoring system functions defeats the major purpose of authoring systems, namely, to quickly disseminate and instruct as great a number of potential software authors as possible in the use of software authoring systems.

The premise of this discussion is that the same mass market that has popularized the modern user interface on personal computers has also created a market for software tools that can be used as components of an authoring system. Mass market economies have recently allowed the offering of very sophisticated authoring system components for between $100 and $600 U.S.; many with features that were previously either non-existant or available only at considerable cost on more powerful computers. Many of these products require no royalty payments on the part of the software author for the software products constructed using these tools.

AUTHORING SYSTEM CONFIGURATIONS

There is no single optimum configuration for an authoring system. The suitability of any particular set of authoring tools or packages is determined by the tradeoff between simplicity of use and flexibility of implementation that any author deems appropriate for the application at hand. Key questions used to make this decision are:

   i) the target audience for the software,
  ii) the degree of author proficiency with various authoring
      systems,
 iii) the degree of freedom desired in designing the user input
      and graphics functions,
  iv) the speed of computation required,
   v) the range of hardware on which the software will run, and
  vi) the legalities of software distribution for software
      written using proprietary software tools.

The author's answers to questions i) and ii) will determine the variety of authoring systems open to meet the software performance goals implied by the answers to the remaining questions.

Figure 2 is a summary of the general classes of presently available authoring systems. The diagonal line below the "type of author" heading (upper left) shows the major impact on the range of authoring system types (from top to bottom) open to authors according to their proficiency with various authoring systems. The adjective "programmer" in this diagram is used to describe author familiarity with traditional computer programming language types such as FORTRAN 77 and C, which are denoted here as development languages. All other language types will be considered collections of the various commands built into the software packages being used as authoring system components.

This broad classification (see the dashed boxes) is meant to quickly categorize the nature of the authoring system environment chosen by a software author. Each of these environments encompass two specific types of authoring systems.

Programming in a Development Language

Development languages are the first of the two authoring systems types, and are most often used by professional programmers as the sole means of controlling computers. Every task that must be performed is coded in this type of language. Only those functions that have been standardized across all implementations of the development language can be used to alleviate the extreme burden of coding that characterizes this software authoring approach. Choosing a particular development language is usually done on the basis of the predominant nature of the programming task. FORTRAN 77 is highly standardized and suitable for algorithmic scientific calculations. C is emerging as the preferred language of those authors wanting the ultimate flexibility in controlling the computer peripherals that maintain the illusion of a user/computer interface.

It is this type of authoring system, in which all program modules are written "in house" by the software author, that has resulted in the high expense and general inaccessability of this method of software authoring. It remains, however, as the most flexible development environment for those software authors who are producing the software tools and packages represented by the remaining three authoring systems.

Specialized programming tools are an exciting new category of programming aids that have arisen largely due to the structured programming developments of the 1970's. Development languages are used to call and control the functions of commercially available subroutines that have been optimized for one of the three authoring system functions. This division of labour, that has been made economic by the mass market for software, has the potential of dramatically decreasing the costs of programming a modern user interface for hydrologic algorithms.

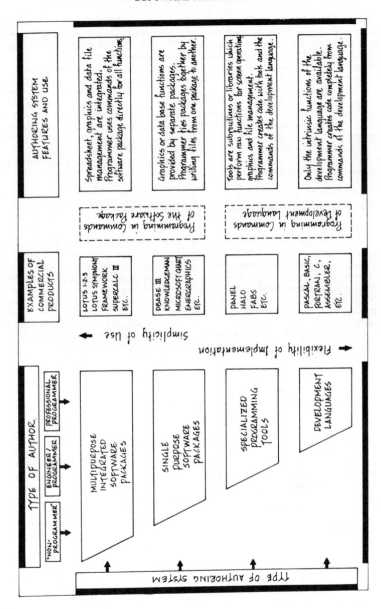

Figure 2. Classification, features and use of authoring systems.

The slight loss of flexibility of implementation inherent in this approach is more than offset by the fact that it is now possible to assemble a proper authoring system for very little cost. Examples of these tools include PANEL (Roundhill Computer Systems, 1984) for text screen manipulation, HALO (Media Cybernetics,1982) for the graphics primitives needed to construct multipurpose graphics modules, and FABS (Computer Control Systems, Inc., 1984) for database functions. These tools are priced for the MS-DOS (IBM personal computers and compatables) market. Similar tools exist for the UNIX software market. A methodology and implementation of two-dimensional graphics known as the Graphical Kernal System (American National Standards Institute, 1984) has recently been standardized for usage in FORTRAN 77, thus allowing the migration of graphics tools into the functions available from the development language.

Programming in the Commands of a Software Package

Single purpose software packages that are user programmable, such as spreadsheets, are largely responsible for the original mass market success of the microcomputer. The spreadsheet metaphor is a very simple but powerful concept that transfers the user's already developed sense of spatial relationships to data manipulation techniques. Very intense competition for this software market, as well as users who have quickly become adept at spreadsheet applications and have demanded more sophisticated programming commands, have caused the spreadsheet to quickly mature to a point where it can now be considered a programming language in its own right, easily taught to a wide variety of users.

While spreadsheets incorporate almost all of the numeric functions found in traditional development languages, they cannot compete with older techniques in terms of computational speed; they simply have too much computational overhead in maintaining the spreadsheet idiom. This is not a drawback for the wealth of useful applications that can still be recognized and written for spreadsheet users, in many cases by "non-programmer" authors. Designing a user input menu in a spreadsheet is accomplished by placing user prompts into cells opposite those which accept user input. Programming the "window" of the spreadsheet to accept user commands that will move it between different areas of the spreadsheet, each of which has been prepared to look like an input screen, is a way in which an interactive "front end" may be quickly constructed. Hence the classification of these packages as legitimate software authoring tools.

The above comments on the adaptability of programmable spreadsheets hold true for other user programmable packages that perform database and graph/chart functions. In addition to programmability, authors of these packages have also recognized that the marketability of their products can be enhanced by allowing them to read data written by other major software packages that a personal computer owner may regularly use. Although the logistics of writing files back and forth between packages that must be loaded or exited as required is a drawback, it still qualifies such a collection of products as a powerful, general purpose authoring system.

Multipurpose, integrated software packages, the fourth category of authoring systems, have arisen from the distinct reponse time advantages of having all elements of an authoring system present in one program. The flexibility of these packages is impressive. They are now programmable and used in a wide variety of business and scientific applications. Although the power of each function - graphics, spreadsheet (read text screen handling and data manipulation), and database - is not always as great as with single purpose packages, they still rank as a significant software authoring system. Fairly lengthy equations can be solved several hundred times and graphically output without losing the instructional value afforded by quick response time. As a result, there are many remaining noncomputationally intensive but extremely useful applications that can now be quickly programmed using these packages. Another advantage of these programs is that they include software to output graphics on a very broad range of hard copy devices.

The use of single purpose software packages as authoring system components should increase greatly when multitasking (executing more than one program at a time) is added to the present generation of personal computers. Multipurpose integrated software packages should become even more popular when more powerful personal computers come into widespread use.

EXAMPLES OF AUTHORING SYSTEM APPLICATIONS

Probabilistic analytical models have been proposed as an alternative to continuous simulation for the planning level analysis of urban drainage system alternatives (Adams and Bontje, 1983). In order to accelerate both the research and educational work in progress in this area, it was felt that a public domain software package with a strong tutorial and graphics component should be written and distributed. An integrated multipurpose software package known as LOTUS 1-2-3 (Lotus Development Corporation, 1983) was chosen to author a package known as SUDS (Statistical Urban Drainage Simulator). Only two man-weeks were required to program the LOTUS spreadsheet so that it presented a complete user environment for this analysis methodology.

The second example application concerns the complete "retrofitting" of a modern user interface for STORM (U.S. Army Corps of Engineers, 1977). STORM is frequently used at the University of Toronto as a planning level continuous simulator that is suitable for evaluating the performance of urban drainage systems as well as familiarizing undergraduate students with the terminology and use of continuous simulation. The formatted input required for this program can be quite complex, especially for multiple catchments with simulations of dry weather flow, erosion, and water quality. A generalized software authoring system known as AUTHOR (Bontje, 1985) was used to build an analysis environment that completely shields the user from STORM input and output files. This project also took two man-weeks to complete.

CONCLUSIONS

A modern user/computer interface is characterized by the extensive use of graphics, simple data entry and program command syntax, and on-line help messages. The mass market for personal computer software has created a demand for the clarity of implementation that such a user interface can provide. This demand is welcome in terms of the greater understanding it can bring to users of water resources programs equiped with such interfaces. However, the expense of coding such programs solely within traditional development language types such as FORTRAN 77 and C has left most water resources program authors unable to fully exploit this aspect of the personal computer. The concepts of software authoring and software authoring systems have been introduced and applied to four types of authoring systems: standard development languages; the use of subroutines optimized to handle details of the user interface; collections of single purpose, programmable software packages; and multipurpose, programmable, integrated software packages. Appropriate use of the last three of these options can dramatically decrease the expense of writing a modern user interface for water resources analysis programs.

ACKNOWLEDGMENTS

The work upon which this paper is based was supported in part by a PRAI Grant from the Natural Sciences and Engineering Research Council of Canada. The authors gratefully acknowledge this sponsorship.

REFERENCES

Adams,B.J., and Bontje, J.B., " Microcomputer Applications of Analytical Models For Urban Stormwater Management ", in Emerging Computer Techniques In StormwaterManagement And Flood Management, W. James, ed., American Society of Civil Engineers, New York, NY, pp. 138 - 162, 1983.

American National Standards Institute, " dpANS GKS X3H3/83-25r3, 5 January 1984 ANSI X3H3 Project 362 ", X3 Secretariat, 311 First Street, N.W., Suite 500, Washington, DC., 1984.

Bontje, J.B., " AUTHOR ", M.A.Sc. thesis, Dept. of Civil Eng., Univ. of Toronto, Canada, 1985.

Computer Control Systems Limited, " FABS ", Lifeboat Associates, 1651 Third Avenue, New York, N.Y., 1984.

Horowitz, E., Kemper, A., and Narasimhan, B., " A Survey of Application Generators ", IEEE Software, Vol.2 , No.1 , January 1985, pp. 40 - 53.

Lotus Development Corporation, " LOTUS 1-2-3 ", Lotus Development Corporation, 161 First Street, Cambridge, MA., 1983.

Media Cybernetics, Inc., " HALO ", Lifeboat Associates, 1651 Third Avenue, New York, NY., 1982.

Roundhill Computer Systems Limited, " PANEL ", Lifeboat Associates, 1651 Third Avenue, New York, NY., 1984.

U.S. Army Corps of Engineers, " Storage, Treatment, Overflow, Runoff Model , STORM ", The Hydrologic Engineering Center, 609 Second Street, Davis, CA., 1977.

UNDERSTANDING LAND AND WATER RESOURCE SYSTEMS AIDED BY GRAPHICS ON MICROCOMPUTERS

Tammo S. Steenhuis,[1] Steven Pacenka,[2] and Keith S. Porter [3]

Background

Over the past ten years, technical assistance has been provided to government and local communities in dealing with groundwater problems (see references). This work has invariably been confronted with two difficulties. The multidisciplinary aspects of groundwater investigations are unusual in their range and complexity. Accordingly, it has been necessary to adopt innovative ways of combining understanding so that balanced holistic evaluations could be achieved which were sufficient for the management purposes to which they were put.

The second difficulty concerned the transfer of this understanding to the recipients or users of the investigations so the results could most usefully be exploited. It was invariably discovered that the integration of scientific understanding from disparate academic disciplines posed conceptual difficulties. However, an even more fundamental impediment is the almost universal absence of reliable intuition about groundwater. The cliche "out of sight, out of mind" is quite literally apt. We cannot see groundwater. Therefore, we do not know exactly where it is, how it flows or in what direction. We have even less sense of the connections between causes of problems and their effects. For example, the detection of a solvent in a sample from a drinking water well may be almost inexplicable in terms of where and when the chemical originated on the land surface.

Unfortunately, the inadequate appreciation of relations between causes of contamination and their occurrence applies to professional as well as lay individuals. In a broad sense we are all lay persons in groundwater investigations since no one can be an expert in all the disciplines that apply. Therefore, we have invested a great deal of effort to develop a basic understanding of groundwater issues.

The involved Cornell faculty and staff have turned to interactive mathematical models running on microcomputers as a key aid for helping both the professional and lay audiences to understand groundwater systems. This paper describes the kinds of software that have proven most useful.

[1] Assoc. Prof. of Agricultural Engineering, Cornell Univ., Ithaca, NY
[2] Research Assistant, Water Research Program, Center for Environmental Research, Cornell Univ., Ithaca, NY
[3] Deputy Director, Water Research Program, Center for Environmental Research, Cornell Univ., Ithaca, NY

The Use of Computer Color Graphics

The most important conceptual basis for understanding groundwater is the temporal and spatial geometry of the system within which it lies. It is then possible to identify the characteristics and properties of this geometrical system about which it is necessary to develop understanding. One can pose the question, what are the important things to measure or about which data should be obtained? Finally, intelligent understanding for management purposes can be gained from the data by analysis using simulations or other appropriate techniques. We and others (Loucks et al., 1985a,b) have found interactive computer graphics to be highly effective for each of these steps. It appears that the dual capability to interactively pose and answer what if questions, combined with clear visual representation of the processes being studied surpasses in efficacy any other means of developing and transferring understanding. This paper describes this kind of software, particularly that including color graphics that has proven most useful.

The Computer and Its Core Software

Our 1981 choice of IBM personal computers for program development was based on not much more than a hint that IBM had developed a good personal computer. Though the early PC's were untested machines for software development, the bandwagon that has developed in IBM's favor since then has ratified our choice.

Today the situation with microcomputers is similar to that with mainframes some years ago; that is once a program has been developed it can be used by many without any modification, because in almost every office there is now an IBM or compatible personal computer. Consequently, programs that are developed can be used by a wide audience for training and design. However, the disadvantage of using personal computers is that the speed of the current PC's is only comparable to that of mainframes in the sixties.

Programs were written in the Pascal language and one in Basic. Pascal was selected above other computer languages because historically it was the first compiler available for the IBM PC and it permits structured programming. As with the choice of the base hardware, Pascal has proven worthwhile; projects involving over 10,000 lines of source code developed by numerous programmers have produced nearly bug-free code.

Three Pascal compilers are being used. At different stages of program development, Microsoft Pascal is used to market the programs because it does not require a runtime system.

Recently IBM announced the availability of a new color board and monitor which overcomes some of the shortcomings of the original board. Our graphics have been designed for the original IBM color/graphics display adapter which has two graphics modes:

Medium and high resolution. In the medium resolution there are 320
horizontal and 200 vertical pixels. The foreground colors are
limited to two palettes of three colors each. A choice of one out
of sixteen background colors is permitted. High resolution has 640
by 2000 pixels which can be either black or white.

Standard Pascal does not include graphics. To avoid royalty
payments we developed a set of routines for graphic display
operations from Pascal. They contain the basic primitives such as
switching between the graphics and the text screens; setting and
reading of pixel colors; drawing lines and filling portions of the
screen with a color. The graphic routines can be used similarly to
other library functions.

The Programs

A set of programs are grouped under the name: "Water And Land
Resource Analysis System" (WALRAS). These programs, all which have
a strong interactive graphics component include:

GERBIL which is a "trainer" for basic ground-water hydrology.
It is designed for the intelligent lay person who has not had prior
training in hydrology. It uses sequences of graphical images to
explain basic terminology, the contents of standard maps, and
qualitative conceptual models of the water cycle near the surface
and the flow of ground water.

SUBDRAIN which uses color graphics designing and evaluating a
subsurface drainage system. Its graphics make the program
especially useful for teaching and demonstrations. The drainage
system consists of laterals connected at any angle to one or both
sides of a single mainline. All laterals are parallel and spaced
at equal distances from each other. The program allows the
analysis of layout schemes with various mainline and lateral
configurations. Slopes, lateral direction and drain spacings can
be altered.

MOUSE which is another kind of trainer, this time for advanced
audiences and covering the subject of contaminant transport. It
simulates the behavior of water and contaminants from the land
surface through the saturated zone. It graphically portrays
aspects of water and chemical cycles near the surface and in ground
water. It has been used in a workshop for professional groundwater
contamination "diagnosticians" and also in an undergraduate
Agricultural Engineering course.

"Spreadsheet" software packages are ideal for building simple
mathematical models of water and chemical cycles. The spreadsheet
routine called **BURBS** fills out an annual water and nitrogen budget
table for a residential area given data about the mix of different
land types, sewage production rates, and a few other parameters.
The spreadsheet package allows the user to change any of the
parameters and quickly see the resulting changes in the budget

table. Such easy "sensitivity analysis" helps the user to learn about the connections between parameters like population density and the resulting quantity and quality of ground-water recharge.

Nitrogen contamination of ground water was a major motivation for providing sanitary sewers on Long Island. We built a set of large computer programs that simulated most aspects of the nitrogen balance near the land surface -- agricultural cropping, turfgrass management, on-site sewage disposal, and other factors -- and employed them in helping to sort out where sewers could reduce the nitrate load being added to ground water. The software called **WAMBAT** previously required a mainframe computer but we converted most of it to run (slowly) on an IBM PC.

Availability

GERBIL has been designed from the start for distribution. We now plan to test its effectiveness with members of a target audience. Subsequently, we intend to distribute the software at as low a cost as possible.

SUBDRAIN has been on the market for one year. It may be obtained from the same organization as **MOUSE**.

MOUSE has been tested with several groups. It can be purchased through the Northeast Regional Agricultural Engineering Service at Cornell University.

BURBS is not suitable for distribution on disk since it requires a particular commercial spreadsheet program for it to operate. However, these models are sufficiently simple that an experienced spreadsheet package user can modify them and reenter them from a paper listing of the formulas.

WAMBAT and its relatives are not yet suitable for general distribution since their data requirements are insufficiently documented.

Close Up of One Computer Software Package

In this section, one of the programs will be discussed in more detail. **MOUSE** was selected for this purpose because this program combines a state of the art model pollutant transport model with interactive computer graphics.

MOUSE is a computer software package that portrays how water and dissolved contaminants behave when underground. It covers the complete path which water and contaminants may follow -- from the land surface where plants and atmospheric processes operate, through the unsaturated soil above the water table, and through the ground water itself.

MOUSE has two intended audiences:

- Persons who wish to learn about general aspects of environmental processes which affect the transport and fate of an introduced chemical (such as a toxic pesticide or a hazardous waste material); and

- Persons who are responsible for assessing the extent and duration of possible ground-water contamination problems which have resulted from the use or disposal of particular chemicals.

Both of these classes of users are assisted by the program's use of color graphical displays on a video screen and by the program's built-in flexibility which allows them to conduct repeated "trial runs" using different assumptions. The intended result for either user is the same: they should develop an appropriate mental model of the way people's activities on the land surface and natural factors join to influence the degree and duration of contamination that can be expected.

MOUSE uses a "divide-to-conquer" strategy. It divides its domain into three parts, accounting for processes within each division and transfers of water and chemicals between the divisions. The atmosphere part considers the effect of climate on the near-surface water cycle. The unsaturated zone part deals with the soil proper, from the surface downward to the water table. The saturated zone part represents the zone from the water table to the eventual discharge of the ground water to a river or to the sea.

Within these zones **MOUSE** follows water and contaminant molecules, keeping close track of the rate at which they move under the influence of gravity and the rate at which the contaminant is converted by chemical or biological processes into simpler substances which are less important.

MOUSE employs **mathematical models** to carry out computations which synthesize data about the soil, the chemical, the weather and other factors into estimates of the patterns of distribution of the water and contaminant. These models consist of arithmetic and "if then" statements which apply basic principles of physics, chemistry, and biology to represent the real world's environmental processes.

Four related models are used.

- The **climate generator** produces a sequence of daily temperatures and rainfall amounts based on historical statistics for a particular weather station.

- The **unsaturated zone water balancer** represents how the falling rain water and any irrigation divide into infiltrated water, evaporated water, surface runoff,

and a change in the amount stored in the soil. The
balance idea is important: all water that comes in
during a time interval must be accounted for in one of
the possible destinations or as a net buildup of the
storage.

- The **unsaturated zone solute transporter** keeps track of
  contaminant molecules with a similar balancing
  technique. (The zone is referred to as **unsaturated**
  because it contains both air and water in its open
  spaces between soil and rock particles.) Anything added
  at or below the surface must either build up, move, be
  degraded by a biological or chemical activity, or be
  removed by plants or evaporation. The model used
  assumes that all water and chemicals move vertically.

- The **saturated zone water and solute transporter** picks
  up where the previous two building-blocks leave off.
  This block traces water and the contaminant from its
  entry at the water table to a zone of outflow, which
  may be a river, lake, or coastal water. The model
  portrays motion in two dimensions: vertically and
  along one horizontal direction.

Utility of Color Graphics for Ultimate Consumers

In multiple projects, compared to other means of information
transfer in which we have provided technical assistance to local
and regional governments, there have been intensive educational
activities. These activities have ransacked the repertoire of
conventional educational techniques. Workshops, presentations
using high quality slide sets or video, multiple reports and
documents written at various technical levels, have all been
prepared and used.

Generally, the efforts were successful. Community by
community, understanding was developed by leaders in the
communities so that well-informed decisions were made. For
example, decisions have been made about the need for sewers,
techniques and criteria have been formulated to determine the
permissible density of residential development consistent with
groundwater protection, the management of fertilizers and
pesticides has been based on the dual need to sustain profitable
crop production while protecting groundwater, etc. In these and
other management questions the communities have been assisted in
responding to existing problems or in avoid new ones.

Unfortunately, all this work has one major limitation: It is
highly labor-intensive over periods which may exceed a year. As a
pattern therefore, for general application to the huge number of
communities in the Northeast dependent on groundwater for their
water supplies, this approach is impractical and unsatisfactory.
Recognition of this serious limitation raised the dual question:
Would it be feasible to provide a means by which communities could

accomplish more using their own technical resources, so that limited number of existing groundwater professionals could be more efficiently and widely deployed?   Second, what means could be developed for this purpose?   The answer arrived at was interactive computer color graphics as a means of fostering more self-sufficiency in communities.   Our experience to date confirms our confidence in the efficacy of this technology compared to more traditional techniques.

References

Bottcher, R.S., T.S. Steenhuis, and M.F. Walter. User Manual for Subdrain. Northeast Regional Agricultural Engineering Service, Cornell University, Ithaca, N.Y.

Hughes, H.B., and K.S. Porter. 1982. Reclamation of a Ground-Water Supply: Clifton Springs, New York. Water Resources Program, Center for Environmental Research, Cornell University, Ithaca, N.Y.

Loucks, D.P., J. Kundler, and K. French. 1985a. Interactive Water Resources Modeling and Model Use. Water Resources Research 21:95-102.

Loucks, D.P., M.R. Taylor, and P.N. French. 1985b. Interactive Data Management for Resource Planning and Analysis. Water Resources Research, 21:131-142.

Pacenka, S. and K.S. Porter. 1981. Preliminary Regional Assessment of the Environmental Fate of the Potato Pesticide, Aldicarb, Eastern Long Island, New York. Center for Environmental Research, Cornell University, Ithaca, N.Y.

Pacenka, S., M.J. Heather, K.S. Porter, K. Hoover, B. Silverman, and L. Maller. 1983. Protecting Ground-Water Supplies in River Valley Communities. A Cornell Cooperative Extension Publication, Miscellaneous Bulletin 131.

Pacenka, S. and T.S. Steenhuis. 1985. User Manual for Model of Underground Solute Evaluation (MOUSE). Northeast Regional Agricultural Engineering Service, Cornell University, Ithaca, N.Y.

Porter, K.S. and S. Pacenka. 1982. Critical Groundwater Areas - A Strategy for Management. Prepared for the New York State Statewide Groundwater Management Program. Center for Environmental Research, Cornell University, Ithaca, N.Y.

Porter, K.S. 1982. Groundwater Information: Allocation and Needs. Prepared for the Long Island Groundwater Management Program. Center for Environmental Research, Cornell University, Ithaca, N.Y.

Steenhuis, T.S., R.E. Muck, and M.F. Walter. 1983. Predictions of Water Budgets for Soils with or Without a Hardpan. In: Advances in Infiltration. Am. Soc. of Agr. Eng. Monograph.

Steenhuis, T.S., M. van der Marel, and S. Pacenka. 1984. A Pragmatic Model for Diagnosing and Forecasting Ground Water Contamination. Proceedings of Practical Application of Ground Water Models. National Well Water Association, Columbus, Ohio. August 1984.

ACCUMULATION OF STREAMFLOW IN COMPLEX TOPOGRAPHY

By Hong-Mo Hong[1] and Robert N. Eli,[2] M. ASCE

ABSTRACT

A proposed synthetic watershed model which simulates the hydrologic process of both overland flow and interflow is presented in this paper. The synthetic model has features designed to be incorporated with digital terrain models. The purpose of the model is to support research investigations into the spatial and temporal accumulation of streamflow over complex topography. A synthetic soil layer overlying an impermeable boundary permits the simulation of interflow, accumulation of soil moisture, and the infiltration/exfiltration process.

INTRODUCTION

Model Purpose - The past decade or two has seen a wealth of watershed model development, ranging from single lumped parameter linear response models to complex parametric or deterministic nonlinear models. These latter models attempt to simulate the surface and subsurface movement of water in great detail. Much argument has been heard concerning the utility of the more complex models in practical applications, especially with respect to the relative improvement in predictive capability as compared to the more simple models. An infinite number of factors influences the accumulation of flow on real watersheds. No existing model would be of practical use if it were not due to the fact that the net result of all of these factors is a retardation of the progress of individual water particles, arriving as precipitation, in their journey to the watershed outlet. Fortunately, the infinite variety of flow paths result in a combined outflow that is effectively an weighted average measure of this infinite variety at any instant in time, or for short segments of time. If all of these flow paths behaved in the same way, independent of time, then lumped parameter linear models would be the best choice. As everyone knows, real watersheds are highly nonlinear in their runoff response. This nonlinearity is due to a vast number of factors, some which are more important than others. The purpose of the research effort, and hence the model being presented herein, is to investigate the relative influence of some of the more important nonlinear factors.

1. Ph.D. Candidate, Department of Civil Engineering, West Virginia University, Morgantown, WV 26506. (304)293-3580
2. Associate Professor, Department of Civil Engineering, West Virginia University, Morgantown, WV 26506. (304)293-3580

The model presented herein is refered to as a synthetic model in an attempt to differentiate it from practical models. It is not intended for practical application, but only to investigate the effects of space and time variant surface runoff, soil moisture, interflow (shallow groundwater flow), and infiltration/exfiltration over real topographic surfaces. The only real world data to be used are digital terrain data.

Use Of A Digital Terrain Model - The digital terrain modeling technique is illustrated in Figure 1. Rectangular grid digital terrain data is first contoured using an automated contouring package. The contour interval is chosen small enough to adequately represent the changing hillside slope, showing slope breaks and divides. The resulting digital contour point strings are next edited, removing excess points, and then stitched together with a triangulated mesh as shown in Figure 1. The reason for selecting an irregular triangulated network digital terrain model is to provide a geometrically more precise representation of a complex surface. The movement of water downslope corresponds to the gradient direction of each triangle lying along the flow path. The combined surface-subsurface model treats each triangle as an equivalent rectangle with equal area and aspect ratio, thereby producing a sequential series of plane surfaces downslope, culminating in a stream segment. The stream segments then accumulate the flow as a drainage tree until the watershed outlet is reached.

Background - Most popular watershed models often used by hydrologists have utilized a Hortonian concept of runoff generation, which states that runoff can be generated when the rate of rainfall exceeds the absorptive capacity (infiltration rate) of the soil. Ground water flow is treated as baseflow, which will respond after a long delay, a few days or weeks after, but not during the storm. Actual observations of rainfall-runoff events (in many cases) contradict this approach,

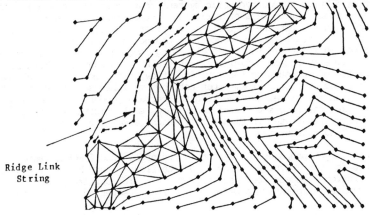

Ridge Link String

Figure 1 Partial Triangulation of a Watershed Segment using Contours

showing a subsurface response within a delay as short as a few minutes, or a fraction of an hour. It appears to be evident that rainfall which exceeds the infiltration rate of the soil will run off, but quick runoff responses are sometimes caused by ralatively light rainfalls that are much lower than the infiltration rate. Therefore, the Hortonian concept can not be generally true and at best draws a partial picture of the mechanisms involved in the rainfall-runoff process.

The mechanisms in the generation of streamflow have been traditionally identified as overland flow, interflow (saturated near-surface flow), and ground water flow (displacement of stored water from upslope) (5,8,10). Overland flow may occur when the rainfall intensity exceeds the infiltration rate of the soil (Hortonian concept), or when the saturation of near-surface zone leads to seepage flow (exfiltration). Hortonian overland flow predominates on those soils having low infiltrability. The upland (hilly) watershed, of major interest here, is likely to have high infiltration rates feeding a shallow subsurface flow (interflow), therefore, simulating runoff by accounting for only overland flow is not appropiate in this situation. It has been suggested that in the small upland catchments, the interflow along soil layers should taken into account (5,8).

The variable (partial) source area concept proposed by Hewlett (1) may be a better way to interpret and explain runoff accumulation from upland watersheds. Many current rainfall-runoff modeling techniques are based on the assumption that a watershed is a lumped hydraulics system. In other words, that streamflow is generated by processes which operate uniformly over the catchment surface, and therefore the catchment has a source area equal to the basin area. Although popular models such as TR-20 (Soil Conservation Service) and HEC-1 (Corps of Engineers) discretize the watershed into several subwatersheds, each subwatershed is still a large lumped hydraulic system that is still not small enough to demonstrate the concept of variable source area. In addition, the foregoing models use the Hortonian concept and do not explicitly account for the subsurface flow component. Shanholtz, et. al. (6), have developed a rainfall-runoff model using smaller subareas which are individual elements in a finite element solution technique. Without the capability of accounting for the interflow, the model can only best describe the overland flow, but not the variable source area. The information contained in the digital terrain model can be used to discretize the watershed into many very small finite elements (as previously illustrated in Figure 1), each element can be treated as a contributing source area.

This paper proposes a synthetic rainfall-runoff model which can account for both overland flow and interflow, and the infiltration-exfiltration process between the two. It utilizes the complex topographic information provided by high resolution digital terrain models.

GENERAL DESCRIPTION OF THE MODEL

Each triangular element in the digital terrain model is assumed to maintain hydrologic and topographic homogeneity within its boundary.

The orientation (flow direction), slope, hydrologic and topographic characteristics of the element are stored in the digital terrain model files. Therefore, the contributing elements to each stream segment can be established. By suitable transformation (as explained earlier), the contributing elements can be treated as a series of planes over or through which the flow passes. Thus the water is routed continuously through a combination of overland flow and interflow from the uppermost element (plane) down to the stream segment.

Kinematic wave routing is used when overland flow occurs, while interflow occurs according to Darcy's law. The storage-discharge history of the entire hillslope system of rectangular elements is based on a water balance (i.e. mass continuity).

Extended Interflow Zone (Subsurface Saturated Flow Zone) - An expandable and shrinkable interflow zone is assumed to adequately represent subsurface flow. The zone thickness will increase or decrease depending on the availability of water supply and the rate of soil moisture draining downslope (a mass balance). The vertical profile of the element is shown in Figure 2. It is assumed that the maximum extension rate of the interflow zone is a function of its thickness and the initial hydraulic conductivity which is equivalent to the infiltration rate of the soil, i.e. :

$$f = f_o EXP(-kH) \tag{1}$$

where f = extension rate of innterflow zone, ft/min
   f_o = extension rate of interflow zone when its thickness is equal to zero, ft/min
   k = a constant (corresponds to initial hydraulic conductivity)
   H = the thickness of interflow zone, ft

The upper bound of the zone is the soil surface and the lower bound is the wetting front which will vary with time. The movement of subsurface water downslope follows Darcy's law which states that the interflow rate

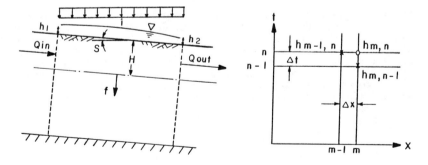

Figure 2 Vertical Profile of Element   Figure 3 Finite Difference Scheme

will depend on the saturated thickness, soil horizontal hydraulic conductivity, and the surface slope (hydraulic gradient), i. e. :

$$Q = KSH \qquad (2)$$

where Q = interflow rate along the slope
K = hydraulic conductivity along the slope
S = surface slope

The possible sources of water input to the subsurface system of each element are the subsurface flow from the upslope element, and availability of overland flow or rainfall for infiltration (treated as lateral inflow). Exfiltrating flow and interflow to the adjacent downslope element are sources of water output. The governing water balance in the subsurface system will determine whether the interflow zone of the present element should extend or shrink, thus determining the lateral inflow rate term on the surface.

Surface Flow - The surface flow is described by the well-known hydrodynamic equations (Saint-Venant) of continuity and momentum. The equation of continuity can be expressed as

$$\frac{\partial h}{\partial t} + u \frac{\partial h}{\partial x} + h \frac{\partial u}{\partial x} = q \qquad (3)$$

and the equation of momentum as

$$\frac{1}{g} \frac{\partial u}{\partial t} + \frac{u}{g} \frac{\partial u}{\partial x} + \frac{\partial h}{\partial x} = S - S_f - \frac{q}{gh}(u-u_x) \qquad (4)$$

where q = lateral inflow per unit length of flow plane
t = time
x = distance along downslope direction
h = depth of overland flow
u = velocity
u_x = x component of the velocity of the lateral inflow
g = acceleration due to gravity
S = surface slope
S_f = friction slope

However, in trying to solve the complete equations, one will encounter a system of non-linear hyperbolic partial differential equations. Due to the complexity and difficulty of solving the full equations, the kinematic wave approximation was applied to the momentum equation. The justification of this procedure is well documented in the literature (2,3,7,9). The kinematic wave approximation requires that there be a balance between the gravitational and frictional forces involved in the momentum equation and it can be represented by a uniform flow equation such as Manning's equation

$$u = \frac{1.486}{n} h^{2/3} S^{1/2} \qquad (5)$$

where n = Manning's n

then the continuity equation can be rewritten as

$$\frac{\partial h}{\partial t} + \frac{5}{3} \alpha h^{2/3} \frac{\partial h}{\partial x} = q \tag{6}$$

where $\alpha = \frac{1.486}{n} s^{1/2}$

The non-linear hyperbolic equation (6) can then be solved by applying backward finite difference scheme in time and x. The scheme is shown in Figure 3, and the difference equation of (6) becomes

$$h_{m,n} = \frac{1}{1+\lambda a} [h_{m,n-1} + \lambda a h_{m-1,n} + q_{m,n} \Delta t] \tag{7}$$

where $a = \frac{5}{3} \alpha_m h_{m,n-1}^{2/3}$; $\lambda = \Delta t / \Delta x$

The linear stability of the scheme is unconditionally stable, which is easily proved by the method of von Neumann (4). Since the initial conditions and boundary conditions of the upmost element are known, the depth of flow on the present element at the current time can be directly computed from the depth of flow on the element at the previous time step and the depth of flow on upstream element at current time step; i. e., the solution can be obtained by propagating downstream. The overland outflow of the element is then calculated by using Manning's equation.

Continuity Check - Before propagating to the next element, the mass balance is checked for the present element, including both overland flow (including lateral inflow), and interflow. If an error correction is required it is needed distributed over the whole element.

The computations continue and advance to the adjacent downslope element until the stream segment is encountered. The accumulation of the streamflow is determined as the sum of the outflows of overland flow and interflow of the last element. The whole procedure is then repeated in the next time step until the maximum time specified. Figure 4 shows the schematic flowchart of the model.

<u>PRELIMINARY RESULTS</u>

A synthetic series of ten planes has been used to test the performance of the model. Two cases of spatial uniform rainfalls are exercised. One of them is a temporal uniform rainfall of 4 inch/hr (10cm/hr) intensity with duration of 20 minutes, the other is a time varied rainfall which has a intensity of 4 inch/hr (10cm/hr) in the first 20 minutes, 6 inch/hr (15cm/hr) in the next 20 minutes followed by 4 inch/hr (10cm/hr) in the last 20 minutes (total duration of 60 minutes). The resulting hydrographs of the streamflows are shown in Figure 5 which indicates a significant contribution of the interflow to the streamflow. Figure 6 shows the saturation history of the sloping soil (exaggerating in the vertical scale). The pocket and band saturations of soil on the hillslope, stated by Hewlett, are produced by the model (Figure 6). It should be noted that saturated conditions are reached first at the concave slope transitions, producing local exfiltration, equivalent to hillside springs observed on real watersheds.

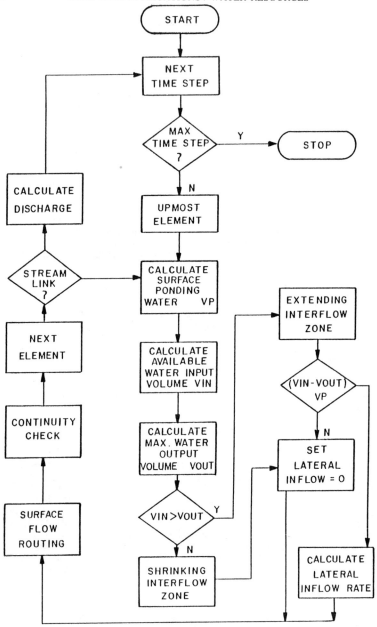

Figure 4 Schematic Flowchart of Model

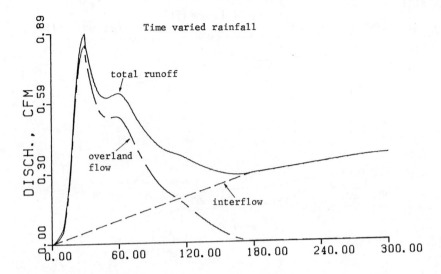

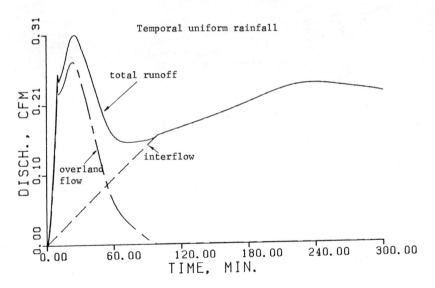

Figure 5 Hydrographs of Streamflows

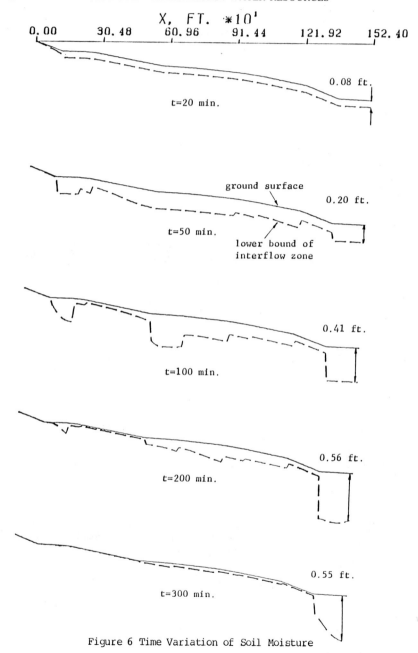

Figure 6 Time Variation of Soil Moisture

FUTURE DIRECTIONS

Although the above results are very preliminary, the model's ability to at least give an appearance of real world watershed behavior is encouraging. It is yet to be shown whether or not the detail behavior of the model is appropriate. The primary goal was to develop a preliminary version of the model that demonstrated the ability to simulate the detail flow behavior observed in actual upland watersheds. The ability of the model to display both spatial and temporal variation of overland flow, interflow, exfiltration, infiltration, and soil moisture has been demonstrated. Future work will involve refinement and proofing the model, plus studies of its efficiency and accuracy when applied to a very large number of triangular elements typically encountered in real watersheds.

KEYWORDS : rainfall-runoff model, digital terrain model.

REFERENCES

1. Hewlett, J. D. and Nutter, W. L., 'The Varying Source Area Of Streamflow From Upland Basins,' Symposium on Interdisciplinary Aspects of Watershed Management, Montana State University, Bozeman, August 3-6, 1970.
2. Kiber, D. F. and Woolhiser, D. A., 'The Kinematic Cascade As A Hydrologic Model,' Hydology Paper No. 39, Colorado State University, March, 1970.
3. Lighthill, F. R. S. and Whitman, G. B., 'On Kinematic Waves, 1. Flood Movement In Long Rivers,' Proc. Roy. Soc., London, 229, May, 1955, pp. 281-316.
4. Mitchell, A. R. and Griffth D. F., '4. Hyperbolic Equations,' The Finite Difference Method In Partial Differential Equations, 1st ed., John Wiley and Sons, Inc., London, 1979, pp. 168-170.
5. Moseley, M. P., 'Streamflow Generation In A Forested Watershed, New Zealand,' Water Resources Research, 15(4), 1979, pp. 795-806.
6. Shanholtz, V. O. and et. al., 'A Finite-Element Model Of Overland And Channel Flow For Assessing The Hydrologic Impact Of Land-Use Change,' Journal of Hydrology, 41(1979), pp. 11-30.
7. Weinmann, P. E. and Laurenson, E., 'Approximate Flood Routing Methods : A Review,' Journal of Hydraulics Division, ASCE, Vol. 105, No. HY12, December, 1979, pp. 1521-1536.
8. Whipkey, R. Z., 'Subsurface Stormflow From Froested Slopes,' Int. Assoc. Sci. Hydro. Bull., 10(2), 1965, pp. 74-85.
9. Wooding, R. A., 'A Hydraulic Model For The Catchment-Stream Problem I Kinematic-Wave Theory,' Journal of Hydrology, Vol. 3, 1965, pp. 254-267.
10. Zaslavsky, D. and Sinai, G., 'Surface Hydrology: I-Explanation of Phenomena, III-Causes of Lateral Flow, IV-Flow in Sloping, Layered Soil, V-In Surface Transient Flow,' Journal of Hydraulics Division ASCE, Vol. 107, No. HY1, Jan., 1981, pp. 1-16, pp. 37-93.

ANALYSIS OF DRINKING WATER SYSTEMS:
A SPATIAL APPROACH

by

Robert M. Clark M.ASCE[a] and James A. Goodrich[b]

ABSTRACT: There has been a growing interest and awareness of the use
of spatial analysis in water supply engineering. Normally, spatial
location and relationships have been considered incidental, although
many engineering activites dealt with the design, construction and
provision of services over geographically diverse locations. This
paper describes recent examples of spatial analyses as (1) a unifying
concept for allocation of costs to various elements of water treatment
and delivery; (2) a link and node (Network) representation of water
supply being integrated with the Water Supply Simulation Model and
maintenance and pipe replacement data to provide a tool for analyzing
"break and leak reports" and (3) to predict water quality at various
locations in a water distribution system. Another far reaching
example of spatial analysis in water supply is the integration of
upstream industrial and toxic dischargers with design decisions in
downstream water treatment.

INTRODUCTION

Many of the subdisciplines of Civil Engineering deal with locating, planning and designing, and analyzing mans' activities. For
example, transportation, surveying, construction hydraulics, and
environmental engineering are in some way involved with the location
of population centers, their characteristics, and are the consequences
of mans' activities. Much of civil engineering is involved in building the infrastructure that provides the basis for fostering and
sustaining population development. Infrastructure generally means the
roads, bridges, sewers, water systems, rail systems, and mass transit
which routinely supply services to the urbanized population of the
United States. A critical portion of this infrastructure development
is the planning, design and construction of water supply systems.

Water systems generally have high fixed costs and are installed
for long design periods. Often water supply facilities are installed
with substantial initial excess capacity, which makes the service
area attractive for development. The treatment and delivery functions
of a water utility represent large economic investments, but the vast

---

[a]Robert M. Clark, Director, Drinking Water Research Division, Water
Engineering Research Laboratory, Cincinnati, OH 45268
[b]James A. Goodrich, Research Environmental Scientist, Drinking Water
Research Division, Water Engineering Research Laboratory, Cincinnati,
OH 45268

majority of expenditures are in the delivery system. Population
projections made in designing water systems frequently become self-
fulfilling. The water utility plays a significant role in community
public health and can also become a determinant of the communities'
growth path.

Traditional thinking in water supply, and in civil engineering,
seldom considers location as a specific factor in engineering analysis.
Normally, spatial location and relationships are considered incidental,
which is suprising since many engineering activities deal with the
design, construction and provision of services over geographically
diverse locations. Properly defined spatial analysis can contribute
another variable that allows for more complete analyses and definition
of system performance.

Recently in water supply engineering there has been a growing
interest and awareness of the use of spatial analysis and a formal
consideration of spatial variations. Many researchers, consultants,
planners and implementers have come to recognize that geographic
location is a common denominator, linking nearly all planning and
engineering data and provides the basis for timely storage, retrieval
and manipulation of data base information, relating to property
ownership and assessment, easements, zoning restrictions, permits,
utilities, transportation and environmental data, housing, schools,
land use, soils, natural resources, crime, fire, etc.

The majority of the spatial considerations that relate directly
to water supply systems are associated with distribution design and
operation. These aspects of spatial analysis along with examples of
completed and ongoing research being conducted by EPA will be discussed in the following sections. Another use of spatial analysis is
in water resources where there is concern for relating industrial and
nonpoint source discharges to influent water quality. Ongoing work
in this area will also be discussed.

SPATIAL ANALYSIS AND WATER DISTRIBUTION SYSTEMS

Design of water distribution systems can be divided into four
major areas. The first is concerned with basic land use and demographic parameters used to determine the preliminary size and shape
of the service area. The second area of concern reflects the natural
features of the service area. The third area of concern is the
capacity requirement of the system as a whole and that of individual
components. The fourth area of concern is that of engineering design
criteria, such as the diameter of pipe, the minimum and maximum
velocities, minimum and maximum slopes, and the flow characteristics
of the pipes themselves.[4,10]

The nature, quantity and locations of water demand can be determined by using spatial analysis as an organizing factor. These
demands can also be determined over time. Once temporally and
spatially varying demands have been established, only then can
capacity limitations and design of the various components of the
system be determined. An example of this approach has been developed
for the Washington Metropolitan Area.[5]

SPATIAL COSTING AND ECONOMICS

The early studies that utilized spatial variation as a key factor
in water supply system performance were a series of case studies
conducted at various utilities together with an in-depth economic
evaluation using the Cincinnati Water Works as a source of data.[1]
This in-depth study incorporated the use of planning permits, zoning
and marginal cost economics as a means of both planning for future
capacity expansion and establishing equitable rates.[7]

In the first series of case studies the waterworks were subdivided into various zones, and then incremental costs were collected
for the zones in an attempt to gain insights as to how costs change
as water moves from the central treatment plant to the various water
demand points within the system. These case studies provided an
empirical basis for development of a spatially oriented cost analysis
system.

This concept provides for allocation of costs, not only to the
specific functions of acquisition, treatment or delivery, but also to
the subfunction level as illustrated in Figure 1. Two types of costs
were identified. Those associated directly with the operating functions of acquisition, treatment and delivery just described, and
those not identified with any specific operating function. This
second type includes billing, accounting and management, and was
placed in a separate category called support services. Figure 1
shows these costs distributed across the entire utility operation.
The cost categories which would normally be the cost items included
in the utilities charts of accounts can be cross-referenced against

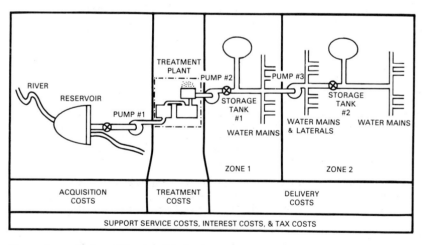

Figure 1.   Water utility simplified schematic.

the utilities functions. Documentation of costs in this format makes it possible to retrieve and display the various levels, or types of information desired. This concept was implemented as a spatial costing system in two water systems. The second example involves development of a more formal analytical approach to evaluating the impact of population density on the cost of water supply. Using this approach the water supply system was separated into two components, the treatment plant and the delivery or the transmission and distribution systems, and it was postulated that each of these components had a different cost function. In the case of the water treatment facility, the unit costs tended to decrease as the quantity of service provided increased. But the delivery system was more directly affected by the characteristics of the area being served. It was hypothesized that the cost tradeoffs between the two components will determine the least-cost service area. Figure 2 illustrates this concept. One can see from the average cost curve in Figure 2 the declining average costs due to the economies of scale in treatment and then the rising average costs as the diseconomies associated with the distribution system predominate.[2]

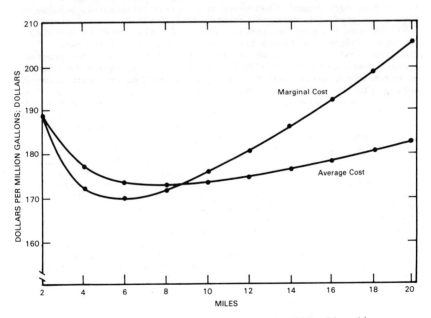

Figure 2.   Unit and marginal cost with distance using 150 gal/cap/day.

A major effort to develop a formal tool to analyze the various factors influencing the cost of water supply was undertaken resulting in the development of a Water Supply Simulation Model (WSSM).

WATER SUPPLY SIMULATION MODEL

The WSSM is based upon the concept of a water utility as a network overlaid upon a spatial distribution of supply and demand. The model explicitly deals with the relationship of delivered water costs to the service requirements of spatially and temporally distributed demand. This spatial representation is based on a characterization of the water supply system as a link-node network. It is assumed that water enters and leaves the system only at nodes, which represent treatment plants, junctions, demand locations, and storage tanks. Water is carried between and among nodes through connecting links. Costs are allocated to the various facilities and system components based on flow in the system.[6]

The WSSM requires that the system be described as a network of pipes, storage tanks, treatment plants, demands and other hydraulic elements. Information concerning the network is stored in a network data base, which also stores additional descriptive or calculated information about each element, such as size of pipe, geographic location of each demand often using state plane coordinates, population associated with a demand, connectivity of pipes, etc. Certain basic information must be stored, in order for the system to operate, but other information is elective, and is a function of the particular uses and analysis to which the WSSM is to be put. Other program modules communicate with the data base through standardized data base access methods, which consist of routines to extract or insert information into the network data base.

The two key modules in terms of system evaluation are the hydraulic and solver algorithms. The current version of WSSM uses both WATSIM and the "Wood Model" as the basis for hydraulic analysis. Both of these algorithms are standards available in the profession and are described elsewhere. The second module SOLVER is a general purpose algorithm that sets up and solves problems relating to mixing in networks, given the network topology and flows.[9] It is used with WSSM for three generic types of problems: (1) determining time required to travel from any source to a node (travel time); (2) determining the concentration of any constituent at any node, given the concentration of the constituent at all sources, and (3) determination of the cost of delivered water at any node, given the individual annualized costs associated with the nodes and links of the system. Ultimately a major objection of the model will be to generate spatial cost variations over the utilities service area as shown in Figure 3.

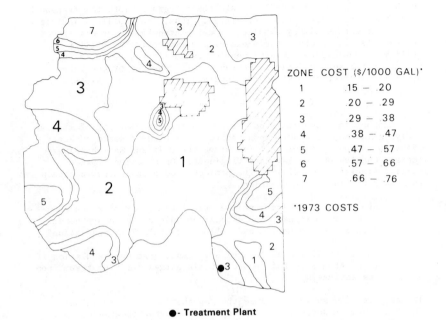

ZONE	COST ($/1000 GAL)'
1	.15 − .20
2	.20 − .29
3	.29 − .38
4	.38 − .47
5	.47 − .57
6	.57 − .66
7	.66 − .76

'1973 COSTS

●- Treatment Plant

Figure 3.   Cost contours for Cincinnati Water Works area, based upon Water Works area, based upon Water Supply Simulation Model.

EXTENSIONS OF MODEL

Currently the use of the WSSM is being extended to test its ability to predict water quality at various locations in a water distribution system. A study is being conducted at the North Penn Water Utility north of Philadelphia to evaluate this concept.

NETWORK RELIABILITY

Research is also being conducted to more fully understand main-tenance and repair information for the water supply distribution network. The key to drinking water supply delivery analysis is the performance of reliability assessments. The critical component of an inventory and water main condition assessment is the geo-spatial coding of data, thus providing a common reference system. The Louisville', Kentucky and Cincinnati, Ohio Water Works are undertaking projects which include (1) an overall description of the system (connectivity, physical characteristics, etc.), (2) structural integrity, (3) quality of service and level of usage, and (4) safety. Each link, node, break and customer complaint can be uniquely identi-fied by its location either in State Plane Coordinates and/or the United States Bureau of Census Dime File code. In this manner, a variety of data such as soil type, land use, traffic load, operating pressure, elevation, etc., can be accessed. Hydraulic analyses using

the WSSM or the "Wood Model" can also be integrated into the framework
since the network is already specified. Thus, "reliability" analyses
need no longer be simply simulations calculated by a hydraulic model,
but can also incorporate socio-economic variables. The ability of a
utility to anticipate, detect, repair, rehabilitate, reconstruct or
replace water supply delivery components is enhanced by the geo-
spatial coding of data which provides a common reference system.

TOXIC SCREEING MODELS FOR WATER SUPPLY

Another more general study incorporating the concepts of spatial
analysis has been a study conducted to predict toxic waste concentrations in community water supplies along the Ohio and Kanawha Rivers
between Charleston, W. Va., and Cincinnati, Ohio, using a water
quality simulation model.[8] The project used a case study approach
to answer the following questions:

° Are those utilities within a specified number of miles downstream from industrical discharges vulnerable to synthetic
   organic contamination and subject to EPA's TTHM regulation?

° Should utilities be granted a variance from the regulation if
   fewer than a certain number of discharges exist upstream from
   its intakes?

The project also sought to close the gap that potentially exists in
the loop between water pollution control and water treatment.
     Through the use of the methodology developed, the study pre-
dicted which communities in the case study area would be vulnerable
to background levels of typical daily discharges. Thus, this study
described who is at risk, their relative levels of risk, and the main
factors contributing to the risk.
     QUAL-II, a water quality simulation model, was used to bring
together the diverse elements of mathematical modeling, fluid
dynamics, organic chemistry, and geography to create an interactive
systems analysis approach that can have an impact of public policy in
drinking water. Though QUAL-II is less flexible than other models in
simulating various flow scenarios and less sophisticated in modeling
dozens of built-in parameters and biological and chemical transformations, the model exhibits a spatial organization that simplifies
thinking and highlights critical variables such as the relative
locations of utilities and dischargers and the time of travel.
     Figure 4 schematically represents the waste loads, tributaries,
and junctions involved in the water quality modeling. The contaminants were routed approximately 200 (322 km) miles at various flow
scenarios to account for seasonal variations in flow. The next step
in the analysis was to develop an inventory and description of existing point sources and communities along the two rivers. To simplify
the project, no attempt was made to identify nonpoint sources. Only
industrial discharges were considered.

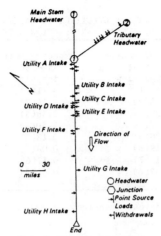

Figure 4. Schematic of the study area

To assess the potential impact on public health, simulated pollutant concentrations for each utility were compared with Water Quality
Criteria, which suggest the concentrations of various pollutants that
could be harmful to human health. The criteria take into account
toxicity, carcinogenicity, or organolepticity (taste and odor) of the
pollutants.

For toxic and organoleptic pollutants, the flow is critical in
determining whether a Water Quality Criteria has been exceeded.
Because vulnerability to carcinogens is evaluated over years of
exposure to pollutants in the drinking water, carcinogenic risk
levels were initially estimated only at average flows. In the event
of a spill, however, the flow characteristics can be important even
to carcinogens, since very high concentrations of carbon tetra-
chloride, for example, can have an acute health effect. Contrary to
conventional wisdom, low flows do not necessarily exhibit higher
pollutant concentrations than high flows because of decreased dilution. As the volume of water increases, so does the mean velocity in
the river channel, thus reducing the time of travel and decay of
pollutants. Utilities well downstream can be at higher risk during
high flows since the river is bringing the pollutants downstream much
quicker and not allowing for decay. Utilities can be vulnerable to
different pollutants at different flows.

Analysis of carcinogenic pollutants is done differently than
that for the toxic and organoleptic pollutants. Actual health hazards
cannot be determined, only risks in terms of expected death rate per
pollutant per year can be estimated. Table 1 lists the results of
the vulnerability analysis.

TABLE 1

VULNERABILITY OF UTILITIES TO CARCINOGENIC
POLLUTANTS AT VARIOUS FLOW RATES

Utility	Expected Death Rate at Average Flow	Expected Death Rate at High Flow	Expected Death Rate at Low Flow
E	6.47(1)*	3.71(1)	19.77(1)
F	5.01(2)	3.14(2)	10.42(2)
G	2.99(3)	2.36(3)	2.35(3)
H	1.57(4)	1.50(4)	0.56(4)
D	0.20(5)	0.13(5)	0.46(5)
B	0.19(6)	0.04(7)	0.44(6)
C	0.18(7)	0.11(6)	0.40(7)
A	0.02(8)	0.01(8)	0.07(8)

*Figures in parentheses indicate ranking.

EXTENSION OF MODEL

    The concept developed in the previous section has been extended
to the Lower Mississippi in the corridor between New Orleans and
Baton Rouge. In this study, data from various EPA and industrial
sources is being used to evaluate water quality as it impacts design
decisions at the New Orleans water supply intake. In this case the
model is being used to structure information needs as they might
effect any major water supply using a surface source. The methodologies described can be used to evaluate the tradeoffs that exist
between various levels of human exposure to toxic and for carcinogenic
chemicals and the cost of water treatment.

SUMMARY AND CONCLUSIONS

    Spatial analysis concepts can provide a useful organizing concept
for analyzing water supply systems. Examples of the concept applied
to design and operation of water distribution systems have been
presented.
    One set of examples deals with the planning, design and opera-
tional aspects of water treatment and delivery. Early studies focused
on the allocation of costs to various elements of the water treatment
and delivery system. Cost functions were developed for treatment and
delivery and a minimum cost point for distribution system size was
developed. A tool for formally analyzing the various elements of the
water supply system was developed in the Water Supply Simulation
Model. The model is based on a link and node (Network) representation
of the water supply system. Currently the network concept is being
used to integrate maintenance, repair and replacement data for the
distribution system with such pieces of information as "colored water
reports", break and leak reports", and repair records. These data
are being organized according to the network and also geo-coded
according to the DIME FILE format.

Another more far reaching example of spatial analysis in water supply is the integration of upstream industrial and toxic dischargers with design decisions in downstream water treatment. The implications for water quality and river basin management are being studied. This approach forces pollution control elements of EPA to recognize their impact on Drinking Water utilities.

The spatial concept in water supply provides a powerful mechanism for analyzing both system and environmental impacts.

APPENDIX A. - REFERENCES

1. Clark, Robert M., Machisko, John A., and Stevie, Richard G., "Cost of Water Supply: Selected Case Studies", Journal of the Environmental Engineering Division, ASCE, Vol. 105, No. EE1, February 1979, pp. 89-100.
2. Clark, Robert M. and Stevie, Richard G., "Analytical Cost Model for Urban Water Supply", Journal of the Water Resources Planning and Management Division, ASCE, Vol. 107, No. WR2, October 1981, pp. 437-452.
3. Clark, R. M., Fender, V. F., and Gillean, J. I., "A Spatial Costing System for Drinking Water" Journal of the American Water Works Association, Vol. 74, January 1982, pp.
4. Clark, Robert M., Stafford, Cheryl L. and Goodrich, James A., "Water Distribution Systems: A Spatial and Cost Evaluation", Journal of the Water Resourcess Planning and Management Division, ASCE, Vol. 108, No. WR3, October, 1982, pp. 243-256.
5. Clark, Robert M., Goodrich, James A., and Gillean, James I., Predicting Future Water Demand, Journal of the Environmental Engineering Division, ASCE, Vol. 108, No. EE6, December 1982, pp. 1248-1264.
6. Clark, Robert M. and Males, Richard M., "Simulating Cost and Quality in Distribution Systems" accepted for publication in The Journal of Water Resources Planning and Management, ASCE.
7. Goddard, Haynes C., Stevie, Richard G., Trygg, Gregory D., Planning Water Supply: Cost-Rate Differential and Plumbing Permits, EPA-600/5-78-008, U.S. Environmental Protection Agency, Municipal Environmental Research Laboratory, Cincinnati, OH 45268, May 1978.
8. Goodrich, James A. and Clark, Robert M., "Predicting Toxic Waste Concentrations in Community Drinking Water Supplies: Analysis of Vulnerability to Upstream Industrial Discharges, EPA-600/2-840112, U.S. Environmental Research Laboratory, Cincinnati, OH 45268, September 1984.
9. Males, Richard M., Clark, Robert M., Wehrman, Paul J. and Gates, William E., "Algortihm for Mixing Problems in Water Systems", Journal of the Hydraulics Division, ASCE, Vol. 111, No. 2, February 1985.
10. Tabors, Richard D., Shapiro, Michael H., Rogers, Peter P., Land Use and the Pipe, Lexington Books, DC Health and Co., Lexington, Mass., 1976.

Automated Data Monitoring
for Disaster Prevention

David C. Leader, P.E., Associate Member ASCE*
David C. Curtis, PhD., Associate Member ASCE

Today, real-time data transportation and analysis are essential in
responding to a variety of rapidly changing environmental conditions.
Vital environmental information delivered in real-time can be used to
save time, money and lives.

A system is now available from International Hydrological Services
for use on micro-computers that will provide real-time environmental
monitoring, analysis, forecasting and control. This system can have
applications in environmental data management, flood forecasts and
warnings, reservoir operation, hydropower production, irrigation
management, frost warning, water supply management and dam safety.

An example of such a system will be installed on a micro-computer
in Emerson, Iowa. This turn-key system will monitor rainfall and river
levels using real-time event radio telemetry. The computer system will
store all data for later display and analysis and it will also issue
warnings and sound alarms if rainfall intensities or river levels
exceed predetermined criteria levels.

Remote warnings will be issued if an alarm condition occurs in this
system. The remote warnings will use radio paging devices. It is
necessary to have the remote warnings sent over radios to avoid the
problem of losing telephone communication lines during severe storms.
This same problem is avoided in data collection by using radio
telemetry.

A river forecasting package is available that will automatically
analyze precipitation and water level reports to prepare river
forecasts. The forecast package also provides the ability to generate
forecasts for potential future precipitation amounts.

The system operators will be able to examine the state of the
system including alarm conditions and sensor values. This information
can be a tremendous aid in making decisions on flood prevention
actions.

*David C. Leader, Vice President Systems Engineering, International
Hydrological Services, 1900 Point West Way, Suite 161, Sacramento, CA
95815.

Today, real-time data transportation and analysis are essential in responding to a variety of rapidly changing environmental conditions. Vital environmental information delivered in real-time can be used to save time, money and lives.

One situation where information transport speed and analysis are important is in flash flood systems. For small watersheds with fast concentration times, a flood potential analysis system must get its information quickly and process it before the crisis occurs. After such a system has determined that a flood crisis is possible, it must issue a warning to inform officials that flood prevention actions must be taken.

A system is now available from International Hydrological Services for use on micro-computers that will provide real-time environmental monitoring, analysis, forecasting and warning. This system can have applications in environmental data management, flood forecasts and warnings, reservoir operation, hydropower production, irrigation management, frost warning, water supply management and dam safety.

An example of such a system will be installed in Emerson, Iowa. This turn-key system will monitor rainfall and river levels using real-time event radio telemetry. The computer system will store all data collected in a database for later display and analysis. It will also issue warnings and sound alarms if rainfall intensities or river levels exceed predetermined criteria levels.

Emerson, Iowa is located on a bend of Indian Creek which flows into the Nishnabotna River, a tributary of the Missouri River. The drainage area above this city is approximately 50 square miles. When heavy rainfall occurs over this basin the creek rises over its banks and floods the main street of the city. To complicate matters, the severe weather often results in telephone communication lines being broken.

The city officials asked the United States Army Corps of Engineers for help in mitigating this flood hazard. The Corps of Engineers studied the situation and decided to use both a structural and non-structural remedy to this problem. The structural part was to construct a levee to help protect the city. Since this would not protect the city from the more extreme flood events, a warning system was included as the non-structural part of the remedy.

To provide the flood warning, it was necessary to place precipitation and water level sensors in the upstream basin. Data from these sensors would then be collected by a base station capable of monitoring the data and sounding warnings if necessary. The use of radio telemetry was required because of the unreliability of telephone lines during severe weather. Event reporting sensors were needed because of the short time to flood peak during heavy rainfall. The sensor packages chosen to meet these specifications are manufactured by Sierra Misco, Inc. (Berkeley, CA).

The base station chosen is a Compaq Plus (IBM PC compatible) micro-computer operating the Enhanced ALERT system. The computer receives the telemetry data through a serial port. This same port is

used to drive the warning system. A second serial port is connected to
a telephone modem for remote user access.

When data is received from a remote sensor it is filed in the
Enhanced ALERT database. This database is stored on the computer's
hard disk. Up to 5000 reports can be stored for each sensor
established in the system. Once data has been stored in the database,
it is available for display and analysis by the Enhanced ALERT
programs.

When a data report is filed in the database, it is checked against
alarm criteria defined for the sensor. Each sensor in the database can
have its own unique alarm criteria. For precipitation sensors, a
precipitation rate is defined as the alarm criteria. If this rate is
met or exceeded, the system issues a warning. For other sensor types
such as river levels, 6 different alarm criteria can be defined. These
criteria are:

absolute value that must be exceeded
absolute value to fall below
positive rate of change
positive rate of change above a threshold value
negative rate of change
negative rate of change above a threshold value

The absolute value and threshold criteria are sensor readings to exceed
or fall below. The rate of change criteria are computed differences in
sensor readings for a specified time period.

A program is supplied as part of the Enhanced ALERT system that
lets the operator define individual sensor alarm criteria. The
operator is also able to define a group of sensors of the same type
(precipitation, water level, etc.) and then set the alarm criteria for
these sensors to the same value. An example of the display output of
this program is shown in Figure 1.

Sensor			Rate of Change			
#	Absolute		Positive		Negative	
type	Max.	Min.	Rate	Threshold	Rate	Threshold
110	8.0 ft	1.0 ft	3.0 ft/hr	4.0 ft	none	none
river	enabled	enabled	enabled	enabled	disabled	disabled
130	10.5 ft	none	2.0 ft/hr	none	none	none
river	enabled	disabled	disabled	disabled	disabled	disabled
220	none	none	4.0 in/6 hr	none	none	none
pcp	disabled	disabled	enabled	disabled	disabled	disabled
134	85 degF	34 degF	none	none	5 degF/hr	42 degF
temp	enabled	enabled	disabled	disabled	enabled	enabled

Figure 1. Example of Sensor Alarm Criteria Display

Sensor	Name	Cause of Alarm	Date	Time
220	Reservoir #	Precipitation rate exceeded	3/2/85	20:19
110	Coffee Creek	Rate of rise exceeded	3/2/85	20:22
130	Broad River	Absolute max. stage exceeded	3/2/85	20:25

Figure 2. Example of Alarm Status Display

When the system determines that an alarm criteria has been met or exceeded, it logs the report for later display and starts the warning process. The Enhanced ALERT system warning process can be tailored to meet a particular installation's needs. In the Emerson system, the local warning will consist of an audio and visual warning on the base station screen. The remote warning will be triggered by sending a signal to a radio paging system to issue a page. Because of the potential loss of telephone lines, a radio paging service directly connected to the computer was required rather than using a modem to call a contracted telephone paging service.

City officials alerted by the paging devices will know to check the status of the flood warning system. A system command is provided that will display the current alarm status log. Each log entry gives the sensor number, the reason for the alarm and the time it occurred. The alarm status command can be executed by an operator at the base station or by a remote user dialing into the system if the local telephone lines are still operable. Knowing what sensor triggered the warning and what caused the alarm will help the city officials decide on the appropriate actions to take. An example of the alarm status display is shown in Figure 2.

In addition to the alarm features, the Enhanced ALERT system provides a variety of data display programs. These displays include single sensor reports, grouped sensor reports, map plots of sensor values and time series plots. All display programs by default display the most recent information available for the system sensors. However, as an option, the operator can request any time period for display of data stored in the database. For systems with graphical and color screens, the plot programs are provided in high resolution and color. These display programs give the operator more information aiding in the decision process. Examples of program displays are shown in Figures 3 and 4.

A river forecasting package is available to operate with the Enhanced ALERT collection and warning system. The forecasting package will perform automated river forecasting and provide alarms based on forecast water surface elevations. To do this the forecast package scans the precipitation and river level files at time steps defined by the user. The time step between forecast updates can be from 5 minutes to 24 hours. For each time step the package generates a new forecast based on current conditions and on up to 5 user definable future precipitation amounts.

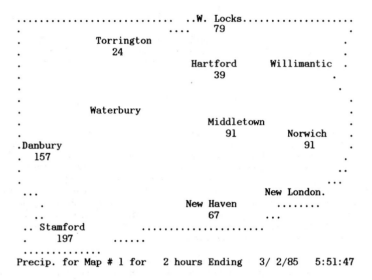

Figure 3. Example of a Precipitation Map Plot

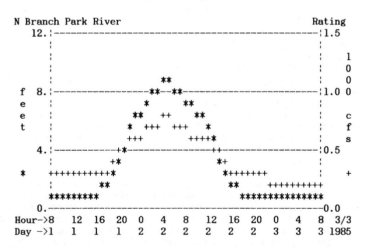

Figure 4. Example of Time Series Plot

The Sacramento Soil Moisture Accounting model is used to compute runoff volumes for the forecast basins. Up to 25 basins can be defined at this time. River routing to downstream points and reservoir inflow forecasting is also available.

The forecast results can be displayed by the operator as a text message or as a hydrograph plot. Figure 5 is an example of a forecast hydrograph plot. The forecast package displays and alarm features give the system operators lead time in knowing the probability of a flood threat due to observed precipitation. The definable future precipitation forecasts extends this lead time even more by computing the results of continuing precipitation.

The warning, display and forecast information provided by the Enhanced ALERT system can be a tremendous aid to officials who must make decisions on flood prevention actions. The system not only increases the lead-time available to initiate the actions but can also releive the official's concerns over whether the actions are necessary or not.

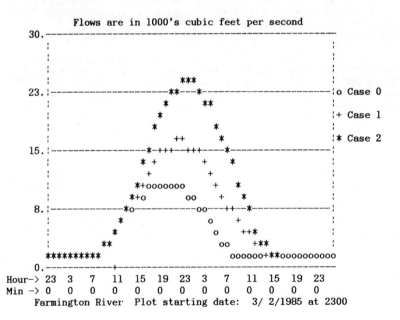

Figure 5: Example of Forecast Hydrographs

Case 0 is the forecast with no additional precipitation.
Case 1 is the forecast with 2 additional inches in 6 hours.
Case 2 is the forecast with 4 additional inches in 6 hours.

Water Quantity Management for a River Regulating Agency

Peter J. Gabrielsen*

Abstract

A river reservoir operations model (RROM) was developed to assist the Hudson River-Black River Regulating District manage flows in the Upper Hudson River Basin. The purpose of the RROM is to give a better understanding of the hydrologic activity in the Basin, and thus improve flow regulation. Combining developed nonlinear regression models, the RROM predicts stream flow responses to precipitation.

The RROM is a user friendly interactive computer program written in the Tektronix version of B-BASIC. The program utilizes the graphics capability of the system and is operational on a Tektronix 4052 micro computer. The simple input required by the RROM includes known hydrologic parameters and estimable meteorologic values.

BACKGROUND

The Upper Hudson River Basin lies in the Adirondack region of New York State, 250 miles (402 km) north of New York City. The mouth of this basin is located at the confluence of the Sacandaga and the Hudson Rivers. The Sacandaga River basin essentially consists of the watershed area controlled by the Conklingville Dam which lies at the outlet of Great Sacandaga Lake (GSL). The Hudson River basin is made up of the Hudson River watershed area above Hadley, New York. Figure 1 shows the major subbasins within the boundaries of the Upper Hudson River Basin. Included are the following subbasins:

Hope - watershed area above USGS stream gauge at Hope, (Hydrologic Unit 01318500 Sacandaga River near Hope, NY), drainage area 491 square miles (1272 sq km).

Stony Creeks - watershed areas upstream from Northville, but excluding the Hope subbasin, drainage area 201 square miles (520 sq km).

Local GSL - watershed area above the Conklingville Dam, but excluding the Stony Creeks and Hope subbasins, drainage area 352 square miles (911 sq km).

*Gabrielsen, M.S. Candidate, State University of New York, College of Environmental Science and Forestry, Syracuse, New York 13210.

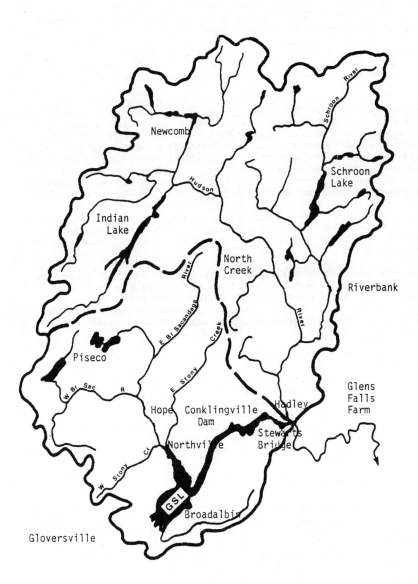

Figure 1   Upper Hudson River Basin

Hadley - watershed area above the USGS stream gauge at Hadley.
(Hydrologic Unit 02020001, Hudson River at Hadley, NY), drainage area
1664 square miles (4,310 sq km). (6).

Great Sacandaga Lake has a normal pool elevation of 768.00 feet (234 m)
(USGS), its surface area is 40.5 square miles (105 sq km), and its conservation storage capacity is 29.6 billion cubic feet (0.83 bcm).

The New York State Legislature created the Hudson River-Black River
Regulating District (The District) in 1955. The District's responsibilities include reducing Hudson River flows caused by excess runoff, and
augmenting river flow in times of drought or other periods when river
flows are low. Specifically, the operational objectives of the Regulating District include maintaining an acceptable water quality and supply,
providing flood protection, hydropower and navigation and general concern for the public welfare. Making these tasks even more challenging
are recreational interests around the GSL that compete for water use.

Flemming (3) states that the regulation of a reservoir is a product
of five considerations: demand, reservoir storage capacity, inflow sequence, downstream flow sequences from other tributary sources and operational rules.

The goals of the Regulating District are twofold with respect to
the Upper Hudson River basin. First, the District aims to produce a
flow on the Hudson River that will satisfy downstream beneficiaries.
Secondly, the District aims to maintain an acceptable GSL elevation to
satisfy seasonal storage requirements and reservoir recreational interests.

Hydrologic modeling was undertaken to develop suitable, contemporary
flow models to be used by the District in managing river and reservoir
flows (4). The utility of resultant models is manifest in a River Reservoir Operations Model (RROM) which was programmed on the District's computer. The purpose of the RROM is to provide the necessary information
to assist in meeting District goals. This includes reliable estimates
for GSL inflow volumes and a hydrograph of mean daily flows (MDF) for
the Hudson River at Hadley for the period of a given event. Knowing
these two quantities provides information to make GSL releases best meet
their operational goals.

RROM PROGRAM DEVELOPMENT

The RROM was developed using a component approach (1). Individual hydrologic models were developed and then cast into a system
framework. The individual models are multilinear regression models
that predict storm related outflows from the individual subbasins identified in Figure 1. Outflows for the subbasins are either estimated as
mean daily flows or volumes for a specified time duration (usually
several days). In both cases the flows are expressed in second-foot-
days (sfd).

The Hope and Hadley models include flow estimates for the peak day
of response to a rainfall event, and for each day of the hydrograph recession beginning at two days after the peak. Total storm related runoff

is also estimated for the Stony Creeks and local GSL watersheds. The
table below lists the models that are incorporated in the RROM.

MODEL	SUBBASIN	DESCRIPTION
MDFP	Hope, Hadley	mean daily flow value (MDF) on the peak flow day
MDF2	Hope, Hadley	the MDF value on the second day after the peak flow day
MDF3	Hope, Hadley	the MDF value on the third day after the peak flow day
MDFr	Hope, Hadley	the MDF values on sequential days of recession flow after MDF2
VOL2	Hope	accumulated volume of runoff (sfd) as measured through the second day after the peak flow day
ISC	Stony Creeks	total inflow from the Stony Creek watersheds
IGSL	GSL	total GSL local inflow for an event

These models are grouped by season; i.e., time of occurrence during
the annual hydrometeorological cycle. The seasons include fall, winter,
spring and summer but are defined as follows: Fall is the period between the rapid decrease in evapotransporation (ET) rates after the
summer season up until winter freeze-up and/or snow cover; winter is the
ensuing cold season period up until the appreciable and continuing rise
in streamflow associated with the onset of the spring and snowmelt
periods; spring is the period between spring snowmelt and full leafout
with the onset of summer temperatures and high ET rates.

The RROM program was written in the Tektronix version of B-BASIC.
A modular approach to programming was used (5). Twelve modules make up
the entire program, each having a separate function. Modular functions
include input/output operations and calculations. The input modules are
portions of the RROM where user input is required. The output modules
include user instructions and calculated output in the form of graphic
and numeric displays. The calculation modules determine flow values and
related statistics for Hope, Hadley, Stony Creek and local GSL subbasins.

A primary level file structure was used to transfer information
from one module to another. These files are accessed, read from,
amended, and filed throughout the RROM program. The files usually transport information that was created in one module to another module. Once
the file has been transported it is usually displayed or used in calculations.

USER MANUAL DEVELOPMENT

The RROM user manual was developed to meet the user's needs. The manual is divided into nine sections, each pertaining to a different aspect of the program. The manual includes sections for the layman, hydrologist, and the computer programmer. These different sections were developed after reviewing the experiences of the HEC-1 User Manual Support Group (2). They made the following suggestion: Any computer model that is developed should be supported through detailed documentation which completely supports the finished model, yet makes its use easy through simple input requirements and comprehensible documentation. The RROM user manual was written with this suggestion in mind.

The presentation of the RROM user manual covers three major areas of concern. First, it discusses the program's architecture, giving the user a complete description of what the program is doing. Second, an input output example is shown and discussed fully. Finally, the program's file structure is explained and the file inventory is listed. A program listing and a brief glossary of terms are also included as sections of the manual.

RROM SAMPLE RUN

Once the Tektronix computer has loaded the program and the hydrologic clock has been set, Figure 2 will be displayed. After the return key is depressed and the screen clears, the program will start asking for input as shown on Figures 3 and 4 (RROM input pages one and two). Page one asks for hydrologic information about the basin; antecedent flow (anteflow), flow on the day before the anteflow, time ordinates, season and date identifiers are required inputs. Page two requires precipitation estimates for selected climatological stations in the basin and information about the current state of GSL. A month counter is also requested.

The output and display section begins with Figure 5; Hope is the first basin that is displayed. This display includes a tabular listing of the storm days and corresponding mean daily flow (MDF) predictions. A graphic display of the simulated hydrograph is also displayed. MDFP, MDF2, MDF3, and VOL2 estimates are shown (in sfd) with their corresponding confidence limits. These estimates, of course, are based on antecedent flow values and rainfall projections. As better estimates are made, or recorded values become available, it may be desirable to ask for a detailed display, new estimates or recorded values for MDFP and MDF2 must be given. A detailed display of such modified flow values and recession flow estimates for the Hope basin includes the flow and day number for each estimate. If a detailed display is not wanted, the next step is the Hadley display shown in Figure 7.

The Hadley displays, Figures 7 and 8, are similar to the ones for Hope except that flow volumes are not estimated for Hadley. Further, if a detailed estimate is not wanted, the program proceeds to the RROM Summary Sheet, Figure 9.

The RROM Summary Sheet is a review of previously listed material; it is a listing of the input data and volumes at various locations. To

```
                    RIVER RESERVOIR OPERATIONS MODEL

                  HYDROLOGIC MODELS AND COMPUTER SOFTWARE WERE
                  DEVELOPED FOR THE HUDSON RIVER - BLACK RIVER
                  REGULATING DISTRICT UNDER A RESEARCH GRANT TO
                  THE STATE UNIVERSITY OF NEW YORK COLLEGE OF
                      ENVIRONMENTAL SCIENCE AND FORESTRY.
                  HYDROLOGIC MODELS WERE DEVELOPED BY PETER
                  GABRIELSEN AND RICHARD McCLIMANS, COMPUTER
                  SOFTWARE WAS DESIGNED AND DEVELOPED BY
                             PETER GABRIELSEN.

                        | RROM PRELIMINARY SETUP |

            UNITS
            ALL FLOW VALUES IN SFD
            ALL PRECIPITATION VALUES IN INCHES
            ALL ELEVATION VALUES IN FEET
            VOLUME VALUES IN BCF AND SFD

            NOTES
            AFTER EACH INPUT PRESS RETURN

            TYPE QUIT TO STOP OR PRESS
            RETURN TO CONTINUE
```

Figure 2   RROM Housekeeping

```
WHICH SEASON ARE YOU WORKING WITH ?                | PAGE 1 |

1 - FALL    3 - SPRING
2 - WINTER  4 - SUMMER
4

INPUT THE DATE OF THE ANTEFLOW (i.e. 4/23/84)
9/22/55

INPUT THE ANTEFLOW FOR HOPE IN SFD
138

INPUT THE ANTEFLOW FOR HADLEY IN SFD
570

INPUT THE HOPE FLOW VALUE THE DAY BEFORE THE ANTEFLOW IN SFD
149

ESTIMATE THE NUMBER OF DAYS FROM THE ANTEFLOW TO THE PEAK FOR
HOPE
2
HADLEY
2

INPUT THE NUMBER OF DAYS AFTER THE PEAK DAY FOR
WHICH THE FLOWS ARE TO BE ESTIMATED (MUST BE > 3)
11

HOW MANY DAYS OF FLOW WILL BE USED TO DETERMINE
UPPER GSL BASIN INFLOW VOLUME (MUST BE > 3) ?
4
                              PRESS HOME PAGE TO CONTINUE
```

Figure 3   RROM Input

```
                                          | PAGE 2 |

INPUT THE PRECIPITATION IN INCHES FOR:

HOPE
2
PISECO
2.9
NORTH CREEK
2.45
INDIAN LAKE
1.91
NEWCOMB
1.80
GREAT SACANDAGA LAKE
2.94

INPUT THE MEAN DAILY LOCAL GSL TEMPERATURE ON 9/22/55
47

INPUT THE GSL ELEVATION ON 9/22/55  (TO THE NEAREST TENTH)
755.1

INPUT THE MONTH NUMBER (i.e. MAY=5, JUNE=6 ...)
9

                            PRESS HOME PAGE CONTINUE
```

Figure 4   RROM Input

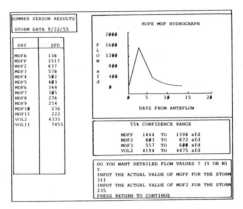

Figure 5 Hope Hydrograph Display

SUMMER SEASON RESULTS | STORM DATE 9/22/55 | PAGE 2

DAY	SFD	55% CONFIDENCE INTERVAL
MDFA	138	
MDFP	311	
MDF2	235	
MDF 3	204	196 TO 212 sfd
MDF 4	140	134 TO 146 sfd
MDF 5	112	108 TO 117 sfd
MDF 6	96	92 TO 100 sfd
MDF 7	85	82 TO 89 sfd
MDF 8	77	74 TO 80 sfd
MDF 9	71	68 TO 74 sfd
MDF10	66	63 TO 69 sfd
MDF11	62	59 TO 64 sfd
VOL2	4335	4194 TO 4475 sfd
VOL11	5247	

PRESS RETURN TO CONTINUE

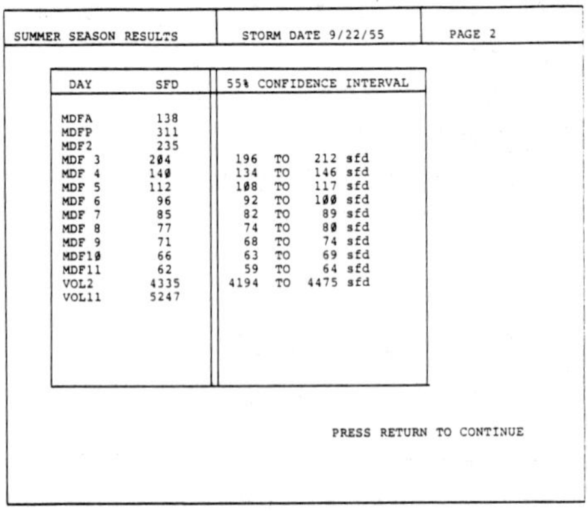

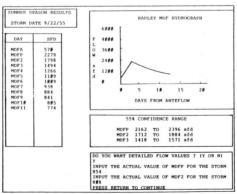

Figure 6 Hope Detailed Display

Figure 7 Hadley Hydrograph Display

```
┌─────────────────────────────────────────────────────────────────────┐
│  SUMMER SEASON RESULTS    │   STORM DATE 9/22/55   │    PAGE 2        │
│                                                                       │
│        ┌──────────────────┬─────────────────────────────┐            │
│        │  DAY      SFD     │  55% CONFIDENCE INTERVAL     │            │
│        │                   │                             │            │
│        │  MDFA     570     │                             │            │
│        │  MDFP     854     │                             │            │
│        │  MDF2     808     │                             │            │
│        │  MDF 3    713     │   693  TO   733 sfd         │            │
│        │  MDF 4    568     │   552  TO   585 sfd         │            │
│        │  MDF 5    498     │   484  TO   512 sfd         │            │
│        │  MDF 6    453     │   441  TO   466 sfd         │            │
│        │  MDF 7    421     │   410  TO   433 sfd         │            │
│        │  MDF 8    397     │   386  TO   408 sfd         │            │
│        │  MDF 9    377     │   367  TO   388 sfd         │            │
│        │  MDF10    361     │   351  TO   372 sfd         │            │
│        │  MDF11    348     │   338  TO   358 sfd         │            │
│        │                   │                             │            │
│        └──────────────────┴─────────────────────────────┘            │
│                                          PRESS RETURN TO CONTINUE     │
└─────────────────────────────────────────────────────────────────────┘
```

Figure 8   Hadley Detailed Display

```
┌──────────────────────────────────────────────────────────────────────────┐
│            RIVER RESERVOIR OPERATIONS MODEL SUMMARY SHEET                   │
│  ┌──────────────┬──────────────┬──────────────────────────────────────┐   │
│  │    HOPE      │   HADLEY     │          INPUT DATA                   │   │
│  │ DAY   Q sfd  │ DAY   Q sfd  │ DATE    9/22/55      GSL ELEV  755.1 ft│   │
│  │ MDFA    138  │ MDFA    570  │ HOPE    2.00 in.     PISECO  2.05 in.  │   │
│  │ MDFP    311  │ MDFP    854  │ NORTH CREEK  2.45 in.  NEWCOMB  1.80 in.│  │
│  │ MDF 2   235  │ MDF 2   808  │ INDIAN LAKE  1.91 in.  GSL  2.94 in.   │   │
│  │ MDF 3   204  │ MDF 3   713  │ LOCAL TEMPERATURE  47 F                │   │
│  │ MDF 4   140  │ MDF 4   568  │                                       │   │
│  │ MDF 5   112  │ MDF 5   498  │          GSL INFLOW VOLUMES           │   │
│  │ MDF 6    96  │ MDF 6   453  │ AT NORTHVILLE   6137   6078 TO 6198 sfd│   │
│  │ MDF 7    85  │ MDF 7   421  │ LOCAL INFLOW    2852   2673 TO 3044 sfd│   │
│  │ MDF 8    77  │ MDF 8   397  │ LOCAL EVAP      295 sfd                │   │
│  │ MDF 9    71  │ MDF 9   377  │ LOCAL PRECIPITATION    2737 sfd        │   │
│  │ MDF10    66  │ MDF10   361  │ TOTAL GSL INFLOW   11432 sfd           │   │
│  │ MDF11    62  │ MDF11   348  │ INPUT GSL RELEASE IN  sfd  5192        │   │
│  │              │              │ CHANGE IN STORAGE     0.54 bcf         │   │
│  │              │              │ ENTER STORAGE AT STARTING ELEVATION IN │   │
│  │              │              │ BCF  30.00                            │   │
│  │              │              │ FINAL GSL STORAGE    30.54 bcf         │   │
│  │              │              │ ENTER GSL ELEVATION FOR FINAL STORAGE  │   │
│  │              │              │ 755.56 ft.                            │   │
│  └──────────────┴──────────────┴──────────────────────────────────────┘   │
│                                          PRESS HOME PAGE TO CONTINUE        │
└──────────────────────────────────────────────────────────────────────────┘
```

Figure 9   RROM Summary Sheet

determine the change in GSL storage, an estimate of flow release for the
storm period is required. If the initial storage is entered the program
will calculate the final GSL storage. If any of the inputs requested on
the Summary Sheet are not known, the appropriate response is zero.

After the RROM summary display section is complete, the program
provides the option of making another run. If another run is not wanted,
the terminal shutdown instructions are displayed.

PROGRAM EVALUATION

An evaluation of the RROM is presented to describe its predictive
capabilities. RROM predictions and historical data for the fall season
will be evaluated. Thirteen randomly selected events were chosen for
analysis from a population of thirty years (water years 1951 thru 1980).
An event can be defined as a single rainfall event producing a storm
hydrograph followed by a long period of basin flow recession.

The RROM has numerous flow prediction capabilities; evaluating all
of them was not a purpose of this paper. Instead, one flow prediction
capability is evaluated to demonstrate model utility. The total GSL
inflow thru three days after the peak (GSL3) was chosen for demonstration. The estimates were determined using the RROM and were compared to
the actual GSL3 inflow which was determined from available USGS data.

Three test statistics were used to examine the validity of the GSL3
inflow estimates, each having its own purpose. The first test statistic
(DIFF) determines the difference between the predicted and observed flow,
the assumption being a perfect prediction would produce a value of zero.
The second statistic (RATIO) determines the ratio of the predicted and
actual inflow volume, this statistic eleminates the bias of high flow
errors masking those of low flows by sheer magnitude. Finally the measure of the percent of absolute error (PERR) was calculated for each
event; this is a standard measure of error in data analysis.

Listed below are the results of the aforementioned statistics for
the GSL3 inflow predictions. Besides the statistics for each storm two
other quantities are listed. Included to provide some insight as to the
hydrolotic state of the basin is the anteflow at Hope (AF). Storm precipitation totals are listed for the Sacandaga River basin above Hope
(PHO), and the local GSL basin (PL). The purpose of these totals is to
quantify the spatial distribution of the storm.

The RROM serves a useful purpose in assisting the Regulating District to meet their operational objectives. It could become a more useful management tool if a data base of estimated and actual flow value
was created. Included in this data base should be temporal and spatial
rainfall distributions for the event as well as the anteflow before the
storm. Gathering this information would provide an understanding of the
prediction capabilities of the program for different hydrologic scenarios. This data could also be used to refine the individual regression
models that are included in the RROM.

GSL3 ANALYSIS FOR THE FALL SEASON

DATE	AF sfd	PHO in.	PL in.	IGSLP sfd	IGSLA sfd	DIFF	RATIO	PERROR
10/17/75	726	2.51	2.36	34777	38451	-3674	0.90	9.6
10/4/55	176	2.84	2.77	16886	15368	1518	1.09	9.8
11/8/66	631	1.10	0.66	10348	12803	-2455	0.81	19.2
10/6/68	132	1.04	0.79	3222	2390	832	1.35	34.8
10/18/66	363	0.48	0.72	3347	5389	-2042	0.62	37.9
11/8/62	615	0.72	1.41	9851	17430	-7579	0.57	43.5
9/28/63	65	0.75	0.94	1761	3260	-1499	0.54	45.9
11/3/57	285	0.22	0.34	1518	3109	-1591	0.49	51.2
9/28/67	197	1.17	0.92	5339	3287	2052	1.62	62.4
10/11/53	251	0.32	0.24	1449	4027	-2579	0.36	64.0
10/2/61	86	0.90	1.66	3316	10764	-7448	0.30	69.2
10/6/56	480	1.25	1.22	10815	6196	4619	1.75	74.5
10/29/76	1700	0.97	0.69	5412	25400	-19988	0.21	78.7

References

1. Dooge, J.C.I. (1977). "Problems and Methods of Rainfall-Runoff Modelling". Chapter 6, pp. 71-108. Mathematical Models for Surface Water Hydrology, edited by T.A. Ciriani, V. Maione, and J.R. Wallis. New York: Wiley.

2. Eichert, W.S. (1978). "Experiences of the Hydrologic Engineering Center in Maintaining Widely Used Hydrologic and Water Resource Computer Models". pp. 229-241. International Symposium on Logistics and Benefits of Using Mathematical Models of Hydrologic and Water Resource Systems, edited by A.J. Askew, F. Greco, and J. Kindler. New York: Pergamon.

3. Flemming, G. (1975). "Computer Simulations in Hydrology". New York: Elsevier.

4. McClimans, R.J.; Eschner, A.R., and Gabrielsen, P.J. (1985). "Hydrologic Modeling for Water Resource Management in the Upper Hudson River Basin". Final Report to the Hudson River-Black River Regulating District. 74 pp. & Appendices.

5. Tektronix INC. (1978). 4907 File Manager Operations, 1978 edition. Beverton, Oregon.

6. United States Geological Survey. (1977). Water Resources Data for New York, Water Year 1977. Volume 1, New York excluding Long Island. United States Geological Survey, Albany, New York 12201.

Computer-aided Drought Operations

Roland C. Steiner, M.ASCE, Daniel P. Sheer, M.ASCE,
and James A. Smith[1]

Abstract

A simulated drought operations exercise is conducted
annually in the Washington, D.C. area. Local water supply
utilities work with the Interstate Commission on the
Potomac River Basin in order to exercise the links
necessary in the event of an actual drought. The
institutional setting for cooperative operations is
established in eight separate agreements singed by the
relevant parties in 1982. They define a coordinated
approach to be adopted during a water supply shortage,
including the duties of those involved. Computer programs
have been developed in order to reduce the manual
computational burden, and to ensure quick, accurate and
consistent results while conducting the exercise. The
programs are used for the three main areas of operational
activity: river flow forecasting, water use forecasting,
and allocation of available resources to meet demands.
Without the programs, it would be impossible to operate in
a real-time interactive mode; the sheer number and
complexity of calculations would be prohibitive.

Introduction

Local water supply utilities in the Washington, D.C. area
participate with the Interstate Commission on the Potomac
River Basin (ICPRB) in an annual simulation of operations
during drought conditions. This simulation is designed to
exercise the links necessary to cooperatively manage the
water resources available to the area. These links are the
same ones that would be used in the event of an actual
drought.

The activities associated with the annual simulation are
referred to as the Drought Operations Exercise. It is
conducted by the Section for Cooperative Operations on the

[1]Respectively: Systems Planning Engineer, Director of CO-OP
Section, and Hydrologist; Interstate Commission on the
Potomac River Basin, 6110 Executive Boulevard, Suite 300,
Rockville, Maryland 20852

Potomac (CO-OP) of ICPRB. Many of the technical and computational functions associated with the Exercise are computerized in the form of mathematical modeling programs. The setting for the Exercises and a discussion of how the models are used forms the basis of the paper which follows.

Institutional Setting

In July of 1982, eight separate agreements were signed among the ICPRB, water utilities and governments in the Washington, D.C. area in order to bring about the coordinated regional operation of water supply facilities.

Operational procedures to be followed in time of drought are set out in the Water Supply Coordination Agreement. This agreement covers a range of subjects and incorporates other documents; it is worth examining in some detail, see Table 1.

TABLE 1.-Water Supply Coordination Agreement, July 22, 1982

Articles:

1. Coordinate operation of water supply systems
2. Maximize local storage during Potomac low flows
3. Agree to releases from Potomac reservoirs
4. Abide by "Drought-Related Operations Manual"
5a. CO-OP to provide services; paid by suppliers
5b. D.C.'s costs consistent with Anti-Deficiency Act
6. CO-OP services may be terminated
7. Creation and duties of CO-OP Operations Committee
8. Consideration is promises in agreement
9. Use of reservoir water regardless of cost-sharing
10. Allocation of additional source costs
11. Litigation of disputes
12. Effective data
13. Agreement to continue as long as systems do

Signed by the U.S.A. (U.S. Army Corps of Engineers), Fairfax County Water Authority, Washington Suburban Sanitary Commission, District of Columbia, and the Interstate Commission on the Potomac River Basin.

The Potomac Low Flow Allocation Agreement (LFAA), dated January 11, 1978, is incorporated by reference into this agreement. The pertinent points of this Coordination Agreement are that the terms of the LFAA and the Drought-Related Operations Manual are reaffirmed and made binding.

The LFAA establishes the institutional mechanism and sets out the formula for allocating water supply withdrawals from the Potomac during periods of low flow. Its structure is outlined in Table 2.

TABLE 2. -- Low Flow Allocation Agreement, Jan. 11, 1978

Articles:

1. Enforcement; establish the post of Moderator, including definition of duties, authority, liability and compensation
2. Administration; establish communication control center, define Alert, Restriction, and Emergency Stages, allocation formula
3. Obligations of the parties; exchange of information and instructions
4. Review Agreement each April and record previous winter's withdrawals
5. Revocation
6. Effective date
7. Severability

Signed by the U.S.A. (U.S. Army Corps of Engineers), Maryland, Virginia, District of Columbia, Washington Suburban Sanitary Commission, and the Fairfax County Water Authority.

The annual Exercises are conducted generally in accordance with the Drought-Related Operations Manual. That manual (incorporated as part of the Coordination Agreement) sets out the duties of CO-OP during periods when the flow in the river at Point of Rocks is less than 2,000 cfs (56 m^3/sec). These duties include the production of monthly long-range water supply outlooks from May through October, and if severe short- or long-term conditions are indicated, to perform the following activities:

1. obtain daily demands from suppliers
2. estimate demands for the following five days
3. make daily forecasts of river flows
4. direct releases from Potomac River reservoirs
5. set water supply withdrawal rates
6. revise withdrawals at mid-day if appropriate
7. if Restriction or Emergency Stages of the LFAA apply, the withdrawal allocation formula will be in effect.

Thus the context, in which the annual drought operations are practiced, is formally and cooperatively established. The lines of communication and functional duties of the parties to the Exercises are shown as a flowchart in Figure 1. This figure indicates the relative timing and relationship of the most important activities among the Baltimore District of the U.S. Army Corps of Engineers (COE), CO-OP, and the utilities.

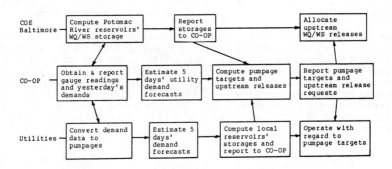

FIG. 1. CO-OP Drought Exercise; Daily Operations Flowchart

Computer-based Mathematical Models

The computer programs were developed in order to reduce the manual computational burden, and to ensure quick, accurate and consistent results. Without them, it would be impossible to operate in a real-time interactive mode; the sheer number and complexity of calculations would be prohibitive.

The programs are used for the three main areas of operational activity: river flow forecasting, water use forecasting, and allocation of available resources to meet demands.

River flow forecasting is based on a conceptual hydrologic model, the Sacramento Soil Moisture Accounting Model (1). Short-term (one to seven days) river forecasts are used for scheduling reservoir releases. Long-term (one to six months) forecasts are used to assess the risk of water supply shortages under a given operation policy. Long-term forecasting is based on the Extended Streamflow Prediction (ESP) procedure developed by the National Weather Service (2).

The Sacramento model provides a conceptual accounting of precipitation input to a drainage basin; precipitation is routed through a series of soil moisture storage zones with ultimate destination either channel inflow or evapotranspiration.   Soil moisture storage is represented in the model by an upper zone and a lower zone.   Each of these zones is further divided into tension water and free water storages.   Traditional components of hydrograph separation can be interpreted as drainage from specific storage zones.   Thus, output from lower zone free water storages can be interpreted as baseflow, while precipitation in excess of the storage and drainage capacity of the upper zone, which is transmitted directly to channel inflow, can be interpreted as overland flow.

The importance of soil moisture storage is illustrated in Figure 2 which shows summer hydrographs of the Potomac River for the years 1951 and 1966.   During the period July–September nearly identical rainfall totals were recorded in 1951 and 1966, yet in 1966 (following three years of abnormally low rainfall) streamflow reached its historical minimum of 547 cfs (15.3 m³/sec), while in 1951 (following a wet Fall and Winter) the minimum daily streamflow was 1170 cfs (32.8 m³/sec).

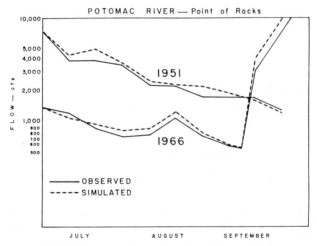

FIGURE 2. -- Flow in the Potomac River

The ESP procedure was developed to exploit information on processes such as soil moisture storage and snow pack for long-range prediction of streamflow.   ESP, as applied to the Potomac River basin, incorporates current information pertaining to soil moisture conditions by using "current" storages in the Sacramento model as the starting point in a simulation of streamflow.   The streamflow simulation procedure is carried out using historical precipitation data. Thus to produce a forecast for the Potomac River near Washington covering the period May 1 to October 1, actual precipitation data are used until May 1 in order to obtain current soil moisture storages. Twenty-four years of historical precipitation (1951-1974) covering the period May 1 to October 1 are then used as input to the Sacramento model to produce 24 simulated hydrographs each of which begins with May 1 soil moisture conditions of the current year.

Table 3 illustrates the main features of the procedure. This table is produced from an ESP forecast of minimum daily flow for the period May 1, 1982 to October 1, 1982. For each of the 24 simulated hydrographs the minimum daily value is selected and shown in Table 3. For comparison, the observed minimum daily value for each year is chosen. Contrasts between the simulated and observed reflect the role of initial soil moisture conditions. From Table 3 it was concluded that the risk of streamflow falling to the levels of the mid-60's during the summer of 1982 was quite small.

TABLE 3. Sample ESP Output From Forecast of Minimum Daily Flow of Potomac River--May 1, 1982 to October 1, 1982

ESP Forecast: Minimum Daily Flow for Potomac River--May 1, 1982 to October 1, 1982

Water Year (1)	Conditional Simulation in CFS (2)	Observed in CFS (3)
1951	1290	1310
1952	1823	2110
1953	1385	1200
1954	1569	1080
1955	2196	1460
1956	1806	1860
1957	1121	806
1958	1420	1810
1959	1208	787
1960	1871	1660
1961	1403	1310
1962	1173	1050
1963	982	880
1964	974	665
1965	1125	734
1966	890	547
1967	1928	1640
1968	1621	1010
1969	1854	885
1970	1405	1480
1971	2183	1810
1972	1989	2160
1973	1640	2270
1974	1560	1740
Mean	1517	1344
Standard Deviation	373	498

(Note: 1 cfs = 0.028 m3/sec)

This information, together with a simulation of demands and reservoir operating rules, can be used to produce probabilistic information regarding the refilling of the reservoirs.

Water demand forecasting is performed by a computer-based mathematical model which relies upon multivariate linear regressions of water use on short-term weather predictions. The model is developed by selecting the most explanatory of several functional forms of daily precipitation and maximum temperature data (3).

Daily data from several recent relatively dry and warm summers are used in deriving and calibrating the water use model. The general form of the model is a multivariate linear regression which incorporates the previous day's water use, and maximum daily temperature and precipitation forecasts as explanatory variables. Counter-intuitively, the raw precipitation data is found to have rather poor explanatory power. An investigation of various transformations found a more useful model variable which represents the number of days since a rainfall of at least 0.10 inch (2.5 mm).

Multivariate regressions of the following form are derived from the data grouped by month and day of week or groups of days of the week for each of the utilities:

$$Z(t) = c_1[Z(t-1)-Zu] + c_2[T(t)-Tu] + c_3[D(t)-Du] + e(t) \quad (1)$$

in which Z = water use (mgd); c = regression coefficient; t = time step (day); u = average for the period (month); T = daily maximum temperature ($^{\circ}$F); D = number of antecedent days with rain <= 0.1 inch (2.5 mm); and e = residual series.

The estimated coefficients for the weather variables have the expected sign in all cases; that is, water use increases with both temperature and number of antecedent "dry" days. The residuals are analyzed and found to possess desirable properties. Occasionally in the shoulder months (May, June, September, October) the coefficients of one or both of the climatic variables are negligible -- reflecting strongest influence in mid-summer. Spatial interpretation of the coefficient values indicates that precipitation explains most variance in the suburbs (presumably due to the greater use of water for lawn and shrubbery maintenance). However in the city, temperature is the dominant independent variable on week days (office building use of air conditioning make-up water) while on weekends, precipitation is more significant (reflecting a return to the dominance of residential requirements).

The model is run to produce water use forecasts for the
Washington Suburban Sanitary Commission (WSSC), Fairfax
County Water Authority (FCWA), and Washington Aqueduct
Division (WAD) of the U.S. Army Corps of Engineers.

Because of the different water using characteristics and
customer profiles, the water use for each of the three
utilities is forecast separately. One-day ahead forecasts
are provided by the model in order to give quantitative
input for daily consideration in the resource allocation
program which follows. Five-day ahead forecasts are
provided to aid in scheduling releases from upstream
river-regulating reservoirs.

<u>Allocation of available resources to meet demands</u> is
performed by a program which schedules daily withdrawals
from the river and local reservoirs. Releases from
upstream reservoirs are not scheduled in the allocation
functions of this program. Instead, they are based upon
the results of the demand forecasting procedure, and
requested approximately 5 days in advance. The program
requires as input: a forecast of the flow in the river, an
estimate of available storage in the local reservoirs, and
the projected demands for each of the utilities. The logic
of the scheduler exhausts the allocatable water in the
river before drawing on water stored in local reservoirs.
The necessity of this logic is apparent, given that there
is no downstream storage capacity available for Potomac
river water, and that a large percentage of supplies
available in local tributary reservoirs must be reserved to
serve parts of the distribution systems that cannot be
served by the Potomac. After producing an initial
withdrawal schedule, the program allows the user to
interactively set some or all of the withdrawals,
afterwhich it recomputes the remaining withdrawals in
accordance with the underlying logic and the new
limitations of the user-specified settings. The resultant
allocations are subject to a number of system constraints,
including: minimum and maximum withdrawal and treatment
capacities of the utilities, and minimum requirements for
flow in the river in order to maintain environmental
habitat.

The programs are interactive to the extent that they query
the user from the screen for input data, allow for
corrections, and provide results to the screen for
immediate interpretation and guidance for alternate runs.
All the results are immediately available for
implementation, and may be directed to magnetic disk file
for future analysis and provision of paper copy.

Conclusions

The use of computers in carrying out the Drought Operations
Exercises replaces rooms full of scribes seated on high
stools performing reams of calculations and checking them
for accuracy and consistency before presenting their
results to the CO-OP staff. Literally, man-days of
calculations are performed before morning coffee break each
day of the Exercises which provide vital information for
water supply operations. The Exercises are conducted with
the wholehearted cooperation of all parties concerned;
their value is unquestioned. As changes occur in the
available resources or withdrawal and treatment capacities,
they are incorporated. Every year sees new improvements in
the way an actual water shortage would be handled in the
Washington, D.C. area.

APPENDIX I. - REFERENCES

1. Burnash, R.J.C., Ferral, R.L., and McGuire, R.A., "A
    Generalized Streamflow Simulation System -- Conceptual
    Modeling for Digital Computers," cooperatively
    developed by the Joint Federal-State River Forecast
    Center and State of California Department of Water
    Resources, March, 1973.

2. Day, Gerald N., "Extended Streamflow Forecasting using
    NWSRFS," Journal of the Water Resources Planning and
    Management Division, ASCE, (forthcoming).

3. Steiner, Roland C., Short-Term Forecasting of Municipal
    Water Use, PhD Dissertation, The Johns Hopkins
    University, Baltimore, Maryland, 1984.

APPENDIX II. - NOTATION

The following symbols are used in this paper:

> c = regression coefficient
> D = number of antecedent days with rain $<= 0.1$ inch
>   (2.5 mm)
> e = residual series
> T = daily maximum temperature ($^{\circ}$F)
> t = time step (day)
> u = average for the period (month)
> Z = water use (mgd)

RELIABILITY OF URBAN WATER SUPPLY RESERVOIR SYSTEM

Les K. Lampe*   J. Darrell Bakken*
M. ASCE   M. ASCE

Abstract

Assessment of the reliability, or risk of failure, of water supply reservoirs is dependent on several factors including reservoir volume, probability of dam failure and drought inflows. A comprehensive evaluation should include analysis of each of these parameters. However, most water supply studies focus only on one or two of the elements. The Indianapolis Water Company recently completed a comprehensive review of its sources of supply that included determination of the volume of its source reservoirs, calculation of the yield of each reservoir on two bases and evaluation of the structural integrity of the two company owned reservoir dams.

Introduction

Indianapolis Water Company (IWC) and its predecessor as investor-owned utilities have furnished public water service to the City of Indianapolis and contiguous Marion County since 1871. From 1881 to 1947 IWC grew along with the City into a compact urban utility. Since 1947 the Company has expanded through marketing and acquisitions to a widespread regional system that provides retail water service to most of what is now metropolitan Indianapolis-Marion County (Uni-Gov) as well as to unincorporated and incorporated areas of three adjoining counties. Estimated population served by IWC has increased from about 445,000 in 1947 to approximately 706,000 by the end of 1984. Daily average water consumption increased from 49.7 MGD (188 x 10^6L/day) in 1947 to 100.2 MGD (380 x 10^6L/day) in 1984, after reaching 103.0 MGD (390 x 10^6L/day) in 1977.

History of IWC Comprehensive Planning

Indianapolis Water has a history (6) of comprehensive engineering and financial planning and decisive management action that has resulted in continuous, unrestricted public water service.

As an investor-owned utility, IWC has had continuity of management, financial and engineering staff to do comprehensive planning in cooperation with its customers, local and state government and community leaders. Extensive planning has also been enhanced because the Company is not limited by artificial political boundaries of many government-operated utilities.

*Les K. Lampe, Black & Veatch, Kansas City, MO
*J. Darrell Bakken, Indianapolis Water Co., Indianapolis, IN

Since 1881 IWC has often utilized the services of prominent
consulting engineers to guide and comment upon in-house long-range
comprehensive plans for water service.

Development of Urban Water Supply System

Our predecessor began water service in 1871 with two wells and a
pump station located in what is now the downtown.(2,8) The pumps were
powered by water from the Indiana Central Canal, purchased by the
utility in 1871. This Company in the 1880's acquired near-downtown
land that is now the location of our general offices, a primary pump
station and another well field. Prior to construction of the well
field a horizontal infiltration gallery was constructed on the
near-downtown site. By the 1890's problems with the gallery and wells
led IWC to wonder if ground water could be the long-range primary
water source. Consulting engineer Allen Hazen was engaged for a water
supply study and in 1896 recommended that surface water become the
primary source. Hazen proposed that White River be used as a source
by means of gravity flow from the Canal and recommended a slow sand
filter plant for treatment. The system was placed in operation in
1904. Earlier, in 1900 IWC bought a dam and grist mill on Fall Creek
to obtain surface water rights on that tributary of White River.

In 1921, Metcalf & Eddy, engineering consultants, commenced a
study (7) of the future water needs of Indianapolis and ultimately
recommended that two reservoirs be built in the ensuing 25 to 30
years. One of these reservoirs was to be located on Fall Creek and
the other on the White River watershed. Acquisition of land for the
Fall Creek reservoir, which later became Geist Reservoir, was
commenced in the late 20's, but the construction program was slowed to
a standstill by the depression. The imminence of World War II caused
the renewal of activity and the reservoir was ultimately completed and
filled on March 17, 1943. Total land and construction cost was
$2,500,000. Geist had an original estimated capacity of 6.9 billion
gallons (26.2 x 10^9L) of water and its initial surface area at full
reservoir was 1,900 acres (770 ha).

Morse Reservoir, also recommended in the original Metcalf & Eddy
report and reaffirmed by a separate 1947 study of an outside
consultant, was completed and filled on February 25, 1956. The first
land for this project was acquired in 1949. Morse Reservoir also had
an original estimated capacity of 6.9 billion gallons (26.2 x 10^9L)
and an initial surface area of 1,500 acres (608 ha). Total land and
construction cost was $6,500,000.

In 1957, after completion of Morse Reservoir, the Company engaged
consulting engineer C. C. Chambers for a site study for a third
reservoir. This study was confirmed in 1958 by an independent review
(1) of three engineering consultants, Abel Wolman, Samuel Morris and
Louis Howson. They recommended the construction of a reservoir on a
tributary of Fall Creek for completion in the 1970's. Land
acquisition started in 1960.

In the meantime, the City of Indianapolis constructed a flood
control and water supply reservoir on Eagle Creek on the western edge
of the city. Starting in 1963, the Company negotiated with the City
for almost eight years for a contract that would provide for raw water
supply from that project. This set back the timetable for the third
Company reservoir until the late 1970's. The proposed project was
announced in 1968 and immediately met with considerable negative
reaction from residents and others in the affected area.

The proposal for a third single purpose water supply reservoir,
after considerable controversy, was set aside in late 1970 in favor of
a city flood control and water supply project, which in turn was
shelved in favor of a joint Corps of Engineers-State of Indiana-local
project known as the proposed Highland Lake. This proposal was
authorized by the Indiana General Assembly but never authorized or
funded for advanced planning by the U.S. Congress.

Reasons For Initiating Comprehensive Analysis

Upon reflection, several unrelated events in the mid-1970's led
IWC to the reservoir comprehensive analysis.

Foremost, the final demise of proposed Federal-State-local
Highland Lake multi-purpose surface water reservoir and either lack of
authorization or deauthorization of every other proposed Indiana
impounding reservoir made it evident that the Company would be
dependent on its existing sources plus new ground water supplies as
yet unknown for the foreseeable future. Indianapolis Water needed to
study both its existing surface sources and explore new groundwater
supplies.

Thankfully, about this time, new reservoir engineering analysis
technology began to appear in the water technical press at the same
time we recognized our existing reservoir design data to be missing,
old or different for each source. New technology included sonar
surveys by boat to obtain reservoir bottom depths, improved surveying
instruments, computer hydrology programs for probabilistic drought
studies and additional such programs for combinations of reservoirs
and/or surface water systems.

The three-stage analysis of reservoir volume, dam safety and
reservoir dependable yield began with the volume studies.

Reservoir Volume Surveys

Company engineers in 1977 discussed with local engineering and
surveying consultants their experience and expertise in impounding
reservoir sedimentation/remaining volume, depth sounding and shoreline
survey studies. Budget work orders were proposed and approved by
management in late 1977 for a 1978 project at Morse Reservoir.

Five local engineering consultants were asked in February 1978 to submit proposals for performing the project based on a stated scope of work. Schneider Engineering Corporation was selected in March based on experience, availability and expected performance.

Residential development on IWC reservoir land began at Morse in 1971 (3). The land use restrictions retained by the Company include broad easement rights on a 20-foot (6.1m) wide strip adjacent to full reservoir water level and the right to cross other land, if necessary to get to the 20-foot (6.1m) strip. We notified involved property owners of our shoreline surveying and water depth measuring project and reminded them of our easement and access rights.

The field work began in April and was completed in August, for 25 cross-sections. The consultant's field data and report were received in September. We then drew up the profiles and new bottom contours. Schneider Engineering performed the volume calculations, finding the current volume was 7.2 billion gallons (27.2 x 10^9L) after 21 years, as compared to the reservoir design consultant's expected volume of 6.9 billion gallons (26.2 x 10^9L).

The Geist Reservoir volume survey work was negotiated with Schneider Engineering in January, 1980 and some shoreline survey work was done in February. Major residential development had not yet begun on Geist land, so few property owners had to be contacted about our project. The field work on 40 cross sections was completed by May and the consultant's field data and report were received in June. We again drew the profiles and bottom contours, and the consultant performed volume calculations. The 1980 volume was 6.1 billion gallons, an 11.6% reduction from the original 6.9 billion gallons (26.2 x 10^9L) of 1943. Total study cost, not including company personnel was about $89,000.

Dependable Yield Calculations, Drought Studies, and Risk Analysis

Three reservoirs, Morse, Geist, and Eagle Creek, constitute the major surface water storage facilities. The locations for these reservoirs are indicated on Figure 1.

The Morse Reservoir-White River source acts as a system. The base flow in the White River is normally adequate to satisfy the water supply needs. During drought conditions, Morse Reservoir is used to make up deficiencies in the White River flows. Water from the White River is diverted to the IWC Canal at the pool created by Broad Ripple Dam. This canal runs past the White River Treatment Plant, and most of the flow in the canal is diverted to the treatment plant. Unless an emergency condition necessitates, some flow must be maintained in the canal downstream from the treatment plant to enhance the aesthetic values of an urban area and a state park.

Although the base flow in Fall Creek is considerably less than the White River, the Geist Reservoir-Fall Creek source also acts as a system. The deficiencies in Fall Creek flows are made up by releases from Geist Reservoir. Water is diverted from a pool behind Keystone Dam and conveyed a short distance to the Fall Creek Treatment Plant.

The third source of surface water for the IWC is Eagle Creek Reservoir. Water is removed from the reservoir through an intake as needed and pumped to the Eagle Creek Treatment Plant.

Previous evaluation of the capabilities of the Indianapolis Water Company's raw water supply system have focused on the 1940-41 drought. Although the most severe historical drought is a valid benchmark for water supply planning, it is always useful to also derive probabilistic estimates of reservoir yields or minimum streamflows. A study was begun in 1984 to 1) refine estimates of drought yields for the components of the raw water supply system, 2) calculate probabilistic drought yields for each of the individual components of the system, 3) estimate both historical and probabilistic drought yields for the entire raw water supply system with coordinated reservoir operation and 4) develop a plan to manage the system of reservoirs to maximize combined drought yield.

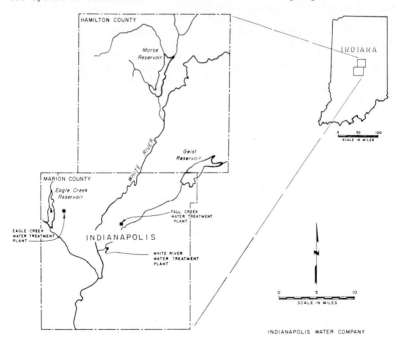

FIG. I-WATER SUPPLY SYSTEM

Previous engineering studies made no attempt to assign a
probability to the yield estimate. These studies estimated the
reliable yields based on the 1940-41 drought, to be:

Source	Net Yield mgd (L x 10^6/day)	
Morse Reservoir-White River	75	(284)
Geist Reservoir-Fall Creek	25	(94.8)
Eagle Creek	12.4	(47.0)
TOTAL	112.4	(425.8)

The first item addressed in the recent study (5)was a reassessment
of the yield estimates based on the 1940-41 drought. New estimates
were based on a recurrence of the hydrologic conditions that created
this drought with reservoir storage volumes and additional upstream
depletions as projected for the year 2000. Projections of storage
reduction due to additional sediment inflows was facilitated by the
hydrographic surveys previously described and recent watershed studies
completed by the Soil Conservation Service.

Major obstacles in the analysis were evalution of the effects of
upstream water users, particularly the cities of Muncie and Anderson,
on drought flows in the White River, estimating streamflows for
ungauged areas tributary to the water supply reservoirs, and
accurately assessing system losses due to a variety of operational
factors that reduce the amount of water available to the IWC. Total
losses, including those for increased upstream water uses, are
estimated to be 16.7 mgd (63.3 x 10^6L/day) for the Morse Reservoir -
White River source, 9.2 mgd (34.9 x 10^6L/day) for the Geist
Reservoir - Fall Creek source, and 5.6 mgd (21.2 x 10^6L/day) for
Eagle Creek Reservoir.

Based on the 1940-41 drought flows, storage volumes available for
gravity release under year 2000 conditions, and the system losses
described above, the net yields for the individual supply components
are estimated to be:

Source	Net Yield mgd (L x 10^6/day)	
Morse Reservoir-White River	87.3	(331)
Geist Reservoir-Fall Creek	27.2	(103)
Eagle Creek	12.5	(47.4)
TOTAL	127.0	(481.4)

Additional storage is available to augment yields in both Geist and Eagle Creek Reservoirs if facilities are installed to utilize this storage. The additional storage from a quarry that may be excavated adjacent to Geist Reservoir could increase the yield during the historical drought for the Geist Reservoir-Fall Creek system from 27.2 mgd (103 x 10^6L/day) to 31.0 mgd (117 x 10^6L/day). In Eagle Creek Reservoir additional storage is available at elevations lower than the IWC's intake structure. Use of this storage could increase the historical drought yield from 12.5 mgd (47.8 x 10^6L/day) to 14.4 mgd (54.6 x 10^6L/day).

Reservoir depletion curves for the three sources during a condition similar to the 1940-41 drought display a critical duration of 16 months for reservoir drawdown, from July 1940 to October 1941.

Yields were also calculated on the basis of probabilistic estimates of river flows during droughts. Calculations were completed for estimates of the 10, 20, 50 and 100-year droughts. Estimates only for 50-year droughts are presented here because this probability level is felt to be most appropriate for public water supply planning.

Based on these statistical determinations of minimum streamflows, year 2000 conditions for reservoir storage volumes and system losses the calculated 50-year net yields of the individual sources were:

Source	Net Yield Gravity Storage mgd (Lx10^6/day)		Net Yield Pumped Storage mgd (Lx 10^6/day)	
Morse Reservoir-White River	87.6	(332)	---	
Geist Reservoir-Fall Creek	28.1	(106)	31.7	(120)
Eagle Creek Reservoir	8.6	(32.6)	10.7	(40.6)

In all of the foregoing yield determinations, based on both historical and probabilistic droughts, values were calculated for the individual sources, but no mention was made of the yield of the system as a whole. Several studies have demonstrated that severe droughts do not affect multiple watersheds as severely as single watersheds, and that the yield of a system of supplies for a given drought is greater than the sum of its parts. This effect has been noted throughout the U.S. but most particularly in studies conducted for basins in Texas, the Kansas River basin, and the Potomac River basin. The case of the Indianapolis Water Company proved to be no different. A program was developed to coordinate withdrawals from the three reservoirs available for use by the IWC to optimize system yield. Withdrawals were allocated among the reservoirs on the basis of the amounts of yield remaining in each as the drought progressed. This ensured that those reservoirs having the greatest yield augmentation capability at any time were the one stressed the most heavily. The benefits of coordinated reservoir operation are apparent if the "without coordination" system yield values are compared to the "with coordination" values, as shown in the following table.

Drought Condition	System Yield Without Coordinated Operation mgd (Lx10⁶/day)		System Yield With Coordinated Operation mgd (Lx 10⁶/day)	
Historical	127.0	(481)	134.6	(510)
50-year	126.8	(481)	139.4	(528)

Hence the IWC may be able to increase its raw water supply capabilities by 7 to 12 mgd (26.5 to 45.5 x 10^6L/day) by making more efficient use of the storage it already owns and operates. The economic benefits of the extra supply are substantial. The cost of the study was $85,000.

Another interesting aspect of the recent study was an attempt to define the probability of the 1940-41 drought, and thus to provide a basis for comparing yield estimates for the historical drought and for probabilistic droughts. This was done first by using the probabilistic yield for each source of supply to develop a plot of yield versus probability. The values of the historical drought yields were then used to enter the yield probability curves to estimate the probability of the historical drought. On this basis, it was estimated that the historical drought had a return period of somewhere between 29 and 45 years. Return periods associated with individual sources were 45 years for Morse Reservoir-White River, 43 years for Geist Reservoir-Fall Creek, and 29 years for Eagle Creek Reservoir.

This comparison has great significance because the Indianapolis Water Company has always used the 1940-41 drought as a basis for water supply planning. As a check on these return periods, 113 years of precipitation data were analyzed. This analysis indicated that the 1940-41 drought was the most severe in more than 100 years, which differs from the evaluation of drought probabilities based on statistical estimates of system yields. A review of both approaches indicates that there is considerable latitude in attempting to define probabilities associated with natural events, and the return period of the most severe event is strongly influenced by the length of record available for analysis. At this point, the conclusion must be that the most severe historical drought has a return period of approximately 100 years.

Dam Safety Evaluations

The IWC owns two dams, Morse and Geist, and is responsible for their safety. Phase I dam safety inspections for Morse and Geist Dams were completed under the auspices of the Louisville District, Corps of Engineers, in 1978. No deficiencies were noted, but annual reports of the Indiana Department of Natural Resources in 1977-80 listed seepage downstream of Geist Reservoir as a possible deficient or serious condition. To alleviate the State's concerns, the IWC conducted a Phase II investigation of Geist Dam in 1981 (4) at a cost of $59,000.

Geist Dam is located on Fall Creek in northeast Marion County (see Figure 1). It is a rolled earthfill dam approximately 1,900 feet(580m) long with a maximum height of 47 feet (14.3m) above stream bed. The dam was completed in 1943. The storage volume at the top of the dam is about 60,000 acre feet (73.3x10^6 m^3) and about 18,500 acre-feet (22.8x10^{6}m^3) at the normal pool elevation 14 feet below the top of the dam. Steel sheet piling, 36 feet (11m) long, were driven to provide a cutoff wall approximately 43 feet (13m) upstream from the center line of the dam. The ogee overflow spillway structure located near the center of the dam is supported by timber piles. The spillway is 500 feet (153m) long with a constant crest elevation of 785 feet. A stilling basin is located on the lower portion of the spillway.

Fall Creek, below Geist Reservoir, flows for a considerable distance through urban areas before it joins the White River near the center of Indianapolis. Based upon the classification requirements set forth in the guidelines established by the Corps of Engineers, the dam is classified as large in size and has a high hazard potential.

Major findings from the Phase II dam safety investigation were that the calculated probable maximum flood can pass through the spillway with essentially no freeboard and that no deficiencies were discovered which affect the dam's stability. It was recommended that the area downstream of the toe of the dam be visually inspected on a monthly basis to note if any pipes or sand boils are forming which may affect the stability of the embankment. The IWC has continued making visual inspections of both Geist and Morse Dams to note any changes in seepage, settlement, sloughing, or other conditions that may require remedial measures.

Summary And Conclusions

A comprehensive evaluation of surface water supply sources involves several elements. The Indianapolis Water Company has conducted a thorough review of its reservoir supplies and this provides an assessment of the reliability of their water supply system. It was found that about 11.6 percent of the water supply storage capacity of Geist Reservoir was lost due to sedimentation from 1943 to 1980 and about 12.9 percent of the Morse Reservoir volume was lost between 1957 and 1978.

A detailed yield analysis indicated that as much as 139.4 MGD (528x 10^{6}L/day) could be obtained on a reliable basis if available storage is fully utilized and the operation of the three reservoirs is coordinated. This compares to previous yield estimates that indicated total capabilities of the system were only 112.4 MGD (426 x 10^{6}L/day). Thus, the IWC may increase available supplies by almost one-fourth by thoroughly reevaluating yield estimates and by developing a plan for coordinating reservoir operations. Cost of the outside consulting engineering studies was $233,000.

The safety of Morse and Geist Dams was evaluated and both were found structurally and hydraulically sound. The IWC continues to monitor the dams to ensure that they remain safe.

Appendix - References

1. Alvord, Burdick and Howson, Engineers; Samuel Morris - Abel Wolman, consultants; Report on Water Supply and Plant Facilities, Indianapolis Water Company. Chicago, Illinois, 1958.

2. Bakken, J. D., "Evolution of a Regional System", Journal American Water Works Association, Vol. 73, No. 5, May, 1981, pp. 238-242.

3. Bakken, J. D., "Residential Development on Indianapolis Water Supply Reservoirs", 1983 Annual Conference Proceedings, American Water Works Association, pp. 123-130.

4. Black & Veatch, Engineers-Architects, Geist Reservoir Phase II Dam Safety Evaluation Report. Kansas City, Missouri 1981.

5. Black & Veatch, Engineers-Architects, Report on Evaluation of Surface Water Supply for Indianapolis Water Company. Kansas City, Missouri, 1985.

6. Giffin, M. G., Water Runs Downhill: A History of the Indianapolis Water Company and Other Centenarians, The Benham Press, Indianapolis, Indiana, 1981.

7. Metcalf and Eddy, Consulting Engineers, The Future Development of The Property of the Indianapolis Water Company, Indiana. Boston, Massachusetts, 1923.

8. Stout, M. C. and Bakken, J. D., "Long Range Planning for Metropolitan Water Service", Water and Sewage Works, Vol. 120, No. 7, July 1973, pp. 65-69.

dBase III, Micros and Water Resource Management

Sheryl L. Franklin

The Brazos River authority is an agency of the State of Texas created to conserve and develop the surface waters of the Brazos River Basin. The Authority has initiated a project to introduce the use of microcomputers into the daily water supply operations and reservoir control of the basin. As a part of this project, a database management system is being developed to reduce the time required for record maintenance and to make information on river and reservoir status more readily available to the decision makers. The commercially available software dBase III was chosen for this purpose. Although dBase III was not expressly developed for water resources applications, it has proved flexible enough to be satisfactory for this purpose.

Introduction

The Brazos River Basin covers approximately 42,000 square miles (110,000 km^2) in a band running NW–SE across the central portion of Texas. See Figure 1 for the location of the basin with respect to major Texas cities. The Brazos River Authority (the "Authority") has water resource management responsibility in twelve major reservoirs in the basin containing conservation storage in excess of 2.1 million acre-feet (2.6 x 10^{9}m^3). Nine of the twelve reservoirs are operated by the Fot Worth District of the U.S. Army Corps of Engineers (COE) with water supply releases and withdrawals controlled by the Authority. In addition to its three reservoirs, the Authority is nearing completion of the feasibility studies on two additional reservoirs, and owns a 200 mile (320 km) canal system in the Houston–Galveston Gulf Coast area. The Authority currently supplies approximately 532,000 acre feet (654 x 10^{6}m^3) of water annually under approximately 80 long term contracts. In addition, there are approximately 100 contracts for short term (one to ten year) supply.

Data management is part of an ongoing project to improve the water management capabilities of the Authority. A companion paper, "Micro Use in the Brazos Basin", describes the additional improvements planned and incorporated.

Data Management Needs

Daily operations were reviewed to determine necessary and desirable capabilities for a data management system.

Water Resources Planner, Brazos River Authority, 4400 Cobbs Drive, Waco, Texas, 76710

The software had to be able to handle a large number of numbers. Daily records of operations for twelve reservoirs, 24 river gaging stations, and all contract releases must be kept, in addition to hydropower generation records, senior water rights accounting and periodic flood operations. This data must be reported in many different forms requiring the data to be accessible to many different reports.

The software had to be able to manipulate data in a fairly sophisticated manner in order to calculate river stage–discharge relationships, gate opening–reservoir–head release relationships, elevation–area–capacity relationships and similar calculations. In-house programming expertise was concentrated in the FORTRAN language so similarity to that logic and structure would make programming faster and easier.

The software had to be flexible enough to permit customizing for the needs of the Authority. Not all of the reservoirs are operated under the same rules and the various water supply contracts contain different provisions and requirements.

The software had to be able to read non–database files into databases. Much of the daily information is retrieved via computer links with the COE or or U.S. Geological Survey (USGS) computers. The Authority did not wish the operators to have to rekey this data.

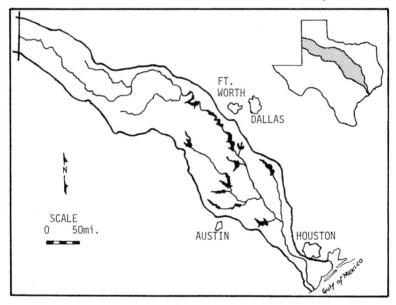

Figure 1 the Brazos River Basin
(1 mi = 1.61 km)

The software had to permit applications programs to generate menu-driven data requests and input to permit the easiest possible data input and retrieval.

The software had to permit the simultaneous use of several databases, permitting the use of a database as a "table lookup". Existing procedure consisted of manual calculations relying heavily on stage-discharge, area-capacity and similar tables. It was decided to retain this format to the greatest extent possible primarily to accommodate the periodic shifts in the tables.

The software had to run on the Authority's 16 bit microcomputers and had to be obtained at a reasonable cost.

DBase III was chosen not only because it would meet the current needs, but also because it was felt it would provide the greatest expansion potential.

User Satisfaction with DBase III

At the time of this publication the database system is not complete, however, major portions are completed and in daily use. The remaining portions do not pose any new conceptual problems.

The experience with the software has, in general, been positive. The few limitations that have been noted are discussed below. The documentation provided with the software is good, and there are numerous third party books describing programming with the dBase language for those who desire additional help. Software support has been satisfactory; a program diskette damaged by a faulty drive was quickly and cheerfully replaced. The dBase language is similar to FORTRAN and BASIC and should be easily understood by anyone familiar with those languages. File structure and the method of accessing and manipulating data within a record is different than in FORTRAN-type languages, but should be understood quickly. This author was totally unfamiliar with the database software, but was creating and manipulating data and databases within a few hours. Within approximately 60 hours, the conceptual problems had been solved, the basic design of the system completed and representative sections of the system successfully programmed.

Two limitations surfaced during the design of the system which were inconvenient, but not impossible to overcome. The maximum size of the databases is extremely large (one billion records with as many as 4000 characters per record) however, by comparison, the maximum program size is surprisingly small (approximately 200 lines of code). Since the software permits the calling of one program within another, and even supports selective parameter passing, one can use subroutines to bypass this limitation. However, this solution may aggravate another limitation; the maximum number of open files is 15. In addition, each database is a file, and any associated index files (necessary for fast searches of the database) increase the number of files in use. Although this has not proved to be a problem so far, some programs have been rewritten to satisfy this limit.

A third limitation which was quickly noticed, and required some thought to circumvent, is the lack of arrayed variables. This limitation was particularly acute in the design of the Authority's system since it was decided to program the currently used tables in tabular, rather than equation, form. The tabular form was necessary due to the nature and frequency of table shifts and adjustments, particularly for the river stage–discharge relationships. The structure of a database file seemed ideal for a tabular design since it is organized in rows (called records) and columns (called attributes) but accessing the appropriate column posed some problem since the columns were not intended to be a dependent variable. The design used was a compromise which tried to balance the storage requirement for the table size, the time requirement to search the database for the appropriate values and numerical manipulation of the data. Depending on the accuracy of the current tables and the required accuracy of the results, databases were designed which tabulated either even foot values or values to the tenth of a foot. Values to the hundredths are linearly interpolated from these tables. Table 1 displays several records of a typical stage–discharge database. The databases were designed with columns for station identifier, even foot value of the independent variable, then ten columns which hold the value of the dependent variable at each tenth of a foot. The value of the independent variable is manipulated using the INTEGER function to determine even foot values and, with appropriate multiplication and division by 10, the appropriate tenth rounded to both the lower and upper tenth. The latter two numbers are converted to characters and appended to the column title to access the appropriate column. For example, from Table 1, a stage of 2.0 at STATION 1 indicates a discharge of 5.62. A stage of 2.05 would be manipulated to indicate EVENFOOT equal to 2, a lower tenth equal to 0, an upper tenth equal to 1, and a hundredth value of 5. The zero and one are converted to character values and appended to the title to indicate attributes TENTH0 and TENTH1. The values corresponding to these attributes are accessed and linearly interpolated. Although the process sounds slightly awkward, it only requires a few lines of code to program.

Table 1 – A Typical Stage–Discharge Database

STATION ID	EVENFOOT	TENTH0	TENTH1	...	TENTH9
STATION 1	1	0.00	0.05	...	5.53
STATION 1	2	5.62	6.04	...	10.14
.	.	.	.	.	.
.	.	.	.	.	.
STATION 2	1	10.02	11.35	...	13.62
STATION 2	2	23.76	28.92	...	35.62
.					
.					
.					

Conclusion

As part of an ongoing project to integrate the use of microcomputers into daily water supply operations and reservoir control, the
Brazos River Authority is developing a database system based on the
commercially-available dBase III software. The system is designed
for ease of data entry and retrieval through the use of menu-driven
applicatons programs. The software has proved satisfactory for the
uses of the Authority; it was found to be flexible, capable of sophisticated data manipulation yet reasonably simple to program and operate.

dBase and dBase III are trademarks of Ashton-Tate.

Modeling Contaminant Fate and
Transport in Ground Water Systems

Cass T. Miller[*] and Walter J. Weber, Jr.[**]

Determination of the fate and transport of contaminants in
subsurface environments has been aided by recent advances in our
understanding of ground water hydrodynamics and subsurface solute
reactions, and by parallel development of innovations in computer
technology. Advanced computational capabilities afford the
application of numerical models which incorporate accurate
representation of complex transport and transformation phenomena,
thus allowing more realistic assessment of contaminant behavior in
ground water systems.

Introduction

Widespread contamination of the nation's ground waters has
resulted from the improper production, transportation, use and
disposal of potentially harmful organic contaminants. National, and
state programs designed to control and eventually eliminate contamination by these substances and to renovate ground waters which have
already been contaminated must be predicated on an accurate understanding of fate and transport processes in subsurface environments.

Mathematical modeling provides a means for translation and
integration of our understanding of the phenomenological behavior of
contaminants into vehicles suitable for use in management and control
programs. The use of mathematical models for this purpose has grown
dramatically in the past several years in response to an increased
awareness of the need to apply more accurate methodologies and the
parallel evolution of advanced computational capabilities.

The appropriate form of a mathematical model to use for
describing contaminant fate and transport in any given circumstance
must be based on an understanding of the physical system in question
and representation of that system in a simplified but meaningful
manner. For many contaminants several fate and transport processes
may operate simultaneously. These include: advection, dispersion,
sorption-desorption, biotransformation, and chemical transformation.
Accurate analysis of contaminant fate and transport in a particular
system requires an accurate treatment of each of the significant
processes operative in that system. This paper presents an overview
of models which can be used to describe several major transport and
transformation phenomena, and of methods which can be used to
facilitate the solutions and application of such models.

*Department of Environmental Sciences and Engineering, The University
of North Carolina, Chapel Hill, NC 27514
**Department of Civil Engineering, The University of Michigan, Ann
Arbor, MI 48109

Hydrodynamics

The movement of ground water and its non-reactive dissolved
components is a function of the properties of the porous media
through which movement occurs and such system stresses or
perturbations as rainfall, evapotranspiration, surface water
interaction and pumped withdrawals or additions. For systems not
subject to density considerations, ground water movement may be
described most simply in terms of hydraulic head (2)

$$S_s \frac{\partial h}{\partial t} = div(K \; grad \; h) \tag{1}$$

where:

S_s = specific storage (1/L);
h = hydraulic head (L);
t = time (t); and
K = hydraulic conductivity tensor (L/t).

Solution of Equation 1, subject to the appropriate boundary and
initial conditions, results in a description of hydraulic head as a
function of time and location within a domain. To assess contaminant
transport it is necessary to translate the hydraulic head
distribution into the corresponding velocity vector field. This may
be accomplished by combining the hydraulic head distribution with
that given by Darcy's law

$$\vec{v} = \frac{K}{\epsilon} \; grad \; h \tag{2}$$

where:

$\vec{v}$ = average velocity vector (L/t); and
ϵ = volumetric void fraction ($L^3 L^{-3}$).

The average velocity vector is a description of the direction and
magnitude of the bulk ground water flow. Determination of the
velocity vector field may be sufficient for a preliminary "quick and
dirty" analysis of non-reactive contaminant transport.

Deviations from average bulk flow are typically described with
the aid of a second rank hydrodynamic dispersion tensor.
Hydrodynamic dispersion is a lumped term used to describe the net
effect of hydraulic dispersion resulting from mixing at the
microscopic (soil grain) size scale, and molecular diffusion
resulting from concentration gradients. Because hydraulic dispersion
is a function of fluid velocity and molecular diffusion is not, the
relative importance of molecular diffusion as a component of the
hydrodynamic dispersion tensor decreases with increasing ground water
velocity. Advection, the product of the average ground water
velocity vector and the concentration gradient, may be combined with
the hydrodynamic dispersion contribution to yield the
advection-dispersion equation

$$\frac{\partial c}{\partial t} = \text{div}(D \text{ grad } C) - \vec{v} \text{ grad } C \qquad (3)$$

where

C = liquid phase concentration of solute (ML^{-3}); and
D = hydrodynamic dispersion tensor $(L^2 t^{-1})$.

The advection-dispersion equation may be solved for a given set of boundary and initial conditions to yield concentration as a function of time and location for non-reactive solutes (2). Figure 1 shows a single spatial dimension concentration profile corresponding to a step concentration input function, for the case of advection alone and for the combined advection-dispersion case. The effect of dispersion is a smearing of the concentration front relative to the sharp front resulting from advection alone.

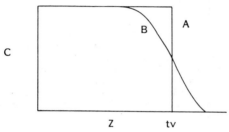

Figure 1.   Concentration Profiles for Contaminant Transport by Advection (A) and by Advection-Dispersion (B).

Reactive Transport

A number of factors additional to advection and dispersion influence the transport and fate of many contaminants in ground water systems. These may include the processes of sorption-desorption, biodegradation, chemical transformation, and radioactive decay. The solute transport equation (Equation 3) may be expanded to include such reaction mechanisms

$$\frac{\partial c}{\partial t} = \text{div}(D \text{ grad } C) - \vec{v} \text{ grad } C - \frac{\rho(1-\epsilon)}{\epsilon} \frac{\partial q}{\partial t} + \left(\frac{\partial c}{\partial t}\right)_{rxn} \qquad (4)$$

where

ρ = solid phase particle density (ML^{-3});
q = normalized solid phase concentration of sorbed solute species (MM^{-1}); and
rxn = subscript denoting biological or chemical reaction of the solute in the solution phase.

Sorption is a process involving the mass transfer of solute from the liquid phase (ground water) to the solid phase (soil). The converse process is termed desorption. The impact of sorption-desorption processes on the fate and transport of solutes in ground

water systems is a function of many variables including the organic
carbon content of the soil, the structure and partitioning
characteristics of the solute, the presence of competing solutes, the
inorganic content and pH of the solution, and temperature. The
linear local-equilibrium model is a common simplified approach to
describing the sorption-desorption process (1). This method assumes
that the rate of sorption-desorption is fast relative to the rate of
ground water movement (i.e., local equilibrium) and that the
concentration of solute in the soil is directly proportional to the
solute concentration in solution (i.e., a linear isotherm). This
condition may be expressed in equation form as

$$\frac{\partial q}{\partial t} = K_p \frac{\partial c}{\partial t} \qquad (5)$$

where
$\quad K_p$ = linear sorption isotherm constant $(L^3 M^{-1})$.

Figure 2 illustrates the impact of sorption on the one-
dimensional solute concentration profile for a linear local-
equilibrium case. It may be observed that the sorption-desorption
reaction delays in time the advance of the solute front. The effect
of dispersion is observed to decreased in time but remain constant in
space for the case of linear local-equilibrium sorption.

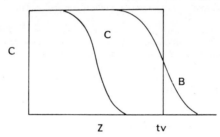

Figure 2.   Concentration Profiles for Contaminant Movement by
            Advective-Dispersive Transport Alone (B) and Coupled with
            Retardation by Linear Local-Equilibrium Sorption (C).

Some solutes undergo biological or chemical degradation in
ground water systems. For modeling purposes it is common to describe
the rate of such degradation in terms of an empirically determined
power function of the solution phase concentration

$$\left(\frac{\partial c}{\partial t}\right)_{rxn} = k_{rxn} c^m \qquad (6)$$

where
$\quad k_{rxn}$ = a reaction rate constant $((L^3 M^{-1})^{m-1} t^{-1})$; and
$\quad m$ = reaction rate order.

Degradation reactions in the environment frequently are described
well by first-order rate expressions in which the reaction velocity
is dependent on the product of the solution phase concentration and a
reaction rate constant. The effect of a first-order reaction on a
solute concentration profile is compared to that of advective-
dispersive transport alone in Figure 3.

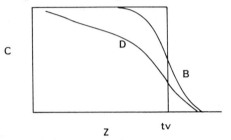

C

D

B

Z   tv

Figure 3.   Concentration Profiles for Contaminant Movement by
            Advective-Dispersive Transport Alone (B) and Coupled with
            a First-Order Degradation Reaction (D).

The magnitude of the reduction in mass is a function of the reaction
rate constant, the solution phase concentration, and the transport
time for the point of reference. It should also be apparent that the
magnitude of the dispersion coefficient impacts the concentration
distribution and therefore the mass reduction as a function of space
and time.

Certain organic solutes are subject to multiple fate mechanisms
involving advection, dispersion, sorption-desorption, and
degradation. For such systems the sorption-desorption and
degradation relationships described in Equations 5 and 6 can be
combined (Equation 4) with the hydrodynamic components of advection
and dispersion to predict a solute profile of the type given in
Figure 4 for a first order reaction.

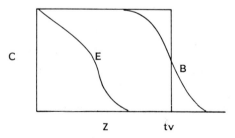

C

E

B

Z   tv

Figure 4.   Concentration Profiles for Contaminant Movement By
            Advective-Dispersive Transport Alone (B) and Coupled with
            First-Order Degradation and Linear Local-Equilibrium
            Sorption (E).

The impact of the combined sorption-desorption and degradation
process relative to advection and dispersion alone is both a

retardation in the rate of solute movement and a decay in mass of the
solute. Because the linear local-equilibrium model of sorption
retards both the velocity and hydrodynamic dispersion as a function
of time, the solute front remains sharper in space than the
equivalent front for a non-reactive system for any given time. For a
reactive system involving both sorption and degradation, the
sharpness of the front effected by the sorption reaction causes a
greater rate of solute mass decay compared to a corresponding case
involving degradation alone for any degradation reaction greater than
zero order.

The above simplified treatment of reactive solute transport
(i.e. linear local-equilibrium sorption and/or first order
degradation) may be readily applied at the field scale. In some cases
the governing equation (Equation 4) may be integrated and an
analytical solution derived. For other cases integrable analytical
solutions do not exist, and numerical methods must be used to
approximate the governing transport and transformation equations.
These cases include problems where hydraulic or reaction coefficients
vary as a function of time or space. Depending on the degree of
accuracy required, representative constant coefficients may be used
to describe a system approximately, although the sensitivity of the
resultant solution to the assumption(s) of constant coefficients
should always be evaluated in such cases.

Nonlinear Reaction Processes

In many cases of reactive transport an accurate analysis of
contaminant behavior is not afforded by the simplified models
described above. For example, the sorption-desorption process has
been shown for many typical systems to approach a nonlinear
equilibrium between the soil and solution phase at a rate
sufficiently slow to be important for field scale systems (7).
These facts of course conflict with the derivative assumptions of the
linear local-equilibrium model discussed earlier and described in
Equation 5.

Sorption equilibrium may be described more generally by a
nonlinear equation isotherm model such as the Freundlich model, which
reduces to a linear isotherm for certain systems

$$q = K_F C^n \tag{7}$$

where
  K_F = sorption capacity constant $((L^3 M^{-1})^n)$; and
  n = sorption intensity constant.

The Freundlich equilibrium model has been used successfully to
describe the relationship between soil and solution phase solute
concentration for many systems (4,7). Ground water transport of a
solute which manifests clearly nonlinear equilibrium sorption
behavior is substantially different than that of a solute whose
sorption may be approximated by a linear equilibrium model (7). As a
further complication, some sorption-desorption reactions have been
shown to exhibit hysteresis. For this condition the function which

describes the relationship between the soil and solution
concentrations for a desorbing solute is a function of the maximum
soil phase concentration achieved.

Several different types of models have been used to describe
rate of sorption for systems in which a local-equilibrium assumption
is not valid (8). One of the more general of these is a dual
resistance model which describes sorption as a process in terms of
two sequential micro-scale mass transfer steps; diffusion through an
external boundary film surrounding a soil particle and diffusion
within a representative fraction (eg. organic matter fraction) of the
soil particle itself. The dual resistance model may be incorporated
in the general reactive transport equation (Equation 4) to yield

$$\frac{\partial C}{\partial t} = \text{div}(D \text{ grad } C) - \vec{v} \text{ grad } C - \frac{\rho(1 - \epsilon)}{\epsilon} \left\{ \frac{3k_f}{\rho R} (C - C_s) \right\} \quad (8)$$

where

  k_f = external (film) mass transfer coefficient (Lt^{-1});
  R = spherical soil particle radius (L); and
  C_s = fluid-phase equilibrium isotherm concentration
    corresponding to the solid (soil)-phase concentration at
    the particle boundary (ML^{-3}).

The solid-phase concentration distribution is given by

$$\frac{\partial q_a}{\partial t} = \frac{D_s}{r^2} \frac{\partial}{\partial r} \left(r^2 \frac{\partial q_a}{\partial r} \right) \quad (9)$$

where

  q_a = normalized solid phase concentration as a function of
    location within the representative soil fraction sphere
    (MM^{-1});
  D_s = solid-phase internal (particle) diffusion coefficient
    ($L^2 t^{-1}$); and
  r = radial particle dimension (L).

The above set of equations, together with the necessary boundary
and initial conditions and an appropriate sorption-desorption
equilibrium equation, provides a description of solute transport in
ground water subject to rate controlled sorption. Solution of these
equations may be facilitated by the application of numerical
approximation methods. Indeed such methods are necessary when the
isotherm equation is nonlinear or hysteretic, or one or more of the
coefficients associated with the hydrodynamic, sorption rate or
equilibrium equations is a function of space or time.

Figure 5 illustrates a typical solute concentration profile for
a one-dimensional solution of the solute transport equation for a
case in which the rate of sorption is defined by the dual-resistance
model and equilibrium between the soil and solution is described by
the nonlinear Freundlich isotherm equation. The effect of a sorption
rate dependence is to smear the concentration front in space and

time. It is important to separate this smearing from that caused by
hydrodynamic dispersion. Failure to properly accommodate such
sorption rate effects in a transport model will result in an
artificially high calibration value for the hydrodynamic dispersion
coefficient by virtue of lumping the effects of such rate phenomena
in a mathematical term which does not accurately describe the
operative physical and chemical processes. This in turn limits the
applicability of the model to the precise circumstances for which it
was calibrated, and seriously compromises its value as a predictive
management tool.

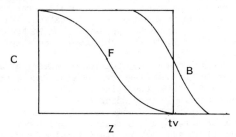

Figure 5. Concentration Profiles for Contaminant Movement by
           Advective-Dispersive Transport Alone (B) and Coupled with
           a Dual-Resistance Rate-Controlled Nonlinear Sorption (F).

The sorption-desorption process is not the only subsurface
phenomenon for which more complex models are often required. For
example, biofilm models have been found more accurate than the simple
rate relationships given by Equation 6 for description of some
biological processes (3). The biofilm model hypothesizes substrate
utilization by a film of microorganisms which surrounds and fills the
interstices of the soil particles. The rate of substrate utilization
by the microorganisms determines thickness of the biofilm. As the
film thickness increases the resistance to diffusive mass transport
of the substrate through the film is increased.

Although strictly chemical reactions such as hydrolysis,
oxidation and radioactive decay tend to be more readily accommodated
by the general chemical reaction rate equation (Equation 6),
combinations of these processes with sorption-desorption reactions
may lead to solution phase and solid phase transformations which
proceed at different rates. In such cases it is necessary to couple
rate relationships describing both the solution and solid phase
transformations with appropriate equilibrium and rate models for the
sorption-desorption process.

Factors which should be reviewed in initial assessment of the
types of transport and transformation phenomena which are likely to
be significant in any given system include the general physical
structure of the subsurface system, such soil properties as particle
size and composition, and such contaminant properties as partitioning
tendencies, degradation potential, volatility and degradation
products. This information may then be used as the basis for field

and laboratory data collection and the selection of appropriate
methods of modeling solute transport and transformation.

Solution Methods

The above discussion presents a brief overview of fate and
transport modeling of contaminants in subsurface environments. Some
of the model equations presented may be solved under sets of
restrictive boundary and initial conditions for systems which are
constant in space. When such analytical solutions are possible they
generally take the form of an exponential integral, error function,
or other solution form requiring numerical integration. Recent
advances in computer technology make approximations to such
analytical solutions a relatively straightforward and simple task.

More complex systems require application of numerical methods to
approximate solutions to the set of governing equations for
appropriate boundary and initial conditions. A wide variety of
numerical methods are available, including the finite difference
method, the integrated finite difference method, the finite element
method, the collocation method, the boundary integral method, the
method of characteristics, and various statistical methods (5). Each
method has associated advantages and disadvantages, and no one
numerical technique is suitable for all applications.

The finite difference method is straightforward in application
and has been used routinely to solve the ground water flow equations
to evaluate ground water velocity fields. In general the method is
sufficiently accurate and quite economical compared to other solution
methods. The finite difference method has difficulty with some
solute transport formulations, notably advection dominated systems,
because of its inability to accurately approximate hyperbolic partial
differential equations.

The finite element and collocation method are more versatile in
terms of their ability to handle irregularly shaped boundaries and
offer some advantages in the solution of advection dominated solute
transport. These advantages are accompanied by a requirement of
increased computational effort, especially for some classes of
nonlinear problems.

The method of characteristics is effective for solution of
advection dominated flow and is reasonably economical. However,
certain classes of nonlinear problems are either not solvable with
the method or involve solutions which are economically unattractive
from a computational perspective.

The boundary integral method is very efficient because it
reduces the spatial dimensionality of a problem. This method is best
suited to steady-state applications in which coefficient parameters
are constant over large areas (6).

Summary

Determination of the fate and transport of contaminants in subsurface environments requires accurate description of all operative processes. These include hydrodynamic transport, sorption-desorption and chemical and biochemical reaction processes. Several models for mathematical representation and approximation of these processes are available. The choice of the particular model to be used in a specific instance should be founded on a thorough knowledge of the contaminant, soil, and aquifer properties, and of all factors likely to impact solute behavior. Numerical methods are generally needed to solve the governing equations. The appropriate numerical method is dependent on the specific problem, with no single method being universally superior.

Appendix I - References.

1. Back, W., and Cherry, J. A., "Chemical Aspects of Present and Future Hydrogeological Problems," Proc. Symp. Adv. Groundwater Hydrol. Amer. Water Resources Assoc., 1976.
2. Bear, J., Hydraulics of Groundwater, McGraw-Hill, Inc., New York, N.Y., 1979.
3. Bouwer, E. J., and McCarty P. L., "Modeling of Trace Organics Biotransformation in the Subsurface," Ground Water, Vol. 22, No. 4, July-August 1984, pp. 433-440.
4. Hamaker, J. W. and Thompson, J. M., "Adsorption," Organic Chemicals in the Soil Environment, Vol. 1, C. A. I. Goring and J. W. Hamaker, ed., Marcel Dekker, Inc. New York, N.Y., 1972, pp. 49-143.
5. Huyakorn, P. and Pinder, G. F., Computational Methods in Sub-Surface Flow," Academic Press, New York, N.Y., 1983.
6. Liggett, J. A. and Liu, P. L-F., The Boundary Integral Equation Method for Porous Media Flow, George Allen and Unwin, London, U.K., 1983.
7. Miller, C. T., "Modeling of Sorption and Desorption Phenomena for Hydrophobic Organic Contaminants in Saturated Soil Environments," dissertation presented to the University of Michigan, Ann Arbor, Mi., in 1984, in partial fulfillment of the requirements for the degree of Doctor of Philosophy.
8. Miller, C. T. and Weber, W. J., Jr., "Modeling Organic Contaminant Partitioning in Ground Water Systems," Ground Water, Vol. 22, No. 5, September-October 1984, pp. 584-592.

MODELING OF MICROBIALLY ACTIVE SOIL COLUMNS

D.S. Kosson, G.C. Agnihotri and R.C. Ahlert
Department of Chemical and Biochemical Engineering
Rutgers, The State University
P.O. Box 909
Piscataway, N.J. 08854

Abstract

A soil-based microbial treatment process for on-site treatment of hazardous industrial wastewaters has been developed. The indigenous microflora of the soil are supplemented by the addition of an inoculum of an acclimated mixed microbial population. Wastewater, balanced with appropriate nutrients, is allowed to percolate through the soil bed. Effluent is collected, in entirety, allowing mass balances to be performed. Daily, batchwise influent additions result in cyclic reaeration and flooding. An aerobic population develops near the surface, while anaerobic organisms dominate at greater depths. Laboratory and pilot-scale field experiments with this system have been conducted over a period of four years. An extensive data base has been developed. Applicability of dispersion models incorporating first-order, reversible adsorption and several forms of a biological reaction term has been examined.

Introduction

In a recent paper, the authors described experiments with high-strength, hazardous industrial wastewaters [3]. These experiments employed biodegradation in beds packed with soil to oxidize organic solutes in waste liquors. Laboratory and pilot-scale bioreactor columns have been used; at both scales, vacuum has been applied at the base of vertical columns to balance capillary forces and mimic so-called "field status". The goal of these experiments is to develop design criteria for in-situ microbial treatment immediately in or adjacent to an uncontrolled dump or spill site.

The approach allows natural selection to control the microbial community as completely as possible. External control is achieved through management of independent parameters such as soil type, depth to groundwater, loading rates, nutrient additions, etc. A mixed microbial population is established in the soil structure. The indigenous microflora of the soil is supplemented through addition, at the soil surface, of an inoculum of a mixed microbial population derived from the secondary sludge of a municipal sewage treatment facility.

The microbial seed propagates through the soil column and permeates the soil structure. Leachate feed is added at the soil surface and is allowed to diffuse through the soil, where it is subsequently adsorbed and/or degraded through aerobic and anaerobic processes.

An experimental field apparatus was designed to examine this treatment process, (1) on a scale suitable for process design, (2) under natural environmental conditions and (3) over a prolonged period of time. To fulfill these goals, a pilot-scale treatment system was installed. The installation consists of six soil columns, termed self-contained lysimeters (SCLs), 60 cm in diameter and 120 cm deep. The SCLs were designed for complete effluent recovery, implanted in the ground and operated in simulation of field conditions. Data for bioreactor modeling was obtained from Experiment 0682, started in June, 1982 and lasting 161 days.

The packed bed bioreactor is a complex system that operates with convective and dispersive flow contributions, physical adsorption and chemisorption, catalyzed non-biochemical reactions and aerobic and anaerobic mixed microbial reactor domains. With the diversity of hydraulic, physical and chemical influences, the development of performance correlation and generalized design criteria is very complex. Fully deterministic modeling is not possible. Thus, a step-by-step approach using incomplete models, as appropriate to limit state operations, was chosen. Ultimately, it is planned to couple these models in a comprehensive design scheme.

Experimental Responses

Soil column responses are the result of three major competing processes: dispersion, adsorption and biodegradation. During operation of the microbially active soil columns, one or more of these processes may control, at different time intervals. Thus, column responses can be seperated into three phases. Phase I is the period of initial operation. Microbial populations are small, and adsorption and dispersion are the processes that dominate TOC reduction. This phase closely resembles a classic adsorption break-through response.

Phase II is the period after the sorptive capacity of the soil has been exhausted. A decline in effluent TOC is generally observed. This results from acclimation, including natural selection, and development of the microbial population. Phase III occurs once the microbial population has developed fully. Sufficient microflora are present to degrade most, if not all, available substrate. A typical response curve is presented in Figure 1. Phase I occurs approximately between Days 1 and 37, Phase II is between Days 37 and 60, and Phase III occurs after Day 60.

Dispersion Model

A dispersion model, assuming negligible radial dispersion, in conjunction with a modified F-statistic was employed by Ahlert, et. al. [1] to estimate packed bed porosity and longitudinal dispersion.

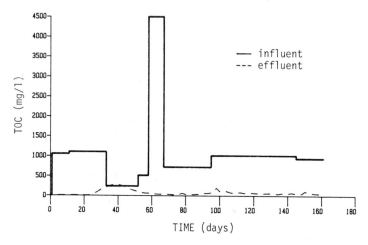

Figure 1. Influent and Effluent TOC (Experimental)

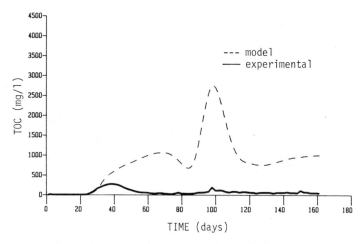

Figure 2. Model with Dispersion and Adsorption, only
(E_z = 6 cm^2/day, R_c = 1.2)

The dispersion model used was:

$$\frac{\partial c}{\partial t} = E_z \left(\frac{\partial^2 c}{\partial z^2}\right) - \bar{u}_p \frac{\partial c}{\partial z} \tag{1}$$

Wen and Fan [6] demonstrated that the boundary conditions required for continuity are:

$$\left(\frac{\partial c}{\partial t}\right)_{z=L} = 0 \tag{2}$$

$$\bar{u}_p c_{z\to 0} = \bar{u}_p c_{z\to 0^+} - E_z \left(\frac{\partial c}{\partial z}\right)_{z\to 0^+} \tag{3}$$

Estimates obtained for packed bed porosity and the dispersion coefficient, E_z, were 40.6% and 6 cm^2/day [6.5 x 10^{-3}ft^2/day], respectively.

Adsorption

An extension of Equation (1) to include first-order reversible adsorption has been presented by Bear [2].

$$\frac{\partial c}{\partial t} = E_z \frac{\partial^2 c}{\partial z^2} - \bar{u}_p \frac{\partial c}{\partial z} - \left(\frac{\rho k'}{\theta_s}\right)\frac{\partial c}{\partial t} \tag{4}$$

or

$$\frac{\partial c}{\partial t} = \frac{E_z}{R_c} \frac{\partial^2 c}{\partial z^2} - \frac{\bar{u}_p}{R_c} \frac{\partial c}{\partial z} \tag{5}$$

where:

$$R_c = \left(\frac{\rho k'}{\theta_s} + 1\right) \tag{6}$$

R_c is frequently referred to as a "retardation factor." Solution of Equation (5) employing the "classic explicit" finite difference approximation described by Lapidus and Pinder [4] results in the algebraic equation

$$c_{i+1,j} = \left(\frac{2E_z h + \bar{u}_p hk}{2R_c k^2}\right)c_{i,j-1} + \left(\frac{R_c k^2 - 2E_z h}{R_c k^2}\right) c_{i,j}$$

$$+ \left(\frac{2E_z h - \bar{u}_p hk}{2R_c k^2}\right)c_{i,j+1} \tag{7}$$

Stability of the numerical solution is assured if

$$h < \frac{R_c k^2}{2E_z} \tag{8}$$

and

$$k < \frac{2E_z}{\bar{u}_p} \tag{9}$$

Assuming adsorption and dispersion are the processes that control Phase I of the reactor operation, an estimate of R_c can be obtained. R_c was estimated to be approximately 1.2; refer to Figure 2.

Biodegradation

Piver and Lindstrom [5] suggested that a first-order rate expression is applicable to biodegradation of landfill leachates in soil systems. Thus, Equation (5) can be extended:

$$\frac{\partial c}{\partial t} = \frac{E_z}{R_c} \frac{\partial^2 c}{\partial z^2} - \frac{\bar{u}_p}{R_c} \frac{\partial c}{\partial z} - \frac{K^*}{R_c} c \tag{10}$$

The same finite difference methodology applied to Equation (5) may be applied to Equation (10). The resulting algebraic equation is

$$c_{i+1,j} = \left(\frac{2E_z h + \bar{u}_p hk}{2R_c k^2}\right) c_{i,j-1} + \left(\frac{R_c k^2 - 2E_z h - k^2 K^* h}{R_c k^2}\right) c_{i,j}$$

$$+ \left(\frac{2E_z h - \bar{u}_p hk}{2R_c k^2}\right) c_{i,j+1} \tag{11}$$

Stability of Equation (11) is assured if

$$h < \frac{R_c k^2}{2E_z + k^2 K^*} \tag{12}$$

and

$$k < \frac{2E_z}{\bar{u}_p} \tag{13}$$

Sensitivity of this model to K^* is described in Figure 3. This model simulates Phase III of soil column responses for $K^* = 0.065$ day^{-1}. Note, this model underpredicts effluent TOC for Phases I and II. A fully developed microbial population is assumed for the estimation of K^*. This assumption is not valid for Phases I and II.

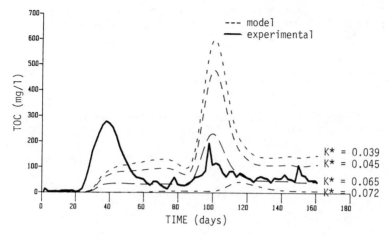

Figure 3. Model Sensitivity to K* (1/day)
$E_z = 6.0 \text{ cm}^2/\text{day}$, $R_c = 1.2$

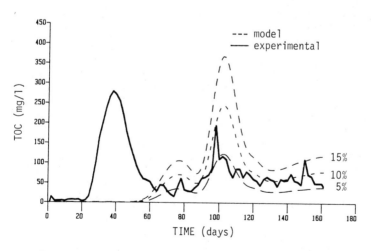

Figure 4. Model Sensitivity to Non-Biodegradable Fraction, A
$E_z = 6.0 \text{ cm}^2/\text{day}$, $R_c = 1.2$

A second approach to the biodegradation term is to assume that the influent TOC is composed of a biodegradable fraction and a non-biodegradable (refractory) fraction, i.e.

$$C = A + B \qquad (14)$$

where: A = non-biodegradable fraction
        B = biodegradable fraction

If the biodegradable and non-biodegradable fractions are assumed independent, such that

$$\frac{\partial A}{\partial B} = 0 \qquad (15)$$

then

$$\frac{\partial C}{\partial t} = \frac{\partial A}{\partial t} + \frac{\partial B}{\partial t} \qquad (16)$$

where

$$\frac{\partial A}{\partial t} = \frac{E_z}{R_c} \frac{\partial^2 A}{\partial z^2} - \frac{\bar{u}_p}{R_c} \frac{\partial A}{\partial z} - \frac{K_A^*}{R_c} A \qquad (17)$$

$$\frac{\partial B}{\partial t} = \frac{E_z}{R_c} \frac{\partial^2 B}{\partial z^2} - \frac{\bar{u}_p}{R_c} \frac{\partial B}{\partial z} - \frac{K_B^*}{R_c} B \qquad (18)$$

Because A is assumed non-biodegradable, $K_A^* = 0$. The finite difference solutions of Equations (17) and (18) are of the same form as the solutions of Equation (11). If the biodegradable fraction (A) is assumed to be completely assimilated during Phase III, the theoretical maximum single pass conversion can be estimated. Sensitivity to this fractional conversion is presented in Figure 4. Note, a 5% non-biodegradable fraction provides a good simulation of the responses observed.

Computational Considerations

The finite difference equations for each model were solved using an IBM personal computer. The programs were written in BASIC and were compiled to reduce execution time. Typical increment sizes were i=0.1 day and j=1.1 cm. Calculated effluent TOCs were averaged over one day intervals, to mimic experimental sampling conditions. Typical execution times were 15 to 30 minutes per trial case.

Conclusions

Several numerical models incorporating dispersion, adsorption and biodegradation have been examined. First-order reversible adsorption combined with a first-order biodegradation (reaction) term provide a good simulation of microbially active soil columns after the microbial population is developed fully (Phase III). A theoretical maximum single pass TOC reduction of 95% has been estimated.

Acknowledgement

The authors with to express their appreciation for the financial support of the Office of Water Policy (U.S. Department of the Interior) and the U.S. Geological Survey, through the New Jersey Water Resources Council.

Notation

A = non-biodegradable fraction of TOC [mg/1]
B = biodegradable fraction of TOC [mg/1]
C = TOC concentration [mg/1]
E_z= axial dispersion constant [cm^2/day]
h^z= time step size [day]
k = spatial step size [cm]
k'= adsorption partition coefficient [1/mg]
$K*$= biological reaction rate constant [1/day]
L = column length [cm]
R_c= retardation factor [1]
t^c= time [days]
$\bar{u}_p$= pore velocity [cm/day]
z^p= axial (vertical) distance from soil surface [cm]
ρ = bulk density of dry soil [mg/1]
θ_s= saturated moisture content of soil [1]

Subscripts

i = increment in time [day]
j = increment in space [cm]

References

1. Ahlert, R.C., D.S. Kosson, E.A. Dienemann and F.D. Ruda, 1984, "The Role of Adsorption and Biodegradation in On-site Leachate Renovation," Management of Uncontrolled Hazardous Waste Sites, HMCRI, Washington D.C., pp. 393-397.

2. Bear, J., 1972, Dynamics of Fluids in Porous Media, Elsevier, New York.

3. Kosson, D.S. and R.C. Ahlert, 1984, "In-situ and On-site Bio-degradation of Industrial Landfill Leachate," Environmental Progress, Vol. 3, No. 3, pp. 176-183.

4. Lapidus, L. and G. Pinder, 1982, Numerical Solution of Partial Differential Equations in Science and Engineering, Wiley, New York.

5. Piver, W.T. and F.T. Lindstrom, 1984, "Simplified Estimation Technique for Organic Contaminant Transport in Groundwater," Journal of Hazardous Materials, Vol. 8, No. 4, pp. 331-339.

6. Wen, C.Y. and L.T. Fan, 1975, _Models for Flow Systems and Chemical Reactors_, Marcel Dekker, Inc., New York.

Two Dimensional Numerical Simulation of Subsurface Contamination
by Organic Compounds - A Multiphase Approach

Linda M. Abriola[*] and George F. Pinder[**]

In recent years, much attention has been focused on the migration
of the soluble portion of an organic contaminant in groundwater
systems. Little work, however, has been directed towards the modeling
of the movement of the non-aqueous phase component of a spill. A two
dimensional mathematical model is presented which is capable of
describing the movement of an organic as both a non-aqueous liquid and
as a component of the water and gas phases. Governing equations are
discretized using a finite difference scheme and the resulting system
of algebraic equations is solved by a Newton-Raphson procedure. In
order to apply this model, a detailed knowledge of matrix and fluid
properties such as relative permeabilities, capillary-pressure
relations, densities, and dispersivities is required.

Introduction

Most previous modeling efforts relating to organic chemical
contamination of the subsurface have focused on the transport of a
soluble contaminant plume in either the saturated or unsaturated
groundwater zones. Models in this category (13)(9)(10)(6)(15) couple
the solution of some type of groundwater flow equation (either
saturated or unsaturated) with the solution of a convective-dispersive
(solute transport) equation. Discretization and solution of these
equations results in a distribution of contaminant concentrations in
space and time. Such models do not attempt to describe the mechanisms
of dissolution which form the contaminant plume and thus, are
restricted in application to far-field contaminant migration or to
situations in which the contaminant is initially introduced in aqueous
form.

In many real contamination situations, however, the organic
chemical enters the subsurface as a distinct non-aqueous liquid phase
which can migrate under its own potential gradients downwards through
the unsaturated zone and spread laterally under the influence of

[*]Assistant Professor, Department of Civil Engineering, University of
Michigan, Ann Arbor, MI 48109-2125.
[**]Professor and Chairman, Department of Civil Engineering, Princeton
University, Princeton, NJ 08544.

capillarity. Much of the chemical may remain trapped at residual
levels in the unsaturated zone due to these same interfacial forces
where it can serve as a source of contamination to infiltrating rain
water or a rising water table. Depending on contaminant density, upon
reaching the saturated groundwater zone the non-aqueous phase organic
may spread laterally along the water table or displace the water and
sink towards some impermeable barrier. Along with this immiscible
phase transport, some of the chemical may also dissolve or volatilize,
forming a plume of contaminated moisture (water) or chemical vapor
spreading out from the initial zone of contamination.

Early efforts at analyzing organic pollution of groundwater as a
two-phase problem were analytical or semi-analytical treatments of the
migration of oil spills (17)(12)(7)(14). These models neglected
capillary effects and were restricted to homogeneous systems. More
rigorous approaches to the two phase flow problem were presented by
Hochmuth (11) for the areal flow of oil on the water table and Faust
(8) for immiscible flow of an organic chemical and water in a vertical
cross-section. Neither of these models incorporated the dissolution
or volatilization of the contaminant.

This paper describes a two dimensional numerical model which is
based on a compositional approach to the modeling of multiphase
contaminant transport. The model is capable of calculating both
concentration and saturation distributions as functions of space and
time.

Governing Equations

The governing equations for this mathematical model are based on a
system of macroscopic mass balance laws which have been obtained by
volume averaging of microscopic balance laws over a representative
volume of the porous medium. The development of these equations is
given in Abriola and Pinder (2). Four distinct phases are considered:
soil, water, organic liquid, and gas. In the derivation of these
equations, the soil matrix is assumed to behave as an elastic medium
and any convective motion of the gas phase is neglected. It is
assumed for modeling purposes that the organic contaminant consists
of, at most, two chemical components, one of which is inert and one
which is reactive (i.e. volatile and/or water-soluble). A modified
form of Darcy's law is used to express fluid velocities in terms of
fluid pressures. Non-advective concentration flux terms are
represented by Fickian-type expressions. The mass fraction of the
reactive organic component in each of the fluid phases is determined
using the concept of local equilibrium between phases.

Resulting governing equations form a system of three non-linear
partial differential equations in five unknowns (two pressures and
three mass fractions) subject to two equilibrium constraints (2):

Water Phase

$$\epsilon \left[\frac{\partial s_w}{\partial P_{ow}} \frac{\partial P_{ow}}{\partial t} + \frac{\partial s_w}{\partial P_{wg}} \frac{\partial P_{wg}}{\partial t} \right] + s_w \beta_w \epsilon \frac{\partial P_{wg}}{\partial t} + s_w \alpha \frac{\partial}{\partial t} (\kappa P_{ow} + P_{wg})$$

$$- \underset{\sim}{\nabla} \cdot (\underset{\sim}{\tau}_w \cdot \underset{\sim}{\nabla} P_{wg}) + \underset{\sim}{\tau}_w \cdot \beta_w \rho^w \underset{\sim}{g} \cdot \underset{\sim}{\nabla} P_{wg} + \rho^w \underset{\sim}{g} \cdot \underset{\sim}{\nabla} \cdot \underset{\sim}{\tau}_w = 0 \qquad (1)$$

Inert Organic Species

$$\omega_1^o s_o \epsilon \left[\beta_o^p \frac{\partial}{\partial t}(P_{ow} + P_{wg}) + \beta_o^1 \frac{\partial \omega_1^o}{\partial t} \right] + \epsilon s_o \frac{\partial \omega_1^o}{\partial t} + \epsilon \omega_1^o \left[\frac{\partial s_o}{\partial P_{ow}} \frac{\partial P_{ow}}{\partial t} + \right.$$

$$\left. \frac{\partial s_o}{\partial P_{wg}} \frac{\partial P_{wg}}{\partial t} \right] - \omega_1^o \underset{\sim}{\tau}_o \cdot \left[\underset{\sim}{\nabla} (P_{ow} + P_{wg}) - \rho^o \underset{\sim}{g} \right] \cdot \left[\beta_o^p \underset{\sim}{\nabla}(P_{ow} + P_{wg}) + \beta_o^1 \underset{\sim}{\nabla} \omega_1^o \right]$$

$$+ s_o \omega_1^o \alpha \frac{\partial}{\partial t} (\kappa P_{ow} + P_{wg}) - \underset{\sim}{\nabla} \cdot \left[\omega_1^o \underset{\sim}{\tau}_o \cdot \underset{\sim}{\nabla}(P_{ow} + P_{wg}) \right] + \omega_1^o \underset{\sim}{\tau}_o \cdot \rho^o \underset{\sim}{g}$$

$$\cdot \left[\beta_o^p \underset{\sim}{\nabla}(P_{ow} + P_{wg}) + \beta_o^1 \underset{\sim}{\nabla} \omega_1^o \right] + \rho^o \underset{\sim}{g} \cdot \underset{\sim}{\nabla} \cdot (\omega_1^o \underset{\sim}{\tau}_o)$$

$$- \frac{1}{\rho^o} \underset{\sim}{\nabla} \cdot \left[\rho^o \epsilon s_o \underset{\sim}{D}_o \cdot \underset{\sim}{\nabla} \omega_1^o \right] = 0 \qquad (2)$$

Reactive Organic Species

$$\rho^w \left[\epsilon s_w \frac{\partial \omega_2^w}{\partial t} + \epsilon \omega_2^w \left[\frac{\partial s_w}{\partial P_{ow}} \frac{\partial P_{ow}}{\partial t} + \frac{\partial s_w}{\partial P_{wg}} \frac{\partial P_{wg}}{\partial t} \right] + \omega_2^w s_w \beta_w \epsilon \frac{\partial P_{wg}}{\partial t} \right.$$

$$\left. - \nabla \cdot (\omega_2^w \underset{\sim}{\tau}_w \cdot \underset{\sim}{\nabla} P_{wg}) + \rho^w \underset{\sim}{g} \cdot \underset{\sim}{\nabla} \cdot (\omega_2^w \underset{\sim}{\tau}_w) + \omega_2^w \underset{\sim}{\tau}_w \cdot \beta_w \rho^w \underset{\sim}{g} \cdot \underset{\sim}{\nabla} P_{wg} \right]$$

$$+ \rho^o \left[\epsilon s_o \frac{\partial \omega_2^o}{\partial t} + \epsilon \omega_2^o \left(\frac{\partial s_o}{\partial P_{ow}} \frac{\partial P_{ow}}{\partial t} + \frac{\partial s_o}{\partial P_{wg}} \frac{\partial P_{wg}}{\partial t} \right) + \omega_2^o s_o \epsilon \left[\beta_o^p \frac{\partial}{\partial t}(P_{ow}+P_{wg}) \right. \right.$$

$$\left. + \beta_o^1 \frac{\partial \omega_1^o}{\partial t} \right] - \omega_2^o \underset{\sim}{\tau}_o \cdot \left[\underset{\sim}{\nabla}(P_{ow} + P_{wg}) - \rho^o \underset{\sim}{g} \right] \cdot \left[\beta_o^p \underset{\sim}{\nabla}(P_{ow} + P_{wg}) + \beta_o^1 \underset{\sim}{\nabla} \omega_1^o \right]$$

$$- \underset{\sim}{\nabla} \cdot \left[\omega_2^o \underset{\sim}{\tau}_o \cdot \underset{\sim}{\nabla}(P_{ow} + P_{wg}) \right] + \rho^o \underset{\sim}{g} \cdot \underset{\sim}{\nabla} \cdot (\omega_2^o \underset{\sim}{\tau}_o) + \omega_2^o \underset{\sim}{\tau}_o \cdot \rho^o \underset{\sim}{g}$$

$$\left. \cdot \left[\beta_o^p \underset{\sim}{\nabla}(P_{ow} + P_{wg}) + \beta_o^1 \underset{\sim}{\nabla} \omega_1^o \right] \right] + \rho^g \left[\epsilon s_g (1 + \omega_2^g \beta_g) \frac{\partial \omega_2^g}{\partial t} \right.$$

$$+ \; \epsilon \omega_2^g \left(\frac{\partial s_g}{\partial P_{ow}} \frac{\partial P_{ow}}{\partial t} + \frac{\partial s_g}{\partial P_{wg}} \frac{\partial P_{wg}}{\partial t} \right) \Bigg\} + \; \alpha (\rho^w s_w \omega_2^w + \rho^o s_o \omega_2^o + \rho^g s_g \omega_2^g)$$

$$x \frac{\partial}{\partial t} (\kappa P_{ow} + P_{wg}) \; - \; \underset{\sim}{\nabla} \cdot (\rho^o \epsilon s_o \underset{\sim}{D}^o \cdot \underset{\sim}{\nabla} \omega_2^o + \rho^w \epsilon s_w \underset{\sim}{D}^w \underset{\sim}{\nabla} \omega_2^w + \rho^g \epsilon s_g \underset{\sim}{D}^g \underset{\sim}{\nabla} \omega_2^g) \; = \; 0$$

$$(3)$$

Equilibrium Constraints

$$K_2^{gw} = \omega_2^g / \omega_2^w \qquad\qquad K_2^{wo} = \omega_2^w / \omega_2^o \qquad\qquad (4)$$

All variables are defined in the nomenclature section at the end of this paper.

Numerical Model Description

A one dimensional numerical model based on equations 1 - 4 has been developed by Abriola and Pinder (3). This model can be extended to handle simulations in two space dimensions (x,y) in a cross-sectional plane. For this case, the gradient operator which appears in equations 1 - 3 is defined as:

$$\underset{\sim}{\nabla} (\;\;) = \frac{\partial}{\partial x} (\;\;) \; \underset{\sim}{i} + \frac{\partial}{\partial y} (\;\;) \; \underset{\sim}{j} \qquad\qquad (5)$$

It is assumed that the principle axes of the intrinsic permeability tensor, k, coincide with the x-y coordinate directions such that this tensor may be represented by the two components k_x and k_y. The dispersion tensor for a given phase is expressed as (5):

$$D_{ij}^\alpha = \begin{pmatrix} D^{m\alpha} + (a_T^\alpha \bar{v}_y^{\alpha 2} + a_L^\alpha \bar{v}_x^{\alpha 2})/\bar{v}^\alpha & (a_L^\alpha - a_T^\alpha)\bar{v}_x^\alpha \bar{v}_y^\alpha / \bar{v}^\alpha \\ \\ (a_L^\alpha - a_T^\alpha)\bar{v}_x^\alpha \bar{v}_y^\alpha / \bar{v}^\alpha & D^{m\alpha} + (a_T^\alpha \bar{v}_x^{\alpha 2} + a_L^\alpha \bar{v}_y^{\alpha 2})/\bar{v}^\alpha \end{pmatrix} \qquad (6)$$

Constraints 4 along with expressions 5 and 6 can be substituted into the governing equations 1 - 3 to form a system of three equations in three unknowns. This system is solved within the model by application of a finite difference discretization scheme. Spatial derivative approximations are centered in space. To enhance stability of the scheme, a fully implicit formulation is used. The resulting system of non-linear algebraic equations is solved using a Newton-Raphson iteration procedure. To limit matrix bandwidth (and

consequently, computer storage requirements), cross-derivative terms
involving the dispersion tensor are lagged one iteration. Velocity
components appearing in the dispersion tensor are calculated by a
finite difference discretization of Darcy's law.

Coefficient matrix structure for the resulting system of equations
is shown in Figure 1(b) for the example grid of twenty nodes pictured
in Figure 1(a). Each box in the figure represents a 3 x 3 matrix. Note
that the matrix structure exhibits a block tridiagonal band with two
off-diagonal bands associated with neighboring nodes on adjoining rows
in the grid.

A banded matrix solver could be used to solve this system of
equations directly. A more efficient approach, however, is to
implement what is known as a D4 numbering scheme. This approach
involves the renumbering of nodes along alternate diagonals and has
been applied to the solution of similar types of equations in the oil
reservoir literature (4). Such a renumbering scheme is given in Figure
2(a). The matrix structure corresponding to this nodal numbering
pattern is given in Figure 2(b). Again, each block in the figure
represents a 3 x 3 matrix. Within the model, matrix solution proceeds
as follows. Nodes are renumbered and forward elimination is used on
the lower half of the matrix shown in Figure 2(b). The lower half of
the resultant matrix equations is then solved for the lower vector of
unknowns using a banded matrix solver. The upper vector of unknowns is
calculated next by inverting the block diagonal matrix in the upper
left quadrant of Figure 2(b) and utilizing the vector of solutions
obtained from the previous step. For a more complete description of
this solver and its computational advantages see Abriola (1).

Before the model described above can be used to simulate a
contamination event, a number of parameters must be evaluated. These
parameters and the ways in which they are handled in the model are
discussed briefly below.

Matrix Properties

Matrix compressibilty and intrinsic permeability are incorporated
into the model as spatially varying parameters which are constant in
time.

Fluid Properties

The compressibility and viscosity of water are assumed constant in
space and time. Organic phase compressibility, however, is treated as
a function of both pressure and composition, based on the assumption
that the phase density can be expressed as the weighted sum of
component densities. Organic phase viscosity and gas phase density are
assumed to depend solely on phase composition and are evaluated using
Arrhenius' equation and the gas law respectively.

Equilibrium Coefficients

These coefficients must be incorporated into the model in
functional or tabular form. Dependency upon pressures and phase

Figure 1: Example Matrix Formulation
    (a)   Example grid structure and node numbering scheme
    (b)   Coefficient matrix structure

(a)

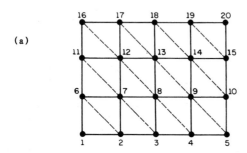

(b)

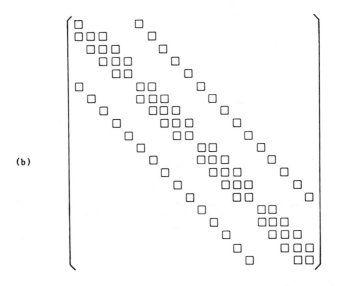

Figure 2: Matrix Formulation Using D4 Ordering
  (a) D4 node numbering scheme
  (b) Coefficient matrix structure

(a)

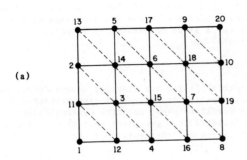

(b)

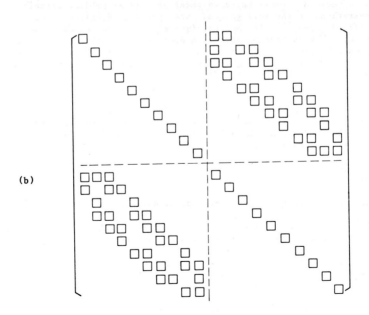

composition is permitted. Coefficients for a given situation can be obtained from Henry's law constants and information on organic chemical solubilities.

Pressure - Saturation Relations

The model assumes fluid saturations can be expressed as unique functions of pressures. Spatial dependence of these functions is also permitted. Functional or tabular forms of these relationships must be incorporated into the model for a given contamination situation. Hysteresis effects are neglected.

Relative Permeability Relations

Liquid phase relative permeabilities are input as unique functions of pressures or saturations. Spatial dependence is also permitted. In the absence of real data for three phase relative permeabilities, these permeabilities are calculated from two phase data by a method developed by Stone (16) for use in oil reservoir modeling.

Summary

In the previous pages, a two dimensional model was presented which is capable of simulating a wide variety of organic contamination scenarios. The model was developed as an extension of a one dimensional multiphase model presented previously (2) (3). It can track non-aqeous organic phase movement as well as predict organic concentrations in the soil gas and water phases. Equations are discretized using a fully implicit finite difference approach and solved by a Newton-Raphson iteration procedure. An efficient solver based on a D4 node renumbering scheme is utilized in the model. Application of the model requires specification of a large number of parameters which have been briefly discussed.

Acknowledgements

This work was supported, in part, by the U.S. Department of Energy under contract DE-AC02-79EV10257 and the Princeton University Industrial Support Group.

Nomenclature
Roman

a_T^α, a_L^α transversal and longitudinal dispersivity

$D^{m\alpha}$ molecular diffusion coefficient for the medium
$\underset{\sim}{D}^\alpha$ macroscopic dispersion tensor for species in α phase
$\underset{\sim}{g}$ gravity acceleration vector
g gas phase
$\underset{\sim}{i}$, $\underset{\sim}{j}$ unit vectors in x and y directions
$\underset{\sim}{k}$ intrinsic permeability tensor

$k_{r\alpha}$ relative permeability of α phase

$K_i^{\alpha\beta}$ species i partition coefficient between phases α and β

o   organic phase

$P_{\alpha\beta}$ capillary pressure - differential between pressures in the α and β phases: $P^{\alpha} - P^{\beta}$

s_{α} saturation of α phase

t time

$\bar{v}^{\alpha}$ average phase velocity

$\bar{v}_x^{\alpha}, \bar{v}_y^{\alpha}$ magnitudes of velocity components in coordinate directions

w   water phase

x,y   spatial coordinates

Greek

α compressibility of soil matrix

β_w compressibilty of water phase

$$\beta_0 = \frac{1}{\rho^o} \left. \frac{\partial \rho^o}{\partial \omega_1^o} \right|_{P^o = const}$$

$$\beta_o^p = \frac{1}{\rho^o} \left. \frac{\partial \rho^o}{\partial P^o} \right|_{\omega_1^o = const}$$

ε void fraction

$\kappa = s_0/(s_0 + s_w)$ weighting parameter

ρ^{α} density of α phase

$\underset{\approx}{\tau}_{\alpha}$ mobility of α phase $= \underset{\approx}{k} k_{r\alpha}/\mu_{\alpha}$

μ_{α} dynamic viscosity of α phase

ω_i^{α} mass fraction of species i in α phase

References

1. Abriola, L. M., "Multiphase Migration of Organic Compounds in a Porous Medium - A Mathematical Model," Lecture Notes in Engineering, Vol. 8, Springer-Verlag, Berlin, 1984, 232p.
2. Abriola, L. M. and Pinder, G. F., "A Multiphase Approach to the Modeling of Porous Media Contamination by Organic Compounds - Part I: Equation Development," Water Resources Research, Vol. 21, No. 1, 1985, pp. 11-18.
3. Abriola, L. M. and Pinder, G. F., "A Multiphase Approach to the Modeling of Porous Media Contamination by Organic Compounds - Part II: Numerical Simulation," Water Resources Research, Vol. 21, No. 1, 1985, pp. 19-26.
4. Aziz, K. and Settari A., Petroleum Reservoir Simulation, Applied Science, London, 1979.
5. Bear, J., Hydraulics of Groundwater, McGraw-Hill, Inc., New York, 1979.
6. Bresler, E., "Simultaneous Transport of Solutes and Water Under Transient Unsaturated Flow Conditions," Water Resources Research, Vol.9, No. 4, 1973, pp. 975-986.

7. Dracos, T., "Theoretical Considerations and Practical Implications on the Infiltration of Hydrocarbons in Aquifers," Proceedings IAH International Symposium on Ground Water Pollution by Oil Hydrocarbons , Prague, 1978, pp. 127-137.

8. Faust, C. R., "Transport of Immiscible Fluids Within and Below the Unsaturated Zone - A Numerical Model," Geotrans Technical Report, 84-01, Herndon, VA, 1984, 15p.

9. Gray, W. G. and Hoffman, J. L., "A Numerical Model Study of Ground-Water Contamination from Price's Landfill, New Jersey - I. Data Base and Flow Simulation," Ground Water, Vol. 21, No. 1, 1983, pp. 7-14.

10. Gray, W. G. and Hoffman, J. L., "A Numerical Model Study of Ground-Water Contamination from Price's Landfill, New Jersey - II. Sensitivity Analysis and Contaminant Plume Simulation," Ground Water, Vol. 21, No. 1, pp. 15-21.

11. Hochmuth, D. P., "Two-Phase Flow of Immiscible Fluids in Groundwater Systems," thesis presented to Colorado State University, at Fort Collins, CO, in 1981, in partial fulfillment of the requirements for the Master's Degree.

12. Mull, R., "Calculations and Experimental Investigations of the Migration of Hydrocarbons in Natural Soils," Proceedings IAH International Symposium on Groundwater Pollution by Oil Hydrocarbons , Prague, 1978, pp. 167-181.

13. Pinder, G. F., "A Galerkin-Finite Element Simulation of Groundwater Contamination on Long Island, New York," Water Resources Research, Vol. 9, No. 6, 1973, pp. 1657-1669.

14. Scheigg, H. O., "Methode zur Abschatzung der Ausbreitung von Erdolderivaten in mit Wasser und Luft Erfullten Boden," Mitteilungen der Versuchsanstalt fur Wasserbau an der Eidgenossischen Technischen Hochschule, Zurich, Nr. 22 (Ger), 1977.

15. Segol, G., "A Three-Dimensional Galerkin Finite Element Model for the Analysis of Contaminant Transport in Saturated-Unsaturated Porous Media," Proceedings 1st International Conference on Finite Elements in Water Resources, Pentech Press, London, 1977, pp. 2.123-144.

16. Stone, H. L., "Estimation of Three-Phase Relative Permeability and Residual Oil Data," Canadian Journal of Petroleum Technology, Vol. 12, No. 4, 1973, pp. 53-61.

17. van Dam, J., "The Migration of Hydrocarbons in a Water-Bearing Stratum," in The Joint Problems of the Oil and Water Industries, P. Hepple, ed., Elsevier Publ. Co., N.Y., 1967, pp. 55-96.

MODELING A WATER DISTRIBUTION SYSTEM

By

Donald R. Jackson, M. ASCE*

Abstract

Problems encountered in modeling the water distribution system for the City of Norwich, N. Y. are discussed and the procedures used to solve each problem are described. The interpretation of results of the modeling is also presented.

I. Purposes of Study

The Susquehanna River Basin Commission was requested by New York Department of Environmental Conservation to conduct an infrastructure study for the City of Norwich, N.Y. The study was completed in July 1983(1).

The City of Norwich is located in southeastern New York, about 50 miles (81 km) north of Binghamton. The 1980 population of the City is 8080. The entire study included modeling the water distribution system, evaluating unaccounted for water, analyzing the financial capability of the system, and recommending improvements. In this paper the focus will be on the problems encountered in the modeling of the system, and on interpretation of the results of the modeling.

II. Description of Water System

The Norwich Water System is municipally owned and operated. The original water system dates back to 1881 and much of the existing distribution system is of 19th century vintage. The system presently serves about 2,500 customers in the City and the surrounding Town of Norwich. The distribution system includes pipes ranging in size from 4 in. (102 mm) to 16 in. (406 mm). There are three separate pressure districts connected only by the pumps which feed a district.

III. Procedures and Problems Encountered

A. System Data

The data necessary to model the system was obtained from water system records. These data included location, size, material, elevations, and dates of installation of all the pipes in the distribution system. It also included pump characteristic curves, pump suction and discharge pressures, tank elevations, measured hydrant pressures, and water usage. A somewhat skeletonized schematic of the entire system is shown in Figure 1.

* Staff Hydrologist, Susquehanna River Basin Commission, 1721 North Front St., Harrisburg, PA. 17102.

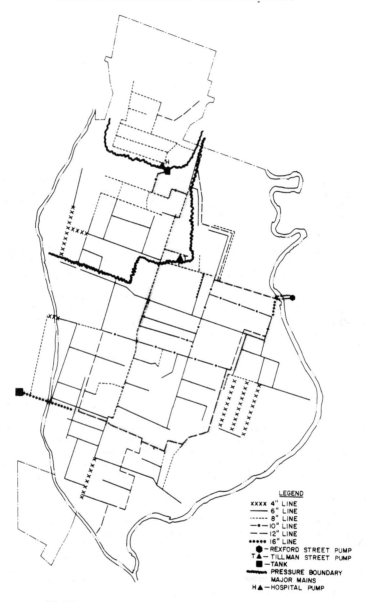

LEGEND
xxxx 4" LINE
——— 6" LINE
----- 8" LINE
—•— 10" LINE
— — 12" LINE
•••• 16" LINE
● — REXFORD STREET PUMP
T▲— TILLMAN STREET PUMP
■ — TANK
━━━ PRESSURE BOUNDARY
MAJOR MAINS
H▲ — HOSPITAL PUMP

FIGURE I. SCHEMATIC OF NORWICH WATER SYSTEM

Note that there are three pumping stations, and two tanks. The three pumping stations are at Rexford St., Tillman Ave., and near the Hospital. The main system input is at the Rexford St. filter plant and adjacent pumps.

The data was used to develop a mathematical model of the system. The program used to model the system was the LIQSS model developed by Stoner Associates, Carlisle, PA., which is a steady state model.

Each of the inputs to the computer model involved a lot of engineering judgement to overcome certain problems. These problems and the procedures developed to overcome them are described in the following sections.

B. Tank Elevations

Since the tanks float on the system, emptying and filling as system demand increases and decreases, the tank elevations are unknown for calibration purposes. A calibration run which reproduces hydrant pressures measured over a period of time will show that the tanks are either filling or emptying. Once certain tank levels are reached the pumps will either turn on or off, and the head within the system will change. Mathematically this results in changing the boundary conditions of the mathematical model, and introduces error into the calibration based on steady state conditions. There is nothing that can be done about the problem except to attempt to assume tank elevations that are as close as possible to those experienced during the period when the calibration measurements were made.

C. Pump Characteristic Curves

The first major problem was with the pumps. The pump pressure data showed that the Rexford St. and Tillman Ave. pumps were not producing as much head increase as the pump curves indicated. The problem at the Rexford St. pumps was ignored, because it was possible to calibrate the system without adjusting pump curves. The pump curves for the Tillman Ave. pumps had to be adjusted in order to calibrate the system.

Since the tanks float on the system, the pumps at this station basically operate at one head and at one flow rate. However the computer model requires the full pump curve.

The problem is shown in Figure 2, which shows the pump curves obtained from the water system records, and the observed operation point. The water system records showed that the impeller size was 6-1/16 in. (154 mm) which is the upper pump curve. Note that the observed operation point was almost exactly on the middle curve. Several different ways were tried to derive a pump curve which adequately described how the system would operate. However the pump curve for the 5 1/2 in. impeller seemed to be the most reasonable and therefore was used.

An effort was made to evaluate whether the hydraulics of the pump intake and discharge were affecting the observed relationship between intake and discharge pressures. Computations showed that the total head loss due to reducing the pump intake line from 8 in. (203 mm) to 2 in. (51 mm), then increasing the size of the discharge line from 2 in. (51 mm) to 8 in. (203 mm), and the loss due to an ell in the discharge line, plus the difference in elevation of the intake and discharge pressure gages accounted for about 2 psi. (14 kPa) of the 12 psi. (83 kPa) difference between the theoretical and observed head increase.

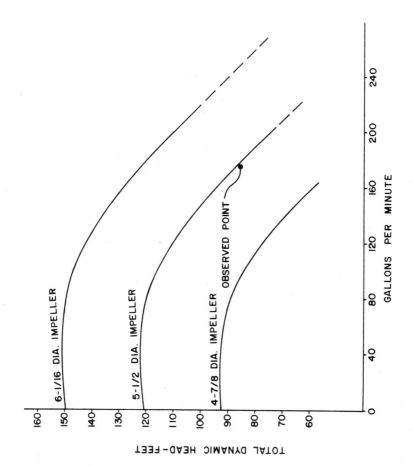

FIGURE 2.—TILLMAN AVE. PUMP CHARACTERISTIC CURVE

D. Flow Distribution

The model calibration was based on pressure measurements made by the water system personnel in 1979 and 1982. The conditions under which these measurements were made are not well defined. Ideally, pressure measurement should be made under controlled conditions or at least conditions which are well defined, but this wasn't possible in this case. In particular the distribution of actual flow rates within the system at the time the measurements were made is unknown. There are private and public organizations which use large quantities of water and whose usage varies over time. Walski (2) recommends using typical daily peak flow rates insofar as possible. However typical peak daily flow rates for individual users are not generally available, and even systemwide daily peak flow rates are difficult to obtain because of the effect of changes in the tank elevations and pumping rates.

According to water system personnel, the hydrant pressure measurements were made approximately between the hours of 9:00 am and 4:00 pm. on certain dates which are shown in the records. The best approximation to actual conditions under which these measurements were made was believed to be an average of the conditions during those daytime hours on the dates on which flow measurements were made. In order to obtain that average condition, the following information was taken from the recording charts for the respective facilities:

    a. Beginning and end of the peak usage period;

    b. Average filter plant production during that peak usage period;

    c. Net change in water surface elevation in the two tanks;

    d. Average flow through the Tillman Ave. pump during that peak usage period.

From that information the average system inflow rate was determined to be 1300 gpm. (82 L/s), compared with an average daily usage of 1181 gpm.(75 L/s). Then the flow was distributed between pressure districts again using the same average conditions. The usage in Pressure District 1 was computed as 960 gpm. (61 L/s), and the usage in Pressure Districts 2 and 3 was computed as 248 gpm. (16 L/s) and 92 gpm. (6 L/s) respectively.

The usage in each pressure district was distributed to each node of the distribution system by identifying the largest users, determining their average daily usage from billing records, subtracting that usage from the pressure district total, and dividing by the number of nodes in the pressure district. Then the individual usage for the large users was added back to the average usage for the appropriate node.

E. Accuracy of Fire Hydrant Pressure Measurements

The only source of inflow to Pressure District 3 is the Hospital pump. The computed discharge pressure at the pump is about equal to that normally experienced, but the pressure at the first node downstream of the pump is overpredicted by 23 psi (158 kPa). Further evaluation showed a difference of 20 psi (138 kPa) between the pressure measurement made in 1979 and the measurement made in 1982 at one node where measurements were made in both years. The 1982 measurement was within 2 psi (14 kPa) of the computed value. Also, the pressures in the western part of this loop were predicted very well, but the pressures in the eastern part of the loop were significantly overpredicted. The pressure measurements in the eastern part of the loop were made in 1979. In order to verify the author's hunch that the 1979 measurements were incorrect, water system personnel made additional measurements in 1983 at two locations in Pressure District 3. These measurements were very different from the 1979 measurements and also compared very well with computed pressures. For these reasons the 1979 measurements in this pressure district were considered invalid and ignored for calibration purposes.

F. Criteria For Model Calibration

Initially, fairly rigorous calibration criteria were established. In particular computed pressures were required to generally agree with hydrant pressure measurements within 2 psi.(14 kPa.) It was determined that this calibration criteria could not be met without a lot of time and computer runs. In view of the uncertainties in the input data it wasn't possible to be sure that the increased effort was really worthwhile. Since the major purpose of the modeling was to evaluate condition of the overall system, rather than the condition of individual pipes, less stringent calibration criteria seemed to be adequate. Walski (2) indicates that calibration to within 5 psi (34.9 kPa) is adequate, and on the average that criteria is met. The locations where it is not met are perceived to represent local problems which will be discussed subsequently.

G. Problems With Use of The Hazen-Williams Equation

The Hazen-Williams equation was used in this study because it is conventionally used in water supply practice. A problem was encountered with the Hazen-Williams equation which, to the author's knowledge, has not been discussed anywhere in the literature. One of the limitations of the Hazen-Williams equation is that it applies only to the turbulent flow regime (3), characterized by Reynold's numbers exceeding approximately 4,000. The computer output from the calibration runs showed very low velocities in certain pipes. The Reynolds numbers were computed for some of these pipes and found to be less than 2,000, which means that the flow regime is laminar rather than turbulent. Reynolds numbers for some pipes were also in the range from 2,000 to 4,000 which indicates a transition flow regime for these pipes. The Hazen-Williams equation does not properly represent head losses in these pipes. Since the calibration run was showing very low C factors, and since the observed pressures were still overestimated, it was thought that the violation of the assumptions of the Hazen-Williams equation might affect the conclusions.

For this reason a run was made using the Darcy-Weisbach equation to represent head losses. The initial values of the Darcy-Weisbach friction factor, f, were computed from the Hazen-Williams C using an equation given by Vennard (3).

The run using the Darcy-Weisbach equation did not converge within specified tolerances within 45 iterations, compared to the runs with the Hazen-Williams equation which converged after about 10 iterations. The results at that stage showed:

a. The computed pressures in general were very close to those obtained using the Hazen-Williams equation;

b. The flow rates in certain pipes were very different between the two runs, due to relatively small changes in hydraulic grade line elevations at the ends of those pipes, and resulting magnitude of the head loss in the pipe;

c. There were a number of problems in the Darcy-Weisbach run which may have been due to lack of convergence.

Since the criteria for calibration was based on comparison of measured and computed pressures and the computed pressure in general did not change very much as a result of the change in the equation used to determine head loss, it was concluded that the solution based on the Hazen-Williams equation was adequate. However additional research seems desireable to determine how to compute head losses when the Reynolds numbers are very low and the Hazen-Williams equation is not appropriate.

IV. Interpretation of Calibration Results
   A. Low C Factors
   The original estimates of C factors were based on pipe age. The pipes in the system are all cast iron.
   Initial calibration runs showed that the pressures in Pressure Districts 1 and 2 were significantly overestimated. Approximate computations based on the equivalent pipe concept suggested that the C factors in Pressure District 1 should be reduced by 30% and that C factors in Pressure District 2 should be reduced by 40%. The calibration run with these reduced C factors showed that pressures on average were still too high. Figure 3 is a histogram of the difference between computed and observed pressures at each node in the system where pressure measurements were used, except for the pump suction and discharge nodes. The computed pressures at the pump suction and discharge nodes are very close to observed pressures. Figure 4 is a histogram of C factor by pipe size and percentage of total length of all pipes in the system. Note that the C factors are at least as low as 30 in some pipes, which implies that 75% of the capacity of those pipes has been lost due to corrosion or deposition.
   B. Low Working Pressures
   New York Department of Health standards state that normal working pressures should be approximately 60 psi. (413 kPa) and not less than 35 psi (241 kPa). The policy of the Norwich water system is to maintain at least 50 psi (345 kPa) working pressure at all points. The model calibration results show that the 50 psi (345 kPa) standard is not met at 16 of the 243 nodes in the system. The 60 psi (413 kPa) standard is not met at 125 of the nodes. If the calibrated pressures were closer to the field measured pressures, there would probably be more locations which do not meet the pressure standards.
   C. High Head Losses
   Certain pipes showed rather high head losses. The author is not aware of any standards for head losses in water distribution systems, so it was arbitrarily assumed that head losses exceeding 1.0 ft/100 ft (1 m/100 m) were excessive. There are 8 segments of the system which have head losses exceeding this arbitrary criterion. These pipes may need early attention in any corrective program. Rehabilitation of these pipes may provide the greatest payoff both in terms of saving energy and in terms of solving problems of low pressures.
   D. Low Velocities
   There is a rule-of-thumb (4) that velocities in water distribution systems should be in the range from 2.0 to 4.0 fps (0.6 to 1.2 m/s). The velocity is less than 2.0 fps (0.6 m/s) in almost all pipes in the Norwich water system, and in most pipes the velocity is

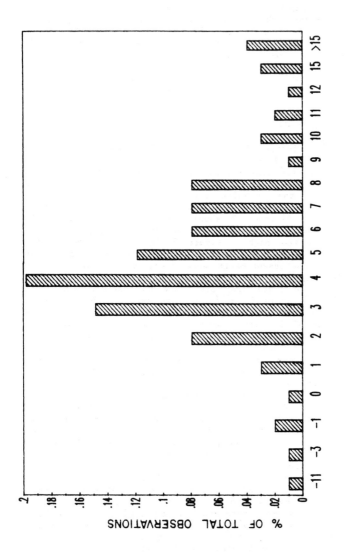

FIGURE 3. HISTOGRAM OF DIFFERENCES BETWEEN COMPUTED AND MEASURED PRESSURES.

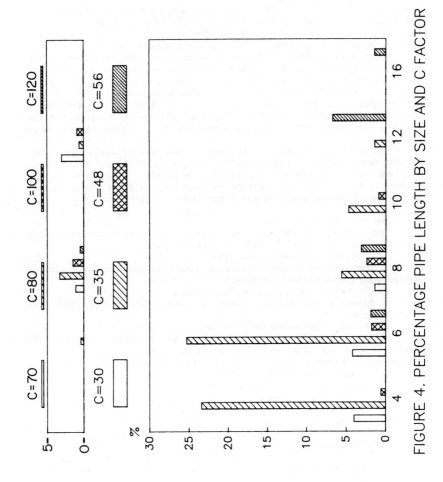

FIGURE 4. PERCENTAGE PIPE LENGTH BY SIZE AND C FACTOR

less than 0.5 fps (0.15 m/s). It is likely that low velocities will
contribute to reduced C values or to reduced pipe diameter due to
corrosion, growth of algae, or deposition.

E. Spatial Variations in Calibration Accuracy
    There are a number of locations where the computed pressures are
significantly different from the measured pressures. These variations
could be due to increased flow or reduced capacity of the pipes
feeding a particular node. These locations were identified and it was
recommended that these pipes be studied further. In particular,
problems affecting the lines feeding the Tillman Avenue pump station
and the potential effect on the operation of the pump station were
noted.
    One area in Pressure District 2 was particularly puzzling,
because one node was substantially overpredicted while an adjacent
node was substantially underpredicted. As a result of pinpointing the
problem area based on the calibration results, water system personnel
were able to locate and repair a large leak in this vicinity.

V. Summary and Conclusions
    The following problems were encountered in modeling the water
distribution system for the City of Norwich, N. Y.
    1. Tanks which float on the system;
    2. Pumps which do not provide as much head increase as indicated
by the pump characteristic curves;
    3. Determination of system flow rates;
    4. Pressure measurements used in model calibration which are
questionable;
    5. Criteria for model calibration;
    6. Low velocities in certain pipes which result in violating
assumptions of the Hazen-Williams equation.
The procedures used to solve these problems have been described.
    Calibration results showed:
    1. Hazen-Williams C factors as low as 30 in certain pipes;
    2. Low working pressures at a number of nodes in the system;
    3. High head losses in certain pipes, which suggest that those
pipes should be considered for early remedial actions;
    4. Extremely low velocities in many pipes, which may contribute
to reduced C factors or to reduced pipe diameter.
    5. Spatial variation in calibration accuracy, which was
perceived as representing localized problems which need further study.

                            Appendix
                      List of References

1. Jackson, D. R. and Seay, E. E., Water Distribution System
Infrastructure Study City of Norwich N.Y., Susquehanna River Basin
Commission Publication No. 79, July 1983.
2. Walski, T. J., "Using Water Distribution System Models", Journal
American Water Works Association, vol. 75, no. 2, Feb. 1983.
3. Vennard, J. K., Elementary Fluid Mechanics, Fourth Ed., New York:
John Wiley & Sons, 1961, p. 303-305.
4. Fair, G. M., and Geyer, J. C. Elements of Water Supply and Waste-
Water Disposal, New York: John Wiley & Sons, 1958. Pp. 142, 165.)

A CASE STUDY - TOMS RIVER WATER COMPANY
TOMS RIVER, NEW JERSEY

G. Matthew Brown, P.E.*

Toms River Water Company provides water service to Dover
Township, the Borough of South Toms River and portions of
Berkeley Township, all in Ocean County, New Jersey. Existing
supply facilities are located throughout the operating area.
Due to rapid growth in recent years, Toms River Water Company
has recognized the need to expand existing facilities and
provide additional source of supply. One such supply source
exists in an area remote to heavy demand locations.

This paper reviews the hydraulic modeling of the system
distribution network to accomodate the proposed supply source.
Illustrations of the problems encountered in balancing a system
of multiple sources of supply are discussed and system design
criteria are presented from data obtained utilizing the computer
model.

INTRODUCTION

Supply for the Toms River Water Company is taken entirely
from wells. Water is pumped directly into the system mains or
into ground level storage or treatment facilities from which
booster pumps take suction and then discharge to the system.
All water is chlorinated prior to system introduction. Distribution storage is provided at five locations to provide supply
to meet peak periods and fire demands. System mains range in
size from 4-inch to 16-inch. Figure 1 illustrates the present
operating area and existing supply and storage facilities.

At year-end 1984, Toms River Water Company served 27,487
customers, an estimated population of 93,450. Average day consumption for 1984 was 7.42 MG, while the maximum day was 15.19
MG.

The proposed source of supply project involves construction
of two new wells in the Berkeley Township area of the distribution network. These wells (Berkeley No. 33 and 34) will divert
3.0 MGD from the Cohansey Aquifer.

Additionally, due to water quality problems, the New Jersey
Department of Environmental Protection has requested abandonment
of Anchorage and Silver Bay Well Fields located in the northeas-

* Assistant Region Engineer, General Waterworks Management &
Service Company, 25 Commerce Road, Newtown, Connecticut, 06470.

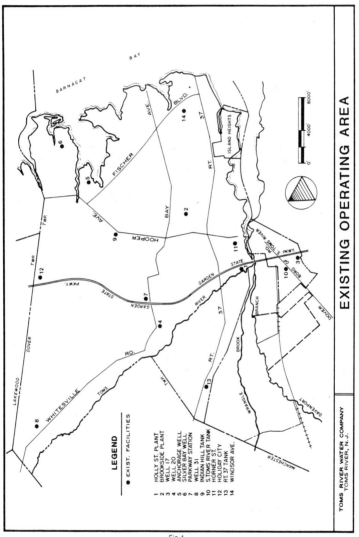

LEGEND

● EXIST. FACILITIES

1   HOLLY ST. PLANT
2   BROOKSIDE PLANT
3   WELL 17
4   WELL 20
5   ANCHORAGE WELL
6   SILVER BAY WELL
7   PARKWAY STATION
8   WELL 31
9   INDIAN HILL TANK
10 S.TOMS RIVER TANK
11 HORNER ST.
12 HOLIDAY CITY
13 RT. 37 TANK
14 WINDSOR AVE.

TOMS RIVER WATER COMPANY
TOMS RIVER, N. J.

EXISTING OPERATING AREA

Fig. 1

tern section of the operating area. Utilization of the proposed
Berkeley Well source in conjunction with the discontinuance of
Anchorage and Silver Bay service will bring the total source of
supply capacity from 15.28 MGD to 17.84 MGD. Projections, as
shown in Figure 2, indicate that maximum daily demand in 1986
will be 16.16 MG. By basing system needs on the premise that
source capacity should be capable of meeting maximum daily
demand, the evidence in support of additional supply is conclu-
sive.

MODELING THE SYSTEM

     The purpose of computer modeling a water distribution
system is to assess the response of the system under various
conditions both quickly and accurately. The first step in the
modeling process is to skeletonize the existing system along
with hypothetical improvements.

     The hydraulic analysis of the Toms River Water Company was
performed utilizing the Liquid Steady-State System (LIQSS)
Version 1.3. The LIQSS system is a proprietary development of
Stoner Associates, Inc., Carlisle, Pennsylvania.

     Skeletonization of the subject system was initiated by
first examining past billing records. A street by street analysis of type and quantity of demands, area elevations and main
sizes provided a basis for loadings and node selection. Working
from a distribution system map, small main sizes (less than
6-inch) were eliminated where possible. Drawoffs from the small
mains were assimilated into larger size or feeder main loadings. Node points were then established based upon inspection
of the reduced model. Node flows were calculated from a summation of area loads. Those drawoffs assigned to sections eliminated in the selection of node points were assigned to the nearest appropriate node in order to ensure that the full system and
skeleton model were similarly loaded.

     Since use of the Hazen-Williams option was intended during
the hydraulic analysis, C values were assigned to each remaining
pipe or node connecting element (NCE). C values were determined
from both actual measurement and estimation based on pipe size,
flow conditions, piping material and age.

     Each supply source was modeled according to existing
facilities. Where wells would pump direcly to the distribution
system, drawdown and capacity data, along with the well pump
curves were included in the model. Booster pumps from ground
storage or treatment facilities were assigned flow values for
the maximum daily demand analysis. For peak hour analysis, the
booster pump curves were provided to allow the computer to
calculate flow requirements.

     Storage tanks were included as node points. During the

Figure 2
Customer and Demand Projection
5-Year

	1984 (Actual)	1985	1986	1987	1988	1989
Total Customers	27,487	28,500	29,500	30,500	31,000	31,700
Avg. Day (MG) Demand	7.42	7.83	8.08	8.30	8.51	8.72
Max. Day (MG) Demand	15.19	15.66	16.16	16.60	17.02	17.44
Peak Hour (MG) Demand	24.16	25.06	25.86	26.56	27.23	27.90
Total Supply (MGD)	15.28	*17.84	17.84	17.84	**19.34	19.34
Total Storage (MG)	6.24	6.24	6.24	6.24	6.24	6.24

* Includes Berkeley Wells No. 33 and 34, and the abandonment of Anchorage and Silver Bay Wells.

** Provides for construction of Berkeley Well No. 35 in 1988.

maximum day analysis, tanks were utilized to establish system pressures. For peak hour analysis the tanks were included to evaluate the impact of each in meeting peak requirements.

Upon establishing a model that appeared adequate, several preliminary computer runs were made at average day demands without the new source. Pressures and flows generated by the program at strategic locations within the system were compared to actual measured values to ensure the validity of the skeletonized model.

In the subject study, results from the preliminary check proved satisfactory. Therefore, the skeleton model was assumed to be correct and a hydraulic analysis of the proposed improvements could commence.

Figures 3a and b provide an example for comparative purposes between the skeleton model and the actual system for an area of the distribution network in South Toms River.

MAXIMUM DAILY DEMAND ANALYSIS

Maximum daily demand is the most important parameter in the design of system supply facilities. The strength of this statement is based upon the aforementioned premise that source capacity must exceed peak day demand.

Of the total number of customers served by Toms River Water Company, 94% are residential. Daily water production in 1984 varied from a minimum of 5.20 MG to a maximum of 15.19 MG, with the average for the year being 7.42 MGD. This wide variation in customer demand is typical for water systems which serve primarily residential customers in temperate climates.

The maximum daily demand for a given year is to some extent a result of coincidence, i.e., more customers watering lawns on a given day, than on the previous or following days. Demands in excess of 90% of the maximum day typically occur only occasionally during the summer months.

For the model simulation of the Toms River system, storage tank elevations were utilized to establish system pressures. However, demands had to be satisfied solely from source capacity.

Flows from ground storage tanks served by wells and dispensed using booster pumps were based upon actual maximum day production measurements for 1984. These flows were assigned as input values at the appropriate node points. Two facilities were utilized during the maximum day analysis, one at the Parkway Station, centrally located; the other at Holly Street Plant, serving the south-central area of the distribution system.

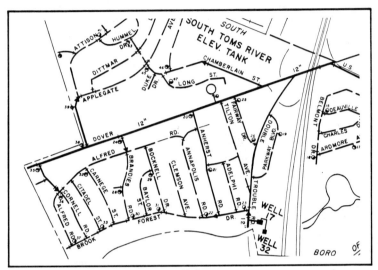

Fig. 3a

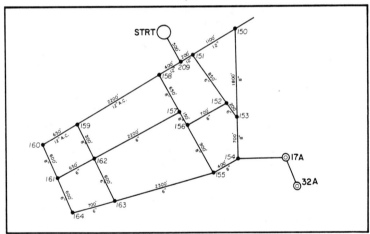

Fig. 3b

Four production wells discharge directly to the distribution system. Two of the wells (Nos. 20 and 31) are located in the northeast portion of the operating area. For the subject analysis, drawdown and capacity data, along with the pump curves for both wells were included in the model. This allowed the simulation to generate production requirements.

The remaining two direct-discharge wells are located in the south-central section of the operating area in a satellite system known as South Toms River. The Borough of South Toms River is a residential area of near-zero growth, being virtually fully developed. Demand loadings were elementary to establish and production capabilities were known. Therefore, flow values could be assigned as input information at a critical node point.

Since the production capacity of the South Toms River wells far exceeded the demand loadings, a forced-flow element transferring water from South Toms River to the remaining system could be included in the model, thus allowing the South Toms River wells to contribute more significantly to meeting peak day demands. In actuality, a booster station is located at the point on the model where the forced-flow element was established. Flows from the booster station are known. This procedure provided further simplification of the skeleton model.

Because the capacity of the proposed supply source was known, the purpose of this exercise was to determine head requirements at peak day demand for well pumps at the new site and to evaluate the impact of the new source on system operation. Both Wells No. 33 and 34 have the capability of producing 1000 gpm or 1.5 MGD each. To meet maximum day demand, it was determined that use of only one of the new wells would be necessary. Again, flow from this well was assigned as an input value at the appropriate node point.

Once system supply information was set, demand loading was adjusted. Since the model contained average day demand information from the preliminary check and because Toms River is so highly residential, a system-wide proportional adjustment could be made to create the higher demand. The 1984 measured maximum day demand was used as criteria for the total system load.

The computer simulation was then initiated. Results from the model analysis are tabulated with those from the peak hour analysis and presented in Figure 4.

From review of the output information, it is evident that Toms River Water Company can meet peak day demands from existing source plus one proposed well. System pressures are adequate to provide satisfactory service at all points in the distribution network without being prohibitively high. Head criteria for the new well pump was noted for comparison with the peak hour analysis.

Figure 4
Simulation Results

Item	Maximum Day Analysis	Peak Hour Analysis
1.) Total System Demand (gpm)	10,610.70	17,500.50
(MGD)	15.29	25.22
2.) Contributing Supply (gpm)		
a.) Well No. 20	494.10	532.50
b.) Well No. 31	558.20	760.00
c.) Well No. 17 (So. Toms River)	700.00	760.00
d.) Well No. 32 (So. Toms River)	700.00	700.00
e.) Parkway Station	4000.00	4681.30
f.) Holly Street Plant	3100.00	3520.70
g.) Proposed Berkeley Wells	1000.00	2000.00
h.) Indian Hill Tank	58.10	215.00
i.) Rte. 37 Tank	—	700.00
j.) So. Toms River Tank	—	235.40
k.) Holiday City Tank	—	1455.70
l.) Windsor Avenue Tank	—	2000.00
Total (gpm)	10,610.40	17,500.60
(MGD)	15.29	25.22
3.) Distribution System Pressures		
a.) High (psi)	110.80	120.50
b.) Low (psi)	25.90	42.00
4.) System Pressure at Proposed Berkeley Well Input Node (psi)	70.90	108.80

PEAK HOUR DEMAND ANALYSIS

Water systems that do not serve large industrial customers typically experience periods of very low and very high demand during any given day. The peak hourly demand is generally much greater than the average flow rate during the day. Peak hours in the Toms River System are historically about 60% higher than the average rate for the day.

For example, if the peak hour requirement were to occur coincidentally on the maximum day; in 1984, the maximum daily demand was 15.19 MG, an average rate of 10,540 gpm. The peak hourly demand was approximately 16,770 gpm.

Peak hours in the Toms River Water Company generally occur between mid and late afternoon of summer days.

To design pumps for the two proposed wells, the units must meet head requirements during a peak hour. The peak hour model was, therefore, adjusted from the maximum day model as follows.

Because Toms River is so highly residential, a system-wide proportional adjustment was made to create the higher demand. The 1984 measured peak hour demand was used as criteria for the total system load.

To meet peak hour demand, both proposed wells were utilized. This flow value was assigned as input information at the appropriate node point.

At Parkway Station and Holly Street Plant, the flow input values from the maximum day model were removed and replaced with the pump curves. Thus, the simulation could generate production requirements.

The five system storage tanks in the model were available for supply contribution. Pressures were specified and flow values requested at two of the tanks, Indian Hill Tank, in the north-central area of the distribution network, and the South Toms River Tank. The remaining facilities are ground storage reservoirs with booster pumping units; the Route 37 Tank, in the south-western section, the Windsor Avenue Tank, in the eastern area and the Holiday City Tank, in the north-central section. Known flow values were input at the critical node for both the Route 37 and Windsor Avenue Tanks. Pump curves for the booster station at Holiday City were included for computer calculation of flow.

Wells No. 20 and 31 were not adjusted. Pump curves were previously included in the maximum day model. Also, the forced-flow element from South Toms River was retained.

The computer simulation was then initiated. Results from

the model analysis are tabulated with those from the maximum day analysis and presented in Figure 4.

From review of the output information, it is evident that Toms River Water Company can meet peak hour demands from existing source and storage plus the two proposed wells. System pressures are adequate to provide satisfactory service at all points in the distribution network without being prohibitively high. System head criteria was established for the two new well pumps. Total Dynamic Head (TDH) can then be calculated through inspection of the well drawdown curve and system head criteria. Thus, the computer model provided the necessary information quickly and accurately to design pumps for the proposed wells and allowed an evaluation of the impact of the new source on system operations.

DISCUSSION

The initial inspection of the output data involved a comparison of all model pump curves with the simulation generated supply values. Flow from each source must be an achieveable figure. If to meet demands, the simulation extended pump curves beyond a reasonable limit, a review of model input information would be warranted before proceeding further. This problem can be especially prevalent when system supplies vary appreciably in capacity and are located sporadically throughout the operating area, as is the case in Toms River. For the subject analysis, calculated flow values were compatible with actual measurements of the capacity at each source. Therefore, confidence in the model was further justified.

With the supply input of the proposed well field a change in the system flow pattern occurred. Head loss through the node connecting elements was reviewed and found to be acceptable. System pressures were within reasonable limits for satisfactory service.

All things considered, the computer model performed within the confidence interval imposed by the equipment and methodology used in measurement. This exercise indicates that a practical degree of accuracy can be attained in modeling distribution networks if careful attention is provided in the skeletonization process. Additionally, computer modeling can be an exceptional tool in the design aspects of water resource engineering.

COMPLICATIONS IN THE DESIGN AND ANALYSIS OF SMALL
WATER DISTRIBUTION SYSTEMS

Joseph H. Shrader*
Associate Member, A.S.C.E.

Introduction

The design and operation of small treatment and distribution
networks can sometimes be more complicated than the design of large
metropolitan systems. More often than not, the use of standard
engineering practices will lead to designs which would not meet
regulatory requirements and would be difficult to operate. For
example, under normal operation, water storage tanks which have
been designed to retain enough water for fire flows could become
stagnant due to the low consumption rates from a small customer base.

In this article, these and other aspects of small water system
design will be investigated and solved through the use of computer
modeling techniques.

Background

At first glance, one might question the economic justification
of small (100-200 customer) municipal water systems. However, some
states, West Virginia in particular, are subdivided into small
entities called Public Service Districts (P.S.D.'s). A P.S.D. may be
no more than one square mile (2.59 km2) in area and have as few as
200 residents, but may apply for funding for $500,000 grants which
in turn may be matched on a dollar for dollar basis on the local
level. As a result, small rural areas which may have been plagued
by polluted groundwater from private wells or seasonal springs are
now in the position to acquire a consultant to design a complete
water system to service their community. Usually, the customer base
for these areas is widespread, and the total grant cost for servicing
an individual residence may be as high as $4,500 to $5,500. Monthly
bills for such systems average $20 to $30 per month, which is quite
high for retired and unemployed persons on fixed incomes. Such is
the case of the Big Four Public Service District located in McDowell
County, West Virginia.

The Big Four P.S.D. is an example of the type of community
described above and will be used throughout this discussion as a
basis for reference. Having a physical area of 1.25 square miles
(3.24 km2) and an estimated population of 300 persons, the P.S.D.

*Office Manager and Project Engineer, Draper-Aden Associates, Inc.,
1407 East Main Street, Princeton, West Virginia 24740

desired to treat and distribute enough water to service approximately
100 customers. A feasibility study illustrated that the most cost
effective system combined drawing raw water through a well from an
abandoned coal mine, treatment through the use of small pressure
filters, and distribution through six inch (152 mm) mains to serve
the system. Other than a small motel and service station, all of
the users in the system are residential.

Tank Design Complications

Several problems surface when designing a small distribution
system with the most problematic being: (1) low fluid flow
velocities in oversized distribution mains, and (2) water stagnation
in storage tanks oversized due to fire flow and emergency storage
requirements. In large systems, the customer base is large enough
to constitute a steady flow through distribution lines and provides
a normal flux in tank level to create adequate mixing of old and new
water.

Most design references estimate that the average water usage for
a normal household with metered service ranges from 100 to 200
gallons per minute (gpm) (379 to 758 lpm).[3] Average design flow
for the Big Four system was set at 150 gallons per capita per day
(gpcd) (569 lpcd). Data derived from recent population surveys
showed 3.11 persons per household, which when combined with the 100
customers, yielded an average daily flow of 46,650 gallons per day
(gpd) (176,804 lpd), or 32 gpm (121 lpm). Since the majority of the
community is composed of retired and fixed income homeowners, both
of these figures were assumed to be sufficient to allow for minor
population growth and for line leakage. Calculation of peak flows
was accomplished by estimating water usage as a percent of average
flow for four individual time segments over a twenty-four hour
period as follows:

Time Interval	Number Of Hours	Estimated Percent Of Total Flow	*GPM (LPM)
6 AM - 11 AM	5	45%	70 (265)
11 AM - 3 PM	4	15%	29 (110)
3 PM - 8 PM	5	35%	54 (205)
8 PM - 6 AM	10	5%	4 (15)

*GPM = (Percent x 46,650)/(# Hours x 60 minutes)

Following the estimation of daily flowrates, the next logical
step in water system design is the calculation of distribution
storage. As mentioned above, one of the most trying design
challenges is the justification of reservoir sizing for a small
system. Illustrated below is a commonly used "normal" design
procedure which just does not work with a small customer base.

Operating Storage (Equalization Requirements)

First, the designer must generate a "hydrograph" which
represents the pattern he feels the system flows will follow. For
the Big Four system, the flowrates derived above were used to
calculate hourly demands and a cummulative demand for the twenty-
four hour period. The average hourly demand (AHD) using this
method was 1,980 gallons (7,504 1).[1]

Second, the cummulative residential demands for each hour are
plotted against a cummulative pumping curve representing the time
period which the water treatment plant is in operation. The result
of the plot graphically produces the amount of storage volume
needed for normal operation of the water system.[1] Our model system
produced a figure of only 25,000 gallons (94,750 1) required for
distribution storage. The water treatment plant was designed to
operate eight hours per day at a constant rate of 120 gpm (455 lpm).
The large flowrate is due to the physical size of the pressure
filters which are used as the filtering media in the treatment
plant. The filters were designed to provide the average daily flow
during an eight hour operating shift.

Emergency Storage Requirements

Requirements for emergency storage for small systems is at
most a quessing game. Due to the unreliability of an abandoned mine
as a raw water source, one must assume the worst conditions when
calculating emergency storage volumes. Other factors which might
affect emergency storage are time delays in shipping replacement
parts for a piece of defective equipment or belated identification
of actual problems with the plant, due to the lack of an operator
being present at the plant during the entire shift. In any event,
the minimum time period for calculating emergency storage was
assumed to be two days. At the average daily flow of 150 gpcd
(569 lpcd), the emergency storage required for the Big Four system
is 93,300 gallons (353,607 1).

Fire Storage Requirements

In small communities, a value of 400 to 600 gpm (1,516 to
2,274 lpm) per hydrant is usually assumed adequate for fire flow.[1]
Fire duration is also an important factor for calculating fire
storage; in Big Four a duration of two hours was selected on the
basis of the actual size and location of the structures in the
system. Meaning that most of the dwellings in the community are not
large enough to burn for two hours and are often separated by a lot
of land, rather than being located extremely close together. Using
a fire flow of 500 gpm (1,895 lpm) and the above duration, the fire
storage required for the system is 60,000 gallons (227,400 1).

Summing all of the above recommended storage volumes yields a
total of 238,300 gallons (903,157 1) required to serve the system or,
in using standard tank sizes, 250,000 gallons (947,500 1). Upon
initial observation, this size tank does not seem uncommon; however,

one must realize that the calculated average hourly demand is only
1,980 gallons (7,504 1). If this hourly demand holds true and,
barring no fires,it would take the community over five days to
utilize all the water in the tank without the treatment plant
supplementing the storage volume. Realistically, for an older
community such as Big Four, the initial flow assumptions are
probably high, along with the persons per residence figure. If
this holds true, the designed tank would not be drained for six
to eight days, which if adequately chlorinated would be safe to
drink but has the posssibility of developing taste and odor problems
from the lack of fresh, aerated water being consistently introduced
into the tank.

At this point in time, the engineer must make the decision on
a realistic storage volume for the tank. Unfortunately, more often
than not economics will dictate tank sizes due to limited funds
available for construction. As in the case of the Big Four system,
in order to construct a distribution system to serve enough
residents to make the project economically feasible, a tank size of
100,000 gallons (379,000 1) was chosen. This size tank is adequate
to handle operational storage, but allows only 75,000 gallons
(284,250 1) for emergency situations.

Line Design Complications

In addition to problems dealing with sizing storage tanks,
small customer bases also lead to problems with fluid flow
velocities in distribution lines. For example, the main
distribution line into the Big Four system from the water treatment
plant is a six inch (152 mm) line. At the plant maximum pumping
rate of 120 gpm (455 lpm), the fluid velocity through the line is
approximately 1.3 feet per second (fps) (.4 mps). The standard
scouring velocity for flow in pipelines is usually recognized as
2.0 fps (.61 mps).[2] Such a low velocity in a distribution main
leads to even lower velocities in six inch (152 mm) service mains
and branch lines which serve fewer residences and thus have lower
flowrates. The major concern over low fluid velocity in water
lines is sediment deposition. Over a period of years, a six inch
line can choke itself and create major operational problems.

Only two possible solutions exist to increase the flow through
water lines. (1) Increase the flow rate, or (2) decrease the pipe
size. The first solution will not work since the plant output is
constant when operational. Due to line size requirements for fire
hydrants, the second solution will not work either. The outcome:
live with the problem. Since neither of the above alternatives are
adequate, sedimentation problems will have to be dealt with on an
operational basis. Regular flushing of distribution lines will
have to be a common occurence for this size system. However, since
there are different flows through different lines, the question
arises of which lines need flushing more often?

Another problem in dealing with a small, single tank network
is low pressure areas at the far reaches of the distribution system.

This is usually not as great a problem in larger systems due to
multiple tanks and booster stations. However, for a total gravity
fed system, placement of the storage tank at the proper elevation
to insure adequate pressures at all points in the system is a major
concern. Spending an immense amount of time churning through
hydraulic calculations is both costly and an inefficient use of
time to the engineer, but what other way is there?

The Solution - Computer Modeling

In the past several years, the use of the computer model has
greatly enhanced the design and operation of water distribution
systems. When the first modeling programs were introduced, most
dealt with only steady-state analysis during a single instant of
time. However, now computer models have advanced to both steady
and transient analyses and allow variation of parameters such as
flowrates, pressures, etc. to fluctuate with time. The result of
such a model allows the engineer to design a system, then observe
how the system will operate under a varying array of conditions.
Output for most programs includes pressures, velocities and
flowrates for pipe lengths and junction points along with tank
levels, pump operating conditions, valve positions, etc.

In order to solve the previous design problems with the Big
Four system, it became necessary to develop a computer model to
answer the following questions:

1. At what elevation should the water storage tank be to
   provide adequate pressures throughout the distribution
   system?

2. Given a variety of flow conditions, which distribution
   mains will have to be flushed the most often due to low
   fluid velocity?

The major point the engineer must take into consideration
during the development of a model is how flowrates from the
customer base will fluctuate during a normal day. Most modeling
programs allow the user to input actual "profiles" which represent
the change in user consumption throughout a normal day. In doing
so, the engineer can watch his system at work, i.e. see tanks
draining and filling, pumps turning on and off, etc.

In the case of the Big Four system, it became necessary to
manipulate the tank overflow elevation to determine the optimum
level at which the entire distribution system would have adequate
service pressures. Also, by manipulating combinations of flow
profiles in conjunction with the plant operation, it was possible
to observe how the tank water level and flow velocities in the
distribution lines were affected. By observing the various
flowrates through the system, it was obvious which distribution
lines would have to be flushed the most frequently. To study fire
flows, computer models allow the user to "open up" hydrants during
the analysis to simulate a fire in one or several different areas

of the community. This capacity allows the designer to further
determine how long the tank will supply water with a fire and normal
consumption flows. During the simulation for this system, it was
noticed that for a prolonged fire it would become necessary to
start up the water plant to supplement flows in the system.

A further example of how a model can be used is the case of
the oversized storage tank. For example, if the Big Four P.S.D.
had adequate moneys and was planning a future expansion to their
distribution system, they could have decided to construct a larger
tank. The previously stated situation with water stagnation in
the tank could become a problem. The computer model could be used
to determine if the water plant would have to be run more often to
supplement aged water in the tank with a fresh supply. This could
be accomplished by watching the tank level during a simulation and
checking to see whether the water volume is receiving an adequate
turnover.

Conclusions

The design and analysis of small water distribution systems
can be more complicated than the design of larger systems. Many
times due to the small customer bases standard design methods and
procedures yield unreasonable figures and lead to systems which are
difficult to operate. However, the evolvement of computer modeling
programs has simplified the design of such small systems to a much
easier task. Engineers may not only use their models to design the
system but also may use field data collected after the project is
constructed to further refine their design and simplify system
operation. Many small systems, such as the Big Four Water System
described throughout this article, could have been left with
oversized distribution lines and insufficient service pressures had
it not been the decision of the engineer to use computer modeling
techniques.

References

1. Clark, John W., Viessman, Warren Jr., Hammer, Mark J., Water
    Supply and Pollution Control, Third Edition, Harper & Row,
    New York, NY, 1977.

2. Merrit, Frederick S., Standard Handbook for Civil Engineers,
    Second Edition, McGraw-Hill Book Company, New York, NY, 1976.

3. Metcalf and Eddy, Inc., Wastewater Engineering: Collection,
    Treatment & Disposal, McGraw-Hill Book Company, New York, NY,
    1972.

Water System Model Brought Improvements
in System Performance

Darrell K. Stapleton, P.E.
Member, ASCE

INTRODUCTION

Analysis of the hydraulic conditions of a multi-pressure zone
water system serving portions of two counties in a mountainous region
of Southwest Virginia was performed using computerized modeling techniques. The model was calibrated by performing selected system operations tests. Problems revealed in the calibration process led to
system improvements resulting in savings in both operation and maintenance costs.

SYSTEM DECRIPTION

In the late 1960's, the need for central water distribution and
treatment facilities became apparent in Buchanan County, Virginia.
Very few of the population of the County were being served by central
systems at that time. The quality of the available water was poor,
having high concentrations of iron and sulphur.

After extensive studies of the area, it was found that a sufficient supply of water for the County's needs was not available within
the County. However, the John Flannagan Reservoir, a flood control
project, in adjoining Dickenson County, had created a supply large
enough to meet the County's needs in the foreseeable future.

The cost effective solution to the problem is what is now called
the Bi-County Water System, shown in Exhibit I, owned and operated by
the Buchanan County Public Service Authority. This system is composed
of approximately 80 miles (50 km) of water pipelines in sizes from 1"
(25 mm) to 16" (406 mm), several pumping stations and tanks. Exhibit
II shows the profile of the main transmission line.

PROBLEM

Initially, the system for transmitting water from Flannagan Reservoir into Buchanan County was designed for the projected water demands
on the system for the year 2020. Therefore, lines, valves, and pumps
were designed for flow rates greatly exceeding initial demands. In
many cases, this meant throttling back pumps to more closely match the
initial capacity of the water treatment plant. Due to extreme elevation differences between ridgetops and valley floors, in-line pressure
reducing stations were required. These stations were also designed for
ultimate system flows.

*Thompson & Litton, Inc., P. O. Box 1307, Wise, Virginia   24293

311

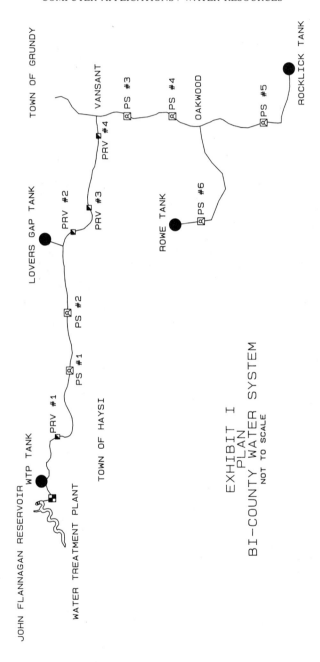

EXHIBIT I
PLAN
BI-COUNTY WATER SYSTEM
NOT TO SCALE

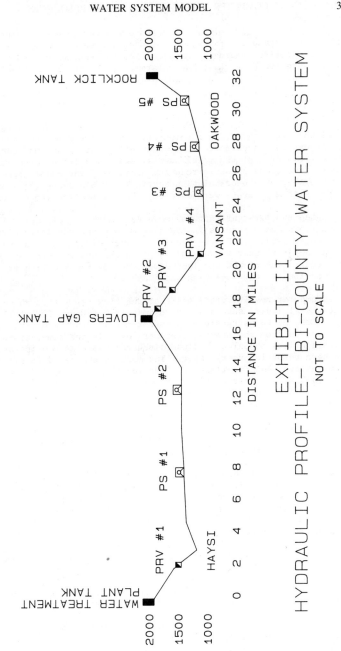

EXHIBIT II

HYDRAULIC PROFILE- BI-COUNTY WATER SYSTEM

NOT TO SCALE

Within two years of system start-up, several recurring problems had become apparent. Excessive amounts of treated water were being lost due to line breakage. Repair costs for replacing gasket sets in pressure reducing valves were large. Also, the local electrical utility rates were increasing rapidly.

SOLUTIONS

At this time, Buchanan County decided to employ an engineer to model the water system on a computer. The purpose of modeling the system was to discover means of reducing operating and maintenance costs. Features of the model used allowed simulating the system's pumps, tanks, and pressure reducing stations. The model chosen for use was LIQVARS, by Stoner Solution Services, in Lancaster, PA. After all of the system elements were entered, the calibration process was begun.

When the first attempt was made to run the model, several of the known flows and pressures in the system were substantially different from those predicted by the model. As each discrepancy was examined, it was apparent that valves and pumps in the system were improperly adjusted. Each of the problems discovered by the modeling procedure is described in the following paragraphs.

Computer results predicted that the flow rates through pumping stations #1 and #2 should be approximately 3,200 gpm (202 1/s). Actual flow with the pumps running was approximately 2,600 gpm (164 1/s). Pump curves from the manufacturer were used in the simulation. Field investigations revealed that the discharge valve at pumping station #2 had been throttled nearly shut. The model was altered to simulate trimming the pump impeller back from 16-1/2" (419 mm) diameter to 13-1/2" (343 mm). After running this simulation, a smaller pump impeller was installed, resulting in significant monthly electrical cost reduction. Wear on the discharge valve was also reduced.

When simulating the portion of the system from the Lover's Gap Tank down into Vansant, solution problems arose in the model. Three 12" (305 mm) diameter pressure reducing stations are installed on this portion of the system. These valves are denoted PRV #2, #3, and #4. Initial flow rates through these stations are less than one-half of the design flow rate. Due to this problem, the 12" (305 mm) pressure reducing valves were operating in the 1 to 2% open range. Excessive wear on leather seats and O-ring seals resulted, causing a high failure rate at these stations. Failure of these stations was causing line breakage and damage to associated equipment. Also, the pressure reducing valves were being overhauled about twice a year. The maintenance costs associated with these three stations were estimated at greater than $30,000 annually.

It was decided to install a smaller diameter pressure reducing valve in a bypass line at each station to solve this problem. The computer model used allows the designer to choose a pressure reducing valve by setting a very small diameter for the new pressure reducing valve. When the model solves the valve, it gives a factor which may be multiplied by the area of the small valve to give the area of the valve to be used. Using this method with the initial flow rates to the system, a 4" bypass valve size was selected. Since installing the 4" bypass pressure reducing valves in stations 2, 3, and 4, no valve failures have resulted.

In the Oakwood area of the system, the suction pressure at pumping station #5 was checked in the field and found to be much lower than the model predicted it should be. This resulted in lower pumping rates and longer pumping times. It was suspected that a valve was partially closed. Field testing was performed to isolate the problem. Pressures were tested at several fire hydrants in the line, and the hydraulic grade line checked against model results. The closed valve was located in this manner, opened fully; and then the model predicted the pressure very accurately.

RESULTS AND CONCLUSIONS

Changes made to equipment and operating techniques resulted in savings of electricity and manpower. Costs for parts replacement and service interruption have also been reduced.

In conclusion, a computer model of a water system aids the hydraulic engineer in pinpointing problems, even when the system is complex with many pressure zones. Calibrating the model requires an understanding of the way in which the system is being operated. Often, this understanding of system operation leads the engineer to conclusions which suggest improvements that may reduce costs. In this case, Buchanan County was able to recover the cost of modeling the system in the first month of operation after installing the proposed changes.

Quantifying Social and Environmental Objectives

Benjamin F. Hobbs[1], Aff. ASCE, and Eugene Z. Stakhiv[2], Aff. ASCE

Abstract: Over the past decade, there have been great improvements in economic and multiobjective techniques for quantifying social and environmental objectives in water resources planning. Nevertheless, problems remain. Among others, they include: application of methods that are inappropriate to the decision making style of the agency; use of value scales and weights in multiobjective analysis that lack the properties that theory requires of them; and inadequate information on the pros and cons of different methods. The purpose of this paper is to give an overview of quantification methods and their use.

Introduction

The National Environmental Policy Act of 1969 dramatically changed the planning procedures of federal agencies. Environmental and social objectives and impacts are now to be given careful consideration in any major federal action significantly affecting the environment. Further, as interpreted by the 1971 Calvert Cliffs' decision (449 F.2d), NEPA mandates that alternatives be compared using "a rather finely tuned and 'systematic' balancing analysis." This has spurred the development of methods for quantifying social and environmental objectives.

These methods have been developed by theorists in economics and multiobjective decision making, with each discipline leaving its distinctive stamp. Economists have refined the techniques of benefit-cost analysis so that many environmental and social effects that were previously ignored in project evaluation can now be monetized. For those effects that are not easily measured in terms of dollars, the tools of multiobjective analysis can help. They enable planners to better understand the tradeoffs that exist between economic and other objectives and to make tradeoff decisions more systematic and defensible.

We believe that a major reason for past misapplication of these methods has been the absence of information on their relative strengths and weaknesses. The purpose of this paper is to give an overview of approaches to quantifying environmental and social objectives, emphasizing methods useful to water planners. Before doing so, criteria for evaluating quantification methods are proposed and the institutional setting for water resources planning is described. We express a number of opinions that are intended to be controversial; our goal is to provoke discussion of the many remaining problems and issues involved with quantification and to alert the reader that quantification is not merely a matter of mechanical application of proven methods.

[1] Assistant Prof., Dept. Systems Engineering, Case Western Reserve University, Cleveland, Ohio 44106.

[2] Senior Policy Analyst, Institute of Water Resources, U.S. Army Corps of Engineers, Ft. Belvoir, Va. 22152.

Criteria for Evaluating Methods: Deciding How to Decide

There is a wide, indeed, a bewildering variety of methods available for quantifying and making decisions with social and environmental objectives. How can, for example, field planners for the U.S. Army Corps of Engineers decide which methods are best for their planning problem? We suggest four criteria [see also 3,9,10]:

1. Appropriateness. Is the method appropriate to the problem in terms of (a) the types of value judgments it asks of decision makers, (b) the types of alternatives it can consider (e.g., discrete vs. a continuous range, few vs. many objectives), (c) the type of data available (e.g., certain vs. uncertain, qualitative vs. quantitative), (d) whether it can accomodate multiple decision makers and viewpoints, and (e) the forms of evaluations it yields? Also, is the method appropriate, considering the dominant decision making philosophy of the organization and where in the planning process the method will be used?

2. Ease of Use. Is the method flexible, allowing use by planners with varying abilities and training? How much effort and knowledge is required to obtain data and apply the method? Are computer codes, if needed, available and inexpensive to use?

3. Validity. Are the underlying axioms of the method consistent with the structure of the decision maker's values and/or with generally accepted theory? Are evaluations of alternatives by decision makers and interest groups accurately predicted by the method? Are the choices made by the method, if any, efficient and the algorithm logically sound?

4. Results Compared to Other Methods. Do the method's results differ significantly from those of other techniques? If so, then considerations of validity become more important.

It is clear that choosing a quantification method is itself a multiobjective problem [3], and a difficult one at that. Methods that perform well under some criteria usually have shortcomings in others. Further, method characteristics that are virtues in some environmental impact assessment situations are often vices in others [25]. Finally, theoreticians disagree among themselves and with practitioners as to which criteria are most important and how the various methods actually perform against them. No wonder practicing engineers often throw up their hands and decide to use whatever method happens to be most convenient!

The last aspect of appropriateness -- consistency with the agency's decision making style -- may be the one most often ignored, leading to misapplication of methods. For this reason, we discuss the institutional setting of water resources planning in the next section. (For an alternative discussion, see Goicoechea et al. [7].)

Federal Water Resources Planning Institutions and Procedures

Since the Flood Control Act of 1936, which declared that no project shall be built unless the benefits, to whomsoever they accrue, exceed the costs, benefit-cost analysis (BCA) has played a central role in water resources planning. To be sure, BCA has not been the most important factor in the planning process -- the dominant force has been, and will continue to be, local objectives ("problems and opportunities"). Nonetheless, BCA set up a hurdle that all projects have had to cross: that the benefit-cost ratio exceed 1. (It must be admitted, however, that prior to 1973 the height of that hurdle was often unfairly shaved by the use of questionable methods, such as the inclusion of secondary benefits but not secondary costs.) BCA also helped improve projects, by showing what modifications of project plans would be economic.

BCA, by its nature, excluded less tangible considerations. The fear that social and environmental objectives were being short-changed lead to the establishment by the U.S. Water Resources Council in 1973 of the "Principles and Standards for Planning Water and Land Resources" (P&S). Consistent with NEPA, the P&S raised Environmental Quality (EQ) to the status of a co-objective with National Economic Development (NED) (i.e., net economic benefits); in addition, Social Well-Being (SWB) and Regional Economic Development (RED) accounts for displaying information on social and local economic impacts were established.

The P&S intended that multiobjective analysis would become the heart of the project evaluation process. But rarely did that actually happen. Environmental impact statements, instead of being the forum for the balancing of objectives, became, for the most part, merely a means for planning mitigation measures. This was because water planners were confused. The first reason for this confusion was the lack of readily available and operational multiobjective methods which were compatible with the diverse needs of water resources planning. The analytical basis for multiobjective evaluation was well-developed [e.g., 3,7,8] but its practical usefulness was not always apparent at the field agency level. A second reason was the proliferation of environmental laws and regulations during the 1970's. Interpretation of these laws was inconsistent among agencies and many new ideas were introduced, making it difficult to absorb and adapt to the rapid growth in requirements. A final reason was the lack of guidance as to how to integrate local goals with the federal planning objectives; Lord [17] found that this problem was one of the key impediments to the under standing and implementation of the P&S.

The adoption of the "Principles and Guidelines" (P&G) [24] in 1983 dethroned EQ as a co-equal objective with NED. Like RED and SWB, EQ is now merely an account. Basically, the final decision rule is: maximize net benefits, as defined by the P&G accounting procedures, subject to environmental constraints.

Nevertheless, the multiobjective approach to quantifying social and environmental objectives has not been thrown on the trash heap. It still plays an important part in the environmental impact statement process. Multiobjective analysis can be used in this preliminary phase of planning to help winnow out alternatives that overly compromise environmental and social objectives. Then, the alternative maximizing net benefits can be chosen from the few remaining options. This win nowing process does not merely consist of the screening of alternatives that would violate environmental laws. Federal water planners have imposed more stringent environmental constraints when they felt it was appropriate. Unfortunately, these constraints have been applied with little consideration as to how they would affect other objectives.

This disregarding of tradeoffs appears contrary to the balancing process envisioned by the Calvert Cliffs' decision. That case concern ed a power plant impact statement written by the Atomic Energy Commis sion. The plaintiffs asserted, among other things, that the state ment did not adequately consider the water quality impacts of the plant because it only noted that the facility would satisfy pollution laws. The judge ruled that the existence of pollution regulations did not excuse the agency from having to weigh carefully all environmental effects against the facility's benefits. It is not enough that a proposed project satisfy environmental laws; the planning process must also have considered any and all significant tradeoffs between environmental, cost, and social objectives. To quote the Council on Environmental Quality [23,Section 1502.23]:

> "To assess the adequacy of compliance ... , the statement shall, when a cost benefit analysis is prepared, discuss the relationship between that analysis and any analyses of unquantified environmental impacts, values and amenities."

This principle is applied by many federal agencies, including the Corps of Engineers, in their regulatory decisions. But federal water project planners have yet to embrace it.

It must be noted that economic and multiobjective methods are not the only formal approaches used to analyze social and environmental objectives. Agencies which regulate health risks, such as the Occupational Safety and Health Administration, the Environmental Protection Agency, and the Nuclear Regulatory Commission, often deemphasize the economic impacts of the standards they set to focus primarily on the health and environmental implications. The Delaney clause, which mandates the banning of any food additive found to cause cancer in animals, is an extreme example of this mode of decision making. There, no compromise with economic objectives is allowed.

Economic Methods for Quantifying Social and Environmental Objectives

"The prime objective of public water resource development is often stated as the maximization of national welfare" [18]. Since "national welfare" is a general, non-measurable term, much as ecosystem stability is, economists have substituted "national income", which at least is partially measurable. Partially, because many less tangible aspects of the 'quality of life' -- including social and environmental goals -- are difficult to measure. If planners and economists are willing to pursue maximization of national income as a measure of national welfare, then the implication is that society is indifferent as to who the recipients of the benefits and bearers of the costs are. If winners could, in theory, compensate the losers, then NED is being maximized -- even though, in reality, such compensation is rarely made.

Economic efficiency is a concept which troubles many environmental scientists charged with the stewardship of public resources. By emphasizing this important, albeit incomplete concern of the Federal interest in resource use and environmental amenities, one gets the impression that the ideas embody a disregard for human concerns and an inherent diminution of natural amenities. By extolling the virtues of efficiency, in economic terms, economists are reflecting the ideal of an allocation of resources or goods which cannot be changed to make some citizens better off while at the same time making no one else worse off. In practice, of course, even efficient policies work to the disadvantage of someone. This should not detract from the overall theoretical evaluation construct, as long as equity, in the form of compensation, is factored into decision making. Compensation can come in four forms: (1) add-on compensation, such as habitat mitigation; (2) direct consideration of equity objectives through, for example, the RED and SWB accounts; (3) delineation of fixed minimal criteria by which investments will be judged; or (4) combination of all three.

Part of the conflict between the attitudes of economists and environmental scientists stems from the promotion of economic efficiency approaches for setting basic standards for water and air quality as well as for health and safety concerns. It is argued that the efficiency approach to environmental regulation fails to consider moral and intangible factors in public decision making. Further, use of BCA as the measurement/accounting arm of an economic efficiency philosophy inherently elevates its role to that of the foremost decision criterion rather than simply as one additional decision-aiding tool, along with, for example, environmental impact assessment [22]. Thus, environmental scientists often feel more comfortable with the setting of absolute standards than with the economic ideas of tradeoffs and efficiency. Such standard setting is consistent with the conservative approach to resources decision making advanced by Ciriacy-Wantrup [2], in which the uncertain possibilities of irreversible damage to critical environmental resources fosters the notion of 'safe minimum standards.'

Economists well recognize that the traditional tools of BCA fail to adequately treat social and environmental objectives. As most economists view it, the problem is not that it is inherently impossible to quantify those objectives monetarily, only that it is difficult, sometimes exceedingly so, to do so. The source of the difficulty is seen as being 'market failure': the inability of the market to provide prices for all goods and services that reflect their true scarcity value to society. The prices for some goods are biased, because of, e.g., the market's failure to force manufacturers to consider the pollution costs it imposes on others in its production decisions. The economist's solution? To adjust price to account for the social cost of the externality. Prices fail to exist for other goods and resources, such as clean water, because of the inability to create efficient markets when it is difficult to assign property rights and exclude nonowners from enjoyment of the good or resource. The economist's solution in that instance? To estimate 'shadow prices' equal to the sum of people's marginal willingness to pay for the resource.

The specific techniques the economist uses to monetize environmental and social goals must often be specifically tailored to the problem. The reader is referred to the articles by Hyman [12] and Fisher and Peterson [5] for excellent reviews of the state-of-the-art. Several general approaches can be noted. All are permitted, if not necessarily widely used, under the P&G. A now classic technique is Clawson's travel cost method for estimating demand curves for recreational resources (see [15] for an application). Another, more recent approach is hedonic pricing, in which the value of a common property resource or service is estimated from statistical analysis of the price of a secondary good, such as real property, that is associated with the resource or service. This approach has been used to evaluate unpriced environmental goods such as clean water and flood control. A problem with this approach, uncovered by Kunreuther [16] in his work on flood control, is that people's perceptions (and thus the market's evaluation) of the environmental risks associated with real property are often badly biased. A third method evaluates the worth of a resource as the cost of the probable alternative -- e.g., the avoided cost of thermal power, which is often used as the benefit of hydropower under the P&G. This principle has been used to help evaluate the opportunity cost of damming the Snake River by defining a probable alternative as river rafting and estimating the worth of that activity [15].

Contingent evaluation is a fourth approach to evaluating environmental resources. It directly quizzes people as to their willingness
to pay for the resource in question. One problem with the approach is
the tendency of people (1) to understate their true valuation of goods
they perceive they might have to pay for and (2) to overstate the worth
of goods whose cost will be borne by others. Several clever strategems
for preventing such 'game playing' have been developed. Yet this
approach still causes psychologists to grind their teeth. To them,
hypothecality and instrumental biases remain a problem. Experiments
have shown that people's expressed preferences, such as willingness to
pay, can be unstable and strongly dependent on seemingly irrelevant
aspects of question phrasing and context. Fischhoff et al. [4] argue
that this is likely to be a severe problem when respondents doen't know
what they want. This, in turn, is probable when problems are non-
routine, complex, and involve strongly held but conflicting values --
which is almost always the case in water resources planning!

An important environmental and social objective that economists
have tried to monetize is human life. Sharefkin et al. [21] have
reviewed the many estimates that have appeared in the literature and
their theoretical and empirical bases. The estimates they found ranged
between $59,000 and $10,120,000 per life. For some decisions, this
range alone may be sufficient to eliminate some alternatives; but for
others, the decision will depend on which technique is used to estimate
the value of life and which value is adopted.

Multiobjective Methods for Quantifying Social/Environmental Objectives

No doubt multiobjective theorists shake their heads at some of the
heroic, but often ineffectual efforts made by economists to monetize
non-market goods such as human life. Multiobjective analysts agree
that the root of the problem is market failure; but they feel that the
economist's cure may make the problem worse by obfuscating the true
nature of the choice. Depending on the problem, the choice is really
between lives and investment cost, or clean water and agricultural
production -- not between dollars and dollars. Converting environmental and social objectives into dollars, it is argued, puts the
decision making power into the hands of analysts who, in a applying a
supposedly 'scientific' method, are forced to make value judgments and
arbitrary assumptions that should rightfully be made by the officials
responsible for the decision. The analyst's role should be one of
describing the tradeoffs that exist among objectives and helping to
structure the decision maker's thinking concerning what tradeoffs are
desirable and which goals are most important.

The multiobjective theorist also disagrees with those who view the
measurement of environmental quality as being 'scientific' and 'objective'. Any index of 'environmental quality' involves many incommen-
surable dimensions -- human life, ecosystem stability, aesthetics, etc.
[20]. Even the creation of an index for a narrowly defined portion of
the environment, such as water quality, necessitates subjective evaluations. The combination of different types of pollutants, each with
different kinds and degrees of effects, into a water quality index is
not merely a factual decision; judgments -- value judgments -- of the
relative importance of health, ecologic, recreation, cost, and aesthetic factors are required. Multiobjective theorists prefer to view the
environmental assessment problem as one of explicating tradeoffs and

making value judgments, preferably quantitative ones.

Multiobjective methods serve two purposes in impact assessment: prescription and description. The object of prescription is to indicate which alternative(s) should be preferred, given the impacts of the alternatives, the values of the decision makers, and presuppositions as to what constitutes rational decision-making. Multiobjective methods are also used to describe tradeoffs between objectives by showing the location of alternatives on plots whose axes are the different objectives. Another important descriptive role is to show what the priorities of different interest groups are and what their choices would be [e.g., 13]. The U.S. Bureau of Reclamation has successfully used multiobjective analysis for this purpose [1].

The multiobjective approach has become an important part of many impact assessments, and many multiobjective methods have been proposed and applied for this purpose [see, e.g, 9,11,19]. They differ widely in terms of the criteria outlined above for evaluating quantification methods. Particularly disturbing is the mounting evidence that which alternative appears best in a multiobjective analysis will often depend on which method is used. Hence, those who use a multiobjective technique in environmental impact assessment should carefully consider which method is most appropriate for their situation. Only a handful of the many methods available can be discussed here; those that seem particularly appropriate to water resources planning are emphasized.

The object of generation methods is to display the tradeoffs among alternatives or between the interests of different societal groups [3]. Although they have found some application to water resources systems, particularly to problems that can be formulated as mathematical programs, what may be called multicriteria or multiattribute methods [7] have been more popular. The latter approaches go beyond simple portrayal of tradeoffs. They are often used to construct indices of environmental quality (e.g., air quality indices) and to choose among options by screening, ranking, or simply picking the 'best' alternative. Each of these methods accomplish three basic tasks. The first is attribute scaling, in which a single impact (e.g., ppm BOD or families displaced) is converted into a measure of value. Also, in some applications, scaling is used to capture decision maker attitudes towards risk. The second is attribute weighting, in which each attribute's 'importance' is assessed. The final task is amalgamation of the weighted and scaled attributes via a decision rule, yielding an indicator of overall value or a ranking of alternatives. Another step that all applications should include, although many fail to do so, is a verification of the assumptions the chosen method makes about the structure of the decision maker's values. As mentioned above, methods are often chosen not because they are most appropriate and valid, but because they are handy and there is little information readily available on the pros and cons of different techniques.

In scaling, either value scaling or utility scaling can be used. Value scaling translates the physical attribute into a measure of value by asking decision makers, in one way or another, for subjective judgments of the worth of different levels of the attribute. In general, it is important that the resulting scales be on an interval level of measurement (i.e., differences between numbers are meaningful). Unfortunately, this property is rarely checked by practitioners. Utility scaling in addition measures decision maker attitudes towards risk by having decision makers choose among hypothetical gambles [see 14]

Attitudes towards risk are important to measure when: (1) decision makers are not risk-neutral (that is, when faced with a situation involving risk, such as possible dam failure, the expected value of a gamble does not provide sufficient information for evaluation); (2) risks are present and have been quantified; and (3) decision makers can respond meaningfully to hypothetical gambles. Unfortunately, risks are not often quantified and people frequently give inconsistent responses that depend strongly on how gamble questions are framed. Therefore, utility scaling is rarely to be preferred to value scaling.

Weights are the means by which many multiobjective methods determine how much of one attribute a person is willing to give up for another. For example, many environmental quality indices are based on the weighting-summation decision rule, in which scaled attributes are weighted and summed to obtain an overall index. Under that rule, if someone is just willing to give up 1 unit of scaled attribute i in order to obtain an improvement of 2 units in scaled attribute j, the weight of i must be twice that of j. If the ratio of the two weights differs from 2, the rule will then incorrectly show that the person is either willing to give up more than 1 unit of i for 2 of j or is unwilling to give up even that 1 unit -- either case being a distortion of that person's preferences. The result can be a decision that is not really preferred based on the tradeoffs that person is willing to make.

Several approaches to weight selection are available. Direct or "magic number" methods ask people to directly assess each attribute's importance (e.g., on a scale of 0 to 10), while other techniques infer weights from tradeoffs people say they are willing to make. A third approach, the holistic method, uses multiple regression or linear programs to solve for weights that best imitate unaided subjective evaluations of alternatives. A number of water resources and environmental studies have used the direct [e.g., 1], tradeoff [e.g., 6,14] and holistic [e.g., 13] approaches. These techniques can differ greatly in their appropriateness, ease of use, validity, and, perhaps most worrisome of all, the weights and decisions they yield [10]. In particular, direct weighting, the most common method, often fails to yield weights that correspond to tradeoffs people are willing to make.

Decision rules amalgamate scaled attributes and weights into a single index or ranking of alternatives. Available rules differ in terms of the assumptions they make about the structure of people's values. For example, some rules , such as weighting summation, focus on tradeoffs people are willing to make, while others, such as goal programming, emphasize minimization of 'distance' from desired goals. Weighting summation is probably the most commonly used decision rule in federal environmental assessments [e.g., 1,11]. Another common rule is exclusionary screening, in which alternatives that are unsatisfactory in any single objective are dropped from consideration. Other rules include the multiplicative form of decision analysis, which can include attitudes towards risk [14] and ELECTRE, a type of concordance analysis [6,7]. In ELECTRE, one alternative is said to 'outrank' another if it is better in a sufficiently large number of attributes without being too inferior in any one of the other attributes. ELECTRE yields a subset of alternatives that are, in a sense, incomparable because each of them is not 'outranked' by any other alternative. In water resources planning, ELECTRE can be useful in the screening phase of analysis; more data can then be collected on the remaining subset of alternatives, which can then be subjected to more careful analysis using, say, weighting-summation or benefit-cost analysis.

Unfortunately, all multiobjective methods, except for generation and display techniques [3], suffer from the same problem that pesters the economist's 'willingness to pay' method: unless the decision is in the 'habitual domain' of the decision makers, they won't know what they want. As a result, weights and value scales will often be unreliable, being more reflective of accidental aspects of question phrasing and context than of the values actually held by decision makers.

Conclusion

We have briefly summarized several methods of economics and multiobjective decision making that can be used to quantify social and environmental objectives in water resources planning. The reader must be warned that our descriptions may be no more than caricatures. Each approach has complications and subtleties that cannot possibly be included a survey as brief as ours. We urge those who are interested to dig into the literature and arrive at their own conclusions as to which methods are best for them. If we have impressed the reader with the diversity of methods available and with the importance of choosing and applying a technique thoughtfully, we have succeeded in our (unquantified!) objective.

Disclaimer

Any opinions expressed are the authors' and are not necessarily those of the U.S. Army Corps of Engineers.

Appendix.--References

1. Brown, C.A., "The Central Arizona Water Control Study: A Success Story for Multiobjective Planning and Public Involvement," Water Resources Bulletin, Vol. 20, No. 4, July, 1984.
2. Ciriacy-Wantrup, S.V., Resource Conservation Economics and Policies, University of California Press, Berkeley, Calif., 1952.
3. Cohon, J.L., Multiobjective Programming and Planning, Academic Press, New York, N.Y., 1978.
4. Fischhoff, B.L., Slovic, P., and Lichtenstein, S., "Knowing What You Want: Measuring Labile Values," Cognitive Processes in Choice and Decision Behavior, T. Wallsten, ed., Erlbaum Associates, Hillsdale, N.J., 1979.
5. Fisher, A.C., and Peterson, F.M., "The Environment in Economics: A Survey," Journal of Economic Literature, 1975, pp. 1-29.
6. Gershon, M.E., and Duckstein, L., "Multiobjective Approaches to River Basin Planning," Journal of Water Resources Planning and Management, Vol. 109, No. 1, 1983, pp. 13-28.
7. Goicoechea, A., Hansen, D.R., and Duckstein, L., Multiobjective Decision Analysis with Engineering and Business Applications, J. Wiley, New York, N.Y., 1982.
8. Haimes, Y.Y., Hierarchical Analyses of Water Resources Systems, McGraw-Hill, N.Y., 1977.
9. Hobbs, B.F., "Choosing How to Choose: Comparing Amalgamation Methods for Environmental Impact Assessment," Environmental Impact Assessment Review, Vol. 5, No. 3, 1985, forthcoming.
10. Hobbs, B.F., "What We Can Learn from Experiments in Multiple Crite-

ria Decision Making: An Example," Decision Making with Multiple Objectives, Y.Y. Haimes and V. Chankong, eds., Springer-Verlag, Berlin, 1985.

11. Hobbs, B.F., Rowe, M.D., Pierce, B.L., and Meier, P.M., "Comparisons of Methods for Evaluating Multiattributed Alternatives in Environmental Assessments: Results of the BNL-NRC Siting Methods Project," Improving Impact Assessment: Increasing the Relevance and Utilization of Technical and Scientific Information, S.L. Hart, G.A. Enk, W.F. Hornick, J.J. Jordan, and P. Perreault, eds., Westview Press, Boulder, Colo., 1984.

12. Hyman, E., "The Valuation of Extramarket Benefits and Costs in Environmental Impact Assessment," Environmental Impact Assessment Review, Vol. 2, 1981, pp. 226-258.

13. Hyman, E.L., Moreau, D.H., and Stiftel, B., "SAGE: A New Participant-Value Method for Environmental Assessment," Water Resources Bulletin, Vol. 20, No. 6, Dec., 1984, pp. 915-922.

14. Keeney, R.L., and Wood, E.F., "An Illustrative Exampe of the Use of Multiattribute Utility Theory for Water Resource Planning," Water Resources Research, Vol. 13, No. 4, 1977, pp. 705-712.

15. Krutilla, J.V., and Fisher, C., The Economics of Natural Environments, Johns Hopkins Univ. Press, Baltimore, Md., 1975.

16. Kunreuther, H., et al., Disaster Insurance Protection, Public Policy Lessons, John Wiley, N.Y., 1978.

17. Lord, W.B., "Conflict in Federal Water Resources Planning," Water Resources Bulletin, Vol. 15, No. 5, 1979, pp. 1226-1235.

18. Marglin, S.A., "Objectives of Water-Resource Development: A General Statement," Design of Water-Resource Systems, A. Maass et al. eds., Harvard Univ. Press, Cambridge, Mass., 1966, pp. 17-87.

19. Nichols, R., and Hyman, E., "Evaluation of Environmental Assessment Methods," Journal of the Water Resources Planning and Management Division (ASCE), Vol. 108, No. WR1, 1982, pp. 87-105.

20. Ott, W.R., Environmental Indices, Theory and Practice, Ann Arbor Science, Ann Arbor, Mich., 1978.

21. Sharefkin, M. Shechter, M., and Kneese, A., "Impacts, Costs, and Techniques for Mitigation of Contaminated Groundwater: A Review," Water Resources Research, Vol. 16, No. 12, 1984, pp. 1771-1784.

22. Swartzman, D., "Cost-Benefit Analysis in Environmental Regulation: Sources of the Controversy," Cost-Benefit Analysis and Environmental Regulations: Politics, Ethics, and Methods, D. Swartzman, R.A. Liroff, and K.G. Croke, eds., Conservation Foundation, Washington, D.C., 1982

23. U.S. Council on Environmental Quality, "Regulations for Implementing the Procedural Provision of the National Environmental Policy Act," 40 CFR, Parts 1500-1508, 1978.

24. U.S. Water Resources Council, "Economic and Environmental Principles and Guidelines for Water and Related Land Resources Implementation Studies," Washington, D.C., 1983.

25. Warner, M., and Preston, E., "A Review of Environmental Impact Methodologies," EPA-600/5-74-002, U.S. Environmental Protection Agency, Washington, D.C., 1974.

Water Development Models For Contemporary Planning

by

Ann S. Bleed, Noel R. Gollehon, Daryoush Razavian
and Raymond J. Supalla

Abstract

A methodology for evaluating water planning alternatives was
developed and applied to the Nebraska Platte River. The methodology
involved a micro-computer based screening model and a multi-objective
optimization model. This procedure was found to be cost effective,
flexible and consistent with the needs of today's socio-economic
planning environment.

Introduction

The growing importance of environmental and budgetary concerns
has made it necessary to use increasingly complex water development
planning processes. In the current political environment effective
water development requires a systems approach which identifies the
most efficient project designs, analyzes tradeoffs and delineates an
equitable financing plan.

The need for a systems approach to water development planning has
been widely recognized and many different methodologies have been
developed. Some of the earliest work focused on the development of
screening models designed to narrow the number of design alternatives
which merited in depth investigation (1, 3). Others have used multiobjective techniques to assess tradeoffs associated with development
options (2). These earlier studies, however, did not incorporate
financing options as part of a systems analysis, and gave limited
attention to flow requirements for wildlife habitat. The purpose of
this study was to develop a technique which begins with reconnaissance
level screening and incorporates all relevant policy tradeoffs,
including those associated with project financing and wildlife
requirements.

*
Authors are listed alphabetically. A. Bleed is Assistant Professor,
Water Resources Center; N. Gollehon is Research Technologist,
Department of Agricultural Economics; D. Razavian is Water Scientist,
Water Resources Center; and R. Supalla is Professor, Department of
Agricultural Economics. All are associated with the University of
Nebraska-Lincoln and may be contacted in care of the Nebraska Water
Resources Center, 310 Ag. Hall, Lincoln, Nebraska, 68583-0710.

Problem Situation

The impetus for this study was a series of long standing issues associated with the use of Platte River water in Nebraska. The Platte River system crosses the entire state from west to east and is an important source of water for irrigation, wildlife and recreation. Current proposals for use of the water substantially exceed the amount available. From a policy perspective, this situation presents three basic questions: (1) what are the tradeoffs between instream uses for recreation and wildlife versus out-of-stream use for irrigation; (2) which of several proposed irrigation projects should receive whatever water is diverted for irrigation; and (3) if Nebraska elects to invest in water development, how should the preferred projects be financed?.

Tradeoffs between instream uses for wildlife habitat and diversions for irrigation are of central importance to policy decisions regarding use of the Platte River. The Central Platte area is a major stopover and feeding location for large numbers of migrating ducks, geese, sandhill cranes, and the endangered whooping crane. The Platte also provides nesting or wintering habitat for the threatened least tern and bald eagle. Although there is no clear consensus on what flows are needed to maintain the habitat, it is clear that large water diversion projects would greatly decrease habitat quality.

The water allocation problem is further complicated by the presence of numerous irrigation development alternatives. Five different entities have proposed diverting water from at least six different diversion points. This means that a development plan must not only determine an allocation between instream and out-of-stream uses, but also determine which irrigation project will receive the diverted water. In addition, since some diversion alternatives involve groundwater recharge, as well as irrigation directly from surface water sources, project economics tends to be a function of aquifer conditions at the time of development. Thus, the relative attractiveness of diversion alternatives varies with when development occurs.

Early in the study process the problem was narrowed for analytical purposes to include only the diversion alternatives which preliminary analyses revealed had reasonable potential for implementation. This resulted in the identification of three development entities, referred to as Little Blue, Central Platte and Big Blue, involving four diversion points, 17 reservoir sites and 5 service or need areas (Figure 1). Also, instream flow considerations were narrowed to three stream reaches based in part on habitat significance and in part on available stream flow data.

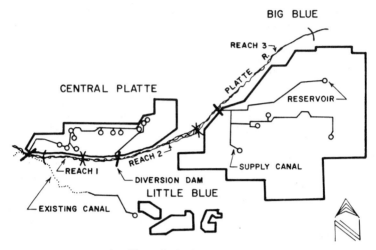

Figure I. Study Area Map

Methodology

The methodology used in this analysis consisted of two major parts: (1) a screening model for determining the most efficient project design configurations; and (2) a multi-objective linear program model for assessing economic, environmental and financing trade-offs. Although it would be conceptually possible to incorporate both the design screening and the tradeoff analysis in a single optimization model, data requirements and computational costs made such an approach undesirable. Moreover, many potential applications of the model involve either a design screening or a tradeoff question, but not both. Thus, a separation of the two components simplifies subsequent applications.

Screening Model

The screening model was designed to eliminate inferior alternatives, as well as provide the necessary coefficients for the multi-objective model. The major design variables incorporated in the model were: diversion points, reservoir sites, canal routes, canal lining type, and irrigation service areas. In addition, the screening model incorporated as inputs all major variables required for computing economic benefits due to surface irrigation, groundwater recharge, flood control and reservoir based recreation. These variables were crop prices, irrigated and dryland grain yields, irrigation requirements, crop production costs and returns, and the relationship between reservoir surface area and reservoir recreation benefits.

The primary outputs from the screening model were the costs and benefits associated with the diversion of a given quantity of water at a particular diversion point, for all alternative project design configurations. These outputs were used to identify the non-inferior project designs for all project sizes associated with a given diversion point. They were also used to compare costs and benefits as a function of project scale and other project design parameters. For further details see Gollehon et al. (This volume).

Multi-objective Model

The multi-objective model was used to determine optimum water development plans from over 1000 development alternatives, with construction occurring over a 25 year time period. Optimums were computed using a linear programming algorithm to maximize the present value of net economic benefits, given specified capital and instream flow constraints. This model also permitted computation of tradeoff curves showing the changes in net present value associated with variations in the instream flow and/or capital constraints.

Instream Flow Constraints. The instream flow constraints used in the model were specified in terms of the average amount of water available for diversion each month at each diversion point.

The total amount of water available in each reach of the river was estimated using a multiple regression model developed by Lee Becker, Nebraska Department of Water Resources. Becker's model was based on historic flows from 1954 to 1978 and used a series of equations which predicted the monthly stream flow at the bottom of the river reach, given the amount of water at the top of the reach, the amount coming in from tributaries, and the amount of water diverted from the reach.

The amount of water available for diversion each month was calculated by subtracting the water reserved for instream use from the water available in each reach. Monthly flows reserved for instream use were not determined by a simple stepwise decline from high to low, but were discrete quantities based on a variety of current ideas of what flows are necessary to maintain certain types of habitat (Table 1). This approach facilitated the interpretation of the impacts of alternative instream flow regimes on the habitat for different wildlife species.

Capital Constraints. The tradeoffs associated with alternative methods of project financing were assessed via alternative specifications of capital constraints. Two types of capital constraints were imposed on the model: appropriated capital and borrowed capital. Appropriated capital was specified as an annual appropriation limit, where the amount available for use at any future point in time was the

Table 1. Instream Flow Definitions

Annual Quantity Reserved

Options	Reach 1	Reach 2	Reach 3	Remarks
	--million of cubic meters--			
A	0	0	0	No instream flows reserved.
B	162	209	224	Low flow level for cranes, no flows for channel maintenance.
C	239	285	300	High level of scouring flow for channel maintenance and low flow level for cranes.
D	400	285	300	High level of scouring flow for channel maintenance; low flow level for cranes; flows for eagles in reach 1.
E	331	485	405	High level flows only for cranes.
F	407	438	482	High scouring flows and high flows for cranes; no flows for eagles or terns.
G	599	490	502	Low scouring flows and low flows for cranes; flows for eagles and terns.
H	601	391	434	Low scouring flows; high flows for cranes; flows for eagles in reach 1; no flows for terns.
I	648	438	482	High scouring flows; high level flows for cranes; flows for eagles in reach 1; no flows for terns.
J	772	669	656	Flows recommended by the Nebraska Game and Parks Commission, No scouring flows.
K	584	612	653	High flows for cranes and flows for terns; no scouring flows or flows for eagles in reach 1.
L	738	613	653	High flows for cranes; flows for terns and eagles, but no scouring flows.
M	614	642	684	High flows for cranes; flows for terns, but no flows for eagles or scouring.
N	661	689	6731	High scouring flows and high flows for cranes; flows for eagles in reach 1, but no flows for terns.
O	814	689	731	High scouring flows and high flows for cranes, flows for eagles and terns.

sum of the annual appropriations plus interest, less any previous construction expenditures. Available borrowed capital was specified as a limit which could not be exceeded.

This approach to specifying capital constraints permitted consideration of all possible combinations of appropriated and borrowed capital which might be used to achieve a given result. From a planning perspective, this meant that one could determine how much capital needed to be appropriated each year to implement a given plan, with and without debt financing.

Results

The results of the analysis can appropriately be discussed in three parts: (1) screening model results; (2) estimated tradeoffs between instream and out-of-stream uses; and (3) estimated tradeoffs between appropriated and debt financing.

Screening Model Results

The impact of scaling and timing differences on economic efficiency was an especially useful result of the screening model. Scale economies were important, because they allowed one to determine the most economic project size, defined in terms of the amount of water diverted. Intertemporal economies were important, because they indicated whether the economic attractiveness of a given development alternative would increase or decline with the passage of time.

Scale economies could be displayed in several different ways, but the essential point is that one wants some measure of economic returns as a function of project size. The measure selected for this analysis was the present value of net benefits relative to the amount of water diverted. Using this measure, it was found that scale economies varied widely between projects (Figure 2). For the Little Blue option the most economic scale was the largest possible (147.6 cubic meters), given available reservoir capacity. For the other two options, however, the net present value per thousand cubic meters increased up to 73.8 million cubic meters and then started to decline. This decline was gradual and consistent for the Big Blue option, but somewhat erratic in the case of the Central Platte option.

The major factors causing variations in scale economies were the canal route, reservoir site, and service area options associated with each case. For that situation where there was a single storage alternative (Little Blue Case), net present value per thousand cubic meters diverted increased across the relevant scale range, primarily because costs per unit storage decreased. For those situations where multiple storage and canal routing options existed (Big Blue and Central Platte), the best storage sites were developed first, resulting in decreasing returns to scale after the capacity levels for the most attractive sites were reached. The scale economy curve was erratic in the Central Platte case, because the addition of new storage sites to increase project size was not efficient until near full capacity was attained.

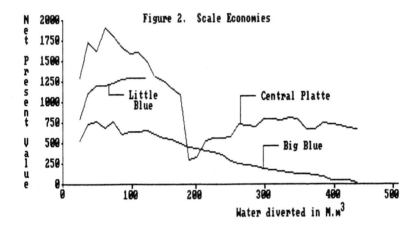

Figure 2. Scale Economies

Net Present Value

Water diverted in M.m^3

Intertemporal economies were measured in terms of the variations over time in net present value per thousand cubic meters diverted, given the optimum scale for each project location. The results were quite similar for each option, with all projects would becoming economically more attractive with the passage of time. The primary factors causing this effect were improved crop yields, which increased irrigation benefits, and deteriorating aquifer conditions, which increased groundwater recharge benefits.

Tradeoffs Between Instream and Out-of-Stream Uses

The tradeoffs between instream and out-of-stream uses were found to be much less significant than expected, although still very important in absolute terms. It was found that the highest instream flow provisions would reduce the present value of net benefits by 120 million dollars, which amounts to approximately 17 percent of the present value which occurred when no instream flow provisions were considered (Figure 3). Perhaps more importantly, the tradeoff curve indicated that about 466 million cubic meters annually could be diverted to out-of-stream uses and still satisfy a very demanding biological opinion regarding instream flow needs. Another significant fact was that most of the instream flow needs associated with the widely quoted opinion issued by the Nebraska Game and Parks Commission (Option J in Table 1) could be met at a reduction in out-of-stream net benefits of only 7 percent or 50 million dollars.

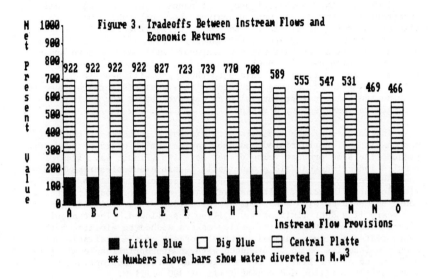

Figure 3. Tradeoffs Between Instream Flows and Economic Returns

These tradeoff results indicated that there were significant opportunities for instream versus out-of-stream compromises, especially when one considered the technical significance of each set of instream flow constraints. The most critical instream flow issue concerned the need for protection of Crane habitat and the findings indicate that one could provide high flows for cranes (option E) with less than a one percent decrease in net present value, relative to the unconstrained case. Although option E requires a reduced annual diversion of 78,000 acre feet, the economic tradeoff was minimal, because the marginal returns to additional diversions were rather small. It is also important to note that the largest tradeoffs corresponding to the most demanding instream flow constraints were due in large part to the possible need for scouring flows. Some experts representing environmental interests contend that with proper habitat management such flows are unnecessary. Thus, it may be possible to reach an instream versus out-of-stream compromise which comes close to meeting the ideal situation of both purposes.

Project Financing Tradeoffs

There are two aspects of project financing which are especially
important to water development planning: how much public money to
allocate to water development; and how to divide the allocation
between current account and debt financing. Financing entirely from
current account means that present taxpayers will pay for development
activities which benefit future generations, while debt financing
shifts at least part of the burden to those who will benefit in future
years. The tradeoff curves provided by this analysis were intended to
provide the political process with an improved basis for making this
intergenerational equity decision.

The results of the analysis were displayed in terms of the
combinations of appropriated and debt capital which could be used to
produce the same present value of net benefits (Figure 4). The
results indicated that all economically feasible out-of-stream uses
could be developed for an annual appropriation of 20 million dollars,
with no debt financing. Alternatively, the same net economic benefits
could be achieved with a minimum appropriation of five million dollars
per year, if a debt limit of 500 million was allowed. The tradeoff
curves also indicated that if policy makers wished to minimize both
appropriated and debt capital, over 95 percent of the available net
economic benefits could be produced with an appropriation level of 10
million and a debt limit of 100 million, or with an appropriation
limit of five million and a debt limit of 300 million.

Figure 4. Tradeoffs Between Appropriated and Debt Capital, No Instream Flow Provisions

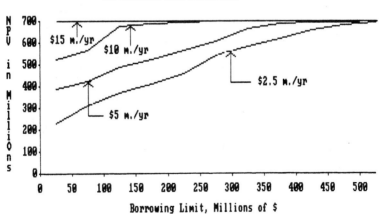

Summary

The increased importance of considering instream as well as out-of-stream uses of surface water, combined with state and federal budgetary pressures, has made water development planning increasingly difficult. The methodology presented in this paper offers a relatively cost efficient method of developing the kinds of information needed for effective water planning in todays socio-economic environment.

The suggested methodology involved: a simulation model to screen the development opportunities associated with a given diversion point; and a multi-objective linear program to develop an optimum development plan for any given set of instream flow and capital constraints. This approach allowed estimates of the kinds of tradeoffs between instream and out-of-stream uses and between appropriated and debt capital that are necessary for well informed planning decisions. The methodology also made sensitivity analyses very cost effective, thus permitting decision makers to examine how results change when parameters which cannot be estimated with certainty are varied.

In applying the methodology to development opportunities involving the Platte River in Nebraska, it was found that the technique was very cost effective. The screening model identified the scale and intertemporal economies associated with each major development option. This permitted decision makers to identify when it might be most desirable to begin a development program, as well as what difference it would make if scale adjustments were made in individual project proposals to accommodate other interests.

From the results of the multi-objective model it was possible to identify opportunities for compromise between instream and out-of-stream uses which would be reasonably consistent with both objectives. The multi-objective model results also indicated the combinations of appropriated and debt capital which could be used to implement a given development plan.

APPENDIX 1. REFERENCES

1. Das, P. and Y.Y. Haimes, "Mulitobjective Optimization in Water Quality and Land Management," Water Resources Research, Volume 15, Number 6, pp. 1313-1322, 1979.
2. Gilbert, D.P., et al., "Development of Quantitative Planning Technology", Working Draft Sponsored by the Upper Big Blue Natural Resources District, Nebraska Water Resources Center, University of Nebraska-Lincoln, Lincoln, Nebraska, Mar. 1981.
3. Goicoechea, A.L., Duckstein and M. Fogel. "Multiojbective Programming in Watershed Management: A Study of Charleston Watershed", Water Resources Research, Volume 12, Number 6, pp. 1085-1052, 1976.

HEC5 HYDROPOWER SIMULATION ENHANCEMENTS

Gary M. Franc*

ABSTRACT

   In 1983, Acres International Corporation (Acres) was granted permission by the Hydrologic Engineering Center (HEC) to modify the U.S. Army Corps of Engineers computer program HEC5. The program is a multi-reservoir, multi-purpose model for simulation of a system of reservoirs operated for flood control, hydropower, and conservation purposes[1,2].

   Acres effort focused on sophisticating the power features to permit the program's use in the general design of hydropower projects. The program has since been successfully used on numerous hydropower studies, and Acres is demonstrating the enhancements to the HEC for possible incorporation into the standard HEC5 simulation model.

INTRODUCTION

   Acres version of HEC5 possesses enhancements in the logic governing conventional hydropower, pumped-storage, and system power simulation. This paper will demonstrate the conventional hydropower capabilities of the program through the use of four test simulations, each using the same hydrologic record, physical site, and turbine characteristic data. To more clearly illustrate the resulting effects on energy production, each test differs only in its power operation policy.

   Capabilities to be demonstrated include: defining head loss as a function of flow; determining turbine efficiency from turbine flow and net operating head; limitation of power operation by head, flow, or cavitation constraints; simulation of multiple unit installations; and simulation of energy generation using different power operating schemes.

OVERVIEW OF POWER OPERATING SCHEMES

   Four types of power operating policies are available in the program. Each type can be individually assigned by reservoir in multi-reservoir simulations.

(a) Run-of-River-Operation - Energy is generated on a 24 hour basis. This policy is used at projects which attempt to maintain a normal reservoir level by matching inflow and outflow. Power is secondary to the primary objective of minimizing reservoir fluctuations.

---

*Hydraulic Engineer, Acres International Corporation, 424 Main Street, Buffalo, New York 14202.

(b) Maximum Energy Operation - Plant factor can vary from a mini-
     mum, input by the user, to 100 percent. When energy production
     is secondary in nature, the turbine settings are based on maxi-
     mizing the energy produced with the given reservoir release.
     When attempting to determine the release required to meet an
     energy demand, the turbine settings are based on producing the
     required energy with the least amount of flow. This policy
     requires the most computing time because a number of turbine
     settings must be analyzed.

(c) Maximum Power Capacity Operation - The plant factor can vary
     from a minimum, input by the user, to 100 percent. When no
     limitations constrain the operation, the turbines are set to
     discharge the total maximum turbine flow.

(d) Partial Peaking Operation - This policy combines aspects of
     policies (b) and (c). The maximum turbine flow for combina-
     tions of turbines are determined. The final turbine settings
     are based on the combination of turbines which maximize the
     energy produced or release the least flow.

GENERAL TEST DEVELOPMENT

     The hydropower project simulated in Tests 1 through 4 is a
fictitious site used to illustrate the hydropower enhancements added
to HEC5. The site and turbine characteristic data were selected to
demonstrate the energy generation aspects of the power routines.
Common aspects of the tests are described below.

     Figure 1 is a partial listing of the HEC5 input data coded for
Test 1. This figure illustrates the input required to define the
common aspects of the project. An abbreviated designation will be
used to refer to specific input parameters. For example, P1.3
refers to the third input parameter on the P1 card.

```
T1 UNAMEIT HYDROELECTRIC POWER PROJECT
T2 HEC5 RUN OF RIVER SIMULATION FOR ONE YEAR OF DAILY FLOWS
T3 NO POWER DEMAND - POWER FLOW SET TO MAXIMIZE ENERGY GENERATION
J1     0     10      4      3      4      2      0      0      0      0
J2     0      0   0.15      8      1      0      0      0      0      0
J3     6      0      0      0      0     20      0      0      0      0
J8  1.09   1.10   1.12   1.22   1.16   1.25   1.33   1.35   1.39   1.40
RL     1   3400   1690   1690   3400  71800
R0     2      1      2
RS     7   1250   1690   2350   3400   4825   6225  71800
RQ     7   3100   3200   3350   3550   3700   3900   6800
RE     7    420    422    425    430    435    440    547
P1     1   4000      0      4      0      0      0      2     66    0.1
P2     0    800      0      0     80     47    800    210     60
P3  71.0 25.650 35.700 45.750 55.800 60.820 65.825 75.830 80.825
P3  83.0 25.700 35.750 45.800 55.850 60.870 65.900 75.910 85.890 100.870
P3 106.0 25.700 35.750 45.800 55.850 60.870 65.900 75.910 85.890 100.870
P3 122.0 25.710 35.770 45.820 55.870 60.890 65.910 75.915 85.895 95.875
P4 19.91      0  12.40  14.76      0    1.0
PR   0.1    0.1    0.1    0.1    0.1    0.1    0.1    0.1    0.1    0.1
PR   0.1    0.1
PQ     0     50    100    167    250    480    970   2000   4000   6000
PT   351  352.3  353.0  353.6  354.0  355.0  356.1  357.7  359.7  361.0
CP     1   6000     23     23
ID LEE KEE DAM
RT     1      2      0                   Figure 1
CP     2   6000                          Example of HEC5 Input
ID DUMMY CONTROL POINT
C1     1    3.5      2
RT     2      0
ED
```

The project is comprised of two vertical Kaplan turbines (P1.8), each rated at a design flow (P2.2) of 400 cfs (11.2 m³/s). Each turbine is capable of accommodating a maximum flow (P2.7) of 400 cfs (11.2 m³/s) and can operate at a minimum flow (P2.8) of 105 cfs (2.9 m³/s). The rated head of each turbine (P1.9) is 66 feet (20.1 m). Net operating head range (P2.6 and P2.5) is 47 to 80 feet (14.3 to 24.4 m).

Each generator is rated at 2 MW (P1.2) and can operate for extended periods of time at 15 percent overload (P1.3).

The overall efficiency of each turbine/generator is dependent on both the turbine flow and net operating head as shown on P3 cards. The percent turbine flow and corresponding efficiency are coded in a combined format with percent turbine flow input to the left of the decimal point. The first P3 card defines the turbine flow vs efficiency relationship corresponding to a net operating head of 46.9 feet (14.3 m) (i.e., 71 percent of the rated head). At this head, the maximum turbine flow through a single turbine is limited to 320 cfs (9.0 m³/s) (i.e., 80 percent of the rated flow). The second and third P3 cards define the turbine flow/efficiency relationship throughout a head range from 54.8 to 70.0 feet (16.7 to 21.4 m). When operating within this head range, the entire rated flow of 400 cfs (11.2 m³/s) can be utilized. The last P3 card defines the turbine flow/efficiency performance for a head of 80.5 feet (24.6 m). The maximum turbine flow is limited to 380 cfs (10.6 m³/s) (i.e., 95 percent of the rated turbine flow). The program will calculate efficiency by performing a double linear interpolation.

Because the power flow is diverted through a branch from the low level outlet tunnel, two loss functions are required to properly simulate the hydraulic loss.

Losses through the low level outlet tunnel can be represented as a function of the total release:

$$HL = 19.91 \text{ E-7} \times Q^2 \quad \text{(see P4.1)}$$

where HL represents the head loss in feet; and where Q represents the total release through the low level outlet tunnel in cfs.

This loss function is valid for total releases up to 2500 cfs (70 m³/s). Releases in excess of 2500 cfs (70 m³/s) are assumed to discharge through a separate flood release tunnel and therefore do not contribute to hydraulic loss. This release policy is simulated in the model by constraining the head loss to a maximum value (P4.3) of 12.4 feet (3.8 m).

The head loss through the power penstocks is represented by:

$$HL = 14.76 \text{ E-7} \times Qu^2 \quad \text{(see P4.4)}$$

where HL represents head loss in feet; and where Qu represents the power flow through a single penstock in cfs.

The tailwater-discharge curve is coded on the PQ and PT cards. All flows released from the reservoir during periods of power operation are assumed to affect tailwater.

At times of non-generation, a continuous minimum release of 23 cfs (0.6 m³/s) must be maintained. This includes periods when flooding is occurring at the downstream control point.

The downstream control point has a safe channel capacity of 6000 cfs (168 m³/s). Whenever the local inflow at this control point exceeds 6000 cfs (168 m³/s), the project will use available flood control storage and the reservoir level will rise at times to levels which cause power head limits to be violated. Flood control storage will be evacuated as soon as possible to return the reservoir to the normal pool level of 430 feet (131.2 m).

Each test will simulate 100 daily time periods with the starting water surface elevation at level 430 (131.2 m). The first twenty five time periods of each test will be displayed in Figures 2-5.

TEST 1 - RUN-OF-RIVER SIMULATION

This test is designed to simulate the project as a run-of-river hydropower facility by requiring all generation to occur on a continuous 24 hour basis (P2.9 = 60/60 minutes). The project has no firm energy requirements (PR.1-PR.12=0) and will generate energy based on using the resulting reservoir release required for other purposes. No generation will occur for releases less than the minimum single turbine flow of 105 cfs (2.9 m³/s).

User designed output displays the reservoir inflow, reservoir outflow, case, average headwater (reservoir) level, energy generated, power capacity, power head, power flow, plant factor, head loss, efficiency, and the number of units operating (see Figure 2).

PER	LEE KEE INFLOW	LEE KEE OUTFLOW	LEE KEE CASE	LEE KEE EL/STAGE	LEE KEE ENERGY G	LEE KEE PEAK CAP	LEE KEE POWER HE	LEE KEE POWER Q/	LEE KEE HEAD LOS	LEE KEE EFFY/UNI
1	100.00	100.00	0.03	430.00	0.00	0.00	0.00	0.00	0.00	0.00
2	70.00	70.00	0.03	430.00	0.00	0.00	0.00	0.00	0.00	0.00
3	50.00	50.00	0.03	430.00	0.00	0.00	0.00	0.00	0.00	0.00
4	40.00	40.00	0.03	430.00	0.00	0.00	0.00	0.00	0.00	0.00
5	209.00	209.00	0.03	430.00	27.37	1140.49	76.05	209.99	0.15	848.01
6	189.00	189.00	0.03	430.00	24.07	1002.82	76.17	189.99	0.12	823.01
7	191.00	191.00	0.03	430.00	24.39	1016.32	76.16	191.99	0.13	825.01
8	180.00	180.00	0.03	430.00	22.63	942.81	76.22	180.99	0.11	812.01
9	151.00	151.00	0.03	430.00	18.20	758.41	76.46	151.99	0.08	776.01
10	152.00	152.00	0.03	430.00	18.35	764.54	76.45	152.99	0.08	777.01
11	166.00	166.00	0.03	430.00	20.45	851.90	76.31	166.99	0.10	795.01
12	1500.00	1500.00	0.03	430.00	96.65	4027.06	68.36	800.99	4.72	870.02
13	657.00	657.00	0.03	430.00	88.14	3672.30	73.58	657.99	1.02	897.02
14	742.00	742.00	0.03	430.00	96.93	4038.89	73.11	742.99	1.30	880.02
15	395.00	395.00	0.03	430.00	51.16	2131.82	74.89	384.99	0.53	875.01
16	388.00	388.00	0.03	430.00	51.16	2131.86	74.90	384.99	0.52	875.01
17	684.00	684.00	0.03	430.00	90.90	3787.58	73.44	684.99	1.10	891.02
18	1500.00	1500.00	0.03	430.00	96.65	4027.06	68.36	800.99	4.72	870.02
19	2550.00	2550.00	0.03	430.00	83.58	3482.37	59.11	800.99	12.64	870.02
20	3780.00	3573.00	0.06	430.72	83.15	3464.54	58.81	800.99	12.64	870.02
21	3930.00	1047.65	2.00	440.72	0.00	0.00	0.00	0.00	0.00	0.00
22	2050.00	23.00	2.00	448.67	0.00	0.00	0.00	0.00	0.00	0.00
23	928.00	23.00	2.00	453.41	0.00	0.00	0.00	0.00	0.00	0.00
24	800.00	23.00	2.00	456.14	0.00	0.00	0.00	0.00	0.00	0.00
25	700.00	3473.76	2.00	452.90	0.00	0.00	0.00	0.00	0.00	0.00

Figure 2
Run-Of-River Simulation Results

The power flow and plant factor are displayed in combined format
with the power flow rounded to the nearest cfs and shown to the left
of the decimal point and the plant factor shown as a decimal fraction. A plant factor of 100 percent can only be displayed as .99.

Efficiency and the number of units operating are displayed
similarly with efficiency shown to the left of the decimal point and
the number of units operating shown as a two digit number.

The power capacity for each time period is calculated from
actual values of turbine flow, power head, efficiency, and the
number of units operating (P1.4=4).

During time periods 1 through 4, no power is generated because
the flow released is less than the minimum turbine flow for a single
unit.

For time periods 5 through 11, the entire reservoir release is
discharged through one turbine to generate energy. Due to flow
limitations, only one turbine is used for power generation. At
least 210 cfs (5.9 m³/s) is required before the program can
attempt to compare generating with one or two units.

In time period 12, the power flow is limited to the maximum
rated flow for two units (800 cfs or 22.4 m³/s). This flow can be
discharged because the power head is between 83 and 106 percent of
the rated head (see P3 cards in Figure 1) and no turbine limitation
occurs. The head loss is based on 1500 cfs (42.0 m³/s) through
the low level outlet tunnel and 800 cfs (22.4 m³/s) through the
two turbines.

Time periods 19 and 20 are similar to time period 12, except
that head loss through the low level outlet tunnel is limited to
2500 cfs (70 m³/s). All flow in excess of 2500 cfs (70 m³/s) is
released through the flood release tunnel.

For time periods 21 through 25, no power is generated; either
the maximum power head limit of 80 feet (24.4 m) or the minimum
turbine flow limit of 105 cfs (2.9 m³/s) is violated. In general,
power is generated on a continuous basis. When turbine flows are
between 105 and 400 cfs (2.9 and 11.2 m³/s), one unit operates.
For available flow in excess of 400 cfs (11.2 m³/s), two units
operate.

This simulation resulted in 5903 MWh of total energy. There
were 10 days when no energy could be generated. The average
capacity when generating was 2733 kW.

TEST 2 - MAXIMUM ENERGY GENERATION SIMULATION

This test is designed to simulate the project as a daily ponding
hydropower facility. The project will be allowed to operate at a
power flow that will maximize energy production. The selection of
this power flow will be constrained by specifying a minimum time of
power generation at 3 hours per day (P2.9=7.5/60 minutes). Additionally, a minimum release of 23 cfs (0.6 m³/s) will have to be
maintained during periods of non-generation. The project has no
firm energy requirement (PR.1-PR.12=0) and will select the power
flow based on the available flow released for another purpose.
Under this scheme, energy can be generated for available daily flows
of 33.25 cfs (0.93 m³/s) and above. This limiting flow is determined as follows:

$$LAF = QMIN + LPLT (LPF-QMIN) = 23 + .125 \times (105-23) = 33.25$$

where LAF = limiting available average daily flow;
      QMIN = minimum downstream flow for non-generation period;
      LPLT = limiting plant factor of 7.5/60 minute per hour;
      LPF = limiting power flow (i.e., minimum turbine flow for one turbine).

The entire reservoir release policy for Test 2 is identical to Test 1, since neither test operates to meet a firm energy requirement (see Figure 3). However, during time periods 1 through 4 of Test 2, energy is generated because the program now selects the plant factor to generate energy most efficiently.

For example, during time period 4, one turbine is operated at minimum turbine flow (105 cfs or 2.9 m³/s) for approximately 21 percent of the day. Note that the operating scheme allows for a continous release of 23 cfs (0.6 m³/s) during the off peak portion of the day.

In the remaining time periods where energy is generated (i.e, time periods 5-20), the power flow selected results in energy equal to or more than that produced in Test 1.

This flexibility in the power operation results in 5969 MWh of total energy, or 1.1 percent more than in Test 1. Test comparisons for an entire year result in 3.7 percent more energy annually for Test 2.

There were 6 days when no energy could be generated due to a violation of either the maximum operating head or the minimum turbine flow. The average capacity was 2876 kW.

PER	LEE KEE INFLOW	LEE KEE OUTFLOW	LEE KEE CASE	LEE KEE EL/STAGE	LEE KEE ENERGY G	LEE KEE PEAK CAP	LEE KEE POWER HE	LEE KEE POWER Q/	LEE KEE HEAD LOS	LEE KEE EFFY/UNI
1	100.00	100.00	0.03	430.00	11.73	1590.02	75.64	274.31	0.26	908.01
2	70.00	70.00	0.03	430.00	7.16	1586.59	75.64	273.19	0.26	908.01
3	50.00	50.00	0.03	430.00	4.01	1335.98	75.15	239.13	0.20	879.01
4	40.00	40.00	0.03	430.00	2.43	487.84	76.92	105.21	0.04	714.01
5	209.00	209.00	0.03	430.00	28.34	1483.82	75.74	257.80	0.23	901.01
6	189.00	189.00	0.03	430.00	25.28	1588.99	75.64	273.66	0.26	908.01
7	191.00	191.00	0.03	430.00	25.58	1596.18	75.63	275.67	0.26	908.01
8	180.00	180.00	0.03	430.00	23.94	1556.65	75.67	268.64	0.25	907.01
9	151.00	151.00	0.03	430.00	19.49	1601.58	75.63	276.51	0.26	908.01
10	152.00	152.00	0.03	430.00	19.64	1604.57	75.62	276.51	0.26	908.01
11	166.00	166.00	0.03	430.00	21.84	1505.73	75.72	260.60	0.23	905.01
12	1500.00	1500.00	0.03	430.00	96.65	4027.06	68.36	800.99	4.72	870.02
13	657.00	657.00	0.03	430.00	88.14	3672.30	73.58	657.99	1.02	897.02
14	742.00	742.00	0.03	430.00	96.93	4038.89	73.11	742.99	1.30	880.02
15	395.00	395.00	0.03	430.00	53.01	3170.51	74.09	557.70	0.73	908.02
16	388.00	388.00	0.03	430.00	52.02	3146.06	74.11	553.69	0.72	907.02
17	684.00	684.00	0.03	430.00	90.90	3787.58	73.44	684.99	1.10	891.02
18	1500.00	1500.00	0.03	430.00	96.65	4027.06	68.36	800.99	4.72	870.02
19	2550.00	2550.00	0.03	430.00	83.58	3482.37	59.11	800.99	12.64	870.02
20	3780.00	3573.00	0.06	430.72	83.15	3464.54	58.81	800.99	12.64	870.02
21	3930.00	1047.65	2.00	440.72	0.00	0.00	0.00	0.00	0.00	0.00
22	2050.00	23.00	2.00	448.67	0.00	0.00	0.00	0.00	0.00	0.00
23	928.00	23.00	2.00	453.41	0.00	0.00	0.00	0.00	0.00	0.00
24	800.00	23.00	2.00	456.14	0.00	0.00	0.00	0.00	0.00	0.00
25	700.00	3473.76	2.00	452.90	0.00	0.00	0.00	0.00	0.00	0.00

Figure 3
Maximum Energy Simulation Results

Test 2 resulted in a better energy generation scheme than Test
1. The project was able to peak flows and operate during periods
when in Test 1, the average daily reservoir release was below the
minimum turbine flow. Additionally, for approximately 1/3 of the
time, operating at a higher power flow and corresponding efficiency
resulted in an increase in energy sufficient to compensate for the
associated reduction in power head due to higher tailwater and head
losses.

TEST 3 - MAXIMUM POWER CAPACITY SIMULATION

Test 3 is designed to simulate the project as a daily peaking
hydropower facility by requiring the turbines to be operated at the
highest possible power flow (P2.9<0). The selection of the power
flow will be constrained by specifying a minimum time for peaking as
3 hours per day (P2.9=7.5). Additionally, a minimum release of 23
cfs (0.6 m^3/s) will be maintained during off-peak hours. The project has no firm energy requirement (PR.1-PR.12=0) and will select
the power flow based on the available flow released for other purposes. This test will closely resemble a "block loading" operation
except that the maximum power flow (i.e., turbine design flow) may
be restricted at times due to turbine limitations as specified on
the P3 cards (see Figure 4).

During periods when generation was possible, the project was
able to peak using two turbines the majority of the time. In time
periods 2 through 4 only one turbine operated. During these 3 days,
the available reservoir release was insufficient to allow for peaking two turbines without violating the minimum plant factor limit of
0.125.

In many periods, including time periods 5 through 11, the total
design flow of 800 cfs (22.4 m^3/s) could not be utilized because
the resulting power head was above 106 percent of the design head
and limitations on flow occurred (see P3 card).

PER	LEE KEE INFLOW	LEE KEE OUTFLOW	LEE KEE CASE	LEE KEE EL/STAGE	LEE KEE ENERGY G	LEE KEE PEAK CAP	LEE KEE POWER HE	LEE KEE POWER Q/	LEE KEE HEAD LOS	LEE KEE EFFY/UNI
1	100.00	100.00	0.03	430.00	10.78	3594.44	73.68	639.13	0.96	902.02
2	70.00	70.00	0.03	430.00	6.65	2121.17	74.76	383.13	0.51	875.01
3	50.00	50.00	0.03	430.00	4.01	1335.98	75.15	239.13	0.20	879.01
4	40.00	40.00	0.03	430.00	2.42	807.88	76.38	159.13	0.09	786.01
5	209.00	209.00	0.03	430.00	24.80	4179.85	72.84	775.25	1.42	874.02
6	189.00	189.00	0.03	430.00	22.13	4179.69	72.83	775.22	1.42	874.02
7	191.00	191.00	0.03	430.00	22.40	4179.70	72.83	775.22	1.42	874.02
8	180.00	180.00	0.03	430.00	20.93	4179.61	72.83	775.21	1.42	874.02
9	151.00	151.00	0.03	430.00	17.06	4179.37	72.83	775.17	1.42	874.02
10	152.00	152.00	0.03	430.00	17.20	4179.38	72.83	775.17	1.42	874.02
11	166.00	166.00	0.03	430.00	19.06	4179.50	72.83	775.19	1.42	874.02
12	1500.00	1500.00	0.03	430.00	96.65	4027.06	68.36	800.99	4.72	870.02
13	657.00	657.00	0.03	430.00	84.62	4184.49	72.92	775.84	1.42	874.02
14	742.00	742.00	0.03	430.00	95.96	4184.49	72.92	775.96	1.42	874.02
15	395.00	395.00	0.03	430.00	49.65	4184.49	72.92	775.49	1.42	874.02
16	388.00	388.00	0.03	430.00	48.72	4184.49	72.92	775.49	1.42	874.02
17	684.00	684.00	0.03	430.00	88.22	4184.49	72.92	775.88	1.42	874.02
18	1500.00	1500.00	0.03	430.00	96.65	4027.06	68.36	800.99	4.72	870.02
19	2550.00	2550.00	0.03	430.00	83.58	3482.37	59.11	800.99	12.64	870.02
20	3780.00	3573.00	0.06	430.72	83.15	3464.54	58.81	800.99	12.64	870.02
21	3930.00	1047.65	2.00	440.72	0.00	0.00	0.00	0.00	0.00	0.00
22	2050.00	23.00	2.00	448.67	0.00	0.00	0.00	0.00	0.00	0.00
23	928.00	23.00	2.00	453.41	0.00	0.00	0.00	0.00	0.00	0.00
24	800.00	23.00	2.00	456.14	0.00	0.00	0.00	0.00	0.00	0.00
25	700.00	3473.76	2.00	452.90	0.00	0.00	0.00	0.00	0.00	0.00

Figure 4
Maximum Power Capacity Simulation Results

Again, no power generation was possible in periods 21 through 25 because of violations of maximum head and minimum turbine flow. Overall, there were 6 days when power generation was impossible.

This peaking simulation results in total energy of 5714 MWh, a reduction of 4.5 percent when compared to the objective of maximizing energy production. However, the average capacity of the project when operating increased by 41 percent to a value of 4058 KW.

TEST 4 - FIRM ENERGY DEMAND SIMULATION

This test is designed to simulate the project as a small base-load hydropower facility required to meet a monthly firm energy of 600 MWh (PR.1 through PR.12=600). This energy requirement is uniformly distributed throughout the month. The selection of the power flow is constrained by specifying a minimum time for generation as 6 hours per day (P2.9=15). A minimum release of 23 cfs (0.6 m³/s) is maintained during all non-generation hours.

The reservoir is operated to attempt to maintain the reservoir level at 430 feet (131.2 m). In satisfying a given energy requirement, the turbine loadings are selected such that the energy is generated by releasing the least possible amount of average daily flow. When reservoir inflows are insufficient to support energy production, the project will supplement power flow from reservoir storage as required, until the reservoir level reaches 422 feet (128.7 m), at which time firm energy shortages are incurred. For periods where releases for other purposes exceed the release to meet the firm energy requirement, the program selects the turbine loadings which result in the most energy.

The user designed output has been modified to display the firm energy requirement for each period in place of the power capacity (see Figure 5).

PER	LEE KEE INFLOW	LEE KEE OUTFLOW	LEE KEE CASE	LEE KEE EL/STAGE	LEE KEE ENERGY R	LEE KEE ENERGY G	LEE KEE POWER HE	LEE KEE POWER Q/	LEE KEE HEAD LOS	LEE KEE EFFY/UNI
1	100.00	150.57	0.10	429.76	19.35	19.35	75.39	275.51	0.26	908.01
2	70.00	151.71	0.10	429.14	19.35	19.35	74.76	276.51	0.26	908.01
3	50.00	153.35	0.10	428.26	19.35	19.35	73.88	277.51	0.27	907.01
4	40.00	155.25	0.10	427.23	19.35	19.35	72.97	257.56	0.23	899.01
5	209.00	155.78	0.10	426.94	19.35	19.35	72.67	258.57	0.23	899.01
6	189.00	155.03	0.10	427.35	19.35	19.35	73.09	257.56	0.23	899.01
7	191.00	154.43	0.10	427.68	19.35	19.35	73.42	257.56	0.23	899.01
8	180.00	153.89	0.10	427.98	19.35	19.35	73.59	277.52	0.27	907.01
9	151.00	153.68	0.10	428.09	19.35	19.35	73.71	277.51	0.27	907.01
10	152.00	153.72	0.10	428.07	19.35	19.35	73.68	277.51	0.27	907.01
11	166.00	153.63	0.10	428.12	19.35	19.35	73.74	277.51	0.27	907.01
12	1500.00	1306.96	0.03	429.09	19.35	97.31	68.83	800.99	3.64	870.02
13	657.00	657.00	0.03	430.00	19.35	88.14	73.58	657.99	1.02	897.02
14	742.00	742.00	0.03	430.00	19.35	96.93	73.11	742.99	1.30	880.02
15	395.00	395.00	0.03	430.00	19.35	53.01	74.09	557.70	0.73	908.02
16	388.00	388.00	0.03	430.00	19.35	52.02	74.11	553.69	0.72	907.02
17	684.00	684.00	0.03	430.00	19.35	90.90	73.44	684.99	1.10	891.02
18	1500.00	1500.00	0.03	430.00	19.35	96.65	68.36	800.99	4.72	870.02
19	2550.00	2550.00	0.03	430.00	19.35	83.58	59.11	800.99	12.64	870.02
20	3780.00	3573.00	0.06	430.72	19.35	83.15	58.81	800.99	12.64	870.02
21	3930.00	1047.65	2.00	440.72	19.35	0.00	0.00	0.00	0.00	0.00
22	2050.00	23.00	2.00	448.67	19.35	0.00	0.00	0.00	0.00	0.00
23	928.00	23.00	2.00	453.41	19.35	0.00	0.00	0.00	0.00	0.00
24	800.00	23.00	2.00	456.14	19.35	0.00	0.00	0.00	0.00	0.00
25	700.00	3473.76	2.00	452.90	19.35	0.00	0.00	0.00	0.00	0.00

Figure 5
Firm Energy Simulation Results

Reservoir releases are made for the first 11 periods to satisfy firm energy requirements (Case=0.10). The power flow is selected to minimize the amount of average daily flow required. In periods 1 through 4, the firm energy is satisfied by slightly supplementing reservoir inflows with available reservoir storage. Reservoir inflows for periods 5 through 11 are sufficient to produce the required energy while storing excess inflow. By the twelfth day, the reservoir has risen to the normal pool level of 430 feet (131.2 m) and all firm requirements have been satisfied.

For periods 13 through 19, all reservoir inflows are released throughout the day to maintain maximum flood control storage capacity (Case=0.03). The turbine settings throughout this period maximize energy production.

There were six days where no energy could be generated due to violation of the maximum head or the minimum turbine flow. This outage resulted in a firm energy shortage of 117 MWh.

This simulation resulted in a total energy of 5993 MWh, 0.4 percent more than in Test 2. This energy increase is directly related to a 0.4 percent increase in power flow, which is a result of supplementing inflows from reservoir storage.

CONCLUSIONS

A critical decision of any hydropower study is the selection of the computer model used to estimate the energy potential. Any deficiency in the simulation process influences the estimate of the energy potential and consequently, effects the project benefits. In today's competitive marketplace, an error of only five percent in the estimate of energy potential is, in many cases, the difference between a profitable venture and a bad investment.

To minimize this risk, a computer model must accurately simulate the reservoir release policy of the project while properly accounting for headwater and tailwater fluctuations. Hydraulic losses throughout the power conveyance system must be adequately determined. The turbine efficiency characteristics and turbine and generator limitations must be incorporated into the simulation. Finally, the model must be able to accurately define the actual power operating policy of the hydropower project.

The revised HEC5 program is one simulation model capable of meeting this objective. The flexibility of the program allows for accurate energy estimates for a wide range of project operations. The program is now an exceptional hydropower operations model as well as a planning tool.

ACKNOWLEDGEMENT

The author would like to express his appreciation to Malcolm Vanderburgh, Hydro and Heavy Civil Deputy Manager, and Angelo Coniglio, Project Engineer, Acres International Corporation, for providing funding support to perform the computer enhancements and prepare this paper.

The Hydrologic Engineering Center is commended for granting permission to modify the HEC5 program and for their supportive attitude of my efforts.

APPENDIX I - REFERENCES

(1) Hydrologic Engineering Center, Davis, CA, "HEC5 Simulation of Flood Control and Conservation System - Programmers Manual", September 1979.

(2) Hydrologic Engineering Center, Davis, CA, "HEC5 Simulation of Flood Control and Conservation Systems - Users Manual", April 1982.

APPENDIX II - NOTATION

The following symbols are used in this paper:

HL   = head loss
Q   = total reservoir release through low level outlet tunnel during period of power generation
Qu   = power flow through a single turbine during period of power generation
LAF = lowest average daily flow which will support daily peaking operations
QMIN = continuous minimum downstream flow requirement
LPLT = minimum allowable plant factor
LPF = minimum allowable turbine flow

AN ECONOMIC AND FINANCIAL PLANNING MODEL

R. B. Allen* and S. G. Bridgeman**

Abstract

A comprehensive computer model for generation planning has been developed and applied to several large-scale power sector master plans. A unique feature of this model is the concurrent consideration of reservoir operations (and the variable nature of the hydrology) with the generation dispatch.

The model monitors the system load demand over the planning horizon and dispatches hydroelectric and thermal generation facilities as required to meet load, on a monthly basis. This process is repeated for each of a series of user specified hydrologic sequences. The system reliability, and economic and financial outcome resulting from each of the sequences, are determined and tabular reports with stastistics are produced.

The economic methods employed are the traditional discounted cash flow analyses. In this case, however, economic outcome is reported for each of a series of hydrologic sequences, as well as the expected value.

The financial projections are summarized by income statements and balance sheets. Full account is taken of debt servicing, revaluation and depreciation of fixed assets, capital works in progress, operating costs and revenues incurred from power and energy sales.

The model can be used to evaluate alternative generation expansion sequences, tariff structures and other key planning variables by successive applications of the model.

Introduction

Many different types of power system planning models are available to aid the generation planner in determining the least-cost investment program for meeting a forecasted load demand over a defined planning horizon. Both simulation models and optimization models have been developed to solve the optimal generation expansion planning problem. Most planning models use a form of discounted cash flow analysis to determine the least-cost investment program. The major,

* Staff Engineer, Acres International Limited, 5259 Dorchester Road, Niagara Falls, Canada, L2E 6W1
**Project Engineer, Acres International Limited, 5259 Dorchester Road, Niagara Falls, Canada, L2E 6W1

recent modification in these models has been concentrated on improving the evaluation of energy production costing and reliability analysis.

Such features as deterministic and probabalistic load stacking have been used to improve the detailed analysis of production costing. With probabalistic load stacking, new definitions of system reliability have become increasingly popular, such as Loss of Load Probability (LOLP) and Expected Unserved Energy (EUE). However, one feature in which most models are inherently weak is their representation of hydropower generation.

The hydropower representation in some models has been improved over the concept of an assigned energy unit by introducing such features as a statistical representation of hydropower energy availability and a multistate representation of hydropower units of each hydro plant for probabalistic stacking. But the hydropower representation in planning models frequently lacks the flexibility to respond in an active mode to a particular load forecast during the load dispatch analysis.

In most planning studies, hydropower generation is predetermined outside the load dispatch mode of the planning model. Hydropower generation is determined by such operational strategies as maximization of firm hydro energy in hydro-dominated systems and maximization of average annual hydro energy in thermal-dominated systems. The communications link between the reservoir operating strategy in the operations model and the system load in the load dispatch model has been broken.

This planning model integrates a reservoir operations model[1] with an investment planning model to maintain this communications link. It greatly improves the hydropower representation and enhances the realism of the planning model to deal with the current system configuration and load pattern.

The financial management of an electric utility requires comprehensive financial planning over a time horizon of 5 to 10 years. The ramifications of alternative policies must be examined before important policy decisions can be made. Studies on expansion plans, tariff structures, rural electrification, imports and exports of energy, and drought recovery depend heavily on financial forecasting to determine their finanical viability. An additional feature of this planning model is that it includes a detailed financial projection of the electric utility for the prescribed expansion development program.

By using a financial forecasting model which accounts for the inherent variability of hydrology, the planner can investigate many options and their financial risk before making any policy decisions. This approach provides a fuller understanding of the range of financial implications of alternative decisions and the impact that hydrological uncertainty has on those decisions.

Model Overview

Traditionally, the generation planning procedure [illustrated in Figure 1(a)] has involved the sequential application of several distinct models, such as

- reservoir operations model to determine hydropower and energy generation

- postprocessor model to statistically process hydroelectric power and energy generation for selected probability levels

- reliability model to analyze the appropriate timing of candidate plants in the selected generation expansion plan

- load dispatch model to determine production costing for both hydro and thermal generation requirements to meet system load demand (using deterministic or probabilistic load stacking)

- economic analysis model to perform discounted cash flow analysis

- financial model to evaluate the financial performance of the selected expansion plan.

In most planning studies this procedure is adequate, but inaccuracies do exist as a result of the lack of communication between the decisions made during the operations phase and the load dispatch phase. For example, this planning procedure cannot handle such operational features as reservoir filling which may extend over several years and limit hydro capability in the early years following commissioning, long drought sequences which are not appropriately represented by statistical hydrology, and the storage of excess hydro energy during years of surplus capability leading up to the year(s) of critical energy supply just before the commissioning of a new power plant.

These operational problems can be modeled very successfully if the operations phase and the load dispatch phase of analysis are integrated to operate concurrently with complete communication between each phase. The generation planning procedure developed in this planning model is designed to achieve this purpose as illustrated in Figure 1(b).

The insertion of the operations model into the load dispatch phase of analysis allows the operational strategy of the hydropower system to respond directly to the current forecasted load demand. The hydropower generation in any load year now depends on the present reservoir storage level and the forecasted load demand.

The operations model simulates a natural hydrological sequence over the entire planning horizon. Many different natural hydrological sequences are analyzed over the planning horizon. This procedure

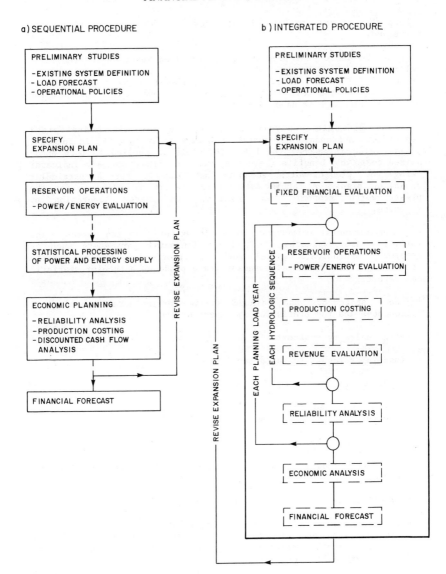

FIGURE I - COMPARISON OF PLANNING PROCEDURES

allows the natural statistical characteristics of the hydrology to be preserved.

At the end of the processing of each load year, the system reliability can be evaluated and compared with a prescribed reliability criteria. The reliability can be calculated using the statisical probability of the full range of hydrological events and not just the critical hydrology as used by most models.

The economic analysis is performed for all hydrological sequences. A standard discounted cash flow analysis (DCF) in constant dollar value is used. The DCF methodology is applied to both annualized costs and benefits (revenues) with the final economic indicator being the present-worth economic net benefit for a particular expansion plan. A tabular statistical report is produced for the present-worth economic net benefit, and energy generation by resource.

The financial performance model is executed in two phases. The initial phase evaluates the 'fixed' financial parameters such as repayment schedules, capital works in progress and fixed assets accounting. The financial forecast phase produces a tabular statistical report of

- income statements and balance sheets for selected hydrological sequences and the statistically expected event

- energy sales by customer

- financial forecast (cash in bank).

Model Structure

As illustrated by Figure 1(b), the model structure is conveniently divided into the following seven phases.

Fixed Financial Evaluation

In the fixed financial evaluation phase the following items are processed

- principal and interest repayment schedules for all existing loans

- construction costs, interest during construction, loan financing, and principal and interest repayment schedules for a prescribed capital works in progress program which includes all new projects in the expansion plan

- fixed assets accounting including assets reevaluation and depreciation

- summary tables of Debt Service Schedule, Capital Works in Progress, Fixed Assets Schedule.

Reservoir Operations

A multipurpose, multireservoir simulation model is used to evaluate the hydroelectric and thermal power and energy generation. An internal network flow optimization algorithm determines the best operating procedure for each month. Energy allocation to meet forecasted load demand is evaluated by deterministic load stacking, thermal plants being stacked in order of least operating costs.

Production Costing

The cost of energy production is evaluated from the dispatch of hydroelectric and thermal energy generation, and is evaluated in both inflated and constant dollar values. The thermal operating costs are adjusted to account for real escalation.

Revenues

Revenues are evaluated by the allocation of energy production to the various customers of the electric utility with different tariff structures. Revenues are calculated by the product of tariff rate and energy supply in both inflated and constant dollar values.

Reliability Analysis

The system reliability can be determined by the analysis of system capability for all hydrological events, and can be compared with the prescribed reliability criteria before proceeding to the next load year of the planning horizon.

Economic Analysis

A discounted cash flow methodology, including both annualized costs and benefits, is used to evaluate the present-worth economic net benefit of each generation expansion plan. The following items are evaluated in constant dollar value

- annualized capital costs
- fixed operation and maintenance costs
- variable operation and maintenance costs
- fuel costs
- insurance
- interim replacement.

Financial Analysis

A detailed financial forecast illustrating the financial performance of the electric utility over the planning horizon is presented in two forms--detailed schedules for particular hydrological sequences and tabular reports of key financial indicators.

Detailed income statements and balance sheets are produced for each selected hydrologic sequence and a composite expected value report. These reports contain the following details.

- Income Statement - total revenues, salary expenses, operating costs, gross assets depreciation, operating income, loan interest payments, income surplus.

- Balance Sheet - fixed assets, capital works in progress, cash in bank, accounts receivable, inventories, total assets, retained earnings, reevaluation reserve, total equity, net long-term debt, accounts payable, interest and committed charges, unpaid dividends, current portion of long-term debt, retention, overdraft, total current liability, total liability and equity.

Tabular reports are produced of key financial indicators such as total revenues, operating income, and cash in bank.

Model Applications

This planning model has been applied successfully in the following types of studies.

Generation Development Planning

Alternative generation development plans can be evaluated by successive applications of the model with the objective of maximizing economic net benefits. The effect of basic parameters used in the analysis can be studied, such as load forecast, sequencing and timing of projects, project costs, construction schedule, economic variables and operating costs.

Financial Forecasting

The financial forecasting component of the model will project the future financial status of a power utility over a planning period of 5 to 10 years, and will give longer range indications if so desired. The model is particularly useful for the execution of tariff studies, both for domestic sales and for export of primary and secondary energy to neighboring utilities.

Reservoir Drought Recovery

In cases where a dry hydrologic sequence has resulted in low reservoir storage and depleted financial resources, the model is a very useful tool for evaluation of joint recovery of the reservoir storage and the utility's cash reserve. Various operational strategies and short-term capital investment programs can be analyzed to determine the most consistent and stable recovery program.

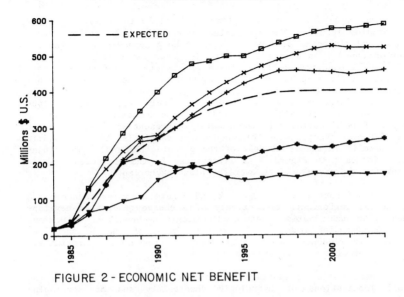

FIGURE 2 - ECONOMIC NET BENEFIT

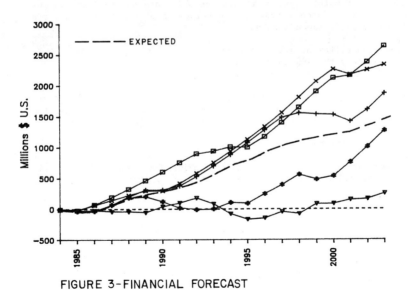

FIGURE 3 - FINANCIAL FORECAST

The application of this planning model to these various types of studies requires the evaluation of the electric utility's economic and financial performance. The likely economic and financial performance of an electric utility is generally described in most planning procedures by the average or expected benefits and costs during the planning horizon. The heavy dashed lines in Figure 2 and Figure 3 show the expected economic performance and the expected financial forecast respectively of a particular generation development plan for a given electric utility. The economic performance in Figure 2 is illustrated by the cumulative present-worth economic net benefit over the planning horizon (and in particular by the economic net benefit in the final year of the planning horizon). The financial forecast in Figure 3 is illustrated by the projected cash in bank for the given utility over the planning horizon.

Also illustrated in Figure 2 and Figure 3 is the economic and financial performance respectively of a chosen generation development plan under various natural hydrologic sequences as determined by the planning model. The results of 5 of the 40 specified hydrologic sequences are plotted, each representing approximately equal probability of occurrence.

These curves illustrate the importance of understanding the full implications of hydrologic uncertainty and of developing additional performance criteria which will capture particular aspects of possible system performance which are not revealed in the expected performance curve. The development of additional measures of system performance such as

- the probability of system failure
- how quickly the system recovers from failure
- how severe are the consequences of failure

will greatly add to the understanding of how the system will perform in the uncertain future and provide additional guidance in the evaluation and selection of alternative development plans.

Appendix I - Reference

1. Sigvaldason, O.T. "A Simulation Model for Operating a Multipurpose Multireservoir System" Water Resources Research, April 1976.

GETTING INFORMATION VIA COMPUTER: SOME BASICS

by Michael R. Walsh[1], M. ASCE

Abstract

The computer and the telephone enable water professionals to
find and acquire information electronically. To take advantage
of this capability water professionals must understand the basics
of "going online", how to find electronic information sources,
and how to transfer the specific information from a remote
computer system to a local microcomputer. Going online requires
hardware, including a microcomputer, serial port, modem, and
telephone and software, including a communications package for
handling data transfer, retrieval and storage and word-processing,
spreadsheet, data base management, and graphics for manipulating
and analyzing retrieved information. Directories are available
to help locate sources of electronic information. Sources of
electronic information include traditional sources of water
information, such as Federal, State and local agencies, and
online service vendors, who maintain database supplied by
producers of all types of information including water related
information. Information is an important resource for the
water professional and going online to retrieve information
electronically may help in acquiring the best possible
information for water related projects.

Introduction

Information is a most important resource for water resource
professionals. With the appropriate information a water resource
planner can use his skill and expertise to develop plans for
water resource developments that are beneficial to society,
without it his plans may go awry. Getting the best information
available is crucial to good planning and the ultimate execution
of water projects.

The combination of the computer and the telephone has
established a new avenue to acquire information. Now it is
easier than ever to gather information electronically by
computer via the telecommunications network. Computerized
information banks have proliferated at an exponential rate in
the last few years, allowing anyone with a microcomputer and a

---

[1]Civil Engineer, Institute for Water Resources, U.S. Army
Corps of Engineers, Casey Bldg., Fort Belvoir, VA 22060-5586

telephone hookup to view bid and ask prices for commodities, find
out about airline schedules, or peruse gourmet recipes. Just
about anything worth knowing and much that would be better
forgotten is available now or will be shortly. One directory
lists about lists about 2,500 computerized, commercial data bases
(1).

Included in this vast expanse of electronic information are
many databases that contain information of interest to water
resource planners and engineers. To tap this information one
must know how to "go online" via computer and telephone. Next,
one must find the sources of information containing the
water-related information and determine how to locate the
specific information needed. Finally, the information must be
either read or a copy transferred back to a personal computer.
This paper describes the fundamentals of going online and getting
information electronically via computer and identifies some
sources of electronic information useful for water professionals.

Fundamentals of Going Online

Going online requires the proper hardware, including a
terminal or computer, a telephone, a modem, and some other
peripheral equipment, and software for communicating with the
computer that stores the information of interest. Making the
connection to the electronic information source involves setting
up the hardware and software, dialing the information source via
the telephone network, selecting the information needed, and
transferring the information back to your hardware.

Hardware. Either a terminal or a computer can be used to
communicate with an electronic information source. Both have
keyboards that can send signals to remote computers and a
display, either a video screen or printer, to show information
received from the remote computer. However, a computer, such
as a microcomputer, offers many advantages in acquiring
information from remote sources. A terminal can not save
information it receives. The information is displayed on the
video screen or printed by the printer. A microcomputer can
store information received from an electronic information
source in its memory or on another storage medium, such a
floppy disk, for later manipulation and analysis. The term
used to describe the transfer and storage of information
via computer is "downloading". When information is
transferred from a local source to a remote computer
the term is "uploading". The advantage of the microcomputer
over the terminal is so significant that the rest of this
paper assumes that a microcomputer will be used to establish
an online connection.

The microcomputer must have a connection called a serial
port that enables it to connect to a modem. Modem is shorthand
for modulator/demodulator. The function of the modem is to
translate the digital signals of a computer to the analog signals

that travel over the telecommunications network and vice versa.
A modem is required at both ends of an online connection
(Figure 1).

   The computer, serial port, and modem are all that are needed
to establish an online connection. However, other peripheral
hardware devices are needed to store and manipulate the
information received from a remote electronic source. A storage
device, such a a floppy disk drive, can be used to transfer
information to floppy disks for later use. A hard disk, with a
storage capability many times that of a single floppy disk, may
be needed to store large amounts of information. A printer is an
output device that can produce a printed record of textual
information received from the online connection.

   Software. The most common form of information transmission
via computer is called asynchronous communication. This form of
transmission works best when using the telephone network to
connect computers. Synchronous communication is another less
commonly used form of transmission. Most of the transfer of
information via computer takes place using asynchronous
communication (3). In asynchronous communication coded data is
transmitted in discrete parts one after the other (serially)
until the entire message is received. There is a standard code
for transmitting information electronically. The standard code
is called the American Standard for Information Interchange
(ASCII). The ASCII code assigns a seven digit binary code to
each letter and number on the keyboard as well as some special
functions, such as a code to signal your computer to make an
audible tone if equipped with a speaker. In order to communicate
online a computer must be able to recognize ASCII.

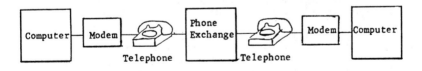

Figure 1. Hardware Setup for Online Connection

The purpose of communications software is to establish the
parameters for communications and send the ASCII codes from your
computer through the serial port to the modem and to receive the
coded information from the remote computer via the
telecommunications network through the modem back to your
computer. Communications software allows the user to set
communication parameters, such as the rate of transmission,
parity, and duplex. A discussion of each of the parameters is
beyond the scope of this paper, however, most good communication
software packages explain the purpose of each parameter and give
example settings. In fact, most communication packages set
default values for parameters that are valid for many connections
to remote computers (2).

Communications software can help you to acquire the
information you want. Once you get that information you will
need other software to manipulate, analyze, and display that
information. There are four other basic types of software that
can assist in using information: 1) Word-processing 2)
Spreadsheets 3) Database Management and 4) Graphics.

Word-processing software can be used to edit textual
information and raw data and incorporate it into your own
reports. Spreadsheet packages are the electronic version of an
accountant's columnar pad. Data from a remote computer can be
entered into a spreadsheet and analyzed in a number of different
ways. As an example, once a total for a column is entered in the
spreadsheet any changes to a value in the column will be
immediately reflected in the total. Data Management packages can
be used to maintain simple list of information or to develop
complex data management systems. The value of these packages is
that it allows a computer user to organize downloaded information
so that it can be retrieved quickly and easily. Finally,
graphics software can be used to turn numerical data into graphs
or charts that convey new or hidden meaning from the information.
Also, graphics can be used to present textual information as
overheads or slides. These additional software are not needed to
acquire information from remote electronic information sources,
but they are important once the information is downloaded.

Making the Connection. Once you have acquired the appropriate
hardware and set up your software it is relatively straightforward to establish an online connection. Access to the
online is made by dialing the phone number of the remote computer
that contains the information you desire. If you have a "smart"
modem you don't have to dial yourself, the computer can have the
modem dial for you. When the remote computer answers you may
hear a high-pitched tone. Depending on your communications
software and the remote computer you may have to hit the
keyboard's return key to establish connection. Once connection
is established you must communicate with the remote computer
using its language. Some systems lead you through your search
with menus, but most require you to communicate through commands

with sometimes exacting syntax. You will have to prepare for
"talking" to the remote computer by reading a manual describing
its language.

To retrieve and store information will require that you
request specific information from the remote computer and use
your communications software to instruct your microcomputer to
prepare to receive the information. For example, to download a
file of information called WATER you will have to instruct the
remote computer to send you the file named WATER. Also, using
your microcomputer software you will inform your microcomputer to
expect a file to be transmitted and to store that file on floppy
disk. You can instruct your microcomputer give the file on
floppy disk the name WATER or another name of your choosing.

To end a session you will sign off the remote computer. The
remote computer will log you off the system and may give you a
summary of the charges for the session you just finished. Upon
exiting from the remote system you would then quit from your
communications software and, then, use one of the other
software packages mentioned above to manipulate and analyze your
downloaded data.

Some Sources of Electronic Information for Water Professionals

Once you understand the basics of communicating with a
remote computer how do you find the one that has the information
that you want. Directories of online databases can aid you in
finding electronic information sources. However, you will find
that the best sources are the traditional sources of the
information for water professionals and commercial online
services.

Finding Electronic Information Sources. The proliferation
of online databases has spawned a number of publications that try
and keep track of what is available online. These directories
are valuable because they describe the type of information that
is available and where to get it (1), (2). Typically, a
directory will include a description of the database that is
available. The description will include the type of information
in the database. It may be bibliographic, numeric, a combination
of numeric and text, or full text. Each database is given a
subject index to aid in identification. The producer is the
organization that develops the database. The online service is
the name of the organization that makes the information available
online. An online service is often used by the producer in order
provide wider access to the information and the online service
can handle the administration of an online system more
effectively than the producer. The conditions, if any, explain
any restrictions on using the information or special costs or
requirements. The content is a brief abstract of the what
information is contained in the database. The language,
coverage, time span and updating are other descriptors used to

define the database. Figure 2 shows a directory listing for the
WATERNET ^{TM} database (1).

Traditional Sources. The most direct source of electronic
information is likely to be the traditional sources of
information used by water professionals. Federal, State,
regional, and local agencies have supplied much information to
water professionals. Many of these sources may be putting their
information online making it available to water professionals via
communications link. As an example the USGS provides the
National Water Data Exchange (NAWDEX) as a service to the water
community to help identify, locate and acquire water information
(4). In your search for water information online you should
first contact sources you have used in the past to inquire if
they now offer online services. Many agencies are just now
developing an online capability.

Another traditional source of information is the
library. Most libraries have the capability to tie into the
telecommunications and look for information. Many libraries use
online services, such as DIALOG, which provide a number of online
databases for use by customers.

Online Services. A library consists of many unrelated books
from diverse sources that are bound together under an orderly
system that allows users to find and retrieve books according to
a set of rules. What the library has done for printed material
the online services organizations are attempting to do for
electronic information. Databases of electronic information can
be derived from many sources. One database may contain the
complete text of all back issues of The New York Times, another
may contain a bibliography of a set ot related technical
journals, still another may contain the history of river levels
at a set of gage stations along a major river. Without some way
to catalog these databases an online search could become an
exercise in frustration (2). Also, if each producer of a
database kept his information apart it would be difficult for a
potential user to find and acquire. An online service can
provide a central point for access to eelctronic information and
can function as an electronic librarian providing order to
electronic information.

There are many online service vendors. Perhaps the largest
is DIALOG Information Systems with more than 200 separate
databases (1). In keeping with their status as an electronic
library DIALOG has provided a more or less uniform search
procedure for accessing information in their databases. Also,
you can access DIALOG through a telecommunications network that
allows you to make a local telephone call to connect to their
computers. Many online service vendors provide these services.

One interesting development related to online service is
the development of microcomputer software that can assist in
accessing electronic databases provided by online service

WATERNET^{TM}

Type: Reference (Bibliographic)

Subject: Environment

Producer: American Water Works Association (AWWA)

Online Service: DIALOG Information Services, Inc.

Content: Contains citations and abstracts to literature on water
quality, water utility management, analytical procedures for water
quality testing, energy-related economics, water system materials,
water and wastewater reuse, industrial and potable uses of water,
and environmental issues related to water. Includes these specific
topics: the drinking water industry, water pollution, health
effects, toxicology, water rates, water conservation, energy costs,
and the history of water supply. Items are selected from books,
conference proceedings, journals, newsletters, standards,
handbooks, water quality standard test methods, and all AWWA
and AWWA Research Foundation (AWWARF) publications, e.g. Annual
Conference Proceedings, Water Quality Technology Conference
Proceedings, Distribution System Symposium Proceedings, Conference
Seminars, and AWWARF Quality Research Newsletter from 1973 to
date. Also covers selected non-AWWA items. Corresponds in part
to the index of the Journal AWWA.

Language: English

Coverage: Primarily U.S., Canada, Mexico, and Latin American,
with some coverage of Europe and Asia.

Time Span: 1971 to date

Updating: Quarterly; about 3000 records a year.

Figure 2. Example of a Directory Listing for an Electronic
Information Source.

vendors. This software simplifies the search procedures required to access information. In addition, since connection to online service networks can be expensive the software can help the user prepare his search request offline and then sending the entire search sequence to the online service network as a bundle when connection is established. This saves connect time charges.

Summary

Getting information via computer can be an effective way to obtain the best available information for the planning, design, and development of water projects. To take advantage of this capability water professionals must understand the basics of "going online", how to find electronic information sources, and how to transfer the specific information from a remote computer system to a local microcomputer. Going online requires hardware, including a microcomputer, serial port, modem, and telephone and software, including a communications package for handling data transfer, retrieval and storage and word-processing, spreadsheet, data base management, and graphics for manipulating and analyzing retrieved information. Directories are available to help locate sources of electronic information. Sources of electronic information include traditional sources of water information, such as Federal, State and local agencies, and online service vendors, who maintain database supplied by producers of all types of information including water related information. All water resource professionals should become acquainted with information retrieval via computer.

Appendix -- References

1. Cuadra Associates, "Directory of Online Databases", Vol. 6,
No. 2, Cuadra Associates, Inc., Santa Monica, CA, 1984.

2. Edelhart, Mike and Davies, Owen, OMNI Online Database
Directory, Macmillan Publishing Company, New York, 1983.

3. Jordan, Larry E. and Churchill, Bruce, Communications and
Networking for the IBM PC, Robert J. Brady Company, Bowie, MD,
1983.

4. Showen, Charles R., Water Information Available from the U.S.
Geological Survey,, Computer Applications in Water Resources,
ASCE Water Resources Planning and Management Division Specialty
Conference, June, 1985.

Appendix -- Bibliography

Daney, Charles, "A Micro-Mainframe Primer", PC Magazine,
Vol. 4, No. 2, January, 22, 1985,

Glossbrenner, Alfred, The Complete Handbook of Personal Computer
Communications: Everything You Need to Go Online with the World,
St. Martin's Press, 1983.

Siegel, Jay, "Moving Data Between PC's and Mainframes", Byte,
Fall, 1984, pp. 248-255.

Water Information Available from the U.S. Geological Survey

Charles R. Showen*

The U.S. Geological Survey investigates the occurrence, quantity, distribution, and movement of the surface and underground waters that comprise the water resources of the United States. The data collected from these investigations are used in determining the adequacy of water supplies and in designing dams, bridges, and flood-control projects; in planning for energy development; and in predicting the potential effects of radioactive waste disposal on water supplies. The number of data collection sites to support these investigations varies as many water-data collection sites are added and others are discontinued; thus, large amounts of diversified data both current and historical, are amassed by the Survey's data-collection activities.

As a part of the Geological Survey's program of releasing water data to the public, two large-scale computerized systems are maintained. The National Water Data Storage and Retrieval System (WATSTORE) was developed to provide more effective and efficient management of data-releasing activities and provides for the processing, storage, and retrieval of surface-water, ground-water and water-quality data. Another service available is providing assistance to users of water data to identify, locate, and acquire needed data. This service is provided by the National Water Data Exchange (NAWDEX), which has the mission to identify sources of water data and to provide the connection between those who acquire and those who use water data.

Introduction

As a part of the field investigations of the U.S. Geological Survey (USGS), a number of data-collection sites are operated each year to support these investigations. The number of data-collection sites operated in fiscal year 1985 are given in Table 1 below. Each year many water-data collection sites are added and others are discontinued; thus, large amounts of diversified data, both current and historical, are amassed by the USGS's data-collection activities. These data are added yearly to the WATSTORE System and the NAWDEX data index.

*Hydrologist, U.S. Geological Survey, Reston, Virginia

Table 1--Number of Data-Collection Sites,
by Source of Funds, FY 1985

| | Number of stations, by source of funds | | | | |
Station Type	Federal Program (Fed)	Federal-State Cooperative Program (Coop)	Other Federal Agency Program (OFA)	Combined Fed Coop OFA	Total Number of Stations
Basic data-collection stations: Surface-water quantity:					
Continuous	570	3,110	1,860	1,870	7,410
Intermittent	90	2,890	360	910	4,250
Surface-water quality:	690	2,050	900	820	4,460
Lake and reservoir contents	20	610	350	250	1,230
Ground-water levels . .	3,250	21,720	1,790	8,980	35,740
Ground-water quality .	240	3,810	480	1,230	5,760
Total	4,860	34,190	5,740	14,060	58,850

The Federal program includes the operation of those sites for which funding is provided by Congress directly to the USGS.

The USGS's Federal-State cooperative program is a partnership for water-resources investigations and the operation of data-collection sites between the USGS and State and local agencies. Details of programs (50-50 matching) are negotiated at State or local level by representatives of USGS and representatives of the cooperating agencies.

The other Federal agencies program includes the operation of data-collection sites for which funds have been transferred to the USGS by the other Federal agency. Included in this program are data sites to support compacts and legal adjudications.

Description of Surface-Water, Water-Quality, and Ground-Water Networks

1. Surface Water

The systematic stream-gaging program began in 1889 at the station on the Rio Grande at Embudo, New Mexico. The base data collected at stream-gaging stations consist of records of stage and measurements of discharge of streams or canals, and stage, surface area, and contents of lakes or reservoirs. In addition, observations of factors affecting the stage-discharge relation or the stage-capacity relation, weather records, and other information are used to supplement base data in determining the daily flow or volume of water in storage. Records of stage are obtained from either direct readings on a non-recording gage, a tape punched at selected time intervals, or by field radios which

transmit data to an earth-orbiting satellite back to a receive
site for distribution.

There are 50 stations (1985) designated as hydrologic bench-
mark stations that provide hydrologic data for a basin in which
the hydrologic regimen will likely be governed solely by natural
conditions. Data collected at a bench-mark station may be used
to separate effects of natural from manmade changes in other
basins which have been developed and in which the physiography,
climate, and geology are similar to those in the undeveloped
bench-mark basin.

2. Water Quality

Water samples are collected and shipped to a laboratory for
analyses that describe the chemical, physical, biologic, and
radio-chemical characteristics of both surface and ground waters.
These samples may be collected at predetermined intervals, i.e.,
monthly, quarterly, semi-annually, etc., or they may be collected
with digital monitors from which the records consist of daily
maximum, minimum, and mean values for each constituent measured.

The routine water sampling program of the USGS began in 1941.

The following special water-quality network is maintained:
National stream-quality accounting network (NASQAN) is a data
collection network designed by the USGS to meet many of the
information demands of agencies or groups involved in national
or regional water-quality planning and management. Both accounting and broad-scale monitoring objectives have been incorporated
into the network design. Primary objectives of the network are
(1) to depict areal variability of streamflow and water-quality
conditions nationwide on a year-by-year basis and (2) to detect
and assess long-term changes in streamflow and stream quality.
There are 500 stations (1985) designated as NASQAN stations.

3. Ground Water

The basic ground-water level network includes observation
wells so located that the most significant data are obtained
from the fewest wells in the most important aquifers. Water-
level measurements are given in feet with reference to either
National Geodetic Vertical Datum of 1929 (NGVD) or land-surface
datum (lsd).

In addition, inventory data about wells, springs, and other
sources of ground water are collected; the data included are
site location and identification, geohydrologic characteristics,
well-construction history, and one-time field measurements
such as water temperature.

The ground-water level network began in 1935.

U.S. Geological Survey Data Stored in Major Data Banks

The water resources data routinely collected by the USGS´s
data-collection programs are stored in the WATSTORE System and, in
addition, are indexed by the NAWDEX System.

1. Description of WATSTORE System.

The WATSTORE System consists of several files in which data
are grouped and stored by common characteristics. Currently,
files are maintained for the storage of (1) surface-water,
quality-of-water, and ground-water data measured on a daily or
continuous basis; (2) annual peak values for streamflow stations;
(3) chemical analyses for surface- and groundwater sites; (4)
water-data parameters measured more frequently than daily; (5)
geologic and inventory data for ground-water sites; and (6)
summary data on water use. In addition, an index file of
sites for which data are stored in the system is also maintained.
A schematic diagram of the system is given in Figure 1.

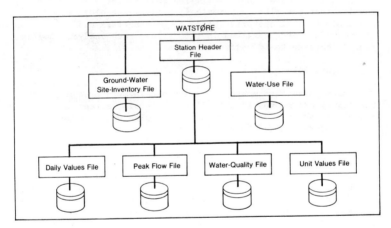

Figure 1.--Schematic Diagram of WATSTORE System

A. Station Header File

The Station Header File contains information pertinent
to the identification, location, and physical description
of over 339,000 sites for which data are stored in the
WATSTORE files. Included in this file are agency codes,
station identification numbers, latitude-longitude, State
codes, county codes, drainage area (for surface water sites),
station names, hydrologic unit codes, geologic unit codes
(aquifer codes), etc.

B. Daily Values File

     All water-data parameters measured or observed either on
a daily or continuous basis and numerically reduced to daily
values are stored in this file. Instantaneous measurements
at fixed-time intervals, daily mean values, and statistics
such as daily maximum and minimum values also may be stored.
The file contains data on streamflow, river stages, reservoir
contents, water temperatures, specific conductance, sediment
concentrations, sediment discharges and ground-water levels.

C. Peak Flow File

     Annual maximum (peak) streamflow (discharge) and gage
height (stage) values at surface-water sites constitute
this file.

D. Water Quality File

     Results of more than 2.7 million analyses of water
samples that describe the chemical, physical, biological,
and radiochemical characteristics of both surface and
ground waters are contained in this file. Each analysis may
contain data up to 185 different constituents.

E. Unit Values File

     Water parameters measured on a schedule more frequent
than daily are stored in this file. Rainfall, stream
discharge, and temperature data are examples of the types
of data stored in the Unit Values File.

F. Ground-Water Site-Inventory File

     This file is maintained within WATSTORE independent of
the files discussed above, but it is cross-referenced to
the Water Quality File and to the Daily Values File. It
contains inventory data about wells, springs, and other
sources of ground water; the data included are site location
and identification, geohydrologic characteristics, well-
construction history, and one-time field measurements such
as water temperature. The file is designed to accommodate
255 data elements and currently contains data for over
900,000 sites.

G. Water Use File

     This file is maintained within WATSTORE independent
of the files discussed above, but is designed to complement
the data on water quantity and quality. The types of data
stored are data on withdrawal, usage, and return flow
(discharge).

2. Description of NAWDEX System

Another service available from the USGS is providing assistance to users of water data to identify, locate, and acquire
needed data. The mission of NAWDEX is to identify sources of
water data and to provide the connection between those who
acquire and those who use water data. This is being accomplished
by establishing better communication among water-oriented
organizations, acquiring as much information as possible on
available water data, and making this information available to
the water-data community. These efforts contribute to the
improvement of the transfer of water data and information
about water data between the collector and end-user communities.

NAWDEX maintains two automated files and a description of
these files is given below:

A. Identifying sources of water data.

NAWDEX has extensive information available that identifies organizations that are sources of water data. This
information is provided through a computerized Water Data
Sources Directory maintained in the USGS´s computer system
in Reston, Virginia, and is accessible by computers or
computer terminals.

The Water Data Sources Directory identifies organizations that collect water data, locations within these
organizations from which water data may be obtained,
alternate sources from which an organization´s water data
may be obtained, the geographic areas in which an organization collects water data, and the types of water data
collected and available. Information has been compiled
for more than 770 organizations, and information on other
organizations is added on a continuing basis.

B. Indexing of water data

NAWDEX, through its Master Water Data Index, provides
a nationwide indexing service. This computerized index
initially identifies more than 441,000 sites for which
water data are available from over 440 organizations. It
gives the geographic location of these sites, the data-
collecting organization, the types of data available, the
periods of time for which data are available, the major
water-data parameters.

It also includes the frequency of measurement of the
parameters and the media in which the data are stored.
Information on additional sites is added on a continuing
basis. The Master Water Data Index is also maintained in
the USGS´s computer system in Reston, Virginia, and is
accessible by computers or computer terminals. A schematic
diagram of the Master Water Data Index is given in Figure 2.

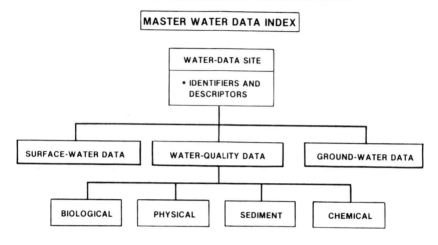

Figure 2.—Schematic Diagram of Master Water Data Index

> The Water Data Sources Directory and Master Water Data Index contain common identifiers that allow them to be used together. For example, the Master Water Data Index may be used to identify water data available in a geographic area and the Water Data Sources Directory may then be used to obtain the names and addresses of organizations from which the identified data may be obtained.

USGS Services to Data Users

Information about the availability of specific types of water data, the acquisition of water data or products, and user charges, can be obtained locally from each of the offices listed in Table 2. Requests may be directed to the NAWDEX Program Office, 421 National Center, Reston, Virginia, 22092, (telephone 703/860-6031 or FTS 928-6031) or to the Assistance Centers in Table 2. NAWDEX provides the requested information or data either from its files or from those to which it has access, or the inquiry is referred directly to the organizations that hold the requested data or information.

In addition, arrangements for direct computer access to the WATSTORE System data files and the NAWDEX directories can be made by the NAWDEX Program Office through the use of a formal memorandum of agreement. The formal agreement provides the user direct access to certain data files for the retrieval of raw data and the use of certain computer programs which are unique to hydrology. Examples of the programs that are unique to hydrology are: flow duration tables, various low- and high-flow sequence summaries, log-Pearson statistics, monthly and annual statistics, annual flood frequency analyses, etc.

Table 2--Location of NAWDEX Assistance Centers for Locating
Sources of Data and WATSTORE Assistance for the
Acquisition of Data or Data Products.

The listed centers offer both types of assistance unless they
are labeled with only "N" for NAWDEX or "W" for WATSTORE.

ALABAMA, Tuscaloosa
ALASKA, Anchorage
ARIZONA, Tucson
ARKANSAS, Little Rock
CALIFORNIA, Los Angeles
  Menlo Park and San Francisco
COLORADO, Lakewood (Denver)
  and Ft. Collins(N)
CONNECTICUT, Hartford
FLORIDA, Tallahassee, Miami(N),
  Orlando(N), and Tampa(N)
GEORGIA, Doraville (Atlanta)
HAWAII, Honolulu (serves
  American Samoa and Guam)
IDAHO, Boise
ILLINOIS, Urbana
INDIANA, Indianapolis
IOWA, Iowa City
  (two locations)
KANSAS, Lawrence
KENTUCKY, Louisville
LOUISIANA, Baton Rouge
MARYLAND, Landover(N)
  Rockville(N) and Towson
  (serves Delaware and
  District of Columbia)
MASSACHUSETTS, Concord, Boston
  (serves Maine, New Hampshire,
  Rhode Island and Vermont)
MICHIGAN, Lansing and
  Ann Arbor(N)
MINNESOTA, St. Paul
MISSISSIPPI, Jackson

MISSOURI, Rolla
MONTANA, Helena
NEBRASKA, Lincoln (two
  locations) and Omaha(N)
NEVADA, Carson City
NEW JERSEY, Trenton
NEW MEXICO, Albuquerque
NEW YORK, Albany and
  Syosset(N)
NORTH CAROLINA, Raleigh
NORTH DAKOTA, Bismarck
OHIO, Columbus
OKLAHOMA, Oklahoma City
OREGON, Portland and
  Salem(N)
PENNSYLVANIA, Harrisburg,
  Malvern(N) and Pittsburgh(N)
PUERTO RICO, Ft. Buchanan
  (San Juan); also serves
  Virgin Islands
SOUTH CAROLINA, Columbia
  (two locations)
SOUTH DAKOTA, Huron
TENNESSEE, Nashville
TEXAS, Austin
UTAH, Salt Lake City (three
  locations) and Logan(N)
VIRGINIA, Richmond, Blacksburg(N)
  and Reston (two locations)
WASHINGTON, Tacoma and Spokane
WEST VIRGINA, Charleston
WISCONSIN, Madison
WYOMING, Cheyenne and Laramie(N)

Services for data-search assistance are provided free of charge to the greatest possible extent by the NAWDEX Program Office and the Assistance Centers. Charges are assessed for services requiring computer costs, extensive personnel time, duplicating services, or other costs incurred when providing services. In the case of direct computer access, the user is responsible for providing the computer terminal or microcomputer, plus the computer charges incurred in processing the request and a small service charge. The computer job cost also includes the telephone charges from a local node on the telecommunication network. If a long distance telephone call is required to access the local network, the user is responsible for these charges also. Charges for processing computer requests for data are generally nominal. Some of the factors that govern these costs are: (1) the amount of data requested, (2) the output format selected, and (3) the time frame required by the requestor.

Summary

The USGS has made a concerted effort to improve the transfer of water data throughout the water-resources community. This effort has improved communication throughout the water-data community, created a better awareness of existing water data, made data-search assistance more readily available to those who need it, reduced the time required to obtain data, increased the utilization of existing water data, and helped reduce redundancy in data collection. We feel that these benefits contribute toward making water-resources programs more effective.

THE NATIONAL GROUND WATER INFORMATION CENTER DATA BASE

Valerie J. Orr*

Abstract: The Research Institute, Education Foundation and
Publishing Company of the National Water Well Association
have long been considered information central for the world's
community of hydrogeologists. Under contract to the U.S.
Environmental Protection Agency's National Center for Ground
Water Research, NWWA's Library has been transformed into a
sophisticated, computerized data base which to date includes
35,000 literary citations indexed in 23 fields of
information.

Research groups, libraries, universities, private consultants
and industrial firms can become regular users of the Library
for a one time fee of $100 which includes the assignment of
an access code, a user manual and personnel training. User
fees for connect time are billed bi-monthly. A competent
searcher can complete a search for under $20. Full detailed
printouts describing desired literature is printed off line
and sent via mail to reduce main computer connect time and
costs.

The National Water Well Association is a Ground Water Research
Institute, Education Foundation, and Publishing Company with a staff
of 55. NWWA is the center of competence for the ground water industry
and is a combined professional society for hydrogeologists and trade
association for water well drillers.

The National Water Well Association Library was initially
conceived to support NWWA's Research Facility, but it has rapidly
evolved into a public library of ground water information.

In 1979, the U.S. Environmental Protection Agency established,
through a cooperative agreement with the National Water Well
Association, the National Ground-Water Information Center -- a
repository of ground-water literature accessible to scientists,
government agencies, business and the public.

The EPA's Ground-Water Research Branch at the Robert S. Kerr
Environmental Research Laboratory in Ada, Oklahoma, through its

*Director, National Ground Water Information Center, National Water
Well Association, 500 West Wilson Bridge Road, Worthington, Ohio
43085.

responsibility for providing technical information upon which
ground-water management decisions can be based, oversees the
activities of the Center.

The NGWIC possesses a ground-water library containing 15,000
volumes. The collection consists of books, journals, newsletters and
other technical holdings. The National Water Well Association began
building the NGWIC Data Base by indexing publications which dealt
specifically with the field of ground water. The NGWIC soon began to
explore literature of related fields of environmental health,
chemistry, agricultural science, irrigation, reservoir seepage, soil
science, and foundations engineering to meet research requirements.
This provides expansion of a more comprehensive library of
publications which deals with underground water and all its facets.

The NGWIC subscribes to nearly 120 technical and trade journals
and newsletters, many of which date back to the initial volumes.
These journals have been indexed retrospectively. Although the
periodical holdings at NWWA are quite extensive (currently numbering
5,000 volumes), thousands more are available from The Ohio State
University libraries for indexing and duplication. A list of
regularly indexed journals follows.

The Center continues to index its existing collection of
significant books, in addition to journals. Government documents with
special emphasis on those reports of projects sponsored by the U.S.
EPA are also indexed. These EPA projects include literature produced
by the National Center for Ground-Water Research (NCGWR), the EPA
Ground-Water Research Laboratory [Robert S. Kerr Environmental
Research Laboratory (RSKERL)] and institutions funded by it,
collections of university reports, esoteric State publications, and
proceedings of national and international conferences and symposia.
General topics include: ground-water quality, monitoring and
protection, aquifer development and restoration, water law, and water
well technology.

In January 1982, we made available to the public, our
computerized retrieval system that searches our extensive
bibliographic data base of references in the areas of hydrogeology and
water well technology.

In order to describe the world's ground water literature, we have
developed a thesaurus of nearly 700 hydrogeologic terms. Three years
of effort with the assistance of some of the nation's leading
hydrogeologists have gone into developing the thesaurus.

The National Ground Water Information Center (NGWIC) under
contract with Battelle Columbus Laboratories is using BASIS, the most
sophisticated computer software available. Basis software permits the
user to: perform proximity searching; search on numeric ranges; scan
the records for terms; use prefix, suffix and infix searching; use the
full compliment of Boolean logic; and save search requests.

NATIONAL GROUND WATER INFORMATION CENTER

Journals Regularly Indexed

Every Issue	Several Times/Yr.	Few Times/Hr.
Canadian Water Well	African and Asian Water and Sewage	AAPG Bulletin
Ground Water		Arab Water World
Ground Water Age	Agricultural Engineering	Civil Engineering
Ground Water Monitoring Review	Agua	Drilling Contractor
Johnson Driller's Journal	Applied and Environmental Microbiology	Earthquake Information Bulletin
Journal American Water Works Association	Drill Bit	
	Engineering News Record	EPA Journal
Journal of Hydrology	Environmental Monitoring and Assessment	EOS
Journal Water Pollution Control Federation	ES & T, Environmental Science & Technology	Garber-Wellington Gazette
Pacific Ground Water Digest	Geothermal Energy	Geology
U.S. Water News	Geothermal Resources Council Bulletin	Geological Society of America Bulletin
Water Resources Bulletin	Irrigation Age	
Water Resources Research	Irrigation Journal	Geotimes
Water Well Journal	Journal of Environmental Engineering (ASCE)	JPT. Journal of Petroleum Technology
	Journal of Irrigation and Drainage (ASCE)	Oil & Gas Journal
	Journal of Soil and Water Conservation	Services Smithsonian
	Journal of the National Water Well Association of Australia	Water Conditioning

continued

Journals Regularly Indexed (continued)

Every Issue	Several Times/Yr.	Few Times/Yr.
	Water Engineering & Management	
	Water International	
	Water Research	
	Water Technology	
	Western Water	

Currently there are 35,000 records in the data base which are indexed by 23 possible fields of information.

References are retrieved by using combinations of indexed fields which include accession number, author, title, source, international standards serial number, international standard book number, publisher, non-U.S. geographic area, State abbreviation, county name, aquifer region, publication date, call number, language, holding library, contents notes (photos, maps, tables, etc.), chemical constituents, thesaurus descriptors, biological factors, author affiliations, and document type. Chemical constituents and biological factors can be searched freely, as all significant chemicals and biological factors are indexed just as they appear in the literature.

Most of these fields are self explanatory but some are rather unique. It is possible to limit searching to foreign countries, particular states, counties or even specific aquifer regions.

When searching using descriptors, they must appear exactly as they do in the thesaurus. Chemicals and biological factors, on the other hand, may be searched freely. They appear in the references exactly as they do in the literature. As a result of this freedom it is suggested that variations in formula, name and spelling be taken into consideration (For example: H_2S, HYDROGEN SULFIDE and HYDROGEN SULPHIDE all appear in the chemical field).

Some of the most commonly used commands in searching are FIND, DISPLAY, and PRINT, but you may SCAN fields, LOOK for terms or BROWSE the thesaurus on-line. Once you have created a document set you may choose to display a full or partial record, or to save on-line computer time you may have the citations printed off-line on a high speed printer and mailed to you from Battelle. An example of a record appears below.

ACCESSION NUMBER	842832474
INDEXER'S INITIALS	MEM
DATE ENTERED INTO DATA BASE	850129
AUTHOR	VALOCCHI A J;ROBERTS P V;
TITLE	ATTENUATION OF GROUND-WATER CONTAMINANT PULSES
SOURCE	JRNL OF HYDRAULIC ENGINEERING (ASCE);V109 N12;P1165-1182
INT'L. STANDARD SERIAL NUMBER	0043-9429
PUBLICATION DATE	12-1984
LANGUAGE	ENGLISH
HOLDING LIBRARY	NWWA
CONTENTS NOTES	FIGURES;TABLES;REFERENCES
CHEMICAL CONSTITUENTS	CHLORIDE;CHLOROFORM
DESCRIPTORS	ATTENUATION;DISPERSION; ANALYTICAL METHODS;SOLUTE TRANSPORT MODELS;OBSERVATION WELLS
AFFILIATE ORGANIZATION	UNIV OF IL;STANFORD UNIV

The data base is accessible from anywhere in the world using a computer terminal with a modem and standard telephone lines. You may dial the data base direct or use TYMNET.

The data base has already proven to be of great interest to government agencies, industry, consultants and those in the academic community concerned with ground water quality and development.

Research groups, libraries, universities, private consultants and individual firms may subscribe to the data base for a one-time $100 fee. For this fee, the user receives a personal user name and passsword and a complete user's manual. After the initial fee, subscribers are only billed for computer time and off-line prints at rates of $75.00 per hour and $1.50 per 500 lines respectively.

Manual and computer searches are performed by the Center staff at a nominal fee for those not wishing to subscribe to the Data Base. A computer printout or list of references is sent to those requesting a search.

If, after reviewing the results of a literature search, the individual requests a copy of the literature, we can either provide a photocopy of the material or arrange to loan the material through interlibrary loan.

Scientists throughout the country are rapidly learning that the NGWIC Data Base is among the most proficient systems available for literature research. It is clearly in a class by itself in the field of ground water science.

COMPUTER APPLICATIONS FOR REAL-TIME OPERATION
OF WATER DISTRIBUTION SYSTEMS

Uri Shamir, M.ASCE*

ABSTRACT. This paper surveys the state-of-the-art in computer assisted real-time operation of water distribution systems. It first examines the reasons and justification for installing computer based control systems, then describes their components and operation. The main part is then devoted to the control system software: demand forecasting, network analysis and simulation, and especially algorithms for optimal control.

Introduction

A recent survey (1, 22) by AWWA's Computer Assisted Design of Water Systems (CADWS) Committee has indicated that many utilities would like to move towards computer controlled or at least computer assisted real-time operation. Many of the utilities are routinely using computer programs for off-line studies of operation and of capacity expansion.

This trend towards real-time control is motivated by some or all of the following factors, in a mix that changes between systems:
(a) Operation of the existing system is becoming increasingly more complex. New facilities are added and the existing ones are further interconnected. Sources of different qualities, reliabilities and costs are introduced. Demands rise and it is more difficult to meet them reliably. All of these require system wide considerations (as opposed to local ones) in setting operating plans.
(b) Retirement of experienced operatores, often not replaced by people of similar capability and/or experience.
(c) Aging systems fail more frequently, leading to difficult operational decisions, which have to be made quickly under stress.
(d) High operating costs justify investments in attempts to optimize.
(e) Control and computer hardware is quite rapidly becoming cheaper, more available, and reliable.
(f) Control systems in plants, power systems and water systems are becoming more common, providing an experience to learn from.
(g) Managers, engineers and operators are feeling more comfortable and less threatened by computers.
(h) Mathematical models, optimization algorithms and control software have developed considerably in recent years.

*Professor, Faculty of Civil Eng., Technion-Israel Institute of Technology, Haifa 32000, Israel; currently Visiting Professor, Dept. of Civil Eng., M.I.T., Cambridge, MA 02139.

This paper will describe systems for computer assisted real-time operation of water distribution systems, concentrating on software, especially algorithms and programs for optimal control. A more detailed description of hardware components and control systems hierarchical structures is given by Shamir (16), and design optimization is presented in Shamir (15). Some practical considerations for selecting and installing control systems on pipelines were presented by an ASCE Task Committee (20).

Control Systems

A computer based control system includes:

(a) Measurement and transmission of field data to a control center.
(b) Pumps and valves which can be controlled remotely from the center.
(c) Computer(s), operators' consoles, displays, printers, other peripheral equipment.
(d) A data base, for historical and current data: network components, water consumptions, operational records, reservoir levels, operating status of pumps, etc.
(e) Software for managing this data base and displaying it in graphic and tabular form for the operators.
(f) Software for analyzing these data, for forecasting demands, and for determining good (optimal, if possible) operating plans. We shall call this the system software.

A system with all but the system software is a SCADA (Supervisory Control and Data Acquisition) system. A SCADA system has software to manage data collection, the data base, graphic and tabular screen displays of the system and data, and to transmit manually imposed controls from the center to the proper locations in the field. Many such systems exist, and more are being installed. The state-of-the-art is distributed systems, which have PLC's (Programmable Logical Controllers) located at the facilities in the field. These have microprocessors and handle data and command traffic. They also perform local protection and control of the facility. Modern PLC's accept downloading of their local control programs from the control center.

We are concerned here primarily with item (f) above--the hydraulic system software, also called control software. Only when such software exists does the system begin to move from a SCADA to computer control. There are many levels of computer control, all the way from occasional off-line analyses of system operation to aid operators in evaluating their actions, up to automatic control, where loops are closed directly from the computer, which determines the operating plan and implements it.

The remainder of this paper will be devoted to the system software. But first, a word about moving from SCADA to computer control. This should be done gradually, with caution. The ultimate degree of automation will vary between systems, depending on many considerations. But even when the final objective is a high degree of automation, this must be approached gradually. First, do the analysis off-line and present the results to the operators, to accept or

reject. When sufficient experience and confidence in the computed
operating plans is gained, one can begin to close loops: first, those
that look safest to delegate to the computer and then, with time, more
and more. This is the way to minimize the chances of doing worse than
the operators did without the computer. Thus, it is recommended to
operate "with-a-person-in-the-control-loop" as long as necessary, possibly always, and automate only proven algorithms.

System Software

To operate the system effectively means to keep operating costs
low, while meeting the demands reliably, maintaining reservoir levels
and system pressures within bounds, and possibly satisfying some practical operating considerations as well. A mathematical definition of
this will be given later. We now describe how various components of
the system software contribute to effective operation.

Demand Forecasting

The first condition for effective operation is to be able to
estimate future demands. Operators do this intuitively, from experience. They use such information as: day of the week, hour of the
day, weather, special events (holiday, a major sporting event), last
day and last hour consumptions, etc.

A demand forecasting program uses past demand data and possibly
additional information, such as weather forecasts, to forecast demands
24 hours ahead (sometimes a weekly forecast is also needed). There
are a variety of techniques which can be used.

Moss (13) reviewed methods previously developed: a Kalman filter
by Perry (14) and a Fourier transform plus exponential smoothing by
Gray (10). Based on these, Moss then developed a six-harmonic Fourier
predictor with triple exponential smoothing, which performs well for
the urban demands supplied by the East Worcestershire Water Co. in
England.

Two simpler time series analysis methods were tried earlier by
Shimron and Shamir (17) to forecast agricultrual demands in Israel.
Other methods are currently being developed and tested in Israel.

It seems that a combination of time-series methods and whatever
direct information can be obtained from consumers and about weather
forecasts is probably the most promising.

Network Analysis and Simulation

Another prerequisite for effective operation is the ability to
know how different controls will cause the hydraulic system to react,
in terms of its physical performance and the resulting cost of operation. Here, too, operators draw on their experience and understanding of the system. A good operator can predict, to a reasonable
approximation, the system's reaction to any control, and how expensive
this control is as compared to others. The prediction may be less

accurate, or even seriously in error, as the hydraulic system becomes more complex, and especially if the system is in a state which is unfamiliar to the operator (for example, due to some major failure).

The software which predicts system response to controls is a network solver. Using a mathematical model of the system, a model which may be modified in real-time to reflect things such as pipe and pump outages, the network solver determines the flows and pressures throughout the system, for a given (forecasted) set of node demands and controls. Many such programs are used for design and operations studies by utilities and consulting firms (1, 22). Not all are suitable for control systems, because they may not be efficient and/or flexible enough to meet the needs. A full discussion of these considerations cannot be accommodated here.

A simulator allows successive network solutions to be linked via the change in reservoir storage. The results at the end of one time period become the boundary and initial conditions for the next. A simulator is thus a simple extension of a network solver. It can also easily total operating hours, quantities produced and supplied, energy used. A simulator is, therefore, a very useful tool for operational studies, to be used in operator training, in aiding real-time decision making, and for investigating system modifications.

Network analysis and simulation can be a very effective tool to aid operators in making decisions. They submit their proposed operating plans and the programs simulate the physical and cost results. The operator can then try different controls and select the best among those tried. This can be done in training sessions, "off-line" so to speak, as well as in real-time.

The Optimal Control Problem

The optimal control problem for a water supply and distribution system is: how to operate the pumps and valves so as to minimize the total cost, while meeting the demands and satisfying minimum pressure constraints.

It is assumed in this formulation that demands are given and must be met. A broader formulation might include the quantities supplied to consumers as decision variables, and the objective would then be to maximize net benefit, i.e., the difference between the benefits resulting from supply and the costs. This might be relevant in irrigation systems, and possibly for industrial consumers, but is outside the scope of this presentation. We deal with urban supply, and assume demands to be exogenous to our decision problem.

The time horizon under consideration is typically 24 hours, since demands repeat approximately on a daily cycle. Occasionally, the weekly behavior must be considered in some way, as well. This occurs when there is weekly storage, i.e., reservoirs which fill, say, over the weekend and are slowly depleted over the week. We shall, however, concentrate on the daily operation problem, since the weekly storage case can be dealt with by a relatively simple modification.

The control problem must be considered for the entire 24-hour period and cannot be separated into individual hourly problems, for a number of reasons. (We shall use one hour time steps, and talk about "the hourly operation," although it is possible to use longer and/or shorter time steps: half an hour is probably the minimum required, and during low demand periods two, four, and even six hour intervals, may be appropriate.) The primary reason is the role of storage, which is the state vector (one component for each reservoir). State transitions, i.e., changes in reservoir storage, link adjacent time steps.

Other reasons for linking the hourly problems over time are: constraints on the minimum time elapsed between turning pumps on, off and on again, to prevent excessive wear, and sometimes also the fact that total operating time and/or energy consumption by a pump may influence costs.

The problem is formulated as an open-loop control for the 24-hour period, with demands at each node given for all hours. The initial state is the reservoir volumes at present, and the final state is assumed known. Frequently, the problem is formulated for a period starting and ending, say, at 6 AM, with all reservoirs assumed to be full at both ends. If a reservoir provides weekly storage, then its final state can be taken lower than the initial by the amount corresponding to one day's withdrawal.

Obviously, the control problem need not be solved for an entire 24-hour period. Given the initial state at any time during the day, the demand forecast for the remainder, and the final state, the control problem can be formulated. Because of the computational burden, as will be discussed later, present control algorithms are solved typically once a day (usually at night), and some have a procedure for modifying the operating plan during the day for the remaining time, if actual conditions deviate form the forecast. This correction is computed by approximate methods which make them feasible for on-line computations.

Solution of the optimal control problem must satisfy constraints of several types:
(a) Demands must be met, as stated above.
(b) Source capacities may have an upper limit. (Assumed to be a limit on instantaneous production; if the total production over the day is to be limited, this introduces an additional state variable in the formulation and complicates it. We shall not deal with this situation here.)
(c) Hydraulic laws of the system must hold: continuity at nodes; head-discharge relations in pipes, pumps and valves; level-storage relations in reservoirs.
(d) Reservoir levels have to be within admissible ranges.
(e) Pressures at nodes have to be within admissible ranges.

The resulting control problem is difficult to solve because:
(a) The problem may be rather large.
(b) Some controls are discrete (pumps on/off).

(c)   The network equations are non-linear, and their solution for each
      time step must be by iterative methods. There is therefore no
      way to obtain explicit expressions for dependent variables, such
      as flows into and out of reservoirs and pressures at nodes, as a
      function of the controls.

      Several approaches exist for dealing with these difficulties, as
will be explained in more detail in the following sections. Among
them:
(a)   Decomposition, aggregation and iterative DP methods to deal with
      problem size.
(b)   When pumps can be operated in a large number of combinations,
      covering rather smoothly the range of possible discharges, the
      corresponding control can be considered continuous rather than
      discrete.
(c)   Network equations are linearized; pressure constraints are
      ignored (with the expectation that the optimal controls will
      anyhow result in feasible pressures).

Solution Approaches and Algorithms

      The control problem can be solved by DP, when its dimension does
not make this computationally impractical. DP can handle all the
aspects of the control problem: discrete control, constraints on the
state variables (reservoir levels) and pressures. Thus, if the number
of state variables is small, DP is the answer. "Small" turns out to
be one, two, possibly three reservoirs, and in special cases maybe
four, but no more.

      Let us first formulate the problem as a DP, and then proceed to
the "tricks" which have to be used to make it solvable. Denote:

$t = 1,\ldots, T$ = time periods (for hourly T = 24);
$D(t)$ = vector of demands at nodes;
$V(t)$ = vector of reservoir volumes at beginning of time t;
$P(t)$ = vector of pressures at nodes;
$U(t)$ = vector of controls for pumps and valves;
$f_t(V,U)$ = cost of operating the system during time period t.

The optimization problem is

$$\underset{\substack{U(t) \\ t=1,\ldots,T}}{\text{Min}} \quad \left\{ \sum_{t=1}^{24} f_t\big(V(t),U(t)\big) \right\} \tag{1}$$

subject to constraints on reservoir volumes (or the corresponding
levels)

$$\underline{V}(t) \leq V(t) \leq \overline{V}(t) \tag{2}$$

where volume changes are given by the network dynamics

$$V(t + 1) = g\big(V(t),\ D(t),\ U(t)\big) \tag{3}$$

and on pressures at some or all nodes

$$\underline{P}(t) \leq P(t) \leq \overline{P}(t) \tag{4}$$

where pressures are given by the network equations

$$P(t) = h\big(V(t), D(t), U(t)\big) \tag{5}$$

The beginning and end states, $V(1)$ and $V(t + 1)$ are given, and $U(t)$ belongs to an admissible set of controls. The recursive equation of the DP algorithm is:

$$f_t^*\big(V(t)\big) = \underset{U(t)}{\text{Min}} \; \{f_t\big(V(t),U(t)\big) + f_{t+1}^*\big(V(t + 1)\big)\} \tag{6}$$

where

$f_t^*(V)$ = The Bellman function = the optimal cost of operating the system from the beginning of time period t, for the rest of the time horizon, starting with state V.

$V(t + 1)$ in Eq. (6) is given by Eq. (3). In searching for the optimal controls, $U_t^*\big(V(t)\big)$, by Eq. (6), all controls which cause violation of constraints (2) or (4) are rejected. This poses no difficulty, since $V(t)$ and $P(t)$ are obtained by a "foreward" solution of Eqs. (3) and (5), respectively.

If the entire Bellman function, $f_t^*(V)$, is stored during computation, then as long as the demands $D(t)$ do not change, there is no need to re-compute when $V(t)$ is found to deviate from the computed optimal trajectory. If the forecast $D(t)$ deviates markedly from that used initially, the optimization for the remaining time may have to be re-run.

Dreizin et al. (8) used this procedure for a relatively simple system. For a larger system, the procedure proved computationally infeasible, and they resorted to an ad hoc search procedure which will not be discussed here. Several systems in Israel are now controlled by ad hoc methods.

Sterling and Coulbeck (18, 19) tried to "push" the DP method to the limit, by simplifying some of the equations, but the results were not very realistic. Coulbeck (4, 5, 6) then developed a different approach, which will be described later.

Cohen and co-workers (2, 3, 11) developed two devices to get around the "curse of dimensionality": decomposition-coordination, and aggregation. Space does not permit a full discussion of the details, so only the principles will be described.

The entire system is divided into non-overlapping sub-systems. Each sub-system must be small enough to be solved by DP (as is, or after some aggregation of its state vector, as explained below), which means one or at most two reservoirs per sub-system. Assume the "cuts" between the sub-systems are in pipes. Then, if the 24-hour trajectory of either head or flow at the cut and the trajectory of cost of the other variable at the same point are given, the sub-network's optimal control problem can be solved. The solution specifies the internal controls of the sub-system and the trajectories of the variables which were free to change at the cut.

For example, consider adjacent sub-systems A and B, and the following assignment of values at the cut between them: A "gives" B the trajectories (24 hourly values) of heads and costs of the flows, B "gives" A trajectories of flows and the costs of heads. Say we fix first the trajectories of flows and head-costs at the cut. Then A can be optimized. The results include a trajectory of heads at the cut. Moreover, the cost of meeting each of the specified flows at the cut can be computed, using the stored Bellman function for the sub-system which was just optimized and a (simplified) estimation of the change in the internal state vector (reservoir storage) due to an incremental change in one value of the specified flow trajectory at the cut. The resulting head and flow-cost trajectories are now passed over to B, which can now be optimized internally.

The results of each sub-systems's optimization are thus trajectories of one physical variable (say, head) at each of its "cut" connections to neighboring sub-systems and of the cost of the other variable (flow) for each hour at the same point. This information is passed on to the neighboring sub-systems, which are similarly optimized. Iterations through the system proceed, until convergence is achieved.

Location of the cuts, and selection of which variable will be computed by each sub-system at the cut, are somewhat of an art, based on mathematical considerations and an understanding of the hydraulics. Suffice it to say that this is far from trivial, and requires experience and judgment aided by acquaintance with the network.

Since decomposition into sub-systems is subject to these considerations, it may turn out that some subs have two or even three reservoirs. A way to reduce the dimensionality of the sub's DP is to aggregate reservoirs. This means lumping two or more into one equivalent reservoir. This can be done without too much loss of accuracy only if the individual reservoirs operate naturally in tandem. This is the case when they are close and strongly connected, but can also occur when the closeness in behavior is less apparent until a hydraulic analysis of the network reveals it.

The coordination process works best when controls are continuous, and when the optimal control of a sub is not too sensitive to the boundary conditions at the cuts.

This procedure by Carpentier and Cohen (2) has been implemented in a regional system west of Paris, France, and is currently being tested. In addition to the computational scheme outlined above, which is carried out off-line every night, it includes a procedure to

correct the operating plan during the day if deviations from forecasts
are noticed. This is done on-line, using the stored Bellman function
from the off-line optimization. Attempts to apply the method to other
systems are under way.

Zessler (23) has used a different iterative DP procedure. Again,
only the principles can be presented, for lack of space. The system
is divided into sub-systems, this time with some overlap between them,
and they are treated iteratively. The time varying problem is solved
by the approximate DP method known as progressive optimality or one-
at-a-time (7, 21). Progressing one time step (hour) at a time, the
starting states $V(t - 1)$ and end states $V(t + 1)$, two time hours
apart, are assumed fixed. Only $V(t)$ is allowed to vary and its optimal value is located by a simple search through the admissible controls. Once it has been determined by the optimization, it is fixed,
together with $V(t + 2)$, and $V(t + 1)$ is optimized. This proceeds
along the time axis, from $t = 2$ to $t = T - 1$, cyclically.

For each pair of time steps, the algorithm goes over the sub-
systems in sequence, optimizing each separately, with the others
assumed fixed. This is again done iteratively.

The whole process is iterative at two levels: over time, and, for
each time step, over sub-systems. Each of these is carried to convergence, which is guaranteed mathematically only if the cost functions
are convex.

The algorithm has been programmed on a very small micro (Sinclair
Spectrum 100, present cost under $100) for a regional water supply
system with 6 subs, and tested extensively. No field installation has
ensued, as of now.

This is the state-of-the-art at present in using DP as the basic
technique.

Fallside and co-workers have developed (9, 14, 13) and installed
(12) a control system for the East Worcestershire Water Co. (EWWC) in
England, which has been operating since the early 1970s and has had
several major updates and improvements. It also has a demand forecasting program (10,13).

The procedure was developed specifically for EWWC, and makes some
a priori assumptions about inter-zonal water transfers. The system is
divided into six zones. In each zone there is one large reservoir and
the entire demand of the zone is lumped into one time varying quantity. System dynamics for zone i are approximated by a simple continuity equation

$$V_i(t + 1) = V_i(t) + U_i(t) - D_i(t) - \sum_j Q_{ij} \qquad (7)$$

where

U_i = pumping (production) in the zone,
D_i = demand of the zone, and

Q_{ij} = transfer from zone i to zone j.

It is assumed that the Q_{ij} are fixed in advance, and are therefore not optimized. This is suitable for the EWWC system, but may not be eleswhere, where inter-zonal transfers are important decisions in the optimization. Having made this assumption, a special purpose optimization process called "pump priority logic" (12) was evolved to determine the optimal controls.

Coulbeck (4, 5, 6) linearized the system equations as follows:

$$V(t + 1) = A_1 V(t) + B_1 U(t) + C_1 D(t) \tag{8}$$

$$P(t) = A_2 V(t) + B_2 U(t) + C_2 D(t) \tag{9}$$

where U is the vector of controls, including valve settings. A_1, $B_1, \ldots, C_2$ are matrices of coefficients, which are obtained through extensive network simulation.

Coulbeck considered in the cost function the variable cost of energy over time and a maximum energy demand tariff. The last component complicates the optimization process.

The Hitachi Co. in Japan has developed a method for determining operating policies such that the resulting pressures throughout the system match closely a prescribed pressure map. This does not seem to fall into the same category of optimization schemes as those discussed above, and since sufficient information about the method and its implementation are not yet available, it is merely mentioned, for completeness.

Conclusions

(a) SCADA systems have in recent years become more readily available and reliable. Costs of hardware and the SCADA software are coming down.
(b) In many cases there is increasing justification for computer assisted control of distribution systems, because the networks are becoming more complex and costly to operate.
(c) Programs for network analysis and simulation are quite common, and can be used effectively to aid in evaluating operating plans.
(d) Methods and programs for demand forecasting are not yet common. While there may evolve some general methods for demand forecasting, it is to be expected that they will have to be adapted and adjusted to the characteristics of each specific demand type.
(e) A few computer controlled systems already exist: EWWC in England; SLEE-RPO near Paris, France; possibly one or more systems in Japan; and a few regional systems in Israel.
(f) Mathematical methods and implemented algorithms for optimal control are still in the development stage. The methods based on DP and decomposition-coordination seem to be the most promising.
(g) If software for optimal control is successfully developed, it should be introduced cautiously, delegating to automatic control

only well tested and proven parts of the overall operational
control.

Appendix I - References

1. American Water Works Association, Computer Assisted Design of
   Water Systems Committe, "Network Analysis Survey--1984," presented
   at the AWWA National Conference, Dallas, Texas, June 1984.

2. Carpentier, P., and Cohen, G., "Decomposition, Coordination and
   Aggregation in the Optimal Control of a large Water Supply Network," Proc. IFAC World Congress, Budapest, July 1984.

3. Cohen, G., "Optimal Control of Water Supply Networks," in S.G.
   Tzafetas (ed.), Optimaization and Control of Dynamic Operational
   Research Models, North Holland, 1982, pp. 251-276.

4. Coulbeck, B., "Optimization and Modelling Techniques in Dynamic
   Control of Water Distribution Systems," Ph.D. Thesis, University
   of Sheffield, 1977.

5. Coulbeck, B., "Optimal Operations in Non-linear Water Networks,"
   Optimal Control Methods and Applications, Vol. 1, No. 2, April-
   June 1980, pp. 131-141.

6. Coulbeck, B. and Sterling, M.J.H., "Optimal Control of Water Distribution Systems," Proc. IEE, Vol. 125, 1978, pp. 1039-1044.

7. Davis, R.E., "Stochastic Dynamic Programming for Multi-Reservoir
   Hydro Optimization," Tech. Memo. 15, Systems Control, Inc., Palo
   Alto, CA, 1972.

8. Dreizin, Y., Arad, N., Shamir, U., and Matmon, H., "Evaluation of
   Energy Savings in Regional Water Systems," (in Hebrew), Report
   131.105, Mekorot Water Co., April 1971.

9. Fallside, R. and Perry, P.F., "Hierarchical Optimization of a
   Water-Supply Network," Proc. IEE, Vol. 122, No. 2, February 1975,
   pp. 202-208.

10. Gray, D.F., "Use of Consumption Predictors," Cambridge University
    Engineering Department, Technical Report 4/78, February 1978.

11. Joalland, G., and Cohen, G., "Optimal Control of a Water Distribu-
    tion Network by Two Multilevel Methods," Automatica, Vol. 16,
    1980, pp. 83-88.

12. Marlow, K. and Fallside, F., "A Planned Strategy for Telemetry at
    the Water Works," Control and Instrumentation, December 1980, pp.
    47-51.

13. Moss, S.M., "On-Line Optimal Control of a Water Supply Network,"
    Ph.D. Thesis, Cambridge University, England, September 1979.

14. Perry, P.F., "An On-Line Optimal Control Scheme for Water Supply Networks," Ph.D. Thesis, Cambridge University, England, 1975.

15. Shamir, U., "Optimization in Water Distribution Systems Engineering," Mathematical Programming Study, North Holland, No. 11, 1979, pp. 65-84.

16. Shamir, U., "Real-Time Control of Water Sypply Systems," in T.E. Unny and E.A. McBean (eds.), Proc. of the International Sysmposium on Real-Time Operation of Hydrosystems, University of Waterloo, Canada, June 1981, pp. 550-562.

17. Shimron, Z. and Shamir, U., "Short Range Forecasting of Water Demands," Israel Journal of Technology, Vol. 11, No. 6, 1973, pp. 423-430.

18. Sterling, M.J.H. and Coulbeck, B., "Optimisation of Water Pumping Costs by Hierarchical Methods," Proc. Institution of Civil Engineers, Vol. 59, 1975, pp. 789-797.

19. Sterling, M.J.H. and Coulbeck, B., "A Dynamic Programming Solution to Optimisation of Pumping Costs," Proc. Institution of Civil Engineers, Vol. 59, 1975, pp. 813-818.

20. Task Committee on Procedures for Management of Control Systems Engineering for Water Pipelines, ASCE, "Management of Engineering of Control Systems for Water Pipelines," April 1978.

21. Turgeon, A., "Optimal Operation of Multi Reservoir Power Systems with Stochastic Inflows," Water Resources Research, Vol. 16, No. 2, April 1980, pp. 275-283.

22. Velon, J.P., Cesario, A.L., and Shamir, U., "Network Analysis of Treated Water Systems," paper presented at the Distribution Systems Conference of the American Water Works Association, Syracuse, NY, September 1984.

23. Zessler, U., "Optimal On-Line Control of Regional Water Supply Systems," M.Sc. Thesis, Dept. of Civil Engineering, Technion-Israel Institute of Technology, May 1984.

Time Series Analysis of Hourly Domestic Water Demand

Judith A. Cronauer[*]

James S. Gidley[+], Associate Member, ASCE

Abstract

Design flows for water supply and sanitary sewer systems are chosen by rules of thumb in the absence of actual data. This research develops two stochastic models of water demand by analyzing a time series of hourly domestic water demand data, in an effort to move towards risk-based design in water and sanitary sewer systems. The best available data yielded hourly flows over a two week period for nine homes; these data were consolidated using the concept of the composite home. A mixed probability distribution was fitted to the data, having a discrete probability of zero flow and a two-parameter lognormal distribution of nonzero flow. The static model treats each hour as independent of all other hours of the week. The dynamic model (Markov mixture model) includes state transitions from hour to hour. Synthetic sequences of water demands were generated by the two models and were compared to the historical data by calculating statistics for both the historical data and the synthetic sequences. The lack of agreement between the synthetic sequences and the historical data indicates that more data is needed to determine the distribution of flows more accurately and to estimate its parameters without large biases. Consolidation of days or hours may be needed also, as well as explicit inclusion of autocorrelation.

Introduction

Design flows for water supply and sanitary sewer systems are chosen by rules of thumb in the absence of actual data. Flow probabilities, risks of system failure, and time variability of flows are usually not explicitly considered, in contrast with storm sewer design, which is often based on stochastic precipitation/runoff models. The development of risk-based design procedures could lead to better alternatives for treatment and disposal of individual household wastewaters, better means of handling peak demands in water and wastewater services for individual homes and small communities, and improved criteria for the sizing of household plumbing, water mains and sanitary sewers (6). For certain design problems with innovative and alternative sewers, a stochastic model of sewage flows from single homes is needed. For example, the work of Donald D. Gray at West

[*] Tech-Law, Inc., 12011 Lee Jackson Highway, Suite 503, Fairfax, Va 22033

[+] Assistant Professor, Civil Engineering Department, West Virginia University, P.O. Box 6101, Morgantown, WV 26506-6101

Virginia University on the probability of failure of pressure sewer systems with centrifugal pumps shows that system performance is highly dependent on which houses have their pumps on at a given moment. The probability of specific pumps being on simultaneously could be estimated by simulation if a good stochastic model of sewage flow from a single home were available. Designers recognize this problem, but they currently deal with it by rules of thumb based on limited experience (8). A stochastic model would also help to solve various other problems in pressure sewer design, such as the sizing of sewer lines, the sequence and duration of timed pumping, and the storage volume to be provided in pump wells (or in septic tanks in septic tank effluent pumping systems). In an effort to improve the handling of such design problems, this research develops two stochastic models of water demand based on time series analysis of hourly water demand data. Some or all of these problems may eventually require a stochastic model generating flows of one minute duration or less, but the present study focuses on hourly flows.

Data Base

To develop an accurate model, a statistically representative set of domestic water demand or sewage flow data is necessary. The data set should be: (1) continuous over an adequate time period; (2) actual flow measurements from a statistically designed sample of users; (3) accompanied by ancillary data on cultural and socioeconomic factors. Several data sets were examined for these desired qualities. Discontinuity of data, loss of data, lack of supplementary data, or inadequate replacement of missing actual flow measurements eliminated many potential data sets (2).

None of the data sets available to the authors was entirely satisfactory, but the best appeared to be a listing of one-minute water demands provided by McPherson (6). The Farmstead Water Study staff of the U.S. Department of Agriculture monitored water demands each minute over a twenty-six day period at eleven individual homes (9). Only six homes generated two weeks of one-minute flows with no missing data. The two weeks occurred from 10/18/64 to 10/24/64 and from 11/1/64 to 11/7/64. Two full weeks of data were obtainable for three other homes by substituting for one missing day in the two-week period with flows from the same day of the intervening week. Thus the data set used by the authors consisted of two weeks of one-minute water demands from nine homes. The discontinuities in the data were ignored in this study. In addition to these continuous flow measurements, the location of the homes, the economic status of the occupants, lists of water-using appliances and the number of occupants per home were provided. The nine homes are situated in a residential subdivision four miles north of Wheaton, Maryland called English Manor (just north of Washington, D.C.). The average market value for the homes in 1965 was $26,000 and lot sizes averaged 13,500 square feet (0.125 ha). All of the homes contained 2-1/2 bathrooms, an automatic clothes washer, and a garbage grinder. Most of the homes contained automatic dishwashers. They were connected to the street by a 3/4 inch (1.91 cm) copper pipe and a 5/8 inch (1.59 cm) service meter located near the street curb. The season in which the data were collected indicates that there was an insignificant amount of outdoor water use, an'd so the data set would be reflective of wastewater flows as well as water consumption (11).

The flows were cumulated into hourly flows and normalized into flows per occupant for analysis. The mean hourly flows for each house ranged from 1.46 to 2.93 gal/cap-hr (5.53 to 11.1 l/cap-hr), the coefficients of variation of hourly flow from 1.11 to 2.67, and the maximum hourly flows from 9.4 gal/cap-hr to 61.8 gal/cap-hr (35.6 to 234 l/cap-hr). Nonparametric methods were used to determine whether all nine sets of flows came from identical populations. The Kruskal-Wallis H test showed that the flows from the nine homes were not from the same population, at the 5% significance level. The Wilcoxon two-sample test was applied to each pair of homes; thirteen of the thirty six pairs were found to be significantly different at the 1% level, and six other pairs to be significantly different at the 5% level. Details may be found in (2). As found by other investigators, there is a great deal of variability between individual households. In particular Witt found that variability between households is more important in determining the water usage than is the season of the year (11). The cross correlations of hourly flows between pairs of homes ranged from 0.01 to 0.33. This also shows that the homes are relatively independent.

Lag-one autocorrelation coefficients were calculated to examine the relationship between flows from one hour to the next (3). The autocorrelations for week 1 ranged from 0.08 to 0.49, and those for week 2 from 0.13 to 0.44. Thus the flow in a given hour is partially dependent on the flow in the hour preceding it. The persistence of zero flows may have a major effect on the values of the lag-one autocorrelation coefficients but no special calculations were made to investigate this. The models developed in this research do not use autocorrelation directly. It will appear later that this is a significant omission.

Model Development

Two different models were developed to generate synthetic hourly flows. Both models treat each of the one hundred sixty eight hours of the week as having a separate flow distribution. The preceding section highlighted the marked variability of the nine homes in the data base. In order to reflect this variability, the models were based on the concept of the "composite home." As mentioned earlier, differences in family habits cause variations in flows from home to home. A given house may contain several different families throughout its existence, and therefore its flow pattern will also vary. The composition of the flow data was accomplished simply by pooling all data for each hour of the week. This composition yielded eighteen observations for each hour of the week (nine homes with two observations each), compensating somewhat for the paucity of data. A composite of the various flow patterns incorporates maximum, minimum and average flow patterns. The composite home has about the same mean as the average home, but covers a much wider range of flows, and therefore has a much larger variance. It is believed that this pattern is a good choice for design purposes, because it includes the variability of flow that may occur over the life of each house. The range and average of hourly flows are shown in Figure 1.

Frequency histograms of the hourly flows were produced for visual observation of the distribution. A large number of zero flows were observed, and the nonzero flows appeared to be distributed lognormally. A discrete probability function can describe the division between zero and nonzero flows. The overall distribution could be described as a mixed probability distribution, having both a discrete and a continuous element. To examine the continuous element further, the Shapiro-Wilk test of normality was performed on the logarithms of the nonzero flows. The null hypothesis of normality was not rejected at a significance level of 5% for the large majority of the hourly samples of the logarithms of the nonzero flows. Thus the use of the lognormal distribution for the nonzero flows appeared to be acceptable. A maximum flow of 70.0 gal. (265 l) per hr. per person was used in both models. This is a conservative estimate of the maximum of 61.8 gal. (234 l) per hr. per person in the historical data, and it prevents the generation of extremely large flows. Whenever the flow generator produces a flow in excess of the maximum, it is simply replaced by the maximum.

The Static Model

The static model is a stochastic process in which all autocorrelations are taken to be zero; that is, each hour is considered to be independent of the hours preceding and following it. To produce a lognormal distribution that will preserve the statistics of the historical flows rather than those of their logarithms, the Matalas transformation equations (5) were solved by Newton's method of approximation to produce the mean and standard deviation of a two-parameter lognormal distribution for each hour:

$$\mu_{xi} = \exp\left[(\sigma_{yi}^2/2) + \mu_{yi}\right]$$

$$\sigma_{xi} = \exp\left[2(\sigma_{yi}^2 + \mu_{yi})\right] - \exp\left[\sigma_{yi}^2 + 2\mu_{yi}\right]$$

where μ_{xi} = sample mean of the historical (nonzero) flows in

hour i

σ_{xi} = sample standard deviation of the historical (nonzero)

flows in hour i

μ_{yi} = corrected mean of the lognormal distribution for

hour i

σ_{yi} = corrected standard deviation of the lognormal

distribution for hour i

Note that these parameters are for the nonzero flows only. In summary, the parameters used in the static model are μ_{yi}, σ_{yi}, and P_{0i}, the probability that the flow equals zero in hour i (estimated as the

relative frequency of zero flows in the historical data), for i=1, 2, ...,
168.

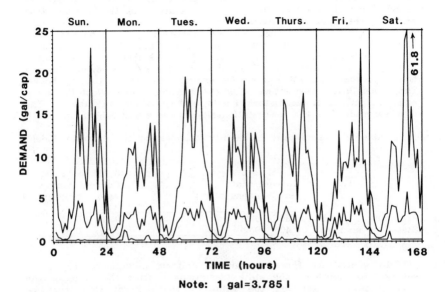

Figure 1. Maximum, Mean, and Minimum Flows of Historical Data

The flows in each hour are generated by a two-stage process. A
random uniform deviate (R_u) between zero and one is generated. If
the random number is less than or equal to P_{0i}, the generated flow is
zero. If the random number is greater than P_{0i}, the process continues
to the second stage, which produces a nonzero flow. A standard
random normal deviate (R_n) is generated and used in the following
equation:

$$q_i = \exp((\sigma_{yi} * R_n) + \mu_{yi})$$

where q_i is the flow value generated for hour i

The static model is considered nonstationary in the weekly
pattern, but stationary with respect to the basic interval (1). The
basic interval in this case is a week. In other words, its properties
are unaffected by a change in time origin, if that change is a multiple
of a week. The model continues generating enough hourly flow values
for a one-week period and then begins the process again using new
random numbers.

The Dynamic Model

In the dynamic model the state of the previous flow is applied to
a transitional probability matrix to determine the state of the current
flow. The dynamic model is therfore a Markov mixture model. This

state transition mechanism provides some autocorrelation in the flows (4). Once the new state is selected, the flow is found in a distribution specific to that state. The transitional probability matrix comprises the probabilities that a process will be in state j in the current time period given that the process was in state i in the previous time period. In this case there are two states, zero and nonzero flows. The frequency histograms indicated that certain hours (11:00PM–6:00AM) tended to have more zero flows than the other hours. Therefore, two transitional probability matrices were used, one for the hours between 11:00PM and 6:00AM and one for the remaining hours. The probabilities were estimated as the relative frequency of the given state transitions in the historical data, and are shown in Table 1. The dynamic model has the same stationarity as the static model.

Table 1. Transitional Probability Matrices for the Dynamic Model

| | | 11 PM to 6 AM Current State | | 6 AM to 11 PM Current State | |
		zero	nonzero	zero	nonzero
Previous	zero	0.80	0.20	0.36	0.64
State	nonzero	0.40	0.60	0.11	0.89

In generating flows, a random uniform deviate on [0, 1] is selected to determine the state transitions. After the state of the current flow is selected the value of the current flow must be determined. If the state of the current flow is zero, the value of the current flow is zero. If the state of the current flow is nonzero, the value of the flow is chosen from the lognormal distribution for the nonzero flows of the current hour, having the same parameters as in the static model. Because of the state transition mechanism, the generated flows would be dependent on the assumed initial state. After some time, however, the effect of the initial state would be negligible; it was calculated that in this case the initial state would have no significant effect after twenty hours. Therefore the state of the last hour generated by the model is used to determine the state of the first hour. The first twenty hours of flow are then regenerated, and so are not biased by the assumed initial state.

Results and Discussion

The models were compared to the historical record using a method similar to that of Srikanthan and McMahon (7). The following statistics were calculated and compared to those of the historical record for both the static and the dynamic models: hourly means, standard deviations and percentages of zero flows, and the overall mean, standard deviation, percentage of zero flows, lag-one autocorrelation, coefficient of skewness and maximum flow. The statistics of each model were estimated as the average of twenty runs, each of a length equal to that of the composite historical record (3024 hours). A comparison of the overall parameters appears in Table 2.

Both the static and the dynamic models produced an overall

percentage of zero flows similar to that of the historical data. However, the dynamic model does not preserve the hourly variation in the percentage of zero flows. Between the hours of 11:00 PM and 7:00 AM the percentage of zero flows tends to be underestimated. There is a consistent overestimation of the percentage of zero flows at 8:00 AM. The dynamic model lags one hour behind the historical data in representing the hours that have a high percentage of zero flows (see Figure 2). If the hours 10:00 PM through 5:00 AM had been chosen for the low flow transitional probability matrix instead of 11:00 PM through 6:00 AM, this one hour lag would probably not have occurred. In addition to the one hour lag, the hourly variation in the number of zero flows is removed because of the consolidation of data. The transitional probability matrices used in the dynamic model did not properly represent each specific hour. The static model, on the other hand, preserves the hourly variation in the number of zero flows (see Figure 2).

Table 2. Overall statistics for historical record and the
static and dynamic models (flows per occupant)

process	mean (gph)	standard deviation	% of zero flows	lag one autocorr.	coeff. of skewness	maximum flow (gph)
Historic	2.05	2.27	29.40	.3320	4.3781	61.80
Static*	2.38	3.22	29.31	.0780	6.2912	69.54
Dynamic*	2.28	3.20	28.25	.0823	6.3427	66.05

* 20 runs averaged. A run is 3024 hours long.
Note: 1 gph = 3.79 liters per hr.

The overall mean in both the static model and the dynamic model is slightly overestimated. Both the static model and the dynamic model tend to overshoot the hourly means, especially in the early morning hours (see Figure 3). In the case of the dynamic model, the errors in modeling the hourly percentages of zero flows explain much of the error in the hourly means: where the percentage of zero flows is substantially higher than that of the historical data, the mean is substantially lower, and vice versa. On the whole, however, there is a tendency to overestimate the hourly means.

Likewise, the overall standard deviation, the overall coefficient of skewness, and the maximum flow are inflated by both models, and the hourly standard deviations tend to be inflated by both models also. Owing to the paucity of data, the coefficient of skewness was not accounted for in the lognormal distribution, but a two-parameter lognormal distribution was used. Therefore, it is not surprising that the skewness of historical data was not reproduced in the synthetic sequences. In fact, with at most eighteen observations with which to estimate the parameters for each hour, pronounced biases are to be

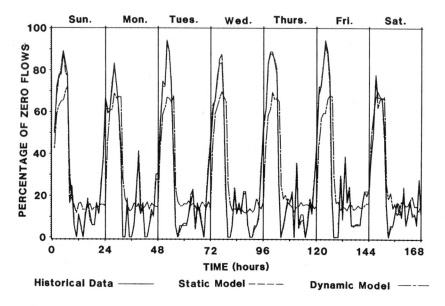

Figure 2.   Hourly Percentages of Zero Flows in the Historical Data,
the Static Model, and the Dynamic Model

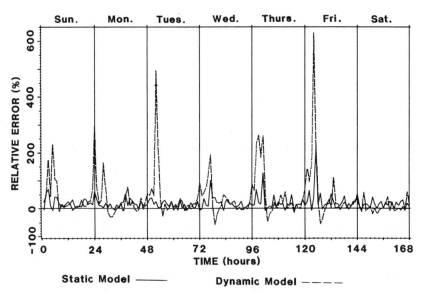

Figure 3.   Relative Errors in Hourly Mean Flows in the Static Model
and the Dynamic Model

expected in the estimates (10). Forty five of the one hundred sixty eight hours had nine or fewer nonzero flows, and two hours had only one nonzero flow. For these hours, no confidence can be placed even in the choice of the lognormal distribution. For none of the hours can one be confident of the parameter estimates.

The overall lag-one autocorrelation is too low in both the static and the dynamic models. The state transition mechanism of the Markov mixture model provided only slightly more autocorrelation than the static model. The autocorrelation in the results of the static model is surely insignificant, because all the hours were treated as strictly independent of each other. Therefore the autocorrelation in the dynamic model is only barely significant, if at all. Neither model came close to representing the autocorrelation in the historical data.

Conclusions

1. The static model and the Markov mixture model reproduce the overall percentage of zero flows.
2. The static model reproduces the hourly percentage of zero flows.
3. The Markov mixture model does not reproduce the hourly percentage of zero flows.
4. The static model and the Markov mixture model do not reproduce the overall mean, standard deviation, skewness, or autocorrelation well. This confirms the statement of Srikanthan and McMahon that binary generators have problems relating to the measure of serial dependence (7).
5. The data set is not large enough to estimate the models' parameters accurately.

Recommendations

1. In future efforts to model hourly water use in individual homes it appears to be absolutely necessary that a large data set should be used. It may be found that the lognormal distribution is inappropriate, but in any case, more data are needed for better parameter estimation. In the dynamic model, several more transitional probability matrices could be used if there are enough data. In the absence of more data, consolidation of days or hours with similar characteristics is necessary.
2. Most likely, a large enough data set does not now exist. Therefore the authors recommend that a large-scale effort in data acquisition should be undertaken so that the design of water and sewer systems can be improved through the use of stochastic modeling. Such data should include the effects of regional, cultural, and economic differences, as well as differences in water conservation efforts.
3. Future modeling efforts should include autocorrelation explicitly. Possibly a lag-one autocorrelation estimated from only the nonzero flows could be used.

Appendix-References

1. Box, G.E., and Jenkins, G.M., Time Series Analysis: Forecasting and Control, 2nd ed., Holden-Day, Inc., Oakland, Calif., 1976, p. 328.

2. Cronauer, J.A., "Time Series Analysis of Domestic Water Demand", problem report presented to West Virginia University at Morgantown, WV in 1984, in partial fulfillment of the requirements for the degree of Master of Science.

3. Fiering, M.B , Jackson, B.B., Synthetic Streamflows, American Geophysical Union, Washington, D.C., 1971, p. 42.

4. Jackson, B.B., "Markov mixture models for drought lengths", Water Resources Research, Vol. 11, No. 1, Feb., 1975, pp. 64-74.

5. Matalas, N.C., "Mathematical assessment of synthetic hydrology", Water Resources Research, Vol. 3, No. 4, Fourth Quarter, 1967, pp. 937-945.

6. McPherson, M.B., "Household Water Use", ASCE Urban Water Resources Research Program Technical Memorandum No. 28, ASCE, New York, NY, Jan. 1976 (available from NTIS as PB 250 879).

7. Srikanthan, R., and McMahon, T.A., "Stochastic generation of monthly flows for ephemeral streams.", Journal of Hydrology, Vol. 47, No. 1, Jan. 1980, pp. 19-40.

8. Tollefson, D.J., and Kelly, R.F., "STEP Pressure Sewers are a Viable Wastewater Collection Alternative", Journal Water Pollution Control Federation, Vol. 55, No. 7, July 1983, pp. 1004-1014.

9. Tucker, L.S., "Sewage Flow Variations in Individual Homes", ASCE Combined Sewer Separation Project Technical Memorandum No. 2, ASCE, New York, NY, Feb. 1967 (available from NTIS as PB 185-995).

10. Wallis, J.R., Matalas, N.C., and Slack, J.R., "Just a moment!" Water Resources Research, Vol. 10, No. 2, Apr. 1974, pp. 211-219.

11. Witt, M.D., Water Use in Rural Homes, Small Scale Waste Management Project, University of Wisconsin, Madison, WS, 1974.

WATER USE FORECASTING
AND
EVALUATING THE EFFECTS OF CONSERVATION MEASURES

By Daniel N. Nvule[1] and David R. Maidment[2]

ABSTRACT

The City of Austin, Texas, instituted mandatory restrictions on water use during a summer drought in 1984 when water use levels beyond 150 million gallons per day stressed the city's water treatment and distribution system. An intervention and transfer function model is used to show the effect of the restrictions as being a reduction in water use of 13 MGD. A 5-day lawn watering cycle for addresses ending in 0-1,2-3,4-5,6-7,8-9 is shown to produce an undesirable 5-day cycle in water use of 4 MGD amplitude, highest for the watering day of 0-1 addresses and lowest for the 8-9 addresses. The impact of announcements by public officials about water conservation averaged 2 MGD on the day of the announcement and 4 MGD the day following, thereafter diminishing. Before the drought struck, possible patterns of 1984 daily water use were constructed as if weather of previous years were repeated. Predictions made from these patterns accurately identified the time when mandatory water use restrictions would be initiated and gave city management an estimate of the likely duration of extreme water use levels if no restrictions were enforced. Daily water use forecasts made throughout the summer using the transfer function model on an IBM-PC in the City's offices enabled management to anticipate short-term water use levels up to two weeks ahead.

1.0 RECONSTRUCTION OF WATER-USE SERIES

Daily water use data for Austin from 1975 to 1983 were adjusted to correspond to the 1984 growth level. If t_o represents the date whose water use should be converted to the 1984 growth level conditions then t^* represents the corresponding date in 1984 . For example if t_o is 2/10/79 then t^* is 2/10/84 and so on. Mathematically, the reconstruction process may be stated as follows. First, the water use W on day t_o is made into a dimensionless water use W_d by the transformation:

1. Graduate Research Assistant, Department of Civil Engineering, University of Texas,Austin,Texas 78712
2. Assistant Professor, Department of Civil Eng. UT,Austin

$$W_d(t_o) = \frac{W(t_o) - W_b(t_o)}{S_p(t_o)} \qquad (1a)$$

where W_b is base use and S_p is peak seasonal use, respectively. Base use is calculated from the minimum monthly use in the winter; seasonal use is total use minus base use. The corresponding reconstructed water use $W_r(t_o^*)$ for day t_o^* is produced by the reverse transformation

$$W_r(t_o^*) = S_p(t_o^*)[W_d(t_o) + W_b(t_o^*)] \qquad (1b)$$

using the values of W_b and S_p at time t_o^*. These transformations have the effect of sliding the past years of data up the trend line of growth in water use while preserving all the response to weather conditions inherent in their daily varying pattern.

After making these reconstructions, the probability of invoking mandatory restraints was computed. Restrictions became mandatory if water use exceeded 150 MGD for three consecutive days or exceeded 157 MGD for one day. The probability of either of these conditions occurring in 1984 was estimated to be:

June	1-10	Less than 1%
	11-20	Less than 1%
	21-30	5%
July	1-10	15%
	11-20	20%
	21-31	15%
Aug	1-10	10%
	11-20	5%
	20-31	5%
Sept	1-10	Less than 1%

The sequence of actual events in 1984 closely reflected these estimates of the relative risk of exceeding high water use levels. Water use first exceeded 150 MGD on June 28 during the first period previously identified as having a significant risk level; mandatory restrictions were required on July 13, shown by the previous analysis to be the highest risk period.

2.0   SHORT-TERM WATER USE FORECASTING

Maidment et al (1985) have modelled Austin's water use as a combination of both long and short memory components. They discuss the methodology and give a mathematical formulation of the WATer-FOREcasting (WATFORE) model. The following shows how the model can be re-formulated for forecasting purposes. In essence, the forecast can be viewed as an aggregate of the various components that make up the water-use with each of these sub-components being forecast separately. These components are:-

(i) Base water-use (winter use)
(ii) Normal seasonal variation in water use due to normal air temperature;
(iii) Water use response to rainfall (negative);
(iv) Water use response to departures of daily maximum temperature from normal;

(v) Adjustment for previous forecast errors.
    Daily water use can be expressed as

$$W(t) = \hat{W}_b(t) + g(t)\,[\hat{W}_p(t) + W_s(t)] \qquad (2.1)$$

where
    W = daily water use, $\hat{W}_b$ = estimated base use, g = trend coefficient
for peak seasonal use, $\hat{W}_p$ = estimated potential water use, a function
of normal air temperature, W_s = short memory water use, t = daily time
index from beginning of series.

A transfer function noise model is formulated for the short memory
series.

$$W_s(t) = \bar{W}_s + \frac{\omega_{01}}{1-\delta_1 B}\,T_1(t) + \frac{\omega_{02}}{1-\delta_2 B}\,T_2(t) + \frac{\omega_{03}-\omega_{13}}{1-\delta_3 B}\,L_1(t)$$

$$+ \frac{\omega_{04}-\omega_{14}}{1-\delta_4 B}\,L_2(t) + \frac{a_t}{1-\phi_1 B-\phi_2 B^2-\phi_7 B^7} \qquad (2.2)$$

where

$\bar{W}_s$ = mean level component of short memory series model

T_1 = transformed daily maximum air temperature for Nov-Feb

T_2 = transformed daily maximum air temperature for Mar-Oct

L_1 = previous day's outdoor water use level if current
          rainfall is below or equal to 0.05 inches

L_2 = previous day's outdoor water use level if current
          rainfall is above 0.05 inches

a = independent normal random variable of zero mean and
        variance σ^2

ω, δ = transfer function coefficients

ϕ_1, ϕ_2, ϕ_7 = autoregressive coefficients of noise model

B = backshift operator

    For forecasting purposes equation 2.2 is decomposed into the
following components:

$$U_1(t) = \frac{\omega_{01}T_1(t)}{1-\delta_1 B}; \quad U_2(t) = \frac{\omega_{02}}{1-\delta_2 B}T_2; \quad U_3(t) = \frac{\omega_{03}-\omega_{13}B}{1-\delta_3 B}L_1(t)$$

$$U_4(t) = \frac{\omega_{04}-\omega_{14}B}{1-\delta_4 B}L_2(t); \quad U_5(t) = \frac{a_t}{1-\phi_1 B-\phi_2 B^2-\phi_7 B^7}$$

The ℓ-step ahead forecasts standing at time "t" are then computed as the following difference equations:

$$U_1(t+\ell) = \omega_{01}T_1(t+\ell) + \delta_1 U_1(t+\ell-1)$$

$$U_2(t+\ell) = \omega_{02}T_2(t+\ell) + \delta_2 U_2(t+\ell-1)$$

$$U_3(t+\ell) = \omega_{03}L_1(t+\ell) - \omega_{13}L_1(t+\ell-1) + \delta_3 U_3(t+\ell-1)$$

$$U_4(t+\ell) = \omega_{04}L_2(t+\ell) - \omega_{14}L_2(t+\ell-1) + \delta_4 U_4(t+\ell-1)$$

$$U_5(t+\ell) = \phi_1 U_5(t+\ell-1) + \phi_2 U_5(t+\ell-2) + \phi_7 U_5(t+\ell-7) + a_t$$

The short term forecast is then computed as

$$W_s(t+\ell) = \sum_{i=1}^{5} U_i(t+\ell) + \bar{W}_s(1-\phi_1-\phi_2-\phi_7)$$

$$a_t = W(t)-\hat{W}(t) \text{ corresponding to a one step ahead forecast error}$$

The complete forecast is then given as

$$\hat{W}(t+\ell) = \hat{W}_b(t+\ell) + g(t+\ell)[\hat{W}_p(t+\ell) + W_s(t+\ell)]$$

where $\hat{W}_b(t) = a_o + a_1 t$ (polynomial function of time) and $\hat{W}_p(t)$ is obtained from the heat-function (a function relating seasonal water use to air temperature during rainless periods) as the seasonal water use corresponding to the normal maximum air temperature for that day. The above scheme was programmed in BASIC for use on an IBM-PC and subsequently used to forecast water use.

3.0   EFFECTS OF CONSERVATION

The purpose of this exercise was to evaluate the effects of the water use restrictions that were imposed during the summer of 1984. Two techniques were employed: regression analysis, and transfer functions with intervention terms. The final conclusions are based on the outcome of the intervention analysis, with the regression analysis results used as a check. The results show that there was a significant decrease in the mean level of water use during the restrictions. Also investigated was the effect of public announcements and the effect of the 5-day watering cycle.

3.1   Regression

3.1.1   Background

         The first use of this technique is attributed to Galton, F.
(1889) who coined the term when he plotted the data of sons' height
against fathers' height. Since then, mathematicians have polished up
the method to cover cases of multiple independent variables. Extensive
treatment of such cases can be found in Draper and Smith (1981). The
method assumes the model errors to be random, independent,
uncorrelated, and also identically distributed. In this study, the
data had to be judiciously manipulated to meet these stringent
assumptions. Regression has traditionally been the premier method by
which water use is modelled, the independent variables usually being
population, number of rainy days, temperature, etc.

3.1.2   Application

         Daily water use data were adjusted to 1984 conditions as in
Section 1.0. This adjusted record was the one that was utilized in the
regression calculations. The three conservation periods May 10-Jul 15,
Jul 13-Aug 17, and Aug 18-Sep 30 were designated as V1, M, and V2
respectively. For each of the three periods, statistics of total water
use (calculated from the adjusted values), the number of degree-days
exceeding 85 degrees Fahrenheit and total number of rain days were
compiled. The symbols for these variables are WU, DD85 and NR
respectively. The actual periods for V1, M, and V2 were of unequal
duration. In the regression analysis, effective periods each of 33
days (equal to the duration of mandatory conservation) were used. This
corresponds to taking "windows" of 33 days in either direction of the M
period. By using accumulated total water use over 33 days rather than
daily water use itself, the regression model errors are no longer
autocorrelated and the analysis is valid. The models derived were of
the form:

$$\hat{WU} = \beta_0 + \beta_1 DD85 + \beta_2 NR \qquad (3a)$$

where:

$\hat{WU}$ = the estimated water use volume (MG)

$\beta_0, \beta_1, \beta_2$ = coefficients determined using reconstructed water use
series and weather data from 1975 to 1983.

3.1.3   Results

         The regression results are given for each of the three
conservation periods. In all three cases the data from which the
regression equations were developed is presented first, then the
equation for that particular period is given and finally an estimate of
the effect of conservation is made utilizing the estimated equation and
the data for 1984. The DD85 values in Table 3A show that 1984 was
second to 1980 as the hottest June 13-July 15 period observed in the
last ten years.

Table 3A: V1 Period (June 13 - July 15)

Year	WU(MG)	DD85(°F)	NR(days)
1975 δ	2738.6	153.0	10
1976 δ	2891.7	130.0	14
1977	3807.6	267.0	6
1978	4664.4	394.0	0
1979	3682.5	249.0	3
1980	4921.5	472.0	1
1981	2790.5	212.0	9
1982	3541.0	309.0	5
1983 δ	3195.0	171.0	10
1984	4390.0	396.0	3

δ omitted when fitting equation due to
distorting effect of high rainfall amount.

The least squares fit for the V1 period is:

$$\hat{WU} = 2991.0 + 4.28 \ DD85 - 112.0 \ NR, \ R^2 = 0.90 \quad (3b)$$
$$(804.1) \quad (1.908) \qquad (55.95)$$
$$S^2 = 58951 \ (3 \ \text{degrees of freedom})$$

The bracketed values under the coefficients are their standard errors.

Expected 1984 water use from equation (3b) = 4349 MG
Amount of water actually used in 1984 = 4390 MG
Amount of water conserved = - 41 MG
Standard error of this estimate = 148 MG

The above standard error makes the conservation estimate insignificant on a two-sided t-test. The variation in the sampling data is of such a magnitude that it is impractical to estimate the effects of conservation by regression for this period.

Table 3b: V2 Period (Aug 18-Sep 19)

Year	WU(MG)	DD85(°F)	NR(days)
1975 δ	3203.2	193.0	9
1976 δ	3311.3	195.0	7
1977	4065.5	341.0	6
1978	3350.6	221.0	10
1979 δ	3516.4	194.0	7
1980	3950.3	330.0	6
1981	3261.8	233.0	10
1982	4407.4	385.0	5
1983	3356.9	274.0	10
1984	4280.5	324.0	3

δ omitted when fitting equation due to effect
of rainfall amount.

The data for DD85 in Table 3b show that 1984 had the fourth hottest

August 18 to September 19 for the last 10 years, exceeded by 1977,1980,1982.
The least squares fit for the V2 period is:

$$\hat{WU} = 3989.0 + 2.52 \text{ DD85} - 129.0 \text{ NR}, R^2 = 0.96 \quad (3c)$$
$$(1102.) \quad (2.19) \quad (59.3)$$
$$s^2 = 9517 \text{ (3 degrees of freedom)}$$

Expected 1984 use from equation (3c)   = 4418.5 MG
Amount of water actually used   = 4280.5 MG

Amount of water conserved   = 138.0 MG
Standard error of this estimate   = 235.0 MG

Again the conservation estimate is insignificant for the V2 period, on a two sided t-test.

Table 3c: M Period (July 16- Aug 17)

Year	WU(MG)	DD85(°F)	NR (days)
1975 δ	3226.6	229.0	7
1976	3434.6	284.0	3
1977	4891.6	415.0	2
1978	4007.4	330.0	7
1979 δ	3141.9	224.0	5
1980	4513.0	408.0	6
1981	4253.0	396.0	3
1982	4871.3	450.0	3
1983	3356.2	278.0	6
1984	3866.8	365.0	6

The data in Table 3c for DD85 show that 1984 had the fifth hottest July 13-August 17 in the last ten years, exceeded by 1977, 1980, 1981, 1982.

The least squares fit for the M period is:

$$\hat{WU} = 931.0 + 8.92 \text{ DD85} - 0.871 \text{ NR}, R^2 = 0.91 \quad (3d)$$
$$(555.5) \quad (1.233) \quad (42.52)$$
$$s^2 = 35,311 \text{ (degrees of freedom)}$$

Expected 1984 use from equation (3d) = 4182.0 MG
Amount of water actually used   = 3833.8 MG

Amount of water conserved   = 315.0 MG
Standard error of this estimate   = 113.4 MG

Statistically, the above estimate is significant at the 95% level of confidence using a two sided t-test.

It is evident that the regression technique has performed poorly for the voluntary restriction periods and shows a significant response of water use for the Mandatory period. For this period, regression predicts that the decrease in the mean level was 9.5 MGD. This result will be used as a check for the intervention analysis results.

3.2   INTERVENTION ANALYSIS

3.2.1   Background

Daily water use data may violate the assumptions for regression analysis because their regression model errors are autocorrelated, thereby rendering classical statistical tests of limited accuracy (e.g., the Student's t-test for detecting differences in mean values). Intervention analysis is a stochastic time series modelling technique suggested by Box and Tiao (1975) and Hipel et al. (1975) for rigorously analyzing whether or not an induced intervention causes a significant change in the men level of a time series. The technique has since been used in water resources to detect changes in sequential streamflow data and water quality records [Hipel et al. (1975) Whitfield and Woods (1984)]. The technique requires the analyst to have a prior knowledge of the behavior of the system and its goal is to quantify the magnitude of the system changes.

3.2.2   Application

The analysis evaluated the change in the mean level of the process during V1, M and V2 periods and also the effect of public announcements and a 5-day lawn watering cycle. The WATFORE model was fitted to the water-use data for the 1st of April through the 22nd of October 1984 (total of 205 days). The functional form of the model employed was:

$$W_s = \bar{W}_s + \frac{\omega_{01}}{1-\delta_1 B} T_1 + \frac{\omega_{02}-\omega_{12}B}{1-\delta_2 B} L_1 + \omega_{03} I_{v1} + \omega_{04} I_{v2} + \omega_{05} I_m$$
$$+ a_t/(1-\phi_1 B-\phi_2 B^2-\phi_7 B^7) \quad (3e)$$

where I_{v1}, I_m, I_{v2} are step function inputs that have a value of 1.0 during the respective conservation periods and zero elsewhere. The rest of the symbols have the meaning described in Section 2.0. The above model was used to investigate the change in the mean level during V1, M and V2 periods.

The model for investigating the effects of public announcements took the following functional form:

$$W_s = \bar{W}_s + \frac{\omega_{01}}{1-\delta_1 B} T_1 + \frac{\omega_{02}-\omega_{12}B}{1-\delta_2 B} L_1 + \frac{\omega_{03}-\omega_{13}B}{1-\delta_3 B} I_p + \frac{a_t}{1-\phi_1 B-\phi_2 B^2-\phi_7 B^7} \quad (3f)$$

In this case I_p was a pulse input with the value of the pulse set to 1.0 whenever there was an announcement in the press that was deemed to have an effect on water use and zero elsewhere. The model employed for the 5-day watering cycle took the following functional form:

$$W_s = \bar{W}_s + \frac{\omega_{01}}{1-\delta_1 B} T_1 + \frac{\omega_{02}-\omega_{12}B}{1-\delta_2 B} L_1 + (\omega_{03}-\omega_{13}B-\omega_{23}B^2-\omega_{33}B^3-\omega_{43}B^4)I_t$$

$$+ \frac{a_t}{1-\phi_1 B-\phi_2 B^2-\phi_7 B^7} \qquad (3g)$$

Where I_t was set to 1.0 on the days when properties with addresses ending in either a 0 or 1 were allowed to water and zero elsewhere.

3.2.3   Results

The results in this case are obtained by estimating the coefficients in equations (3e) to (3g). In estimating these coefficients, the actual lengths, i.e., May 10-Jul 15, Jul 13-Aug 17, and Aug 18-Sep 30 for the V1,M and V2 periods were utilized. The rest of the parameters in equations (3e) to 3g) were comparable to those of Maidment et al. (1985) estimated prior to 1984. The intervention parameters were estimated as:

Direct Effects on water use, equation (3e)

Period	$\omega_o I$ (MGD)
May 10-Jul 15 (V1)	- 2.77 (4.14)
Jul 13-Aug 17 (M)	-13.45 (6.8)
Aug 18-Sep 30 (V2)	- 1.27 (1.9)

The bracketed terms are the standard errors of the estimates.

Thus, by intervention analysis, it is estimated that conservation reduced water use by 2.77 MGD during the V1 period, by 1.27 MGD in the V2 period and by 13.45 MGD during the M period after weather departures from normal conditions have been accounted for in these periods.

Public Announcements, equation (3f)

Coefficient	Value	(standard error)
ω_{03}	-2.207	(1.78)
ω_{13}	2.230	(1.81)
δ_3	0.934	(0.032)

It is concluded from these data that there was an immediate drop of 2.2 MGD in response to a public announcement, increasing to 4.4 MGD the day after, then diminishing with time. While the data do show that the citizens response to public announcements, the figures should not be interpreted literally because the model they were estimated from (Eq. 3f) does not have any intervention terms (such as I_m in Eq. 3e) to account for the "background" effect the conservation program would have had independent of the public announcements. In effect, all conservation effects are being attributed to public announcements in Eq. 3f.

5-day watering cycle, equation (3g)

Address ends in	Coefficient	Value (MGD)	(Standard error)
0-1	ω_{03}	2.3548	(4.801)
2-3	ω_{13}	-0.8821	(4.891)
4-5	ω_{23}	1.3545	(4.937)
3-7	ω_{33}	3.2195	(4.893)
8-9	ω_{43}	4.4175	(4.804)

The conclusion from this analysis is that the 5-day watering cycle introduced a cyclical pattern into the water use data. When compared to the 5-day average water use over the cycle, watering for addresses ending in 0-1 increased usage 2.4 MGD, for 2-3 increased usage 0.9 MGD, for address 4-5 decreased usage 1.4 MGD, for addresses 6-7 decreased usage 3.2 MGD and for addresses 8-9 decreased usage 4.4 MGD. When comparing the numbers tabulated above, the signs in front of the ω terms in Eq. 3g have to be taken into account to determine whether usage decreased or increased for each variable.

3.3 EVALUATION OF CONSERVATION ESTIMATION METHODS USED

It is intended in this section to evaluate the performance of the analysis strategy by comparing both the regression and intervention analysis results. Table 3d below shows the estimates for the decrease in the mean due to conservation by the two methods.

Table 3d.   Regression and Intervention Results
           Decrease in the mean of the series

Period	Decrease by Regression (MGD)	Decrease by Intervention (MGD)
V1	-1.24	2.77
	(4.5)	(4.1)
M	9.5	13.45
	(3.4)	(3.8)
V2	4.2	1.27
	(7.1)	(1.9)

(bracketed terms are standard errors)

It is evident that it is difficult to estimate the effect of the voluntary water conservation measures. The impact of mandatory restrictions is clearly delineated by either method.

4.0 REFERENCES

Box, G. E.P. and G.C. Tiao (1975). Intervention Analysis With Applications to Economic and Environmental Problems. Journal of American Statistical Association 70:70-79.

Draper, N. and H. Smith (1981). Applied Regression Analysis. John Wiley and Sons, New York.

Galton, F. (1889) Natural Inheritance. Macmillan, London.

Hipel, K.W., W.C. Lennox, T.E. Unny, and A.I. McLeod (1975). Intervention Analysis in Water Resources. WRR 11: 855-831.

Maidment, D.R., S.P. Miaou and M.M. Crawford (1985). Transfer Function Models of Daily Urban Water Use. Water Resources Research (in press).

Whitfield, P.H. and P.F. Woods (1984). Intervention Analysis of Water Quality Records. Water Resources Bulletin 20: No. 5 357-338.

INCORPORATING GRAPHICS IN WATER DISTRIBUTION ANALYSIS

by

S. Sarikelle,* K.E. Mehrfar** and Y.T. Chuang**

Abstract: One area that has currently been receiving attention is the
presentation of hydraulic analysis results utilizing computer graphics
to display pipe network and pressure values in graphical form.

The study presented herein deals with the development of a computer model related to the plotting of pipe network and pressure contour
lines for a given water distribution system. The use of the model is
described with several applications based on results obtained from
computer simulations.

Introduction

Computer Graphics plays an important role in supporting the decision making processes that managers and engineers go through in the
planning and analysis of water supply systems. Although hydraulic analysis programs provide the basic information (flow, velocity, pressure) related to the performance of a given system, coupling this information with graphics provides the managers with the visual representation that leads to a better assessment of system performance
under various design and operating conditions.

In order to utilize the advantages that a graphic system can
bring to the design environment a software package was developed for
analyzing water distribution systems. This paper summarizes the various components of the model and its application to Water Distribution
Systems.

Model Capability

The model is designed to generate a plot of the pipe network and
pressure contour lines (also hydraulic grade line contours and fire
flow contour lines) based on values obtained from simulation studies.
The size and identification number of each pipe is labeled in accordance with the pipe network data and is shown on the plot. The node
whether it is a hydrant, reservoir, pump station or a street junction
is also identified. Figure 1 shows a portion of a distribution system
showing the pipe network and pressure contour lines.

---

*   Professor, Department of Civil Engineering, The University of
       Akron, Akron, Ohio 44325

**   Research Associate, Department of Civil Engineering, The Univer-
       sity of Akron, Akron, Ohio 44325

412

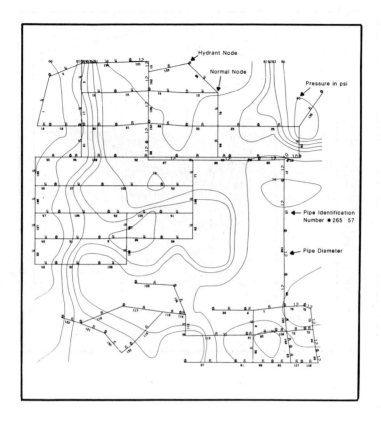

Figure 1. Plot of Pipe Network and Pressure Contours

For a given pipe network and node pressures a three dimensional plot of the pressure diagram can also be produced. The pressure diagram can be rotated and viewed from different angles and reproduced by the copier or plotter at selected positions. Figure 2 shows the three dimensional pressure diagram for a pipe network where points on the diagrams represent the pressure values at each of the nodes including hydrant nodes.

Program Structure and Operation

The graphics model consists of a digitizing program and a plot program. The digitizing program establishes the data base for the pipe distribution network. The plot program generates the drawing of the pipes, pressure contour lines and three dimensional pressure diagrams using information generated by the digitizing program and the hydraulic analysis program (not presented here).

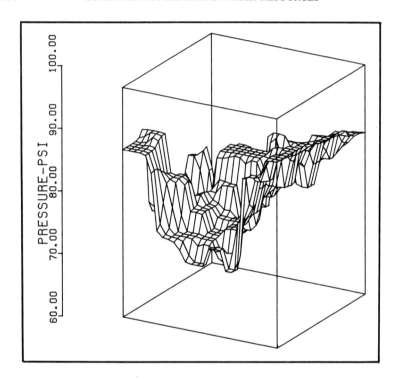

Figure 2. Three Dimensional Pressure Diagram

(a) Digitizing Program

The digitizing program consists of 24 subroutines (1500 source statements) and is the first program to be activated in a series of operations to obtain the plot of the pipe network and pressure contour lines. It is used with a digitizing board and a graphic display monitor supported by a central processor. The pipe network information is obtained from existing maps such as underground record maps or original design drawings. These maps (or sketches drawn to scale) are placed on the digitizing board and the X,Y location of each node is electronically registered by the use of a stylus and tied to a reference coordinate system. Additional information regarding each node whether it is a hydrant or a street junction, pipe and node identification numbers, pipe diameters are entered by the use of a menu which is activated at a convenient location on the digitizing board. The process of establishing this data can be accomplished either in an interactive mode or batch mode. Best results are obtained in an interactive mode, since it is faster and each entry is established in a sequential manner as prompt messages appear on the video display monitor accompanied by an acoustic signal. Some examples of messages are-

"enter node location" "enter node number", etc. If the entry is made
in the batch mode the X,Y location of each node must be measured and
typed in along with related information. In either case when all data
is entered the program is run to obtain a summary of processed data
and is used to check entry and related errors. At this point titles,
street names, pump and tank information are also entered. The data
is then stored to be used by the plot program to obtain pipe network
and pressure contours (or HGL contours).

(b) Plot Program

     The plot program is composed of 33 subroutines (4,500 source
statements) and is designed to obtain a plot of the pipe network, pressure contour lines and three dimensional pressure diagrams. Once activated the program seeks and reads the data and information generated
by the digitizing program. The program then goes through a series of
prompts and requests information from the operator regarding the various details to be generated. These include the scale to be used, line
type, color, pressure contour line increments, whether all pipes will
be plotted and whether pressure contour lines will be superimposed on
the pipe network plot. The program then draws the pipe network on the
graphics terminal. If a plot of pressure contour lines is being requested, the pressure values at each node is supplied (as determined
by the hydraulic analysis program) in a separate file to be read by the
plot program. Once the computations are completed, the pressure contour lines are drawn on the monitor. The copier attached to the monitor is used to obtain copies of the images displayed on the screen.
This is extremely helpful since adjustments can be made before the
final plots are routed to the ink plotter. In the case of three dimensional plots the Z axis represents the pressure scale and the X,Y
coordinates establish the location of each node.

Applications

     The program was used to plot City of Avon Lake Water Distribution
network. This system was composed of 1,020 pipes and 926 nodes of
which 700 are hydrants nodes. The original underground record drawings
of the city were composed of twelve maps each consisting of 24 x 36 in.
(60.96 x 91.44 cm) sheets drawn to a scale of 1" = 200' (1 cm = 24 in).
A general schematic of the twelve maps and their relative position is
shown in Figure 3. The water lines are shown as solid lines with hydrant locations indicated by special symbols. The size of each pipe,
street location of pipe junctions and ground elevations are also documented.

     The transfer of data from these maps started with the digitizing
process. Map numbers were used to specify the file identification
where pipe and node data along with X,Y coordinates of each node was
stored. The digitizing of maps for the Avon Lake System was established by first assigning identification numbers to each of the nodes and
pipes. The numbering of the nodes and pipes can also be established
during the digitizing and entered by the operator as the location of
each node is established.

REFERENCE
MAP

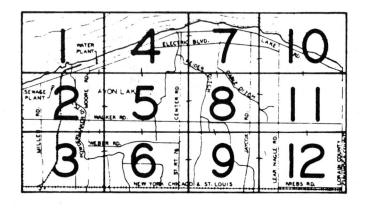

Figure 3. City of Avon Lake Underground Map Reference Numbers

Regardless of which numbering scheme is used, the identification numbers for the nodes and pipes must be compatible with the numbers used in the hydraulic analysis program. Once the node and pipe identification numbers are established, the pipe segment joining the nodes, its degree of curvature, size and type are also established. The plot for the pipe network was stored on twelve separate files each indexed according to the original map sequence. These files were then used to produce plots of the system or portion of the system by merging the files.

Application I

Figure 4 shows the pipe network and pressure contour line plot for the City of Avon Lake Water Distribution System.

The contour lines shown represent pressures that were obtained by the analysis program for average demands imposed on the system by the various class of users. This condition is also referred to as the "Static Condition". The pressure values presented were confirmed by field measurements at 28 hydrants. The pressure at four of the hydrants were recorded by chart recorders during the test period. In this simulation the pump operating point at the water plant is determined to be 78 psi and represents conditions during the test period.

Examination of the pressure patterns obtained from this simulation shows pressure values along Miller Road going south drop to 50 psi (344.5 kPa). At this point the system is supplying water to areas outside the city limits at the rate of 3,000 gpm (0.432 m³/sec).

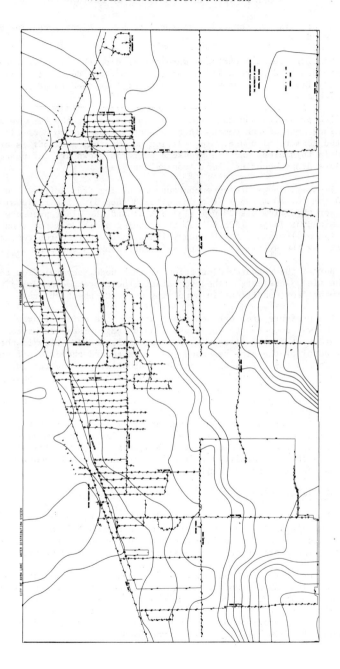

Figure 4. Avon Lake Water Distribution System and Pressure Contour Lines

Portion of this draw-off is also supplied by an eight inch line along Moore Road.

Similar pressure patterns were obtained on the line located along Avon-Belden Road where a 1,300 gpm (0.187 m^3/sec) demand is applied at the city limits. The pressure at this point dropped to 48 psi (330.7 kPa).

The pressure changes in the eastern portion of the city were minimal since most of the demand in this section was due to domestic and limited commercial usage. In addition no external draw-off is experienced in this area, and the pressure patterns shown are influenced by pressure drops occuring along Avon-Belden Road.

Figure 5 shows pressure contours resulting from a fire flow of 4,500 gpm (0.280 m^3/sec) at node No. 3113 (Map 3). The residual pressure for this flow was 20 psi (137.8 kPa) and the plant pressure is maintained at 76 psi (523.6 kPa) by bringing additional pumps on line. The figure also shows the boundary lines that separate the twelve maps comprising the system along with reference numbers for each section.

Before the computer simulation at this node, several flow tests in the field were established to balance the system, especially to determine flow conditions in supplying water to the test area.

The pressure drop between the plant and the point of draw-off for this run was computed to be 56 psi (385.8 kPa). Pressure contour lines indicate most of this loss occurs along Miller Road. Flow in the lower end (south) of the pipe reverses and flows toward the draw-off node. Again this pattern is visible as the contour lines converge and wrap around the draw-off node No. 3113 (Map 3) from both directions.

Similar fire flow applications can be obtained for all the fire hydrants in a given water distribution system. The results can be given in the form of fire flow contour lines as shown in Figure 6. As will be noted this map is a segment of a larger system consisting of 4,500 nodes of which 3,000 are fire hydrants. Such results are used to assess the availability of fire flow at a specified location under various system operating conditions.

Hardware Requirements

The model is designed to be used with a Tektronix graphics terminal and digitizing tablet attached to an HP1000-A900 computer. The maps drawn on the video display screen are copied using an ink jet copier. The plots in ink are generated by a Calcomp plotter.

The pressures and hydraulic grade lines at the nodes are computed using a HP1000-A900 computer or an IBM 3033 U computer. The results are kept in storage and subsequently used by the plot program to obtain pipe network, pressure contours, HGL contours and fire flow contours. The programs are written in FORTRAN language and utilize Tektronix PLOT-10 graphics library routines.

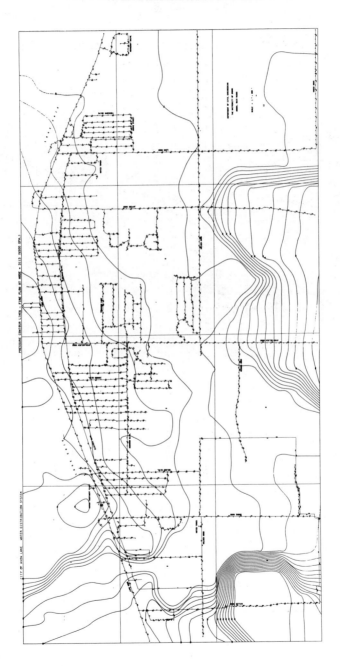

Figure 5. Results of Fire Flow Simulations at Node 3113 (Map 3)

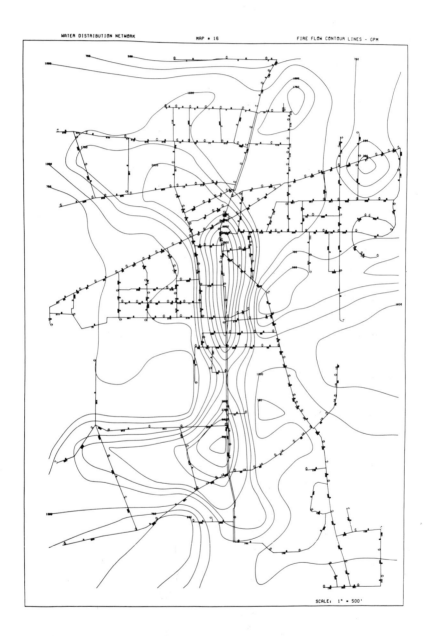

Figure 6. Fire Flow Contour Lines @ 20 psi

Conclusions

The software developed as reported herein offers an excellent means of evaluating the performance of water distribution systems. The interactive capability of the program and the quick turn around time of the computer allows the engineer to view the results for various design alternatives under considerations without going through an extensive and time consuming study of the outputs obtained from the analysis program.

Further copies of the (plot) images drawn on the video screen can be made economically by the hard copy device, and results can be compared to previous runs before a final set of alternatives are presented and analyzed in detail.

References

1. Davis, A. L. and Jeppson, R. W., "Developing a Computer Program for Distribution System Analysis", AWWA Journal, Vol. 71, No. 5, May, 1979, pp. 236-241.

2. Foley, J. D. and Dam, A. V., "Fundamentals of Interactive Computer Graphics", Addison-Wesley Publishing Co., Reading, MA, 1982.

3. Giloi, W. K., "Interactive Computer Graphics", Prentice-Hall, Englewood Cliffs, NJ, 1978.

Acknowledgements

The authors wish to express their appreciation to John W. Kniepper Director of Utilities, City of Avon Lake for his continued interest and support during the development of the model.

WATER QUALITY MODELING OF DISTRIBUTION SYSTEMS

By Ivan Metzger, Fellow, ASCE[1]

ABSTRACT: Computer modeling of hydraulic conditions in distribution
systems has been widely applied over the past decade for design and
operation of systems. Conversely, little attention has been given to
the use of computer models for water quality studies and management
of distribution systems.

This paper presents highlights of computer-aided studies directed by
the author over the past 15 years and selected to show the extension
of hydraulic modeling to water quality modeling of distribution
systems. Applications include evaluation of carrying capacity,
blending of sources, settling and scouring, and pipeline reaction.

HYDRAULIC MODELS

Procedures

Hydraulic conditions in water distribution networks are described by
a system of flow (continuity) and headloss (energy) equations. These
equations are satisfied when the calculated flows are in balance at
each junction, and when the algebraic sum of the headlosses around
all closed loops equals zero. In the computer-aided studies reported
herein, the equations were solved using an iterative technique of
over-relaxation, applied at junctions.

Analysis is initiated with the preparation of an appropriately
skeletonized network schematic showing junctions and pipes, or
hydraulically-equivalent substitutions. System configuration is
defined for computational purposes by numbering the junctions and
pipes, but in the programs no regard to sequence is needed in the
assignment of these numbers.

Although in principle the degree of skeletonization depends upon the
purpose of analysis, in practice it remains a matter of judgment.
Detailed studies made by the author for several grid-like systems
showed that system-wide flows and pressures calculated from skeletons

---

[1] Staff Consultant, Birdsall Engineering, Inc., 1700 "F"
Street, South Belmar, New Jersey 07719.

containing pipe substitutions with as few as 20 percent of the actual
pipes compared well with results using all of the actual pipes. In
the studies reported herein, all pipes were included only in
situations where localized flows and pressures were required;
frequently this was done by a computational "overlay" of the skeleton
in selected areas whereby boundary conditions from the skeleton were
used for input to the localized section.

For the computer programs used in these studies junction information
for the skeletal systems is assembled as shown below:

EXISTING SYSTEM JUNCTION INFORMATION

JUNC NO	JUNC TYPE	DEMAND GPM	HGL FEET	ELEV FEET	PRESS PSI	CALC DEM GPM
89	0			3212.0		
76	0			3191.0		
91	0			3210.0		
75	0			3185.0		

Junction types are coded according to whether they represent demand,
storage, pumping, or pressure-reducing locations. Elevations and
pressures are at ground level. The calculated demand ("CALC DEM" is
printed to show convergence status of the solution.

Pipe information is assembled as shown below:

EXISTING SYSTEM PIPE INFORMATION

PIPE NO	PIPE TYPE	LENGTH FEET	DIA INCHES	C	JUNCTIONS FROM	TO	FLOW GPM	VEL FPS	LOSS FT/1000
99	0	2430.	16.	60.	125	119			
506	0	4430.	16.	60.	64	125			
505	0	3080	40.	60.	56	54			

Pipe types are classed for convenience according to the specific
situations. The remaining column headings are self-explanatory.

For model verification, at least two test conditions are selected --
a high demand condition and a low demand condition. For each,
estimated demands are allocated and assumed hydraulic grade lines are
assigned, as illustrated below:

MODEL VERIFICATION - HIGH DEMAND

JUNC NO	JUNC TYPE	DEMAND GPM	HGL FEET	ELEV FEET	PRESS PSI	CALC DEM GPM
89	0	2422.	3291.2	3212.0		
76	0	2422.	3291.0	3191.0		
91	0	2422.	3292.8	3210.0		

An advantage of using the junction solution, mentioned above, instead of a loop solution, is that an initial flow balance is not required for the network. Only arbitrary junction heads (hydraulic grade lines -- HGL) are needed initially.

Computer computation is initiated for test conditions. The sample output below illustrates the flow imbalance after the first iteration (compare Demand with Calculated Demand).

MODEL VERIFICATION (HIGH DEMAND) - JUNCTION RESULTS

JUNC NO	JUNC TYPE	DEMAND GPM	HGL FEET	ELEV FEET	PRESS PSI	CALC DEM GPM
89	0	2422.	3291.2	3212.0	34.3	6168.2
76	0	2422.	3291.0	3191.0	43.4	1179.1
91	0	2422.	3292.8	3210.0	35.9	222.3

As the solution progresses, the operator interacts to prescribe the accuracy desired in the flow balance; when reached, the calculated hydraulic grade lines (HGL) appear in the appropriate column.

Calculated hydraulic grade lines are then compared with measurements made in the field under test conditions. Adjustments are made to friction factors and demand allocations, as necessary, but only over a limited range, so that calculated results match field measurements. Model validation is achieved when a single set of adjusted friction factors can be used to reproduce all test results with reasonable accuracy.

Pipe results are illustrated below:

MODEL VERIFICATION (HIGH DEMAND) - PIPE RESULTS

PIPE NO	PIPE TYPE	LENGTH FEET	DIA INCHES	C	JUNCTIONS FROM	TO	FLOW GPM	VEL FPS	LOSS FT/1000
99	0	2430.	16.	60.	125	119	782.	1.2	1.7
506	0	4430.	16.	60.	64	125	1211.	1.9	3.7
505	0	3080.	40.	60.	56	54	11241.	2.9	2.7

Notice, as with junction results, the output is in exactly the same format as the input, with the completed columns containing results. This feature permits ready checking of input and results.

Hydraulic applications of the model require a return through several data handling and model verification steps to make appropriate modifications for examining study situations. Modifications may be made in any number of items such as in water demands, using estimates for future development, or in network data, to account for any proposed pipe cleaning. Computer runs are then made to test the

revised system, especially during extreme conditions, against
velocity and pressure criteria, tank filling and pump capability,
fire demands, etc..

Localized Hydraulics

A localized hydraulic analysis was made for a 975-dwelling
development to be served by a network designed to complete a "loop"
in an authority's distribution system. In addition to meeting
domestic demands, the authority required that stipulated fire
requirements be met with minimal impact on system integrity beyond
the connections to the overall system. Since the authority would pay
the marginal cost of protecting system integrity, the chief purpose
of the analysis was to provide a basis for cost negotiations.

The domestic and fire requirements were imposed on alternative
networks, and hydraulic grades were obtained at the development
connections and somewhat beyond. These grades for each alternative
were tallied along with estimated costs. The authority selected the
network based upon minimizing external impacts, and paid the marginal
cost above the "basic" alternative.

Of course, pre-construction studies of this general type provide no
opportunity to validate the computer model used for analyses.
Although dimensions of proposed systems are known, and fire flows so
dominate domestic requirements that water demands essentially are
known, the weakest link is estimating friction factors. These
factors are likely to change over the years as a result of water
quality, bacterial slimes, and related factors.

Recognizing the weakness mentioned above, spot measurements were made
to determine friction factors in existing adjacent pipes which carry
the same water supply. These measurements covered pipes ranging in
age from 10 to 30 years and were used for the assignment of friction
factors along with results from other studies.

Generalized Hydraulics

A computer model was developed for generalized hydraulic analyses of
a tunnel system serving a community of 8,000,000 people. The
existing system comprises some 50 miles of tunnel sections ranging in
diameter from 10 to 24 feet. The purpose of the analyses was for
preliminary examination of alternatives to provide "bypass security"
of the older sections and future needs. A separate step in model
verification was conducted for selected tunnel sections to check the
applicability of the Williams-Hazen flow formulation over the range
of velocities anticipated. Flows and pressures were predicted fairly
well by both the Williams-Hazen and the Darcy-Weisbach formulations
and, although either can be used in the computer programs, the
Williams-Hazen formula was employed in this and other studies
reported herein because of the more widely quoted Williams-Hazen
friction factors.

The overall model verification was accomplished by calculating
pressures at selected shaft risers and at a large tank which rides
the system, and by comparing the results with field measurements.
The resulting model reasonably represented field conditions and
reasonably reproduced results reported in more extensive earlier
modeling efforts. The generalized hydraulic model was employed for
simulating a number of hydraulic conditions.

EXTENSION OF HYDRAULIC MODELS TO WATER QUALITY

Carrying Capacity

Before improvement, a system serving some one million persons was
characterized by a tree-like arrangement, with the larger pipes
forming trunks from the single source and the smaller ones branching
out for supply. Tanks were located at the perimeter of the system,
connected to some of the larger branches. As water demands increased
over the years, the rather obvious problem developed -- tanks failed
to fill, peak demands could not be met, and pressure drops become
serious. A computer model of the system was initially assembled, and
verification was attempted using easy-to-measure flows, tank levels,
and pressures. Initial estimates of the carrying capacity of the
trunk lines were repeatedly adjusted downward, Williams-Hazen "C"
values between 75 and 80 for 10-year old pipes, to reproduce the
results of field measurements. Measurements at both high and low
demand conditions were used, and were repeated; yet adjustment to the
same low carrying capacities was required.

A set of computer model runs was conducted to plan a strategic
pattern for field pipe tests. Field results corroborated the
estimated carrying capacities and showed bacterial slimes as the
likely cause, an observation reported elsewhere.

Further computer analyses were conducted to estimate the improvements
in carrying capacity and the savings in power likely to result from a
program of pipe cleaning/relining. Pipe cleaning was one remedial
step implemented.

Blending

A single-source surface system serving some 300,000 people was slated
for expansion by integrating a groundwater source, located on the
opposite side of the city from the first source. The grid-like
elongated distribution system, then, would be reinforced and served
by sources on opposite ends. With different costs for each source,
and different elevations and distances, crucial hydraulic questions
included the best allocations, storage locations, and pumping
arrangements, to meet peak demands and ensure fire reserves.

Model set-up and verification for the existing system was straight
forward and the system model matched field conditions closely.
Alternative well locations and system additions were added to the

model and tested under extreme conditions, including failure at one
source. Cost studies were made for anticipated routine operation. A
final balance was cast between well locations and system additions to
minimize annual costs.

The difference in water quality between the existing surface source
and the proposed groundwater source prompted an extension of the
computer model to predict the characteristics of the blended water in
parts of the distribution system. For this purpose, the assumption
was made that complete mixing takes place at junctions, and computer
routines were prepared according so that both hydraulic and
concentration conditions were met to a prescribed accuracy. Junction
and pipe results are illustrated below:

JUNCTION WATER QUALITY

JUNC NO	JUNC TYPE	DEMAND GPM	CHLORIDE MG/L
89	0	2422	40
76	0	2422	60

PIPE WATER QUALITY

PIPE NO	PIPE TYPE	FLOW GPM	CHLORIDE MG/L
99	0	782.	55
506	0	1211.	48

Although the assumption on complete mixing could not be verified in
these pre-design studies, subsequent studies elsewhere on a
two-source system showed it to be reasonable. In these subsequent
studies the sources differed considerably in temperature and somewhat
in mineral content. Temperature was used at the "tracer" to check
the mixing assumption.

Settling and Scouring

Prior to recent treatment plant renovation, a coastal community
experienced considerable "red water" problems resulting from
iron-bearing wells and treatment problems. The elimination of
treatment problems focused more attention on the removal of
iron-bearing sediments from the distribution system and the
maintenance of sediment-free conditions.

The community has a year-round population of 5,000 which expands to
15,000 on summer weekends. Seasonal water demands vary accordingly,
with average daily demands in summer running twice the winter
consumption. The 3-hour maximum demands cover a 10-fold range over

the year with resulting system velocities frequently changing from
settling to scouring conditions. The most dramatic impact on water
quality occurs as summer approaches and the wintertime accumulation
is scoured by sustained high velocities on holiday weekends. A
flushing program was designed to induce even higher velocities under
controlled flushing conditions to clean the system before the season.

The development of the flushing program was guided by a computer
model originally verified for system evaluation. Model additions
included coding of valves and hydrants. A closed valve is coded as
two separate dead-ended pipes if there is a demand near the valve,
otherwise as a "missing" pipe. Flow from fully opened hydrants is
calculated in the model using head-discharge relationships
established for the system hydrants. Illustrative results are shown
below:

FLUSH #15 - JUNCTION STATUS

JUNC NO	JUNC TYPE	DEMAND GPM	REMARK
89	2	2200.	Open Hydrant
76	0	120.	Background
91	0	0.	Valve Closed

FLUSH #15 - PIPE STATUS

PIPE NO	PIPE TYPE	LENGTH FEET	JUNCTIONS FROM	TO	FLOW GPM	VEL FPS	REMARK
99	1	2430.	125	119	0	0	Valve Closed
506	0	4430.	64	125	2000	4	Scouring
505	0	3080.	56	54	100	1	Background

A detailed procedure was developed, employed, and documented in a
manual for systematic flushing of the distribution system such that
scouring velocities were achieved and water flowed from
previously-flushed to unflushed areas throughout the stepwise
procedure. This was achieved by strategic manipulation of system
valves in conjunction with hydrant openings. Frequently, mains were
flushed in one direction and then the other.

A significant finding was that flushing as typically done accom-
plishes little more than cleaning hydrants. Adequate pipeline
flushing requires far more time and water. However, the results have
been appreciated and reflected by customer compliments rather than
complaints.

Pipeline Reactions

An extension was made of a hydraulic model for the analysis of the impact of pipeline reactions on water quality in an asbestos-cement distribution system. The system serves a community with a residential pipulation of 18,000 which uses water during the summertime at rates some 135 percent of annual averages. Water is supplied from four sources which are somewhat aggressive and need pH adjustment. Two sources are treated for iron removal. A hydraulic model was prepared to evaluate: the capability of the distribution system under near- and long-term demands; and the prospects of strategic deployment of water sources for energy conservation. Since localized pipes were sized adequately for fire requirements, the focus of the model was on overall water movement and source deployment. For these purposes, water demands at selected "demand centers" were estimated using a computer program designed to "load" the network model. These demand centers were connected by actual or equivalent pipes to complete the network skeleton.

The model was also used to investigate the system response with various pressures maintained at the four sources. Computationally, hydraulic grades were assigned at sources within reasonable tank operating ranges and pump discharge pressures and inflow patterns were determined. The computations were repeated to determine source inflows over a range of conditions, and with various combinations of sources. From this, system deployment plans were developed for energy conservation and other purposes.

One purpose was to adapt the hydraulic model to predict water quality conditions resulting from the reaction of corrosive waters on asbestos- cement pipes, and to develop interim measures to mitigate adverse impacts on water quality until planned facilities are operational for the reduction of corrosivity. Two approaches were evaluated: the addition of a polyphosphate with temporary equipment to form a metal complex on the pipe surfaces; the strategic deployment of sources and lines to minimize contact with asbestos-cement pipes.

Observed alkalinity and pH changes along the asbestos-cement lines outward from the source were used to roughly check a preliminary model of pipeline reaction aimed at predicting the rate of solution of pipe materials. Although within the range of rates estimated little could be accomplished by alternate system deployment, the model did serve as a guide to temporary and permanent installations for chemical addition of sequestering chemicals and lime, respectively.

CONCLUSION

Water quality modeling of distribution systems can be useful in understanding problems and guiding remedial measures. More consideration should be given to the application of models to water quality studies in distribution systems and to the exchange of ideas related thereto.

ADAPTING A PIPE NETWORK ANALYSIS COMPUTER PROGRAM

BY TERRY L. TANNER, M. ASCE[1]/

Abstract

The Metropolitan Water District of Southern California (Metropolitan) has developed a mathematical simulation model for a key portion of its distribution system. Metropolitan is a wholesaler of water for domestic, municipal, agricultural, and groundwater replenishment uses and serves an area of 5,200 square miles (13,500 km^2) with a population of nearly 13 million people, including the Los Angeles and San Diego urban areas. The distribution system has more than 750 miles (1200 km) of pipeline with diameters as large as 20.5 feet (6.3 m) and delivers an average of 1.3 million acre-feet (1.6 x 10^9 m^3) per year. The system operates with throttled flows as the rule rather than the exception, generates electricity with in-line turbine/generators, and blends water from two primary sources that are very different in hardness. The large number and complexity of the hydraulic calculations, the difficulty of estimating energy costs and revenues, and the necessity of tracking the blend of the water through the system have made it imperative to develop a practical computer model that can be used by system operators, planners, and engineers. A representative portion of the distribution system was selected to develop the fundamental modeling and programming concepts and to incorporate the needs of the eventual model user prior to modeling the entire system. This paper discusses the unique hydraulic constraints of this system and the adaption of a standard pipe network analysis computer program to simulate it.

Introduction

Metropolitan chose the network analysis computer program developed at the University of Kentucky (1) as the foundation for the hydraulic simulation model. This network analysis program was selected primarily for its convergence reliability and self-starting characteristics. The fundamental approach has been to minimize the modifications to the foundation program by using external subroutines to do specific enhancements. The program was converted from FORTRAN IV, G Level to FORTRAN 77 and is run on an IBM 4341 computer with a Virtual Machine operating system. The Virtual Machine has made it possible for the user to work interactively with the program to selectively monitor intermediate results and to simulate operational changes during an analysis.

---

1   Engineer, Operations Division, The Metropolitan Water District of Southern California, Box 54153, Los Angeles, CA 90054

The presently modeled portion of the system contains 12 flow control structures, two filtration plants, 15 topographic controls, one reservoir, three reaction and two impulse turbines, and 150 miles (240 km) of pipe that varies in diameter from 4 feet (1.2 m) to 13 feet (4 m). A schematic diagram and profile of a portion of the modeled system is shown in Figure 1.

Adaptions

The most significant adaption is the checking of a hydraulically balanced solution against the physical and operational constraints of the distribution system. An example of constraint checking is comparing the hydraulic grade line (HGL) elevation at a specific point against a minimum and/or maximum allowable HGL. If a constraint is not satisfied, the program logic makes appropriate changes in the system configuration. The network analysis, constraint check, and configuration change cycle is repeated until the constraints are satisfied. In effect a system that can have reaches of open channel flow is being reconfigured into an equivalent system operating under full pressure.

The following are descriptions of the specific hydraulic features and how they are handled in the hydraulic simulation model:

Flow Control Structure -- In a supply system, the most common case is to deliver a set flow at a particular point in the distribution system. This is usually accomplished with an energy dissipation structure that consists of massive valves. The percent open settings of the valves are adjusted until the desired flow is obtained. The model handles this with an upstream and a downstream node connected by a closed pipe. The desired flow is set as a demand leaving the system on the upstream node and as a demand entering the system on the downstream node. The network analysis calculates the HGL elevations at the upstream and downstream nodes. The constraint logic takes the upstream HGL elevation, subtracts the headloss through the valve structure as if the valves were wide open, and compares this hypothetical downstream HGL elevation with the actual HGL elevation. If the hypothetical is greater than the actual, the constraint is satisfied; otherwise the valve is opened and the demands are removed so that the actual maximum possible flow can be determined by another pass through the network analysis.

Topographic or High Point Control -- At several locations in Metropolitan's system it is possible to calculate negative pressures at high points. In actuality these high points are vented and can act like a spillway crest that causes a reach of open channel flow downstream. The constraint logic checks these high points and if a negative pressure is found determines if the flow rate is controlled at either the upstream or downstream end of the pipeline. For downstream control, the desired flow rate is too large and the constraint logic reconfigures the system by closing the pipe downstream of the high point and opening a pipe leading to an open water-surface elevation that represents the minimum allowable HGL elevation

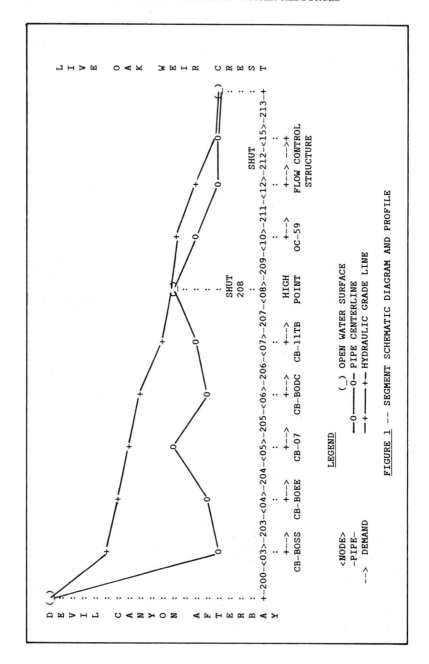

FIGURE 1 -- SEGMENT SCHEMATIC DIAGRAM AND PROFILE

at the high point. The reconfigured system is sent through the network analysis to determine the reduced flow rate over the high
point. For upstream control, the constraint logic increases the HGL
elevation of all upstream nodes by the absolute value of the negative
pressure. In both cases the water cascades away from the high point
in open channel flow until it descends to the HGL that has been
calculated from a downstream control elevation under pressure flow.

Reservoirs -- The initial reservoir water surface elevation is
assigned and thereafter the water surface elevation can be either
fixed or allowed to vary between assigned maximum and minimum
operating water surface elevation limits. For multiple time period
simulations the ending water surface elevation is computed using
tabled elevation-storage relationships, the net inflow or outflow,
and the difference in time. If the elevation is fixed by the user or
reaches an operating limit, then the inflow and outflow are equated.
The reservoir can be of any shape since the elevation-storage
relationship is defined by a table. The foundation network analysis
program is limited to tanks of constant horizontal cross-sectional
area.

Hydroelectric Turbine/Generators -- The upstream and downstream HGL
elevations and the flow through the hydroelectric plant are determined in the network analysis in the same manner as a flow control
structure. The available head is computed. Knowing the flow and the
available head, the efficiency is interpolated from a turbine
characteristic table that is derived from operational or theoretical
data and the power output is calculated. The turbine characteristic
table also defines the operating envelope of the turbine/generator.
The constraint logic is developed for both reaction and impulse
turbines. The foundation program does not model turbine/generators.
This same concept is readily adapted to simulating pumps when the
characteristics need better definition than in the foundation network
analysis program.

Pipe Headloss -- The headloss in each pipe reach is computed by the
product of a coefficient and the square of the flow rate. The coefficient combines the headloss as computed by the Manning equation and
the minor losses into a convenient single term. The use of this
single coefficient eliminates the diameter, pipe length, and minor
loss term from the computation of headloss and also simplifies the
calibration process since the coefficient is calculated directly from
field measured flow rate and headloss data. The Manning equation and
the single loss coefficient have proven to be satisfactory in over
forty years of use on the distribution system. The foundation
network analysis program uses either the Hazen-Williams or
Darcy-Weisbach equation.

Segmentation of the Distribution System -- The distribution system is
divided into segments that are interdependent with respect to the
flows that cross from one segment to another but are otherwise
hydraulically independent. Segmentation improves computational
efficiency by limiting the network analysis system balancing to small
portions of the system directly affected by the particular constraint

logic. The results for the nodes (demands and HGL elevations) and
for the pipes (open water surface elevations, open/closed status, and
flow rates) are stored for use by subsequent segments. Segmentation
also makes it possible to run only a portion of the system for
special or localized studies.

Interactive System Operation -- The user has the option of selecting
specific segments and specific time periods for interactive system
operation. After the network analysis for the initial conditions,
the program is halted and displays on the terminal screen a summary
of the results, lists constraint violations, shows the user the input
values that can be changed, and allows the user to change the input
values through the terminal. If the user makes changes, they are
taken as new initial conditions. Otherwise, the default logic makes
the necessary changes to satisfy the constraints. A typical
interactive screen display is shown in Figure 2.

Output - The hydraulic simulation model retains all node input and
results (demands and HGL elevations) and all pipe input and results
(open water surface elevations, open/closed status, and flow rates)
in a database. This makes possible the flagging of changes made by
the constraint logic when the routine detailed output is desired;
this also makes it possible to access specific information about the
simulation run without modifying the hydraulic simulation model
program and rerunning it. The output database, the system parameter
database that contains pipe lengths, diameters, headloss
coefficients, and node elevations, and any other related database can
readily be accessed by separate programs to produce specific
summaries of a simulation in numeric and/or graphical form. The
normal output from the simulation run is written to a separate file
rather than printed directly. The user has the option of getting a
printed copy of all or a portion of the output after he has reviewed
it on the display screen. This is significant when a normal run of
Metropolitan's entire system on a multiple time period simulation can
produce more than 500 pages of output. A sample of routine detailed
output is shown in Figure 3.

User-Friendliness - The input, interactive, and output phases of the
hydraulic simulation model have been designed with the user in mind.
The dependence upon a network schematic diagram has been reduced by
displaying a description along with the node and pipe numbers. The
service connections are identified by the agency name and connection
designator. In the figures, CB-BOSS describes Chino Basin Municipal
Water District Blow-Off at San Sevaine Creek. The input and output
phases will be even more user-friendly with the application of a
fourth-generation programming language as a database manager. The
database manager will be used for creating new and modifying existing
input files, and will generate the specialized summaries of
simulation run results. The database management application is
currently being developed. Considerable effort has gone into making
the programming of the constraint logic programmer-friendly as well.
Several utility subroutines for accessing and changing values in the
internal network analysis arrays have simplified the constraint logic
programming. The capability of outputting intermediate values while

```
***    WIDE OPEN PCS VALVES LIMIT FLOW TO LIVE OAK RESERVOIR    ***

     THE DEMANDS THAT YOU CAN CHANGE IN EPS # 1 AT 0.00 HOURS ARE:

NODE  DEMAND  DESCRIPTION                       LOCATION  HGL ELEV  HEAD (FT)
----  ------  -----------                       --------  --------  ---------
 3     15.0   CB-BOSS  30. CFS CAPACITY  ||  CB-BOSS   1763.0    206.0
 4     25.0   CB-BOEE  30. CFS CAPACITY  ||  CB-BOEE   1720.7    150.7
 5      5.5   CB-07    7.5 CFS CAPACITY  ||  CB-07     1681.0     37.5
 6     20.0   CB-BODC  30. CFS CAPACITY  ||  CB-BODC   1654.9     85.1
 7     27.0   CB-11TB  40. CFS CAPACITY  ||  CB-11TB   1595.3    -15.8
10    115.0   OC-59   150  CFS CAPACITY  ||  OC-59     1524.5    -77.0
15    590.9   RESERV.  INFLOW DEMAND     ||  RESERV.   1567.0      0.0

   :: INPUT Q : ACTUAL Q ::  CLEARS ::  CLEARS : OUTFLOW ::
   :: LIVE OAK : LIVE OAK ::  PCS BY ::  TOPO BY : DEVIL CN ::
   ::   590.9 :   590.9 ::  -121.4 ::  -113.0 :   798.4 ::

===> ENTER THE NUMBER OF CHANGES YOU WANT TO MAKE
     (ZERO FOR NONE, NEGATIVE TO TERMINATE)
         FOLLOWED BY THE PAIR(S) OF NODE NUMBER & DEMAND
              (EXAMPLE: 2   5 3.   15 300. )

0_
```

Figure 2 - Typical Interactive Screen Display

PERIOD NO. = 1 -- TIME FROM INITIATION OF SIMULATION = 0.00 HOURS

SEGMENT NO. 1 -- CONSTRAINTS SATISFIED

---- SUMMARY OF PIPE INFORMATION ----

PIPE NO.	LOCATION	STATUS 0=OPEN 1=SHUT	OPEN WATER SURFACE EL (FEET)	FLOW RATE (CFS)
200	DEVIL CN	0	1930.0	681.3
203		0	0.0	666.3
204		0	0.0	641.3
205		0	0.0	635.8
206		0	0.0	615.8
207		0	0.0	588.8
208	TOPO D.C	1	1644.0	
209		0	0.0	588.8
211	PCS INFL	0	0.0	473.8
212	VALVE	1	0.0	
213	RES INFL	0	0.0	473.8
215	WEIR EL.	0	1567.0	0.0

---- SUMMARY OF NODE INFORMATION ----

NODE NO.	LOCATION	DEMAND (CFS)	HGL ELEV (FEET)	STATIC HEAD (FEET)
3	CB-BOSS	15.0	1808.4	251.4
4	CB-BOEE	25.0	1777.8	207.8
5	CB-07	5.5	1749.4	105.9
6	CB-BODC	20.0	1730.8	161.0
7	CB-11TB	27.0	1688.7	77.6
8	TOPO CON	0.0	1644.0	0.6
10	OC-59	115.0	1639.5	38.0
12	PCS U/S	473.8<*	1598.6	19.1
13	PCS D/S	-473.8<*	1567.0	0.0
15	RESERV.	473.8<*	1567.0	0.0

NOTE: '<*' INDICATES THE CONSTRAINT LOGIC HAS ADJUSTED THIS VALUE

Figure 3 - Typical Detailed Segment Output

progressing through the constraint logic calculations and comparisons
has also simplified program logic verification.

An Example

The following figures illustrate the capabilities of the hydraulic
simulation model. Figure 1 shows the schematic diagram for one of
the simpler hydraulic segments. Figure 2 shows an interactive screen
just after the network analysis of the original input data. Note
that violations of hydraulic constraints (negative clearances) are
indicated at the flow control structure (PCS) and at the topographic
control. The user indicated that he wanted to make no changes in the
service connection demands and the default logic determined the
maximum inflow to the reservoir. Figure 3 shows the routine detailed
segment output. This network analysis took two trials to solve for
the original input. It then took five trials to solve for the
maximum flow through the wide open flow control structure, and the
constraint at the topographic control was not satisfied. It took
five trials to find the maximum flow over the topographic control and
then two more trials to analyze the previously found flow rate
through the segment. Note that the demands at nodes 12, 13, and 15
are flagged, indicating that they have been changed by the constraint
logic from the input reservoir inflow of 590.9, shown in Figure 2, to
473.8, shown in Figure 3. The HGL for the constraint satisfying
system configuration is shown on Figure 1.

Conclusions

Metropolitan has been able to successfully adapt a standard network
analysis program to simulate a distribution system that has many
features not modeled in the original program. The adaption was
accomplished with minimum modification of the original program by
using external subroutines as much as possible. The adaption was
made utilizing in-house engineering staff for the conceptual
development and the programming of the adaption. The needs of the
system operators, planners, and engineers that will be using the
hydraulic simulation model have been addressed throughout the
adaption process.

Appendix I. -- References:

1. WOOD, D. J., User's Manual -- Computer Analysis of Flow in Pipe
    Networks Including Extended Period Simulations, Office of
    Engineering Continuing Education, University of Kentucky,
    Lexington, KY 40506, 1980.

Modelling Complex Water Distribution Systems

John F. Shawcross[*]

Abstract

A program previously used for the analysis of hundreds of water distribution systems was successfully modified to provide the features needed for the extended simulation of large complex water systems.

Extended simulation of water distribution systems allows a time step analysis through several days of operation. It is particularly useful in sizing storage tanks and pumping stations. The program should be able to react to conditions normally acted on by an operator or handled by system instrumentation.

Each area of a water system has a unique pattern of operation and water use. The program should be able to provide individual demand curves to different areas of the water system.

Modelling the primary water distribution system for Austin, Texas is described. The preprocesser programs used for the manipulation of population and water use data are also described. Additional refinements to the program are proposed.

Introduction

Fifteen years ago, Metcalf & Eddy[**] developed a program (WADSY) for water distribution system analysis. This program has been used by the company to analyze hundreds of water distribution systems. The program has been improved several times to take advantage of improvements in computer technology and in response to the needs of engineers using the program. This paper describes the most recent change which was to provide extended simulation suitable for use in large complex water systems. Reference is made to use of the improved WADSY-D program and preprocesser programs for the analysis of the City of Austin water system.

---

[*] Project Director, Metcalf & Eddy, Inc.
   P.O. Box 4043, Woburn, MA 01888-4043
[**] Metcalf & Eddy, Inc., 10 Harvard Mill Square, Wakefield, MA.

438

Background

WADSY uses a modified Newton-Raphson solution technique and was designed to run on the smaller computers of the 1960's. Most use of the program has been on a DEC PDP 11/70 accessed by in-house terminals and from regional offices. Later versions of the program were modified to run on a DEC VAX VMS.

A close relationship has continued between the engineers using the program and the programmers writing and improving the program.

The added features are in four categories.

1. Improvements to make the computer output more useful to the engineer. Examples of this are improved format, graphical output, and plotting capabilities.

2. Preprocesser programs to assist in preparing the data for analysis. An example of this type of program is (GRIDNODE) which distributes water demand recorded in specified areas to the nodes of the model.

3. Extensions to the program to provide new features. An example of this are a (DESIGN) function which sizes new pipes in accordance with criteria established by the engineer. Another example is (WADSY-D), an extended period simulation which is described in this paper.

4. Postprocesser programs designed to use the output of WADSY plus additional information to provide new results. An example of this type of program is WADSY-Q, which tracks water quality from several sources through the water system. The program WADSY-Q is described in another paper at this conference.

Need for Extended Period Simulation

The original WADSY program provided solutions to instantaneous point-in-time problems. This type of analysis is normally sufficient to solve most distribution system problems. Average and extreme rates of flow can be analyzed on a number of computer runs. Pipes, pumps and tanks can be sized accordingly. Occasionally, a large system with multiple tanks, pumps and pressure zones however, makes it necessary to track a series of runs to determine whether pumps and tanks are adequately sized. This can be very time consuming so that few alternatives can be economically considered. For large complex water systems, therefore, the use of an extended period simulation is essential.

Decision to Improve WADSY

Two factors contributing to the decision to add extended period simulation to WADSY instead of buying available programs with this capability were:

1. The preprocesser programs and other features developed for WADSY over more than ten years of use are needed even more in a large complex system than in a small system. Enhancement of WADSY would retain these features.

2. Development of the program would permit the incorporation of advanced features more closely simulating operation of a real water system.

Features Included

Significant features included in the program are as follows:

1. The ability to operate for 24 to 168 time periods with tank water elevations computed at each time step.

2. The ability to change system demands in each time period with different patterns of change in different areas.

3. The ability to have pumps stop and start at predetermined times, at predetermined tank levels or at predetermined system pressures.

4. An ability to close an altitude valve on a full tank and to stop water feeding the system on an empty tank.

The 24 to 168 time step period was chosen to coincide with one day to one week of continuous operation based on a one hour increment.

The change of system demands in different areas according to different patterns is essential in large water systems. Downtown and suburban use patterns are very different. Different patterns occur dependent on affluence of suburb, distance from the center of the city, and climatic factors. Up to 50 different user defined pattern types can be specified in WADSY-D for each time period.

The ability to model stopping and starting of pumps is essential in a large water system. In a real water system, the operator or instrumentation does not allow a tank to empty or overflow if a pump can be started or stopped to correct the condition. Similarly, if pressure is low in an area, the operator will start a pump. The program, therefore, includes a choice for each pump to stop and start according to time or tank level or pressure at a point in the distribution system. Correct simulation of closed altitude valves or empty tanks is essential to obtain valid results. System pressures under these conditions are very different than if water is assumed to continue entering a full tank or feeding from an empty tank.

Example of Use of WADSY-Q

The primary water system of the City of Austin, Texas was modelled in 1984/85 using WADSY-D. The model included all pipes greater than 20 inches (508 mm) in diameter and included proposed new facilities needed through 2005.

To model this system typically required 60 pumps in operation, 1,000 pipes, 750 nodes, 600 boundary nodes and 23 water storage facilities. The water system is complex. Water is pumped from water treatment plants to storage near the boundary of pressure zones and from there it is repumped to higher elevation zones. Water may be pumped and repumped as many as five times between the treatment plant and the consumer. There are a substantial number of operator choices to decide which combination of treatment plants and pumps to use to meet the demand. Water use patterns vary widely throughout the water system. Table 1 shows 12 of 32 diurnal demand factors (peaking factors) used in a typical 24 hour period throughout the area. Water demands ranged from 0.4 of average to 7.5 of average at extreme low and high demand periods, but peaks occurred at different times in different areas. Figure 1 shows the distribution of peak hour demand by pressure zone.

Figure 2 demonstrates 24 hour plots of contrasting patterns of demand on water storage tanks. These present typical results during the analysis phase of the work.

Brushy Creek, shows a reservoir where insufficient water is provided to meet the demand. Later runs corrected this problem by increasing pumping into the area and enlarging pipe sizes.

Jollyville, shows the opposite extreme, a reservoir that fills and then remains full. This problem results from excessive supply from a new source at a higher pressure. This problem was corrected by reducing pumping.

Davis Lane, demonstrates a better level variation where the reservoir remains within the desired limits and at the end of the day, has returned to approximately the same level as at the start of the day.

Water Use Allocation

The accurate, but efficient, allocation of water use throughout the distribution system is a substantial challenge. The method used for large systems in general is to utilize a program (GRIDNODE). This program accepts data on geographic areas and then distributes a calculated water demand to nodes listed as being in the area or in nearby areas. There are a number of advantages to this technique.

TABLE 1. DIURNAL DEMAND FACTOR CURVES

Initial Time .... TZERO = 0
Time Increment .... DELT = 1
Final Time .... TFINAL = 24

Time:	0	1	2	3	4	5	6	7	8	9	10	11	12	13	14	15	16	17	18	19	20	21	22	23
DM: CENTRAL3	0.8	0.6	0.6	0.6	0.7	0.7	1.1	2.4	2.6	2.5	2.5	2.2	2.1	1.9	2.0	2.0	2.4	2.7	3.2	3.4	4.3	2.9	1.9	1.3
DM: NORTH 4	1.2	1.1	1.1	1.1	1.5	1.5	1.9	2.5	2.6	2.5	2.6	2.6	2.1	1.7	1.6	1.5	1.3	1.2	1.8	2.2	3.0	2.4	1.9	1.5
DM: NWA5	1.2	0.9	1.2	1.2	1.3	1.3	1.5	2.2	2.3	2.4	2.5	2.6	3.3	1.9	0.9	1.2	1.7	1.9	2.2	2.4	3.8	2.6	1.4	1.1
DM: NWB1	2.2	1.9	1.3	1.2	1.3	1.5	2.9	6.5	5.6	5.1	4.9	4.8	4.3	3.9	3.9	3.5	4.5	4.8	5.4	5.8	7.5	5.5	3.9	2.9
DM: SWB	1.6	1.0	0.5	0.6	0.6	0.8	1.0	1.7	2.3	2.5	2.6	2.6	2.1	1.9	1.8	1.8	1.8	1.9	2.3	2.9	4.0	2.8	1.7	2.2
DM: NWA3	1.1	1.1	1.1	1.0	1.3	1.5	1.6	2.0	2.0	2.1	2.3	2.1	1.9	2.1	4.3	2.3	2.1	2.0	1.8	1.6	1.5	1.5	1.3	1.2
DM: SOUTH	1.1	0.8	0.9	0.9	1.0	1.0	1.6	2.4	2.4	2.2	1.8	1.8	1.9	1.8	1.7	1.7	2.3	2.4	2.8	3.0	3.8	2.9	2.2	1.7
DM: SWA1	0.8	0.7	0.7	0.7	0.8	0.8	2.8	4.6	4.3	3.0	1.8	1.8	1.6	1.5	1.4	1.3	1.3	1.4	1.5	4.7	6.0	1.8	1.2	1.0
DM: SOUTHRED	0.9	0.9	0.9	0.9	1.1	1.4	2.1	2.7	2.8	2.3	2.2	2.0	2.1	2.1	2.0	1.9	1.9	1.8	2.1	2.4	3.1	2.3	1.9	1.4
DM: SWA3	1.0	1.5	0.8	0.4	0.4	0.4	2.9	3.0	2.2	1.8	1.7	1.8	1.5	2.6	2.7	1.8	1.9	2.2	2.6	3.3	5.0	3.2	2.5	1.9
DM: CENTRAL7	0.9	0.7	0.6	0.5	0.5	0.5	1.0	3.1	3.8	2.8	2.5	2.3	1.9	1.7	1.8	1.8	2.2	2.2	2.8	3.4	3.4	3.2	2.3	1.7
DM: SOUTH2	0.8	0.7	0.7	0.9	1.0	1.2	1.7	2.1	2.0	2.2	2.2	2.2	2.0	2.0	2.0	1.9	2.2	2.4	3.1	3.1	3.7	2.7	2.0	1.4

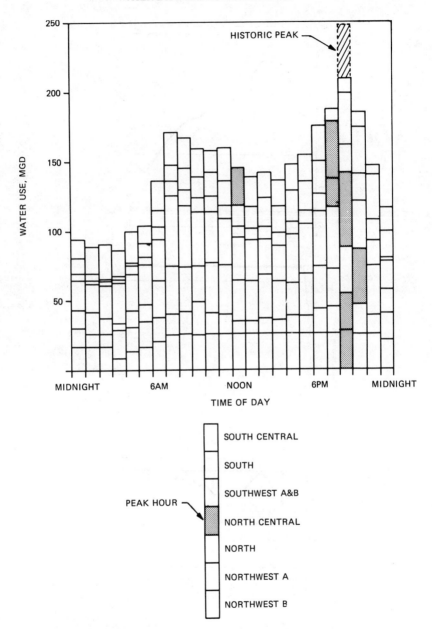

FIGURE 1 MAXIMUM DAY WATER USE BY PRESSURE ZONE

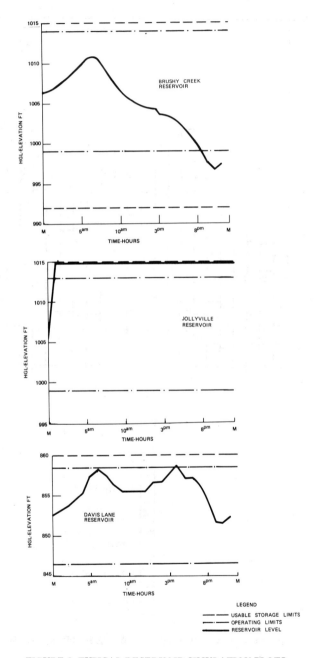

FIGURE 2. TYPICAL RESERVOIR SIMULATION PLOTS

1. Once the water demand of an area has been determined, the allocation to model nodes is an automatic process which results in the generation of a water demand file suitable for input to WADSY or WADSY-D.

2. When new pipes and nodes are added to the model reallocation of demand is easily achieved.

3. GRIDNODE can accept population and per capita data in place of water use which makes demand projections easier. The population in each geographic area can be divided into use types dependent on housing quality and different per capita use rates can be allocated to each housing type.

Water Use Allocation in Austin

For the Austin project, data was available on water use and population by census tract. It was appropriate, therefore, to use groups of census tracts as the basic geographic areas for the distribution of water demand. From these data, existing per capita information were developed. Use of these data and population projections through 2005 permitted the efficient distribution of water demand to the nodes of the model. It also established a system for future water demand updates for when new census data are available and when per capita water use trends have been further defined.

Additional Refinements

As a result of recent use of WADSY-D, two desirable refinements were identified.

. Improved plotting of results.

. Pumps reacting to both suction and delivery tank elevations.

In reviewing computer results regarding changes of levels in tanks the following data should appear on the graphical output.

. The computed water level and top and bottom tank elevations and control limits.

. Tank capacity and volume per unit depth.

. Details on pumps pumping in or out of the reservoir.

An example of a desirable graphical output is presented as Figure 3.

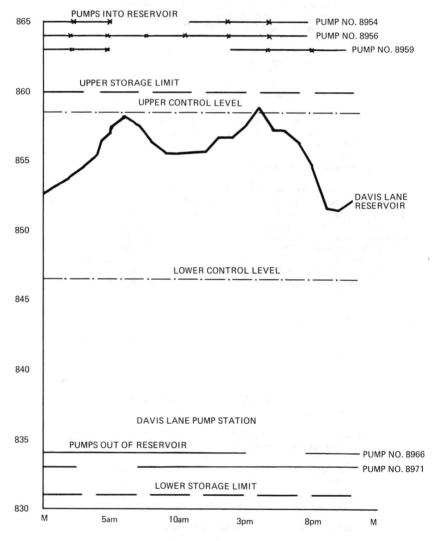

FIGURE 3.
PROPOSED GRAPHICAL DISPLAY FOR RESERVOIR AND PUMP OPERATION

Summary and Conclusions

For the analysis of large complex water distribution systems, the choice of a program should consider:

.   The availability of extended period simulation.

.   The ability of the program to model operator and instrumentation reaction to events such as full tanks and low pressure in the distribution system.

.   The availability of preprocesser programs to manipulate vast amounts of data particularly relating to water use.

.   The clarity of the computer output.

The WADSY-D program successfully meets these criteria although additional refinements in the presentation of graphical output and pump controls are desirable.

Computer Modeling of Distribution System Water Quality

by Douglas G. Chun[1] and Howard L. Selznick[1], Associate Member, ASCE

ABSTRACT: The WADSY-Q computer program was developed as a tool to analyze water quality patterns in water distribution systems with multiple sources. The program calculates the concentrations of conservative parameters at any point in a modeled network, for steady-state conditions and known source concentrations. The program requires a prior hydraulic solution of the network so that mass balance equations can be derived and solved for each pipe node. In the application of WADSY-Q to a municipal water system, the program provided results which closely approximate actual field measurements. The program provides an efficient means of evaluating the water quality impacts of supply alternatives being considered to meet future demands. This information helps provide a more complete picture of benefits and costs so that prudent management decisions can be made.

INTRODUCTION

Managers of larger water distribution systems are commonly faced with the challenge of how to best utilize multiple water sources. Typically, the decision as to which combination of sources should be used is based on the capacity of each source and its associated cost of operation. A reasonably precise method has been lacking for projecting distribution system water quality when a particular combination of sources is used. Often, the only means to evaluate alternative source management schemes has been in situ testing, requiring actual operation of the system in a particular mode, and taking and analyzing water samples from throughout the system.

WADSY-Q, for WAter Distribution SYstem Analysis - Quality, is a computer program developed by Metcalf & Eddy to provide an efficient, desktop aid for making better water supply management decisions. For a distribution system network with known hydraulic conditions and source characteristics, the program is able to calculate the steady-state concentrations of conservative parameters at each pipe node. From these results, the influence zones of each source can be determined. Of greater significance is the ability to quickly assess how influence lines are shifted when available sources are used to a greater or lesser degree. Such application is valuable not only for day-to-day management decisions, but also for long-range planning decisions when substantial capital investment may be at stake.

---

1. Senior Project Engineer, Metcalf & Eddy, Inc., 290 Santa Ana Court, Sunnyvale, CA 94086

PROGRAM DESCRIPTION

WADSY-Q is a user-friendly program designed to be used by those who do not have detailed knowledge of computers or programming. Data are input through program-generated prompts or independently by the user and printed output is simply formatted and easily interpreted.

Use of WADSY-Q requires a completed run of WADSY, a base program developed by Metcalf & Eddy, which is used for hydraulic network analysis. WADSY-Q uses as input the output of WADSY, including pipe flow and nodal demand data. Descriptions of how WADSY and WADSY-Q are formulated are provided in the following paragraphs.

WADSY Formulation

WADSY simulates the operation of a water distribution system under steady-state conditions. The distribution system is abstracted in terms of nodes, lines, and boundary conditions. Nodes are pipe intersections, reservoirs, tanks, wells, pump suction and discharge points, and other points where the system characteristics change, such as change of pipe size or material, or where major users are served. Lines connect nodes and are sections of pipeline or pumps. Lines can contain check valves or pressure reducing valves. Boundary conditions are flows, pressures, or elevations in the system as specified by the user for each node. Flow data are both demands on the system and inputs into the system from wells or reservoirs.

Data Requirements. WADSY requires two general classes of data for its input file: (1) the physical system, i.e., pipe characteristics, pump curves, reservoir and tank elevations, ground elevations at nodes, pressure settings, etc.; and (2) flow demands on the system.

How WADSY Works. For a given input of pipe characteristics (Hazen-Williams "C" coefficient, and check valves or pressure reducing valves, if any), pump curves, and boundary conditions (flow demands on the system and given elevations and/or pressures), WADSY computes flow and headloss in each section of pipe and the hydraulic grade elevation (pressure plus ground elevation) for each node in the system. The results are for a steady-state condition for the system described by the input data. The system's behavior can be simulated under various conditions, such as average daily flow, peak hourly flow, etc.

The WADSY algorithm used is a modified Newton-Raphson technique that solves a system of nonlinear equations by an iterative process. The method of solution is predicated on the continuity of flow at each node, i.e., the sum of the flows into a node must be zero. The procedure used to form the system of equations results in a nonsingular coefficient matrix (i.e., the system of equations is linearly independent). Thus, the user cannot specify a set of boundary conditions that will result in a set of equations that cannot be solved.

WADSY Output. The WADSY output file consists of three tables: (1) system connectivity, (2) pipe data, and (3) node data. The system connectivity table lists each node and the lines into and out of the

node. This table is used to check the accuracy of the input data. The
pipe table includes the following information: pipe number, node at
each end of the pipe, pipe length, pipe diameter, Hazen-Williams "C"
factor, flowrate, direction of flow, total headloss, and slope of the
hydraulic gradient. In the nodes table, gradient elevations are given
as total hydraulic gradient (pressure head plus elevation) and pressure
head or static pressure in both feet and pounds per square inch. WADSY
also lists on the nodes table the flow for all nodes that have specified
boundary conditions. This includes demands on the system and sources
for the system (i.e., reservoirs and wells).

WADSY-Q Formulation

WADSY-Q is literally an extension of the water distribution system
simulation achieved by WADSY. To ensure the validity of WADSY-Q
results, it is essential that the WADSY results used as input be
correct. This validation is most easily carried out by comparing
simulated and actual pressures at representative points throughout the
system.

Data Requirements. WADSY-Q requires two input files: (1) a WADSY
output file, and (2) a concentration file. The first file is generated
by a WADSY run. The concentration file consists of chemical
concentrations at each source, e.g., wells, reservoirs. Concentrations
can be entered either after a set of program-generated prompts or
modifying existing data. In the former case, WADSY-Q automatically
selects the sources from the WADSY output file.

In the case of reservoirs or storage tanks where concentrations are
not known, a WADSY-Q run can be made using a WADSY output which has
these reservoirs or tanks filling. The results of this run will
determine the quality in the reservoirs or tanks. WADSY-Q can then be
run with a WADSY output in which these reservoirs or tanks act as
sources from a water quality standpoint.

How WADSY-Q Works. WADSY-Q solves for the chemical concentrations in a
piping network by constructing mass balance equations at each node. The
general equation for mass balance is given by (1)

$$\Sigma\,(QC)_{in} = \Sigma\,(QC)_{out} \tag{1}$$

Where Q = flow
       C = concentration

This equation when applied to an actual network is generally immediately
solvable for C at the source node, as illustrated in Figure 1 for node
44. The equations for nodes 45, 47, and 52 can be solved immediately.
However, node 4 cannot be solved until the concentration of a second
flow input (of 252 gpm) is known. This concentration is eventually
found by successive solution of nodal equations which are determinate.
WADSY-Q works in a similar fashion by solving each nodal equation one at
a time. When a mass balance equation is solved, its effect on the
unknown of other nodes is accounted for in the next iteration. WADSY-Q
continues to look at all the nodes in the network until all the chemical
concentrations are known. The algorithm determines directly an exact

solution at each node and does not use a technique which successively approximates and converges on the final result.

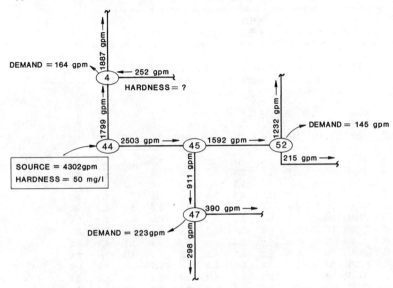

FIGURE 1. WADSY-Q NETWORK SOLUTION EXAMPLE

WADSY-Q Output

WADSY-Q results are based on the assumptions that (1) there is complete mixing at the nodes (i.e., all water leaving a node is assumed to have the same concentrations); (2) the chemicals being considered are conservative (i.e., do not degrade or chemically change while flowing through the piping network); and (3) network hydraulic conditions area steady-state.

The actual printed output may include any of the following tables:

● Percent flow from each source at each node (see Figure 2 for sample output)

● Total concentration of input chemicals at each node (up to 6 chemicals may be evaluated for any one run)

● Influence each source has on each node chemical concentration

● Nodes which have concentrations within a given range, e.g., are less than or equal to a given concentration, between two given concentrations, or greater than or equal to a given concentration

The variety of formats in which results are displayed is convenient

for plotting areas of influence for sources, contouring lines of
constant water quality, and the like.

```
================================================================================
                                % FLOW
        PERCENT OF VOLUME FLOW OUT OF A NODE FROM EACH SOURCE: NODE - ALL
§================================================================================
```

NOTE: This is a characteristic of flow and stays constant for
any chemical and any amount of chemical input into the
same system.

NODE	DEMAND FLOW (GPM)	SOURCE NODES (% flow) 44	118	288	349	670	671	701	805	807	817
4	164.120	100.0	0.0	0.0	0.0	0.0	0.0	0.0	0.0	0.0	0.0
6	336.590	100.0	0.0	0.0	0.0	0.0	0.0	0.0	0.0	0.0	0.0
11	787.810	100.0	0.0	0.0	0.0	0.0	0.0	0.0	0.0	0.0	0.0
19	781.160	96.6	0.0	0.0	3.4	0.0	0.0	0.0	0.0	0.0	0.0
33	327.740	100.0	0.0	0.0	0.0	0.0	0.0	0.0	0.0	0.0	0.0
38	72.940	100.0	0.0	0.0	0.0	0.0	0.0	0.0	0.0	0.0	0.0
43	0.000	100.0	0.0	0.0	0.0	0.0	0.0	0.0	0.0	0.0	0.0
44	0.000	100.0	0.0	0.0	0.0	0.0	0.0	0.0	0.0	0.0	0.0
45	0.000	100.0	0.0	0.0	0.0	0.0	0.0	0.0	0.0	0.0	0.0
47	222.760	100.0	0.0	0.0	0.0	0.0	0.0	0.0	0.0	0.0	0.0
52	145.150	100.0	0.0	0.0	0.0	0.0	0.0	0.0	0.0	0.0	0.0
54	239.030	93.9	0.0	0.0	6.0	0.0	0.0	0.0	0.0	0.0	0.0
56	165.350	100.0	0.0	0.0	0.0	0.0	0.0	0.0	0.0	0.0	0.0
61	0.000	100.0	0.0	0.0	0.0	0.0	0.0	0.0	0.0	0.0	0.0

**FIGURE 2. WADSY-Q OUTPUT TABLE-PERCENT
FLOW CONTRIBUTION BY SOURCE**

APPLICATION OF WADSY-Q

The WADSY-Q program was used in the analysis of a municipal water
supply system as part of a long-range master planning study for the
Alameda County Water District (ACWD), Fremont, California. The District
serves about a 97-square mile area within the corporate limits of the
cities of Fremont, Newark, and Union City and provides water to some
57,000 customers through over 625 miles of pipeline. Historically,
residential water demand has accounted for greater than 70% of total
demand, which amounted to an average 36.7 mgd in 1984. Ultimate water
demands are projected to grow to 60 mgd by the year 2010 due to (1) an
increase in population from 228,000 to an estimated 294,000 at buildout
(a 29% increase), and (2) substantial industrial/business park
development, principally "high tech" research and development and
manufacturing operations.

Source Water Quality

The District is served by three sources of water supply. These
include (1) South Bay Aqueduct (SBA) water from the State Water Project,
(2) groundwater, and (3) San Francisco Water Department (SFWD) water

taken from the Hetch Hetchy Aqueduct. To meet drinking water
regulations and historical concerns for water hardness, treatment
includes complete filtration SBA water and split stream, ion-exchange
softening of groundwater. All 3 sources are chlorinated and
fluoridated. Typical values of conservative parameters for each source
as delivered to the water distribution system are given in Table 1.

Table 1. ACWD SOURCE WATER QUALITY

Constituent	Typical concentration, mg/L		
	SBA	Groundwater	SFWD
Hardness (as CaCO$_3$)	135	119	50
Total dissolved solids	170	540	46

System Modeling

The District's water distribution system was reduced to a simplified
network consisting of 166 interconnected pipelines and 134 pipe
junctions or nodes. Pipelines modeled were generally 12 in. in diameter
and larger except for areas where pipelines down to 6 in. in diameter
were included for adequate representation of the network. Water demand
and supply data were derived from actual consumption and production
records. Pipeline lengths and Hazen-Williams "C" factors were provided
by District engineering staff. This input to the WADSY hydraulic
network analysis program resulted in calculated flow and pressure data
that compared favorably to field measurements for average and peak day
conditions after trial runs and model calibration adjustments had been
made.

System Quality Simulation

After the hydraulic analysis of the system was performed using the
WADSY program, the input was prepared for running the WADSY-Q program.
Hardness was chosen as the parameter to characterize the quality of each
source, including distribution storage reservoirs. This parameter is
significant to the District because of customers' concern over "hard"
water in the groundwater supply which may result in (1) increased soap
usage and (2) formation of scale in hot water pipes, hot water heaters,
boilers, and other heat exchange surfaces. Runs were completed for
three periods of time including one day for which intensive distribution
sampling was performed. Hardness concentrations as calculated by the
program and as actually determined from laboratory analysis of samples
were used to evaluate the validity of the WADSY-Q results; these
comparisons indicated good agreement overall.

Source influence plots are given by Figures 3 and 4. Influence
boundary lines delineate areas where the quality of one particular
source predominates. Figure 3 indicates the system water quality when
each of the three available sources are used. This water quality
pattern would typify the conditions generally experienced throughout the
year. In Figure 4, groundwater sources were not used and the area of
influence for remaining surface water sources increased in proportion to
use as indicated. In both cases, the influence boundaries between

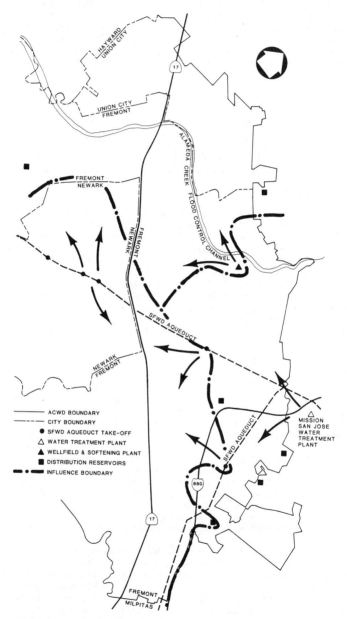

FIGURE 3. ACWD DISTRIBUTION SYSTEM WATER QUALITY PROFILE FOR APRIL 11–14, 1983 – THREE SOURCES OF SUPPLY

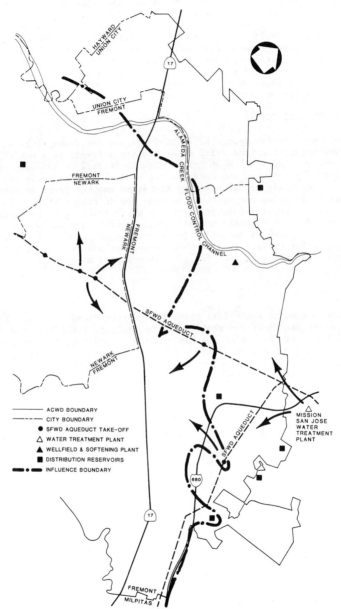

FIGURE 4. ACWD DISTRIBUTION SYSTEM WATER QUALITY
PROFILE FOR FEBRUARY 10–17, 1983 –
TWO SOURCES OF SUPPLY (NO GROUNDWATER)

sources were well defined; this finding was confirmed by the results of sampling and laboratory analyses.

Additional simulations are to be conducted for modified conditions which will reflect future water supply-demand scenarios. Water quality changes will be determined for situations in which one source may be off-line for reasons of maintenance or emergency. These results will facilitate decisions regarding system isolation or valving to ensure consistent water quality to customers.

SUMMARY AND CONCLUSIONS

Computer modeling using the WADSY-Q program has shown to be an efficient method for predicting water quality patterns in a municipal water system. Application of the program is helpful in modeling what changes take place when the contribution of each source is varied. The ease and flexiblity of the modeling technique enables rapid assessment of water quality impacts without the need for in situ testing. Such testing may be precluded in applications where tracking of groundwater pollution (such as volatile organic contaminants) into the water distribution system is desired. In conclusion, WADSY-Q is a useful for analyzing water quality in distribution systems and provides a valuable operations and planning tool for the water supply manager.

ACKNOWLEDGMENTS

The authors wish to thank Karl Ngan, Engineering Manager of the Alameda County Water District, and members of the District staff for providing helpful input and review of the application of WADSY-Q; John Shawcross and Bill Mahlum of Metcalf & Eddy, for development of the program itself, and review of the manuscript; and Franklin Burton of Metcalf & Eddy for his editorial comments.

WELCOME TO THE WONDERFUL WORLD OF DATA BASES
(LESSONS FROM AN ENGINEER TURNED MIS)

by

Gerald Greener, M. ASCE[1], Major Steve Lockhart[2],
Russell Epps [3]

ABSRTACT: The paper describes some of the problems
and solutions surrounding the National Dredging
Data Management System (NADDAMS). By an analysis
of these problems and solutions, the authors
develop some basic principles for data base design
and discuss how an engineering background can help
in utilizing computers. The subjects of getting
started in computing, buying hardware and software,
and a warning about disorganization are also
discussed.

The authors close with a detailed discussion of how
NADDAMS was designed to provide easy data transfer
to and from engineer/managers with micro and
personal computers for local use or file updating.
This discussion will include a section on how to
convert non computer users into computer activists.

The primary function of U.S. Army Corps of Engineers is
in the area of construction management. To properly
manage an activity, one needs to compile information on
the subject. The Corps of Engineers has, during the
course of its long history, devised many reporting

---

[1] Civil Engineer, Dredging Division, Water Resources
Support Center, Corps of Engineers, Casey Building, Ft.
Belvoir VA 22060-5586

[2] Assistant Director, Water Resources Support Center,
Corps of Engineers, Casey Building, Ft. Belvoir VA
22060-5586

[3] Computer Scientist, Dredging Division, Water
Resources Support Center, Corps of Engineers, Casey
Building, Ft. Belvoir, VA 22060-5586

procedures that are of use to the individual project
manager as well as to the Headquarters elements who
report to Congress. These reporting procedures have
evolved from simple hand written notes, to the
extensive use of standard forms reporting formats, to
that of electronic data bases that are shared by the
end user and the headquarters elements. This evolution
has been at times slow and tedious.

The old manual system that was the mainstay of the
Corps and the rest of government prior to computers was
extremely slow and cumbersome. With all the Corps
districts sending in their many required reports, the
system at the national level quickly bogged down. The
amount of paper reports collected just in the Dredging
Division over the past several years would fill a 10 ft
by 20 ft room from floor to ceiling. This amount of
paper quickly overwhelmed a manager trying to find a
specific piece of information on a particular project.
Senior managers quickly realized that a better, less
manpower intensive system had to be devised. Hence, the
development of the Dredging Division's own data base,
NADDAMS.

The road from the old paper reporting system to that of
a computer data base was not a smooth one. When
computers were first used, the spreadsheet programs
attempted to make sense of all the information
available. These were chosen because they were
relatively easy to use, and most of the managers did
not know how to use computers. These managers were
typically in their mid 50's. When they were in
college, computers did not exist. They accomplished
their work using ledger paper and slide rules. The
spreadsheet programs tended to duplicate the ledger
paper and had a built-in calculator. For the first few
months of operation, novice users usually found the
spreadsheet adequate. As the user became more
sophisticated and increased his data volume, he started
to reach the limits of the spreadsheet. At this point
the managers had to turn to other methods of achieving
their desired result, that of being able to store and
retrieve vast amounts of information in a useable form.

At present there are many programs on the market for
computers called Data Bases Managers that can
accomplish this desired goal. Until recently, these
have been on large, centrally located mainframe
computers. There have been problems in using the
services of these large computers. First, they were
not user friendly and they did not always provide an
easier method of handling information for the manager.
The real problem was that of not having the right
information formated in such a way that met everyone's
needs.

Generally, when a data base was designed, a group
of data processors got together with the various
managers and tried to find out how they could help each
other. The data processing personnel tended to be more
introverted and did not understand people and people's
needs very well. On the other hand, the managers,
whose job was that of accomplishing the job through
people understood people very well but not computers.
The problem with the central data base tended to be one
of communications between the people involved.

Today with the micro and mini computers in a price
range where each manager/engineer can have one on their
desk, the managers are having the opportunity to expand
their knowledge of data bases and find new uses for it.
The personal and mini computers sold by some companies
are really management tools, especially those which
include bundled software and the new lap portables.
Because of their learning disciplines and analytical
background, engineers seem to have a lower degree of
fear of the unknown and thus are more willing to accept
new tools. Sensitivity to cause-effect relationships
allows them to discover new applications. Trained to
search out "better ways" of doing things, engineers
readily adapt and are more willing to try the computers
in their work.

The design of a data base that would be used by all the
dredging managers throughout the Corps was not an easy
task. First it needed to have a useful function for
them as well as provide the required information at the
national level. In the development of this system, even
small seemingly insignificant items when not precisely
defined can cause havoc in the overall function of the
data base.

One part of the National Dredging Data Management
System (NADDAMS) was designed to record when a dredge
was on the job, the length of time it was there, and
the actual number of hours spent dredging. If the time
the dredge arrived on the job was recorded and the time
it left the job was also recorded, then one could
calculate the time the dredge was available for
dredging. From existing contract information, the
actual work time was already available. By combining
these three elements together, the physical length of
time for dredging was known. However, many people
thought that the date a contract was completed was the
same date that the dredge left the job; this was not
correct. Many Corps officials were saying that the two
ending dates were repetitive, but an examination of the
descriptions of the two dates revealed the following
differences:

Dredge ending date - date the dredge left the dredging site after completion of the work.

Contract ending date - date the contract was officially completed, i.e., all paper work was completed and final payment made.

We can see that the importance of designing a data base cannot be overstressed. Just as you would not think of constructing a building without a careful examination of the soils and the preparation of a design for the foundation, the data base designer has to construct his foundation by defining the data elements carefully. Mistakes made at the data element design stage can threaten the total project, much as a faulty foundation threatens the collapse of a building.

During the development of NADDAMS, we did not want to over burden the field by having to report the same information to different offices. So we looked for elements that were being reported to another data base or recorded on some existing report for which detailed instructions on developing the "proper" value were already in existence. The effort was extensive and involved not only the data processing contractors hired to establish the system but also the various dredging managers from around the Corps. Where possible, the data elements from other systems was used as input to NADDAMS. The real driving force was to create a system that would make the manager's job easier, provide useful information and meet the needs of the Dredging Division in providing information that goes to Congress.

The process above was a rather lengthy explanation of a rather simple, if not easy, process. As engineers, most of us like to simplify the steps in any equation to a clear and precise set of words or numbers. The basic steps in creating a data base are as follows:

1. Data element definition.

2. Development of logic relationships.

3. Testing the data base.

4. Deployment of the data base.

In the attempt to move from the age of paper reporting to that of data bases handled by computers, our managers had many new things to learn. Since most of our managers are in the same age group as those in the field, mid 50's to early 60's, they too had used slide rules in college. The computer generation was still a dream in someone's garage. Not only did they have to learn about the structure of a data base but also how to procure the necessary machines or hardware to "run" the system on. Trying to decide on the "right" type of hardware was not an easy task since the only ones who really knew anything about computer hardware were the same data processing people who are more into machines than into people. The data processors have a tendency to look for the latest and greatest in the selection of equipment, and they generally use their frame of reference instead of looking for easier ways of managing.

Here are some tips on how you as managers can avoid making this mistake:

1. Decide what you want to do with the computer equipment in the near term.

2. Purchase only hardware and software for your immediate needs. With this limited equipment and software, growth will still occur.

3. Once you can no longer do what you need and know how to do, you should consider upgrading to more powerful hardware and software.

4. Never buy much above your current level. By the time you reach your top level as a user, there will be much better equipment available.

5. More expensive does not mean better.

6. Fewer commands in your software means smaller memory required both in the machine and human operator.

7. Consumer beware.

The Dredging Division of the Water Resources Support Center has and will continue to strive for excellence in the way its work is accomplished. In today's world of declining resources this means that we must continue to seek better ways of doing our jobs, since our "real" job is that of processing and analyzing dredging information and then making decisions on how to keep the nations waterways open for the least cost to the taxpayer. The efforts undertaken to upgrade and modernize the way we handle information at all levels is already paying off for us.

WATER DATA BANK OF THE HASHEMITE KINGDOM OF JORDAN

By Zuhair A. Heyasat[1] and David V. Maddy[2]

ABSTRACT

The Hashemite Kingdom of Jordan and the United States of America have jointly undertaken an investigation of the ground-water resources of Northern Jordan. An initial step in the investigation was the procurement of a Digital Equipment Corporation minicomputer, model PDP-11/44, through an Agency for International Development grant Number 278-0243. The Water Data Bank of the Hashemite Kingdom of Jordan is contained on the minicomputer which is located in the Water Authority of Jordan under the direction of His Excellency, Engineer Mohammad S. Kilani, President of the Water Authority.

A major goal of the investigation was the improvement of water resources planning and management techniques through the development and use of a water data bank. The Water Data Bank contains information about rainfall, evaporation, wells, aquifer tests, well lithology, discharge from springs, surface water runoff to wadis and rivers, and water quality. The availability of these various kinds of water data will give management officials and water resources planners the information necessary to evaluate options during decision-making activities.

In addition to the data in the Water Data Bank, the Water Data Bank has an extensive array of software to be used in data presentation and data analysis. The software ranges from data tabling, graphing, and mapping programs to programs for ground-water flow modeling and statistical analysis. The coupling of the software and the data of the Water Data Bank will give the Hashemite Kingdom of Jordan effective tools to use in the management and the planning for future development of natural resources.

Introduction

The Hashemite Kingdom of Jordan is a mainly arid country of rocky deserts, rolling plains, and mountains, situated between the Red Sea and the Mediterranean Sea.

1.   Act. Ch., Water Authority Water Data Bank, Amman, Jordan
2.   Hydrologist, U.S. Geological Survey, Amman, Jordan

(see figure 1.). Jordan is part of the ancient land known as the
Fertile Crescent and has a Mediterranean climate. The rainy season
occurs from November to April, during the period of lowest
temperatures, and the remainder of the year is very dry. Average
rainfall in Amman is about 16 in (400 mm) and the temperature ranges
from an August average of 90 degrees Farenheit (32 degrees Centigrade)
to a January average of 50 degrees Farenheit (10 degrees Centigrade).
The recent increase in population, especially in the urban centers, has
been accompanied by an increased in demand for water to be used for
domestic, agricultural, and industrial purposes.

Unfortunatly the available water resources are not near these
areas of increased demand, so in September 1980, under Section 532 of
the Foreign Assistance Act. the Hashemite Kingdom of Jordan Groundwater
Resources Investigation, Project Grant Number 278-0243, was authorized
at an obligation level of $5,000,000. The Project, to be administered
by the Agency for International Development (AID), covers the Azraq
Basin, the Zarqa Basin, the Yarmouk Basin, and the upper Jordan Valley
Basin (see figure 2.). An initial step in the investigation was the
proqurement of a Digital Equipment Corporation (DEC) minicomputer,
model PDP-11/44.

The minicomputer is used to store the Water Data Bank of the
Hashemite Kingdom of Jordan. The minicomputer, and the Water Data
Bank, is located in the Water Authority of Jordan under the direction
of His Excellency, Engineer Mohammad S. Kilani, President of the Water
Authority. The Water Authority was established by Cabinet approval of
Water Authority Law Number 35 on December 15, 1983, to centralize the
management of water resources for the entire Kingdom.

Staff

The present staff of the Water Data Bank Section consists of an
Acting Chief, Zuhair Heyasat, a computer engineer, a computer
programmer, a computer operator, seven data-entry technicians, and a
section aide. David Maddy has been assigned to the Investigation as a
Technical Advisor in computer techniques since March 1984. Three of
the data-entry technicians are assisting the computer engineer in
checking data entered into the Water Data Bank, a quality assurance
process.

Hardware

The Water Data Bank computer system consists of a Digital
Equipment Corporation (DEC) minicomputer, model PDP-11/44, two Control
Data Corporation (CDC) 80-mega-byte magnetic disk drives, two Kennedy

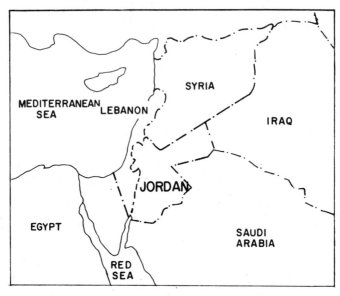

Figure 1 -- Map of Jordan and surrounding area

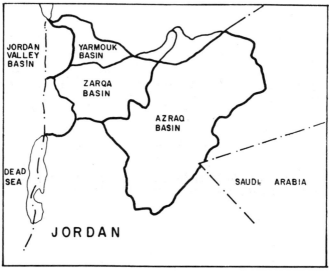

Figure 2 -- Map of North Jordan Project area

magnetic tape drives, a Printronix 300-line per minute line-printer, an
ALTEK digitizer, a CALCOMP plotter, a TEKTRONIX 4014-1 graphic display
terminal, a ZENTEC bilingual Arabic-English display terminal, a
Decwriter operator console, and six DEC VT100 visual display
terminals. The computer system is located in a restricted-access room
in which temperature and humidity are controlled by a Liebert five-ton
air-conditioning unit. The electrical system is protected by a TOPAZ
voltage regulator and power conditioner and the minicomputer is
equipped with a DEC battery backup unit. This equipment was installed
and tested in September-October 1983. At present the central
processing unit (CPU) consists of 512 kilobytes of memory. An
additional two megabytes of memory has been ordered and should be
installed soon. An additional multiplexor also has been ordered and
will allow the operation of up to sixteen more terminals, six of which
are on order.

The system is operated such that an incremental backup is
performed daily (saving on tape only the files which have changed since
the last backup) and a full-system backup is performed weekly. Disk
packs are cycled such that they are used on both disk drives, in online
and backup roles. This operation serves to increase the operational
life of the disk drives and the disk packs.

Software

The Water Data Bank computer system software consists of an
RSX11-M PLUS operating system, a FORTRAN-77 compiler, and
Datatrieve-11. The operating system supports a combination of
multiuser terminals and realtime applications. The FORTRAN-77 compiler
gives the personnel using the Water Data Bank the flexibility to write
application programs as needed. Datatrieve-11 is a simple, but
powerful, inquiry language and report-writing system which also
provides record management services.

Datatrieve-11 allows an effective system of data entry to be
developed using system prompts, data validation techniques, and
description tables. Datatrieve-11 provides a capability to retrieve
data using commands which range from extremely simple to exceptionally
complex. Datatrieve-11 has report-writing features such as headings,
control groups, statistics, and summaries. Datatrieve-11 files may be
sequential or multiply keyed. Sequential output files may be created
with either longer of shorter record lengths.

Data Files

At present the Water Data Bank has twelve basic files with data in four categories, meteorological, surface water, water quality, and ground water. The organization and structure of the Water Data Bank files are shown on figure 3. The structure is basically hierarchical with the site identification number providing the linkage from the Master Record File to the other files. The Master Record File contains data about a site, including name, ownership, location, altitude, drainage basin, water use, and records available. The file presently contains almost 2500 site records. With the records available and the site identification number, the linkage to the other files is complete. Master Record File forms are completed and checked by other sections before being given to the Water Data Bank Section for entry.

The meteorological data files include the Rainfall Record File and the Evaporation Record File. The rainfall record consists of daily rainfall amounts with codes to indicate estimated values, partial sums, and periods of missing records. The file presently contains almost 90,000 records. FORTRAN programs have been written to produce tables of rainfall data as shown on figure 4. The evaporation record consists of daily readings of maximum and minimum temperatures, humidity parameters, wind direction and velocity, and evaporation parameters. The file presently contains almost 20,000 records. Daily rainfall and evaporation records from field observation sheets are given to the Water Data Bank Section for entry.

The surface water data files include the Surface Water Record File, the Surface Water Discharge Measurement Record File, the Suspended Sediment Record File, and the Spring Discharge Record File. The surface water record contains the mean daily flow for rivers or wadis. The file presently contains almost 15,000 records. The surface water discharge measurement record contains data about individual measurements of flow at a river or wadi, including the date, time, gage height, width, maximum depth, area, and discharge. The mean depth and mean velocity are calculated, but not stored. Presently this file contains over 1500 records. The suspended sediment record contains data about conditions in a river or wadi when a sediment sample was collected, including the date, time, gage height, width, depth, and water temperature. The spring discharge record contains measurements of spring discharges and the measurement date. The file presently contains over 25,500 records. Surface water data on field observation sheets are given to the Water Data Bank Section for entry.

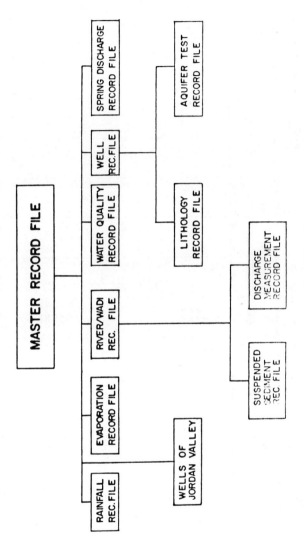

Figure 3 -- Organization and structure of the Water Data Bank files

Figure 4 -- Output of rainfall data program

DAILY, MONTHLY, ANNUAL RAINFALL RECORD (MM)

WATER AUTHORITY

WATER RESOURCES DIVISION

SITE IDENTIFICATION NO: AL0022 (AL22) OWNER NAME: AMMAN HUSSEIN COLLEGE   LATITUDE : 31.5800   LONGITUDE : 35.5600

GOVERNERATE : 1   ALTITUDE (M) : 834   PALESTINE GRID: NORTH :152. 000   EAST: 238. 200

WATER YEAR : 66/67

DAY	OCT	NOV	DEC	JAN	FEB	MARCH	APRIL	MAY	JUNE	JULY	AUG	SEP
1												
2												
3					3.0	28.0						
4					2.6	36.5						
5						8.8						
6	.3					3.0						
7	6.2						.7					
8				.9			.8					
9		8.5	1.9									
10					1.2							
11		8.7	9.3									
12			1.7									
13												
14					5.5							
15					3.0							
16			13.0	30.0	18.5	5.6						
17			46.0	34.0	1.6							
18			17.5	25.0	.2							
19			82.5									
20			21.6									
21					.2							
22												
23	.7		1.9	6.5		13.0						
24	5.8			61.0		6.0	1.5					
25				27.0		30.0	2					
26						55.0						
27						17.5						
28						.4						
29												
30												
31												
M. TOTL	13.0	17.2	195.4	184.4	35.8	203.8	1.5					
R. DAYS	4	2	9	7	9	11	2					

ANNUAL TOTAL : (651.1)

ANNUAL RAINY DAYS : 44

SYMBOLS: $: PARTIAL SUM   X : NO RECORD   ( ) : ESTIMATED VALUE.
          * : STARTING NO RECORDS. ** : ENDING NO RECORDS. *** : INCOMPLETE RECORD.

Figure 5 -- Output of water quality hydrograph program

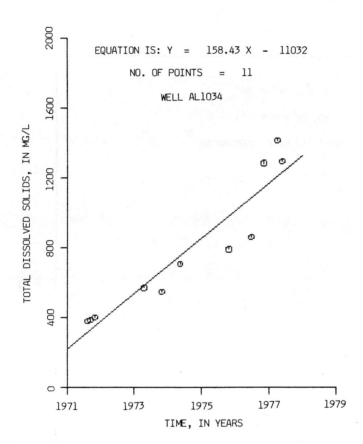

Figure 6 -- Output of groundwater plotting program

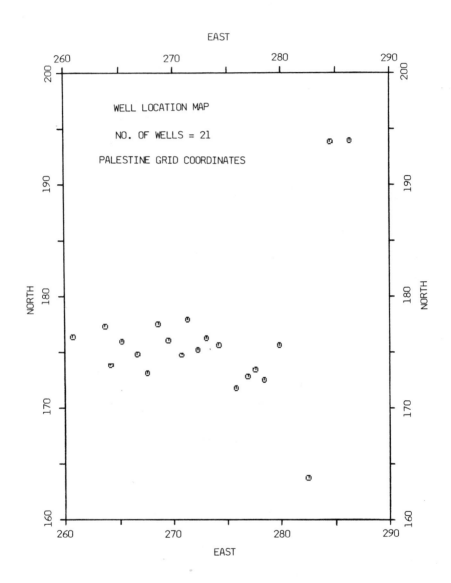

The Water Quality Record File presently contains data from over 3000 water quality analyses. The records consist of the sampling date, time, depth, water temperature, electrical conductivity, total dissolved solids, pH, major anions, major cations, sodium adsorption ratio, irrigation classification, and total hardness. FORTRAN programs have been written to assist hydrologists in analyzing water quality data, including the production of hydrographs of total dissolved solids as shown on figure 5. Summaries of laboratory results are given to the Water Data Bank Section for entry.

The ground water data files include the Well Record File, the Aquifer Test Record File, the Well Lithology Record File, and the Jordan Valley Well Record File. The well record contains data about a well, including the owner, name, driller, drilling type, drilling date, depth, well use, water use, casing, screen, lift, power, and available logs. The aquifer test record contains data about a test at a well at a particular date, including the well yield, salinity, temperature, duration of test, static water level, pumping water level, drawdown, and aquifer properties such as transmissivity and storage coefficient. FORTRAN programs have been written to produce plots of well locations such as shown on figure 6. Ground water data forms are completed and checked by other sections before being given to the Water Data Bank Section for entry.

Water Resources Management

One goal of the investigation was the improvement of water resources planning and management techniques through the development and use of the Water Data Bank. As the amount of data available increases and the use of various types of data analysis programs accelerates, management techniques will become more automated. Decisions, and their results, can be tested through computer models and the use of statistical analysis will provide a sound basis for those decisions. The coupling of software and data of the Water Data Bank gives the Hashemite Kingdom of Jordan effective tools to use in the management of existing natural resources and the planning for the future development of those resources.

State-of-the-Art Design of Databases for Water Related Data

Harold T. Glaser, A.M.[1] and Philip A. Naecker, A.M.[2] ASCE

Introduction

Civil engineers working in water related fields today are being called upon to collect, measure and sample massive amounts of data. The profession is moving toward the use of increasingly sophisticated computerized tools for the analysis and solution of increasingly complex engineering problems. The advent of modern instrumentation for collection and production of raw data has shifted engineering decision support from a basis which was largely qualitative in the past to a much more quantitative basis today. As a result, project engineers are faced with managing data as a major project task. Decisions are now based on statistical analyses, graphics, tables, reports and most recently, predictions from mathematical models. Considerable investment is often made in data collection and manipulation. Therefore it is imperative that civil engineers be cost effective in collecting, managing and evaluating water related data.

Fortunately, coupled with the shift toward more intensive data analysis, a revolution in information management technology has taken place. The costs per unit of resource in computer processing power, physical memory and disk storage have dropped logarithmically over the past several years and the trend shows every indication of continuing in the foreseeable future. Powerful new hardware, software and programming tools are available at an attractive cost which extend the capabilities of analysis and presentation to project engineers. Decision making and alternative selection are no longer bounded by human ability to assimilate or process large quantities of data. New software products provide the tools for analysis and presentation to the engineering professional who does not desire to be a computer specialist.

This paper presents an overview of techniques for design and application of databases to water related data. The intent is to introduce new concepts to the practicing engineer who has a need to manage water related data for a variety of projects. The concept of a computerized project database is presented as a vehicle for managing data. New tools for working with data are also available including database management systems (DBMS) and interactive query and report languages as well as techniques for designing the project database such as norm

1. Supervising Software Engineer, James M. Montgomery, Consulting Engineers, Inc., P.O. Box 7009, Pasadena, California, 91109-7009.

2. Manager of Information Services, James M. Montgomery, Consulting Engineers, Inc., P.O. Box 7009, Pasadena, California, 91109-7009.

alization.   The software engineering approach for designing and
building the database is presented as a framework for software development through the application of engineering principles in managing
the development process.

Project Database Concept

Given the problem of vast amounts of data and a need for improved
analysis and productivity, engineers must now develop a methodology
for managing the data resource.   In our experience, the best approach
has been to use what can be termed the "Project Database Concept."
When managing water related data, it is useful to start by building a
project database as the foundation to the solution of the engineering
problems at hand.

Exactly what is a Project Database?   Briefly, it is a self-contained
system of programs and data that will aid in the completion of the
assigned engineering tasks.   It is useful to think of the Project
Database as more than just all of the data collected relevant to the
project. The data must be carefully organized to be a database. A
collection of books isn't really a library until it has been cataloged
and thoughtfully arranged.   It is useful to consider the concept of a
Project Database as including a "toolkit."   The toolkit contains
special purpose programs, graphic display utilities, and statistical
analysis systems that work together with the database in a coordinated
fashion. Similarly to the database, the toolkit is available to the
entire project staff for consistent analysis and display of the data.

The Project Database generally becomes the crossroads of the entire
project. All project data flows into the database, and all project
outputs flow out of the database.   It is most practical if the database is stored in a computer, but other than that it might be a series
of simple data files, a spreadsheet program, indexed files, a relational database management system, or any of a number of other specific data storage and management schemes.   What is important is not
the specific details of the database management system, but rather the
concept of coordinated and controlled storage of data and provision of
a common set of tools for managing and analyzing that data.   There are
a number of advantages in implementing the Project Database Concept:

   o   Shared Data. All project staff members have access to the
       same data, simultaneously.   Furthermore, there is never any
       question as to the location of the data - it's always in the
       database.

   o   Access Control. Hand in hand with the concept of shared data
       is the concept of access control. The database must provide a
       means of managing access to different users. For example,
       only certain individuals may have the right to add or modify
       data, whereas other individuals may only be able to view the
       data and not change it.

   o   Quality Assurance. By establishing a project database, imple-
       menting a program of quality assurance is much easier. A

requirement that all data entries are approved before they
enter the database can be stated. In more sophisticated databases, different levels of "quality" can be assigned to the
data, so that the engineer analyzing the data will know if
they are working with preliminary information, confirmed data,
etc.

o   Efficiency. The major advantage of a computerized database is
    the speed and efficiency with which many typical data manage-
    ment tasks can be performed. Standard reports can be program-
    med to be generated automatically, data can be sorted and
    searched efficiently, and powerful statistics and data-reduc-
    tion techniques can be applied to vast quantities of data.

    Perhaps the most important advantage of the project database
    concept is the improvement in the effectiveness of the engi-
    neer. Instead of studying the project data, the engineer can
    use the tools provided as part of the Project Database to
    analyze the information contained in the data. This point is
    discussed in more detail in the next section of this paper.

o   The Toolkit. As stated previously, the Project Database
    should be considered hand-in-hand with a "toolkit" of all
    utilities, programs and procedures used in managing the data.
    There are several advantages to providing a toolkit as part of
    the Project Database. First, it improves the effectiveness of
    engineers by helping them to avoid writing their own programs
    every time they want to analyze the data in a particular way.
    They can simply use the software already provided in the tool-
    kit which may have been built and placed in the kit by another
    engineer or by specially trained staff supporting the data-
    base.

    Second, using tools improves the quality and consistency of
    the analysis. Because the tools are standardized, everyone
    using them will get comparable and consistent results. And
    because the toolkit is part of the project database, it's
    contents are subject to the same quality assurance measures as
    the data itself. By storing all of the tools in a central
    location (the project database), it's easy to present the
    methods used in managing the data. The tools may be reported
    on and revealed to reviewing peers to help define the method-
    ology used in the study, just like the data itself.

Database Management Systems

Once all project related data has been collected in the project database, the engineer is faced with the task of managing this data.
Fortunately, there are a number of powerful software systems available, for virtually every kind of computer, to aid in the management
of data. These systems are generally termed a Database Management
System (DBMS) and provide a number of features useful to the engineer
dealing with water related data. While the details of a DBMS as
applied to an engineering project are too complicated to be addressed
here, the following will provide a brief overview so that the reader

may see how Database Management Systems are currently being used to manage water related data.

Database management systems were first created approximately twenty years ago as an outgrowth of the need for reliability in banking transaction processing systems. A true DBMS will provide protection against data loss due to computer system hardware or software failure by using sophisticated mechanisms such as recovery-unit journalling, volume-shadowing, rollback, and so on. DBMS's also provide concurrency control, or the ability of many users (such as all the tellers in all the branches of a bank) to simultaneously access the same data without getting in one-anothers way or losing track of any of the data. The DBMS will ensure, for example, that you can't simultaneously remove your entire account balance from each of 10 bank branches! A DBMS will also provide access control, or the protection from unauthorized access to your account's records.

Engineers managing water related data have some requirements that are similar to a banker's needs, but also some that are different. It is useful to consider a few basic assumptions about the needs of an engineer from a database used to manage water-related data.

o   Information vs Data. Generally speaking, for an engineer the data itself is of little concern. Engineers are more likely to be interested in the information which can be extracted from that data. For an engineer working with a water related database, the point of the analysis is to be able to better understand the problem by management and analysis of the data, thereby turning the data into information. Therefore, an engineering DBMS must include tools for data analysis. This differs, for example, from the banking application where the accuracy and completeness of the data is the greatest concern, and analysis of the data is secondary.

o   Traditional DBMS Concerns. Some of the engineer's needs are similar to the banker's. The engineer would like ensure that the data will not be lost or compromised by a computer hardware failure. It is also important that it be available to many users simultaneously, and that only authorized users be able to change the data.

o   Rapid Access. Another concern is rapid access to data. If a database contains thousands or even millions of records (which is not at all uncommon in even medium-size projects today), even a fast computer can take a long time to find the handful of records of interest for a particular engineering analysis. There are many different methods of improving the performance of databases, but they can all be thought of much like a card catalog system at a library. The various portions of a database contain indices, much like the tabs on the top of the index cards in a card catalog. By looking up just the indices, the computer can rapidly find the records of interest without performing an exhaustive or complete search of the data. Of course, this method works only if the database is designed using the right keys. For example, a library

card catalog is not much help if you want to find books based
upon the publisher, rather than the author or the subject.

o   Time Dependent Data.   Most   water   related data is concerned
    with some sort of physical   process,   such as rainfall, flow,
    etc. Therefore, the data has an inherent temporal component.
    An engineering DBMS must be able to deal consistently and
    flexibly with time as part of   the data. This is especially
    important because the frequency of sampling is rarely regular.

o   Range of Data.   Engineering   data are typically expressed in
    many different units and with absolute values over a very
    large range. Concentrations may be measured in micrograms per
    liter, flows in cubic feet per second, microbiological counts
    in millions per milliliter, etc.   An engineering DBMS must be
    able to deal with both the absolute numeric range of the data
    and with the   various   units used to express the parameters.
    Furthermore, real-world data may have many values that cannot
    be expressed numerically.   For instance, microbiological
    values might be expressed as "Too Numerous to Count", and
    organic contaminants as "Below Detection Limit."   The DBMS
    must be able to deal consistently and rigorously with these
    special kinds of values.   Note again how different this is
    from a banking application where in most cases, dollars and
    cents is the predominant data type and the range is well-
    defined.

o   Flexibility. Whereas the needs of a banking application tend
    to change relatively slowly, an engineering database might
    change frequently as new aspects of the problem are studied,
    new kinds of data are collected, more sites are added to the
    study, etc. It is important that an engineering DBMS provide
    the flexibility to change the structure of the project data-
    base easily and efficiently.   When changes are made to accom-
    odate new requirements, they   should not cause previous
    programs or applications using the database to fail.

o   Normalized Data Storage. Normalization is one attribute of a
    DBMS that differentiates it from other means of storing data
    on a computer. In its simplest form, normalization refers to
    the removal of redundant data from the storage format. This
    reduces the amount of information that must be stored. It
    also simplifies changes, because a change must be made to only
    one data item instead of many.

It should be stated that not all DBMS's can provide all of the above
functions, and different software may perform faster or slower depending upon the exact method of implementation and the needs of the engineering problem being solved. There are a number of components to any
well-structured database management system, including the file system
(where the data is stored), the query-language (what the engineer uses
to ask questions of the database), graphics software, statistics software, a report-writer (to help analyse the data) and so on. Selection
of a DBMS for a particular project should be conducted after a careful
analysis of essential features and available alternative systems. The
following discussion of software engineering suggests an approach for

selecting the DBMS and further development of the software tools
required to implement the Project Database.

Software Engineering

Once a decision has been made to adopt the project database concept,
the recommended approach for implementing the decision is through
software engineering. Software engineering is a managed process for
development of computer programs and systems to meet the user's needs
and objectives. It is an approach to software development which has
been proven successful in the data processing industry because it
ensures an end product which meets the user's needs by involving them
in the development process through close interaction and frequent
technical reporting and review. In improperly managed software development, the sad result is a computer program often delivered on the
final day of the project that is a disappointment to the user. This
is typically the result of poor programmer interaction with the user
during software development. In the past, the approach to developing
software for civil engineering projects was to begin programming immediately, and through an iterative process of comparing the product
to the user's needs continue working on the program until it performed
the required functions. The software engineering approach emphasizes
the thinking process first before a line of software code is written.

The overall process is analogous to the feasibility study, predesign
report, detailed design, construction and startup approach used by
engineers for water resources projects. At each major step, the owner
or client has an opportunity for review, comment and correction. In
this manner, mid-course corrections are made to suit the user's wishes
and the cost and risk of changes is reduced at each step which ensures
the user of a satisfactory end-product and a cost-effective investment. The tasks conducted during the software engineering process are
as follows:

   o   Requirements Analysis. The requirements analysis is the first
       step in the software engineering process. While it is a step
       that is often overlooked or bypassed by many, it's importance
       cannot be overstated. The tasks completed during a require-
       ments analysis include the operations/systems analysis, user
       requirements definition, technical support approach, concep-
       tual design and report preparation.

       In the operations and systems analysis, basic documentation
       covering user organization, functions, workflows, reports,
       forms and files is prepared. Interviews are conducted with
       project team members to obtain input on day to day functions.
       In addition, detailed analyses are conducted to understand
       exception processing, impact of incomplete reports, quality of
       existing files and information, controls used to identify and
       correct errors, relevant policies, operating constraints and
       current levels of system performance.

       The user requirements subtask produces a detailed definition
       of the proposed system's end products. It is critical that
       these requirements reflect the essential functions and

strengths of existing operations and resolve current system shortcomings. The user needs for reports, graphics, hardcopy, calculations and adhoc online query needs are also determined. The technical support approach defines the technical environment in which the proposed system must operate. The emphasis here is on hardware and non-application system software. This software might include the operating system, database management system and communications control programs. Alternative technical approaches are created and evaluated in terms of technical staff requirements, benefits, costs, education requirements and project schedule impacts.

The conceptual design translates the user requirements into a conceptual application approach for their implementation. Conceptual design activities include determining the electronic data processing functions and flows required to relate all inputs, outputs and data element groups previously identified in the user requirements step. These flowcharts are not intended to identify every program that may eventually be developed, but only to depict the required primary processing functions. The design effort also includes documenting approaches for security, privacy and control constraints.

The requirements report is the culmination of efforts in the entire requirements analysis. Technical and systems approaches are evaluated and finalized in report form and a detailed project plan for subsequent development is prepared. This includes a revised economic evaluation with estimated costs. The analysis is presented in written form to the user for review and comment.

o   Predesign. The purpose of the predesign step is the preparation of a functional specification for the software. The functional specification should spell out what the system is going to do for the user in plain language (as opposed to computer jargon). It describes every input the user can introduce to the system, both valid and invalid, and the response of the system to each possible input. In those cases where introduction of input into the system causes the production of output, the functional specification should describe how the input is manipulated to produce the output. The functional specification is be presented to the user in writing for review and comment. This is a key milestone for midcourse corrections, along with user approval and sign off.

o   Design. In the predesign task, an agreement is reached with the user as to what the system will do. The purpose of the design task is to determine how to construct the system so that it will perform as specified in the functional specification. Because there are generally many ways to design a system so that it functions as specified, it is important to consider alternative designs so that the optimum needs of each user is satisfied. Reports are presented, in writing, at the end of the two major components of design (external and internal) for user review and comment.

The external design presents the capabilities of the system as
they will appear to the user. The emphasis is placed on the
overall structure of the database management system, menu and
screen layouts, data element definitions and general usage
definitions. The external design does not define how tasks
will be performed by the computer and its data management
system. Rather, those details are presented in the next task,
the internal design.

The external design report is directed toward two audiences.
One audience is the proposed system user. The report allows
the user to understand what the system will look like and how
it will perform the functions established in the functional
specification. Screen and hardcopy report layouts are presented allowing the future user to check them for completeness.
Depending on the size and complexity of the proposed system,
the external design may also specify a documentation plan
and/or a training plan for the system.

The second audience is the designer who will perform the internal design. Data element format definition, menu hierarchy, information flow and valid and invalid data names must
be established prior to the initiation of internal design.
The internal design report presents detailed programming specifications for the system. These specifications are developed
based on the external design report.   The internal design
defines how tasks will be performed by the computer and its
software. This includes decisions regarding the languages
used for software construction, the integration of software
packages, designation of command and system procedures and
detailed data access, storage and reporting methods. Design
standards for screen, subroutine and data access methods are
also established. This is basically a technical task, and
does not require a great deal of interaction with the user.

o   Construction.   The construction step involves the actual
    system assembly based on the results of the internal and ex-
    ternal design. Modular components of the software are cons-
    tructed by applications programmers and unit tested sepa-
    rately. Test data and expected outputs are prepared in
    advance to ensure that each module is correct. Once each
    module has been tested, the overall system is assembled and
    tested as a whole.   Any debugging required is performed in
    this step.

Written documentation of the system is prepared for the user
which includes a manual for input/output, data files, system
access, file maintenance and recovery.   User procedures are
developed for normal operations, manual backup, error correction and terminal operation. Documentation is prepared for
all system operation needs as well as the technical details.
Normally, if the approach of requirements analysis, predesign
followed by design are followed, this often overlooked task is
simplified considerably because the written reports from
previous tasks form the basis for the final documentation.

o   Installation. Once software construction is complete and the
    system has passed all tests, it can be installed on the user's
    system. Any conversion of old files or programs is completed
    as described in the conversion plan written during the cons-
    truction phase. The system is tested by the user under each
    of the conditions set forth in the functional specification to
    ensure expected performance. Minor debugging or fine tuning
    is also accomplished at this time.

    Training utilizes the completed documentation to prepare users
    for system testing and subsequent implementation and oper-
    ation. It includes preparation of a training program which
    will be tailored to the needs of the user. Normally, this
    involves a mixture of classroom time and online one-on-one lab
    work with users.

Conclusions

1. The concept of a project database is useful for implementing
    the difficult task of managing project data. The advantage of
    a Project Database is that it enforces the concept of coord-
    inated and controlled storage of data and provision of a
    common set of tools for managing and analyzing that data.

2. Powerful Database Management Systems are available which offer
    tools and design techniques borrowed from the data processing
    industry for managing water related data. They simplify many
    of the tasks involved in setting up and maintaining the
    Project Database.

3. Software engineering is a managed process for development of
    computer programs and systems to meet the user's needs and
    objectives. It is the recommended method for implementing the
    Project Database and selection of a Database Management System
    for water related data.

In future papers, we hope to address each of the above techniques and
tools in greater detail. Case studies from a variety of water related database systems will be used to illustrate the power and value
of the techniques.

Development of a State Information Clearinghouse

Shaw L. Yu[1], A.M. ASCE and Achyut M. Tope[2]

Abstract: The University of Virginia is conducting a study on the feasibility of establishing the Virginia Water Resources Information System (VWRIS). Objectives of the study are: 1) Documenting the need for and expected benefits of VWRIS and determining what data should be stored in the system; 2) Examining existing national and state data base systems in terms of organization, hardware/software systems, mode of operations, accessibility to state users, etc.; and 3) Analyzing the institutional, organizational, and financial arrangements that would be needed to operate a clearinghouse.

Introduction

The Virginia Water Resources Research Center (VWRRC) in 1983 issued a problem statement concerning the need for the development of a water resources information clearinghouse for Virginia:

"Easy access to existing water resources information would improve the state's ability to develop a water resources management plan and would increase the potential for reducing water data collection costs by eliminating unnecessary duplication of effort.

Large amounts of information exists in Virginia. However, it is in a variety of forms and media. The information stored in a federal system is often not as detailed as the information found in a university researcher's data base. A good deal of information never finds it way into any data system; it gets no farther than a file cabinet or box."

In August 1983, the University of Virginia was selected by the Virginia Water Resources Research Center to conduct a study on the feasibility of establishing the Virginia Water Resources Information System (VWRIS).

A two-phase work plan was devised for the development of VWRIS. Phase one involved the formation of a task force committee to provide guidance and a review of the existing water resources information systems. Institutional and financial arrangements were also examined. Phase two of the work plan deals with a detailed review of system

[1]Assoc. Prof., Dept. of Civil Engineering, Univ. of Virginia, Charlottesville, VA 22901
[2]Grad. Research Asst., Dept. of Civil Engineering, Univ. of Virginia, Charlottesville, VA 22901

software/hardware selections and the identification and documentation of water data collectors in the state of Virginia.

Formation of the VWRIS Task Force Committee

A 16-member Task Force Committee (TFC) was formed with representation from state and local agencies, federal water information systems, and state universities. The main charge of the TFC is to guide the development of a plan for the implementation of VWRIS.

Existing Water Information Systems

A nationwide search of recent documentations on water data information systems was made. The search includes both federal and state or local systems. Those systems which are considered most important and relevant to the proposed Virginia system are briefly described below.

1. Federal data systems

    A. STORET (STOrage and RETrieval system: EPA)

    STORET is a computerized data base utility maintained by EPA for the storage and retrieval of water quality data taken from more than 200,000 collection points throughout the nation. STORET is a comprehensive system which is capable of performing a broad range of reporting, statistical analysis and graphic functions.

    B. NAWDEX (NAtional Water Data EXchange: USGS)

    NAWDEX was established by USGS in 1976 to serve as a national program for cataloging and indexing water data that are available throughout the nation and to improve access to these data. The system contains two computerized data bases: Water Data Storage Directory (WDSD), and Master Water Data Index (MWDI).

    WDSD identifies organizations (over 400) that are sources of water data or other environmental data pertinent to water resources activities, while MWDI identifies individual sites (over 370,000) for which water data are available.

    C. WATSTORE (National WATer data STORage and retrieval system: USGS)

    The WATSTORE system contains files for the storage of surface and ground water quantity as well as quality data. In addition, there are files containing peak flow data and groundwater site inventory. WATSTORE can provide a variety of data products such as complex statistical summaries and graphics.

    D. NEDRES (National Environmental Data Referral Service: NOAA)

    NEDRES is maintained by the National Oceanic and Atmospheric Administration. NEDRES is a publicly available service which identifies the existence, location, characteristics, and availability conditions of

environmental data sets held by organizations throughout the United
States. Types of environmental data referenced by NEDRES include
climatological and meteorological; oceanographic; geophysical and geological; geographic; and hydrological and limnological through
interfacing with NAWDEX and OPDIN, the Ocean Pollution Data and Information Network.

2. State and local data systems

A. TNRIS (Texas Natural Resources Information System)

TNRIS was established in 1972 under the guidance of a task
force committee with representation from thirteen state agencies. The
primary objective of TNRIS is to tie together the information systems
already in existence in the state and elsewhere to make the data more
easily accessible. As of 1984 TNRIS provides access to hydrological,
meteorological, geological, biological and socioeconomic data which
are stored in more than 350 automatic files. TNRIS is also in interface with NAWDEX, WATSTORE, STORET, and some other major data systems.

B. CDB (Commonwealth Data Base: Virginia Department of Budget and
Planning)

The CDB system documents and maintains an inventory of the
data bases, in manual or automated form, that store socioeconomic
(some water) information throughout Virginia. The February, 1983 CDB
catalog lists 79 files of data, of which 23 contain water resources
related information.

C. Chesapeake Bay Data System

At least twelve different institutional data systems exist with
various purposes, computer equipment, software and compatibility.
Examples of these systems are the Hydro Data Base and the Marine
Environmental Resources and Research Management System (MERRMS) maintained by the Virginia Institute of Marine Science (VIMS), and the
data bank maintained by the Chesapeake Bay Institute (CBI).

Comparative Features of Commonly Used Data Base Management System
(DBMS) Packages

A survey of the commercially available Data Base Management Systems (DBMS) was conducted. Some of the commonly used DBMSs, especially
by the water community, are identified, discussed, and compared below.

1. DRS: DRS is a flexible, nonprogrammer oriented data base/data
management system that possesses all of the features of a total
information management system. In addition to incorporating many
arithmatic and logical data handling facilities, the system is
geared to handle textual data. It possesses the ability to accommodate relatively large data bases and even multiple data bases.
The system offers hirarchical, network and bill of materials data
structures, a report writer, a host language interface, a video
data terminal (VDT) control language, and data base graphics.

2. **DMS 1100**: DMS 1100 is CODASYL-oriented DBMS . It interfaces the operating system for many of the DBMSs facilities. It provides data independence, representation of a variety of data relationships without redundancy, concurrent updating of shared data, and mapping of data base to multiple files. DMS includes utilities for data base initialization, dumps/restores, display/modification, analysis and for auditing the contents of journal files.

3. **IDMS/R**: IDMS is a combined network and relational data base. It can be used interchangeably as a network DBMS for production applications, or as a relational DBMS addressing end user data base requirements. It is an integrated data base management system conforming to the CODASYL DBTG specifications. Interfaces allow it to be used with most of the commercially available telecommunications monitor systems.

4. **MODEL 204**: Model 204 is primarily oriented toward rapid multikey accessing of data. It uses a proprietary implementation of the inverted approach called Inverted File Access Method (IFAM). Model 204 files can be accessed either through the system's User Language or through a host programming language.

5. **SYSTEM 2000**: System 2000 is a full-feature data base management system that supports both on-line and batch data processing. The system supports a Programming Language Extension (Plex) feature which allows the programmer to access System 2000 data base from a Cobol, Fortran, PL/1, or Assembler application program. A high powered query/update language (Quest) is also available for programmers and end users.

6. **TOTAL**: Total provides facilities to generate a data base that enables data to be automatically related and cross-referenced in a predetermined manner. Access to the data base is possible from conventional application programs written in Cobol, Fortran, PL/1, Assembler and RPG II.

7. **ADABAS**: ADABAS is a large scale, general purpose data base management system. It is multithreaded and incorporates a number of utility programs that are used for data base generation and access. The system uses a variety of reportedly high-efficiency data management techniques and provides a multi-data base, file-coupling capability to give the user unlimited file access.

8. **SIR**: SIR provides data management of non-rectangular scientific data files, particularly update and retrieval procedures; methods for retrieving data sets in either batch or interactive mode. SIR has a formatted report generating facility; performs limited statistical routines such as simple descriptive statistics and line printer plots.

9. **SAS**: SAS is an integrated system for data management and is capable of performing statistical analysis, forecasting, graphics and data entry, and editing. It can handle unlimited types of input from any input device and produce a wide variety of reports, graphs and charts.

Of the data base packages described above, System 2000 is used by NAWDEX, STORET and WATSTORE and is one of the most popular data management systems. DMS 1100 is used by TNRIS.

A comparison of some of the specific features of the above data management systems is given in Table 1.

Inventory of Water Data Sources in Virginia

A survey was made to identify the water data collectors or sources in Virginia. The survey was conducted by way of a newsletter survey; direct mailings; phone inquiries, and personal visits. As of March, 1985, 95 data sources have been identified, of which 18 are federal, 33 state agencies, 42 university sources, and 2 private groups. Detailed information of the data sources, such as parameter coverage; geographic coverage; sampling frequency, time span; status of data base; and data availability are documented. The data source inventory will be updated on a continuous basis for the duration of this project.

Institutional Aspects

The following is a summary of the general consensus of the TFC members regarding institutional aspects of VWRIS:

1. The primary function of VWRIS is to provide maximum availability of water resources information to Federal, State, regional, local and private entities.

2. VWRIS should be developed in a progressive manner, beginning with a small-scale operation such as indexing water resources data by one person and gradually grow to an eventual central facility which houses and disseminates water resources information.

3. VWRIS should be designed to suite Virginia's needs. It should not duplicate features of existing systems.

4. A feasible approach to the development of VWRIS is to have it built as a subsystem of an existing system such as the Commonwealth Data Base.

5. A standing advisory committee consisting of representatives from various user groups should be formed to oversee the actual implementation of VWRIS.

6. Initial funding and support must come from the 'hides' of the state agencies. Once the system is established and the benefits of having VWRIS are justified, separate funding from the legislature may then be solicited.

7. Once VWRIS is in operation, user fees and membership fees could be collected to supplement its budget.

System	DRS	DMS 1100	IDMS/R	MODEL 204	System 2000	Total	ADABAS	SIR/DBMS	SAS (Data Dictionary System)
Current # of users	250+	-	1400+	250+	1000+	5800+	1000+	350	8000+
Initial Installation	1970	1971	1973	1971	1970	1969	1971	1977	1970
CPU Supported	370,303x, 308x,43xx, DEC,VAX, PDP11	Sperry 1100 Series	370,303x, 308x,43xx	370,303x 308x,43xx	370,303x, 308x,43xx, CDC Cyber; Sperry 1100	IBM; DG; CDC;WANG; DEC;Prime; Sperry	370,303x, 43xx, DEC VAX, Siemens 4004,7000	CD Cyber; NOS(BE); 370,30xx, 43xx, VM/CMS, Sperry 1100,90	370,30xx, 43xx, DEC VAX; Data General; Prime 50 Series
Operating Systems	VM/CMS; VMS,RSX	OS 1100	DOS, DOS/VS(E), MVS,VM	MVS,DOS, DOS/VS(E), NOS, NOS/BE; OS 1100	MVS,NOS, VM/CMS, DOS/VS(E), NOS/BE; OS 1100	All assoc. operating systems	DOS, DOS/VS(E), VM/CMS, VMS; B1000/ 2000	Hon:GCOS; Prime, Gould, DEC 10/20, VAX;Cray; HP9000	MVS; DOS/VS(E), VM/CMS; VMS; PRIMOS
Minimum Memory	32KW	15KW +buffer	70K + buffer pools & control tables	250K	IBM:256K, CDC:22K, Sperry: 32K	30K	Mainframe: 165K + buffers; VAX: .5MB	Machine dependent	Minimum 512KB to 2MB
DB Organization	Network, Relational, Hirarchical	Network, Hirarchical	Network, Relational, Hirarchical	Network, Relational, Hirarchical	Network, Hirarchical	Network, Hirarchical	Network, with full inversion	Network, Relational, Hirarchical	

Table 1 Comparative Features of Some of the Major Commercial DBMSs (After Datapro Research Corporation 1984)

System	DRS	DMS 1100	IDMS/R	MODEL 204	System 2000	Total	ADABAS	SIR/DBMS	SAS (Data Dictionary System)
Application Languages	Cobol, Fortran, Assembler, Pascal, PL/1	Cobol, Fortran, PL/1	Cobol,PL/1, Fortran, RPGII, Assembler	Cobol, Fortran, Assembler, PL/1	Fortran, Cobol, PL/1, Assembler	Cobol, Fortran, PL/1, Assembler, RPGII, Pascal	Cobol, Fortran, PL/1, Assembler	Fortran, Assembler, Cobol, PL/1	Fortran, PL/1
Concurrent Batch/On-line	Yes	Yes	Yes	Yes	Yes	Yes	Yes	Yes	–
Concurrent Application Prog.Access.	Yes	Yes	Yes	Yes	Yes	Yes	Yes	Yes	Yes
Micro/Mini Computer Link	Yes	No	Yes	Yes	Yes	Yes	Yes	Yes	–
Report Generator	DRS Report Writer II	Cobol & Query Report Writers	Culprit, EDP/Auditor	User language; Access/204	Yes	Socrates, Interface to more report writers	Adacom Included	Simple & Complex Report Writers	Report
Tele-communication Interface	Yes	Yes	IDMS-DC, CICS, & most other monitors optional UCF	Self-contained, interfaces to VTAM, TCAM, BTAM	CICS, TSO, TONE, CMS	Environ/1, CICS, Task/ Master Intercomm; depends on system	Com-plete, CICS,TSO, Taskmaster Others	TSO	Under TSO, CMS
Price (Basic System)	$60,000	Varies according to config-uration	$27,000 -$72,000	$150,000 to $235,000	$45,000 -$60,000	$13,500 to $79,500	Mainframe: $106,000 to $142,000	$6,000 to $60,000	Varies according to configura-tion

Table 1 (Continued)

Conclusions

1. VWRIS should be developed to house water resources data that are
    not stored in existing systems such as NAWDEX and STORET. VWRIS
    should interface with such systems to provide certain information
    needed by a user.

2. VWRIS should be developed in a progressive manner and should be part
    of an existing system as the CDB. Being a subsystem of a federal
    system such as NAWDEX should also be a possibility.

3. VWRIS should begin with providing indexing services. It may
    actually store information as it grows.

4. Questions regarding hardware/software requirements, system input/
    output formats, interfacing with other systems, etc., will need to
    be examined.

5. Management of state agencies should be invited to future TFC meet-
    ings so that financial and institutional matters can be discussed
    more formally.

6. A standing advisory committee should be formed to oversee the actual
    implementation of the VWRIS when the TFC's mission is complete.

Appendix - References

1. Datapro Research Corporation, "A Buyer's Guide to Data Base Manage-
    ment Systems," Reports No. 70E-010-61a-Software, May, 1984. No.
    70E-132-01a-Software, June, 1984;No.70E-027-01a-Software, July,
    1984; No. 70E-195MM-101-Software, Nov., 1984; No. 70E-782MM-101-
    Software, Feb., 1985, Delran, N.J.

2. Yu, Shaw L., and Tope, Achyut M., "Development of a Water Quality
    Clearinghouse for the Commonwealth of Virginia," Report No.
    UVA/530288/CE85/101 to Virginia Water Resources Research Center,
    August, 1984.

REAL-TIME CONTROL OF WATER RESOURCE SYSTEMS
by
John W. Labadie
Professor of Civil Engineering
Colorado State University
Fort Collins, CO 80523

ABSTRACT

With dramatic advances in communication and computational hardware and software technology, the stage may be set for widespread application of automation and real-time control to complex water resource systems. Successes in industry and manufacturing and preliminary experiences in the water resources field have documented the productivity and performance benefits obtainable with application of real-time computer control. The architecture of real-time control systems is summarized, followed by discussion of a selection of actual case studies taken from the areas of municipal water supply, hydrogeneration, wastewater management, and irrigation scheduling. The importance of moving into more sophisticated control logic for maximizing performance benefits and reliability is stressed for current and future applications.

INTRODUCTION

Many feel that the era of traditional water systems planning is at an end. In the past, management and operations tended to take second place to capital improvement involving heavy expenditures. The public no longer seems willing to make such economic and financial commitments and are now asking the question: how can we make better use of existing facilities or how can we more effectively include operational considerations directly in the planning process in order to reduce capital expenditures for new or upgraded projects. The success of automation and real-time control technology in industry and manufacturing both in the U.S. and abroad has provided encouragement that this technology can be applied to water resource systems for improving reliability and reducing costs of both existing and planned systems.

The term "real-time control" actually refers to a subset of the higher levels of automation. Automation can be defined as the process of rendering systems self-measuring, self-adjusting, or self-controlling without direct human intervention. It is a relative term since it represents a dynamic process and is implemented in degrees. The various aspects of automation include:
* instrumentation and measurement devices
* pneumatic, hydraulic and electromechanical control devices, such as the "little man" controller for stabilizing irrigation canal water levels (USBR, 1973)
* computerized telemetry and data base management
* supervisory direct digital computer control
* localized closed loop automatic control
* system-wide integrated automatic control

489

In a sense, each level builds upon the previous, but there are currently few examples of the highest levels of automation in water resource system management. Control in "real-time" implies that the computer is performing direct on-line functions during actual time of the operational process. Real-time control systems may actually be imbedded within broader scoped computerized decision support systems designed to provide off-line strategic guidelines on optimal system management and operations for on-line computer control systems.

Some of the specific types of water resource system components where the introduction of automation and real-time control can improve productivity and performance include:
* municipal raw water supply and conveyance systems, including conjunctive use of groundwater and surface water.
* multipurpose, multireservoir systems for flood control, water supply, hydropower, water quality maintenance, and other benefits.
* water treatment plant operation
* municipal water distribution systems
* urban storm drainage and combined sewer systems
* wastewater treatment and reuse
* irrigation water supply: distribution system control and application scheduling
* groundwater basin management, including management of overdrafted aquifers and artificial recharge
* pollution control in rivers and estuaries
* pollution control in groundwater, including waste disposal and salinity management
* navigation systems, particularly where a series of locks and dams are regulated to provide additional benefits of add-on run-of-the-river hydropower.

Though automation and real-time control can be beneficial when applied to these individual components, more substantial gains can be made if a true systems approach is taken and several interacting components are integrated together for control purposes. However, integrated system-wide control requires a higher level of sophistication of control system logic than is currently being used in most implementations. The software is available, but a major effort is needed to incorporate it into existing and planned automation and water control systems.

Based on experiences with automation and real-time control outside of the water resources field, and based on limited documented experiences within the field, the following is a list of benefits that can be expected with "appropriate" application of real-time computer control:
    1. reduction in labor and energy costs associated with system operation and maintenance
    2. increased reliability and reduced influence of human error
    3. greater precision in meeting water supply demands so as to reduce waste (i.e., deliveries above the actual demand and system losses), as well as shortages. This is similar to effectiveness criteria where it is desired to maintain apriori standards and targets

as closely as possible. For hydropower production, this could be related to minimizing power-only releases in order to meet energy
requirements
    4. more rapid and effective response to emergency situations and
breakdowns
    5. general reduction in operations and maintenance costs -- such
as controlling pressure in certain portions of water distribution systems to minimize leakage and the probability of breakage
    6. possible reductions in capital investment and debt service with
better incorporation of real-time control systems at the planning and
design level
    7. better documentation of operational experience through the data
logging activities normally associated with real-time control
    8. a natural leading to expert system development to help make up
for shortages in experienced operational manpower
    9. possible increases in revenues such as increased hydrogenera-
tion capacity and firm energy contracting, or expanded agricultural
production
    10. relieving manpower of tedious tasks so that more time can be
spent in productive endeavours in improving system performance.

    There are a number of reasons why the stage may be set for sig-
nificant advances in implementation of automation and real-time control
for water resource systems:
    1. the explosion in computer technology over the past two decades
is an American success story. Advances in computer hardware have placed
the potential for powerful, low cost computer systems in every engineering office, large or small.
    2. communication systems and data base management systems have
likewise advanced considerably for the efficient telemetering, processing and organizing of data. Many water-related agencies such as the
U.S. Army Corps of Engineers and the Bureau of Reclamation have been in
the process of implementation of comprehensive, computerized data acquisition and management systems. The stage is set for linking this
data processing technology with realistic system models for direct
supervisory or even closed loop control.
    3. software continues to lag behind hardware advances, but sig-
nificant contributions have been made.
    4. there appears to be more realism and care taken in systems
modeling in water resources.
    5. the advent of expert systems indicates a change in philosophy
by system scientists in respecting the experience of practitioners and
actually attempt to model it.
    6. there are some documented successes in application of automa-
tion and real-time control to water systems, some of which are described
subsequently.
    7. advances in user-friendly interactive systems and graphical
display have increased the attractiveness of this technology to water
control staff.

STRUCTURE OF REAL-TIME CONTROL SYSTEMS

    A real-time control system is composed of the following elements in
varying degrees of emphasis:

1. measuring instruments and sensors such as rain gages, water level gages, pressure gages, flow meters, soil moisture probes, and water quality analyzers

2. control instruments such as regulators, gates, weirs, valves, and pumps

3. telemetry system such as leased phone lines, line-of-sight radio, meteorburst VHF radio, microwave, satellite UHF transmission, and associated repeater and power boasting equipment if needed, for both receiving data and alarm information as well as transmitting control signals to the control elements

4. centralized computer hardware and operating system for integrating possible remote microprocessors, receiving and processing data, displaying system status, including alarm and emergency information, and computing and sending control signals

5. simulation model software for predicting flows, pressures, water quality, energy output, etc. in the system, given certain measured or forecasted inputs

6. forecasting models for forecasting random inputs such as rainfall, runoff, or meteorological data affecting evapotranspiration and water consumption

7. multivariable control strategy, including:
   * open loop control, where predefined operational policies are implemented without including feedback adjustments to compensate for errors and target derivations
   * closed loop or feedback control which can monitor system output and produce corrective action in real-time (this is also referred to closed loop reactive or myopic control since forecasts are not directly employed)
   * feedforward control, which instead of waiting for measured errors and target deviations, attempt to forecast anomalies and take anticipative corrective action (this could also be referred to as an adaptive, anticipitory, or fully dynamic control)
   * optimal control, which involves the use of on-line optimization algorithms in any of the above control modes
   * stochastic optimal control, which recognizes the inherent randomness and errors in measurements and models, and attempts to find risk averse, reliable strategies

8. system redundancy in computation and instrumentation

9. I-O equipment -- CRT, plotters, printers, etc. for the critical human-machine interfacing. The control software must be designed for effective human interface with the computing and control equipment. This must be an integral part of the software design, and not just an add-on.

There are innumerable possible combinations of system hardware. There exist today much more low cost, commercially available control system hardware than ever before. However, some customizing of equipment may be necessary depending on the application and the "hostility" of the environment where equipment is to be placed (e.g., subsurface combined sewer regulators represent a difficult environment for control system hardware installation and maintenance). Equipment should be selected with proven records of success and reliability in other areas. It is probably best to use a consistent, compatible family of processors and equipment. This will simplify implementation of the system and training of staff. Software developed on one processor can then easily be implemented on another of the same family.

Another basic decision, depending on the complexity of the application, is whether to use centralized control or decentralized, distributed control. Distributed processing may be important if speed is a critical factor. That is, if control decisions must be made within a matter of seconds or minutes, the simultaneous, parallel computations available in distributed or multi-processing may be necessary. Replacing a single large Central Processing Unit (CPU) with several small ones may in fact be less costly and more reliable. By assigning specific processors to specific tasks, if a CPU fails, the remaining CPUs can continue to function. If one large CPU is used, its failure can be disastrous. Duplexing the centralized CPU of course increases reliability, but also doubles the cost.

Microprocessors available today are fully capable of performing the complex calculations that may be required in water system control implementation. Currently available 16 bit processors will probably suffice in most applications, and instruction sets now available are quite robust. Modern microprocessors are characterized by internal speeds and architecture comparable to the minicomputers of less than a decade ago.

Even with the acquisition of commercially available hardware, software development for specific data acquisition and control functions will represent the greatest challenge to the operational staff. Of course, there are firms available which can help design both hardware configurations and system software. For in-house development, however, there are some newly emerging, low-cost alternatives.

Jensen (1985) reports on a new software package for simultaneous control of digital, analog, and servo signals called MIDICS (Modular Interactive Distributed Intelligence Control System). This package is reportedly designed for the novice, but appears to be extremely powerful. It can link 4,096 processing modules and has the capability of learning and adapting through artificial intelligence methods during process control. Software development is greatly simplified through a high level, symbolic Dynamic Interactive Programming System (DIPS) which can be used to design all direct control functions with no need for additional programming. This package reportedly can be interfaced with existing FORTRAN code for system operation and is available for the IBM PC microcomputer. Jensen (1985) claims that the package is powerful enough to control the workings of an entire metropolitan city.

SELECTED APPLICATIONS

Municipal Water Treatment and Distribution

The following information on the current status of computer control applications to municipal water supply in the U.S. has been compiled by Neil S. Grigg, Department of Civil Engineering, Colorado State University.

The Denver Water Board has maintained a consistent interest in automation and computer control of their water treatment and distribution facilities. They currently have remote supervisory control of all treatment plants and pump stations. There are no sophisticated computer simulation or optimizing models in use for operating the systems but the Process Control Section appreciates the potential for them and will consider these advances in the future. Practical problems of control such as equipment maintenance and reliability, cost, and employee reaction continue to be large factors in decisions about computerization (Fellows, 1984).

The City of Philadelphia Water Department reports a continued interest in automation. They have contracts completed for automation of two filter plants. Controls will be distributed and based on microprocessors. They anticipate completion of the projects in 1985 (Cairo, 1984).

Dallas continues their interest in computers and automation but has not implemented closed-loop automatic control with use of prediction models. They do have some direct digital control loops in their treatment plants. They continue their interest in off-line analysis by modeling and the application of scientific techniques to water system operation (Brock, 1984).

Overseas, Miyaoka and Funabashi (1984) report on a successful application of a real-time control system for Takamatsu City, a city of 300,000 in Japan. The water distribution system is composed of 486 nodes and 654 links representing reservoirs, control valves, pump stations, pressure observation points, demand points, and pipes exceeding 200 mm in diameter. A sophisticated hierarchical control scheme utilizing nonlinear programming and network flow theory is utilized. A process computer performs all data analysis, control computation, and signal transmission. The speed of the processing allows controls to be updated every 5 minutes. Though the system is fully automated, operators check all computed controls before they are exercised. It is believed this checking can eventually be abandoned as the system reliability is further verified. The real-time control system has alleviated high pressures in portions of the system threatened with breakage and resulted in a 22% reduction in water leakage throughout the system.

ENR (1984) reports that "when Singapore's water schemes are complete...the tiny country may well have the most sophisticated water-management system in the world." This $300 million water supply management system will allow Singapore to sever its dependence on Malyasia for water supply through integrated, computerized operation of several small ponds collecting urban runoff which will in turn supply two larger reservoirs. Totally integrated computer control of water collection, reservoir operation, treatment, pumping, distribution, and eventually, wastewater operations is planned. It is estimated that Singapore will save $200,000 per year in labor costs for pump station operators alone. It is noted that "the project could have been very conventional but the government pushed for a high tech approach."

Integrated optimal operations is a key element in maximizing the benefits of computerized water supply management systems. Labadie and Lazaro (1983) showed through extensive network modeling studies that the reliability of both the proposed Southern Conveyor Project for the Island of Cyprus and the existing Vasilikos-Pendaskinos water supply project could be greatly enhanced if the two systems were linked together and operated in an optimal, integrated fashion.

Hydropower Systems

An industrial hydroelectric system owned by the Great Northern Paper Co. in Maine is currently being operated under integrated automatic computer control in real-time (Firlotte, et al, 1983). The system is composed of 19 dams with six of the projects capable of producing hydropower. Total storage capacity is over one million acre-feet, with a base load of 114 MW and an average annual energy production of 1400 gigawatt-hrs. Since installation of the computer control system, Firlotte, et al (1983) document that there has been a 7.5% increase in station power for the same waterflow and a 3% increase in annual energy production. This has been accomplished with substantial reduction in labor cost since only one dispatcher is needed to operate the entire system. An optimization procedure is used to maximize total energy production levels subject to given total power releases by maintaining the highest possible efficiencies in each project through balanced operations. The authors report that accurate instrumentation and attractive man-machine interfaces were key elements in the eventual acceptance of the computerized system.

Wastewater Management

Milwaukee completed the installation of two 16-bit minicomputers at its South Shore Water Treatment Plant in 1977. As of this date, they have nine control loops in operation, ranging from raw sludge pumpage and dissolved oxygen control to sampler flow pacing. They report consistent improvement of plant performance without increased manpower. Observations about necessary conditions for successful computerization include: effective instrumentation, coordination of data transmission with instrumentation, simple control loops (at least initially) and good definition of control set-points (Dedinsky, et al, 1982).

The situation with combined sewer overflow (CSO) control is, as always, the most complex. In spite of the enthusiasm with which some agencies approached computerized CSO control in the 1970's, the lack of federal funds combined with a relaxation of regulatory tensions has resulted in little progress with automation and computer control.

The best success story encountered so far continues to be Seattle. They were known in the 1970's for their innovative CSO approach and their story was highlighted in many reports and papers as well as at least one film. They currently continue to operate the CSO system with compuer control of 20 key regulator stations. The control uses the rule curve approach. Work on more sophisticated prediction models has been halted and they currently see no advantage in the more complex models. At the present time, they are considering upgrading their control hardware, but financial analyses are still underway and federal support has not been secured. One important factor in Seattle's success was the vision and drive of the Executive Director when the system was being implemented. They have documented that the $3.1 million system has saved the City $70 million in construction costs for an alternative separated sewer system. Stormwater overflows have been reduced by 80% since its 1973 installation by simply making better used of in-line storage capacity in the sewers through controlled regulators (Brown and Caldwell, 1978).

No reports appear to be available on the use of models to control other CSO systems such as Minneapolis-St. Paul. San Francisco has not yet moved ahead with its plans for computer control and automation as of this date. It seems safe to say that any actual use of prediction models to operate CSO systems is still in the future.

Previous work by Trotta et al (1977) has shown that urban runoff control is most effectively accomplished on a totally integrated, city-wide basis. Labadie et al (1980) have emphasized the importance of including fully dynamic hydraulic system modeling in computer control schemes. Trotta et al (1977) have demonstrated the importance of in-cluding rainfall forecasts and anticipated storm flows into real-time decision making which considers the inherent stochasticity of the con-trol problem and the risks associated with control decisions. Morrow and Labadie (1980) have attempted to demonstrate how these elements can be integrated together through a software development called the Stormwater Control Package that can be used for operational planning as well as possibly adapted for actual real-time control. Labadie et al (1981) have gone a step further and actually documented the value or "worth" of real-time storm inflow forecasting in computer control systems. It was found that attempts to forecast can be valuable, even in the presence of somewhat large forecast errors. Though the City of San Francisco has served as the primary case study for most of this research, attempts have been made to generalized the software develop-ment for use in other cities.

What this research has shown is that real-time computer control and decision support systems, even in the presence of prediction uncer-tainties, can enhance the performance of urban drainage and flood control systems. Again, this has implications both in an operational and a planning content. At the operational level, it means maximizing performance of existing facilities, and hence improving cost effectiveness. In a facilities planning content, it means that incor-poration of these control concepts into capital improvement alternatives can possibly reduce sizing requirements.

Irrigation Scheduling

A fully automated computer control system has been installed by Dale Heerman and Harold Duke of the Agricultural Research Service, USDA to regulate a center pivot irrigation system at the Condon Ranch near Crook in Northeastern Colorado. The goal is to give the crops enough water but not overwater, while attempting to minimize energy costs. The computer system is designed to (i) moniter the soil moisture status of the fields and the state of the 15 pivots, (ii) control pumps supplying water to the pivots, (iii) schedule irrigations, (iv) regulate energy consumption, and (v) perform all data acquisition and processing. All of these functions can be controlled by the farmer at his ranch office, or left in an automatic mode. An automated weather station sends temperature, relative humidity, wind conditions, and solar radiation to microprocessor by radio transmitter. An on-line modified Penman evapotranspiration model is used to predict soil moisture status in the fields. Each pivot is actually outfitted with its own rain gage, which are also checked every 15 minutes by the microprocessor.

According to Duke, "Bill Condon...used to spend all day checking his pumps. Now, with this system, he runs it once a day." Any emergencies or pump failures are clearly displayed so that the farmer can know exactly where the problems are (Sheevers, 1983).

Trava et al (1977) report the use of a supervisory control system for surface irrigation that utilized linear programming for developing real-time irrigation schedules at the Northern Colorado Research Demonstration Center near Greeley, Colorado. The objective was to meet crop water requirements while minimizing labor costs and inconvenience due to night and weekend scheduling. The linear programming solution was updated on a weekly basis during the 1975 irrigation season, with daily schedules provided to the irrigators. For comparative purposes, a simulation model was used during the previous season with no optimizing capability. Results show that use of optimization in the supervisory control scheme reduced the need for weekend irrigations by 70%. Additional studies at the Greeley farm were conducted by Buchleiter, et al (1982) to estimate labor cost savings through use of optimization, in contrast with standard scheduling practice, when interrupts in water supply occur during the week due to energy peak load control schemes. The savings were 13% when the load control was anticipated and 29% when unanticipated by the irrigators. This optimization procedure used dynamic programming. Refinements on the procedure with inclusion of more realistic labor cost evaluation are given by Pleban, et al (1984).

APPENDIX I. - REFERENCES

1. Brock, D., Dallas Water Utility, personal communication, 1984.
2. Brown and Caldwell, Inc., "Municipality of Metropolitan Seattle's Computerized Stormwater Control System," Project Highlights, No. 5, 1978.
3. Buchleiter, G., D. F. Heermann, J. W. Labadie, and S. Pleban, "Optimal Irrigation Scheduling Under Engergy Constraints," Proceedings of Water Forum '81, ASCE Specialty Conference, San Francisco, California, August 10-14, 1981.
4. Cairo, P., General Manager, Planning and Engineering Division, Philadelphia Water Department, personal communication, 1984.
5. Dedinsky, H., J. Grinker, R. Meagher and J. Schlintz, "What is Needed to Successfully Automate a Wastewater Treatment Plant," Central States Water Pollution Control Association, May 1982.
6. Engineering News Record, "Computer Magic Aids Singapore's Water Search," March 15, 1984.
7. Fellows, R. J., Superintendent of Process Control, Denver Water Board, personal communication, 1984.
8. Firlotte, P., M. Cuddy, and J. Ziegler, "Computer Control and Optimization of an Industrial Hydro-Electric System," Proceedings

of Waterpower '83, International Conference on Hydropower, Knoxville, Tennessee, pp. 998-1005, September 18-21, 1983.

9. Jensen, J., "A User Directed Control System," Simulation, Vol. 44, No. 2, p. 102, 1985.

10. Labadie, J. and R. Lazaro, "Computer Simulation Results for Proposed Phase I Integrated VPP-SCP Project, Cyprus," Technical Report for the World Bank, February 1983.

11. Labadie, J. W., R. C. Lazaro, D. M. Morrow, "Worth of Short-Term Rainfall Forecasting for Combined Sewer Overflow Control," Water Resources Research, Vol. 17, No. 6, pp. 1594-1604, October 1981.

12. Labadie, J. W., D. M. Morrow, and Y. H. Chen, "Optimal Control of Unsteady Combined Sewer Flow," Journal of the Water Resources Planning and Management Division, ASCE, Vol. 106, No. WR1, pp. 205-223, March 1980.

13. Miyaoka, S. and M. Funabashi, "Optimal Control of Water Distribution Systems by Network Flow Theory," IEEE Transactions on Automatic Control, Vol. AC-29, No. 4, pp. 303-311, April 1984.

14. Morrow, D. M. and J. W. Labadie, "Urban Stormwater Control Package for Automated Real-Time Systems," AGU Symposium on Urban Hydrometeorology, Toronto, Ontario, Canada, May 26-27, 1980.

15. Pleban, S., D. F. Heerman, J. W. Labadie and H. R. Duke, "Real-Time Irrigation Scheduling via Reaching Dynamic Programming," Water Resources Research, Vol. 20, No. 7, July 1984.

16. Sheevers, H., "The Future: Computers and Irrigation," Colorado Economic Issues, Cooperative Extension Service, Colorado State University, Fort Collins, Colorado, October 1983.

17. Trava, J., D. F. Heermann and J. W. Labadie, "Optimal On-Farm Allocation of Irrigation Water," Transactions of the American Society of Agricultural Engineers, Vol. 20, No. 1, pp. 85-88, 95, 1977.

18. Trotta, P. D., J. W. Labadie, and N. S. Grigg, "Automatic Control Strategies for Urban Stormwater," Journal of the Hydraulics Division, ASCE, Vol. 103, No. HY12, pp. 1443-1459, December 1977.

REAL TIME CONTROL OF COMBINED SEWERS

by

Wolfgang Schilling
Visiting Scientist
Department of Civil Engineering
University of Ottawa
770 King Edward
Ottawa, Ontario, Canada, K1N 9B4
on leave from:
Institut fuer Wasserwirtschaft
Universitat Hannover
Callinstrasse 32, 3000 Hannover 1
West Germany

Abstract

After an introduction on the scope of urban drainage and water pollution control problems static solution approaches are shortly described
and their disadvantages are lined out. The potential of real time control for combined sewer systems is evaluated. State-of-the-art control hardware and software is described. The wide gap between research and applications of systems control concepts is discussed. Physical and administrative criteria are assessed. Some descriptions of
actually implemented systems illustrate the findings.

Introduction

The economical scope (i.e. investment, operation and maintenance cost,
social costs) of urban drainage in general and of downtown combined
sewer systems (CSS) in particular tremendous. Graham (1979) documents
that in the United States in the 60's and 70's far more money was spent
for urban drainage than for water distribution and wastewater treat-

ment together. Most of the European cities and more than 1000 in the
United States are at least partly served by combined sewer systems
(CSS). Urban drainage costs a lot of (tax) money so the question
should be allowed whether the benefits are the maximum possible.
These benefits are to avoid flooding and pollution. The evident operational requirement should be to avoid these troubles unless the entire
upstream system is at capacity. For systems which are not actively
operated this requirement is only fulfilled is one situation namely
when the (one) design storm occurs. For the infinite number of other
storms they necessarily perform suboptimal which means that combined
sewer overflows (CSO) or flooding occur although part of the system
still have idle capacities. Widely known as "best management practices" a number of "low-cost-high-committment" techniques for pollution and flooding abatement exist; (Lager and Smith, 1974; Lager et al,
1977; GAO, 1979). One is particularly attractive : use to a higher extent what is already there by actively controlling it. It is almost
15 years ago when in that era of general high expectations a number of
demonstration projects on real time control (RTC) of CSS were started,
(see for example Callery, 1971; Leiser, 1974; Watt et al, 1975).
Most of these systems were successful, are maintained and some were or
will be expanded. However, the sparks of successful demonstrations
did not ignite the whole scene as sometimes forecasted in the early
70's. Sewage flows in the vast majority of collection systems are
still operated in the same mode as 50 years ago, namely not at all.

Drawbacks of Passive Control

Solutions to above adverse impacts of CSS such as surcharging, back
watering and pollution shock loads to treatment plants and receiving
waters, have traditionally been of a "passive" or "static" kind.
Apart from separation, which is very expensive and also debatable in
its environmental effects, additional storage (both in-line and off-
line) is widely applied. Although still expensive, detention is conceptually simple and therefore usually works. But to what extent?
The concept of a gravitationally governed in-line detention tank in
Fig. 1 not only demonstrates that static orifice control of the outflows requires a larger volume of storage but that the tank is also
less available for the next storm.

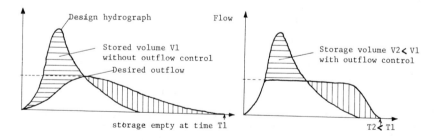

Fig. 1   In-Line Storage Without and With Outflows Control.

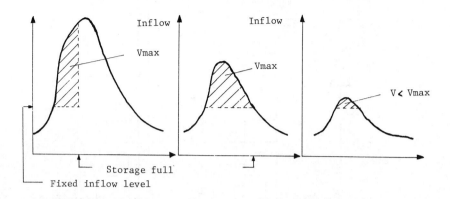

Fig. 2 Effectiveness of Off-Line Storage With Fixed Inflow Level.

For a given tank volume, Fig. 2 shows that even if the outfall gate
can be controlled actively to meet a prespecified flow there is only
one hydrograph (the second) for which the available storage volume is
mobilized with maximum success. For a larger storm the peak flow remains the same (compared to "no storage") and for a smaller storm only
a small amount of water is stored and the tank is never full. Consider
finally a cascade of two tanks each of them controlled to not release
more than maximum downstream conduit capacity. Fig. 3 shows that this
"local" control policy (with fixed release) results in downstream over-
loading (here : CSO) whereas a better "global" or "systems" control policy exactly avoids this. Mind that for better performance no additional capacities are needed. The only requirement is to tie together
all available hydraulic information and use some intelligence to find
the best control policy.

The Potential of Real Time Operation for Combined Sewer Systems

A water system (i.e. CSS) is said to be operated in "real time" if
current process data (i.e. rain, flow levels, etc.) are used to operate regulators (i.e. gates, inflatable dams, pumping stations, etc.) to
achieve better performance (i.e. less CSO, less flooding, etc.) during
the ongoing process (i.e. storm flow). If data allows to determine
the current state of the entire system and if operation is based on
this knowledge, "systems" or "global" control is applied. "Optimal"
control is achieved if any other control policy than the one applied
yields worse performance. In an "automatic control system" the operational decisions are taken by machines rather than man. In a "computer control system" this machine is a programmable computer. A "supervisory control system" is an automatic control system where a human o-
perator can take over decisions at any time (by "manual control"). In
a RTC system at least one of each of the following elements has to
exist :

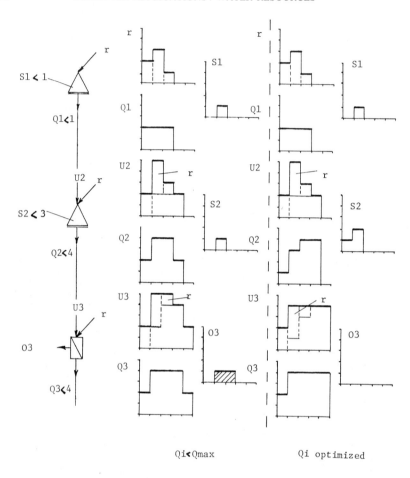

Qi< Qmax   Qi optimized

Fig. 3   Advantages of Systems Control for Storage Cascade

- a sensor which measures the ongoing process,
- a regulator which manipulates that process,
- a controller that decides whether and how to exert that regulator, and
- a telemetry device that carries the field data from the sensor to the controller and the instructions of the controller back to the regulator.

These four elements form a "control loop" with is common to every RTC system.

What makes CSS so attractive for RTC application?

1. CSS do create problems : After Giggey and Smith (1978) CSO contributes BOD loads in the order of 30% to 60% of secondary treatment
   plant (TP) effluent loads. Suspended solids from CSO even are
   80% to 170% of TP effluent loads. With higher levels of dry weather treatment these CSO problems become even more visible. Flooding hazards of CSS -the second important problem- are always increasing since urbanization is never be reversed.

2. Nobody wants to pay the bill to reduce CSO pollution to acceptable
   levels using traditional techniques like additional storage and
   treatment. Sullivan et al (1977) estimated $42 billions for the
   United States to reduce BOD pollution caused by CSO to 15% of the
   loads.

3. There is probably no water system other than CSS that has such a
   large discrepancy between design and operating conditions. Roughly at 90% of the time CSS carry only flows of less than 10% of
   their transport capacity. This difference between design and operating conditions is the RTC "potential" that is waiting to be
   tapped.

Real Time Control Hardware.

The hardware development in the past two decades seems to have converged to some proven designs for each element of the control loop. As
for sensors in CSS mainly raingages ("tipping bucket" or "weighing" types) and flow level sensors exist. The latter are mostly "bubbler",
"pressure cell" or "sonic" devices. Although each of those sensor
types is not perfect, hundreds of them are implemented in CSS and perform with acceptable accuracy, durability and maintenance requirements.
The author is not aware of any routine application of flow rate measurement in CSS. Flows usually have to be computed from levels which,
of course, can create quite an error especially if backwatering occurs.
Like flow rate sensors also quality sensors are not routinely used in
CSS. Important, although not so versatile, are a number of on/off
sensors like the "mercury switch" for high flow level detection or the
"proximity sensor" to detect closed tide gate positions.
      The old APWA (1970a; 1970b) reports discuss regulator problems
in detail and seem to be still valid today. Clogging was reported one
of the major problems which for unmonitored regulators results in extended periods of raw sewage diversions, backwatering, additional sedimentation, etc. Consequently APWA recommended RTC of regulators, not
to create additional problems but to make them work at all. Modern
remotely controllable regulators are remarkably different from the old-
style designs in the sense that :
      - the parts exposed to sewage and the sewer atmosphere are dras-
tically simplified and corrosion resistant (stainless steel);

      - fail-safe devices and emergency alarms are included (by-passes,
redundant emergency switches, etc.);

- sensitive parts are placed in an appropriate environment (extra hydraulic machinery and electronic vaults).

Particularly attractive for trunk flow regulation are inflatable dams
which are less expensive and fail-safe by their design. Some are installed now for more than ten years and still perform well (i.e.Mineapo-
lis - St-Paul, Detroit and Cleveland). Pumping stations have proven
their performance for a long time now and are widely used regulators.

Leased (dedicated) telephone lines are normally used for signal
transmission, although some form of wireless communication (UHF radio,
microwave, etc.) is at least considered. Dialled lines should be considered as a cost-effective means for rainfall data transmission. Sometimes public agencies own their own telephone networks which relieves
from a large fraction of operational costs. Data transmission should
include error checking procedures (parity bit, double transmission,
etc.). To prevent loss of data and allow for post-event checking of
transmission quality limited data storage should be provided at each
measurement site.

The most dramatic changes have occured to the element that ties
all information together namely the controllers. They determine the
timing and magnitude of regulator actuation to reach and hold a prespecified "set point". Traditionally only available as analog (pneumatic, mechanic) devices which operate independently and were cumbersome
to adjust a major step forward has been the advent of "direct digital
control" (DDC) where a central computer was used to function as a controller for a number of loops. DDC systems, however, were prone to
outage because of their centralist layout. The present state-of-the-
art is distributed control where a local loop (i.e sensor/regulator
unit) is controlled by an on-site micro-processor and systems control
(adjustments of local set points) is performed by a central minicomputer. A second minicomputer ("front end/host" configuration) can take
over at any time and furthermore be used to run simulation/optimiza-
tion routines. User friendly input/output devices such as high resolution color CRT'S, programmable keybords (providing "control menus"),
light pen, etc., allow instant manual takeover to modifiy the current
automatic control. Furthermore they can be used to conveniently modifi-
fy the dynamics of the remote on-site controllers (remote programming
of the microprocessors)

In a RTC system there necessarily is a need for more maintenance
and a different kind of maintenance staff (with knowledge in electric,
electronic and hydraulic equipment) at ultimately higher cost. The result , however, is a system that is controlled in the true sense of
the word and mastered at high performance by the operational staff rather than a system that randomly yields indications of malfunctions
through events such as flooding and fishkills.

Software for Systems Control

Whereas the hardware for RTC of CSS experienced slow but steady development applied software for systems control ("control concepts", "policies", "strategies", "rules") is still primitive compared to what
should be feasible today. With the first demonstration projects in the
early 70's control concepts were envisioned which soon turned out to be
too far-reaching. The term "optimal control" was already discussed
when the bulk of the work with the new systems was still hardware deve-

lopment and trouble shooting. Since in a RTC system (first) the hardware has to function and (second) the controllers for local regulator
loops have to be calibrated before (third) a systems control concept
can be applied, the latter practically has never been achieved anywhere,
let alone optimized. However, unless this last step is taken the ultimate benefit of RTC cannot be reached. In a complex RTC system the online adjustment of regulator set points becomes a necessity to "cut off
the hydrographs" in the right moment (see Fig. 2). How can that be a-
chieved? Obviously one needs some sort of forecasting if the control
center is manned the operator can simply look at the incoming data
and, based on his experience,decide upon what to do. An alternative
would be to feed the data into an on-line simulation model, try out a
control decision, compute the result, try another one, compute again,
etc. If satisfactory performance is simulated the control decisions
are finally executed. With this methodology one gets an idea of the
behavior of the entire system at the additional cost of the simulation
software.

     If automatic systems control is desired (only 20% of the time
is covered by normal working hours) again two approaches can be considered. The conceptually easier way is a sequence of "if-then-else" decisions which are executed by a central computer (i.e. "if rain intensity at A is X and if flow level at B is Y then set regulator C to Z").
Obviously, this method is relatively inflexible unless it incorporates
a multitude of "if-then-else". If one wants to make sure that really
the best control decisions are taken an optimized control scheme can be
used. The operational objectives have to be formulated in mathematical
terms (i.e. minimize CSO) and the physical constraints of the controlled system specified (i.e. flow capacities, storage volumes, etc.). An
algorithm is then executed during a storm that automatically finds the
best control sequence for all regulators (i.e. "linear programming",
"dynamic programming", see for example Labadie et al, 1975; Labadie et
al, 1980).

Applications in the United States and Canada

Based on a 1984 survey (questionnaire and personal communication,
Schilling, 1984) CSS in the United States and Canada are discussed with
respect to RTC. Since CSO and flooding abatement techniques are not
routinely applied the low percentage of RTC applications for one reason
can be explained by the low percentage of CSO/flooding abatement approaches whatsoever. Tab. 1 shows how different cities recognize their
past and present CSS problems (mostly in ranked sequence). Infiltra-
tion/inflow and dry weather CSO are mentioned quite often thus indicating basic upgrading and treatment capacity needs. In Tab. 2 the approaches to solve these problems are listed. According to this (non-
representative) survey separation, additional storage and RTC of the
existing systems are the more frequently applied approaches. Table 3
gives a comprehensive overview on some characteristic numbers of existing RTC systems. Surprisingly these systems have almost nothing in
common. Successful RTC systems do exist for a wide range of catchment
sizes,available storage as well as population served. Apparently RTC
is feasible and effective for a wide variety of CSS.

Table 1. Problems with Combined Sewer System

CITY	FLOODING	SEDIMENTATION	STRUCTURAL	SEPTIC.CONDITION	INFILTR. / INFLOW	STORAGE INEFFECT.	CORROSION	OVERDESIGNED	DRY WEATH. OVERFL.	WET WEATH. OVERFL.
Detroit, MI	5	3	7	6	4		8	9	2	1
San Francisco, CA										1
Grand Rapids, MI	2				3	4				1
Cleveland, OH	3								2	1
Boston, MA	6	3	4		2				1	
Toledo, OH	1	4			2				3	
Rochester, NY	1	4	3							2
Philadelphia, PA	x	x	x		x				x	
Vancouver, BC	x		x							1
Indianapolis, IN	2		3		4				1	
Omaha, NE	5	4	3						1	2
Akron, OH		1			2					3
Albany, NY	1	3			2					1
Ottawa, Ont.										x
Milwaukee, WI									2	1
Chicago, IL	x									x
Providence, RI	6	3	2	8	4	7	9		5	1
Lima, OH	1	4			3					2
Hamilton, Ont.	3	1	1	1	1		1	1	2	3
Washington, DC	3								2	1
Minneapolis-St. Paul, MN	3				4				2	1
Seattle, WA	3								1	2
Evansville, IN	1	4	3	5	6				2	7
Edmonton, Alta.	1				3				4	2
St-Louis, MO		2	2		2				1	2
Montreal, Que.	3				4				1	2

Table 2. Problem solution

CITY	SEWER SEPARATION	NEW SEWER MAINS	~W/FIXED REGULATORS	NEW DETENT. BASINS	FLUSHING PROGRAM	WET WEATH. TREATM.	SOURCE CONTROLS	SURFACE FLOW ATTENUAT.	REAL TIME CONTROL	SEWER GROUTING	BETTER MAINTENANCE
Detroit, MI									x		
San Francisco, CA		x				x			x		
Grand Rapids, MI			x	x					(x)		
Sacramento, CA	x	x				x					
Cleveland, OH									x		
Boston, MA	x	x		x		x	x				x
Toledo, OH	x			x		x	x	x			
Rochester, NY		x	x				x		x		
Philadelphia, PA		x			x				x		x
Vancouver, BC			x						(x)		
Indianapolis, IN					x		x		(x)	x	
Omaha, NE	x	x	x						(x)		
Akron, Oh											x
Albany, NY	x	x	x	x				x	x		
Ottawa, Ont.	x		x			x					
Milwaukee, WI	x	x							x		
St-Louis, MO									(x)	x	x
Chicago, IL		x							x		
Lima, OH									x		
Hamilton, Ont.		x				x					
Washington, DC		x				x			x		
Minneapolis-St.Paul, MN	x								x		
Seattle, WA									x		
Evansville, IN									x		
Edmonton, Alb.		x	x	x							
Montreal, Que.	x	x							x		

Table 3. Statistics of Real Time Control Systems

City	Minneapolis-St. Paul	Seattle	Detroit	Cleveland	Lima
Total Area (km^2)	4100	840	1675	432	n.a
CSS Area (km^2)	80	53	635	185	15
Population(1000)	1700	n.a	3200	1300	47
Outfalls	120	81	110	500	5
Volume of Contr. Storage ($1000m^3$)	n.a	120.4	530	n.a	34
(in m^3/ha)	n.a	22.7	8.3	n.a	22.7
Rain Monitors	9	11	41	25	0
Level Monitors	44	70	247	100	13
Outstations	38	36	n.a	69	9
Data Points	139	800	475	1500	300
Central Computer	DEC PDP-9	XEROX SIGMA-2	CDC SC 1700	n.a	n.a
Back-up Comp.	no	no	no	yes	yes
Rapid Access Storage (KB)	24	45	24	n.a	52
Remotely Contr. Regulators	6	16	10	34	8
Remotely Contr. Pumping Stations	0	21	17	0	1

(1 km^2 = 0.38659 miles; 1 ha = 2.47 acres; 1 m^3 = 35.7 cu ft)

Prospects and Constraints for Implementation

At present, there is hardly any flow meter routinely applied in combined sewers that has reasonable cost, range, accuracy, robustness and head losses. The alternative of converting level into flow rates is not satisfactory since backwatering (which is one method of flow control) drastically disturbes the conversion accuracy. The lack of water quality sensors is a comparatively minor problem since the monitoring of quality parameters (concentrations) only makes sense if flow rates are known well enough. Regulator designs are highly site specific, however, some general guidelines have evolved such as use of non-corrosive materials, simplified and fail-safe layout, etc. Major progress will continue within the telemetry and computing environment. Computer hardware, 15 years ago a major cost portion of the RTC demonstration projects is now almost negligible. Telemetry (i.e telephone) cost might not drop so drastically but fiberoptics might eventually be an interesting alternative to standard telephone lines. Provided the appropriate software the so-called "heart of the control system", the control center, might eventually disappear completely. Computing tasks might be carried out through the distributed network of jointly operating on-site microprocessors whereas the supervisory equipment might become so small that it could be carried away and hoocked up to any telephone be it at the operator's home.

In the last 15 years consultants, universities and a few water agencies developed digital simulation models to a sophistication that the question seems reasonable whether models are "better" than related measurements. Those models run on one of the new powerful microcomputers bring the drainage system the desk. Thereby finally computer modeling might become as popular as it was (wrongly) foreseen shortly after the first models were developed. How can computer models help to provide a solution for the RTC problem? A real time stormwater model will use all available on-line measurements, interpolate what is going on between measurement sites and extrapolate to downstream and into the future, respectively. It will automatically account for measurement errors (i.e. stage and discharge relation) or complete failure of data transmission. Thus a full scale picture of the flows in the entire system is continuously provided.

Is there a certain kind of CSS that is particularly attractive to be controlled in real time? Such properties as large systems, much in-line storage, loops, interconnections, diversions, already existing regulators and pumping stations, receiving waters of different sensitivity, already existing central monitoring system, excess flooding hazard, sedimentation problems, inflow problems, all favor the implementation of a RTC system. However, those are neither necessary nor sufficient conditions to render RTC beneficial as can be seen from the table 3. Apparently there is no physical system data that disqualifies some CSS from RTC. So why do RTC systems exist in these few and only in these few municipalities? The answer seems to be simple: there are some people who like it. In fact, the survey indicated that the success of a RTC system goes proportional with the enthusiasm of a dedicated group of engineers which is
  - small in number,
  - eager to communicate vertically (i.e. with the public, the regulatory agency, executives, and operators),
  - as well as horizontally accross divisions such as planning, design, and operations,
  - backed by executives,
  - persuasive towards operating staff,
  - willing to look "over the borders" (i.e. treatment, river quality management).

RTC is an agency-wide task. All divisions are involved and therefore communication is essential. Since it is a complete systems approach operation can hardly be broken down to multiple and isolated sub-group responsibilities. Since there is no such thing as a turnkey RTC system from the shelf" this high level of commitment is a necessary condition for a successful application of the RTC concept. Unfortunately but obviously this is not an engineering problem .

Appendix I-References

1. APWA, "Combined Sewer Regulation and Management-A Manual of Practice", Fed. Wat. Qual. Administ., Report No. 11022 DMU 08/70, Washington, DC, July 1970 a.

2. APWA, "Combined Sewer Regulator Overflow Facilities", Fed. Wat., Qual. Administr., Report No. 11022 DMU 07/70, Washington, DC, July 1970 b.

3. Callery, R.L., "Dispatching System for Control of Combined Sewer Flows", US EPA Report No. WQO-11020-FAQ-03/71, 1971.

4. GAO, "Large Construction Projects to Correct Combined Sewer Overflows are Too Costly", Comptroller General, Us General Accounting Office, Report No. CED-80-40, Dec. 1979.

5. Giggey, M.D.; Smith, W.G., "National Needs for Combined Sewer Overflow Control", J. Env. Eng. Div., ASCE, Vol. 104, No. EE4, 1978, pp. 351-366.

6. Graham, P.H. "1978 Needs Survey-Cost Methodology for Control of Combined Sewer Overflow and Storm Discharges", US EPA, Report No. 430/9-79-003, Feb. 1979.

7. Labadie, J.W.; Grigg, N.S.; Bradford,B.H., "Automatic Control of Large-Scale Combined Sewer Systems", J. Env. Eng. Div., ASCE, Vol. 101, No EE1, Feb. 1975, pp.27-39.

8. Labadie, J.W.; Morrow, D.M.; Chen, Y.H., "Optimal Control of Unsteady Combined Sewer Flow", J. Wat. Res. Plann. Man. Div., ASCE, Vol. 106, No. WR1, Mar. 1980, pp.205-223.

9. Lager, J.A.; Smith, W.G., "Urban Stormwater Management and Technology: An Assessment", US EPA, Report No. 670/2-74-040, Dec. 1974.

10. Lager, J.A.; Smith, W.G.; Lynard, W.G.; Finn, R.M.; Finnemore, E.J., "Urban Stormwater Management and Technology: Update and User's Guide", US EPA, Report No. 600/8-77-014, Sep. 1977.

11. Leiser, C.P., "Computer Management of a Combined Sewer System", US EPA, Report No. 670/2-74-022, Jul. 1974.

12. Schilling, W. "Application of Real Time Control in Combined Sewer Systems", Interim Report, Dept. Civil Eng., Colorado State Univ. Ft. Collins, CO, Dec. 1984.

13. Sullivan, R.H., et al, "Nationwide Evaluation of Combined Sewer Overflows and Urban Stormwater Discharges", US EPA, Report No. 600/2-77-064, Sep. 1977.

14. Watt, T.R.; Skrentner, R.G.; Davanzo, A.C.,"Sewerage System Monitoring and Remote Control", US EPA, Report No. 670/2-75-020, May 1975.

YAKIMA SUPERVISORY REAL-TIME MONITORING AND CONTROL SYSTEM

William H. Casola[1] A.M.ASCE, Onni J. Perala[2] M. ASCE,
and Daniel W. Farrell[3]

ABSTRACT

The Yakima Remote Control System is a case study application of supervisory control and data acquisition (SCADA) concepts for the operation and monitoring of a large water resources project. The remote control system allows centralized control and monitoring of a series of water storage and diversion dams along the Yakima River which provide irrigation water and hydropower to the Bureau of Reclamation's Yakima Project in south-central Washington. The system controls operating gates and other devices at the water storage and diversion dams using line-of-sight radio telemetry. The project involved both software and hardware development and is highlighted by a menu-driven program and graphics package that allow monitoring of the system and scheduling of control events to be executed in a real-time framework. The system monitoring includes an array of alarms that can be generated by both the remote sites and the central computer. An unusual feature of the project is the automatic paging system for the alarms which utilizes a voice-synthesized telephone answering system. Project personnel are automatically paged by beepers when alarms are generated and can call in to the central computer with a touch-tone telephone, listen to a synthesized identification of the problem, and acknowledge the alarm.

INTRODUCTION

The Yakima Remote Control System (YRCS) is a supervisory control and data acquisition (SCADA) system designed for the control of remote hydraulic structures. The system consists of a Digital Equipment Corporation VAX minicomputer as the central controller and five remote water storage and diversion dams that are monitored and controlled using a line-of-sight radio communications link. The YRCS was

----

1. Water Resources Engineer, Sutron Corp., Herndon, VA

2. Chief, Hydrology Division, Yakima Project Office, Bureau of Reclamation, Yakima, WA

3. Vice President, Sutron Corp., Herndon, VA

installed by the Sutron Corporation for the Bureau of Reclamation in
Yakima, Washington to aid in the management of irrigation water,
instream flow uses, and hydropower production. The system provides a
comprehensive set of functions for monitoring remote dam operations,
computing new gate settings, raising and lowering gates, controlling
operating machinery, and detecting and announcing alarms. A
user-friendly interactive program provides the operator interface to
the system. The menu-driven program provides color graphics displays
to help water managers monitor the system.

THE PROJECT

The YRCS operates part of the Yakima Project which provides
irrigation water to over 450,000 areas in the fertile areas along 175
miles of the Yakima River. Information critical to reservoir release
operations are provided by a network of hydromet stations which report
stream levels, reservoir levels, precipitation, and snowpack data over
the same radio link used by the YRCS.

The hydrologic data is sorted and stored as part of the Yakima
Hydromet System and is subsequently passed on to the Boise-Minidoka
Hydromet System and finally to the Columbia River Operational Hydromet
Management System (CROHMS). Real-time data from twenty-two hydromet
stations in the Yakima Basin are accessed by the YRCS from the Yakima
Hydromet System database.

Three storage dams located high in the Cascade Mountains are
controlled by the YRCS. The dams are over an hour-and-a-half drive
from the project office in good weather. Until recently, a full-time
dam tender stationed at one of the reservoirs made operational changes
to all three of the dams. Now the project has the capability of
making gate changes from the project office.

Farther down the river system, two powerplants which are power drops
off canals produce hydroelectric power for pumping stations and for
marketing by the Bonneville Power Administration. Changes in power
demand and river flows previously required operating personnel at the
powerplants to drive to the diversion dams and adjust operating gates
in order to change flows in the power canal. Each of the powerplants
is ten miles from its source of water at the diversion dams.

The Yakima Hydromet System was installed in 1977 to automate
collection of hydrologic data. The hydromet system greatly enhanced
the water managers daily overall view of the hydrologic aspects of the
project. The hydromet stations provide data on river, canal, and
reservoir levels, and weather data such as precipitation, air and
water temperature, and snow pillow pressure. However, site visits and
phone calls were still necessary to obtain operational data at the
dams such as gate settings and status checks. Recently, operations
budgets have tightened as water uses have grown more critical. For
example, water managers have contended with the drought in 1977 and
operations for fish spawning and incubation in more recent years. As

a result, the Bureau of Reclamation contracted for a SCADA system to aid in project operations.

The remote control system installed does not replace operating personnel. The dams still require regular visits for checks on operations and for mechanical maintenance. Instead, the remote control allows for more efficient use of the available water. In effect, the YRCS buys better water service for the project. Operators can now schedule operating changes at nights or on weekends. The ability to make immediate changes to operating gates at the dams from the project office instead of waiting the hour or two it might take for someone to be dispatched to the dam greatly improves the flexibility of the water managers to respond to system needs.

Figure 1   YRCS Manager Using Tektronix Color Graphics Terminal
at Bureau of Reclamation Project Office

DATA ACQUISITION AND MONITORING

The YRCS alleviates many of the problems faced by operations personnel by placing the burden of data acquisition and problem detection on the central computer. The YRCS collects data on the state of the system, comparing new data received with previous data. The remote sites are polled on a regularly scheduled basis for current data and the data received from each poll is checked against current data to determine if changes have occurred. Automatic polls around-the-clock can be scheduled by the managers. Data on current gate setpoints, gate openings, gate limits, a list of system status values, gate status values, and data on remote site hardware are provided in each poll message from each dam.

The remote sites use random reporting over the radio link to transmit messages to the central computer whenever the remote detects a change which has been flagged by the operator for such notification. The remote continues to send these messages until a reply is received from the central computer.

The VAX-based YRCS maintains a list of alarms which describe various problems that have occurred at the remote dam sites, or which have occurred because the computer detects a problem with the progress of operations or with the failure of a remote site to report. All alarms are maintained active until an operator at a terminal acknowledges the alarm. The alarm is deleted only if the problem has been resolved. Two hundred fifty-six (256) alarms are provided for each dam site. Currently, however, fifty-nine (59) alarms are active. Of these fifty-nine, sixteen (16) are system alarms monitoring electrical contacts for electric power, smoke and intruder alarms, high and low reservoir levels, (future) earthquake sensors, and other devices. Eight (8) alarms for each operating gate include sets of limits on the gate stem (physical limits of gate movement) and the shaft encoder (thumbwheel switches at the dam changeable by operators) which measures the gate opening to prevent out-of-bounds gate movements. Other gate alarms monitor hydraulic pressure switches for the hydraulic pumps which move the gates, and the gate opening to determine if the gate creeps off the setpoint. Finally, nineteen (19) alarms are generated by the central computer for such problems as failure of the remote site to communicate, failure of a gate change to produce the desired change in flow from the dam, failure of the central computer to perform a scheduled function, etc.

Operators can generate a screen display of current data at any site using normal CRT's (cathode ray tube) and printing terminals. However, color graphics displays are drawn for users logged in on Tektronix 4100 series terminals. A sample of the graphics display is shown in Figure 2.

The reservoir level in the color graphics is displayed by filling in a rectangle at the top left of the screen. Hydromet gaging stations are represented by small houses and gage heights are drawn as float symbols on vertical axes. The operating gates are drawn as rectangles with the current gate position labeled as "CP". The various sets of gate limits are shown by shading different portions of the gate rectangle different colors. The bottom of the Tektronix screen is called the dialog area and can be scrolled up or down to show buffered information. The information contained in the dialog area is the same information shown on a terminal without Tektronix graphics capabilities.

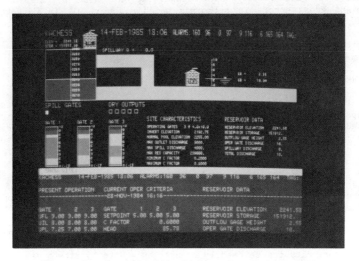

Figure 2   Graphics Site Display for Kachess Dam

SUPERVISORY CONTROL

The crux of the control operations are gate setpoints. Operators can schedule gate setpoints to occur in real-time up to 72 hours in the future. The 72-hour figure is operator-selectable. Gate setpoints are defined by control operations as the proper gate opening. Gate limits are provided as a check on operator controls. The gate limits disallow any setpoint choices made by the operator which are out of an adjustable range.

In order to choose new gate setpoints, a computation format is provided to choose new operating conditions. The YRCS prompts for new operating constraints and then computes the new required setpoint. The operator can select new values of discharge and anticipate reservoir level changes.

When the operator schedules the gate change to be made, a value for desired total dam discharge is included in the scheduling. The total discharge is used to compute a check on the operation after the gate change has been completed. Data from hydromet stations near the dam are used to compare the actual discharge to that desired by the operator. If the difference not within pre-set limits, an alarm is generated to notify the operator.

Several gate limit check mechanisims are used by the YRCS to prevent gross errors in setpoints which might result in dangerously high outflows. One set of limits is used by the central computer to prevent out-of-limit gate setpoints. The other two sets of gate limits are maintained at the remote site to provide backup protection from error.

ALARM FUNCTIONS

Alarms can be generated at both the dam sites and by the central computer as described previously. Each alarm is assigned a priority based on its importance to normal operation by the river operator. The project office is not manned 24-hours a day. During non-attended hours, when alarms of a specified threshold level are generated, the YRCS operators are notified immediately by portable pocket beepers. The operators can then call into the central computer using a touch-tone telephone and receive a voice-synthesized code of the alarm. The operator can turn the paging off by using buttons on the phone to acknowledge the alarm.

The threshold priority for alarm paging is one of the parameters personnel can easily change using the YRCS VAX software. The minimum paging priority can be readily changed on a site-by-site basis so that only selected essential alarms will interrupt managers during nights and weekends.

SUMMARY AND CONCLUSIONS

The Yakima Remote Control System is a computerized SCADA system used to monitor and operate a large water resources project for irrigation, instream flow uses, and hydropower production. The system is integrated with an existing hydrologic data collection system to allow managers to schedule real-time operational changes. The system enhances the ability of water managers to provide for more efficient use of available water through quicker response to weather and demand changes.

ANALYSIS OF RESERVOIR OPERATIONS ON THE IBM-PC

Dapei Wang[1] and Barry J. Adams[2], M. ASCE

ABSTRACT

The optimization of reservoir operations is a major economic concern. This paper contributes a computer software package, SPORO, written for the IBM-PC, for the stochastic optimization of reservoir operations. The software is based on the recent developments in reservoir operations analysis made at University of Toronto (Chen and Adams, 1983; Wang, 1983; Wang and Adams, 1985 a, b).

The hydrological uncertainty, seasonality and serial correlation of reservoir inflows as well as the multiple services provided by reservoir operations and the reliability of these services are considered in the optimization. The computational efficiency of the stochastic optimization procedure for reservoir operations presented herein provides the opportunity to implement the optimization procedure on the IBM-PC. The implementation of the integrated, stand-alone software package on a PC allows for in-situ utilization of the optimization methodology in the field of real-time reservoir operations. Computing experience and demonstrations are also presented.

----

[1] Ph. D. Candidate, Dept. of Civil Eng., Univ. of Toronto, Toronto, Canada, M5S 1A4. (on leave from the Wuhan Institute of Hydraulic and Electrical Eng., Wuhan, China)

[2] Associate Professor, Dept. of Civil Eng., Univ. of Toronto, Toronto, Canada, M5S 1A4.

INTRODUCTION

Reservoir operations require the determination of release volumes during successive time periods in accordance with certain economic criteria, which are usually to maximize the expected total rewards from the long run operations subject to meeting reliability constraints on the multiple services provided by the reservoir. For real-time operations, the release decisions should be determined at the beginning of the current time period with the information of the current reservoir storage volume and the historical inflow records up to the current time period. The main difficulty involved in determining release decisions is due to hydrological uncertainty -- that the inflows during the current time period and during subsequent future periods cannot be predicted with certainty.

In general, the methodologies available for reservoir operations can be grouped into three categories: (i) conventional rule curves determined from some selected representative inflow sequences; (ii) deterministic optimization with some representative inflow sequences or some representative statistics of the inflow records such as mean values or some selected quantiles of the records; and (iii) stochastic optimization in recognition of the hydrological uncertainty and seasonality of the inflow processes, in the form of both explicit and implicit stochastic optimization.

Since the optimization of reservoir operations is a major economic concern, the subject has been studied extensively. Unfortunately, to date most of the computer programs in this field are problem-oriented. The applications of optimization methodologies to reservoir operations are greatly limited by the requirements of intensive studies needed to develop an efficient computational procedure and a suitable computer code for applying these methodologies. The recent development of powerful personal computers has created opportunities for effective technology transfer from the researcher in this field to the hydro industry and for the in-situ implementation of these optimization technologies, provided that the optimization procedures are computationally efficient.

This paper presents a computer software package, SPORO, comprised of integrated, general purpose programs for real-time stochastic optimization of reservoir operations written for the IBM-PC. The software is based on recent developments in the field of explicit stochastic optimization of reservoir operations made at University of Toronto (Chen and Adams, 1983; Wang, 1983; Wang and Adams, 1985 a, b). The software was coded for flexibility of use and with an interactive user interface for application to a wide range of reservoir operations problems with only limited computer expertise on the part of the user.

The technical background of the optimization procedure, on which the software package is based, is presented subsequently, followed by the organization of the modules and the interface between the modules and the user. An example of the implementation of this software is then demonstrated. The complete software package and a detailed users' manual are available from the authors.

ANALYSIS TECHNIQUES

The availability of an integrated microcomputer software package for problems of reservoir operation optimization arises in part from the computational efficiency of the optimization procedure proposed. Recent studies on reservoir operations analysis conducted at the University of Toronto have resulted in procedures for explicit stochastic optimization of reservoir operations with improved computational efficiency. The software package presented herein was based on these developments. The technical background of the procedures is presented briefly below. For a more detailed discussion, the reader is referred to Wang and Adams (1985 a, b).

The probabilistic analysis of inflow processes provides the basis for operations optimization and guides the selection of the proper optimization models to be used. The first step of inflow analysis is the statistical analysis of the historical seasonal inflow records, where the definition of a 'season' may be one-month, one-week or any other period of time as appropriate. The seasonal inflows are fitted to selected theoretical probability distributions. The three-parameter Log-Normal distributions are recommended and applied in the software, based on their applicability to hydrological data, fitting flexibility and computational efficiency. The estimation of distribution parameters is by the method of maximum likelihood. The acceptance of the fitting to a particular inflow record is based on the percentage fitting error. If there is lack of fit for the Log-Normal distribution, the Normal distribution may be used instead.

Supported by experience with streamflow analysis, reservoir inflows are described as periodic Markov processes with annual cycles in recognition of hydrological uncertainty, seasonality and serial correlation of the streamflows. The quantiles and the limiting probability distributions of the seasonal inflows are derived based on the fitted distribution. An effective procedure based on synthetic streamflow formulas given by Fiering and Jackson (1971) is proposed for deriving practically usable inflow transition probability matrices from the available inflow records with limited length (e.g., less than 100 years). (Appendix A, Wang and Adams, 1985b).

The multiple services provided by a multipurpose reservoir and the reliabilities of these services are considered in the optimization procedure. Particularly, the prespecified reliabilities for providing flood control and low flow maintenance with some predetermined values and for producing firm power are incorporated in the procedure. These requirements are presented in the form of probabilistic constraints. A set of operational targets concerned with the reservoir storage states and power production levels are established. Penalty values are incorporated into the reward function of the optimization procedure to account for the violation of these targets, corresponding to the degree of violation, so as to make sure that the relevant requirements on the reliabilities are met. A set of deterministic optimization models, using the inflow sequences as the proper quantiles of the seasonal inflows in accordance with the relevant levels of reliabilities, are employed to derive these operational targets and the associated penalty values (Wang and Adams, 1985b; Wang, 1983). These are the preliminary studies for the optimization.

The steady-state operation describes the convergent nature of the prospective operations which occur in the future time periods. In the steady-state optimization model, the seasonal inflows are represented by the annual cycle of the limiting probability distributions of the seasonal inflows. The optimization of steady-state operations is a problem of periodic Markov decision processes, where only one state variable, the reservoir storage state, is involved (Wang and Adams, 1985b). The optimal steady-state operating strategy consists of the optimal release decisions for every storage state at the beginning of each season. The optimization of steady-state operation is implemented by means of the generalized Howard's policy iteration procedure and the generalized White's method of successive approximations (Wang and Adams, 1985a). In general, convergence of the policy iteration can be achieved within five iteration cycles of successive approximations.

In recognition of the serial correlation between the inflows in successive seasons, first-order Markov chains are used to describe the inflow processes, supported by the results of inflow analysis. For the optimization of real-time operation, two state variables, the current storage state and the previous inflow, are involved. By using the steady-state optimization as the interim step, the value iteration procedure for deriving the real-time optimal operation decisions can be performed over only a few time periods and an algorithm to use the updated data can be applied (Wang and Adams, 1985b). The computational efficiency of the proposed explicit stochastic optimization procedures makes it possible to implement the optimization of reservoir operation on a microcomputer.

Simulation studies with historical inflow records and with synthetic inflows are used to assess the operational characteristics of the derived optimal operating strategies and to evaluate these strategies.

The reservoir active storage volumes are discretized into a number of discrete states according to Savarenskiy's scheme and the level of discretization can be adjusted accordingly by the users. The seasonal inflow and release volumes are discretized with unique increments in accordance with the storage states where the ratio is also adjustable as appropriate. Similarly, the time periods (i.e., seasons) can be user-defined as appropriate.

ORGANIZATION OF THE SOFTWARE PACKAGE

The software package SPORO consists of five separate modules, each of which is contained on a floppy disk and assigned some specific utilities and can be used independently or collectively according to the users' preference.

Module 1. IWANA — Probabilistic analysis of inflow records and the determination of the inflow limiting probability distributions and the inflow transition probability matrices;
Module 2. PRESD — Preliminary studies of reservoir operation optimization to identify the various operational targets, parameters

and penalty values used in the single-stage reward functions;

Module 3. STOP -- Stochastic optimization of the steady-state reservoir operations with periodic Markov decision processes;

Module 4. RLOP -- Determination of the optimal real-time operating strategy based on the updated inflow information, which is used to rule the real-time operation of a multipurpose reservoir; and

Module 5. SIMUL -- Simulation studies for the assessment of the operational characteristics and for the evaluation of the operating strategies.

Each of the modules contains a few program files. One is for the main program, supplied as source code for the adjustment of the sizes of some arrays used in the program. Others are for subroutines, supplied as object code for the convenience of the users; however, the source codes for all the modules are stored on the sixth disk -- the reference disk, as a reference for users. All of the subroutines are written in adjustable form so that there is no need to adjust and recompile them in the implementation of the modules. Each module also has a few I/O files. The input data files, named with an extension (.DAT) and given in the formal forms, are adjustable with respect to the data in the particular applications. The files named with an extension (.IND) are used to transfer data between the modules. The output files named with extensions (.OUT) and (.GRA) are used to present the results of implementing a module.

INTERFACE AND EXECUTION

The programs in this package are coded with high flexibility such that they can be applied to a wide range of reservoir operation problems, and the adjustments required by the applications to particular reservoir operation problems are easily performed. Most of the required adjustments can be achieved by changing the values of parameters in the data input. The formal forms of the input data files display the definition, notation, and format of all input data such that enough information is available to instruct the user to adjust the input data. The only adjustment necessary to the program is to change the sizes of the arrays in the main programs of each module according to the data available to the users. This is also easily performed since all the necessary information is provided in the specification blocks of the programs in the form of comments just above the specification statements involved to instruct the user to perform the required adjustments.

The successive implementation of modules produces the necessary data for the subsequent modules. The internal data files are used to perform the data transfers between the modules. The output files named with an extension (.OUT) are employed to provide detailed, well-documented output for the results of the implementation of the modules. The output files named with an extension (.GRA) are intended to provide a video-graphic presentation of the analysis results by using the utility programs supplied with the software as parts of the system disks.

The software runs with the IBM-PC MS-DOS operating system (version 2.0 or 3.0) and the Microsoft MS-FORTRAN compiler (version 3.2) (Microsoft Corporation, 1984). All of the utility programs can be organized

on three master system disks. The compiling, linking and executing of
the software requires only the presence of the system disks. The basic
hardware requirements include an IBM-PC with 512 kbytes of RAM, the
8088 processer and the 8087 co-processor, two 360 kbyte floppy disk
drives and a Hercules graphics card (Hercules Computer Technology Inc.,
1983) for high-resolution monochrome graphics display; however, installation of the software on an IBM-PC/AT with hard disk will significantly accelerate the execution of this package.

The master system of the package consists of three system disks.
Users can organize their own software into two system disks in the
following manner for convenience:

The first system disk is COMPILER.
It consists of the following utility programs:
    COMMAND.COM, AUTOEXEC.BAT, EDLIN.COM, PRINT.COM,
    (the above comes from the IBM-PC MS-DOS)
    FOR1.EXE, PAS2.EXE,
    (the above comes from the MS-FORTRAN compiler)
    one text processing program, e.g., WS.COM or SEE.EXE

The second system disk is LINKER.
It consists of the following programs:
    COMMAND.COM, AUTOEXEC.BAT, FORTRAN.LIB,
    MATH.LIB   - (renamed from 8087.LIB),
    LINK.EXE   - (renamed from LINK.V2)

The third system disk is AUTHOR, which is an integrated, general
purpose authoring system recently developed at University of Toronto
for providing full-screen editing, general interfacing and various
graphing features for Microsoft FORTRAN users (Bontje et al, 1984).
This authoring system is available from the authors together with the
software package SPORO.

EXAMPLE RESULTS

To demonstrate the performance of the software package SPORO, the
results from an example problem of reservoir operation optimization are
presented. The reservoir in this problem is proposed to provide services of downstream flood control, power generation, upstream water
diversion and downstream lowflow augmentation. The reservoir active
storage volume is discretized into twenty-two storage states and thirty
years historical monthly inflow records are available. The optimization involves twelve decision periods (months). This problem is a
reasonably complex practical application. For solving the optimization
problem, the package SPORO was utilized on both the IBM-PC and the IBM-
PC/AT with a 20 MB hard disk.

The execution times for each of the modules are presented in Table
1 to provide information on the performance of the package. Here, the
real-time optimization was implemented for each of the twelve months,
where the number of the previous inflow states for each month varies
from five to twenty-three. It should be noted that such a 'universal'
real-time optimization is not necessary in practical applications and,

instead, the updating implementation of real-time optimization, i.e., optimization for a given previous inflow state and for a particular season, is often sufficient. The execution time for the updating implementation of Module RLOP on the IBM-PC is only about three minutes.

Table 1.   Execution Times for the Modules

Module	IBM-PC	IBM-PC/AT
IWANA	2 min. 20 sec.	50 sec.
PRESD	14 min.	6 min.
STOP	61 min.	32 min.
RLOP	146 min.	75 min.

The results of simulation studies for evaluating the relative merit of the derived optimal operating strategies are presented in Appendices 1 and 2. The results show that significant improvements on the economic impacts of the reservoir operations are achieved through the application of the stochastic optimization procedures provided in the software package.

CONCLUSION

The optimization of reservoir operations is a major economic concern. However, the problem-oriented nature of current optimization programs limits the application of these optimization methodologies. The availability of low-cost, high powered personal computers and the computational efficiency of optimization procedures recently developed at the University of Toronto provided the opportunity to develop an integrated software package for the stochastic optimization of reservoir operations.

This software package is coded with high flexibility and convenient interfacing for users such that it can be used for a wide range of reservoir operation problems. This package consists of five separate modules, each of which is stored on a floppy disk. These modules can be run independently or collectively to implement a complete analysis for the stochastic, real-time optimization of reservoir operations.

The software package is executed with IBM-PC MS-DOS operating system (version 2.0 or 3.0) and the Microsoft MS-FORTRAN compiler (version 3.2). The basic hardware requirement for the software package is the IBM-PC; however, better performance can be achieved on the IBM-PC/XT or IBM-PC/AT. The implementation of this software package on all of the above systems is deemed satisfactory.

The availability of this software package is expected to provide professional engineers responsible for reservoir operations with a useful tool for the in-situ utilization of the optimization methodology in the field of real-time reservoir operations.

ACKNOWLEDGEMENT: The work reported herein was supported in part by a scholarship awarded to the first author by the Government of the People's Republic of China and in part by a grant awarded to the second author by the Natural Sciences and Engineering Research Council of Canada. The technical assistance of Mr. John B. Bontje in programming matters is greatfully acknowledged.

REFERENCES

Bontje, J.B., Ballantyne, I.K., and Adams, B.J., (1984): User interfacing techniques for interactive hydrologic models on microcomputers, Proceeding, Stormwater and Water Quality Management Modeling Conference, Burlington, Ontario, Canada, Sep., 1984, pp.75-89.

Chen, H.Y., and Adams, B.J., (1983): Stochastic optimization and reliability analysis for optimal seasonal control of a reservoir, Publication 83-04, Dept. of Civil Eng., Univ. of Toronto, Toronto, Canada.

Fiering, M.B., and Jackson, B.B., (1971): Synthetic streamflows, Water Resources Monograph No.1, AGU, Washington, D.C.

Howard, R.A., (1960): Dynamic programming and Markov processes, MIT Press, Cambridge, Mass.

Klemes, V., (1977): Discrete representation of storage for stochastic reservoir optimization, Water Resour. Res., Vol. 13, No.1, pp. 149-158.

Wang, D., and Adams, B.J., (1985a): Generalization of Howard's policy iteration procedure to periodic Markov decision processes, Paper submitted for review, Water Resour. Res.

Wang, D., and Adams, B.J., (1985b): Optimization of real-time reservoir operation with Markov decision processes, Paper submitted for review, Water Resour. Res.

Wang, D., (1983): Optimization of real-time reservoir operation with Markov decision processes, M. A. Sc. thesis, Dept. of Civil Eng., Univ. of Toronto, Toronto, Canada.

White, D.J., (1963): Dynamic programming, Markov Chains, and the method of successive approximations, J. Math. Anal. Appl., Vol.6, pp. 373-376.

Appendix 1. Results of Simulation Study with Historical Inflows

-- Statistics of Historical Simulation Study --

	Rule Curves IS= 1	Det. Opt. Sy. IS= 2	Steady State IS= 3	Real Time Sy. IS= 4	Retrosp. Opt.
AN.AV.REWARD (M$)	88.53	100.78	107.11	108.69	122.48
RELATIVE VALUES	100.00 %	113.83 %	120.99 %	122.77 %	
AN.AV.ENERGY (BWH)	4370.	4517.	4577.	4564.	4862.
RELATIVE VALUES	100.00 %	103.35 %	104.73 %	104.43 %	
NO. OF LOW FLOW VIOLATION	0	0	3	0	0
NO. OF BANK FULL FLOWS	43	31	15	17	0
NO. OF HIGH FLOW VIOLATION	11	7	5	4	0
NO. OF EXTREMELY HIGH FLOW	1	1	0	0	0
NO. OF OCCURRENCE OF SPILLS	61	51	28	25	6
NO. OF FIRM POWER SHORTAGE	51	28	40	54	15
NO. OF MINIMUM POWER SHORTAGE	24	7	18	14	1
NO. OF UPPER STATE VIOLATION	45	32	17	14	0
NO. OF LOW STATE VIOLATION	0	0	0	0	0
ENDING STORAGE STATE	15	15	14	13	20

Appendix 2. Results of Simulation Study with Synthetic Inflows

```
*** Final Results of Simulation Studies ***
*********************************************
No. of Simulation Runs : 10
Length of Each Run : 300 years
```

-- Statistics of Simulation Study --

	Rule Curves IS=1	Det. Opt. Sy. IS=2	Steady State IS=3	Real Time Sy. IS=4
AN.AV.REWARD (M$)	77.17	89.31	95.06	96.05
RELATIVE VALUES	100.00 %	115.73 %	123.18 %	124.47 %
AN.AV.ENERGY (BWH)	4316.	4488.	4525.	4506.
RELATIVE VALUES	100.00 %	103.97 %	104.84 %	104.39 %
PR. OF LOW FLOW VIOLATION	.0001	.0000	.0067	.0010
PR. OF BANK FULL FLOWS	.1154	.0633	.0391	.0389
PR. OF HIGH FLOW VIOLATION	.0269	.0245	.0175	.0173
PR. OF EXTREMELY HIGH FLOW	.0123	.0114	.0089	.0088
PR. OF OCCURRENCE OF SPILLS	.1679	.1269	.0728	.0623
PR. OF FIRM POWER SHORTAGE	.1307	.0791	.1039	.1481
PR. OF MINIMUM POWER SHORTAGE	.0568	.0068	.0268	.0147
PR. OF UPPER STATE VIOLATION	.1276	.0818	.0354	.0332
PR. OF LOW STATE VIOLATION	.0000	.0000	.0004	.0006

IMPLEMENTATION OF A MICRO-CADD SYSTEM

David C. Wheelock, P.E., Associate Member ASCE*
John N. Furlong, P.E., Member ASCE**

INTRODUCTION

Computer-aided-design-and-drafting (CADD) systems utilize computer technology to aid the engineer in his work. CADD systems are designed to process graphics with speed and accuracy to greatly enhance the productivity and analytical ability of engineers. CADD systems utilize graphic input devices, graphic display screens, and graphic output devices to produce accurate scaled drawings for engineering applications.

Some of the advantages of implementing a CADD system in an engineering office are:

* Drawings can be produced in less time.
* Drawings are precise.
* Drawings can be edited on screen - no erasing.
* High quality drawings are produced.
* Editing ability allows the engineer to analyze multiple design alternatives.
* Engineers spend less time with routine drawing production.
* Number of errors are reduced.
* Drawings and details are easily and completely standardized.
* Some aspects of "systems drafting" can be performed on screen, thereby producing higher quality product.
* Greater flexibility of design firms to ride market swings is achieved.
* Proper implementation produces computer assistance in work, not computer constraints.
* Allows engineer to design at a CADD work station screen and produce a high quality product. This also bypasses the draftsman, further reducing the chance of errors.

An engineer is often constrained with too little time to analyze all of the possible alternative solutions to a project. In parallel with this situation, an engineer often cannot consider alternative solutions to the detail that available data may allow. CADD systems, with the intrinsic ability to handle large amounts of information, present the information in infinite format variations, and make compu-

*Associate, Gebhard Engineers, 5750 Balcones Drive, Suite 210, Austin, TX 78731.
**Principal, Furlong Engineering, 8705 Shoal Creek Blvd, Suite 108, Austin, TX 78759.

tations quickly, now allow the engineer to study alternate solutions and available data in detail.

Another important aspect of CADD systems is their innate feature of reducing errors in drawings. The precision with which information is displayed and the normal method of entering data in an organized and logical sequence (typically from calculation sheets or coordinate geometry output) precludes many errors. Errors that are entered into the machine are noticed quickly on the screen due to illogical displays. Examples of this type of data checking are presented in the section discussing site plan preparation. Errors are further reduced by the requirement that the personnel operating the CADD systems are more highly qualified technicians. Better trained personnel with computer aptitude are needed to efficiently operate the CADD system due to its intrinsic job quality. Thus, errors are recognized as they are entered rather than during the engineers' review.

Micro-computers have become ubiquitous in engineering offices, performing word processing, accounting, computations, and time-sharing tasks. With the emergence of micro-computers and their widespread implementation, the cost of even the most advanced machine has come within reach of all engineering offices. Additionally, peripheral equipment for the micro-computer has become very advanced and reasonably priced. Peripherals that support CADD systems were specialized pieces of equipment available from only a few sources. Plotters and digitizers have traditionally been expensive pieces of equipment designed to work with mainframe computers, and, consequently, the market was small. Recently, peripherals manufacturers have realized the potential of the micro-computer market and have developed plotter, digitizer, and graphics screens for this market.

Recently, two small consulting engineering firms in Austin, Texas, have implemented micro-computer based CADD systems. Both firms practice in the general area of water resources, including detention design, small scale hydro-power, hydrology, hydraulics, and land development.

CADD SYSTEM ACQUISITION

A primary constraint of a small office in acquiring a CADD system is the cost. A small firm cannot afford an Intergraph or an IBM CADD system in which a single work station may cost $60,000, not including the central processing computer. With the recent price drops of micro-computers, and a corresponding drop in the cost of peripheral equipment, the total price of a micro-computer based CADD system is under $15,000.

Having seen demonstrations on a micro-based CADD system in 1984, the authors investigated the capability of available systems. It was quickly learned that micro-CADD capability is hardware independent; i.e. some thirty (30) different computers are capable of running CADD software, of which there are at least three (3) products available. The CADD software that the authors investigated was initially developed on IBM-PC's or IBM compatibles and then modified for Tandy, TI, and other computers. Without a doubt, the largest availability of software, peripherals, information, and general support is available for the IBM-PC and the most popular IBM compatibles.

With the choice of hardware made, analyses of software was made. Three micro-CADD packages were analysed. A detailed discussion of the capabilities of each package is not presented for one simple reason; our analysis was made in mid-1984, and, the quality of the micro-based CADD software is improving rapidly.

For civil engineers, some suggested criteria for analyzing a micro-CADD software package are:

* Entry of points by rectangular and/or polar coordinates.
* Ability to handle site layouts in actual dimensions, not scaled coordinates.
* Availability of planimeter command.
* Interface with COGO program.
* Ability to insert standard details from external files.
* Floating point versus integer coordinates.
* Ability to use a multi-pen plotter.
* Linetype shown on screen.
* Ability to customize screen menus.
* Unit specifications.
* Ability to use a variety of text styles.
* Dimensioning capability.
* Availability of cross-hatching patterns.
* Ability to interface with a 24 inch by 36 inch digitizer.
* Fillet commands.
* Ability to digitize topographic data.

While these are features that are important to civil engineers, there are significant other capabilities that CADD systems must possess to enable efficient drawing production, regardless of the engineering discipline of the drawing. These required features include editing commands, drawing manipulations, machine speed, layering, maximum drawing size, and ease of digitizer input.

After selecting the software, hardware that works efficiently with the software and is capable of utilizing all of the features of the software must be chosen. Discussions with the software vendor, the technical support staff at the software developer, and with users are recommended before purchasing hardware.

Currently, the authors use three (3) configurations for the CADD software:

Computer	Monitor	Graphics Card	Disk Drives	Digitizer	Plotter
IBM PC	MicroVitek Color	Tecmar	2-Floppy	Hitachi	Houston Instruments
IBM PC	Zenith Color	Tecmar	2-Floppy	Mouse Systems	Numonics
Compaq	Compaq Monochrome	____	2-Floppy 10 MB-Fixed	Microsoft Mouse	____

IBM machines were chosen due to the availability of software in every area and from every source. This advantage has been repeatedly affirmed.

GETTING STARTED

Once the CADD system has been chosen, interconnected, plugged in and is operating, a learning process begins that can require a great deal of hard work and patience. The technicians who will use the system must genuinely be interested in mastering it. They must be willing to put forth the effort to devise an operating procedure for the AutoCAD system that will increase production of higher quality drawings and also save time. The cost in time for learning and efficient implementation is high.

A systematic organization of drawing files that are used repeatedly must be devised to gain the full benefits of the CADD system. Computer programming is not necessary, but only an understanding of the capabilities of the CADD system. AutoCAD is an interactive program; that is, the user responds to a command prompt by choosing items from several menus that are available. The learning process involves developing an understanding of how each menu item "acts" on the drawing. During this initial learning process, the production of useable drawings will be slower than pencil or ink drawing. The small engineering firm must be willing to sacrifice some productivity "today" so that production and drawing quality will be increased "tomorrow".

Usually all projects are on a tight budget and time schedule, and during the initial learning stages, it may not be practical or cost effective to try and produce a complete drawing with the CADD system. The authors have found that portions of drawings can be produced at first by using the AutoCAD system and completed by hand. As the technical staff gains experience with the CADD system, a greater portion of each drawing can be done with AutoCAD until it becomes cost effective to completely produce drawings with AutoCAD. Each drawing or portion of a drawing can be used as a "building block" for future drawings. Details drawn can be reused and modified very rapidly from one drawing to another. The authors have found that drawing can even be fun! A technician may even want to practice drawing on his own time, so he can spend less time on the boards.

APPLICATION OF CADD TO CIVIL ENGINEERING

Computer-aided-design-and-drafting can be applied to all phases of civil engineering involved with graphical representations of physical things. Our offices have applied CADD to drainage projects, land development, site planning, hydrologic analysis, and small-scale hydroelectric power plant design.

Small Scale Hydro Electric Plant Design

The firm of Gebhard Engineers has applied the CADD software, running on an IBM-PC, to small scale hydroelectric plant design and to hydrologic analysis of rivers. The application of micro-CADD to small scale hydro begins with digitizing the site configurations and existing facilities. Digitizing refers to overlaying a scale drawing on a special electronic work surface (a digitizing tablet) that records the movements of a stylus as the operator traces the lines on the drawing. Digitizing creates an electronic record of the drawing that can be edited, scaled up or down, or inserted in other files. The digitizing process can be tedious and is often left to technicians to complete. The economical (under $1500) digitizing tablets available for use with micro-computers typically have a working surface of 11 inches by 11 inches. This size tablet is a constraint if digitizing is to be performed on a regular or daily basis.

Once existing information is digitized, the remainder of drawing preparation is electronic. The digitized information can be edited, text can be added, areas can be calculated, and computations made - all on the computer screen. Design survey information can sometimes be entered directly out of the field book, or one may have to go through an intermediate step of coordinate geometry calculations. The CADD software allows entering data as polar coordinates, rectangular coordinates, or as relative displacements from the previous entry. Often, survey information must be reduced to rectangular coordinates, using a coordinate geometry program (COGO). Currently, the firm does not have software that interfaces between the COGO program and CADD. Such interfaces exist and would be helpful by eliminating the manual re-entry of coordinates from the COGO program to the CADD package.

Once existing information and survey data is entered, the design phase can begin. A powerful feature of micro-CADD programs is the ability to "layer" drawings. Just as drawings are created using a pin-register system, with certain items of a drawing on each sheet, CADD programs allow this, but with much more flexibility. With CADD, the number of layers allowed in a drawing is unlimited. Topographic information, easements, property lines, concrete structures, mechanical equipment, and notes can each be placed on a separate layer. This is useful in allowing creation of multiple drawings from the same base drawing; i.e., a mechanical layout, structural layout, electrical layout, site grading. When a change must be made, it automatically is updated on every layer or drawing, saving the time of correcting many

originals, and eliminating the potential error of not updating every
sheet.

Another strong advantage of using a micro-CADD system on an application such as a hydro-electric plant design is in developing the
mechanical drawings and details. Any mechanical equipment that is
symmetrical, such as hydro-electric turbines, can be quickly drawn
using the CADD's ability to create mirror-images, and multiple shapes
in circular or rectangular patterns. Once a piece of equipment is
drawn, the CADD software can be told to remember it as a separate
entity, and it can then be inserted anywhere in the current drawing or
other drawings. The inserted detail can be recreated at any vertical
or horizontal scale to fit exactly in the required space. Portions of
other drawings on file can be extracted and placed in the current
drawing, thereby making it unnecessary to draw any detail more than
once.

The CADD software includes features such as cross-hatching and
user-defined line types that create a superior quality finished
drawing. Cross-hatch patterns available include all ANSI standards,
concrete, grass, and checkered plate.

Hydropower Hydrologic Analysis

A recent unexpected application of a CADD system arose in the
Gebhard Engineers' office. Gebhard had been retained to perform the
hydrologic analyses of a proposed hydro-electric power plant to be
installed on the Colorado River at Austin, Texas. The site is downstream of two (2) storage reservoirs that provide irrigation water for
eight (8) months each year. During the remaining four (4) months, the
water passing the power plant site came only from the contributing
area downstream of the reservoirs. Additionally, the upstream dams
have hydro-electric stations that operate on an irregular basis. The
combination of the irrigation water release schedule and the irregular
hydro-plant releases caused the available USGS flow-duration data to
not be accurate enough for our purposes. It was determined that a
detailed look at monthly flow-duration data must be done for three (3)
separate gages and for differing time periods. The micro-CADD system
enabled us to load all of the data available, without regard to the
required final graphical output. Each separate curve, whether for
monthly data, gaging stations, or time periods, was placed on a unique
layer. With the layering features, flow duration curves were quickly
compared on the screen, without ever having sketched or drawn a curve
on paper. With the planimeter command, areas under the flow-duration
curves were quickly measured on screen - without the errors associated
with a mechanical planimeter. When a significant comparison of curves
is made and an exhibit is needed for presentation, the CADD system
quickly produces a plot at any scale and of extremely high quality.
This method of analyzing hydrologic data allowed us to make expedient
comparisons of 64 flow-duration curves.

Site Plan Preparation

First, a draftsman/technician should study the site in the field, the architectural site plan, topographic information and areas where ponding may be developed on the site in a cost effective way. Second, a draftsman/technician should think through completely what parts of the drawing need to be included for a site. Third, he should see what parts of the drawing should be calculated (i.e. building corners, parking area, or street and property lines). Fourth, some parts of the drawing will obviously be repetitive such as general notes, North arrows, signature or approved blocks, scales, and title blocks. Other repetitive items would be details like headwalls, driveways, sidewalks, and drainage channels. The respective parts can be stored on a standard file and later be inserted as a block into a drawing.

Flood Plain Studies

Furlong Engineering has applied micro-CADD in the area of flood plain studies. Furlong currently uses HEC-1 and HEC-2 on a Compaq micro-computer.

Typical HEC-2 run times for a "small" flood plain study (ten to twelve cross sections with one bridge routine and three to four multiple profiles) may take two to three minutes. It may take anywhere from five to eight minutes to print the summary input, intermediate results and summary output. Naturally, as the number of ground points goes up, or the number of cross sections goes up, or the number of multiple profiles increases, the run times get longer. The "utility" of the Compaq is a strong point in its favor due to its portability.

Once the results of the flood plain study are known, we use the CADD system to plot the profiles and cross sections as a check of the output data.

Flood Plain Reclamation

A CADD system is also useful in plotting and presenting cut/fill quantities or volume calculations for doing remedial flood plain work in a flood fringe area. Oftentimes, developers will ask to what extent can they perform work in a flood plain. Usually these questions can only be answered by determining the value of the reclaimed land versus leaving the land "as is". The first issue is an economic constraint, the second issue is a technical question, best answered with a hydraulic model. We have used CADD to plot cut/fill volumes and HEC-2 to model the developed condition.

Subdivision Drawing

The production of street and drainage and water and wastewater construction plans can be accomplished with a CADD system. The preparation of these plans usually involves the drawing of several sheets for various purposes at different scales showing portions of the project.

Because CADD can display and plot at any scale, the entire project can be drawn on a single scale and then portions can be manipulated, copied and rotated as necessary to produce construction drawings. Once the proper sequence of CADD commands is mastered by the technical staff, the drawings can be structured in such a way that changes in the plans can be made rapidly without erasing and the sheets redrawn. Excellent quality drawings can be generated at the end of the project. In fact, "new" originals can be generated anytime since the information is stored on a disk.

Plotting

Plotting a drawing created with a CADD system can be a rewarding experience, especially when a drawing so exact has been created in a short time. The plotting process can take anywhere from a few minutes to over an hour, depending on the complexity of the drawing being generated. It is suggested that CADD users plan to plot drawings while other office activities can be tended to, i.e. lunch, phone calls. With two computers, one can be dedicated to plotting while the other is used as a CADD work station.

CONCLUSIONS

Micro-computer based CADD systems offer engineering offices the advantages of producing precise, high-quality drafting without a drafting staff. CADD systems enable an engineer to sit at a work station and produce final drawings as the design is developed. Cost savings occur in an engineering office due to the increased speed available from a CADD system and from the reduced need for a drafting staff.

A CADD system can literally make you lazy. The ease with which revisions and corrections can be made is beneficial to. As Murphy's Law states "If something can change, it will, and at the worst (or usually last) possible moment." Once a CADD system is learned proficiently, Murphy's Law has less significance.

The authors have found that a CADD system is an asset to a civil engineering office active in the water resources field. However, the proper implementation of the machine in the design process can be time-consuming and painful to project budgets. Adapting the complex software to a specific field of practice requires a dedication by the operator to learn the machine and understanding by the managers of the amount of time needed before the "break even" point is reached on the learning curve.

A typical consulting engineering office performs a variety of projects. Each type of project requires a different implementation of a CADD system. With each new type of project, a learning curve is natural, regardless of the amount of experience gained on other projects. An office that practices in a wide range of fields may have an extremely long and costly learning process before the CADD system is fully utilized and before the office productivity reaches pre-CADD levels.

However, automation of the engineering office is inevitable, and firms that wait to invest in CADD will be behind in general technical ability, knowledge of current computer practices, and general productivity.

COMPUTER CONFERENCING FOR MANAGERS

by

Major Stephen C. Lockhart[1] and Gerald Greener, M, ASCE[2]

ABSTRACT: The authors will describe a computer conferencing/message system called Confer II currently being utilized by the U.S. Army which they have implemented among dredging managers in the U.S. Army Corps of Engineers.

The capability of such a computer conferencing/ message system to provide ongoing discussions without requiring participants to travel or be available at specified times will be presented. The authors will explain how Confer II can locate critical expertise effectively, reduce the time spent communicating, and increase the productivity of an engineer/manager.

The United States has shifted emphasis from production of manufactured goods to an information economy. A study done in 1967 showed that 46 percent of the Gross National Product (GNP) was derived from information-related jobs and more than 53 percent of the earned income came from information-related jobs. Since then the explosion of information in this country has accelerated at an ever faster pace. For example, in 1977 only 50 stores catered to computer hobbyists; by 1982 there were 10,000!

This shift to an information economy has created many new ways of doing business. Increased availability of computers and the need to streamline the information processing capability have led to many new application software programs. This paper discusses Confer II as one that has been very useful to the Dredging Division of the

---

[1]Executive Officer, Water Resources Support Center, Corps of Engineers, Casey Building, Ft. Belvoir, Virginia 22060-5586

[2]Civil Engineer, Dredging Division, Water Resources Support Center, Corps of Engineers, Casey Building, Ft. Belvoir, Virginia 22060-5586

Water Resources Support Center. It is designed to
facilitate ongoing discussions among many people located
throughout the world and at a time that is convenient to
each individual.

The U.S. Army Corps of Engineers is no exception to the
rest of the world in terms of information processing. In
fact, the real work of the Corps has been, for many years,
that of construction management. This is especially true
in the area of dredging where until 1978 the Corps had the
only sea going hopper dredges (15) in the United States and
a total fleet of 40 dredges to keep the navigable waters in
the United States open to maritime traffic. With the
passage and implementation of PL 95-269 in April 1978, the
Corps was directed to drastically reduce its fleet to the
minimum required to meet the national defense and emergency
requirements and to accomplish the majority of the dredging
by contract. Currently, the Corps has only 12 operating
dredges in its inventory, and over 80 percent of this
Nation's Federal navigation projects are dredged by private
contractors. Again, we see a clear and significant shift
from constructing/manufacturing to that of
managing/informing.

The real change, other than transferring Federal jobs to
the private sector, is that Corps managers of the dredging
program must do much more intensive planning, managing, and
performance monitoring, to accomplish the necessary work in
light of declining resources ($). To aid in this task,
many are turning to the computer to get better, more timely
management information.

WRSC Dredging Division prepares testimony for OCE managers
who testify before Congress and at times, give testimony
directly. The Division also assists in allocating work
allowances and dollars; briefing senior Civil Works
managers weekly on key dredging issues around the nation;
and answers congressional inquiries for information.
Therefore, the primary function of the Dredging Division's
management role is that of information processor and
analyzer.

Dredging managers in the Corps districts have many
different data bases at their disposal to help in managing
their dredging programs. Through their years of experience in gathering pertinent information and solving their
particular problems, they have developed an intuition for
anticipating problems and reacting to them before they
become crises. This capability is very difficult if not
impossible to capture in a conventional data base, since
data bases are generally designed to provide facts and
figures with the user providing the analysis, in this
instance.

At the national level, the need for raw data does exist,
but the need for the analysis of the raw data is probably
more important. Hence, the need for having face-to-face
meetings or telephone calls to distant points. The request
is seldom for raw data but usually a query as to "what does
all this mean?" This type of information exchange also
provides the opportunity to build inter- personal
relationships that are crucial to business.

The task of how to get the necessary information from those
we know and trust in a world on the move has not been an
easy one. The Dredging Division searched for a system that
would allow for communications from various parts of the
organization, would not depend on both parties being
present at a communicating device at the same time, would
be easy to use, and would be convenient to the managers.
Confer II, a computer-based communications system was
selected because it met these criteria.

However, the real power of Confer II is its similarity to a
group meeting where a central idea is generated by one of
the participants and written on a chart pad. Others add
their comments to this central idea, and these too are
added to the chart pad. As the meeting progresses, an idea
is expanded, explored, changed, and/or synthesized until a
statement of the problem/solution is agreed upon by most if
not all in attendance.

As many of you who have attended meetings know, the process
is not quite that simple. There never is just one idea
generated at a time, nor do you progress to a solution of
one issue before another is added to the chart pad. Also,
two or more participants will get together during coffee
breaks to discuss the issues at hand in private. When the
meeting is finally over and everyone goes home, there are
always issues that require further work or study.

With Confer II, a meeting or a "net" like the one described
above can be called but no one has to board an airplane to
attend. First, as with a regular meeting, an attendee or
"user" list is prepared and user ID's are sent out. The
users gain access to the mainframe computer running Confer
II software with their ID's, a terminal, and a telephone
modem.

The individual users can sign on the net anytime they
choose. Each user has the power to express any original
idea as an "item" or he can make a "response" to someone
else's item, just as he would do in a regular meeting. A
user can also send a private "message" to one or more users
of the net, similar to the coffee break discussions.

Basically, the real advantage of Confer II is that a
face-to-face meeting can be held to discuss a particular

topic and the items that are left unresolved can be
continued with Confer II at a later time. The system, as
used by the Dredging Division, gets the personal opinion of
the various dredging managers in the field, but not the
"official position" of the command. This is useful for a
major headquarters trying to establish policy.

This network does on occasion create a problem for the
intermediate managers who are being bypassed by the
informal chain of command. The truth is that the same
people expressing their personal views are the same ones
the intermediate managers go to for advice on a dredging
matter. The problem is, therefore, one of perception.

A workable solution is to carry out the informal
discussions on Confer II, devise the appropriate policy or
position, then staff it through the formal chain of
command. This process usually shortens the approval
process because the managers who actually review the policy
helped to shape the wording by using the Confer II system.

The Confer II net used in the Dredging Division is called
Dredgenet, and it has proved quite valuable to the dredging
program for the Corps. There are many examples of how this
communication medium has saved time and provided a means to
gather more complete information. The following is an item
that was pulled off the net. The information gathered from
the various dredging managers will be used by the personnel
office to try and keep a law in force that saves the Corps
money and is favored by the employees involved.

DO NEXT? i 35 date

Item 35 16:47 Feb22/85 7 lines 1 response

ADAM HEINEMAN:
COMPRESSED WORK SCHEDULE LAW EXPIRATION:
We have been told that the compressed work schedule law
expires 30 June 85. This would create havoc for our dredge
work schedules. We would have to go back to the 10 and 4
or some other 8 hour day alternative. I'm sure we would
lose a lot of our good young officers. Recommend you
investigate what we can do to have the law renewed. We
also have hydro crews working 4- to 10-hour days for
efficiency.

1 response

Feb27/85 08:06
1) Chuck Hummer:
I'll check with Office of Counsel and Personnel to confirm
if the compressed work week law does expire on 30 June 85.

Will report back when I have info. Thanks for the
heads-up, Adam.

RESPOND, FORGET, OR PASS: p

DO NEXT? i 38 date

Item 38 13:41 Feb27/85 8 lines 12 responses
Chuck Hummer:
COMPRESSED WORK WEEK LEGISLATION:
Compressed work week legislation- Current law which
provides for the compressed work week expires on 30 June
85. OCE personnel office reports that the Office of
Personnel Management (OPM) is aware of the expiration and
expects hearings to be held by the Congress in March. OPM
apparently has not developed a position either for or
against extension of the current provisions and will await
the hearings before taking any firm action. OCE labor
relations officer has been made aware of this issue and has
promised to keep on top of it.

12 responses

Mar01/85 07:34
1) Chuck Hummer:
OCE personnel office called on 28 Feb 85 to report GAO has
asked Corps for statistics and background on use of
alternate work schedule law to allow them to recommend a
position to the Congress. Request you provide benefits of
using the law (compressed work week dredge crew schedules)
in terms of overtime/FTE (manpower) savings. Also look at
the effect of changing the present credit hour carry over
to 24 hours a pay period. Need an estimate of savings in
dollars and FTE on basis of 24-hour carry over. Need a
ballpark estimate by NLT next Tuesday, 5 Mar 85. Thanks.

Mar01/85 14:30
2) Barry Holliday:
The snagboat Snell is presently working a 10 hour-4 day
week. The cost savings are difficult to estimate but we
are convinced that the efficiency of this type of work is
greatly enhanced by the compressed work week.

Mar04/85 07:06
3) Chuck Hummer:
Barry, give a wag on savings. Something is better than
nothing.

Mar04/85 13:57
4) Barry Holliday:

After looking into it some more and discussing it here, we would save at least $25,000 per FY. I could get more detailed if you need it and can give me a few days.

Mar04/85 14:04
5) Henry Schorr:
NOD uses compressed work schedules for hired labor construction forces when working in remote areas, in SWP from 9 Jul to 15 Oct the savings amounted to $31,000. During warm months (daylight saving time) aquatic growth control crews work a compressed work week because of remote work sites. Savings in FY 84 were approx. $70,000. The crew of the dredge Wheeler works 14 days on and 14 days off. Savings in overtime amount to approximately $18,000 annually; however, the biggest factor is crew morale and the fact that the compressed work schedule makes us competitive in recruiting quality people with an industry working a similar schedule. Total dollar savings in NOD should exceed $120,000 annually for all work.

Mar04/85 17:21
6) Chuck Hummer:
Thanks for the info to date, but I need to hear from the others.

Mar05/85 09:59
7) Ron Kreh:
Officers of dredge McFarland are presently on 16/12 schedule which is required by negotiated labor agreement with MMP and MEBA. Unlicensed crew have elected to stay on 10/4 schedule. Reverting back to 10/4 schedule would cause significant morale problem with officers. McFarland works entire east coast, and present 16/12 schedule cuts personnel travel costs and travel time in half. OT savings of 16/12 are negligible, and this schedule does not effect FTE's. Regarding credit hour carryover, present carryover is already 24 hours per pay period to our knowledge.

Mar05/85 19:37
8) HOPMAN REDLINGER:
Compressed work week legislation. If NPD minimum fleet dredges had to revert back to a 10-4 schedule from the 8-6 schedule, about $250,000 in overtime would be required. There would also be an approximate 40% reduction in production, meaning that some 4 to 5 MCY of dredging would have to be done by other means at a cost of about $10 million (conservative rough estimate). Worse yet, some dredging might not get done. Equally important, the U.S. moorings could not provide shore side support to the dredges with only 4-day maintenance periods. Currently dredges work only 230 days annually and then go into seasonal tie-up with moorings crew in conjunction with ship's crew performing most of required maintenance. Another big factor, as adequately stated by Henry Schoor

and Ron Kreh, crew morale would be diminished to such a
degree that dredge officers and perhaps crew would find
employment elsewhere, putting the Corps in the untenable
position it was several years back without sufficient
dredge staffing. As the saying goes "they would abandon
ship like rats." Replacements would require training which
would further accentuate the costs of reverting back. On
the other hand, it would not have an appreciable effect on
FTE's.

Mar06/85 11:29
9) HOPMAN REDLINGER:
NPS will provide additional comments on subject matter
later today regarding hydrographic survey and field crews.

Mar06/85 15:57
10) BECHLY HEINEMAN:
5 of our hydro crews work 10-hour days, with FTE limits we
could not return to 8-hour days and get work done. Would
go to OT. Cost about $75,000/yr to get same work.

Mar06/85 17:36
11) Leonard Juhnke:
We will be into our third year of using a 5-4-9 work
schedule for our two hydro crews starting next week. In
1983 we only used this for two months, but realized a 2,300
cost savings and a productivity increase of about 10%. In
84 we went from March through October. Our savings were
limited due to a 50% increase in contract dredging.
Probably around 5,000. Did see a 51% reduction in sick
leave use as most people scheduled appointments on day off.
This year the crews will get the advantage of the day off
creating four long weekends. (At their pay and what they
have to put up with, it's the least we can do!!)

RESPOND, FORGET, OR PASS: p

DO NEXT?

As you can see from the above, a good deal of information
can be obtained in a short period of time. The information
was not really detailed cost analysis but an analysis of
the problem by each of the dredging managers and the impact
of the law on their operations. This sort of dialog is
where Confer II can pay for itself.

This explosion of information and information exchange has
its own set of problems to overcome. For example, in the
above Confer II session it took Chuck Hummer 5 days to
answer Adam. Chuck was out of town on business and did not
have a computer terminal with him. When managers are
required to travel, a means must be established to keep
them in touch with the systems and people in the
organization.

We now have briefcase, battery-powered computer terminals
on order. The actions that our senior managers fail to
take in a timely fashion cost money and time. The portable
computers will pay for themselves in a relatively short
period of time by keeping our high-priced managers in touch
with the organization and with the tools they need to
conduct business.

The Dredging Division of the Water Resources Support Center
has found a tool in Confer II that greatly accelerates the
exchange of information with the dredging managers in the
Corps of Engineers. To them the Confer II system may seem
a panacea; to others it's just Big Brother watching. The
truth probably lies somewhere in between.

In conclusion, this shift in the economy of the United
States from manufacturing to information and information
processing should not be regarded with fear. The use of
computers has drastically changed and will continue to
change the way we communicate with each other and
accomplish work in the future.

See you at the Do Next?

Optimizing Computer Aided Planning

Lynn Jeffrey Bernhard, PE[1]
Member ASCE

Abstract

Computer aided planning may fail if new or untried computer programs or new equipment is used when time is limited. Eleven leadership skills helped the Utah Projects Office, U.S. Bureau of Reclamation, use new equipment and programs meet critical deadlines when a major portion of the Central Utah Project was reformulated. These leadership skills helped create a positive environment where individual creativity and responsibility were broadly exercised.

Introduction

Computers--the mention of the word in today's planning, engineering, and business climate evokes images of "state-of-the-art technology" at the service the professional. It also harrows up memories of monumental failures of machines and programs to meet the needs of those whom they were intended to serve. New or unproven systems may spawn disasters when the results are most needed. More important than hardware predictability, however, is human ingenuity--that eternal quality which is so essential to productivity. Employee creativity is strongly influenced by 11 characteristics of successful leaders. Attention to detail and careful application of these leadership principles can significantly enhance the probability for success in using modern computer technology to plan water resource development projects.

Water resource planning managers, team leaders, and professionals have firsthand knowledge of the validity of "Murphy's Law" and its many corallaries. Water resources planning activities somewhat resemble the medium which they seek to control and use; in that, on the surface the flow of work appears smooth and orderly, yet like a stream plunging relentlessly towards the sea, planning activity, too, encounters rapids, where outside constraint or influence causes feverish releases of energy. When beset by such acceleration of the traditional planning process, managers often look to tools or methods which, while speeding up the end product, still allow for responsible professional analysis of the issues, mechanics, and constraints of the project.

Modern technology has provided a powerful tool which, when appropriately used, enables planners to accomplish the thorough analysis which they feel responsible to deliver. Before computers appeared in the planning scene, Murphy's Law worked at relatively slow

[1]M, ASCE; Chief, Engineering Branch, Bureau of Reclamation, P.O. Box 1338, Provo, Utah 84603

rates. "What may go wrong, will" occurred on a basis that could be charted on a calendar. Computers have changed this forever. Now "What may go wrong, will; MUCH FASTER" in the bane of those trying to apply computer technology to planning activities under pressure. New computer equipment or programs have a tendency to not perform well when they are most needed.

The Utah Projects Office (UPO) of the United States Department of the Interior faced a significant reformulation of the Central Utah Project early in the summer of 1984. UPO had just taken delivery of an on-site mini-computer system. Economic analysis of the preferred plan and shifts in estimated project hydroelectric power demands led to the decision to reconfigure a large number of project features to reflect the reduced hydroelectric generation capacity needed under the new guidelines. A schedule had been established earlier for the issuance of an environmental statement (ES) covering the original features. The decision was made to retain the original ES schedule, but revise the proposed plan. Activities needed to complete the task were scheduled using a precedence scheduling computer package called PROPLAN. The critical activities were clearly identified.

The first "no float" activity involved the revision of planning designs and cost estimates. The Engineering Branch completed their task 3 days early, without using any of the planned overtime work which had been allocated to them. The atmosphere was busy, but not crisis. The engineers and technicians in the Engineering Branch were all young. They made extensive use of the available computer resource. They completed their task early and, in fact, several took leave to take advantage of Utah's superbly beautiful Wasatch Mountains' summer weather. Other work units had similar experiences.

It was remarkable that a young staff could complete such a complex task and have time to go on vacation in the very midst of a major crisis. The work environment and management styles of the managers, supervisors, and employees were evaluated to determine what led to their group success. Their success was due, in large part, to a healthy work environment which encouraged personal creativity and performance. Eleven leadership principles, none really original or startling, were applied by all levels of management. Effective leadership, while it had no direct involvement with or use of computer resources, established a positive environment where professionals could integrate the manipulative and computational power of the modern computer with their personal expertise.

Each of these 11 skills will be discussed individually with application to the use of computers in water resources planning. The 11 skills are:

1. Knowing the resources of the group
2. Communication
3. Understanding the individual and group needs
4. Management's representing the group to others
5. Planning

6. Effective teaching and training
7. Evaluating performance
8. Controlling the group and its activities
9. Sharing leadership
10. Feedback and counseling
11. Management setting the example

Some of these elements were much more evident during the actual project reformulation phase. Management had built a foundation of trust, responsiveness, creativity, and employee skill by having earlier practiced the skills.

Each of these leadership skills is taught by corporate trainers, agency trainers, educational institutions, and an army of consultants. Alone, they are valuable, but practiced together they produce synergism—that most cherished attribute of any planning organization. It is difficult to practice one skill to the exclusion of the others. The value of their individual practice comes when they are interrelated in application.

Water resource planning in the Bureau of Reclamation is accomplished by interdisciplinary teams led by a team leader who has no line supervisory responsibility for the team members themselves. Traditional line and staff organization exists for administrative control, but the real planning work at the Utah Project Office is accomplished by the planning teams. Supervisors and managers create the environment that the professional staff function within.

Knowing the Resources of the Group

The manager or supervisor must know what he has available to meet his goals. Computers, but more importantly, those who use the computers must be known. In some organizations, computers are seen as fast adding and accounting machines of little use to the broader needs of water resource planners. When skills, knowledge, experience, interests, and abilities are understood, managers may make work assignments with reasonable certainty that the task will be completed.

Recent developments in the computer industry and its broad based popularity have made the populace in general, interested in computers. Salesmen and promoters have been known to promise computer and software performance that their products simply cannot attain under field conditions.

Comprehension of both human and electronic resources is the foundation of effective utilization of computers in planning. "Garbage in-Garbage out" is true. The quality of computer aided planning depends, in large measure, on the integrative creativity of those who use the machines. Managers need to have a strong foundation of fact so that their expectations for computer aided planning will be met.

Communication

Human behavaioralists stress the critical importance of effectual interpersonal communication. Water resource planning is an inter-disciplinary art. Computers add new dimensions to cross discipline interchange. Often computer support professionals lack exposure to the social, natural, and political sciences, resulting in ineffective com-munication with resource planners. It is incumbent on planning mana-gers and supervisors to be literate in computer terms and expressions, to have a general knowledge of what computers can and importantly, can-not do. Even more important is encouraging planning professionals and computer specialists to share ideas and concepts. Most vital, however, is the personal contact between the planning leaders and their colleagues. Not just "telling" and "order giving", but two-way com-munication with feedback. Extensive writings are available to help the manager improve his communication skills. They need to be continually honed to insure accurate interchanges.

Understanding Group and Individual Needs

Water resource plans are made by people--not computers. People have varying needs; much has been written by human behavioralists about the "hierarchy of needs"[2] and other models.[3] Computer aided planning requires synergistic performance from people. The manager must understand his unique mix of people and personalities so that optimum performance may be possible. Understanding needs is not analogous to catering to needs. The individual is part of the group. The planning team or office has overall goals, but the informed, sensitive manager can meet both the individuals needs and the group. The group and indi-vidual need, among many other things--security, adequate tools or equipment, understanding of group goals, personal fulfillment, oppor-tunities to grow professionally, healthy emotional climate, recogni-tion, and praise.

Representing the Group

Everyone has a boss. Everyone has peers. Managers represent their staff in many situations. Group credibility and even the group's self image are partly established by how their leader represents them to others. Rare is the planner who functions so independently that he/she is solely responsible for the final plan or study. Private consultants represent their planning group to clients and regulatory agencies. Governmental planners at all levels represent their groups to the public and other regulatory bodies. Accurate portrayal of group com-puter aided planning skills and lack of skill to outside groups is a key to establishing schedules and expected results.

Planning

Success in computer aided planning results from careful analysis of what is to be accomplished, the resources available, and available time. Planning for success in using computers is identical to other task planning processes. Constraints are delimited, resources identified, personnel and equipment allocated, goals written, estimates of time and cost prepared, responsibility and accountability defined, authority delegated, and performance reported.   Planning computer studies requires a working knowledge of true capabilities that exist within the organization. While an experienced computer aided planning team could develop a new ground water recharge model in short order, another group may flounder due to inadequate computer expertise or equipment. Unanticipated costs can quickly become astronomical. Key schedule dates can be missed. Careful, thorough planning depends on managerial leadership and example.

Effective Teaching and Training

While this skill may not seem germane, to highly skilled water resource planning professionals it is vitally important. True learning occurs in very few institutional training programs. The most effective teaching and training occurs when trainees can develop and maintain relationships with those who have skills and expertise. Mentors are needed to transfer computer skills effectively. Such mentors are best found among a trainees peer work group. Classroom or formalized training is valuable for overviews and presenting of large amounts of information. Applying new knowledge and skill in the work environment is a much surer way to encourage deep understanding of the power of computers. For example, no one understands water resource economic analysis better than those who actually do it. They quickly find applications for computer technology to their unique specialty. Learning by doing, combined with the teaching of skills and techniques is an exceptionally effective way to elevate planner's computer expertise.

Evaluating Performance

Performance evaluation is not only necessary, but is desirable. Computer aided planning is dynamic. Only by regular evaluation of goals, accomplishments, problems, and successes can the group grow and imporve. This provides the building blocks of future planning activities. Performance evaluation provides a time to build personal relationships and communicate goals. Computer aided planning activities can quickly get out of hand. If CAP isn't meeting the needs of the planning study, it needs to be reassessed and abandoned, if necessary. Constant monitoring, coupled with knowledge of reasonable expectations, will identify problems.

Controlling the Group

Another management skill that is contributatory to positive use of computers in the water resource planning process is controlling the efforts of group's members. The manager needs to know what is going on within his group. It is his place to redirect effort, reorganize working groups, or adjust direction. This skill relies on many of the previous skills. Computer aided planning can become misdirected if the manager doesn't control its overall activity. A word of caution: One cannot be intimately involved in every activity that occurs under their direction. Rather, the overall thrust of the group must be directed.

Sharing Leadership

Leadership styles vary from autocratic to reclusive. There are certainly situations which require autocratic leadership. But, planning professionals are generally self-directed and self-motivated. Simple delegation does not meet the needs of self-fulfillment which many planners feel. The group, when properly trained, can assume much of the responsibility traditionally held by supervisors. Managers cannot abrogate their authority and ultimate responsibility. Personal involvement in group decisions, communication of peer goals and constraints, and seeking feedback from the group establish the manager's role in allowing group members to share the group's leadership. Managers should participate in group decision making. A manager's responsibility for meeting schedules, legal conformity, budget, etc., cannot be shared. The manager, in these cases, serves as a restraint on shared leadership. A manager cannot hope to be master of all the skills needed to successfully use computers for water resources planning. He must rely on others for the actual expertise.

Feedback and Counseling

Seemingly unrelated to specific computer aided planning is another communication skill, feedback and counseling. Effective feedback encourages employees accountability for their own actions. Problems with worker performance can be corrected before they seriously impact the overall planning project. Managers can use these counseling/feedback sessions to add new ideas to the project analysis. Study approaches can be monitored. Importantly, effectiveness of computer modeling, engineering, and design efforts can be ascertained.

Example Setting

The most important of all these skills is example setting by the manager. Positive leadership example is easily followed by subordinates. They see the results of the attitudes and skills demonstrated by their leaders. Managers can set the example in using computers in planning work by identifying and using appropriate computer hardware and software in their own work. Office automation packages are readily available. Computer based scheduling is widely used in business. The manager need not become an expert user, but they should know the strengths and limitations of the data processing equipment available to them. Professional contacts, reading of current literature, acquisition of appropriate skills, and encouragement of subordinates creative application of computer technology to planning tasks are ways that a manager sets the example to his coworkers. Negative examples are also closely followed.

Each of these 11 skills can be practiced independent of the others. Synergy occurs when they are integrated into a management style and philosophy. Each skill complements others and in turn is complemented by others. Experience has shown that positive leadership prepares a climate where planners can apply modern computer technology to their fields of expertise.

Computers are a tool that modern science and technology has provided. We have the opportunity to significantly change the way we do our work. Computers are not a panacea for planning problems, rather they are a tool to be mastered. By freeing the professional from rote tasks, their minds can be loosed to practice creative problem solving.

Bibliography

1. Bloch, Arthur. Murphy's Laws and Other Reasons Why Things Go Wrong! Price/Stern/Sloan, 1981.

2. Maslow, Abraham H., Motivation and Personality, 2nd Edition, Harper and Row, Publishers, Incorporated, 1970.

3. MacGregor, Douglas, The Human Side of Enterprise, McGraw-Hill Book Company, 1960.

Computers: Water Resources Models in Latin America

Medardo Molina*

ABSTRACT

Ninety-six national institutions dealing with planning, irrigation,
water supply, and hydropower generation in twenty-six Latin American
and Caribbean countries were surveyed between February and April,
1984, to assess their status in computer and modeling technologies.
Some findings are:
   a) Eighty-five percent of the institutions utilize one or more
      computers. Of these: 17% are mainframe, 43% mini, and
      38% micro-computers.
   b) The computers are used for a wide variety of data processing,
      the most popular being statistical and rainfall/runoff analysis.
   c) Forty-six percent of the mathematical models in use were
      developed locally, while 26% originated in the U.S.A.
The main conclusion of the survey is that the Latin American and
Caribbean national authorities in water resources are aware that microcomputers and modeling can help them improve their jobs. But training and access to the most recent hardware and software sources is
urgently needed to accomplish that task.

1. Introduction

As is usually the case anywhere in the world, the water resources
in Latin America and the Caribbean region are not evenly distributed
in space or time. This situation makes it difficult to satisfy the water
needs of the 130 million people(1) who suffer frequent droughts and
floods that further their already weak economies.

In 1982 and 1983, for example, the "El Nino" phenomenon triggered
floods of one thousand years frequency in many parts of the region(3)
while concurrently, in other areas, a persistent drought was causing
misery and death to thousands of people.

There is nothing we can do to change the natural conditions. But
we can improve the management of this resource through a better

*Medardo Molina, Ph.D. Hydrology Consultant and former Regional
Adviser in Water Resources for the United Nations Economic Commis-
sion for Latin America, Santiago, Chile. 176 Elm Drive, Hollister,
California 95023.

understanding of the historic events, and it is here where computer
technology can come to our assistance.

However, it is important to realize that the application of new technology is almost never inexpensive or simple. Nor is it readily acceptable or rapidly applied. A new frame of mind, newly-trained personnel,
and the approval of the decision-makers are prerequisites for the success
of any new technology.

To discern, therefore, the actual status of computer technology in
this important region of the world, a survey was carried out in twenty-
six Latin American and Caribbean countries. The main findings of the
survey are:

   a) Computer technology is known and accepted in the technical
      and professional communities.
   b) There is adequate knowledge of computer modeling and use
      of mathematical models.
   c) For this technology to be effectively used, the countries
      urgently require training of engineers and other professionals
      in the development and operation of models, plus access to the
      most recent computer hardware and software.

2. Data Collection

   A special questionnaire was sent out to ninety-six water resources
authorities in twenty-six countries in Latin America and the Caribbean.
Thirty-three institutions from seventeen countries replied to the questionnaire between April and June of 1984. Table 1 shows the number of
institutions that replied per country. Table 2 shows the economic sectors in which the replying institutions develop their main activities.

Table 1

Country	Institutions Contacted	Institutions Replying	Percentage
Argentina	6	1	16.7
Bolivia	5	1	20.0
Brasil	6	1	16.7
Chile	2	1	50.0
Colombia	5	5	100.0
Costa Rica	5	2	40.0
Ecuador	8	2	25.0
El Salvador	6	2	33.3
Honduras	4	1	25.0
Mexico	4	2	50.0
Nicaragua	4	2	50.0
Panama	3	1	33.3
Peru	9	6	66.7
Dominican Republic	4	1	25.0

Table 1, continued

Country	Institutions Contacted	Institutions Replying	Percentage
Trinidad Tobago	2	1	50.0
Uruguay	6	2	33.3
Venezuela	2	2	100.0
Other countries	15	0	0.0
Totals	96	33	

Table 2.

Economic sector	Number	Percentage
Agriculture	13	17.6
Energy	9	12.1
Planning	16	21.6
Water Supply	13	17.6
Data collection and processing	11	14.8
Watershed Management	10	13.5
Industries	1	1.4
Others	1	1.4
Totals	74	100.0

3. Results

3.1 Use of Mathematical Models

Table 3 shows the different disciplines in which mathematical modeling is being applied. It can be observed that the most popular models are those for rainfall/runoff and statistical and probabilistic analysis.

Table 3.

Fields	Number of answers	Percentage
Hydraulic structures	11	8.8
Rainfall/runoff analysis	18	14.4
Droughts and Flooding	10	8.0
Statistics and Probability Analysis	22	17.6
Linear Programming	11	8.8
Operation of reservoirs	12	9.6
Groundwater	12	9.6
Watershed Management	12	9.6
Sediment Transport	8	6.4
Others not specified	9	7.2
Totals	125	100.0

3.2 Origin of Mathematical Models in Actual Use

It was considered important to know the sources of the mathematical models that are being used at present by the different institutions related to water resources in this region. Table 4 shows that 46.1% of models have been developed by the institution itself while 25.6% have been developed in the U.S.A.

Table 4.

Model Developed	Number of answers	Percentage
By institution itself	18	46.1
By other national institution	3	7.7
In the U.S.A.	10	25.6
In European countries	7	18.0
In other Latin American countries	0	0.0
In Israel	1	2.6
In socialist countries	0	0.0
Totals	39	100.0

3.3 Why Mathematical Models are Not Used

The institutions were also asked to state their reasons for not using a mathematical model when they thought they should. It is revealing to see in Table 5 that the only reason why nine of the institutions are not using any mathematical model at the moment of the study is lack of knowledge about the proper technology.

Table 5.

Reason	Times mentioned	Percentage
Don't know how to operate them	6	37.5
Don't know how to develop them	5	31.3
Don't know where to get them	4	25.0
Don't need them	0	0.0
No reason stated	1	6.2
Totals	16	100.0

3.4 About the Computers

The institutions were asked to itemize their computers, differentiating them by size and name of manufacturer. Table 6 shows the number of computers that are being used, indicating their RAM. It can be observed that there are slightly more minicomputers than micro-computers.

Table 6.

Size of Computer	Times mentioned	Percentage
Mainframe More than 1 MB of RAM	19	16. 7
Minicomputers 48 to 764 KB of RAM	52	45. 6
Micro-computers Up to 512 KB of RAM	43	37. 7
Totals	114	100. 0

Concerning the actual use of the computers, Table 7 shows that they are mostly used for Data Processing, with Management being the second most popular usage.

Table 7.

Activity	Numbers mentioned	Percentage
Management	19	31. 7
Word processing	8	13. 3
Data processing	28	46. 7
Others	5	8. 3
Totals	60	1 00. 0

The most popular use of Data Processing includes all the tasks related to the fields listed in Table 3. Personnel Management, the second most popular use, includes payroll and budgeting. Word Processing is not yet very popular.

The list of microcomputers in use includes known names such as Apple, IBM, Radio Shack TRS-80, and Hewlett-Packard, among others. Table 8 shows the number of each name brand in actual use in the Latin American/Caribbean region.

Table 8.

Name	Number
Radio Shack TRS-80	9
Hewlett-Packard	8
Cobra	8
Apple II	5
Wang	2
Texas Instruments	2
NCR	2
CROMENCO	2
Other names, one each	5
Total	43

3.5 Training and Personnel

The efficient use of any new technology requires personnel trained in its application. This is particularly true in computer technology, mainly because of its rapid and continuous development.

Table 9 shows the situation in Latin America and the Caribbean concerning training of the personnel in the use of computers. Table 10 indicates where the training actually took place. The fact that 32 out of 33 respondents feel the need for more training in programming and modeling is an obvious comment on both the quantity and quality of their present computer users.

Table 9.

Situation of Training	Yes	No	Total
Have trained personnel in computer programming	29	4	33
Have trained personnel in mathematical modeling	24	9	33
Would like updating and more training	32	1	33

Table 10.

Place of Training	Number	Percentage
Own country	27	51.9
Other Latin American country	7	13.6
U.S.A.	10	19.2
Socialist country	1	1.9
Europe, Occidental	6	11.5
Canada	1	1.9
Totals	52	100.0

4. General Projections and Conclusions

The following are qualitative projections based on the author's experience in the area and the replies to the questionnaires.

The interest in the use of computer technology by the different economic sectors involved in the use of water is reflected in Table 2. But at the present time the energy sector is by far the biggest user of computer technology. They have well-trained personnel, good computer facilities, and well-developed programs to handle their data.

Water supply services will require the most immediate assistance in computer technology. Their need is becoming urgent in view of the increasing demand for water from rapidly increasing Latin American populations, which, in turn, require improved efficiency in managing the service that computers can provide. Fortunately, at present, some monetary resources for this purpose are available: the International Water Supply and Sanitation Decade, sponsored by the United Nations(2), have attracted some funding, mainly from the World Bank.

There will be increasing need for software for irrigation management. Approximately 12.5 million acres (5 million hectares) of agricultural lands are irrigated in this region, and it is becoming clear that one way of augmenting the production is through better management of the water, which can now be attained with the help of computer technology.

It is not anticipated that the computer modeling use in different aspects of water management shown in Table 3 will change in the near future. But it is to be expected that linear programming will be increasingly applied as people learn that the best way to increase the amount of useful water is to manage it better.

The proportions of computer use shown in Table 6 will probably change rapidly and drastically in the near future. Many institutions have funds to acquire large numbers of micró-computers and establish national computer networks. Colombia and Peru are countries that have such a plan. (4)

The big countries, such as Brasil, Mexico, and Argentina, are more likely to develop their own software and even hardware, and thus they will become less dependent on other countries for their computer technology development.

All countries, however, are eager to receive technical assistance in this field. The countries most receptive and ready to assimilate this technology seem to be Chile, Peru, Ecuador, Colombia, Panama, and Venezuela.

There are difinitely countries where the introduction of intensive computer technology will not be speedy or easy. But if some international agency promotes and funds the introduction of this technology, the gap can be filled quickly and efficiently.

APPENDIX I. -- REFERENCES

1. Ceres, "Cada vez se gastan mas en armas, no tanto mas en producir alimentos," Vol. 15, No. 1, Jan.-Feb. 1982, p. 7.

2. Dieterich, Berndt, "Water Decade is not a Numbers Game," World Water, A special reprint of articles during 1982, p. 3.

3. Molina, M., "Analisis de la frecuencia de lluvias de 1982-1983 en Guayaquil, Ecuador," Informe Sobre las Inundaciones Producidas por el Fenomeno del Nino, Economic Commision for Latin America, Santiago, Chile, May, 1983.

4. Molina, M., "Ordenamiento de Recursos Hidricos y Modelos Matematicas en America Latina y el Caribe," presented at the Fourth National Hydrological Seminar, Lima, Peru, September 26 -30, 1983.

State-of-the-Art Pipe Network Optimization

Thomas M. Walski*, M. ASCE

Abstract

Within the next decade water distribution system optimization models should become everyday tools of practicing engineer. This paper examines existing models and discusses some of the hurdles that must be overcome for them to be widely accepted.

Introduction

People have been building water distribution systems for several hundred years. Customers in most parts of the developed world can be fairly certain that when they open their taps, water, under adequate pressure, will flow. No one, however, can say with certainty that any water distribution system is the least costly system that could have carried the water.

With the development of the high speed digital computer and powerful optimization techniques in the 1950's, it appeared to be only a matter of time before engineers could supply some simple data to a computer and the computer would determine the optimal pipe network. (Optimal in this paper will refer to least costly in terms of life cycle cost, although much of what is said also pertains to optimality in terms of reliability or minimizing only capital costs.) To this date, the problem of optimally sizing pipes in networks remains largely unsolved. It is not as if researchers have not been diligently working on the problem. Dozens of papers containing "solutions" to pipe network optimization problems have been prepared. However, one would indeed have to diligently search to find practicing engineers who actually use these optimization techniques to solve pipe network problems. Rules-of-thumb and trial-and-error remain the primary tools of choice for practicing engineers faced with the problem of selecting water distribution systems components.

In the early 1980's, pipe network optimization programs are in a position similar to that of network steady state simulation programs in the late 1960's. The mathematics of the problem have been addressed in theoretical papers and some programs have been written and, in a few instances, applied to real problems. However, pipe network optimization is not considered a standard engineering tool and user friendly programs are just becoming available.

---

* Research Civil Engineer, U. S. Army Engineer Waterways Experiment Station, Vicksburg, Miss. 39180.

The purpose of this paper is to summarize the state-of-the-art in pipe network optimization. This is done by first presenting a classification of problems followed by a brief description of work to date. Finally, the problems in developing a practical, general program for pipe network optimization are discussed.

Classification

Pipe network optimization problems can be classified in numerous ways. The two most meaningful classifications concern: 1. whether the flow distribution is initially fixed (fixed vs. variable flow pattern) and 2. whether the system's energy is provided by gravity or pumping (gravity vs. pumped systems).

Systems in which the flow distribution is initially fixed and only one constant head node (e.g. tank, pump) exists are fairly easy to handle because the flow pattern does not change when the diameter changes. Branched systems and long pipelines with occasional withdrawals (e.g. closed conduit irrigation systems and rural water systems) fall into this category.

Most water distribution systems, however, contain loops and multiple sources of supply, some of which may be constant head nodes while others are pumps. As a result the flow in any pipe is determined by the diameter in that pipe and the diameter of all other pipes in the network. Solving this type of problem is much more difficult because of interactions among pipe sizing decisions.

The approaches used also differ between gravity and pumped systems. In gravity systems, the least costly piping system will dissipate all excessive head thus keeping pipe size, and hence cost, to a minimum. In pumped systems, the available head is not fixed but can be altered by changing pump head with the associated changes in energy and pumping equipment costs.

Work to Date

Traditional Approach. The approach traditionally used by design engineers to size pipes for fairly complicated systems is to first construct and calibrate a mathematical model of the system. Future demands and emergency situations are then simulated using the model. This enables the engineer to identify problem areas in the system. To identify workable solutions, alternative pipes, pumps, tanks and valves are tested using the model. The costs for some of the better alternatives are then calculated to arrive at a recommended solution.

In this process the design engineer is generally armed with a few rules-of-thumb to arrive at a practicable solution. These include:

1. Velocities less than 8 ft/sec at peak flow;
2. Velocities on the order of 2 ft/sec at average flow;
3. Pressures between 60 and 80 psi under normal conditions;
4. Pressure at least 20 psi during fire conditions;
5. Diameters at least 6 in. for systems providing fire protection;

6. Diameters at least 2 in. for systems without fire protection;
7. Adequate pumps such that design flow can be delivered with one pump
    out of service;
8. No dead end mains.

Armed with a good model and the above rules, engineers have been
able to design workable distribution systems at reasonable cost.

Field Pattern-Gravity. The first work on optimizing gravity systems dates back to Camp (11). Cowan (17), Swamee, Kumar and Khanna (64)
Deb (19), Chiplunkar and Khanna (15) and Walski (66) presented methods
that rely essentially on classical, constrained optimization techniques--
in particular Lagrangian Multipliers. Canales-Ruiz (12) proposed a
method which relies on Pontryagin's Maximum Principle. The MAPS (Methodology for Areawide Planning Studies) (U. S. Army Corps of Engineers
(65)) and MAINS (Koh and Maidment (37)) computer programs use trial-and-
error techniques.

When the problem becomes sufficiently complicated, as is the case
for highly branched systems, classical optimization techniques and brute
force trial-and-error become unworkable. In those cases, linear programming (LP) can be used to select optimal pipe sizes. Actually, since
costs are a linear function only of length, it is the length of pipe of
a given diameter that is determined by the program. Karmeli, Gadish and
Meyers (33), Lai and Schaake (38), Gupta, Hussan and Cook (28), Calhoun
(10), Robinson and Austin (55) and Bhave (6) developed LP solutions for
systems with known flow patterns.

Oron and Karmeli (48) developed a method that combines generalized
geometric programming with a branch-and-bound technique to solve the
problem. Buras and Schweig (9), Liang (40), Sathaye and Hall (58) and
Kareliotis (32) used dynamic programming to optimize branched systems.
Kettler and Goulter (34) offered a method that accounts for reliability
of looped systems, but it is based on a fixed initial flow pattern.
Mandl (42) summarized available techniques for optimizing branched
systems.

Fixed Flow Pattern-Pumped. When pumping is allowed or required in
the system, optimization of pipe sizes can be viewed as a tradeoff
between capital and energy costs subject to head constraints. Babbitt
and Doland (4), Camp (11), Osborne and James (49), ASCE Committee on
Pipeline Planning (3), Dancs (18), Deb (21), Deb (22), and Walski (66)
have developed manual methods for finding optimal pipe sizes. The
PIPEOPT (Ainsworth (1)), MAPS (U. S. Army Corps of Engineers (65)) and
MAINS (Koh and Maidment (37)) programs use trial-and-error solutions to
arrive at optimal pipe size. Walski (66) also developed nomograms from
which it is possible to directly read pipe diameter given peak and average flow, energy cost, and construction cost index.

Pernold (51) presented a method for sizing pumped irrigation systems with varying demands based on heuristic rules. The approach of
Chiplunkar and Khanna (15) includes pumping cost in a Lagrangian formulation. Nolte (46) described several pipe optimization techniques used
in the chemical process industry.

In general, methods that rely solely on tradeoffs between capital and energy cost tend to predict smaller pipe sizes than customarily used. It is important that pipe sizes selected by such methods be checked to insure they are hydraulically feasible without requiring excessive initial heads.

Variable Flow Pattern. In most real systems, the flows in the pipes are not fixed beforehand but vary with the pipe sizes selected. Shamir (59, 60) summarized the approaches developed through the 1970's and Stephenson (62) gave procedures for applying some methods. de Neufville, Schaake and Stafford (24) discussed pipe optimization in a broader framework than simply minimizing cost.

Most of the methods used for solving problems with variable flow patterns involve first fixing the flow pattern and finding the optimal solution, then adjusting the flow pattern using a gradient search approach. Kally (31), Shamir (59), Alperovits and Shamir (2), Shamir (60), Quindry, Brill and Liebman (52, 53) and Mays (43) have suggested variations in this type of approach. Smith (61) combined random sampling and linear programming. Bhave (7) and Kikacheishvilli (36) also developed methods incorporating linear programming.

Other researchers have used a combination of non-linear programming techniques and heuristic algorithms. Pitchai (50) used a random sampling technique. Jacoby (29) used a gradient, random experience approach. Cembrowicz and Harrington (13) suggested using a combination of graph theory and heuristic rules while Lam (39) proposed what he called a "discrete gradient optimization."

Deb and Sarkar (23) proposed a method for determining pipe sizes based on equivalent pipes. Swamee and Khanna (64) pointed out that this method essentially fixes the hydraulic gradient. Deb (20) extended the equivalent pipe approach to determination of inlet heads. Watanatada (67) used a sequential, nonlinear programming technique. Rasmusen (54) used a gradient search based on critical node(s) in the system.

Bhave (5) proposed an iterative manual approach which is based on breaking the system into a system with fixed flows by fixing flow or diameter in "non-primary" links. Cenendese and Mele (14) used a heuristic procedure to determine optimal pipe sizes. Kher, Agarwal and Khanna (35) proposed an iterative method that uses the Univariate method to adjust diameters. Ormsbee and Contractor (47) used a modified Box-Complex optimization.

Gessler (26) and Gessler and Walski (27) used an efficient enumeration technique to identify not only optimal but several nearly optimal systems as well as taking into account pipe rehabilitation. Featherstone and El-Jumaily (25) fix a constant hydraulic gradient to optimize a network. Conbere and Jeppson (16) used a line search among discrete variables. Stoner Associates added a heuristic pipe selection technique to an existing network simulation model.

Rowell (56) and Rowell and Barnes (57) presented a two-step procedure for determining pipe layout as well as pipe sizes. Morgan and

Goulter (44, 45) used linear programming to determine optimal layout while Bhave and Lam (8) used "Steiner trees" to identify optimal layout for branched systems.

Problem Areas

The most common trait of the models mentioned above is that they are not available for engineers. Only the programs of Gessler and Walski (27) and Jeppson (30) are readily available for use by practicing engineers and well supported with user's guides and program documentation. These programs contain optimization techniques which are less elegant than many of the other techniques described above. In Jeppson's program, no formal optimization occurs, but pipes or pumps can be sized by specifying minimum pressures as well as demands at nodes. Why has much of the sophisticated technology described above not been transferred to practicing engineers?

A major problem is that optimizing water distribution systems is a difficult, if not impossible, problem to solve. None of the programs developed can solve real world optimization problems. In a discussion of the paper by Cenendese and Mele (14), Lischer (41) stated:

"In this writer's opinion, based on a lifetime of experience in the water supply field, the optimum design for most new systems, and for improvement of old systems, cannot be achieved by mathematical or computer exercise alone. Experienced judgement will be necessary to select the options and system operational methodology before computer techniques and network analysis are applied.

"To emphasize the complexity of the problem and not to misguide the naive into oversimplification, it is appropriate here to list some, and hopefully most, of the parameters entering into public water supply system design:

"1. Water usage and demand: (a) Pattern of water use for various types of customers; (b) location of customer demand; (c) fire flow requirements; and (d) future trends.

"2. Storage considerations: (a) Reserve; (b) peaking; (c) elevated storage; (d) ground storage, with pumping; and (e) site determination to best obtain optimum design of whole system.

"3. Minimum pressure requirements: (a) Residential areas; (b) high value districts; and (c) industrial areas.

"4. Population distribution: (a) Future trends.

"5. Topographic: (a) Need for separate pressure districts; (b) need for pressure reducing controls; and (c) available sites for storage.

"6. Reliability considerations: (a) Looping; (b) standby power for pumping operations; (c) limitations and cost of attended operations; (d) system size; (e) practicality, maintainability, and reliability of automatic controls; and (f) cost of storage.

"7. Pumping options: (a) Outdoor or housed; (b) vertical; (c) horizontal split case; (d) submersible; and (e) booster pumping.

"8. Pipe options: (a) Material, as affecting cost life and depreciation; (b) carrying capacity; (c) structural properties; (d) reliability; (e) means and ease of repair as affecting maintenance cost; and (f) cost.

"9. Economic consideration: (a) Value of money; (b) depreciation; (c) capital recovery; and (d) inflation or deflation effects.

"10. Energy options: (a) Electric; and (b) other power."

Other factors not mentioned by Lischer contribute to the complexity of the problem. For example, pipes are only available in specific discrete sizes. Most optimization methods assume the existence of continuously variables pipe sizes which are later rounded off.

Most of the models are oriented toward optimal pipe size selection but pipe size selection is only one facet (albeit a complicated one) of the overall water system design problem. Engineers must also select pumps and decide how to operate them, choose locations and settings for PRVs and determine tank heights and volumes. These decisions are tied closely with pipe sizing decisions.

Systems are not static, but rather grow over many years. None of the methods allow for staging of construction. The carrying capacity of existing systems can be increased by cleaning with or without cement mortar lining. Few programs consider this option. Few of the programs allow for realistic cost functions (i.e. costs expressed as a function of more than merely diameter).

Most of the methods proposed handle one or only a handful of loadings. Yet most systems must be able to operate over a fairly wide range of conditions. Fires may occur at many locations in the system; valves and pumps may malfunction; pipes may break. The number of conditions that must be considered for a thorough analysis can be staggering.

This does not mean that practicing engineers are doing any better than models in adequately addressing the problem today. However, in standard practice, overdesign and redundancy are commonly used to minimize the impact of uncertainty. Optimization methods result in cost savings by reducing redundancy and overdesign.

The engineer trying to optimize water systems is also faced with ambiguous design and performance criteria for the system. State standards usually contain criteria terms such as: "maintain 20 psi under all conditions," "peak velocities must be less than 10 (or 8) ft/sec" or "all pipes must be 6 in. or larger." When trying to enter data in to a computer program, the engineer realizes just how vague these performance criteria actually are. The engineer must decide: Are the tanks full, half-full, almost empty? Are all pumps running, one pump per station out, all pumps without standby power off? How large of a fire must be fought, or should there be several simultaneous fires? Should any of

the pipes be out of service? Should the water use be average day-
average hour, average day-peak hour, peak day-average hour, peak day-
peak hour? Should water use correspond to current year, 2000, 2030? If
10 engineers were asked to answer these questions, they would probably
give 10 different sets of answers. More precise methods for analyzing
water systems highlight the need for more precise performance criteria.

Summary

Because of the complexity of real systems, models which appear to
be attractive in journal articles tend to cough and sputter when fueled
with real data. The situation is only improving slowly since university
faculty members and students are rewarded for preparing and publishing
reports, not necessarily for producing programs that will be used by
practicing engineers. The challenge before the engineering profession
is to develop tools that can be used by practicing engineers to design
real systems.

References

1. Ainsworth, S. C., 1979, Water Pipeline Optimization Program, U. S.
   Dept. of Energy Conference on Energy Conservation, New
   Orleans.
2. Alperovits, E. and U. Shamir, 1977, Design of Optimal Water
   Distribution Systems, Water Resources Research, Vol. 13,
   No. 6, p. 885.
3. American Society of Civil Engineers, Committee on Pipeline Planning,
   1975, Pipeline Design for Water and Wastewater, ASCE, New York,
   NY.
4. Babbitt, H. E. and J. J. Doland, 1931, Water Supply Engineering,
   McGraw Hill, New York.
5. Bhave, P. R., 1978, Noncomputer Optimization of Single-Source
   Networks, J ASCE EED, Vol. 104, No. EE4, p. 799.
6. Bhave, P. R., 1979, Selecting Pipe Sizes in Network Optimization by
   LP, J ASCE HYD, Vol. 105, No. HY7, p. 1019.
7. Bhave, P. R., 1983, Optimization of Gravity Feed Water Distribution
   Systems, J ASCE EED, Vol. 109, No. EE1, p. 189.
8. Bhave, P. R., and C. F. Lam, 1983, Optimal Layout for Branching
   Distribution Networks, Journal of Transportation Engineering,
   ASCE, Vol. 109, No. 4, p. 534.
9. Buras, N. and Z. Schweig, 1969, Aqueduct Route Optimization by
   Dynamic Programming, J ASCE HYD, Vol. 95, No. HY5, p. 1615.
10. Calhoun, C. A., 1971, Optimization of Pipe Systems By Linear Pro-
    gramming, In. J. P. Tullis, Control of Flow In Closed Conduits,
    Colorado State University, Ft. Collins, Co.
11. Camp, T. R., 1939, Economic Pipe Sizes for Water Distribution
    Systems, Transactions ASCE, Vol. 104, p. 190.
12. Canales-Ruiz, R., 1980, Optimal Design of Gravity Flow Water Con-
    duits, J ASCE HYD, Vol. 106, No. HY9, p. 1489.
13. Cembrowicz, R. G. and J. J. Harrington, 1973, Capital Cost
    Minimization of Hydraulic Network, J ASCE HYD, Vol. 99,
    No. HY3, p. 431.
14. Cenendese, A. and P. Mele, 1978, Optimal Design of Water
    Distribution Networks, J ASCE HYD, Vol. 104, HY2, p. 237.

15. Chiplunkar, A. V. and P. Khanna, 1983, Optimal Design of Branched Water Distribution Systems, Journal of Environmental Engineering, Vol. 109, No. 3, p. 604.
16. Conbere, W. and R. W. Jeppson, 1984. Pipe Network Optimization under Time Varying Demands, ASCE Urban Water '84, Baltimore, MD.
17. Cowan, J., 1971, Checking Trunk Main Designs for Cost-Effectiveness, Water and Water Engineering, Vol, 75, No. 908, p. 385.
18. Dancs, L., 1977, Sizing Force Mains for Economy, Water and Sewage Works, Reference Number, R-127.
19. Deb, A. K., 1973, Least Cost Design of Water Main in Series, J ASCE EED, Vol. 99, No. EE3, p. 405.
20. Deb, A. K., 1976, Optimization of Water Distribution Network Systems, J ASCE EED, Vol. 102, No. EE4, p. 837.
21. Deb, A. K., 1978, Optimization in Design of Pumping Systems, J ASCE EED, Vol. 104, No. EE1, p. 127.
22. Deb, A. K., 1981, Optimal Energy Cost Design of a Pipeline, Journal of Pipelines, Vol. 1, p. 191.
23. Deb, A. K., and A. K. Sarkar, 1971, Optimization in Design of Hydraulic Network, J ASCE SAN, Vol. 97, No. SA2, p. 141.
24. de Neufville, R., J. Schaake and J. H. Stafford, 1971, Systems Analysis of Water Distribution Network, J ASCE SAN, Vol. 97, No. SA6, p. 825.
25. Featherstone, R. E. and K. K. El-Jumaily, 1983, Optimal Diameter Selection for Pipe Networks, ASCE Journal of Hydraulic Engineering, Vol. 109, No. 2, p. 221.
26. Gessler, J., 1982, Optimization of Pipe Networks, International Symposium on Urban Hydrology, Hydraulics and Sediment Control, University of Kentucky, Lexington, KY.
27. Gessler, J. and T. M. Walski, 1984, Selecting Optimal Strategy for Distribution System Expansion and Reinforcement, ASCE, Urban Water '84, Baltimore, MD.
28. Gupta, I., M. Z. Hassan, and J. Cook, 1969, Linear Programming Analysis of a Water Supply System, Trans. AIIE, Vol. 1, No. 1, p. 56.
29. Jacoby, S. L. S., 1968, Design of Optimal Hydraulic Networks, J ASCE HYD, Vol. 94, No. HY3, p. 641.
30. Jeppson, R. W., 1982, User Manual: Pipe Network Simulation Analysis Computer Program, Utah State University, Logan, Utah.
31. Kally, E., 1971, Automatic Planning of Least Cost Water Distribution Network, Water and Water Engineering, April, p. 148.
32. Kareliotis, S. J., 1984, Optimization of a Tree-Like Water-Supply System, J. of Hydrology, Vol. 68, p. 419.
33. Karmeli, D., Y. Gadish and S. Meyers, 1968, Design of Optimal Water Distribution Networks, J ASCE PL, Vol. 94, No. PL1, p. 1.
34. Kettler, A. J. and I. C. Goulter, 1983, Reliability Considerations in the Least Cost Design of Looped Water Distribution Systems, International Symposium on Urban Hydrology, Hydraulics and Sediment Control, University of Kentucky, Lexington, KY.
35. Kher, L. K., S. K. Agarwal and P. Khanna, 1979, Nonlinear Optimization of Water Supply Systems, J ASCE EED, Vol. 105, No. EE4, p. 781.

36. Kikacheishvili, G. E., 1984, Optimization of Hydraulic Parameters of a Pipeline System, Journal of Pipelines, Vol. 4, p. 31.
37. Koh, E. S. and D. R. Maidment, 1984, Microcomputer Programs for Designing Water Systems, J AWWA, Vol. 76, No. 7, p. 62.
38. Lai, D. and J. C. Schaake, 1969, Linear Programming and Dynamic Programming Applied to Water Distribution Network Design, MIT Hydrodynamics Lab Report 116, Cambridge, Mass.
39. Lam, C. F., 1973, Discrete Gradient Optimization of Water Systems, J ASCE HYD, Vol. 99, No. HY6, p. 863.
40. Liang, T, 1971, Design Conduit System by Dynamic Programming, J ASCE HYD, Vol. 97, No. HY3, p. 383.
41. Lischer, V. C., 1979, Discussion of Optimal Design of Water Distribution Networks (Cenendese and Mele), J ASCE HYD, Vol. 105, No. HY1, p. 113.
42. Mandl, C. E., 1981, A Survey of Mathematical Optimization Models and Algorithms for Designing and Expending Irrigation and Wastewater Networks, Water Resources Research, Vol. 17, No. 4, p. 769.
43. Mays, L., 1984, A Review and Evaluation of Reliability Concepts for Design and Evaluation of Water Distribution Systems, Draft Miscellaneous Paper, U. S. Army Engineer Waterways Experiment Station, Vicksburg, Miss.
44. Morgan, D. R. and I. C. Goulter, 1982, Least Cost Layout and Design of Looped Water Distribution Systems, International Symposium on Urban Hydrology, Hydraulics and Sediment Control, Lexington, KY, p. 65.
45. Morgan, D. R. and I. C. Goulter, 1985, Optimal Urban Water Distribution Design, accepted for Water Resources Research.
46. Nolte, C. B., 1979, Optimal Pipe Size Selection, Gulf Publishing, Houston, TX.
47. Ormsbee, L. and D. N. Contractor, 1981, Optimization of Hydraulic Networks, International Symposium on Urban Hydrology, Hydraulics and Sediment Control, Lexington, KY, p. 255.
48. Oron, G. and D. Karmeli, 1979, Procedure for Economic Evaluation of Water Networks Parameters, Water Resources Bulletin, Vol. 15, No. 4, p. 1050.
49. Osborne, J. M. and L. D. James, 1973, Marginal Economics Applied to Pipeline Design, J ASCE Transportation Division, Vol. 99, No. 3, p. 637.
50. Pitchai, R., 1966, A Model for Designing Water Distribution Pipe Networks, Ph.D. Thesis, Harvard Univ., Cambridge, Mass.
51. Pernold, R. P., 1974, Economic Pipe Sizing in Pumped Irrigation Systems, J ASCE IRR, Vol. 100, No. IR4, p. 425.
52. Quindry, G. E., E. D. Brill and J. C. Liebman, 1979, Water Distribution System Design Criteria, University of Illinois, ENG-79-2003.
53. Quindry, G. E., E. D. Brill and J. C. Liebman, 1981, Optimization of Looped Water Distribution Systems, J ASCE EED, Vol. 107, No. EE4, p. 665.
54. Rasmusen, H. J., 1976, Simplified Optimization of Water Supply Systems, J ASCE EED, Vol. 102, No. EE2, p. 313.
55. Robinson, R. B., and T. A. Austin, 1976, Cost Optimization of Rural Water Systems, J ASCE HYD, Vol. 102, No. HY8, p. 1119.

COMPUTER APPLICATIONS / WATER RESOURCES

56. Rowell, W. F., 1979, A Methodology for Optimal Design of Water
    Distribution Systems, Ph.D. Dissertation, Univ. of Texas,
    Austin, TX.
57. Rowell, W. F. and J. W. Barnes, 1982, Obtaining Layout of Water
    Distribution Systems, J ASCE HYD, Vol. 108, No. HY1, p. 137.
58. Sathaye, J. and W. A. Hall, 1976, Optimization of Design Capacity of
    an Aqueduct, J ASCE IRR, Vol. 102, No. IR3, p. 295.
59. Shamir, U., 1974, Optimal Design and Operation of Water Distribution
    Systems, Water Resources Research, Vol. 10, No. 1, p. 27.
60. Shamir, U., 1979, Optimization in Water Distribution Systems
    Engineering, Mathematical Programming, No. 11, p. 65.
61. Smith, D. V., 1966, Minimum Cost Design of Linearly Restrained Water
    Distribution Networks, M. S. Thesis, MIT, Cambridge, Mass.
62. Stephenson, D., 1976, Pipeline Design for Water Engineers, Elsevier
    Scientific Publ.
63. Swamee, P. K., V. Kumar, P. Khanna, 1973, Optimization of Dead End
    Water Distribution Systems, J ASCE EED, Vol. 99, No. EE2,
    p. 123.
64. Swamee, P. K. and P. Khanna, 1974, Equivalent Pipe Method for
    Optimizing Water Networks - Facts and Fallacies, J ASCE EED,
    Vol. 100, No. EE1, p. 93.
65. U. S. Army Corps of Engineers, 1980, Methodology for Areawide
    Planning Studies, Engineer Manual 1110-2-502, Washington, D. C.
66. Walski, T. M., 1984, Analysis of Water Distribution Systems, Van
    Nostrand - Reinhold, New York, NY.
67. Watanatada, T., 1973, Least-Cost Design of Water Distribution
    System, J ASCE HYD, Vol. 99, No. HY9, p. 1497.

Optimization of Looped Water Distribution Networks

E. Downey Brill, Jr., Jon C. Liebman, Members ASCE,
and Han-Lin Lee, Student Member ASCE*

The optimization algorithm developed by Quindry et al. (2,3) can be used to obtain a least cost pipe network for a looped water distribution system. A solution is obtained under steady state design conditions. Such a solution provides insights for a particular design problem. Although a solution does meet the looping requirements imposed, the level of redundancy provided is typically less than desired for municipal water systems. The algorithm will be used to explore the example problem to be provided by the session chairman, and the results will be presented at the conference.

Review of the Algorithm

Since a mathematical presentation of the algorithm has already been published (2,3), only an overview is provided here. It was shown by Lai and Schaake (1) in 1969 that linear programming can be used to obtain a least cost solution for a looped pipe network if the head at each node in the network is known. For a complex network, however, the heads at the nodes are not known in advance.

The proposed algorithm is based on a step where linear programming is used to solve the network problem for a particular set of values for the heads at the nodes. The set of values is then changed and another linear programming problem is solved. This procedure continues iteratively; a new set of values is determined and the new linear programming problem is solved. The important feature of the algorithm is that cost information is used in the determination of each new set of node heads. The procedure terminates when the set of values of the heads cannot be changed to produce a less costly solution.

The cost information that is used is the mathematical gradient of the network cost with respect to each of the fixed values of the heads at the nodes. Thus the fixed values are changed to produce a series of less costly solutions until an improved solution cannot be obtained.

The algorithm has been demonstrated using three example problems: 1) the New York system of supply tunnels considered by Lai and Shaake (21 links), 2) a residential distribution system with multiple demand patterns (55 links), and 3) a skeleton system for a medium sized city (253 links).

*Professor of Civil Engineering and Environmental Studies, Professor of Environmental Engineering, and University Fellow, respectively, Department of Civil Engineering, University of Illinois at Urbana-Champaign, 208 N. Romine St., Urbana, IL 61801.

Several of the more detailed points about the algorithm are:

1) Pipe diameters are the variables, and they are assumed to be continuous. Thus, to obtain a practical solution it is necessary to convert a length of pipe of an unavailable size to two segments of pipes of available sizes.

2) The cost function for each pipe must be approximated by a linear function; a fixed cost can be taken into account. If pipe diameters may vary widely, the linear approximation that is used may be adjusted as the algorithm proceeds.

3) The solution obtained at each iteration is hydraulically balanced.

4) Water demands are specified at nodes. Multiple sets of demands can be considered. One constraint is required in the model for each node for each demand.

5) The algorithm has been implemented using a FORTRAN program to calculate the mathematical gradients and to prepare the input for the APEX code that was used to solve each linear program on a Control Data Corporation CYBER 175 computer. (The input format is similar to the MPSX format used for numerous other codes.) The program is shown in reference (2), and it is available from the authors of that work. It is a research level program; although it is documented, it is not a user oriented code.

Limitations of the Algorithm

One limitation of the algorithm is that it may not produce a global optimum. This limitation is not very important if the method is used mainly to explore alternative designs and to identify potential improvements in designs obtained using other methods.

The main limitation of the procedure is that the solutions obtained are looped but often only to the extent required by the constraints. If only one set of water demands is imposed, a typical solution is really a branched network with the loops formed by the addition of pipes with the minimum diameter allowed by the mathematical formulation. Thus, such solutions obtained using the model do not reflect the real redundancy concerns that underlie the use of loops in conventional design practices. On the other hand, if multiple loadings are imposed while using the formulation, many of the loops may not contain a pipe with the minimum diameter. By selecting the multiple loadings carefully it may even be possible to obtain looped networks that do provide the desired type of redundancy to some extent.

Such mathematical procedures provide tools for gaining insights about a particular problem. They may suggest network links that may be desirable main trunks in a distribution system. Extra links can even be added to the mathematical formulation and given lower limits of zero. The algorithm could then be used to identify potentially attractive layouts. The use of the algorithm as a tool will be explored using the example problem to be provided by the session chairman, and the results will be presented.

Appendix I-References

1. Lai, D., and Schaake ,J., "Linear Programming and Dynamic Programming Applications to Water Distribution Network Design," Report 116, Department of Civil Engineering, Massachusetts Inst. of Tech., Cambridge, Mass., 1969.

2. Quindry, G., Brill, E. D., and Liebman, J., "Water Distribution System Design Criteria," Department of Civil Engineering, University of Illinois at Urbana-Champaign, Urbana, Ill., 1979.

3. Quindry, G., Brill, E. D., and Liebman, J., "Optimization of Looped Water Distribution Systems," Journal of the Environmental Engineering Division, ASCE, Vol. 107, No. EE4, Proc. Paper 16439, Aug., 1981, pp. 665-679.

Pipe Network Optimization by Enumeration

Johannes Gessler, M. ASCE

ABSTRACT: The paper describes a procedure for the optimization of pipe networks which is executed entirely in the discrete pipe size/cost domain. The technique is based on exhaustive enumeration. To keep the computational effort to a minimum two tests were built into the enumeration loop, one on cost and one on pipe sizes. Only if both tests are passed is it necessary to determine the pressure distribution for a pipe size combination. The proposed procedure guarantees the global minimum within the user specified constraints and can generate a queue of Pareto optimal solutions.

Introduction

Today pipe network optimization is about at the same point as was network simulation some ten years ago. Many practicing engineers insist that network optimization is not feasible. But the critique is about as well founded as the one heard in regard to pipe network simulation some time ago. Availability of user friendly software, which is reasonably flexible in regard to the constraints the engineer would like to impose, and which uses an optimization technique the engineer can comprehend, will lead to general acceptance of computer optimization.

The purpose of an optimization program can only be to guide the engineer toward a solution; it is not to provide the final solution. Every optimization program requires the specification of constraints. The user will need to experiment with various sets of constraints, to compare potential solutions, and to incorporate into the final solution aspects which cannot be phrased as constraints for the optimization. An optimization program will help to perform the first step toward finding a final solution.

Needs for Optimization

It is rare that very large and complex networks are designed in one step. It is much more typical that only the pipes of a relatively minor addition to a network need to be sized. For instance the main supply grid of an existing city water distribution system is given. New developments, covering perhaps an area of a square mile, require the sizing of the main grid in the area to be developed. Somewhere around 10 to 15 miles of pipes need to be sized. Cost of the part of the system which is to be sized may be in the range of a few million dollars. The sizing of the pipes within the subdivisions is typically not part of such an optimization.

Associate Professor, Department of Civil Engineering, Colorado State University, Fort Collins, CO 80522

A second example of needs for pipe network optimization is the improvement of an existing distribution system. Due to increased per capita water usage, or due to the continuous addition of more and more subdivisions to an existing grid, pressure conditions in a network may become unsatisfactory. It is desired to reinforce the existing main grid to meet the projected needs. An interesting alternative to adding new pipes to the main grid may be the cleaning and possibly lining of existing pipes. Typical project cost may start around the one million dollar range and may reach tens of millions of dollars.

Gessler (2) discussed several reasons why engineers may think optimization is not necessary. Here the New York City water supply tunnels may serve as an example to illustrate how essential optimization may be. The optimization by Lai and Schaak (4) lead to total system cost of 73.3 million dollars for the required improvements. The optimization by Quindry et al (5) reduced this figure (using the same demands and minimum pressure requirements) to 63.6 million dollars. Gessler (2) showed that there was indeed a technically feasible solution for 41.2 million dollars (all amounts in 1969 dollars). There are even less expensive solutions, yet the additional savings are relatively minor and operational considerations (redundancy) make the solutions less attractive. The fact that engineers overlooked significantly less expensive solutions points out how unreliable the intuition is in regard to recognizing an optimal solution and how non-trivial the optimization process must be.

Reasons which Make Optimization Difficult

There is a number of reasons which cause difficulties in the optimization procedures. Some are listed here.

* The pipe size variable is discrete. Many standard optimization procedures require that the variable to be selected be continuous. A simple rounding off to the nearest available pipe sizes can lead to solutions which are not optimal or which may not meet the requirements.
* The cost function is discrete. Because of the arbitrary character of this function, mathematical approximations are difficult. Convenient approximations over small ranges of sizes can lead to entirely wrong answers.
* The cost function of looped pipe networks may have several local minima. The value of the cost function at these minima can differ significantly from each other.
* The optimization must be carried out under more than one loading pattern because the pressure requirements for various loading patterns may differ from each other. This may make it difficult to say a priori which loading pattern controls the solution.
* If pumping cost are part of the optimization such cost can only be determined if the pump head and pump discharge are known, that is the pressure distribution in the system must be known.
* Pipe cleaning as an alternative to adding new pipes as part of a system reinforcement poses difficulties because this approach is conceptionally different from the problem of pipe sizing.

The above list may be incomplete. What causes difficulties also depends on the particular optimization procedure employed. The list includes items which are of concern in most optimization methods. The last two items, related to pumping cost and pipe cleaning respectively, may be of lesser concern, depending on the kind of systems to be optimized.

Requirements for Optimization Programs

These requirements are closely related to the above list of aspects causing difficulties in the optimization. They are listed roughly in the order of importance as viewed by this author.

* Pipe sizes must be treated as discrete variables.
* The algorithm should guarantee the global minimum within a set of user specified constraints.
* No restrictions should be imposed on the unit cost function for the discrete sizes. It can be assumed that the cost function always increases with increasing pipe size.
* The optimization procedure must be able to guarantee that the solution meets all requirements for more than one loading pattern.
* The user should be able to decide at what points in the system a pipe size can be changed.
* The procedure should be able to account for pumping cost.
* The algorithm should be able to consider cleaning of existing pipes as an alternative to adding new pipes.

An additional set of requirements for an optimization procedure relates to the amount of control the user retains over the design. It is desirable for the user to control to some degree which pipes become part of the major conveyance system. The user should be able to prevent the program from offering solutions which show an apparently 'random' selection of pipe sizes without displaying a clear pattern of major conveyance lines. The discrete character of the pipe size variable can indeed lead to such undesirable solutions.

Finally it is desirable that the algorithm provides not only a single solution but a list of alternative, Pareto optimal solutions. It is not uncommon that just a slight increase in total cost can generate a significantly better pressure distribution, or a minor relaxation of the pressure requirement can result in very significant savings.

Optimization by Exhaustive Enumeration

Most gradient search techniques operate with the pipe size as a continuous variable. After an optimal solution is found the program needs to search for the nearby least expensive discrete solution which meets the requirements. This procedure requires an exhaustive search in the neighborhood of the local or, hopefully, global minimum. Because the final solution in the discrete space will in general not coincide with this global minimum, it is possible that the least expensive solution with discrete pipe sizes in the vicinity of the global minimum is more expensive than the least expensive solution with discrete pipe sizes in the vicinity of a local minimum. Since exhaustive search in the discrete pipe diameter space is a major component of any optimization routine which uses continuous pipe sizes in the first part of the algorithm, it is logical to investigate the possibility of using exhaustive search exclusively.

The feasibility of such exhaustive search hinges on two major aspects:

* Because the pressure distribution must be evaluated many times, the algorithm used to calculate the distribution must be most efficient.
* The program must be able to recognize 'obviously inferior' pipe size combinations without the need of computing the pressure distribution.

Gessler (2) discussed the importance of an efficient algorithm. Because pressure and its accuracy are of primary concern, the most efficient algorithm is based on a node method. Such an algorithm was described by Gessler (1).

The second item above relates to the fact that in its most general formulation such an exhaustive search is NP-hard, that is to say that computer time increases exponentially with system size. This observation deserves two comments.

First, the fact that an algorithm is NP-hard does not automatically exclude it from consideration as a useful tool. It may simply limit its use to 'relatively small' systems. In the opening paragraph it was pointed out that it is rarely necessary to optimize very complex systems. The fact that such an exhaustive search resulted in finding a solution which saved about $ 22 millions dollars or about 34% relative to the previously best known solution (1), may serve as proof that such a technique can serve as a valuable tool.

Second, for practical reasons it may be undesirable to pose the problem in its most general formulation in which each pipe is sized individually. Such a formulation can lead to solutions which do not display a clear conveyance concept. The lack of such a concept can only result in great difficulties in daily system operation. It may be preferable to identify groups of pipes (in series or in parallel) which all will be assigned the same diameter in the final solution. In most systems, even if they are quite complex, it seems to be possible to group the pipes to be sized such that one needs not more than some 6 to 10 groups. Also it is quite possible to limit the range of candidate pipe sizes in each group to a relatively small number, say some 4 to 6 sizes (including perhaps the possibility of eliminating a group or cleaning pipes parallel to a group instead of adding the new pipes). If there is in deed an upper bound for the number of groups and number of candidate pipe sizes in each group the problem is no longer NP-hard, and computer time increases only with system size (number of nodes) to some power less than two (if the algorithm for calculating the pressure distribution accounts for sparseness in the coefficient matrix of the node equations.)

Description of the Algorithm

A similar algorithm was previously described by Gessler (2) and

Gessler and Walski (3). A number of refinements have increased the efficiency considerably.

Data Input. The user will need to identify all pipes to be sized. This list may include all pipes of the system when optimizing a new system or can be limited to only those pipes to be added to an existing system. Each of the pipes to be sized must be assigned to a group. All pipes in the same group will be assigned the same pipe size. For each of the groups a list of candidate pipe sizes needs to be specified. This list may include elimination of the group as an alternative and/or cleaning of the old pipes which run parallel to the new pipes. In addition the user will need to identify which cost function should be used for each pipe. The program has several cost functions on file, representing various conditions related to construction cost. For instance one cost function may represent typical downtown conditions; another one can represent suburban conditions where the pipe is very deep in the ground; etc. The pipes within one and the same group can be assigned to different cost function. In a final set of data the user enters the required output at all nodes and the pressure which needs to be maintained. If necessary, such data can be specified for a number of different loading patterns (e.g. for the testing of various fire flow locations.)

The program will then enumerate all possible combinations of pipe sizes. A schematic flow chart of the procedure is given in Fig. 1.

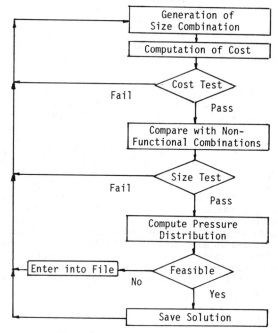

Figure 1. Schematic Flow Chart

Cost Test. For each pipe size combination the program will first calculate the total cost (excluding pumping cost). If the construction cost is already more than the total cost of a previously found and functional solution, the program will disregard this combination and proceed with the next one.

Size Test. During the enumeration process the program maintains a file of pipe size combinations which failed to meet the pressure requirements. It will not be necessary to calculate the pressure distribution for a combination in which all sizes are equal or less than the sizes of the corresponding pipes in a combination stored in this file because it could not meet pressure requirements either.

Size combinations which are less expensive than the so far best solution and which cannot be excluded in the size test, require computation of the pressure distribution. The pressure distribution is calculated for each of the loading patterns. The accuracy to which the pressure distribution is calculated depends on how close the pressures are to the required minimum. It is usually sufficient to carry out only 2 or 3 iterations.

Non-Functional Solution. As soon as a pressure of sufficient accuracy is encountered which falls below the minimum required at the node, pressure computations can be terminated. In this case the combination is entered into the file of non-functional combinations and the program proceeds with the next size combination.

New Best Solution. If the pressure requirement is met in all combinations (and there are no pumps present) the algorithm has found a solution better than any other one previously encountered. It is stored as the new best solution and the program proceeds with the next size combination. If there are pumps present, the present worth of the pumping cost is added to the construction cost. If the total cost is more than the cost of the so far best solution the combination is disregarded and the next size combination is tested. If the total cost is less than the total cost of the so far best solution the solution is stored as the new best solution.

The procedure continues until all combinations have been enumerated. It is clear that for the constraints specified the final best solution guarantees the global minimum in the cost function.

Cost and Size Tests

The efficiency of this optimization procedure depends heavily on the efficiency of the cost and size test. It is therefore important to find early in the optimization procedure a functional and inexpensive solution. Even if the size combination is not optimal it will be effective in eliminating a large number of combinations from consideration. The program combines the search for such an inexpensive and functional solution with the search performed for various size tests explained in the next paragraph.

In order to reduce the total number of possible combinations the program will test whether the smallest pipe size in each group can meet the pressure requirement when combined with the maximum sizes of all other groups. It is also advantageous to initialize the file of non-functional combinations. In order to have these combinations as effective as possible in screening out other combinations it is beneficial to have one group at its maximum size while all other sizes are at a smaller size. The searches performed for these tests, especially for the second one, locating non-functional solutions, will encounter relatively inexpensive, functional solutions which will be useful in the cost test.

Pareto Optimal Solutions

A queue of Pareto optimal solutions has the characteristic that no size combinations can be found which will provide higher pressure at less cost for any of these combinations. The function of minimum pressure vs system cost for Pareto optimal is continuously increasing. The program allows the user to specify two parameters relative to this queue. A percentage of total system cost will test and retain size combinations which are within that percentage from the presently best solution, even though they are more expensive than the present best solution. A pressure tolerance is also specified such that solutions are saved even if they fail the pressure test, but are within this tolerance from the required minimum pressure. The resulting list of alternative solutions will be extremely useful in the search for a final solution.

Example

The following example illustrates the procedure. The layout of the system is sketched in Fig. 2. The solid lines represent the present

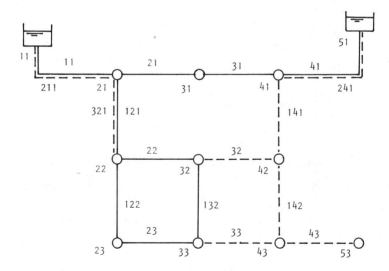

Figure 2. Network for Example.

system. The dashed lines represent the system expansion to be sized in order to meet pressure requirements under three loading patterns. Group 1 includes pipes 211 and 321. They are in parallel to lines 11 and 121 both of which have relatively low Hazen-Williams coefficients. Therefore cleaning of these two pipes is an alternative to be considered instead of adding these two pipes. The same is true for group 2 which includes pipe 241. Both groups, 1 and 2 are to be considered for elimination since the optimal solution will most likely need only one of these addition. The remaining pipes are to be sized, and no other lines should be eliminated. It is assumed that the cost of providing water from one or the other source is the same. The system data are provided in Table 1.

Table 1. System Data

Node Data

Node No.	Elev. Ft.	Output Gpm	
11	1200.0		Reservoir
21	1050.0	160.	
22	980.0	240.	
23	950.0	160.	
31	1070.0	160.	
32	970.0	300.	
33	950.0	240.	
41	1090.0	0.	
42	960.0	300.	
43	960.0	300.	
51	1120.0		Tank Height: 100.0 Ft.
53	950.0	200.	

Pipe Data

Pipe No	B Node	E Node	Diam. In.	Length Ft.	Coef
11	11	21	14.0	15840.0	75.
21	21	31	10.0	5280.0	80.
22	22	32	8.0	5280.0	100.
23	23	33	8.0	5280.0	100.
31	31	41	10.0	5280.0	80.
32	32	42	12.0	5280.0	120.
33	33	43	12.0	5280.0	120.
41	41	51	10.0	21120.0	80.
43	43	53	12.0	5280.0	120.
121	21	22	10.0	5280.0	80.
122	22	23	10.0	5280.0	80.
132	32	33	4.0	5280.0	100.
141	41	42	12.0	5280.0	120.
142	42	43	12.0	5280.0	120.
211	11	21	12.0	15840.0	120.
241	41	51	12.0	21120.0	120.
321	21	22	12.0	5280.0	120.

The cost functions for the new pipes and for cleaning of the old pipes are given in Table 2 as cost functions 1 and 2 respectively. A summary of the optimization parameters appears in Table 3. The program

Table 2. Cost Functions

	Price Functions	
Size	1	2
6	15.1	14.5
8	19.3	15.7
10	28.9	16.8
12	40.5	17.7
14	52.1	18.5
16	59.4	19.2

will then enumerate 405 combinations out of the total of 900 possible combinations. 495 combinations are eliminated because in group 5 the 6" size can be eliminated and in group 2 pipe elimination and cleaning can be eliminated. By the time the program has carried out the search for pipe size eliminations it has initialized the file for combinations which are not functional with the 5 combinations listed in Table 4. And

Table 3. Optimization Parameters

Group #	Pipes in Group		Candidate Pipe Sizes					
1	211	321	E	C	12	14	16	(E=Elimination)
2	241		E	C	12	14	16	(C=Cleaning)
3	141	142	8	10	12			
4	32	33	6	8	10			
5	43		6	8	10	12		

Loading Patterns

Pattern #	Load Min. Press. 1		Load Min. Press. 2		Load Min. Press. 3	
Node #						
21	200.	40.0	200.	20.0	200.	20.0
22	300.	50.0	300.	20.0	300.	20.0
23	200.	50.0	200.	20.0	200.	20.0
31	200.	25.0	200.	20.0	200.	20.0
32	300.	50.0	1300.	15.0	300.	20.0
33	300.	50.0	300.	20.0	300.	20.0
41	0.	25.0	0.	20.0	0.	20.0
42	300.	50.0	300.	20.0	300.	20.0
43	300.	50.0	300.	20.0	300.	20.0
53	200.	50.0	200.	20.0	800.	15.0

the program has as the so far best solution the combination E, 16", 12",10", and 12" at cost of $ 2,201,232. In this example the exhaustive enumeration procedure excludes 81% of the combinations in the cost test, and 13% are eliminated in the size test. This will leave 6% of the 405 combinations for which the pressure distribution needs to be evaluated. The optimum solution has the following pipe sizes:

Group #	1	2	3	4	5
Pipe Size	E	14	12	8	8

at a total cost of $ 1,833,744.- . The minimum pressure is 2.1 psi above the required minimum. The program was instructed not to produce a queue of Pareto optimal solutions.

Table 4. Initial Entries in File for Non-Functional Solutions.

Group #	1	2	3	4	5
Sizes	12	12	8	6	12
	12	12	8	10	8
	C	12	12	6	8
	12	16	8	6	8
	16	12	8	6	8

If the program is requested to provide a queue of Pareto optimal solutions it offers the following alternatives if the cost factor is set at 5% and the pressure tolerance is set at 5 psi.

Group #	1	2	3	4	5	Min. Pressure psi	Cost $
E	16	12	10	12		13.4	2,201,232
E	16	12	8	12		13.1	2,099,856
E	16	10	10	12		10.1	2,078,736
E	14	12	8	10		2.1	1,884,432

The minimum pressure refers to the smallest pressure difference between actual pressure and required pressure at any node in any loading pattern. There is no negative value in the minimum pressure column, indicating that the search did not find a combination which failed the pressure requirement, yet which would have been within 5 psi from the required pressure. With the cost and pressure margins relatively large, the program needed to balance 22% of all combinations, in order to generate the Pareto optimal solutions.

Conclusion

The proposed procedure may lack mathematical elegance. But it provides a great deal of flexibility. It guarantees the global minimum in the discrete pipe diameter/cost space. And it offers a set of alternative solutions which are Pareto optimal. The program also allows for easy incorporation of additional considerations, like maximum velocities, or cost of providing water at different supply points.

REFERENCES

1 Gessler, J., 1981, Analysis of Pipe Networks, Chapter 4 in Closed Conduit Flow, edited by M. H. Chaudhry and V. Yevjevich, WRP.
2 Gessler, J., 1982, Optimization of Pipe Networks, International Symposium on Urban Hydrology, Hydraulics and Sediment Control, University of Kentucky, Lexington, KY.
3 Gessler, J. and T. M. Walski, 1984, Selecting Optimal Strategy for Distribution System Expansion and Reinforcement, ASCE, Urban Water '84, Baltimore, MD.
4 Lai, D. and J. C. Schaake, 1969, Linear Programming and Dynamic Programming Applications to Water Distribution Network Design, Report 116, Department of Civil Engineering, MIT, Cambridge, MA.
5 Quindry, G. E., E. D. Brill and J. C. Liebman, 1981, Optimization of Looped Water Distribution Systems, J. Environmental Engineering Division ASCE, Vol. 107, No. EE4.

Water Distribution Design with Multiple Demands

D.R. Morgan[1]
I.C. Goulter, A.M. ASCE[2]

An iterative procedure for the layout and design of new looped water distribution systems is presented . The procedure is also applicable to the expansion of existing systems. The approach consists of a linear programming formulation linked to a network solver. A wide range of demand pattern and pipe failure combinations can be handled explicitly by the approach. Applications of the model to different types of problems encountered in water distribution design are discussed.

Introduction

A major weakness in many of the available optimization approaches for pipe network design is that they tend to design what Templeman (6) has described as inflexible systems. In his discussion of Quindry et al. (4), Templeman asserted that optimization has a tendency to eliminate redundancy by removing all spare capacity not required by a specific design loadings. Templeman then suggested that flexibility to serve fire fighting demands at all nodes must be incorporated in the design criteria.

Most of the models described in previous studies consider only one demand pattern and therefore tend to converge on quasi-branched systems with minimum size redundant pipes connecting the end nodes. A few of the models recognized the flexibility issue by considering more than one demand pattern. However, in these cases only a few of the many possible demand patterns were able to be analyzed, a condition that falls far short of Templeman's recommendation of a separate demand pattern for a fire flow at each node. The inability to handle this type of flexibility is more than an academic concern. It is perhaps one of the primary reasons practising engineers are uncomfortable with fully utilizing the available methods in design.

The model described in the following sections is directed towards the joint consideration of multiple demand patterns and pipe failures

[1]MacLaren Engineers, 640-5 Donald Street, Winnipeg, Manitoba R3L 2T4, Canada.

[2]Dept. of Civil Engineering, University of Manitoba, Winnipeg, Manitoba, R3T 2N2, Canada.

in both the layout and design of new systems and the expansion of existing systems.

Model Description

The approach itself is based upon a linear programming formulation linked to a network solver. A complete theoretical description of the approach is given in Morgan and Coulter (3). This discussion will therefore concentrate on the significant features of the technique and give a descriptive summary of some of the theory behind the approach.

Features of the Technique: The technique was developed to address the following specific points.

1. The system must deliver a certain flow at a specified pressure to any node in the system when one of the key pipes in the system is not functioning. This implies that at least two independent and adequate paths from a source must be provided.

2. The system must deliver severe fire flow demands at adequate pressures. While these fire flow demands occur infrequently throughout the system, they may, however, be the limiting factor in the design of the system.

3. The methods should be efficient enough to be applied to large systems.

4. The techniques used to solve the problem should be widely available.

5. The method should be applicable to expansion of existing systems as well as design of new systems.

6. The method should incorporate a realistic cost function, preferably using standard unit costs as given by suppliers, i.e., cost per length.

The major innovation of this technique is its ability to handle efficiently as many demand or loading patterns as there are links within the system. This ability is a direct response to the recommendation of Templeman that design criteria incorporate a flow pattern for a fire flow demand at each node. With such a feature the model represents a significant improvement over many of the previous models, e.g., Schaake and Lai (5), Alperovits and Shamir (1), and Quindry et al. (4).

Furthermore, the technique permits a different failed pipe to be associated with each demand pattern so that the redundancy of the system can be considered implicitly. The flexible way in which the failed pipe to be associated with each demand pattern is chosen permits the selection of the most critical link as the failure candidate for that load pattern.

The complete specification of the head loss constraint set required to ensure that all nodes have adequate pressures under all loading patterns makes solution by a linear programming formulation unrealistic. The constraint set is therefore reduced to a manageable size using a technique described in detail in Morgan and Goulter (3). In essence the reduction technique requires the specification of a critical node for each loading pattern. Head loss constraints are developed for the critical node associated with each loading pattern. After solution by the linear program, the pressures at all nodes are checked and the necessary adjustments made to the linear programming formulation. This process is described in more detail under the section on application of the model.

The way in which the constraints for the wide range of demand patterns to be considered are reduced to a manageable size, together with the way in which the link which a failure is considered for a given flow pattern is selected, requires that the approach be classified as heuristic. However, experience with the approach has shown that it does converge upon a 'reasonable pragmatic' optimum.

This approach is easily adapted to analysis of expansion or upgrading of existing systems. While this is not the primary task for which the model was developed, it does demonstrate its flexibility and usefulness while providing another basis for comparison with a number of earlier studies. The extension of the model to analysis of existing systems is described in more detail in a later section.

Application of the Model to Design of New Systems

The model itself is divided into two distinct stages; a pipe diameter modification stage, and a network solving stage. The procedure begins with the design engineer selecting an initial design which should contain 'deliberately' oversized pipes. The initial design should also include all possible candidate links, i.e., all the realistic node to node connections. The object at this point is not to design as low a cost of solution as possible but to specify as many link options as possible.

The next step is to develop as many loading conditions as possible. The maximum number of loading conditions that can be considered simultaneously during the optimization depends on the size and complexity of the problem and is equal to the maximum number of candidate links in the system. These loading conditions include peak daily demand, fire flow requirements and times when major pipes are under repair. Each combination of these events constitutes a single design loading condition. Morgan and Goulter (3) describe the application of the model to a problem with 37 design loadings.

The flow pattern assumed with each loading pattern is determined for the assumed layout using the network solver. Assuming that the flows in each link are constant for each loading pattern, head loss constraints are developed for each of the 'critical' nodes. The pipe diameters are then selectively increased or decreased by the linear program to reduce the overall system cost while maintaining adequate pressures at the 'critical' nodes under the loading combinations.

The flows in the network must now be balanced in order to conform to the new pipe configuration determined by the linear program. This flow modification step is required as the hydraulic consistency head constraints, i.e., the constraints requiring the head losses around each loop to sum algebraically to 0.0, are dropped as part of the heuristic reduction of the size of the head loss constraints. The new flow pattern determined by the network solver is then returned to the linear program and the pipe modification step repeated using the previous linear program solution as the 'assumed' or 'initial' design. As the model progresses through each iteration the magnitudes of the changes in diameters (and therefore the flow corrections) become smaller. When these changes become insignificant in terms of effects upon the overall system cost, the model is considered to have converged upon a solution.

An important feature of the whole technique is that the decision variable is the selection not of the length of a particular diameter but rather the length of existing diameter that should be replaced by an equivalent length of smaller or larger diameter pipe, without violating any of the head constraints. This 'replacement' or 'modification' as opposed to 'selection' type of decision variable not only permits the model to design new systems and expand existing systems, but it also permits, without any additional complexity, the inclusion of pipe rehabilitation as part of network upgrading or expansion. This issue is described in more detail later in the paper.

Removal of 'Inefficient' Pipes

As it is described above the model is not capable of completely eliminating inefficient pipes from the complete set of candidate or potential links. The removal of inefficient pipes is performed as follows.

As stated earlier the initial pipe layout should contain as many possible pipe connections or links as possible. As the engineer develops an optimal solution many of these links can be removed at substantial savings without jeopardizing overall system reliability. These pipes can be identified by their relatively low contribution to the carrying capacity of the system. The relative magnitude of the contribution of a link to the overall carrying capacity of the system is defined by the use of a 'weighting' factor which is calculated as follows.

For a given loading condition the percentage of the total demand at the 'critical' node that is carried by each pipe in the system is calculated using a simple algorithm described in Appendix A of Morgan and Goulter (3). These percentages are determined for every pipe under each of the loading conditions. Pipes which are found never to carry a significant portion of the demand at any node under any of the loading conditions are given a low 'weighting'. In more specific terms, the weighting for each pipe is set equal to the largest flow percentage identified for that pipe under any flow condition. The links with the lowest weighting are candidates for removal from the network as they can be eliminated without significantly lowering pressures are degrading overall system performance.

The flows within the system are then redistributed on the basis of the new network and the linear program run again. If the new solution, with the inefficient pipe removed, is less expensive than the previous solution, then it becomes the new 'base' solution. If it is more expensive than the previous solution, it is dropped and the previous solution with its links and the corresponding flow distribution is returned to the pipe modification stage as discussed earlier. The general form of the linkage between the network solver and the linear program pipe modification stage is shown in Figure 1.

Extension of Model for Analysis of Expansion or Upgrading of Existing Systems

While the model was developed primarily for analysis of new systems it is, however, easily extended to the analysis of existing systems. The design engineer selects suitable locations for reinforcement of pipes (i.e., installation of pipe parallel to existing pipes) and installation of new connecting pipes. As with new systems these pipes are 'deliberately' oversized in the initial iteration. The 'existing' pipe diameters which constitute the 'initial' pipe configuration for the procedure, are assigned zero cost per unit length. The cost of the system must therefore increase if the existing pipe diameter is 'replaced' by either a smaller or larger diamter. It is obvious, however, that the model will not select a smaller pipe, as such a selection would both increase cost and reduce capacity.

Other than this relatively simple modification the procedure operates in the same fashion as for the layout and design of new systems. Morgan and Goulter (3) have shown that use of the model in this way produces, in a relatively efficient manner, a very good solution to the New York Tunnels problem used in previous studies (4,5).

Discussion of Model Capabilities Relative to the General Objectives of a Network Distribution Model

In his review of the current state of water distribution network optimization Walski (7) asserts that none of the programs currently available can really 'solve' real world optimization problems. While this issue is of concern, it is unrealistic to expect a single model, used in isolation to be able to provide all the answers to all the question. Each model has its own strengths and weaknesses. In evaluating models the appropriate question should perhaps be "If a program is used as a design tool, does it help to design an effective system at a lower cost?" Using this philosophy many, if not all, optimization approaches have some use. However, the number of

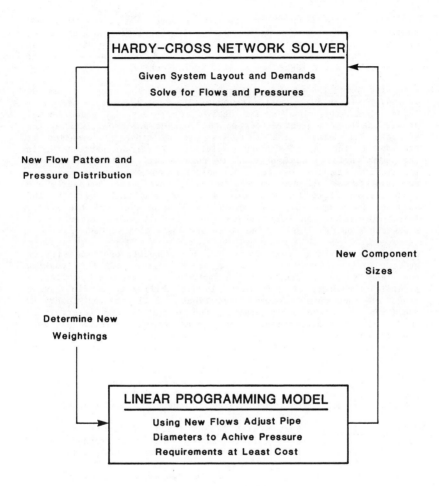

Figure 1. Linkage Between the Network Solver and Linear Program (Source: Ref. 3)

important parameters that a model can address and the ease in which these parameters are handled, does provide one means of assessing the relative usefulness of a particular approach.

The primary issues for which this model has been developed, namely multiple demand patterns, pipe failures, layout and design of new systems, and expansion of existing systems, have been discussed in detail earlier. This section reviews how the model can be used to address some of the issues enumerated by Lischer (2).

Effective Reduction of Demand Requirements: Water usage and demand, including individual customer and fire requirements, are very important in the planning and design of systems. A reduction of demand can have a great effect on the cost of a system. One of the strengths of linear programming is the additional information it provides in the way of the dual solution. As linear programming is the optimization technique used in this model, information on the sensitivity of the cost of the solution to changes in pressure requirements at each node is available. However since pressures are dependent on flows implicit information on the sensitivity of the solution to changes in flow demands is also provided by the model. This information can help locate the nodes at which water demand reduction should be implemented to reduce costs efficiently.

Reservoirs: Although this model does not directly optimize size of storage reservoirs, operation of reservoirs used for peaking requirements can be handled by the approach. As mentioned earlier, a significant feature of this model is its ability to handle a wide range of independent loading conditions. Inclusion of reservoir operation is achieved by considering the node at which a reservoir is to be located as a demand node during some loading condition and as a supply node during day peak loading conditions. The differences between the conditions when the reservoir is supplying flows and when it is being filled will be reflected directly in the flow patterns associated with those loading conditions. Additional checks external to the model are, however, necessary to ensure that the reservoir has sufficient time to be filled during the off-peak hours. The cost of the reservoir must also be calculated outside of the model proper.

Reliability of the System with Broken Pipes: Reliability of the system is explicitly considered through the wide range loading conditions that can be handled by the model. Each loading pattern can be developed on the basis of one or more major pipes being out of order. The specific pipes which are chosen to be out of order can vary with each loading condition.

Pumping: The consideration of pumping requires that the present value energy cost of maintaining a certain pumping pressure over the life of the system be determined. The model should be run until the trade-offs between pumping pressure and total pumping (capital and energy) costs are determined. The cost of the pipe network in terms of the pumping pressures can then be compared to the pumping costs and the overall optimum point identified.

Pipe Rehabilitation: Pipe rehabilitation is an important option in the upgrading in of an existing system. Consideration of this option can be handled with only slight modifications to the existing model. Since the Hazen-Williams friction coefficient is assumed constant or standard for all pipes in the network, the existing 'deteriorated' pipe is represented by a 'new' pipe of the same length with an equivalent smaller diameter. This new equivalent diameter is allocated such that the head loss through the 'new' pipe with the standard Hazen-Williams coefficient is the same as the head loss for that same flow through the existing deteriorated pipe with its larger Hazen-Williams coefficient. Then, as in the basic upgrading model, the existing diameter is assigned a zero cost per unit length. The next largest pipe in the set of candidate pipe is the rehabilitated existing pipe and it is assigned a cost per unit length corresponding to cost of rehabilitation per unit length. A separate set of candidate diameters and corresponding prices is thus defined for each link in the system.

Construction Staging: The staging of construction is an important consideration in the economic design of a system. The pipes in the second stage of a construction, perhaps several years in the future, have a different present value than those installed at the present time. The model can be modified to allow for pipes of the same diameter to have different costs depending upon when they are staged to be installed. The system can be modelled for all construction stages by allowing a set of loading patterns for each stage. If a group of pipes is not installed during a given loading condition those pipes are considered 'broken' for that loading. In this way these 'future' pipes will remain in the solution at their future 'discounted' values without being selected to contribute (at an artificially low cost) to the required flow capacity in the earlier stages of development.

Summary

The model represents an efficient approach for layout and design of new systems and expansion of existing water distribution systems under multiple demand patterns. The loading conditions used can incorporate both variation in demand with the location of the fire flows and the simultaneous occurrence of broken or failed pipes. The model can be extended to consider both pipe rehabilitation and construction staging without any additional complexity. Pumps and reservoirs can be handled by approach but, as with many other models, their consideration requires iterative use of the overall approach.

Appendix - References

1.   Alperovits, E. and Shamir, U., "Design of Optimal Water Distribution Networks", Water Resources Research, Vol. 13, No. 6, Dec. 1977, pp. 885-900.

2.   Lischer, V.C., "Discussion of 'Optimal Design of Water Distribution Networks' by Cenedese and Mele", Journal of the Hydraulic Division, ASCE, Vol. 105, No. HY1, Jan. 1979, p. 113.

3.   Morgan, D.R., and Goulter, I.C., "Optimal Urban Water Distribution Design", to be published in Water Resources Research. .

4.   Quindry, G., Brill, E.D., and Liebman, J.C., "Optimization of Looped Water Distribution Systems", Journal of the Environmental Engineering Division, ASCE, Vol. 107, No. EE4, Aug. 1981, pp. 665-679.

5.   Schaake, J.C., and Lai, D., Linear Programming and Dynamic Programming Application to Water Distribution Network Design, Hydrodynamics Laboratory, Massachusetts Institute of Technology, July 1969, Report No. 116.

6.   Templeman, A.B., "Discussion of 'Optimization of Looped Water Distribution Systems' by Quindry et al.", Journal of the Environmental Engineering Division, ASCE, Vol. 108, No. EE3, June 1982, pp. 509-602.

7.   Walski, T.M., "State-of-the-Art Water Distribution Pipe Network Optimization", Proceedings of the ASCE Speciality Conference "Computer Applications in Water Resources", June 11-15, 1985, Buffalo, New York.

A Review of Artificial Intelligence

Richard N. Palmer,[1] A.M. ASCE

ABSTRACT: This paper presents a brief history and overview of the field of artificial intelligence (AI), describes the architecture of an expert system, and discusses the logic procedures used in their development. The paper also discusses programming techniques and programming languages developed for AI. Successful applications of AI and expert systems are given, including two developed for water resources. An argument is presented for the use of AI techniques in water resource applications and the parallels between the development of AI and developments in the use of computers in water resouces are made.
KEYWORDS: Artificial intelligence, Expert systems, Water resources, Computer application, Decision making, HYDRO

Introduction

The purpose of this paper is to provide a brief history and overview of the fields of artificial intelligence (AI) and expert systems and to explore their potential application to problems in the field of water resources. The paper begins with several definitions of artificial intelligence, emphasizing the breadth of the field. The concept of computers "thinking" is introduced and a classic test for such behavior is reviewed. A brief history of AI is then presented with a categorization of problem areas to which it has been successfully applied. The architecture of expert systems, a subset of AI is then presented with a description of predicate calculus, which is used as a formal logic, and search procedures, which are used to limit the range of solutions investigated. Languages that have been developed for the implementation of AI techniques are discussed together with a description of computer software available for the development of AI and expert system solutions. Four examples of expert systems are reviewed, two which are extremely successful and two which make direct application to water resources. AI is then contrasted to computer techniques that are typically applied in Civil Engineering systems and the applicability of AI discussed. Finally, the future of AI techniques in Civil Engineering and water resources is discussed.

Definitions of Artificial Intelligence

Because the field of AI is new it is appropriate to begin with a simple definition. However, in review of the AI literature, it becomes

---

1. Assistant Professor, Department of Civil Engineering, University of Washington, Seattle, Washington, 98195

obvious that no simple definition exists. Rich (8) defines AI as the
process of, "How to make computers do things at which, at the moment,
people are better at." Winston (17) suggests that AI has two goals.
"The primary goal of Artificial Intelligence is to
make machines smarter. The secondary goals of Artificial Intelligence
are to understand what intelligence is ... and to make machines more
useful." Barr and Feigenbaum (1) define AI as the "part of computer
science that is concerned with designing intelligent computer systems,
that is, systems that exhibit the characteristics that we associate with
intelligence in human behavior such as understanding languages,
learning, reasoning, solving problems, and so on. These experimental
systems include programs that 1) solve some hard problems in chemistry,
biology, geology, engineering, and medicine at human-expert levels of
performance, 2) manipulate robotic devices to perform some useful,
repetitive, sensory motor tasks, and 3) answer questions posed in simple
dialects of English (or French, Japanese or any other natural
language)." What is suggested by these definitions is that computers
and computer programs will be used in an entirely different fashion than
before; that is, they will assume attributes that in the past we have
associated only with human cognitive processes.

Central to any discussion of AI is the fundamental question, "Can
a machine think?" This question has been correctly answered both in the
affirmative and the negative, depending upon the definitions selected
for machine and think. Turing (15), in his seminal paper on computing
machinery and intelligence, stated that this question "was too
meaningless to be answered" and proposed instead an experiment known as
the "Imitation Game." This game is played with a man, a women, and an
interrogator who is kept apart from the other two. The purpose of the
game is to determine if the interrogator can, through a series of
questions posed over a teletype (terminal), determine which unseen
individual is a man and which is a women. If the woman is replaced by a
computer, and the interrogator is unable to discern which is the man and
which is the machine with a greater frequency than before, Turing
considers the machine to have won the game. In addition, he suggests
that the machine has demonstrated many of those qualities that we
associate with the process of thinking. He suggested, some thirty five
years ago, that "by the end of the century the use of words and general
educated opinion will have altered so much that one will be able to
speak of machines thinking without expecting to be contradicted."

A piece of evidence supporting the proposition that computers
cannot and will not be able to think is the opinion that a computer
"simply does what it is told to do and no more. Surely such activity
can not be considered thinking." Simon (12) suggests that such a
statement is "intuitively obvious, indubitably true, and supports none
of the implications that are commonly drawn from it." He suggests that
people think because of their biological endowment and their
interactions with their environment. "If a computer thinks, learns, and
creates, it will be by virtue of a program that endows it with these
capabilities. Clearly this will not be a program - any more than the
human's is - that calls for highly stereotyped and repetitive behavior
indepedent of the stimuli coming from the environment and the tasks to
be completed. It will be a program that makes the system's behavior
highly conditional on the task environment - on the task goals and on

the clues extracted from the environment that indicate whether progress
is being made toward these goals. It will be a program that analyzes,
by some means, its own performance, diagnoses its failures, and makes
changes that enhance its future effectiveness."

If these suggestions appear to be unrealistic, one has only to
turn to recent developments to see the fruits of the efforts made by
these early pioneers. Computer programs have been developed that
perform tasks which, by most measures, exhibit powers of reasoning. One
example, reported by Schank (10), concerns a program designed to read
newspaper articles, determine their relevence to specific researchers,
and summarize their contents. The summarizations are not based upon
"key words" but rather upon "key concepts." The program is designed to
draw inferences rather than to simply condense.

What does the field of AI and the techniques it has developed
hold for water resource engineers? The answer is, a great deal. Much
of what is accomplished in Civil Engineering, especially water resource
engineering, is based upon past experiences, both successes and
failures. Sriram et al. (13) suggest that "Civil Engineering consists
of subfields where knowledge is largely empirical and heuristic" and
that it "takes many years to gain expertise in these subfields." A
primary research effort in AI has been how to best capture the expertise
of individuals and to translate it into a context that can be understood
by others and effectively applied to new problems. Any tool that can
aid in the transferal of expertise to the novice is of value. In
addition, in the application of AI techniques, problems are approached
in a different manner than that typically used in water resource
engineering. One of the results of the techniques used in AI is that
the analyst is often more likely to discover surprises and
idiosyncrasies of the system under investigation than if other
techniques are used. Finally, AI techniques attempt to model decision
making as a human activity, rather than as mathematical operations.
This shift in emphasis is more likely to result in solutions that
represent actual decision making than the techniques traditionly used by
water resource engineers. We will return to the question of the
relevence of AI in water resources at the conclusion of this paper.

History and Areas of Application

The development of AI has been attributed to developments in two
fields, mathematical logic and symbol processing. Researchers such as
Bertrand Russell (9) developed mathematical logic to illustrate that
reasoning could be formalized in a relatively simple framework.
Advances in the field of symbolics and computations provided means by
which mathematical logic could be executed on computers. With the
availability of these tools, researchers began to discover areas of
application. In the initial phase of AI research emphasis was directed
towards general laws of reasoning. This was followed by a search for
theories of knowledge representation and the development of narrow
domains of specialized knowledge.

In a tongue in cheek history, Winston (17) described the history
of AI in five stages, Prehistory (before 1960), Dawn (1960 - 1965), the
Dark Ages (1965 - 1970), the Renaissance (1970 - 1975), and the era of

Partnerships (1975 and beyond). Prehistory is defined to be that period
of time in which people wished to work on a computational approach to
understanding intelligence and decision making but had no computers.
During the Dawn, computers became available and people began to predict
that computers would soon be as intelligent as people. Although the
Dawn did have success stories, some of which will be described below,
the predictions made in the Dawn led to the Dark Ages. During this
period, the true level of difficulties that faced researchers became
apparent. During the Renaissance, several highly successful AI programs
received attention and once again interest increased. This increased
interest has lead to the Era of Partnerships in which alliances were
made not only between groups of researchers, such as between computer
scientists, linguists, and psychologists, but also between researchers
and entrepreneurs.

Currently, AI has been successfully applied to a wide variety of
fields. Barr and Feigenbaum (1) have categorized these areas as: 1)
Problem Solving - games such as chess and backgammon but includes any
problem requiring the ability to look ahead, to search, and to do
problem reduction, 2) Logical Reasoning - primarily mathematical proofs,
algebraic reductions, and manipulations, 3) Language - understanding
natural languages, human voice, and translation, 4) Programming -
developing automatic programs that write programs based upon
descriptions of requirements, 5) Learning - developing systems that
exhibit explicit cognitive behavior, 6) Expertise - knowledge
engineering in which an expert's knowledge and a data base are used to
arrive at a solution, and 7) Robotics and Computer Vision - instructions
to machines to make them perform repetitive tasks.

AI techniques can be considered to differ from other forms of data
processing more familiar to water resource engineers in that it deals
with symbolic represention, symbolic logic, and heuristic search. Waltz
(16) suggests that "one of the constant themes of artificial
intelligence has been how to best explore the range of possible actions
in the pursuit of well defined goals. In most artificial intelligence
programs heuristic principals, or informal rules of thumb, are
incorporated so that the most promising actions are selected for future
examination in the search and less promising ones are eliminated from
full scale consideration." Numerical values and mathematical
manipulations may not be considered in the solution to a problem but
rather are replaced by more generic symbols (linguistic expressions) and
symbolic logic. Specific techniques have been developed for each of the
seven areas mentioned above. Although all of these areas of application
are fascinating, detailed discussion here will be limited to that area
most closely related to water resource engineering applications, expert
systems. This area of AI will be discussed in detail below.

Architecture of Expert Systems

An initial goal of AI was to develop a formal problem solving
theory which, when coupled with extremely powerful computers, would
produce superhuman powers of problem solving. Known as general purpose
problem solvers, these techniques proved to be poor at solving specific
problems of significant complexity (6). Recognizing the limitations of
these general problem solvers, researchers pursued work in more defined

and narrow applications. From these efforts came the development of
expert systems, also noted as knowledge base engineering. This field is
defined as that which "investigates methods and techniques for
constructing man-machine systems with specialized problem-solving
expertise. Expertise consists of knowledge about particular domains,
understanding of domain problems, and skill at solving these problems"
(4). This field has focused on the use of knowledge itself rather than
on formal reasoning methods as was earlier AI research. Hayes-Roth et
al. (4) have suggested three reasons for this emphasis: 1) Most of the
difficult and interesting problems do not have completely tractable
algorithmic solutions because of the complex situations from which they
arise, 2) Human experts do often achieve outstanding performance because
they are knowledgeable. If a machine can be made to embody this
knowledge, then it should also be able to perform well, and 3) Knowledge
has intrinsic value. Extracting it from experts and making it available
for others provides an efficient use of knowledge as a limited resource.
Expert systems differ from other types of AI approaches in several ways.
Most importantly, expert systems attempt to separate knowlege from
reasoning and maintain this separation throughout the problem. Another
important characteristic of expert systems is their transparency. The
rules and knowledge for a conclusion are made evident to the user so
that they may determine whether or not they concur with the path by
which the conclusion is made.

Fundamental to the development of expert systems, or knowledge
engineering, are two concepts; search procedures and symbols and their
manipulation through predicate calculus. Search procedures are those
algorithms that limit the universe of potential solutions that must be
investigated. Simon (12) suggests that symbols can be defined as
"physical patterns (e.g., chalk marks on a blackboard) that can occur as
components of symbol structures (sometimes called expressions)." Simon
also suggests that "a physical symbol system is a machine that, as it
moves through time, produces an evolving collection of symbol
structures." To manipulate these symbols and symbol structures a formal
logic is needed and the logic chosen is that of predicate calculus.

Predicate calculus is a formal language of symbol structures that
can be used for representation on a computer (14). Essential to the
calculus is a precise syntax. Symbol structures are written to describe
items or individuals and predicates to describe their relationship.
Stefik et al. (14) propose the following example: Suppose three blocks
(A, B, and C) sit on a table. Block B rests on Block C. Blocks A and C
rest directly on the table top, denoted by D, which is supported by
table legs F and G. One can easily develop functional connectives to
describe the locational relationships of these objects. For example if
TOP-OF is defined to be a functinal symbol, then (TOP-OF D) denotes on
the table. Expressions and formulae can be combined through the use of
connectives. Examples of such connectives include "©" for the
conjunction and, "v" for the disjunction or, and − for implication.
The formulae "Either block A is on table D or it is on block B" can be
expressed as: ON (AD) v ON (AB).

By utilizing predicate calculus and imbedded parentheses for
qualification, much more complex operations can be generated. What
makes the formality of predicate calculus attractive is the strength of

the inferences that can be derived from it. Let ALL be a functional that means "all elements of." ABOVE can then be defined as:

$$(ALL(x)(ALL(y))((ON\ x\ y\ )\ -\ (ABOVE\ x\ y\ ))))$$

or "If x is on y, then x is above y."

Inferences are drawn using predicate calculus by examining the paths that lead to conclusions. Two methods exist for this procedure. "Forward chaining," or data directed search, is defined as the process of going from established facts and proceeding to a specific goal. Unfortunately, one can not determine which of the established facts are necessary to reach the goal and superfluous information becomes a difficulty. "Backward chaining," or goal directed search, is defined as beginning with a hypothesis and, using a rule set, examining facts to determine if the hypothesis can be supported. These state-space problems are familiar to water resource engineers acquainted with dynamic programming. AI researchers have considered solving the graphs that result in a variety of ways (14). In most situations the combinatorial size of the problem makes blind searches that require exhaustive enumeration infeasible. Often, the range of the problem must be reduced by applying simple rules of thumb that represent locally optimal advances toward an objective.

Throughout its development, an expert system can be considered to consist of five components: an expert, a knowledge engineer, a data base, an inference engine, and a user. From the expert a series of operational rules are derived. This is done by the aid of a knowledge engineer or by a computer program developed specifically for this purpose. The rules derived from the expert and any available supplemental knowledge are placed into the data base. Access to the data base, manipulation of the data base, and solution heuristics are contained in the inference engine. In an ideal system, a potential user can execute the expert system, gaining insight into their particular interest with a minimum of assistance.

Languages of Artificial Intelligence

Although other computer languages, such as Fortran or Pascal, could be modified to address the specific needs of AI, several specialized languages have been developed that deal directly with predicate calculus and symbolics. In addition, these languages have typically been interactive to allow ease in the development and use and possess a flexible structure to facilitate both recursion and parallel decomposition of problems (8).

The first AI computer language was developed by McCarthy (5) for mathematical functions in the late 1950's. LISt Processing (LISP) treats both data and procedures as list which make it possible to integrate declaritives and procedural knowledge into a single structure. The most natural control structure in the language is recursion, which is very appropriate for most problem solving. A family of functions exist that operate on the lists of the problem. A serious drawback to LISP is that no standard form has been adapted and standard functions and features vary from one version to another. A popular dialect of

LISP is known as INTERLISP. This language has a variety of additional
features that makes program development and debugging much easier than
in traditional LISP. In addition, it features a tree processing
structure that allows for co-processing of programs.

In addition to these primary languages, a number of others have
appeared. SAIL was developed as a COBOL derivative and is most useful
in those settings in which more traditional computing is required.
PROLOG is a language based upon production rules. Rules are written to
prove relationships and the program's interpreter tries to find proofs
of the truth of each specific relationship. Other languages developed
include PLANNER and KRL. The characteristics of each are described by
Rich (8). Hardware and software have been designed specifically for use
in AI. Most notable among the software is KS 300 designed by
Teknowledge, Inc. for the XEROX 1100 series and M.1 for the IBM PC. VAX
operational software is also available. This is an area in which new
software and hardware is being introduced at a rapid pace.

Application of Expert Systems

Table 1 presents a list of computer programs developed from the
application of AI and expert systems techniques. As the table
indicates, AI has found application in a wide variety of fields. Four
of the programs listed in the table will be discussed here. Two
programs, MYCIN and PROSPECTOR, are discussed because they represent
programs that have receive significant recognition as being successful.
Two others are presented because they are directly related to water
resources.

Table 1

Science	Medicine	Education	Automatic Programming
TERIRESIAS	MYCIN	SCHOLAR	PSI
DENDRAL	CASNET	WHO	CHI
CRYSALIS	PRESENT ILLNESS	SOPHIE	SATE
MACSYMA	PROGRAM	WEST	PROGRAMMER
SRI CBC	DIGITALIS THEORY	WUMPUS	APPRENTICE
PROSPECTOR	ADVISOR	GUIDON	PECOS
HYDRO	IRIS	BUGGY	DEDALUS
	EXPERT	EXCHECK	NLPQ
			LIBRA

MYCIN (11) is the best known example of an expert system. It was
developed to give expert advice in the identification of bacterial
diseases. Knowledge is represented in the form of production rules
involving certainty factors which are incorporated into the program in a
form similar, but not identical, to probabilities. The logic used in
MYCIN is backward chaining, reasoning backwards to clinical data from
its goal of finding significant disease causing bacteria. Rich (8)
presents the following example of the rules incorporated into the data
base:

    If: (1) the stain of the organism is gram positive, and
        (2) the morphology of the organism is coccus, and

```
          (3) the growth conformation is clumps,
     Then there is suggestive evidence (0.7) that the identity of the
     organism is staphylococcus.
```

The LISP interpretation of this statement is:

```
     PREMISE: ($AND (SAME CNTXT GRAM GRAMPOS)
                    (SAME CNTXT MORPH COCCUS)
                    (SAME SNTXT CONFORM CLUMPS)
     ACTION:  (CONCLUDE CNTXT IDENT STAPHYLOCOCCUS TALLY .7)
```

MYCIN has been extensively tested and shown to produce results similar to those obtained from physicians given the same clinical data.

PROSPECTOR (3) is an expert system very similar in structure to MYCIN developed by Stanford Reseach International designed to give expert advice on discovering ore deposits based upon geologic data. The knowledge base in PROSPECTOR is divided into two parts, one for knowledge relative to the general problem and one for knowledge specific to a problem in question. PROSPECTOR contains a knowledge acquisition program (KAS) to facilitate generation of the knowledge base. The program compares information provided by a user for a specific site against its knowledge base, requests additional information that improves the certainty of its conclusion, and provides the user with a summary of its results. PROSPECTOR makes use of Bayesian decision analysis in determination of likelihood ratios. Currently PROSPECTOR has about 1600 rules and makes use of both forward and backward chaining as solution strategies.

The most successful application of expert systems to a water resource problem is HYDRO (7). This program is an extension of PROSPECTOR. HYDRO was developed to aid in the calibration of a large hydrologic watershed model (HSPF) developed by Hydrocomp, Inc. HYDRO uses watershed chacteristics to calculate initial parameter values. HYDRO's knowledge base consists of inference networks that capture an expert's knowledge concerning how to estimate parameter values. The model prompts the user to answer questions concerning the physical characteristics of the watershed such as soil type, vegetation, precipitation, runoff, and temperature. Because of the inherent uncertainty associated with these values, the user may either: 1) enter the information as a range of values or 2) enter a single value with a certainty factor. The user's responses to the questions are propagated through the inference engine and HYDRO calculates the "most likely" value for the parameters together with a certainty factor. A unique feature of HYDRO is that the user may specify how the certainty factors associated with the parameters are manipulated. Through an INTERLISP interface the user can determine the consistency of the values calculated and, if not acceptable, they can be overridden by the user.

A recent example of the application of expert systems to water resources is given by Cuena (2). Cuena reports the development of an expert system designed to operate flood control dams during emergencies and to plan for civil defense in flood prone areas. The system includes a series of simulation models that predict the hydrologic condition of a watershed and allow experts to provide guidance on operation based upon updated, predicted conditions. The system is driven by a set of physical rules (such as rain, inflow, and flood level rules) and a set of operation rules (such as civil defense and dam operation rules).

AI in Water Resources

Computing in water resources has evolved dramatically in the past three decades. At least three eras have have occurred; the Era of Hostile Computers (the 1950's and 1960's), the Era of Interactive Computers (1970's), and the Era of User Friendly Computers (the 1980's to date). During this period of transition the major themes that have emerged are that users of computers expect their interactions with the computer to be convenient, that they want to understand what tasks the computer is performing, and that they desire the capability to modify programs for their specific needs. This trend is especially relevent since the use of computer graphics and interactive programming have been shown to aid in the resolution of conflicts and enhance the probability that a solution resulting from a quantitative analysis can be understood by appropriate decision makers and the public.

It is interesting to note that many of the characteristics now desired in water resource computing are those that are possessed by AI techniques. Perhaps the most important of these characteristics is the interaction between the developer of a AI program, an expert in a given discipline, and potential users of the program. This close interaction results in programs whose logic and underlying assumptions can be easily understood. This is not to suggest that AI offers a panacea to all problems. Many of the larger computational problems in water resources are inappropriate for AI applications.

Conclusions

The topics of artificial intelligence and expert systems have been reviewed in this paper. The review indicates that these techniques have found wide application in a variety of problems settings. The strength of the techniques include their effectiveness in capturing the essential characteristics of expertise, in modeling decision making as a human activity rather than simply a mathematical exercise, and in making the logic of their structure transparent to the user. These qualities are valuable in all decision making, including that required in water resource management such as that demonstrated by the HYDRO expert system. The successes attained by AI in the past and its general applicability suggest that it will find a significant role in water resource management in the future.

Acknowdgements

This research was funded under NSF Grant CEE-8304069. The author would like to express his appreciation to the other members of the research team for there helpful support and advice. These individuals are Dr. Colin Brown, Douglas Johnston, and Jay Lund.

References

1. Barr, A., and Feigenbaum, E.A., eds, The Handbook of Artificial Intelligence, Vol. 1, William Kaufman, Los Altos, California, 1981.
2. Cuena, J., "The Use of Simulation Models and Human Advice to Build An Expert System For the Defense and Control of River Floods, Proceedings of the Eighth International Joint Conference on Artificial Intelligence, Vol. 1, 1983, pp. 246-249.
3. Duda, R.O., Hart, P.E., Barrett, P., Gaschnig,J., Konolige, K., Reboh, R., Slocum, J., "Development of the PROSPECTOR Consultation System for Mineral Exploration," Final Report, SRI Projects 5821 and 6415, Artificial Intelligence Center, SRI International, Menlo Park, CA, 1978.
4. Hayes-Roth, F., Waterman, D.A., and Lenat, D.B., "An Overview of Expert Systems," Building Expert Systems, F. Hayes-Roth, D.A. Waterman, and D.B. Lenat, eds., Addison-Welsley Publishing, Reading, Mass., 1983.
5. Newell, A., and Simon, H.A., "GPS: A Program That Simulates Human Thought," Computers and Thought, E.A. Feigenbaum and J.A. Feldman, eds., McGraw Hill, New York, NY, 1963, pp. 279-293.
6. McCarthy, J., "Programs with Common Sense," Proceedings of the Symposium on Mechanisation of Thought Processess, D.V. Blake and A.M. Uttley, eds., National Physics Laboratory, Teddington, England, London, 1959, pp. 75-84.
7. Reboh, R., Reiter, J., and Gaschnig, J., Development of a Knowledge-Based Interface to a Hydrological Simulation Program, SRI International, Menlo Park, CA, May, 1982.
8. Rich, E., Artificial Intelligence, McGraw Hill, New York, NY, 1983.
9. Russell, B., History of Western Philosophy, Simon and Schuster, New York, NY, 1940.
10. Schank, R., "Intelligent Advisory Systems," The AI Business, P.H. Winston and K.A. Prendergast, eds., The MIT Press, Cambridge, Mass., 1984.
11. Shortliffe, E.H., Computer-Based Medical Consultation, American Elsevier, New York, NY, 1976.
12. Simon, H.A., The Sciences of the Artificial, 2nd ed., The MIT Press, Cambridge Mass., 1981.
13. Sriram, D., Maher, M.L., Bielak, J., and Fenves, S.J., "Expert Systems for Civil Engineering - A Survey," Deparment of Civil Engineering, Carnegie Institue of Technology, Carnegie-Mellon University, Pittsburg, PA, July, 1982.
14. Stefik, M., Aikins, J., Balzer, R., Benoit, J., Birnbaum, L., Hayes-Roth, F., and Sacerdoti, E., "Basic Concepts for Building Expert Systems," Building Expert Systems, F. Hayes-Roth, D.A. Waterman, and D.B. Lenat, eds., Addison-Welsley Publishing, Reading, Mass., 1983.
15. Turing, A.M., "Computing Machinery and Intelligence," Mind, Vol. 59, Oct., 1950, pp. 433-460.
16. Waltz, D., "Artificial Intelligence", Scientific American, Vol. 24, No. 4, Oct., 1982, pp. 118-133.
17. Winston, P.H., "Perspective on Artificial Intelligence", The AI Business, P.H. Winston and K.A. Prendergast, eds., The MIT Press, Cambridge, Mass., 1984.

DIAGNOSIS OF WASTEWATER TREATMENT PROCESSES

Douglas M. Johnston*

This paper presents an approach to the development of an expert system for aiding the operation of an activated sludge wastewater treatment facility. The expert system incorporates a diagnostic model of the treatment process defined by an expert in the operation of a metropolitan facility in Seattle, Washington. The system is developed from elements of fuzzy set theory to facilitate the incorporation of approximate reasoning and imprecision endemic to complex systems. The paper details the logic structure, the development of a knowledge base specific to the operation of a wastewater treatment facility and their integration in a microcomputer based interactive program. Information characterizing the state of input elements is evaluated against the model and the program requests additional information to resolve inconsistencies. After evaluation, control strategies are produced. Preliminary findings are reported and directions for future efforts presented.

INTRODUCTION

The operation and control of large, complex processes is frequently dependent on the knowledge and intuition of the operator(s). In deterministic operation, precise control is possible through complete knowledge of process elements and the behavior of the system itself. Under most practical circumstances this ideal state is weakened by the presence of uncertainty in either process inputs or in their effect on system performance. Such systems typically require the presence of an expert operator who has achieved complex understanding of the system primarily through experience. Control by a human expert is frequently enabled through the application of both quantitative information and expert judgment.

Quantitative information is obtained from instrument readings or laboratory tests. Qualitative information is derived from observations of the behavior of process parameters or associations with historical behavior. The application of judgment is typically through the use of "rules-of-thumb" or heuristics. Heuristics are used to guide a problem toward a feasible solution without the need to consider all possible solutions. Heuristics may take a form such as "If the temperature of the mixture is very high, then make a medium negative adjustment to the fuel supply rate." In developing and applying a set of heuristics to a control problem, the operator is implementing a flexible solution strategy.

While a human operator is effective in many situations, the complexity of a system under abnormal conditions may limit performance. In such

*Research Assistant, Department of Civil Engineering, University of Washington, Seattle, Washington, 98195.

situations, control responses may be inadequate. Methods exist that
could assist the operator in improving process operation. Several
approaches within the field of expert systems have been proposed to
provide such a method in diagnosis and control. This paper examines the
potential role of an expert system in the diagnosis of municipal waste
water treatment problems with an emphasis on representing uncertainties
inherent in the relationships between symptoms, diagnoses, and
treatments.

EXPERT SYSTEMS

An area of artificial intelligence, expert systems are concerned with
the development of computer programs that represent human knowledge and
utilize that knowledge to solve complex problems within a specific
domain. Substantial success in the development and implementation of
expert systems has been achieved over the last decade. Successful
implementations have occured in areas including: medical diagnosis
(11), mineral prospecting (2), computer configuration (7), and model
parameter estimation (8), to mention a few.

Like artificial intelligence in general, expert systems typically
differ from traditional data processing approaches in that they utilize
symbolic representation, symbolic inference, and heuristics (5). Expert
systems are typically composed of a knowledge base containing facts and
rules elicited from an expert, a processing element (inference engine),
a "blackboard" containing intermediate results, and some form of user
interface. The emphasis in developing expert systems is on the
accumulation and efficient representation of knowledge.

Diagnosis involves the determination of a cause of failure in a system
inferred from a set of symptoms or observations. Diagnosis is hindered
by incomplete or unreliable data, and inconsistent or complex
relationships between symptoms and diagnoses. Thus any expert system
dealing with diagnosis must possess the ability to represent not just
knowledge but uncertain and incomplete knowledge.

Production Rules for Knowledge Representation.- Existing techniques
for representing knowledge contained in expert systems include
propositional and predicate logic, inference nets, frames and production
rules (9). Production rules are a very common method in existing expert
systems because they allow the knowledge base to be represented
independently of the inference engine and they describe procedural
knowledge, such as that found in diagnostic and some design problems,
efficiently.

Production rules define the paths by which an input into a system can
reach a goal state. For example, given the state of a particular
symptom within a system, a production rule can result in the
determination of a diagnosis (or of some sub-hypothesis leading to a
diagnosis). Production rules typically are of the form of conditionals,
defining the relationship between parameters. These rules may generally
be expressed in terms of a premise and action as

    IF <premise1> <premise2> ... <premiseN>
    THEN <action1> ... <actionM>

Examples of production rules applied to wastewater treatment diagnosis
and control are provided in figure 1.

The execution of production rules suggests that there is complete certainty in both the premise and the action. As indicated, such conditions limit the applicability of production rules to trivial problems. Formal methods of incorporating uncertainty into production rules are therefore necessary. There are two forms of uncertainty that might be evidenced in a production rule. These are uncertain premises and inexact causal relationships between the premise and the associated action. Uncertain premises may arise from incomplete data, or the premise may be itself composed of an uncertain hypothesis.

IF (influent color is abnormal) OR (pH levels are abnormal)
THEN (there is suggestive evidence that metals are present in the influent)

IF (oxygen uptake decreases) AND (mixed liquor settleability remains the same) AND (flow remains the same)
THEN (there is suggestive evidence that toxic organics are present in the influent)

IF (toxic organics are present in influent) AND (detention not possible)
THEN (discharge after primary treatment)

FIG. 1.- Sample Production Rules for Activated Sludge Diagnosis

Many techniques are available for representing uncertainty in production rules including nonmonotonic reasoning, probabilistic reasoning, and fuzzy logic. Probabilistic reasoning is appropriate when variations in the field of interest can be attributed to randomness or appears random in small samples. A strict application of probabilistic reasoning through the use of Baye's theorem is provided in the expert system PROSPECTOR (3). A more ad hoc approach based on Bayesian techniques is utilized by MYCIN (1). An application using fuzzy logic will be developed in this paper.

Fuzzy Relations for Knowledge Representation.- In spite of the popularity of the model of inexact reasoning utilized in MYCIN there are problems with the effect of inconsistency in rules and limitations in the representation of uncertainty. Other approaches may be considered. The relationships between symptoms of process malfunction and diagnosis of causal elements, and between causal elements and remedial or mitigating responses, may be represented through the use of fuzzy relations. The modeling of causal relationships has been described by Sanchez (10) in the context of medical diagnosis, and by Tsukamoto and Terano (12) using the example of automobile trouble diagnosis.

The relationship between a symptom (or process state) and a diagnosis (or cause of failure) can be expressed using logical implication. A brief overview of logic operations and fuzzy set theory pertinent to the discussion is provided here. For more detailed information, the reader is referred to works by Gaines (4), and Zadeh (13).

In classical two valued logic there exist two modes of reasoning with respect to implication, modus ponens and modus tollens. The modus ponens conclusion of "q" is derived from the premises "IF p THEN q" and "p". Relating to the diagnosis problem at hand, modus ponens states that if there is a relationship between a symptom and a diagnosis, then

if a symptom p has been observed, then a fault q has occured. Modus
tollens is derived from the premises "IF p THEN q" and "NOT q" yielding
the conclusion "NOT p". In other words, if a fault did not occur then a
related symptom would not be observed. Under these classical modes the
conclusion that a fault did occur given that a symptom was not observed
is not permitted. This would be a desirable conclusion given the
possibility that an operator fails to observe a symptom. Classical or
binary logic does not represent well this and much human reasoning.

Multiple valued logic permits the valuation of the truth of a
proposition on a continuous scale rather than the true-false requirement
of classical logic. Thus for implication, given a truth value of the
relation $p \longrightarrow q$ and the truth value of p, the problem becomes one of
finding a consistent truth value of q. There are several operators in
multiple valued logic, but the operator defined by Lukasiewicz

$$p \longrightarrow q = \min(1, \ 1 - p + q) \dots\dots\dots\dots\dots\dots\dots\dots\dots\dots\dots \ (1)$$

will be utilized here. The operator supports modus ponens for binary
logic.

The theory of fuzzy sets is based on the premise that there can exist
partial membership of an element to a class. This capability has been
shown to be useful in representing linguistic variables and uncertainty
(6). A fuzzy set is a mapping of the degree of membership of a group of
elements over a discourse of interest. A fuzzy relation is formed from
a composition of fuzzy sets. Production rules have been expressed by
relations (6) in the manner

IF S THEN X = S x X = R

where S x X denotes the fuzzy cartesian product

$$R = S \ x \ X = \min(s,x) \quad \forall \ x \in X, \ s \in S \dots\dots\dots\dots\dots\dots\dots\dots \ (2)$$

In expert system applications, the relation R is the knowledge base
relating symptoms to diagnoses and can be obtained from experts or other
sources.

With respect to the generation of automatic diagnoses, the diagnoses
associated with a set of observed symptoms can be inferred by solving:

$$x \ = R \circ s \dots\dots\dots\dots\dots\dots\dots\dots\dots\dots\dots\dots\dots\dots\dots\dots\dots\dots\dots\dots \ (3)$$

where:
    x is the (fuzzy) set of observed symptoms,
    s is the (fuzzy) set of induced diagnoses, and
    R $\circ$ s denotes the max-min composition between R and s.

Both Sanchez and Tsukamoto and Terano provide similar approaches to
the solution of Eq. 3. The latter propose two propositions relating
causes (diagnoses) and symptoms:

$$P_j : \quad X_j \text{ implies } (\ \exists \ i \ (R_{ij} \text{ and } S_i)), \ 1 \leq j \leq n \dots\dots\dots\dots\dots \ (4a)$$

$$P_{ij} : \quad S_i \text{ implies } X_j, \ 1 \leq i \leq m, \ 1 \leq j \leq n \dots\dots\dots\dots\dots\dots \ (4b)$$

The first proposition (Eq. 4a) indicates that if a symptom is observed,
then there must be at least one cause (diagnosis) that can be inferred

from R and S. The second proposition (Eq. 4b) states that the determination of a cause implies there exists a symptom that has been observed. While the first proposition is always true (assuming the knowledge base encompasses the observed symptoms), the second proposition is much less likely to be true in that a faulty diagnosis might occur. Such an error could occur from faulty interpretation of causality or simply because a symptom was not recognized. The latter condition will be discussed in more detail in a later section.

The propositions (Eq. 4a and Eq. 4b) can be expressed as:

$$P_j \longrightarrow 0 \leq x_j \leq \max_i (\min (r_{ij}, s_i)) \qquad 1 \leq j \leq n \dots\dots\dots\dots (5a)$$

$$P_{ij} \longrightarrow 0 \leq s_i \leq \min (1, x_j + 1 - t_{ij}) \qquad \forall \ i \in S, \ j \in X \dots\dots\dots (5b)$$

Given the set of observed symptoms and the causal relations, the solution for s_i is desired. Eq. 5b provides the upper bound on the solution for s_i while Eq. 5a provides the lower bounds on the solution. This solution requires the consideration of the inverse problem $(X = R \circ S, \ S = R^{-1} \circ X)$. Letting $e_{ij} = [0, \min(1, x_j + 1 - t_{ij})]$, the solution can be expressed as:

$$\max_j (\inf(w_{ij}(k'))) \leq s_i^k \leq \min_j (\sup(e_{ij})) \dots\dots\dots\dots\dots\dots\dots\dots (6)$$

$$\text{for}^j k' \in \left[k^j \mid \max_j (\inf(\tilde{w}_{ij}(k))) \leq \min_j^j (\sup(e_{ij})) \right] \text{ and } k \in K \dots\dots (7)$$

$\text{Sup}(e_{ij})$ is from the multivalued logic definition of implication:

$$v(T \longrightarrow X) = \min(1, 1 - T + X)$$

or the degree to which a symptom can be induced from the knowledge base. To solve the inverse problem, Tsukamoto and Terano introduce two compositions on numbers valued in the interval $[0,1]$:

$$p \ \omega \ q = \begin{cases} q & \text{if } p > q \\ [q,1] & \text{if } p = q \\ [0,1] & \text{if } p < q \end{cases} \dots\dots\dots\dots\dots\dots\dots\dots\dots\dots\dots (8)$$

$$p \ \omega \ q = \begin{cases} [0,q] & \text{if } p > q \\ [0,1] & \text{else} \end{cases} \dots\dots\dots\dots\dots\dots\dots\dots\dots\dots\dots (9)$$

The compositions (Eq. 8) and (Eq. 9) are derived from fuzzy implication operators described previously. The investigators further define two matrices U and V whose elements are respectively defined by:

$$u_{ij} = r_{ij} \ \omega \ x_j \text{ and,}$$
$$v_{ij} = r_{ij} \ \omega \ x_j \qquad \forall \ i, j \dots\dots\dots\dots\dots\dots\dots\dots\dots\dots\dots\dots (10)$$

The combinations of the u_{ij} and v_{ij} elements define the elements of the jth column of the matrices W as:

$$w_{ij} = \begin{cases} u_{ij} & \text{for } \exists! \ i \in \left[i \mid \inf (u_{ij}) = x_j \right] \\ v_{ij} & \text{for other } i's \dots\dots\dots\dots\dots\dots\dots\dots\dots\dots\dots (11) \end{cases}$$

The solution for the entire problem is provided by Eq. 6 conditioned by a test of consistency between solutions (Eq. 7). The condition simply states that the kth combination is consistent if for a given element, its lower bound is not higher than its upper bound. Finally, the set of possible values of s_i are defined by:

$$s_i = \bigcap_k s_i^k \quad k \in K \dots\dots\dots\dots\dots\dots\dots\dots\dots\dots\dots\dots\dots\dots\dots\dots (12)$$

It is possible that no solution will exist indicating there is an inconsistency between the observed symptoms and the relation connecting symptoms to diagnoses. An inconsistency could occur when an operator fails to observe an existing symptom (the set x is deficient). In this case it is desirable to identify the deficient symptom so that the operator can be notified and sufficient consideration is given to the symptom.

APPLICATION OF AN AUTOMATIC DIAGNOSIS ALGORITHM

A wastewater treatment facility will be examined to illustrate the use of fuzzy relations in the diagnosis of possible faulty conditions occuring in process control. The sets of diagnoses (S) and symptoms (X) are given in figure 2. Some of the symptoms can be mechanically monitored (pH and DO, for example) while others require subjective interpretation by the operator (e.g. color of influent). Furthermore, the causal relationships between a symptom and a failure (diagnosis) will, in most cases, require some subjective interpretation in that a symptom may only partially contribute to a diagnosis or may be causally linked to several possible failures. Subjective interpretations and ambiguity in causal relationships can require the application of fuzzy sets.

SYMPTOMS (X)

x_1 = change in color of the influent
x_2 = abnormal increase in dissolved oxygen (DO) levels in the aeration tanks
x_3 = abnormal decrease in dissolved oxygen (DO) levels in the aeration tanks
x_4 = abnormal change in pH levels in the aeration tanks

CAUSES OF FAILURES (DIAGNOSES) (S)

s_1 = presence of abnormal levels of heavy metals in the influent
s_2 = extreme change in temperature of the influent
s_3 = presence of substance with undesirable pH levels in the influent
s_4 = extreme peak loading conditions
s_5 = presence of abnormal levels of toxic organics in the influent

FIG. 2.   Sample Symptoms and Diagnoses for the Detection of Toxic Substances in Influent

The sets of possible diagnoses and symptoms are pertinent to the problem of the detection of toxic substances in the influent. The relations were identified by a process control expert. The relational matrix T is derived from pairwise comparisons of symptoms to each diagnosis. The values obtained for the T matrix are shown in Table 1.

T CAUSE	SYMPTOM x1	x2	x3	x4
s1	.39	.09	.09	.43
s2	.11	.40	.40	.09
s3	.15	.05	.05	.75
s4	.08	.08	.76	.08
s5	.16	.07	.68	.09

TABLE 1.- Values of Relation Between Symptoms and Diagnoses.

Assume the process operator observes abnormal conditions in the system and assigns values representing the operator's degree of certainty in the presence of observed symptoms to the set (X) as

$$X = (0.9, \ 0.0, \ 0.3, \ 0.6)$$

indicating that the operator has recognized a definite change in the color of the influent, no abnormal increase in dissolved oxygen levels, a possibly significant decrease in the dissolved oxygen levels in the aeration tanks, and a moderate change in pH levels. The assignment of values is somewhat controversial. One method is to apply pairwise comparisons as discussed above.
The upper bound solution of possible diagnoses is found from Eq. 5b to be (.91, .60, .85, .54, .62). The lower bounds of the solution are found as

$$\max_j (\ \inf(\ w_{ij})) = (0.9, \ 0.0, \ 0.3, \ 0.6, \ 0.0).$$

In testing for consistency (Eq. 7) it is found that s_4 is inconsistant (0.6 > 0.54). The consistent solution of the lower bounds therefore becomes

$$S = (0.9, \ 0.0, \ 0.3, \ 0.0, \ 0.0).$$

The intersection of the lower bounds with the upper results in the solution set defined by Eq. 12 as

$$s_i = ([0.9, \ 0.91] \ [0.0, \ 0.6] \ [0.3, \ 0.85] \ [0.0, \ 0.54] \ [0.0, \ 0.62])$$

The diagnostics induced imply that the presence of heavy metals in the influent is most certain with significant support for a substance with undesirable pH levels in the influent. The presence of the other substances are much less strongly implied.

Resolution of Inconsistency.- It was suggested in a previous section that in situations where no solution exists to the above problem, it is desirable to identify deficient symptoms so that additional information might be obtained. The negation approach presented by Tsukamoto and Terano results in the identification of possibilities of diagnoses not occuring given insufficient symptom observations. Assume the supports for the observations of symptoms given in the previous problem are:

$$x_j = (0.0, \ 0.9, \ 0.0, \ 0.0).$$

The upper bound of the solution set is (.57, .60, .25, .24, .32). The
lower bounds of the solution are found to be (0.9, 0.9, 0.9, 0.9, 0.9).

It is seen that there is no solution to this problem. The negation
algorithm may now be applied. Letting the negation of

$$x_j \ (\bar{x}_j) = 1 - x_j = \quad (1.0, \ 0.1, \ 1.0, \ 1.0),$$

the negation of possible diagnoses obtained from the solution of the
inverse problem results in the set

$$\bar{s}_i = (1.0, \ [0.1, \ 0.7], \ 1.0, \ 1.0, \ 1.0).$$

The solution indicates that there is full support that the diagnoses of
heavy metals, undesirable pH, extreme peak loading, or toxic organics
could not be implied from the observed symptoms. The remaining support
of $[0.1, \ 0.7]$ for a change in temperature would indicate that this
diagnosis cannot be eliminated from consideration as a possible cause of
the observed symptom. This result should come as no great surprise.
Upon examination of the relation matrix T, it is seen that between the
symptom "increase in dissolved oxygen levels" and the set of possible
diagnoses, the strongest implication is with the diagnosis "extreme
change in temperature."

It would be of interest to be able to derive the set of symptoms that
should be considered in greater detail in order that a feasible solution
to the problem might be obtained and a set of supports for diagnoses
obtained. Tsukamoto and Terano do not extend their methodology beyond
the negation algorithm described above.

A possible algorithm for seeking additional information from the
process operator when insufficient evidence is presented may be derived
from the existing algorithm. The propositions identified in Eq. 4 may
be rewritten to reflect the negation operations:

$$P_j: \quad \bar{x}_j \ \text{implies} \ (\ \exists i \ (R_{ij} \ \text{and} \ \bar{s}_i), \quad 1 \leq j \leq n \dots\dots\dots\dots \quad (13a)$$
$$P_{ij}^j: \quad \bar{s}_i \ \text{implies} \ \bar{x}_j \dots\dots\dots\dots\dots\dots\dots\dots\dots\dots \quad (13b)$$

In this case the proposition (Eq. 13a) indicates that if a symptom
cannot be eliminated from consideration then there must exist at least
one diagnosis that also cannot be eliminated as a possible cause. The
second proposition (13b) indicates that being unable to eliminate a
diagnosis suggests that a symptom must be considered. Expressing the
second proposition as in Eq. 8b, the bounds on the diagnoses are defined
as:

$$0 \leq \bar{s}_i \leq \min(\ 1, \ \bar{x}_j + 1 - t_{ij}) \dots\dots\dots\dots\dots\dots\dots \quad (14)$$

which states that if a failure s_i does not occur then there is a
possibility that a symptom x_j need not be observed. Given the negation
diagnoses $\bar{s}_i$, the $\bar{x}_j$ are sought that satisfies Eq. 14. The lower bound
of the $\bar{x}_j$ are found such that

$$\bar{s}_i \leq \sup(\ \min(\ 1, \ \bar{x}_j + 1 - t_{ij})).$$

Recalling that $\bar{s}_i = (1.0, \ 0.1, \ 1.0, \ 1.0, \ 1.0)$ the x_j satisfying the
above equation are (.39, .09, .76, .75). From Eq. 14 the upper bound of

the solution is $x_j = 1$. Therefore, the final solution of the negation of possible symptoms is

$$x_j = ([.39, 1.0] \quad [.09, 1.0] \quad [.76, 1.0] \quad [.75, 1.0]).$$

The solution implies that given that the diagnosis "extreme change in temperature" cannot be eliminated, there is very strong support that the symptom "increase in DO" cannot be rejected (which should come as no surprise as this symptom was the only one observed in the first place) and there is somewhat strong support that the symptom "change in color of the influent" cannot be rejected as a possible source of important information. The other two symptoms provide low support for the possibility that they may be importantly related to the derived diagnosis.

Given notification that another symptom(s) may provide an important contribution to diagnosis, the operator may reevaluate existing observations on the state of the system. Although the negation solution seems to provide a viable feedback mechanism in the case of insufficient evidence provided by the operator, it is possible that the operator is providing as much information as possible with still no solution to the problem. Another source of restriction to the automatic diagnosis of process faults arises from limitations in the knowledge base itself. If the knowledge base is incomplete or incorrect in its causal relations, no solution may result. In a manner identical to the inference of diagnoses given observed symptoms, the set of possible treatments or actions may be derived from a knowledge base containing relations between diagnoses and treatments.

CONCLUSIONS

This paper surveys applications of expert systems and applies a method based on fuzzy set theory to the diagnosis and treatment of problems associated with the operation of an activated sludge wastewater treatment plant. The system is comparable to some existing expert system methodologies in its ability to represent uncertain knowledge. Advantages of the system described include the ability to resolve inconsistencies in the knowledge base and efficiencies in knowledge representation. A disadvantage is a lack of an explanation capability in which the system is able to trace and report its reasoning process. It is significant that few systems have this capability.

The implemation of a fuzzy set based expert system may easily be accomplished through an interactive, microcomputer based program. Over a period of time, a knowledge base can be expanded to include more comprehensive and complex relationships. The system can also be expanded to include greater representation of judgmental relations including the use of linguistic variables. This capability is a distinct advantage over production rule systems. In its full capacity, an expert system could provide valuable assistance to a process operator.

ACKNOWLEDGEMENTS

Funding for this research was provided by the National Science Foundation, NSF Grant No. CEE-8304069. The patience and expertise of Richard Finger, Process Control Supervisor, METRO, Seattle, WA, and Dr. David Stensel, University of Washington; and the guidance and suggestions of Dr. Richard Palmer and Dr. Colin Brown, University of Washington, are greatly appreciated.

APPENDIX.- REFERENCES

1. Buchanan, B. G., and Shortliffe, E. H., "A Model of Inexact Reasoning In Medicine," Mathematical Biosciences, Vol. 23, pp. 351-379, 1975.
2. Duda, R. O., Hart, P. E., Konolige, K., and Reboh, R., "A Computer-Based Consultant for Mineral Exploration," Technical Report, SRI International, Sept. 1979.
3. Duda, R. O., Hart, P. E., and Nilsson, N. J.," Subjective Bayesian Methods for Rule-Based Inference Systems," AFIPS 1976 National Computer Conference, pp. 1075-1082, 1976.
4. Gaines, B.R., "Foundations of Fuzzy Reasoning," International Journal of Man-Machine Studies, Vol. 8, pp. 623-668, 1976.
5. Hayes-Roth, F., Waterman, D. A., and Lenat, D. B., (Eds.), Building Expert Systems, Addison-Wesley, Reading, MA, 1983.
6. Mamdani, E. H., and Assilian, S., "An Experiment in Linguistic Synthesis With a Fuzzy Logic Controller," International Journal of Man-Machine Studies, Vol. 7, pp. 1-13, 1975.
7. McDermott, J., "R1: A Rule-Based Configurer of Computer Systems," Artificial Intelligence, Vol. 19, No. 1, 1982.
8. Reboh, R., Reiter, J., and Gaschnig, J., "Development of A Knowledge-Based Interface to a Hydrological Simulation Program," SRI International, May, 1982.
9. Rich, E., Artificial Intelligence, McGraw-Hill, NY, 1983.
10. Sanchez, E., "Resolution of Composite Fuzzy Relation Equations," Information and Control, Vol. 30, pp. 30-48, 1976.
11. Shortliffe, H., MYCIN: Computer Based Medical Consultations, Elsevier, NY, 1976.
12. Tsukamoto, Y., and Terano, T., "Failure Diagnosis By Using Fuzzy Logic," Proceedings IEEE Conference on Decision Control, Vol. 2, pp. 1390-1395, 1975.
13. Zadeh, L. A., "Fuzzy Sets," Information and Control, Vol. 8., pp. 338-353, 1965.

INTEGRATED KNOWLEDGE-BASED SOFTWARE
FOR FLOOD AND WATER POLLUTION MANAGEMENT

William James, M. ASCE and Alan R. Dunn*

Abstract

Our group has been active in several areas related to advanced
software. Our new software is: a) intended for use by end-users,
b)database-management centered, and c) non-procedural. The following
are the software design criteria: 1. Monitor drainage system
behaviour. 2. Starting with rain and given situations, infer likely
consequences. 3. Take observed data and explain its meaning by
inferring the problem. 4. Infer malfunctions from observed irregularities. 5. Plan remedies for malfunctions. 6. Design a set of
actions to produce a desired outcome. 7. Interpret data, predict
behaviour, formulate plans, execute the plans, and monitor their
execution. 8. Develop a configuration which satisfies all applicable
constraints.

Our aim is to develop a comprehensive city-wide system to control
both flooding and pollution. This system provides information on the
sewer system with regard to: storm intensity, storm speed and direction, flows within the sewer system, pollutant concentrations in the
drainage network, status of diversions and storages, and pollutant
levels in the receiving waters. Allowable control of the drainage
system is through on-line storage and diversion structures which
direct excess flows to off-line storage (or parts of the receiving
waters where the risk of infection is lower), by-pass of the Sewage
Treatment Plants and by closure of affected beaches.

An artificially intelligent control package that ensures a correct modelling approach is described. The system distils the
experiences of several "experts" for model verification, sensitivity
analysis, calibration and validation.

Introduction

The Computational Hydraulics Group (CHG) at McMaster University
has been active in several areas related to advanced software. The
areas are briefly as follows:

(a) Special instrumentation and software has been developed for

-- --- ---- ------ --- ---- --- ---- --- ---- -- ---- ------- --- -------

*Computational Hydraulics Group, McMaster University, Hamilton,
Ontario, Canada L8S 4L7, Phone: (416) 527-6944

rainfall gauging in urban areas.

(b) Special algorithms have been developed for pollutant accumulation on street surfaces and rooftops in the interstorm dry weather,

(c) Wash-off and transport of contaminants through the sewer network has similarly been studied.

(d) Continuous models have been developed for IBM-PC compatibles, mostly based on the Stormwater Management Model (SWMM),

(e) Continous modelling in turn has required the development of special time-series management systems.

(f) The pollutants overflow at diversion structures to outfalls, so algorithms have been developed to predict diverted flows and pollutant dispersion in the nearshore zone.

(g) Finally, hardware and software for real-time control of sewer flows such that hazardous contaminants are stored during overflow events have been developed.

Our new software is:

(a) intended for use by end-users, usually untrained in traditionaldata processing disciplines,

(b) data-base management centered, combining a DBMS with retrieval or applications-development language, and

(c) non-procedural; the language tells a computer what task to perform, but not the steps necessary to accomplish it.

The following are the general software design criteria (not all software meets all the criteria):

1. Monitoring: Monitor drainage system behaviour and compare the observations to the planned behaviour to determine malfunctions.

2. Prediction: Starting with rain and given situations, infer likely consequences.

3. Interpretation: Take observed data and explain its meaning by inferring the problem.

4. Diagnosis: Infer malfunctions from observed irregularities.

5. Repair: Plan remedies for malfunctions.

6. Planning: Design a set of actions to produce a desired outcome, e.g. provide flood control capacity and storages.

7. Control: Interpret data, predict behaviour, formulate plans, execute the plans, and monitor their execution.

8. Design: Develop a configuration which satisfies all applicable constraints, e.g. flood storages.

Microcomputer Control of Sewer Networks

Real-time control of urban stormwater may be achieved by onsite microcomputers rather than by a single, central computer. The microcomputers need not be expensive; in fact, $30 hand-held Z-80 based microcomputers having BASIC in ROM are more than sufficient at each control site. The site will generally include:

1) a sensor to measure flow, water level, rainfall and/or pollutant concentration,
2) circuitry to transform the signal into information meaningful to the microcomputer,
3) a small, replaceable microcomputer running a model derived from statistical or similar analyses of data relevant to the control site,
4) circuitry to drive the electrical control mechanism, and
5) a data logger recording all incoming information, the control action, and the precise date and time.

Flood and pollution control may be effected by:

a) diverting overflows to storage, directly to receiving waters or to some other sewer network,
b) pumping or draining overflows from detention storage,
c) warning for timely closure of underpasses, and/or
d) computing the extent of the swimming or recreational areas which should be evacuated.

Suitable microcomputers and associated circuitry, for onsite control, and inexpensive raingauges measuring rainfall intensity, have been developed by CHG. The real-time control software (RTCONTROL) has been based on Transfer Function Models (TFM's) of synthetic long-term flow and pollution at each control site. The TFM is easily coded into the data logging program, written in BASIC. The whole package is called DASUTIL, is menu-driven and has, among other attributes, data communication software, so that the data may be automatically transferred to a central database.

Because potential real-time control sites may exist at many locations in a large metropolitan sewer system, the long-term flow and pollutant records are synthetically generated using an elaborate, deterministic computer model such as the U.S. Environmental Protection Agency's Stormwater Management Model (SWMM). Version 3 of SWMM has been adapted by our group to run on IBM-PC compatible machines, so that a complete, very large and intricate model can now be run on a computer costing less than $3000. There are no serious drawbacks using PCSWMM3 in this environment. We have supplied this package to a significant number of users, and the existing large SWMM user group infrastructure assures wide-ranging, continuing support and interest in this product. User Group Meetings are held twice a year, alternately in Canada and the U.S.A. The package is used world-wide.

PCSWMM3 has many advanced capabilities not available in other models in use today, e.g. continuous modelling, water quality, diversion structures, sedimentation and scour, snow management, costing, statistical summaries, to name a few. Nevertheless the package is easy to use, having simple direct menu-driven input and graphical output. Probably the most important attribute is continuous modelling, since this removes all the intrinsic shortcomings of the design storm approach - all flows are ranked directly, giving correct probabilities and risks. Difficulties due to the management of large amounts of input and output data are eliminated by our special data base management software (CHGTSM), also specially written for IBM-PC compatible environments.

The TFM software is derived directly from the synthetic long-term time series generated by continuous PCSWMM3 at each site. It predicts expected flow and pollution in the vicinity of the control site a few minutes ahead (enough time to complete a control action). There is a risk, in some drainage systems, that bad timing of diversions could cause flows to coincide downstream such that flow conditions become worse than they need have been. In these cases it is necessary to run the continuous simulation for the overall drainage system with all constituent control software at each site simulated. This is why an elaborate overall deterministic model is necessary. PCSWMM3 also allows the full range of other stormwater management strategies (separation of roof leaders, tile drains, etc.) to be evaluated.

There are important benefits that accrue from a dense network of field stations. Perhaps the best example occurs in storm modelling. It should be obvious that urban flooding often results from the short, sharp, local thunderstorms that are so common in warm weather. These storms are much smaller in area than the catchments and have surprisingly short lives, typically 30 minutes or so. Our software RAINPAC analyses data from a network of synchronized raingauges to compute storm speeds, directions, growth and decay. Output from RAINPAC is fed directly into PCSWMM3 to compute flood flows and pollution loads that are demonstrably more accurate than any other hydrologic package known to us. This is to be expected: the better the input, the better the results.

Modelling in Perspective

The whole system may sound unduly complex, but runs very effectively on IBM-PC compatibles. To summarize again, the components of the technology in place are as follows:

1. Establish a network of field stations.
2. Use CHGTSM to manage the data.
3. Build a PCSWMM3 model of the drainage system.
4. Use the observed data to properly validate the model.
5. Transpose a nearby continuous rain record and compute long term flows at control sites.
6. Derive TFM's for each site.
7. Simulate the TFM's in the continuous PCSWMM3 model to validate the control strategies.
8. Install the real-time controllers at each site.

This should result in:

a. timely diversion of first-flush polluted water to storage,
b. timely treatment of diverted stormwater,
c. timely diversion of relatively clean second-flush stormwater to receiving waters,
d. timely temporary storage of hazardous sanitary effluents at point-of-origin,
e. timely warnings of flooding,
f. timely warnings of desirable beach closures.

It should be noted that the system can also be installed on in-line storage tanks at all factories or other institutions (such as hospitals) that may contribute hazardous contaminants to a combined-sewer or overflowing sewer network. In-storm storage at source will be an effective control method, provided that the know-how is properly shared between the authorities and the industry concerned. That's the catch. The microcomputer may only cost $30 (excluding the interface and control hardware), but the study could last a whole summer.

Intelligent, Expert Modelling

Because model users are one step removed from the internals of the model, they seldom meticulously address model validation. We are devising an automatic methodology for systematic verification, sensitivity analyses, calibration and validation, that appears to work smoothly and faultlessly. Of course, adequate field data is essential. (Our inexpensive raingauges and data loggers render it easy to collect sufficient summer thunderstorm activity in one or two months during the period May–October to satisfy most critical modelling situations. The same instrumentation is used in the real-time controllers – this points to the advantages of considering an integrated microcomputer-compatible system from the outset).

Uncertainties pervade every step in water quality modelling, from model building to inference. Model prediction errors result from several sources: imperfect model structure, parameter estimation errors, numerical solution errors, and uncertainty in initial conditions and model inputs. The logical structure of a model imperfectly represents the real world; either because the processes are not completely understood or because a better representation is too costly to implement.

Uncertainty in model structure affects parameter estimation, compensated for by adjusting the parameters to optimize some goodness-of-fit criterion. Final parameter estimates are affected also by uncertainty in the measurements, which may take the form of unrepresentativeness, measurement errors, or incompleteness (1).

Accuracy is of overriding importance. If the required accuracy can be established early in the study, it would make the selection of the algorithms and determination of the level of discretization for the model an easier task. In a sense the accuracy level predetermines the level of disaggregation to be used. There seems to be a mismatch between the accuracy of the results demanded from the computer and those obtainable from field observation or laboratory analysis. Both the systematic and the random sources of error should be investigated, as part of the selection process, for both the model (concepts, solution methods, computational accuracy, input data, etc.) and the field equipment. There is little point in producing simulation results for validation that are many times more accurate than the observations which are used to validate the model.

A series of verification, validation, and sensitivity tests can be designed to produce sufficient information to satisfy a wide range of advanced questions about a model's performance. The tests should also help to detect certain types of error (5). Some of these tests are described below:

1. Verification Tests: Verification tests use some specific conditions for which the model response can be exactly predicted to check if indeed the model has been structured and coded as intended. Verification tests are not conducted by comparison of model responses with those of the actual system to be modelled; rather, comparisons between model responses and theoretically anticipated results are made in as many cases as possible. The input data need not be physically reasonable. Verification must be done at least once on receipt of the model, ahead of the first design application on any new hardware.

An intelligent program should include a standard data file for verification tests. For stormwater models, for example, a hypothetical system comprising two simple, square subcatchments, of say one acre (0.4 ha) each would be suitable. The subcatchments are joined by a pipe of standard diameter and simple form. The hydrograph from the first subcatchment should be attentuated in the pipe. At the downstream end of this pipe the hydrographs from both subcatchments are superimposed. At the outlet of the pipe the combined hydrograph is routed through a simple, standard, perhaps rectangular, storage tank. The purpose of such a verification data set would be to test the algorithms for:

(1) the generation of the overland flow hydrograph;
(2) routing in the pipes;
(3) the superposition of two hydrographs; and
(4) storage routing in storage tanks.

A special algorithm and data file is built into the program such that when the "auto-verify" option is requested the model automatically carries out a series of verification tests.

2. Calibration and Validation Tests: Calibration implies the comparison of model simulation results to field measurements, to another model known to be accurate, or to some other adequate criterion to ensure that the model of the system is producing accurate information. If these comparisons indicate that the model results are not sufficiently accurate, the model of the system is altered, usually by

adjusting one or more program parameters, and the procedure is repeated. This process generally involves several iterations before a satisfactory confidence level is achieved. Techniques used in calibration include:

(1) comparison of results against field observations;
(2) cross-correlation of continuous model results with those of another proven (usually discrete event or process) model; and
(3) some combination of field observations and modelling.

Validation implies testing the model of the system with a data set not used in the calibration procedure. The most accurate method of validation is the comparison of output from the calibrated model against a corresponding set of independent field measurements. Tests which can be used in assessing the degree of fit of the system model to the physical system are outlined in the literature (3; 2; 7).

The calibration and validation process should be limited to the most important or sensitive parameters, and to the range of parameter values applicable to the normal operating conditions of the system. First, acceptable tolerances must be established. They should be related to achieveable field observations and to the accuracy of the field equipment. The degree of fit must take into account the errors associated with field measurements. Then, emphasis should be placed upon those critical parameters that have the greatest effect on the performance of the system model. Reasonable assumptions may be satisfactory for less critical parameters. Hence, calibration tests are closely related to sensitivity analysis, discussed subsequently.

Once verified, calibrated, and validated, the model can be applied with confidence to the evaluation of the real system. A recent paper describes the process for combined quantity and quality modelling (6).

3. Level of Discretization: The procedure for systematic disaggregation has been described in an earlier paper (4). Disaggregation implies modelling more subspaces of smaller size using a finer time step.

4. Sensitivity Analysis: Sensitivity analysis proceeds by holding all parameters but one constant at their expected values, and perturbing that parameter within reasonable expected limits such that the variation of the objective function can be examined. If apparently small perturbations of the parameter produce large changes in the objective function, the system is said to be sensitive to that parameter. The user must obtain a measure of how accurately that parameter must be represented in his model. If the objective function is not sensitive to the perturbed parameter, then the parameter need not be accurately represented. If the system is insensitive to the perturbed parameter, the parameter and its associated process is redundant and the process should be deleted. The tests are done using the full design problem input data set. It must be stressed that the

actual values of the constant parameters may affect the sensitivity
analysis and so their values should be typical of the conditions being
modelled.

Here again algorithms within the program permit the user to
easily conduct a sensitivity analysis. When this "auto-sensitivity"
option is selected, the program requests the user to identify the
parameter whose sensitivity is to be tested, and the range of perturbed values. The system data file is then automatically rebuilt and
the tests carried out. All output response functions, such as hydrographs, should be plotted on the same family of curves in order to
present the impact immediately to the user. It is critically important
to rank environmental parameters that affect the important components
of your response function for your model in this way.

5. Control of Errors: Having carried out the required verification,
calibration, validation, and sensitivity analyses at various levels of
discretization, the results have to be presented in the report in a
way which ensures that the purposes of the tests have been achieved.
The verification tests must be shown to produce expected results,
thereby demonstrating that there are no errors in the coding of the
program. The calibration and validation results must be shown to be
reasonably accurate.- The trends resulting from the sensitivity
analysis must be shown to make sense in the light of the actual design
problem, and will indicate whether the level of effort put into
estimating the individual parameters is appropriate, based on their
significance in affecting model results.

Conclusions

The procedures are close to those of MODELER, written by Walker
(8). Using the program's data management functions, MODELER employs
sensitivity and error analysis techniques to assess the effects of
input variable uncertainty or variability on output values. To account for uncertainty, input is specified in terms of means and
standard deviations. Sensitivity is carried out by estimation of a
matrix of sensitivity coefficients for any set of input x and output
y, where a sensitivity coefficient $S(I,J)$ is defined by the change in
$Y(J)$ induced by a given change in $X(I)$, expressed in absolute or
percentage terms. Error analysis is carried out by estimation of
variance and confidence ranges for any set of output variables, as
induced by variance in the input variables, using a first-order estimation procedure.

Such model manager programs may truly be said to ensure that the
model is applied with expertise, perhaps approaching that of the
original model authors. The lack of confidence or credibility on the
part of the users is compensated for by artificially coding into the
management program the inherent modelling approach of intelligent
experts. For the sake of obfuscation, the program may be termed an
"Intelligent, Artificial Stormwater Model Manager"!

References

1. Bowles, D. S. and Grenney, W.J., 1984. "Uncertainties in the Water Quality Modelling Process". 1984 Fall Meeting of the American Geophysical Union (not published).

2. Garrick, M., Cunnane, C., and Nash, J.E., 1978. "A Criterion of Efficiency for Rainfall - Runoff Models". Journal of Hydrology, 36, pp. 375-381.

3. Jacoby, S.L.S., and Kowalik, J.S., 1980. "Model validation and use". In Mathematical modelling with computers. Prentice - Hall Inc., Englewood Cliffs, NJ, pp. 215-242.

4. James, W., 1972. "Developing simulation models". Journal of Water Resources Research, 8(5), pp. 1590-1592.

5. James, W. and Robinson, M., 1981. "Standard terms of reference to ensure satisfactory computer-based urban drainage design studies". Canadian Journal of Civil Engineering, Vol. 8, No. 3. pp. 294-303.

6. Jewell, T.K. et al., 1978. "Methodology for calibrating stormwater models". Proceedings, Stormwater Management Model User's Meeting. Published by the USEPA, Athens, Georgia, pp. 125-173.

7. Overton, D.E., and Meadows, M.E., 1976. "Model optimization techniques". In Stormwater modelling. Academic Press, New York, pp. 169-191.

8. Walker, William W., 1982. "A Sensitivity and Error Analysis Framework for Lake Eutrophication Modelling." Water Resources Bulletin, Vol. 18, No. 1, February 1982, pp. 53-60.

Data Base Management Principles

N. Scott Kukshtel[*]
Associate Member, ASCE

Abstract

The rapid growth of computing power available in desktop micro and mini computers has placed at the disposal of individual scientists and engineers a very powerful set of tools designed specifically for information management. This tutorial provides an introduction to these tools, commonly known as data base management systems, or DBMS. The basic concepts of data base management are presented, including typical data models, query and data retrieval methods, and the types of user interface available. The common features and advantages of DBMS software are discussed, and criteria for DBMS selection are outlined.

Introduction

The study of water resources has always been a very data-intensive science. Hydrologic simulations, hydraulic modeling, statistical analyses, and even strategic planning all rely to one degree or another on the accurate and comprehensive tracking of a number of variables, i.e. management of a data base. Improvements in automated data collection techniques have provided research projects with the means to easily collect large quantities of raw data, but have not addressed the problems of data reduction, qualification, and summarization.

A computerized data base system is one method of addressing these problems. Before discussing specific approaches to computerized data base management, let us define a few terms and concepts.

What is a Data Base?

A **data base** is a collection of data organized in such a manner as to make searching and retrieval of the data as efficient as possible.

A **data base system** is a combination of computer hardware and software which provides the tools necessary to make search and retrieval possible.

A **data base management system (DBMS)** is a general purpose software package that is used to construct a data base system.

----

*Programmmer/Analyst, Powerbase Systems,Inc. 12 West 37th Street, New York, NY 10018.

Common Data Base Terminology

Data – the entire set of information of interest.

Field – a variable of interest, its values being a particular subset of the data. Fields usually have assigned names or labels for identification purposes.

Record – a grouping of one data value from each of a set of fields. The combination of fields contained in a record determines the **record type.**

File – a collection of records of the same type. A file can also be thought of as a two-dimensional matrix, with fields along one axis, and record numbers along the other.

In order to illustrate these concepts, consider the data a researcher may collect for a unit-hydrograph analysis. The variables of interest would be time, precipitation, and runoff. In building a data base, these variables would become the fields. The values of all three variables at each sampling time would comprise a record. The records would then be grouped into a file whose structure can be modeled as a two-dimensional matrix of the form:

Record #	Time	Precip.	Runoff
1	$t(1)$	$p(1)$	$r(1)$
2	$t(2)$	$p(2)$	$r(2)$
3	$t(3)$	$p(3)$	$r(3)$
.	.	.	.
.	.	.	.
n	$t(n)$	$p(n)$	$r(n)$

The records in this file can be sorted into a different order, edited, added to, deleted, or retrieved. At retrieval time, individual or multiple records may be accessed by specifying a value or range of values for one or more fields. In addition, only selected fields may be retrieved for each record. These requirements can be stated as a series of logical equations, and are referred to as the **search criteria** for the retrieval request.

Advantages of Data Base Management Software

Anything that is done using a data base management system can also be done using a standard programming language, such as BASIC or FORTRAN. In fact, the earliest DBMS packages were simply a set of subroutines or functions callable by one of these languages. The advantage of a DBMS is that the user no longer has to be concerned with internals of the data files, such as record length, field type, and field offsets within a record. All of these parameters are stored in a **data dictionary** and retrieved automatically by the system as needed.

Many of the most popular DBMS packages today still contain a procedural language with specialized data base function commands, and the user must learn the language in order to build a usable system. However, new packages are now providing more sophistication in the areas of screen and report generation and data base query and retrieval, so that procedural programming is in many cases unnecessary.

Some of the advantages of using a data base system can be categorized as follows:

Multiple Views of the Data

- When using a data base system, data can be entered once and then retrieved in a variety of formats. In a data base system which is accessed by multiple users, each individual or class of users can be shown only the data of interest to them, in a format specially customized for their use. In fact, it may be that no single user will ever see the complete set of raw data as it was input to the system, but instead, each will have a subset of the data pre-processed for their own purposes.

Non-Redundancy and Integrity of Data

- In any data management system, it is likely that a large portion of the data will be used for more than one purpose. For example, in a streamflow gauging data base, certain physical parameters for a gauging station may be used to determine the actual flow at that station as well as to describe that station in a station summary report. In a manual system, this means that as data is entered and/or changed, multiple entries must be made, and these must be cross-checked and validated numerous times. Using a computerized data base system, data need only be entered once, stored, and then referenced as needed. This significantly reduces the volume of data actually stored in the system as well as insures accuracy and integrity of the data.

Data Validation

- As data is entered into the system, it can be validated against already existing data. Range and data type checking are the simplest methods of validation. In a system with multiple file capability, the value can be checked against existing data in another file, with validation made on the basis of value and/or relationship to another variable. Calculations on the entered value may also be performed and the result then used in a validation check.

Flexible Retrieval

- A good data base management system will provide the user with a variety of data retrieval methods. Instead of retrieving all of the records in a file, the user may want only an individual record or a subset of the records, based on specific criteria. In an analogous manner, perhaps only a subset of the fields in a file may be desired. The user may want to reorder the data in various ways, sorting the output by the values of one or more fields. Multiple-file data base systems usually allow operations such as **join**, **union**, or **intersect**, in which records or fields from one file are combined in a particular manner with those from another file. In this manner, a variety of relationships between the data can be established and studied.

Common Data Models

Data base systems are usually classified according to which type of data model they best fit. A data model is nothing more than a conceptual basis for describing the data: it provides a set of structures for holding the data and a set of operations for manipulating the data. It is usually not necessary to become overly involved in the semantics of describing your data base, but some familiarity with the terminology and concepts will help in determining the best approach to building a data base to meet your needs. Some of the most common data model types are described below.

Single-file Models

The example two-dimensional data structure presented above is a single-file data base; that is, all information of interest is kept in one file. Data base management systems which handle only the single-file model are often more commonly referred to as list managers. Because of their simplicity, these systems are often very popular for small projects, but do not offer the full range of features necessary to properly handle large amounts of data.

Relational Models

Relational data base systems allow data to exist in more than one file. The grouping of fields into files is a flexible process, and in fact is done primarily for convienience in storage. Fields can be added, moved to other files, or removed at will in order to examine various patterns in the data. It is for this reason that the relational model is often referred to as a **data-level model**. A purely relational data base by definition does not contain any predefined associations between fields or files; instead, all relations are specified at the time of data base access. This provides maximum flexibility in the system, but also extracts a price in the form of reduced system speed and response due to the overhead required to set up and establish the requested relationships before acting upon the data itself.

Hierarchical and Network Models

The hierarchical and network models are called **file-level** models because the data base system contains very distinct definitions of the relationships between files. Records in two or more files may be related based on one or more matching field values in each file. The predefined relationships are established basically for efficiency - the data storage and retrieval can be optimized based on the overall structure of the data base.

In the case of the hierarchical model, the relationship between files is a very ridgidly structured, "many children-to-one parent" relationship: like the branches of a tree, each file has one (and only one) "parent" file, but may have any number of "child", or dependent, files. The network model is similar except that the relationships are less rigid: many-to-one, one-to-many, and even many-to-many relationships may occur.

Data Base Query and Information Retrieval

Sorting and Indexing

The most important function of a data base system is to bring order to the data and present it in a logical manner. This is done using either sorting, indexing, or a combination of the two.

Sorting is a process which is simple in concept, but often very slow and unwieldy in execution. It consists of physically arranging the records in a file in an order determined by one or more of the fields in the record. The sort fields are often referred to as the **keys.** Generally, sorting the records in a disk file is done by creating a second copy of the file on the disk, so that sorting even a medium-sized file can be taxing to the system in terms of both time and system resources. In addition, each time a record is added or a key field modified, the file must be resorted.

Indexing is a much more complex process, but it eliminates the sorting required after each change in the data. Instead, a separate file is created, called the **index,** which acts as a cross reference to the main data file. Each record has an entry in the index file which contains the values of the keys for that record as well as the physical location of the record in the data file. Instead of keeping the data sorted and retrieving it directly, the index file constantly keeps track of each record's proper logical position, and points to its physical location in the data file for use in a retrieval request. The smaller size of the index file and its special structure make indexing a much more efficient process. A variety of methods are available which seek to minimize the frequency of index reorganization required.

Ad Hoc Inquiries

Ad hoc inquiries are casual, one-time, non-programmed queries of the data base in which a set of selection criteria is specified and the data base system returns all records meeting those criteria. This is the most common type of query made when a data base system is being used in

the interactive mode. Ad hoc inquiries provide instant data access,
allowing the user to examine the results and, if desired, either broaden
or narrow the search criteria until the desired results are obtained.

Formal Reporting

     More structured access to a data base system usually involves some
type of formal reporting. Criteria for queries which are made at
regularly scheduled intervals or in specific formats are defined once
and then stored, to be accessed as needed. Most data base management
systems provide facilities for building custom reports, extracting data
from one or more files, and incorporating report-specific data, such as
date, time, and summary statistics.

Criteria for Selection of a Data Base Management System

     In planning a data base system, it is most important that the
selection of a DBMS be application-oriented; that is, the software must
be fitted to the application, and not vice versa. An application which
is force-fitted to the wrong software package can become inefficient,
cumbersome, and inflexible. Fortunately, the wide variety of DBMS
software available on the market today makes it possible to find a
suitable package for almost every application. Some guidelines to
follow in selecting a DBMS package are:

Purpose of the Data Base

  - What type of data base will the DBMS be used to construct?
          Simple   single-file applications   will probably require
     nothing more than an interface for entering data and simple
     tools to sort, select, and retrieve it. However, careful
     attention must be paid to the structure of the application; what
     may at first appear to be a suitable single-file application can
     often benefit greatly from multiple-file capabilities. If the
     data includes a number of relatively constant parameters
     associated with a single data item, such as the parameters of a
     streamflow monitor or the time, date, location and duration of a
     rainfall event, these can be stored in a separate file and
     "looked-up" as needed by the other data files. Having less data
     in each file will also speed up sorting and retrieval and
     facilitate easier data handling overall.
          The appropriate data model to consider depends on the size
     of the data base and the amount of flexibility desired. For
     maximum flexibility of data associations and retrievals, the
     relational model may be appropriate, whereas more efficiency in
     operation will be achieved using a hierarchical or network model
     that has been specifically customized to the application.

Ease of Application Development and Maintainence

- How much work am I willing to do now, and will the data base system be changing in the future?
    First, examine the capabilities of the staff that will be building the data base. Can they program a complete system, or should a "canned", fully programmed application be considered? Perhaps a system with automatic data definition and screen building functions can be used to speed development. In terms of future plans, how difficult is it to redefine one or more parts of the data base system once data has been entered? If the original staff constructing the data base will not be available when future enhancements are implemented, how difficult will it be for new staff to learn the system well enough to make the necessary changes? Also consider the documenting capabilities of the DBMS. A self-documenting system will aid greatly in tracking and recording changes in the data base over time.

Data Base Size

- How much data will I be storing?
    Most microcomputer-based DBMS systems are capable of handling records numbering in the tens of thousands; data quantities above that are best handled on a minicomputer or mainframe system. Generally, if the data is properly structured and multiple files are allowed, the number of fields allowed per record or the absolute record size will not be as limiting as the allowable number of records in a file. What will also be of concern in large applications is speed and efficiency of retrieval. Indexed access and retrieval is a must in any large application, and multiple file capability is necessary to minimize data redundancy.

Special Data Types and Their Requirements

- What type of data will I be storing?
    Numeric data and short alphanumeric descriptions can be handled by almost all DBMS software. Scientific and engineering calculations will require a larger degree of precision than financial applications; not all systems can handle scientific notation. Built-in trigonometric and statistical functions may be a plus. Large amounts of textual information will require a DBMS with text handling capabilities. Features to look for in a text-oriented DBMS include word-processing capabilities (editing, formatting, etc.), sufficient allowable field sizes, and variable length records. The provision of other special data types, such as money, date, time, and phone number, or the ability to define them yourself, makes data entry and editing more convenient.

Hardware Requirements

- <u>What type of hardware is needed to run the system?</u>
  Existing hardware may constrain the size and type of data base system possible, but planning for any significantly-sized system should include careful consideration of the hardware requirements. For microcomputer-based systems, a hard disk drive may be required to handle the amount of data involved and to speed up data access and retrieval. Spreadsheet veterans should remember that, unlike spreadsheets, most data base systems keep the data on disk and retrieve it one record at a time, so that disk drive performance is a much more speed limiting factor than the size of core memory. If access is required by more than one user at a time, some type of microcomputer network or a multi-user minicomputer may be required.

Modes of Data Access

- <u>How will data be entered, edited and retrieved?</u>
  The type of user interface incorporated in a data base system will affect the usefulness and efficiency of the query and retrieval process. A user who is intimately familiar with the data base system°s structure and programming concepts may find a command-oriented interface a sufficiently flexible and efficient approach, while one who is less familiar or uses the system less frequently may prefer a menu-driven system. One concept for data retrieval which is gaining popularity is known as Query By Example, or QBE. In this procedure, the user specifies the data base search criteria via a "fill-in-the-blanks" interface, and the logical search specification is built automatically.

Data Presentation Capabilities

- <u>What formats for data presentation will be desired?</u>
  Quick listings will be useful for ad hoc inquiries of the data base, whereas more formal reports will be required for presentation purposes. If you need to use a standard form for reporting data, the system should have a "free-formatting" feature which allows you to position output anywhere on the page. For a multiple file system, make sure that the report writing feature can handle data from more than one file. Also, examine the options a system offers for translating data into other formats. Special presentations or post-processing of the data may be best handled by another package, such as a word processor or spreadsheet, or by a custom-written program.

Data Security

- <u>Will any of my data need to be protected from unauthorized access?</u>
    Data security is usually needed in two cases - to prevent access to sensitive data, and to prevent unauthorized changes from being made to certain portions of the data. Various levels of security are available in which data can be protected at the file, record, or field levels. Passwords or some other type of security checks are usually used to authorize access to the proper data. In multi-user and networking applications in which a common data base is shared by many users, some type of security will be necessary to prevent simultaneous modification of the same data.

Vendor Support

- <u>What type of support is available for the DBMS?</u>
    Vendor and/or software dealer support in areas such as technical support, maintainence, and training are important factors to consider, especially if you will be building the data base system yourself. If you are buying a "canned" application, find out if custom programming services are available to meet the special needs of your application.

Conclusions

Data base systems are highly efficient tools which, when implemented properly, can provide more accurate and flexible management of information. The wide variety of data base management software available provides the scientist and engineer with an array of potential solutions, but at the same time may cause confusion and frustration for those without an adequate understanding of both the capability of DBMS software and the particular problems of their own data base application. A thorough understanding of the purpose of the data base system, the characteristics of each data element and the relationships between all elements under consideration is the number one priority in evaluating data base management software; only after this understanding is reached can a proper fit be made between the DBMS software and the application to be developed.

Managing A Water Control Database

Scott W. Boyd*, A.M. ASCE

ABSTRACT

The management of a Water Control Database is important to the usability of the database. Three areas of importance in the management of a database are: 1. good management practices, 2. management tools, and 3. data identification. Items that make for good database management are discussed, and examples of how these are used in the management of the CROHMS (Columbia River Operational Hydromet Management System) Database are presented.

INTRODUCTION

The proper management of a Water Control Database is just as important as the design of the database. A database that is not properly managed will fail to meet the needs of the users of the database even if it is a well designed one. This paper will cover the areas which have shown to be significant in a well managed database. Three topics that have demonstrated their importance in making a database well managed will be covered: 1. good management practices, 2. management tools, and 3. data identification. This paper is based on the author's experience at the North Pacific Division, U.S. Army Corps of Engineers in the Pacific Northwest. This experience includes working with the different versions of the CROHMS (Columbia River Operational Hydromet Management System) Database. The problems which the Corps has experienced, along with the solutions that the Corps has developed as they relate to good database management will be presented.

CROHMS DATABASE

The CROHMS Database is an integral part of the management of the Columbia River basin. The Columbia River drains an area of 259 thousand square miles (670.8 thousand square kilometers). CROHMS is an inter-agency agreement which was established in 1970 to better manage hydromet data from the Columbia River Basin. In the agreement, seven different government agencies agreed to share their hydromet data to avoid duplication and reduce expense (1). The current version of the CROHMS Database has been in existence for five years. The Corps is currently reorganizing the CROHMS Database in order to improve it, based on the experience of the last several years.

*Chief, Data Management/CROHMS Unit, Reservoir Control Center, Army Corps of Engineers, North Pacific Division, P.O. Box 2870, Portland, OR 97208

The CROHMS Database currently contains data from approximately 1100 different locations. There are over 5000 different identifiable pieces of data in the database. Approximately 44,000 items of data are added to the database each day around the clock.

GOOD MANAGEMENT PRACTICES

Management practices that make for a well managed Water Control Database are: 1. the need to have a well defined method of resolving differences of opinion about the management of the database, 2. the need to maintain consistency in the database, 3. the benefits of having a written plan for the use of the database, 4. the need to keep the users informed about the database (especially about changes in the database), and 5. the need to coordinate with other agencies.

When there are many different groups of people using a Water Control Database there will be differences in opinion on how the database should be managed. A method needs to be established to handle these differences and to make decisions on how the database is managed.

In order to resolve disagreements and make decisions about the CROHMS Database, a three level group of committees has been created. The first level committee consists of the people from the main agencies concerned with the database who work with the database on a day to day basis. The second group is comprised of their supervisors. The third level consists of the second group's supervisors. Most of the problems have been resolved in the first level committee. A few have been resolved in the second. The third level committee has not had to be used yet.

Consistency is one of the most important aspects of a well managed database. This particularly applies in the area of data identification. A database that is consistent in the way it operates makes it easier for users of the database to locate the data that they need. If the database is not consistent, data will be hard to find, thus reducing the usability of the database. A large part of the problems we have had in the Pacific Northwest with the CROHMS Database has been due to the lack of providing this consistency in regard to data identification. In order to achieve control of the database one person or a group of people must be responsible for the management of the database. For the CROHMS Database, the database manager is responsible for maintaining consistency.

A third important item in managing a Water Control Database is proper planning. A plan should be developed for the database. The most important item of this plan is stating the purpose of the database. Some of the questions that should be answered are: 1. what are the data in the database to be used for, 2. should all water management data be kept in one or many databases. 3. how long should data be kept, and 4. how should data in the database be identified.

If these items are not decided upon, the different groups using the database will have their own set of assumptions concerning the purpose of the database. This can lead to-conflicts over how the database is to be managed and used. The result is that each group of users bases their work with the database on their perception of the database's goals. The database manager(s) needs a plan to guide the decisions that are made regarding the database. Without a plan to guide the manager the manager's decisions will have to be made based on the manager's perceptions of the purpose of the database. This could lead to mismanagement. The CROHMS Database does not have a formal plan about the operation and function of the database. Problems have surfaced because of the lack of a formal plan.

A Water Control Database is not static. Changes are going to occur. New data will be added and existing data will be changed. One of the items that has to be provided for in a well managed database is a clear method to keep users informed about changes in the database. For the CROHMS Database, a form has been developed that must be filled out before changes to the database can be made. This form is circulated to the different users of the database before the changes are made. This has helped solve the problem of keeping the users informed about changes in the database. Another idea being considered is making changes in the database only at a set time. Maybe once a month would be adequate so the users could limit the changes they make.

Along with keeping users informed about changes to the database, information about how the database functions must be sent to the users. One effective method to keep users informed is to develop a users manual. The users manual should cover such items as: 1. how to access data in the database, 2. where data are located in the database, and 3. some general idea of how the database is run.

Unfortunately, a users manual for the CROHMS Database has not been produced. Because of this, one of the problems that has occurred is that users do not use the database to its fullest potential. They say it is "hard to use". Hopefully in the future a manual will be produced.

Recently, a CROHMS Database bulletin has been started to keep users informed about current developments. The bulletin's primary purpose is to keep users informed about the upcoming changes. It informed them about the new version of the CROHMS Database. In addition, information was included on how to use the new database. More of these bulletins are planned for the future.

It is important to coordinate with other agencies in your locality that are involved with water control data. In this day of limited resources, an agency needs to take advantage of other agencies' data and other database management items. Included are such items as software and data identification systems. Fewer problems will arise when dealing with other agencies if the system is well coordinated.

MANAGEMENT TOOLS

Good management tools are essential to the proper management of a database. The tools that are being developed to help in the management of the CROHMS Database are concerned with database documentation. This documentation is used to help manage the information stored in the database. This system of documentation was developed to help the database manager; however, the documentation is also available to the users of the database.

Database documentation is a tool that can assist the proper management of a database. This documentation includes: 1. information on what data are in the database, 2. where the data come from, and 3. where data are stored in the database. It is helpful to both the database manager(s) and the users if this documentation is available both in written form and via an on line computer system.

This documentation serves two purposes. The first is to help the users find the data that they want. Also, this allows them to determine where data are coming from so that if there is a problem with the data they can notify the proper person to solve the problem. The second purpose of the documentation is to help the database manager(s) keep track of the data and avoid duplication of location and parameter identification.

If this documentation is not available or maintained on a current basis the users become dependent on their memories to get needed information. In a large database system no one can remember all of the needed information. There is also the possibility of not properly assigning data identifications. Proper documentation also allows the manager to keep track of what is in the database. Questions can be answered regarding what data identification elements are being used in the database: How many stations are there? How often do data come in? An advantage of keeping the documentation on line is that users of the database can have easier access to it and the documentation can be kept more current.

The CROHMS Database is currently being reorganized. While this is being done, a "master file" of the database was developed in order to provide the type of documentation mentioned above. This "master file" was principally developed as a tool for the database manager to use in setting up the new CROHMS Database. However, provisions have been made so the data in the "master file" are accessible in an easy to use format for the users. The "master file" is a separate data file from the database itself. In the future, the "master file" is planned to be a part of the database. The advantage of having the "master file" as part of the database is to make it easier for the users to access the "master file" at the same time they are accessing the database.

The "master file" currently includes information on most of the data that are stored in the database. For observed data there is information on which agency sends in the data, how often the data come into the database, where the data are stored in the database, and what parameter codes the data are identified by before they are posted to the database. For each location the following information is stored: 1. the station code, 2. the station name, 3. the station number, 4. the latitude and longitude, 5. the elevation, and 6. if it is a GOES station, the GOES platform i.d.

For processed data, such as calculated inflows, the method that is used to make the calculation is stored along with what information is used in the calculations. Similar information will be stored when forecast data is put into the database. In the future, additional information will be added to the "master file" such as basin identification and additional hydrologic information. The information in the "master file" will be used to generate manuals for our system.

Along with the documentation in the "master file", notebooks are being kept with information concerning each group of data that is entered into our system. Copies of the files that control such functions as compressing the data, translating the data and other processing that is done to the data are kept in the notebooks. In addition, information is kept on when data records are added to the database and the calculations which determine the amount of space assigned. Along with information on each group of data, a separate record is kept for each physical location. For each physical location or station the following information is kept: 1. the parameter codes for that station in the database, 2. who sends in the data, and 3. a record of any changes. In the future, some of this information will be added to the "master file". The purpose of this documentation is to have all the information the database manager needs readily available.

DATA IDENTIFICATION

The proper identification of data in a Water Control Database is one of the most critical management jobs. When data are properly identified, the users of the database are able to obtain the data they need. If data are not properly identified, the database will be very difficult to use and will not function up to its full potential.

Proper identification of data in a Water control database consists of two elements. The first element is location, or station identification. This element lets the user know where, physically, a piece of data is from. The second element of data identification is parameter identification. Parameter identification tells the user what the piece of data is. Developing the proper system of parameter identification has been one of the biggest problems with the CROHMS Database. On the other hand, the system of location or station identification used in the CROHMS Database has been very successful.

A good system of location identification should uniquely identify every location in the database. The location identifier should be easily recognizable and there should be some method behind the system that is used. The system used in the CROHMS Database has been very successful and can be used as an example of a good system.

The CROHMS Database location system has been in use in all versions of the database. All locations are identified by a three or four letter station code. Stations with three letter codes are dam sites. All the rest of the locations have a four letter code. The last letter of the four letter code identifies the state the station is in; O stands for Oregon, W for Washington and so on. Stream gages located directly downstream from a dam are identified by the three letter code of the dam followed by the letter of the state identifier. For example, Cougar dam in Oregon has the station code CGR and the downstream gage has the station code CGRO.

There have not been any major problems with this system. A few minor questions have been raised in the last several years. One of the questions that has surfaced is how big an area does one station identifier cover. How far apart can two gages be before a new identifier should be assigned? A set answer has not yet been determined. Generally the decision has been made by judging each case by itself. At dams any measurement taken at the project has used the location identifier of the project. This system for the dams has worked well in the past. However, problems are starting to arise with water quality data where recordings of water temperature and dissolved gas measurements are taken at several places at the dam. The problem has been dealt with by assigning nonstandard location identifiers. In the future, the problem will be handled by the use of vector data parameters (where several parameters can be assigned to each reading, such as water temperature and depth).

Another minor problem concerns use of the three letter station identifiers for dams. These identifiers do not fit in with the National Weather Services Handbook 5 system. (4)   The Handbook 5 system specifies that station identifiers are four letters plus a number. The last letter and the number refer to the state. For example, data in Oregon would end in 03 (Oregon is the third state alphabetically which starts with the letter O). For example, the downstream gage below Cougar dam, given above, would have the code CGRO3. It is simple to transform CGRO to CGRO3 in the CROHMS system because of the use of a different letter for each of the states. This simple transformation does not work with the three letter dam identifiers since CGR cannot be simply transformed by changing it to CGRO3 which is not the same location in the CROHMS system as CGRO. A solution to this problem has not been worked out yet.   The CROHMS Database gets a large amount of data from the Weather Service. If the CROHMS Database was being designed today it might have been better if only four letter station identifiers had been used to maintain compatibility with the Weather Service system.

A good system of parameter identification should have several important features: 1. it should clearly identify the data, 2. it should be easy to use, and 3. it should be able to handle all the types of data that are planned to be stored in the database. One system that meets these needs is the SHEF (Standard Hydrologic Exchange Format) system of parameter codes. This is the system that is currently being used in the newest version of the CROHMS Database. SHEF has been adopted by the National Weather Service and the Corps of Engineers as the preferred method of interagency hydrologic data exchange. Consequently, using SHEF parameter codes in the CROHMS Database has the added benefit of being compatible with data that are transmitted in the SHEF format. SHEF was developed by the Portland River Forecast Center of the National Weather Service and the North Pacific Division, U.S. Army Corps of Engineers based on the experience gained from using the CROHMS system.

The SHEF parameter code system is the third system of parameter identification that has been used in the different versions of the CROHMS Database. The following discussion will describe each of the three systems used: their good points and the reasons for going to a different version. All of the versions previous to SHEF were well thought out. However, these versions had problems that arose due to the changing nature of the CROHMS Database. These problems are a good example of problems that can occur with parameter identification.

The first system of parameter identification was developed from the CBT (Columbia Basin Telecommunications, formerly known as CBTT) (2) method of data transmittal. This is still being used as the primary method of data entry into the CROHMS Database. The CBT method of data transmittal system was designed for data collection over the CBT network. Data on the CBT network are manually entered and are identified by a two letter parameter code. For example, some parameter codes are: FB for forebay, GH for gage height, and TW for tailwater height. This system of parameter identification is very simple and most of the heavily used data measurement parameter codes are visually recognizable. The system works quite well for common hydrologic measurements. Where this sytem runs into trouble is when parameter codes are set up for variations of the common measurements such as processed values and forecast values. For an illustration, look at flow data parameter codes. Instantaneous flow at a point has the CBT parameter code of Q. One of the items that is stored in the database is daily average flow. That has a CBT parameter code of QD. Other data items are 6 hourly average flow (parameter code QQ) and maximum and minimum flow for the day (parameter codes QX and QN). When one starts to consider all the variations that can be thought of for flows alone (the CBT manual lists over 50 parameter codes for flow) it can be seen how it would be hard to remember all of the parameter codes. The system also loses the visual recognition the parameter codes. As an illustration, estimated daily maximum discharge has the parameter code of HZ. In order to overcome these problems the CROHMS parameter code system was developed.

The CROHMS parameter code (3) was designed as a structured code. Each element in the parameter code gives different information about the datum. There are five elements in the CROHMS parameter code system. The parameter code is six letters long with all elements except the first, which is two letters long, one letter long. The structure of the CROHMS parameter code is represented by PCTDEP. The five elements are:

1. PC-parameter code (or physical element) which identifies the type of data that is being measured such as gage heights, air temperature, and flow;

2. T-type which identifies the type of data such as forecast, observed, visual and telemetered;

3. D-duration which identifies the time period of the data such as instantaneous, daily and weekly;

4. E-extremum which identifies if the datum is maximum or a minimum for a certain time period such as maximum for the day, average for the month, and minimum of a six hour time period;

5. P-probability which identifies for forecast data the probability of the value being exceeded.

While each individual parameter code is longer than the equivalent CBT parameter code, the number of items that one has to remember is fewer because each letter has a meaning based on the element. The user knows that when there is a D in the fourth letter of the code that the datum is a daily value no matter what the other letters are. When there is a QR in the first two letters, the parameter code is a flow measurement of some type. Additional examples are:

1. QRZIZZ (Z is a filler in any element) is an instantaneous flow measurement,

2. QRZQZZ is a six hourly average flow,

3. QRZDZZ is a daily average flow. Only one element is changed to indicate the different types of flow data.

This system has worked very well except for one problem area, and it is the basis for the SHEF parameter code system. The problem is in the second element (T-type). In the CROHMS system some data which are otherwise identical comes into the database along several different paths. In a few cases, there are as many as four different paths. The data from different paths needs to be assigned different parameter codes to store them separately in the database. Storing them separately helps in determining where problems are coming from. Furthermore, sometimes two readings taken at the same time can have significantly different values. In one case, gage heights taken at the same location, differ by 50 feet due to different datums. In the definition of the CROHMS parameter codes only two letters were assigned to differentiate between different paths for observed data in the type element (Z for Filler and T for telemetered data). There was not a way provided to differentiate between data that was telemetered over two or more different paths. When the SHEF parameter code system was developed this problem was solved.

The SHEF parameter code system (5) is a direct development of the CROHMS parameter code system. The only changes that were made were that one additional element was added and the location of another element was changed. The additional element was the source element. The type element in the SHEF parameter code system only identifies the type of data, such as forecast or observed. The new source element allows for a further differentiation among each type. The duration element was moved after the physical element (or parameter code) because the duration is of more significance than the type and source elements. This was also done to facilitate the use of "minimum keys" in database retrieval. The six elements of the SHEF code are represented PEDTSEP. The six elements are: 1. PE-physical element same as PC in the CROHMS parameter code, 2. D-duration same as D in the CROHMS parameter code, 3. T-identifies type of data such as observed, forecast, 4. S-source a further refinement of the type element, 5. E-extremum same as E in the CROHMS parameter ccode, and 6. P-probability same as P in the CROHMS parameter code.

The use of a "minimum key" is a key feature of the SHEF parameter code system. The purpose of "minimum key" is to cut down on the number of elements entered by people who ask the system for data. Each physical element has a standard set of defaults for each of the other five elements in the SHEF code. These defaults are chosen to represent the most common data that the users will want for that physical element. For example, to obtain an instantaneous gage height, all a user would have to enter is the physical element HG. The software will translate it to HGIRAZZ which is the full SHEF code for an instantaneous observed gage height. In another example, to get daily precipitation amounts the user would have to enter only PP which is the physical element for precipitation amount. In this case the duration would default to D for daily instead of I in the example above because a daily value would be the one that users would most likely want.

One feature that the SHEF code has is dual use of the source value (S). The source value can rank the value of measurements of the same type but come in over different paths. As an example, the best gage height reading at a location would have the source code of A, the second best B, and so on down to D. The source value can also be used to indicate the path the data took. For example, the source G indicates the data came from the GOES system, the code R indicates that the data came over a radio network. This feature allows users of the database to retrieve data by either method depending on their needs.

CONCLUSION

From the discussion above, it is easy to see that as much, or more, effort needs to be put into managing a Water Control Database as is put into the design of the database. A well managed database will provide better data to the users of the database, which is the primary purpose of the database. It will also reduce the work of the people who have to manage the database. The effort put in will be will rewarded by the results.

APPENDIX. -- REFERENCES

1. Columbia River Water Management Group, "Interagency Memorandum of Understanding for Task Force on Operational Hydromet Data Management", Portland, Oregon, June 1970.

2. Corps of Engineers, U.S. Army, North Pacific Division, "CBTT Users Manual", Portland, Oregon, September 1980.

3. Corps of Engineers, U.S. Army, North Pacific Division, "CROHMS Programming Guide", Portland, Oregon, August 1980.

4. National Weather Service, U. S. Department of Commerce, "National Weather Service Communications Handbook No. 5", NOAA/NWS Location Identifiers, Silver Spring, Maryland, March, 1977.

5. National Weather Service, U.S. Department of Commerce, Northwest River Forecast Center, "Standard Hydrologic Exchange Format (SHEF) Version 1", Portland, Oregon, November 1982.

Hydrological Database Management

By Evangelos Paleologos[1] and Mohammad Karamouz[2], A.M. ASCE

Introduction

Development of hydrological database management is investigated in this study. Lotus 1-2-3, a commercially available database, which makes use of spreadsheet has been used to solve a broad range of hydrological problems on microcomputer. Through the use of the database, any change in data or modifications can be made interactively and globally at a glance. It gives the user the versatility to structure the data in the most convenient way. Thus the data can be presented either in the most detailed way or in a very compact form (4).

The spreadsheet format gives the user the advanatage of seeing the intermediate results that lead to the final evaluation, thus enhancing the understanding of the relationships that create and influence the end result. Originally, spreadsheets were used by accountants and managers and they proved to be a powerful tool for financial and budget analysis. However, nowadays they are used by such a large spectrum of professionals, that a survey conducted by the market research firm Software Access found that only 39 percent use it for the purpose originally designed (1). It has already been proven to be highly effective in the solution of engineering problems (15), (16). The use of the spreadsheet in database management can only be fully utilized through the use of "Macros", a stored sequence of keystrokes.

This article explains how database can be applied to hydrological problems. Special emphasis is placed upon the spreadsheet and the macros, their potential to fully automate the use of the database as well as their limitations. Applications are drawn to problems such as hydrograph analysis, backwater calculations, river and reservoir routing, water quality and even some stochastic hydrology problems. In most of these problems a step by step procedure should be followed. Furthermore, tables should be constructed by manipulating a series of columns of data through simple arithmetic calculations. Solution of many hydrological problems involves trial and error selection of parameters and graphical observation of several alternatives, and this makes the use of the spreadsheet embeded in a database even more attractive.

1 Graduate Student, Department of Civil and Environmental Engineering, Polytechnic Institute of New York, Brooklyn, N.Y. 11201

2 Assistant Professor, Department of Civil and Enviromental Engineering, Polytechnic Institute of New York, Brooklyn, N.Y. 11201

Database And Spreadsheet

A database can be defined as a system whose base, whose key concept, is simply a particular way of handling data (8).

The data inserted in a database can be of any type: They can be
numbers, a set of names, addresses or other information, codes, or
pieces of text. Through the database the data are processed (9),(10).
This means that they can be manipulated and transformed to a new piece
of information. They can be stored in a suitable form, retrieved as a
whole or as parts rearranged, compared according to different criteria,
combined with other data, manipulated mathematically or statistically,
used to generate new data or they can be entirely transformed (7).

What is an electronic spreadsheet?

A spreadsheet is nothing but a grid or table, displayed on the
video screen. It is arranged in rows and columns. The most popular
spreadsheet software used today are VisiCalc, Multiplan, Peachcalc and
Lotus 1-2-3. Lotus 1-2-3 is perhaps the most advanced one containing
256 columns and 2,048 rows. It also has the advantage over the other
packages by providing a programming language with many special commands, and allowing much flexibility in its use (5).

The information provided by the Lotus 1-2-3 can be divided as
follows:

1. Basic skills for the use of Lotus: This consists of information
   having to do with the different keys of the keyboard. Another
   important aspect is the creation of a cell entry which may be a
   number, a label, or a formula.

2. Commands. These can determine the overall appearance of the
   worksheet-columns widths and overall display formats. They can
   determine the way in which the formulas are calculated. They can
   make large-scale changes to the worksheet's contents, such as
   moving whole ranges of data, or inserting empty rows and columns.

3. Functions. These are built in formulas. The most important, from
   an engineering point of view, are the mathematical, the logical
   and the statistical ones. However these are mostly of an elementary level due to its general-purpose orientation.

4. Macros. Macros are one of the most essential and important parts
   giving the spreadsheet a new dimension (3). A keyboard macro is
   nothing but a stored sequence of keystrokes. This means that
   instead of executing the keystrokes manually, they are recorded as
   a label entry in a certain cell or range of cells in the spreadsheet. The cell or range of cells that contain the above information is then assigned to a letter key. But a macro can be much
   more than just a collection of keystrokes (2). Inside the macro
   decisions can be made based on the values in the spreadsheet or on
   actions taken by the user during macro execution.

Applications

Lotus 1-2-3 is applied to river routing, backwater profile calculations, hydrograph analysis, and water quality problems. Other applications are also discussed. A TI-PC Microcomputer with 256K memory is used this study.

Application 1: The Muskingum Method

The Muskingum method is employed to predict the outflow hydrograph from a watershed subjected to a known amount of precipitation (12). It employs two equations:

1) The equation of continuity: $I - O = \dfrac{dS}{dt}$

   where I : inflow rate to reach.

   O : outflow rate from reach.

   $\dfrac{dS}{dt}$: rate of change of the storage in the reach.

2) A relationship between the storage and the dischange within the system.

$$S = K \left[xI + (1-x)O \right]$$

   where K : storage time constant for the reach

   x : a weighting factor for the given river section.

Four different macros are used in this application. The first macro puts the titles, arranges the form of the problem and stops for the data to be inserted. The second calculates the main body of the table up to the storage and sets the directions for the graphs. The third evaluates the $[xI + (1-x)O]$ for a value of x and plots this quality versus the storage S. Since the storage is a linear expression of $xI + (1-x)O$ the most linear graph is associated with the best x value. The fourth macro estimates the parameters needed for the least-squares line and finds the value of K as the reciprocal of the slope. The advantages of using Lotus 1-2-3 in this application are as follows:

1) The entire process is interactive, both the tabular and the graphical results are available on the screen

2) The process of finding a satisfactory value of x can be done quickly. Furthermore the improvement of this value can be carried on to a desirable accuracy.

3) By changing values in the data, the whole table is recalculated instantly and the effect of these changes is presented both in numerical and graphical forms.

Tables 1, 2 and Figures 1,2 demonstrate this application $x = .35$ produces the best linear graph. Then the K value of 28.60 can calculated by the least square macro.

Table 1 - Muskinghum Method for X = 0.2

Inflow	Outflow	(I1+I2)/2	(O1+O2)/2	S2	X= 0.2
36	58			0.00E+00	53.60
43	46	39.50	52.00	0.00E+00	45.40
121	42	82.00	44.00	1.64E+06	57.80
346	61	233.50	51.50	9.50E+06	118.00
575	149	460.50	105.00	2.49E+07	234.20
717	326	646.00	237.50	4.25E+07	404.20
741	536	729.00	431.00	5.54E+07	577.00
612	674	676.50	605.00	5.85E+07	661.60
440	681	526.00	677.50	5.19E+07	632.80
328	560	384.00	620.50	4.17E+07	513.60
251	437	289.50	498.50	3.27E+07	399.80
196	341	223.50	389.00	2.55E+07	312.00
153	272	174.50	306.50	1.98E+07	248.20
124	218	138.50	245.00	1.52E+07	199.20
101	180	112.50	199.0C	1.15E+07	164.20
84	150	92.50	165.00	8.36E+06	136.80
71	124	77.50	137.00	5.79E+06	113.40
60	104	65.50	114.00	3.69E+06	95.20
52	86	56.00	95.00	2.01E+06	79.20
46	73	49.00	79.50	6.91E+05	67.60
41	62	43.50	67.50	0.00E+00	57.80
37	52	39.00	57.00	0.00E+00	49.00

Table 2 - Muskinghum Method for X= 0.35

Inflow	Outflow	(I1+I2)/2	(O1+O2)/2	S2	X= 0.35
36	58			0.00E+00	50.30
43	46	39.50	52.00	0.00E+00	44.95
121	42	82.00	44.00	1.64E+06	69.65
346	61	233.50	51.50	9.50E+06	160.75
575	149	460.50	105.00	2.49E+07	298.10
717	326	646.00	237.50	4.25E+07	462.85
741	536	729.00	431.00	5.54E+07	607.75
612	674	676.50	605.00	5.85E+07	652.30
440	681	526.00	677.50	5.19E+07	596.65
328	560	384.00	620.50	4.17E+07	478.80
251	437	289.50	498.50	3.27E+07	371.90
196	341	223.50	389.00	2.55E+07	290.25
153	272	174.50	306.50	1.98E+07	230.35
124	218	138.50	245.00	1.52E+07	185.10
101	180	112.50	199.00	1.15E+07	152.35
84	150	92.50	165.00	8.36E+06	126.90
71	124	77.50	137.00	5.79E+06	105.45
60	104	65.50	114.00	3.69E+06	88.60
52	86	56.00	95.00	2.01E+06	74.10
46	73	49.00	79.50	6.91E+05	63.55
41	62	43.50	67.50	0.00E+00	54.65
37	52	39.00	57.00	0.00E+00	46.75

n=	22
E(Y)=	236.91
	39386.42
VAR(Y)=	41261.97
E(X)=	1.87E+07
	3.80E+14
VAR(X)=	3.98E+14
COV(X,Y)=	3.86E+09
K=	28.607516

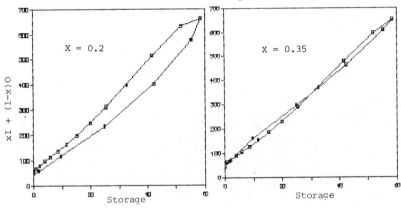

Fig. 1 Muskinghum Method   Fig. 2 - Muskinghum Method

X = 0.2   X = 0.35

xI + (1-x)O

Storage   Storage

Table 3 - The Direct Step Method

Q=	400
b=	20
z=	2
n=	0.025
So=	0.0016
a=	1.1
yc=	2.22
yn=	3.36
g=	+32.17
START:	5
STEP:	0.2
STOP:	3.2

y	P	A	R	R(4/3)	V	aV(2)/2g	E
5.00	42.36	150.00	3.54	5.40	2.667	0.1216	5.1216
4.80	41.47	142.08	3.43	5.17	2.815	0.1355	4.9355
4.60	40.57	134.32	3.31	4.93	2.978	0.1516	4.7516
4.40	39.68	126.72	3.19	4.70	3.157	0.1703	4.5703
4.20	38.78	119.28	3.08	4.47	3.353	0.1923	4.3923
4.00	37.89	112.00	2.96	4.24	3.571	0.2181	4.2181
3.80	36.99	104.88	2.84	4.01	3.814	0.2487	4.0487
3.60	36.10	97.92	2.71	3.78	4.085	0.2853	3.8853
3.40	35.21	91.12	2.59	3.55	4.390	0.3295	3.7295

DE	Sf	Sav.	So-Sav.	Dx	x
	0.000371				
0.1861	0.000432	0.000401	0.001199	155	155
0.1839	0.000506	0.000469	0.001131	163	316
0.1813	0.000596	0.000551	0.001049	173	491
0.1781	0.000708	0.000652	0.000948	188	679
0.1742	0.000846	0.000777	0.000823	212	890
0.1694	0.001021	0.000934	0.000666	254	1144
0.1634	0.001242	0.001131	0.000469	349	1493
0.1558	0.001527	0.001384	0.000216	722	2215

Application 2: The Direct Step Method

The direct step method is used for the computation of gradually - varied-flow profiles (11). It employs:

1)   The energy equation in the form: $\Delta x = \dfrac{\Delta E}{S_o - S_f}$

2)   The Manning formula: $S_f = \dfrac{n^2 \, v^2}{2.22 \, R^{4/3}}$.

where: y : the depth of flow.
            v : the mean velocity.
            α : the energy coefficient.
            S_o : the bottom slope
            S_f : the friction slope
            S_{av} : the average value of S_f
            R : the hydraulic radius
            E : the specific energy $(E = y + \alpha \dfrac{v^2}{2g}$).

     The vertical increment, for the depth of flow can be chosen by the user to any degree of accuracy and a sensitivity analysis can be easily performed. Any changes in discharge, slope, Manningn, energy coefficient can be incorporated and the difference in the water surface profile can be observed interactively. The result of this application are shown in Table 3 and Figure 3.

Application 3: Total Hydrograph - Direct Runoff

     In this application the water-stage and its relationship with the discharg are know.

     In order to separate the base flow from the total hydrograph, the direct runoff is terminated a fixed time after the peak of the hydrograph. This time N is calculated using the formulas: $N = 0.8 \, A^{0.2}$ where A: the drainage area in square Km and N is given in days.

     After the base-flow line is established the direct runoff can be estimated. The graphs for the total hydrograph and the direct runoff are shown in Figures 4, 5. The whole problem is done is S.I. units (see Table 4). For this particular problem $Q = 30 \, (Z-475.0)^{2.5}$ where Z: the gage reading.

Application 4: Dissolved-Oxygen Sag

In order to evaluate the oxygen deficit D in time t the equation:
$$D = \frac{K_1 Lo}{K_2 - K_1} \, (e^{-K_1 t} - e^{-K_2 t}) + Do \, e^{-K_2 t}$$

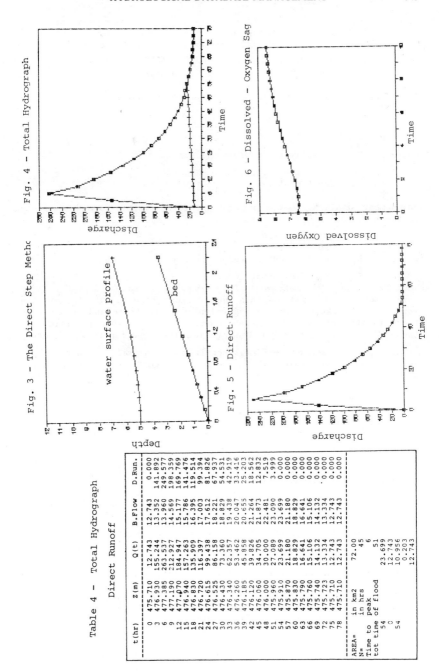

Fig. 4 - Total Hydrograph

Fig. 3 - The Direct Step Method

Fig. 5 - Direct Runoff

Fig. 6 - Dissolved - Oxygen Sag

Table 4 - Total Hydrograph

is used, where: Do : initial oxygen deficit at the point of waste
                          discharge.
                    Lo : initial concentration of the organic matter.
                    K_1 : coefficient of deoxygenation
                    K_2 : coefficient of reaeration

The K_2 is calculated with the O'Connor and Dobbins formula (6).

$$K_2 = \frac{(D_L V)^{\frac{1}{2}}}{H^{3/2}}$$

where D_L : diffusivity of oxygen in water.
            V : velocity of flow.
            H : depth of flow.

Adjustment of K_1, K_2 to the temperature of the mixture is made according
to the formula:

$$K_T = K_{20} \; 1.047^{T-20}$$

where K_T : coefficient at temperature T
            K_{20} : coefficient at 20°C.

Three macros are used in this application. The first arranges the
format of the table. The second calculates the table and sets directions for the graph. This second macro stops its execution twice: at
the value of K_2 (at 20°C) thus giving the opportunity of directly
changing its value and perform a sensitivity analysis. It also stops,
for the saturation value of O_2 to be inserted. And the third macro
presents the graph.

    The sensitivity analysis based on the different values of the
characterisitics of the wastewater is performed very effectively, and
is presented in both numerical and graphical form (see Table 5
and Figure 6).

Other applications

    Other applications include the:

1. Reservoir Routing where the discharge is a function of the water-
    surface elevation. The elevation-storage curve and the elevation-
    discharge curve as well as the curves of $S - \frac{O \Delta t}{2}$ and $S + \frac{O \Delta t}{2}$ ver-
    sus the elevation can be plotted (13).

2. Manipulation and analysis of the precipitation data can be done
    very effectively. The use of the double-mass curve, the least-
    squares line, the handling of precipitation data as a time series
    and the derivation of synthetic data are some examples where Lotus
    1-2-3 can be applied very effectively.

3.   The application of the S-curve method, the derivation of unit
     hydrographs from simple and complex storms or via-versa are also
     applicable.

4.   The problem of evapotranspivation from an area with the approach
     of Penman, Thornthwaite, Blaney-Griddle etc.

5.   Stochastic Hydrology Modeling and the generation of synthetic data
     (14).

6.   Water quality modeling.

Summary and Conclusion

A database is most suitable in handling the large amount of data
usually required in hydrology. The use of spreadsheet further facilitates the organization, transformation and manipulation of hydrological
data. Lotus 1-2-3, an advanced database-spreadsheet package, is very
effective in dealing with problems of river and reservoir routing,
hydrograph analysis, backwater calculations, water quality modeling,
water resources systems modeling and even stochastic modeling.

Table 5 - Dissolved - Oxygen Sag

	RIVER UPS.	WASTEWATER	RIVER DOWNS.
V(fps) =	1.300		
H(ft) =	10.000		
Q(cfs) =	161.000	34.810	195.810
L(mg/1) =	1.800	19.000	4.858
D.O.(mg/1) =	7.620	1.400	6.514
T(Cel.) =	21.200	26.100	22.071
K1(base e)at 20C=	0.230	0.450	0.269
K2(base e)at 20C=			0.467
K1(mix. temp) =			0.296
K2(mix. temp) =			0.514
Csat.(mix.temp) =			8.790
Initial Def.=			2.276
TIME(days)	DIST.(mi)	DEFICIT(mg/1)	D.O.(mg/1)
0.0	0.000	2.276	6.514
0.5	10.636	2.347	6.443
1.0	21.273	2.322	6.468
1.5	31.909	2.233	6.557
2.0	42.545	2.104	6.686
2.5	53.182	1.952	6.838
3.0	63.818	1.790	7.000
3.5	74.455	1.626	7.164
4.0	85.091	1.466	7.324
4.5	95.727	1.314	7.476
5.0	106.364	1.171	7.619
5.5	117.000	1.039	7.751
6.0	127.636	0.919	7.871
6.5	138.273	0.810	7.980
7.0	148.909	0.713	8.077
7.5	159.545	0.625	8.165
8.0	170.182	0.547	8.243
8.5	180.818	0.478	8.312
9.0	191.455	0.417	8.373
9.5	202.091	0.364	8.426
10.0	212.727	0.317	8.473
T(critical) =	0.591		
Def(min) =	2.349		

Appendix-References

1. Foster, E., "Building Simple Spreadsheets," Personnel Computing, Vol. 9, No. 1, January 1985, pp. 61-67.

2. Strehlo, K., "Streamlined Spreadsheeting With Keyboard Macros," Personal Computing, Vol. 8, No. 5, May 1984, pp. 123-130.

3. Bonner, P., "Stretch Your Spreadsheet To Its Limit," Personal Computing, Vol. 8, No. 4, April 1984, pp. 139-144.

4. Sehr, R., "Saying It With Spreadsheets," Personal Computing, Vol. 8, No. 8, August 1984, pp. 79-87.

5. McCarthy, M., "Getting The Most Out Of Your Spreadsheet," Personal Computing, Vol. 8, No. 6, June 1984, pp. 136-149.

6. Clark, W.J., Viessman, Jr., Hammer, J.M., "Water Supply and Pollution Control," Harper and Row Publishers, Inc., New York, 1965.

7. Cook, R., "Conquering Computer Clutter," High Technology, Vol. 4, No. 12, December 1984, pp. 60-70.

8. Deakin, R., "Primer: An Easy-To-Understand Guide To Database Management Systems," A Plume Book, New American Library, New York and Scarborough, Ontario, 1984.

9. Greene, G., "Database Manager In Microsoft Basic," Tab Books, Inc., Blue Ridge Summit, P.A., 1983.

10. Date, C.J., "Database: A Primer," Adison-Wesley Pub. Co., Reading, MA, 1983.

11. Chow, V.T., "Open-Channer Hydraulics," McGraw-Hill Book Co., Inc., New York, N.Y. 1959.

12. Viessman, W., Knapp, W.J., Lewis, L.G., Harbaugh, E.T., "Introduction To Hydrology," Harper and Row Publishers, Inc., New York, 1972.

13. Linsley, R., Kohler, A.M., Paulhus, L.H.J., "Hydrology For Engineers," McGraw-Hil Book Co., Inc., New York, N.Y. 1958.

14. Karamouz, M., Delleur, J.W., "Statistical Analysis For Evaluation of Reservoir Operating Rules," CE-HSE-82-7, Purdue University Publications, June 1982.

15. Schmidt, W., "Material Balances On A Spreadsheet," Chemical Engineering, December 1984, pp. 67-69.

16. Selk, S., "Spreadsheet Software Solves Engineering Problems," Chemical Engineering, June 1983, pp. 51-53.

COMPUTER-AIDED REAL-TIME RESERVOIR OPERATION METHODS

by Walter O. Wunderlich, M. ASCE

Introduction

Over the years many mathematical models have been developed with potential application to computer-aided real-time reservoir operations. Only a few of these models have been practically used. Some reasons for this lack of implementation will be discussed. Also, a review is given of the types of models that have found use in real-time operations, ranging from basic simulations using only the physical constraint equations to hierarchical multiple-purpose optimization models. Future developments will be aided by the availability of cheap and plentiful computer power combined with more and more sophisticated software including the use of artificial intelligence. A major challenge for the future will be improving short-term inflow and other input forecasting.

Development and Implementation Problems

Real-time operation of reservoirs involves the daily or shorter time step setting of reservoir levels and releases to achieve stated objectives, such as hydropower production and flood control. This process is based on predicted inflows, power demands and system characteristics (unit availabilities) and, thus, requires a certain amount of contingency planning to safeguard against uncertainties in these predictions. By its very nature, real-time reservoir operation requires repetitive calculations until an acceptable schedule for implementation is found. The entire process including input data acquisition and processing as well as the schedule calculations, must be carried out within a very limited period of time. Therefore, reservoir operations has been a prime target for computer application. Over the past 20 years, numerous mathematical models have been developed for simulating reservoir operations and for calculating daily or longer range operation schedules. But only a few of these models have seen practical real-time use. Many reasons have been given for this discrepancy between development effort and practical use (Helweg, et al., 1982; Schultz, 1982; US-OTA, 1982). One reason is that the development effort is not matched by a corresponding implementation effort, simply because the implementation effort is not recognized by developers, users, and managers as a very complicated process that depends on the cooperation of many. Model development and implementation should be considered as integral parts of a total methodology enhancement

*Civil Engineer, Tennessee Valley Authority, P.O. Drawer E, Norris, TN 37828

process. While model development requires the solution of technical problems by developers, implementation involves a special effort by the users to replace existing methods by new ones. Such a changeover usually must be accomplished in addition to the normal workload. Since the new methods must also satisfy management policies, special management support may be required until the new procedures are established. So, unless there is a good working relationship between developers, managers, and users based on an entrepreneurial spirit for exploring new frontiers, the developed tools may not see practical use. But fast advancing computer technology and an upcoming new generation of computer-trained engineers will continue to push for the use of advanced methods. Similarly as the curse of dimensionality in model development is defused by decomposing a multi-state problem into a series of simpler problems at the expense of time, so the model implementation problems may be solved by simple procedures leading the way for more complex ones over time. Therefore, it would be premature at this moment to conclude that advanced water resource management methods have failed. It is more appropriate to say that their potential has not been realized. But this will not remain so in the future. Advanced management methods which have a policy-finding capability based on the optimization of a prespecified operation objective have been successfully applied in areas where the proper incentives existed for their use. For example, since the 1950's, the classical Lagrange (or the variational) approach to optimizing a constrained objective function has become the standard method worldwide for achieving cost minimization in power system operations (Kirchmayer, 1959). Also, commercially available computer software that can tackle complicated optimization problems can be applied with almost no additional development effort (Giles and Wunderlich, 1984).

In principle, one would expect that advanced methods faster executed by computers will produce more alternatives, better contingency plans, and thus, more benefits than simple methods. However, real-time reservoir operations are carried out in the face of a triple uncertainty of input into the system, demand to be met by the system and performance of the system's components. This lack of knowledge or the improper use of the available limited information about the future can produce too conservative or too optimistic schedules. Thus, uncertainty reduces the benefits that can be reaped by advanced methods and masks the losses incurred by the use of simple methods. It has the tendency to level off the difference between the use of good and poor methods. The weakness in making a case for using better methods is, therefore, to some extent due to the weakness of prediction methods for inputs over the near future, from several days up to one or a few weeks ahead.

In the following, a brief review will be given of where we stand and where we most likely will go with computer-aided real-time reservoir operations methods.

Real-Time Operation Tools

Reservoir scheduling consists of two major components: input data prediction and water level and release calculation.

Undisputably, the computer has become the enabling tool in both areas. Disputable are only the methods that are presently being used or not used in both areas. At first scheduling methods will be discussed followed by a discussion of inflow prediction methods.

Physical Process Simulation Models

These models mathematically simulate physical processes, such as the runoff from a watershed for a given rainfall, the downstream channel flow, and stages for a given upstream release, water quality development in streams and reservoirs for given inputs and environmental conditions, etc. These models are based on physical laws and there is usually no decision making necessary inside these models since they are based on strict satisfaction of equalities. Examples of mathematical models for such processes are the mass balance equation, the constituent balance equation, and the force balance equation. For one-dimensional flow in x-direction (i.e., no gradients in the other directions) one can write:

mass balance: $\partial(\rho V)/\partial t = (-\partial(\rho Q)/\partial x + \rho q_0)dx$ (1)

constituent balance (here for heat):

$$d(\rho VcT)/dt = (\partial(k\partial(\rho cTA)/\partial x)/\partial x + h_0)dx \qquad (2)$$

momentum balance: $d(\rho Vu)/dt = fg + fp - fr$ (3)

with ρ being the density of the fluid (water), V the volume of the (water) parcel considered, dt the time step, Q the flowrate, dx the distance step, ρq_0 the source (or sink) of mass, cT the amount of constituent per unit mass (here heat per mass), A the flow area, k the diffusivity of the constituent; h_0 the source (or sink) of constituent; u the velocity of the water in flow direction; and fg, fp, and fr the weight, pressure and resistance forces in flow direction. Note that the substantial differential quotient on the lefthand sides includes local and convective changes, i.e.,

$d(\cdot)/dt = \partial(\cdot)/\partial t + u\partial(\cdot)/\partial x.$

Specific examples of physical process simulation models based on the above equations are:

- Quasi-steady reservoir routing models based on Equation 1; use relatively large time and distance steps (e.g., 6 hours and more and the entire length of a reservoir); release or ending storage determined by operator.

- Muskingum-type flow routing models based on Equation 1; for unsteady non-uniform flow; use empirical release rule, usually based on water storage in reach as a proxy for dynamic equation; relatively large time and distance steps.

- Dynamic flow routing models using Equations 1 and 3 (also known as St. Venant equations); for rapidly changing flows in rivers and shallow reservoirs; for local stage and discharge predictions by hourly (or shorter) time steps.

- Water quality models; steady-state transport models based on Equation 2 and unsteady state models based on Equations 1 to 3. Instead of heat "concentration," cT (in kJ/kg), any other constituent C (in kg/kg) may be substituted. Usually, Equation 2 can be solved independently of 1 and 3. In slow moving water bodies, buoyancy may be non-negligible which leads to stratified flow and requires the simultaneous solution of all three equations due to coupling via a density-temperature (or constituent) function $\rho = \rho(T)$.

- Conceptual watershed models based on Equation 1 applied to various underground storage reservoirs combined with special input and output models (for infiltration and evapotranspiration) and streamflow routing models; use empirical hydrographs for short time step distribution of calculated (daily) runoff.

Now let us look in some detail at Equation 1 and its use in day-to-day reservoir operation models. Applied to daily time steps and one reservoir as a space step, Equation 1 takes the form:

$$\Sigma S_{ij+1}^{u(i)} + R_{ij} = \Sigma S_{ij}^{u(i)} + \Sigma F_{ij}^{u(i)} \tag{4}$$

S_{ij+1} being the storage in reservoir i at the end of period j; S_{ij} being the storage at the beginning of period j; R_{ij} and F_{ij} being the release from and the local inflow to reservoir i during period j; u(i) is the subset of reservoirs that includes reservoir i and all its upstream (direct and indirect) neighbors. For example, a five reservoir system consisting of three serial and two parallel reservoirs may consist of u(1)=(1); u(2)=(2); u(3)=(1,2,3); u(4)=(1), u(5)=(1,2,3,4,5). The sums in Equation 4 are taken over all the reservoirs in the subset.

For period j=1, the right hand side of Equation 4 is known. It contains initial reservoir elevations and local inflows. The left-hand side usually contains two unknowns, storage and release for each reservoir. Hence a subset u(i) of equations contains $2U_i$ unknowns with U_i being the number of reservoirs in the subset. In Equation 4, the equations for all upstream reservoirs have been used to express the upstream releases in terms of upstream ending storages. But, there are still $2U_i-(U_i-1)=U_i+1$ unknowns left in Equation 4. These are the U_i ending storages plus the release from the most downstream reservoir. Hence, a total of U_i assumptions are needed to solve the U_i equations for $2U_i$ unknowns. The solution obtained may violate constraints not included in the set of continuity equations, such as reservoir level or release limits. By iteratively modifying the assumed unknowns, an implementable operation schedule can be obtained. Achieving optimality for a specified performance criterion (e.g., maximum hydro benefit or minimum flood stage exceedance) will be laborious and not very likely. Especially in a multi-reservoir and multi-period simulation, this approach quickly becomes bogged down by the curse of dimensionality, even if computer-aided. Heuristic rules may then be introduced for setting releases and reservoir levels, thereby generating additional equations with the effect of reducing the number of variables that need to be fixed. The solution may proceed in a top-down fashion, reservoir by reservoir. An implemented version of such a model for TVA's daily reservoir scheduling is described by Goranflo (1981). A flood routing version of an hourly time step model based on Equations 1 and 3 is described by Goranflo (1982).

Advanced Simulation Models

These models are based on an expanded constraint set that describes the system operation policy as accurately as possible. This includes all limits on reservoir elevations and releases, any (a priori) fixed release or operation rules, any minimum hydropower requirements, admissible flood stages, etc. The aim of such a model is to produce feasible ranges of reservoir levels and releases. Within these ranges, selected reservoir levels and releases satisfy all known operation constraints. Furthermore, these constraints may be satisfied in some order of prespecified priority which assumes that the most important constraints are satisfied before an attempt is made to satisfy the less important ones. For example, the highest ranking constraint, such as not exceeding a flood stage, may be satisfied immediately after a feasible solution of the physical constraints, as expressed by Equation 4 and augmented by maximum and minimum reservoir storages and non-negative releases, has been found. The additional information in this case would be of the form

$$R_{ij} \leq RX_i \qquad\qquad (5)$$

This means the release from reservoir i must not exceed a maximum flow RX_i, which could be a downstream channel capacity. This additional information is appended to the already existing constraints of the type of Equation 4 in m variables as

$$\max \; d_{m+1,j}$$

$$\text{subject to} \quad R_{ij} + d_{m+1,j} = RX_i; \qquad \overline{SN} \leq \overline{S} \leq \overline{SX}; \qquad (6)$$

$$\overline{Ax} = \overline{b}; \qquad\qquad \overline{R} \geq \overline{RN}$$

where $\overline{x}$ represents the vector of ending storages and releases, $\overline{b}$ the vector of known inputs in the continuity equations, SN and SX the vectors of the allowable minimum and maximum levels of all reservoirs, RN the vector of the allowable minimum release, which must be no less than zero and $d_{m+1,j}$ the deviation of R_{ij} from the target RX_i; A is the incidence matrix of the continuity equation set.

If a solution to Equation 6 can be found in the form $d^*_{m+1,j} \geq 0$, then Equation 5 can be satisfied; otherwise, the constraint cannot be satisfied and the maximization, which in this case produced $d^*_{m+1,j} < 0$, assures that a minimum violation has been determined by which RX_i must be adjusted. The equation added to the equation system (6) is then

$$RX_i' = RX_i - d^*_{m+1,j}.$$

This process continues with one constraint added at a time and a feasible solution being sought without allowing any violation of previously satisfied constraints until all constraints have been considered. Such a scheme based on linear programming has been implemented in TVA's weekly scheduling model (Gilbert and Shane, 1982). To obtain a final policy, the operator must in the end again specify target levels or releases. In the model mentioned they are historical median reservoir levels. The model then meets those targets with minimum deviation, subject to all previously satisfied constraints. The result is an assured feasible solution.

Optimization Models

From the previously discussed model it is only a small step to the optimization model. While the previously described model already uses optimization techniques to achieve constraint satisfaction, the optimization model includes one more significant objective to be achieved on top of those so that no direct target setting is required by the operator. The objective function is a more or less complex formulation expressing a system objective in a quantitative form. An example of such a function is the cost formulation for a hydrothermal power system. It requires the model to search for those water levels and releases within all previously satisfied constraints so that the total operation cost to meet a given system load is minimized (Giles and Wunderlich, 1981 and 1983).

Decomposition/Coordination

This approach can be explained as the mathematical simulation of the coordination of individual subsystems toward achieving a common goal (Haimes, 1977). It can be used, for example, for the calculation of a schedule of steam and hydropower production in a hydrothermal system to meet a total system load while minimizing operation costs and meeting all hydro system and thermal system constraints. In essence, a Lagrangian is formed which coordinates all objectives, the cost objectives as well as the meeting-of-constraint objectives, through Lagrange multipliers. Manipulation of the Lagrangian reveals submodels, such as a thermal system submodel, a hydro system submodel, and possibly others, which can be solved independently in the decomposition step for Lagrange multipliers previously determined by the coordination step. The iteration between the two steps continues until the constrained optimum is reached. An implementation of this concept for the daily dispatch of the Electricite' de France power system has been described by Merlin and Sandrin (1983) and Monti, et al. (1984).

Input Forecasting

Planning for real-time operation usually requires the consideration of not just one time step but of a sequence of time steps, called a planning period. The number of time steps in a planning period depends on the length of the individual time steps, the length of the period for which input can be forecast with reasonable accuracy and on the lead time for commitments that need to be made for future time steps. In addition, unless the planning period is very long, additional guidance is required at the end of the planning period. This guidance is usually specified in the form of a target state of the system (or individual reservoirs) or by an economic function or other quantitative measure related to the system target states. A desirable length of the planning period is usually one that covers some periodicity, such as a day for hourly scheduling or a week for daily (or hourly) scheduling. Depending on the variability of inflows and demands, meaningful prior commitments can be made, such as for on- or offpeak hydro generation, pumped-storage operations or water supply scheduling within such a planning period. The decision arrived at for the time step to be implemented is sensitive to the forecast information used in the planning period. The schedule may show an optimistic or pessimistic bias if too much or too little information is used. Therefore, simulating the right amount of information available to the operator is an important aspect that cannot be over-emphasized in real-time operations planning. Computer-aided real-time operating can make a contribution here by allowing contingency planning for input scenarios that have reasonable probability of occurrence. For each scenario a best policy can be obtained which in turn is used as target policy in each of the others. Such an approach is meaningful if each scenario has about equal likelihood of occurrence and the differences between them are not extreme. One can then expect sufficient closeness in the operations suggested for the first time step to be implemented.

Without doubt, improving forecasts is the key for improving real-time operation and for reaping full benefits from advanced computerized methods. In a comparison of a simple regression-type rainfall/runoff model and a conceptual rainfall/runoff model it was found that, while the storm was in progress, the conceptual model did not have a decisive edge over the regression model. However, the conceptual model was considerably more reliable in predicting the depletion of the basin after the peak flow (Shiao and Wunderlich, 1983). Improved short-term forecasting could produce considerable dollar savings through anticipative flood operations by advanced reservoir drawdown at turbine capacity followed by reduced spill during the storm (Shane, 1983). Usually such drawdowns are not made because of the low reliability of the rainfall forecasts.

Present quantitative precipitation forecasts do not provide sufficiently accurate information beyond one hour (AGU, Committee on Precipitation, 1984). Thus, real-time operations usually must rely on precipitation on the ground or on generalized guidance on approximate amounts of precipitation and location of rainfall areas. But also the amount of rainfall on the ground is not easily determined either with conventional or advanced technology. Point rainfall measurements, while suffering from relatively minor catchment errors (~10%), may be only weakly correlated to areal rainfall given the usually rather sparse station networks (100 and more square miles per station) and during localized events. Remote sensing techniques by radar and satellites, while achieving better areal coverage, are subject to a wide variety of technical errors (AGU, 1984). Improvements of accuracy in areal rainfall determination, and providing this information in time for streamflow prediction, usually requires cooperation between various collection and processing agencies; to accomplish it is one of the great challenges of the future next to solving the physical problem of rainfall formation itself. For the foreseeable future, the operator must continue to rely on contingency planning for the most likely precipitation scenarios and his tool kit of streamflow prediction and scheduling models. The undisputable support that these models can provide is an improved "tracking" capability which allows continued updating of schedules as fast as new input information develops.

Expert Systems

Attempts to make computers more useful in finding solutions to messy real world problems through so-called expert systems have found wide publicity in recent years (Fenves, et al., 1984; Gevarter, 1984; Hayes-Roth, 1984). Messy real world problems are characterized by complexity, uncertainty, and ambiguity. The search for alternative solutions for such problems quickly gets bogged down by combinatorial explosion of the number of pathways that need to be examined. Artificial intelligence (AI) has become the buzz-word for methods used to constrain the search by making all available knowledge accessible in what is called a knowledge base (KB). Engineering problems are usually well described by mathematical formulations, in contrast to less structured problems, such as the interpretation of experience and data in diagnostics where expert systems so far have mostly been applied. Advanced search algorithms for structured problems already exist in the form of mathematical programming techniques. So, complexity here is already tackled to some extent by what one could call intelligent algorithms (IA). However, extensions of what is already there are seen in efficient knowledge representation (KR) and making knowledge readily accessible in a knowledge base. The next step then is to make logical inferences based on this KB by reaching conclusions through automated theorem proving. Such inferences would include subjective reasoning in situations of uncertainty or ambiguity, based on the expert's attitude toward risk, for example.

Many expert systems have already been built, but (there we go again!) few have actually been used. No application is presently known in water resources. But this is most likely a temporary situation because the application potential is too great to be ignored. Some possible applications are: data interpretation; reservoir system real-time operations; planning of operations; diagnosis of situations, such as various degrees of flood threat; emergency decision making in crises, e.g., dam failures, extraordinary hydrologic events, major industrial accidents or other unusual circumstances; and automated subsystem operation. The development and implementation of expert systems will pay off by cost savings through best use of available resources, increased efficiency of manpower use, more satisfying decisions by sure use of accumulated expert knowledge, increased safety and reliability of systems, decreased dependence on the availability of the human expert, improved consistency of decisions and last but not least preservation of expertise beyond an individual expert's demise. Expert systems for industrial use are predicted to be mass produced by 1990, probably at the expenditure of several hundred million dollars per year.

CONCLUSIONS

Developers have prepared a tremendous menu of tools for every user's delight. Computers have become so available that it is awfully hard to resist the temptation of using them. Wherever computerized use has been made of even simple methods, no case has been reported of reversion to more primitive procedures. Hence, the only way to go is forward to more and more sophisticated methods. Besides, they are just too attractive to be ignored.

REFERENCES

AGU, Committee on Precipitation, Hydrology Section, "A New Interdisciplinary Focus on Precipitation Research," EOS, Transact. Am. Geoph. Union, June 5, 1984.

Fenves, S. J., M. L. Maher, and D. Sriram, "Expert Systems: CE Potential," Civil Engineering, ASCE, October 1984, pp 44-47.

Gevarter, W. B., "Artificial Intelligence, Expert Systems, Computer Vision, and Natural Language Processing," Noyes Publications, Park Ridge, New Jersey, 1984.

Gilbert, K. C., and R. M. Shane, "TVA Hydro Scheduling Model: Theoretical Aspects," J. Water Resources Planning and Management Division Proceedings, ASCE, Vol. 108, No. WR1, March 1982.

Giles, J. E., and W. O. Wunderlich, "Weekly Multipurpose Planning Model for TVA Reservoir System," J. Water Resources Planning and Management Division, ASCE, Vol. 107, No. WR2, October 1981.

Giles, J. E., and W. O. Wunderlich, "Experiences with a Mathematical Hydropower Representation," Water Power '83, Conference Proceedings, Vol. II, pp 1016-1025, 1983, TVA, Knoxville, Tennessee 37902.

Giles, J. E., and W. O. Wunderlich, "Hydro System Planning of the TVA," Water Power and Dam Construction, London, July 1984.

Goranflo, H. M., "User's Guide for Operational Version of the Daily Main River Routing Model from Fort Loudoun Through Pickwick," Report No. WR28-2-500-138, Norris, March 1981.

Goranflo, H. M., "User's Guide for Main River Hourly Dynamic Routing Model," Report No. WR28-2-500-149, Norris, August 1982.

Haimes, Y. Y., "Hierarchical Analysis of Water Resources Systems," McGraw-Hill, New York, 1977.

Hayes-Roth, "Knowledge-Based Expert Systems," IEEE, October 1984, pp 263-273.

Helweg, O. J., R. W. Hinks, and D. T. Ford, "Reservoir Systems Optimization," J. Water Resources Planning and Management Division, Proc. ASCE, Vol. 108, No. WR2, June 1982.

Kirchmayer, L. K., "Economic Control of Interconnected Systems," J. Wiley & Sons, New York, 1959.

Merlin, A., and P. Sandrin, "A New Method for Unit Commitment at Electricite' de France," IEEE Transactions of Power Apparatus and Systems, Vol. PAS 102, No. 5, May 1983.

Monti, M., P. Sandrin, and J. P. Gonot, "Pumped Storage Peak Generation or Operating Reserve," Water Power and Dam Construction, London, August 1984.

Schultz, G. A., "Real-Time Operation of Hydro Systems - A Short Note," Experience in Operation of Reservoirs, T. E. Unny and E. A. McBean, Editors, Water Resources Publication, P.O. Box 2841, Littleton, Colorado 80161, 1982.

Shiao, M. C., and W. O. Wunderlich, "River Forecast Using the Computed Hydrograph Adjustment Technique," TVA, P.O. Drawer E, Norris, Tennessee 37828, 1983.

Shane, R. M., "A Proposed Method to Improve 3- to 5-Day Quantitative Precipitation Forecasts," Report No. WR28-2-500-116, TVA, Norris, 1983.

US-OTA, "Use of Models for Water Resources Management, Planning and Policy, Lib. of Congress Cat. Card No. 82-600556, U.S. Government Printing Office, Washington, D.C. 20402, 1982.

Computerized Operation of
California State Water Project

James Q. Coe and M. Hossein Sabet* M. ASCE

ABSTRACT

Hydraulic and electrical schedules for the California State Water Project are determined and dispatched from the Project Operation Control Center (POCC) in Sacramento. The dispatched schedules are executed by five Area Control Centers (ACCs). POCC has juridiction of the SWP facilities and can take the control of all the facilities at any time. Each of the facilities, such as pumping plants, generating plants, and check structures, are monitored and controlled by a dedicated mini-computer. The schedules for operation of the SWP facilities are determined using several hydraulic models and an electrical network model. These models have been in use since April 2, 1983. A large-scale simulation/optimization model is being developed for optimal operation of water and power for the SWP, and will replace the existing ones when testing is completed. It consists of hydraulic network programming components to meet the storage objectives at all the reservoirs, a linear programming component to determine the schedules at pumping and generating plants, an elecrical network programming coomponent to balance electrical loads and resources, and a number of other simulation components.

INTRODUCTION

Description of State Water Project.-The California State Water Project (SWP), shown in Fig. 1, consists of a series of reservoirs linked by rivers, pumping plants, canals, tunnels, and generating plants(5). Near Oroville in Northern California, the Feather River flows into Lake Oroville, the Project's principal reservoir. Also located at Oroville are the Hyatt and Thermalito Pumping/Generating Plants providing approximately 900 megawatts (MW) of hydroelectric generation capacity. Releases from this reservoir flow through natural channels of the Feather and Sacramento Rivers to the Delta. In the south Delta, the Banks Pumping Plant with an ultimate capacity of 850 acre-feet/hour lifts water into Bethany Reservoir. From this small reservoir, some water is lifted again by the South Bay Pumping Plant to the South Bay Aqueduct, which serves Alameda and Santa Clara Counties.

The California Aqueduct is the principal water conveyance structure of the SWP. Most of the water from Bethany Reservoir flows into the Aqueduct, which winds along the west side of the San Joaquin Valley to O'Neill Forebay. From this point, water can be pumped to San Luis Reservoir. This 2.04 million acre-foot (2.51 cubic dekameter) reservoir(1) was built and is operated jointly by the California Department of Water Resources and the U. S. Bureau of Reclamation.

---

*Respectively; Chief of Modeling Support Section, and Water Resources Engineer, Department of Water Resources, Sacramento, California 95082.

Fig. 1.-The California State Water Project

Water from either San Luis or the Delta flows south through the
Aqueduct, down the valley, and is raised 969 feet (295.54 meters) by
four more pumping plants before reaching the foot of the Tehachapi
Mountains and then Southern California.   In the lower San Joaquin
Valley, the Coastal Branch of the aqueduct serves agricultural areas to
the west. On the main aqueduct at the Tehachapis, the A. D. Edmonston
Pumping Plant raises the water 1,926 feet (587.43 meters) in a single
lift to   enter 10 miles of tunnels and siphons. From the Tehachapi
Crossing, the water flows into the Antelope Valley, where the Aqueduct
divides.   The East Branch carries water through the Antelope Valley
into Silverwood Lake in the San Bernardino Mountains. From Silverwood,
the water enters the San Bernardino Tunnel and drops 1,418 feet (432.49
meters) through Devil Canyon Powerplant. Then the water flows in a
buried pipeline to Lake Perris, the southernmost terminus of the
Project, 444 miles (714.84 kilometers) from the Delta where the
aqueduct begins.   Water in the West Branch flows through Warne
Powerplant into Pyramid Lake in Los Angeles County, then through the
Angeles Tunnel, into the Castaic Powerplant and into Castaic Lake,
terminus of the West Branch.

Operation Objectives of the SWP.-The fundamental operation objective of
the SWP is to provide water service in accordance with the existing
contracts.   In the early 1960s, the DWR entered into 75-year water
contracts with 31 local agencies serving areas throughout California.
Under the contracts, the Department promises to make all reasonable
efforts to most economically operate the facilities, and make
deliveries within contractual entitlements. The contractors promise to
pay their respective shares of the costs the Department incurs for such
efforts.

Associated with the fundamental objective are certain legislative
mandated responsibilities (such as providing for recreation and fish
and wildlife at project facilities and maintaining water quality
objectives in the Delta) and contractual obligations such as providing
flood damage protection in cooperation with the U. S. Army Corps of
Engineers. The service of entitlements, however, is foremost of the
Department's SWP responsibilities.

The Department as an Electric Utility.-Operation of the pumps in the
SWP requires a considerable amount of electrical energy --approximately
3 percent of the California total use. Project load consists of 13
pumping plants which pump the water throughout the system. The maximum
load of these plants is approximately 2,400 MW. To this date the
maximum coincidental peak demand has been 1,514 MW which occurred in
January 1978. Since the project began operation in 1967, the highest
annual energy use has been 5.3 billion Kwh which occurred in 1981.

Until March 31, 1983, energy required for SWP operation in excess of
that generated by power recovery plants on the aqueduct system was
purchased by the Department from four major California utilities. At
that time, the contract for supply of the required energy expired and
the Department began balancing its loads and resources and buying and
selling energy on the general market, like an electric utility.

There are two major factors which are unique in operation of the SWP as an electric utility. First, SWP does not have its own transmission lines connecting its loads with its generation sources. It must use contracted transmission services of either Pacific Gas and Electric Company (PGandE) or Southern California Edison Company (SCE). Second, it has control over its loads. The SWP load is determined by the water and power operation model and can be modified if energy resources change. Utilities ordinarily do not have load reduction capability except in response to some system disturbance or overload. In the performance of its power operations, the SWP is expected to conform with the rules of the North American Electric Reliability Council (NERC).

PROJECT CONTROL SYSTEM

The Project Operations Control Center (POCC), located in Sacramento, has the responsibility for scheduling all of the SWP facilities. These facilities are remotely monitored and may actually be operated from the POCC. However, under normal conditions, the project is operated from Area Control Centers (ACCs) under instructions from the POCC. The project is geographically subdivided into five areas, with all of the facilities within an area being remotely monitored and controlled from an ACC located within the area. Each ACC operates its respective area of the Project independently of the other ACCs(2).

Area Control Centers.-The Oroville ACC, located at the Hyatt plant switchyard, controls the Hyatt and Thermalito plants and the other facilities within the Oroville area. The remaining four ACCs cover the Aqueduct facilities. The Delta ACC, located near the Banks Pumping Plant, controls the facilities from Clifton Court Forebay to the inlet to O'Neill Forebay. The San Luis ACC, located near San Luis Dam, controls the San Luis Pumping-Generating Plant, the Dos Amigos Pumping Plant, and the California Aqueduct through Check 21, located between Dos Amigos and Buena Vista Pumping Plants. The San Joaquin ACC, located near the Wind Gap Pumping Plant, controls the facilities from Check 22 through the Tehachapi Afterbay, including the Buena Vista, Wheeler Ridge, Wind Gap and Edmonston Pumping Plants. Tehachapi Afterbay is the pool immediately after Edmonston Pumping Plant. The facilities of the Coastal Branch Aqueduct are also controlled from this ACC. Finally, the Southern California ACC, located near the Castaic Dam, controls all the facilities on both the West Branch and East Branch.

Data Communication.-Data communications between the various remote facilities and the ACC/POCC are digital because a large number of points over a long distance have to be monitored, and a high degree of accuracy is required. All communications between facilities are accomplished by exchange of commands, interrogations, and data, status, and alarm messages.

Backup communications exist to each major site from the control center. This is an active backup and is accomplished by approaching each site with communication lines from two geographically separate directions. A primary or "A" line is routed to each site in turn from the control center by the most direct route, usually along the

Aqueduct. A backup or "B" line is routed to the end of the aqueduct section and, starting with the last site, comes into each site in reverse order and from the opposite direction.

OPERATION CONTROL CAPABILITY AND EQUIPMENT

Within each of the control areas of the SWP, capability of complete remote control is provided from the control console located in each ACC. Capability for control of each individual aqueduct site or plant is provided locally from a site control panel for aqueduct facilities or from a plant control room for pumping and power plants. In addition, at plants, a level of control is provided from the unit control boards. A general summary of the capabilities from each level of control is as follows:

Unit Control Board.-The unit control board provides for manual operation of pumping and generating plants. The plant operator has the capability of monitoring the unit to ensure its proper performance. Displays are provided by indicating meters.

Plant Control Room.-The plant control room consolidates the operation of all units, switchyard, station service, and plant auxiliary function from a single location within the plant. (Note that each plant may consist of several units.) The plant control equipment provides complete start and shutdown sequencing of the units with monitoring and alarming capability.

Local Check Structure Control.-Each check structure may be operated from the adjacent control building. Capability is provided to monitor and control all functions at a check structure. Gate positions are controlled and monitored, and water levels are monitored and recorded. All control is possible without dependence on any signals from the ACC.

Turnout Control.-Major turnouts are provided with both monitoring and control capabilities. A major turnout is the one with a design capacity greater than 5 percent of the capacity of the aqueduct pool in which it is located, or 200 cubic feet per second, whichever is less. Minor turnouts have the monitoring capability only.

Other Site Control.-Other facilities, including dams, reservoirs, flow measuring stations, and water quality monitors are monitored locally, and in some cases also from the ACCs.

Area Control Center.-The ACC consolidates operation of all remotely conrolled sites within the area. Data monitoring is provided to the level necessary to ensure proper operation and surveillance of all facilities.

Project Operation Control Center.-The POCC is provided with capability for complete monitoring and dispatching of project operation, complete jurisdictional control, and back-up control for any aqueduct ACC. Status of all the SWP facilities are monitored by a graphic wall display, and screens. The POCC control room is shown in Fig. 2. Part of the graphic wall display between Buena Vista Pumping Plant and Warne

Fig. 2.-The Project Operation Center, Control Room

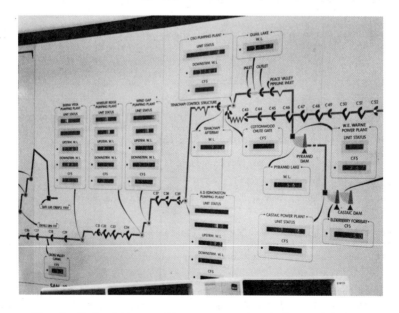

Fig. 3.-Part of the Graphic Wall Display at the Control Room

Powerplant is enlarged to demonstrate the type of information displayed(Fig. 3).

ELECTRICAL METERS

Revenue meters are provided for monitoring the power and energy at points of interconnect in the electrical system. The points of interconnect are points at which the electrical energy is delivered or received. To enhance the operation of the SWP as an electric utility, meters are being installed to provide SCE and PGandE with the capability of reading KW and Kwh data at points of interconnect.

COMPUTER SYSTEM

At the POCC a UNIVAC 1100/60 computer is used for controlling the SWP facilities. It has two control processing units of 1000k words (36bit) each. At the ACCs computer systems vary in size from 24k to 32k words of 16 bit core memory. All have secondary storage in the form of magnetic disk or drum. The amount of secondary storage varies from 262k to 512k word (16-bit). The computers are of the type designed as general purpose minicomputers. At check structures the basic element of the control system is a small, general purpose, digital computer system. This computer interfaces with the communication terminal equipment, the local operator control panel, and various measuring and control devices. At most check structures this computer has a 4k memory.

The UNIVAC 1100/60 computer at the POCC is also used for running the optimization models which determine the schedule for operation of the SWP facilities.

OPTIMIZATION MODELS

Until April 1, 1983, the SWP was operated by a hydraulic model designed for meeting long-term objective of the Department. This model was designed to supply water to contractors considering contractual, environmental, and physical constraints. Energy was purchased six years in advance in accordance with estimates provided by a long-range optimizing procedure which minimized power cost by minimizing pumping during periods of peak power demand and by equalizing required electrical capacity over a period of 50 years. After April 1, 1983, when the long-term energy contracts expired, the Department was required to minimize the actual cost of energy use in its operations. A large-scale model, designed for optimal operation of water and power, was being tested at that time. An interim operations model was put to use on April 2, 1983. The interim model consisted of the hydraulic models being used prior to that date, and a power allocation network developed from the large-scale water and power model.

The power allocation network is designed to provide SWP schedules for sales, purchases, and exchanges of power with its sister utility companies. The network represents the contracts, power sources, power loads, and transmission lines used for electrical energy on a periodic basis. The solution of this network provides hourly schedules of energy generation at SWP powerplants, energy use at   pumping plants, and sales and purchases.

The large-scale simulation/optimization model will determine optimal schedules for operation of pumping plants, generating plants, check structures, and reservoirs. It will also provide schedules for power generation, use, sales, and purchases. The model consists of seven major components:

-- A linear programming(4) component for minimizing operation cost and providing hourly schedules at Dos Amigos, Buena Vista, Wheeler Ridge, Wind Gap, Edmonston, Oso, and Pearblossom Pumping Plants, and Alamo and Warne Generating Plants.

-- A Network Programming Component (NPC) for determining flow volumes (total of all the hours), and the reservoir storages for Lake Oroville, Hyatt Generating Plant, Thermalito Forebay, Thermalito Generating Plant, and Thermalito Afterbay, minimizing deviation from given target storages and flows.

-- A NPC for calculating total plant flow volumes and reservoir storage on the California Aqueduct from Banks Pumping Plant to Lake Perris and Castaic Lake in Southern California, minimizing deviation from target storage for reservoirs in its system.

-- A NPC for checking the operation of O'Neill Forebay for overflows and overdrafts on an hourly level. It modifies the schedules of Banks Pumping Plant, Dos Amigos Pumping Plant, and San Luis Pumping/Generating Plant to eliminate out-of-range conditions.

-- A NPC for checking Quail Lake for operation within storage range for each hour. It modifies the Warne Generating Plant schedule to eliminate overflows and overdrafts at Quail Lake.

-- A NPC called the Power Allocation Network for scheduling power operation as explained earlier.

-- A simulation model for checking hydraulic feasibility of the hourly energy schedules provided by the power allocation model at Hyatt and Thermalito Generating Plants. It makes modifications to the energy schedules when required for hydraulic feasibility.

The algorithm used to solve the networks for optimum flows is called SUPERKIL. It was first developed by the Texas Water Development Board(7). It was modified by Barr, Glover and Klingman as an improved version of the "out-of-kilter" algorithm of Ford and Fulkerson(3). The linear program is solved by the dual simplex algorithm using the nonproprietary XMP package(6).

Reports of the results of the optimization model take from 30 seconds to 3 minutes to be prepared depending on the degree of detail required. They may be printed or displayed on a computer terminal.

STATUS

The large-scale simulation/optimization model is currently being tested. It sucessfully provides hourly schedules for operation of the SWP. Minor modifications are underway. The interim model has been used for providing schedules since April 2, 1983.

Control systems designed and executed for monitoring and controlling the SWP facilities have been in use for over a decade. Computers intalled for controlling the check structures, pumping, and generating plants have worked well. State-of-the-art of the equipment and control system suggest replacement of some of the equipment used in the system.

Control of aqueduct facilities from the ACCs based on the schedules developed at the POCC has been effective. However, with the completion of the large-scale model the Department has the option of controlling the entire SWP from the POCC in Sacramento. Centralized operation is technically feasible. It may be achieved by designing a new control and communication system. This will require new equipment and replacment of some of the existing equipment. Economics and political feasiblity will decide the question of adoption of a centralized and fully automated system. The Department is likely to make this decision within a year from February 1985.

APPENDIX I.-REFERENCES

1. "Basic Facts Booklet, California Water Project", Division of Operations and Maintenance, Department of Water Resources, the Resources Agency, State of California.

2. Cosper, Alan L., and Papathakis, George L., "Bulletin No. 200 California State Water Project Control Facilities". Vol. V. State of California, The Resources Agency, Nov. 1974.

3. Ford, L. R., Jr., and Fulkerson, D., Flows in Networks, Princeton University Press, Princeton, N.J., 1976.

4. Hadley, G., Linear Programming, Addison-Wesley Publishing Compnay, Inc., Reading, Mass., 1962.

5. Kahrl, W.L., The California Water Atlas, Department of Water Resources, State of California, 1978, 1979.

6. Marsten, R. E., "The Design of the XMP Linear Programming Library", ACM Transactions on Mathematical Software, Vol. 7, No. 4., December 1981, pp. 481-497.

7. Texas Water Development Board, Economic Optimization and Simulation Techniques for Management of Regional Water Resources Systems, July, 1972, pp. 83-106.

AUTOMATED DATA COLLECTION FOR RESERVOIR REGULATION

By Jeffrey R. Weiser*
AND
John Gauthier, M. ASCE*

ABSTRACT: Various regulation changes in the Lake Winnebago basin have been proposed regarding the protection of wetlands and assurance of adequate outflows for water quality. To implement these proposals, it became apparent that additional sampling sites, parameters and a more timely transmission system was required. Data collection systems are compared and a remote satellite based collection system was developed. Automatic data retrieval is being accomplished and future direct data input into regulation models is planned.

The Lake Winnebago drainage basin (Figure 1) is located in the northeastern portion of Wisconsin and has a total drainage area of 6,430 square miles (16,650 km^2). The two main tributaries to the lake, the Fox and Wolf Rivers, have a combined drainage area of approximately 4,400 square miles (11,400 km^2). The lake is about 28 miles (45 km) along its north-south axis and 11 miles (18 km) across its east-west axis. The Wolf and Fox Rivers join above Oshkosh and enter Lake Winnebago through a series of shallow, marshy lakes. Winnebago and these smaller upstream lakes have a low water surface area of 265 square miles (690 km2), increasing to 320 square miles (830 km^2) during high water. Lake Winnebago drains into the Lower Fox River through two channels, one at Neenah and the other at Menasha, which join above Appleton. The Neenah channel is controlled by a dam with five sluice gates, a spillway and nine needle gates. This dam is privately owned, but is operated according to the Corps' directions. The Menasha Dam, which is federally owned, has six sluice gates and a spillway section. Together, the Neenah and Menasha Dams control the total outflow from the Lake Winnebago pool.

Regulation of Lake Winnebago's stage was historically necessary in the interest of navigation and to protect the private rights of waterpower and riparian interests. During the navigation season, the limits of regulation under existing laws is from the crest of Menasha Dam to 21 1/4 inches (540 mm) above the crest. An additional drawdown of 18 to 24 inches (460 to 610 mm) is allowed during the winter. Observance of the upper limit, without unnecessary waste of water, gives water-power interests on the lower Fox River all the water to which they are entitled under the laws and the deed of transfer to the United States, without interfering with private rights. The River and Harbor Act of 8 August 1912, provides that water shall not be drawn from any pool to such an extent as to lower the surface of the pool below the crest of the dam which retains that pool.

*Hydraulic Engineer, U.S. Army Engineer District, Detroit, Michigan.

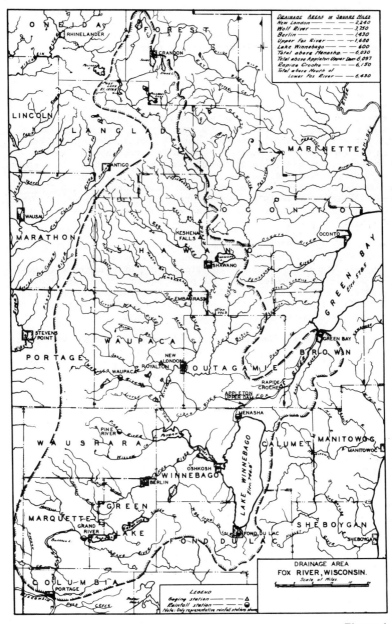

Figure 1

Until 1970, data collection in the Lake Winnebago basin remained virtually unchanged for almost 100 years. Data were collected by observers using staff gages to measure water levels and calibrated buckets to estimate precipitation. Crude methods of collecting snow depths and water equivalents were utilized. After these data were collected, the observer would record them and mail the information to the regulator on a daily basis. This resulted in a three or four day lag time between the data being collected and its use in regulation. During normal hydrologic periods, this time lag was not significant. However, during periods of drawdown, storms, flooding or drought, system management suffered due to a lack of real time data. Though more recently, near real time data could be obtained via telephone from the gage observer, problems frequently arose when the gage observer was not available or the phone lines were out due to a storm. Since 1970, telemark gages were installed on the two main feeder streams to Lake Winnebago and then later on two other critical up-stream locations. In 1978, an accounting model was developed to store these data and to compute and display inflows and outflows for Lake Winnebago.

During the late 1970's, the Wisconsin Department of Natural Re-sources (WDNR) formulated modifications to the existing manner in which Lake Winnebago had been regulated. This proposal came to be known as the Linde Proposal for its prime author, Mr. Arlyn Linde, of the WDNR. The proposal called for numerous operational changes for the benefit of marsh stability, vegitation, and flood control, while complying with existing legislative restrictions.

The Linde Proposal advocated greater drawdown during the winter to provide for better control of the spring runoff, a delay in the rise of the pool to protect marsh vegetation from ice damage, more constant summer and fall levels to protect marsh vegetation and the associated wildlife habitat, and a dealy in the drawdown until ice cover forma-tion to further protect the marsh habitat. In addition to lake stage goals, the Linde Proposal also included a minimum flow requirement for the Lower Fox River to help industry meet water quality standards (see Figure 2).

To test the hydrologic realities of the proposed regulation changes, the WDNR and the Fox Valley Water Quality Planning Agency (FVWQPA) contracted with the United States Geological Survey (USGS) to model the proposed changes against the period of record inflow conditions. The results of the modelling effort were documented in the USGS pub-lication "Hydrologic Effects of Proposed Changes in Management Practices, Winnebago Pool, Wisconsin", by William R. Krug (6).

Mr. Krug's study showed that the Linde Proposal's apparently con-flicting alteration of stage and flow objectives could be achieved under certain idealized circumstances. The model did not consider operational constraints or the limited data available during the course of actual regulation.

The Krug study has been used as basis of communication for the Corps of Engineers, the WDNR, and the FVWQPA in attempting to add the

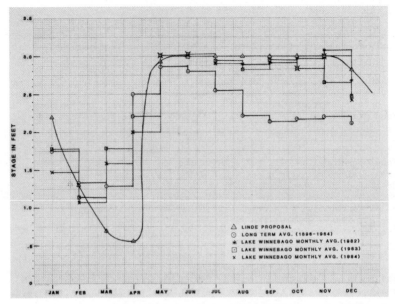

IMPACT OF LINDE PROPOSAL   **Figure 2**

Linde Proposal's enhancements to the Lake Winnebago Regulation Plan.

In attempting to satisfy the Linde Proposal, the limited data available to the regulator became critical to fulfill the needs of the regulator, an expanded data collection system including real time data collection and dissemination was necessary. Several key data needs had to be addressed prior to selection of any total system. First, since water level information was sparse, additional water level sites had to be identified to enable the total inflow entering the lake to be determined. Outflows from the lake were derived using outdated equations, so an improved method for determining outflows was also needed. Another area of concern was in determining the water level of Lake Winnebago. The regulator had to evaluate the lake status based upon an instantaneous stage reading from the west side of the lake (Oshkosh). Due to the shape of the lake and prevailing wind conditions, a stage differential of four to six inches (100 to 150 mm) between the east and west lake shores was not unusual during periods of strong winds. Therefore, gaging on the lake had to be expanded to accurately define its average level. To evaluate the rainfall/runoff process and its impact in inflows, a basinwide network of real time rainfall and snow water equivalent sites had to be designed.

Once all these data were collected in the field, they needed to be relayed to the regulator on a real-time basis in a form he could use with a minimum of manual effort. The methods and hardware used to fulfill the above data then became input for defining the requirements for the total data collection and dissemination system.

As a first step, in fulfilling the data needs, the areas of ungaged supply to the system were located. After this was accomplished, actual site availability for gage installation was identified in the field. The Corps' Cold Regions Research and Engineering Laboratory (CRREL) did a field investigation and subsequent report (1). The study they compiled has been transformed into a standard operating procedure for data collection siting. Site selection was based upon an opti-mized combination of site availability, hydrologic significance and existing institutional constraints.

To attempt to determine a more accurate lake level, a single addi-tional location was selected. This site, at Stockbridge, provided a balance along the lake's east-west axis with the Oshkosh site. The addition of the Stockbridge gage to the data collection network made an immediate impact in the regulation activities, since the lake level was now determined by averaging the Oshkosh and Stockbridge water levels. Figure 3 shows the difference in lake stage across the east-west axis for November 1984. The difference between averaging the gages, or using one or the other would not be as significant if the only objective of regulation was to maintain the lake level within the allowed limits. However, the addition of consideration of water quality flow augmentation has the impact of increasing the long-term consequences of each regulation decision.

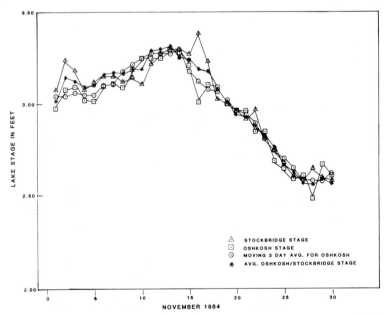

Figure 3

The lake stage is of great significance to the regulation because of the ways in which it is used to represent the status of the basin and because of decisions based upon these representations. The inflow is computed from the previous days outflow and the change in storage, which is a function of stage. Since the lake is extremely flat, small errors in stage result in large errors in storage. To determine the gate settings on the Neenah and Menasha dams, a regression equation (4) was developed by relating outflow to lake stage and gate setting. This relationship also relies heavily on the accuracy of lake stage.

Once gage sites were selected, a system of data collection had to be chosen. Several options were evaluated for capital cost, timeliness, maintenance, real estate requirements, data reliability and future expansion. Table 1 shows the data collection systems evaluated and lists the advantages and disadvantages of each.

Based on the above, it was determined that utilizing data collection platforms (DCP's) to obtain basinwide data would be the best alternative. Initially, a test DCP was installed at the only existing site on Lake Winnebago (Oshkosh). This site provided six, four-hour readings of water level, wind speed and direction and air temperature on a daily basis. To test data needs, two new sites, Waupaca and Royalton, were installed with water level telemarks to begin to quantify the total supply to the lake. The water levels from the dams in the lower river were telemetered into the on site project office,

TABLE 1. - Comparison of Data Collection Systems

Data Collection System	Advantages	Disadvantages
Telemarks	-inexpensive capital costs -low maintenance $	-phone line dependent -instantaneous data -manual data storage
Line-of-sight (LOS) radio	-more reliable than phone lines	-higher capital costs -instantaneous data -manual data storage -data not available to other users
Telemeter	-can store data -can be interrogated by computer	-phone line dependent
Data collection platform (DCP)	-satellite based -can store data -random reporting -high data reliability -can support many parameters	-higher maintenance $ -requires training -new technology risks

to allow round-the-clock real time knowledge of downstream conditions
for dam and lock operations. The new DCP's and sensors were then
procured and the field sites prepared. Table 2 shows the final site
selection and the parameters to be measured at each site. Currently,
DCP's have been installed in Oshkosh, Royalton, Waupaca, Berlin,
New London and Stockbridge. DCP's are set to be installed in the
remainder of the sites this spring.

The next step was to allow for automatic data collection and dissemination. A small microcomputer was purchased to initially handle
this task. Later this year, a minicomputer will be procured to automatically interrogate, store and evaluate these data.

In 1976, prior to the recent regulation changes, it was recognized
that the system could be better regulated if reservoir inflow were
more accurately determined. At that time, a study (5) was conducted
to attempt to fit computed historic inflows for high inflow periods
with various regression equations using the tributary flows as the
independent variables. The study provided inflows equations of the
following form:

$$\text{Total Inflow} = C_1 + C_2 F_B + C_3 F_{NL}$$

where: C_1, C_2 and C_3 are constants,

       F_B is the river flow at Berlin in c.f.s.

       F_{NL} is the river flow at New London in c.f.s.

TABLE 2. - Lake Winnebago DCP Sites

Location	Data Collected
Embarrass River @ Embarrass	Stage
Fox River @ Berlin	Stage
Lake Winnebago @ Oshkosh	Stage, wind speed and direction, air temperature
Lake Winnebago @ Stockbridge	Stage, precipitation, air temperature
Little Wolf River @ Royalton	Stage, precipitation, air temperature
Lower Fox River @ Menasha	Stage
Lower Fox River @ Neenah	Stage, precipitation, air temperature
Lower Fox River @ Area Office	Stage
Waupaca River @ Waupaca	Stage
Wolf River @ New London	Stage

This study was helpful in providing inflow approximation equations for periods of high inflow, but was limited by the existing data collection system, particularly the problems associated with using only one lake gage. The analysis it provided could not be reasonably expected to be more accurate than the data the existing system could provide. Figure 4 shows gaged inflows and lake stages for November 1984.

The completed data collection system as shown above, is expected to provide the data necessary to develop and maintain a near-real time inflow forecast model that would be based on precipitation and then verified at each gaged point along the major tributaries. This inflow model (2) would be calibrated for accuracy throughout the range of potential flows. Once the model is complete, it could be used to provide input into a reservoir regulation model (3) that could evaluate pool conditions, inflows, outflow objectives and stage, and then determine the best possible outflow for various periods into the future.

The development of these models will serve to provide both a much more systematic basis for evaluating the basin status and the opportunity to avoid floods and droughts through early detection of potentially hazardous conditions, as well as providing for the enhancement of the environment.

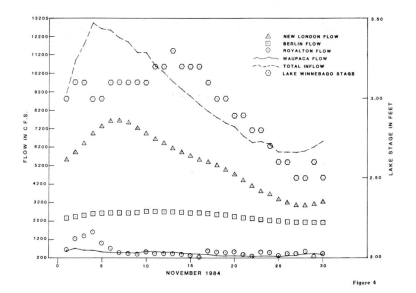

Figure 4

Acknowledgments

   The authors would like to acknowledge the contributions to this effort made by Timothy Pangburn, Bruce Brockett and Harlan McKim of the Corps' Cold Regions Research and Engineering Laboratory in Hanover, NH.

Appendix. - References

1. Brockett, B., and Pangburn, T., "Evaluation of Proposed Sites for the Installation of Sensor and Data Collection Platforms to Monitor Watershed Hydrologic and Meteorologic Parameters", Technical Note, U. S. Army Cold Regions Research and Engineering Laboratory, 1983.
2. Hydrologic Engineering Center, "HEC-1 Flood Hydrograph Package", U. S. Army Corps of Engineers, 1981.
3. Hydrologic Engineering Center, "HEC-5, Simulation of Flood Control and Conservation Systems", U. S. Army Corps of Engineers, 1979.
4. Hydrologic Engineering Center, "Multiple Linear Regression Program", U. S. Army Corps of Engineers, 1970.
5. Hydrologic Engineering Center, "Special Projects Memo No. 466, Lake Winnebago Inflow Study", U. S. Army Corps of Engineers, 1976.
6. Krug, W. R., "Hydrologic Effects of Proposed Changes in Management Practices, Winnebago Pool, Wisconsin", U. S. Geological Survey, 1981.

SUCCESSIVE APPLICATION OF RESERVOIR SIMULATION MODELS--A Case STUDY

By Francis I. Chung[1], M. ASCE and Robert H. Zettlemoyer[2], M. ASCE

ABSTRACT

Reservoir simulation models are sequentially applied 1) to generate inflows and diversion requirements deriving from smaller water basins and 2) to operate the main frame of the system utilizing the generated hydrology and demands. Replacement of the conventional method of generating hydrology by a well established reservoir simulation model renders enormous amounts of flexibility and savings in computation time. The linkage that connects the generated hydrology to the input data required for the subsequent model execution is a data bank that contains a large number of data files representing varying assumptions and operational criteria. The subsequent simulation of the main frame of the system is preceded by the selection of the pertinent data sets from the established data bank through an automated procedure. The whole process is currently being used by the California Department of Water Resources for various statewide planning studies. A case study of the American River Basin and the California State Water Project is presented along with the descriptions of the models.

INTRODUCTION

The computer simulated operation of a water system requires two essential components: the model and the data. The model in the context of this paper is defined as a set of integrated instructions in a language recognizable by a computer. The model is designed to depict the responses of the prototype to the desired degree of accuracy. The data is a collection of impulses to the model so that when the model is executed utilizing the data in a computer, the behavior of the prototype is predicted.

The enhancement of one component does not warrant better accuracies in the final prediction without the improvement of the other component to the same degree. Input data currently being supplied to a reservoir simulation model developed by the California Department of Water Resources (2,4) for the simulated operation of the entire California Central Valley is being improved through the application of a similar model replacing the conventional way of generating the hydrologic data.

---

[1] Systems Analyst, Department of Water Resources, State of California, Sacramento, California.

[2] Senior Engineer, Department of Water Resources, State of California, Sacramento, California.

The "HEC-3" model (4) is first applied to a smaller upper basin and the resulting outflows from the basin become the inflow data to the succeeding model. This mechanism renders more flexibilities so that the resulting basin outflows can readily reflect any changes both in the configuration and in the operation criteria of the water system in the basin. These features are very advantageous in a typical planning study where various levels of future developments along with a number of alternatives at a given level are being analyzed.

DWR SIMULATION MODEL

A detailed river basin simulation model has been developed by the California Department of Water Resources to simulate the combined operation of two major water project systems in California; namely the Central Valley Project (CVP) operated by the U.S. Bureau of Reclamation, and the State Water Project (SWP) operated by the California Department of Water Resources (DWR). Barnes and Chung (2) present the detailed description of the model; however, in order to stress the developments important to our purpose here, and for completeness, a brief discussion of the model seems justified.

The "HEC-3" model (4) developed by the U.S. Corps of Engineers' Hydrologic Engineering Center (HEC) in Davis, California has been adopted as a basic tool for reservoir releases and channel routings. The original HEC-3 model has been extensively modified and enhanced to provide more modeling flexibility and features and to account for the special characteristics of the CVP-SWP system. The model accounts for the CVP and SWP and provides unique capabilities for conducting studies not possible with the original HEC-3 model. The model developed is now called the DWR Planning Simulation Model (DWRSIM) and is being used for many planning studies by the California Department of Water Resources to analyze possible future additions or changes to the CVP-SWP system. DWRSIM is a simulation model designed to operate on a monthly time basis for purpose of water supply, recreation, instream flow augmentation, and hydroelectric power generation. Changes in configuration of surface reservoirs, groundwater reservoirs, river diversions, power generating plants, pumping plants, and conveyance facilities can be incorporated by changes in data entry to the program rather than modifying the model. In addition, various operating criteria such as reservoir operating rules or Sacramento-San Joaquin Delta outflow requirements can be easily changed by data entry as well.

General locations of the major impounding and transport facilities are presented in Figure 1. Table 1 describes major CVP and SWP storage facilities shown in Figure 1. DWRSIM represents the actual CVP-SWP system by a network of control points depicting surface reservoirs, groundwater reservoirs, river diversions, tributary stream inflow points, pumping plants, and power generating plants. The control points are connected by links representing rivers or canal reaches. Schematic representation of the entire California Central Valley is available elsewhere (2,3).

Figure 1.—General Locations of Major Central Valley Project and State Water Project Facilities

TABLE 1.- Major CVP and SWP Storage Facilities

Reservoir (DAM)	Capacity (TAF)	Purpose	50-Year Average Annual Inflow (TAF)
Shasta Lake	4552	W,P,F,R	5752
Clair Engle Lake	2448	W,P,R	1270
Whiskeytown Lake	241	W,P,R	250
Folsom Lake	1010	W,P,F,R	2627
New Melones	2400	W,P,F,R	1119
Lake Oroville	3538	W,P,F,R	4429
Silverwood Lake	75	S,R	--
Lake Perris	132	S,R	--
Pyramid Lake	171	S,P	--
Castaic Lake	324	W,S,P,R	--
San Luis	2039	S,P,R	--

Note: W-Water Supply, P-Power, F-Flood, R-Recreation, S-Reregulatory Storage, 1 TAF = 1.23 x 10^6 m^3.

DEPLETION ANALYSIS MODEL

Inflows and diversions are developed in two major steps, namely consumptive use studies and depletion analysis studies. In order to perform these two studies for the whole Central Valley, the Central Valley is divided into 35 smaller water basins called Depletion Areas (DA's). Table 2 provides the major characteristics of each Depletion Area. Figure 2 shows the general location of the 35 DA's. Figure 3 depicts how these two analyses are conducted in each DA. Potential evapotranspiration, soil mositure criteria, land use patterns and precipitation are supplied into the consumptive use model which produces the historic and projected depletions of irrigated crops, and the consumptive use of replaced native vegetation within the DA. This will generate a modification to the historic flow due to land use changes. The final step of developing inflows is the depletion analysis model execution. In this step, the historic flows are combined with the land use modifications and with other basin modifications, and with flow requirements to produce projected flows for each DA. In this step, a theoretical groundwater operation is sometimes produced to meet demands. This ground water represents only the new groundwater required to meet projected demands, since the historic flow already includes a historic groundwater supply.

The most complex and time-consuming component of the above development is the local storage operation. This is especially true when a basin has a number of local storages and varying rules of operation. For example, a reservoir may be built by a local district to meet future water supply for the district. In the early years of the project's life, while the ultimate project demand is not fully developed, the reservoir could operate primarily for the power generation, but in later years of the project's life when the ultimate designed water supply is required, the operation of the same reservoir must be

TABLE 2. - Year 2000 Land Use and
Annual Precipitation of Selected Depletion Areas

Drainage Area	Total Area(Acres) x1000	Irrigated Area(Acres) x1000	Urban Area(Acres) x1000	Percentages Of Developed To Total Acreage	Annual Precip (inches)
10	806	203	17	27	20.9
12	914	343	5	38	17.5
13	635	318	26	54	21.8
15	351	240	2	69	15.9
21	840	262	119	45	23.4
23	467	273	21	63	20.0
59	976	380	41	43	16.9
55	682	407	43	66	13.6
49	2947	1622	93	58	10.9
60	11000	3726	173	35	8.3

Note: 1 Acre = 0.405 ha, 1 inch = 25.4 mm

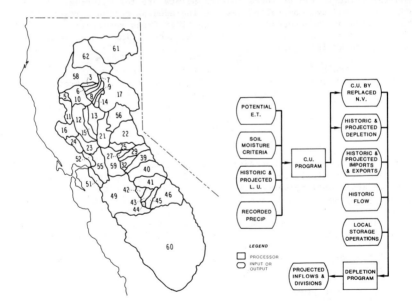

Figure 2.-Thirty-Five Depletion Areas
in the Central Valley, California

Figure 3.-Consumptive Use and
Depletion Programs

substantially altered. As a remedy, a reservoir simulation model
(HEC-3) has been applied on a selective number of DA's replacing the
depletion program and the local storage operations. The outputs of
these simulations are projected inflows and diversions which in-turn
are readily supplied to the DWRSIM. The first DA chosen to apply a
reservoir simulation model replacing the conventional depletion
analysis model is the American River Basin DA (Figure 1). Resulting
outflows from this DA become the inflow data to DWRSIM.

AMERICAN RIVER BASIN MODEL

The American River Basin drains an area of 1888 square miles (4890
km^2) and varies in elevation from 71 feet (22 m) at the Fair Oaks
gage to near 10,000 feet (3050 m) at the highest points. There are six
agencies operating water projects within the basin: Placer County Water
Agency, Sacramento Municipal Utility District, Georgetown Public
Utility District, Pacific Gas & Electric Company, El Dorado Irrigation
District and the U.S. Bureau of Reclamation. Combined storage of
thirteen existing reservoirs is 1,840,000 acre-feet (2.26 x 10^9 m^3)
and unimpaired runoff for the period 1922 through 1980 averaged
2,570,000 acre-feet (3.16 x 10^9 m^3) per year.

The HEC-3 model representation of the American River requires 54
control points. Ten of these control points are for existing
reservoirs and two control points are included as optional reservoirs
for studies of the proposed Auburn and Alder Creek Reservoirs. Several
minor reservoirs are not simulated in the model. The schematic of the
basin is shown in Figure 4.

The simulation model sequentially considers the water requirements at
each control point in the system, beginning at the most upstream point
and moving downstream. The release needed at a reservoir to meet these
requirements for all pertinent purposes is determined by evaluating
each operational requirement and all physical and operational
constraints at every downstream control point.

After instream requirements and diversion requirements have been met at
all control points (or shortages declared if water is not available in
upstream reservoirs), system requirements are examined to determine
whether additional releases will be needed to satisfy the system
demands. If so, the additional needs are proportioned among projects
in the system. These additional releases are added to the previously
computed releases for meeting at-site requirements; thus the system and
at-site requirements are met (or system available). This process is
repeated for each period of the study, with the ending state
(condition) of the projects in the system for the current period being
the beginning state for the next period.

RESULTS OF SIMULATION

The American River Model (1) can be used in two basic modes: As a
stand alone model for in-basin studies or as an input model for the
DWRSIM. DWRSIM normally requires inflows for up to 30 years into the
future. The American River Model is executed at three discrete levels
of future

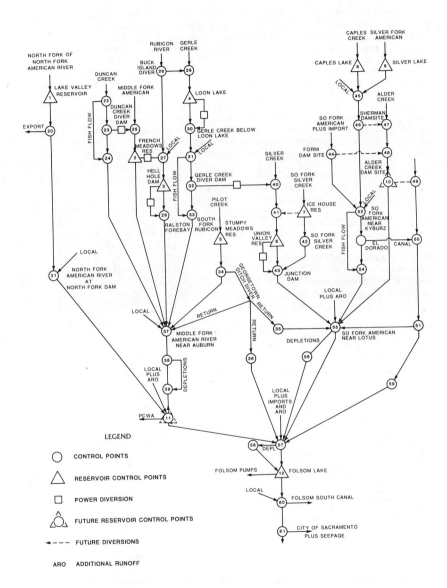

Figure 4.–Schematic Representation of the American River Basin

development, namely 1980, 2000, and 2010. Fifty nine years of the
historic flows are first converted into the natural flows via the
aforementioned consumptive use model. Then the natural flows are
adjusted for different levels of future development through the use of
the American River Basin Model. Figure 5 shows the monthly average
flows of the natural, historic and three future levels of development
over the 59-year period at the mouth of the American River Basin (Fair
Oaks gage). From the figure, it is noted that the high summer peaks of
natural flows have been shifted to augment the low winter flow
through the historic operation of the storage facilities in the basin.
Similar trend is observed as the 1980 level flows are compared with the
historic flows. The losses experienced from natural to historic
development can be attributed to the consumptive uses from the

TABLE 3.- Annual American River Flows
1922-1980 Averages in TAF

	Historic	1980	2000	2010
Natural Flow at Fair Oaks . .	2,574	2,574	2,574	2,574
Imports	+151	+162	+162	+162
Exports	−78	−132	−584	−768
Net Irrigated Lands	−33	−23	−28	−29
Reservoir Evaporation	−25	−58	−56	−54
Reservoir Storage Decreases .	−21	−2	−2	−2
Impaired Flow at Fair Oaks. .	2,568	2,521	2,065	1,882
In CFS . .	3,540	3,480	2,850	2,600

Note: 1TAF= 1.23 x 10^6 m^3; 1 CFS = 0.028 m^3

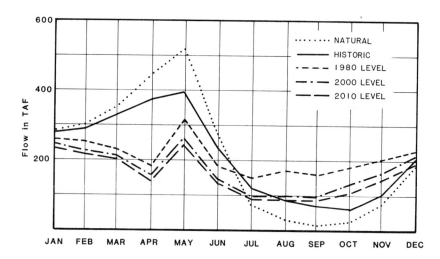

Figure 5.-American River Historic and Simulated Flows

irrigated crops. Table 3 shows the yearly totals of the monthly flow
averages at natural, historic and three different levels of
development. Both Figure 5 and Table 3 describe the reduction in the
impaired flow at Fair Oaks as the amounts of exports to other DA's are
being increased.

MANIPULATION OF DATA SETS

Figure 6 describes how the DA models along with the update model
prepare the input data for the final DWRSIM. Each data set generated
by the DA models reflect different sets of operational criteria at
different levels of future developments. These sets are, then, stored
in a data bank. The update model upon receiving the user specified
instructions such as level of hydrology and assumed mode of operating
facilities selects the pertinent data sets from the bank and merges the
selected sets in the acceptable form to DWRSIM.

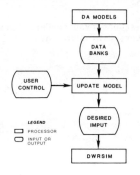

Figure 6.- Generation and Selection
of Data Sets

SUMMARY AND CONCLUSION

The "HEC-3" model developed by the Hydrologic Engineering Center at
Davis, California has been used to simulate the operation of a
reservoir system in a smaller basin. The resulting outflows from the
basin become the inflows to the succeeding model that simulates the
operation of water facilities in a very large area--the entire
California Central Valley. Compatible degrees of accuracy and
flexibility can be attained through the use of the similar models both
in the generation of the data and in the subsequent execution of the
model.

Through the use of the developed DA model, the interactions of various
storage facilities owned and operated by several different agencies can
be closely analyzed. Futhermore, the integrated operation of the
storage facilities may produce preferable basin outflows while meeting
each agency's objectives. Much time and effort in data preparation is
saved through the use of the update model where the required data decks
are selected from the data bank and integrated in the appropriate
format via a facilitated utility program.

ACKNOWLEDGEMENT

The authors are grateful to Price Schreiner and Jan Sweigert for their generous effort on the development of the model and data. The skillful typing of the manuscript by Terrie Brown is also appreciated.

APPENDIX--REFERENCES

1. "American River Watershed Model," Central District Memorandum Report, Department of Water Resources, State of California, March, 1984.

2. Barnes, George W. Jr. and Il Whan Chung, "Use of Simulation Models for Water Resources Planning for California," Journal of Water Resources Planning and Management Division, ASCE, Vol.____, No._____

3. Chung, Il Whan and Otto J. Helweg, "Modeling the California State Water Project," Journal of Water Resources Planning and Management Division, ASCE, Vol. 111, No. 1. January, 1985.

4. "HEC-3" Reservoir System Analysis for Conservation-Users Manual," 723-030, Hydrologic Engineering Center, U.S. Army Corps of Engineers, July 1974.

Models for Lake and River Basin Analysis

Darrell G. Fontane*, M. ASCE

Abstract

This tutorial describes basic concepts, purposes and issues of mathematical models for lakes and river basins. Simulation and optimization models are discussed and their structure and uses are contrasted. Specific concern is directed towards reasons that these models are not being used to their full potential. Suggestions for increasing and improving the use of mathematical models for lakes and river basins are offered.

Introduction

The use of mathematical models to analyze lakes, reservoirs, and river basins has become a common practice in water resource engineering over the past decade. However the application of mathematical models in analyzing and solving actual problems is nowhere near the potential for the use of these techniques. During the ASCE National Convention in San Francisco, CA, in October 1984, numerous papers addressed the question of why these techniques were not receiving more use. In particular this question was directed towards optimization models. A paper presented at the convention by Ford and Davis (1) addressing the practical role of system analysis models served as the inspiration for the format of this tutorial.

It is impossible to describe how to develop and use models for lake and river basin analysis in a 30 minute tutorial. That description is the basis for numerous texts, university graduate courses, and professional training courses. Rather, this tutorial will reexamine some of the basic purposes for using these models at all. If mathematical models are not being used as much as the model developers feel they could or should, then maybe we should look right to the beginning of the process to attempt to discover why.

There are a tremendous variety of mathematical models. Water quantity models range for simple mass balance computations to detailed unsteady flow routings. When water quality considerations are addressed, the hydrodynamics with the lake and reservoir often require description in addition to the interactions between reservoirs. Time scales may vary from hours to years and spatial scales from feet to miles. Models are called simulation models if their structure is primarily descriptive, that is, they convert system inputs to system

---

*Assistant Prof., Dept. of Civil Engineering, Colorado State University, Fort Collins, Colorado 80523

outputs. Optimization models extend this concept by measuring the
system outputs against some performance goal and then modifying
appropriate system parameters to attempt to achieve optimum system
performance.

The availability of a large variety of models has inevitably led
to the question of "which model is best?" Unfortunately there is no
answer to this question since almost every analysis of a lake, reservoir, or river basin involves different purposes. An analogy is the
set of tools used by a carpenter in building a house. Questions such
as "what is the best tool to use to build the house?" or "is a hammer
better than a saw?" are obviously meaningless. Mathematical models
are tools just like carpenter's tools, and similar comparisons can be
just as meaningless. Perhaps much more important than the selection
of a tool, is the ability to use it. A skilled carpenter with a hand
saw can do a much better job than an unskilled worker with a power
saw, even though one could develop a convincing argument that a power
saw is inherently better than a hand saw.

This tutorial will focus on a general description of the purposes
and structure of simulation and optimization models. The session
papers will illustrate specific examples of these models in more
detail. It is assumed for this tutorial that a basic purpose of using
any model, regardless of type, is to provide input for decision
making. Models can be used to purely represent the response of a
"system" to a given input. However, the nature of water resource
engineering is such that engineers and managers are interested in
system responses as a mechanism to determine how to alter or improve
the outputs of a system to achieve specific objectives. Therefore, an
engineer or manager is essentially always judgemental in the analysis
of mathematical model studies. As such water resource engineers have
focused their modeling activities on controllable man-made reservoirs
and systems of these reservoirs, rather than on natural lakes where
control options are minimal or nonexistent. This tutorial will also
focus on controllable reservoir systems.

Simulation Models

Simulation models use mathematical equations to represent the
physical interactions of a river-reservoir systems. They allow the
user to assess the impact of a given input (such as a dam failure) on
the system without having to actually experience that event. A common
terminology is that simulation models allow the user to ask "what if"
questions. Generally these models are easy to use and the outputs can
be directly related to the users knowledge and experience with the
real system. The user can often determine by inspection whether or
not the model output is reasonable. By comparison to optimization
models, simulation models have received a much wider acceptance and
use.

In addition to using simulation models to predict the impact of
various scenarios on the system, simulation models provide other
useful services. These models identify the type of data that is
needed to describe the system and provide a convenient means by which
to store this data. In addition to the physical and hydrologic data,

the simulation model usually contains operational, legal, and institutional information about the system. Development of simulation models helps to identify physical and institutional relationships and interactions that are not adequately understood and leads to needed research. Finally simulation models are an excellent training mechanism to allow inexperienced personnel to gain understanding about the characteristics of a water resource system by allowing these users to "experience" a wide variety of potential scenarios.

Simulation models of single reservoirs are usually based upon mass balance. For example, these models would determine reservoir releases based upon storage, inflow, and specific operating criteria. By evaluating the computed release against desired release levels, the performance of the specified reservoir operating criteria can be measured. The addition of water quality to the simulation model usually requires a more precise definition of the hydrodynamics within the reservoir and a smaller simulation time increment, however, the basic concept is similar.

River basin models provide a means to link various reservoirs together and also evaluate the conditions in the river below and between the reservoirs. Generally a node-link concept is used to represent significant physical aspects of the system such as reservoirs, diversion points, and confluence points. The links represent the river segments connecting the nodes. Again mass balance is the primary characteristic of the system and the model preserves mass balance at all nodes in the system. The output of these models is a summary of reservoir storages, releases, energy produced, and any shortages at various points throughout the river basin.

Under the assumption that a simulation model will be used to assist decision making, the user employs a trial and error procedure. A specific scenario is evaluated against the results of alternative scenarios for hydrologic conditions of interest. If the model use is for planning or design, scenarios might include number, location, and sizing of reservoirs. If the model use is for operations, scenarios might include operational policies within and between reservoirs. By comparison of model output between alternative scenarios, the user can select a "best" alternative or determine a potential better alternative to evaluate.

Optimization Models

Optimization models are essentially simulation models with a built-in mechanism to generate and evaluate alternative scenarios in a systematic fashion so as to identify the "best" alternative strategy. As described by Loucks, et al. (3), the number of alternatives that the user of a simulation model might have to generate and test can be enormous, particularly if the system is complex. A user, specifically one not familiar with the system, could easily select a best solution by a trial and error method that was far from the optimum performance achievable by the system. Conceptually optimization models eliminate or minimize this difficulty.

Optimization models have to essentially represent by mathematical equations, the judgement processes of the human brain. While the

impossibility of that task is obvious, further consider that mathematics is limited to optimizing scalar functions. Usually a single
objective is optimized, for example, maximizing hydropower production
from a system. Other objectives such as flood control or recreation
might be specified as limits or constraints. One objective is maximized while providing at least a certain amount of other specific
objectives. Further, consider the difficulty in writing a mathematical equation to maximize even a single objective such as hydropower
production. Merely maximizing hydropower could conceivably result in
enormous hydropower production in some months and no production in
others. Maximizing hydropower implies spatial and temporal attributes
that must be explicitly described in mathematical terms for the
optimization model to yield desirable results. The development of a
descriptive objective function is a skill that must be developed
through training and experience. Considering all of the above difficulties it is not surprising that optimization models have not been
as widely used as simulation models. However, as discussed by Hall
and Dracup (2) the fact that real systems can not be completely
treated by systems analysis models does not imply that these techniques are not useful.

Just as simulation models help to identify the important interactions within a water resource system, optimization models help to
identify the important purposes for the system. A basic premise of
this paper is that all modeling is done for the purpose of improving
the system. How do we define "improving"? Optimization models
require that the user explicitly define his purposes or objectives in
sufficient detail to allow mathematical representation. The articulation of those purposes, both by definition and ranking of importance,
define the basis for comparison in determining the performance of the
system. This articulation may be more valuable in fact than all of
the results of the model studies.

Optimization models are generally more mathematically complex
than simulation models. In addition to incorporating the simulation
model as the system description, the optimization model must have a
mathematical algorithm to generate and discriminate among alternatives. Depending upon the nature of the objectives and the systems,
techniques such as linear programming, non-linear programming or
dynamic programming algorithms might be employed. Effective use of an
optimization model requires knowledge of both the physical system
being simulated and the solution characteristics of the optimization
technique employed.

Optimization models can be used in a trial and error fashion
similar to simulation models. The alternative scenarios evaluated now
focus on project objectives. For example, one objective is maximized
or minimized with other objectives being set at specified limits.
Those limits are altered and a new optimum is found. Perhaps one of
the objectives specified as a limit is now made the objective to be
optimized. The process is continued until the user has found a "best"
satisfaction of project purposes. An interested benefit of an
optimization study may be the identification of the "constraints" most
limiting the overall performance of the water resource system. Often
these constraints are not physical but institutional and the impact of

these constraints can be put in perspective with overall system objectives and goals.

Summary

The purpose of using both simulation and optimization models is to aid decision making to improve reservoir or river basin operations. Simulation models help the engineer to better understand the system and optimization models help to better articulate the objectives. In fact the models actually overlap since the use of simulation models requires objectives and the use of optimization models requires system description. Simulation and optimization models are simply two different tools much like the hammer and saw of the carpenter's toolbox. One tool is not better than the other, one tool is not necessarily used before the other. Depending upon the task they are used together or separately to accomplish the job.

If simulation and optimization models are valuable tools for the water resource engineer then why aren't they used more? Ford and Davis (1) suggest some reasons including the observation that there are academic goals and practical goals for model development. Academic research is most often oriented toward developing new and improved model techniques usually increasingly mathematically complex. This is partly by nature to want to build a "better" model and certainly reinforced by academic and professional journal pressure to develop something new. Training users to effectively employ these models is a worthy but much lower esteemed academic function.

It is the opinion of the author that the lack of adequate training in the "effective" use of these models is the primary reason for their limited acceptance. As mathematical modelers we have equated the ability to make a model run on a computer system with the ability to "use" the model. That is no more reasonable than equating the ability to start a car with the ability to drive it. The use of mathematical models is a skill that must be acquired through adequate training and experience.

Recommendations

A key issue is the most effective means of providing adequate training for the users of mathematical models of reservoirs and river basins. Unfortunately a key ingredient is experience time with the models. If a user could participate in a concentrated two week to four week training course he could develop a high level of proficiency. However this is a large time committment from both the employee and the engineering organization. The use of intense training seminars should be developed, although, this mechanism will probably not be used by the majority of practicing engineers.

A second suggestion would involve the development of programmed courses for individual self study. Basically these courses would go beyond a user manual and include a text with progressively difficult example problems to be implemented and tested with the mathematical models. The examples could be developed to illustrate advantages and pitfalls of the models. An extension of this concept would involve developing the self-study courses for use on microcomputers. The software could include the models, their documentation, and the programmed text materials. This concept could even be combined with a one or two day introductory workshop, to introduce the user to the models and their underlying concepts. The primary difficulty of this approach is the time and effort required to develop these programmed courses and still be able to sell the courses at a price that is affordable to the general water resource engineer or manager.

A final suggestion would involve an active campaign to get more practical application papers into appropriate professional journals. The concept is skill development much more than technical understanding of mathematical relationships. The focus should be on how the use of mathematical models helped or hindered the conduct of actual water resource engineering studies. The journal would be a forum to share experiences among actual users and promote communication between modelers. This experience would also be invaluable to model developers. They could use this input to determine the most needed improvements in modeling techniques and focus future research.

In conclusion it is the sincere hope of the author that the use of mathematical models for reservoirs and river basins will be greatly expanded in the future. This will require an understanding from both the model users and model developers that these models are very sophisticated tools that will require a significant technology transfer effort. The mechanisms to effect the technology transfer and the nature of the personnel to be involved in the process need innovative thought.

References

1. Ford, D.T. and Davis, D.W., "A Practical Role for Systems Analysis in Water Resources Planning", paper presented at the ASCE Annual Convention, Oct. 1-3, 1984, San Francisco, CA.

2. Hall, W.A. and Dracup, J.A., Water Resources Engineering, McGraw Hall, 1970.

3. Loucks, D.P., Stedinger, J.R., and Haith, D.A., Water Resource Systems Planning and Analysis, Prentice-Hall, Englewood Cliffs, New Jersey, 1981.

OPTIMAL OPERATION OF A SYSTEM OF
LAKES FOR QUALITY AND QUANTITY

by

Bruce Loftis[1], M. ASCE; John W. Labadie[2], M. ASCE;
and Darrell G. Fontane[3], M. ASCE

Abstract

A methodology is presented combining simulation and optimization techniques for determining operation strategies for a system of lakes in the presence of quality and quantity constraints. The objective of the methodology is to determine release flow rates from each lake in a system of lakes such that downstream quality targets are met as nearly as possible and specified quantity constraints are satisfied.

The methodology involves separating the quality and quantity aspects into distinct subproblems and iterating between the subproblems until some measure of convergence is reached. A one-dimensional numerical model is used to simulate the temporal and spatial water quality characteristics within the lake. Changes in water quality characteristics with depth an with time are described with the theory of stratified flow. An important component of the simulation model is the capability of accurately modeling the hydraulic characteristics of a multi-level outlet structure. Output from the simulation model includes daily downstream quality characteristics for a specified set of daily release flows. The release quality characteristics are used as input to the optimization module.

The optimization module is used to solve a quantity subproblem. Given a set of daily release quality characteristics specified by the simulation model, the optimal release flow rates from each lake are determined such that a performance index based on downstream quality is minimized and quantity constraints are satisfied. Output from the

---

1. Senior Scientist, Institute for Computational Studies, Colorado State University, Fort Collins, CO 80523

2. Professor, Department of Civil Engineering, Colorado State University, Fort Collins, Colorado 80523

3. Assistant Professor, Department of Civil Engineering, Colorado State University, Fort Collins, Colorado 80523

694 COMPUTER APPLICATIONS / WATER RESOURCES

optimization subproblem includes a set of optimal daily release flow rates for each lake in the system. The release flow rates are then used as input into the simulation model to determine updated values of release quality characteristics. Iteration between simulation and optimization proceeds until convergence is reached. A procedure for decomposing the optimization problem into a sequence of smaller and thus more tractable subproblems was developed.

A case study is presented illustrating the value of the technique in determining optimal release flow rates from a system of lakes. The large-scale characteristics of this problem are illustrated with results obtained on the CYBER 205 at Colorado State University.

Introduction

Impoundment of a river or stream results in change to the physical and chemical characteristics of the water resources system. Evaluation and management of the changed system are important challenges in Water Resources Engineering. Operation of multi-purpose lakes to meet water quality objectives is fundamentally a matter of tradeoffs between a variety of seemingly noncommensurable objectives. Some of these tradeoffs and considerations are the following.

In a density-stratified lake, concentrations of water quality constituents vary with elevation. Operation of projects with a multi-level intake structure requires evaluation of tradeoffs between ports to determine which ports should be opened and what the flow rate should be for each open port in order to meet downstream water quality requirements.

Operation of a lake to meet goals for several water quality parameters may result in conflict. Satisfying both temperature and dissolved oxygen targets is often not possible.

Deviations from water quality targets can be allocated over time. It is possible to operate a lake optimally on a day-to-day basis with no anticipation of future conditions. Such operation will often result in small deviations from target water quality objectives on some days and possibly severe deviations on other days. If future conditions are known or can be estimated, dynamic-optimal operation can smooth out the daily deviations over time to achieve an overall lower level of deviation. The principle behind dynamic-optimal operation is that a large number of small deviations can have a less damaging impact on the ecosystem than a smaller number of large deviations.

Another type of tradeoff requires making decisions relating to total flow released from a lake in order to claim water quality benefits in conjunction with benefits or demands from other project purposes such as flood control or hydropower production.

A final consideration is related to the operation of a system of lakes and connecting streams to achieve overall water quality requirements at specified locations throughout the system. Individual lakes in a system of lakes have particular requirements to be satisfied such as maintaining pool elevation at a particular level. And there may be characteristics such that particular project purposes can best be satisfied with releases from particular lakes. Operation of a system of lakes such that constraints for each lake are satisfied and objectives defined by project purposes for the system are met is a significant water resources challenge.

The purpose of this paper is to present a brief discussion of a procedure for determining operation strategies for a system of lakes in the presence of water quality and water quantity constraints. A case study is used to demonstrate that the procedure can be used to determine release flow rates from a each lake in a system of lakes such that water quality and quantity requirements are satisfied.

An important contribution of the research discussed herein is demonstration that a lake operation problem with quantity and quality considerations can be solved by separating the quality and quantity aspects into distinct subproblems. The subproblems can be solved nearly independently with iteration between the subproblems yielding convergence. There is potential for extension of the techniques to larger systems, longer time frames, more quality parameters, and more project purposes.

Problem Description and Solution Approach

The problem under consideration is to identify strategies for operation of a system of lakes such that quality and quantity constraints are satisfied. Complexity exists in the problem because of the large number of interrelated decisions. Daily release flow rates must be determined for each lake of a system. The water resources problem of interest in this discussion is the daily operation of a system of lakes such that benefits from the various project purposes are maximized, related costs are minimized, and constraints on the system are satisfied. It is desired to determine strategies for operation of a single lake or a system of lakes such that all water quantity constraints are satisfied and the highest level of water quality is attained.

Decisions in operation may be constrained by any of the following water quantity considerations. The minimum release flow from a lake for every day may be specified. The minimum flow passing a control point downstream of a lake or system of lakes may be specified. The daily pool volumes may need to be maintained within an allowable range of a specified volume-day guide curve throughout a period of interest. The hydraulic characteristics of selective withdrawal structures offer flexibility with respect to the vertical location in a lake from which water is withdrawn, but there are limits with respect to quantity and quality of water that can be released from a particular vertical location.

The solution or answer to the problem is a set of release flow rates from each lake in the system for every day of the period of interest. Thus, for one year and a two-lake system, there are 730 daily release flows to be determined. This is a large problem computationally, but actual daily operation is significantly more complicated. If a particular lake has a multi-level outlet structure, then there are many ports from which water can be withdrawn. The quality of water released downstream is dependent on the vertical location of open ports and the flow rate passing through each open port. The characteristics of water released from a port in a stratified flow environment are a function of the flow quantity released through the port. Changing the total release flow or changing the allocation of the release flow to open ports will change the downstream quality characteristics. Thus, the decisions to be made for each day of interest for each lake are the total flow released from the lake and also the allocation of that total flow rate to the various selective withdrawal ports. In the presence of a multi-level outlet structure. the determination of optimal operation strategies can be seen to be an exceedingly complex task.

The lake operation problem under discussion is one with many lakes, many quality parameters, many time steps, and many selective withdrawal ports. A direct formulation and solution of the complete large-scale problem would challenge even the fastest of current computers. But the large intractable problem can be decomposed into a sequence of smaller subproblems which can be solved quickly with sufficient accuracy. The problem as described requires determining daily operational strategies to provide the best, in some sense, water quality while satisfying many quantity constraints. The problem then is not one of making subjective tradeoffs between quality and quantity, but rather determining the best water quality that can be achieved within the bounds specified by the quantity constraints.

The solution approach is a combination of simulation modeling and mathematical optimization. Conceptually, a quantity subproblem and a quality subproblem can be formulated. The quantity subproblem is a determination of release flows from each lake such that constraints are satisfied and water quality resulting from the operational decisions is maximized. The quality subproblem is determination of the quality of water released from a lake when the release flow from the lake is known. With the overall problem formulated as quantity and quality subproblems, there is a need for iteration between the subproblems in order to effect convergence to an overall solution. The quantity subproblem is solved with optimization techniques. The quality subproblem is solved primarily with simulation modeling. Iteration between subproblems is a powerful approach because quantity and quality aspects are separated, and the many of the interactions which cause the complexity in operational decision-making are eliminated. A schematic of the iteration process between simulation and optimization is shown in Figure 1.

Quality Simulation Model

The WESTEX model provides a procedure for examining the balance of thermal energy imposed on an impoundment. This energy balance and lake hydrodynamic phenomema are used to dynamically simulate vertical temperature profiles and release temperatures.

The model includes computational procedures for simulating heat transfer at the air-water interface, advective heat transfer of inflow and outflow, and the internal dispersion of thermal energy.

Additionally, there is an optimization procedure for determining which ports should be open and what flow rate should pass through each open port in order to minimize deviation of the predicted release qualities from specified downstream target qualities. The model is conceptually one-dimensional based on the division of the lake into discrete horizontal layers of uniform thickness. One-dimensional models are in general acceptable if the important output from the model is the release characteristics from the lake.

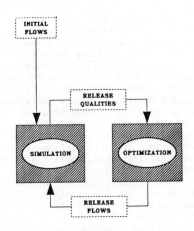

Figure 1   Iteration Between Simulation and Optimization

The simulation model is primarily a heat budget model. That is, temperature is the fundamental water quality parameter under consideration. However, the model is capable of performing a simple routing of conservative water quality constituents. The actual budgeting of conservative constituent concentrations is performed in a manner similar to the budgeting of heat. Details of the simulation model are presented by Loftis (1).

The purpose of the quality simulation model to determine daily release quality characteristics from a lake for a specified set of daily release flows and to determine the proper port operation strategy to minimize deviations from specified water quality targets. The model developed for the research effort reported herein is a temperature model with conservative constituent routing. Because the simulation model is essentially independent of the optimization model, a different temperature model or a comprehensive ecosystem model could also be used to predict the release quality characteristics.

Quantity Allocation Model

A general formulation of the quantity allocation model could include tandem lakes and parallel lakes, numerous water quality parameters, and control points downstream of each lake and throughout the rest of the system. A general formulation could also include

hydrologic routing of flows and quality constituents through the river
reaches. Hydrologic routing and identification of changes in water
quality as water released from a lake flows through a downstream river
reach could be an important consideration in a system where lakes are
geographically far apart, and significant time elapses between the time
the water is released from the lake and the time the water passes the
downstream control point.

The objective of the quantity allocation problem is to determine
release flows from each lake such that water quality target concentrations at downstream control points are most nearly met. The objective
function for the quantity allocation problem is a scalar measure of how
well a particular decision strategy meets the downstream target quality
concentrations. Calculation of the least-squares objective function
chosen for this research effort is as follows: a) for each water
quality constituent under consideration, evaluate daily quality concentration passing a control point, b) determine the daily differences
between computed quality concentration and target quality
concentration, c) square the differences, d) sum the differences over
the time period of interest, e) add the sums of squared differences for
each quality parameter. The contribution to the objective function by
each of the water quality constituents can be weighted to account for
specific project characteristics.

The constraint set for the quantity allocation problem can take
the form of constraints on release flow from each lake and at each
downstream control point, constraints on end-of-day lake volume, and
constraints on downstream quality concentrations. Downstream quality
constraints can effect a non-feasible optimization problem and are thus
more properly handled in the objective function.

Nonlinear programming offers a convenient formulation for the
optimization problem. An important disadvantage of nonlinear programming techniques is that the computational requirements increase
exponentially with increasing problem size. That is, solving the
quantity allocation problem for two lakes and 365 days would be beyond
the limits of all but the very largest computers. However, there are
techniques to decompose large problems into sequences of smaller
problems. There are a number of nonlinear programming algorithms which
could be used to solve the quantity allocation problem. Gradient
projection techniques are among the most effective methods for dealing
with linearly constrained problems with nonlinear objective functions.

The quantity allocation problem has been formulated for solution
with the gradient projection algorithm. However, direct application of
the solution method to this formulation is difficult because of the
size of the problem. The typical time frame of interest for problems
pertaining to operation of lakes for water quality purposes is a year.
A phenomenon known as fall turnover occurs in many lakes, after which
the lake is completely mixed and stays mixed throughout the winter
months. The mixing leaves the water quality concentrations homogeneous
from top to bottom. Because of this mixing, for water quality analyses
it is convenient to consider each calendar year to be independent of
other years. The quantity allocation problem under discussion, for 2
lakes for a period of 365 days would have 730 decision variables, which
are the release flow rates from the 2 lakes and a constraint matrix

with (5x365) rows and (2x365) columns. Computer memory requirements
for just the constraint matrix would be 1,330,000 words. Additional
memory is needed for other matrices and for the computer code itself.
Such memory requirements are beyond the limits of all but the largest
computers. It is possible, however, to decompose the quantity allocation problem into a sequence of smaller subproblems, such that the
accuracy of the solution is acceptable, and the computer resources
required are significantly less.

Decomposition of the quantity allocation optimization problem into
a sequence of smaller problems includes the following steps.

a. Consider the one year time frame to be composed of many
optimization weeks.

b. Solve the quantity allocation problem with gradient projection to determine the optimal release flow rates from each lake for
each optimization week. The solution to this problem is the set of
total flow rates from each lake for each optimization week.

c. Solve a sequence of single-week problems. For each single-
week problem, the total flow from each lake for the week is known. The
problem is then to allocate the total flow for the week to each of the
days of the week. The same formulation and the same solution technique
are used.

Details of the formulation of the optimization problem and the
procedure for decomposing the large problem into a sequence of smaller
tractable problems are presented by Loftis (1).

Case Study -- Background

The purpose of the application of the concepts described herein
was to identify operational strategies that would best satisfy water
quality requirements downstream of the confluence of the North Branch
Potomac River (NBPR) and the Savage River (3). The confluence of these
two rivers is at Luke in western Maryland (Figure 2).

Bloomington Lake is located on the NBPR upstream of the confluence
with the Savage River. The purposes of Bloomington Lake are to provide
water quality control, flood control, municipal and industrial water
supply, and recreation. The Bloomington watershed is heavily mined,
and the NBPR is quite acidic. The water in the NBPR is of very poor
quality. Primary sources of pollution include coal mine drainage from
abandoned deep and surface mines and to a lesser extent, poorly treated
wastes from municipalities and industries scattered throughout the
basin. The prominent characteristics of mine drainage are sulphuric
acid, heavy metals, high dissolved solids, and copious precipitates.
Acid mine drainage has a devastating impact on aquatic life. It makes
water undesirable for municipal and industrial water supplies and all
but eliminates water-borne recreation. The total acid load in the
NBPR has declined somewhat in recent years, but acid mine pollution is
still the most degrading component of the water flowing into
Bloomington Lake. Any bacteriological problem that might exist
upstream of Luke is effectively eliminated by the low pH of the water.

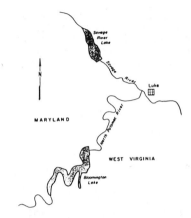

Figure 2   Location of Bloomington and Savage River Lakes

Bloomington Lake is expected to have water quality ranging from poor to
fair, but it will be aesthetically pleasing due to the absence of algae
and macrophytes (2).

    Savage River Lake and Dam are located on the Savage River upstream
of the confluence with the NBPR.   The Savage River has very little
mining activity, and the quality of the water is quite good. Project
purposes for Savage River Lake and Dam are to augment streamflows, to
supply sufficient water for industries, and to reduce pollution.

    The purpose of the application was to determine an operational
strategy to balance   the relatively poor   quality releases from
Bloomington Lake with the high quality releases from Savage River Lake
in order to satisfy water quality objectives for downstream users. The
study was accomplished with simulation modeling to evaluate the impact
of any proposed operational strategy and mathematical optimization
techniques that systematically generate operational strategies until a
strategy that is best by some criterion is identified.

Results

    Two sets of results are presented. The first results presented
are from the execution of the simulation model alone with no attempt to
make optimal release flow decisions based on future hydrological and
meteorological conditions.   These simulation results provide a basis
for assessing results from the combination approach of simulation and
optimization. These are, in a sense, the best results that the simulation model alone can produce. Operation of the two lakes is similar to
the way the projects might be operated in a real-time mode. A volume
guide curve is maintained for every day except when minimum flow constraints require that more flow should be released. The decisions with
respect to which Bloomington Lake ports should be opened are made
optimally given that release flows are specified. The release charac-

teristics for one quality parameter with a constant target value are
presented in Figure 3.

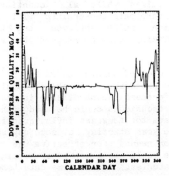

Figure 3   Downstream Quality -- Simulation

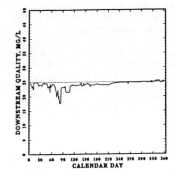

Figure 4   Downstream Quality -- Simulation and Optimization

Figure 4 shows the predicted downstream quality concentration for
the optimal flow strategy. There is a period of time in the spring for
which the predicted downstream quality is as much as 5 mg/l below the
target quality, but for most of the year the predicted downstream
quality is within 1 mg/l of the target quality. This figure can be
compared with the results from the simulation model alone. It can be
seen that much better release flow strategies can be developed using a
combination of simulation and optimization than by using only
simulation.

Conclusions and Recommendations

An important aspect of these results is the demonstration that
quality and quantity aspects can be considered in the same problem.

The separation of the quality and quantity aspects into distinct sub-problems allow optimal release flow rates to be computed such that water quality is maximized while all quantity constraints are satisfied. Stringent hydrologic constraints will limit the maximum water quality level which can be achieved, but the water quality benefit gained from relaxing constraints can be assessed with the methodology.

The methodology presented herein could be of significant value when used as a real-time procedure. Capability would need to be added to the methodology to forecast uncontrollable inputs into the future. Statistical time-series techniques could be used with the approximately 25 years of available data to forecast inflow quantities and qualities for the remainder of the year starting at some day when conditions are known. Another extension needed for effective use of the methodology as a real-time procedure would be a method of evaluating the value of suggested operating strategies. A real-time data base would need to be developed accumulating water quality conditions in the lakes, pool levels, inflow conditions, suggested operation strategies, actual operation, predicted downstream quality, and measured downstream quality. The data base could then be analyzed continually with results used to systematically modify the suggested operation strategies from the simulation-optimization methodology.

It was shown that it is possible to achieve good water quality downstream of Bloomington Lake and still satisfy constraints imposed on the system. And, significantly, the suggested operation strategies provide acceptable water quality levels consistent with requirements for the larger Potomac River Basin.

References

1.   "Optimal Operation of a System of Lakes for Quality and Quantity", Ph.D Dissertation, Civil Engineering Department, Colorado State University, 1984.

2.   Master Manual for Reservoir Regulations, Potomac River Basin, Volume I - North Branch Potomac River, Appendix A, Bloomington Lake, May 1981. U. S. Army Engineer District, Baltimore. Baltimore, Maryland.

3.   Palmer, R. N., Wright, J. R., Smith. J. A., Cohon. J. L, and ReVelle, C. S. October 1977. "Policy Analysis of Reservoir Operation in the Potomac River Basin, Volume 1 - Executive Summary", Technical Report No. 59, Water Resources Research Center, University of Maryland, College Park, Maryland.

MODELING OF RESERVOIR OPERATIONS FOR
MANAGING ECOLOGICAL INTERESTS

By Marshall Flug,[1] M. ASCE; Dennis Morrow,[2] M. ASCE;
Darrell G. Fontane,[3] M. ASCE

ABSTRACT:

   A network simulation model is applied to a three reservoir system
to analyze the effects of alternative operating policies in response to
such seasonal water demands as hydropower, pollution abatement, recreation, fish spawning, and wild rice propagation. The model (MODSIM)
employs an out-of-kilter optimization technique embedded within the
network simulation. Water throughout the river basin's collection of
nodes (reservoirs) and links (river channels) is sequentially allocated
on a monthly basis, subject to system constraints. A monthly optimum
allocation is based on minimizing the pseudo-costs (priorities)
assigned to each objective which include target lake levels and river
flows. An application to Lake of the Woods Basin along the Minnesota-
Canadian border, which encompasses Voyageurs National Park, is provided. Present-day regulation is in compliance with rule curves
established under authority of the International Joint Commission. The
simulation model is used to analyze the effects of changes to these
rules of regulation.

INTRODUCTION

   Lake of the Woods Basin, located along the Minnesota-Canadian
border, is a complex network of lakes, rivers, portages, and dams.
Numerous lakes fill glacier-carved rock basins and extend into bogs,
marshes, and beaver ponds. Three major lakes of the basin are quantitatively described in Table 1. The active lake depths are a result of
current regulation policy. Note the size of Namakan and Rainy Lakes
and the corresponding 3:1 relationship in active depths. Namakan
Reservoir, known as the Namakan Chain of Lakes, includes Kabetogama,
Namakan, Sand Point, and Crane Lakes. Namakan and Rainy Lakes together
contribute about two-thirds of the total inflow to Lake of the Woods.
The international boundary follows the eighteenth century fur traders'
route between Lake Superior and Lake of the Woods; Voyageurs National
Park adjoins a 56-mile (90 km) stretch of that Voyageurs Highway
through both Namakan and Rainy Lakes.

---

[1]Hydrologist, Water Resources Lab, National Park Service, Colorado
State Univ., Ft. Collins, CO 80523.
[2]Staff Scientist, Institute for Computational Studies, Colorado State
Univ., Ft. Collins, CO 80523
[3]Assistant Professor, Civil Engrg., Colorado State Univ., Ft. Collins,
CO 80523.

Table 1. Lake Characteristics (1)

Subbasins	Active Depth ft (m)	Lake Area mi^2 (km^2)	Drainage Basin Area mi^2 (km^2)
Namakan Lake	11 (3.4)	100 (259)	7,440 (19,270)
Rainy Lake	4 (1.2)	345 (894)	7,460 (19,320)
Lake of the Woods	6 (1.8)	1,485 (3,846)	5,700 (14,760)

Why is there interest in studying the regulation of lake levels in this drainage basin? The hope is that through better management and operation of the existing regulated reservoir system, a larger variety of interests will be accommodated. An act by the United States Congress in 1971 (3) created Voyageurs National Park which was established in 1975 to preserve the natural environment, and native plant and animal life, for the benefit of future generations. These management functions of the National Park Service are harmonious with directives of the Organic Act (4) which established the National Park Service. Although both Namakan and Rainy Lakes existed as natural water bodies, the present-day reservoirs are larger and regulated to satisfy many specific concerns. Around the lake shores groups are primarily concerned with lake levels and include resort owners, tourist outfitters, wild rice harvesters (including native people), pulp and paper companies, municipal water suppliers, commercial and sport fishermen, and commercial and recreation navigators. However, apparent conflicts exist because some interests prefer higher lake levels when others desire lower lake levels, particularly during the spring and summer months. Additional concerns include navigation and pollution abatement which are dependent on reservoir outflows.

Authority granted by an Act of Congress and of the Canadian Federal Parliament permitted construction of the dam and powerhouse on the Rainy River between 1905-1909. This action paved the way for development of forest products mills which in turn created communities at International Falls, Minnesota and Fort Frances, Ontario; a transition from fur-trading posts to small urban communities. This dam at the outlet of Rainy Lake, as well as the two upstream parallel dams at the outlet of Namakan Lake (i.e., Kettle Falls Dam and its sister, the Canadian Dam) are privately owned and operated to provide water storage for hydropower generation and processing in the pulp and paper mills. Rainy Lake also supplies domestic water as well as high grade process water for the industrial mills.

HISTORICAL LAKE LEVEL REGULATION

In 1909 the Boundary Waters Treaty between the United States and Canada was created and established the International Joint Commission (IJC), to prevent disputes regarding use of boundary waters and to provide for adjustments and settlements of questions regarding common surface waters, and to provide a framework for cooperation on questions relating to air and water pollution, as well as the regulation of water levels and flows. The IJC appoints International Boards of Control which perform in both a technical capacity and ensure compliance with IJC orders. Natural flows and lake levels are a thing of the past in most of the Rainy Lake Watershed. Artificially regulated levels have existed on Rainy Lake since March, 1909 and on Namakan Lake since March, 1914. Naturally occurring lake levels and discharges (i.e., river flows) are quite variable with time in an uncontrolled system as compared to a regulated system. This difference has strong implications on the conservation of scenery, natural objects, and wildlife and preservation in an unimpaired state for future generations.

In 1938 a convention between both Canada and the U.S. was initiated which empowers IJC to determine when emergency conditions exist in the Rainy Lake Watershed and to adopt rules of regulation deemed proper with respect to existing and future dams or control works. A primary objective was to secure most advantageous use of waters for combined purposes of navigation, sanitation, domestic water supply, power production, recreation, and other beneficial purposes. Noteworthy actions of this convention included: 1) a field investigation and technical studies of the hydrology of the watershed by the International Rainy Lake Board of Control; 2) identification on Namakan Lake of a natural high-level outlet called Bear Portage, which was partially obstructed by a crude timber and rock-fill barrier constructed without authorization from IJC; and 3) the holding of public hearings to allow all interested parties to be heard and present evidence addressing questions raised by the Convention. These actions eventually led to the IJC Order of 1949 which established criteria for flow releases and desirable surface water levels at both Namakan and Rainy Lakes on a monthly basis. This order specifically recognized the interests of the pulp and paper mills which owned and operated the dam and powerhouses at International Falls and Fort Frances. In addition, impacts of regulated lake levels on riparian lands, shore properties, erosion of banks, flooding, creation of unsightly and unsanitary conditions, recreational use, and damaging high flow discharges were recognized concerns of individuals and the general public in both the U.S. and Canada.

Besides the initial 1949 order, major Amendments were added in 1957 and 1970 which changed the rules of operation and temporary modifications allowed in 1976 and 1977. In brief, the 1957 and 1970 Amendments modified the timing at which full reservoir levels were achieved, adjusted the low level in April to improve fish spawning, replaced the rule curve with a maximum and minimum rule band, redefined "emergency conditions," provided greater flood reserve capacity, and established minimum discharges for downstream pollution abatement. These Orders, Amendments, and rules of regulation were implemented by IJC in response to natural hydrologic events that overtaxed the system of operation in place at the time and due to resulting outcries from various interests along the lake shores. The objective in these rules of regulation remained: to secure most advantageous use of waters for several combined purposes including power production, recreation, sanitation, navigation, and other beneficial public purposes.

MODELING THE RIVER BASIN NETWORK

Given that violations of the established rules of operation are a natural phenomena which have occurred in the past, and considering the multitude of concerns surrounding the lake and shoreline, the National Park Service became interested in evaluating alternative rules of operation. This was inspired by their late arrival on the scene and the subsequent intensive involvement in biologic studies to evaluate management policies and the effect on preservation of the natural environment. A mathematical simulation model of the multi-lake watershed seemed an obvious approach for management to evaluate if slight modifications of the regulated rules of operation could reduce adverse effects on Park aquatic and riparian life without conflicting with other authorized uses of water. Figure 1 portrays the hydrologic system for the Lake of the Woods Basin in a flow chart format. The system as depicted is merely a representation of inputs, outputs, controls, constraints, and hydrologic connections of the real water resource system.

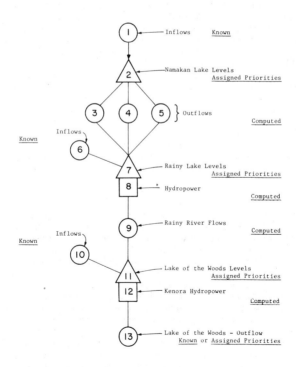

Figure 1. Lake of the Woods Basin Network Model

The flow chart of the drainage basin network shown in Figure 1 is interpreted as a series of nodes which are linked by mathematical relationships. A mass balance model simulates the lake system by maintaining continuity between reservoirs in the system such that:

Inflows = Outflows + Change in Storage

where, Inflows serve as the input data (i.e., the independent variable); Outflows are computed at each node (i.e., dam outlet); and the Change in Storage is computed for each reservoir.

A mathematical simulation model was desired for this study that could rapidly and easily evaluate many alternative management schemes. For example, to preserve higher lake elevations in one reservoir as opposed to another (e.g., Namakan Lake instead of Rainy Lake); or to maintain a larger minimum outflow from a particular dam (e.g., International Falls-Fort Frances outflows). The simulation model selected, MODSIM(2), represents the real river basin system as a circulating network. Priorities (or costs) are assigned to each link of the network on a monthly basis and an out-of-kilter optimization algorithm is used to minimize a weighted objective function. By assigning a different set of priorities, the simulation behaves in an alternative fashion while maintaining continuity. The assignment of priorities changes the weights of the objective function and thereby forces the optimum simulation to operate in the desired alternate mode; for example, increased discharges or higher lake elevations can be given higher priorities. In addition to continuity, various constraints are included in the model which represent physical or legal limitations of the reservoir system. These constraints include maximum outflows through existing outlet works, minimum flow requirements for water pollution, both maximum and minimum lake levels, and others as appropriate. As used in this study, the model routes mean monthly inflows through the system; and is not intended for daily operation of the reservoirs in real time. Modeling of a real river system by simulation and optimization has a distinct advantage of routing inputs (i.e., inflows) of a known quantity, whereas in the real system, reservoir releases are made in response to estimated inflows.

The computer model is calibrated using "back calculated" inflows with historical lake levels to calculate outflows. This procedure hopefully reproduces the historical outflows and thus tests the model to simulate the real lake system. At this time, monthly lake level priorities are assigned. These priorities encourage the simulation to operate in the desired fashion (e.g., according to past practices for calibration). Priorities are assigned for each lake on a monthly basis.

The desired data for evaluating this lake system consist of long-term records of lake levels, outflows, and most importantly river inflows. Ideally, inflows, outflows, and lake levels are known and then continuity relationships are used to compute losses or other ungaged fluxes to the system. A lack of inflow data exists, however, both upstream and tributary to the Rainy River. To overcome these data deficiencies and keeping in perspective the initial intention of this study, daily measured lake levels and outflows (i.e., discharges) are used as independent variables. A "back calculation," to determine mean monthly inflows, is performed using the continuity relationship and working upstream from Lake of the Woods outflow, using end of month lake levels for calculation of lake storage and mean monthly discharges. The "back calculation" procedure is used to generate a representative sequence of monthly inflows that accurately portray the naturally occurring hydrologic time series. The same set of inflows are used in all model simulations for analyzing modified rules of operation.

There are occasions when lake levels are not contained within the prespecified rule curves. The simulated levels fall significantly below the minimum rule curve during late summer and fall of 1976, spring and summer of 1977, and the summer of 1980, a phenomena that actually occurred on both Namakan and Rainy Lakes. In fact, all the simulated results correspond almost identically to the historically observed lake levels, for the respective time period. These results demonstrate that under extreme hydrologic events (e.g., droughts and floods) the reservoir system cannot maintain strict compliance with the current rules of regulation (i.e., IJC Order). This difficulty is due in part to a lack of meteorologic and hydrologic forecasting which would provide information useful to anticipate runoff and inflows. Forecasting of expected inflows provides lead time to regulate reservoirs to help dampen the impact of extreme hydrologic phenomena. Violations of the rule curve raise the concerns of various groups having interests in and near the lake shores. As a result, new calls for alternative rule curves and regulation policies are requested and from time to time implemented.

ALTERNATE RESERVOIR REGULATION

Discontent by various groups regarding lake levels and discharges is formally expressed by a call for changing the operating rules for both Rainy and Namakan Lakes. One alternative rule curve is presented in Figure 2 for Namakan Lake and likewise in Figure 3 for Rainy Lake. The cyclic pattern for each of these rule curves results from the five year period plotted (i.e., each rule curve repeats every year). These alternative rules of regulation vary from existing IJC rules of operation and are assumed more responsive to needs for preserving natural conditions. These alternative rules are presented only as one example and represent target levels for each lake, not a rule band as for the 1970 IJC Amendements. Specific concerns incorporated into these alternate target curves include timing of peak lake elevations and drawdown to low reservoir levels as occurred under the natural regime, preservation of a summer flood reserve capacity in each reservoir, and reducing the range of lake levels between high and low conditions.

Specifically, the naturally occurring peak lake levels occur around June 1 and this point is reflected in the alternate targets shown in Figures 2 and 3. Approximation of the natural peak allows for a more natural transition from low lake elevations in closer harmony with naturally occurring fluctuations. Additionally, by controlling the peak level in Namakan Lake to 1117.5 feet (340.8 m), an additional 1 foot (0.3 m) of flood reserve is provided, whereas only 0.5 feet

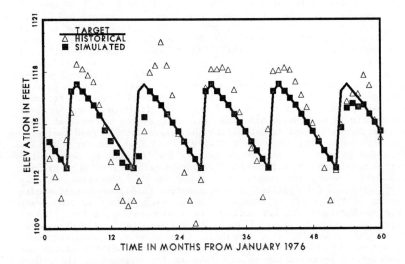

Figure 2.   Namakan Lake Levels, 1976-1980

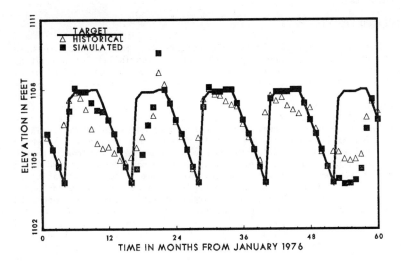

Figure 3.   Rainy Lake Levels, 1976-1980

(0.15 m) is currently reserved. The desire for a general decline in water levels from June to October simulates the natural hydrologic cycle, and therefore provides improved habitat conditions for walleye and northern pike spawning activity. By gradually lowering lake eleva- tions there is a reduced potential for flooding shore, island, and marsh bird nests, as well as greater opportunity to provide wave washed gravel, prime walleye pike spawning habitat. The fall through winter drawdown is further limited to only an additional four feet (1.2 m) [i.e., minimum 1112.5 feet (339.3 m)] on Namakan Lake, whereas present- day drawdowns are about 6 feet (1.8 m). This limit provides for less adverse effects on aquatic and riparian life. Beaver and muskrat along the lake shores become isolated from the lake and their food source by large drawdowns, when lodges and dens are left high and dry. Aquatic plants and animals are adapted to natural fluctuations by sensing the natural magnitude of water level drawdowns and accordingly prepare their nests, dens, and lodges in response to this phenomena. Exces- sively regulated fluctuations tend to simulate flood and drought condi- tions on an annual cycle; thus creating a yearly 9 feet (2.7 m) level change on Namakan Lake, in contrast to a more natural 6 feet (1.8 m) fluctuation. This increased fluctuation has resulted in the disappear- ance of once extensive wild rice beds. Furthermore, a new rule curve for each of Namakan and Rainy Lake can eliminate any preference for protection or preservation on one lake at the expense of the other; that is, both lakes should be equally responsive to the enhancement of natural conditions. In the past, Namakan Lake experienced greater fluctuations in favor of more responsive regulation and stabilization on Rainy Lake.

SIMULATED RESULTS

The above described alternate targets for lake levels are used within the simulation model to determine the feasibility of regulating the reservoir system in compliance with this alternate set of rules. Figures 2 and 3, respectively, show the simulation results for Namakan and Rainy Lakes for a five year period, 1976-1980. As described else- where in this paper, "back calculated" monthly inflows for this five year period are used as model inputs. The simulation then attempts to satisfy prespecified target lake levels while maintaining mass balance relationships between inflows, outflows, and lake storages. As shown by the close fit of the simulated elevations with alternate target rules in Figues 2 and 3, the reservoir system can accommodate modified operating schemes under normal hydrologic events. Close observation of Figures 2 and 3 indicate two time periods in which the simulated condi- tions (i.e., levels) deviate from target elevations, the 1977 and 1980 low spring runoff years. In addition, a single summer storm in 1977 actually resulted in the one high lake level shown for the simulated Rainy Lake levels in Figure 3. These violations (i.e., levels differ- ent from the target) shown for the simulated lake elevations are also experienced under the current operating rules (i.e., IJC Order) and were really observed in 1977 and 1980. Lake elevations observed in the real system are also plotted on Figures 2 and 3. These violations point to the inability of the physical reservoir system to respond to every natural hydrologic series of events, particularly without fore- casting inflows. Emergency regulations were implemented in 1976 and

1977 to permit reduced flow releases from the reservoirs in a last minute attempt to alleviate some of the consequences of the drought. Similar deviations from the rule curves have occurred at other times in response to both high and low water inputs (i.e., runoff). Without good predictions of meteorologic conditions, little can be done to lake storages in anticipation of runoff inputs, particularly runoff resulting from thunderstorm activity and not snowmelt.

The simulated lake levels shown in Figures 2 and 3 are only slightly different than the historically observed elevations. However, these simulated levels are more responsive to additional aquatic and riparian interests and yet have little, if any, negative impact on other beneficial uses of water including hydropower. Analysis of the hydropower produced from Rainy Lake and Lake of the Woods shows some differences in the timing of hydropower produced. For example, power produced at the outlet of Rainy Lake on a given month is often considerably different in the simulated scenario as compared to that historically observed. This is due in part to the priorities of the simulation and the use of an alternate target policy. However, the net change in power produced for the ten-year period, 1972-1981, is less than 2 percent for Rainy Lake, and the net difference for Rainy Lake and Lake of the Woods combined is less than one-half percent. Much of the reason that no significant differences are found in hydropower generation for example, is because the alternative target elevations are no more than 3 feet (0.9 m) different than current operating policy. Therefore, the "head" available for power production is similar to historic levels. Additionally, the outflows at the downstream end of the system (i.e., Lake of the Woods outflow) are constrained to match the actual historic releases, and this also strongly influences the discharges at International Falls and Fort Frances (i.e., from Rainy Lake).

SUMMARY AND RECOMMENDATIONS

Dams constructed in the early 1900's are regulated for the primary purpose of hydropower generation. Reservoir operating rules, which primarily specify desired lake elevations but also define limited discharge constraints, evolved over the years with changes periodically implemented in response to various lake shore interests and due to difficulties in operating the physical system in adherence to the existing rules of regulation. Interest groups continue to voice their concerns for more natural lake level fluctuations, different timing of peak and low lake elevations, increased flood storage reserve, navigation, and improved water levels for fish (e.g., walleye pike), wild rice, nesting birds, and other aquatic and riparian life, as well as individuals and resort owners with vested lake shore interests. Of late, the National Park Service (circa 1975) was given the responsibility to conserve natural objects and wildlife, and to leave them unimpaired for future generations. This alone is a formidable task for a system that was regulated for over half a century. However, Voyageurs NP is actively pursuing and cooperating with other groups to quantify aquatic and riparian biotic needs and is most supportive of this modeling study of the lake system. The Park Service is interested in management options for regulating lake levels and reservoir outflows to accommodate all beneficial uses of these waters. An optimizing simulation model is used to assess the impact of alternate reservoir operating rules on various lake shore interests. An analysis of impacts on specific beneficial uses of these waters is quantifiable by simulation modeling. Such an effort supplies sound information for evaluating management options. As new data become available, from ongoing aquatic and riparian studies, alternative reservoir target elevations can be modeled. The results provide valuable information for fruitful discussions and negotiations between Federal, State, international, and private interests, and hopefully can lead to mutually agreeable solutions for continued beneficial use of water. Use of a simulation model and the associated output provides concrete indications as to what changes are possible and goes a step beyond idle rhetoric of what are and are not realistic management options.

APPENDIX - REFERENCES

1.   Lake of the Woods Control Board. "Managing the Water Resources of the Winnipeg River Drainage Basin." Hull, Quebec, Nov. 1982.

2.   Shafer, J. M., Labadie, J. W. and Jones, E. B., "Analysis of Firm Water Supply Under Complex Institutional Constraints," Water Resources Bulletin, Vol. 17, No. 3, June 1981, pp. 373-380.

3.   United States Code. Act of January 8, 1971 (84 Stat. 1971), 1971.

4.   United States Code. Act of August 25, 1916 (39 Stat. 535), 1916.

MODELING WATER RESOURCES SYSTEMS FOR WATER QUALITY

by

R. G. Willey[1], M. ASCE, D. J. Smith[2], A.M. ASCE
and J. H. Duke[3], M. ASCE

ABSTRACT

A reservoir system analysis computer model has been recently developed with the capability to simulate up to 10 reservoirs, 30 control points and 8 water quality parameters. With this model the user can evaluate a "best" system operation analysis for multipurpose reservoir regulation to obtain target water quality conditions at user specified control points.

The model uses a linear programming algorithm to evaluate the "best" system operation among all the reservoirs and a nonlinear routine for operation of multilevel intakes at each reservoir in the system. The user may select to operate the system for a balanced reservoir pool operation and its associated water quality or to allow for a modified flow distribution between reservoirs to improve the water quality operation.

This model, HEC-5Q, has been applied to the 10,000 square mile (26,000 square kilometers) drainage area of the Sacramento River System. The Sacramento system includes two tandem reservoirs, three parallel reservoirs and 400 miles (640 km) of stream channel network.

INTRODUCTION

The U.S. Army Corps of Engineers is responsible for the operation of hundreds of multiple purpose reservoirs in addition to maintenance of hundreds of miles of non-reservoir projects (e.g., levees and navigation channels). Management of reservoir releases can be analyzed to determine the best operation with any of the numerously available reservoir computer programs (2,3,5,6,7). With river analysis programs, the impact of specified reservoir releases can be evaluated at downstream points of interest.

[1]Hydraulic Engineer, U.S. Army Corps of Engineers, Hydrologic
   Engineering Center, 609 Second Street, Davis, CA. 95616.
[2]Resource Management Associates, 3738 Mt. Diablo Blvd., Suite 200,
   Lafayette, CA. 94549.
[3]Consulting Water Engineer, 5303 Pony Chase, Austin, TX. 78759.

The problem with using single project models is the difficulty of coordinating releases among projects which impact on a single location. This is particularly obvious in Figure 1 where the operation of both Reservoirs A and B impact on the amount and quality of water at City A (i.e., control point 3). As the system is expanded further downstream, the computations necessary to provide a best operation of Reservoirs A through D for control point 7 obviously require a comprehensive system approach.

MATHEMATICAL MODEL

"HEC-5Q, Simulation of Flood Control and Conservation Systems (Including Water Quality Analysis)" computer model (4) has been developed specifically for evaluating the type of problem shown in Figure 1. The model is capable of evaluating a reservoir system of up to ten reservoirs and up to thirty control points. The model will define a best system operation for water quantity and quality; evaluating operational concerns like flood control, hydropower, water supply, and irrigation diversions. Since the computer program users manual (4), and several technical papers (1,8,9) adequately document the details of the model concepts and the input description, only a brief overview is provided below.

Flow Simulation Module

The flow simulation module was developed to assist in planning studies for evaluating proposed reservoirs in a system and to assist in sizing the flood control and conservation storage requirements for each project recommended for the system. The program can be used to show the effects of existing and/or proposed reservoirs on flows and damages in a complex reservoir system. The program can also be used in selecting the proper reservoir releases throughout the system to minimize flooding as much as possible while maintaining a balance of flood control storage ("balanced pool") among the reservoirs.

Water Quality Simulation Module

The water quality simulation module is capable of analyzing water temperature and up to three conservative and three non-conservative constituents. If

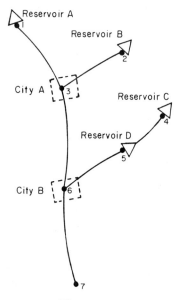

Figure I

TYPICAL RESERVOIR
SYSTEM SCHEMATIC

at least one of the nonconservative constituents is an oxygen
demanding parameter, dissolved oxygen can also be analyzed.

The water quality simulation module accepts system flows generated
by the flow simulation module and computes the distribution of all the
water quality constituents in up to ten reservoirs and their
associated downstream reaches. The ten reservoirs may be in any
arbitrary parallel and tandem configuration.

Gate openings in reservoir multilevel withdrawal structures are
selected to meet user-specified water quality objectives at downstream
control points. If the objectives cannot be satisfied with the
previously computed "balanced pool" flows, the model will compute a
modified flow distribution necessary to better satisfy all downstream
objectives. With these capabilities, the planner may evaluate the
effects on water quality of proposed reservoir-stream system
modifications and determine how a reservoir intake structure should be
operated to achieve desired water quality objectives within the system.

RESERVOIR SYSTEM DESCRIPTION

The Sacramento Valley reservoir system consists of four major
reservoirs as shown in Figure 2. Shasta and Keswick Reservoirs are
located on the Sacramento River in northern California about 240 miles
(390 km) north of Sacramento. Below Shasta and above Keswick,
inter-basin water transfers enter the Sacramento River through Spring
Creek. Along the Sacramento River, Cow Creek and Cottonwood Creek are
major inflowing tributaries and the Anderson-Cottonwood,
Tehama-Colusa, Corning and Glenn-Colusa Irrigation District Canals are
major irrigation diversions.

Oroville Reservoir is located on the Feather River in the Sierra
foothills about 100 miles (160 km) north of Sacramento. Major
tributaries entering the Feather River include the Yuba and Bear
Rivers. Major diversions are located immediately below Oroville Dam
from the Thermalito Afterbay. The Feather River flows into the
Sacramento River near Verona.

Folsom Reservoir is located on the American River in the Sierra
foothills about 30 miles (50 km) east of Sacramento. The American
River below Folsom Reservoir is leveed with no major tributaries
entering before its confluence with the Sacramento River at Sacramento.

The Sacramento River continues to flow south towards the San
Francisco Bay. This study's lower boundary is located near Hood about
20 miles (30 km) south of Sacramento.

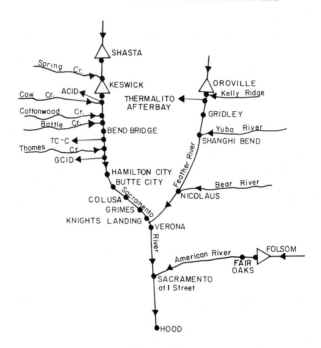

Figure 2
SACRAMENTO VALLEY RESERVOIR SYSTEM SCHEMATIC

APPLICATION PROCEDURE

The application of the HEC-5Q model to the Sacramento Valley reservoir system, or to any other system, includes data assembly, model execution and interpretation of results.

Data Assembly

The HEC-5Q model data requirements are similar to those of most comprehensive water quality models. The data to be assembled are categorized into three types; time independent, required time dependent and optional time dependent.

The time independent data include: physical description of the reservoir (i.e., elevation vs. volume, surface area and discharge capacity; and vertical reservoir segmentation), physical description of the river (i.e., river mile vs. cross section and channel discharge capacity; and river reach segmentation), control point desired and required flows, model coefficients (i.e., flow routing; reservoir diffusion; physical, chemical and biological reactions rates) and initial conditions for the start of the simulation. The required time

dependent data include: evaporation, meteorology, diversions, inflow
quantity and quality for all reservoir and river tributaries,
discharge quantity from reservoirs, and control point target water
quality conditions. The optional time dependent data include:
reservoir storages; river flows at other than control points; and
reservoir and river water quality profiles. These data are used as
checks on the model output in contrast to the previously mentioned
data which are required to make the model work.

Sources for the data categorized above are numerous. In general,
they include all water-related agencies at the federal, state, local
and private levels. Meteorological data are readily available from
the U.S. Weather Service, local airports and universities. The
primary data source is the NOAA's National Weather Service (NWS)
office in Ashville, North Carolina.

Tributary inflows, diversions and reservoir discharges may be
readily available from WATSTORE and STORET data systems. WATSTORE is
managed by the USGS and contains streamflow data. STORET is managed
by the EPA and contains water quality data. These computer data
systems can often provide the necessary tributary inflow quantity and
quality data.

Model Execution

The model simulation for the Sacramento Valley system used
temperature, specific conductance (sometimes called electrical
conductivity), alkalinity, carbonaceous biochemical oxygen demand
(BOD), ammonia (NH3) and dissolved oxygen (DO). These specific
parameters were chosen based on the availability of at least limited
data.

The model can be used for existing and/or proposed reservoirs. If
an existing condition is being simulated, usually the objective is to
reproduce historical events through model calibration. Selection of
the calibration option, can significantly decrease computer time by
not using the time-consuming linear and non-linear programming
algorithms in the model.

Once the model has been calibrated, the objective may be to modify
an existing reservoir operation pattern or to evaluate the impact of
proposed new reservoirs or channel modifications. This analysis
requires the use of the linear and non-linear programming algorithms.

The simulation mode discussed above can be used either to evaluate
the best water quality that can be provided throughout the system for
given reservoir discharges (obtained either external to the simulation
or determined by the HEC-5 quantity part of the model) or to evaluate
the best water quality operation without preconceived discharge
quantities. The former operation is referred to as a balanced pool
operation and the latter as a flow augmentation operation.

When using the balanced pool operation, the HEC-5Q program simply
evaluates the best vertical level for withdrawal (assuming multiple
level intakes are available) at each reservoir to meet all downstream

water quality targets for the given reservoir discharge determined by
the flow simulation module.

The flow augumentation operation allows the model to relax the
balanced pool concept and to decide how much flow should come from
which reservoir and at which vertical level in order to meet
downstream water quality targets. Sometimes downstream water quality
improvements require significantly increased discharge rates to obtain
only small improvements in water quality. This flow augumentation
operation is the most-costly mode of execution.

For this application, the input data set was executed using the
calibration option. Application of this option allows the user to
define the exact level of the intake structure operated. This is the
normal method of model application when calibrating the model to
observed historical data.

Interpretation of Results

The Sacramento Valley reservoir system was executed and produced
results which were compared to observed water quantity and quality
data in the four reservoirs and at all downstream control points. The
data for comparison purposes consisted of discharge rates at most
control points as well as water temperature at many of the same
locations. Other water quality parameters are less available but were
compared where they are available. Selected portions of the graphical
display of these results are shown in Figures 3-6 for the reservoirs
and at selected locations along the stream network.

These plots satisfactorily demonstrate the capability of HEC-5Q to
reasonably reproduce observed reservoir and stream profiles on large
systems. The legends at the bottom of the reservoir temperature plots
define simulated and observed data for various dates. Shasta,
Oroville and Folsom Reservoirs have sufficient observed temperature
data to be useful for calibration purposes. Sufficient observed data
for the other parameters were not available. (Only data for Shasta
Reservoir are shown due to space limitations) Considering the model
limitation of having only one weather station for the entire system,
it is the authors' opinion that the reproduction is quite good.
Perhaps some further refinement could be achieved with additional
trials but the acceptability of the model can be demonstrated with
these results.

The legend at the bottom of the stream profile plots defines the
various observed and simulated water quality parameters for the study
period. Simulated constituents 1 and 2 are specific conductance (or
EC) and alkalinity. Unlike the simulated data, the observed data
points are often more than one-day apart. Some caution should be
applied to interpretation of the connecting line between observed data
points further apart than one or two days.

In general, the calibration of the model is quite good along the
Sacramento River for all the observed parameters down to Hamilton City
inclusive. (Only data for Hamilton City are shown due to space
limitations.) Butte City and Colusa measured temperatures show

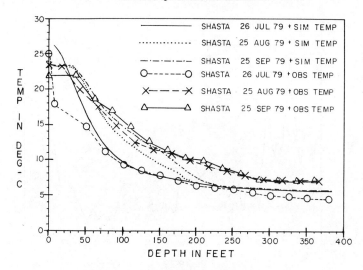

Figure 3

SHASTA RESERVOIR TEMPERATURE PROFILES

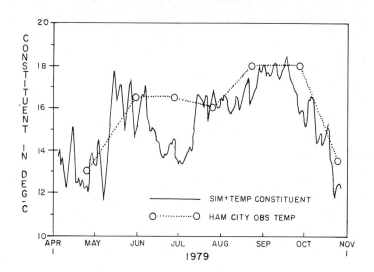

Figure 4

SACRAMENTO RIVER AT HAMILTON CITY – WATER TEMPERATURE

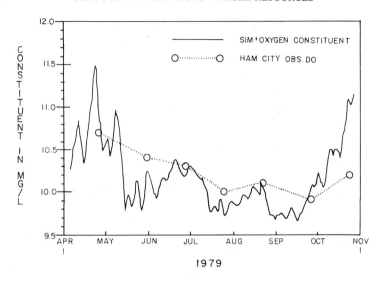

Figure 5

SACRAMENTO RIVER AT HAMILTON CITY-DISSOLVED OXYGEN

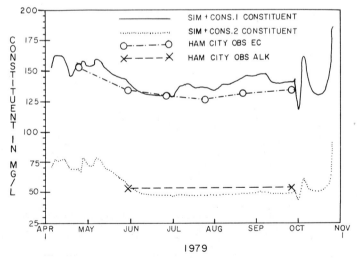

Figure 6

SACRAMENTO RIVER AT HAMILTON CITY – SPECIFIC

CONDUCTANCE (EC) & ALKALINITY

significant warming of the reach of the Sacramento River takes place at least during the Spring (April and May 1956). This temperature consideration, in addition to the lack of sufficient simulated quantity of flow at Butte City and Colusa (compared to accurate simulation of flow at Bend Bridge), suggests that the undefined return flows on the Sacramento River between Hamilton City and Knights Landing are sufficiently large and need to be evaluated.

The Feather River below Oroville and the American River below Folsom lack sufficient water quality data to provide adequate information for calibration purposes.

Since the Sacramento River below Sacramento is the combination product of all three river systems, the inaccuracies already discussed are also apparent at this location. Careful interpretation and evaluation of all these results lead the authors to encourage the continued application of this model to help develop understanding of the workings and operation of any stream system.

SUMMARY

HEC-5Q model is capable of simulating the effects of the operation of as many as ten reservoirs and the stream network of the basin. Each reservoir may be operated to satisfy a number of objectives, including flood control, low flow maintenance, hydropower production, water conservation and water quality control. The water quality portion of the model will simulate temperature and seven other constituents including dissolved oxygen. The model will internally determine the water quality needed from all reservoir releases to meet specified downstream water quality objectives and will determine the gate openings in each reservoir that will yield the appropriate reservoir release water quality.

REFERENCES

1. Duke, James H., Donald J. Smith and R.G. Willey, 1984, "Reservoir System Analysis for Water Quality," Technical Paper No. 99, Hydrologic Engineering Center.

2. Hydrologic Engineering Center, 1972, "Reservoir Temperature Stratification," Computer Program Description.

3. Hydrologic Engineering Center, 1978, "Water Quality for River-Reservoir Systems," Computer Program Description.

4. Hydrologic Engineering Center, 1984, "HEC-5Q, Simulation of Flood Control and Conservation Systems (Including Water Quality Analysis)," Draft Computer Program Users Manual.

5. Loftis, B., 1980, "WESTEX - A Reservoir Heat Budget Model," Draft Computer Program Description, Waterways Experiment Station.

6. U.S. Army Corps of Engineers, Baltimore District, 1977, "Thermal Simulation of Lakes," Computer Program Description.

7. Water Resources Engineers, 1969, "Mathematical Models for the Prediction of Thermal Energy Changes in Impoundments," Report to the Environmental Protection Agency.

8. Willey, R.G., 1982, "River and Reservoir Systems Water Quality Modeling Capability," Technical Paper No. 83, Hydrologic Engineering Center.

9. Willey, R.G., 1983, "Reservoir System Regulation for Water Quality Control," Technical Paper No. 88, Hydrologic Engineering Center.

PRACTICAL OPTIMIZATION OF LOOPED WATER SYSTEMS

Roland W. Jeppson M. ASCE[1]

INTRODUCTION

Water distribution represents an enormous investment. The approximately 40,000 water services in the U.S. today have invested about $200 billion in facilities alone. Each year over $2 billion are spent for construction of new water systems. Nearly 15 million miles of pipeline are used to transmit and distribute this water to practically every home, business, commercial and public building in this country. A large fraction of engineering consulting is associated with municipal and city water facilities. Energy and construction costs are escalating while public and regulatory commissions insist that cost of water be minimized. Engineers, researchers, and applied mathematicians have devoted much effort to develop methods for optimizing pipe network design. While this effort, coupled with the widespread use of computers, has resulted in better design recently, the engineer responsible for the design of a new water system, or the expansion and improvement of an existing system, must still rely on "rules-of-thumb", and his best professional judgment in selecting the network's layout, the location of facilities such as pumping stations and storage tanks, and even to a lesser extent, in selecting pipe sizes. This state of affairs is partly caused by the non-linearity and resulting difficulties of solving optimization formulations of the problem, but is due more to the lack of knowing how the optimization problem should be defined. Furthermore, charging engineering fees as a fraction of the construction costs, the desire on the part of most clients to keep costs for engineering services minimal, and liability concerns on the part of engineers are all disincentives for realizing a least cost, or optimally designed water system in practice. Questions are seldom raised about overdesign because that can be for future growth and expansion, but lack of capacity is equated to incompetence.

Even if incentives are present for attempting to design the "least cost" system, there are many important considerations beyond the economics and hydraulics of the system that have a direct bearing on the problem that make an optimal design virtually impossible to guarantee. Without including political, environmental and social concerns some of these are: 1. What will the future demands be, and what magnitude and pattern should be used over the useful life of the system, 2. What will the future costs of energy be; what interest rate is appropriate to use, should construction be phased, etc., 3. How extensive, or what type of surge control should exist, 4. What are the impacts of future technologies on the operation and control of the system, 5. How large, where, and for how long should fire fighting and other emergency flows be designed for, or should a dual system exit, 6. Will the system be operated in the same manner that is anticipated in its design, and if such operation is critical, how will proper operation and maintenance be insured, 7. How stable are sources of supply, i.e. if the water is pumped from groundwater, how much will pumping lifts increase with time, will brackish waters be drawn into fresh water aquifers or if the supply depends on precipitation, will droughts deplete the inflow, and are the water rights available, 8. Should design include special features to prevent freezing of pipe lines during extremely cold winters, and 9. What type or types and/or class of pipe should be used.

For most of these items no quantitative data are available. For some statistical correlations and/or projections are available. With these and a host of other possible special, but important concerns, that should be considered the optimum design of a large water system falls into the category of an academic exercise that is relevant only to the extent that all important items are included.

[1]Professor of Civil & Environmental Engineering, Utah State University, Logan, UT 84322

Those individuals, with a comprehensive working knowledge of the system and the host of conditions it needs to perform satisfactory under, are in a better position to watch-dog that the important items are adequately examined in the proposed design than individuals who develop software packages designed to efficiently converge to an optimum solution after the decision variables are defined and constraints imposed, etc. If the design engineer does not have such a working knowledge, he should be forced to acquire it. He will not acquire this knowledge if he is lead to believe that all he needs to do is come up with input required by the computer program, and the output will provide the optimum design. The individual with an intimate knowledge of the system needs to be able to readily pose "what if" questions, and obtain answers easily. If he does not have the appropriate questions to ask, then a means should be provided to assist in posing meaningful questions.

During the last decade a number of easily used and powerful software packages have been developed that allow the practicing engineer to easily acquire answers to how a water system will respond to various conditions. However, more needs to be done in this area. Effective graphics can assist in this process. Not only should he be supplied answers to flow rates and pressures that a completely specified water system will produce, but he should also be able to request that the solution size pumps and pipes to meet specified flowrates and pressures.

This paper describes one such tool that might be part of a package to assist a design engineer in sizing pipes, determining ideal locations for booster pumps and their heads, determining heads that source pumps should supply, and establishing water surface elevations of storage tanks or reservoirs to achieve a near minimum cost network based on appropriate cost parameters. A very limited amount of assistance is provided in establishing the layout of the system. The assumption is that water must be pumped and this costs energy. Therefore, a least cost, or near least cost, water distribution system will be one in which the pressures throughout the system are close to the minimum pressure allowed under the peak, or near peak demands. Once such a near least cost system is tentatively established, its adequacy needs to be verified by analyses covering typical current and future conditions, including time dependent solutions over such periods as 24 hours.

LEAST COST SLOPE OF HGL VERSUS FLOWRATE RELATIONSHIP

In achieving a least cost, or near least cost, design of a piping system, knowledge of what the optimum slope, S, that the hydraulic grade line (HGL) should have as a function of the flowrate, Q, will be helpful. With such a optimum S-Q relationship the least cost branched system can readily be designed by beginning at the downstream branches and working toward the main upstream trunk. At every node, the flowrate in pipes can be determined. From these flowrates, the lengths of the pipes and the optimum S-Q relationship, the head losses can be computed, and therefrom the least cost diameter computed. While it is not practical to develop such a optimum S-Q relationship in algebraic form with the usual form of cost data, particular for pipes, a discrete relationship can be obtained and used in table look-up and interpolation techniques. Means for developing such a table of optimum S-Q values is provided below. In this discussion, only the three major costs of: (1) pipes and their installation, (2) energy for pumping, and (3) reservoir capacity and head are included, but other costs can be considered in a similar manner.

Pipe Costs

Costs for pipe are most readily available as some dollar amount per unit length as a function of the pipe diameter, D or,

$$C_p = F(D) \quad . \quad . \quad . \quad . \quad (1)$$

in which C_p is the dollars per unit length, and can include common appurtenances and maintence over the life of the system as well as the capital investment of buying the pipe and installing the system. To illustrate the methodology that will be used, Table 1 contains such a table of discrete pipe costs for standard pipe diameters.

Table 1. Capital Costs of various sizes of pipe for Water distribution.

Pipe D(in.)	4	6	8	10	12	15	18	20	24	30	36	42	48	54
dollars/ft	3.67	5.33	7.67	10.67	16.67	24.0	43.33	56.67	80	100	120	145	170	200

A hydraulic flow equation establishes the relationship between these costs and the slope of the HGL. Because the use of the Darcy-Weisbach equation is most difficult, it is selected. If the Darcy-Weisbach equation is solved for the pipe diameter, then

$$D = \left[\frac{fQ^2}{2gS(\pi/4)^2} \right]^{0.2} \quad \cdot \quad \cdot \quad \cdot \quad \cdot \quad \cdot \quad (2)$$

in which the friction factor f can be obtained from the ColeBrook-White equation as a function of the Reynolds number, $Re = VD/\nu$ (ν = the kinematic viscosity of the fluid) and the relative roughness of the pipe wall e/D.

$$\frac{1}{\sqrt{f}} = 1.14 - 2 \log \left[\frac{e}{D} + \frac{9.35}{Re\sqrt{f}} \right] \quad \cdot \quad \cdot \quad \cdot \quad (3)$$

With Q and S fixed, Eqs. 2 and 3 must be solved simultaneously for f and D. The Newton method can be utilized for this purpose, but an even simpler technique converges rapidly that consists of iterating between Eqs. 3 and 2. Once D is obtained, the cost can be determined by interpolation from pipe cost data as in Table 1. This interpolated value is multiplied by an appropriate capital recovery factor, crf, obtained from the interest rate, and life of the pipe, so that the costs are on a comparable basis to the other annually reoccurring costs. Repeating this solution with S varying produces the pipe cost curve shown in Figure 1.

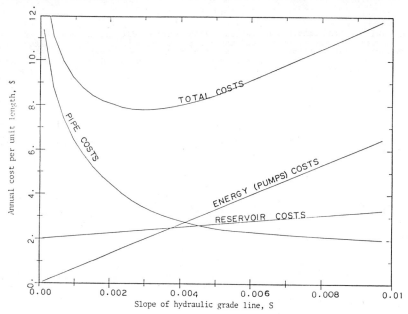

Figure 1. Several costs as a function of the slope of the HGL of pipes.

Energy Costs

For networks with all or part of their water pumped, the cost of the electrical energy can be included in the optimum S-Q relationship by noting that annual energy costs equal the unit cost of energy, R, ($/kilowatt-hr or other appropriate amounts) times the electrical power consumed by the pumps, P, times the time, t, that the pump operates per year. Since other costs are expressed per unit length of pipe, the head, h_p produced by pumps that is dissipated per unit length in any pipe is S X L, where S is the slope of the HGL, and L is the pipe length. Whether all pump energy is dissipated through fluid friction or some simply increases the head throughout the network, the costs are the same. Therefore, the cost of energy C_e per unit length of pipe is,

$$C_e = R(\gamma QS/C)t/e \quad . \quad . \quad . \quad . \quad . \quad (4)$$

in which C depends on the units used, γ is the specific weight of water and e equals the efficiency.

One curve on Fig. 1 shows such energy costs as a function of S assuming R = $.0556/killowatt-hr, t=24 X 365 hours per year and e = 0.556. In addition to the above, capital recovery costs may be added that vary with Q to accommodate acquistion and installation of pumps.

Reservoir costs

Costs associated with reservoirs and how these costs can be expressed as a function of the slope, S, of the HGL varies, depending upon the operation of the reservoir. If all water in reservoirs is pumped, then these costs are identical to energy costs above, with the possible exception that the rate may be different depending upon when the pumping occurs. Alternately, or in addition to, the assigment of costs to reservoirs may recognize that costs are related to both capacity, i.e. volume of the reservoir, and the head of the water surface in the reservoir. Capacity costs generally consist of discrete values, therefore, the following might be used.

$$C_r = crf \left[CAP(Q) + C_o(S-S_o) \right] \quad . \quad . \quad (5)$$

in which CAP(Q) consists of tabular values that handle the capacity costs as a function of the flowrate, and the other term accommodates costs of requiring higher water surfaces. A reasonable means for obtaining CAP(Q), i.e. relating costs to flowrate is by dividing a tank's volume by the time it normally supplies water. The term $C_0(S - S_0)$ requires that C_0 and S_0 be given to reflect the costs of increasing the water surface in the reservoir divided by the length of pipes used to convey this water to a central location within the network.

The minimum of the total costs on a graph such as Fig. 1 gives one point of the optimum S-Q relationship. Repeating the procedure for other flowrates that cover the range expected in pipes of the network provide the relationship desired. If the wall roughness of pipes varies considerably, it may need to be repeated for different values of e. The optimum S-Q relationship will be used subsequently herein to assist in obtaining a near least cost network.

PROCEDURE FOR IMPROVING DESIGN OF NETWORKS

A means of assisting in improving upon the design of an existing looped water system, or designing such a new system is described below. The assumption is that the layout, or a proposed layout, of the system is given that includes the sources of supply as well as the lengths and locations of pipes, some of which may be eliminated. The procedure consists of separating the network into a primary branched system, and additional loop forming pipes. The method can be described in the following six steps.

1. Identify the two most dominant sources of supply for the system. A criterion for selecting these two dominant sources, that can easily be implemented in a computer program as a default, consists of sources with the potentially largest total heads, as given by the input data describing the network. Next, connect these two most dominant sources of supply by the shortest path of pipes between them. For subsequent descriptions of the methodology this path will be referred to as the "dominant path". All other paths of the branched system that will be defined will ultimately terminate at one of the nodes of

this dominant path. If only one source of supply exists, this dominant path is
not defined.

2. Connect the other sources of supply to one of the nodes of the dominant path by the shortest path of pipes. These additional paths will be referred to as primary paths. In selecting the node of the dominant path on
which a primary path terminates, preference is given to nodes closer to the
dominant source with the largest total head, however, all such primary paths
may terminate on the same node. A default order in forming primary paths can
be according to the descending magnitude of the total head available at the
sources. Any such primary path is terminated when it intersects a previous
primary path. Should only two sources of supply exist they constitute the
dominant sources and this step is omitted.

3. Connect the remaining nodes of the network that are not included in
the dominant path or any primary path by the shortest path of pipes to one of
the nodes of the dominant path. Whenever this path intersects a node in a
previous path it is terminated. These paths of pipes will be referred to as
secondary paths. The order in which these secondary paths are formed is first
from nodes of degree 1, i.e. dead end pipes, next from nodes of degree 2,
i.e. that have only two connecting pipes, etc. The order in which nodes are
selected within a given degree is according to their descending elevations.

In completing the above three steps a branched system of pipes is formed
that includes all nodes of the network and presumably contains the pipes that
will convey the vast majority of the flow from the sources of supply to the
various demand points throughout the network. Those pipes not included in
this branched network are identified as additional loop forming pipes. Their
diameters are specified arbitrarily, and if not specified otherwise, are equal
to the minimum diameter permitted.

4. Establish an appropriate head at each node of the network. The procedure for doing this consists of working through paths in the reverse order
of their formation. By ignoring the carrying capacity of the additional
loop-forming pipes the flowrate in each pipe of the branched system
is determined. At the beginning node of each path, the total
head is equated to the minimum allowable pressure head plus the elevation of
the node. Proceeding from this node to succeeding nodes of the path, the
total heads are established by utilizing the optimum S-Q relationship corresponding to the flowrate in the pipe. If this node's head was previously
assigned, then the currently computed head is compared with the previous
head and the larger of the two selected. Also, should any pressure head be
less than the minimum then all previously assigned HGL values along that path
are raised. Should the pressure head exceed a maximum specified amount that
merits inclusion of a booster pump, then a pipe that might contain the pump
and an appropriate head for that pump is suggested. Also a list of consecutive pipes and nodes in which the pressure head exceeds the maximum specified
amount are listed. The user can accept the suggested pipe and head or give
another pipe and/or head. The total head at nodes upstream from the pipe in
which a booster pump is placed is reduced by the amount of head supplied by
the pump. This process of identifying pipes that should contain booster pumps
continues whenever the pressure head exceeds the specified maxiumum pressure
head.

When this procedure for establishing HGL elevations advances back to the
primary paths, it is necessary to have a flowrate that reservoirs supply, or
receive in order to determine the flowrates in the pipes of these primary
paths. Appropriate rules might be used which are based on the available heads
of the sources as given in the input to provide these flowrates, or the user
requested to supply a fraction of the total demand, either positive of negative, that this source supplies. Besides the flowrate requirement, however,
the total heads are established at nodes along primary paths in the same
manner as along secondary paths.

5. The total heads at nodes of the dominant path, that have not been assigned previously are determined last by a process designed to not only
allow for optimum, or near optimum sizing of pipe, but also to assist in
determining allowable heads that the two dominant sources of supply
should have. To assist in describing how these heads are determined it will
be assumed that N_d nodes exist along the dominant path, excluding the two dominant sources of supply. Figure 2 shows a sketch in which N_d is 3. N_d different cases are examined that assume the flow is directed toward the N_d nodes
from both sides. For case 1 the hydraulic grade line (HGL) must slope from
both directions toward the node #1 that is closest to one of the dominant
sources; for case 2 the HGL slopes from both directions to the next node, etc.

until for the N_d-th case the HGL slopes toward the node closest to the other dominant source. The elevations of the HGL for each case starts at the node at either the minimum head, Hmin above the elevation of the node, or at the head, H that may have been established during step 4. The slope, or gradient, of HGL is based on the optimum slope corresponding to the flowrate carried by the pipe. These flowrates can be determined since the flowrates, or demands, leaving from each of the nodes of the dominant path are now known in completing step 4. When at the starting node for each case, the demand at this node can be distributed by some rule such as the ratio of how many pipes this node is away from the dominant source that it receives the water from to N_d+1. Should the HGL fall below the minimum head, Hmin or the total head, H required from step 4, which ever is larger, then the entire HGL is raised so as not to fall below any required head. Raising of the HGL is illustrated in case 2 and 3 of Figure 2. For each case, i, the required total heads from the two dominant sources of supply H_{1i} and H_{2i} are computed. The case that produces the minimum sum of these source heads is selected, i.e. the case of minimum $(H_{1i} + H_{2i})$ is used to establish the total head for all nodes along the dominant path unless the user wished to assign other heads at these sources of supply. The heads given for these two dominant sources of supply in the original data are adjusted to agree with those as determined above. If this dominant source is a reservoir, then the water surface of the reservoir is altered, or if this source is a pump, then the head supplied by the pump is altered.

It should be noted that this procedure not only changes the heads of the dominant sources, but also the water surface elevations of the other sources at the beginning of the primary paths.

6. With the total heads and flowrates known for each pipe in the branched system as a result of steps 1 through 5, the diameter of each pipe is next computed. These diameters may be determined from any of the frictional head loss equations. If the Darcy-Weisbach equation is selected, then the equation is,

$$F(D) = h_L/L - (f/D)(Q^2/2gA^2) = 0 \quad . \quad . \quad (6)$$

or if the Hazen-Williams equation is used, then

$$D = \left[UQ^{1.852}/(SC^{1.852}) \right]^{0.2053} \quad . \quad . \quad . \quad (7)$$

or if the Mannings equation is used, then

$$D = \left[Un^2 \, Q^2/S \right]^{.1875} \quad . \quad . \quad . \quad (8)$$

in which h_L is the headloss, i.e. the difference between the total head at the end nodes of the pipe, Q is the flowrate, L is the length of the pipe, A is the cross-sectional area of the pipe, C is the Hazen-Williams coefficient, n is Mannings roughness value, U is a constant dependent upon the units used and equation being used (U = 4.73 or 10.7 respectively depending upon whether SI or ES units are used in the Hazen-Williams equation, U = 1 or 1.49 respectively depending upon whether SI or ES units are used in the Mannings equation), and f is the friction factor defined through the implicit Colebrook-White Eq. 3.

The diameters computed can be changed to standard diameters that are either: (a) closest to the computed diameter, (b) the next larger standard size, or (c) the next smaller standard diameter depending upon the desires of the user.

After standard pipes in the network have been established as described above, the network is ready to obtain solutions for other demand patterns, or to determine how it will perform under time-dependent demand patterns over some desired simulation period. If desired, this solution might be used as a guide in specifying flowrates from/to primary sources and the entire process repeated

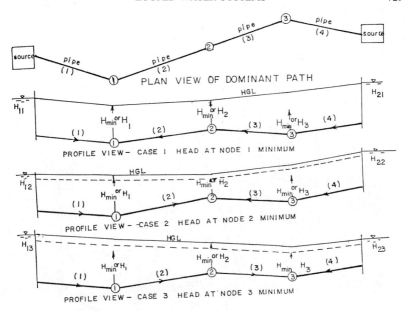

PLAN VIEW OF DOMINANT PATH

PROFILE VIEW— CASE 1 HEAD AT NODE 1 MINIMUM

PROFILE VIEW – CASE 2 HEAD AT NODE 2 MINIMUM

PROFILE VIEW— CASE 3 HEAD AT NODE 3 MINIMUM

Figure 2: Illustration of determining the HGL elevation for the dominant path.

SIMPLE ILLUSTRATIVE EXAMPLES

Figure 3 contains a sketch of a small 23 pipe, 20 node network that is supplied by a source pump and a reservoir. The demands shown on this figure represent the peak hourly demands that will be used as the basis for redesigning the network using the procedure described above. A somewhat different feature of this system is that the elevation across the two nodes at the ends of pipe 16 changes from 250 ft (76.2m) to 100 ft (30.5m). Table 2 contains the solution to the original system as proposed. The lowest pressure is 46.8 psi at node 3 and the pressure at the lower elevation nodes exceeds 100 psi. The source pump produces 189.9 feet of head and supplies 108.8 kilowatts of power to 6.77 cfs of the total demand of 9.59 cfs. Based on the capital costs of pipe given in Table 1, a 50 year life, energy costs of $0.0557/kilowatt-hour and a combined motor pump efficiency of 0.557, a 365 day per year operation, and the assumption that the costs associated with reservoir water are equivalent to that of pumped water from a base elevation of 290 ft, and a power cost of $0.08/killowatt-hour the total costs per year come to $146,970 as shown at the bottom of Table 2.

Using the procedure described earlier, the pipe sizes and reservoir water surface elevations and pump heads were redesigned, but no pipes were eliminated. The solution to the redesigned network is given in Table 3. The designing procedure used a minimum pressure head of 93 ft. After the rounding of pipes to the nearest standard diameter, the solution gives a minimum pressure of 39.1 psi. In this redesigned network, pipe 16, whose diameter was taken equal to 6 inches, dissipates 60.7 feet of head to help reduce the pressure at the lower elevation portion of the network. A better design to control the pressures in this lower elevation zone, while still providing for fire, or other large emergency flows, might consist of installing a pressure reduction valve in pipe 16, and keeping its diameter larger. The annual costs for operating this redesigned network equals $72,051, or a cost of 49 percent of the costs of the original network. (Note since these analyses are based on peak hourly demands the actual annual costs would be reduced.)

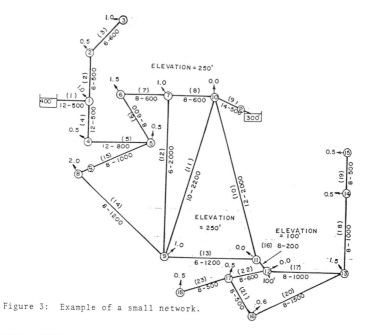

Figure 3: Example of a small network.

TABLE 2. SOLUTION OF THE ORIGINAL SMALL NETWORK

PUMPS:

PIPE	HEAD	FLOW	HORSEPOWER	KILOWATTS	KWATT-HRS
9	189.9	6.77	145.88	108.83	2611.84
15	48.2	2.82	15.42	11.51	276.12

PIPE DATA :

PIPE NODES LENGTH DIA. FLOW HEAD L.

NO.	FR	TO	ft	in.	cfs	ft
1	19	1	500	12	6.33	9.77
2	1	2	500	6	1.50	20.93
3	2	3	600	6	1.00	11.30
4	1	4	500	12	3.83	3.63
5	4	5	800	12	3.33	4.42
6	5	6	600	8	0.01	0.00
7	7	6	600	8	1.49	5.59
8	10	7	600	8	2.08	10.75
9	20	10	500	8	6.77	91.32
10	10	11	2000	12	3.51	12.25
11	10	9	2200	10	1.18	4.14
12	9	7	2000	6	0.41	6.62
13	9	11	1200	6	0.59	8.11
14	8	9	1200	8	0.82	3.48
15	5	8	1000	8	2.82	32.52
16	11	12	200	8	4.10	13.64
17	12	13	1000	8	1.96	15.95
18	13	14	1000	8	1.00	4.27
19	14	15	500	8	0.50	0.56
20	16	13	1500	8	0.54	1.93
21	17	16	500	8	1.14	2.73
22	12	17	600	8	2.14	11.29
23	17	18	500	8	0.50	0.56

NODE DATA:

NODE	DEMAND	HEAD	HGL
NO.	cfs	ft	ft
1	1.0	140.23	390.23
2	0.5	119.33	369.33
3	1.0	108.03	358.03
4	0.5	136.60	386.60
5	0.5	132.19	382.19
6	1.5	132.19	382.19
7	1.0	137.77	387.77
8	2.0	147.87	397.87
9	1.0	144.39	394.39
10	0.0	148.53	398.53
11	0.0	136.28	386.28
12	0.0	272.64	372.64
13	1.5	256.68	356.68
14	0.5	252.42	352.42
15	0.5	251.85	351.85
16	0.5	258.61	358.61
17	0.5	261.35	361.35
18	0.5	260.78	360.78
20	-6.8	239.85	489.85
19	-6.3	110.00	400.00

SUMMARY OF COSTS

TYPE	PRESENT WORTH	SERIES AMOUNT
ELEC.	1045126.	105410.55
PIPE	188740.	19036.13
RESER.	223354.	22527.33
TOTAL	1457220.	146970.01

TABLE 3. SOLUTION OF THE ORIGINAL SMALL NETWORK

PUMPS:

PIPE	HEAD	FLOW	HORSEPOWER	KILOWATTS	KWATT-HRS
9	49.53	3.82	21.46	16.01	384.18
15	45.39	5.83	30.01	22.39	537.31

PIPE DATA :

PIPE NODES LENGTH DIA. FLOW HEAD L.

NO.	FR	TO	ft	in.	cfs	ft
1	19	1	500	14	9.28	9.36
2	1	2	500	8	1.50	4.70
3	2	3	600	6	1.00	11.30
4	1	4	500	14	6.78	5.04
5	4	5	800	12	6.28	15.40
6	6	5	600	8	0.05	0.01
7	7	6	600	10	1.55	1.90
8	10	7	600	10	2.21	3.81
9	20	10	500	12	3.82	3.61
10	10	11	2000	10	2.36	14.42
11	9	10	2200	12	0.75	0.70
12	9	7	2000	6	0.33	4.51
13	9	11	1200	8	1.74	15.11
14	8	9	1200	10	3.83	22.38
15	5	8	1000	12	5.83	16.60
16	11	12	200	6	4.10	60.71
17	12	13	1000	12	3.03	4.61
18	13	14	1000	8	1.00	4.27
19	14	15	500	6	0.50	2.44
20	13	16	1500	6	0.53	8.28
21	17	16	500	6	0.07	0.06
22	12	17	600	6	1.07	12.83
23	17	18	500	6	0.50	2.44

NODE DATA:

NODE	DEMAND	HEAD	HGL
NO.	cfs	ft	ft
1	1.0	110.64	360.64
2	0.5	105.94	355.94
3	1.0	94.64	344.64
4	0.5	105.60	355.60
5	0.5	90.20	340.20
6	1.5	90.21	340.21
7	1.0	92.11	342.11
8	2.0	118.99	368.99
9	1.0	96.61	346.61
10	0.0	95.92	345.92
11	0.0	81.50	331.50
12	0.0	170.79	270.79
13	1.5	166.18	266.18
14	0.5	161.92	261.92
15	0.5	159.48	259.48
16	0.6	157.91	257.91
17	0.5	157.96	257.96
18	0.5	155.52	255.52
20	-3.8	99.53	349.53
19	-9.3	80.00	370.00

SUMMARY OF COSTS

TYPE	PRESENT WORTH	SERIES AMOUNT
ELEC.	333480.75	33634.60
PIPE	217169.34	21903.48
RESER.	163722.63	16512.93
TOTAL	714512.72	72051.01

As a second illustrative example, a small existing water system in western Nevada will be used that consists of 66 pipes, 56 nodes, 2 source pumps, and 4 booster pumps, which from a preliminary examination of its performance would appear to be a well engineered system since all peak demands are satisfied with adequate pressures. An often occurring feature of this system is that water elevations for the source pumps are lower than the elevations where major demands exist. The ground elevation is 4532 feet in the area of the pumps and gradually increases into the area being served until at the furthest point, where the demand is the largest, the elevation is 4805 feet.

Using the design procedure described above, three instead of four booster pumps are proposed in different locations. The heads of the source pumps are reduced, but the heads of booster pumps increased. Table 4 summarizes a few important differences between the existing and redesigned system's performance under peak demands. The redesigned system has a more uniform pressure throughout. The energy required from the two source pumps has been reduced to 57 percent of that of the existing system, and the total energy required by booster pumps has been increased only 4.5 percent resulting in a savings of $19,059, or 19 percent, in energy costs per year. By reducing some pipe sizes, but increasing other sizes, the annual cost associated with recovery of the investment in pipes per year is reduced by $14,093, or 34 percent. Actually, in this redesigned system a further reduction in pipe costs could be achieved by elimination of a number of pipes that according to the analysis are conveying very small flowrates.

Table 4. Comparison of some features of existing and redesigned network of example 2.

| | max. pres psi | min. pres psi | Energy, kilowatt-hours per day | | | | | | | Annual Costs | | |
| | | | source pump | | booster pumps | | | | | elec. $ | pipe $ | total $ |
			1	2	1	2	3	4	tot.			
Exist.	122.2	45.8	1220	1221	504	700	367	862	2433	98,980	41,158	140,138
Redes.	87.2	41.9	694	698	76	1338	1131		2545	79,921	27,065	106,986
Difference			526	523					-112	19,059	14,093	33,152

While these savings are impressive considering that a major cost is associated with lifting the water from the supply location to higher elevation demand areas, it would be unwise to accept the revised design without additional analyses, such as low demand conditions, fire fighting-emergency demands, etc. that should ultimately include the simulation of the network performance over several different 24 hour time periods using typical demand patterns that may exist during different seasons of the year, and or projected future requirements. Such studies may show that considerations of various time varying demand patterns might be more economically satisfied by adding a storage tank at a higher elevation to receive water during times when the demand is small and supply water when the demand is large.

SUMMARY AND CONCLUSIONS

The design of the most cost effective large looped water distribution system, that is supplied by several sources of supply, is a major problem for which only partially satisfactory methods exist today. Methods are developed in this paper that assist the engineer in designing a network so that pressures are keep near the minimum allowed at all nodes throughout the network for the demand pattern that is selected. The method also indicates where booster pumps should be located, and what heads they should produce. Optimal water surface elevations of supplies are also determined.

While the methods can substantially reduce the total costs associated with water distribution systems when implemented in their design, they are not a substitute for engineering judgement from a competent individual who has become thoroughly familiar with the water system from both on site experience and study of computer anaylses that cover the range of conditions the real system is likely to experience.

A METHODOLOGY FOR OPTIMAL NETWORK DESIGN

Kevin Lansey, Student Member, and Larry Mays, Member, ASCE*

Abstract

A methodology is developed to optimize the design of water distribution networks using reduced gradient techniques with a network simulator. The problem is reduced in complexity by incorporating a network
simulator into the optimization model. This allows a more general problem to be solved including pipe sizing for new and expanding systems,
pump sizing, valves, and storage facilities. In addition, the reduced
problem can consider large networks under a number of loading conditions.

Introduction

A water distribution network is a complex system in which flow
patterns are described by nonlinear equations. These flow and loop
equations include terms defining the flow within a pipe as well as those
representing pumps, valves, storage tanks, and other network components.
This high degree of nonlinearity causes great difficulty in determining
an optimal design of the network. The problem is further complicated by
the fact that the present manner in which proper redundancy, i.e., reliability, is introduced is to analyze the system under more than one set
of demands. Thus, instead of a single set of n nonlinear equations being
considered, there are (n x number of loads) equations. The technology to
determine optimal solutions to very large highly nonlinear mathematical
programming problems is just becoming available.

This paper proposes a methodology using this technology. The solution technique is based upon the concepts of optimal control theory in
which the generalized reduced gradient method makes up the overall optimization framework along with a simulation model used to perform function evaluations at each iteration of the optimization. In other words,
the nonlinear problem will be solved but reduced in complexity by incorporating a network simulator to solve the flow and loop constraints.
Such a methodology allows very detailed analysis of the system components, various emergency loading conditions, and reduces the constraint
size so that very large water distribution systems with thousands of
components can be designed for new systems and/or analyzed and operated
for existing systems.

---

*Research Assistant and Associate Professor, respectively, Department of
Civil Engineering, The University of Texas at Austin, Austin, Texas.

Problem Statement

The overall optimization problem for water distribution system design and analysis can be stated as functions of the heads, H, and design parameters, D, as:

Objective:
Minimize Cost

$$\text{Min } f_c(D,H) \quad (1)$$

Subject to:

a. Conservation of flow constraints ⎱
b. Energy equation (Loop equations) ⎰ $g(H,Q) = 0$ (2)
c. Head bounds $\underline{H} \leq H \leq \overline{H}$ (3)
d. Design constraints $\underline{D} \leq D \leq \overline{D}$ (4)

where D is the vector of decision variables which are defined for each component (and link) in the system and represents the dimension of each component, such as diameter of the pipe links, pump size, control valves, storage facilities, etc. The vector H are the heads at specified locations in the system with $\underline{H}$ and $\overline{H}$ being their lower and upper bounds.

The above general problem could be stated as minimizing costs subject to the constraint set. The problem is nonlinear with both nonlinear constraints and a nonlinear objective function. This model can result in very large nonlinear programming problems to be solved. As a result, previous investigators have either simplified the problem by linearizing, making it unrealistic but easier to solve, or have used iterative methods that are cumbersome and non optimal and can only solve small problems because of the difficulty in solving the nonlinear problem.

Solution Technique

The proposed solution methodology reduces the problem in the same manner as applied to discrete time optimum control problems (Lasdon and Mantell, 1978; Norman, Lasdon and Hsin, 1982). In this case, the variables H and D are terms as "state" (dependent) and "control" (independent) variables, respectively. They are also referred to as basic and nonbasic variables in mathematical programming. The reduced problem is formulated by writing the state variables in terms of control variables resulting in smaller problems in terms of a number of decision variables and number of constraints. The reduced problem, which contains a new objective function and constraints only on variable bounds is then solved by the existing large-scale NLP codes. This approach was successfully applied by Lasdon et al. (1982) to the problem of optimum management of oil and gas reservoirs using the GRG2 (Lasdon and Warren, 1979) to solve the reduced problem. The approach has been used to develop a general ground water management model by Wanakule, Mays, and Lasdon (1984) that has been applied to both the localized problems such as aquifer dewatering problems and to large scale regional problems such as the management of large regional aquifers. A ground water simulation model was used to solve the ground water flow constraint set and the reduced problem was solved using the generalized reduced gradient technique along with the augmented Lagrangian technique.

Formulation of the Reduced Problem

For a given set of control variables, D, and initial conditions of state variables, H_o constraint set (2) can be solved which determines H as an implicit function of D. By the implicit function theorem (Luenberger, 1973), H(D) exists if and only if the basic matrix of the system of equations (2) is nonsingular. Thus, given any set of D there is always a solution of H which satisfies (2), implying that H can be written in terms of D, H(D). In a similar manner the objective function can be written as

$$F(D) = f\left[H(D), D\right]$$ (5)

which is generally called the reduced objective function. Then, the general problem is transformed to a new problem which contains the above objective function but does not include constraint set (2).

This reduced problem is much smaller than the original problem, but contains the implicit functions F(D) and H(D). Any algorithms for solving the reduced problem, however, will require values of the functions. The values of H(D) can be computed for a given set of D using a water distribution simulation model to solve equation (2) (i.e., the unique node heads are calculated for the given network configuration and demand pattern). Once the values of H(D) are known, the value of F(D) can be evaluated.

Considering the conservation and energy equations, the Jacobian matrix of g(H,D), which is defined as the first partial differential matrix of g(H,D) with respect to the vector (H,D), is given by

$$J(H,D) = \left[\partial g/\partial H, \; \partial g/\partial D\right] = \left[B,C\right]$$ (6)

where $B = \partial g/\partial H$, is nonsingular at all points, and is known as the basic matrix. F(D) and H(D) are differentiable but are not known in closed forms. However, the gradients of F(D) and H(D), called reduced gradients, can be computed efficiently using the two step schemes described in Lasdon and Mantell (1978). These gradients supply directions to change the design parameters which will reduce the cost of the network, thus moving toward the optimal values.

Solving the Reduced Problem

The reduced problem is nonlinear so that one of several NLP algorithms can be applied. The most likely codes that can handle a large matrix are (1) a Generalized Reduced Gradient code called GRG2 (Lasdon and Warren, 1979), (2) a Successive Linear Programming (SLP) code (Palacios—Gomez, et al. 1982), and (3) a Successive Quadratic Programming (SQP) code (under development by Prof. Lasdon of the University of Texas). GRG2 is one of the best codes available for small to medium size problems (Shittkowski, 1980), while SLP and SQP are capable of solving large problems, i.e. containing hundreds of constraints. However, GRG2 is used widely in various fields such as econometrics (Lasdon and Mantell, 1978), optimum control and chemical blending, hydrology (Mays and Taur, 1982, and Mays and Unver, 1984), water reuse planning (Ocanas and

Mays, 1981, a, b) etc. Both SLP and SQP have performed well in computational tests (Shittkowski, 1980) and SQP is generally acknowledged to be one of the leading NLP algorithms today (Powell, 1978 and Shittkowski, 1980).

Augmented Lagrangian Methods

In solving the reduced problem by the NLP codes, the problem may arise of retaining feasibility of the new point at each iterative step. This is due to the simple head bounds (3) not being explicitly determined at each iteration. Most of the NLP codes handle simple bounds through governing the step size of moving to a better point at each iteration, and this is done on the nonbasic (control) variables. Unfortunately, if the basic (state) variables are violated, more iterations are needed to cut back the step size so that the new point is satisfied by both bounds. This may reduce the efficiency of the overall algorithm. A solution tactic that may be useful in solving the reduced problem is to incorporate the head bounds (3) into the objective function using an Augmented Lagrangian (AL) type of penalty term (Hsin, 1980). One would then solve a sequence of problems in which the head bounds would be violated until convergence occurred. Such an approach was used by Hsin (1980), and is similar in spirit to the relaxation tactic mentioned earlier in this section.

The Augmented Lagrangian function for minimization (1) resulting from head bound constraints (3) can be given as (Powell, 1978)

$$\text{Min } L_A(H,D,\mu,\sigma) = f(H,D) + \tfrac{1}{2} \sum_i \sigma_i \, \min\left[0, (c_i - \frac{\mu_i}{\sigma_i})\right]^2 - \sum_i \frac{\mu_i^2}{2\sigma_i} \quad (7)$$

where i is an index to each inequality constraint set (3), μ_i and σ_i are respectively, the penalty weights and the Lagrange multiplier associated with the i-th head bound. Since only lower or upper head bounds can be violated at a time, the following are defined:

$$c_i = \min (\underline{c}_i, \overline{c}_i); \quad \underline{c}_i = H_i - \underline{H}_i; \quad \overline{c}_i = \overline{H}_i - H_i.$$

When the reduced gradient method is applied to the above modified objective function (7), the new objective function is

$$\text{Min } \Lambda_A(q,\mu,\sigma) = F(D) + \tfrac{1}{2} \sum_i \sigma_i \, \min\left[0, c_i(q) - \frac{\mu_i^2}{\sigma_i}\right] - \sum_i \frac{\mu_i^2}{2\sigma_i} \quad (8)$$

This objective function and remaining constraints (4) and (5) can be solved by an NLP code such as GRG2. The reduced gradient required by the NLP code is then computed based on this new objective function (8), by the scheme previously discussed. A general flow chart of the algorithm is presented in Figure 1.

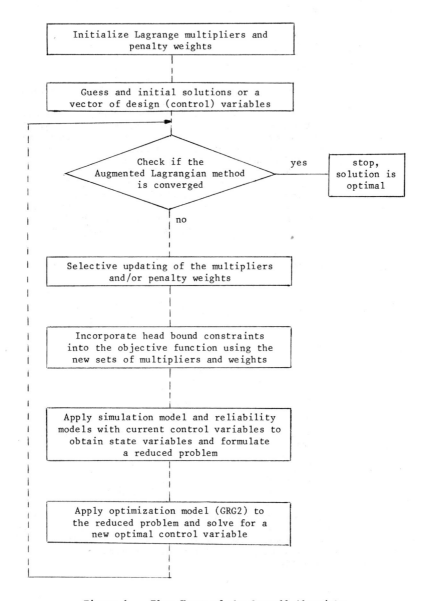

Figure 1.   Flow Chart of the Overall Algorithm

Network Simulator

Any efficient simulation model can be incorporated into the optimization model. However, the limitations of the overall scheme are those of the network simulator, i.e., the optimization procedure can determine least cost design or best operation only of components which can be evaluated by the simulation model. For this reason, the proposed simulator is the University of Kentucky model developed by Don J. Wood. The program, acquired by over 1000 engineering firms, carries out simulations of steady state pressure and flow in pipe distribution systems. The pipe hydraulic equations (2) are solved directly using a linearization scheme and sparse matrix methods. This technique allows the inclusion of such components as pressure regulators, pumps, storage tanks, etc. Thus since this widely accepted simulator is capable of efficiently evaluating most major components of a distribution system, it allows the comprehensive design of the entire network by the optimization model.

Conclusion

The methodology described here is very general in the sense that it can handle nonlinearities and dimensionality problems, both in the network size and number of loads considered, incurred in modeling large scale water distribution systems. It is also general in the context of management and/or design objectives (pipe diameters, pump sizing, etc.) and constraints which depend on user requirements. A computer model based upon the techniques outlined in this paper is presently in the development stages.

Appendix I

Hsin, J.K., "The Optimal Control of Deterministic Econometric Planning Models," Dissertation, Department of General Business, The University of Texas, Austin, Texas, August 1980.

Lasdon, L.S. and Mantell, J., "A GRG Algorithm for Econometric Control Problems," Annuals of Economic and Social Management, Vol. 6, No. 5, 1978.

Lasdon, L.S. and Waren, A.D., "Generalized Reduced Software for Linearly and Nonlinearly Constrained Problems," in Design and Implementation of Optimization Software, H. Greenberg, ed., Sigthoff and Noordoff, pubs., 1979.

Lasdon, L.S., Coffman, P.E., MacDonald, R., and McFarland, J., "Optimal Management of Oil and Gas Reservoirs," Internal Report No. 81/82-3-4, Department of General Business, The University of Texas, Austin, Texas, March 1982.

Luenberger, D.G., Introduction to Linear and Nonlinear Programming, Addison-Wesley Pub. Co., Inc., Menlo Park, California, 1973.

Mays, L.W. and Taur, C.-K., "Unit Hydrographs via Nonlinear Programming," Water Resources Research, Vol. 18, No. 4, pp. 744-752, August 1982.

Norman, A.L., Lasdon, L.S., and Hsin, J.K., "A Comparison of Methods for Solving and Optimizing a Large Nonlinear Econometric Model," Discussion Paper, Center for Economic Research, The University of Texas at Austin, Texas, 1982.

Ocanas, G. and Mays, L.W., "A Model for Water Reuse Planning," Water Resources Research, American Geophysical Union, Vol. 17, No. 1, pp. 25-32, February 1981.

Palacios-Gomez, F., Lasdon, L.S., and Engquist, M., "Nonlinear Optimization by Successive Linear Programming," Management Science, Vol. 28, No. 10, 1982.

Powell, M.J.D., "Algorithms for Nonlinear Constraints that Use Lagrangian Functions," Mathematical Programming, Vol. 14, No. 2, 1978.

Schittkowski, K., "Nonlinear Programming Codes—Information, Tests, Performance," Internal Report, Institute fur Angewandte Mathematic and Statistik, Universitat Wuzburg, Am Hubland, D-87, Wuzburg, West Germany, 1980.

Unver, O. and Mays, L.W., "Optimal Determination of Loss Rate Functions and Unit Hydrographs," Water Resources Research, AGU, Vol. 20, No. 2, pp. 203-214, February 1984.

Wanakule, N., Mays, L.W., and Lasdon, L.S., "Development of a Model for Determining Optimal Pumping and Recharge of Large-Scale Aquifers," Proceedings, American Water Resources Association Meeting, October 1983, San Antonio, Texas, to be published 1985.

Wood, Don J., "Computer Analysis of Flow in Pipe Networks including Extended Period Simulation - User's Manual," Office of Engineering Continuing Education and Extension, University of Kentucky, Lexington, Kentucky, 1980.

OPNET: A Nonlinear Design Algorithm for Hydraulic Networks

Lindell Ormsbee, Associate Member ASCE[*]

Since the distribution system is often the major investment of a municipal water works, it is important that any design satisfy system requirements at a minimum cost. In current practice, the designer will usually employ a trial and error procedure to obtain a hydraulically feasible solution using some method of hydraulic analysis. He may then, by trial and error, obtain another feasibile solution (i.e., one that satisfies flow and pressure constraints) and then compare the costs of the two solutions to obtain a least cost design. This process may be repeated a number of times until the designer is satisfied with the final design. Such a procedure can be very tedious and time consuming and requires a great deal of engineering judgment. It also suffers from the disadvantage that the designer can never really be sure that he has obtained the true or globally optimal solution.

The author has developed a general computer program OPNET to be used in the optimal design of hydraulic networks. The computer program can be used to optimize three basic variables; tank elevation, pump head, and discrete pipe diameter sizes. A modified Box Complex optimization technique is used to minimize a nonlinear objective function while the linear method of hydraulic analysis is used in the evaluation of the network system constraints.

Introduction

In recent years, several authors have introduced various mathematical optimization techniques to be used in the solution of the hydraulic network design problem. The employed techniques have included linear programming, dynamic programming, nonlinear programming and general heuristics. A comprehensive review of several of the algorithms has been provided by Walski (4).

The author has developed a general computer program OPNET to be used in the optimal design of hydraulic networks. The computer program can be used to optimize three basic variables: tank elevation, pump head, and discrete pipe diameter sizes, all for a single flow realization. The general computer program uses a nonlinear search algorithm (1) along with a hydraulic analysis subroutine for use in checking any flowrate, velocity, or pressure constraints imposed on the system. The hydraulic analysis subroutine uses the linear method (5) for solving the system of network equations.

*Assistant Professor, Dept. of Civil Engineering, University of KY, 212 Anderson Hall, Lexington, KY 40506-0046

Formulation of the Problem

Any problem investigated in an optimization analysis will have as its objective the improvement of the system or systems. In analyzing the problem, it is usually necessary to express the objective in a mathematical form called the objective function. In the formulation of an objective function to describe a water distribution system, it is assumed that the basic network geometry is fixed along with the location of the basic network components (i.e., pipes, tanks, pumps, etc.). Thus the problem is to determine the optimal sizes of the basic network components that yield a minimum cost while still satisfying all the basic variable and system constraints. The overall optimization problem involves three different sets of decision variables. These include pipe diameters D_p, pump heads H_m, and tank elevations E_t.

The general optimization problem may be expressed in mathematical form as follows:

Minimize

$$F(D,H,E) = \sum_{p=1}^{P} PC(D_p) + \sum_{m=1}^{M} (POC(H_m)*USPWF + PIC(H_m)) + \sum_{t=1}^{T} TIC(E_t) \quad (1)$$

Subject To

(1) Explicit Variable Constraints

   (a) Explicit Diameter Constraints

   $$D_p \ \varepsilon \ \{\text{Discrete Pipe Sizes}\}; \ p=1,\ldots,P \quad (2)$$

   (b) Explicit Pump Head Constraints

   $$HMIN_m \leq H_m \leq HMAX_m; \ m=1,\ldots,M \quad (3)$$

   (c) Explicit Elevation Constraints

   $$EMIN_t \leq E_t \leq EMAX_t; \ t=1,\ldots,T \quad (4)$$

(2) Implicit System Constraints

   (a) Implicit Flowrate Constraints

   $$QMIN_p \leq Q_p(D_p,H_m,E_t) \leq QMAX_p; \ p=1,\ldots,P \quad (5)$$

   (b) Implicit Velocity Constraints

   $$VMIN_p \leq V_p(D_p,H_m,E_t) \leq VMAX_p; \ p=1,\ldots,P \quad (6)$$

   (c) Implicit Pressure Constraints

   $$PMIN_j \leq R_j(D_p,H_m,E_t) \leq PMAX_j; \ j=1,\ldots,J \quad (7)$$

Cost Functions

The pipe cost function $PC(D_p)$ is evaluated by means of a cost graph generated by the computer[p]program. In using the proposed computer program, the user supplies a desired range of discrete pipe diameter sizes and the cost per foot of pipe for each size. The computer program then uses the values to construct a cost graph relating pipe diameter to cost per foot of pipe. In evaluating the pipe cost function for each pipe, the program utilizes the internal graph to obtain the cost per foot of pipe and then multiplies this value with the pipe length to obtain the cost of an individual pipe. These individual pipe costs are then summed to obtain a total cost for the pipe network.

The cost of any pumping facilities depends on an initial installation cost and subsequent operating costs. Any variable initial cost (cost related to the size of the pump as a function of pump head) may be included in a variable installation cost factor $PIC(H_m)$. The operating cost of any pump facility is related to the horsepower requirements for the facility. Horsepower requirements for any pump are related to the flow through the pump and the hydraulic head generated. The energy requirement for a pump is usually expressed in terms of kilowatts. Thus the basic operating cost of any pump for any period is simply the cost of one kilowatt hour times the number of kilowatt hours used. The basic operating cost for each pump is included in the objective function via the $POC(H_m)$ term which is then multiplied by a uniform series present worth factor (USPWF) to discount the extended operating cost back to the present.

In formulating a cost function for a storage reservoir, a variable cost factor, $TIC(E_t)$ is included which can account for the cost per vertical foot of storage. Given the total elevation of the tank, the cost of the tank can be obtained by multiplying the elevation of the tank with the cost per vertical foot.

Problem Constraints

There are two basic types of constraints on the decision variables of the optimization problem. The first type of constraint is an explicit constraint of the form $X_1 \leq X_i \leq X_h$ where X_i is a decision variable; X_1 is the lowest value that the decision variable may assume, and X_h is the highest value that the decision variable may assume. Constraints of this type may be directly imposed on the decision variables of pipe diameter, pump head, and tank elevation.

The second type of constraint on the decision variables are implicit constraints of the form $Y_1 \leq Y(X_i) \leq Y_h$ where Y is a system variable which is a function of one or more decision variables, Y_1 is the lowest value that the system variable may assume, and Y_h is the highest value that the decision variable may assume. Constraints of this type may be imposed on the system variables of flowrate Q_p, pipe velocity V_p, and junction node pressure R_j.

Design Algorithm

The general water distriution problem as formulated in equations
1 thru 7 involves the minimization of a nonlinear objective function
subject to linear and nonlinear explicit and implicit inequality
constraints. In order to solve the mathematical formulation of the
water distribution design problem, a general design algorithm has been
developed. The general algorithm employs the Complex method of Box
(1) along with the linear method (5) of solving the basic hydraulic
network equations. Although various other nonlinear optimization
algorithms are available, the Box Complex method was chosen because
(1) the method is conceputally simple (2) no derivatives are required
(3) the method is directly applicable to problems involving nonlinear
inequality constraints, i.e., no transformations are required (4) the
method is easily applied to problems involving complex implicit
constraints and (5) the method may be applied to problems with
nonconvex solution spaces.

The Complex method of Box (1) is a direct search method. The
method handles constraints by use of a flexible mathematical figure,
called a complex, which can expand or contract in any or all
directions and can extend around corners. In this method k>n+1 points
are used, where n equals the number of function variables. Each point
in the complex corresponds to a single design. Associated with each
point (design) are n coordinates, with each coordinate corresponding
to an individual design variable in the objective function. In
addition to allowing nonlinear inequality constraints on the solution
space the method also allows explicit limits on the values of the
decision variables.

In order to generate the initial complex an initial point
(design) must be given or determined that satisfies both the explicit
and implicit constraints. The further (k-1) points required to set up
the initial complex are obtained one at a time by the use of random
numbers and ranges for each of the independent variables which are
based on the explicit constraints. A point so selected will thus
satisfy the explicit constraints but not necessarily all the implicit
constraints. In order to evaluate the implicit constraints a
hydraulic analysis must be performed for each trial design. If an
implicit constraint is violated the trial point is moved halfway
towards the centroid of those points already selected (where the given
initial point is included). Ultimately a satisfactory point will be
found. Proceeding in this way, the (k-1) points are found which
satisfy all the constraints. Once the initial complex has been
formed, further progress is then made through expansion or contraction
of the complex. These two operations can be visualized as follows:

At each stage of movement the objective function is evaluated at
each of the points in the complex, and the vertex of the greatest
function value determined. The complex is then expanded away from
this worst point, P high, through the centroid of the remaining points
to yield a new point P new. The objective function is then evaluated
at this new point P new. If the new point yields an objective
function value which is better than the worst point P high, then the
high point P high is discarded and replaced by P new. In this way the

complex moves in the direction of function minimization. If, however, the value of the new point is worse than P high, then the new point is contracted back toward the centroid and another new point generated.

This dual process of expansion and contraction continues until some constraint is violated or some tolerance level reached. If an independent variable X_i of a new point i violates some explicit constraint then that variable is reset to a value just inside the constraint. If the new point violates some implicit constraint, the point is moved halfway towards the centroid of the remaining points. Ultimately a permissible point will be found. The search finally terminates when consecutive function evaluations have yielded the same result, indicating that the complex has collapsed into the centroid (2).

In applying the Box Complex method to the water distribution design problem, two modifications have been made. The first modification concerns the feasibility of the complex centroid. In applying the Box Complex method it is implicitly assumed that the solution space is convex. A general analysis of the problem formulation has indicated that the resulting solution space may be nonconvex. As a result it is possible that the complex centroid could move into an infeasible region such that continued contraction would fail to produce a feasible point. In order to circumvent this problem the centroid is tested for feasibility during each contraction phase. If the centroid is feasible then the new point is sought between it and the violating point; otherwise the new vertex is sought between the current worst feasible vertex and the centroid.

The second modification to the Box Complex algorithm concerns the generation of discrete (noncontinuous) values for selected decision variables such as pipe diameters. Using an initial feasible solution the design algorithm generates an initial complex. Progress toward the optimum component values is achieved by expansion and contraction of the complex. During each trial a new nondiscrete point (design) is generated. Once the explicit constraints have been checked, a hydraulic analysis is run and the implicit constraints are evaluated. If an explicit constraint is violated, the variable (or variables) is reset within the acceptable region. If an implicit constraint is violated, the point is contracted halfway back toward the centroid (assuming the centroid is feasible) and the process repeated until an acceptable point is found. Once an acceptable nondiscrete point has been obtained, a discrete point (corresponding to the discrete values of the continuous point) is generated by rounding the results to the nearest preselected discrete value. The new discrete point (design) is then compared with the current minimum discrete point (design) to determine which point yields a lower value for the objective function. If the new point proves to be the better point then it replaces the old point. However, if the old point is better then it is kept and the new point discarded. This entire process is then repeated until a selected level of tolerance has been reached. A flow chart of the hydraulic network optimization program, OPNET, is shown in Figure 1.

Application

    To demonstrate the mechanics of OPNET the design algorithm was
applied to the simple network illustrated in Figure 2. The sample
network consists of 7 pipes, two storage tanks and a single booster
pump. Pipe 1 has a length of 1000 ft (305 m), pipe 2 has a length of
400 ft (122 m), pipe 3 has a length of 600 ft (183 m) and pipes 4 thru
7 have lengths of 500 ft (152.5 m). The roughness of each pipe is
described by a Hazen-Williams coefficient of 100. Tank A and pipe 1
are assumed to be existing components of the system while pipes 2 thru
7, Tank B, and the booster pump are to be designed. In designing the
various components of the system, flow demands of 1 cfs (0.028 m/s)
are to be supplied to junction nodes 2 and 3 while pressures in excess
of 20 psi (138 kPa) are to be maintained at all four junction nodes.
In addition, a flowrate in excess of 1.5 cfs (0.042 m^3/s) is to be
delivered to tank B. The ground elevation of tank B is assumed to be
equal to 100 ft (30.5 m).

    In selecting the values of the decision variables for the system
the pump head was constrained between values of 50 and 150 feet, (15.3
and 48.8 meters) the tank elevation was constrained between values of
60 and 100 feet, (18.3 and 30.5 meters) and the diameters were
selected from a set of discrete sizes ranging from 6 to 16 inches (15
to 41 centimeters). In evaluating the objective function for the
design a variable cost of $500/ft ($1639/m) was used for the storage
tank while a variable cost of $400/ft ($1,311.5/m) was used for the
pump. In addition, a project life of 20 years along with an interest
rate of 10% and a kilowatt rate of $0.05/kwh were used for determining
the operating cost of the pump. The costs of the various pipes are
given in Table 1.

    To begin OPNET an initial feasible design must be provided. For
the example network this design was obtained by setting all pipe
diameters equal to 12 inches (30.5 centimeters), the pump head at 100
ft (30.5 m) and the tank elevation at 70 ft (21.4 m). The results for
the initial feasible solution are provided in Table 3 while the
optimal results are provided in Table 4. The optimal solution was
obtained in 60 iterations which required 90 seconds of CPU time on a
PRIME 850 computer.

Summary and Conclusions

    OPNET has been found to yield very good results in an accurate
and expeditious manner. Although the computer program can greatly aid
in the optimal design of water distribution systems, it must of course
be recognized that there are many more variables to this problem than
have been dealt with here. Factors such as storage considerations,
water usage and demand, system reliability considerations, pumping
options, pipe options, and energy options have not been fully
addressed. As pointed out by Lischer (3) some engineering judgement
will always be needed. While this may be true, the author feels that
OPNET still provides a powerful tool for any such analysis.

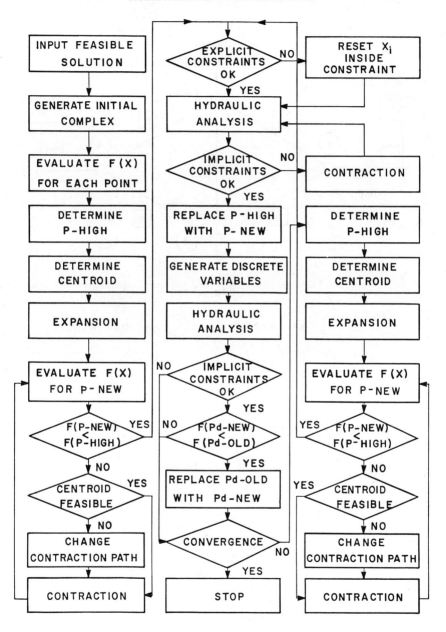

FIGURE 1. FLOWCHART OF OPNET

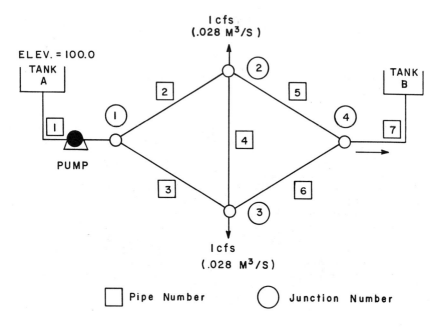

FIGURE 2. EXAMPLE NETWORK

TABLE 1. PIPE COST DATA

DIAMETER (INCHES)	COST/FOOT (DOLLARS)
6.0	12.0
8.0	16.0
10.0	20.0
12.0	26.0
14.0	32.0
16.0	40.0

TABLE 2. INITIAL NETWORK FLOW RESULTS

TOTAL COST = $ 243356.00

PIPE	LENGTH (FEET)	DIAMETER (INCHES)	FLOWRATE (CFS)	HEADLOSS (FEET)	COST (DOLLARS)
1	1000.00	12.00	5.413	-78.6639	0.00
2	400.00	12.00	2.991	2.8452	8800.00
3	600.00	12.00	2.422	2.8865	13200.00
4	500.00	12.00	0.270	0.0412	11000.00
5	500.00	12.00	1.721	1.2784	11000.00
6	500.00	12.00	1.691	1.2371	11000.00
7	500.00	12.00	3.412	4.5403	11000.00

JUNCTION	DEMAND (CFS)	ELEVATION (FEET)	GRADE (FEET)	PRESSURE (PSI)
1	0.0	100.00	178.66	34.09
2	1.0	100.00	175.82	32.85
3	1.0	100.00	175.78	32.84
4	0.0	100.00	174.54	32.30

TANK ELEV (FEET)	TANK COST (DOLLARS)	PUMP HEAD (FEET)	PUMP COST (DOLLARS)
70.0	35000.00	100.0	142356.00

TABLE 3. OPTIMUM NETWORK FLOW RESULTS

TOTAL COST = $ 150803.00

PIPE	LENGTH (FEET)	DIAMETER (INCHES)	FLOWRATE (CFS)	HEADLOSS (FEET)	COST (DOLLARS)
1	1000.00	12.00	3.504	-75.4928	0.00
2	400.00	10.00	2.332	4.3595	6400.00
3	600.00	8.00	1.173	5.4292	6000.00
4	500.00	6.00	0.253	1.0697	4000.00
5	500.00	8.00	1.079	3.8773	5000.00
6	500.00	6.00	0.425	2.8076	4000.00
7	500.00	8.00	1.504	7.1754	5000.00

JUNCTION	DEMAND (CFS)	ELEVATION (FEET)	GRADE (FEET)	PRESSURE (PSI)
1	0.0	100.00	175.49	32.71
2	1.0	100.00	171.13	30.82
3	1.0	100.00	170.06	30.36
4	0.0	100.00	167.26	29.14

TANK ELEV (FEET)	TANK COST (DOLLARS)	PUMP HEAD (FEET)	PUMP COST (DOLLARS)
60.08	30040.00	85.03	90363.00

Appendix I. - References

(1) Box, M. J. "A New Method of Constrained Optimization and a Comparison with Other Methods," The Computer Journal, Vol. 8, 1965, pp. 42-51.

(2) Box, M. J., Davies, and Swann, W. H., Monograph No. 5: Nonlinear Optimization Techniques, Oliver and Boyd, Great Britain, 1969.

(3) Lischer, V. C., Discussion of "Optimal Design of Water Distribution Networks" by A. Cenedese and P. Mele, Journal of Hydraulics Division, ASCE, Vol. 105, January 1979, pp. 113-114.

(4) Walski, T. M., "State-of-the-Art Water Distribtuion Pipe Network Optimization" Proceedings Computer Applications in Water Resources, Buffalo, New York, June 10-12, 1985.

(5) Wood, D. J. and Charles, C. O. A., "Hydraulic Network Analysis Using Linear Theory," Journal of the Hydraulics Division, ASCE, Vol. 98, No. HY7, Proc. Paper 9031, July 1972, pp. 1157-1170.

Appendix II. - Notation

where D_p = pipe diameter of pipe p

H_m = pump head of pump m

E_t = tank elevation of tank t

R_j = pressure at junction node j

Q_p = flowrate in pipe p

V_p = velocity in pipe p

P = number of pipes

J = number of junction nodes

M = number of pumps

T = number of tanks

$PC(\ )$ = pipe cost function

$POC(\ )$ = pump annual operating cost function

$PIC(\ )$ = pump installation cost function

$TIC(\ )$ = tank installation cost function

$USPWF$ = uniform series present worth factor

CATCHMENT RESPONSE MODELS IN THE COMPUTER AGE

By Walter T. Sittner * - Fellow, A.S.C.E.

ABSTRACT: The paper deals with catchment response models and addresses the question - - - what do we know when we know a model? The history of catchment modelling over the last seventy five years is described. The end result has been computerized conceptual models and "black box" models. The advantages, the capabilities and the limitations of each type are discussed.

HISTORY OF CATCHMENT MODELLING

One who observes the field of catchment modelling today encounters a bewildering array of models and model terminology. Words such as deterministic, stochastic, conceptual, black-box, empirical, lumped and distributed input, lumped and distributed parameter, linear and non-linear systems, convolution integrals, etc., etc. abound. One is likely to receive the impression that this is a very complex and hard to understand subject. Such is not the case, and while no effort will be made to define all of the foregoing terms it is hoped that the following discussion will place in perspective the present state of the art in catchment modelling. To understand the present, it usually helps to understand how it came about - - - and to this end, the history of catchment modelling must be considered. This history, spanning some three fourths of a century, can be divided into four phases, or "eras":

First era (1910 - 1930) - - The "crude" era:

In the decades, or perhaps centuries, prior to this time, people had some interest in hydrologic processes and had methods by which they could infer conclusions about the response of rivers to meteorological phenomena. But - - - it was in this period that the first attempts were made to actually analyze and quantify those processes. What were sought were very simple relationships between the principal causative variable and its ultimate effect. One such approach was to observe, for a number of events, the quantity of rainfall at some point in the catchment - - usually the outlet - - and the amount by which the stage of the river increased and to then plot "precipitation" versus "rise in stage". A smooth curve drawn through the points presumably showed the relationship between the two.

Another very early - - - and very simple approach is called the "rational method". In it, the maximum rate of outflow from a catchment is equated to the product of three quantities, the rainfall intensity, the catchment area, and a coefficient. It is assumed that the rain continues at the stated intensity until the maximum flow is reached, an equilibrium condition. Obviously, if a rain storm maintains a constant intensity until equilibrium is reached - - - and if the correct value of the coefficient is known, the method will yield a correct value of

* Consultant - Annapolis, Maryland

peak discharge. Just as obviously however, storms do not maintain constant intensity until equilibrium and - - - since the coefficient reflects the effects of so many variables, its value can never be known. Although guidelines exist which relate the value to physical conditions they are very rough - - - and, in a paper published in the year 1915, Charles B. Buerger [2] wrote of the method - - - "in its application there will usually be as many results (differing widely from each other) as the number of men using it.".

Second era (1930 - 1945) - - The "theoretical" era:

After the crude methods had been thoroughly exploited and after it was realized that the physical process is really much more complicated than this, investigators began to turn to what they felt were more scientific approaches. Work done during the theoretical era was characterized by attempts to *understand* the processes and to represent them mathematically. Typical of the period was the work of Horton [6],[7], [8] and others in analyzing the infiltration process. Horton - - - we can imagine - - - had been out of doors during a storm, looked at the ground and noticed - - - as we have, that some of the rain drops soak into the ground. And, those which do not soak in, seem to run over the ground, presumably finding their way to the river and contributing to the flow. The solution to the problem was obvious; determine how much water soaked into the ground, subtract this from the total rainfall and the remainder was what went to the river. The key to the whole thing was the *infiltration* process. *This* was what should be studied.

Much work was done in this general area. Not only was the problem studied in light of what was known of the properties of water movement through porous media, but a great deal of laboratory work was done with physical models in an attempt to learn just what rules controlled the way drops of water worked their way through and between the particles of soil.

Third era (1945 - 1965) - - The "empirical" era:

It eventually became evident that the methods developed in the theoretical era did not - - - for some reason - - - give very good results and some investigators then turned to more empirical methods. The word, empirical, is defined as - - - "relying upon or derived from observation or experiment". By this definition, everything is empirical because every theory stems originally from someone having observed something and then having gone through a reasoning process based on that observation. In *this* context however it means that the investigators of the empirical era decided that the reason the theoretical approach did not work well was that no one really did understand the rainfall-runoff process and that the mathematical relationships based on this false understanding were *wrong*. Consequently, any attempt to fit observed data to such formulations was doomed to failure. The *right* way to handle the problem then was to observe, for many events, the magnitude of rainfall, of river response, and of any other factors which were logically thought to be involved in the process. And then - - - experiment with different types of mathematical, or graphical, relationships until one is found which causes everything to "fit together". That is, let the *data*, rather than theory, dictate the form of relationship to be used. The most notable example of this philosophy is the work of Kohler, et al [9],[11] in the late 1940's with a coaxial graphical rainfall-runoff relationship employing the now well known "Antecedent Precipitation Index" or "API". This method soon proved to be quite suitable for various types of hydrologic studies and has been very popular for the last thirty years. During that time many hydrologists have devised variations on the basic procedure [13],[14]. Some of these are valid adaptations or improvements and others, unfortunately, simply reflect a lack of understanding of the method on the part of the person trying to modify it.

Fourth era (1965 –   ) – – The "conceptual" era:

The conceptual era of catchment modelling began with the publication by Linsley and Crawford of the Stanford Watershed Model [5] in 1966. Their approach was new at the time and, to the best of the author's knowledge, original with them. It consists of writing mathematical formulations which represent the modeller's concept of all of the processes taking place in and on the soil profile, and in the vegetation and lower atmosphere just above the ground, putting all of these formulations together and then computing, on a continuous basis, over a long period of time, the movement of water through all parts of the catchment.

It is quite clear that this era of modelling came about as a result of the advent of electronic computers. Computers became available to hydrologists in the late 1950's and one of the first uses made of them was the automation of existing hydrologic techniques, not only the hydrologic analysis methods but data reduction tasks as well. The products of such computerized operations were no better nor worse than those which had resulted from manual computation but they were obtained much faster and more easily.

At the same time, some investigators – – – among them Linsley and Crawford – – – saw the opportunity to develop *new* modelling techniques, to do things which *cannot* be done without a computer simply because those things involve a tremendous volume of computation. In this way, the computer made it possible to develop the new techniques and, through the repeated testing, revising and refining of the model structure, which such development involved, to acquire new knowledge of hydrologic processes.

Since 1965, other hydrologists – – – either having been "shown the way" by the work done at Stanford, or independently, but with similar motivation – – – have produced a number of other conceptual catchment models. Notable among these are the Sacramento Model [3],[4], the Japanese Tank Model [17],[18] and the Swedish HBV Model [1].

Is there a fifth era (1975 –   ) – – The "black box" era?

The "black box" approach to catchment modelling was introduced by Wallis and Todini in 1973 in the form of the "Constrained Linear System", or "CLS" Model [12]. It involves the use of a computer to correlate great masses of input and output data using mathematical formulations having little or nothing to do with hydrologic processes but which result in outputs which resemble a catchment's output – – – a hydrograph. Some observers feel that black box modelling is a new era in hydrology. Others view it as nothing more than a return to the empirical era but using modern, very powerful computing equipment.

ADVANTAGES OF CONCEPTUAL MODELS OVER EARLIER METHODS

When the Stanford Model was introduced it was greeted with some degree of skepticism. Were the originators simply playing games with the computer? Was the model nothing more than a high powered curve fitting technique or was it real hydrology? It was obvious that this model - - - and others of the same category which followed - - - had some *dis*advantages. Principal among these was their complexity. The use of such a model requires a degree of computing power which was not available to most practitioners fifteen to twenty years ago. It was obvious that conceptual models could supplant earlier methods only if they had some overwhelming advantage - - - and that the only thing of which this advantage could possibly consist would be - - - a greater accuracy of simulation.

In the late 1960's and early 1970's a number of studies were made to compare the accuracy of conceptual models with that of the simpler methods [15],[16],[19], and some hydrologists are still making such investigations. The results of those studies were, at first, confusing. Many simulations were made in many catchments and numerous types of statistical error functions were computed. These error analyses however seemed to indicate that there was no appreciable difference in simulation accuracy between the conceptual models and the older methods.

When some investigators looked more closely however, when they looked beyond the statistical summaries and studied individual events, they saw that *occasionally* there were great differences in simulation accuracy but these cases were so rare that their effect on the statistical summaries - - - involving thousands of errors - - - was slight. When these investigators studied the inner workings of the models to find out *why* these differences occurred, they learned something very interesting. The earlier methods analyzed only one or a very few of the many processes taking place in the soil profile and in the catchment, making implicit assumptions about the boundary conditions which related those processes to the ones which were not actually analyzed. The conceptual model treats *all* of the processes and is continuous with respect to time. Thus, when *unusual* combinations of state variables exist the boundary conditions assumed in the earlier methods are not valid and the model cannot simulate the catchment response - - - the conceptual model *can*. As most of these studies were made by people who had *river forecasting* responsibilities, this capability was deemed to be very important. A forecaster works with one event at a time and the forecast user who suffers a loss due to a gross error in a forecast is not impressed by the fact that the *average* error of all forecasts issued is small.

Another phenomenon noted in some of these studies was related to the ability of conceptual models to use, as input, real time evapotranspiration data, although they can operate without it - - - using a normal evapotranspiration curve - - - when such data are not available. It was found that when long term (a few years) departures from climatological normals took place, a continuous model not using real time evapotranspiration data - - - and the earlier models *cannot* use it - - would generate long term yield figures significantly different from the observed. A conceptual model - - - using such data - - - was able to "track" such trends quite nicely. This is of course an important consideration in studies involving the long term yield of rivers.

These then are the advantages of conceptual models and the reasons for them. This also explains why the pseudo-conceptual approach of the "theoretical" era did not work. What has been learned from the work with conceptual models is simply this:

WE CANNOT DO A GOOD JOB OF MODELLING RUNOFF EVENTS UNLESS WE ALSO DO A GOOD JOB OF MODELLING THE LOW WATER PERIODS BETWEEN THEM AND WE CANNOT DO A GOOD JOB OF MODELLING THE LOW WATER PERIODS UNLESS WE DO A GOOD JOB OF MODELLING THE RUNOFF EVENTS - - - WE CANNOT DO A GOOD JOB OF MODELLING SURFACE RUNOFF, INFILTRATION AND OTHER THINGS TAKING PLACE AT THE SURFACE OF THE GROUND UNLESS WE ALSO DO A GOOD JOB OF MODELLING GROUNDWATER FLOW AND WE CANNOT PROP-ERLY MODEL GROUNDWATER FLOW UNLESS WE PROPERLY MODEL WHAT IS GOING ON AT THE SURFACE. EVERYTHING IN THE RAINFALL-RUNOFF PRO-CESS IS RELATED TO EVERYTHING ELSE IN TIME AND IN SPACE; EVERY-THING AFFECTS EVERYTHING ELSE AND IS, IN TURN, AFFECTED BY EVERY-THING ELSE. IF A MODEL IS TO SIMULATE ANY ONE OF THESE PROCESSES ADEQUATELY IT MUST SIMULATE ALL OF THEM AND ITS MATHEMATICS MUST REPRESENT ALL OF THE INTERRELATIONSHIPS WHICH EXIST IN NATURE.

This knowledge has rendered a lot of earlier hydrologic thinking quite obsolete.

CONCEPTUAL MODELS VS. BLACK BOX MODELS

There is a great and fundamental philosophical difference between these two approaches to catchment modelling. Some people find it hard to understand the convolution integral until it is explained that it is simply a mathematical representation of the physical process which a unit hydrograph represents graphically - - - others find it hard to understand the unit hydrograph until it is pointed out that it is nothing more than a graphical representation of a convolution integral. Because the world contains such different kinds of people, there can probably never be a meeting of the minds in this area. Suffice to say then that the objective of the black box modeller is prediction of the result and the objective of the conceptual modeller is the gaining of an understanding of the rainfall-runoff process. It has been said that a good conceptual model is the best tool available for teaching hydrology.

A claimed advantage of black box models is the ability, when being calibrated on poor quality historical data, to "filter out" random errors in the data thereby producing a set of parameters which accu-rately represents the hydrologic characteristics of the catchment. This concept however is not universally accepted.

CAPABILITIES AND LIMITATIONS

Capabilities:

Catchment response models are created for the purpose of simu-lating - - - or predicting - - - the quantity of outflow from a catch-ment. In the case of a black box model it is clear that this is exactly what it can do, nothing more - - - nothing less. The properties of a conceptual model, on the other hand, suggest additional possibilities. The term, conceptual model, has been defined by the World Meteor-ological Organization (WMO) [19] as:

" - - - those which represent(ed) a concept of either the whole
or a part of the physical process of the hydrological cycle, expressed by either simple or complex mathematical formulations."
While this is an accurate definition it is perhaps understandable only
to those who already know what a conceptual model is. In order to
facilitate communication in the workaday world - - - and to clarify the
distinction between these models and the earlier types - - - it has
been necessary to devise a more pragmatic definition. Thus:

A conceptual model is one in which the various parameters and
state variables represent actual and identifiable volumes of
water - - - rather than being indices to those volumes.

Such a definition suggests some alternative uses for this type of
model. The user of the model has available a continuous accounting of
the volumes of water present in all parts of the soil profile. If he
were interested in say, water temperature modelling, he could presumably write heat transfer equations between the water and its environment in all the places through which it passes, and incorporate those
equations into the model. A similar thing might be done with water
quality modelling. Another possibility is the combining of a hydrologic
catchment model with a conceptual (dynamic) routing model to solve
problems such as bank loss and bank storage during floods. While these
possibilities are seen by some as a great opportunity to solve water
resources problems, very little research of this type has been done to
date, perhaps because such activities would involve more than one academic discipline.

Along similar lines, Leader et al [10] reported in 1983 on an
investigation by the U.S. National Weather Service in cooperation with
the U.S. Geological Survey in which it was learned that the occurrence
of landslides - - - in one area of California - - - was closely related
to the quantity of free water in the upper soil layer. It was found
that when upper zone free water contents, as computed within the Sacramento Model, approached 95% of the zone's capacity, as specified by a
model parameter, that landslides - - - in the area under study - - -
had a very strong likelihood of occurrence. They stated that it is
planned to explore this phenomenon more fully in the future with an eye
toward the development of a landslide forecasting capability.

Limitations:

The foregoing is a rather optimistic outlook in regard to peripheral products and side benefits which may accrue to one who uses a
conceptual model for the purpose of simulating catchment outflow. There
are rather definite limits to such things however.

In using a catchment model for real time river forecasting, one of
the continuing problems is the reconciling of model output with
observed concurrent river discharge. When the two fail to agree within
acceptable limits it is highly likely that one or more of the model's
intermediate computed state variables is in error by an excessive
amount. It therefore follows that if the value of such a variable could
be observed, that information could be used to correct the computed
value - - - thus correcting, at least partially, the discharge being
generated by the model. One example is the continuing effort by those
engaged in remote sensing from satellites or aircraft to measure soil

moisture. It is proposed that such data could be used as described above. The problem is that even if reliable soil moisture could be obtained in this manner, and even though any conceptual model does contain one or more state variables which supposedly represent the actual quantity of water in such storage, the user of the model simply would not know just where to "plug in" the observed value. These models are quite complex. But, in comparison to the physical process which they purport to represent, they are gross oversimplifications. Stated more succinctly, the models are conceptual but they are not *that* conceptual.

The situation is summarized by the World Meteorological Organization in Sec. 6.5.10 of Volume II of their "Guide to Hydrological Practices", a section dealing with forecast adjustment techniques:

"Adjustment need not be based only on the output of the model, but may also be accomplished by using measurements of state variables for comparison with the values generated by the model. For example, one such technique uses observed measurements of the water equivalent of the snow cover as a means of improving the seasonal water supply forecasts derived from a conceptual model [41]. It would be incorrect to directly substitute field measurements for numerically generated values of the internal variables of the model. This is because, in practice, model simplifications result in slightly non-physical values."

SUMMARY AND CONCLUSIONS

Modern catchment response models, those which make full use of the capabilities of computers, are the results of three fourths of a century of evolution. They fall into two categories, black box and conceptual. Some types of accuracy advantage are claimed for black box models but these have not been demonstrated convincingly. Conceptual models have not been shown to be more accurate than the simpler types when simulating typical hydrologic events. They are however able to simulate non-typical events which simpler models cannot. This capability results from their multi-level moisture accounting and the fact that they operate continuously with respect to time.

While a conceptual model is supposedly a mathematical representation of the modeller's concept of a physical process, the experimentation necessary to develop a successful model verifies and/or revises these concepts. Thus, when one "knows" such a model, he also "knows" the physical process. But - - - this is a simplified version of the process.

The conceptual qualities of a model make it possible to use it for purposes other than streamflow simulation. The simplifications in the structure of the model however place definite constraints on such usage.

APPENDIX I. - REFERENCES

1. Bergström, S., "The Development and Application of SMHI Run-off Model HBV-2", *Hydrological Report No. 22*, Swedish Meteorological and Hydrological Institute, Stockholm, 1973.

2. Buerger, C.B., *Transactions*, American Society of Civil Engineers, 78:1139, 1915.

3. Burnash, R.J.C. and Ferral, R.L., "A Generalized Streamflow Simulation System", Presented at the fifteenth general assembly of the I.U.G.G., held at Moscow, 1971.

4. Burnash, R.J.C., Ferral, R.L. and McGuire, R.A., "A Generalized Streamflow Simulation System - Conceptual Modelling for Digital Computers", United States Department of Commerce, National Weather Service and State of California Department of Water Resources, March, 1973.

5. Crawford, N.H. and Linsley, R.K., "Digital Simulation in Hydrology - Stanford Watershed Model IV", *Technical Report No. 39*, Department of Civil Engineering, Stanford University, Stanford, California, July, 1966.

6. Horton, R.E., "The Role of Infiltration in the Hydrologic Cycle", *Transactions*, American Geophysical Union, Vol. 14, 1933, pp. 446-460.

7. Horton, R.E., "Determination of Infiltration in the Hydrologic Cycle", *Transactions*, American Geophysical Union, Vol. 18, 1937, pp. 371-385.

8. Horton, R.E., "An Approach Toward a Physical Interpretation of Infiltration Capacity", *Proceedings*, Soil Science Society of America, Vol. 5, 1940, pp. 399-417.

9. Kohler, M.A. and Linsley, R.K., "Predicting the Runoff From Storm Rainfall", *U.S. Weather Bureau Research Paper 34*, United States Weather Bureau, 1951.

10. Leader, D.C., Burnash, R.J.C. and Ferral, R.L., "An Incident of Serious Landslide Occurrences Related to Upper Zone Soil Wetness as Computed With the Sacramento Streamflow Model", Presented at the Sept., 1983 International Technical Conference on Mitigation of Natural Hazards Through Real-Time Data Collection Systems and Hydrological Forecasting, held at Sacramento, California by the World Meteorological Organization, the United States National Oceanic and Atmospheric Administration and the California Department of Water Resources.

11. Linsley, R.K., Kohler, M.A. and Paulhus, J.L.H., "Relations Between Precipitation and Runoff", *Hydrology for Engineers*, 3rd ed., McGraw Hill Book Company, New York, N.Y., U.S.A., 1982, pp. 242-247.

12. Natale, P. and Todini, E., "A Constrained Parameter Estimation Technique", *Mathematical Models for Surface Water Hydrology*, T.A. Ciriani, U. Maione and J.R. Wallis, eds., John Wiley and Sons, Inc. London, U.K., 1977.

13. Němec, J. and Sittner, W.T., "Application of the Continuous API Catchment Model in the Indus River Forecasting System in Pakistan",

Proceedings, International Symposium on Rainfall-Runoff Modelling, held at Mississippi State University, Mississippi State, Mississippi, May, 1981.

14. Sittner, W.T., Schauss, C.E. and Monro, J.C., "Continuous Hydrograph Synthesis With an API Type Hydrologic Model", *Water Resources Research*, Vol. 5, No. 5, Oct., 1969.

15. Sittner, W.T., "Modernization of National Weather Service River Forecasting Techniques", *Water Resources Bulletin*, American Water Resources Association, Aug., 1973.

16. Sittner, W.T., "WMO Project on Intercomparison of Conceptual Models Used in Hydrological Forecasting – – Report by WMO to the International Symposium on the Application of Mathematical Models in Hydrology and Water Resources Systems, Bratislava, 11 September, 1975", *Hydrological Sciences Bulletin*, International Association of Hydrological Sciences, Vol. 21,1, Mar., 1976.

17. Suguwara, M. et al., "Tank Model and its Application to Bird Creek, Wollombi Brook, Bikin River, Kitsu River, Sanaga River and Nam Mune", *Research Notes*, National Research Center for Disaster Prevention, No. 11, Tokyo, Japan, 1974.

18. Suguwara, M. et al., "Tank Model With Snow Component", *Research Notes*, National Research Center for Disaster Prevention, No. 65, Tokyo, Japan, 1984.

19. World Meteorological Organization, "Intercomparison of Conceptual Models Used in Operational Hydrological Forecasting", *Operational Hydrology Report No. 7*, Secretariat of the World Meteorological Organization, WMO No. 429, Geneva, Switzerland, 1975.

Data Transforms on USGS Surface Water Records

Lowell W. McBurney, Lawrence B. Schoch,
Peter J. Gabrielsen and Richard J. McClimans*

Abstract

Surface water records compiled and stored by the United
States Geological Survey (USGS) on machine readable tape are
transformed and analyzed by computer methods to enable visual
inspection of data and statistical relationships, and to
facilitate hydrologic modeling efforts. The work involves
(a) constructing a disk data set from a machine readable USGS
tape of mean daily flow (MDF) or gauge elevation (GE) values
for the period of record for a given gauging station; (b)
formatting the resultant values to Julian calendar days for
each year, and displaying such data; (c) developing average
MDF or GE and other statistics, for the Julian days of record;
and (d) graphing average MDF or GE and other statistics, as
a function of Julian calendar days beginning on October 1.

Research and development of valuable computational tools for the
water resource engineer was recently completed at the State University
of New York, College of Environmental Science and Forestry, Syracuse,
New York. The work included development of hydrologic models to aid
management efforts of the Hudson River-Black River Regulating District.
During this study, the need for easily accessible surface water records
was realized. Currently, the United States Geological Survey (USGS) (3)
catalogs and produces publications of these records on a regional basis.
In addition, the surface water records compiled by the USGS are stored
on machine readable computer tape. The USGS surface water publications
proved to be too cumbersome in the detailed analyses required of the
modeling studies. Efforts were then directed toward a procedure to retrieve and analyze information residing on the USGS magnetic tapes for
increased computational efficiency. The result of this procedure is a
formatted tabular representation of data (Figure 1) similar to the USGS
publications which are presented in a Julian calendar format and a graphical rendering of various statistical relationships (Figure 2) which are
presented in a water year calendar format. The advantage of this procedure is that the user has the freedom to select the gauging station(s)
and the year(s) of record under consideration, thus eliminating extrane-
ous information. Indeed this procedure possesses more utility than required of this single, independent research study since the construction

*McBurney, B.S. Forest Engineering, 1985; Schoch, M.S. 1984; Gabrielsen,
M.S. Candidate; McClimans, P.E., Member ASCE, Senior Research Associate,
State University of New York, College of Environmental Science and
Forestry, Syracuse, New York 13210.

MEAN DAILY FLOW VALUES, HUDSON RIVER AT HADLEY, (CFS)

---------------------------- YEAR=1980 ----------------------------

DAY	OCT	NOV	DEC	JAN	FEB	MAR	APR	MAY	JUN	JUL	AUG	SEP
1	1100	1900	7130	2300	1200	800	6640	6280	1280	926	991	628
2	1040	1870	5940	2100	1190	700	6590	5780	1610	1210	963	958
3	893	2400	5220	1800	1140	700	6180	5410	2020	1210	930	1240
4	1040	3210	4710	1600	1090	760	6470	5020	3730	1110	916	1190
5	1020	3200	4300	1570	1100	800	7860	4630	4390	976	883	1070
6	2860	2950	3960	1520	1000	873	7380	4290	3870	910	927	919
7	5880	2740	3750	1420	1000	859	6340	4000	3410	833	1290	792
8	4750	2630	3590	1300	1000	863	6490	3820	3110	867	1670	705
9	3770	2530	3270	1300	1000	882	8640	3720	2760	1020	1570	640
10	3280	3110	3070	1400	1000	957	21000	3620	2610	1260	1320	610
11	2970	4070	2940	1470	1000	950	18000	3420	2390	1270	1140	573
12	2800	4040	2870	2190	1000	961	13000	3240	2140	1150	989	556
13	3040	3620	2990	2570	1000	797	10900	2980	1920	1040	894	533
14	3140	3240	3080	2550	1000	848	10000	2860	1740	938	848	550
15	2960	2960	2870	3040	929	800	10700	2850	1570	854	834	586
16	2940	2740	2400	2800	702	912	11200	2630	1540	816	799	642
17	3010	2560	2000	2470	684	910	9550	2480	1500	745	810	776
18	2790	2430	1700	2360	740	1370	8110	2400	1340	689	772	845
19	2690	2330	1600	2200	800	1730	6860	2700	1190	661	727	876
20	2610	2240	1600	2100	922	1870	6100	3050	1140	612	680	965
21	2520	2160	1700	2020	1020	2810	5670	3120	1200	624	633	925
22	2470	2110	1700	1730	998	11000	5300	2850	1340	715	590	850
23	2380	2090	1800	1700	907	8610	4920	2570	1380	814	552	867
24	2280	2110	1970	1600	968	6930	4480	2320	1290	963	523	881
25	2460	2210	2370	1480	980	7120	4300	2130	1180	1040	501	835
26	2510	3090	3800	1500	900	6510	4870	1940	1080	995	479	918
27	2380	14700	4190	1500	800	5740	5240	1760	969	887	461	881
28	2230	14300	3700	1500	740	5450	5110	1610	867	948	451	1010
29	2120	10800	3260	1400	760	5900	6270	1500	807	1090	440	1160
30	2050	8640	2980	1300	0	7210	6790	1390	786	1110	468	1080
31	1970	0	2720	1230	0	7170	0	1290	0	1040	570	0

Figure 1

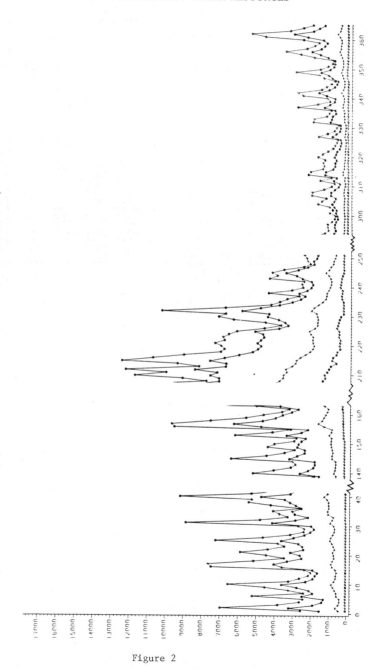

30-YEAR MEAN DAILY FLOW DATA (CFS), HOPE GAGE (WY 1951 – 1980)
WITH MEAN, MINIMUM AND MAXIMUM FLOW VALUES
(MEAN PLUS 2 STANDARD DEVIATIONS PLOTTED IN RED)

Figure 2

of the data base format is similar for all watersheds monitored by the
USGS. A standardized version would serve a diverse number of interests
in the field of water resource engineering. The basis of this report is
to describe the general procedures which were developed on an academic
mainframe computer system to satisfy project objectives.

The data transformation procedure is based on a series of interrelated computer programs. The data, consisting of the USGS surface
water records, is transformed into a usable format and subsequently
analyzed using various statistical functions. Relevant information for
this procedure on the USGS tape is mean daily flow (MDF) for stream
gauges and gauge elevation (GE) for reservoirs. In sequential order,
the steps of the data transformation include (a) the construction of a
disk (storage medium) data set from the raw information on the USGS
tape of MDF or GE for a given gauging station and the corresponding
period of record; (b) formatting the data into a suitable arrangement
for tabular representation similar to that published by the USGS; (c)
conversion from a Julian calendar to a water year calendar for plotting
purposes; (d) statistical analyses of information; and (e) graphical
representation of statistical relationships as a function of a water
year calendar. The IBM Conversational Monitoring System (CMS) (1) provided an operating environment for the analyses of the hydrologic data
using the Statistical Analysis System (SAS) (2).

The first step of the data analysis is accomplished by a program
entitled GETFLOW written using a combination of the system's job control
language (JCL) and SAS. The program's JCL statements provide batch processing information for data input and output, and SAS provides indexing, data formatting, and computational capabilities. The program
GETFLOW creates a disk data set by reading the USGS tape for a selected
gauging station and for a specified number of years. Desired selection
is achieved by modification of the GETFLOW program using the CMS line
editor. It seems useful to point out that the user need not have to
possess an intimate knowledge of the entire structure of the mechanics
and development of this software. A general understanding of CMS, the
computer programming environment, and the nature of the required program
modifications are necessary for efficient use of this data transformation procedure. Once GETFLOW has been executed, a data set containing
information in a proper, usable format is created on a system disk.
Generally, it is recommended that GETFLOW be performed for the period of
record for a given station. All of a station's available information
will then reside on disk storage at one location within the system and
only the desired period of record need be accessed as necessary for this
particular station. Each disk data set created by GETFLOW has a unique
identifier assigned to the stations by the modification of a three
letter acronym. Once GETFLOW has addressed all the stations and the
respective periods of record, the need for the tape is eliminated. All
the data has been catalogued and is on a system disk for future use.
Use of GETFLOW allows for the temporary procurement of the USGS tapes,
subsequent transfer and formatting of data, thereafter the tape can be
returned to its owner.

With specific reference to procurement of data, a user can contact
USGS and submit a request for data from specific gauging stations. Depending upon regional policy, the USGS will then prepare a transient

tape with the requested information and forward it to the user on a temporary loan basis. Use of GETFLOW creates the disk data sets from the data contained on the borrowed tape and places these files in storage for retrieval at a later date for further analyses. Subsequently the tape is returned to the USGS.

The next step is the production of a tabular representation of the USGS stream or reservoir data such as presented in Figure 1. TABLE2 is the title of this JCL-SAS program. TABLE2 requires and utilizes the system disk data set created by the program GETFLOW in the initial step of this procedure. Operationally TABLE2 is similar to GETFLOW, slight modifications of the station and year parameters are necessary to produce tables of the desired data. Also, appropriate changes in a title statement for the tables is necessary. The utility of performing GETFLOW for the entire record period only once is now evident. If all of a station's data is currently contained on a system disk data set, the user need only specify the desired years for which tabular output is required by use of the program TABLE2. An overall savings of computer processing time is realized by performing these programs in this more efficient manner. For example, assume GETFLOW has been previously performed for gauging station X for the calendar years 1920-1980, the station's entire period of record. User A desires tabular data for the years 1970-1975 for this station. This person would modify the station identifier in TABLE2 accordingly by specifying the assigned acronym for the disk data set for station X and change the year parameters to those desired. Upon execution of TABLE2, the program retrieves the previously created disk data set for station X and is only concerned with the years 1970-1975 in producing the tables of data. At a later date, user B requires tabular data for the same station but for the calendar years 1930-1950. User B would simply be required to change the year parameters in TABLE2, and the same disk data set would again be accessed by the program, but only for the years specified.

The third, fourth, and fifth steps are all accomplished by the same program. Entitled PLOTFLOW, this program is also written using a combination of JCL and SAS statements. The data used by PLOTFLOW is contained in the same system files originally created by GETFLOW. PLOTFLOW addresses these disk data sets for each individual station in the same manner as TABLE2. A title statement modification is once again necessary for the graphical output produced by this program. The format of the data up to this point has been on a Julian calendar year. For graphical purposes, a water year format was deemed more appropriate. PLOTFLOW transforms the format of the data into a water year calendar for this reason. Once the data has been converted to the water year calendar, PLOTFLOW performs a statistical analysis of the data. The program calculates for the specified period of record the mean, maximum, minimum, and the mean plus two standard deviations for the flow values concerned. PLOTFLOW continues by plotting these calculated statistics with the flow values (stream gauges) or elevation values (reservoirs) on the ordinate and water year days on the absissca. The plots produced by PLOTFLOW offer a pictorial representation of the hydrological activity of a particular gauging station throughout the course of a typical water-year for the specified period of record.

This data transformation process was developed using the available resources at the Syracuse University Academic Computing Center (SUACC). The utility of this procedure is indeed great, however the practical application as described is limited by the availability of the vast computational resources such as those offered by a large institution such as Syracuse University. In practice, the professional engineer probably does not have access to such resources. A user convenient and universal version of this procedure would allow greater freedom in data acquisition and analysis. The logical extension of this work, therefore, is to develop such a version.

A private consulting engineer has recently employed one of the authors to develop software for application of this procedure utilizing an IBM-PC-XT microcomputer. The goal of the work is to be able to deliver the USGS tape to a vendor equipped with a tape drive, then using a telecommunications software package, transmit and download the USGS data into the microcomputer unit where subsequent processing occurs. The need for the tape and a tape drive are still present, but the dependence upon a large main frame computer system has been removed. This application greatly improves the procedures reported herein.

References

1. International Business Machines Corp. (1980). "IBM Virtual Machine/ System Product: CMS User's Guide" 1980 edition. IBM Programming Publications. Endicott, New York.

2. SAS Institute Inc. (1979). "SAS Users Guide" 1979 Edition. SAS Institute Inc., Cary, North Carolina.

3. United States Geological Survey. (1977). Water Resources Data for New York, Water Year 1977. Volume 1, New York excluding Long Island. United States Geological Survey, Albany, New York 12201.

Real-Time Data Verification

Kevin J. O'Brien,[1] AM. ASCE, and Thomas N. Keefer,[2] M. ASCE

Abstract

Recent improvements in the real-time acquisition of hydro-meteorological data have raised concerns regarding the quality of the data received. Water users having practically instant access to conditions in the field, are making water control decisions whose impact could be devastating if invalid data are used. This paper presents several techniques used in the verification process and reviews their performance. The discussion is limited to real-time data verification; thus, the techniques used are without the aid of human intervention via graphic analysis or complete time series statistical analysis. The real-time analyses described are already operational at over five locations throughout the United States.

Introduction

Data base management of large, satellite-based, hydro-meteorological (hydromet) data collection systems involves collecting and transmitting data values in the field, receiving and decoding (processing) the data at a central site, and archiving the data for use by water managers. Because such a system allows users instant access to data, data verification must be performed in real-time. Real-time data verification refers to the quality control analyses of individual, or unit, data values the instant the value is received. To ensure timely performance of data processing, the data verification is performed during the decoding/processing step.

Data verification is an extremely important tool in the management of a hydromet system. Large hydromet systems often involve over 200 remote sites (or stations) each day collecting over 100,000 unit values. The manual evaluation of these data values is an enormous task even with the aid of graphic analysis. However, the quality of the data available is extremely important in the modeling of hydrologic processes, and data verification must be performed. Figure 1 illustrates the difficulty encountered when data verification is not

----

1. Water Resources Engineer, The Sutron Corporation, 2190 Fox Mill Road, Herndon, VA 22071.

2. Vice President, Water Resources Division, The Sutron Corporation, 2190 Fox Mill Road, Herndon VA 22071.

performed. The values of temperature, in degrees fahrenheit, for February 21, 1985 are shown with and without data verification. Without verification, the minimum observed temperature would be archived as approximately -95 °F (200 K). With verification, the minimum observed temperature is approximately -12°F (250 K). Real-time flood forecasting for snowmelt-prone areas is often handled by an index model based primarily on daily temperature fluctuations (2). The incorrect minimum temperature of -95 °F (200 K)degrees would seriously affect a forecast based upon a daily average temperature technique.

FEB. 21, 1985

TEMPERATURE IN°FARENHEIT

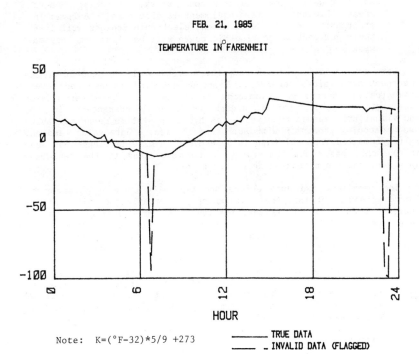

Note: K=(°F-32)*5/9 +273

_____ TRUE DATA
_____ _ INVALID DATA (FLAGGED)

FIG. 1.-REAL-TIME VERIFICATION FOR JACKSON WYOMING TEMPERATURE DATA

The cause of such an error in a unit value is typically either of the following:

o Data communication errors. The primary source of errors lies with the quality of the data transmission. Typically, data are lost completely during a transmission failure. Occasionally, the loss of a digit in a unit value occurs.

o Sensors and recording equipment errors. Errors are often caused in the field by improper operation of equipment. In the case of a stream gage, floats become stuck, intakes at stilling wells clog, float tapes break, or drive chains break. Electronic field equipment is also a major culprit in equipment errors. Quite often, electronic sensors will lose their calibration or electric power will be lost or become weak.

Data communication errors comprise approximately 98 percent of the incorrect data values received. A proper decoding package can detect communication errors by examining the length of the transmission received, or detect parity errors or illegal characters in the individual unit values received. The hydromet systems described above use a decoding processor with such capabilities; a data value (and any values computed from it) that is determined invalid is flagged as such in the data base, and therefore, is not subjected to the real-time data verification processes described below.

The remaining two data errors are typically caused by sensor or recording equipment failures. Alexander (1) details the United States Geological Survey's (USGS) verification plan for hydrologic data for detecting these errors. The plan is based on a combination of traditional manual-verification procedures and three techniques for use in real-time, namely: upper and lower exceedance limits, rate-of-change checks, and instrument deadband or no-change checks. The three real-time techniques are presently utilized in a real-time data verification analysis of hydromet data for several agencies including the State of Colorado, Omaha District of the Corps of Engineers (COE), Utah State University, and the Northern Colorado Water Conservancy District.

Data Verification Techniques

Multiple data verification techniques must be used to completely define the occurrence of invalid data, because of the variability in error sources previously discussed. The techniques mentioned above, upper and lower exceedance limits, rate-of-change checks, and no change checks, are described in more detail below.

A high/low limit (LIM) implies that an upper and lower window (or limit) are allowed on a variable. If a value is greater than (or less than) some predefined limit, that value will be flagged. This is the simplest data verification technique and also the most useful.

The rate-of-change limit (ROC) compares a value with its previous value, and computes the difference between the two. The difference is then divided by the number of minutes between the values. The rate of change can then be compared against an upper and lower (negative rate of change) limit. This analysis is particularly useful when evaluating randomly transmitted data.

A continual no-change (NOC) limit watches a value to detect the occurrence of a prolonged period in which a value has not changed. This technique is particularly useful in catching stuck floats. A deadband can be supplied (e.g., 0.01 feet for a stream gage) to allow for minor fluctuations in the value.

Quite obviously, an important factor in using any of these techniques is the knowledge of the proper verification criteria to be applied for each unit value. Alexander (1) states that the primary problem with computerized verification is how to store and use the verification criteria once they are developed. He also states that these criteria must be allowed to change with time (or at least season). Lystrom (3) suggests using a curve fitting-procedure to express the criteria as a function of time using polynomial equations. The hydromet data management system described above uses a master configuration file (MCF) to control the limits for each station's data verification. The controlling limits are routinely adjusted (system wide) to allow for monthly, weekly, or even daily updates on system data verification limits criteria.

Real-Time Data Verification Results

The two bad values of temperature shown in Figure 1 were detected as invalid by a LIM function and flagged as appropriate. This station, at Jackson, Wyoming, had a lower limit of -50°F (230 K). The upper limit of temperature at this station was set at +60°F (290 K). These limits will be shifted upwards by approximately 50°F (280 k) during the coming summer season.

Reasonable limits on a rate-of-change function are difficult to define for temperature variations during a 15-minute time interval. This function can more aptly be applied to stream gage height or discharge. Figure 2 illustrates the use of the ROC function on discharge data from a stream-gaging station on the Owyhee River near Rome, Oregon. The rate-of-change limits were set at 100.0 cfs (2.80 m³/s) for both increasing and decreasing rates of change.

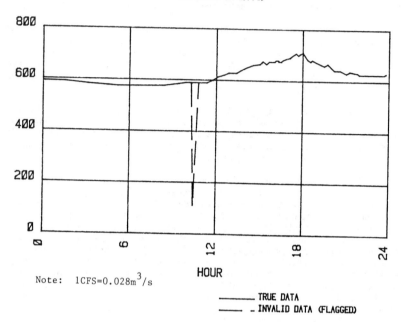

Note: 1CFS=0.028m^3/s

FIG. 2.-ROC LIMIT EXCEEDANCE AT ROME, OREGON

During winter seasons, ice jams often distort stream gage data. The NOC function can be applied to a station's data to determine the occurrence of continual repetition of a value which might be caused by such a jam. Figure 3 shows the use of the NOC on the Snake River near Alpine, Wyoming. Inspection of the figure shows that the NOC function did not detect (and therefore flag) all of the bad data, but only that which exceeded a counting limit of 24 unit values without changing. No additional ROC or LIM checking was performed; thus, the inverted spike at approximately 08:00 AM was not flagged as invalid. The counting was reinitialized following the spike, and approximately 6 hours later, the NOC function began flagging the data. The NOC function is primarily useful for notifying the system manager of the possibility of ice jams or other sensor problems.

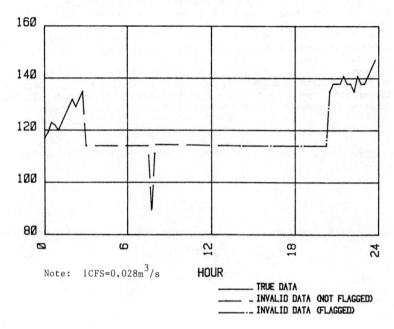

Note: 1CFS=0.028m³/s   **HOUR**

———— TRUE DATA
——— _ INVALID DATA (NOT FLAGGED)
———.._ INVALID DATA (FLAGGED)

FIG. 3.-NOC LIMIT EXCEEDANCE AT ALPINE, WYOMING

    The three techniques shown could easily be applied to a variety of
data values. The analysis could have been performed by comparing data
from different sources (interstation comparisons), such as LIM
function on the difference in cumulative precipitation between two
weather stations that behave the same meteorologically.

Summary

    The basic components of a real-time data verification scheme have
been successfully applied to several large hydromet systems, and shown
to be an effective tool for system data management. The need for
real-time data verification is clearly evident to any system manager
responsible for the quality of a data base. The three techniques
shown each represent a specific response to the wide variety of
problems which occur in connection with real-time data collection.

Appendix A - References

1. Alexander, C. W, "Verification Plan For Hydrologic Data," Report No. 82-374, United States Department of the Interior, Geological Survey, Portland, Oregon, 1982, pp. 1-22.
2. Bend, D. H., and McBean, E. A., "River Flow Forecasting Model For Sturgeon River," Journal of Hydraulic Engineering, ASCE, Vol. 111, No. 2, Feb., 1985, pp. 315-333. 3.
3. Lystrom, D. J., "Analysis of Potential Errors in Real-Time Streamflow Data and Methods of Data Verification by Digital Computer," Open-File Report, United States Department of the Interior, Geological Survey, Reston, Virginia, 1972, pp. 1-41.

Program Monitoring by Database Management

Jonathan P. Deason,* M. ASCE

Abstract: Management of the water resources programs of the Army Corps of Engineers, with its $3 billion annual budget, 27,000 employees, and decentralized organizational structure, is obviously a difficult task. Fortunately, however, recent advances in computer-based management information systems are enabling top managers to increase significantly the timeliness, accuracy, and relevance of information used for decision-making. One very recent application of this new technology uses the database management approach to monitor the hundreds of formal contracts and agreements the Corps negotiates annually in carrying out its water resources programs. This new management information system, developed under the direction of the Assistant Secretary of the Army (Civil Works), enables top managers to track 13 key data elements on 21 categories of agreements, from water supply contracts to historic preservation agreements, as they proceed through various stages of negotiation and approval.

Introduction

How does one manage a Federal government organization with 27,000 employees, a $3 billion annual budget, and a worldwide geographic disperion? "With great difficulty," one might respond. Although this rather cynical response may still have a lot of truth in it, it is less true now than in the past.

Recent advances in computer-based management information systems are enabling top managers to increase significantly the timeliness, accuracy, and relevance of information used for decision making. One very recent application of this new technology uses the database management approach to monitor the hundreds of formal contracts and agreements the Army Corps of Engineers negotiates in carrying out its water resources programs.

To describe the application, an explanation of the database management concept is presented initially. Then a statement of the problem is set forth, followed by a description of the new database management system that was used to solve the problem. This paper is intended to help other potential users understand the benefits of database management systems so that they might take advantage of the concept to improve their own management systems.

*Special Assistant for Water Resources, Office, Assistant Secretary of the Army (Civil Works), Room 7126, 20 Massachusetts Avenue, N.W., Washington, D.C. 20314

What is a Database Management System?

Perhaps the best way to explain the database management concept is to use an example. Suppose a certain organization decides to place its personnel records into one or more computer files. Finding this to be a success, it later chooses to automate its payroll, followed by its training program files, security clearance files, work scheduling files, and other functions. Having thus completed automating all of its files concerning personnel actions, however, the organization would still be faced with the task of updating many files every time an employee obtained a promotion, changed jobs, changed a home address, or experienced any of a number of conceivable changes that could affect more than one file.

Database management systems are designed to overcome such inefficiencies. Under the database concept, only one master file, containing all the information needed for any planned application, is maintained. Thus, even though a piece of information, such as an employee address, is needed for multiple applications (e.g., payroll and alert rosters), it is kept in only one file. A computer program called a database management system (DBMS) allows the user to retrieve information from the master file to satisfy all planned applications. Generally, the master file is referred to as a database and the software needed to permit selective sorting and retrieval is called a DBMS. A fully developed system to meet identified management needs may be referred to as one type of a management information system (MIS).

Not only does the database concept eliminate effort wasted in updating duplicative data, it also makes it far easier to sort data into desired order, extract certain data buried in a large file (separate the "wheat from the chaff"), and combine data that previously may have been scattered among a number of files. One can readily imagine many applications of the database concept: inventory control, real estate sales, and medicine, just to name a few. It is no wonder that DBMS software has proliferated in recent years as microcomputers with sufficient power to handle them have come within the grasp of many businesses. These literally number in the hundreds and some, such as dBase III, Condor, VisiFile, PFS:File, and InfoStar, are becoming household names.

A Water Resources Program Management Problem

Effective execution of the missions assigned to the Army Corps of Engineers requires the negotiation of many types of formal agreements with other Federal agencies, state and local governments, foreign nations, private industries, and other parties. These agreements cover such disparate subjects as cost sharing, historic preservation, dredged material disposal, and law enforcement services.

The wide geographic dispersion and decentralized organizational structure of the Corps dictates that most of the agreements should be negotiated at the field level. However, many of these agreements have significant policy implications and almost all are unique in some respects. A continuing problem has been insuring that commitments made in these agreements are consistent with national policies, without causing top managers to become buried in an avalanche of details.

In October 1982, the Assistant Secretary of the Army for Civil Works saw a need to provide closer management oversight to these agreements. Toward that end, he asked the Chief of Engineers to provide a quarterly report of the status of all agreements concerning the Civil Works programs. The manual reporting system that grew out of that request, while useful to top management, proved to have a number of disadvantages:

Excessive volume - The large number of entries on the quarterly report greatly reduced the usefulness of the document. Most applications were limited to specific areas. For example, some uses of the report were concerned only with functional areas (e.g., water supply contracts); others focused on geographic areas (e.g., agreements affecting the Tulsa District); others were concerned only with agreements in certain stages of review (e.g., those that had reached Division level in the review process); and still others were limited to specific time frames (e.g., agreements approved within the last year). However, the compilation of all agreements into a single report made the document so lengthy (typically about 35 pages long) that use was discouraged.

Insufficient Detail - The amount of information provided about each agreement was insufficient to meet the needs of top management. However, increasing the level of detail would have exacerbated the problems of excessive volume, noted above.

Lack of Timeliness - Since the report was compiled on a quarterly basis and took some time to process through the organizational structure, much of the information it contained was out of date by the time it was available to top management.

Expense - Compilation of the quarterly report and processing it through the organizational hierarchy required an inordinate commitment of human resources.

A New Database Management System

To overcome these problems, the Assistant Secretary directed in June 1984 that the manual system be replaced by a computer based management information system. This new system, which became fully operational in May 1985, uses a software product called INFO 921, which is a relational database management system marketed by Henco Software, Inc., of Waltham, Massachusetts. The system resides in a Harris 500 minicomputer located in the Office of the Chief of Engineers in Washington, D.C. It is accessible via modem by terminals and microcomputers from all Corps Division and District offices throughout the world. During the course of its development, the new MIS acquired the name Memoranda of Agreement Tracking System, or "MOA."

The MOA format allows 13 types of information (fields) to be entered into the system for each agreement that is tracked. These are listed in Table 1. The system has the capability of sorting and retrieving based on information in six of the fields, which are marked with asterisks in Table 1. For example, one user may wish to see only those agreements currently under negotiation by the North Central Division, and thus would

Table 1. MOA Information Fields

Item Name	Description	Example	Type & No. Characters
Agreement Name	Brief name or subject of agreement	-	100 AN
Agreement Type*	Water supply contract, FWCA agreement, etc.	WS	10 A
File Number*	Unique # assigned by originating office	LMK001	6 AN
Status & Date*	Reflects status and date of milestone	K 6-12-83	10 AN
Implementation*	Likely or projected date of implementation	Late 1984	10 AN
FOA contact	Last name, phone number of field contact	Watterson 202-272-0118	25 AN
State*	State in which project is located	WA	10 A
Corps Project	Name of Corps project	Stonewall Jackson L&D	50 AN
Army Signer	Proposed signer in HQDA or USACE	SACW	25 A
Other Signer	Other agency signer or signature level	WA DOT	25 A
Proponent*	Organization symbol of submitting office	DAEN-CWR-W	10 A
Last Update	Date file was last updated	1-26-84	8 AN
Remarks	Space for additional comments		100 AN

sort on the "Proponent" field. Another user might wish to see only those agreements under negotiation that relate to projects in Oklahoma, and would sort on the "State" field.

All of the fields in Table 1 are self-explanatory, except for the "Agreement Type" and "Status and Date" fields. Table 2 lists the 21 possible entries in the "Agreement Type" field. These correspond to the

Table 2. Types of Agreements

Acronym	Definition
ADM SUPP	Administrative support
ARCH	Archeological preservation
DREDGE	Dredged material disposal site
EVAC	Evacuation procedure agreement
FED ENGR	Federal Engineer agreement
FLOW	Flow control agreement
FWCAA	Fish & Wildlife Coordination activity
HIST PRES	Historic preservation
HP	Hydropower(includes FERC licensing)
JOINT O&M	O&M sharing with another agency
PERMIT	Regulatory activity
PLAN	Agreement for feasibility phase and DPR
POLICE	Law enforcement procedure agreement
R&D	Reimbursable R&D work by laboratories
REC	Recreation contract
REIM	Reimbursable work for others
SECT 14	Section 14 agreement
SECT 221	Section local cooperation agreement
WS	Water supply contract
MULTI	More than a single type
OTHER	None of the above (use remarks)

21 types of agreements that are tracked by the MIS. Table 3 lists the 13 possible entries in the "Status Code" portion of the "Status Code & Date" field. These 13 entries represent the 13 stages through which agreements proceed from conception to implementation.

It is not difficult to imagine a wide variety of ways in which the sorting and retrieval capabilities of MOA are being used. One application, for example, may be concerned only with municipal and industrial water supply contracts in the southeastern region of the Nation that have not yet reached the Washington review level. Another application may involve retrieval of all regulatory agreements under development in the eastern half of the United States, sorted alphabetically by state.

MOA has the capablitiy of providing three levels of output displays. The lowest level ("quick list") simply provides a listing of record numbers and agreement names. The middle level ("short list") provides record numbers, status codes, dates, agreement types, and agreement names. The highest level ("full display") displays all fields for each record requested.

Figure 1 provides an illustrative example of a typical use of the "short list" output display. This list was compiled by MOA in response to a request for all Fish and Wildlife Coordination Act agreements in the master database under some stage of negotiation in the North Atlantic Division of the Corps of Engineers, sorted according to status code.

Table 3. MOA Status Codes

Status Code	Status Description
A	Preliminary discussion stage only
B	Discussions have commenced with second party, but no draft agreement has been provided
C	Proponent has developed a draft agreement
D	Draft agreement has been reviewed by other party
E	Draft agreement has been submitted to respective Division Office for comment
F	Draft agreement has been reviewed by OCE
G	Draft agreement has been reviewed by OASA(CW)
H	Final agreement has been prepared by CE proponent, but it has not yet been approved
I	Final agreement has been signed by second party
J	Final agreement has been signed by respective District Office
K	Final agreement has been approved by respective Division Office
L	Final agreement has been approved by HQUSACE
M	Final agreement has been approved by OASA(CW)

Figure 2 provides an example output display of another typical application of MOA. The listing in Figure 2 was compiled by MOA in response to a request for a listing of agreements of all types with status code "K", sorted by date. This provides a listing of all agreements that have been approved at Division level, and which are awaiting action by Headquarters, Office of the Chief of Engineers. The sorting by date enables the program managers to focus on those that have been awaiting action the longest period of time.

The advantages of MOA over the manual reporting system it replaced are easy to identify. The output displays illustrated in Figures 1 and 2 can be created by a manager in only a matter of minutes from the time the power switch on the terminal is activated. This compares with an hour or more that may have been required to compile a similar list from the 35 page hard-copy report previously used. The typical user requires less than an hour's training to operate the new user-friendly management information system efficiently.

In addition to greatly increased speed of retrieval, MOA provides significantly more information in its 13 information fields than the five entries of the hard-copy report used previously. Since one of the fields contains the name and telephone number of a field-level point of contact for each agreement, additional information can be readily obtained at any time.

```
FILE *STATUS AND*   TYPE   *AGREEMENT
NUMBER*  DATE   *AGREEMENT *  NAME
--------------------------------------------------------------
NAP004 D  1- 9-85 FCWAA     HARBOR OF REFUGE SCOPE OF WORK
NAN303 J 12-14-84 FCWAA     KILL VAN KULL - NEWARK CHANNEL CP&E
NAN505 K 10-25-84 FCWAA     SAWKILL CREEK FLOOD CONTROL PROJECT
NAN508 K 10-31-84 FCWAA     NEW YORK HARBOR & ADJACENT CHANNELS
NAN517 M 11- 8-84 FCWAA     PASSIAC RIVER MAINSTEM
NAN617 M 10- 1-84 FCWAA     RAMAPO BEACH RESTORATION
NAN717 M 10- 1-84 FCWAA     THIRD RIVER
NAN817 M 10- 1-84 FCWAA     ROCKAWAY BEACH RESTORATION
```

Figure 1. Short List Display Example 1

```
FILE *STATUS AND*   TYPE   *AGREEMENT
NUMBER*  DATE   *AGREEMENT *  NAME
--------------------------------------------------------------
NPP004 K  2-10-84 MULTI     KILLS CREEK LAKE RESOURCE MANAGEMENT
NED001 K  7- 1-84 HP        DEWEY MILLS PROJECT (CONST + STUDIES)
POD002 K  7-24-84 WFOD      SAIPAN RIVER DOCK FACILITY
NEDP04 K 10- 1-84 WFOD      NERR CORRIDOR UPGRADE, NEW LONDON, CT
NAN505 K 10-25-84 FCWAA     SANKILL CREEK FLOOD CONTROL PROJECT
NAN508 K 10-31-84 FCWAA     NEW YORK HARBOR & ADJACENT CHANNELS
NCD100 K 12-14-84 WFOD      DOE NUCLEAR WASTE DEPOSIT IN SALT SITES
POD003 K  1- 4-85 WFOD      KEKAHA SHORELINE REVETMENT
POD004 K  1-25-85 WFOD      ANJOTA ISLAND REVETMENT
POD001 K  1-26-85 WFOD      NANPIL RIVER HYDROPOWER
```

Figure 2. Short List Display Example 2

A third advantage of MOA involves timeliness of information. MOA is a real-time management information system in that entries are available to all levels of management as soon as they are entered into the system. This is a distinct improvement over the manual reporting system in which information may have been a month old or more when first made available to top management.

Finally, use of MOA instead of the hard-copy reporting system has greatly reduced the level of manpower required to provide the information. A single entry at any level of the organization is sufficient to make the information available immediately to the entire organization. This eliminates many levels of review and handling previously required in data compilation and updating. Although these savings have not been quantified, it is clear that they far outweigh the costs of developing and implementing the new management information system.

Conclusion

This relatively simple case study illustrates one application of the database management concept in a major Federal water resources program. This new information management technique has a wide array of potential uses in water resources information systems. Hopefully, this straightforward example will help other potential users to understand the benefits of database management systems and encourage them to take advantage of recent explosive advances in information technology to improve their own management systems.

Microcomputer-Based Monthly Treatment Reporting
Richard R. Noss, A. M., ASCE and Kevin T. Lautz*

Abstract:

    Massachusetts wastewater treatment plants must file monthly
operating reports with the Massachusetts Division of Water
Pollution Control. The current form is four pages long and must be
filled out by hand.

A microcomputer-based monthly reporting system has been developed
to replace the current handwritten forms. The system includes:
(1) interactive software which will allow plant operators to enter
and store data using a microcomputer, (2) a communications program
to accomplish data transfer (via telephone) to the Division's computer, and (3) software for the Division's engineers to review the
monthly data. The Division's software package includes report generation, compliance checking, performance evaluations and graphical
presentations of selected parameters.

This paper presents the overall system and reports on an ongoing
pilot implementation of the system at three treatment plants.

INTRODUCTION

    Each wastewater treatment plant in Massachusetts must submit a
monthly report of operational data to the appropriate regional office of the Massachusetts Division of Water Pollution Control
(MDWPC). These reports are used for several purposes. The MDWPC
checks the effluent data for compliance with the plant's National
Pollutant Discharge Elimination System (NPDES) Permit. In addition, the monthly operating reports are reviewed by MDWPC engineers
to assess plant performance and determine the degree of plant
utilization. The monthly data can also be used for preliminary
troubleshooting of plants that are performing poorly and to identify other plants with sub-optimal performance.

---

*Assistant Professor and Graduate Research Asst., respectively,
Environmental Engineering Program, Dept. of Civil Engineering,
Univ. of Massachusetts, Amherst, MA 01003.

The current data management system begins with tabular monthly operating reports prepared by the treatment plant operators. The MDWPC provides a four page monthly operating report form for this purpose, but many treatment plant operators prefer to use their own forms. As a result, the MDWPC receives over 100 operating reports with a variety of different formats each month. Report contents vary from the 81 parameters required by the MDWPC to more elaborate forms with additional parameters and diagnostic evaluations.

After a required check of regulatory performance requirements, the most important task of the Division engineers is to "troubleshoot" treatment plants which are operating poorly. Due to budget cutbacks and an ever-increasing number of permit holders, Division Engineers find they do not have time to fully process all of the report forms.

The Division has recognized that the current system is inadequate. It is too time consuming and wastes staff abilities on routine performance checks that could be automated. Furthermore, the handwritten forms are poorly suited to subsequent use of the data in performance evaluation modeling or even for statistical purposes.

OPTICAL SCANNING FORMS

In an attempt to remedy this situation, research began in June, 1974, by DiGiano et al. on a computer program to analyze treatment plant data ("Diagnostic Testing of Efficiency by Computerization of Treatment Reports" [DTECTR]). This work is reported in references 1 and 2.

DiGiano et al. developed an optical scanning form which was to be filled out by the treatment plant operators instead of the MDWPC's tabular report form. The optical scanning forms could then be read automatically and the data entered directly to computer files. This would eliminate keypunching the data, a task which is often a major bottleneck and a major source of errors in computer data management systems.

The old optical scanning form handled four days of data per sheet for a very limited number of parameters (see Figure 1). Two days of data were tightly fit onto each side. No decimal points were present to help the operator place significant figures. Instead of a circle response or bubble sheet, the form used fill-in bar responses. This type of optical scanning form is now obsolete and cannot be processed.

A pilot scale study of implementation of the optical scanning form-DTECTR program system was conducted at three wastewater treat-ment plants. Plant operators involved in the study completed

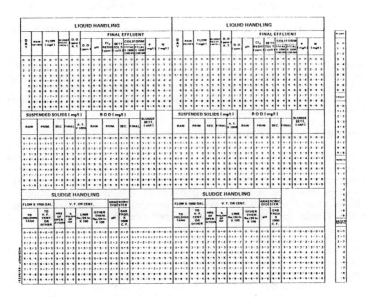

Figure 1. Previous Optical Scanning Form

the forms for processing and were then asked to comment on the format of the forms.

The operators found the op-scan forms more cumbersome to fill out than the tabular form. Furthermore, since the op-scan forms did not have space for all the parameters customarily reported, the operators found that they were filling out both the old form and the op-scan form. Despite the objections and additional work involved, the operators were supportive of the MDWPC's objectives and felt that the long range benefits would justify the inconvenience.

Unfortunately, the work begun in 1974 was not maintained and, as of 1981, both the program and the optical scanning form were out of date, leading to the initiation of the work conducted by the authors.

The original intent of the work that began in 1981 (again funded by the MDWPC) was to rework the data processing program,

DTECTR, and to prepare an optical scanning form that could be read
by currently available equipment.

The revised optical-scanning form included more parameters,
built-in decimal points and space to write in the parameter values
above the columns of circles, and space for handwritten comments.
Unfortunately, because of the changed technology each form would
hold only one day's data. It soon became apparent that full scale
implementation of this approach would involve handling a ton of
paper (literally). Nonetheless, the monthly reporting/evaluating
process with the op-scan forms and the DTECTR model was estimated
to be 35 percent cheaper than the status quo. Furthermore, most of
the savings was in MDWPC personnel time - time which therefore
would become available for troubleshooting and technical assistance
to treatment plant operators.

MICROCOMPUTER BASED REPORTING

The most attractive feature of the op-scan form system was the
ability to go directly from the operator's completed monthly report
to a computer data file. The difficulty was to accomplish this via
a procedure that the operators would accept and use without the
procedure itself causing mistakes and errors. As mentioned above,
even the simple op-scan forms encountered operator resistance.

Terminals connected via modem to a central computer were
briefly considered as an alternative to the op-scan form. Computer
terminals would also allow data to be entered directly into the
computer from the operators without an intervening data transcription step. This alternative was rejected because operator
acceptance was doubtful. In many respects terminals are the
epitome of black box technology.

About this time, Apple, Osborne and IBM were revolutionizing
the microcomputer market. Microcomputers became self contained,
thereby eliminating a lot of the high-tech phobia engendered by
terminals. Microcomputers are versatile - a microcomputer in a
treatment plant could be put to many uses (operator training, inventory management, process evaluation/simulation, maintenance
records, scheduling, and accounting as well as management of
operating data). They are relatively inexpensive. And most importantly, they are "user-friendly", i.e. a minimum amount of
specialized training is required to use them.

Furthermore, discussions with a sample of wastewater treatment
plant operators indicated that microcomputers would be well
received by the operators. They recognized the many ways microcomputer based software could assist their operations. In fact many
of the operators commented that they were trying to convince their
superintendents and town councils to include a microcomputer in
their next budget.

Accordingly the decision was made to adapt the data collection
system to microcomputers and pilot-test it at treatment plants that

already possessed microcomputers. For the pilot testing program, operators periodically entered the data using a "user-friendly" data collection program, which would concurrently store the data onto a diskette. After all the data for one month was collected and stored, the operator would then transfer the diskette files electronically to a VAX 11/780 minicomputer (located on the University of Massachusetts/Amherst campus). The DTECTR program (which resides on the VAX) would then access these files to process the data and generate a report.

The data collection software has been written entirely in BASIC. Commercially available software such as spreadsheet and data base management programs provide more efficient and flexible data entry and editing capabilities - but they are machine-specific. The software described here is generic, that is, it will run on all of the machines currently owned by the local treatment plants. (We use a vended software package to rewrite the programs on properly formatted diskettes for use on other machines.) Standardization, which is highly desirable from the state agency's point of view, is achieved by using "lowest common denominator" programming since the hardware is not standardized.

SYSTEM DESCRIPTION

The DTECTR system has three main components: data collection, data transfer, and data processing.

Data Collection. This component, located on the premises of each treatment plant, consists of a microcomputer (e.g. IBM-PC, Apple II, Rainbow 100, etc.) and specialized software which will guide the plant operator in entering and storing the data for eventual transfer to the data analysis component of the system.

The hardware requirements consist of a microcomputer/personal computer (128K memory is adequate) with video display, keyboard, and two 5 1/4" diskette drives, all of which are standard equipment for the better quality machines. A printer, although useful, is not required.

The data collection software package consists of seven "subprograms" linked together by a main program. These "subprograms" are as follows:

DAILY   for entering daily operational data.

BODSS   for entering BOD and suspended solids data.

ACTSLDG for entering activated sludge data.

SLUDGE   for entering sludge processing data.

EDITOR   for reviewing and editing previously entered data.

FORMAT   for formatting the data so that it is consistent with
          the input requirements of the data analysis
          component; used prior to data transfer.

STARTUP   for initializing data files prior to entering a new
          month's data.

The entire package is user friendly, i.e., it requires minimal
formal training on the part of the operator. To run the package,
all the operator needs to do is "load" program MAIN from the BASIC
interpreter of his or her particular machine, and "run" it. A main
menu and several sub-menus are used to move between and within the
seven options. Requests for information or responses are clear,
yet concise, and have error-trapping capabilities which will issue
a message to the operator informing him or her that the input is
unacceptable and then allow the data to be reentered.

The data input and output sections are both organized into
four main groups: daily operational data, BOD/suspended solids
data, activated sludge data, and sludge processing data. Within
each main group are one or more subgroups, each containing closely
related information. For example, within the daily operational
group, there are subgroups for weather and flow data,
chlorination/coliforms data, wastewater characteristics, and
nutrient data. Data may be viewed on the screen, edited, or routed
to a printer at any time. When all the data is entered for a particular month, it can be formatted for transfer automatically using
the FORMAT procedure.

In addition, several more features are currently under
development, including routine calculations (parameter averages and
medians), data archiving, and trend analysis using low-resolution
graphics. These features will be included in an updated version of
the data collection package.

Data Transfer. Once the data is formatted, it may be sent
electronically to the data analysis location using telephone lines
and the appropriate hardware and software. Elements of this component will be found both at the local treatment plant and the data
analysis location.

Hardware requirements for this component consist of an
asynchronous communications adapter, a modulator-demodulator
(modem), and a telephone at the treatment plant, with analogous
equipment at the receiving end. A "communications" software
package is required to coordinate the transfer of data files and
verify their integrity at the receiving end. For the purposes of
the pilot implementation, a public domain program called KERMIT was
used.

The data transfer procedure involves establishing a telephone
link with the computer on which the data analysis component resides
(through the asynchronous adapter and modem), and then using KERMIT

to actually transfer the files. Once the files are transferred, they may be accessed directly by the data analysis component.

Data Analysis. The DTECTR data analysis program uses appropriate calculations and modeling approaches, as well as graphical and statistical analyses, to turn raw data into meaningful information. This information would be used by MDWPC engineers for compliance checking and problem solving. This component would tentatively be located in each of the MDWPC regional offices, as well as in a central (archive) location to be determined by the Division.

The hardware requirements for this component include a mini-computer (e.g. VAX 11/750, IBM System 32) for the central location, and microcomputers with large memory capabilities (e.g. DEC 350 w/hard drive or IBM-PC XT) for the regional offices. While the mini-computer specified as the Division's central computer will be much more than adequate for handling the compliance checking and review activities, it is anticipated that the system will be used for other activities, such as water quality modeling, record-keeping, and word processing. Prior to acquisition of its own system, the Division could access DTECTR at its current location, a VAX 11/780 on the University of Massachusetts campus.

The data analysis program is a rewritten and modified version of the original DTECTR program. DTECTR prints a standard monthly operating data report form, does special analyses of BOD and suspended solids removals and the sludge handling system, checks and reports compliance with NPDES permit conditions and selected plant design parameters, and prints selected graphs for visual comparison of trends, including multi-year trends making use of historical data that is stored on each plant's permanent data file. A scaled down version of DTECTR has been written in BASIC and will also be implemented on the individual plant's microcomputers. Figures 2, 3, 4, and 5, in the Appendix present portions of the first four sections of output generated by DTECTR. Further modification of DTECTR is underway to improve the utility of the program, through better file handling and storage capabilities, more readable tables and graphs, more analytical capabilities (including statistical and modeling subroutines), and by allowing greater interaction on the part of the engineer operating the program.

Implementation Issues

In many respects the software development, though requiring significant effort, is only a small part of the overall implementation of a system using distributed microcomputers for monthly treatment plant reporting.

Software compatibility. Each of the programs that make up the reporting/data analysis system has undergone several rounds of testing and evaluation by treatment plant operators and/or MDWPC staff. The system, to be successful must: 1) run by itself and 2) provide more and/or better information than the current system. If

the software cannot be used by the operators without extensive or
continuous assistance from MDWPC engineers, then its advantages
will be cancelled and perhaps even outweighed, by the time consumed
in its operation. Similarly, the data analysis software has been
revised and refined to produce the information and analyses the
MDWPC engineers want and in the form that is most useful to them.
It is expected that that revision process will be ongoing as more
and more calculations and analyses are identified and added to the
program. Adding additional analyses will not make the program more
cumbersome to use because its menu-driven nature gives the user the
ability to generate only the information wanted.

Human factors. The many advantages of the microcomputer-based
reporting system over the current system do not guarantee its implementation and acceptance. A system which imposes additional
burdens on the operators may never be accepted, no matter how great
the advantages to the MDWPC. The pilot implementation, at plants
receptive to the use of new technology, provided important feedback
on the organization and sequencing of data entry procedures. Of
special interest were operators' suggestions for calculations, etc.
the software could do for them. (One operator said he would do
anything if the program would calculate monthly averages for him.)
As a result the data entry program may be augmented by a scaled-
down, microcomputer-based version of DTECTR, for use by the
operators themselves. Hopefully the report generation and analysis
capabilities of the DTECTR model will make clear the advantages to
the operators themselves of implementing the system.

Hardware Standardization. The requirement that any software
developed be implementable on any microcomputer has been a very
limiting constraint on this work. Yet there is no way to standard-
ize the hardware involved unless the MDWPC purchases the
microcomputers and gives them to the local treatment plants (an option that is not financially feasible at present). Even then,
because of state bidding procedures, there appears to be no way to
anticipate the the model to be purchased ahead of time; that is, it
is not possible to develop machine-specific software (making use of
vended software) in advance of the actual purchase of the
microcomputers. Nonetheless, the ability to incorporate the power,
flexibility and versatility of some vended software is very appealing and every effort is being made to identify a means of
standardizing the hardware in the local treatment plants.

Legal Issues. The submission of monthly reports and signed attes-
tations of their accuracy are legal requirements. One advantage of
the data transfer software is that it verifies that the monthly
data has beenn received by the MDWPC's host computer. Perhaps
passwords and encryption will satisfy the need to provide proof of
origin and protection against tampering.

Appendix - Sample DTECTR Output

SECTION I I

TABULATION OF DAILY OPERATIONAL DATA

PLANT NUMBER 1 : MODIFIED ACTIVATED SLUDGE

DAY	RAINFALL (inches)	AVE. FLOW (mgd)	PEAK FLOW (mgd)	RECYC FLOW (mgd)	DO: AER TANK (mg/l)	MLSS (ml/l)	SVI (ml/g)	F/M RATIO (/days)	CHLORINE RESIDUAL (mg/l)	TOTAL COLIFORM (/100 ml)	FECAL COLIFORM (/100 ml)	PHOS (mg/l)	AMM NIT (mg/l)	NO3 NIT (mg/l)
1	0.00	3.06	4.10	0.00	0.0	2240.0	0.00	0.00	0.60	95.0	0.0	2.4	7.8	0.51
2	0.02	3.14	4.40	0.00	14.4	2235.0	0.00	0.00	1.40	0.0	0.0	0.0	0.0	0.00
3	0.06	3.10	4.40	0.00	0.0	0.0	0.09	0.00	1.30	0.0	0.0	0.0	0.0	0.00
4	0.01	3.01	[illegible]	[illegible]			[illegible]	[illegible]	2.30	0.0	0.0	0.0	0.0	0.00

Figure 2. Output for daily operational parameters.

SECTION III

DAILY BOD, SS LOADINGS, AND PERCENT REMOVALS

DAY	DAILY BOD (mg/l)		DAILY SS (mg/l)		BOD LOADING (PPD)		SS LOADING (PPD)		PERCENT REMOVALS	
	Influent	Effluent	Influent	Effluent	Influent	Effluent	Influent	Effluent	BOD	SS
1	85.50	2.80	133.30	2.80	2181.99	71.46	3401.87	71.46	.97	.98
6	91.50	6.60	101.30	6.00	2411.43	173.94	2649.70	158.13	.93	.94
8	99.00	4.50	133.10	5.40	2666.88	121.22	3590.86	145.47	.95	.96
10	[illegible]					[illegible]	2951.56	252.20	[illegible]	

Figure 3. Output for BOD and suspended solids parameters.

SECTION III:

TABULATION OF SLUDGE TREATMENT PARAMETERS

METHOD: DIGESTION

DAY	FLOW TO DIGESTER (100 GAL)	INFL. PERCENT SOLIDS (mg/l)	GAS PRODUCED (Cf-3)	DETENTION TIME (MIN)	PH	VOL. SLUDGE PRODUCED (YR-3)	% SOLIDS SLUDGE
1	13.200	0.0	0.0	50	5.2	20.0	27.0
8	15.100	0.0	0.0	75	2.9	24.0	25.0
15	14.100	0.0		40	4.7	25.0	26.0

Figure 4. Output for sludge treatment parameters.

SECTION IV :

COMPARISON OF OPERATING PERFORMANCES
WITH PERMIT AND DESIGN LIMITS

	MAXIMUM VALUE	PERMIT LEVEL	NO. TIMES PERMIT EXCEEDED
DAILY BOD (mg/l)	2.40	8.40	0
MONTHLY BOD (mg/l)	3.86	10.00	0
DAILY SS (mg/l)	4.50	8.00	0

Figure 5. Output for NPDES compliance checking.

Summary

Regulatory requirements for periodic reporting of operating or performance data are common in the environmental field, and elsewhere. For wastewater treatment plants, the state regulatory agency uses the data to check compliance with discharge permit provisions (a legal obligation) and would like to use the data for performance evaluations, troubleshooting, report generation, etc. All of these tasks would be greatly simplified and enhanced by computer-based manipulation of the data. The problem has been getting the data into the computer's memory in the first place. Typically the handwritten reports have been reviewed for compliance, and most of the rest of the tasks have been let slide.

A pilot test is now underway in Massachusetts on the use of distributed microcomputers for monthly wastewater treatment plant report generation. Interactive data entry software is being tested at treatment plants which already own microcomputers. The locally created data files are transferred to the MDWPC's host computer via modem. The data is then analyzed with a third program, DTECTR. DTECTR generates hard copy monthly reports, checks compliance with NPDES Discharge Permit limitations, performs selected diagnostic computations, and generates graphical presentations of daily and historical parameters, as desired.

Initial results indicate acceptance of the software based reporting system by the local operators. The analyses and tabulations performed by the DTECTR model will greatly increase the efficiency of regulatory agency personnel in reviewing the monthly reports, thereby making time available for troubleshooting and attention to poorly operating plants. Furthermore the data will be available in the computer's storage for other analysis and tabulation uses in the future.

Full scale implementation to the more than 100 publicly owned wastewater treatment plants in the state has not been finalized. Full scale implementation would require some means of providing microcomputers to all treatment plants - a feat which is beyond the Division of Water Pollution Control's budget at present. For the short term, implementation will be on a case by case basis as individual treatment plants purchase microcomputers on their own.

APPENDIX - REFERENCES

1. DiGiano, Francis A., Roland J. DuPuis, and Peter J. Williams, "Computerized Monthly Reports; Cost-effective Alternative?", Water and Sewage Works, Dec. 1975.

2. DiGiano, Francis A., and Enrique J. La Motta, "Computerized Review of Monthly Treatment Plant Operating Reports", Prog. Wat. Tech., Vol. 9, No's 5 & 6, Pergamon Press, 1977.

REAL-TIME RESERVOIR OPERATIONS BY QUADRATIC PROGRAMMING

Emre K. Can[*], A.M. ASCE

ABSTRACT: A quadratic programming model is developed for real-time reservoir operations. It is assumed that convex penalty functions that relates the deviations of storage levels and downstream control station flows (or releases) from their targets or desired performance levels to an amount of penalty, exist. The optimal operation is determined by minimizing the sum of penalties incurred over the horizon. A solution to the model is attained by solving the Kuhn-Tucker conditions using an efficient and easily programmable complementary pivot method. The quadratic programming model offers a new alternative to a solution of an important problem. The construction of the model and the determination of the required parabolic penalty functions are easier and the size of the problem is considerably small compared to some earlier models. The complementary pivot method guarantees to find an optimal solution.

INTRODUCTION

Small changes in the operation of an existing reservoir system may result significant increases in benefits and/or decreases in damages. Accordingly, the problem of optimal real-time operations of reservoir systems has been subject to many research projects and many models have been developed. Yeh (14) reviews the available methods and gives extensive, comparative bibliography. Some of the recent works dealing with real-time operation of reservoirs is reported in (2, 4, 5, 6, 12, 13, 15).

It has been suggested (11) that the operating manual for every project should be reviewed and revised once every decade in light of newly available data and analysis techniques. In order to achieve this, the newly developed or the modified existing models should be easily perceived, adopted and efficiently programmed. Models with different assumptions and solution techniques enable the decision makers to choose from a broad range of alternatives.

In this paper, a new quadratic programming model is proposed for real-time operations of reservoir systems. The objective of the model is to minimize the sum of penalties incurred over the operating horizon due to deviations in the suggested operation from the ideal conditions. It is assumed that the convex penalty functions are parabolic. The model developed here is expected to be solved

*Assistant Professor, School of Engineering, Lakehead University, Thunder Bay, Ontario, P7B 5E1, Canada.

at the beginning of each time period with updated forecast information
and initial conditions. The algorithm suggested for the solution of
the developed model, complementary pivot method, guarantees to find
the optimal solution and can be easily programmed.

REAL-TIME OPERATIONS MODEL

The optimal real-time operation of reservoir systems requires
the determination of the "best" reservoir releases (and computing
corresponding reservoir storages and downstream control station flows)
to satisfy the objectives of the system and the restrictions on
operations due to physical constraints. The decisions are based on
the short-term, limited forecast information. Inflows to the
reservoirs, precipitations, evaporation from the reservoir surfaces,
seepage from the reservoirs, and uncontrolled tributary flows at
downstream of reservoirs are forecasted. It is shown that (1,3)
a model's performance is highly correlated with the reliability of
these forecasts. Therefore, a trade-off has to be made between the
forecast reliability and the operating or forecast horizon to be
used in the real-time operations model.

The real-time reservoir operations model will be defined for
an optimal daily operation of a simple single reservoir, one downstream
control station systems as shown in Figure 1. The decisions are
based on the inputs of the model, i.e. initial storage of the
reservoir, previous reservoir releases, and forecasted effective
reservoir inflows (inflow + precipitation - evaporation - seepage)
and effective tributary inflows for the operating horizon.

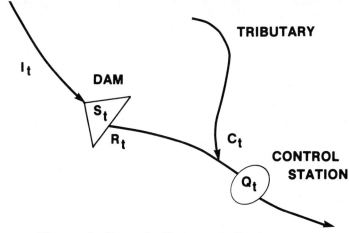

Figure 1. Sample Reservoir System

The objective of the model is to minimize the sum of penalties
incurred over the operating horizon due to deviations in the suggested

operation from the ideal operations. This objective implies that
some targets or desired performance levels for the system operations
exist and the deviations from these targets result in losses or
penalties. An ideal operation then corresponds to an operation where
all the targets are hit and it results in zero penalty. Equations 1-7
define such a mathematical model. This model is a general model, not
a quadratic programming model, since the functions in Eq. 1 are not
yet defined.

Minimize

$$Z = \sum_{t=1}^{T} [\lambda \, f(S_{t+1}) + (1-\lambda)g(Q_t)] \tag{1}$$

Subject to

$$S_{t+1} - S_t + R_t = I_t \quad t=1,2,\ldots,T \tag{2}$$

$$Q_t - aR_t - bR_{t-1} = C_t \quad t=1,2,\ldots,T \tag{3}$$

$$|R_t - R_{t-1}| \leq RDIF \quad t=1,2,\ldots,T \tag{4}$$

$$SMIN \leq S_{t+1} \leq CAP \quad t=1,2,\ldots,T \tag{5}$$

$$RMIN \leq R_t \leq RMAX \quad t=1,2,\ldots,T \tag{6}$$

$$Q_t \geq QMIN \quad t=1,2,\ldots,T \tag{7}$$

in which S_t = expected reservoir volume at the beginning of day t;
S_1 = initial storage volume; R_t = suggested reservoir release during
day t; R_0 = last day's release; Q_t = expected flow at downstream
control station; I_t = forecasted effective reservoir inflow during
day t; C_t = forecasted efficient tributary flow; $f(S_{t+1})$ = penalty
function based on the expected storage; $g(Q_t)$ = penalty function
based on the expected flow at downstream control station; RDIF =
maximum allowable fluctuation in releases; CAP = storage capacity of
the reservoir; SMIN = minimum allowable storage volume; RMAX, RMIN =
maximum and minimum allowable release rates; respectively; QMIN =
minimum allowable control station flow; T = operating and forecast
horizon; t = index of days in the forecast or operating horizon;
λ = weighing factor between zero and one; a,b = channel routing
coefficients.

Equations 2-7 are the constraints of the problem. Eq. 2
represents the continuity of the reservoir storage volume from the
beginning of the current day through the next T days. Eq. 3 is the
routing equation relating the reservoir releases, tributary flows
and the flows at the downstream control station. For simplicity,
the routing equation is chosen to be a linear function of the current
and the previous days' releases and current effective tributary
inflow. Eq. 4 indicates that the rapid and drastic changes in the
reservoir release from one day to next is avoided. Eq. 5-7 ensures
that the operation will satisfy the physical constraints of the
system. The objective function, Eq. 1 is the minimization of the
weighted sum of penalties associated with the anticipated reservoir
storages and flows at the downstream control station.

In actual operation, the mathematical program is solved at

the beginning of each day with a limited forecast information. The
solution of the model comprises suggested optimal releases and the
corresponding anticipated reservoir storages and downstream control
station flows. However, the only implemented portion of this
solution is the suggested optimal release of current day, R_1^*. At the
beginning of the next day, the model is reconstructed with revised
forecast information and the actual beginning storage for that day
(which is not to be the same as model computes unless the inflow
forecasts have 100% reliability). Then, the model is resolved and
optimal release for that day is made.

The mathematical program constructed above consists of 3T
variables (S_{t+1}, R_t and Q_t), 4T constraints (one constraint for
every equation of type 2 and 3, and two constraints for every equation
of type 4) and 5T bounds (equations 5-7).

QUADRATIC PROGRAMMING MODEL

The mathematical program in Eqs. 1-7 is formulated with an
objective of minimizing the weighted sum of penalties associated
with storages and downstream control station flows over the horizon
if the suggested operation is implemented. This objective assumes
that some targets or accepted ranges are known and that the deviations
from these result in penalties. The shape of the penalty functions
is convex, implying that as operations deviate further from their
targets or accepted ranges, the marginal penalty associated does
not decrease, i.e. the slope of the penalty function increases as
deviations increase. Figure 2 illustrates a typical nonlinear
penalty function for reservoir storages and flows at downstream
control station flows. For illustration purposes it is assumed that
a target storage (STAR) exists for reservoir storages while a range
of flows (Q1 to Q2) describes the ideal operation for control station
flows.

The quadratic programming model assumes that the nonlinear
penalty functions shown in Figure 2 are (or can be approximated to
be) parabolic functions. Then, the penalty functions $f(S_{t+1})$ and
$g(Q_t)$ of the objective function can be expressed as:

$$f(S_{t+1}) = \alpha(S_{t+1} - STAR)^2 \tag{8}$$

$$g(Q_t) = \begin{cases} \beta(Q1 - Q_t)^2 & \text{if } Q_t \leq Q1 \\ \gamma(Q_t - Q2)^2 & \text{if } Q_t \geq Q2 \\ 0 & \text{otherwise} \end{cases} \tag{9}$$

The nonnegative constants α, β and γ in the above equations have to be
determined. In practice, these may be obtained from experienced
reservoir operators (13) or from an economic analysis of the reservoir
operations. Eq. 9 can not be included in the mathematical programming
problem in its present form. After introducing three new variables,
$X1_t$, $X2_t$ and $X3_t$ as defined below:

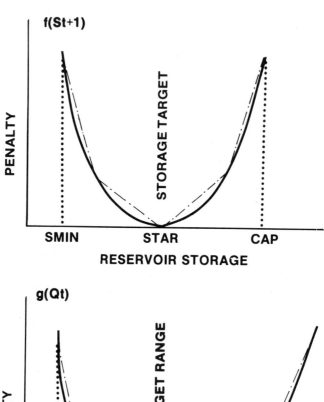

Figure 2. Typical Penalty Fuctions

$$\text{if QMIN} \leq Q_t \leq Q1 \quad X1_t = Q1 - Q_t \quad X2_t = X3_t = 0 \tag{10}$$

$$\text{if Q1} \quad \leq Q_t \leq Q2 \quad X1_t = X2_t = 0 \quad X3_t = Q_2 - Q_t \tag{11}$$

$$\text{if } Q_2 \quad \leq Q_t \quad X1_t = 0 \quad X3_t = Q2 - Q1 \quad X2_t = Q_t - Q2 \tag{12}$$

one can replace Eq. (9) with the following equations:

$$g(Q_t) = \beta \ X1_t^2 + \gamma \ X2_t^2 \tag{13}$$

$$Q_t - X1_t + X2_t + X3_t = 0 \tag{14}$$

$$X3_t \leq (Q2 - Q1) \tag{15}$$

Then, the objective function of the Eq. 1 can be replaced by:

$$\text{Minimize} \qquad Z = \sum_{t=1}^{T} [\lambda\alpha(S_{t+1} - STAR)^2 + (1-\alpha)(\beta X1_t^2 + \gamma X2_t^2)] \tag{16}$$

The complete quadratic programming model consists of the objective function given by Eq. (16) and the constraints (2) to (7), (14) and (15). Therefore, the model has 6T variables (S_{t+1}, R_t, Q_t, $X1_t$, $X2_t$ and $X3_t$) and 11T constraints and bounds.

A general quadratic programming (QP) problem is an optimization problem involving a quadratic objective function and linear constraints (7,10). In vector form, it can be stated as:

$$\text{Minimize} \qquad Z = YX + X' \ D \ X \tag{17}$$

$$\text{Subject to} \qquad AX \geq B \tag{18}$$

$$X \geq 0 \tag{19}$$

where A is an (mxn) matrix of constraint coefficient, B is an (mxl) column vector, Y is a (lxn) row vector, D is an (nxn) matrix of quadratic form and X is an (nxl) vector of decision variables.

The region of feasible solutions is defined over a set of linear constraints, thus it is convex. Then, if the objective function, Z is convex, it is known that if a local minimizing solution exists to the QP problem it will also be a global minimizing solution. The quadratic objective function is convex, provided that the matrix D in the objective function is positive definite or positive semidefinite.

In the QP model of real-time reservoir operations defined above, the constraints are linear and the matrix of quadratic form can be written as shown in Table 1 (for simplicity the operating horizon, T, is assumed to be 2).

The matrix in Table 1 has zero off-diagonal elements and non-negative diagonal elements. One way to determine whether a symmetric matrix is positive (semi)definite is through the leading determinants. A symmetric matrix is positive semidefinite if all the diagonal elements and all the leading principal determinants are nonnegative

TABLE 1. MATRIX OF QUADRATIC FORM FOR QP MODEL.

$D =$

	S_1	S_2	$X1_1$	$X1_2$	$X2_1$	$X2_2$	$X3_1$	$X3_2$	R_1	R_2	Q_1	Q_2
S_1	$\lambda\alpha$											
S_2		$\lambda\alpha$										
$X1_1$			$(1-\lambda)\beta$									
$X1_2$				$(1-\lambda)\beta$								
$X2_1$					$(1-\lambda)\gamma$							
$X2_2$						$(1-\lambda)\gamma$						
$X3_1$							0					
$X3_2$								0				
R_1									0			
R_2										0		
Q_1											0	
Q_2												0

ALL OFF-DIAGONAL ELEMENTS ARE ZERO

(positive definite if they are positive). It is clear that for the quadratic form matrix of the proposed model, Table 1, the first 6 leading principal determinants are positive (since α, β, γ are positive and $0 < \lambda < 1$) and the remaining 6 (3T in general) diagonal elements and leading principal determinants are zero. Hence, the matrix is positive semidefinite and the objective function is convex. Therefore, an optimal solution for the model can be obtained by quadratic programming.

An efficient and simple method for solving the QP problems with convex objective functions is the complementary pivot method developed by Lemke which is based on solving the Kuhn-Tucker optimality conditions (7,10). This method guarantees to find an optimal solution for quadratic programming problems with positive semidefinite quadratic form matrices. It is shown (9) that the complementary pivot method is computationally more attractive than most of the methods available for solving QP problems when the matrix of quadratic form is positive semidefinite. The complementary pivot method can easily be programmed in Fortran language within 320 executable statements. A computer program for the method is given in Ravindran (8).

If a target flow (QTAR), rather than a range of flows describes the ideal operations for control station flows, then the flow penalty function (Eq. 9) would be similar to the storage penalty function given in Eq. 8 and a need for introducing new variables and constraints (Eq. 10-15) ceases. The quadratic programming model for this case (QP1) consists of objective function (20) and constraints 2-7.

$$\text{Minimize} \qquad Z = \sum_{t=1}^{T} [\lambda\alpha(S_{t+1} - STAR)^2 + (1-\lambda)\theta(Q_t - QTAR)^2] \qquad (20)$$

In the above objective function, since λ, α and θ are all constants, they all can be replaced by a single weighting factor, μ, i.e.

$$\text{Minimize} \qquad Z = \sum_{t=1}^{T} [\mu(S_{t+1} - STAR)^2 + (1-\mu)(Q_t - QTAR)^2] \qquad (21)$$

The only parameter to be estimated in the QP1 model is the weighting factor μ, indicating the relative importance of the storage and flow penalties with each other. If the model is to be used in reservoir operation studies to investigate alternative operating policies by generating a trade-off curve between the storage and flow penalties, then the model does not need any parameter estimation.

If the mathematical program in Eqs. 1-7 is formulated as a linear program (LP), then the penalty functions have to be given as piecewise linear convex functions (13) as shown (in dashed lines) in Figure 2. In this case, the size of the problem increases considerably. A new variable and an upper bound for this variable is added for every zone (line with different slope) in the penalty function, and for every time step. In addition, zone constraints (similar to Eq. 14) are required. The number of variables (n) and number of constraints and bounds (m) of an LP for the sample problem for NS storage and NQ flow zones are:

$$n = (3 + NS + NQ)T; \quad m = (11 + NS + NQ)T \qquad (22)$$

For example, for 5 storage and flow zones, an LP model consists of 13T variables and 21T constraints. Comparing these with 6T (3T) variables and 11T (9T) constraints of QP (QP1) model, it is clear that the problem size of the quadratic programming model could be less than 50% of the LP model.

Table 2 presents a comparison of the dimensions of the problem for an extension of the simple model given in Eqs. 1-7 to NRES reservoirs and NCS control stations. The numbers given in brackets are for a hypothetical daily reservoir system operation consisting of 3 reservoirs and 7 control stations. For this system, it is assumed that the operating horizon is 3 days; and 4 storage, and 5 flow zones represent the convex piecewise linear penalty functions for the LP model.

Table 2.   Comparison of problem dimensions.

Model (1)	Variables (n) (2)	Constraints (m) (3)
QP1	$(2NRES + NCS)T$ [39]	$(7NRES + 2NCS)T$ [105]
QP	$(2NRES + 4NCS)T$ [102]	$(7NRES + 4NCS)T$ [147]
LP	$\{(2+NS)NRES + (1+NQ)NCS\}T$ [180]	$\{(8+NS)NRES + (3+NQ)NCS\}T$ [276]
NRES: Reservoirs [3] NCS: Control stations [7] T: Operating horizon [3]		NS: Storage zones [4] NQ: Flow zones [5]

SUMMARY AND CONCLUSIONS

The use of quadratic programming for real-time reservoir system operations has been proposed. The objective of the quadratic programming model is to minimize the sum of expected penalties over the operating horizon due to deviations in the suggested operations from ideal conditions. Penalty functions for reservoir storages and control station flows are expressed as parabolic functions. It is shown that the objective function is convex, thus a global optimum can be obtained by solving Kuhn-Tucker conditions. An efficient and computationally attractive complementary pivot method is suggested for the solution algorithm. The model and the solution method is easy to understand and apply. Increase in the number of available models with different assumptions and solution techniques is believed to broaden the use of systems analysis techniques for real-time reservoir operations which would expand the benefits from existing reservoir systems.

APPENDIX: REFERENCES

1. Can, E.K. and Houck, M.H., "Reliability of Forecasts in Real-Time Reservoir Operations", presented at the May 29-31, 1984, ASCE National Specialty Conference, "Urban Water '84 - A Time for Renewal", held at Baltimore, Maryland.
2. Can, E.K. and Houck, M.H., "Real-Time Reservoir Operations by Goal Programming", *Journal of Water Resources Planning and Management*, ASCE, Vol. 110, No. 3, July, 1984, pp. 297-309.
3. Datta, B. and Burges, S., "Short-term, Single, Mutliple-Purpose Reservoir Operation: Importance of Loss Functions and Forecast Errors", *Water Resources Research*, Vol. 20, No. 9, September, 1984, pp. 1167-1176.

4. Datta, B. and Houck, M.H., "A Stochastic Optimization Model for Real-Time Reservoirs Using Uncertain Forecasts", *Water Resources Research*, Vol. 20, No. 8, August, 1984, pp. 1039-1046.
5. Houck, M.H., "Real-Time Reservoir Operation by Mathematical Programming", *Water Resources Research*, Vol. 18, No. 5, October, 1982, pp. 1345-1351.
6. Orlovski, S., Rinaldi, S., and Soncini-Sessa, R., "A Min-Max Approach to Reservoir Management", *Water Resources Research*, Vol. 20, No. 11, November, 1984, pp. 1506-1514.
7. Phillips, D.T., Ravindran, A., and Solberg, J.J., *Operations Research: Principles and Practice*, Wiley, New York, 1976.
8. Ravindran, A., "A Computer Routine for Quadratic and Linear Programming Problems", Algorithm 431, *Communications of the Association for Computing Machines*, Vol. 15, No. 9, pp. 818-820, 1972.
9. Ravindran, A., and Lee, H., "Computer Experiments on Quadratic Programming Algorithms", *European Journal of Operations Research*, Vol. 8, No. 2, pp. 166-174, 1981.
10. Reklaitis, G.V., Ravindran, A., and Ragsdell, K.M., *Engineering Optimization: Methods and Applications*, Wiley, New York, 1984.
11. Sheer, D.P., and Meredith, D.D., "Improve Operation or Build New Projects", *Journal of Water Resources Planning and Management*, ASCE, Vol. 110, No. 3, July, 1984, pp. 351-355.
12. Wasimi, S.A., and Kitanidis, P.K., "Real-Time Forecasting and Daily Operation of a Multireservoir System During Floods by Linear Quadratic Gaussian Control", *Water Resources Research*, Vol. 19, No. 6, December, 1983, pp. 1511-1522.
13. Yazicigil, H., Houck, M.H., and Toebes, G.H., "Daily Operation of a Multipurpose Reservoir System", *Water Resources Research*, Vol. 19, No. 1, January, 1983, pp. 1-13.
14. Yeh, W. W-G., "State of the Art Review: Theories and Applications of Systems Analysis Techniques to the Optimal Management and Operation of a Reservoir System", *Report UCLA-ENG-82-52*, University of California, Los Angeles, 1982.
15. Yeh, W. W-G, and Becker, L., "Multiobjective Analysis of Multireservoir Operations", *Water Resources Research*, Vol. 18, No. 5, October, 1982, pp. 1326-1336.

INTEGRATED OPERATION OF THE OTTAWA RIVER SYSTEM

Denis Béchard and Daniel Richard

ABSTRACT

Several years ago, an integrated operating process was developed in response to specific problems on the Ottawa River. The operating process involves several public-sector organizations working together to ensure maximum satisfaction for the users of the river. It includes inflow forecasting, optimization, and hydraulic simulation models. The object of this paper is to describe the strategy and its application, comment on its effectiveness and suggest improvements.

INTRODUCTION

The Ottawa River system presents particular operating difficulties. First, a large number of control structures and hydroelectric power stations have been built on the river and its tributaries. Second, several municipalities and industries located along the river use the water for a variety of purposes in addition to hydroelectric power generation. Third, spring freshet causes damages to homes and public infrastructures. And, last, management of the river system is complicated by the presence of several agencies owning facilities along the river. All these factors add up to make the Ottawa River an extremely complex system to operate.

In 1976, after serious flooding occurred on the river, the governments of Canada, Ontario and Québec decided to take joint action to improve the situation. A committee made up of the main parties concerned was created to study possible solutions to the problems of the Ottawa River. This committee recommended the application of an integrated operating strategy as well as the creation of an operating committee whose main function would be to coordinate the river operation. The recommendations were adopted several years ago.

This paper describes the operation of the Ottawa River system during the freshet period, first giving the main components of the operating process and then describing how information is communicated.

Planification des mouvements d'énergie, Hydro-Québec, 75 ouest, boul. Dorchester, Montréal, Qué., H2Z 1A4

THE OTTAWA RIVER SYSTEM

Characteristics: The catchment area basin is located in the two eastern Canadian provinces of Ontario and Québec. In fact, most of the length of the main stream constitutes the border between these two provinces. The basin has an area of about 56,000 mi^2 (145,000 km^2), 65% of which lies in Québec and 35% in Ontario (Fig.1).

OTTAWA RIVER BASSIN

FIGURE I

The river flows over a distance of about 720 mi (1160 km), with a total drop of 1345 ft (410 m) from the Dozois head reservoir to the outlet at Deux-Montagnes Lake.   The lake in turn empties into the St. Lawrence River, Mille Iles River and Des-Prairies River. The main tributaries of the Ottawa River are the Montreal, Kipawa, Petawawa, Coulonge, Madawaska, Gatineau and Du Lièvre rivers.

Hydrology: The size and topography of the catchment area basin give rise to extremely varied climatic conditions. The time lag in the flow from the main tributaries, combined with wide temperature variations, produce two different peak flood periods in the spring. The first originates in the southern tributaries, which are practically unregulated. The second results from the snowmelt in the northern tributaries. This second flood, which is partly regulated, usually occurs three weeks after the first. The annual average flow is 69,000 ft^3/s (1950 m^3/s) at the outlet.

Physical system: The Ottawa River is one of the most densely populated basins in Canada and also one of the most important in terms of hydroelectric power generation, with 43 power stations and an installed capacity of 3500 MW. Annual production is 8.4 TWh on the Québec side and 6.0 TWh in Ontario.

The basin contains some 30 reservoirs with capacities of more than 1 bcf (28 hm³), for a total storage capacity of over 500 bcf (14,000 hm³). About 50% of this capacity is concentrated in the northern part of the basin, 40% in the middle and 10% in the southern part.

Interests involved: The principal uses or needs involving the water in the Ottawa River basin are hydroelectric power generation, flood protection, low water, residential water supply, recreation, and log driving. Of these uses, some are compatible while others are contradictory: for example, flood protection is usually ensured at the expense of power generation. It would appear, then, that integrated operation is the only way to serve the interests of the users as a whole.

SYSTEM OPERATION

The Planning Committee: After two serious floods in the 1970s, the federal and provincial governments created the Ottawa River Regulation Planning Committee (ORRPC). Its mandate was to recommend regulation criteria with consideration to the interests of all users, and to apply these criteria to real-time operation (5).

Seven organizations are represented in the ORRPC: the federal departments of the Environment, Public Works and Transportation, the Québec Ministry of the Environment, Hydro-Québec, the Ontario Ministry of Natural Resources, and Ontario Hydro.

The Operating Committee: The ORRPC recommended the formation of an operating committee to coordinate daily operations and to establish regulation practices and procedures in conformity with the ORRPC's general policies. The operating committee, called the ORRC, reports to the ORRPC and consists of representatives from the operating agencies: Hydro-Québec, Ontario Hydro, Public Works Canada and Environnement Québec. Figure 2 shows each agency's responsibility as a percentage of the total reserve and installed capacity. It should be noted that the agencies have every power in the management of their own facilities, and that the only role of the ORRC and ORRPC is to promote discussion.

FIGURE 2

THE OTTAWA RIVER OPERATORS	STORAGE CAPACITY CONTROL		POWER INSTALLED CAPACITY	
	109 m3	%	MW	%
DEPARTMENT OF PUBLIC WORKS, CANADA	3.22	23	0	0
ONTARIO HYDRO	1.72	12	1 588	43
HYDRO-QUEBEC	6.91	50	1 680	45
MINISTÈRE DE L'ENVIRONNEMENT, QUÉBEC	1.71	12	0	0

Decision-making process: Decisions as the releases from reservoirs are made according to an integrated process, as shown in Fig. 3. In the next pages we shall describe the principal steps in this process as well as the flow of information from one step to the next.

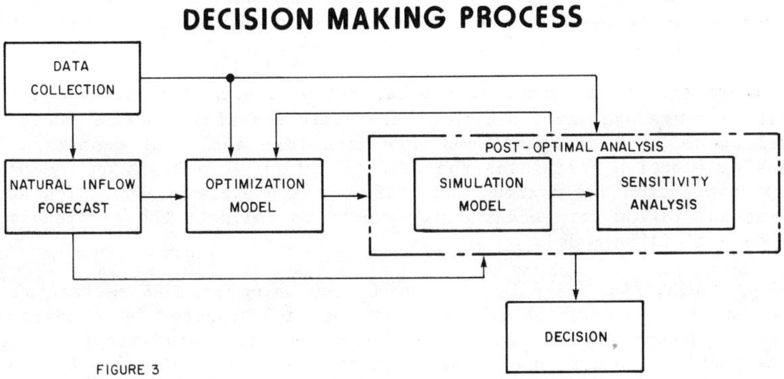

DECISION MAKING PROCESS

FIGURE 3

DATA COLLECTION

Information needed for hydrosystem operation is essentially: (1) the state of reservoirs; (2) last day's discharges; and (3) natural inflows. This information serves as input for the operating process. State of reservoirs and last days' discharges are deduced directly from collected data, while figures on natural inflows result from calculations involving the first two sources of information.

Water level measurement: The state of reservoirs is usually estimated from the stage-storage relation according to the water level. The water level is measured daily (in most cases) by the local operator with the help of a limnimeter. The information is transmitted to the utility's regional operator and/or central operator.

Flow calculation: Water takes a certain time to flow from one structure to the next. As a result, there is a large volume of water in transit that must be taken into account in operations. River water not only takes time to flow from one point to the next, but it is also deformed on the way.
The discharge flow of a site is the sum of the flows of all its outlets. For each outlet, this flow is estimated from the opening of the gates using a pre-established formula in which the size of the gates and the water level are known. The flow data are transmitted to the utility's operating centre in the same way as the water-level measurements.

Inflow calculation: To calculate the natural inflow to a site, it is necessary to know the reserves (if applicable) at the beginning and end of the period in question, the total outflow during the same period, and the effective flow from upstream sites. The calculation is carried out by a hydraulic simulation program. In addition to calculating the inflow, the program also provides a "snapshot" of the system.

INFLOW FORECASTING

Based on meteorological data on precipitation and temperatures in the basin, the natural inflow forecasting model gives the statistical distribution of future runoff. The runoff forecasting model is divided into two separate operations: creation of a runoff simulation bank and probabilistic analysis of these simulations to determine expected runoff distribution (2).

To create the runoff simulation bank, meteorological forecasts and climatic data are used as input to a parametric transfer function (deterministic model), which transforms them into time series of runoffs. The transfer function calculates the natural inflow of a basin on the basis of precipitation and maximum and minimum temperatures. The calculation of natural inflow for recent days is used to validate the parameters of the deterministic model.

The probabilistic analysis of results is based on the estimation of error due to inaccuracies in the input data and transfer function parameters. Through statistical processing of the simulated runoff series, it is possible to obtain a probabilistic runoff forecast. For a specified probability level, it is possible to extract a forecast of daily runoff, volume of inflow, the beginning or end date of the flood period, and so on. These data will be used mainly to verify the impact of a variation in expected inflow if our release decisions are maintained (sensitivity analysis).

OPTIMIZATION MODEL

Operation of the Ottawa River system involves the use of ORRMS (1), an optimization model developed under the auspices of the ORRPC with the active participation of most of the agencies concerned. Although the model can be applied to other river basins, it was designed around the specific needs of the Ottawa River. It was begun in 1977 and put into application during the 1980 freshet period.

The purpose of ORRMS is to provide guidelines for hydrosystem operation. The criteria used in the search for a solution are (1) maximization of hydroelectric power generation and (2) minimization of damages caused by flooding. As these two criteria are often contradictory, the model reaches a compromise between them according to their respective monetary values. ORRMS uses linear programming in separable variables. This technique was chosen because of its ease of use and the availability of software packages. The software selected was IBM's MPSX program (3).

Hierarchical approach: Optimizing the operation of the Ottawa River system is a major problem, partly because of the large number of control structures in the system. Furthermore, operation requires long-term decisions on energy production as well as daily decisions on flood control. With some 40 sites, operations on a day-to-day basis, and a horizon of at least a year, the problem was beyond the scope of existing methods. A hierarchical approach was therefore used to divide the problem into interconnected subproblems. The divisions were drawn on a temporal basis, as follows:

	Horizon	Time period
Long-term	1 year	1 month
Mid-term	3 months	1 week
Short-term	10 days	1 day

The link between the various subproblems is established by means of targets. For example, at the end of its horizon, the mid-term must reach the state prescribed by the long term. The same applies to the short term in relation to the middle term.

Application strategies: ORRMS showed several deficiences that had to be corrected before the model could be applied. The most important difficulty was the fact that optimization models do not give any answer when the problem is unsolvable. In this case, with the model being used every day and taking up considerable CPU time, a non-solution situation was unacceptable. The model's constraints therefore had to be relaxed to ensure that a "reasonable" solution was always given, even when the problem was unsolvable. To accomplish this, a penalty (cost) was applied whenever certain constraints were violated, the violation cost depending on the importance of the constraint.

The second difficulty had to do with reservoir outflow. The model gives an optimum solution with sequential flows in a saw-tooth form. However, it would be unthinkable to operate the system this way; not only would it be harmful to the environment, but the cost of daily operations would be prohibitive. This problem was solved by the smoothing of outflows over time, a strategy that is directly included in the model. In other words, excessive variations in outflow were penalized. This strategy takes us away from the optimum in the sense of the criteria defined earlier, but at least it makes the solution more realistic.

For each site and each period of the horizon, ORRMS produces the value of the flow (turbining and spilling), the resulting state of reservoirs and the amount of power generated.

ORRMS was test-run during the 1980 flood period in parallel with the existing operating procedure. Like most models, it experienced some initial difficulties. There was strong resistance from the operators at first, but this was gradually overcome, and the model is now regarded as a guide with all its qualities and faults.

Evaluation of ORRMS: The model's most serious shortcoming is its deterministic nature. It treats the inflow forecast as a fact without considering the possibility of a variation. And since inflow varies greatly and is difficult to forecast, the model is continually basing its decisions on false information.

Another important problem lies in its formulation of optimization criteria. ORRMS uses the monetary value of energy production versus claims for damages caused by flooding. The value of the energy is much greater than the cost of flood damages; however, since the latter has a social and political impact, it was necessary to increase its value in order to compare it with the energy produced. Because we had no way to estimate

the real dollar value of the damages, we used the model to simulate historical cases several times, applying different values until a satisfactory estimate was obtained.   This procedure is, of course, highly subjective.

POST–OPTIMAL ANALYSIS

Post-optimal analysis refers to the mechanisms applied in order to
reach a decision based on the information received from the optimization
model and on other information that could not be integrated into the
model. The latter category of information includes :

1. technological uncertainties: those related to modelling (physical
   aggregation of the system, large time period, time lag between
   sites, etc.);

2. strategic uncertainties: those related to the actual definition of
   the problem to be solved. Does the objective function exactly represent the goal we want to attain? Are the penalties applied to the
   softbound constraints an accurate reflection of their order of importance?

3. hydrological uncertainties: those related to runoff forecasting.
   What is the possible variation in the forecast volume or peak?

The post-optimal analyses carried out in the decision–making process
are hydraulic simulation and sensitivity analysis.

Hydraulic simulation: The optimization techniques applied to hydrosystem operation usually give rather approximate results (i.e. release decisions). Daily operation requires a higher degree of accuracy. For
the Ottawa River system, we use Streamflow Synthesis and River Regulation (SSARR) (8) following the application of ORRMS. A simulation of
release decisions serves to refine the physical, economic or other consequences arising from the application of optimization results.

Sensitivity analysis: Natural runoff sensitivity analysis is another
tool that enables the operator to determine the possible consequences
of a given scenario. It indicates the system's sensitivity to variation
in runoff and points out critical situations in a release scenario (6,
7). These situations may include :

• serious flooding caused by early rapid filling of a reservoir or by
  excessive streamflow or river water level;

• a drop in energy production or low water problems, due to partial
  filling of the reservoirs.

The methodology for this analysis was generalized so it could be applied
to all reservoirs where critical situations might occur. The results of
the sensitivity analysis and the hydraulic simulation are important
steps in the decision–making process.

FLOW OF INFORMATION

Data collection: Each agency must collect streamflow and water level data for its own facilities. It collects and validates them every morning and estimates the missing values. The transmission of the data from sites to the agency's head office uses various means. Some data are transmitted by computer and some by telephone, while a few sites are still using limnimetric tapes.

Transmission of data and declarations: Each agency's basic data serve as input to the optimization and simulation models. But in addition to these data, flow declarations are needed for the simulation model. These declarations or decisions are made by the agencies in light of the results of the optimization model, which is run during the night with data from the day before. Toward mid-morning, each agency transmits its data by telecopier to the Montreal head office of Hydro-Québec, which is responsible for overall data collection.

Inflow forecasts: Once all the data are centralized, they are used to calculate the previous day's natural inflow. Ideally, this calculation should include an automatic estimate of the missing data, a data Hydro-validation module, and a routing model. At the end of the morning, the Québec computer uses the resulting figures to draw up inflow forecasts.

Operations simulation: Once the data has been collected, validated and centralized and the inflow forecast is available, the processing of operations as such can begin. For the Ottawa River, two models are used: the ORRMS optimization model and the SSARR simulation model. SSARR is run in Montreal, usually during the lunch hour, on the same computer that does the inflow forecasts.

Access to simulation results: By the end of the lunch hour, the SSARR results are usually ready, and each agency can use them to provide instructions to its operators. All the participating agencies access the results through a small DECwriter terminal.

Adjustments: Operating a hydrosystem like the Ottawa River often presents difficulties. Because of the wide variations in inflow, it often happens that one or more participants are not happy with the simulation results. When this happens, the dissatisfied agencies can request adjustments; however, all the other partners must be consulted, since their decisions are interconnected. This is usually accomplished through telephone conference calls. When a consensus is reached, SSARR is re-run with the requested adjustments.

Transmission of ORRMS data: ORRMS is managed by the ORRC in Ottawa and is run on the computer of a private consulting firm, also located in Ottawa. The model is run at night because of the CPU time it takes. Normally, it should be run before the simulation model, but its lengthy execution time prevents this. Nevertheless, it is used as the first link in the chain, but with data from the day before. The results from the previous day's optimization model determine the declarations of the operating organizations. Data are transmitted directly from Montreal to Ottawa by two computers using IBM's "Host Remote Node Entry System" (HRNES) (4) via a conventional telephone line. HRNES turns the Hydro-

Québec computer in Montreal into a terminal for the host computer in Ottawa. The data are transmitted to Ottawa in the early afternoon.

Access to optimization results: Once the optimization model has been run, the results are transmitted in the same way as the SSARR results, via a DECwriter.

Data transmission flow chart: Fig. 4 shows the flow of information as described in this section.

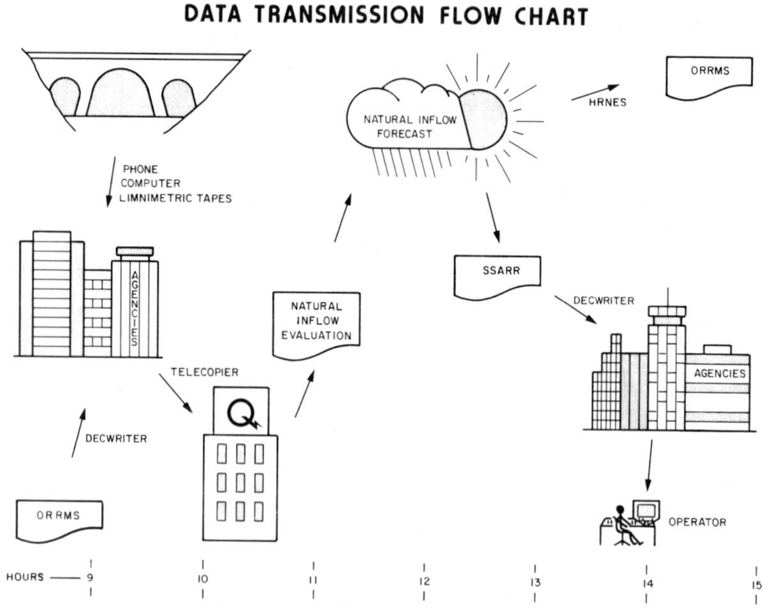

DATA TRANSMISSION FLOW CHART

FIGURE 4

CONCLUSION

A complex but effective procedure: Given the flow of information involved in this integrated operating system, it is no exaggeration to say that it is an extremely complex procedure. We can nevertheless affirm that it has been thoroughly run in and is now functioning quite well. Still, because of its complexity, the procedure requires a lot of operations and therefore considerable effort from the operators.

Possible improvements: One way of improving the system would be to centralize operations in a single location. However, this would involve transferring not only the three models used at the operating centre but also the employees of each participating agency. While this solution offers undeniable advantages, it also has major drawbacks. The possibility of centralizing operations was recently studied by the committee and was rejected because of its cost.

Another solution, easier to apply than the first, would be to use more efficient means of data transmission. This would involve the automatic acquisition of level and flow data by the participants and the installation of data-transmission connections between their computers. Such modifications would greatly accelerate data handling and would reduce response times; on the other hand, the advantages would not be as great as for the first solution.

APPENDIX I – REFERENCES

1. Béchard, D. et al., **The Ottawa River Regulation Modelling System (ORRMS)** , Proceedings of the International Symposium on Real-Time Operation of Hydrosystems, Waterloo, June 1981.

2. Bisson J.-L., Charbonneau R., Richard D., Roberge F., **Gestion des systèmes hydriques à Hydro-Québec** . To be published, 1985.

3. IBM, **Mathematical Programming System Extended (MPSX)** , 1974.

4. IBM, **Host Remote Node Entry System** , 1982.

5. Ottawa River Regulation Planning Committee, **Final Report** , 1980.

6. Rassam J.-C., Richard D., **Sensitivity Analysis** , Ottawa River Regulation Planning Board, 1983.

7. Rassam, J.-C. **Flood and Drought Management of the Ottawa River System,** Second Iraqi Hydrological Conference on hydrological problems of arid and semi-arid regions, Beghdad, Iraw, 1984.

8. U.S. Army Engineer Division, North Pacific, **Streamflow Synthesis and Reservoir Regulation (SSARR)** , Portland, Oregon, 1972.

USER-FRIENDLY RESERVOIR ROUTING ON MINICOMPUTERS

H. Morgan Goranflo, Jr., A.M. ASCE*

Two models for routing reservoir releases and computing reservoir elevations for the TVA reservoir system are described. The models are designed for use on a 16-bit minicomputer with a floating point processor. The models are provided as tools to enable the reservoir operators to quickly evaluate alternative operation schemes so that appropriate operating decisions can be made. The utility of the models is determined by their accuracy, turnaround time, and overall "user-friendliness."

The first model uses a daily time step. It can best be described as using a "quasi spreadsheet" approach in that all essential data for up to eight reservoirs are displayed in matrix form on the screen at once. The user can specify target releases or elevations for each day of the routing period for each reservoir. The model then reads the screen, performs indicated computations, and displays the results back to the screen. The output data, after modifications, become the input data for successive runs. The model uses simple flat pool routing for most reservoirs, with provisions for profile storage included for larger, shallow main river reservoirs.

The second model is a dynamic routing model which uses an explicit finite difference solution technique to solve the St. Venant equations. Basic models of this type (incorporating various solution schemes) have abounded for many years, but data input requirements, turnaround time, and complexity of use have often precluded their use for supplying information for real time reservoir operation. The model uses hourly input data and provides hourly output, although the computational time step is much smaller due to stability constraints. Several data management concepts and algorithms, in conjunction with terminal hardware and software, enable the model to be run and provide output on a timely basis. This model simulates transient flow regimes more accurately than the daily model and provides detailed information at any location along the reservoirs which can be extremely useful during flood control operations.

TVA Reservoir System

The reservoirs in the TVA system may be broadly classified into two types: tributary, and main stream. The tributary reservoirs are generally deeper and provide the majority of the flood control storage above Chattanooga. The main river reservoirs are all on the Tennessee River, and for the most part are wider and shallower than the tributary reservoirs, and form a continuous chain of navigable reservoirs from near Paducah, Kentucky, to Knoxville, Tennessee. A schematic view of the system is shown in Figure 1.

* Head, Hydropower Planning Section, TVA Water Systems Development Branch, Post Office Drawer E, Norris, Tennessee, 37828.

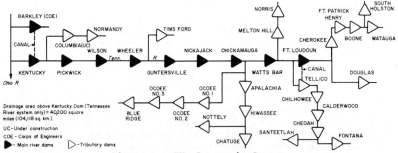

Figure 1.- TVA Reservoir System

TVA Reservoir Operations

Each day, TVA must schedule and implement releases from 34 major reservoirs for a variety of purposes including flood control, navigation, and power, and secondary objectives as provided by the TVA Act. The Reservoir Operations Branch (ROB) is responsible for overall scheduling and management of the reservoir system, and coordinating the scheduled releases with the Division of Power Systems Operations, who integrates hydropower production with the thermal system and is responsible for economic dispatch for the entire power system.

Daily, ROB projects future reservoir operations for a time horizon of up to 4-10 days. During periods of continuing rainfall or rapidly changing streamflows and system demands, these projections, or forecasts, may be updated several times each day as new information is received. These projections are required to determine necessary operation schedules, including turbine releases and spillway and sluice releases, and to provide timely information to river and reservoir users.

The two models described in this paper were developed for ROB use, to allow the evaluation of several alternative schedules within a relatively short time, thus providing for better contingency planning and allowing the selection of the most attractive schedule to meet operating criteria.

Model Selection

A wide variety of flow routing techniques is available for simulating river and reservoir flows and elevations. The decision as to which method is "best" for a particular application must be based on several factors:

* the hydraulics of the network, i.e., the range of flows to be simulated; the complexity of the channel network; the presence or absence of rapidly changing flow conditions and surges; and the number of control points
* the type of results needed, i.e., reservoir headwater elevations; elevations and flows at various points along the water courses
* the accuracy of the results needed

* the available computer hardware
* amount of time available for simulation
* manpower requirements for the method selected
* the amount, type, and quality of input data available
* the development effort required to produce the necessary software

For ROB applications it was decided to implement a two stage approach. First, a daily model would be implemented, based on manual computation procedures already in place. This model allowed rapid data entry and trial simulations for the entire system in a very timely manner, providing adequate detail of information for routine operations. Second, a dynamic routing model would be implemented for all the main river reservoirs, where more complex hydraulic conditions and heavier development along the river indicated a need for more accurate and detailed information. Both models are purely descriptive simulation models, performing no optimization. Experienced personnel are required for providing input and interactive use of the models.

Daily Reservoir Routing Model

Scheduling of the reservoir system varies from day to day depending on projected power loads, predicted streamflow, and predicted rainfall. The model was designed to allow the user flexibility in specifying combinations of target headwater elevations and daily releases to be analyzed. The routing of each reservoir depends on three basic decision variables once all forecasted inflows have been set. These are reservoir release, reservoir headwater elevation and upstream reservoir release (except for uppermost reservoirs on each subsystem). Two of these variables must be known for the third to be computed. The model user can choose which of these variables are to be set for each day.

The model is structured so that all commands required to invoke various file management routines and run instructions are initiated by using pre-programmed function keys. Therefore, there is a minimal opportunity for the user to destroy files inadvertently or interfere with other computer functions, and also minimizes the number of keystrokes required. Computer language expertise is not required since all commands and procedures are pre-programmed. Skill and dexterity in using the terminal keyboard and familiarity with the model options are desirable.

The method of computation selected for this model is a simple volumetric water balance approach, using level pool storage assumptions except on the main river where provisions for profile storage are included. Wave travel time between reservoirs is taken into account by "lagging" upstream releases. Results from the model are daily midnight headwater elevations and/or daily reservoir releases. There are generally no provisions for results on a less than daily interval, although six-hourly release changes may be input along the main river. Computation time for any subset of reservoirs (up to eight) is generally two seconds or less, with total turnaround time being on the order of 30 seconds, depending on the size of the subsystem.

The model calculations are based on a water balance for each reservoir. The storage change in each reservoir during the time step equals the total inflow minus outflow for that reservoir

$$ST(I,J) - ST(I,J-1) = TI(I,J) - QQ(I,J) \tag{1}$$

where I represents the reservoir number, J the current day, ST the midnight reservoir storage, (ft³/s) day, TI total daily inflow into the reservoir, (ft³/s) day, and QQ the total daily average outflow from the reservoir, (ft³/s) day.

Generally, the total daily inflow may be expressed by

$$TI(I,J) = TL(I,J) + AJ(I,J) + \overset{\{L\}}{\Sigma}AR(I,J,K) \tag{2}$$

where TL represents the total daily local inflow, AJ represents adjustments to inflow due to surges and known or suspected discharge errors, AR is the daily "arrival" from upstream reservoir K, all values in (ft³/s) day, and L is the set of numbers indicating which upstream reservoirs flow into reservoir I. If desired, the total daily local inflow may be broken down into inflows from smaller subareas to aid in predicting their value with watershed models.

The concepts of "arrivals" and "carryovers" are used because of the non-negligible travel time associated with the releases from some reservoirs. Arrivals are computed

$$AR(I,J,K) = QQ(K,J) - CO(K,J) + CO(K,J-1) \tag{3}$$

where K is a reservoir whose release flows into reservoir I, and CO is the carryover, the amount of release from reservoir K which because of travel time does not reach reservoir I until the next day, (ft³/s) day. The estimation of carryovers is subjective in that the forecaster must anticipate during which portion of the day water may be released from reservoir K. Estimates of hourly releases from the project may be available for the current day, but changes in anticipated power loads due to temperatures, day of the week, and availability of water must be taken into account for succeeding days of the forecast period. For some reservoirs, arrivals are the daily release from the upstream reservoir due to negligible wave travel time.

A mathematical relationship must be established between the headwater elevation and storage for each reservoir. For tributary reservoirs, a cubic spline interpolation procedure was used to fit available data. For main river reservoirs, a more complex relationship exists. As flow velocities increase in these reservoirs, the storage becomes not only a function of the headwater elevation but also of the flow in the reservoir, due to wedge or profile storage. A flow "parameter" is introduced to establish a relationship between storage and headwater elevation. An example of such a relationship is shown in Figure 2. A statistical analysis package was used to fit a mathematical relationship for these curves for model purposes. When using these flow parameter curves, a flow value must be available to enter the curves with. The choice of the flow parameter is often subjective, but is usually characterized by the flow at the upstream end of the reservoir. The selection of the proper parameter is most difficult during periods of transient flow, since the curves are usually based on steady flow assumptions.

The user invokes the model by requesting a working file to be displayed to the terminal screen. This could be a blank file, or yesterday's file lagged one day. At this time, the file is in the terminal memory, and all modifications to the file are only made to the terminal. This means the central processor is not tied up during the editing stage. The user then inputs or changes data as required

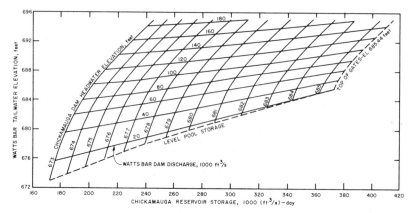

Figure 2.- Profile Storage Relationship

to specify his target operation. The CPU then reads the terminal memory, performs the calculations, and displays the results back to the terminal. If the routing was successful, (no glitches in transmission), a backup file is also made in case problems with the terminal occur before the next run. Thus the routing procedure is somewhat like some of the better known spreadsheet type procedures, except tailormade for specific reservoir systems and subsystems. An example of a simple screen display for a two-reservoir subsystem is shown in Figure 3. The largest subsystem modeled is an eight-reservoir subsystem, but the size is limited only due to TVA requirements and the current terminal memory capability.

Other reservoirs may have more or fewer entries than Norris. All main river reservoirs have additional rows of input for the flow parameter and six-hourly breakdown of releases. In addition to the numeric fields in the files, there are also alpha fields as illustrated in Figure 3. These characters allow the user to indicate whether that variable is specified or whether the variable is to be computed, (X's indicate the value is specified, C's indicate that value and all following values on that line are specified at a constant level unless otherwise indicated).

When the input file is processed, the model first scans the entire file, determining how much information has been specified by the user. It then determines the proper sequence of calculations (it may solve from downstream to upstream or vice versa, depending on the information available). Each time the model is run, all reservoirs are routed for each day. It was determined that this was faster than trying to determine where changes had been made and recomputing only those variables which would differ because of those changes. Other model options, capabilities, and model structure are described by Goranflo and Granju (1), and Goranflo and Myers (2). In applications such as this, close cooperation between the developer and the end users is required to fully exploit the capabilities of the hardware to make model use as easy and failsafe as possible.

TIME	8/30	8/31	9/1	9/2	9/3	9/4	9/5	9/6
10:07	MON	TUE	WED	THU	FRI	SAT	SUN	MON
------	------	------	------	---NORRIS---	------	------	------	------
ADJUST		-.40C	-.40	-.40	-.40	-.40	-.40	-.40
. TAZWLL		.90	.80	.70	.50	.40	.30	.00
ARTHUR		.20	.20	.20	.20	.20	.20	.00
SM LCL		.70	.70	.70	.60	.60	.60	.00
TOT LO	.953	1.80	1.70	1.60	1.30	1.20	1.10	.00
TOT IN		1.40	1.30	1.20	.90	.80	.70	-.40
DEL ST		-6.40	-6.70	-6.80	-7.10	-6.10	-6.20	0.00
STORAG	639.89	633.49	626.79	619.99	612.89	606.79	600.59	0.00
ELEVAT	993.30	992.8	991.6	991.6	991.1	990.5	990.0	0.00
POWER		2262	2320	2320	2320	2001	2001	0
FACTOR		290C	290	290	290	290	290	290
TURB Q		7.80X	8.00C	8.00	8.00	6.90	6.90	0.00
OTHR Q		0.00C	0.00	0.00	0.00	0.00	0.00	0.00
TOTL Q		7.80	8.00	8.00	8.00	6.90	6.90	0.00
RATIO		.28	.28	.28	.28	.28	.28	.28
CRYOVR	1.97	2.17X	2.27X	2.27X	2.27X	1.97X	1.97X	0.00
------	------	------	---MELTON	HILL---	------	------	------	------
NR ARR		7.60	7.90	8.00	8.00	7.20	6.90	1.97
ADJUST		.60C	.60	.60	.60	.40X	.40X	0.00
TOT LO	.968	.30	.30	.30	.30	.30	.30	0.00
TOT IN		8.50	8.80	8.90	8.90	7.90	7.60	1.97
DEL ST		-.60	0.00	.10	.10	0.00	0.00	0.00
STORAG	56.39	55.79	55.79	55.89	55.99	55.99	55.99	0.00
ELEVAT	793.55	793.3	793.3	793.4	793.4	793.4	793.4	0.0
POWER		774	748	748	748	672	646	0
FACTOR		85C	85	85	85	85	85	85
TURB Q		9.10X	8.80C	8.80	8.80	7.90X	7.60X	0.00
OTHR Q		0.00C	0.00	0.00	0.00	0.00	0.00	0.00
TOTL Q		9.10	8.80	8.80	8.80	7.90	7.60	0.00

Figure 3.- Example Screen Display

Using Norris Reservoir as an example, rows are defined as follows:
ADJUST--Adjustments to inflow, as described previously, user entered;
TAZWLL,ARTHUR,SM LCL--Inflows from smaller subwatersheds, user
entered;
TOT LO--Sum of subwatershed inflows, computed;
TOT IN--Sum of all inflows, computed;
DEL ST--Change in reservoir storage content, computed;
STORAG--Reservoir content, computed;
ELEVAT--Reservoir elevation, user entered or computed;
POWER--Generation (MWh), user entered or computed;
FACTOR--Generation/water conversion ratio (MWh/1000cfs-days), user
entered;
TURB Q--Daily turbine release, user entered or computed;
OTHR Q--Daily sluice, spill, or leakage, user entered or computed;
TOTL Q--Sum of TURB Q and OTHR Q, user entered or computed;
RATIO--That portion of the release which is carried over the next
day, user entered;
CRYOVR--Release volume that day which arrives downstream the
following day, user entered.

Hourly Dynamic Routing Model

This model was developed for the entire main river chain of reservoirs, from Fort Loudoun-Tellico through Kentucky-Barkley. The purpose of the model is to simulate reservoir hydraulics for a varying range of flow regimes ranging from turbine pulses resulting in surges and reverse flows to flood control releases resulting in backwater profile differences of 40 feet (12 meters) or more. A finite difference solution technique applied to the St. Venant equations is the computation method used in the model. The St. Venant equations can be written

$$\partial Q/\partial x + \partial(A+Ao)/\partial t - q = 0 \qquad (4)$$

$$\partial Q/\partial t + \partial(Q^2/A)/\partial x + gA(\partial h/\partial x + Sf) - qVx + B\ Wf = 0 \qquad (5)$$

with
x and t the distance and time,
Q and h the discharge and water surface elevation,
A and Ao the cross section area of flow and off-channel dead storage,
q and Vx the lateral inflow per unit distance and its velocity in the channel direction,
g the gravity acceleration,
Sf the friction slope expressed by (6)
B the channel width
Wf the wind effect per unit surface area,

$$Sf = n^2\ V|V|/(2.21\ R^{4/3}) \qquad (6)$$

with
n the Manning's roughness,
V the flow velocity,
R the hydraulic radius

There are many well-discussed solution techniques which have been used to solve these equations, including implicit and explicit finite difference schemes, method of characteristics, etc. The user should carefully select the scheme based on the needs of the particular application. For this case, since a detailed grid was necessary to allow sharp definition of sudden boundary changes, the explicit scheme was chosen. Details of the differencing scheme used are presented by Granju (3).

Equally important as turnaround time and computation time considerations is the ease of model use. Since the model was designed to be used as an interactive tool to aid in reservoir operating decisions, it was necessary to ensure that the data input and output routines were structured so that the user could concentrate more on making reservoir operating decisions than on managing the large amount of data normally associated with models of this type. A brief description of the types of input data and the way they are managed is included below.

Local inflows--These may be derived from watershed models and reported streamflows. They are made up of both gaged and ungaged inflows into the reservoir. The model has provisions for including varying inflows into each computational reach. The user generally inputs lumped regional locals into a file, and a preprocessor disaggregates that flow into reach inflows based on relative drainage areas. Major tributary inflows may be input separately.

Boundary conditions--These may be either discharges or elevations at the boundaries (upstream and downstream dams for each reservoir). The data is entered in an hourly format by the user. A preprocessor is used to aid in data entry by repeating hourly values when desired, or linearly interpolating between specified values. The preprocessor also checks data ranges, so that by the time the routing program is invoked, most input data errors have already been detected and corrected.

Initial conditions--Internally, initial conditions consist of elevations and discharges at each computational cross section at the beginning of the routing period. For a typical reservoir, there may be 20-40 cross sections, and usually gaged information is not available for all these points. Three options have been provided to the user to aid in establishing initial conditions: (1) the option of interrogating the output file from a previous simulation, using computed values to begin a new simulation; (2) similar to (1) above, except the user can adjust the previously computed discharges and elevations using available gaged data which a preprocessor uses to distribute discrepancies in the computed data; and (3) the option of "cold starting" the model, whereby the user enters observed gage elevations and discharges where available and the preprocessor computes starting profiles and discharges using a steady flow backwater routine.

Like the previously described daily model, this model uses preprogrammed function keys to invoke all commands and procedures. All data editing is done on "forms" displayed to the screen, in a full screen edit mode. Preprocessor programs are usually run when the user saves data at the end of the edit session. Three files for each boundary, local inflow, and output for each reservoir are available to the user for use in storing data and running alternate operation schemes.

The routing program stores hourly elevations and discharges into an output file during the simulation. In addition to the routine output displayed onto the terminal screen during the simulation, the user can interrogate the output file to construct plots or listings of elevations and discharges at any point within the reservoir. One such plot is a profile plot at a given instant which shows the elevation along the entire length of the reservoir. Another useful plot is the hydrograph of discharges or elevations at a given location for the course of the simulation. The ability to retrieve data at any site (linear interpolation is used to estimate the data between adjacent computational cross sections) is an important advantage of using this type of model as compared to models where curves or relationships are established only for preselected sites.

The model was structured to allow the simulation of one reservoir at a time. The output from an upstream simulation can be used as the input into the downstream reservoir, etc., so the reservoirs can be chained together in this manner. This type of flexibility allows the user to route only certain reservoirs if so desired rather than the entire main river system.

The Kentucky-Barkley reservoir subsystem is the most common application of the model by ROB. This system is shown in Figure 4. Kentucky Reservoir is 184 miles (296 km) in length, and Barkley Reservoir is 118 miles (190 km) in length. Forty computational cross sections are used on the Kentucky side, while 21 are used for

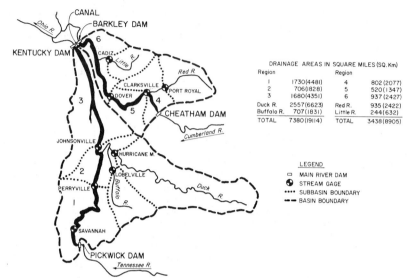

DRAINAGE AREAS IN SQUARE MILES (SQ. Km)

Region		Region	
1	1730(4481)	4	802 (2077)
2	706(1828)	5	520(1347)
3	1680(4351)	6	937 (2427)
Duck R.	2557(6623)	Red R.	935 (2422)
Buffalo R.	707(1831)	Little R.	244(632)
TOTAL	7380(19114)	TOTAL	3438(8905)

LEGEND

☐ MAIN RIVER DAM
◉ STREAM GAGE
•••• SUBBASIN BOUNDARY
▬ ▬ BASIN BOUNDARY

Figure 4.- Kentucky-Barkley Reservoir Subsystem

Barkley. Reach lengths between cross sections vary from 2 miles (3.2 km) to 10 miles (16 km), with closer definition generally being in the upper ends of each reservoir where smaller cross sections and higher velocities are prevalent. The two reservoirs are connected by a free-flowing canal. A simple steady flow rating curve is used to determine the canal flows. At the end of each computational time step, the simulated reservoir elevations at each end of the 1.2 mile (1.9 km) long canal are used to determine the canal flow and that value is used as a local inflow (or outflow depending on direction) for the next routing step. A limit both in absolute and relative change is set to avoid fluctuation in the flow which would not be physically possible, acting as a damper or filter of sorts. A computational time step of 5 minutes is used in the model. The run time requirements for the routing program are approximately 1 minute per day of simulation. Requirements for other main river reservoirs are proportional to the number of cross sections and inversely proportional to the time step used.

The model is run practically every day in ROB. A continuing simulation based on observed (actual) discharges is updated each morning using data for the previous day. The simulation results are reviewed and adjustments made based on intermediate gage locations on each reservoir (corresponding to gages shown on Figure 4). The results of this updated simulation are used as the initial conditions for all forecast simulations that day. After updating the initial conditions, the model user spends considerable time forecasting local inflows for the local watershed areas. After these are entered into the model, preliminary simulations may be performed using previous predictions of boundary releases (discharges at Cheatham and Pickwick Dams), and target operations (discharges or elevations) at Kentucky

and Barkley Dams. Later, revised forecasts for releases at Cheatham
and Pickwick are received, and additional simulations are made based
on this information. The model prints results at all gage locations
and scans for minimum and maximum elevations during the course of
each day's simulation.

Extensive calibration and verification are required for models of
this nature. Several historical events covering the range of flows
expected to be encountered during future operations must be used.
Space limitations here do not allow presentation of calibration
results, but they have been documented in a report by Granju (3).

Conclusions

Two models have been described which have been implemented for
daily use by TVA's Reservoir Operations Branch. The models are
different both in the amount of detail required for input, and in the
amount of information available as output. They both serve useful
functions, and serve to complement each other, the simpler model
being used for routine applications, and the more detailed model
being used as a followup when greater detail is needed. The hourly
model for main river reservoirs other than Kentucky-Barkley is used
much less frequently, probably due to two reasons: (1) experienced
personnel can obtain satisfactory results most of the time using the
simpler model, and (2) even with the extensive data entry aids which
have been provided, the model requires an extensive amount of effort
to prepare the input. This is compounded by the fact that since the
model is not used routinely (except for Kentucky-Barkley), personnel
are not as familiar with the model options and capabilities.
Hopefully, this can be remedied as more and more data becomes
available in digital form, requiring less effort by model users.

Acknowledgments

I would like to thank several colleagues at TVA for their support
in the development and implementation of these models: Walter
Wunderlich, for his direction and ideas; Jean-Pierre Granju for his
calibration and verification support; James R. Myers for his
expertise in designing the I/O capabilities; and the personnel in ROB
for their patience and interaction in the implementation stages.

Appendix 1. - References

1. Goranflo, H. M. Jr., and Granju, J. P., "Daily Main River Routing
   Model from Fort Loudoun Through Pickwick, Operations Version,"
   Report No. WR28-1-500-130, TVA Water Systems Development Branch,
   Norris, Tennessee, March, 1981.

2. Goranflo, H. M. Jr., and Myers, J. R., "Daily Tributary Reservoir
   Routing Model (Including User Guide)," Report No. WR28-1-500-157,
   TVA Water Systems Development Branch, Norris, Tennessee, March,
   1983.

3. Granju, J. P., "Kentucky-Barkley Dynamic Routing Model," Report
   No. WR28-1-500-140, TVA Water Systems Development Branch, Norris,
   Tennessee, May, 1981.

Savannah River Basin Flood Management Decision Support

George F. McMahon[1], Annette H. Taylor[2], and Terry M. Darragh[3]

Introduction

The Savannah District Army Corps of Engineers has constructed and now operates three multipurpose reservoirs on the Savannah River. Hartwell, the most upstream of the three projects, is located approximately 89 miles above Augusta, Georgia. The project drains an area of approximately 2,088 square miles and installed generation capacity is 344 MW. The next project, moving downstream, is the Richard B. Russell Dam and Lake, a pumped-storage facility with a 300 MW conventional installation and an ultimate additional 300 MW of pump-turbine capacity (a total of eight units). This project is located 63 miles above Augusta, Georgia, and drains approximately 812 additional square miles below Hartwell. Finally, the Clarks Hill Project is located on the Savannah River approximately 22 miles above Augusta, Georgia, draining an incremental 3,244 square miles below the Russell Dam, for a total drainage area of 6,144 square miles. Clarks Hill has an installed capacity of 280 MW and two station service units with 2 MW. Combined flood control and conservation storage of the three projects is nearly 5 million acre-feet.

Because these three tandem projects are used for flood control, hydropower, recreation, and water supply, they are operated as a system. Releases from upstream projects, runoff, and downstream impacts are considered when scheduling reservoir releases. Real-time and predictive determinations of flood discharges and stages are required for water control management decisions. A computer model to provide water control management decision support has been developed, and permanent and updatable datasets have been developed for all three reservoirs.[1,2,3] This software, known as the BRASS (Basin Runoff and Streamflow Simulation) Model, was developed in 1981 by the Savannah District Corps of Engineers.[5] The model was designed to combine some aspects of continuous and single-event hydrologic simulation with dynamic streamflow routing, and in fact combines previously-developed software developed by Savannah District with the National Weather Service DWOPER (Dynamic Wave Operational) Model.[4] Component modules are linked by a command program using "problem-oriented language" (POL) input.

Flood management decision support is provided by BRASS in the form of a hydraulic/hydrologic model with the following capabilities: (1) Continuous simulation of the infiltration potential of subbasins with-

[1]Supervisory Civil Engineer, U.S. Army Corps of Engineers, Savannah District , Savannah, GA
[2]Hydrologic Technician, U.S. Army Corps of Engineers, Savannah District
[3]Hydraulic Engineer, U.S. Army Corps of Engineers, Savannah District

in a watershed; (2) continuous simulation of subbasin baseflow; (3) generation of storm-event runoff hydrographs for subbasins using infiltration potential, baseflows, areal and temporal rainfall distributions, and user-specified unit hydrographs; (4) storage routing of subbasin outflows including both controlled and uncontrolled releases; and (5) dynamic streamflow routing for combining subbasin outflows and determining stage, discharge, and velocity histories at points throughout a river system.

The BRASS model is designed to permit the most effective use of data commonly available in regional flood forecasting in providing a degree of determinism consistent with economy of measurement. Stated simply, BRASS provides for more detailed analysis of hydraulic, geo-metric and system boundary data while employing a simpler hydrologic model, because in most cases hydraulic data are more readily obtained than hydrologic data; in many operational or design studies hydraulic considerations are paramount. BRASS was developed primarily for large watersheds where river routing considerations are significant, although it may be used for small watersheds employing only the hydrologic computations, or using both hydrologic computations and river routing if desired. BRASS is designed to be effectively used by project operators, designers, or planners not having hydrologic expertise. This is because once the model has been calibrated, only parameters related to alternatives under investigation need be changed, and the input data structure is designed to facilitate such changes.

Because of the complexity of the model, the large amounts of data required, and the limitations imposed by DWOPER on handling of internal boundary conditions, BRASS is normally applied to one reservoir at a time; reservoir releases are then used as upstream boundary data for subsequent downstream reservoirs. A typical application of BRASS to the Clarks Hill Reservoir for simulation of runoff potential for a seven-month period, and simulation of rainfall, runoff and streamflow for a six-day storm at the end of this period is described. Considera-tions in using the model, problems encountered, and comparisons with observed data are provided. An assessment of the practicality of using the model for day-to-day reservoir operations and flood management is provided.

Real-Time and Predictive Model Application

Two general datasets for the Clarks Hill Lake drainage area had been previously developed.[1] One set was developed for continuous runoff potential and baseflow simulation, and the other for single-event rainfall-runoff-streamflow simulation. For both datasets, the Clarks Hill watershed was subdivided into 54 principal subareas, com-prising river boundary sources, point lateral tributary sources, and distributed lateral inflow sources. Hydrologic data for each subarea required for single-event simulations are runoff potential (in the form of Soil Conservation Service curve numbers), baseflow, unit hydrographs, rainfall, and connectivity with the dynamic routing system. Curve numbers at the start of single-event simulations are developed by continuous simulation using long-term rainfall and evapo-ration records and physical characteristics of each subarea including land use, impervious area, and seasonal variation in soil moisture capacity. Baseflow is developed for each subarea using recorded data as available and variable-rate exponential decay. Baseflows can be updated throughout the simulation using available data, and runoff potential increases during periods of rainfall are provided for in the model. Calibration coefficients affecting curve number and baseflow variation over time and by season were determined as part of the basin dataset development, and were not modified for real-time simulation efforts; this is the basic philosophy behind model development - that it should be readily useable by water control managers.

To update curve number to current (pre-storm) conditions, daily rainfall data at gages affecting the watershed were used as input to the model; because the simulation period was considered to be representative of a drought condition, errors endemic to assumed initial conditions were minimized by starting with low (antecedent moisture condition (AMC) -1) curve numbers in all subareas. The BRASS model provides for distribution of recorded rainfall on subareas, augments missing rainfall data, and can handle both recording (hourly) and non-recording (daily) gages. The continuous simulation period extended from July 1, 1984 through January 31, 1985, distributing daily rainfall from 17 gages. Typical variation in curve number for one subarea over the period is shown in Figure 1.

Baseflow decay coefficients had been determined during initial database development by analysis of unit discharges (cfs per square mile) for five years of record at eight streamflow gaging stations. During single-event simulations, baseflows for all subareas are held constant by the BRASS model.

Simulation of rainfall and reservoir release events uses a permanent channel geometry (DWOPER) database updated and rewritten through POL and computed subarea runoff. Typical modifications to this database are upstream and downstream boundary releases or rating curves on the main channel and tributaries, subarea connectivity, computational time step, length of simulation, and output and data debugging control. The permanent database had been calibrated for reach lengths, Mannings "m" values and storage volumes using recorded streamflow data and known reservoir data. Together with the coefficients affecting curve number and baseflow variation, and with actual reservoir releases from Richard B. Russell and Clarks Hill, the model was verified for recorded floods of significant magnitude.

The model permanent datasets were updated with basin rainfall data from both recording and nonrecording gages, initial stage at Clarks Hill, initial backwater profile computed by the model, curve number and baseflow simulation results, and actual reservoir releases from Richard B. Russell and Clarks Hill for a six-day flood event beginning February 1, and extending through February 6, 1985. Observed and simulated stages at Clarks Hill Dam are plotted in Figure 2.

Conclusions

As shown in Figure 2, computed stages are in good agreement with observed stages throughout the simulated period, with a standard error of about 0.21 feet and a maximum error of approximately 0.35 feet.

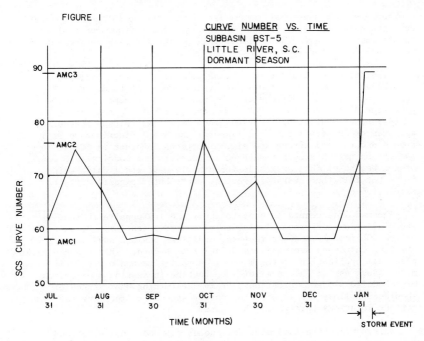

FIGURE 1

CURVE NUMBER VS. TIME
SUBBASIN BST-5
LITTLE RIVER, S.C.
DORMANT SEASON

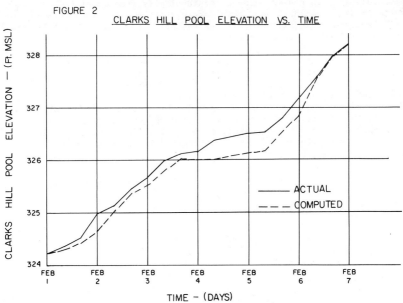

FIGURE 2

CLARKS HILL POOL ELEVATION VS. TIME

Limitations in dimensional array size for reservoir release boundary conditon data prevented continuous running of the flood event after end of rainfall; array size limits will be increased in subsequent versions of the model.

Simulation results for the rising limb of the stage hydrograph show slightly lower computed inflow volume than observed. Possible sources of error are differences in initial stages computed by the backwater algorithms in DWOPER from actual, errors in calculated initial baseflows, simplifications made in actual release schedules, differences in actual rainfall temporal and areal distribution from recorded data, and errors and simplifications inherent in SCS curve number and unit hydrograph subarea rainfall-runoff modeling. Because of the wealth of data available for dynamic wave model calibration, it is not felt that hydraulic routing contributed significantly to simulation error.

The model is generally easy to apply and inexpensive to run, especially in continuous simulation of runoff potential. Because of the POL input command structure, modifications and additions to existing databases are easily made and interpreted. This was the first practical application of the model in a real-time and a predictive mode. Such use of the model will be routine in testing the results of scheduled project operations, or in determining what schedules should be followed in maintaining target stages or discharges at various locations throughout the system.

This application indicated some needs for model upgrading and improvements. Increased array dimension limits (the model incorporates variable dimensioning), and preprocessing software for automatic entry of telemetered rainfall data will be essential for routine application of the model to all three reservoirs.

This application does indicate the model can be successfully applied by water control management personnel and produce accurate results. Typically, it is envisioned that continuous curve number and baseflow simulation will be updated weekly for all three projects, requiring less than two hours for a hydraulic engineer or hydrologic technician. Storm event runs will require approximately two man-hours per reservoir per week of real-time simulation; this estimate could be reduced significantly by automated rainfall data transcription into model databases.

Appendix - References

1. "BRASS Database - Clarks Hill Lake Drainage Basin," U.S. Army
Corps of Engineers, Savannah District, September 1984.

2. "BRASS Database - Hartwell Lake Drainage Basin," U.S. Army Corps
of Engineers, Savannah District, December 1983.

3. "BRASS Database - Richard B. Russell Lake Drainage Basin," U.S.
Army Corps of Engineers, Savannah District, September 1984.

4. Fread, D.L., "NWS Operational Dynamic Wave Model," Verification
of Mathematical and Physical Models in Hydraulic Engineering,
Proceedings, 26th Annual Hydraulic Division Specialty Conference,
ASCE, College Park, Md., Aug., 1978, pp. 455-464.

5. McMahon, George F., Fitzgerald, Robert and McCarthy, Brent,
"BRASS Model: Practical Aspects," Journal of Water Resources Planning
and Management, ASCE, Vol. 110, No. 1, Paper No. 18503, January, 1984,
pp. 75-89.

6. National Engineering Handbook, Section 4, "Hydrology," Soil
Conservation Services, U.S. Department of Agriculture, Aug., 1972.

COMPUTERIZED DESIGN AND SELECTION
OF PUMPING SYSTEMS

David G. Van Arnam, P.E., Associate Member ASCE*
Richard J. Metzger, Associate Member ASCE**

ABSTRACT

As with the dramatic increase in energy costs over the past decade, the potential for energy cost savings has significantly expanded relative to water and wastewater pumping units. To maximize the savings of cost reduction alternatives, detailed evaluations must consider the total life cycle cost of new or replacement pumping units, and operational modifications.

Three computer models have been applied in the evaluation, design and selection of a high-lift pump station upgrading program developed for the City of Poughkeepsie, New York. The three models evaluate system hydraulics, pump performance and energy costs, and total pumping system energy costs. A broad range of alternatives were evaluated. The lowest total cost alternative, utilizing a staged pump replacement program, high-efficiency motors, and pump control valves has been implemented.

INTRODUCTION

Water purveyors have seen energy costs increase dramatically over the past ten years. United States Department of Energy and Edison Electric Institute statistics indicate that electric cost have increased 330% between 1970 and 1981[1]. As a result of these increased energy costs, power requirements have often become the largest, single portion of the total water system operating budget. Although potential energy cost savings are significant, detailed evaluations must consider the total life cycle cost of new or replacement pumping units, and operational modifications.

The need for a mechanism to effectively and efficiently evaluate the alternatives available for minimizing pumping energy costs is emphasized by several factors:

1. Each hydraulic network in which the pumping system is located has unique hydraulic and boundary (head and flow rate) characteristics.

---

* Managing Engineer, O'Brien & Gere Engineers, Inc. 1304 Buckley Road, Syracuse, NY 13221

** Project Engineer, O'Brien & Gere Engineers, Inc. 1304 Buckley Road, Syracuse, NY 13221

2. Each pump design has its own unique performance characteristics (only in rare instances will two different pump manufacturers have units with identical design characteristics).

3. Numerous pumping unit drives and control systems are available.

To perform detailed evaluations on a large matrix of options, three computer models have been applied for a high-lift pump station upgrading program developed for the City of Poughkeepsie, New York, to evaluate energy saving alternatives. The three models evaluate system hydraulics, pump performance and energy costs, and total pumping system energy costs.

HYDRAULIC NETWORK MODELING

Computerized hydraulic network analyses allow for rapid and efficient solution of large and complex networks under a variety of conditions. Consideration of the full range of potential conditions is necessary for a complete assessment of system operation and for the evaluation of potential improvements to the system.

The analysis of water system hydraulic characteristic utilizing computerized solutions have been available for over 25 years. Currently, there are numerous programs available for hydraulic analyses[2]. The methods most commonly utilized in the solution of these equations are the Hardy-Cross Method and the Newton-Raphson Technique.[3]

Development of the network model involves a three step process. First, data on the physical characteristics of the infrastructure (size, location and configuration of pipes, pumps, tanks, and valves) is collected and a system schematic is developed. Data on the system's operational characteristics, including consumption, pump operations, and storage utilization, are collected for use in calibration of the model and assessment of current operations. Thirdly, the mathematical model is calibrated and verified.

The Poughkeepsie hydraulic network model was used to develop the system curves used in the design and selection of the pumping system up-grading plan. Recognizing, that the City has limited usable storage, the system curves have been bracketed around the condition where the pumping rate equals the consumptive rate (no charge in storage). Based on a statistical evaluation of previous storage and pumping data, a conservative estimate of the peak storage filing and withdrawal rate was made. The maximum and minimum head at any flow represents a demand either from, or provided by, storage of approximately 35 percent.

The hydraulic network model was also used for other evaluations including:

1. Evaluation of the capacity and efficiency of the existing transmission system under current conditions.

2. Evaluation of the effects of proposed transmission system modifications and capital improvements.

3. Determination of optimal storage capacity needs and optimal utilization of existing capacity.

4. Location and analysis of trouble areas, such as high or low pressure areas, closed valves or main breaks.

5. Development of plans for system operation under emergency situations.

PUMPING ENERGY MODEL

Each pump manufacturer has a slightly different pump design applicable to the specific flow and head requirements of any one pumping application. In general, the manufacturers may have the same type of unit (i.e. double-volute, single-stage design) however, the size, configuration and mechanical efficiency of each manufacturer's impeller, casing and other internal components results in performance characteristics unique to each pump manufacturer.

To establish the optimal sizing, resulting in the lowest operating costs, four major manufacturers were selected and a detailed evaluation was performed to establish the optimal sizing of the two proposed replacement pumps at the Poughkeepsie High-Lift Pump Station (HLPS).

In addition to the unique performance of different pump designs, the performance of the pump drive unit and the control system must be evaluated to determine the cost-effectiveness of the various alternatives.

The pumping energy model was developed to assess the energy costs associated with the operation of individual pumps and drives, and combinations thereof, under varying system conditions. The process of the pumping energy model is diagrammed on Figure 1. Pump and drive unit performance data may be obtained from published data for proposed units or from pump performance testing of existing units.[4] Data required includes total dynamic head (TDH) and efficiency versus flow rate (Q) for the pumps; motor efficiency and power factor versus percent of full load for the drives. From the resulting plot of the unit power required versus the flow rate, the optimal pumping schedule (based on power consumption) is established. The optimal pumping unit(s) (pump plus drive) for operation is the unit which has the lowest unit power consumption at a given flow rate. An example data output and a unit power consumption plot are shown on Table 1 and Figure 2, respectively.

For the Poughkeepsie HLPS design, the following alternatives were evaluated:

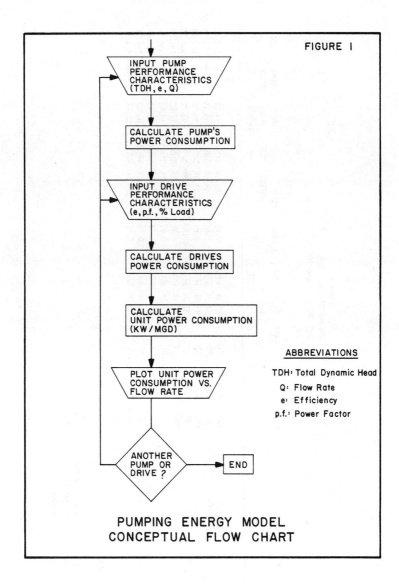

FIGURE 1

INPUT PUMP PERFORMANCE CHARACTERISTICS (TDH, e, Q)

CALCULATE PUMP'S POWER CONSUMPTION

INPUT DRIVE PERFORMANCE CHARACTERISTICS (e, p.f., % Load)

CALCULATE DRIVES POWER CONSUMPTION

CALCULATE UNIT POWER CONSUMPTION (KW/MGD)

PLOT UNIT POWER CONSUMPTION VS. FLOW RATE

ANOTHER PUMP OR DRIVE?

END

ABBREVIATIONS

TDH: Total Dynamic Head
Q: Flow Rate
e: Efficiency
p.f.: Power Factor

PUMPING ENERGY MODEL
CONCEPTUAL FLOW CHART

TABLE 1
POUGHKEEPSIE H.L. P.S.
UNIT ENERGY EVALUATION

PUMP	MODEL	MOTOR hp	TDH ft	PUMPING RATE gpm	MGD	EFFICIENCY %	BHP hp	% LOAD %	MOTOR EFFICIENCY %	POWER USE kW	UNIT POWER kW/MGD	POWER FACTOR	KVA
No. 4 NEW	18x14x28 26.3"IMP.	800 (HI EFF)	280	8540	12.31	87.4%	691.27	0.86	94.6%	545.87	44.39	0.868	629.03
			285	8260	11.90	87.5%	679.77	0.85	94.6%	536.97	45.14	0.866	619.91
			290	8000	11.53	87.5%	669.92	0.84	94.5%	529.36	45.95	0.865	612.18
			295	7840	11.30	87.5%	667.84	0.83	94.5%	527.75	46.75	0.864	610.56
			300	7560	10.89	87.4%	655.65	0.82	94.5%	518.37	47.62	0.862	601.13
			305	7360	10.61	87.2%	650.43	0.81	94.5%	514.35	48.53	0.861	597.12
			310	7000	10.09	87.1%	629.48	0.79	94.4%	498.29	49.43	0.857	581.23
			315	6590	9.50	86.5%	606.35	0.76	94.2%	480.65	50.65	0.852	564.02
			320	6000	8.65	84.7%	572.74	0.72	94.0%	455.16	52.68	0.844	539.56

NOTES:

Kilowatts = 0.747 x Horsepower (hp)
Meters = 0.3048 x Feet (ft)
Liters/second = Gallons/minute x 0.0631

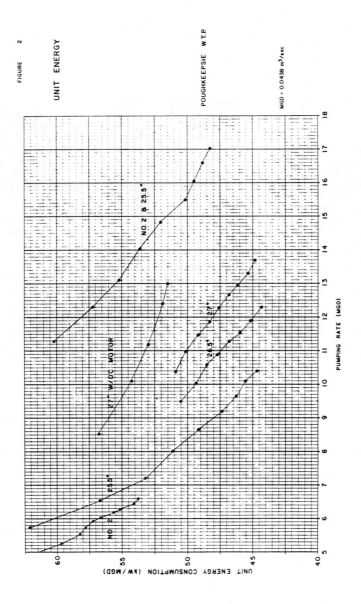

FIGURE 2

UNIT ENERGY

POUGHKEEPSIE W.T.P.

MGD = 0.0438 m³/sec

    a.   Different pumps and manufacturers;
    b.   Standard motors;
    c.   High-efficiency motors;
    d.   Two speed and variable speed drives;
    e.   Power factor correction; and
    f.   Pump control valves.

COST ANALYSIS MODEL

To enable the cost-effective analysis of each alternative a third
model was utilized. The cost analysis model considers the optimal
pumping unit(s) and its unit cost of operation within a specific flow
range and the estimated annual hours of operation within the flow
range to project the annual operating cost of an alternative. The
estimated annual hours of operation at a specific flow rate was
established for the projected replacement units design life based on a
statistical analysis of past flows. The optimal pumping schedule and
unit power consumption was developed with the use of the pumping
energy model. The total estimated annual power cost of each
alternative was then calculated based on this information. The cost
model was developed using commercially available spread-sheet
software. An example of the output for the analysis of one
alternative is presented on Table 2.

The least cost alternative was selected following a present worth
analysis of alternatives using the annual operating cost projected
from the cost analysis model.

STUDY RESULTS

The results of the cost-effective analysis for the Poughkeepsie HLPS
design found that a staged replacement program, initially replacing
two of the four high-lift pumps was the least cost alternative. The
study also concluded that high-efficiency motors with pump control
valves have a lower present worth than standard efficiency, variable
speed, or two speed motors when applied to the Poughkeepsie water
system. Power factor correction was determined not to be cost-
effective.

Total energy savings of the lowest cost alternative, as compared to
continued operation with the existing system, was projected to be
$50,000 per year (approximately 18 percent of the annual energy
costs), as shown below:

	Annual Pumping Energy (KW-hrs)	Annual Pumping Energy Cost
Existing Units	5.62×10^{6}	$284,000
Least-Cost Alternative	4.62×10^{6}	$234,000

The estimated pay-back period of the first phase pump replacement is
between four and five years.

TABLE 2
EXAMPLE COST ANALYSIS MODEL OUTPUT

ANNUAL PUMPING ENERGY COST ESTIMATE

ALTERNATIVE No. 2

(A)	(B)	(C)	(D)	(E)	(F)
INTERVAL MID-PT	PROB OF OCCURENCE	OPTIMAL PUMP(S)	UNIT PUMPING ENERGY	DEMAND	ESTIMATED POWER CONSUMPTION
(MGD)	(%)		(kW/MGD)	(kW)	(kWhrs)
7.3	0.00	25.5"	53.0	387	0
7.5	0.14	25.5"	52.5	394	4,832
7.7	0.30	25.5"	52.0	400	10,530
7.9	0.50	25.5"	51.5	407	17,832
8.1	0.70	25.5"	51.0	413	25,349
8.3	1.10	25.5"	50.0	415	40,017
8.5	1.40	25.5"	49.5	421	51,636
10.1	7.40	27"	52.0	525	340,689
10.3	7.90	27"	51.0	525	363,778
10.5	7.90	27"	50.7	532	368,660
10.7	7.70	27"	50.5	540	364,727
10.9	7.60	27"	50.3	548	365,266
11.1	6.20	27"	50.0	555	301,638
11.3	4.90	27"	49.5	559	240,260
11.5	4.00	27"	49.2	566	198,392
11.7	3.20	27"	48.6	569	159,505
11.9	2.80	27"	48.3	575	141,076
12.1	2.20	27"	48.0	581	112,008
14.5	0.30	#2& 25.5"	52.7	764	20,096
14.7	0.26	#2& 25.5"	52.4	770	17,556
14.9	0.20	#2& 25.5"	52.0	775	13,584
15.1	0.18	#2& 25.5"	51.5	778	12,270
15.3	0.14	#2& 25.5"	50.7	776	9,520
15.5	0.10	#2& 25.5"	50.1	777	6,807
15.7	0.08	#2& 25.5"	50.0	785	5,505
15.9	0.06	#2& 25.5"	49.7	790	4,156
16.1	0.04	#2& 25.5"	49.7	800	2,806
16.3	0.00	#2& 25.5"	49.7	810	0

TOTAL kWHRS/YR   4,649,423
TOTAL ENERGY $ $234,889

PUMPING UNIT ACQUISITION

To assure the acquisition of the lowest total cost (capital plus operational) pumping equipment, the cost-effective analysis was incorporated in the competitive bidding procedure. The pumping units were bid separately from the installation contract to assure the acquisition of the lowest total cost equipment. Each pumping unit bidder was required to complete the necessary bid information by calculating the present worth of his proposed pumping units based upon the operational data provided by the City. This cost-effective bidding format was successfully implemented. The selected low bid required an additional initial investment of $5,600 over the low capital cost only bid; however, annual energy costs are projected to be $9,000 per year lower. Thus, the additional initial investment will be returned in less than one year, or over the 20-year life-cycle of the units will result in a present-worth cost savings to the City of approximately $80,000.

REFERENCES

1. Sillian, John O. "Future Directions in Electric Rates" In American Water Works Association 1984 Annual Conference Proceedings: (June 1984).

2. Walski, T.M. Using Water Distribution System Models. Jour. AWWA 75:2:58 (February, 1983).

3. Shamir, U. and Howard, C.D.D. Engineering Analysis of Water-Distribution Systems. Jour. AWWA 68:9:510 (September, 1977).

4. VanArnam, D.G., Heckathorne, J.R., and Metzger, R.J. "Our Water System Infrastructure: Planning Now for the Twenty-First Century" In American Water Works Association 1984 Annual Conference Proceedings. (June 1984).

Integrated Design Methodology for Urban Stormwater
Detention Facilities

Stephan J. Nix, A.M. ASCE*

Abstract

Detention systems are commonly used to abate urban runoff flooding
problems. In fact, they are probably the most popular technique
in use today. A review of current design wisdom reveals an almost
exclusive use of methods based on the "design storm" concept. While
the venerable nature of this concept is substantial, it is quite
dated and rooted in the environment of the pre-computer age. Its
deficiencies are fairly well known. Given the recent advances in
computer technology and accessibility, the time has come to
re-evaluate the methods based on this concept and explore the use
of modern computational technology to derive more effective techniques.
The objective of this paper is to present the core of a design methodology that avoids the pitfalls of the design storm concept by using
a microcomputer algorithm to estimate the long-term response of detention systems. The algorithm consists of three modules: (1) a stochastic runoff event generator, (2) an event "shaper" (for estimating
intraevent variations), and (3) a detention basin model. These modules
are part of a larger effort to produce a viable design methodology.
Future extensions will include a module to guide the detention basin
model in estimating flood control capability over a large matrix
of design variations and an optimization module to locate the most
cost-effective design.

Introduction

Urbanization results in increased flow rates and volumes from
stormwater runoff events. The concept of detention storage is the
technique most commonly applied to abate the problems caused by this
phenomenon (1, 2, 3, 6, 17). In a 1980 survey, the American Public
Works Association found 12,683 detention systems in use in 325 communities throughout the United States and Canada. Since this survey
relied on the participation of those surveyed and represents only
a fraction of all communities in the U.S. and Canada, the true number
is undoubtedly much higher. The more common detention system types
reported in this survey were dry basins, parking lots, wet ponds,
rooftop storage, and underground storage. In many localities, detention systems are required by regulation or statute. A cursory review
of the literature leaves little doubt that detention storage is considered to be a highly effective means of controlling urban runoff
quantity problems.

*Assistant Professor, Dept. of Civil Engineering, Syracuse University
Syracuse, NY 13210

A review of current design wisdom for urban stormwater facilities
reveals a nearly exclusive reliance on methods based on the design
storm concept (1, 23, 25 and many others). These methods are popular
because of their relative simplicity and their explicit or implied
inclusion in numerous state and local regulations. While the venerable
nature of the design storm concept is substantial, the idea is quite
dated and rooted in the environment of the pre-computer age. At
a recent American Society of Civil Engineers (ASCE) symposium devoted
to the subject of urban detention systems (2), it was noted that
one of the most pressing research needs was to review available design
techniques and assess their relative strengths and weaknesses. The
author also believes that the time is right for a new perspective
on the problem. Given the recent advances in computer technology
and accessibility, the time has come to re-evaluate these methods
and explore modern computational capabilities in an attempt to derive
more effective techniques. To date, the principal use of computers
in this field has been to automate the traditional methods. Very
little effort has been directed toward the application of computers
to the comprehensive analysis of historical records, costs, benefits,
and various designs in order to create unique, cost-effective solutions for local stormwater problems.

The use of the design storm concept has several widely recognized
drawbacks, including those listed below:

(1)   The design storm technique does not adequately consider
      the interactions of the total system, i.e., the watershed,
      detention basin, and receiving stream. This includes the
      effect of antecedent moisture conditions.

(2)   The rainfall intensity-duration-frequency curves from which
      storm volumes are taken can not provide any information
      concerning the time history of the event.

(3)   The return period of the design rainstorm is not necessarily
      the same as the return period of the resulting runoff event.

(4)   The design storm technique ignores the possibility that
      a sequence of smaller events or a less intense storm with
      a longer duration might place more stress on the system.

While the deficiencies listed above are serious, the design
storm method has one particularly debilitating problem -- it does
not readily allow comprehensive investigations into the cost-effectiveness of alternative designs. Regardless of the relative merits
or demerits of the design storm concept, it has been misused in the
sense that the design storm should be the result of an engineering
exercise rather than the criterion from which the engineer begins
his work. Such an exercise looks at a wide range of events and selects
the one that minimizes the sum of the system costs and damages to
society (see Fig. 1). This simple fact seems to have been lost in
a maze of statutory design storms that seem to have little justification behind them. While some attention may be paid to economics
in the promulgation of these regulations, they are generally not
site-specific and, as a result, they are probably overly conservative
for most applications.

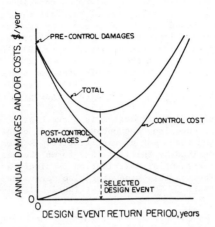

Figure 1.   Selection of a Design Event.

The objective of this paper is to present some initial thoughts
on a design method that avoids the pitfalls of the design storm concept
by treating the runoff pattern and detention basin in a comprehensive,
long-term manner. The methodology is microcomputer-based and currently
consists of (1) a stochastic runoff event generator, (2) an event
"shaper," and (3) a detention basin simulator.   The entire program
is written in BASIC. Future extensions will include a module to
guide the detention basin model through a matrix of design variations
and an optimization module capable of selecting the most cost-effective
system designs.

Basic Approach

    One of the most severe criticisms of the design storm concept
is the fact that it only looks at an isolated storm developed from
a rather primitive set of assumptions. An obvious way to circumvent
this problem is to use a computer model to produce long-term continuous simulations. However, there are problems with this approach
(16). The most pressing problem is the fact that most computer models
capable of long, continuous runs are generally limited to hourly
time steps. In addition, published rainfall data from first-order
precipitation stations are in an hourly format. For intense, short
duration storms the use of an hourly time step is inadequate because
the true peak runoff flow will be underestimated in the subsequent
simulation. Another major problem associated with the use of continuous simulation is the large amount of data that must be gathered
and processed. There appears to be a limited number of options in
handling the time discretization and input data magnitude problems,
especially if one wants to keep the final methodology as practical
as possible. At present, the following general approach seem plausible.

    The gamma and exponential distributions have been used to describe
such rainfall and runoff event characteristics as duration, average

intensity, volume, and interevent times (5, 7, 12, 13, 15). These distributions are certainly not the only ones capable of representing these characteristics. Distributions of rainfall and runoff event characteristics are skewed; i.e., there are many smaller observations and few large ones. The lognormal and Weibull distributions are also capable of representing such populations (7, 9). Nevertheless, the gamma and exponential distributions have been used extensively in studies concerning the performance of detention systems (5, 8, 12, 13, 15, 19) and because of this they will be used in much the same capacity in this preliminary approach to the problem.

The first module of the algorithm is a stochastic runoff event generator used to produce long sequences of runoff events from the statistics describing the event characteristics. A gamma random deviate generator derived by Phillips (22) forms the heart of the module. Since the exponential distribution is simply a special case of the gamma distribution this generator also serves as an exponential random deviate generator. The gamma distribution is given below:

$$p(x) = (\kappa/\bar{x}) \; \frac{x^{\kappa-1}}{\Gamma(\kappa)} \; \exp(-\kappa x/\bar{x}) \dots\dots\dots\dots\dots\dots (1)$$

where $p(x)$ = gamma probability distribution function of x, $\kappa = 1/\nu^2$, ν = coefficient of variation, $\bar{x}$ = mean of x, and $\Gamma(\kappa)$ = gamma function with argument κ. The coefficient of variation is defined as the standard deviation divided by the mean. As can be seen in Eq. 1, the gamma is a two-parameter distribution requiring estimates of the mean and standard deviation (or coefficient of variation).

The gamma random variate generator was structured to first produce a sequence of interevent times given values for the mean and coefficient of variation. The exponential distribution is commonly used to describe the time between independent events of many types including rainfall and runoff events (7, 8, 12, 13, 15). In fact, this distribution has been used to define sequences of independent rainfall and runoff events (15). If the exponential distribution is used to produce a sequence of interevent times the coefficient of variation is set equal to 1.0. Inspection of Eq. 1 shows that when $\nu = 1.0$, the exponential distribution results (i.e., $\kappa = 1$, $\Gamma(1) = 1$).

Following the interevent times, the generator produces a sequence of average event flow rates given values for the mean and coefficient of variation. Subsequently, the event durations are generated. The three sequences are merged into a single sequence of events with each event defined by its antecedent dry period (i.e., the interevent time), mean flow rate, and duration. The entire generation process stops when a preselected time limit is equalled or exceeded. The sequence is stored on a floppy disk.

The stochastic model described above only produces a sequence of events with varying durations and average flow rates -- no within-event variations are mimicked. Possible remedies might include using a single hydrograph shape or deriving a set of shapes representing variations due to the season, event duration, event average intensity,

etc. The effectiveness of either approach could be checked against
actual records or records derived from simulations using highly
detailed rainfall records. The rather simple approach used here assumes
a triangular hydrograph for each runoff event. The module developed
for this task is run separately from the runoff event generation
module: it only requires the specification of the time to peak flow
(expressed as a fraction of the event duration) and the time step
used to discretize the hydrograph. The module prepares a complete
runoff hydrograph by interspersing the appropriate dry interevent
periods between the runoff events. The resulting long-term hydrograph
is stored in an independent disk file. The contents of the event
and hydrograph files are maintained separately to allow multiple
runs without completely re-executing all portions of the algorithm.

The third module consists of a detention basin simulator. This
simulator was adapted from the Storm Water Management Model (SWMM)
Storage/Treatment Block (14, 19) and is essentially a computerized
version of the modified Puls method of level-surface reservoir routing
(24). The reader is referred to the indicated references for details.
The version used here requires a hydraulic description of the basin
via a set of depth-discharge-storage data triplets and the initial
state of the basin (i.e., initial values for water stored, inflow,
and outflow). The module produces an outflow series in response
to the inflow series produced by the previous module. This series
is also stored in an independent disk file.

The three modules described above represent a limited version
of what the author hopes will be a comprehensive design tool. What
has been described provides a way to generate a long-term record
of detention basin performance. However, it is not complete, for
it does not answer at least two obvious questions:

(1) Where are the runoff statistics to come from?

(2) How are the results produced by the detention basin simula-
     tor used to design a detention system?

The first question is an important one for seldomly are there
runoff records of sufficient length to produce good estimates of
the required statistical parameters. However, there seems to be
several possible approaches. First, one could use a well-calibrated
rainfall-runoff model to produce a lengthy, sufficiently detailed
runoff record (assuming a lengthy rainfall record is available).
There are some obvious caveats, not the least of which is the bias
that the model, by its very structure, gives the simulated runoff
record. However, if the model was well calibrated it seems reasonable
to expect that the statistics gleaned from the simulated record would
be representative. An obvious question at this point would be "Why
not just use the simulated runoff record as the input to a detention
basin model?" Recall that a historical record, whether it be real
or simulated, is only one possible sequence of events from an infinite
number of possibilities. However, that sequence can give us the
information we need to learn of the probabilistic nature of runoff
at a particular site. With this information, a very long sequence
(many times longer than the longest historical record) can be produced

via a stochastic model. This sequence, if its credibility is good, can lead to more reliable designs than those based on the frequency of events occurring during a 10, 20, or 50 year period.

Another possibility for establishing representative runoff event statistics is the development of relationships between the rainfall and runoff event statistics. Rainfall records are more available than runoff records, thus, there is obvious advantage in developing such relationships. A few simple relationships were hypothesized in earlier attempts to characterize the performance of stormwater storage/treatment systems (12, 13, 15).

Ideally, the statistics required for this method, or some variation thereof, could be developed for a wide variety of locations in much the same way that intensity-duration-frequency curves can be found for many locations around the United States. This would allow local engineers and planners to use the method without having to develop the necessary statistics.

The second question is not simple to answer. However, it is certain that the answer will deal with designing a system that meets certain performance levels at the least possible cost. Essentially, performance can be expressed as some measure of reliability (18, 19). Pertinent forms include occurrence-based reliability (the probability that a failure will not occur more than a given number of times in a given time period), time reliability (the portion of time that a given objective is satisfied), and volume reliability (the total volume of water captured by the system). Each of these can play a role depending on the level of the analysis (preliminary screening, planning, design) and the objectives of the system (peak flow control, volume control, etc.). Regardless of the measure of performance, it is convenient to use production functions to depict performance as it relates to various design parameters (i.e., basin volume, outlet characteristics, etc.). Production theory and production functions have been applied by several investigators in the analysis of detention systems (8, 10, 11, 12, 19, 21). Given the technical information summarized by a production function it is possible to locate the least cost design for any level of performance. A graphical technique has been proposed by the author for handling this type of problem (19, 20, 21). Such a technique is amenable to execution by a computer graphics software package. Future extensions will produce the necessary production functions and search for the least-cost designs.

Application

The methodology was applied to a hypothetical scenario involving a simple detention basin receiving runoff from a drainage area of 640 acres (259 ha). The basin was given vertical sides and a rectangular surface area of 45,000 sq ft (4,181 m^2) at all depths. The basin width, length, and depth were 150 ft (45.7 m), 300 ft (91.4 m), and 12 ft (3.66 m), respectively. The storage capacity (450,000 cu ft or 12,743 m^3) corresponded to 0.194 in. (0.492 cm.) over the drainage area. The outlet structure consisted of a 3 ft (0.914 m)-diameter orifice located at the base of the basin and a weir along the width

of the basin at the outlet side. The base of the weir is at the
10-ft (3.05 m) level. The orifice was assumed to behave according
to the well-known equation

$$Q = CA(2gH_o)^{\frac{1}{2}} \dots\dots\dots\dots\dots\dots\dots\dots\dots\dots\dots\dots\dots(2)$$

in which Q = discharge (cubic feet per second); C = orifice coefficient
(dimensionless); A = orifice cross-sectional area (square feet);
g = acceleration due to gravity (32.2 ft sec^{-2}); and H_o = depth from
the water surface to the center of the orifice (feet). For simplicity,
C was assumed to be 1.0. The weir was assumed to behave according
to

$$Q = 3.3 \ L \ H_w^{3/2} \dots\dots\dots\dots\dots\dots\dots\dots\dots\dots\dots\dots\dots(3)$$

in which L = width of the weir (feet) and H_w = depth from the water
surface to the base of the weir (feet).

The Runoff Block of SWMM was used to generate a year of hourly
runoff flows. The model was driven with the 1969 hourly precipitation
record for Atlanta, Georgia. This particular year was selected on
the basis of a frequency analysis performed by Heaney et al. (10)
in which the record for 1969 was deemed to be the most representative
of a longer record (1948-1972). This is obviously a very short time
period but it will suffice for illustrative purposes. The imperviousness
of the watershed was assigned a value of 27% and the watershed width
was assumed to be 2000 ft (609.6 m). The ground slope was assigned
a value of 0.005. Evaporation rates were taken from Heaney et al.
(10). All other surface characteristics related to the runoff simulation were described by default values found in earlier versions of
SWMM. The latest version supplies very few default values (14).

The flows generated by the SWMM Runoff Block were routed through
the detention basin described above. This particular step was accomplished by the SWMM Storage/Treatment Block. In addition, the flows
discharged by the detention basin were analyzed by the Statistics
Block of SWMM to produce a cumulative frequency curve for comparison
with the results produced by the microcomputer modules. This curve
is shown in Fig. 2.

The runoff produced by the Runoff Block was also analyzed to
determine the mean and coefficient of variation of the event mean
flows, duration, and interevent times. Seventy-six independent events
were defined by assuming a minimum interevent time of 6 hours. The
results are given below:

	Mean	Coef. of Variation
Flow	0.0637 in/hr	2.559
Duration	25.1 hrs	0.702
Interevent Time	89.6 hrs	0.943

The stochastic event generator was set-up with the statistics given
above. It generated seventy-seven events with the following statistics:

	Mean	Coef. of Variation
Flow	0.0780 in/hr	2.664
Duration	26.7 hrs	0.700
Interevent Time	86.2 hrs	1.012

These events were converted to a series of triangular hydrographs in which it was assumed that the peak flow occurs at one-third of the event duration. The entire series was routed through the detention basin simulator. The simulator produced a cumulative frequency of discharges. This information is depicted in Fig. 2. The results produced by the deterministic runoff flows and those generated by the algorithm proposed here demonstrate poor agreement. This was to be expected, for little effort was spent to determine the appropriateness of the distributions used or the adequacy of the assumed hydrograph shape. Additionally, the length of time over which the comparison was conducted increased the likelihood that the stochastically generated runoff sequence would not mimic the deterministically generated series.

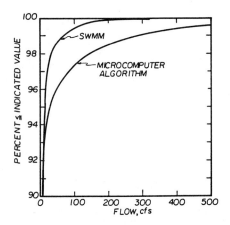

Figure 2. Application Results.

Conclusions

In spite of the rather poor results shown above, it seems clear that the general approach has merit and that it begins to address some of the deficiencies of the design storm concept. Unfortunately, many other questions arise. These can only be answered by lengthy study. However, it also seems certain that the art of detention basin design could be advanced by using present-day computer technology in a way that truly takes advantage of its power and potential.

References

1. American Public Works Association, "Urban Stormwater Management," Special Report No. 49, APWA, 1981.

2. Degroot, W., ed., Proceedings of the Conference on Stormwater Detention Facilities, Henniker, New Hampshire, ASCE, New York, 1982.

3. Delleur, J.W., "Recent Advances in Urban Hydrology in the USA," Proc. International Symposium on Urban Hydrology, Hydraulics, and Sediment Control, Univ. of Kentucky, Lexington, Kentucky, July, 1983, pp. 1-10.

4. Delleur, J.W. and G. Padmanabhan, "An Extended Statistical Analysis of Synthetic Nonpoint Urban Runoff Quantity and Quality Data," Proc. International Symposium on Urban Hydrology, Hydraulics, and Sediment Control, Univ. of Kentucky, Lexington, Kentucky, July, 1981, pp. 229-237.

5. DiToro, D.M. and M.J. Small, "Stormwater Interception and Storage," Journal of the Environmental Engineering Division, ASCE, 105(EE1), Feb., 1979, pp 43-54.

6. Donahue, J.R., R.H. McCuen, and T.R. Bondelid, "Comparison of Detention Basin Planning and Design Models," Journal of the Water Resources Planning and Management Division, ASCE, 107(WR2), Oct., 1981 pp. 385-400.

7. Eagleson, P.S., Dynamic Hydrology, McGraw-Hill, New York, 1970.

8. Goforth, G.F.E., J.P. Heaney, and W.C. Huber, "Comparison of Basin Performance Modeling Techniques," Journal of Environmental Engineering, ASCE, 109(EE5), Oct., 1983, pp. 1082-1098.

9. Haan, C.T., Statistical Methods in Hydrology, Iowa State Univ. Press, Ames, Iowa, 1977.

10. Heaney, J.P., W.C. Huber, M.A. Medina, M.P. Murphy, S.J. Nix, and S.M. Hasan, "Nationwide Evaluation of Combined Sewer Overflows and Urban Stormwater Discharges," EPA-600/2-77-064b, USEPA, Cincinnati, Ohio, Mar., 1977.

11. Heaney, J.P., S.J. Nix, and M.P. Murphy, "Storage-Treatment Mixes for Stormwater Control," Journal of the Envirnomental Engineering Division, ASCE, 104(EE4), Aug., 1978, pp. 581-592.

12. Howard, C.D.D., "Theory of Storage and Treatment--Plant Overflows," Journal of the Environmental Engineering Division, ASCE, 102(EE4), Aug., 1976, pp. 709-722.

13. Howard, C.D.D., P.E. Flatt, and U. Shamir, "Storm and Combined Sewer Storage-Treatment Theory Compared to Computer Simulation," Grant No. R-805109, USEPA, Cincinnati, Ohio, Oct., 1979.

14. Huber, W.C., J.P. Heaney, S.J. Nix, R.E. Dickinson, and D.J. Polmann, "Storm Water Management Model, User's Manual, Version III," EPA-600/8284-109a&b, USEPA, Cincinnati, Ohio, 1984.

15. Hydroscience, Inc., "A Statistical Method for the Assessment of Urban Stormwater," EPA-400/3-79-023, USEPA, Washington, D.C., May, 1979.

16. James, W. and M. Robinson, "Continuous Models Essential for Detention Design," Proc. Conference on Stormwater Detention Facilities, Henniker, New Hampshire, ASCE, New York, 1982, pp. 163-175.

17. Jones, J.E. and D.E. Jones, "Essential Urban Detention Ponding Considerations," Journal of Water Resources Planning and Management, ASCE, 110(WR4), Oct., 1984, pp. 418-433.

18. Kritskiy, S.N. and Menkel, M.K., "Computational Methods for Water Resources," Gidrometeoizdat, Leningrad, USSR, 1952 (from Klemes, V., "Applied Stochastic Theory of Storage in Evolution," Advances in Hydroscience, Vol. 12, Academic Press, New York, 1981, pp. 79-141.

19. Nix, S.J., "Analysis of Storage/Release Systems in Urban Stormwater Quality Management," Ph.D. dissertation, Univ. of Florida, Gainesville, Florida, 1982.

20. Nix, S.J., "Graphical Design Optimization," Civil Engineering for Practicing and Design Engineers, Pergamon Press, 3(4), Apr., 1984, pp. 311-325.

21. Nix, S.J., J.P. Heaney, and W.C. Huber, "Analysis of Storage/ Release Systems in Urban Stormwater Quality Management: A Methodology," Proc. International Symposium on Urban Hydrology, Hydraulics, and Sediment Control, Univ. of Kentucky, Lexington, Kentucky, July, 1983, pp. 19-29.

22. Phillips, D.T., "Generation of Randon Gamma Variates from the Two Parameter Gamma," AIIE Transaction, Vol. III, No. 3, Sept., 1971.

23. Poertner, H.G., "Practices in Detention of Urban Storm Water Runoff," Special Report No. 43, American Public Works Association, Chicago, Illinois, June, 1974.

24. Viessman, W., J.W. Knapp, G.J. Lewis, and T.E. Harbaugh, Introduc tion to Hydrology, 2nd ed., Harper and Row, New York, 1977.

25. Wanielista, M.P., Stormwater Management--Quantity and Quality, Ann Arbor Science Publishers, Ann Arbor, Michigan, 1978.

Storm Sewer Computer-Aided Design and Uncertainty

William P. Gilman[1], M. ASCE and Mitchell J. Small[2], M. ASCE

A micro-computer based storm drainage model is presented which facilitates urban storm sewer design on fast tracked construction projects.
The model is an interactive Basic program using a time-lagged Rational
Method to compute design flows, required pipe diameters, sewer appurtenances, and estimated project costs. For design rainfall intensities the
model incorporates a new generalized rainfall intensity-duration-frequency formula. A sensitivity/uncertainty analysis is conducted on the model
to determine the range of possible design solutions and associated costs,
and to identify which design input parameters most significantly affect
this range. The model is replicated using a Latin hypercube sampling
scheme, and regression and rank order correlation are used to identify
the parameters most important to the resulting design cost.

Introduction

The design of a storm drainage system for a site development project involves the estimation of several design input parameters. The
level of accuracy in estimating these parameters can have a significant
influence on the system's constructed cost. Presented here is a model
developed to provide computer aid to the design of an urban storm sewer
system. The model is an interactive BASIC program, written for an IBM-
PC, which prompts the user for general and elemental site information.
A modified Rational Method is used to route storm water steady flows
through the system with time-lagged hydrographs (10). The method of Chen
(4) is used to predict rainfall intensity-duration relationships for
specified return periods. The model's format is an abbreviated version
of the Storm Drainage Design Summary in ASCE Manual No. 37 (1).

A sensitivity/uncertainty analysis is conducted on the model outputs
to determine the range of possible design solutions and associated costs,
and to identify which design input parameters considered in this study
most significantly affect this range. The uncertain input parameters
considered include drainage area characteristics: runoff coefficients,
times of concentration, and tributary areas; the conveyance properties:
Manning's n and slope; and the meteorological inputs: the 10-year 1-hour
rainfall depth, the 10-year 24-hour rainfall depth, and the 100-year 1-
hour rainfall depth used in the Chen method. A Latin hypercube stratified sampling scheme (7,9) is used to randomly select the model inputs for
each replication. Model output is summarized by a total project cost.
A partial rank order correlation and multivariate linear regression are
used to identify the uncertainties that exhibit highest influence on the
resulting design cost and to determine how sensitive the cost is to each

[1] Professional Engineer and Graduate Student, Department of Civil Engineering, Carnegie-Mellon University, Pittsburgh, Pa. 15213.
[2] Assistant Professor, Civil Engineering and Engineering & Public Policy,
Carnegie-Mellon University, Pittsburgh, Pa. 15213.

parameter. The model and uncertainty analysis are demonstrated using
test data taken from an industrial storm sewer system recently constructed on a 250 acre (101 ha) site in Ohio.

Model Computations

Model operations are shown in the conceptual flowchart illustrated
in Figure 1. The model prompts the design engineer for an estimate of
the design inputs contained in three categories: drainage area parameters which define the physical and hydraulic characteristics of each elemental watershed; rainfall parameters in the Chen method; and conveyance
parameters including the type of pipe and roughness factors.

Model simulation begins with the determination of composite drainage
area characteristics for each junction. Each elemental watershed is divided into various land use categories for which runoff coefficients are
assigned. The tributary areas in these watersheds are then used to develop a composite runoff coefficient, C, and a value for the time of
concentration.

Rainfall depth relationships are next computed and used in a generalized rainfall intensity-duration-frequency formula developed by Chen (4).
This formula computes the average rainfall intensity for any duration and
return period using the following relationship:

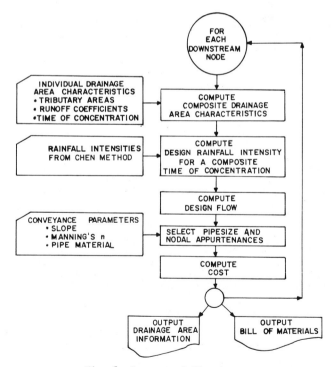

Fig. 1. Conceptual Flowchart

$$r_t^T = \frac{aR_1^{10} \log(10^{2-x} T^{x-1})}{(t+b)^c}$$

where: r_t^T = average rainfall intensity (inches/hour) for a time of concentration, t (minutes), and return period, T (years);

R_Υ^I = rainfall depth values determined from rainfall records or interpolated from appropriate isopluvial maps, e.g. (6), for duration, Υ (hours), and return period, T (years).

a, b, c = standard storm parameters approximated by a table look-up subroutine based on values of x and y:

x = depth-frequency ratio = R_1^{100} / R_1^{10} ;

y = depth-duration ratio = R_1^{10} / R_{24}^{10} .

The resulting average rainfall intensities are comparable to those determined from more detailed analysis of rainfall records, as indicated in Figure 2 for the study area in Ohio, though short duration rainfalls are somewhat underestimated. Peak flows in the watershed are calculated using the Rational formula:

$$Q = Cr_t^T A$$

where A is the drainage area.

The drainage model completes the design by considering conveyance characteristics. Manning's equation is first used to compute the required pipe size; then, the model converts to the smallest commercial pipe diameter available that will still provide free-surface flow in the sewer. Partial-flow hydraulics for the sewer (2) are computed using a table look-up subroutine. The partial-flow characteristics are used to develop a

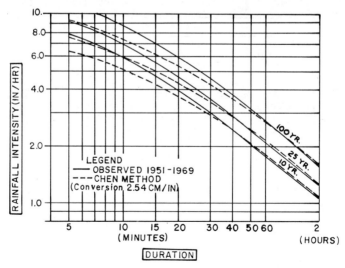

Fig. 2. Observed Rainfall Intensity-Duration Relationship to that Predicted by the Method of Chen for the Study Area.

hydraulic grade line and to determine the lagged flow time in the sewer. Finally, the cost of each installed pipeline and its appurtenances are computed from unit cost data for material and labor.

The model program is written in IBM-PC Advanced Basic. Minimum requirements to operate are: 64K RAM, one disk drive, video display, and DOS version 1.10. The program features input and output to random access disk files, a screen mask (overlay) to facilitate interactive manipulation of data, and cursor control by locking values into cells and windows. Model outputs can be viewed either on the video display or on printed documents.

Two outputs are generated, drainage area information and a Bill of Materials. The drainage area information, Figure 3, consists of the physical characteristics of each elemental watershed, the resulting partial-flow hydraulics, the rainstorm parameters and the design cost of the pipeline. The Bill of Materials, Figure 4, consists of the total length of each commercial pipesize required, the quantity of appurtenances, and the total cost for the system.

```
Record #  41

            From: MH108                      To: MH107
   Invert Elev.:1069.17           Invert Elev:1068.23
        Length: 420.0               Comments: LONGEST RUN

         Slope:0.0024       Total Tributary Areas:  17.85
          Flow:  36.60      Composite Runoff Coef.:0.432
 Pipe Diameter: 42                Type of Pipe:CONCRETE
   Mannings n:0.0130            DEPTH OF FLOW: 2.13
      Velocity: 5.97           Velocity Head:0.55
Time of Concen: 11.92            Energy Head: 2.68

      Intensity: 4.744          Design Period: 10
   10yr-1hr Depth: 1.75      100yr-1hr Depth: 2.55
  10yr-24hr Depth: 3.55     Cost of Pipeline:  $10,920.00
```

Fig. 3. Drainage Area Information

```
******************* BILL OF MATERIALS **********************
     12 inch Diameter Pipe - Total Length in Feet   5,869.3
     15 inch Diameter Pipe - Total Length in Feet   2,292.9
     18 inch Diameter Pipe - Total Length in Feet   2,660.7
     21 inch Diameter Pipe - Total Length in Feet   1,133.3
     24 inch Diameter Pipe - Total Length in Feet   1,118.5
     27 inch Diameter Pipe - Total Length in Feet   1,145.9
     30 inch Diameter Pipe - Total Length in Feet     360.0
     33 inch Diameter Pipe - Total Length in Feet   1,233.0
     36 inch Diameter Pipe - Total Length in Feet   1,643.3
     42 inch Diameter Pipe - Total Length in Feet   1,924.0
     48 inch Diameter Pipe - Total Length in Feet     674.5
     54 inch Diameter Pipe - Total Length in Feet     480.5
     60 inch Diameter Pipe - Total Length in Feet     505.4
     66 inch Diameter Pipe - Total Length in Feet     200.0
     78 inch Diameter Pipe - Total Length in Feet     378.0

  Amount of Catch Basins and Small Manholes            116
  Amount of Junction Boxes                              13
  Total Quantity of inlets, manholes & junction boxes  129

  Total Project Cost   * * * * * * * * * *   $1,089,289.00
```

Fig. 4. Bill of Materials

Sensitivity/Uncertainty Analysis

The objective of a sensitivity study is to assess the effect of different modeling assumptions on overall model output. The objectives of an uncertainty analysis are to measure the uncertainty in a dependent variable and to partition that uncertainty among the contributing independent variables (5). The key factor in the current study is that the model developed is for the purpose of design, and as such, sensitivity or uncertainty analyses are addressed to the design process.

The model presented in this study is used to determine the physical design of the storm system; quantity of pipes, pipe diameters and cost. The model is unlike commercially available programs; such as, HEC, SWMM, and STORM (3) which are performance models. Given a design, these models route storms through the system to determine how well the system performs. The model presented in this paper is based on a much simpler hydraulic representation, but allows development of a working design. However, this design is dependent on the specification of a set of input parameters; and a change in these input parameters results in a different design. To conceptualize the uncertainty analysis performed, consider different engineers who are to design the same industrial storm sewer system using identical unit costs. They are likely to determine or select slightly different values for each input parameter, resulting in a number of different system designs. A sensitivity/uncertainty analysis is conducted to determine the range of possible design solutions and associated costs, and to determine how sensitive this range is to the design input parameters selected.

Value ranges for the input parameters were estimated and expressed as triangular probability distribution functions. A triangular distribution allows specification of a range of possible values as well as a most likely, or best guess estimate. Input values from each distribution were independently sampled and the model analyzed. A Latin hypercube stratified sampling scheme was used to select these input values (7,9). In this sampling scheme, the input distribution is divided into as many intervals as model simulations. The width of each interval is determined so that each interval in the distribution has the same probability of occurance. Random re-ordering of values is performed resulting in an array of uncorrelated input vectors, allowing for independent analysis of the model's output with respect to each input parameter. The determination of input distributions for each parameter is now considered.

Literature values for Manning's roughness factor were used to develop the input distribution with values for concrete pipe ranging from 0.010 to 0.016. The selection of different values among design engineers is somewhat judgemental; for instance, if the design engineer is concerned about slime build-up, he might choose a higher, more conservative value. The most likely choice, however, and most frequent literature value, is 0.013. The input distributions for slope, area, and time of concentration were developed by analyzing the test data for the particular application site. The ranges of uncertainty in determining these parameters were estimated for the current study to be 17%, 5%, and 28%, respectively. All values for slope, area, or time of concentration in the drainage system are modified by the multipliers sampled from within these ranges.

The determination of runoff coefficient ranges requires a more sophisticated parameterization of uncertainty. Runoff coefficients for largely impervious surfaces are relatively certain. For undeveloped areas, however, soil type, rainfall intensity, slope, design frequency, and surface roughness create variations in C yielding greater ranges of uncertainty (8). The ranges of runoff coefficients for different land use categories in this study were developed by literature research and experience. These ranges were plotted against a typical value for C for each land use category used in the design of an industrial storm sewer system (Fig. 5). The values on the x-axis, C_i, represent an initial best guess estimate based on site characteristics. The fitted envelope represents the range of runoff coefficients which may actually be appropriate for design. Transformed values of C are generated using the formula:

$$C = b + mC_i \quad \text{if } 0.05 < b + mC_i < 1.00$$
$$= 0.05 \quad \text{if } b + mC_i <= 0.05$$

where: b = transformation parameter selected by Latin hypercube sampling; and
        m = 1-b.

The parameter b is sampled from a triangular distribution with range -0.30 to 0.30 and midpoint 0.0, representing the range of uncertainty reflected in Figure 5. Note that runoff coefficients in all subasins increase or decrease depending on the value of b. Slopes, areas, and times of concentration similarly increase or decrease uniformly across all subasins. Thus the uncertainty is reflective of variation in input parame-

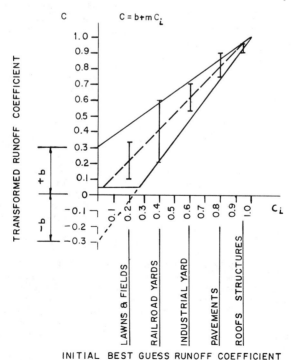

Fig. 5. Range of Uncertainties in Runoff Coefficient.

ters for the total system.

The uncertainties in the meteorological inputs are created by the limited observation records at weather stations, the limited observation period in TP 40 (6), or errors in reading values from the isopluvial maps. The values of R in the Chen method used in the current study are sampled from triangular distributions with the following ranges:

R_1^{10} from 1.7 to 1.8; R_{24}^{10} from 3.5 to 3.6; R_1^{100} from 2.5 to 2.6.

Wider ranges may in fact be more representative of the level of uncertainty in these inputs.

Results

Model replications were conducted on the test data using the 10-year, 25-year, and 100-year return period as the basis for design. Model simulations for the 5- and 50-year storms were also conducted to determine maximum and minimum values for the range of design costs. A partial correlation analysis was performed on the ranks of the input parameters and model outputs and a linear regression was performed on the actual input and output values. The results for 32 model simulations are summarized in Table 1. The results indicate that design costs in this example are most significantly influenced by values for runoff coefficient and Manning's n as indicated by the large partial rank correlation coefficients for these parameters. This result is consistent with observations from other studies (8) and provides a quantitative estimate of how sensitive the cost is to each parameter. For instance, a significant unit change in the value of b for runoff coefficients, of 0.1, affects the median value for total project cost by 3%. Likewise, a significant unit change in Manning's n of 0.001 affects the median value for total project cost by approximately 1.5%. For the remaining six parameters, a lower influence on model response is observed. The parameters in Table 1 are listed in relative order of significance for each parameter studied. Note that the use of wider uncertainty ranges for rainfall inputs would have resulted in a larger influence on model results.

Table 1. Results of Partial Rank Order Correlations on Model Inputs and Outputs and Linear Regressions on Input and Output Values.

Variable	Partial Correlations			Slopes of the Regression Line		
	10	25	100	10	25	100
b-Values for Runoff Coef.	0.839	0.840	0.839	44,680	46,980	37,840
Manning's n	0.563	0.564	0.556	21,530	23,380	19,770
Slope	-0.268	-0.278	-0.270	-1,540	-1,730	-1,170
Time of Concentration	-0.225	-0.243	-0.267	-750	-530	-940
10-yr 1-hr Rainfall Depth	0.236	0.229	0.215	-1,910	960	-450
100-yr 1-hr Rainfall Depth	0.202	0.227	0.237	-1,260	1,790	660
10-yr 24-hr Rainfall Depth	0.050	0.052	0.061	150	120	1,440
Tributary Area	0.067	0.044	0.049	4,750	4,440	5,030

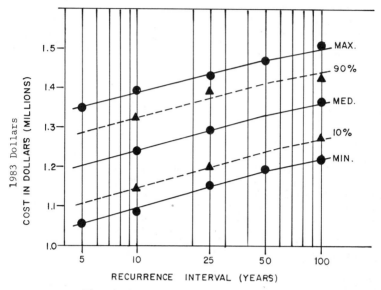

Fig. 6. Range of Uncertainty in Model Response.

The range of uncertainty in design cost resulting from the uncertain model input is of interest. Figure 6 depicts the range of model response for each return period simulation and confidence intervals for
each design period. It is interesting to note that this uncertainty is
comparable in magnitude to the cost of changing the design to the next
larger return period. The range of uncertainty in a design is approximately 20% of the median cost; whereas, the change in project cost associated with a change in return period, from 10-year to 25-year or from
25-year to 100-year, is approximately 5%. Uncertainties in input selection may thus be at least as important as the selection of a design
period.

Figure 6 can also be used to evaluate storm sewer system designs as
a method of identifing out-liers on bidding curves. If an estimate falls
within the range, reasonable design assumptions are likely to have been
made. If, however, the estimated cost deviates significantly from the
indicated range, the design is suspect. Of course, this is predicated on
all designs employing identical or similar unit costs. Uncertainties in
unit costs could also be considered in further model studies of this type.

In addition to the overall system cost, it is useful to characterize
the distribution of pipe sizes for alternative designs (Fig. 7). As expected, increasing cost is associated with a shift towards larger pipe
sizes. This is particularly evident for the smallest pipe used (12 inches,
30 cm.), as well as the largest outlet pipe diameter which increases from
78 inches (198 cm) in the least costly design to 102 inches (259 cm) in
the most costly design. The distribution of required lengths notably
shifts towards diameters larger than 42 inches (107 cm). This information,
taken directly from the Bill of Materials (Fig. 4), provides a succinct
summary of alternative designs.

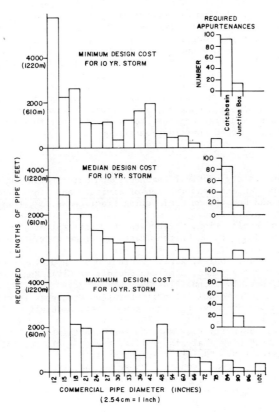

Fig. 7. Characterization of Pipe Sizes and Lengths in Resulting
Designs of the 10-year Return Period.

Summary and Conclusions

This study has presented a storm drainage computer model which can
be used as an aid in the design of storm sewer networks. The model is
developed using a steady-flow routing method with time-lagged hydrographs. A new generalized rainfall intensity-duration-frequency formula,
developed by Chen, is used to predict rainfall intensities used in the
Rational Method. A sensitivity/uncertainty analysis is conducted on model outputs to determine the range of uncertainty in the resulting designs
and associated costs, and to determine which design input parameters
most significantly affect this range. A Latin hypercube sampling scheme
is employed for model response analysis.

The results show that model output is most sensitive to runoff coefficients and Manning's n, though this is somewhat dependent on the uncertainty ranges assumed for this example. The effects of a unit change in
values for these parameters results in a change in the median design cost

for the model simulation of approximately 3% and 1.5%, respectively. The range of uncertainty in the design cost is equal to about 20% of the median design cost for each return period analyzed. The results from this sensitivity/uncertainty analysis illustrate that consistency of design estimates could be significantly improved by better definition of runoff coefficient values and Manning's roughness factors.

In addition to the sensitivity/uncertainty study, the model presented can be an effective tool in an ongoing design process. Its ability to iterate through design changes, and rapidly determine new designs and costs, enables a design engineer to track the multitude of changes that occur on fast-tracked construction projects.

Appendix 1. - References

1. American Society of Civil Engineers and Water Pollution Control Federation, Design and Construction of Sanitary and Storm Sewers, ASCE Manuals and Reports on Engineering Practice No. 37, Fourth Printing, New York, N.Y., 1976.
2. Bureau of Reclamation, United States Department of the Interior, Design of Small Dams, United States Government Printing Office, Washington, D.C., 1977.
3. Cassidy, J.J., Tonias, E.C., "Hydraulic and Hydrologic Computer Applications," Proceedings, American Society of Civil Engineers, Vol. 108, No. TC2, Nov. 1982, pp. 214-225.
4. Chen, C.L., "Rainfall Intensity-Duration-Frequency Formulas," Journal of Hydraulic Engineering, American Society of Civil Engineers, Vol. 109, No. 12, Dec., 1983, pp. 1603-1621.
5. Cox, D.C., Baybutt, P., "Methods for Uncertainty Analysis: A Comparative Study," Risk Analysis, Vol. 1, No. 4, 1981, pp. 251-258.
6. Hershfield, D.M., "Rainfall Frequency Atlas of the United States," U.S. Weather Bureau Technical Paper No. 40, 1961.
7. Jaffe, P.R., Ferrara, R.A., "Modeling Sediment and Water Column Interactions for Hydrophobic Pollutants. Parameter Discrimination and Model Response to Input Uncertainty," Water Resources, Vol. 18, No. 9, 1984, pp. 1169-1174.
8. McCuen, R.H., Bondelid, T.R., "Relation Between Curve Number and Runoff Coefficient," Proceedings, American Society of Civil Engineers, Vol. 107, No. IR4, Dec., 1981, pp. 395-400.
9. McKay, M.D., Conover, W.J., Beckman, R.J., "A Comparison of Three Methods for Selecting Values of Input Variables in the Analysis of Output from a Computer Code," Technometrics, Vol. 21, No. 2, May, 1979, pp. 239-245.
10.Yen, B.C., Sevuk, A.S., "Design of Storm Sewer Networks," Journal of the Environmental Engineering Division, American Society of Civil Engineers, Vol. 101, No. EE4, Paper 11503, Aug., 1975, pp. 535-553.

COMPUTER AIDED DESIGN USING "CORPS"

by A. J. Reese[1] M. ASCE and J. J. Ingram[1] AM. ASCE

Abstract

The Hydraulic Analysis Division, Hydraulics Laboratory, U. S. Army Engineer Waterways Experiment Station (WES) has the responsibility for developing and disseminating hydraulic guidance for the Corps of Engineers. A portion of this guidance is currently in the form of interactively accessible computer programs known as the Conversationally Oriented Real-Time Programming System (CORPS). In this system is a family of hydraulics applications software. This paper presents one of these programs in order to highlight some of the capabilities of this system.

Part I - System Description

Since 1952 the Hydraulic Analysis Division, Hydraulics Laboratory, U. S. Army Engineer Waterways Experiment Station (WES), has had the responsibility of developing and disseminating hydraulic design guidance for the Corps of Engineers. This program has been a continuous effort with guidance published in the form of "Hydraulic Design Criteria," "Engineer Manuals," "Engineer Technical Letters," etc. In the last 15 years, a computer-aided design system, Conversationally Oriented Real-Time Programming System (CORPS), has been developed and is operational which supplements these guidances. This system provides quick and accurate numerical solutions to design problems. The CORPS system provides software in a number of different disciplines including coastal engineering, surveying, mathematics, structural engineering, soils engineering, and hydraulic engineering.

Presently, 75 computer programs for hydraulic design (listed in Table 1) are available to Corps offices through district Harris computers, the WES DPS-8 System, and the CDC CYBERNET system. Areas covered by these programs are: spillways, stilling basins, outlet works, locks, closed conduit flow, open-channel hydraulics, stable channel design, and sediment transport. Documentation for each program is prepared according to standards established by the Office, Chief of Engineers (OCE), with emphasis on the step-by-step engineering rationale of each program. A copy of the documentation, when approved by OCE, is filed in the WES Engineering Computer Programs Library (TP-C) and is available on request.

The CORPS system has many advantages: (a) the programs are written for engineers by engineers, thus providing a means of computer

---

[1]Research Hydraulic Engineer, U. S. Army Waterways Experiment Station, Vicksburg, MS 39180.

communication in the user's own disciplinary language; (b) all programs can be run interactively in real-time providing immediate results; (c) the programs are stored in machine language, thus eliminating compilation and debugging time; (d) most of the system's programs provide a "RERUN" option in which data can be selectively changed and the program rerun without beginning from the start; (e) a graphics capability is available on many of the programs; (f) most of the programs can be easily downloaded to a micro-computer with minor modifications; and (g) the programs are available to all Corps offices through district computer facilities and are supported through the WES Automation Technical Center (ATC).

A potential user of CORPS can easily run any of the hydraulic design programs if he is able to access the CORPS library. A special information or master program is available from which the following information may be retrieved:

- a description of CORPS

- a listing of the available programs

- a brief description of any of the programs in the system

- an execute command for any of the programs.

A sample run demonstrating the use of a typical CORPS program is presented in the next section of this paper.

Part II - Design Example

Program H1108 "Crest and Upper Nappe Profiles for Elliptical Crest Spillways" has been selected to demonstrate some of the capabilities of the CORPS system. Details of the design theory can be found elsewhere (1, 2) and will only be summarized here.

The upstream quadrant of the overflow spillway is proportioned according to an equation for an ellipse as

$$\frac{x^2}{A^2} + \frac{y^2}{B^2} = 1 \tag{1}$$

where x and y are the horizontal and vertical coordinates of the upstream quadrant and A and B are constants. These constants were determined experimentally to be a function of the approach depth (P) and the design head (H_d) (2). They have since been verified by an extensive physical model study program at the Waterways Experiment Station. Any upstream face slope can be incorporated into the design by simply attaching the upstream face tangent to the ellipse.

The downstream coordinates are expressed by

$$x^{1.85} = K \, H_d^{0.85} \, Y \tag{2}$$

where K is an experimentally determined constant dependent on P and

H$_d$. These coordinates are calculated to the point where the downstream face slope is tangent to the downward sloping curve expressed by Equation 2. The parameters A, B, and K then fully define the crest shape.

Experimentally determined upper nappe profiles have also been incorporated into H1108 to facilitate gate placement and sidewall height calculation. These profiles are calculated both with and without piers.

Figure 1 shows the input sequence for H1108. User inputs are typed after an "=" prompt. Notice that limits of accuracy are provided to the user. Because of the practice of "under designing" spillway crests to take advantage of the negative pressures thus generated (and higher discharge coefficients), the user has the ability to input both the design head and the actual head present (inputs AC and AH).

Figure 2 shows the tabular output for this design problem. All the input data is output as well as tangent points for both the up- and downstream faces, crest coordinates, and upper nappe coordinates. Figure 3 shows graphical output for this design.

The program then asks the user if he would like to rerun the design. If the user responds affirmatively a special subroutine is called which allows the user to selectively alter various input values and rerun the program. This feature allows for rapid design changes without the need to reinput unchanged data. Figure 4 shows the rerun sequence. The upstream face slope is changed from vertical to 1V:1H and the actual head is changed to 10 feet. By hitting a carriage return at the next prompt the program automatically reruns with the new value(s) replacing the original value(s). The output is similar to that presented in Figures 1-3 with the necessary changes for the 1V:1H face. Figure 5 shows the graphic output for the new design.

H1108 is part of a family of programs used in the design of this type of spillway. Other programs in the family calculate the stage-discharge curve, pressures on the crest, energy losses along the crest to the stilling basin, and flow velocity and depth entering the stilling basin.

Conclusion

CORPS provides a library of hydraulic design programs which can aid an engineer in design calculations. Use of this system is interactive and the capability of CORPS is enhanced with the provision of a rerun option for each program giving the user the ability to quickly evaluate alternate solutions.

Acknowledgment

The tests described and the resulting data presented herein, unless otherwise noted, were obtained from research conducted under the Civil Works Program of the U. S. Army Corps of Engineers by the Waterways Experiment Station. Permission was granted by the Chief of Engineers to publish this information.

TABLE 1

Conversationally Oriented Real-Time Programming System

(CORPS) Hydraulics Programs

H0001	-Graphics Program for Corps H-Files
H0011	-Kinematic Viscosity of Water-effects of Temperature
H0114	-Bridge Pier Loss-Rect or Trap Sect-Any Flow Class
H0910	-Computation of Particle Fall Velocity by Shape Factor
H0920	-Total Sediment Transport Rate in Sand Bed Streams by Colby's Method
H0921	-Bed Load Transport in Rivers by Einstein's Method
H0922	-Total Sediment Load by Modified Einstein Procedure
H0923	-Bed Load Transport Rate by Meyer-Peter Muller's Method
H0924	-Computation of Sediment Discharge in Rivers by Shen and Hung's Method
H0925	-Total Sediment Discharge by Yang's Method
H0926	-Sand Discharge by Toffaleti's Method
H0941	-Stable Channel Design from Five Methods
H1102	-Standard High Spillway Crest Coordinates
H1103	-Stage-Disch Relation for Standard Spillway (Ungated)
H1105	-Stage-Disch Relation-Spillway Crest-Uncontrolled Flow
H1107	-Stage-Discharge Relation for Elliptical Crest Spillway
H1108	-Crest and Upper Nappe Profiles for Elliptical Crest Spillways
H1109	-Pressure Distribution for Elliptical Crest Spillway
H1110	-Spillway Energy Losses
H1111	-Standard Spillway Crest Water Surface Elev-High Dam
H1116	-Standard Shape Spillway Crest Pressure-High Dam
H1121	-Spillway Basin Design for a Free Overflow Spillway
H1170	-High Spillway Crest Coordinates- 3-1 Upstream Face
H1180	-High Spillway Crest Coordinates- 3-2 Upstream Face
H1190	-High Spillway Crest Coordinates- 3-3 Upstream Face
H2030	-Disch-Pressure Conduits-Darcy-Weisbach Formula
H2035	-Disch-Pressure Conduits-Manning Formula
H2040	-Geometric Elements of a Horseshoe Conduit
H2041	-Geometric Elements of a Rectangular Conduit
H2042	-Geometric Elements of an Oblong Conduit
H2043	-Discharge in Horseshoe Cond (Man or Dar Form)
H2044	-Discharge for Rect. Conduit (Dar or Man)
H2045	-Disch in an Oblong or Circ Conduit-Mann or Dar Form
H2050	-Analyses of Slug Flow in Circular Outlet Conduits
H2250	-Reservoir Storage Drawdown Time
H2251	-Outlet Works Loss Coeff. From Prototype Measurements of Drawdown
H2261	-Stilling Basin Design for Conduit Outlet Works
H3106	-Standard Disch Relation-Tainter Gate on Curve Crest
H3201	-Disch for Partly Open Vertical Lift Conduit Gates
H5310	-Surges in Navigation Channels
H5320	-Lock Fill and Empty--Symmetrical Systems
H6001	-Geometrical Elements-Trap, Rect, Tria-Channel
H6002	-Geometric Elements of Circular Conduit
H6005	-Geometric Elements of a General Channel, Cross-Sect
H6110	-Normal Depth-Trap, Rect, Tria Sect-Manning Formula
H6111	-Normal Depth and Velocity-Circ Conduit-Mann Formula

H6112	–Normal Discharge– Manning Formula
H6113	–Normal Depth–Trap, Rect, Tria Sect–Manning Formula
H6114	–Normal Discharge– Chezy Formula
H6115	–Normal Depth and Velocity–Circ Conduit–Chezy
H6116	–Normal Discharge–Colebrook White Formula
H6117	–Normal Depth–Trap, Rect, Tria Sect–Colebrook White
H6118	–Normal Depth and Vel–Circ Conduit–Colebrook White
H6122	–Conjugate Depth–Circular Section
H6123	–Conjugate Depth–Trap, Rect, Tria–Section
H6124	–Specific Force and Energy–Trap, Rect, Tria–Sect
H6125	–Specific Force and Energy–Circular Section
H6140	–Critical Depth and Velocity–Trap, Rect, Tria Sect
H6141	–Critical Depth and Velocity for Circular Conduit
H6201	–Friction Slope–Any Flow Sect–Manning, Chezy, or Colebrook White Formula
H6208	–Flow Profile–Prismatic Channel–Manning, Chezy, or Colebrook White Formula
H6209	–Flow Profile–Prismatic Channel–Manning, Chezy, or Colebrook White Formula
H6210	–LDR–I Backwater Profiles
H6602	–Spiral Banked Curve–Supercritical Flow–Rect, X Sect
H7010	–Riprap Requirements for Open Channels
H7011	–Riprap Design by Four Methods
H7012	–The Alpha Method
H7220	–Erosion at Culvert Outlets and Riprap Requirements
H7221	–Culvert Sizing and Inlet Design
H7222	–Culvert Rating Curves
H7780	–Wave Runup and Wave Setup, Computational Model
H8000	–Development Program for HROHP
H9110	–Flow Resistance Over Movable Beds by Einstein's Method
H9111	–Flow Resistance by the Method of White, Paris and Bettess
H9121	–River Regime by the Method of White, Paris

```
*******************************
*  CORPS PROGRAM  #  H1108  *
*        VERSION  # 14/10/84 *
*******************************


     H1108 WILL DESIGN AN ELLIPTICAL UPSTREAM QUADRANT SPILLWAY AND
PROVIDE BOTH UP- AND DOWNSTREAM CREST COORDINATES. THE RE-
QUIRED INPUT IS: AVG. APPROACH DEPTH (AB), DESIGN HEAD (AC)
UP- AND DOWNSTREAM FACE SLOPES (AD AND AE),
X INCREMENT (AF),   WHEATHER OR NOT PIERS ARE PRESENT (AG),
AND THE ACTUAL HEAD ON THE CREST (AH).
-------------------------------------------------

H1108 WILL ALSO PROVIDE COORDINATES FOR THE UPPER NAPPE SURFACE
OF SPILLWAYS DESIGNED USING THE ELLIPTICAL UPSTREAM QUADRANT
DESIGN PROCEDURE.
EXPERIMENTAL VALUES WERE DETERMINED AT P/HD=0.25,0.5, AND 1.0
AND H/HD VALUES OF 0.5,1.0 AND 1.5. NO 1.5 VALUE IS AVAILABLE FOR P/HD
LESS THAN 0.5.

H1108 WILL INTERPOLATE AND EXTRAPOLATE  LINEARLY FOR OTHER VALUES
OF P/HD AND HE/HD


LIMITS ARE: 0.2<P/HD AND 0.25<HE/HD<2.0
            EXCEPT WHEN P/HD<0.5 HE/HD MUST BE LESS THAN 1.34
            AND WHEN HE/HD>1.0 P/HD MUST BE GREATER THAN 0.33
-------------------------------------------------

DO YOU WANT GRAPHICS? (Y OR N)
-Y
AA-INPUT THE NAME OF THE SPILLWAY DESIGN
-DESIGN EXAMPLE
AB-INPUT AVG. CHANNEL APPROACH DEPTH-P (FT)
   (DIFFERENCE BETWEEN CREST ELEV. AND APPROACH CHANNEL ELEV.)
-20
AC-INPUT DESIGN HEAD-HD (FT)
-15
AD-INPUT THE UPSTREAM FACE SLOPE (V,H) (1,0-VERT)
-1,0
AE-INPUT THE DOWNSTREAM FACE SLOPE (V,H)
-1,1
AF-INPUT THE X (HORIZONTAL) INCREMENT-XINC (FT)
-1
AG-DOES THE SPILLWAY HAVE PIERS? (Y OR N)
-Y
AH-ACTUAL HEAD ON CREST-HE(FT)
-20
HARDCOPY IF DESIRED-THEN RETURN
-
```

FIG. 1.--H1108 input sequence

OUTPUT FOR:DESIGN EXAMPLE

FOR CREST COORDINATES: +X TO THE RIGHT AND +Y DOWNWARD

```
APPROACH DEPTH (FT)= 20.00
DESIGN HEAD (FT)= 15.00
UPSTREAM FACE SLOPE= 0.  V: 1.00H
DOWNSTREAM FACE SLOPE= 1.00V: 1.00H
A AND B IN ELLIPSE EQUATION= 4.123  2.433
K IN D.S. EQN= 2.002
```

COORDINATES OF UPSTREAM TANGENT POINT (X,Y)= -4.12, 2.43

COORDINATES FOR DOWNSTREAM TANGENT POINT (X,Y)= 16.46, 8.90

UPSTREAM COORDINATES

X	Y
0.	0.
-1.000	0.073
-2.000	0.305
-3.000	0.764
-4.000	1.842
-4.123	2.433
-4.123	20.000

DOWNSTREAM COORDINATES

X	Y
0.	0.
1.000	0.050
2.000	0.180
3.000	0.382
4.000	0.650
5.000	0.982
6.000	1.376
7.000	1.830
8.000	2.342
9.000	2.913
10.000	3.540
11.000	4.222
12.000	4.959
13.000	5.751
14.000	6.596
15.000	7.494
16.000	8.444
16.456	8.895
17.000	9.439
18.000	10.439
19.000	11.439
20.000	12.439
21.000	13.439
22.000	14.439
23.000	15.439
24.000	16.439
25.000	17.439
27.561	20.000

    LINEAR SLOPE BETWEEN LAST TWO D.S. POINTS

UPPER NAPPE OUTPUT

```
DESIGN HEAD (FT)=    15.000
ACTUAL HEAD (FT)=    20.000
APPROACH DEPTH (FT)=  20.000
P/HD=  1.3333
HE/HD=  1.333
```

THE ORIGIN OF THE WATER-SURFACE ELEVATION COORDINATES IS LOCATED
AT THE CREST WITH +X TO THE RIGHT AND +Y UPWARD.

UPPER NAPPE ELEVATIONS WITH PIERS(FT)

X	BAY C.L. Y	ALONG PIERS Y
-15.00	17.075	17.805
-12.00	16.805	17.625
-9.00	16.415	17.315
-6.00	15.925	16.920
-3.00	15.260	16.375
0.	14.440	15.660
3.00	13.385	14.735
6.00	12.015	13.620
9.00	10.435	12.245
12.00	8.560	10.600
15.00	6.220	8.525
18.00	3.505	6.050
21.00	0.535	3.200

FIG. 2.--H1108 tabular output

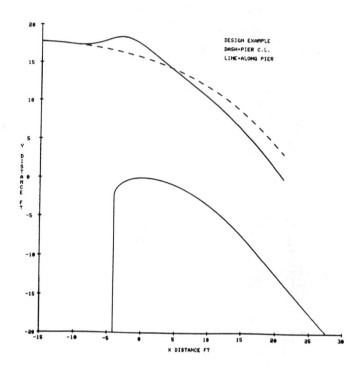

FIG. 3.--H1108 graphics output

```
WANT TO RERUN? (Y OR N)
=Y
RERUN OPTION PERMITS YOU TO CHANGE ANY OR ALL INPUT VARIABLES.
AT >>>= QUE TYPE IN THE TWO LETTERS(AA,AB,ETC.) CORRESPONDING
TO THE VARIABLES YOU WISH TO CHANGE.  THEN AT NEXT = QUE, ENTER
THE NUMERICAL VALUE.  TO TERMINATE DATA ENTRY, TYPE A CARRIAGE
RETURN AT >>>= QUE.
>>>
=AD
AD-INPUT THE UPSTREAM FACE SLOPE (V,H) (1,0=VERT)
=1,1
>>>
=AH
AH-ACTUAL HEAD ON CREST-HE(FT)
=10
>>>
=
HARDCOPY IF DESIRED-THEN RETURN
=
```

FIG. 4.--CORPS rerun sequence example

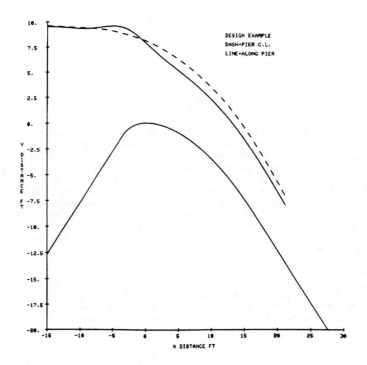

FIG. 5.--H1108 graphics output after rerun

Appendix I - References

1. Melsheimer, E. S., and Murphy, T. E. 1970. "Investigations of Various Shapes of the Upstream Quadrant of the Crest of a High Spillway," Research Report H-70-1, U. S. Army Engineer Waterways Experiment Station, Vicksburg, MS.

2. Murphy, T. E. 1973. "Spillway Crest Design," Miscellaneous Paper H-73-5, U. S. Army Corps of Engineers Waterways Experiment Station, Vicksburg, MS.

GREAT LAKES WATER DIVERSION: LEGAL ISSUES

Dean T. Massey*

ABSTRACT: State/provincial, regional and federal institutions and laws
in the United States and Canada, as well as international treaties, are
concerned with Great Lakes water. The governors and premiers of the
Great Lakes states and provinces signed a Great Lakes Charter providing
that each would seek and implement legislation establishing programs to
manage and regulate diversions. Legislation permitting diversion of
Great Lakes water may be challenged by a private citizen on the basis
of the public trust doctrine, or by another state on the grounds of
damage to riparian rights. Statutes prohibiting interstate transfers
are subject to examination under the commerce clause and must regulate
evenhandedly to effectuate legitimate local public interests. The local benefits from the prohibition must outweigh the effects on interstate commerce, and the local purpose cannot be better achieved by alternative means.

INTRODUCTION

Population growth and industrial and agricultural expansion in
Western water-scarce regions increase demands on these regions' already
strained water supplies. Agricultural production in many of these regions, dependent largely on irrigation, is depleting water supplies
faster than they can be replaced. Therefore, as water supplies in the
West diminish, and as pumping costs increase due to the greater depth
of wells, users will be looking outside their regions for alternative
supplies. The Great Lakes, with their abundant supply of water, may be
a prospective source (3).

States have primary responsibility for managing water within their
boundaries, responsibilities generally related to allocation among competing users. The federal government has historically demonstrated reluctance to impinge upon states' rights in this area, except in exer-
cising constitutional responsibilities that have an impact on water
policy, such as the commerce clause (21). Largely because of the
states' primacy in water management, the federal government has never
developed an affirmative national water management policy (3).

The Great Lakes states as a group have begun to act more aggressively to protect their water resource base. Concern emerged in 1981
when a coal slurry pipeline company was studying a plan to move
Wyoming coal to the Midwest by using Lake Superior water. The Council

*General Attorney, Natural Resource Economics Division, Economic
Research Service, U.S. Department of Agriculture; and Lecturer, Law
School, University of Wisconsin, Madison, Wisconsin 53706.

864

of Great Lakes Governors, in an attempt to regulate interstate diversions of water from the Great Lakes, adopted a major policy resolution
in 1983 in which the governors agreed to support federal legislation
protecting the water and to promote state legislation prohibiting any
diversion of Great Lakes water within their boundaries for use outside
their states without concurrence of the other Great Lakes states and
the International Joint Commission (2).

This article deals with state/provincial, regional, federal and
international legal issues involved with protecting Great Lakes water.
First, the article describes the institutions and laws available for
that purpose at the various levels of government in both the United
States and Canada. The article then describes the legal and constitutional issues involved with state legislation that permits diversions
of Great Lakes water or prohibits such diversions.

INSTITUTIONS AND LAWS CONCERNED WITH GREAT LAKES WATER

United States Institutions and Laws

Four Great Lakes states, Illinois (5), Indiana (6), Minnesota (8)
and Ohio (11), have legislation relating to Great Lakes water diversions. Indiana's statute prohibits diversion of water from that part
of the Great Lakes drainage basin within Indiana for use in a state
outside the basin, unless the diversion is approved by the governor of
each Great Lakes state (5).

The other three states permit limited diversions. The Illinois
Department of Transportation may divert water from Lake Michigan for
domestic purposes and to maintain water quality in the Chicago Sanitary
and Ship Canal, provided steps are taken to conserve and manage the
water resources. Illinois' Level of Lake Michigan Act prohibits the
department from diverting Lake Michigan water for use outside the state
without prior approval of the other Great Lakes states and the International Joint Commission (6).

Minnesota requires appropriation permits for water withdrawals in
excess of 10,000 gallons (37,900 liters) per day or one million gallons
(3.79 million liters) per year, and the water must be used in accordance with state, regional and local water management plans. Also, diversions for use in other states are discouraged (8). Ohio requires
a permit from the Department of Natural Resources to divert more than
100,000 gallons (379,000 liters) per day out of the Lake Erie or Ohio
River basins to another basin. Permit applicants must provide information on the quantity to be diverted, purpose of the diversion, and
life of the project for which the water is to be diverted (11).

The Great Lakes Commission is the only regional organization in
the United States mandated by statute to represent the collective views
of the Great Lakes states. The commission gained congressional consent
in 1968 with the Great Lakes Basin Compact, and is comprised of representatives appointed by the governors and legislatures of the eight
Great Lakes states (23). The primary goal is to promote the orderly,
integrated and comprehensive development, use and conservation of the
water resources in the Great Lakes Basin (23). However, the commission

lacks legal authority and the administrative structures to effectively manage and regulate water uses in the basin (3).

Though not a congressionally approved regional organization, the Council of Great Lakes Governors, a private, nonprofit corporation, was started in 1982 by the governors of Illinois, Indiana, Michigan, Minnesota, Ohio and Wisconsin to work cooperatively on common public policy issues. The council's 1983 resolution recommending federal and state legislation to regulate Great Lakes water diversion also established the Task Force on Water Diversion and Great Lakes Institutions to explore means by which the states and Canadian provinces could protect the waters of the Great Lakes (2). That task force, composed of representatives from all the states and provinces bordering the Great Lakes, was to develop recommendations for strengthening the Great Lakes Compact and for improving institutional arrangements and the effectiveness of regional organizations (3). The task force prepared the Great Lakes Charter that was signed by all the Great Lakes governors and premiers in February 1985 (4). Each state and province is to seek and implement legislation establishing programs to manage and regulate the diversion and consumptive use of Great Lakes water, and to prohibit diversions that would have any significant adverse impact on lake levels, in-basin uses and the ecosystem. The charter also provides that no state or province will approve or permit any major new or increased diversion or consumptive use of Great Lakes water exceeding an average of 5 million gallons (18.95 million liters) per day without notifying and seeking the consent and consurrence of all affected states and provinces (4).

The Great Lakes, being national waters, are subject to control by the federal government under the commerce clause of the U.S. Constitution (21). Congress, acting under this clause, has ultimate authority over interstate transfers and the power to both forbid and require them. No federal laws explicitly prohibit diversions of water from the Great Lakes Basin; however, at least two statutes could provide a basis for federal intervention to prevent large-scale diversions. Section 10 of the Rivers and Harbors Act requires that any facility or structure built on the bed of navigable water receive prior approval from the Corps of Engineers (20). Similar Corps' approval is required for crossing navigable water with a pipeline that diverts water (20). The requirement in the Coastal Zone Management Act that federal activities be consistent with state coastal zone management programs may furnish states with CZMA approved programs another avenue for protection (19).

Canadian Institutions and Laws

The Canadian Parliament has exclusive legislative jurisdiction over navigation on watercourses of any significant size. The Canada Water Act authorizes the federal government to enter into arrangements with the provinces to establish intergovernmental committees to formulate and implement water policies and to coordinate existing provincial and federal water programs (1). Under this act, the federal government and a province could jointly authorize a Great Lakes interbasin transfer by finding the transfer to be an efficient development and an optimum use of Great Lakes water (1).

The Ontario Ministry of the Environment, under the Ontario Water Resources Act, has major legislative authority over water supply, and requires permits for withdrawing more than 10,000 Imperial gallons (50,000 liters) of water (14). Under the Environmental Assessment Act, the ministry also reviews and approves assessments of withdrawals that may have a significant effect on the environment (12). The Lakes and Rivers Improvement Act empowers the Ontario Ministry of Natural Resources to regulate the construction and operation of dams and diversion works (13). The Quebec Environmental Quality Act requires authorization from the Ministry of the Environment before establishing or modifying any water diversion (16). In addition, the Watercourses Act requires a permit from the Quebec Cabinet for the construction of dams or dikes on public or private watercourses and for the construction of any structures on public watercourses (17).

International Institutions and Laws

The Boundary Waters Treaty of 1909 was entered into by Canada and the United States to regulate the shared use of the Great Lakes water and to resolve disputes along their common frontier (22). The treaty created the International Joint Commission (IJC) and gave it the power to approve or withhold approval of applications for the use, obstruction or diversion of boundary waters on either side that would affect the natural level or flow on the other side. Further uses or diversions on either side, whether temporary or permanent, that affected the natural level or flow of boundary waters on either side of the line were prohibited under the treaty, except by authority of the United States or Canada within their respective jurisdictions and with approval of the IJC (22).

DIVERSION OF GREAT LAKES BY STATE

Illinois, Minnesota and Ohio statutes permit diversions of a limited amount of Great Lakes water under certain conditions. Other Great Lakes states, except Indiana, do not have statutes specifically governing Great Lakes water diversions. A state permitting diversions could face challenges from its own citizens or from another Great Lakes state. At the present time, there are five major diversions, two in the United States (Lake Michigan Diversion at Chicago and New York State Barge Canal Diversion) and three in Canada's Ontario Province (Ogoki, Long Lac and Welland Canal diversions) (3).

Private citizens may challenge legislation enabling water diversions in a state court on the basis of the "public trust doctrine" developed under common law. The state, as trustee under this doctrine, must manage the water of the state in the best interest of all of its citizens (9). A state would have to show that public benefits exceed the public harms resulting from the diversion. The economic losses suffered by the public because of reduced shipping, recreation, tourism and shoreline land values, in addition to the environmental damages, would probably exceed the benefits to the public from a large-scale diversion.

A Great Lakes state may also seek an injunction in a federal court to prohibit another state from diverting Great Lakes water. Since the

1920s, several Great Lakes states have been challenging the authority of Illinois and the Sanitary District of Chicago to divert Lake Michigan water into the Chicago River to reverse the river's flow, removing Chicago's sewage from the Port of Chicago and providing the city with a navigation link to the Mississippi River. Permission to divert water was granted in 1899 by the Secretary of War under the Rivers and Harbors Act (20).

Wisconsin and other states brought an action against Illinois in 1922, seeking an injunction to restrain the permanent diversion of Lake Michigan water and the dumping of sewage into the Port of Chicago, claiming that the diversion was damaging public and private riparian rights, shipping and interstate commerce, and that sewage made the port unnavigable and unsanitary (24). In finding in favor of Wisconsin and other plaintiff states, the U.S. Supreme Court held that the Secretary of War could not make local sanitation a basis for continuing a diversion. The protection of navigation on Lake Michigan was the sole justification for the permitted diversion, not to protect Chicago from its own sewage or to enhance the navigational opportunities of Chicago or the Mississippi or other rivers. Therefore, the secretary was forced to issue a temporary permit for diversion to protect the interest of navigation within the Port of Chicago. Any future diversions not authorized by Congress, but permitted by the secretary, must take into account the maintenance of navigation on the Great Lakes for interstate commerce; also, navigation on the Great Lakes cannot be diminished to enhance or create interstate commerce elsewhere (24). Under this case, Western states would not appear to have any interest in Great Lakes water based on enhancing their interstate commerce claims, and any diversions out of the Great Lakes to the West would need congressional approval.

STATE LEGISLATION PROHIBITING DIVERSION OF GREAT LAKES WATER

Legal conflicts may arise if a Great Lakes state adopts legislation similar to Indiana's (6) that prohibits diversion out of the Great Lakes. The U.S. Supreme Court held in Sporhase vs. Nebraska (18) that water is an article of commerce and, as such, is subject to the commerce clause of the U.S. Constitution (21). That case, which dealt with the constitutionality of a Nebraska statute restricting interstate transfers of ground water (10), established guidelines for testing the constitutionality of such statutes on commerce clause grounds (18). The guidelines for testing entail evaluating whether the statute has a legitimate local purpose, whether the statute regulates evenhandedly, whether the local benefits outweigh the incidental effect on interstate commerce, and, assuming a legitimate local purpose, whether the purpose could be better achieved by alternative means with less discrimination against interstate commerce (7, 15, 18).

The purpose of the Nebraska statute was to conserve and preserve the state's diminishing ground water supplies (10), which is important and a legitimate exercise of a state's police power to protect the public welfare and health (7, 18). Indiana's statute prohibiting diversions out of the Great Lakes Basin asserts that such diversions would impair or destroy the Great Lakes (6). At issue in this statute is whether it is a valid exercise of the police power to protect a

legitimate local purpose, such as public welfare, or whether its purpose is only for an invalid economic protection. As in Nebraska, where
public welfare would be harmed by diminishing ground water, the public
in Indiana depends upon an adequate water level in the Great Lakes to
protect navigation, fisheries and shoreline environments. Therefore,
Indiana can use its police powers to regulate diversions to protect the
public welfare from potential damages from reduced Great Lakes water
levels, as Nebraska did in regulating diversions to protect its ground
water supplies.

The second part of the test requires an analysis of the "evenhand-
edness" between intrastate and interstate transfers. If both are
equally restrictive, then interstate commerce has not been unreasonably
burdened. Conversely, if restrictions on interstate transfers are more
severe, then the burden is on the state to show why interstate commerce
should be so heavily burdened. Disparities in treatment of in-state
and out-of-state users are permissible, but only if legitimate reasons
exist (7, 15, 18). In the case of Great Lakes water transfers, no apparent rationale exists for why out-of-state water use would cause
greater harm than using the water in the state. Significantly, the
Indiana statute does not treat intrastate and interstate transfers
evenly, as it forbids transfer to states not at least partially within
the Great Lakes Basin and allows transfer out of the Great Lakes Basin
as long as the transfer is within a Great Lakes state. Indiana's statute may be ruled unconstitutional as being burdensome to interstate
commerce.

The third test requires weighing of local benefits against the
burden imposed on interstate commerce by the statute. Statutes will be
upheld unless the burden imposed on interstate commerce is clearly excessive in relation to the local benefits (7, 15, 18). Indiana must
show that prohibiting diversions is the only way to insure an adequate
water level in Lake Michigan, and that the local benefits derived from
fisheries, interstate navigation and recreation, and the maintenance of
shoreline environments due to an adequate water level outweigh the burden placed on interstate commerce. A court would probably find in favor of the statute on this test.

Under the fourth test, a state with a restrictive statute would
have to show that the statute's purpose could not be promoted with an
alternative that would be less restrictive to interstate commerce.
Indiana's statute may fail this test because it is overly restrictive
in accomplishing its purpose of preventing destruction to the Great
Lakes. A less restrictive statute accomplishing the same purpose could
establish a minimum water level below which the Great Lakes could not
fall without damage to the public welfare, and then prohibit diversions
that lowered the level below the designated minimum. The Indiana statute does not allow diversions to states outside the Great Lakes drainage basin even if the water level is above the minimum necessary to
achieve the statute's purpose. A prohibition against transferring excessive water to a neighboring state was one reason for declaring a
portion of Nebraska's statute unconstitutional (7, 18).

SUMMARY AND CONCLUSIONS

Western water-scarce regions are beginning to look at the Great Lakes as a prospective source of water. Great Lakes states and Canadian provinces have begun to act more aggressively to protect their water resources from being diverted out of the basin. The governors and premiers of the Great Lake states and provinces signed a Great Lakes Charter providing that each state and province is to seek and implement legislation establishing programs to manage and regulate the diversion and consumptive use of Great Lakes water.

In the United States, states have primary responsibility over water management; four states have legislation relating to Great Lakes diversions. The Great Lakes Commission is the only regional organization with a statutory mandate to represent the collective views of the Great Lakes states. Traditionally, the federal government's interest in the Great Lakes has been to protect navigation; there are no federal laws explicitly permitting or prohibiting diversions. Federal control of navigable waters is primarily through the commerce clause of the U.S. Constitution. In Canada, the Parliament and two provinces have statutes regulating diversion of Great Lakes water. The Boundary Water Treaty, which created the International Joint Commission, was entered into by Canada and the United States to regulate the shared use of the Great Lakes water and to resolve disputes arising along their common frontier.

On the basis of the public trust doctrine, private citizens may challenge state legislation enabling a diversion of Great Lakes water. The diverting state would have to show that public benefits exceed the public harms resulting from diversion before the statute could be upheld.

Conflicting results could exist when challenging state legislation either permitting or prohibiting water diversions from the Great Lakes in federal courts under the commerce clause of the U.S. Constitution. A Great Lakes state may seek an injunction to prohibit another from diverting Great Lakes water on grounds of damages to public and private riparian rights. The U.S. Supreme Court held that water could not be taken from the Great Lakes, thereby reducing navigation on those lakes for interstate commerce, for the purpose of enhancing or creating interstate commerce elsewhere without authorization from Congress.

State statutes prohibiting interstate transfers of water are also subject to analysis under the commerce clause of the U.S. Constitution. Guidelines for testing the constitutionality of such statutes entail an evaluation of whether the statutes have a legitimate local purpose, whether the statutes regulate evenhandedly, whether the local benefits outweigh the incidental effect on interstate commerce, and, assuming a legitimate local purpose, whether the purpose could be better achieved by alternative means with less discrimination against interstate commerce. Embargo type statutes, such as Indiana's, may be unconstitutional because they do not treat intrastate and interstate transfers evenhandedly, and because the statutes' purposes could be promoted with less restriction on interstate commerce.

APPENDIX -- REFERENCES

1. Canada Revised Statutes, Chap. 5 (1st Supp., 1970, as amended).

2. Council of Great Lakes Governors, Resolution on Great Lakes Water
    Diversions, November, 1983. (Reprint in reference 3)

3. Council of Great Lakes Governors, Final Report and Recommenda-
    tions: Great Lakes Governors Task Force on Water Diversions and
    Great Lakes Institutions, Madison, Wis., January, 1985.

4. Council of Great Lakes Governors, The Great Lakes Charter,
    February, 1985. (Reprint in reference 3)

5. Illinois Annotated Statutes, Chap. 19, Secs. 119 to 120.11 (Smith-
    Hurd 1972 & Cum. Supp. 1984-1985).

6. Indiana Code Annotated, Sec. 13-2-1-9 (Burns Cum. Supp. 1984).

7. Massey, D. T., Hong, A. C., and Szilogyi, A., "Interstate Transfer
    of Colorado Water for San Marco Slurry Pipeline," Oklahoma Law
    Review, Vol. 36, No. 1, 1983, pp. 41-52.

8. Minnesota Statutes Annotated, Sec. 105.41 (West 1977 & Cum. Supp.
    1984).

9. Muench vs. Wisconsin Public Service Comm'n, 261 Wis. 492, 53 N.W.
    2d 514 (1952).

10. Nebraska Revised Statutes, Sec. 46-613.01 (Reissue 1978).

11. Ohio Revised Code, Sec. 1501.30 (Page Supp. 1984).

12. Ontario Revised Statutes, Chap. 140 (1980).

13. Ontario Revised Statutes, Chap. 229 (1980).

14. Ontario Revised Statutes, Chap. 361 (1980).

15. Pike vs. Bruce Church, Inc., 397 U.S. 137, 90 Sup. Ct. 844 (1970).

16. Quebec Revised Statutes, Chap. Q-2 (1977, as amended).

17. Quebec Revised Statutes, Chap. R-13 (1977, as amended).

18. Sporhase vs. Nebraska, 458 U.S. 941, 102 Sup. Ct. 3456 (1982).

19. U.S. Code, Title 16, Sec. 1456 (1982).

20. U.S. Code, Title 33, Sec. 403 (1982).

21. U.S. Constitution, Article I, Section 8, Clause 3.

22. U.S. Statutes at Large, Vol. 36, p. 2448 (1910).

23. U.S. Statutes at Large, Vol. 82, p. 414 (1968).

24. Wisconsin vs. Illinois, 278 U.S. 367, 49 Sup. Ct. 163 (1928).

MULTI-OBJECTIVE PLANNING: GREAT LAKES WATER POLICY ISSUES

Jonathan W. Bulkley*   Member: ASCE
L. A. Zimmerman**   Student Member: ASCE
Paul Schmiechen***
Pat Langeland***

Abstract

Water resource management is more complex as diverse demands are placed on water resource systems. Conflicting objectives may impact adversely on the water resource. A need exists for the analysis and display of information to assist in more effective and efficient allocation of limited resources to meet these diverse demands and potentially conflicting objectives.

Multi-objective planning (MOP) is one method which can be used to assist decision-makers in the evaluation of policy options. It is anticipated that the techniques of multi-objective planning will have a wide application to diverse water policy issues in federal, state, regional, and other governmental agencies.

This paper reports upon the development of computer algorithms for multi-objective planning for Great Lakes water policy issues. Sample applications are presented for the control of phosphorus loadings to western Lake Erie, Saginaw Bay, and Lake Ontario. A further example is presented of using MOP techniques to present the results of a previously performed detailed study regarding expansion of the St. Lawrence Seaway. In all of these applications, the effort has been directed toward presentation of information to better inform decision-makers regarding the tradeoffs between different objectives.

Introduction

The Great Lakes constitute one of the largest masses of liquid surface fresh water on earth, and are jointly shared by the United States and Canada. The States and Provinces which border the Lakes and their connecting waterways are the trustees of these critical water resources. These Lakes have provided transportation routes, hydro-electric power production, water supply for both municipal and industrial needs, valuable fisheries, a sink for waste disposal, and important recreational amenities. Mankind's intervention in the use

---

*Professor of Civil Engineering/Professor of Natural Resources, The University of Michigan, Ann Arbor, MI 48109-1115.
**Graduate student, Department of Civil Engineering, The University of Michigan, Ann Arbor, MI 48109-1115.
***Graduate students, School of Natural Resources, The University of Michigan, Ann Arbor, MI 48109-1115.

873

of these unique resources has provided benefits to persons not only living in the region through employment but also nation-wide and world-wide as others have made productive use of goods which are derived from the Great Lakes and its industrial, mining, agricultural, and forestry sectors. Mankind's intervention in the use of these unique resources have also resulted in critical stresses being placed upon the Great Lakes. These anthropogenic stresses have primarily occurred within the last 100 years.

The Second National Assessment of the nation's water resources identified a number of Great Lakes water policy issues including the following (10):

1. Water Quality Degradation

     This deterioration of water quality results from municipal and industrial point source discharges, agricultural non-point source discharges, toxic substances, and nutrient enrichment.

2. Low Lake Levels

     Natural fluctuations of water elevations occur within the Great Lakes. Increased consumptive use acts to decrease the lake levels. Low lake levels have adverse impacts upon production of electrical energy, navigation, and critical habitat areas. Low lake levels do result in decreased erosion from shore lands during these time periods.

2. Water Diversion/Consumptive Use

     Certain areas adjacent to the Great Lakes but outside of the drainage basin have relied upon groundwater as a source of supply for both municipal and industrial purposes. Overdraft of the existing groundwater resources in these areas may increase the pressure to use Great Lakes water through diversion. More speculative is the use of Great Lakes water to compensate downstream users for major intra-basin diversions of the High Plains Region of the United States (1,5).

4. Erosion/Sedimentation

     Wind-driven wave action plus high lake levels may cause the erosion of over 400 million metric tons/year (1 metric ton = 1.102 U.S. tons) of materials into the Great Lakes. Certain land areas are particularly susceptible to soil erosion caused by rain on agricultural areas. The subsequent loss of soil, nutrients, and chemicals from the land surface and into the Lakes poses a threat to water quality in certain regions -- especially in Saginaw Bay in Lake Huron and the western basin of Lake Erie. Furthermore, the erosion and sedimentation process contributes to the requirement for continued dredging to maintain navigation at critical points in the waterway.

5. Flooding

The Great Lakes and its drainage areas are subject to periodic flooding from two sources. First, storms in the Lakes may be especially destructive of adjacent low-lying shore areas during periods of high lake levels. Secondly, flooding in the drainage basins of the Lakes themselves following severe storm events.

It is beyond the scope of this paper to address each of these problem areas with the techniques of multi-objective planning. This study has applied MOP techniques to an issue of water quality degradation and to an issue of navigation which is related to lake levels. However, it is our belief that the application of MOP techniques may provide a useful tool for the decision-makers required to manage all of these problem areas. The resulting analyses will assist in the sustained use management of the water resources of the Great Lakes for present and future generations. The subsequent application of MOP techniques is particularly important in the Great Lakes as a consequence of the Federal Governments of the United States and Canada as well as the Great Lakes states and provincial governments having endorsed the need for ecosystem management in the Great Lakes.

Ecosystem Management

The International Joint Commission of the United States and Canada endorsed the concept of ecosystem management for the Great Lakes. The 1978 Water Quality Agreement between the two countries formally incorporated ecosystem management as one means to provide more effective resource management in the Great Lakes. The art of managing complex ecosystems such as the Great Lakes is in the process of development (6).

"The ecosystem approach -- means looking at all implications of choices -- both in the natural and inter-linked societal systems. This approach should incorporate the activities, stresses, needs, and institutions of humans as endogenous rather than external to the strategic model" (7).

In short, the ecosystem approach as applied in the Great Lakes and elsewhere requires a means to recognize and incorporate relationships and interactions among key elements in resource policy decisions. It is our contention that one method of formalizing the ecosystem management is the application of the techniques of Multi-Objective Planning to resource policy issues.

Multi-Objective Planning (MOP)

The MOP concepts which have been utilized in this research effort have been formulated after Cohon's work (4). In this application the multi-objective planning involved first describing the system with a set of linear equations, secondly using an integer version of the simplex method in order to find the solution that satisfies the constraints, and thirdly using the epsilon constraint method to optimize for more than one objective. A significant potential for the application of MOP to Great Lakes water policy issues occurs in the generation and evaluation of alternatives for problem mitigation. In particular, those techniques of MOP which are classified as generating methods and result in the preparation of a set of non-inferior solutions or trade-off curves appear to be most useful as an aid to display information to decision-makers. The non-inferior set arises from the fact that one is seeking to optimize more than one objective. With a single objective problem, the optimum solution usually represents a unique solution in decision variable space which satisfies all of the problem constraints. Alternative optima may exist but each will produce the same value for the objective function. However, in multi-objective planning, this unique concept of optimality needs to be discarded. Rather one has a situation in which what is optimal for one objective may not be optimal for any of the remaining objectives. The non-inferior set provides a representation of solutions to the problem which dominate all other solutions and which define a trade-off region between objectives. Any gain in value for one objective is only reached by trading-off or reducing value for another objective.

Figure 1 displays a set of non-inferior solutions for a case of two-objective optimization. The ordinate represents annual cost of nutrient reduction. The abscissa represents the probability of occurrence of an eutrophication in the water body. It is necessary to reduce nutrient loadings in order to reduce the probability of occurrence of eutrophication in the water body. The MOP analysis thus is to minimize cost and to minimize the probability of observing the specified trophic condition. The curve shown in Figure 1 represents the trade-offs between the two objectives. One may only reduce the probability of occurrence of eutrophication by increasing nutrient removal and thus incurring increased annual costs for such removal.

For example, Point A in Figure 1 represents a feasible solution for nutrient removal whose annual cost is 240 million dollars. The associated probability of occurrence of eutrophication is .76. Point B dominates Point A because for the same investment one obtains a probability of occurrence of eutrophication of .65. Finally, Point C lies in the infeasible region beyond the boundary of possible solutions.

The non-inferior solution which is selected as the preferred alternative may be designated the best compromise solution (4). It represents the values of the decision-maker(s) at the time the decision is made. A different group of decision-makers (with different values) could be expected to choose a different non-inferior solution as their preferred alternative. The task before us is to apply the techniques of MOP in order to generate sets of non-inferior solutions or trade-off curves which decision-makers may find useful as they consider the choices before them.

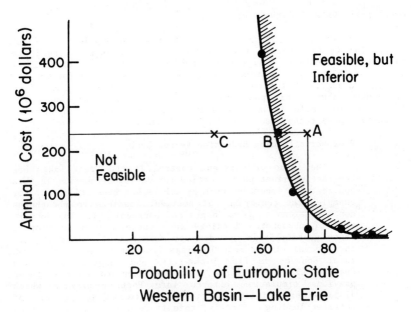

Figure 1

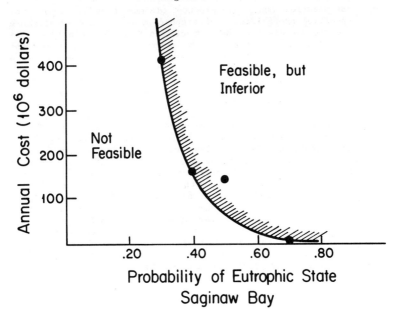

Figure 2

Great Lakes Water Policy Issues

Three issues were initially chosen to test the application of MOP techniques to Great Lakes water policy. These issues included the following: reduction of phosphorus loadings to reduce the probability of undesirable trophic states; the optimal depth decision for the St. Lawrence Seaway; and the policy options to control the Sea Lamprey in the Great Lakes. This paper will provide a brief report upon the first two of these issues and illustrate the application of two-objective (MOP) techniques to the policy issues.

1. Phosphorus Loading Reduction Versus Cost

The issue of nutrient control in the Great Lakes has been an important policy choice for decision-makers. In this application, important work by others has been utilized. For example, the conversion of nutrient loadings to phosphorus concentrations is from Chapra and Sonzogni (2). The conversion of phosphorus loadings and concentrations to trophic state probabilities was done by Walker (9). The cost data for removal of nutrient loadings from municipal, urban, and rural sources is from Wicke (11) and Chapra, Wicke, and Heidtke (3). Our first task has been to combine these previous simulation efforts into Fortran program which displays probability of trophic state as a function of nutrient loading. Finally, this trade-off or delta function information is utilized by a standard linear programming optimization model to produce minimum cost solutions for specified probabilities of trophic state. These results are plotted to display the set of non-inferior solutions. It should be noted that for the purpose of this example, the models are steady state annual loading models. The probability results output from Walker's model reflect in part the uncertainty associated with using the total phosphorus concentration in a water body to predict the resulting trophic state. An integer model is utilized to choose least cost combinations for nutrient reduction from municipal point source discharge, urban non-point source discharges, and agricultural non-point source discharges. In any event, the MOP results should be viewed primarily as examples of the technique and not, as yet, as information ready for decision-makers to use. Figure 1 shows the trade-off between cost of nutrient removal versus probability of eutrophic conditions in the Western Basin of Lake Erie. Figure 2 shows a similar display for Saginaw Bay. Note that Figure 1 indicates that regardless of the funds expended, it is unlikely that one may reduce the probability of eutrophic conditions in this location much below .60. This is due to the nutrient loadings to western Lake Erie being dominated by agricultural non-point source loading.

2. St. Lawrence Seaway -- Depth/Length and Fleet Size

In researching the history of the decision to build the St. Lawrence Seaway, it became clear that the decision process proceeded through a complex set of interactions in both the United States and Canada. Historically, it appears that little serious consideration was given at the time of the initial decision to evaluating a full range of alternative depths and lock-sizes for the Seaway. In fact, the size of existing key facilities such as the Welland Canal appear to have been major determinants of the initial Seaway size configuration. As a result, our study focused upon the application of MOP techniques to problems of expansion of the existing Seaway System. Accordingly, sources in the Department of Naval Architecture at the University of Michigan provided the results of a U.S. Army, Corps of Engineers' (8) study which investigated the costs and benefits of increasing the capacity of the Great Lakes-St. Lawrence Seaway system. This study considered thirteen different plans (length of ship/width of ship for both the upper Great Lakes and the St. Lawrence Seaway system). Each of the different plans was further evaluated for four (4) different depths. Our approach incorporated the cost and benefit information for each of the separate plans and each of the separate depths. Figure 3 displays the set of non-inferior solutions for maximizing net benefits versus depth. One clearly observes that the set of non-inferior solutions is very sensitive to depth. Increased draft is the most significant determinant of economic performance of the vessel itself (8). However, for the upper Great Lakes and the St. Lawrence Seaway System, the increase in draft generates rapidly increasing costs. In part this is because of the increased requirements for dredging to maintain the deeper depth throughout the navigation channel.

A total of fifty (50) separate plans were evaluated. The 25.5' (1 foot = .305 meters) depth represents the present nominal draft of 27' maintained throughout the Great Lakes. The 25.5' depth is the limit for vessels passing through the locks on the upper Great Lakes and the St. Lawrence Seaway. This is the maximum depth that a vessel may draw in the locks; otherwise, the vessel would strike the bottom of the lock as it accelerates out of the lock.

The four plans identified as the set of non-inferior solutions included the following:

Plan A12 25.5' depth: Extended navigation season in place: 1000' x 130' vessels to trade on the entire system: 1200' x 103' vessels operating above the Welland Canal.

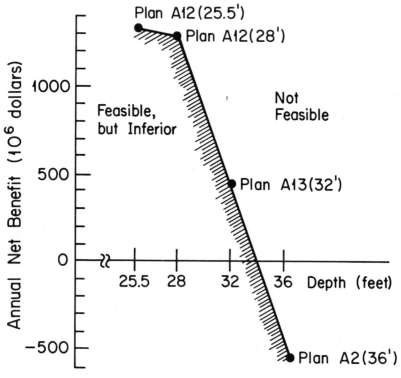

Figure 3

Plan A12 28.0' depth: Same as A12 above except depth now extended to 28.0'.

Plan A13 32.0' depth: Extended navigation season in place: 1000 x 130' vessels to trade on the entire system: 1300' x 130' vessels operating above the Welland Canal.

Plan A2 36.0' depth: Extended navigation season in place: 1000' x 130' vessels on the entire Great Lakes-St. Lawrence Seaway System.

These four plans define the boundary of the set of non-inferior solutions shown in Figure 3. From a decision-maker's perspective the MOP result shows the trade-off of net benefits versus depth for the expansion of maximum ship size on the Great Lakes-St. Lawrence Seaway System.

Observations

The applicability of MOP techniques to water policy issues in the Great Lakes has been demonstrated. The generation of sets of non-inferior solutions provides insight for the decision-maker(s) regarding consequences of choice. The results from MOP serve to clarify actual trade-off decisions which need to be made.

The next step is to apply the techniques of MOP to an ongoing issue that is currently being considered by Great Lakes decision-makers. One possibility may be the new directions for control of the Sea Lamprey. Originally physical barriers and mechanical/electrical devices were designed to control the Sea Lamprey. Once chemical treatments were devised, emphasis switched from physical devices to chemical treatment of key rivers used by the Sea Lamprey for spawning. Recently, renewed interest has been shown in applying the techniques of integrated management to control the Sea Lamprey. It is our expectation that the techniques of MOP may be of assistance to decision-makers as they consider more cost-effective means to be implemented for control of the Sea Lamprey.

Acknowledgments

This publication is a result of work sponsored by the Michigan Sea Grant College Program, Grant Number (NA-80AA-D-00072), Project Number (E/GLE-7), from the National Sea Grant College Program, National Oceanic and Atmospheric Administration (NOAA), U.S. Department of Commerce, and funds from the State of Michigan. The U.S. Government is authorized to produce and distribute reprints for governmental purposes notwithstanding any copyright notation appearing hereon.

References

1. Bulkley, J. W., S. J. Wright, and D. Wright. "Preliminary Study, The Diversion of 283 m^3/sec (10000 cfs) from Lake Superior to the Missouri River Basin." Journal of Hydrology.

2. Chapra, S. C. and W. C. Sonzogni. "Great Lakes Total Phosphorus Budget for the Mid-1970's." Journal, Water Pollution Control Federation, Vol. 51, No. 10, October 1979.

3. Chapra, S. C., H. D. Wicke, and T. M. Heidtke. "Effectiveness of Treatment to Meet Phosphorus Objectives in the Great Lakes." Journal, Water Pollution Control Federation, Vol. 55, No. 1, January 1983.

4. Cohon, Jared L. Multi-Objective Programming and Planning. Academic Press, New York, 1978.

5. De Cooke, B. L., J. W. Bulkley, and S. J. Wright. "Great Lakes Diversions - Preliminary Assessment of Economic Impacts." 36th Annual Conference, Canadian Water Resources Association, Saskatoon, Saskatchewan, June 21-23, 1983.

6. Harris, Hallett J. et al. "Green Bay is the Future -- A Rehabilitative Prospectus." Technical Report No. 38, Great Lakes Fishery Commission, September 1982.

7. Olson, E., Q. C. Richmond, and Commissioner International Joint Commission. "The Estate of Citizen and Its Manifestation in an International Institution: The International Joint Commission." University of Windsor, February 1983.

8. U.S. Army, Corps of Engineers. "Maximum Ship Size Study - Great Lakes St. Lawrence Seaway." North Central Division, October 1977.

9. Walker, W. W. "A Sensitivity and Error Analysis Framework for Lake Eutrophication Modelling." Water Resources Bulletin, American Water Resources Association, Vol. 18, No. 1, February 1982.

10. Water Resources Council, U.S. 1978. The Nation's Water Resources: 1975-2000. Vol. 4: Great Lakes Region. Second National Water Assessment.

11. Wicke, H. D. "Risk Analysis and Water Quality Management: Lake Ontario." Ph.D. Thesis, School of Natural Resources, University of Michigan, Ann Arbor, Michigan, 1983.

Legal Constraints on the Transport of Water

William E. Cox*

Abstract: Transport of water from areas of relative abundance to
areas of scarcity traditionally has been a basic water management
tool, but transport is subject to a substantial array of legal
constraints. Constraints may exist with respect to movement
across both hydrologic and political boundaries. An example
involving hydrologic boundaries is the riparian doctrine's prohibition against interbasin transfer. Constraints with respect to
political boundaries exist at many levels and in many forms.
Area-of-origin statutes and mandated local approvals for water
development can be a major factor in relatively short distance
transfers within a single state. Constraints on interstate
transport are limited by the commerce clause of the U.S.
Constitution, but recent court decisions appear to have left
adequate flexibility for carefully drafted controls. Proposals
to transfer water across international boundaries are especially
complex undertakings due to the sovereignty of individual
nations. Legal constraints on water transport are based on
legitimate concerns for protecting the future interests of the
area of origin, but such constraints sometimes appear overly
restrictive in view of actual water needs likely to arise in the
area of origin. Improvement of the existing condition can be
achieved by modification of existing institutional arrangements
to enhance negotiation and through development of better data
concerning future water demands and impacts of water transfer
proposals. These modifications are an important aspect of
improved water resources management since proposals for water
transfer will continue to arise as water demand increases over
time.

Introduction

   Transport of water, as well as other resources, from areas of
natural occurrence to areas of demand is a basic management tool.
Neither water nor population is distributed uniformly, and the areas
of concentration do not always coincide. In some cases, areas of
greatest population concentration occur in areas of relatively scarce
water supply. If water supply availability were the major determinant
of growth, this situation would be unlikely to develop. However,
several other factors are at least as important as water availability,
and growth may be stimulated to such an extent that local water

* Associate Professor, Department of Civil Engineering, Virginia
   Polytechnic Institute and State University, Blacksburg, VA 24061

supplies become inadequate. When such conditions develop, a
significant incentive to transport water from other areas is created.

History provides many examples of significant water transport.
Within the United States, the development of water supplies for the
southern California region provides a primary example. Movement of
water within Colorado from the western slope of the Rocky Mountains to
the areas of population concentration on the eastern slope provides
another major example. The diversion of water from Lake Michigan at
Chicago is a third example. An eastern example is provided by the
water supply system for New York City involving transport of water
from the western boundary of the state.

Although the examples of water transport cited above were controversial when implemented, each would face substantially greater
opposition if proposed today. In fact, the question of whether any of
the particular transfer projects could be implemented at present is
debatable. Both the legal mechanisms for offering opposition and the
vigor with which opposition is expressed have increased.

Types of Legal Constraints

Legal constraints on the transport of water exist at multiple levels
and involve several types of boundaries that must be considered during
the transport process. The first boundary of potential concern is
that separating parcels of private property. A second is that of the
hydrologic unit where the water is initially captured. A variety of
political boundaries also may constrain movement, including local,
state, and national boundaries. The following sections describe the
types of constraints imposed at these different levels.

Property Boundaries. - Property boundaries can be important with
respect to water transfer due to their use in defining private water
rights. They achieve their greatest prominence under the riparian
doctrine where water rights arise by virtue of ownership of riparian
land and must be exercised on riparian land. Although the transfer of
a riparian right separate from the land to which it originally
attached is generally recognized, the right of the riparian landowner
to transfer the riparian right for exercise on nonriparian land has
not been completely defined in many of the riparian states. This
right would appear to be limited due to the general principle that the
restrictions attaching to a property interest are conveyed to the new
owner upon transfer. The restrictiveness of the prohibition of
nonriparian use, as well as other riparian doctrine constraints, is
mitigated by the fact that is is not enforceable if surplus water over
the needs of riparian landowners is available (3, Vol. 7; 4).

The appropriative doctrine generally is considered to offer fewer
constraints to the transfer of water rights among individual land-
owners and the transport of water away from its natural source. Even
here, however, property boundaries can serve as obstacles.
"Appurtenancy" requirements attaching the appropriative right to a
specific parcel of land may hinder transfer in some cases although
this constraint is not a major problem in most states. More
significant is the restriction concerning transfer of established

water rights under conditions where return flows are altered. Appropriative law constrains such transfers to protect other water rights holders, including those with junior rights (3, vol. 5; 11; 14).

Watershed Boundaries. - In the case of watershed boundaries, the riparian doctrine again offers the most obvious example of a significant constraint. Riparian law is considered to prohibit interbasin transfer since riparian land generally cannot extend beyond the boundaries of the watershed, even where a tract of riparian land in single ownership extends beyond such boundary (5).

Appropriative law contains no general prohibition of interbasin transfer. The greater meed for transfer in the water-scarce West is often seen as a reason for rejection of the riparian doctrine in favor of the appropriative doctrine. But constraints on interbasin transfer can have other origins such as state statutes that impose limitations on water movement in addition to those traditionally contained in appropriative law (9,13).

Local Political Boundaries. - Local political boundaries usually are not significant factors with respect to water rights determinations but may constrain water transport whenever local governments are given authority over water resource development. The extent of local authority in this area depends on state policy and varies among the states. In some cases, local authority can be substantial. In Virginia, for example, a local government desiring to develop a water supply within the boundaries of a second jurisdiction must obtain permission from that jurisdiction. If approval is denied, an appeal to a specially constituted court is authorized (12).

State Boundaries . - State boundaries traditionally have constituted an important impediment to water transport. One of the common forms taken by constraints on interstate water movement has been the legislative reciprocity rule that prohibits export of water to any state not allowing water transfer in the opposite direction between the two states. Such state-imposed constraints on interstate water transport are limited by federal authority regarding regulation of interstate commerce. Attempts by states to impose restrictions potentially can be invalidated as infringement on the federal power. This action has been taken in a variety of cases extending over the history of the Nation, but only recently has the federal power undergone extensive interpretation regarding applicability to state constraints on interstate water movement (1).

The most significant development of law in this area occurred in the 1982 U. S. Supreme Court case of Sporhase v. Nebraska (10). This case involved water-use by the owners of adjoining land in Colorado and Nebraska. Water pumped from a well on Nebraska land was used to irrigate land in Colorado. No permit for the groundwater use had been requested and would not have been available since Nebraska law concerning export of water required reciprocity from the other state involved, a condition not satisfied by Colorado law. The Supreme Court held that a reciprocity requirement not tailored to a legitimate state resource conservation issue is inconsistent with federal authority over interstate commerce and therefore invalid.

Although the <u>Sporhase</u> decision imposes limits on the power of states to control interstate transport of water, not all power of control is negated. In fact, remaining state powers appear considerable. First, the Supreme Court suggested that the power to restrict export of water during times of severe shortage, a condition not demonstrated in the <u>Sporhase</u> case, would likely be recognized. Second, the court indicated that restrictions on export generally would be valid if closely related to legitimate water conservation efforts. The court suggested that, with proper evidence, the necessary means-end relationship might be found between a total ban on exportation and the conservation of water. Thus, the <u>Sporhase</u> decision, while holding that state laws categorically discriminating against out-of-state water users are invalid, has preserved substantial flexibility for restricting export where such action is closely related to valid water management objectives.

Another recent conflict over interstate water transfer to be brought to the federal courts involves the attempt by the City of El Paso, Texas to use New Mexico groundwater as its source of supply. The City's application to the State of New Mexico to appropriate the groundwater in question was denied due to New Mexico legislation prohibiting groundwater export. This prohibition was determined to be unconstitutional in a 1983 decision by the federal district court for New Mexico (2). However, this decision was vacated on New Mexico's appeal to the Tenth Circuit Court of Appeals, and the case was remanded to the district court for reconsideration of the case in light of New Mexico's modification of applicable law. The statutory ban on export has been repealed and a new provision enacted to govern transport of water for use outside the state. This case should further delineate state powers to control interstate water movement when finally resolved.

International Boundaries. - Boundaries between sovereign nations pose major obstacles to water transport due to limited institutional mechanisms for conflict resolution. Unlike conflicts involving boundaries of lower level political units, international conflicts generally cannot be resolved by referral to higher authority. Conflict resolution generally must be achieved by negotiation, a process responsible for various agreements but often unsuccessful and usually quite time consuming.

The United States has negotiated treaties involving water management with both Mexico and Canada. In the case of Canada, the principal example is the Boundary Waters Treaty of 1909, which created the International Joint Commission as a continuing international body. The 1944 treaty with Mexico concerning use of the waters of the Colorado, Tijuana, and Rio Grande rivers created the International Boundary and Water Commission as a continuing body to oversee operation of the treaty.

Existing treaties focus primarily on management of international impacts of development activities within hydrologic systems shared by the two countries involved. For the most part they have not focused on the direct transport of water across national boundaries. Approval of any proposal for such transfer (such as the various schemes for developing water supplies of western Canada for use in the arid regions of the United States) would require individual negotiation. The existing treaties may provide a framework for such negotiations but do not provide international institutional mechanisms for reaching a solution binding on the individual countries involved. Approval of transfer on the basis of negotiation generally requires the identification of mutual benefits for both parties.

Evaluation of Existing Constraints

Constraints on the transport of water traditionally have been established to protect the economic interests of residents of the area of the water's origin. Diffused environmental interests have been added to these geographically based interests as concern for values associated with water in the natural state has grown. To the extent that economic and environmental concerns are based on realistic projections of associated water needs, constraints on the transport of such water appear to be justifiable expressions of the collective will.

However, such constraints sometimes appear excessive in view of realistic economic and environmental demands for water. Proposals for movement of water almost always encounter opposition and are often among the most controversial of natural resource development activities. This situation arises form several factors, two of which are information deficiencies and institutional disincentives.

Information Deficiencies. - Misconceptions concerning water appear widespread. The fact that water is essential to life and plays a role in most economic activities may lead to an exaggerated perception of its overall role in socio-economic development. Most detailed studies have indicated the role of water to be less important than is often assumed (6,8). However, the fact that data concerning future water use in a given area are often incomplete or unavailable results in the translation of commonly held perceptions into the belief that all available water will be needed for local economic growth. The same patterns appear to occur with respect to environmental needs. The potential for environmental harm tends to lead to adoption of a worst-case scenario associated with any proposed water transfer in the absence of definitive information.

An example is provided by a case involving proposed interbasin transfer of water to expand the supply of the metropolitan Norfolk-Virginia Beach area of southeastern Virginia. Opponents have expressed concern over major lake drawdowns causing interference with use of recreational property and boating facilities, destruction of sportfisheries, disruption of the recreation-based regional economy, and limitation of future economic growth in the region. Analysis of the anticipated impact of the proposed transfer indicates a maximum lake drawdown of about 4 in (10 cm) in the typical year (7). While these impacts may in fact be significant, this case demonstrates the tendency for common perceptions to differ substantially from the actual factual situation.

Institutional Disincentives Affecting Negotiation. - Persons in the area of origin for a proposed water transfer are encouraged to offer uncompromising resistance to any such proposal by commonly prevailing institutional arrangements. Several inherent characteristics of these institutions serve as disincentives to consideration of negotiated solutions with potential for mutual gain. One important disincentive is the uncertainty associated with water rights. Well defined property interests are a necessity for negotiation in order for the participants to be able to proceed with confidence that negotiation will produce enforceable rights. Uncertainty in the relevant property interests undermines the fundamental basis of negotiation.

Water rights under alternative allocation systems differ in the nature and extent of uncertainty, but no system totally eliminates this problem. The greatest uncertainty exists under the riparian doctrine where water rights are not quantified but must be defined through a case-by-case application of the reasonable-use standard when water-use conflicts occur.

Another characteristic of water-rights systems potentially acting as a disincentive to voluntary negotiation regarding proposed water transfer is the status of surplus water, which is often the focus of transfer proposals. Property interests in water are rights of use, limiting enforceability of rights in water not being put to use. In the case of riparian rights, unexercised rights are legally recognized but generally cannot be asserted to bar other water use unless a realistic prospect of harm to the unexercised right exists. The absence of substantive legal rights in surplus water largely eliminates the possibility of compensation for such water, thereby providing a major disincentive for resolution of water-transfer conflict through negotiated settlement. The only rational action for those in the area of origin is to oppose any proposed transfer of the surplus since no incentive to negotiate exists.

This naturally occurring opposition is facilitated by the current institutional framework due to the diversity of independent decision points provided by the substantial number of approvals necessary from local, state, and national governments. Each of these approvals provides a potential veto based on consideration of a particular aspect of the proposal. While each of the individual approvals is based on legitimate concerns, a question can be raised as to whether this fragmented approach, which provides little opportunity for comprehensive consideration of transfer proposals, is the most desirable decision-making process (4).

Conclusion: Recommendations for Improvement

Constraints that prevent socially undesirable transport of water certainly should be maintained, but those that obstruct objective evaluation of potentially useful transport should be examined for possible elimination or modification. Constraints imposed by information inadequacies are subject to direct mitigation by improved data collection and interpretation to provide better insight into water demands and impacts of water development activities. Such information in part is a public good that should be developed through traditional public sector programs, but the party proposing water transfer must be prepared to make a substantial contribution to this effort. Impact assessment requires thorough understanding of the behavior of hydrologic systems and may involve development of predictive models. This activity often will require significant time for completion and generally must be initiated substantially in advance of the planned date for implementation of water transfer.

The problem of excessively restrictive institutions is likely to be difficult to resolve. These constraints are a reflection of an increasingly negative attitude toward large scale water development projects. However, institutional change to facilitate more effective evaluation and resolution of the transfer issue is possible. Two types of changes appear to have promise. First, some consolidation of the numerous independent decision processes appears desirable. This approach has the greatest potential application within the boundaries of individual states. In states with a significant degree of local control and relatively weak or decentralized state controls, consolidation to achieve a more centralized approach may provide a better forum for effective management of the transfer issue. Such consolidation could take the form of comprehensive state controls over water use or more selective measures such as an institutional mechanism limited to control of certain types of water transfer. In either case, reduction in the degree of fragmentation of decision processes would allow a more comprehensive view of transfer proposals and improve the quality of the decision process. Consolidation of decision processes is less feasible for water transport across state or national boundaries due to the increasing levels of sovereignty involved; however, improved management of intrastate water transport would be a significant development since the greatest number of water transport cases are in this category.

A second type of change to facilitiate effective resolution of conflict associated with water transport is expanded use of compensation within related decision processes. The inability of the area of origin to receive compensation for transfer of surplus water is a major source of opposition to water transfer. The prospect of compensation would reduce opposition to transfer of water objectively determined to be in excess of reasonable economic and environmental needs of the area of origin. Such compensation should be paid by the water transferrer, with the amount of compensation to be calculated as a portion of transfer benefits. These benefits could be determined by comparing the costs of water transfer to the costs of the next best alternative source of supply. Implementation of such a compensation mechanism would require development of special institutions, but this approach has potential to reduce conflict and facilitate agreement in cases of socially desirable water transfer (4).

The issue of improving decision-making processes associated with water transport deserves serious attention because the need for water transport will continue to arise. The incorporation of demand management into water supply planning will reduce development of new supplies, but continued growth in population and human activity will require some measure of continued supply development. This additional development in some cases will involve proposals for water transport,

and even short-distance transport may require the crossing of boundaries that activate legal constraints. Timely and efficient resolution of the resulting conflict will continue to be a major function
of the water management process.

Appendix. - References

1. Barnett, P. M., "Mixing Water and the Commerce Clause: The
    Problems of Practice, Precedent, and Policy in Sporhase v.
    Nebraska," Natural Resources Journal, Vol. 24, 1984, pp. 161-194.

2. City of El Paso v. Reynolds, 563 F. Supp. 379 (D.N.M. 1983).

3. Clark, R. E., Waters and Water Rights, 7 Vols. The Allen Smith
    Co., Indianapolis, Ind., 1967-1976.

4. Cox, W. E., and Shabman, L. A., Virginia's Water Law: Resolving
    the Interjurisdictional Transfer Issue," Virginia Journal of
    Natural Resources Law, Vol. 2, 1984, pp. 181-234.

5. Farnham, W. H., "The Permissible Extent of Riparian Land," Land
    and Water Law Review, Vol. 7, 1972, pp. 31-61.

6. Howe, C. W., "Water and Regional Growth in the United States,
    1950-1960," Southern Economic Journal, Vol. 34, 1968, pp. 477-
    499.

7. "Lake Gaston Water Supply Project Environmental Report," CE
    Maguire, Inc., Virginia Beach, VA, 1983.

8. Lewis, W. C., Andersen, J. C., Fullerton, H. H., and Gardner, B.
    D., Regional Growth and Water Resource Investment, Lexington
    Books, Lexington, KY, 1973.

9. Robie, R. B., and Kletzing, R. R., "Area of Origin Statutes - The
    California Experience," Idaho Law Review, Vol. 15, 1979, pp.
    419-441.

10. Sporhase v. Nebraska, 102 S. Ct. 3456 (1982).

11. Trelease, F. J. and Lee, D. W., "Priority and Progress -- Case
    Studies in the Transfer of Water Rights," Land and Water Law
    Review, Vol. 1, 1966, pp. 1-76.

12. Virginia Code Annotated, sec. 15.1-37 (1981).

13. Weatherford, G. D., "Legal Aspects of Interregional Water Diver-
    sion," UCLA Law Review, Vol. 15, 1968, pp. 1299-1346.

14. Williams, S. F., "Optimizing Water Use: The Return Flow Issue,"
    University of Colorado Law Review, Vol. 44, 1973, pp. 301-321.

Conceptual Framework for Regression Modeling of Ground-Water Flow

Summary

Richard L. Cooley*

Ground-water flow models have been used to estimate hydrogeologic parameters, such as transmissivity and storage, and predict dependent variables, such as hydraulic head and fluxes, for more than 50 years. Early models, such as the Theis equation, were simple and based on analytic solutions. As electric-analog models and, finally, general mathematical (digital computer) models were developed, the models became increasingly complex. Within the last 5 to 10 years there has been a trend toward adding stochastic components into models. This has resulted partly from recognition of errors and uncertainties in all types of data used for input and calibration of models, and partly from recognition that all of the complexities, such as small-scale variations in transmissivity, cannot be incorporated into models.

We will examine here the uses of ground-water flow models and which classes of use require treatment of stochastic components. We will then compare traditional and stochastic procedures for modeling actual (as distinguished from hypothetical) systems. Finally, we will examine the conceptual basis and characteristics of the regression approach to modeling ground-water flow.

Three classes of use of ground-water flow models may be distinguished. The first class is the model for conceptualization. Its objective is to examine the effects of selected factors (such as parameter values, boundary conditions, and configuration of transmissivity zones) on the resulting flow system, as measured by, for example, distribution of hydraulic head and magnitudes of fluxes. The main characteristic of this class is that the model is strictly deterministic; because there are no actual data, there are no errors or uncertainties in the input or output. The second class is the model for flow-system synthesis. Its objective is to integrate a preliminary conceptual model of an actual present-day or past flow system and the various data collected from it in order to improve understanding of the flow system. Because the flow system and the data obtained for it are not hypothetical, any deterministic model is in error. A critical point is that the error cannot automatically be ignored; it is as much a part of the model as any other component, such as variations in recharge rate or transmissivity. The third class is the model for prediction. Its objective is to predict the

* U.S. Geological Survey, P. O. Box 25046, MS 413, Federal Center, Lakewood, CO 80225

results of future applied stresses, or other events, on an actual flow system. Models for prediction are usually based on (or derived from) models of present-day or past flow systems. Thus, they share with the second class the characteristic of containing errors. However, this third class has the added complexity that errors of prediction, derived from uncertainties in future behavior of the system, are added to the errors and uncertainties inherited from the model of the present or past system (the class-two model). Note that although the three classes of models are based on use, the models for each class actually differ from one another because of the presence, absence and types of error components.

While it is widely recognized that models of actual systems contain errors, most model studies have not formally taken the errors into account. Most studies have been based on models developed as if they were deterministic, for which the best conceptual model and parameters (such as transmissivities, storage coefficients, leakage coefficients, recharge rates, discharge rates, boundary fluxes, and boundary hydraulic heads) were derived by trial and error calibration procedures. Because the model was developed as if it were deterministic, uncertainties in the model (class-two model) or a predictive model derived from it (class-three model) are only qualitatively known. Sensitivity analysis may be used to help quantify the uncertainties, but evaluation of the effect of joint changes in parameters or predictions is difficult with sensitivity analysis.

To consider the full effect of input errors and uncertainties on model output, we need to use interval estimation and prediction. Input errors are formally taken into account by specifying that parameters are stochastic quantities, having a joint statistical distribution. Output from the model is then stochastic, having a joint statistical distribution. Three statistical methods that have been used are the Monte Carlo method, the geostatistical method, and regression. For the Monte Carlo method, the model equations are used to generate numerous realizations of the dependent variable based on statistically generated realizations of the parameters. In the geostatistical approach, hydraulic heads and parameters are considered to be distributed as a joint probability density function for which covariances of hydraulic heads and parameters are obtained from perturbation linearizations of the model equations. The best joint density function is then fitted using maximum likelihood estimation. Stochastic variability of parameters and measurement errors can both be approximately accounted for using this method. Regression methods fit the model equation and computed parameters to observed (that is, measured) hydraulic heads and observed (measured or computed independently of the model) parameters using either maximum likelihood or least squares estimation. Stochastic variability and measurement errors can again be taken into account, but in contrast to the geostatistical approach, no linearization of the model equations is involved.

The statistical approaches allow testing the extent to which the errors and uncertainties in input have propagated into the output. One may test whether the input data are compatible with the mathematical model, and whether values of parameters observed independently of the model are compatible with those obtained by calibrating the model. One also may derive confidence and tolerance regions and intervals on parameters computed by the model and on values of dependent variables computed by the model. In some circumstances where both the model to be used for prediction and the error structure for this model are known, one also may derive prediction regions for predicted dependent variables. Hence, the extent to which the objective of the class-two models (that is, improving understanding of the flow system) has been met during a study can be determined in a much more quantitative manner than with deterministic methods. Furthermore, some components of the errors in predicting future systems can be quantified.

In this writer's opinion, of the presently available methods, regression is the most ideally suited as a robust and economical statistical modeling method. To apply regression procedures one must translate a sound conceptual model into a practical deterministic mathematical model, then specify how the various errors and uncertainties contribute to error in the principal dependent variable (generally, hydraulic head). The two most common ways are the additive error:

$$h_i = f_i(\xi_1, \xi_2, \ldots; \beta_1, \beta_2, \ldots) + \varepsilon_i$$

and the multiplicative error

$$h_i = f_i(\xi_1, \xi_2, \ldots; \beta_1, \beta_2, \ldots) \varepsilon_i$$

where h_i is observed hydraulic head at point i, $f_i(\xi_1, \xi_2, \ldots; \beta_1, \beta_2, \ldots)$ is the hydraulic head at point i computed by the deterministic mathematical model, $\xi_1, \xi_2, \ldots$ are the independent variables of the model, $\beta_1, \beta_2, \ldots$ are the parameters of the model (transmissivities, storage coefficients, leakage coefficients, recharge rates, discharge rates, boundary fluxes, and boundary hydraulic heads), and ε_i is the error in h_i. Because the multiplicative-error equation can be transformed into the additive-error equation by taking logarithms of both sides, only the additive-error type is considered further here.

Three major assumptions are usually made involving the model and the errors: (1) The deterministic model is correct; (2) the model is unbiased (that is, $E(\varepsilon_i) = 0$, where E signifies expected value); and (3) $Cov(\varepsilon_i, \varepsilon_j)$, where Cov signifies covariance, is known to within a constant multiple.

Observations (as measurements or computations) of the parameters made independently of the model are termed prior information. These data may be entered into the model analysis in one of two ways, either classical or Bayesian. Because classical and Bayesian approaches usually yield the same regression solution, Bayesian approaches are

not considered further here. In the classical approach, the prior
information is specified by a model equation written for observations
in a manner exactly analogous to the equation for hydraulic head, h_j.
For example

$$p_j = g_j(\xi_1, \xi_2, \ldots; \beta_1, \beta_2, \ldots) + \eta_j$$

where p_j is prior information at point j; g_j is the model equation for
prior information at point j; and η_j is the error in p_j. Direct prior
information on some subset of parameters is specified by setting $g_j =$
β_j where β_j is a parameter on which there is prior information.
Another possible example of specifying prior information is if a total
model flux, such as total flux across some boundary, is known and the
β_j are individual fluxes across sections of the boundary. In this
case, g_j would be a linear combination of the β_j. Classical use of
prior information requires the assumption that $E(\eta_j) = 0$ and that
$Cov(\eta_j, \eta_k)$ is known. Usually it also is assumed that $Cov(\varepsilon_j, \eta_j) = 0$.
Solution of the regression problem may be obtained by using either
maximum likelihood estimation or generalized least squares. The
result of the solution is estimates $\hat{b}_1, \hat{b}_2, \ldots$ of parameters
$\beta_1, \beta_2, \ldots$ and estimates of computed dependent variables f_j and g_j.

Prior information also may be incorporated in the case where
$Cov(\eta_j, \eta_k)$ is unknown. This is accomplished by constraining the
regression solution using the elliptical constraint

$$\sum_i \sum_j (\hat{b}_i - p_i) \, a_{ij} \, (\hat{b}_j - p_j) = c^2$$

(where c^2 is a given constant and $\{a_{ij}\}$ is a known positive definite
matrix) in place of the model equation for p_j. It can be shown that
for an assumed matrix $\{a_{ij}\}$ an optimum value of c^2 exists such that
the mean square error in estimated parameters is minimized. Matrix
$\{a_{ij}\}$ usually is assumed to be either the identity matrix or a
diagonal scaling matrix intended to emphasize certain components of
the quadratic form, c^2. The optimum value of c^2 cannot be found
directly, but may often be approximated.

One of the more important aspects of formulating regression
solutions to ground-water flow problems is understanding the origin
and structure of errors ε_j and η_j. These stochastic components are
simply an attempt to represent processes that cannot be modeled
deterministically. Hence, they are related not only to the existence
of measurement errors but to complexities of ground-water physics and
hydrogeology as well.

Because parameters β_j represent quantities such as transmissivities, storage coefficients, leakage coefficients, and rates of
ground-water recharge and discharge, they are inherently variable in
space and often in time as well. Small-scale fluctuations of these
parameters cannot be incorporated into a flow model. Therefore, the
quantities used as regression parameters in the regression model must
be regarded as lumped (or effective) parameters.

To formulate a regression model where the error ε_j in observed hydraulic head h_j, resulting in part from small-scale variability in parameters, can be considered additive to a deterministic hydraulic head f_j requires generalization of the idea of an observation point. The theory of regression modeling requires that an observation point be defined so that a repeated observation at the point will sample all sources of variability in ε_j. A single well drilled into a flow system will not accomplish this, because it does not sample local spatial variability in parameters. Thus, the idea of a point must be generalized to become a volume of aquifer material just large enough to sample all sources of variability in ε_j, and this includes variability resulting from various measurement errors as well as variability resulting from small-scale, random-appearing fluctuations in parameters. Local model biases resulting from lumping parameters are converted into a psuedo-random component.

Lumped parameters need to be physically interpreted in order to physically interpret the regression solution. This is especially important because it is necessary to know if the parameters in the model equation for h_j and the parameters in the model equation for p_j are actually the same quantities, so that the two models can be used conjunctively. However, at the present time, knowledge is limited concerning effective values of the various parameters under general conditions involving the model equations and local parameter variability. Thus, we must rely on statistical tests for compatibility of parameters in prior (p_j) and sample (h_j) models.

Large-scale variability of parameters can be defined by zones of constant parameter values or by models defining the trends in parameters. A particularly useful model is a finite element discretization of large scale variation of a quantity such as transmissivity, with regression parameters being the values at nodes. This specification of parameter variability is then imbedded in the deterministic flow model. Prior information could be given directly on the nodal parameter values, or in some other manner as on combinations of nodes as discussed previously.

An important consequence of errors and uncertainty in modeling ground-water flow concerns the appropriate level of model complexity for a given model study. Because of errors in observed hydraulic heads and parameters, combined with lack of sensitivity of computed hydraulic heads to changes in some parameters, a complex model may yield a computed hydraulic head distribution that is not different enough from the computed hydraulic head distribution resulting from a simpler model to warrant inclusion of the complexities. In this instance the complexities may be present, but they are not manifested to a large enough degree to allow estimation of reliable values for parameters. To delineate significant controls on flow system behavior, we need to determine if the difference between two models could result solely from random fluctuations in errors in observed data. If this possibility is accepted, then the added complexities would not seem to be important in comparison with data errors. No exact methods are available for this test, but an approximate test can be derived by considering that one model is derived from another by constraining the parameters of one in such a way as to produce the other. If the addition of the constraints produces a significantly less accurate model in terms of the fit of h_j to f_j and g_j to p_j (as determined statistically), then the models can be considered to be different. It is important to recognize that insignificant parameters for a present-day (class-two) model may become important when the flow system changes in the future, as predicted by a class-three model.

Prior Information in the Geostatistical Approach

Peter K. Kitanidis*, Member, ASCE

Abstract

An overview of recent work on the geostatistical approach to the inverse problem of groundwater modeling is presented. A method which allows utilization of prior information about the drift coefficients and the covariance-function parameters is described.

Introduction

The inverse problem of groundwater modeling is defined, in the strict sense, as the determination of permeabilities or transmissivities from measurements of the piezometric head. However, in a more general sense, the inverse problem may be defined as the estimation of model parameters, such as transmissivities, leakage coefficients, and boundary conditions, given observations of the parameters as well as of related quantities such as piezometric head, pumping rates, and tracer-test concentrations.

The study of the inverse problem has attracted much attention in the last twenty years because groundwater models have heavy data requirements but direct measurements of hydrogeologic properties are scarce. The most common approach is based on the minimization of a fitting criterion. The problem of parameter estimation has been defined as follows [18]:

"Determine the groundwater model parameter values which give the closest correspondence (or best "fit") between measured hydrologic variables (such as water table elevations obtained at available well locations) and simulated hydrologic variables (computed from the model)."

However, earlier efforts were stymied by the fact that many different sets of property estimates may provide satisfactory and essentially indistinguishable data fits. In particular, as discussed in [5], estimation of transmissivities from piezometric head has been shown to be a mathematically not well posed problem which does not admit a unique and stable solution. In practice, the problem is addressed by introducing prior information about the parameters or the smoothness of the unknown field in papers such as [1], [2], [3], [7], and [17].

*Associate Professor, St. Anthony Falls Hydraulic Laboratory, Department of Civil and Mineral Engineering, University of Minnesota, Mississippi River at Third Avenue Southeast, Minneapolis, Minnesota 55414

897

This paper will present an overview of a rather new methodology, called the geostatistical approach to the inverse problem. Then, it will be shown how prior information may be used in the context of the geostatistical approach.

The Geostatistical Approach

The geostatistical method for the solution of the inverse problem involves two main steps.

1. The structure of the property field is identified. In essence, at this step the modeler determines how much spatial variability is small-scale (compared to the smallest separation distances between measurements) and how much can be explained through measurements at neighboring points. Furthermore, a mathematical model is selected to describe how two property measurements are correlated as a function of their location.

2. The probabilities of point or block-averaged estimates of the unknown property are obtained conditional on available measurements.

The first step is equivalent to "model estimation" in time series and to "structural analysis" in geostatistics (e.g., [6].) The structure of the field may be represented through drifts (or trends) and covariance functions or variograms. Structure identification is applied in an iterative fashion with three substeps: model selection, parameter estimation, and model validation or diagnostic checking. The representation through drifts and covariance functions, although mathematically not generally complete, is convenient and adequate for most practical purposes. The model is selected and fitted using all available measurements of the property of interest and input-output variables, and prior information, if available. The second step, which is equivalent to prediction in time-series analysis, uses linear estimation theory to yield unbiased minimum mean square error estimates of the property field given all available information.

The geostatistical approach to the inverse problem is founded on the assumption that the aquifer property and system variable distributions can be considered to be realizations of some random field or random function. It is important to recognize that this is only a convenient and extremely general way to describe geometrically the spatial variability of hydrogeologic properties. It is similar to but much more realistic and powerful than the assumption of the formation consisting of many homogeneous blocks. If the characteristics of the random functions can be determined from the available observations, then estimates of the actual fields can be obtained conditional on all available measurements.

Methods used to derive head variability ("geostatistical direct problem") include, but are not limited to, Monte Carlo techniques [16] and small perturbation or Taylor's series expansion analysis allowing linearization of flow equations [4, 15, 17]. These studies provide a statistical description of the hydraulic head given a statistical description of the log-conductivity or log-transmissivity field.

The geostatistical approach was tested extensively [11] through simulations on a simple one-dimensional case for which the small perturbation method yielded analytical solutions to the direct problem. Maximum likelihood estimates of variogram parameters were obtained using all available information, including measurements of hydraulic head and permeability. Logpermeability measurements were then obtained using cokriging. The obtained estimates of logtransmissivity were found to be remarkably stable and well-behaved. The estimated field is a smoothed approximation of the actual field while small-scale variability is statistically described. As the number of measurements increases and measurement error decreases, the procedure reproduces more features of the original field.

References [8] and [9] presented extensions of this methodology to two-dimensional steady flow problems using numerical methods to determine the first two joint moments of log-transmissivity and piezometric head. Cokriging was then used to yield point or block-averaged estimates of log-transmissivity as well as piezometric head. The authors tested their approach through simulations and applied it to a case study with favorable results.

Another author who extended the methodology of Kitanidis and coworkers was Dagan [5]. Dagan is in favor of approximate analytical solutions which, unlike numerical methods, are not affected by discretization error but are restricted to simple problems. Furthermore, Dagan recommends classical linear (or conditional Gaussian) estimation instead of cokriging used by Kitanidis and coworkers. The results of classical linear estimation were compared to cokriging in Reference [9]. In the framework of the geostatistical approach to the inverse problem in steady two-dimensional flow, it was found that prediction variances calculated using classical linear estimation are too low compared to corresponding actual mean square errors of estimation when drift coefficient are unknown a priori. Cokriging, however, was found to be unaffected by such a bias. As will be discussed later, cokriging is the appropriate procedure to use for a priori unknown drift coefficients.

Ordinary cokriging is invariant to estimates of drift coefficients. The only requirement is that the expected value of the data be a linear function of the unknown drift coefficients. In groundwater modeling this condition is generally not met. For example, even if the log-transmissivity drift is assumed linear in the unknown coefficient, the piezometric head usually turns out to be a nonlinear function of these parameters. An extended form was developed in Reference [9] for such cases. Extended cokriging is an iterative procedure which yields estimates which are invariant to small errors in the estimated drift coefficients.

For the estimation of structural parameters, such as variances and integral scales, two useful procedures are restricted maximum likelihood [13] and minimum variance unbiased quadratic estimation [12]. The first procedure relies on the maximization of the likelihood function of data increments which are invariant to unknown drift coefficients. The Gauss-Newton method is likely the most computationally efficient method for the solution of this optimization problem. Reference [12] describes the conditions under which minimum-variance unbiased estimation of variance components can be obtained. For the useful class of covariance functions which are linear in the parameters, estimates can be obtained which are unbiased and invariant to drift coefficients. Furthermore, if the data can be considered to be generated according to a Gaussian model (or any other known model, for that matter) minimum variance estimation can be achieved subject to the constraints of unbiasedness and invariance to drift coefficients.

Use of Prior Information

This section describes how prior information about drift coefficients or covariance-function parameters can be utilized in the geostatistical approach to the inverse problem. Only the general methodology will be presented here, while the proof of the main result and case studies are presented elsewhere.

To be specific, consider the case of steady two-dimensional flow in an aquifer with head ϕ and log-transmissivity $\underline{Y} = \ell nT$ (such as the case described in References [8] and [9]). To simplify the analysis further, assume that only log-transmissivity is unknown. A general way to describe the "structure" of the regionalized variable Y is to assume that it is a realization of a random function with drift which is linear in the parameters and a given covariance function. That is,

$$Y(\underline{x}) = \sum_{i=1}^{p} f_i(\underline{x})\beta_i + \varepsilon_Y(\underline{x}) \tag{1}$$

where $\underline{x}$ is the vector of spatial coordinates; β_i , $i=1,\ldots,p$ are (generally unknown) drift coefficients; $f_i(\underline{x})^i$, $i=1,\ldots,p$, are known function of the spatial coordinates, usually taken as polynomials; and $\varepsilon_Y(\underline{x})$ is a zero-mean spatial random function with a covariance function which is known except for some (partially unknown) parameters, $\underline{\theta}$. Using the flow equations, generally after a linearization, the piezometric head at a point with spatial coordinates $\underline{x}$ may be given by

$$\phi(\underline{x}) = \phi_o(\underline{x}) + \sum^{p} g_i(\underline{x})\beta_i + \varepsilon_\phi(\underline{x}) \tag{2}$$

where $\phi_0(\underline{x})$ is a known function of $\underline{x}$, $g_i(\underline{x})$ are known functions of $\underline{x}$, and $\varepsilon_\phi(\underline{x})$ is a zero-mean process with covariance function which depends on $\underline{\theta}$ and, sometimes, on $\underline{\beta}$. Reference [9] presents an iterative method which leads to a result of the form of Equation 2. To simplify the analysis, the dependence of the covariance matrix of $\varepsilon_\phi(\underline{x})$ on $\underline{\beta}$ will be neglected. Our computational experience suggests that this assumption is reasonable in some cases (for example, it is valid for the case examined in Reference 11) but will need to be reexamined in the future. Note that $\varepsilon_\phi(x)$ is correlated with $\varepsilon_Y(\underline{x})$. The covariance function of $\varepsilon_\phi(x)$ and the cross-covariance of $\varepsilon_\phi(\underline{x})$ and $\varepsilon_Y(\underline{x})$ may be expressed as known functions of using analytical [5, 11] or numerical methods [8, 9].

Let $\underline{z}$ be nx1, the vector of measurements, consisting of log-transmissivity measurements, $Y(\underline{x}_i)$, and piezometric-head measurements, $\phi(\underline{x}_j) - \phi_0(\underline{x}_j)$, where $\underline{x}_i$ and $\underline{x}_j$ give the coordinates of locations where measurements are available. Then

$$\underline{z} = X\underline{\beta} + \underline{\varepsilon} \tag{3}$$

where $\underline{\beta}$ is the vector of drift coefficients, X is a known nxp matrix, and $\underline{\varepsilon}$ is a vector with zero mean and covariance matrix Q_{zz} known except for a few unknown parameters $\underline{\theta}$. Under the common assumption of normality (see discussion in Reference [10]), the probability of $\underline{z}$ given $\underline{\beta}$ and $\underline{\theta}$ (or the likelihood function of $\underline{\beta}$ and $\underline{\theta}$ given $\underline{z}$) is

$$p(\underline{z}|\underline{\beta},\underline{\theta}) = L(\underline{\beta},\underline{\theta}|z)$$

$$= (2\pi)^{-n/2}|Q_{zz}|^{-1/2}\exp(-\frac{1}{2}(\underline{z} - X\underline{\beta})^T Q_{zz}^{-1}(\underline{z}-X\underline{\beta})) \tag{4}$$

where $|\ |$ denotes determinant.

Let $p'(\underline{\beta},\underline{\theta})$ describe the prior joint probability density function (pdf) of $\underline{\beta}$ and $\underline{\theta}$. This may be written as

$$p'(\underline{\beta},\underline{\theta}) = p'(\underline{\beta}|\underline{\theta})p'(\underline{\theta}) \tag{5}$$

It is assumed that $p'(\underline{\beta}|\underline{\theta})$ is Gaussian with mean $\underline{b}$ and covariance matrix V_b . The posterior pdf is given through Bayes' theorem

$$p''(\underline{\beta},\underline{\theta}|\underline{z}) = cL(\underline{\beta},\underline{\theta}|\underline{z})p'(\underline{\beta},\underline{\theta}) \tag{6}$$

where c is a constant such that the expression of Equation 6 describes an appropriate pdf. However, the main problem of interest is not how to derive the posterior pdf of the parameters, but to derive the Bayesian distribution of the logtransmissivity at any point given only these measurements and prior information. This distribution accounts for inherent as well as parameter uncertainty. Let z_o be an mx1 vector of point- or block-averaged values of log-transmissivity.

$$\underline{z}_o = X_o \underline{\beta} + \varepsilon_o \qquad (7)$$

where X_o is a known mxp matrix and ε_o is a zero mean vector with covariance matrix Q_{oo}. Furthermore, the cross-covariance matrix between ε_o and $\underline{\varepsilon}$ is Q_{oz}, an mxn matrix. Both Q_{oo} and Q_{oz} are known except for parameters $\underline{\theta}$. It is shown in Reference [14] that the Bayesian pdf of $\underline{z}_o$ given $\underline{z}$ and $\underline{\theta}$, $p(\underline{z}_o|\underline{z},)$, is Gaussian with mean vector and covariance matrix which can be readily calculated from the following formulas:

$$\tilde{E}(\underline{z}_o|\underline{z},\underline{\theta}) = (X_o - Q_{oz}Q_{zz}^{-1}X)(V_b^{-1} + X^T Q_{zz}^{-1}X)^{-1}V_b^{-1}\underline{b}$$

$$+ [Q_{oz}Q_{zz}^{-1} + (X_o - Q_{oz}Q_{zz}^{-1}X)(V_b^{-1} + X^T Q_{zz}^{-1}X)^{-1}X^T Q_{zz}^{-1}]\underline{z} \qquad (8)$$

$$\tilde{V}(\underline{z}_o|\underline{z},\underline{\theta}) = (Q_{oo} - Q_{oz}Q_{zz}^{-1}Q_{zo})$$

$$+ (X_o - Q_{oz}Q_{zz}^{-1}X)(V_b^{-1} + X^T Q_{zz}^{-1}X)^{-1}(X_o - Q_{oz}Q_{zz}^{-1}X)^T \qquad (9)$$

The marginal posterior pdf of $\underline{\theta}$ given $\underline{z}$ and prior information is given by

$$p''(\underline{\theta}|\underline{z}) = cL_\theta(\underline{\theta}|\underline{z})p'(\underline{\theta}) \qquad (10)$$

where c is a constant required to make the integral of $p''(\underline{\theta}|\underline{z})$ over all possible values equal to one and $L_\theta(\underline{\theta}|\underline{z})$ is the marginal likelihood ($p(\underline{z}|\underline{\theta})$, with the effects of $\underline{\beta}$ averaged out). The marginal likelihood of the covariance function parameters given the measurements is found in [14] to be

$$L_\theta(\underline{\theta}|\underline{z}) \alpha |Q_{zz}|^{-1/2} |(V_b^{-1} + X^T Q_{zz}^{-1} X)^{-1}|^{1/2}$$

$$\exp[-\frac{1}{2}(\underline{z}^T(Q_{zz}^{-1} - Q_{zz}^{-1} X(V_b^{-1} + X^T Q_{zz}^{-1} X)^{-1} X^T Q_{zz}^{-1})\underline{z}$$ (11)

$$- 2\underline{b}^T V_b^{-1} (V_b^{-1} + X^T Q_{zz}^{-1} X)^{-1} X^T Q_{zz}^{-1} \underline{z} + \underline{b}^T V_b^{-1} \underline{b})]$$

Then the prediction problem is equivalent to finding the Bayesian distribution of $\underline{z}_o$ given only the data and prior information

$$\breve{p}(\underline{z}_o|\underline{z}) = \int_\theta \tilde{p}(\underline{z}_o|\underline{\theta},\underline{z})p''(\underline{\theta}|\underline{z})d\underline{\theta}$$ (12)

The integration can generally be achieved only numerically, at a high computational cost, or analytically after some approximations. Some results are given in Reference [14]. A suboptimal procedure which is consistent with common practice in linear estimation or kriging is to obtain some point estimates of θ and then use them as shown in Equations 8 and 9. The estimates which maximize $p''(\theta)$ of Equation 11 are called maximum aposteriori probability or MAP estimates and account for prior as well as sample information.

Discussion

If no prior information is available about the drift coefficient $(V_b^{-1}=0)$, then: a) Equations 8 and 9 are identical to the kriging equations and, b) the marginal likelihood function is the same with the restricted likelihood function used in [8], [9], [11], and [13], i.e., the probability of any complete set of data increments which are invariant to drift coefficients.

On the other extreme, that of a priori known drift coefficients: a) Equations 8 and 9 correspond to Gaussian conditional mean or linear estimation equations such as those used in [5] and, b) the marginal likelihood function has the same form as the likelihood function of Equation 4 except that the elements of $\underline{\beta}$, instead of being parameters to be estimated, are a priori known.

This methodology is, thus, a natural generalization of the work of [5], [8], [9], [11], and [13]. Prior information on both drift and covariance-function parameters is utilized without substantially increasing the computational cost. The effect on estimates of log-transmissivity of uncertainty in drift coefficients is taken into account. Furthermore, the distortion of covariance-function parameters which is caused when drift coefficients are calculated simultaneously, e.g., through the joint probability function of covariance function and drift parameters, is reduced or, in some cases, completely eliminated.   This distortion could be quite significant for nearly nonstationary fields.

Concluding Remarks

This paper has presented an overview of the geostatistical approach to the inverse problem and an extension which allows using prior information about drift coefficients and covariance-function parameters.   The methodology is computationally efficient, yields generally undistorted estimates of covariance-function parameters, and accounts for the effect of uncertainty in drift coefficients on the estimates of logtransmissivity.

APPENDIX I.   REFERENCES

1. Clifton, P. M., and Neuman, S. P., "Effects of Kriging and Inverse Modeling on Conditional Simulation of the Avra Valley Aquifer in Southern Arizona," Water Resources Research, Vol. 18, No. 4, 1982, pp. 1215-1234.

2. Cooley, R. L., "Incorporation of Prior Information on Parameters into Nonlinear Regression Groundwater Flow Models: 1. Theory," Water Resources Research, Vol. 18, No. 4, 1982, pp. 965-976.

3. Cooley, R. L., "Incorporation of Prior Information on Parameters into Nonlinear Regression Groundwater Flow Models: 2. Applications," Water Resources Research, Vol. 19, No. 3, 1983, pp. 662-676.

4. Dagan, G., "Stochastic Modeling of Groundwater Flow by Unconditional and Conditional Probabilities: 1. Conditional Simulation and the Direct Problem," Water Resources Research, 18, No. 4, 1982, pp. 812-833.

5. Dagan, G., "Stochastic Modeling of Groundwater Flow by Unconditional and Conditional Probabilities: The Inverse Problem," Water Resources Research, Vol. 21, No. 1, 1985, pp. 65-72.

6. Delhomme, J. P., "Spatial Variability and Uncertainty in Groundwater Flow Parameters: A Geostatistical Approach," Water Resources Research, Vol. 15, No. 2, 1979, pp. 269-280.

7. Emsellem, Y., and de Marsily, G., "An Automatic Solution for the Inverse Problem," Water Resources Research, Vol. 7, No. 5, 1971, pp. 1264-1283.

8. Hoeksema, R. J., and Kitanidis, P. K., "An Application of the Geostatistical Approach to the Inverse Problem in Two-Dimensional Groundwater Modeling," Water Resources Research, Vol. 20, No. 7, 1984a, pp. 1003-1020.

9. Hoeksema, R. J., and Kitanidis, P. K., "The Geostatistical Approach to the Inverse Problem in Two-Dimensional Steady State Groundwater Modeling," IIHR Tech. Report No. 282, University of Iowa, Iowa City, 1984b.

10. Hoeksema, R. J., and Kitanidis, P. K., "Analysis of the Spatial Structure of Properties of Selected Aquifers," in press in Water Resources Research, 1985.

11. Kitanidis, P. K., and Vomvoris, E. G., "A Geostatistical Approach to the Inverse Problem in Groundwater Modeling (Steady State) and One-Dimensional Simulations," Water Resources Research, , Vol. 19, No. 3, 1983, 677-690.

12. Kitanidis, P. K., "Minimum Variance Unbiased Quadratic Estimation of Covariances of Regionalized Variables," J. of Mathematical Geology, Vol. 17, No. 2, 1985, pp. 195-208.

13. Kitanidis, P. K., and Lane, R. W., "Maximum-Likelihood Parameter Estimation of Hydrologic Spatial Processes by the Gauss-Newton Method," in press in Journal of Hydrology, 1985.

14. Kitanidis, P. K., "Parameter Uncertainty in Estimation of Spatial Functions: Bayesian Analysis," Unpublished Report, 1985.

15. Mizell, S. A., Gutjahr, A. L., and Gelhar, L. W., "Stochastic Analysis of Spatial Variability in Two-Dimensional Steady Groundwater Flow Assuming Stationary and Nonstationary Heads," Water Resources Research, Vol. 18, No. 4, 1982, pp. 1053-1067.

16. Smith, L., and Freeze, R. A., "Stochastic Analysis of Steady State Groundwater Flow in a Bounded Domain: 2. Two-Dimensional Simulations," Water Resources Research, Vol. 15, No. 6, 1979, pp. 1543-1559.

17. Wilson, J. L., Kitanidis, P. K., and Dettinger, M., "State and Parameter Estimation in Groundwater Models," in Applications of Kalman Filter to Hydrology, Hydraulics, and Water Resources, ed. by C.-L. Chiu, University of Pittsburgh, 1978, pp. 657-679.

18. Water Resources Engineers, "Investigations of Alternative Procedures for Estimating Groundwater Basin Parameters," Report prepared for OWRT, U. S. Department of the Interior, January 1975.

19. Yeh, W. W.-G., and Yoon, Y. S., "Aquifer Parameter Identification with Optimum Dimension in Parametrization, Water Resources Research, Vol. 17, No. 3, 1981, pp. 664-672.

Forecasting Water Use: A Tutorial

John J. Boland*

Abstract: In spite of 4,000 years of public water supply system construction, designs have been customarily based on forecasts of future water use only during the last 100 years. Choices among available forecasting methods are based on issues and criteria developed during that 100 years of forecasting experience. These issues and criteria are examined by reviewing the historical development of forecasting methods, by considering general principles of forecasting, and by incorporating the insights of recent water use research. Topics discussed include the importance of disaggregation in forecasting, the role of price and income, the consequences of changes in household and employment characteristics, and weather normalization.

Introduction

If the forecasting of water use is an important activity, it has become so only recently. Societies wholly ignorant of water use forecasting methods built water supply systems more than 4,000 years ago (3). Travellers on the shores of the Mediterranean, or in the Near East, can see water supply works built by the Romans 2,000 years ago, some still serving their original purpose. Yet the Romans not only did not forecast water use, they lacked a valid concept of volumetric flow (8).

After an early start in the mid-seventeenth century, the development of public water supply systems in the U.S. and Canada progressed slowly. By 1860 there were only about 136 water systems in the U.S., and another ten in Canada (4). In many cases, these were investor-owned systems serving a portion of an urban area: the area served depended upon the capability of the source. Since there was no obligation to supply water to the entire population, present or future, there was no need to forecast the demand which any particular population could impose.

After the U.S. Civil War, however, water planning changed dramatically. The rebuilding and industrialization of North American cities was accompanied by construction of thousands of new water systems, most intended to serve all local residents and businesses and even to provide for anticipated future population. The motivation for this expansion came from two distinct concerns: (1) the need for readily available water for fire suppression (the advent of steam-powered fire equipment promised the eventual end of periodic disastrous urban fires) and (2) a desire, nearer the end of the nineteenth century, to provide safer drinking water to cities suffering from endemic typhoid and cholera.

*Professor of Geography and Environmental Engineering, The Johns Hopkins University, Baltimore, MD 21218.

These concerns introduced a new element to water supply planning: the quantity of water supplied would be determined by the needs of the population, not the capability of the source. Needs would have to be determined first, then sources would have to be found to meet the needs. Engineers responsible for the design of water systems, both large and small, were now required to consider, for the first time in a systematic way, the nature and behavior of water use.

But, after 3,900 years of building water systems without forecasts, the engineering profession had little to offer those designing supply systems in the last half of the nineteenth century. Today's engineers are more fortunate, having access to the accumulated experience of the past 100 years. A recent study esimates that about $8.5 billion dollars (in 1982 dollars) are spent on water and wastewater facilities in the U.S. each year, much of that investment driven by and predicated on water use forecasts (5).

In spite of the obvious economic importance of sound forecasting techniques, many if not most water supply projects are based on quickly prepared, simplistic forecasts (7). This practice suggests that the perceived importance of forecasting has not changed greatly over the history of the water supply industry.

The choice of an appropriate forecast method is not a simple one. Many approaches are possible, and they differ substantially with respect to data requirements, analytical complexity, and the characteristics of the resulting forecast. It is the purpose of this paper to examine and place into perspective the experience of the past 100 years, and to highlight various issues and criteria which affect choices among water use forecasting methods.

Principles

Most simply, a forecast is a statement about the future. The most general term for such statements is "prediction," but not all predictions are forecasts. Forecasters (engineers and water planners in the present example) are unable to make unqualified statements about the future: that is the work of seers and psychics, not those trained in technical disciplines. A forecast is, instead, a conditional prediction, a statement about what is expected to happen if various assumptions turn out to be valid. Discussions of forecasting, then, are as much about assumptions as they are about forecasting itself.

The term "forecast" implies nothing about the method or the assumptions used. Many forecasts, however, rely on a set of assumptions which include continuation of at least some past trends and/or relationships. Such forecasts are called projections. Some forecasts are based on assumptions which consist entirely of continuation of past trends; these are usually termed "extrapolations." This paper discusses forecasting in the most general sense although it should be understood that, in practice, most forecasts are projections (they incorporate at least some reliance on past trends/relationships).

Some wonder whether forecasting should thought of as a subjective or an objective enterprise, or, similarly, whether the act of forecasting

is an art or a science. In this case, "objective" refers to something
based on facts and verifiable while the exercise of "science" is to use
a technique derived from a body of systematized facts. The answers
follow directly from the distinctions made above. Since a forecast is a
statement about the future, and since the future does not exist (is not
a fact), forecasting is inherently and unavoidably subjective. Forecasting is therefore art, not science.

But this is not the whole story. Forecasting, though subjective,
has substantial objective content; it is art based on science. That
this is so can be demonstrated by dividing the act of forecasting into
two stages: explanation and prediction. Explanation occurs when forecasters study past experience (facts) in order to understand (e.g.) past
water use patterns and the factors that caused those patterns. Explanation is wholly objective and scientific in nature. The knowledge obtained by studying the past can be used to determine appropriate assumptions and relationships for the future, which lead to the forecast
itself. The application of objective knowledge to this task, applying
past trends and relationships to the future, lies in the realm of subjective judgment ("art"). The dependence of subjective methods on
objective analysis suggests another definition: forecasts are the judgment (a subjective act) of experts (those with objective expertise).

The procedures and conventions used to analyze past water use (explanation) and to apply resulting knowledge to the future (prediction)
are known as forecasting methods. Researchers are engaged in the development of methods and practitioners must choose among them. All are
faced with the problem of comparing and evaluating methods, of deciding
which are best in individual situations, or which are in need of improvement. These comparisons require some criterion which defines
"best" and "worst" methods.

If a single criterion is to chosen, the most obvious candidate is
doubtless accuracy. It can be assumed that most forecasters intend
their predictions to be accurate, and accuracy would seem the appropriate basis for comparing the work of various forecasters, or for comparing the methods which they use. Unfortunately, data on accuracy are not
usually available, and accuracy itself is an incomplete criterion (2).

In order to understand the limitations on accuracy as a criterion,
it should be recalled that water use forecasts, based on assumptions,
are themselves assumptions in the water supply planning process. As
such, they are useful only to the extent that they provide the needed
information and are believed: that must be complete, persuasive, author-
itative, credible, etc. These characteristics do not necessarily follow
from objective accuracy alone; they are better related to a perception
of accuracy. It can also be noted that an exclusive focus on accuracy,
coupled with the mistaken impression that being not wrong is the same as
being right, can lead to vague, hedged forecasts. Such results are
unlikely to be persuasive or useful to planners.

Accuracy is not only an incomplete criterion, there are circumstances where it is inappropriate as well. These include cases where
the forecast audience has incentives to alter the trends that are being
forecast. These are "self-fulfilling" or "self-defeating" forecasts,

and they cannot be reasonably expected to be accurate. In fact, if they are done well, inaccuracy is guaranteed. Another situation is more common: forecasts which are "right for the wrong reasons." Key assumptions underlying a particular forecast may turn out to be seriously in error, yet the forecast value itself is essentially correct. This can only occur when other assumptions are also in error so that the errors counterbalance one another. Such a result, while narrowly accurate, should not reflect favorably on the forecaster or the method.

How, then, are forecasts and forecast methods to be judged? Ascher speaks of two methods: the "insider's approach" and the "outsider's approach" (2). The "insider" systematically reviews assumptions and details of method, relying on correlates of accuracy--techniques or characteristics which have been associated with accurate forecasts in the past. The "insider" is concerned with sound practice, on the assumption that such practice is more likely to lead to accurate forecasts. The "outsider", on the other hand, is pragmatic. Important considerations to an "outsider" are the credibility and track record of the forecaster and, to a lesser extent, the forecast method used.

The "insider" focuses on details of analysis and mathematical procedures (the objective or explanatory aspects) while the "outsider" is more concerned with institutional and disciplinary biases as well as past performance (as they affect the subjective, predictive phase). Taken together, these perspectives provide the most comprehensive alternative to reliance on a desirable but unrealizable criterion--demonstrated accuracy.

Explanation--Early Experience

When the problem of determining the water supply needed to serve a given population first presented itself, it seemed natural to review water use experience elsewhere. By the early years of the twentieth century, water use data for a number of communities in the U.S. and Europe had appeared in the literature. In order to facilitate comparison, these data were commonly presented as per capita water use. Table 1 lists examples of data published at that time.

TABLE 1.--Early Observations of Per Capita Water Use

Year	Location	Gallons per capita per day	Year	Location	Gallons per capita per day
(1)	(2)	(3)	(4)	(5)	(6)
97	Rome	38	1913	U.S.:	
1550	Paris	0.25		Dallas	56
1885	Philadelphia	72		New York	129
1890	Paris	65		Chicago	275
1895	Philadelphia	162		Europe:	
	Baltimore	95		Vienna	14
1900	"National average"	90		London	40
	"Typical city"	100		Paris	98
	"Industrial city"	150			

An indication of the uncertain state of affairs for water use forecasting can be gained from the following discussion, taken from a report published in 1897 (11):

> It has been shown that the present water consumption approaches the amount of one hundred gallons per head of present population. This is believed to be adequate for future requirements. Whilst the tendency in the past has been to increasing consumption per head, it is not thought that this will continue. . . . Nevertheless, in estimating the volume . . . it has been deemed prudent to add thirty per cent. to the present consumption per head . . . we thus have one hundred and twenty-five gallons per head . . . it has nevertheless been deemed prudent by the Consulting Engineers from the information supplied to them to provide for 150 gallons per head.

As this extract implies, the water use forecast was performed by the simple expedient of choosing a per capita water use level for the future, then multiplying that per capita coefficient by the projected population. Given the uncertainty regarding then-current levels of per capita use, or expected trends, there was a tendency to adopt rules of thumb, such as the 150 gal/day figure finally decided upon. In fact, that figure continues to be mentioned in textbooks to this day, and is doubtless in wide use.

Whether this is an adequate approach to explaining and predicting water use is another matter. A survey of 768 cities conducted in 1970 by the American Water Works Association found per capita use rates ranging from 31 to 552 gal/day, with fully 77 percent of the observations almost uniformly distributed over the 100-300 gal/day range (1). Aside from the cross-sectional variation, individual cities may display increasing, constant, or decreasing per capita use rates over time; year-to-year differences may be large. It seems apparent that factors other than population have important impacts on water use.

Explanation--Recent Developments

An early critique of the per capita explanation of water use is contained in an extraordinary article published in 1926 by Leonard Metcalf (10). Using data from 30 cities, he examined possible reasons for the observed variation in per capita use coefficients, and reported that city size, degree of industrialization and prices faced by various sizes of users were significant determinants. Metcalf was the first to offer empirical evidence for the price elasticity of water. He also argued that water use should be recorded and analyzed on a sectorally disaggregate basis.

Metcalf, it seems, was far ahead of his time. No further substantial empirical studies of this subject were reported in literature for almost 30 years, until the late 1950's. Once the subject was introduced again, however, interest grew rapidly. The rate of appearance of new studies grew steadily through the 1960's and 1970's until, by the mid-1980's, there is a considerable literature. As a result of this research, the ability to explain, and thus to forecast, water use has been markedly improved. It is also worth noting that Metcalf's findings of

60 years ago have proved fundamentally sound.

Among the inescapable conclusions which can be drawn from the past 30 years of water use studies is that urban water use can only be satisfactorily explained if use sectors (e.g., residential, commercial, industrial, public) are analyzed separately. This disaggregate approach has characterized virtually every recent study, and the results make clear that quite different sets of explanatory variables apply to different sectors.

Most research has been directed to the residential sector, and most of that effort has been concerned with water use in detached single-family homes. Relatively less is known about other residential categories (e.g., semi-detached housing, apartments, house trailers, etc.), or about commercial, institutional and industrial users. Still, some studies are available for virtually every category of urban water use and, taken together, the results go far beyond per capita methods in explanatory power. Some of the factors which have been associated with water use in the various sectors are listed as Table 2.

TABLE 2.--Partial List of Explanatory Variables

Water Use Sector (1)	Explanatory Variables (2)	
Residential	No. household units Persons/household Household income Marginal price Housing value	Irrigable area Potential evapotranspiration Precipitation Total bill size
Commercial/Institutional	Employment Per capita income Marginal price	Building area Temperature/humidity Business volume
Industrial	Employment Marginal price Cost of alternative supply	Value of shipments Value added Degree of recycling

Public/Unaccounted	Population
	Acres of public
	  parks, etc.
	No. of hydrants
		Size of distribution
		  system
		Age of distribution
		  system

Population, it can be noted, appears only in the Public/Unaccounted sector. It is implicit, of course, in the residential sector which includes no. of housing units and the number of persons per unit. This reflects the finding that water use is much better correlated with the number of household units than with total population; residential per capita water use is a declining function of household size. This result would be unimportant if household sizes thought to be constant. The fact that average household size has fallen dramatically since the turn of the century, and continues to fall, lends importance to this insight into residential water use.

Weather variables are essential in explaining differences in water use from one city to another; they also permit a fuller understanding of seasonal and year-to-year variation at the same location. One of the more successful formulations is the "moisture deficit" variable popularized by Howe and Linaweaver, equal to potential summer evapotranspiration reduced by effective summer precipitation (usually 60 percent of actual summer precipitation) (9).

The usual economic variables of price and income have their usual role in explaining the use of water. Other things being equal, water use declines as marginal price increases, and increases with increases in income, as measured by household income or as proxied by housing value. The income effects of alternative rate structures can be captured by introducing a bill difference variable (calculated from total bill size, marginal price, and water use per billing period). Since the rate structure effect, though small, is correlated with price, most recent demand studies include a bill difference variable in order to avoid biases in the price coefficient.

The existence of measurable price elasticity for water has long been a subject of needless controversy. Because the response to a change in price is relatively small in most instances, develops slowly over time, and occurs simultaneously with changes in other explanatory variables (e.g., weather), casual observation of water use data almost always fails to reveal a consistent response to price. Careful econometric analysis is required to control for the effect of time and other variables, isolating and measuring the price response. A recent review found 53 significant studies of the relationship between water use and price, and concluded that differences in reported price elasticities were due to differences in the type of water use analyzed or to estimation bias.

Forecast Methods

Table 3 lists, in general terms, some of the approaches that have been taken to water use forecasting. Each approach implies a particular kind of explanation of past water use; the deficiencies of the various approaches usually derive directly from the deficiencies of the implied explanatory technique.

Consensual methods avoid explicit explanation and focus on pure prediction. Objective content, therefore, is minimal and little can be said of the reliability of such methods. Methods in the next category--time extrapolation--rest on the notion that changes in water use can be explained by the passage of time. This is a useful method for some short-term forecasting applications but unlikely to give accurate predictions beyond a few years.

Single coefficient methods, which include the traditional per capita approach, provide some objective content, but limit explanation to that which can be accomplished by a single variable. Accuracy is improved if water use is disaggregated and an appropriate unit use coefficient asso-

TABLE 3.--Water Use Forecasting Approaches

CONSENSUAL METHODS

    Simple judgment
    Collective judgment
    Structured judgment (e.g., delphi methods)

TIME EXTRAPOLATION

    Simple extrapolation
    Time series analysis
    Other time extrapolation

SINGLE COEFFICIENT METHODS

    Per capita requirements
    Per connection requirements
    Unit use coefficient approaches

MULTIPLE COEFFICIENT METHODS

    Requirements models
    Econometric demand models

ciated with each sector, but a number of potentially useful variables must be excluded. Multiple coefficient methods permit inclusion of all potentially important variables, and econometric methods offer rigorous tests for causality, avoidance of bias, and completeness of the specification.

    In addition to the methods named on Table 3, many kinds of combinations and variants are possible. Among these are the application of probabilistic techniques, such as the use of contingency trees (with any type of basic forecast) and stochastic methods (e.g., in conjunction with time series analysis).

Conclusions

    Water use forecasts, like most other forecasts, are conditional predictions which derive from a method having both objective and subjective components. The objective component consists of explaining past levels and patterns of water use, while the subjective component is the application of the resultant knowledge to the future. Forecasts are, therefore, based on both judgment and expertise.

    While nearly all forecasts are intended to be accurate, demonstrated accuracy is neither available nor adequate as a criterion for judging forecasts or forecast methods. Instead, a combination of objective examination (focusing on methods and characteristics associated in the past with accurate forecasts) and subjective appraisal (assessing the reputation and biases of the forecaster and the method chosen) can be used.

Most water use forecasts use a method first applied approximately 100 years ago: an assumed per capita use coefficient is multiplied by projected population. Experience shows, however, that per capita water use varies widely from place to place, and from time to time at the same place. If the per capita coefficient is an inadequate method of explaining past water use, then, it must be an inadequate technique for forecasting future use.

More recent research has demonstrated that water use can only be effectively explained on a sectorally disaggregate basis, and that quite different sets of explanatory variables are required for each sector. Population appears only in implicit form as number of households and population per household assume independent roles in explaining residential water use. Price and income, as well as climate and weather, also are important variables in explaining both residential and non-residential water use.

A wide variety of forecasting techniques have been devised and applied, ranging from simple consensual methods to disaggregate econometric demand models. These techniques are more than adequate to incorporate all of the knowledge of water use gained in the past 100 years, providing the most accurate possible explanation of the levels and patterns of use. When models of this kind are used to forecast, the resulting predictions are likely to demonstrate all of the characteristics sought in a forecast, including accuracy.

Appendix.--References

1. American Water Works Association, "Operating Data for Water Utilities 1970 & 1965," AWWA Statistical Report, (undated).

2. Ascher, W., Forecasting: An Appraisal for Policy-Makers and Planners, The Johns Hopkins Press, Baltimore, MD, 1978.

3. Babbitt, H.E., and Doland, J.J., Water Supply Engineering, McGraw-Hill, New York, 1929, p. 1.

4. Baker, M.N., The Quest for Pure Water, American Water Works Association, New York, 1948, p. 125.

5. Boland, J.J., "Water/Wastewater Pricing and Financial Practices in the United States," Tech. Report 1; MMI 19-83, MetaMetrics Inc., Washington, DC, Aug. 1983, p. 1.5.

6. Boland, J.J., et al., "Influence of Price and Rate Structures on Municipal and Industrial Water Use," Contract Report 84-C-2, Institute for Water Resources, U.S. Army Corps of Engineers, Fort Belvoir, VA, June 1984.

7. Boland, J.J., Baumann, D.D., and Dziegielewski, B., "An Assessment
    of Municipal and Industrial Water Use Forecasting Approaches," Con
    tract Report 81-CO5, Institute for Water Resources, U.S. Army Corps
    of Engineers, Fort Belvoir, VA, May 1981, pp. IV-4, IV-5, IV-6.

8. Frontinus, S.J., The Two Books on the Water Supply of the City of
    Rome, translated by Herschel, C., Dana Estes & Co., Boston, 1899.

9. Howe, C.W., and Linaweaver, F.P., "The Impact of Price on Residen-
    tial Water Demand and its Relation to System Design and Price Struc-
    ture," Water Resources Research, Vol. 3, No. 1, 1967, pp. 13-32.

10. Metcalf, L., "Effect of Water Rates and Growth in Population upon
    Per Capita Consumption," Journal American Water Works Association,
    Vol. 15, No. 1, Jan., 1926, pp. 1-20.

11. "Report of the Sewerage Commission of the City of Baltimore," to the
    Mayor and City Council of Baltimore, MD, 1897.

FORECASTING DEMAND FOR URBAN WATER

Duane D. Baumann*
James E. Crews** - Member ASCE

ABSTRACT

The potential savings from precision to estimating future urban water use are obvious. And, because of the need to predict the effectiveness of potential water conservation measures, new and more responsive approaches of disaggregated demand forecasts are mandatory.

The purpose of this study is to assess current water use forecasting practice in the U.S. Army Corps of Engineers and to recommend those additional approaches which best satisfy current requirements. To accomplish these objectives, this report presents the findings of a three-prong investigation: 1) identification of current needs for improved forecasting approaches in light of the current requirements; 2) review and assessment of current forecasting approaches; and 3) recommendation of the most appropriate forecasting approaches which meet the identified needs and satisfy current requirements. Data were obtained from personal interviews with field planners in 6 districts and 3 divisions, from a questionnaire to 35 districts and 11 divisions, and from the analysis of 27 Corps studies that had forecasted demand.

Introduction

Long range forecasts of future water use are indispensable to the efficient management of municipal water supply systems. Forecasts, and the planning activities which use them, determine the investments which water utilities make, or forego. Miscalculations in preparing or applying forecasts are always serious. They may result in the over-commitment of large amounts of money, diverting it from other critical needs, or, on the other hand, the failure of a water supply system to meet its demand. Although forecasting is admittedly a risky business, it is more important today that forecasts be made with greater accuracy, and that they be made with the best information and techniques available to reduce the cost of error.

This report examines current needs for improved forecasting approaches in light of current planning requirements; reviews and assesses current forecasting approaches; and recommends the most appropriate forecasting approaches to meet identified needs. It also includes a discussion of a highly disaggregated computer forecasting

*Professor, Department of Geography, Southern Illinois University, Carbondale, IL 62901.
**U.S. Army Corps of Engineers, Institute for Water Resources, Casey Building, Ft. Belvoir, Virginia 22060.

model known as the IWR-MAIN System.

Data for this study were obtained from personal interviews, from questionnaires to federal water planners, and from the analysis of 57 water supply studies that had forecasted water demand (1).

Assessment of Existing Approaches

Many different approaches have been used or proposed for water use forecasting (3). Furthermore, specific forecasts may incorporate the use of several distinct approaches. In order to provide an evaluation of forecasting approaches, therefore, a limited number of prototypical methods were chosen for discussion and evaluation. Each prototype was evaluated according to the following criteria: 1) SCOPE – any limitations imposed by the approach: 2) DISAGGREGATION – suitability of the approach for use in preparing sectorally and geographically disaggregated forecasts; 3) MULTI-VARIATE MODELS – choice of explanatory variables used; 4) ALTERNATIVE FUTURES – ease of incorporating alternative assumptions regarding future conditions; 5) CONTINUITY ASSUMPTIONS – nature of the assumed underlying process as to its stability; and 6) COMPATIBILITY – approaches must be compatible with the planning process, field conditions, skill requirements, etc.

The prototypical approaches fall into six broad categories, with each category containing a range of specific techniques having similar characteristics. The categories are: 1) per capita methods; 2) per connection methods; 3) unit use coefficients methods; 4) multivariate requirements models; 5) multivariate demand models; and 6) probabilistic methods. The first three categories are all single coefficient methods: each employs a single explanatory variable. The fourth, and fifth categories are multiple coefficient methods, using more than one explanatory variable. The sixth category use probabilities in conjunction with one of the above methods (2).

Forecasting Methods

Per capita coefficient – is the most widely used water used water use forecasting method: future water use is estimated by multiplying expected future population by an extrapolated water use coefficient. The method is simple, requires little data, and the data are easily obtained. Yet, in spite of its popularity, this approach has serious shortcomings in the fact that results are insensitive to most trends and changes known to affect urban water use, and provides minimal information to those wishing to plan future facilities or management strategies.

Per connection coefficient – expresses future water use as a product of the expected future number of customers connections and a per connection water use coefficient. The value of the coefficient is usually extrapolated from past experience. The major advantage of this method over the per capita approach is that historical data on number of connections to a water system is likely to be more readily available and more accurate than data on past population served. Also, number of connections is well correlated with aggregate water use.

Unit use coefficient - uses a single explanatory variable other
than population or number of customer connections. Unit use coefficients differ from the per capita and per connection techniques,
however, in that they are more often used in the context of sectorally disaggregated forecasts.

Multivariate requirements models - incorporate more than one
explanatory variable and fall into one of two categories: those
employing requirements models and those using econometric demand
models. Requirements models include variables observed to be significantly correlated with water use, not necessarily those suggested
by a priori economic reasoning. The number of explanatory variables
may range from two to several dozen, and the dependent variable may
be aggregate (total) or sectoral water use. Data requirements can be
considerable, depending upon the number of explanatory variable used,
and data are sometimes comparatively difficult to collect. Data
collection efforts must be balanced against potential improvements in
the accuracy and usefulness of the forecast.

Multivariate demand models - are based on economic reasoning, and
include only variables which are expected to be causally related to and
found to be significantly correlated with water use. Demand models
consider price and income, as well as other variables. The number and
nature of the explanatory variables actually used may vary greatly from
one application to another, according to data availability, required
accuracy, local conditions, etc.

Probabilistic methods - provide a means for considering uncertainty
in a water use forecast. Ordinarily, this approach requires that a base
forecast be prepared, using one of the methods mentioned above. Possible sources of uncertainty regarding future water use levels are
identified, and subjective probabilities are estimated for each possible outcome. The base forecast is modified to reflect the effects of
all possible combinations of the uncertain factors, one combination at
a time, and the joint probability of each of the combinations is
associated with the forecast water use expected to result from the
combination.

Each of these approaches are used to varying degrees. Some
approaches enjoyed wide use and acceptance, others are applied in
isolated cases, or have been adopted in the recent past.

The techniques were tabulated against the earlier described needs
to determine which approaches best satisfied specific needs. Particular
attention was given to approaches that have been applied under actual
planning conditions. These evaluations applied to the capabilities of
the forecasting approaches, and not the characteristics of the forecast
which they might produce. The evaluations were necessarily of a summary
nature, touching on major issues and considerations.

Table 1 presents a comparison of the needs and capabilities of the
various approaches. Although actual forecasting techniques may differ
from those shown in one or more details, the prototypical approaches
represent realistic possibilities along the continuum of all possible
forecasting approaches.

TABLE 1

Comparison of Existing Approaches to Planning Needs

Planning Need	Simple Time Extrapolation	Single Coefficient Methods		Unit Use Coefficient	Multiple Coefficient Methods		
		Per-Capita	Per-Customer		Requirements	Demand	Con-tingency
Permits prediction of various measures of water use	+	+	+	+	+	+	+
Suitable for medium range forecasts	+	+	+	+	+	+	+
Suitable for long range forecasts	-	+	+	+	+	+	+
Facilitates sectoral disaggregation	-	-	+	+	+	+	n.a.
Facilitates geographic disaggregation	-	+	+	+	+	+	n.a.
Includes adequate explanatory variables	-	-	-	-	0	0	+
Requires reasonably available data	+	+	+	+	0	0	0
Provides detailed planing information	-	-	-	-	0	+	+
Demonstrated under existing conditions	+	+	+	+	+	+	n.f.

Legend: + = Yes - = No 0 = Unknown n.a. = not applicable n.f. = not found in survey

Table 2 summaries some general observations about the application characteristics of the seven forecasting approaches studied. The need to evaluate possible water conservation measures, is best obtained by appropriate application of unit use coefficient methods, multiple coefficient methods, and the probabilistic method. On the other hand, the three simplest forecasting approaches, plus the unit use coefficient method are likely to remain a part of various preliminary planning efforts. The small quantities of data required, and the ease of obtaining such data, argue for their continued use in appropriate applications.

Need For Improved Approaches

Water use forecasts are employed in a wide variety of planning studies conducted. Forecasts are frequently used by the Federal Government in planning the water supply purpose of a multiple purpose water resource project. Federal engineers also use water use forecasts to reallocate a major impoundment. Most forecasts are used by water utilities as the basis of design of water supply facilities and are of the longer-range type of projections.

The most commonly employed forecasting technique today relies on an aggregate description of water use, which is a forecast based on a single use coefficient (usually water use per capita) whose value may or may not be permitted to change during the forecast period.

Aggregate forecasts, however, are insensitive to changing sectoral patterns in developing communities, including differential growth rates for multi-unit and single-unit housing. Specific water conservation measures, which often selectively alter water use by user sector, is difficult to consider with the absence of sectoral disaggregation.

Since most variables known to affect water use are omitted (such as price, income, family size, irrigable area, weather, levels of commercial and institutional activity, etc.), aggregate forecast are insensitive to any changes from past relationships existing among these variables. In particular, the sensitivity of future water use to alternate planning assumptions cannot be determined.

It should be noted, however, that attempts to develop disaggregated forecast have been hampered by the general inability of water utilities to produce the analyses of billing records needed to support the development of the necessary forecasting models. Further, the inclusion of additional explanatory variables creates the requirement to forecast future values for those variables, multiplying data requirements in areas where data may not be readily available.

Conclusions

This survey disclosed a wide range of forecasting methods actually in use, including all approaches defined above except the probabilistic method. Some approaches now in use are not widespread, but they have been applied.

Generally forecasting approaches now in use do not facilitate

TABLE 2
Application of Forecasting Approaches

Application Characteristic	Simple Time Extrapolation	Single Coefficient Methods			Multiple Coefficient Methods		
		Per Capita	Per Customer	Unit Use Co-efficient	Requirements	Demand	Con-tingency
Facilitates forecasts consistent with Principles and Guidelines	no	no	no	when used in disaggregate forecasts	when used in disaggregate forecasts	when used in disaggregate forecasts	yes
Facilitates evaluation of water conservation measures	no	no	no	"	"	"	yes
Suitable for reconnaisances type studies	yes	yes	yes	yes	no, too complex	no, too complex	no, too complex
Suitable for detailed planning	no	no	no	when used in disaggregate forecasts	when used in disaggregate forecasts	when used in disaggregate forecasts	yes
Data Requirements:							
quantity of data needed	very little	very little	very little	moderate	moderate to large	moderate to large	depends on application
difficulty of obtaining needed data	low	low	low	low to moderate	moderate to high	moderate to high	depends on application
Adequacy of training and experience of field planners	adequate	adequate	adequate	adequate	further training required	further training required	further training required

disaggregation by user sector, or by season and are not usually multivariate, as they depend primarily on population to explain future water use. Alternative futures is not assisted by current methods and most underlying assumptions are implicit and may not be known to the planner or the intended audience. Current methods rely heavily on the assumption of continuity of past trends, and provide relatively little information to the planning process.

In addition, the two areas were identified where additional experience would be helpful. The first is the forecasting approach which introduces a probabilistic dimension to water use forecasts and greatly increases the amount of information which the forecast can convey to the planning process. The second area for further development is the use of flexible, computerized forecasting systems which allow an array of forecasting methods, combined with necessary data management procedures.

Computerized Forecasting System

An existing computerized forecasting system developed by Hittman Associates, Inc. (4), known as the MAIN II System, has been modified by the U.S. Army Corps of Engineers Institute for Water Resources for use by its field planners and anyone else who wishes to use the model (5).

The IWR-MAIN System considers four major sectors of water use: 1) residential; 2) commercial/institutional; 3) industrial; and 4) public/unaccounted users. Each sector is further disaggregated as needed for forecasting purposes. As many as 284 individual water use categories can be used. Water use models included in the IWR-MAIN System include econometric demand models (residential categories), unit use coefficient models (commercial/institutional and industrial categories) and per capita models (some public categories). The structure of the IWR-MAIN System is shown in Table 3.

For each future time period, water use is calculated as a function of a set of projected parameters or explanatory variables. Four alternative methods are available for predicting future levels of these parameters: 1) projection by internal growth models; 2) projection by extrapolation of local historical data; 3) use of projections made external to the model and provided as input by the user; and 4) any combination of the above.

The IWR-MAIN System is capable of preparing highly disaggregated forecasts of future water use, based on a moderate quantity of good quality data. This is especially true of base year data, where the greatest detail is required. Inaccuracies in base year data may alter subsequent forecasts in complex and subtle ways, not readily apparent to the analyst.

This forecasting program has received wide application in utility contexts and was tested on independent sets of data. Retrodictions or "backcasts" of water demand by customer class were generated for communities based on known historical values of explanatory variables. The results are presented in Table 4.

TABLE 3
Internal Structure of the IWR-MAIN Model

Sector	Category

Residential	Metered and Sewered
	    Domestic Use (winter and summer)
	Mastered Meter Apartments
	    Domestic Use
	Flat Rate and Sewered
	    Domestic Use
	    Sprinkling Use[a]
	Flat Rate with Septic Tanks
	    Domestic Use
	    Sprinkling Use[a]

Commercial/
Institutional
	Subdivided by type of establishment:
	    up to 50 categories available
	    -28 categories provided

Industrial	Subdivided by 3- and 4-digit SIU
	    Code:
	    -200 categories provided

Public/
Unaccounted
	Subdivided by type of water use:
	    up to 30 categories available
	    -2 categories provided

[a]Separate sprinkling water use models provided for east and west U.S.

More recently, the model was tested against two cities with the results generally the same as before even though water use characteristics and trends have changed over the last twenty years. These results are presented in Table 5.

The IWR-MAIN System is currently undergoing some dramatic changes and no longer resembles its earlier brother. All of the current water use models have been revised to more accurately reflect today's water use patterns. Next, the growth (or projection) models are revised. Plans are also underway to incorporate water conservation evaluations into the model.

The program is available for mainframes as well as IBM PC's. The micro-computer version is a greatly enhanced version and easier to use than the mainframe version.

Summary

Traditional forecasting procedures, for the most part, were developed during a period when water supply planner's responsibility did not extent beyond the provision of water supply storage. However, changes in the world economic environmental and social policy, as well

TABLE 4
Application Experience with the IWR-MAIN System

	Actual Demand (MGD)	IWR-MAIN Estimate (MGD)
Baltimore, Maryland (1963 data)		
Residential	97.3	95.2
Public-Commercial	19.6	19.2
Industrial	42.0	45.1
Total	158.9	159.5
Park Forest, Illinois (1959 data)		
Residential	1.68	1.49
Commercial	0.15	0.15
Park Forest, Illinois (1961 data)		
Residential	1.70	1.58
Par, Forest, Illinois (1962 data)		
Commercial	0.18	0.15
Park Forest, Illinois (1963 data)		
Residential	1.72	1.58
Commercial	0.19	0.17
Park Forest, Illinois (1965 data)		
Residential	1.91	1.75
Commercial	0.21	0.19
Park Forest, Illinois (1967 data)		
Residential	1.91	1.84
Commercial	0.21	0.20
Baton Rouge, Louisiana (1965 data)		
Residential	n/a	14.0
Commercial	n/a	5.20
Public & Unaccounted	n/a	4.36
Total	23.8	23.6
Kings Heights District		
Anne Arundel County, Maryland (1968 data)		
Residential & Commercial	0.31	0.32

n/a - not available

TABLE 5
Recent Application Experience with the IWR-MAIN System

	Actual Demand (MGD)	IWR-MAIN Estimate (MGD)
Chester, Pennsylvania (1980		
Residential	5.0	7.52
Commercial/Industrial	1.45	3.20
Industry	12.02	11.13
Public/Unaccounted	5.24	2.05
Total	23.71	23.85
Springfield, Illinois (1980)		
Total	19.7	19.6

as needs to make utility systems more reliable, stimulated increased concerns to improve water supply planning techniques. Planners are required now to apply new forecasting techniques, and to collect types of data that have not been required in the past in order to reduce the cost of forecast error. Forecasting methods are destined to become more complex and sophisticated at the same time accuracy becomes more critical. Tools, such as the IWR-MAIN System, are now becoming available to aid the analyst in providing a more accurate and reliable forecast.

References

1. Boland, John J., Baumann, Duane D., and Dziegielewski, Benedykt. An Assessment of Municipal and Industrial Water Use Forecasting Approaches, Institute for Water Resources, U.S. Army Corps of Engineers, Ft. Belvoir, Virginia, 1981.

2. Boland, John J., et al. Forecasting Municipal and Industrial Water Use: A Handbook of Methods, Institute for Water Resources, U.S. Army Corps of Engineers, Ft. Belvoir, Virginia, 1983.

3. Dziegielewski, Benedykt, Boland, John J., and Baumann, Duane D. An Annotated Bibliography on Techniques of Forecasting Demand for Water, Institute for Water Resources, U.S. Army Corps of Engineers, Ft. Belvoir, Virginia, 1981.

4. Hittman Associates, Inc. Forecasting Municipal Water Requirements. Vol. I, the MAIN II System. Report No. HIT-413. Columbia, Maryland, 1969.

5. U.S. Army Corps of Engineers. Forecasting Municipal and Industrial Water Use: IWR-MAIN System User's Guide for Interactive Processing and User's Manual, Institute for Water Resources, U.S. Army Corps of Engineers, Ft. Belvoir, Virginia, 1983

Practical Water Demand Forecasting

G.K. Young[1], M. ASCE, R.T. Kilgore[2], M. ASCE and K.G. Saunders[3]

Abstract

The authors describe their experience in designing, building, and applying a water demand forecasting model for the Denver metropolitan area. In the presence of incomplete and sometimes inconsistent data, a method is presented through which adversarial interests may participate in the building and ultimate acceptance of the model and its corresponding forecasts. The model itself is a two-tiered approach to forecasting in which use factors are applied to demographic variables (for example, households and population) for a first approximation of forecast demand. Then, through regression analysis of various socio-economic variables (for example, lot size and price), the preliminary estimates are fine-tuned.

Introduction And Objective

Water demand forecasting in a real world environment having conflicting interests and limited data imposes conditions on the forecaster not present in academic case studies. Limited - or apparently conflicting - data require that the forecaster use "best professional judgment" to bridge data gaps and to weight the contribution of various data sources. With data inadequacies, informed parties affected by the forecasting outcome are able to focus criticism on elements of a forecast that are adverse to their interest.

This was the environment in which the authors built and used a water demand forecasting model for the Denver metropolitan area. In addition to the technical requirements of deriving reliable demand forecasts, two major interests were in conflict. The water providers desired the forecasts to be as high as possible so that planned water supply projects could be justified and built insuring both a comfortable margin of safety and perfection of existing conditional water rights. An environmental coalition desired the lowest possible forecasts to prevent development in wilderness areas and to preserve available water for potential use without an interbasin transfer to the Denver area.

[1] President, GKY & Associates, Inc., 5411-E Backlick Rd., Springfield, VA 22151
[2] Staff Engineer, GKY & Associates, Inc.
[3] Research Associate, GKY & Associates, Inc.

Given this environment, the technical objective was to develop
an accurate, disaggregated method of forecasting water demand, unbiased by opposing interests. The need for accuracy is self-evident.
Disaggregation by use sector and water provider was necessary for two
separate reasons. First, disaggregation by water provider was required
to allow each provider a basis for planning future needs. This presented the problems of weighting data. As shown in Fig. 1, there
are over 70 water providers serving demands ranging from less than
1% to 58.1% of the total Denver area water demand. The second element of disaggregation was by water use sector: residential, (multi
and single family), commercial and industrial, and public. These
distinctions were necessary to perform a subsequent analysis of a
range of conservation measures applicable to particular sectors.
With this objective in mind, a two-tiered model was developed.

Model Development

The first tier was represented by use factors for different
sectors of water consumers. These use factors incorporated average
or typical water demand and were used to make respectable first
approximations of demand forecasts. Total water demand for a water
provider was, therefore, primarily driven by demographics: the number
of households, the number of employees, and the total population.

The second tier of logic recognized differences in socioeconomic
characteristics (for example, lot size and family income) of water
districts which affect water demand. This observation allowed
fine-tuning of the first approximation estimates. This tier was
added to the model by regression analysis of household level data.
The model was developed using several data sources at the water
provider level and the household level covering the period 1974
through 1982 (1). Discussion of the two tiers follows.

Use Factors

Use factors for each of the five water consuming sectors-single
family metered (SFM), single family flat (SFF), multi-family (MF),
commercial and industrial (CI), and public use (P) - were developed
representing typical average use for the particular sector in the
absense of any conservation programs.

SFM households typically demand water at a rate of 478 gal/hh/day
(1,812 L/day) and account for approximately 42% of the total demand
in the Denver area. Forty-six percent of this demand is estimated
to be used indoors and 54% outdoors, primarily during the summer
months. Similiarly, SFF households demand water at a higher rate
of 630 gal/hh/day (2,388 L/hh/day) and account for 23% of the total
demand. However, only 37% is indoor use. The final residential use
sector, MF households, demands water at a rate of 217 gal/hh/day
(822 L/hh/day) and represents 16% of total demand. Eighty-three percent of this is used indoors.

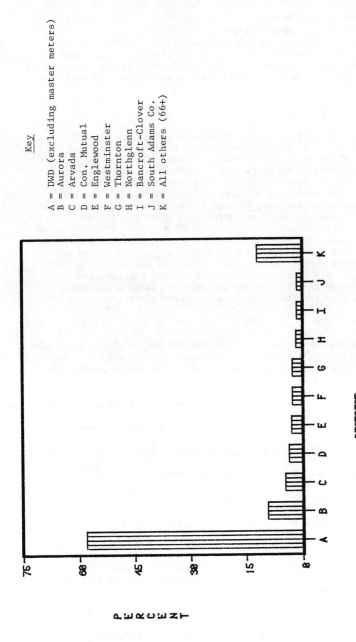

Key

A = DWD (excluding master meters)
B = Aurora
C = Arvada
D = Con. Mutual
E = Englewood
F = Westminster
G = Thornton
H = Northglenn
I = Bancroft-Clover
J = South Adams Co.
K = All others (66+)

Figure 1. Distribution of Water Demand Among Providers (1974-1982)

The two nonresidential sectors account for smaller portions of the total demand. Commercial and industrial users require 12% of the demand at a rate of 45 gal/employee/day (171 L/employee/day). Similarly, public use accounts for 7% at a rate of 14 gal/person/day (53 L/person/day. Neither of these factors were divided into indoor and outdoor use. (The distribution of demand by use sector is shown in Fig. 2.)

Socioeconomic Characteristics

The second portion of the model development was to incorporate individual district characteristics (lot size, family income, marginal price, household size) which would contribute to variations in water demand from provider to provider. However, this analysis was only performed for the largest sector: SFM households. It is reasonable to suspect that analogous adjustments might be made to the other four use factors: SFF, MF, CI, and P. However, it is less certain that improvements in model sophistication would justify additional analysis. Such analysis on the SFM use factor was justified because this sector of consumers demanded more water (42%) than any other. Furthermore, the relative absence of data in the literature for the other consumer sectors support the claim that these are difficult to analyze. This, combined with their smaller contributions to current area demand, led to the decision not to go beyond simple demographics in the model for these consumer sectors.

Model Formulation

Combining the two analyses yielded the following model formulation for predicting the demand of an individual water provider by estimating use by each sector. Total water demand is derived by summing the individual provider's demands.

The variables used in the formulation are defined as the following:

1. SFM is the number of single family households (metered).

2. SFF is the number of single family households (flat-rate).

3. MF is the number of multi-family households.

4. E is the number of employees.

5. P is the population.

6. f is the SFM use factor (gallons per household per day).

7. f_o is the base SFM use factor (gallons per household per day - 550 for Denver City and County; 469 for suburban providers).

8. A is the mean lot size ($\overline{A}$ = 0.241 acres).

9. dP is the mean marginal price ($\overline{dP}$ = $1.17/1,000 gal).

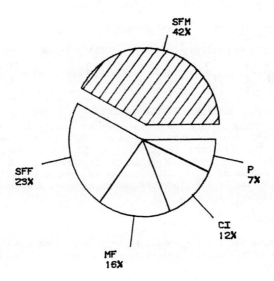

Figure 2. Distribution of Demand By Use Sector

10. I is the median household income ($\overline{I}$ = $20.6 thousand).

11. HH is the mean household size ($\overline{HH}$ = 2.71 people).

12. a_i is the coefficient adjustment for using different data sources (dimensionless).

13. D is the district demand (gallons per day).

The district demand is expressed as:

$$D = f(SFM) + 630(SFF) + 217(MF) + 45(E) + 14(P) \tag{1}$$

$$\text{where } f = f_o + \left[350(a_1)\right] (A - \overline{A}) - \left[118.7(a_2)\right] (dP - \overline{dP}) + \left[3.59(a_3)\right] (I - \overline{I}) + \left[31.2(a_4)\right] (HH - \overline{HH}) \tag{2}$$

The model is applied by first calculating the SFM use factor (f) using Eq. 2. This adjusts the factors for the particular socioeconomic characteristics of a district. This factor, along with those for the other consumer sectors, are applied to the demographic projections of households, employment, and population to arrive at a forecast provider demand using Eq. 1. The demands are summed for all providers arriving at the projected water demand at a given time for the entire Denver area.

Model Reliability

The motivation for the model was to produce a reliable water demand forecasting model. The reliability of the model is shown by the following:

1. The model was developed from a diverse data base utilizing sound professional judgment.

2. The coefficient of determination (R^2) is 0.998, indicating that it explains 99.8% of the variation in water demand from provider to provider.

3. The model predicts the total area demand within 1.4% of the actual demand over the 1974 through 1982 period.

4. The model predicts demand for Denver City and County, which represents over 45% of the total demand, within 3.8% of the actual demand. The average departure from the actual provider demand for all districts is 21.9%.

Observations

In addition to the technical merits of a forecasting model, a real world environment demands more of the modeler and the model before implementation and acceptance can occur. The model described in this paper was accepted immediately by all parties while it remained abstract. The key to its ultimate acceptance was the iterative process of product, review, and revision. At several

stages during the development of the forecasting model, progress was
documented and distributed to all interested parties for review and
comment. This accomplished three objectives.

1. Thorough assessment of the "weak" elements of the model.

2. Provision of additional data from commentors.

3. Gradual acceptance of the model as significant and valid
    contributions from interested parties were incorporated into
    the model.

Because of this process and the modeler's experience, the model
was successful in achieving its technical objectives as indicated by
its reliability. In its completed state, its format is simple which
tends to belie the analysis effort required to merge and extrapolate
diverse and sometimes contrasting data bases. The model was also
successful in finding acceptance from diverse interests in the
Denver area. By allowing for outside participation at frequent
intervals, the model and its corresponding forecasts now form the
basis for water supply planning in the Denver metropolitan area.

Appendix - References

1. "Systemwide/Site-Specific Environmental Impact Statement -
    Metropolitan Denver Water Supply," Appendix 2, U.S. Army Corps
    of Engineers, Omaha District, Dec., 1984, 290 pp.

EPA Supported Wasteload Allocation Models

Thomas O. Barnwell, Jr.[1], Member, ASCE
D. King Boynton[2]

ABSTRACT

Modeling is increasingly becoming a part of the Wasteload Allocation Process. The U S EPA provides guidance, technical training and
computer software in support of this program. This paper reviews the
support available to modelers through the Wasteload Allocation Section
of EPA's Office of Water Regulation and Standards and through the
Center for Water Quality Modeling of EPA's Office of Research and
Development. The paper also looks to the future of water quality
modeling and the prospect for principles from Artificial Intelligence
increasing the accessibility of these tools to practicioners.

INTRODUCTION

As part of the national effort to implement the Clean Water Act,
water quality planners and managers in the United States have increasingly used mathematical models to analyze water quality problems.
These models are used in conducting evaluations of waste loads from
point and nonpoint sources and in pollutant exposure assessments. To
encourage the wider application of these techniques, EPA supports two
activities that provide technical assistance and methodologies in support of wasteload allocation.

OFFICE OF WATER REGULATION AND STANDARDS

The Wasteload Allocation Section of the Monitoring and Data
Support Division in EPA's Office of Water Regulation and Standards
provides national policy and guidance for the program and provides
technical training and assistance in support of Wasteload Allocation.
These guidance documents, part of the **Technical Guidance Manual for
Performing Wasteload Allocations**, are summarized in Table 1 and discussed below. The documents are available by writing:

> Wasteload Allocation Section (WH-553)
> Monitoring and Data Support Division
> U S EPA
> Washington, DC   20640.

A monthly newsletter is circulated that gives the status of the guidance documents and discusses other wasteload allocation related subjects.

---

1. Environmental Research Laboratory, U S EPA, Athens, GA 30613
2. Monitoring and Data Support Division, U S EPA, Washington, DC 20460

Table 1. Summary of Wasteload Allocation Guidance Status (March 1985)

BOOK	CHAPTERS	STATUS
I. The TMDL Process		In Preparation
II. Streams and Rivers	BOD/DO Impacts	Available
	Nutrients/Eutrophication	Available
	Toxic Substances	Available
III. Estuaries	BOD/DO Impacts	In Review
	Nutrients/Eutrophication	In Review
	Toxic Substances	In Review
IV. Lakes and Impoundments	BOD/DO Impacts	In Planning
	Nutrients/Eutrophication	Available
	Toxic Substances	In Preparation
V. Design Conditions	Stream Flow	In Review
	Temperature	In Review
	pH	In Review
	Effluent Flow	In Preparation
	Rate Constants	In Planning
VI. Permit Averaging		Available
VII. Screening Manual	Toxic Organics/ Conventional Pollutants	Available
	Toxic Metals	In Review
VIII. Innovative Wasteload Allocations		In Review
IX. Toxics Control		In Review
X. Program Guidance		In Review

Book I. The TMDL Process, currently in planning, will provide a general description of the TMDL (Total Maximum Daily Load) process for those waters where technology based effluent limitations are insufficient to protect and maintain the designated water uses. This document will describe the steps of the process and show how they interrelate.

Book II. Wasteload Allocations for Streams and Rivers consists of three chapters. Chapter 1 provides methods for establishing BOD and ammonia wasteload allocations, chapter 2 provides methods for establishing nutrient wasteload allocations, and chapter 3 provides methods for toxic substances. These three chapters are currently available.

Book III. Wasteload Allocations for Estuaries also consists of three chapters that parallel the subject matter for streams and rivers. These three chapters are currently under review.

Book IV. Wasteload Allocations for Lakes and Impoundments also parallels the streams and rivers' subject matter. Chapter 2, nutrient wasteload allocations, is currently available, and chapter 3, toxic substances, is in preparation.

Book V. Design Conditions develops rational methods for selecting design conditions for each of the major environmental and effluent variables involved in steady state modeling. These variables include stream flow, temperature, pH, effluent flow, concentration/loading, and rate constants. Chapter 1 (stream flow) is in the final revision stage and will provide a method for establishing a stream design flow for water quality modeling based upon the acute and chronic toxicity of the pollutant and the low flow variability of the receiving stream. Chapters 2 (temperature) and 3 (pH) are also under review and will provide methods for establishing design conditions that represent the stream's critical event. Site-specific design conditions are developed through a simulation modeling approach. Chapter 4 (effluent flow, concentration and loading) is in the early stages of preparation and will include techniques to develop normalized curves for these variables on a monthly and seasonal basis. The normalization will be done with respect to the POTW (Publicly Owned Treatment Works) design flow, concentration and loading. Chapter 5 is in planning and will include statistical techniques for making the best water quality-based choice of various rate constants.

Book VI. Permit Averaging Periods, currently available, provides a rational basis for selecting the most appropriate NPDES permit averaging period (1-, 7-, or 30-day) for any industrial or POTW effluent. The technique considers the site-specific variability of receiving stream and the effluent.

Book VII. Screening Manual (14) , also available, provides desktop analysis techniques for use with hand-held calculators for assessing the loading and fate of both conventional (temperature, BOD/DO, nutrients and sediment) and toxic pollutants (from the 129 priority pollutants list) in streams, impoundments and estuaries. An addendum describing procedures for metals is in the final stages of review.

Book VII. Innovative Permits, now in review, provides guidance for the issuance of innovative permits based on sound wasteload allocations. It presents the principles behind standard and innovative permits and emphasizes seasonal permit limits for BOD and nitrogen.

Book IX. Technical Support Document for Water Quality-Based Toxics Control, now under review, provides procedural recommendations for identifying, analyzing, and controlling adverse water quality impacts caused by discharge of toxic pollutants. This document supports implementation of the U S EPA's national policy for the development of water quality-based permit limitations for toxic pollutants (16).

Book X. Guidance for State Water Monitoring and Wasteload Allocation Programs, to be available in early summer 1985, defines the process that the States and EPA Regional Offices use in developing monitoring and wasteload allocations under sections 106 and 303(d) of the Federal Water Pollution Control Act.

The Monitoring and Data Support Division has also sponsored technical seminars for State and EPA Regional Office personnel. These seminars have presented basic modeling principles, theory, and case studies for BOD/DO and toxic pollutant modeling. Workshops on implementation of Book IX, the Technical Support Document for Water Quality-Based Toxics Control, have also been conducted. These workshops included recommendations on how to conduct near- and farfield modeling for individual toxicants and whole effluent toxicity. Both steady-state and dynamic modeling techniques were discussed. By September 1985, three workshops will be conducted on toxic wasteload allocation models that have been successfully calibrated for rivers, lakes and estuaries. Model theory and structure will be described and example model applications will be presented. Future seminars will deal with permit averaging and design conditions, innovative wasteload allocations, and estuary modeling.

OFFICE OF RESEARCH AND DEVELOPMENT

EPA's Office of Research and Development established the Center for Water Quality Modeling to provide a focal point for water quality modeling activities. The Center for Water Quality Modeling is located at EPA's Environmental Research Laboratory in Athens, Ga, which has long been involved in the development and application of mathematical models that predict the transport and fate of water pollutants. For selected water quality and pollutant loading models, the Center provides a central file and distribution point for computer programs and documentation. In addition, the Center sponsors workshops and seminars that provide both generalized training in the use of models and specific instruction in the application of individual simulation techniques.

The modeling packages currently available through the Center were selected from many candidate models by experienced users in EPA regulatory and regional offices and by the Center staff. Selection criteria included model utility and effectiveness, availability of adequate documentation, degree of acceptance and application by users, and the Center staff's experience with the software. A wide range of analysis techniques is provided, ranging from simple desk-top techniques suitable for screening analysis through computerized steady-state models to sophisticated, state-of-the-art continuous simulation models for detailed planning. Modeling packages currently supported by the Center are:

Water Quality Assessment: A Screening Procedure for Toxic and Conventional Pollutants (14) -- a collection of formulas, tables and graphs that planners can use for preliminary assessment of surface water quality in large river basins. These desk-top procedures are appropriate for hand calculators. The manual includes a discussion of the environmental chemistry of synthetic organic chemicals and metals; a chapter on waste source estimation techniques; and simple methods for assessment of pollutant fate and transport in rivers, lakes and estuaries. Stream analysis techniques include conservative substances, water temperature, biochemical oxygen demand, dissolved oxygen, total suspended solids, coliform bacteria, nutrients, and toxic organic chemicals. Lake analysis procedures include thermal stratification, sediment accumulation, toxic organic chemicals, phosphorus budget, eutrophication potential, and hypolimnion dissolved oxygen. Estuarine analyses include estuarine classification, temperature, biochemical oxygen demand, dissolved oxygen, turbidity, sediment accumulation, and non-conservative substances. This manual has been adopted as Book IX of the agency's National Wasteload Allocation Guidance.

Exposure Analysis Modeling System (EXAMS) (2) -- a steady-state model designed for rapid evaluation of the behavior of synthetic organic chemicals in aquatic ecosystems. Starting from a description of the chemistry of a toxicant and relevant transport and physical-chemical characteristics of the ecosystem, EXAMS computes <u>exposure,</u> the ultimate expected environmental concentrations resulting from a long-term steady pattern of pollutant loadings; <u>fate,</u> the distribution of the chemical in the environment and the fraction of the loadings consumed by each transport and transformation process; and <u>persistence,</u> the time required for effective purification of the system once the loadings cease. EXAMS is an interactive program and allows the user to store the properties of chemicals and ecosystems, modify the characteristics of either via simple English-like commands, and conduct rapid, efficient evaluations of the probable fate of chemicals.

MEXAMS is an extension of the EXAMS model for heavy metals that incorporates **MINTEQ,** a thermodynamic equilibrium model that computes aqueous speciation, adsorption and precipitation/dissolution of solid phases (9). This model permits the user to examine the equilibrium distribution of heavy metals along with transport and fate in various aquatic systems. This information is important because different species of a metal may cause differing biological effects.

Stream Water Quality Model QUAL-II (15) -- a steady-state model for conventional pollutants in branching streams and well-mixed lakes. It includes conservative substances, temperature, coliform bacteria, biochemical oxygen demand, dissolved oxygen, nitrogen, phosphorus and algae. QUAL-II is widely used for waste load allocation and permiting in the United States and other countries. It has a 15 year history of application and is a proven, effective analysis tool.

Storm Water Management Model (SWMM) (11) -- a comprehensive model for simulation of urban runoff quantity and quality. All aspects of the urban hydrologic and quality cycles are simulated including surface runoff, transport through the drainage network, and storage and treatment (including cost). Alternative techniques are available for simulation of sewer systems -- a kinematic wave procedure for most problem assessments and a full-equation routing method for surcharged systems. SWMM can be used both for single-event and continuous simulation. It has been used in a planning context as well as for detailed design studies. SWMM also has a long history of use in the United States and Canada for urban drainage assessment and design.

Agricultural Runoff Management (ARM) (5) and **Non Point Source (NPS)** (6) -- techniques for assessing agricultural and urban nonpoint source loadings. The models use the Stanford Watershed Model for the water balance and extend it to the assessment of nonpoint source pollution from agricultural and urban areas. ARM can be used to study pollutants from agricultural lands such as sediment, nutrients and pesticides and includes detailed process descriptions for nutrient and pesticide fate on the land surface. NPS contains simpler algorithms and can be used on both urban and agricultural lands.

Hydrological Simulation Program - FORTRAN (HSPF) (12) -- a comprehensive package for simulation of watershed hydrology and water quality for both conventional and toxic organic pollutants. HSPF incorporates the watershed-scale ARM and NPS models into a basin-scale analysis framework that includes fate and transport in stream channels. Simply put, the model uses such information as the time history of rainfall, temperature, and solar radiation; land surface characteristics, use patterns and soil properties; and land management practices to simulate the processes that occur in a watershed. The result of this simulation is a time history of the quantity and quality of runoff from an urban or agricultural watershed. Flow rate, sediment load, and nutrient and pesticide concentrations are predicted. The program takes these results, along with information about the stream network and simulates instream processes to produce a time history of water quantity and quality at any point in a watershed -- the inflow to a lake, for example. HSPF includes an internal data base management system to process the large amounts of simulation input and output. A user-friendly editor to aid in developing input for the program is also available (13) as well as a comprehensive application guide (8).

Water Analysis Simulation Program (WASP) (4) and its extension to toxic contaminants, **TOXIWASP** (1) -- a generalized modeling framework for contaminant fate and transport in surface waters. Based on the flexible compartment modeling approach, WASP can be applied in one, two, or three dimensions. A variety of water quality problems can be addressed with the selection of appropriate kinetic subroutines that may either be selected from a library or written by the user. WASP is designed to permit easy substitution of user-written routines into the program structure. Problems that have been studied using WASP include biochemical oxygen demand-dissolved oxygen dynamics, nutrients and eutrophication, bacterial contamination, and toxic chemical movement. TOXIWASP combines a kinetic structure adapted from EXAMS with the WASP transport structure and simple sediment balance algorithms to predict dissolved and sorbed chemical concentrations in the bed and overlying waters. WASP has been used in the Great Lakes and the Potomac estuary to assess eutrophication problems. TOXIWASP has been applied in Mississippi and in the Delaware estuary to examine fate and transport of toxic contaminants. **WASTOX** (3) is similar to TOXIWASP in that it includes additions to WASP to assess the fate and transport of toxic chemicals in the environment. WASTOX is also being used as a research tool to investigate the fate of chemicals in the aquatic food chain.

ANNIE (13) -- an interactive model input editor under development in conjunction with the United States Geological Survey. ANNIE is a FORTRAN program designed for mini- and microcomputers to help the user interactively create, check, and update input to hydrologic and water quality models. For models that require access to data bases, ANNIE can be used to reformat, store, list, update and plot these data. Each model has an information file that is used to display questions and check the responses against acceptable values. When all input has been prepared, the model is then submitted for processing. Eventually, ANNIE will also help the user interpret model output by printing, plotting and statistically analyzing the output. ANNIE is a general software package that can be applied to any model. It was first applied to EPA's HSPF water quality model (see above) and two USGS rainfall/runoff models.

Further information on the software described above can be obtained by writing:

Center for Water Quality Modeling
Environmental Research Laboratory
U S EPA
Athens, GA   30613

The Center also maintains a mailing list of persons interested in the subject, sponsors a Users Group that meets twice a year, and sponsors periodic training on supported software.

APPLICATIONS OF ARTIFICIAL INTELLIGENCE AND EXPERT SYSTEMS TO MODELING

To further the usability of these computerized models, the Athens Environmental Research Laboratory is beginning a research program in the application of artificial intelligence/expert systems technology to environmental modeling. Preliminary investigations have shown this technology to be very promising in enhancing the ease-of-use of environmental models (10).

Modeling, in its computerized form, is becoming a key component of decision-making in EPA. The problems facing the agency increasingly involve more complex interactions between elements of the environment. Large, multi-media modeling systems must be built to understand these interactions. Artificial intelligence is an important methodology that can assist in building, using, and interpreting these models. Several of the concepts from artificial intelligence can be of benefit to environmental modeling. They include:

* A different perspective on decision-making.
* Programming languages that can reason as well as compute.
* Improved man-machine interaction.

There is a fundamental dichotomy in modeling and regulation. Modeling is directed at predicting the consequence of an action, e.g., the environmental concentration resulting from a waste discharge. Regulation, however, focuses on limiting the range of actions in order to protect the environment from adverse consequences. Regulation can be directed at either the environmental concentration or the waste discharge. Traditionally, technological standards have been set on the waste discharge but this regulatory strategy must be extremely conservative to be protective. To be more efficient and cost-effective, regulation must be directed at site-specific environmental concentrations. However, this strategy requires that an inverse problem be solved, i.e., the regulator must infer an allowable waste discharge from a target environmental concentration. In a system with complex environmental interactions and multiple waste sources, this problem is nontrivial and the solution is usually not unique. Problem-solving in this context can be viewed as a search for optimal solutions and notions from Artificial Intelligence about search spaces and search strategies have important implications to efficient decision making.

Modeling, as currently practiced, uses a rigid algorithmic language such as FORTRAN as the fundamental way of representing knowledge. The concept of the knowledge base or knowledge representation in Artificial Intelligence is much broader and includes ways to deal with incomplete or uncertain data. Knowledge can typically be divided into two classes: factual or causal knowledge and empirical associations or rules. For example, an algorithmic processor deals with causal relationships and may ask for a single value for an input variable. A knowledge-based expert system will allow input of an upper and lower bound for the variable as well as the degree of certainty in that variable. The process by which an experienced modeler evaluates parameter values can also be made part of the model.

In artificial intelligence methodology, premise-action rules are selected by a knowledge processor, or inference engine. The processor also has the capability to explain why particular rules are chosen and used. This explanation feature is important in dealing with ill-structured or ill-defined problems because it documents the system's reasoning process. This feature will be extremely important in a regulatory framework that makes extensive use of computer technology because it clearly presents and documents the information used in making a decision.

Large, complex models require extensive human interaction for their successful implementation. A major barrier to this interaction is the paucity of most computer languages compared to natural languages. An expert system can act as an intelligent front end to a complex simulation model, relieving the user of the tedium of preparing rigidly formatted model input and advising the user on selection of appropriate parameter values, especially under conditions of uncertainty. Such a system might include alternate parameter estimation techniques and provide advice on the estimate with which the system has highest confidence. An expert system with these capabilities has been developed in prototype form for 16 important hydrologic parameters in EPA's Hydrologic Simulation Program - FORTRAN (HSPF) (10). The availibility of a knowledge-based expert system containing the experience and expertise of model developers and skilled users would be of enormous benefit to those skilled in the physical and biological sciences but less skilled in the art of interacting with the computer.

The addition of extended modeling capabilities such as uncertainty and sensitivity analysis would facilitate model calibration and verification. Inclusion of this capability in models will be facilitated by an expert system that can aid the user both in the model calibration/ validation stage and in the model interpretation and decision making process.

As mentioned above, EPA is cooperating with the United States Geological Survey in the development of ANNIE, an input data preparation system and data base for hydrologic models that includes rudimentary artificial intelligence concepts. This system has the potential to provide basic public domain tools that can be used to further implement artificial intelligence concepts in modeling. This system now aids model input preparation and will increase access to models for many users. Software design for a general hydrologic model data base is underway. However, an important part of modeling that has not yet been addressed by these "intelligent" systems is the interpretation of model output.

It is expected that most of the developmental work specific to environmental modeling will focus on model output interpretation and completing the feedback loop for the calibration/verification process. Preparing model input is conceptually analogous to data base preparation and it is expected that the literature will be very rich in these concepts because of their commercial utility. One concept that will be considered is an intelligent interface that can "learn" a user's jargon and preferences for model input. Such an interface could make a user much more comfortable when first using a new model. Much of the effort in learning a new computer program goes into learning the syntax and input formats preferred by the software. This part of the learning curve, at least, might be put on the software and not on the user.

Methods for interpretation of model output and the calibration/verification process, however, are not as well developed. To the extent that this process involves optimization, the AI literature in pattern recognition may prove fruitful but it is expected that this part of the project will involve considerable developmental work.

SUMMARY

In this paper, we have discussed the support available for waste-load allocation available from the U S EPA. This support ranges from general technical guidance available from the Office of Water Regulation and Standards to specific software available from the Athens Environmental Research Laboratory. We have also discussed prospective research using expert systems directed at improving the usability of this software.

REFERENCES

1. Ambrose, R B, S I Hill, and L A Mulkey (1983) **Users Manual for the Toxic Chemical Transport and Fate Model TOXIWASP: Version I** EPA-600/3-83-005, U S EPA, Athens, Ga 30613.

2. Burns, L A, D M Cline and R R Lassiter (1982) **Exposure Analysis Modeling System (EXAMS)** EPA-600-3-82-023, U S EPA, Athens, Ga 30613.

3. Connolly, J P and R P Winfield (1984) **A User's Guide for WASTOX, A Framework for Modeling the Fate of Toxic Chemicals in Aquatic Environments** EPA-600/3-84-077, U S EPA, Gulf Breeze, FL 32561.

4. Di Toro, D M, J J Fitzpatrick and R V Thomann (1983) **Water Quality Analysis Simulation Program (WASP) and Model Verification Program (MVP) - Documentation** EPA-600/3-81-044, U S EPA, Duluth, Mn 55804.

5. Donigian, A S et al. (1977) **Agricultural Runoff Management (ARM) Model Version II: Refinement and Testing** EPA-600/3-77-098, U S EPA, Athens, Ga 30613.

6. Donigian, A S and N H Crawford (1976) **Modeling Non Point Pollution from the Land Surface** EPA-600/3-76-083, U S EPA, Athens, Ga 30613.

7. Donigian, A S et al. (1983) **Project Summary: Application of Hydrological Simulation Program - FORTRAN (HSPF) in Iowa Agricultural Watersheds** EPA-600/S3-83-069, U S EPA, Athens, Ga 30613.

8. Donigian, A S et al. (1984) **Guide to the Application of the Hydrological Simulation Program - FORTRAN (HSPF)** EPA-600/3-84-065, U S EPA, Athens, Ga 30613.

9. Felmy, A R, S M Brown, Y Onishi, S B Yabusaki, R S Argo, D C Girvin, and E A Jenne (1984) **Modeling the Transport, Speciation, and Fate of Heavy Metals in Aquatic Systems** EPA-600/S3-84-033, U S EPA, Athens, Ga 30613.

10. Gasching, J, R Reboh, and J Reiter. **Development of a Knowledge-Based Expert System for Water Resourses Problems** SRI Project 1619, Artificial Intelligence Center, SRI International, Palo Alto, CA

11. Huber, W C et al. (1984) **Storm Water Management Model User's Manual Version III** EPA-600/2-84-109a,b, U S EPA, Cincinnati, Oh 45268.

12. Johanson, R C et al. (1984) **Users Manual for the Hydrologic Simulation Program - FORTRAN (HSPF): Release 8.0** EPA-600/3-84-066, U S EPA, Athens, Ga 30613.

13. Lumb, A M and J L Kittle (1984) "ANNIE - An Interactive Processor for Hydrologic Models," in **Emerging Computer Technology in Stormwater and Flood Management,** American Society of Civil Engineers, New York, NY 10017, pp 352-365.

14. Mills, W B et al. (1982) **Water Quality Assessment: A Screening Procedure for Toxic and Conventional Pollutants** EPA-600/6-82-004, U S EPA, Athens, Ga 30613.

15. Roesner, L A, P R Gigure and D E Evenson (1981) **Computer Program Documentation for the Stream Water Quality Model QUAL-II** EPA-600/9-81-014, U S EPA, Athens, Ga 30613.

16. _____ (1984) "Development of Water Quality-Based Permit Limits for Toxic Pollutants", <u>Federal Register,</u> Vol. 49, No. 48, March 9, 1984, page 9016.

FUTURE TRENDS IN SOFTWARE DEVELOPMENT

By Elizabeth Southerland[1], A.M. ASCE and Charles S. Spooner[2]

ABSTRACT: USEPA's Office of Water has set program goals of improving the productivity and technical quality of wasteload allocation modeling and water quality-based permitting in the States and Regions. Interactive programming and artificial intelligence techniques are being employed to implement these goals and will be the basis of most future software developments. Current efforts in interactive programming concentrate on applying the pre-processing and post-processing capabilities of this type of software to facilitate the execution, calibration, and verification of wasteload allocation models. Future efforts will be directed at developing interactive computer graphics programs to display model predictions in an understandable way for water quality managers. Current efforts in applying artificial intelligence methods concentrate on developing knowledge-based expert systems that contain NPDES permit writing procedures, the requirements of effluent guidelines, and screening analyses for the identification of areas needing water quality-based permit limits. A prototype expert system uses the wasteload allocation that has been developed for these areas to devise appropriate permit limits and to automatically print a draft permit fact sheet. Future applications of expert systems in permitting will await the results of field studies intended to test their cost effectiveness.

INTRODUCTION

As the deadline for installation of Best Available Technology (BAT) draws near, the U.S. Environmental Protection Agency is emphasizing the need to go beyond BAT wherever necessary to meet applicable water quality standards. The emphasis on water quality-based treatment is, in turn, increasing interest in wasteload allocation modeling since this predictive tool is used to link pollutant discharges to target concentrations in receiving waters. Since the emphasis on water quality-based treatment extends to toxic pollutants as well as conventional ones, State and Regional EPA personnel are faced with the need to learn new models and to deal with new concerns about the duration and frequency of water quality violations.

---

[1]Environmental Engineer, USEPA, Monitoring and Data Support Division, 401 M Street S.W., Washington, D.C. 20460

[2]Environmental Engineer, USEPA, Water Policy Office, 401 M Street S.W., Washington, D.C. 20460

In the past, wasteload allocation modeling was generally performed for conventional pollutants using steady state models with a design low flow condition. The design receiving water flow was whatever the State had established by precedence or by regulation as the cut-off point for water quality standard compliance. This year, however, EPA will publish new criteria for toxic pollutants that specify an allowable duration and frequency of compliance. Wasteload allocations to meet these criteria must either employ dynamic modeling techniques or must use design conditions for steady state modeling that ensure the appropriate duration and frequency of compliance.

The advances in computer models that deal with the complexities of allocating wasteloads and data management will dramatically improve the ability to project impacts and to impose more precise limits on discharges, but advances in this area alone will not necessarily improve the overall ability to implement these refinements. EPA must be careful to see that the administrative systems for permitting keep pace with these technical advances. The permitting process itself must be streamlined in order to eliminate the backlogs that have long plagued the system and to impose future permit limits consistently.

The Office of Water (OW) has set program goals of improving the productivity and technical quality of wasteload allocation modeling and water quality-based permitting in the States and Regions. The Monitoring and Data Support Division (MDSD) in the OW is channeling its initial efforts into developing a variety of interactive programs to facilitate wasteload allocation modeling. The immediate office staff of OW is applying artificial intelligence methods to use these techniques and, more generally, to develop permit limits from wasteload allocations. A summary of these two programs follows.

PURPOSE OF INTERACTIVE PROGRAMMING

The overall goal of MDSD's efforts in interactive programming is to improve the productivity and technical quality of wasteload allocation modeling. Designed so that users will not need a strong background in computer programming in order to use the models, the programs perform one or more of the following functions: preprocessing of model input data, post-processing of model output data, and data presentation.

A number of tasks come under the category of preprocessing data. Interactive programs can be used to format data for model input and to store, list, update, and plot these data. This function eliminates the tedium and errors in keypunching fixed format input data for wasteload allocation models. Interactive programs can also be designed to synthesize input data for dynamic models using stochastic techniques and Monte Carlo procedures. The pre-processor can provide default values for a specific model and check all user-supplied data against acceptable ranges of values. In addition, pre-processors can include a tutorial session on how to use the model by explaining options, variables, parameters, and commands.

The post-processing functions of interactive programs can facilitate model calibration and verification. An interactive program
can be used to plot simulated and observed data to provide visual
evidence of goodness-of-fit and to provide statistical tests of
error. Post-processors can also be designed to analyze model predictions for alternative treatment scenarios. As an example, plots
of concentration-frequency curves can be created to illustrate the
predicted duration and frequency of toxic criteria violations.

Interactive programs for data presentation can be designed to
generate charts, graphs, and maps that compare model predictions
for various treatment schemes. Computer graphics can also be used
to show the dynamic movement of pollutants predicted by surface and
ground water quality models.

CURRENT INTERACTIVE PROGRAMMING PROJECTS

ANNIE is a general interactive program that can be applied to
any model (5). In association with EPA's Center for Water Quality
Modeling, MDSD is applying ANNIE to a version of the Qual-II model.
Qual-II is one of the most popular steady state wasteload allocation
models for conventional pollutants (7). The purpose of this project
is to make Qual-II easier and faster to use by providing interactive
processing. ANNIE is being used to create a formatted input run
stream for Qual-II and to modify existing input during a "question
and response" interactive session. At the request of the user,
ANNIE will provide definitions of input variables and parameters.
ANNIE will detect errors in input data by checking against acceptable
values, prompt the user for modification of out-of-range values, and
provide default numbers when necessary.

MDSD has also developed a TOXWLA set of subroutines for ANNIE
(4). The purpose of this project is to facilitate the use of dynamic
modeling techniques to predict the frequency and duration of toxic
criteria compliance. TOXWLA is designed: 1) to perform dynamic
wasteload allocation modeling for discharges to rivers using dilution
or first-order decay equations and 2) to generate dynamic effluent
data as input to more sophisticated fate and transport models for
discharges to rivers, lakes and estuaries. TOXWLA is written in
three levels of detail ranging from a very concise question-response
form for experienced users to a step-by-step explanation for new
users. TOXWLA consists of three main subroutines--one designed for
continuous simulation, one for Monte Carlo simulation, and one for
lognormal probabilistic analysis.

The continuous simulation subroutine in TOXWLA creates daily
timeseries data for effluent flows and effluent concentrations from
the observed values supplied by the user. A daily timestep is used
because EPA's new toxic pollutant criteria specify maximum 1-day
durations for acute values and 4-day durations for chronic values.
If the existing effluent database is fairly complete, the user can
select a linear interpolation scheme for filling in missing data. If
the observed data are inadequate, however, the user can choose a

lag-one Markov stochastic approach for synthesizing daily effluent
values. The lag-one Markov option uses the mean, standard deviation,
and daily correlation coefficient of the observed data to generate
daily timeseries for any specified period of time. If seasonal
differences in treatment efficiency are significant or if batch process
operations are used, a "multi-period" Markov option is provided to
synthesize effluent data that follow the appropriate pattern. The
subroutine displays the final input data in graphs or plots so the
user can see what has been generated.

The user can write the daily input data to a separate file in
the proper format for the fate and transport model selected for the
wasteload allocation. Alternatively, the user can do continuous
simulation modeling within this subroutine, but he is limited to
dilution or first order decay analyses of discharges to rivers only.
For these simple analyses, the subroutine uses the STORET daily
streamflow data from the nearest USGS gage; adjusts flows according
to known point source contributions, water withdrawals, and drainage
area ratios; and makes daily calculations of receiving water concentrations. Time-of-travel must be specified for each reach if the
first-order decay option is selected. The user can also read in
STORET water quality data to provide upstream boundary conditions.
The subroutine can then display the predicted daily instream concentrations in frequency plots and provide statistical analyses of these
values.

The Monte Carlo subroutine in TOXWLA characterizes each input
variable with a statistical distribution or empirical histogram.
Input variables include stream flows from STORET, boundary concentrations from STORET, effluent flows, and effluent concentrations.
A random generating function is then used to select multiple sets of
these input variables to run iteratively in a wasteload allocation
model. If some of these input variables are correlated, a "multi-
period" analysis can be performed or a cross-correlation coefficient
can be used to preserve this linkage during dataset selection. The
user can write the randomly selected datasets to a separate file in
the proper format for the fate and transport model selected for the
wasteload allocation. Alternatively, the user can do Monte Carlo
modeling within this subroutine, but he is limited to dilution or
first order decay analyses of discharges to rivers only. Guidelines are provided on how many times these equations must be run
before the solutions converge on a concentration-frequency distribution. The same adjustments in stream flow that are described for
the continuous simulation approach are also made in this subroutine.
In addition, the Monte Carlo subroutine uses the same display of predicted instream concentrations in frequency plots and the same statistical analyses of these values.

The lognormal probabilistic subroutine in TOXWLA characterizes
each input variable as a lognormal distribution. Input variables
include stream flows from STORET, boundary concentrations from STORET,
effluent flows, and effluent concentrations. If some of these input
variables are correlated, a "multi-period" analysis can be performed
or a cross-correlation coefficient can be used to preserve this

linkage. The lognormal subroutine displays the input distributions in plots so the user can see how well the observed data fit the lognormal assumption. The user can do lognormal probabilistic modeling within this subroutine, but he is limited to dilution analyses for a single river discharger. The assumption of lognormality is not accurate for concentrations downstream of a discharger, so analysis of multiple dischargers is not recommended in the subroutine. The lognormal distributions of input data are used to calculate the downstream concentration-frequency distribution using numerical solution techniques (2). The same adjustments in stream flow that are described for the continuous simulation approach are also made in this subroutine. Model output is presented in tables that list the downstream concentration predicted at the specified duration and frequency.

FUTURE INTERACTIVE PROGRAMMING PROJECTS

MDSD has plans to develop interactive programs for several new purposes. An interactive program is proposed to perform the analyses necessary to select design conditions for steady state wasteload allocation models of rivers. The program will calculate the design stream flow, instream pH, instream temperature, and effluent flow that should be used in steady state models to ensure that the recommended duration and frequency of criteria compliance are met. A second proposed project involves an interactive program that can select the appropriate biochemical processes, spatial and temporal scales necessary to model a site-specific water quality problem. The program will direct the user to MDSD guidance on the available wasteload allocation models that have these capabilities for rivers, lakes, or estuaries. A third potential project involves the use of interactive computer graphics to display digitized environmental information and to illustrate model predictions for water quality managers.

THE PURPOSE OF ARTIFICIAL INTELLIGANCE

Artificial intelligence (AI) is the general field of computer science that uses computers to represent human understanding of problems. The goal of AI systems is to go beyond numeric applications to use their power in applications where numbers themselves are not as important as procedures, rules, and interpretation. The field of AI encompasses robotics, game playing, the automated translation of language, and a major sub-discipline, called expert systems.

Expert systems, also called knowledge based systems, guide an informed program user through the logic of a problem, asking questions, apply rules, and performing calculations in order to solve that problem. Well constructed systems appear to contain the wisdom that comes from the natural intelligence of an expert.

By using an expert system to assist in solving a problem, a user employs a programmed logic sequence, data bases, computational subroutines and knowledge used in interpretation that he or she may know exist, but which would require unavailable time and effort, and sometimes skill to assemble and use.

Expert systems are not new, but their use has begun to grow as systems for developing them have been refined. Existing systems have been designed to interpret data, predict, control and teach. They have been built -- many in academic environments -- to plan, design, and debug as well as to monitor and diagnose. Work on civilian systems has been centered in medicine under the decade-old sponsorship of the Department of Health and Human Services. The system called MYCIN diagnoses infectious diseases and its use compares favorably with the judgements of physicians who specialize in such diseases. Other systems have been built for medical and biochemical uses.

The use of expert systems in industry is also growing. A system called CATS-1 diagnoses problems with General Electric's diesel-electric locomotives. The Digital Equipment Company uses a system called R-1 to configure its VAX computers, saving engineering time to customize orders. This system employs over 1300 rules and is regarded as one of the most advanced expert systems.

Government use of expert systems is also growing. PROSPECTOR was developed by USGS to guide mineral exploration. This program is credited with finding a $100 million molybdenum deposit. The Department of Labor has experimented with a system that judges the validity of unemployment compensation claims.

At least two expert systems exist within EPA, and others are being prepared. The first, developed by EPA's Office of Research and Development, used Integrated Pest Management techniques to suggest ways to control aquatic weeds. Another was developed by the Office of Pesticide Programs to check responses to requests for information in their data bank. While much of the information in this data bank is public, EPA cannot release certain confidential statistics, nor data from which confidential information can be inferred.

These systems are used to enhance productivity by providing what is otherwise limited expertise to those who must solve specialized technical or administrative problems routinely. It is in this context the OW is exploring their use as an aid to NPDES permitting.

CURRENT APPLICATIONS OF ARTIFICIAL INTELLIGENCE

The objective of the Office of Water Expert System Test is to explore the feasibility of using expert systems to prepare NPDES permits and to evaluate their utility for water programs in general. It is hoped that the project will demonstrate that an automated system can increase permit writing productivity, produce more consistent permits, and help train new permit writers more quickly. The first phase of that work has been completed.

The NPDES permits are at the center of the country's clean water program. They are the means used to implement each phase of our control programs for industrial and municipal dischargers. Issuing

them efficiently is essential to the integrity of our regulatory
program. Statistics show, however, that we have not fully overcome
the technical and administrative problems involved in permit issuance.

There are over 63,000 NPDES permits. Each permit lasts for five
years. We estimate that about 26,000 have expired and must be re-
issued if we are to impose new requirements and make adjustments
reflecting the results of new wasteload allocation model runs. About
6,800 permits will expire in each of the next three years, adding to
this workload.

Permit writing is an activity EPA's ten regions share with 38
states. EPA and States devote about 500 staff-years to this effort,
at a cost of about $15 million annually. These figures demonstrate
why our interest in permit writing efficiency is not only a matter
of preserving the system's integrity, but one of cost-effectiveness.

Permit issuance has been the subject of several studies in EPA.
One of these studies revealed that problems with permit consistency
may extend beyond the site-specific considerations we know many
permits must reflect. Another study identified technical assistance
to States in permit writing as a major need (1). There is widespread
concern that permit writers may suffer more than the usual rate of
staff turn-over in pollution control programs. This may drain programs
of valuable experience and be a factor contributing to many of the
other problems.

In Phase 1 of the OW project, two expert systems were designed to
prepare permits in each of two permit categories---steam electric
power generation and municipal wastewater treatment. Together these
two categories comprise about 16,000 permits, or about a quarter of
the permit total. Before designing the systems, OW conducted a
review of the software tools that facilitate building, editing, and
using expert systems. The selection of a software system was constrained by its specialized hardware needs, an issue of importance
to the decentralized applications planned by OW The assessment of
available tools concluded that the product KES, "Knowledge Engineering
System" (8) was a reasonable initial choice for use in this project.
The products "TIMM" (3) and RuleMaster (6) also show promise for future
use.

OW classified the general permit writing procedures to be encoded
as either "horizontal" or "vertical" steps. The horizontals were the
sequence of procedures used from start to finish during permitting,
while the specialized steps in which very technical knowledge was
needed, such as wasteload allocations, were verticals nested within
these horizontals.

Verticals are potentially useful components of many horizontal
permit writing systems. In the steam electric horizontal, we encoded
two verticals, the "ash pond test", described in EPA's "Draft Guidance
on Establishing Permit Limitations for Steam Electric Power Generating
Facilities", and the whole effluent tiered testing procedures, described
in the "Technical Support Document for Water Quality-Based Toxic

Control." The whole effluent tests will also be used in the municipal permitting system, and can be transported to other expert systems in the future.

The steam electric expert system prototype has been completed. It contains 250 rules and automatically performs over 150 calculations. It completes the work in about 15 minutes of interaction with a permit writer. The system first assigns the appropriate technology-based effluent limits to the discharge and uses a simple dilution equation to compare projected in-stream concentrations with water quality standards for individual pollutants and whole effluent toxicity. Next the system reviews available data on whole effluent toxicity, and recommends additional data collection when necessary.

This system stops short of writing a full permit, but produces a three page fact sheet containing a summary of the BPT and BAT requirements or the water quality-based limits that are appropriate. The system allows the operator to suspend the permit writing session and to automatically write a letter to the permit applicant to request further information. This feature will be added to several other points in the program. The system has been reviewed by EPA's steam electric expert in Region IV, as well as other experts in EPA's Headquarters, and they have verified that it functions accurately. The municipal expert system has not been developed as extensively as the steam electric, although considerable progress has been made. A detailed logic flow diagram containing about 60 major decision points has been prepared and is being peer reviewed. It will then be encoded into the KES shell. This will involve delineating specific decision rules for each of the steps. The logic now allows the rapid review of a standard secondary treatment permit, but also allows the permit writer to deal with the various special considerations, such as a 301 (h) waiver or the new definition of secondary treatment. This flexibility should allow the resulting municipal system to be used for both major and minor municipal permits.

FUTURE PROJECTS

The completion of these two systems will allow Phase 2 of the project to proceed. In Phase 2, OW will assess whether such systems can provide benefits which exceed predicted development costs. During this phase, we will examine the extent to which the two prototypes can improve permit writing productivity, aid in training, and contribute to permit consistency.

Potential additional uses of expert systems within EPA might include diagnosing POTW performance problems to help ensure compliance; designing systems to insure compliance with current regulations; establishing bio-monitoring requirements for NPDES discharges; specifying pretreatment requirements for indirect discharges; automating grant reporting systems; estimating costs or risks at Superfund sites; and issuing RCRA permits.

APPENDIX 1. - REFERENCES

1. "Assessment of State Needs for Technical Assistance in NPDES Permitting", U.S. Environmental Protection Agency, Washington, D.C., April 25, 1984.

2. DiToro, D., "Probability Model of Stream Quality Due to Runoff", Journal of the Environmental Engineering Division, ASCE, Vol. 110, No.3, June, 1984, pp. 607-623

3. General Research Corporation, "TIMM™ Tuner User's Manual", General Research Corporation, McLean, Virginia, July, 1984.

4. LimnoTech, Inc., "Users Manual for TOXWLA Portion of ANNIE", U.S. Environmental Protection Agency, Washington, D.C., March, 1985.

5. Lumb, A.M., and Kittle, J.L., "ANNIE-An Interactive Processor for Hydrologic Models", Proceedings of Emerging Computer Technology in Stormwater and Flood Management, American Society of Civil Engineers, 1984, pp. 352-365.

6. Radian Corporation, "Rulemaster User's Manual", Radian Corporation, Research Triangle Park, North Carolina, 1984.

7. Roesner, L.A., Gigure, P.R., and Evenson, D.E., "Computer Program Documentation for the Stream Water Quality Model QUAL-II", EPA - 600/9-81-014, U.S. Environmental Protection Agency, Athens, Georgia, September, 1981.

8. Software Architecture and Engineering, "Knowledge Engineering System - Knowledge Base Author's Manual", Software Architecture and Engineering, Arlington, Virginia, November, 1983.

Tampa Bay 205J Water Quality Impact Study

Scott McClelland*

Introduction

Tampa Bay is a complex estuarine system located in west central Florida (see Fig. 1). The Bay is one of the nation's largest phosphate shipping ports as well being valued for swimming, boating and sport fishing. It is also experiencing poor water quality: algal blooms occur periodically which result in a depletion of the dissolved oxygen resources and subsequent fish kills. For these reasons, Tampa Bay was identified by the State of Florida Department of Environmental Regulation (FDER) as the top priority for an impact study using federal 205(j) grant funding.

The study was divided into two steps: first, since there are various uses of the Bay, and the state regulations do not define a numerical nutrient standard (Rule 17-3, Florida Administrative Codes), nutrient related target concentrations were developed; second, predictions of the relative impacts of point and non-point sources of nutrients were considered with the use of mathematical modeling. Studies in both of these areas is still ongoing; however, preliminary results are presented here (11).

Nutrient/Chlorophyll a Targets

The water quality problems in Tampa Bay appear to be related to nutrient enrichment. High concentrations of chlorophyll a frequently occur in the lobes of the Bay with associated depletion of dissolved oxygen (DO), fish kills and possibly the restriction of sunlight to seagrasses. The primary concern of this part of the study was, therefore, to relate acceptable values of DO and sunlight to chlorophyll a and subsequently to nutrients. The state standard for DO requires 4 mg/l as a minimum and a 5 mg/l daily average, the former believed to be more critical in Tampa Bay.

Historical Data. Water quality data since 1967 were available from various sources, the majority of which were collected by the Hillsborough County Environmental Protection Commission. Simple statistics performed on these data showed that chlorophyll a was related to orthophosphorus (R^2 = 0.65), but not to nitrogen. It should be noted that Tampa Bay is phosphorus rich: in July of 1983, the average concentration of total phosphorus in Hillsborough Bay was

----
* Environmental Scientist, Camp Dresser & McKee Inc., One Tampa City Center, Suite 1750, Tampa, FL 33602

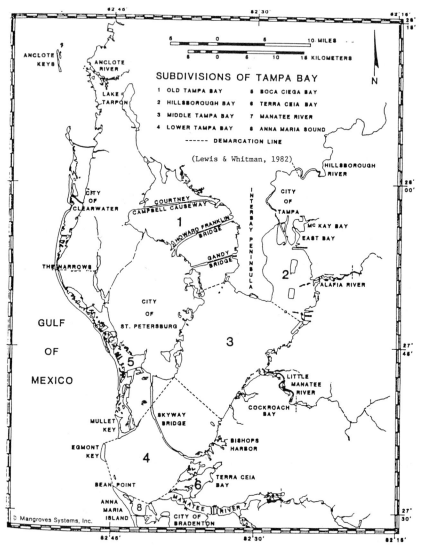

Figure 1 - The Tampa Bay Study area (9).

0.60 mg/l and in the whole Bay was 0.52 mg/l; much higher than the half saturation value for phytoplankton growth (about 0.005 mg/l, (15)). Also, algal assays (2, 7) and the ratio of nitrogen and phosphorus (0.21, (11)) indicated the potential for growth limitation by nitrogen but not phosphorus. The relationship between phosphorus and chlorophyll a was, therefore, an artifact. During high flow seasons, both nitrogen and phosphorus loads increase to the Bay. The nitrogen loads are "immediately" converted into biomass, but since there is so much already, increased phosphorus loads simply increase the water column concentration. It was clear then that a usable relationship between nutrients and chlorophyll a could not be derived using the historical data.

Seagrass/Light Penetration Data. Operationally defining health as long-term persistence, seagrass distribution maps were prepared by Continental Shelf Associates for c.1940, c.1963, 1972, 1979, and 1983. Using only the general outline of the beds, the areal coverage of seagrasses was determined for each map and compared to the earliest distributions. About 50% of the coverage was lost between 1940 and 1963; while water quality deterioration may have caused some of this loss, shoreline modification and dredging also contributed. Since 1963, some loss was noted in Old Tampa Bay but overall the whole Bay showed only a 2% loss.

Such a small loss is very misleading. The areal coverage was based upon the general outline of the grass: while the total area of the bed may remain the same, the density of seagrasses may decrease indicating poor health. Indeed, Lewis et al (8) has indicated decreasing grass beds in many areas of Tampa Bay, the decrease resulting from shoreline modification and dredging, as well as decreased water quality and light availability. Unfortunately, very little data on structural changes to Tampa Bay was collected so that the study ultimately concluded water quality-grassbed loss relationships could not be generated since the impact of the structural changes could not be isolated.

Relative to sunlight requirements for seagrasses, the Tampa Bay study did not conclusively determine a reasonable value either as a percentage of the surface irradiance (S.I.) or as an absolute value. Limited literature research (3, 4) yielded minimum light requirements from 5 to 50% S.I. The study considered 1% S.I. since this value is defined by stated rule as the compensation point (Rule 17-3.021(6)). Preliminary results on further work in this area appears to support a value of about 15% S.I. for the minimum requirements for seagrasses.

The minimum light requirement was used to generate a chlorophyll a target through the extinction coefficient, K_e. Based upon data collected during intensive water quality surveys of Tampa Bay in July and August, 1983, the extinction coefficient was statistically related to the chlorophyll a concentration ($R^2 = 0.5$):

$$K_e = 0.5787 + 0.0393 \text{ (chl a)}; \qquad (1)$$

where the units are 1/m for K_e and ug/l for chlorophyll a. From the Beer-Lambert law (15):

$$I/I_0 = \exp(-K_e z); \qquad (2)$$

where I/I_0 is the ratio of the irradiance at depth z and the surface irradiance, I_0. Thus, setting I/I_0 to the light requirement for seagrasses gives

$$Z = 4.605/K_e \text{ for } I/I_0 = 0.01, \text{ and} \qquad (3)$$

$$Z = 1.897/K_e \text{ for } I/I_0 = 0.15. \qquad (4)$$

Solving for chlorophyll a and noting that maximum depth at which seagrasses occur is about 2 meters (12), target chlorophyll a values can be derived: 43.9 ug/l for 1% S.I. and 9.4 ug/l for 15% S.I. Clearly the exact minimum light requirement is critical.   The Tampa Bay study concluded that further study in this area was required in order to use the target derived by this method for regulatory purposes.

Diurnal Dissolved Oxygen.   Since the previously described attempts did not result in targets, the cholorophyll a relationship to DO was considered as a last resort.   The chlorophyll a concentration, C, can be related to the maximum photosynthetic oxygen production, P_s, and subsequently, P_s to the average production, P_a, as follows (15):

$$P_s = 2.67 \, u_m \, A_{cp} \, (1.066)^{T-20} \, C, \text{ and} \qquad (5)$$

$$P_a = \frac{ef}{K_e H} [\exp(-ab) - \exp(-b)] \, P_s; \qquad (6)$$

where 2.67 is the stoichiometric constant relating carbon and DO, u_m is the maximum specific growth rate, A_{cp} is the carbon to chlorophyll a ratio, T is the water temperature, $e \cong 2.718...$, f is photoperiod as a fraction of a day, H is the water depth, "a" is the ratio of irradiance at depth H to irradiance at the surface (=$\exp(-K_e H)$), and

"b" is the ratio of average daylight light intensity and the saturated intensity. Finally, the average production was related to the diurnal variation of DO (10):

$$d = \frac{[1-\exp(-K_a f)][1 - \exp(-K_a (1-f))]}{fKa[1-\exp(-K_a)]}, \qquad (7)$$

where K_a is the reaeration coefficient.   Combing equations 5 through 7 and using results from the sampling and modeling efforts (13) it was determined that for the whole bay system d = 0.095C.   The DO standard given above require that the worst case is when the daily average DO is 5 mg/l and the minimum is 4 mg/l; i.e. d/2 = 1 mg/l which yields a target chlorophyll a of 21 mg/l.   Consideration of the survey data and the modeling indicated that the target was more likely about 30 mg/l based upon the diurnal DO: it was this value that was ultimately used.

A word of caution is warranted at this point. For estuarine waters, the target of 30 mg/l chlorophyll a seems very large: a value on the order of 5 - 10 mg/l is more reasonable. Use of the 15% S.I. minimum light requrement to set the target may be promising for this reason. Also, the modeling effort predicted time-dependent DO values so that the diurnal variation was known independent of the chlorophyll a: the chlorophyll a target was therefore redundant. The model, however, predicted vertically-averaged values and the problems in Tampa Bay include large DO gradients over depth during the summer: studies have been initiated to relate chlorophyll a to the vertical gradient of DO.

Water Quality and Quality Models

Nutrient Budget. Using historical measurements and literature rates, nutrient storage and flux rates between pools were defined (13). The overwhelming amount of nutrient storage was contained in benthic deposits (over 80% of the total storage); a distant second was the water column. Also, the flux rates for nitrogen indicate a balance between algal settling/mangrove detritus (the former dominating) and benthic release and between tidal exchange out of the Bay and nitrogen loading from point and non-point sources. The budget implied then that the dominant cycle for nitrogen was organic nitrogen input to the sediments via planktonic detritus, conversion from organic to inorganic nitrogen and subsequent release to the water column in an assimilatable form. This picture may be complicated by potential denitrification in the sediments (14) although rather large nutrient flux rates were observed in Tampa Bay (5, 6).

Dynamic Box Model. Developed by Dr. Bernard E. Ross at the University of South Florida, the box model is predicated upon a long-term accounting of water fluxes at the boundaries with the use of the 2D hydrodynamic model. This information was used in a water quality model which considered the Bay as a single box. The resulting simulation required much less computer time to simulate a long time period (1 - 2 months) than a conventional two-dimensional, FD model.

An example output of the box model is shown in Fig. 2 (13). Various constitutent boxes list the starting and ending mass in million pounds and arrows indicate the accumulated mass transferred in or out of the component. This simple representation indicated whether a constituent increase or decreases with time and where the mass accumulates.

The dynamic box model was used to simulate all of the point source alternatives defined for the study. Since the model represented general features of the Bay and the point sources were not the major load as identified by the nutrient budget, there were very few differences in the box model results. One result was significant: all of the point source treatment levels tested results in an increase in ambient DO except secondary treatment. Indeed, after 40 days of simulation with secondary treatment, the ambient DO had not reached a minimum. Based upon these results, the study concluded that secondary treatment was insufficient to maintain the DO standards in Tampa Bay.

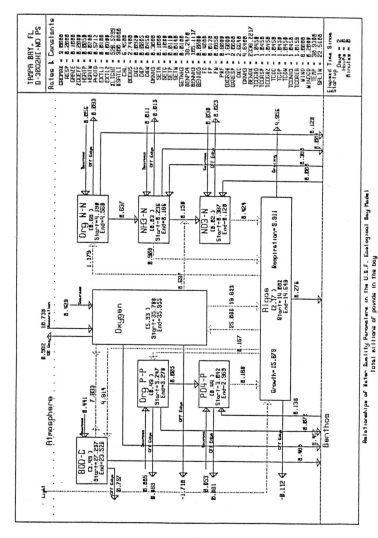

Figure 2 – Example dynamic box model output showing starting and ending constituent masses (boxes) and flux rates (arrows) (13).

Finite Difference (FD) Model. The Tampa Bay Study employed a set of models developed over the last 15 years. Documented in detail elsewhere (15), the models can be used for well-mixed, dynamic, two-dimensional water flow and quality. The mass balance equations are listed in Table 1. The water quality equations allow for the following features:

o   settling of CBOD, organic P, organic N and ammonia N,
o   organic N and P increases due to algal respiration,
o   nitrogen and phosphorus limited growth via Monod kinetics
o   preferential consumption of ammonia over nitrate,
o   benthic sources of ortho P, ammonia and nitrate and sink of DO,
o   algal DO production (consumption) by photosynthesis (respiration),
o   light limitations,
o   self-shading of algae,
o   wind generated reaeration, and
o   low-DO kinetics.

The equations were solved numerically using split-time, staggered grid, explicit finite difference methods with stability criteria of $dt < dx/[2gH_m]^{1/2}$ for the hydrodynamics and $dt_w < dx/V_m$ for the water quality where dt is the time step, dx is the grid size, g is gravitation acceleration, H_m is the maximum grid depth, dt_w is the water quality time step and V_m is the maximum average transport expected over the time step. For the Tampa Bay model, these criteria resulted in dt = 30 sec. and dt_w = 600 sec. for a 68 x 48 grid system with dx = 805 m (0.5 miles). The algorithm was coded on a PRIME 750 minicomputer in FORTRAN 77.

The FD model calibration was accomplished using data collected during July and August, 1983. The hydrodynamic results appeared to be well calibrated: the maximum errors between the predicated and observed tide heights were generally less than 10%. On the other hand, the water quality results varied in error: in the northern portions the error was greatest (at times exceeding 100% for an individual observation) while in the southern region near the Skyway Bridge the error was 25% or less for an individual observation. This is due to the fact that Tampa Bay has a less varying bathymetry in the south than the north.

Model Application to Tampa Bay

Future Flow and Loading Conditions. Based upon long-term USGS stage records, tributary flow inputs were estimated for 2-year, 5-year, 10-year and 20-year recurrence intervals and 7-day, 14-day, and 30-day periods for the duration of averaging (1). This allowed for the testing of numerous flow conditions, such as the classic low flow condition, $_7Q_{10}$ (7-day, 10-year). It was ultimately decided that

Parameter	Decay Rate(K)	Source/Sink(R)
ALGAE(A)	$\rho_G + \rho + \dfrac{\sigma_A}{D} - \mu$	$\emptyset$
CBOD(C)	$f_1 K_C + \dfrac{\sigma_C}{D}$	R_C
ORGP(P_1)	$K_{P_1} + \dfrac{\sigma_P}{D}$	$R_{P_1} + \alpha_p \rho A$
ORTHO-P(P_2)	$\emptyset$	$R_{P_2} + K_{P_1} P_1 - \alpha_p \mu A + \dfrac{S_{P2}}{D}$
ORGN (N_1)	$K_{N_1} + \dfrac{\sigma_{N1}}{D}$	$R_{N_1} + \alpha_n \rho A$
AMMONIA-N (N_2)	$f_2 K_{N_2} + \dfrac{\sigma_{N2}}{D}$	$R_{N_2} + K_{N_1} N_1 - \Delta \alpha_N \mu A + \dfrac{S_{N2}}{D}$
NITRATE-N (N_3)	$\emptyset$	$R_{N_3} + f_2 K_{N_2} N_2 - (1-\Delta)\alpha_N \mu A + \dfrac{S_{N3}}{D}$
DISS. O_2 (O_x)	K_O	$K_O O_x + (\alpha_{OG} \mu - \alpha_{OR} \rho)A - f_1 K_C C$ $-f_2 \alpha_{ON} K_{N_2} N_2 - \dfrac{S_B}{D}$

Basic Equation:

$$\frac{\partial CD}{\partial t} + \frac{\partial CU}{\partial x} + \frac{\partial CV}{\partial y} = \frac{\partial}{\partial x}\left(E_x \frac{\partial CD}{\partial x}\right) + \frac{\partial}{\partial y}\left(E_y \frac{\partial CD}{\partial y}\right) + RD - KCD$$

Terms:

ρG = grazing rate
ρ = respiration rate = $\emptyset.1\,\mu'$
σ_A = algae settling rate
μ = local specific growth rate
K_D = deoxygenation rate
f_1 = $O_x/(O_x+\emptyset.\emptyset1)$
σ_C = settling rate of CBOD
K_{P_1} = reaction rate of Organic P
σ_{P_1} = settling rate of Organic P
α_p = ratio of phosphorus to biomass
S_{P_2} = benthic source rate of Ortho-P

K_{N_1} = hydrolysis rate of Organic N
σ_{N_1} = settling rate of Organic N
α_N = ratio of nitrogen to biomass
K_{N_2} = nitrification rate·
f_2 = $O_x/(O_x+\emptyset.5)$
σ_{N_2} = settling rate of ammonia
Δ = $\emptyset.9N_2/(\emptyset.9N_2+\emptyset.1N_3)$
S_{N_2} = benthic source rate of ammonia
S_{N_3} = benthic source rate of nitrate
K_O = reaeration rate
O_S = DO saturation
α_{OG} = photosynthic oxygen production rate
α_{OR} = oxygen consumption rate by respiration
α_{ON} = oxygen uptake per unit nitrification = 4.57

Supplementary Equations:

$$\mu = \mu'\left(\frac{N_2+N_3}{N_2+N_3+K_N}\right)\left(\frac{P_2}{P_2+K_P}\right)L$$

where:

μ' = maximum specific growth rate
K_N = half saturation value for inorganic N
K_P = half-saturation value for inorganic P
L = $\dfrac{ef}{K_e D}\left(\exp(-ab) - \exp(-b)\right)$
e = 2.718...
f = photoperiod (fraction of day)
K_e = extinction coefficient = $\dfrac{1}{H_s'} + \emptyset.\emptyset52A$
H_s' = algae-free secchi depth
a = $\exp(-K_e D)$
b = I_A/I_s
I_A = avg light intensity over daylight hours

I_s = saturation light intensity
K_O = $11.61\emptyset1\,U^{0.969}D^{-1.673} + K_{ow}\dfrac{W}{D}$
K_{ow} = wind coefficient for reaeration
W = wind speed
C_L = chlorophyll-a concentration = $\alpha_{CL}A$
α_{CL} = ratio of chlorophyll-a to biomass

Table 1 - Mass balance equations for the USF Tampa Bay Model (11).

two conditions would be used. For low flow, a 10-year recurrence interval was chosen with a 30-day averaging preiod. On the other hand, for high flow, a 50% probability, 2-year recurrence interval was used.

Constituent loading information was also generated (1) based upon future land use estimates and nonpoint source controls. The scenarios included no BMP's, urban and agricultural BMP's and phosphate mine limits. The first of these represented no controls while the sum of the rest represented the best of controls.

Future Point Characteristics. The list included eight facilities with a total of up to 167.5 mgd of treated wastewater. Three different treatment characteristics were tested: Secondary (CBOD5 = 25 mg/l, TN = 20 mg/l, TP = 8 mg/l), Advanced Secondary Treatment (AST; CBOD5 = 8 mg/l, TN = 10 mg/l, TP = 8 mg/l), and Advanced Waste Treatment (AWT; CBOD5 = 8 mg/l, TN = 5 mg/l, TP = 8 mg/l).

NPS Model Scenarios. Baseline water quality was simulated by inputting the various nonpoint source (NPS) control scenarios without the point source inputs at both low and high flow conditions. In these scenarious and the others discussed below, the dynamic box model was run for up to 40 days before the full 2D model was used. Also, while the full constituent set was simulated, only DO and chlorophyll a were considered.

The first and possibly most dramatic result of the simulations was that neither DO nor chlorophyll a concentrations met the targets during high flow conditions while both were better than the targets at low flow conditions. The former was true even with the NPS controls imposed. The high flow condition was run again with reduced benthic releases: ambient DO was greater than 4 mg/l and chlorophyll a was less than 30 mg/l. Clearly the benthic loading controlled the results. Further simulations are being done to consider benthic loads in more detail.

Point Source Model Scenarios. Since the NPS model runs showed that Tampa Bay would not maintain the targets even under strict controls, the point source alternatives were judged based upon the change caused relative to the NPS control simulations. Very little change was observed. Even tabulating the change in the area covered by a certain concentration did not show large changes although chlorophyll a varied more than DO. It was concluded that greater detail was required to consider the localized impacts.

Conclusions

The Tampa Bay 205(j) Water Quality Impact Study is not finished. Both the target concentrations and the model simulations require further work. Nevertheless, the study allowed for a level of understanding to be reached of Tampa Bay and of general aspects of impact studies.

The nutrient dynamics in Tampa Bay are dominated by a plankton-sediment cycle. The vast amount of nutrients (in particular, nitrogen) stored in the sediments indicate that the cycle will continue for many years to come. Unless the release is reduced, water quality problems experienced today will continue.

It is for this very reason that further effort should have been provided in the study to more completely define the sediment demand

and nutrient release. While other estuaries may not have as large a
release as Tampa Bay, more careful consideration of sediment loads
appears warranted in all estuarine impact studies. Also, the use of a
number of different types of models were necessary to refine the
understanding of the sediment's contribution and, more generally,
those of point and non-point sources.

References

1. Camp Dresser & McKee, "Tributary Streamflows and Pollutant Loading
    Delivered to Tampa Bay," Annandale, VA, January, 1984.
2. City of Tampa, "Results of Phytoplankton Bioassay Experiments,"
    Department of Sanitary Sewers, Tampa, FL, June, 1983.
3. Continental Shelf Associates, "Annotated Bibliography of Seagrass
    Research Conducted in Tampa Bay, Florida," Tequesta, FL, June,
    1983.
4. Continental Shelf Associates, "Annotated Bibliography of Published
    Research Dealing with Light/Seagrass Relationships," Tequesta, FL,
    July, 1983.
5. Environmental Protection Agency, "Sediment Oxygen Demand (SOD) and
    Nutrient Exhange Rate (NER): Hillsborough Bay, Florida,"
    Ecological Support Branch, Athens, GA, February, 1983.
6. Environmental Protection Agency, "Suppliment to February 1983
    Report: August, 1983 Measurements," Ecological Support Branch,
    Athens, GA, January, 1984.
7. Florida Department of Environmental Regulation, "Limiting Nutrient
    and Growth Potential Algal Assays of Hillsborough Bay and Manatee
    River, Florida," Biological Section, Tallahassee, FL, April, 1983.
8. Lewis, R. R. III, Durako, J. J., Moffler, M. D., and Phillips, R.,
    "Seagrass Meadows of Tampa Bay - A Review," presented at the Bay
    Area Scientific Information Symposium, University of South
    Florida, May, 1982.
9. Lewis, R. R., III, and Whitman, R. L., "A New Geographic
    Description of the Boundaries and Subdivisions of Tampa Bay,"
    presented at the Bay Area Scientific Information Symposium,
    University of South Florida, May, 1982.
10. O'Connor, D. J. and Mueller, J. A. (eds.), "Quality Models of
    Natural Water Systems," Manhattan College, NY, 1983.
11. McClelland, S. I., "Draft Tampa Bay 205(j) Water Quality Impact
    Study," Water Quality Technical Series, Vol. 2., FDER,
    Tallahassee, FL, September, 1984.
12. Phillips, R. C. "Observations on the Ecology and Distribution of
    the Florida Seagrasses," Professional Papers Series, Florida Board
    of Conservation, No.2, October, 1960.
13. Ross, B. E., Ross, M. A., and Jerkins, P. D., "Wasteload
    Allocation Study: Tampa Bay, Florida", U.S.F. Center for
    Mathematical Modeling, Tampa, Vols. I-V, March, 1984.
14. Seitzinger, S. P., Nixon, S. W., and Pilson, M. E. Q.,
    "Denitrification and nitrous oxide production in a coastal marine
    ecosystem", Limnol. Oceanography, Vol. 29, No. 1, 1984, pp 73-83.
15. Zison, S. W., Mills, W. B., Deimer, D., and Chen, C. W., Rates,
    Constants and Kinetics Formulations in Surface Water Quality
    Models, USEPA (ORD) EPA-600/3-78-105, December, 1978.

Optimization of Flood Control Projects

Terry Meeneghan *
Mohammad Karamouz ** A.M.ASCE

ABSTRACT

Project optimization analysis techniques have become indispensable tools for the design, management, and administration of flood control improvements. The increasing complexity of engineering designs and requirements has given engineers a new role in the decision making process. The use of computer technology for optimization analyses allows the engineer to make objective choices between alternative project components and ultimate project scopes. This paper will utilize an actual case study to illustrate how computerized analyses were used to determine an optimum engineering solution for a specific flood problem area.

INTRODUCTION

Every year hundreds of communities around the country are subjected to flooding. When the flooding is severe the financial and personal loss to communities is unmeasurable, and flooded residents take strong action to protect themselves from future events. Community leaders ultimately turn to government agencies for help. Difficult decisions have to be made and several questions arrise. With many communities throughout the country having flood relief needs, how does one allocate limited funds fairly? Many diverse opinions will be dogmatically expressed as to what should be done for a specific community; how does an engineer determine the "best" solution or determine if a cost justified solution even exists?

The answer to these key questions can be obtained from the proper utilization of computerized optimization analysis techniques. Flood damage information can be gathered in the field and analyzed on a computer to accurately weigh the flood relief needs of each community, thus providing the factual data necessary to make fair, unbiased decisions. Computer analyses allow the engineer to formulate and screen alternative solutions, determine the most efficient improvement configurations, and compare the cost efficiency of alternative proposed plans. This paper will demonstrate how optimization analyses were effectively used in the design of improvements for a flood problem area in northeastern New Jersey (figures 1 and 2.)

* Civil Engineer, Leonard Jackson Associates, Consulting Engineers, 26 Skylark Drive, Spring Valley, NY 10977.
** Assist. Professor, Dept. of Civil and Environmental Engineering, Polytechnic Inst. of New York, Brooklyn, NY.

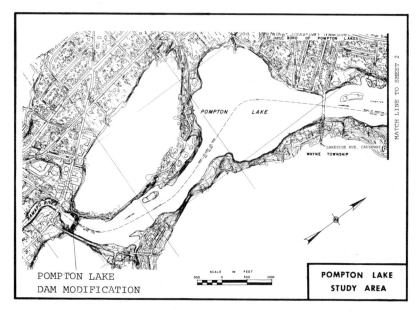

POMPTON LAKE
DAM MODIFICATION

POMPTON LAKE
STUDY AREA

FIGURE 1

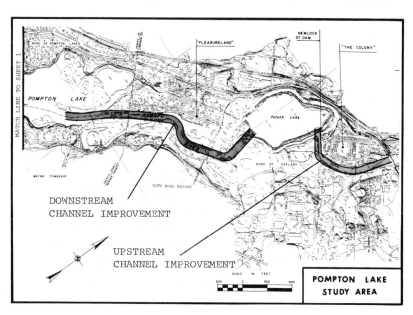

DOWNSTREAM
CHANNEL IMPROVEMENT

UPSTREAM
CHANNEL IMPROVEMENT

POMPTON LAKE
STUDY AREA

Figure 2

WATER RESOURCES PLANNING PROBLEMS

At the municipal level, site selection, project scopes, and levels of protection for flood control projects are often improperly determined. The selection of problem areas for the implementation of flood control improvements is often determined by which interest group complained the loudest or carried the most political clout. Site selections which are not based on proper engineering analyses will often result in tax money being spent in a way that does not maximize the total public benefit. Needs may go unmet because available funds were exausted on improperly selected projects. Project limits are often hastily or improperly set based on inaccurately perceived needs. Without proper analyses some flood control needs may be overlooked, and improvement projects may extend beyond where they are warranted. Levels of protection for projects are often dictated by specific design storms that have been adopted into local ordinances. These design storms were usually legislated as a planning tool, yet they are often inappropriately applied to flood control designs. If proper optimization analyses were performed, it might be discovered that a substancially higher level of protection could be provided with only a modest increase in project cost. It might also be discovered that if a modest decrease in the level of protection were allowed, project costs could be substancially reduced.

At State and Federal levels, funding policies often dictate design standards for flood control projects. Many state and federal agencies will not fund a flood control project unless it provides a 100 year level of protection (meaning that in any given year there is a 1% chance that flood flows will exceed the design capacity of the improvement and cause damage.) Communities seeking financial aid for their local protection projects are thus forced to meet state and federal design standards whether or not these standards are cost justified for the local project.

The improper determination of project sites, scopes, and levels of protection for proposed flood control projects can cause unnecessary wasting of public funds. Tax payers are thus required to shoulder the financial burden of funding proposed flood control projects without their tax revenues providing an optimal solution to their flooding problems.

WATER RESOURCES PLANNING OPPORTUNITIES

The application of computer technology to optimization techniques and problems has opened up many opportunities for water resources engineers to provide valuable consultation services. By assessing and quantifying both past flood losses and potential flood damages, engineers can provide an accurate priority assessment of flood problem areas so that sound decisions between alternative projects can be made. Computer analyses can be applied to provide an effective and efficient plan of action to alleviate flood problems. Areas where cost effective solutions are not possible would be identified and unfeasible alternatives would screened out early, thereby preventing the waste of engineering time and money. Project scopes, levels of protection, and improvement configurations providing maximum flood reduction benefits can be developed, analyzed, and presented to the public for funding.

Once optimization analyses have been completed, flood problem areas have been prioritized, optimal improvement plans have been designed, and project costs have been determined, then a longe range plan for implementation can be formulated. These plans, called flood control master plans, are valuable planning tools that water resource engineers can provide, thereby insuring that improvements can be funded and constructed in an organized and efficient manner.

The PROJECT OPTIMIZATION PROCESS

The process of optimizing flood control projects can be described in terms of these five basic steps (figure 3).

1. Identification of Flood Problems: Talk with community residents and leaders to identify existing and potential flood problem areas.

2. Preparation of a Preliminary Report: The tasks required to prepare this report are described briefly below.
a) Gather preliminary flood damage data. Interview community residents and officials to quantify flood damages.
b) Determine oppertunities, objectives, and constraints. Oppertunities associated with lakes and streams such as recreation, aesthetic beauty, and future development should be determined. Specific flood control goals and objectives should be established. Legal, environmental, social, and physical constraints should be identified to prevent unforseen negative impacts from the implementation of proposed plans.
c) Develop a list of alternative solutions.
d) Prepare a rough estimate of costs and benefits: Determine the approximate project costs and flood reduction benefits associated with the alternative solutions developed.
e) Screening: Flood problem areas and alternative solutions are analyzed by comparing project costs and benefits, and by applying the stated oppertunities, objectives, and constraints. Physically feasible and cost effective flood control projects are identified. Unfeasible and inefficient alternatives are ruled out.

3. Preparation of Input Data: Input data must be prepared for the optimization analysis process. The usual input requirements are described below.
a) Detailed flood damage assessment: Community residents and businessmen are interviewed to accurately inventory potential flood damage to structures within the flood plain. Computer analyses are utilized to process this field data into flood depth versus flood damage curves.

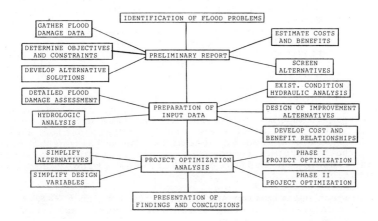

FIGURE 3.

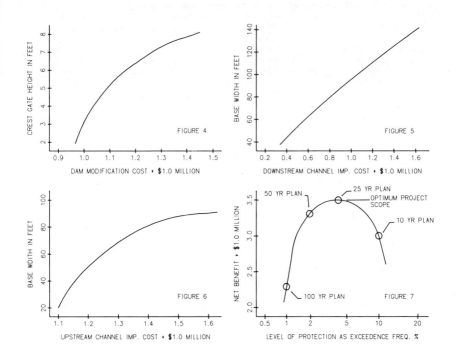

b) Hydrologic analyses: Flow versus frequency relationships are determined. Gaged and synthetic flow data is analyzed, and hydrologic simulation models are created to determine peak discharges and their chance of occurrence.

c) Existing condition hydraulic analyses: Hydraulic computer models are prepared to compute flood profiles. Flow versus stage relationships are thus determined and causes of flooding are thus readily identified.

d) Design of improvement alternatives: The hydraulic and hydrologic computer models are then used to develop and design alternative project configurations and levels of protection.

e) Development of cost and benefit relationships: Computer models are prepared to determine the relationship between alternative project components, their corresponding material quantities and costs, and their resulting flood damage reduction benefits.

4. Project Optimization Analyses: Once the input relationships have been prepared, an optimal flood control solution can be determined. This process is summarized below.

a) Simplify alternatives: The design configuration alternatives must be simplified as much as possible. Not more than 3 or 4 levels of protection should be analyzed, and improvement projects must be reduced to their basic components. The number of design parameter options to analyze should be limited. Once the total project is reduced to its basic design components and the components are in turn reduced to a limited number of design variables, optimal solutions providing the selected levels of protection can be determined.

b) Phase I project optimization: For each level of protection, the impact of each of the selected design variables on flow versus frequency, flow versus stage, and stage versus damage relationships, their corresponding project costs, and their flood reduction benefits are simaltaneously analyzed untill an optimal value is determined for each of the design variables.

c) Phase II project optimization: The optimized plans providing each of the selected levels of protection are then analyzed to determine a single optimal solution. The trade-offs between improvement costs and flood reduction benefits thus become readily apparent.

5. Presentation of Findings and Conclusions: All findings and conclusions should be presented in a clear, concise report. Planning officials can use this report to encourage community support for the proposed flood control projects, and make the necessary plans for funding and construction.

CASE STUDY

The purpose of this paper is to show how computerized optimization analyses can be applied to specific flood control needs. An actual case study will be used to illustrate how these five steps were used to develop an optimal solution for a specific problem area. The study area is a segment of the

Ramapo River located in Bergen and Passaic Counties in north-eastern New Jersey (figures 1 and 2.) The study area begins at the Pompton Lake Dam, a concrete wier that creates a 200 acre lake used for water supply and recreation. The study reach continues upstream for approximately 3.5 miles (5.6 km) where the river passes through several residential communities. There are approximately 340 homes and 18 businesses susceptable to inundation by flood flows. The proceedures and analyses applied to this study area are described below.

1. Identify Flood Problems: The study area has experienced significant flooding. Every year the Ramapo River tops its banks causing extensive damage for area residents and businessmen. The largest floods of record resulted from storms occurring in May 1968 and in November 1977. The 1968 storm caused an estimated $1.5 million in damages, and damages from the 1977 storm were in excess of $3.9 million.

2. Prepare a Preliminary Report: Several preliminary studies have been conducted to determine the feasibility of providing flood protection for this area (reference 9.) In those reports the needs and oppertunities of the area were studied, and five plan objectives were determined.

1) Reduce the flood hazzard, and the associated flood damages along the Ramapo River.
2) Insure the structural stability of the Pompton Lake Dam.
3) Maintain the existing water supply capabilities at the Pompton Lake Dam.
4) Enhance the fish and wildlife resources of the existing stream and lake environments.
5) Maintain existing open space areas and recreational oppertunities in the study area.

Several constraints were discovered for the project area. The North Jersey Water Supply Commission withdraws water from the Pompton Lake at the dam site and diverts it to the Wanaque Reservoir for distribution throughout northeastern New Jersey. Any proposed improvements to the dam would require that either the normal pool elevation of the lake be maintained, or modifications to the intake structures be provided. The Pompton Lake is also used as a recreation facility. Area residents enjoy boating, fishing, and swimming as well as the aesthetic beauty the lake provides, and proposed plans must maintain the recreational quality of the lake. The Pompton Lake and its surrounding marshes provide a habitat for many forms of life, and proposed improvement plans must minimize the disturbance to these areas and maintain existing environmental quality.

Several alternative solutions were developed for feasibility analyses. Channel and dam improvements were considered to increase the conveyance capacity of the river. The use of detention sites to reduce flood peaks was analyzed. The use of levees and floodwalls was considered to confine flood flows to the channel. Non-structural measures such as

floodproofing and relocation were also studied. Rough
estimates of project costs and flood reduction benefits were
prepared for each of the proposed alternatives to determine if
it was physically and economically feasible. It was concluded
that flood control improvement plans are feasible and
economically justified for the Ramapo River, but of all the
alternative measures analyzed, the use of channel and dam
improvements was the only feasible and efficient alternative.

3. Preparation of Input Data:

a) Flood Damage Assessment: Detailed field surveys and interviews were conducted to estimate potential flood damage for
structures within the flood plain. Flood elevation versus
damage relationships were thus developed for the study area.

b) Hydrologic Analyses: A USGS crest gage with 63 years of
record is located at the Pompton Lake Dam. A Log-Pearson Type
III flood frequency analysis (references 1 and 10) was performed to determine discharge versus frequency relationships.

c) Hydraulic Analyses: The HEC-2 computer Program (reference
6) was utilized to prepare a hydraulic model for the computation of the water surface profiles. Overbank cross sections
for input into the model were obtained using photogrammetry.
Channel sections, dams, and bridges were field surveyed. The
constructed computer model was calibrated to an historic flood
event by adjusting the mannings n values, expansion and
contraction coefficients, and effective flow area delineations.
The calibrated model can then be used to develop stage versus
flow relationships throughout the study area for all selected
recurrence intervals.

d) Simplification of Alternatives: In order to determine an
optimal flood protection plan, it was necessary to limit the
number of plan configurations considered. To reduce the number
of alternatives, it was decided to analyze only those plans
providing 10 year, 25 year, 50 year, and 100 year levels of
protection. To further simplify the optimization analyses,
improvement activities were grouped into three basic components.

The first component was the lowering of the crest of the
Pompton Lake Dam during flood peaks. From preliminary investigations it was concluded that an eight foot operating height
was the maximum that was physically feasible. It was also
decided to analyze the lowering of the crest in increments of
one foot. Thus the height of the dam crest lowering became the
first design variable to be optimized.

The second component was a downstream channel improvement
extending approximately 4000 feet (1200 m) from the top of
Pompton Lake to the bottom of Potash Lake. To simplify the
optimization analyses for this component, it was decided to
optimize only a single design variable. A fixed invert, slope,
and allignment was set. A trapezoidal channel with 2.5 on 1

side slopes was selected that would have a constant base width
for its entire length. This base width would be the second
design variable to be optimized.

The third project component was an upstream improvement
extending approximately 2200 feet (650 m) upstream from the top
of Potash Lake. The channel allignment, invert, slope, and
shape would also be fixed, and the base width would be the
third design variable to be optimized.

e) Design of Improvements: It was determined that the use of
movable spillway crest gates was the best dam modification
alternative that met all the planning objectives. These gates
would remain in the closed or up position during low flows and
would open or lower during flood peaks. Hydraulic analyses
were conducted to determine flow versus depth relationships for
the gates, and structural analyses were performed to assure the
structural stability of the proposed designs.

For the downstream channel improvement, an allignment was
determined that would minimize excavation quantities and the
disturbance to existing homes and wildlife areas. A channel
invert was selected that was consistant with that of the
Pompton Lake, and a slope was selected to minimize channel
erosion and sedimentation. A trapezoidal channel section with
grassed 2.5 on 1 side slopes was selected to facilitate
construction and insure stable channel banks.

For the upstream channel improvement, an invert was
selected to maintain adequate depths for boating and swimming
during periods of low flow. A computerized erosion analysis
was performed (reference 8), and it was determined that
hazardous channel velocities could occur during peak flows.
The proposed channels would therefore be lined with riprap to
prevent erosion.

f) Development of Cost Relationships: In order to compare
alternative plans in terms of their cost it is necessary to
develop cost curves relating the size of the project component
to its cost. For this project analysis costs had to be
determined for each of the three project components. Costs for
the proposed modifications to the Pompton Lakes Dam were
determined as a function of the crest gate height and are shown
graphically in figure 4. Costs for the proposed upstream and
downstream improvements were determined as a function of the
base width and are shown in figures 5 and 6.

g) Development of Benefit Relationships: In order to compare
alternative project configurations in terms of thier benefits,
it is necessary to analyze the reduction in expected annual
flood damage provided by each alternative. This reduction is
known as the innundation reduction benefit. The HEC-EAD
computer program (reference 7) was used for this analysis. The
program requires the input of flow versus frequency, stage
versus flow, and stage versus damage relationships along the

study reach. Different improvement plans alter these relationships in different ways, providing different innundation
reduction benefits. The EAD model was used to compare the
relative flood damage reduction capabilities of each of the
alternative project configurations.

Phase I Project Optimization:

During this first phase of the project optimization
process, the impact of each of the three design variables on
flood reduction benefits and project costs was analyzed to
determine an optimal size for each of the plan components.
This process was utilized to determine optimum projects
providing each of the four selected levels of protection.

The first category of improvement plans to be optimized
was those plans providing a 10 year level of protection. A
series of trials was performed on the HEC-2 hydraulic model to
develop combinations of design variable sizes that convey the
10 year design storm. The results are summarized below:

GATE SIZE	D.S. CHANNEL BASE WIDTH	U.S. CHANNEL BASE WIDTH	PROJECT COST
2 FT (0.6 m)	80 FT (24 m)	20 FT (6 m)	$2.88 Mil.
3 FT (0.9 m)	60 FT (18 m)	20 FT (6 m)	$2.67 Mil.
4 FT (1.2 m)	40 FT (12 m)	30 FT (9 m)	$2.72 Mil.

From this series of trials, an optimum 10 year improvement
plan can be determined. Since all of the alternative
configurations provided identical levels of protection and
therefore yielded identical innundation reduction benefits, the
plan with the lowest cost was the most efficient. It was thus
determined that the second alternative improvement plan was the
most economical means of providing a 10 year level of
protection along the Ramapo River.

The other three categories of improvement plans to be
optimized were those plans providing 25, 50, and 100 year
levels of protection. Additional series of trials were
performed on the HEC-2 hydraulic model to develop alternative
combinations of design variable sizes. Using the same
procedure as was described above for the 10 year plans, optimal
improvement plans providing 25, 50, and 100 year levels of
protection were determined and are summarized below.

LEVEL OF PROTECTION	GATE SIZE	D.S. CHANNEL BASE WIDTH	U.S. CHANNEL BASE WIDTH	PROJECT COST
10 YEAR	3 FT (0.9 m)	60 FT (18 m)	20 FT (6 m)	$3.9 Mil.
25 YEAR	6 FT (1.8 m)	80 FT (24 m)	50 FT (15 m)	$4.6 Mil.
50 YEAR	7 FT (2.1 m)	110 FT (34 m)	70 FT (21 m)	$5.5 Mil.
100 YEAR	8 FT (2.4 m)	140 FT (43 m)	90 FT (27 m)	$5.8 Mil.

5. Phase II Project Optimization:

In phase I of the optimization analysis process, improvement plans providing 10, 25, 50, and 100 year levels of protection were optimized on the basis of their being the cheapest means of providing the desired levels of protection. In Phase II of the optimization analysis process, each of the four optimized plans will be further analyzed to determine a single optimal improvement configuration for the study area.

A direct comparison of the four alternative flood protection plans can be made. The total project benefit for each plan was computed as the present worth value of the average annual innundation reduction benefits. The total project cost for each plan was computed as the sum of the construction costs and the present worth value of the average annual maintenance costs. The net benefit was calculated for each of the plans by subtracting the total present worth costs from the total present worth benefits.

The relative efficiency of each of the four alternative plans was determined by comparing the net benefit values. The optimal improvement configuration is one that provides the maximum net benefits. To compare the net benefits provided by each of the alternative plans, they were plotted against the levels of protection provided. The resulting curve (figure 7) is concave down, and the optimal level of protection corresponds to the highest point on the curve.

From this phase II optimization analysis, it was determined that an improvement plan providing a 25 year level of protection provided the maximum possible net benefits for the project area. From the previous phase I optimization analysis it was determined that the optimal means of providing a 25 year level of protection to the Ramapo River study area was an improvement plan consisting of a modification to the Pompton Lake Dam involving the installation of six foot crest gates in conjunction with a downstream channel improvement with an 80 foot base width and an upstream channel improvement with a 50 foot base width.

Conclusion:

Computerized optimization analyses have become indispensable tools for the design, management, and administration of flood control projects. They allow the engineer to formulate and screen alternative solutions, make objective choices between alternative components and ultimate project scopes, design efficient improvement configurations, and compare the cost effectiveness of alternative plans. Long range flood control master plans can then be prepared so that improvements can be funded and constructed in an organized and efficient manner.

REFERENCES

1. Beard, Leo R., _Statistical Methods in Hydrology_, U.S. Army Corps of Engineers, Sacramento, Ca., January 1962.

2. Brater, Ernest F., and King, Horace W., _Handbook of Hydraulics for the Solution of Engineering Problems_, Sixth Ed., McGraw-Hill Company, New York, 1976.

3. Chow, Ven Te, _Handbook of Applied Hydrology_, McGraw-Hill Company, New York, 1964.

4. Goodman, Alvin S., _Principals of Water Resources Planning_, Prentice Hall, Inc., Englewood Cliffs, New Jersey, 1984.

5. Hydrologic Engineering Center, _HEC-1 Flood Hydrograph Package_, Users Manual, U.S. Army Corps of Engineers, Davis, Ca., September 1981.

6. Hydrologic Engineering Center, _HEC-2 Water Surface Profiles_, Users Manual, U.S. Army Corps of Engineers, Davis, Ca., September 1982.

7. Hydrologic Engineering Center, _Expected Annual Damage Computation_, Users Manual, U.S. Army Corps of Engineers, Davis, Ca., February 1984.

8. Maynord, Stephen T., _Practical Riprap Design_, Misc. Paper H-78-7, Army Engineer Waterways Experiment Station, June 1978.

9. Passaic Basin Study Group, _Interrum Report on Flood Protection Feasibility on the Ramapo River_, Phase I General Design Memorandum, U.S. Army Corps of Engineers, New York, march 1984.

10. United States Geologic Survey, "Flood Frequency Analysis for Gage #01388000, Ramapo River at Pompton Lakes, N.J.", Water Resources Division, Trenton, N.J., 1984.

COMPUTER USAGE IN OBTAINING ALTERNATE OPTIMAL SOLUTIONS FOR WATER RESOURCES OPTIMIZATION PROBLEMS

G. Padmanabhan,[*] M.ASCE
and
Ramey O. Rogness,[*] M.ASCE

ABSTRACT

Among many Mathematical Programming techniques Linear Programming formulations are abundantly used for obtaining optimal solutions in water resources planning and management. However more than one optimal solutions may exist for these problems. Typically commercially available computer codes indicate only one of them. The likelihood of alternate optimal solutions is even greater when the bounds of problems are less tight. In this paper, alternate optimal solutions of a few example LP problems are obtained using a computer routine developed for the purpose. The routine is capable of generating at least a few, if not all, of the alternate optimal solutions. The program permits the decision maker to select the alternate optimal solution that he desires in terms of the decision variable values or for other non quantifiable reasons.

INTRODUCTION

For many optimization problems in water resources planning and management, there may exist more than one optimal solution for the same objective function value by having different values for decision variables. Less tight the bounding constraints are, more is the likelihood that alternate optimal solutions exist. However, because of the combinatorial nature of the problem total generality is not

---

* Assistant Professor, Department of Civil Engineering, North Dakota State University, Fargo, North Dakota 58105

assured. While in terms of the objective function value, there is no advantage of these alternate solutions, the different possible decision variable values of the alternate optimal solutions may allow the decision-maker to pick one in preference to the other optimal solution based on considerations other than the objective function used for optimization. This may permit secondary goals or factors to be considered in decision variable value determination. Also the effort to effect a physical change in the decision variable values may be a major undertaking in the field. So the existence and knowledge of alternate optimal solutions (let alone near-optimal solutions) can be important in the decision process.

For example, consider an engineering optimization problem dealing with optimal selection of four combinations of stages for a system. There are three possible sizes and levels. The sizes represent three increasing allocations of time to be split among the levels. The levels represent three different flow arrangements for the stages. There are four sequential stages for the problem. Considering the several different sizes for the optimization problem and the number of levels, the number of alternate optimal solutions obtained for each combination (out of a total of 256 possible solutions, i.e., four things taken four at a time) are as shown in Table 1.

Generally, as the level is increased in value, the problem is less tightly bound. Thus, the less restrictive

Table 1
Number of Alternate Optimal Solutions

	Level 1	Level 2	Level 3
Stage 1	1	16	21
Stage 2	9	4	12
Stage 3	1	3	4

TABLE 2. OPTIMAL SOLUTIONS FOR EXAMPLE 1

Variable	Solution presented in ref. 1	Alternate optimal solution
h_1	101.25	100.00
h_2	102.50	102.50
h_3	103.75	105.00
w_1	0.00	250.00
w_2	0.00	0.00
w_3	500.00	250.00
Z(obj. function value)	307.50	307.50

(tight) the bounds are there appears to be more likelihood of alternate optimal solutions. However, the combinatiorial nature of the problem precludes total generality, as is shown with the effect of the value of size on the number of alternate optimal solutions. In terms of this illustration, the presence of no alternate optimal solutions for some combinations and the presence of a number (21) of alternate optimal solution gives an indication of what might occur in an engineering optimization problem. Also the decision variable values may not necessarily be close together.

Linear Programming (LP) formulation is an important class of Mathematical Programming optimization techniques widely used in water resources planning and management. In general a LP problem has either a unique optimal solution or a number of them. Enumerating all of the optimal solutions is extremely difficult, if not impossible. Nevertheless, the knowledge of the presence of even a few of the alternate optimal solutions is important for the decision - maker. Typically commercially available computer codes indicate only one of the several possible optimal solutions, although by inspecting output generated by these codes, it is possible to detect the presence of alternate optimal solutions. However, to obtain these alternate solutions using this information successively is tedious. In this paper, an experimental computer code is used to obtain alternate optimal solutions of a few example

LP formulations of water resources problems. The optimal solutions and the alternate optimal solutions obtained from a commercially available code and from the developed code respectively are presented.

COMPUTER CODE

In general a LP problem has either a unique optimal solution or a number of them. To reduce the dimensionality of the problem it is reasonable to think in terms of finite extreme point optimal solutions. Enumerating all the extreme point optima corresponds to enumeration of all extreme points lying on a hyperplane--a convex polyhedrom of dimension one less than that of the convex polyhedral feasible region. Thus the computational complexity of the problem is the same order of magnitude as that of generating all extreme points of a convex polyhedron which is known to be a significantly hard problem. Many approaches to generate all of them have not been successful computationally (2,3). Sadagopan (4) developed a computer program to generate at least some of the extreme point optima.

In this method, an optimal solution to the problem is determined first. If alternate optimal solutions exist, then one of the alternate optimal solutions is determined using a nonbasic variable with zero relative cost as the incoming variable. Using pivot operation the tableau corresponding to the new optimal solution is determined. This tableau is in turn used to generate alternate optima

that have not been generated previously. This procedure is
continued until no new optimal solution can be generated by
one step pivot operation. Since only pivot operations are
involved as in the Simplex procedure, the method works
efficiently. However, this procedure is not capable of
generating all the alternate optimal solutions. As pointed
out earlier, computational burden involved in generating
all of them using currently available methods is enormous.
Nevertheless Sadagopan's code enables the decision - maker
to choose from a set of alternate optimal solutions instead
of being forced to choose only one among them.

EXAMPLES

Three examples in the area of aquifer management from
ref. 1 are shown herein to have at least one alternate
optimal solution each. Complete problem descriptions and
the formulation of LP may be had from the original
reference. In the examples chosen the objective was to
maximize the sum of hydraulic heads in the interior wells
of the flow domain. For brevity only the solutions are
presented.

1.   The   LP   problem for the   case of a
one-dimensional confined aquifer with fixed head boundaries
at both ends under steady state conditions is chosen as the
first example. Using the same numerical values as in ref.
1 for m=500, the code indicated one alternate optimal
solution as shown in Table 2. (L=40 ft. Δx =10 ft
T=10000 sq ft/day h_o=100 ft h_4=110 ft   m=500 ft/day).

2.   The case for the steady-state two-dimensional confined aquifer with fixed head boundaries is chosen next for the required total productions of 0.04 and 0.4 ft/day (m=0.01 and m=0.10). The solutions are presented in Table 3.

(T=10000 sq ft/day Δx=1000 ft h_p=20 ft for p=2,3,5,8,9, 12,13,16,17,20,22,23).

3.   The case of transient one-dimensional linear example of confined aquifer with fixed head boundaries is taken next.   The code generated the solutions shown in Table 4.

(L=40 ft Δx=10 ft   t=0.0001 day   T=10,000 sq ft/day $h_{1,0}$=110 ft $h_{2,0}$=120 ft $h_{3,0}$=130 ft $W_{1,0}=W_{2,0}=W_{3,0}=0$ ft/day m_1=150 ft/day m_2=100 ft/day).

In example 1, while the solution presented in ref. 1 indicated W_3 to be the only pumping well, Sadagopan's code generated an alternate solution in which W_1 and W_3 were found to be pumping wells. The change of pumping wells can be exploited advantageously depending on the water requirements in the immediate vicinity of the corresponding wells. This is the same case with example 2. W_{18} and W_{19} are interchanged as pumping wells in the two solutions for both the cases of m=0.1 and m=0.01. Even intuitively, this was evident from the pattern of disposition of wells and the boundary conditions.   In example 3, the alternate optimal solution has the production of the permissible lower limits of the first and second time steps from node 1

TABLE 3. OPTIMAL SOLUTIONS FOR EXAMPLE 2

Variable	m=0.1		m=0.01	
	Solution in ref. 1	Alternate Optimal Solution	Solution in ref. 1	Alternate Optimal Solution
W_6	0.1	0.1	0.01	0.01
W_7	0.1	0.1	0.01	0.01
W_{10}	0.0	0.0	0.00	0.00
W_{11}	0.1	0.1	0.01	0.01
W_{14}	0.0	0.0	0.00	0.00
W_{15}	0.0	0.0	0.00	0.00
W_{18}	0.0	0.0	0.00	0.01
W_{19}	0.0	0.1	0.01	0.00
h_6	15.57	15.59	19.56	19.56
h_7	15.15	15.14	19.51	19.52
h_{10}	17.13	17.23	19.50	19.73
h_{11}	15.05	14.96	19.72	19.50
h_{14}	17.92	18.35	19.84	19.74
h_{15}	17.90	17.46	19.75	19.81
h_{18}	16.64	18.72	19.87	19.67
h_{19}	18.63	16.54	19.65	19.87
z(obj. function value	133.99	133.99	157.40	157.40

TABLE 4. OPTIMAL SOLUTIONS FOR EXAMPLE 3

Variable	Solutions in ref. 1	Alternate Optimal Solution
h_{11}	109.08	109.08
h_{21}	119.47	119.47
h_{31}	129.76	129.76
w_{11}	150.00	150.00
w_{21}	0.00	0.00
w_{31}	0.00	0.00
h_{12}	109.07	109.52
h_{22}	119.32	119.32
h_{32}	129.65	129.20
w_{12}	100.00	0.00
w_{22}	0.00	0.00
w_{32}	0.00	100.00
$Z=h_{12}+h_{22}+h_{32}$	358.04	358.04

and node 3 respectively, whereas in the solution reported in the reference it was always from node 1. Correspondingly there is a change in the head distribution too.

CONCLUSIONS

Though it is well known that the optimal solutions given by many commercially available LP package programs may not be unique, not many have attempted to seek and present the alternate optimal solutions for LP formulations of water resources optimization problems. The computer program used in this paper is capable of generating at least a few of the alternate extreme point optimal solutions for LP problems. Though not exhaustive, they do provide additional possibilities for the management leaving the final choice to the decision maker based on possible secondary objectives. Examples used in this paper are intentionally chosen to be simple to be illustrative. The code is being tested for large scale real life problems.

APPENDIX-REFERENCES

1. Aguado, E. and I. Remson, "Groundwater Hydraulics in Aquifer Management", Journal of Hydraulics Division, ASCE, Vol. 100, HY1, pp. 103-118, January 1974.

2. Balinski, M. L., "An Algorithm for Finding all Faces of a Convex Polyhedron", Jl. Soc. Ind. App. Math., Vol. 9, No. 1, pp. 72-88, 1961.

3. Murty, K. G., "Solving the Fixed Charge Problem by Ranking the Extreme Points", Operations Research, Vol. 16, pp. 268-279, 1968.

4. Sadagopan, S., "On Ranking the Extreme Points of Convex Polyhedra", unpublished Master's Thesis, School of Industrial Engineering, Purdue University, December 1977.

Optimizing Nonpoint Source Pollution Reduction Costs

John G. Garland III and Frank S. Tirsch, A. M. ASCE*

ABSTRACT: This study demonstrates diminishing marginal returns for spending to reduce nonpoint source pollution in Hampton, Virginia. A linear optimization program selected the best combination of management practices to minimize the cost of removing five nonpoint source pollutants -- total nitrogen, total phosphorus, suspended solids, fecal coliforms and five-day biochemical oxygen demand. Management practice options were grass swale roadways, porous pavers, detention basins, ponds and fertilizer management. A sensitivity analysis was conducted for total phosphorus to determine how sensitive overall nonpoint source pollution control costs were to key management practice data used in the linear optimization problem. Significant diminishing marginal returns occurred above 40.0 percent removal for nitrogen and 50.0 percent removal for phosphorus, suspended solids and fecal coliforms. Overall pollution reduction cost was most sensitive to the pollution removal data for grass swale roadways and ponds.

Introduction

In a recent United States Environmental Protection Agency report to Congress on nonpoint source (NPS) pollution, six of ten Agency regions specified NPS pollution as the principal cause of water quality problems (11). This report also listed urban NPS pollution as one of the most commonly cited problems. Urban NPS pollution presents a special challenge to water quality managers, because the many available pollution removal and treatment options (management practices) have cost and pollution removal characteristics which vary with land-use. This complicates selecting optimum treatment practices and spending levels. The focus of this study is on a factor which influences decisions on spending levels -- diminishing marginal returns. Diminishing marginal returns occur at the point where less pollution removal occurs per dollar spent.

This study's objectives were to find out if diminishing marginal returns would occur for spending on management practices in Hampton, Virginia and to evaluate how sensitive the point of diminishing marginal returns was to the management practice and land-use data in the problem. The sensitivity of the results to the data was evaluated to determine the importance of data accuracy. This information is essential to evaluate the reliability of the results and the effect of data assumptions.

* Master of Science Civil Engineering Degree Candidate P.O. Box 889 Langley AFB, VA 23665 and Assistant Professor of Civil Engineering Old Dominion University Norfolk, VA 23508-8546 respectively.

To achieve the diminishing marginal return objective, a linear optimization problem was created for each pollutant. These problems included the cost and pollution removal characteristics of every management practice in every land-use area. The data for the allowable pollution was set at the desired level and the problem was solved. The problem solution contained the overall cost of achieving the pollution level and a cost breakout, i.e., a list of the management practice area recommended in each land-use that contributed to the overall cost. The allowable pollution was reduced in 10.0% increments from 10.0% to 60.0% pollution reduction. This systematic adjustment provided cost and management practice data for a range of pollution removal which was used to analyze diminishing marginal returns. These results are reported in a graphic presentation of percent pollution removal and cost. The results are also presented in the form of cost per percentage pollution removal.

The sensitivity of the problem to the data was evaluated using a single pollutant. The approach was to change one data element and solve the linear optimization problem again at each of the pollution removal increments. The difference between the new (modified data) cost and the previous cost was the result of the data element change. These differences are reported for 50.0% pollution removal in the results.

Linear optimization has been used as a water quality management tool in the past. Anderson and Day (2) minimized the regional operating costs of conventional point source waste treatment with linear optimization. Revelle et al. (7) compared linear programming results to dynamic programming to show both techniques yielded essentially the same result. Smith and Morris (9) optimized water-use goals and management options using point sources as the modified management practice and dissolved oxygen as the water quality constraint. Monteith et al. (5) illustrated how to use linear programming to minimize the cost of reducing point and NPS pollution flowing into a water body.

Linear optimization model

The linear optimization approach was to minimize the cost of NPS pollution control subject to land-use and water quality constraints. The land-use constraints required the sum of all the management practices and the land where there was no recommended management practice to equal the total area in each land-use category. Water quality constraints set limits on the NPS pollution permitted in each land-use area. Without water quality limitations, no management practices were necessary and all the urban NPS pollution reached the receiving water. Making the water quality constraints more stringent, i.e., requiring larger reductions in pollutants, caused the program to select a land-use area and management practice for implementation to reduce pollution.

The objective function (Eq. 1) minimized the total cost (C) of implementing area in each of the management practice options (X_{ij})

with individual costs (Cij). The management practice options were
represented by subscript j, and the land-use categories were
represented by subscript i.

$$\text{Minimize } C = \sum_{i=1}^{m} \sum_{j=1}^{n} C_{ij}X_{ij} \quad \dots\dots\dots\dots\dots\dots\dots(1)$$

The land-use constraints required the sum of the management
practices in each land-use area i to equal the area in i (Ai) (Eq. 2).

$$\sum_{j=0}^{n} X_{ij} = A_i \quad \text{for } i = 1,2,\dots,m \quad \dots\dots\dots\dots\dots\dots(2)$$

Each hectare (ha) of management practice Xij was assigned a
fixed amount of NPS pollution that would be generated yearly (Lij).
The sum of LijXij for each land-use area was a water quality
constraint equation (Eq. 3). (This formulation creates a water quality
limitation on each of the land-use areas to more equitably distribute
the NPS reduction. A less restrictive formulation -- not used -- would
require one water quality constraint on the double summation for i and
j of LijXij.) The right side of the water quality constraint (w.q.)
was set at fixed increments. Non-negativity constraints required Xij
be greater than zero ($X_{ij} \geq 0$) because negative area was not feasible.
A detailed formulation of the problem is described by Garland (3).

$$\sum_{j=1}^{n} L_{ij}X_{ij} \leq \text{w.q.} \quad \text{for } i = 1,2,\dots,m\dots\dots\dots\dots\dots(3)$$

The result of these equations was a linear programming problem
with 40 variables and 16 constraints for each pollutant. This problem
was solved using the Linear Interactive Discrete Optimizer (LINDO) by
Shrange (8). LINDO, depending on the host computer, can solve problems
with as many as 800 constraints and 4,000 variables.

Management practice data

The management practice options were grass swale roadways
(GSR), porous pavers (PP) -- a composite management practice including
porous pavement and modular pavement, detention basins (DB), ponds
(PO) and fertilizer management education programs (FM). The land-use
categories were commercial strip, heavy industry, light industry, high
density residential, multi-family residential, central business
district, low density residential and open land.

The assigned cost of each management practice ($/ha) was based
on the management practice cost and the different characteristics of
each land-use area (Table 1). Land-use influenced cost because most
management practices could only be applied to a fraction of the total
land-use area. Other land-use factors which affected cost were length
of roadway, percentage of impervious area and dwelling unit density.

TABLE 1.--Management Practice Cost Summary in 1984 Dollars per Hectare

	Land-Use	Area[a] (ha)	Grass Swales	Porous Pavers	Pond[b]	Basin[b]	Fert. Mgt.
i\j			1	2	3	4	5
1	Comm. Strip	811	...	44,702	11,577	36,964	...
2	Heavy. Ind.	333	911	38,935	4,787	15,284	...
3	Light Ind.	249	911	27,399	4,532	14,472	...
4	High Den. Res.	700	911	38,935	22,519	71,894	141
5	Multi-Fam. Res.	109	319	12,256	22,373	71,427	469
6	Low Den. Res.	5,760	190	...	15,875	50,679	32
7	Cen. Bus. Dist.	67	...	47,587	75,582	241,312	...
8	Open Land	2,663	...	...	1,820	5,812	...

SOURCES: Hampton Roads Water Quality Management Plan (4) and Tourbier and Westmacott (10).
NOTE: Costs include equipment, material, installation, capital and maintenance factors (3). Costs converted to January 1984 dollars using the Department of Commerce Composite Cost Index. Infeasible combinations "...". No management practice options (Xi0) have no cost.
[a] Land-use data from Hampton, Virginia. 1 hectare = 2.47 acre.
[b] Volume determined by fixed inflow to area ratio. Price increased by a real estate factor in each land-use category.

These factors influenced GSR, PP and FM costs respectively.

GSR for example, can only be applied to roadways in certain land-use areas because they require wider right-of-ways and are not feasible on main highways with a high number of access roads. This led to the assumption that GSR were not applicable in commercial strip and central business districts, and they were only feasible on 20% of industrial land. GSR were not considered a management practice option for open land, because limited roadways would only provide very limited overall pollution reduction. The cost ($/meter) for GSR was obtained from the Hampton Roads Water Quality Management Agency (4). The length of roadway in each hectare (m/ha) for each land-use was multiplied by the cost ($/m) and feasible area (e.g., 0.20 for industrial land) to calculate the GSR cost per hectare.

Both the rate of pollution generation and the ability of the management practice to remove the pollutant for each land-use area were needed to create the water quality constraint. Pollution loading data was obtained from a 1978 STORM (Storage Treatment Overflow Runoff Model) analysis of the Hampton area conducted by the Hampton Roads Water Quality Agency (4).

Management practice effectiveness was expressed as the amount of pollution which would remain (kg pollution loading/ha) after the management practice was implemented. Literature values provided figures for how effective each management practice was, but the literature did not detail how extensively the management practice could be applied in each land-use hectare. For example, porous pavers (PP) are 100% effective at removing surface runoff in a parking lot by infiltration if properly designed. However, PP are not 100% effective at removing NPS pollution on a hectare of any land-use category because they can not be applied to the entire area. The PP treatable percentage of each land-use category had to be estimated based on the impervious area of the land-use categories. The effectiveness data is displayed in Table 2. For example, in Table 2 the pond (PO) management practice applied to commercial strip land-use will remove 50% of the total P, SS and FC; 40% of the total N and 20% of the BOD_5.

Both PO and DB were assumed to be applicable to all of the area in every land category. Pollution removal effectiveness was based on the removal rate of three PO systems in the local area

TABLE 2.--Management Practice Pollution Removal Effectiveness (%)

Land-Use	Poll.	GS	PP	PO	DB	FM	Land-Use	Poll.	GS	PP	PO	DB	FM
Comm. Strip	Total P	..	62	50	80	..	Multi-Family Resid.	Total P	50	17	50	80	10
	Total N	..	62	40	57	..		Total N	65	17	40	57	10
	BOD_5	..	62	20	63	..		BOD_5	73	17	20	63	..
	SS	..	62	50	70	..		SS	77	17	50	70	..
	FC	..	62	50	70	..		FC	77	17	50	70	..
Heavy Ind.	Total P	10	54	50	80	..	Low Density Resid.	Total P	50	..	50	80	10
	Total N	13	54	40	57	..		Total N	65	..	40	57	10
	BOD_5	15	54	20	63	..		BOD_5	73	..	20	63	..
	SS	15	54	50	70	..		SS	77	..	50	70	..
	FC	15	54	50	70	..		FC	77	..	50	70	..
Light Ind.	Total P	10	38	50	80	..	Cent. Bus. Dist.	Total P	..	66	50	80	..
	Total N	13	38	40	57	..		Total N	..	66	40	57	..
	BOD_5	15	38	20	63	..		BOD_5	..	66	20	63	..
	SS	15	38	50	70	..		SS	..	66	50	70	..
	FC	15	38	50	70	..		FC	..	66	50	70	..
High Density Resid.	Total P	50	54	50	80	10	Open Land	Total P	..	..	50	80	..
	Total N	65	54	40	57	10		Total N	..	..	40	57	..
	BOD_5	73	54	20	63	..		BOD_5	..	..	20	63	..
	SS	77	54	50	70	..		SS	..	..	50	70	..
	FC	77	54	50	70	..		FC	..	..	50	70	..

SOURCE: Anderson et al.(1).
NOTE: Infeasible combinations "..".
[a] GS -- grass roadway swales, PP -- porous pavers, PO -- ponds, DB -- detention basins and FM -- fertilizer management.

examined by Anderson and coworkers (1). These researchers showed PO needed a 53 m³/inflow hectare ratio (0.21 acre-inch/inflow acre) in order to achieve a 50% SS reduction. A 50% removal rate for SS for DB corresponded to a storage volume to inflow ratio of 170 m³/inflow hectare (0.67 acre-inch/inflow acre). FC were assumed to behave as particles, because most bacteria are attached to suspended solids.

FM programs were assumed to be applicable only in the residential areas since this management practice is directed toward the reduction of P and N pollution caused by excessive fertilizer application practices. The effectiveness assigned to this management practice was a 10.0% reduction in the total N and total P runoff.

Results

The plots of the data for cost and percentage of pollution removal are shown in Figs. 1 and 2. A visual inspection of the plotted data revealed linear segments in the relationships between cost and percentage pollution removal. For BOD_5, the linear range extended from 10.0% to 60.0%. Total P, SS and FC appeared linear between 10.0% and 50.0%, and linear at a new slope between 50.0% and 60.0%. Total N appeared linear from 10.0% to 40.0% and then linear at a new slope above 40.0%.

A best fit line was developed for each segment with linear regression and the slope used to calculate the cost per percentage pollution removed ($/1%). This data is shown in Table 3. When the points being measured represented costs from the same set of recommended management practices the correlation coefficient equaled 1.0, indicating that there was a perfect correlation of the data. When the correlation dropped slightly, e.g., to 0.9999, this indicated a region where a new management practice was added to the treatment set or one of the management practices was no longer recommended.

No feasible solution was possible above 57.0% removal for total N because none of the management practice options would remove more than 57.0% of the pollution load for industrial and open land.

TABLE 3.--Pollution Removal Costs (1984 Dollars)

Pollutant	Range (%)	Cost/Percent Removal ($/1%)	Pollutant	Range (%)	Cost/Percent Removal ($/1%)
BOD_5	10-60	992,603	Total N	10-40	526,510
SS	10-50	427,460		40-60	2,364,271
	50-60	1,996,428	Total P	10-50	592,273
FC	10-50	429,938		50-60	12,735,077
	50-60	2,006,944			

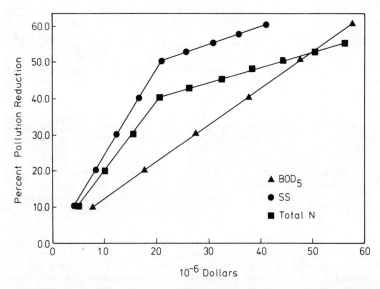

FIG. 1. Pollution Reductions Costs for BOD$_5$, Suspended Solids and Total Nitrogen in 1984 Dollars.

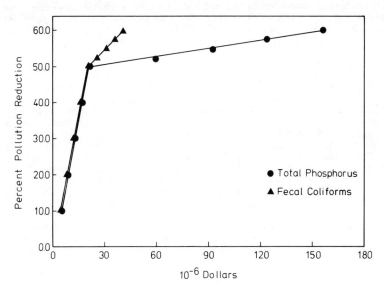

FIG. 2. Pollution Reduction Costs for Total Phosphorus and Fecal Coliforms in 1984 Dollars.

BOD_5 was the most expensive pollutant to remove in the 10.0% to 50.0% removal range, costing about 1.5 times the removal cost of the other pollutants. BOD_5 cost more to remove due to the low effectiveness of PO. Because PO were only capable of removing 20.0% of the initial BOD_5, the DB management practice had to be used in some land categories for removals higher than 20.0%. DB cost between three and four times as much per hectare as PO creating the high cost for BOD_5 pollution removal.

Above 40.0%, total N removal costs also increased due to the switch in recommended management practices to DB instead of PO and GSR in industrial areas. For SS, FC and total P, DB were not selected until above 50.0% pollution removal.

The extremely high cost of total P removal above 50.0% was caused by the requirement to implement DB in residential areas while all the other pollutants were still removed by GSR management practice. DB cost from 70 to 270 times the cost of GSR per hectare in residential areas.

The cost sensitivity analysis results are shown in Table 4. The increases in overall cost caused by the 10.0% drop in the management practice effectiveness of PO and GSR (19.56% and 154.38% cost increase respectively) at the 50.0% pollution removal level was caused by a switch in management practices. For example, to achieve a 50.0% total P pollution removal level, PO capable of removing 50.0% of the pollution could be implemented on all the land-use area (Table 2). If PO effectiveness is reduced to 45.0%, another more effective and more expensive management practice (DB) must be selected in order to achieve 50.0% pollution removal. When DB was selected to augment PO or GSR at the 50.0% pollution reduction level the cost increased greatly for each percentage of pollution removal.

At the total P removal levels examined, the greatest overall cost change was caused by changing PO cost. Increasing PO costs had a greater effect than other cost sensitivity changes because the PO fraction of the overall cost was greater. For example, for 50.0% total P removal, 4,106 ha of the total 10,642 ha were to be managed by PO and 6,444 ha by GSR. Given the distribution of these areas throughout the city and the differing costs of implementing the practices in each area (Table 1), PO cost 62.74% of the total costs and GSR 6.20%. FM was not selected at 50.0% pollution removal, so the change in FM cost had no impact on overall cost. Below 50.0% pollution removal, a 10.0% increase in FM cost changed overall cost by approximately 1%, e.g., at 10.0% pollution removal a 0.65% overall cost change occurred as the result of a 10.0% increase in FM cost.

An additional sensitivity analysis raised the effectiveness of GSR in residential areas to 80.0% for total P. The purpose of this analysis was to simulate the lack of diminishing marginal returns shown by BOD_5 with another pollutant. One of the main differences between BOD_5 and the other pollutants was GSR removal effectiveness.

TABLE 4 .--Sensitivity Analysis Summary for 50.0% Total P Removal

Mgt. Practice/ Variable	Change to All Land-Use Areas	Total Cost % Increase
Grass Swale Roadways	Lower effectiveness 10%	154.38
Ponds	Lower effectiveness 10%	19.56
Ponds	Increase cost 10%	13.57
Open Land	Raise area 20% and decrease other areas fractionally	1.45
Porous Pavers	Increase cost 10%	0.86
Grass Swale Roadways	Increase cost 10%	0.62
Open Land	Raise area 10% and decrease other areas fractionally	0.53
Fertilizer	Raise cost 10.0%	0.00
Management	Lower effectiveness 10.0%	0.00

GSR are 73.0% effective for removing BOD_5 in residential areas. Improving the GSR effectiveness to 80.0% for total P eliminated the need to recommend any other management practices in the residential land categories. This switch to one management practice for the residential areas did cause a reduction but not a complete elimination of diminishing marginal returns between 40.0% and 50.0% pollution removal. The results were similar to those shown for BOD_5 (Fig. 1).

The fraction of the open land land-use area was examined to see how sensitive the results were to errors in land-use data collection caused by using zoning data. This type of data error would occur if a 10 ha area zoned commercial strip was in fact 8 ha of commercial strip and 2 ha of open land.

Increasing open land area increased removal cost in the 10.0% to 50.0% pollution removal range and decreased removal cost above 50.0%. This occurred because the average cost of treatment of open land below 50.0% pollution removal exeeded the average cost of treatment in other land-use areas. However, above 50.0% removal the recommended practices on open land (DB and PO) were less expensive than the management practices recommended on other land-use areas.

Conclusions

Significant diminishing marginal returns did occur for all pollutants except BOD_5 at spending levels between $20 and $28 million. This spending level is too high to effect Hampton's expected NPS pollution control program, because it represents approximately 25% of the city's total expenditures.

Pollution removal costs were the sum of the costs of the management practices in each land-use category. As additional hectares of a set of management practices were added to meet the more rigid water quality criteria, a linear relationship was formed between cost and pollution reduction.

A new set of management practices was selected when the old set would no longer achieve the desired amount of pollution removal. This occurred at 40.0% pollution removal for total nitrogen and 50.0% removal for total phosphorus, suspended solids and fecal coliforms. New management practices were introduced causing a change in the cost and pollution removal relationship. Each new set of management practices was capable of removing less pollution per dollar spent than the previous management practice set thereby creating diminishing marginal returns.

The five-day biochemical oxygen demand cost per percentage removal remained approximately the same from 10.0% to 60.0% pollution removal levels. A sensitivity analysis showed this situation was caused primarily by the assumptions making grass swale roadways inexpensive and highly efficient at removing biochemical oxygen demand through 73.0% removal levels.

In general, pollution removal effectiveness was the most sensitive input variable. Decreasing management practice effectiveness caused an increase in pollution removal costs due to the increase in management practice area which had to be implemented to achieve the desired pollution reduction. In some cases the decrease in management practice effectiveness made it necessary to select a new, more expensive, set of management practices.

While this study focused on spending levels for treating urban nonpoint source pollution, linear programming is a potentially valuable tool for selecting the optimum combination of acreage for application in each management practice option. The optimum set of management practices under the assumptions of the study were similar for all pollutants. Ponds and detention basins were recommended for commercial strip. Porous pavers were recommended for central business districts. For industrial areas, grass swale roadways were recommended below 10.0% pollution removal. Between 10.0% and 50.0% pollution removal, a combination of ponds and grass swale roadways was recommended. Where five-day biochemical oxygen demand was the pollutant, detention basins were recommended instead of ponds in the 20.0% to 50.0% pollution removal range to compensate for poor biochemical oxygen demand removal by ponds. A combination of ponds and detention basins was recommended for all pollutants above 50.0% pollution reduction. The management practice recommendation below 50.0% removal for residential areas was grass swale roadways. Above 50.0% pollution reduction, a combination of detention basins and grass swale roadways was recommended. Open land treatment was by ponds below 50.0% pollution removal and a combination of ponds and detention basins above 50.0% pollution removal.

APPENDIX 1.--REFERENCES

1. Anderson, G. F., Neilson, B.J.; and Campbell, D.H., "Management Practice Evaluation for Urban Areas in Hampton Roads Vicinity," Virginia Institute of Marine Science College of William and Mary, Gloucester Point, Virginia, Aug. 1982.

2. Anderson, M. W. and Day, H. J. ,"Regional Management of Water Quality -- A Systems Approach,"Journal of Water Pollution Control Federation, Vol.40, Oct, 1968, pp. 1679-1687.

3. Garland, J. G. III, "Selecting Optimum Urban Nonpoint Source Pollution Management Practices Using Linear Programming Computer Modeling," thesis presented to Old Dominion University, at Norfolk Virginia, in 1985, in partial fulfillment of the requirements for the degree of Master of Science.

4. Hampton Roads Water Quality Agency , Hampton Roads Water Quality Management Plan, Hampton Roads Water Quality Agency, Virginia Beach, Virginia, 1978.

5. Monteith, T. J., Sullivan, R. A. C. and Heidtke, T. M., Watershed Handbook -- A Management Technique for Choosing Among Point and Nonpoint Control Strategies,EPA-905/9-84-002, Great Lakes National Program Office, Chicago, Il., Aug. 1981, pp. 50-58.

6. Northern Virginia Planning District Commission, Guidebook for Screening Urban Nonpoint Pollution Management Strategies, Metropolitan Washington Council of Governments, Wash., D.C., 1979.

7. Revelle, C. S.,"Linear Programming Applied to Water Quality Management," Water Resource Research, Vol. 4, Feb. 1968, pp. 1-9.

8. Schrange, L., Users Manual for LINDO, Scientific Press, Palo Alto, California, 1981.

9. Smith, E. T. and Morris, A. R., "Systems Analysis for Optimal Water Quality Management," Journal of Water Pollution Control Federation, Vol. 41, pp. 1635-1646.

10. Tourbier, J. T. and Westmacott, R., Water Resources Protection Technology: A Handbook of Measures to Protect Water Resources in Land Development, Urban Land Institute, Wash., D.C., 1981.

11. Environmental Protection Agency, Report to Congress: Nonpoint Source Pollution in the U.S.,436-672/879, U.S. ·Government Printing Office, Washington, D.C., 1984.

OPTIMIZATION IN WATER RESOURCES PLANNING

Lee G. Baxter, Associate Member A.S.C.E.[1]

ABSTRACT

The ability of digital computers to quickly and efficiently process complex mathematical computations has proven invaluable in engineering analysis. Heretofore, however, computer applications have largely been confined to analysis. Planning and design have generally been human functions, to be followed only later by computer aided analysis. Recently developed optimization software represents significant first steps toward the application of the digital computer as a design and planning tool. This software has recently been successfully applied to two planning studies; a power generation facility, and an irrigation distribution system. The results of these studies indicate that significant cost and time savings can be realized through application of digital computer capabilities early in the planning process.

INTRODUCTION

The ability of digital computers to rapidly process complex, and often tedious, mathematical computations has proven to be an invaluable asset to engineering analysis. The past decade has seen phenominal strides in both hardware and software development, making possible increasingly detailed analysis of more and more complex engineering systems. Modern, digitally aided, finite element and finite difference techniques make an excellent example. This software provides us with the capability to do a level of analysis that, in years past, was not only economically unjustifiable, but literally beyond conception.

This proliferation of software, however, has been largely confined to increasingly sophisticated analysis packages. Engineering design and planning have generally been reserved as human functions, to be followed only later by computer aided analysis.

Engineering design can be thought of as an iterative process. Given a problem, a designer will identify three things. First, there will be one or more objectives to either minimize or maximize. In structural applications, cost, or weight are generally objectives to be minimized. For transportation applications, it may be more important to maximize capacity. Second, a designer must identify a set of parameters that can be altered or varied to achieve the stated objective. Dimensions are probably the most common example of these parameters;

---

[1]Utah Projects Office, U.S. Bureau of Reclamation, 302 East 1860 South, P.O. Box 1338, Provo, Utah 84603

the diameter of a pipe, or the thickness, or amount of steel, for a concrete slab, for instance. The third item identified by the designer is a family of constraints that limit the fluctuation of the above mentioned parameters. Maximum allowable stress or deflection, for example, or possibly a minimum plant factor in an electrical generation facility. The design process, then, consists of selecting and iteratively varying appropriate design parameters such that the objective is minimized (or maximized) and the constraints are not violated.

Water resources planning conceptually follows a similar process. Objectives could be to maximize a benefit/cost ratio, maximize net benefits, or to minimize overall project cost. Design parameters, or variables, might be features sizes (dams, pipelines, powerplants, etc.). Constraints could be minimum (or maximum) allowable feature size, plant factor, environmental impacts, or return on investment. The task of the planner is then twofold. First, design parameters must be selected that yield a feasible solution. Once a feasible solution has been obtained, these parameters can then be varied in order to maximize or minimize the objective, all the while keeping the project feasible.

In the past, the nebulous nature of Water Resources planning has generally precluded the use of digital computer capabilities until relatively late in the planning process. A project is conceived, roughly sized, and then parceled out to various designers for final design and sizing. It is only here that digital computer capabilities begin to be seriously used, and once again, only for the analysis portion of the design process.

Regional water resources planning, however, tends to have such a large number of interrelated variables that visualization of the impact of any one on the overall project becomes very difficult. Optimal planning and design is impeded because of the sheer number of possible features and sizes. Those experienced in the application of digital computers, however, can readily see the potential for applying these tools to this semi-iterative process, if only the objective could be adequately represented by a mathematical expression.

COMPUTER AIDED OPTIMIZATION

In recent years, software packages have become available that allow the conversion of the digital computer from an analysis tool to a design and planning tool. These packages have the ability to intelligently vary the above-mentioned design parameters, thus independently driving anlaysis software toward optimal solutions. These packages represent significant first steps in moving digital computer techniques from the analysis realm into actual planning and design applications.

The author has recently been involved in the successful application of one of these commercially available packages, OPTDES.BYU, to two relatively dissimilar Water Resources planning projects.

OPTDES.BYU is an interactive, general purpose optimization program written by the Design Optimization Group of Brigham Young University[1]. OPTDES requires that the user provide what is termed an analysis subroutine. This subroutine essentially consists of a digital computer model of the design to be optimized. The subroutine must be capable of computing values for the objective and the constraints of a problem, given a family of design variables and design constraints. The variables, objective, and constraints may be related through explicit expressions, or through equations which are solved numerically (e.g. finite element techniques). The program can handle linear or nonlinear objective functions, and can deal with equality or inequality constraints. Unconstrained problems can also be accommodated. OPTDES will guarantee a global optimum for linear problems, however only local optima are guaranteed for non-linear problems. Non-linear algorithms which guarantee global optima do not presently exist.

OPTDES gives no specific limit on the number of design variables or constraints that can be used. The complexity of the mathematical relationship between the objective, the variables, and the constraints, with the resulting impact on computation time, tends to be the only limiting factor.

OPTDES follows a "directed trial and error" procedure in optimizing an objective. Design variable values are selected and fed to the analysis subroutine, which provides a value for the objective function. Various mathematical algorithms are then used to select new values for the design variables. This process is continued until a family of design variables yielding a more optimal objective function, or solution, cannot be found. For the optimization techniques to work, the objective and constraints must be assumed to be continuous and differentiable.

One significant capability of OPTDES is its capacity to use existing analysis routines. An engineer may have already developed a finite element program to analyze a particular structure. This existing program can be interfaced with OPTDES relatively easily.

OPTDES contains four optimization algorithms. Each has individual strengths and weaknesses, and will perform differently on different types of problems. The user may select any one or combination of these algorithms in optimizing a design. The algorithms correspond to a Modified Simplex method, a Generalized Reduced Gradient method, a Feasible Directions method, and an Exterior Penalty Function method. Discussion of these methods is beyond the scope of this presentation, but can be found in most modern texts on optimization theory.

---

[1]Utah Projects Office, U.S. Bureau of Reclamation, 302 East 1860 South, P.O. Box 1338, Provo, Utah 84603

OPTIMIZATION EXAMPLE

A simple example of the above process is given in OPTDES training material. Consider the problem of determining the required amounts of alloying elements to produce a steel that will minimize the cost per ton and give a specified amount of hardenability. From acquired data for this particular steel, it is known that the cost per ton is given by the following expression:

Cost($/ton) = 150 + 9.52*Mn + 20.41*Mo + 2.0*Si + 47.37*Ni + 42.64*Cr

Where Mn, Mo, Si, Ni, and Cr are the percent amounts of Manganese, Molybdenum, Silicon, Nickel, and Chromium, respectively.

The hardenability of steel can be expressed as:

Hardenability (units of critical diameter) =
    0.201 * (1. + 0.711*Si) *
    (1. + 2.18*Cr) * (1. + 3.04*Mo) *
    (1. + 3.9*Mn - 1.13*Mn**2 + 0.6977*Mn**3) *
    (1. + 0.604*Ni - 0.273*Ni**2 + 0.0814*Ni**3)

In this example, the objective function is cost per ton, the constraint is hardenability, and the design variables are the percent amounts of the various alloying materials. It is conceivable that other constraints may be the maximum (or minimum) percent amounts of the alloying ingredients.

If these two equations were written as a subroutine, passing in the variables Si, Cr, Mo, etc. and passing out the values of cost and hardenability, as well as any other constraints, the subroutine could then be linked to OPTDES. OPTDES would determine the optimum mix of alloying materials that would provide the least cost per ton, subject to some constraint on the hardenability. As mentioned above, this constraint could be a minimum value, a maximum value, or an equality.

While this example is somewhat simplistic, it does give an indication of the potential complexity of the interaction between design variables, as well as the difficulty of quickly selecting an optimum set of design variables if one is faced with any significant number of constraints.

As mentioned above, OPTDES has been successfully applied to two water resource projects. These projects, as well as the results of the optimization process, are outlined below.

THE SIXTH WATER POWER SYSTEM

The first of these projects was a hydro-electric power generation facility known as the Sixth Water Power System. The Sixth Water complex, located in Sixth Water Creek of north-central Utah, is a component of a large water resource development known as the Central Utah Project. This project, being planned, designed and built by the U.S.

Bureau of Reclamation, is to provide water for the agricultural, municipal, and industrial needs of 12 counties in northern and central Utah. The Sixth Water System develops the hydro-electric potential provided by the 2,600 foot (790 m) drop between the primary storage facility in the project and the delivery area.

Shown in Figure 1, the Sixth Water System consists of a series of pipelines, tunnels, reservoirs, and powerplants connecting the Enlarged Strawberry Reservoir and the Spanish Fork River. The system will provide approximately 166 megawatts of hydro-electric power, as well as facilitate the annual conveyance of nearly 200,000 acre-feet (250,000,000 m3) of water from its source in the Uinta Mountains (Colorado River Basin) to the population centers of the Wasatch Front of Utah (Bonneville Basin). The total annual energy output of the system is estimated to be 362,000 megawatt-hours.

The Sixth Water System is designed to provide peaking power capacity for the Intermountain West. This peaking capacity would be integrated into the Colorado River Storage Project system, which currently has a total generating capacity of about 1,500 megawatts. The purpose of the optimization study was to determine the ideal capacity of the Sixth Water Power System, weighing increased construction costs against the increased benefits resulting from greater capacity.

In order to apply the optimization process to this system, it was necessary to first determine the objective, the design variables, and the constraints. It was determined that the objective would be to maximize the annual net benefits, defined as the total annual benefits less the total annualized costs.

Due to previous decisions, it was decided that the only practical design variables in this exercise would be the pipeline, tunnel, and penstock capacities and diameters. Midway through the study, it was determined that active capacity of the lower reservoir, Monks Hollow, could also be considered a design variable. This gave a total of 13 design variables.

As mentioned above, the objective and constraints must be able to be expressed and calculated as functions the design variables. This necessitated the development of relationships to determine the size of a powerplant given only the related conduit size and capacity. This was not as difficult as it may seem, since the static head and the flow pattern could be assumed, again based on previous information. Given plant capacity, flow patterns, and calculated system losses, it was possible to compute the plant factor, energy production, and hence, the expected revenue, or benefits. It was also possible to compute the construction, operation, and maintenance costs for each feature, enabling the calculation of a total annualized cost of the system.

As it turned out, there were few significant constraints. Tunnel and pennstock velocities were restricted to 20 and 30 fps (6 and 9 m/s), respectively, and minimum allowable plant capacity factors were established for each powerplant.

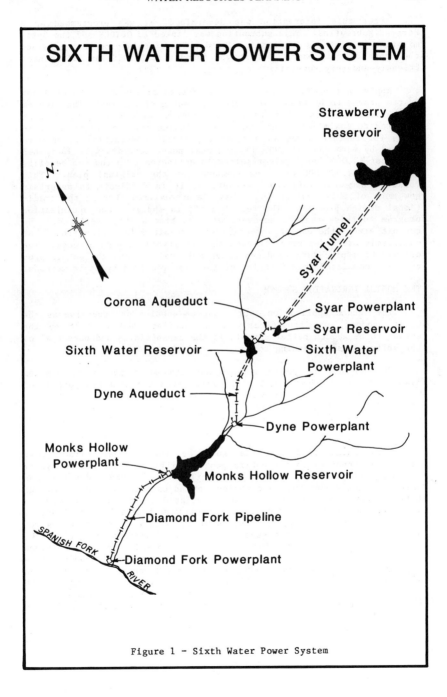

SIXTH WATER POWER SYSTEM

Figure 1 – Sixth Water Power System

After this information was determined, it was programmed as a Fortran subroutine. This subroutine was linked to OPTDES and the optimization process was completed. The details of this process are beyond the scope of this paper, but it was found that OPTDES was fairly user friendly and very versitile.

Applying the OPTDES optimization program to the Sixth Water Power System proved to be productive from a planning standpoint. The program did provide a resulting family of design variables (sizes) that appeared to maximize the net benefits. Taking original planning estimates for feature sizes as a baseline, total construction costs were lowered by more than $12,000,000. Annual power benefits were increased by almost $3,000,000. This resulted in an increase in the net benefits of almost $4,000,000/year, as compared to the original plan. This value is somewhat inflated, however, as it is difficult to ascertain how much of this savings would have been realized through the traditional design process. The real benefit in applying the optimization program to this project, however, was the time savings realized. The conduit sizes (the design variable) were required in a time frame that completely precluded going through the traditional design process. The optimization procedure produced acceptable values, and the entire process was completed in a fraction of the time required by other methods.

THE MOSIDA IRRIGATION SYSTEM

The second application, while not as massive or expensive as the power project, was considerably more detailed, and is felt by the author to be a much better example of the capabilities and potential of the software as a planning tool.

The Mosida Irrigation system consists of a series of pumping plants and canals designed to lift water from the southern portion of Utah Lake to farms and orchards near the western shore. Mosida is a part of the irrigation distribution system for the Central Utah Project, described above in conjunction with the Sixth Water Power System.

The Mosida lands provide some of the highest direct cost irrigation benefits in the entire project, therefore the Mosida system is essentially used to absorb and beneficially use any and all excess water available due to minor changes or adjustments elsewhere in the total distribution system. This translated to a need not only to determine where to put the water for maximum beneficial utilization, but to also determine which portions of the system to construct, given a less than complete water supply. This was to be done not only once, but conceivable dozens of times as planning proceeded on other portions of the project. As can be seen from Figure 2, the system involves five pumping plants, four main canals, one short canal, and has been approximated by providing for 35 canal turnouts. The weighted average pump lift for the entire system is about 180 feet. As defined, each turnout has the capability of using the water for up to three different crops, with a different benefit for each crop.

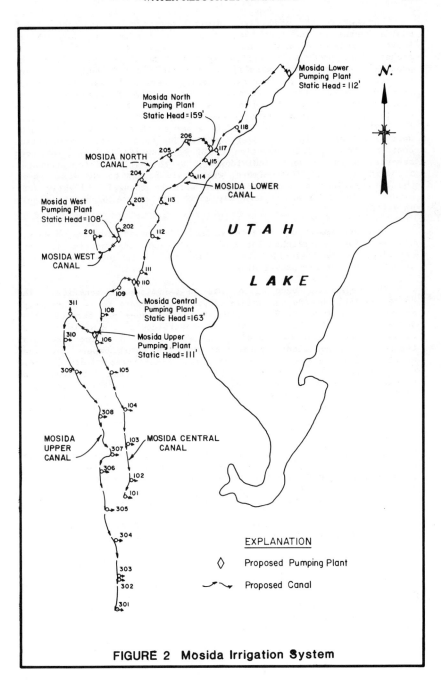

FIGURE 2 Mosida Irrigation System

The key to the need for a digital optimization approach to the Mosida system is the fact that as one goes further up the sidehills above the lake, the pasture and farm ground gives way to orchards. The orchard land produces significantly higher benefits, but due to its proximity to the water supply, requires more canal construction and maintenance, as well as increased pumping costs. Whereas there exists over 100 possible irrigation demands, the problem of determining which combination would yield the maximum annual net benefit becomes very complex. Are the higher benefits available for the orchard lands worth the higher marginal cost to get the water to them, or is it more economical to settle for the lower benefits due to the lower construction cost required? This question could be answered for one, or even several, of the turnouts individually, but the entire system presented a formidable task. Furthermore, what would happen to the analysis if the total volume of available water were to change? Slightly less water available to an orchard may make that entire orchard's supply unjustifyable.

The development of a digital model of the Mosida complex, however, was relatively straight foreward. Although the system is very detailed, it is logically ordered, and fits well into the language structure of Fortran programming.

The objective, once again, was to maximize net benefits. The design variable became the volume of water to release to each crop type at each canal turnout (35 turnouts * 3 crop types per turnout = 105 design variables). Each variable was constrained by the maximum amount of water capable of being used by the specific crop at the particular turnout. An additional constraint was the total amount of water available for the system. The individual canal turnout volumes, computed from the values of the design variables, then determined the required feature sizes for the canals and pumping plants. These could then be used to determine all construction, operation, maintenance, and pumping energy costs. Benefits, of course, were a relatively simple function of the volume of water applied to the specific crops.

Once the model was constructed, the determination of the optimum system configuration for a given volume of available irrigation water was a relatively simple matter. The available water volume was set as a constraint, and OPTDES was allowed to distribute that water in the most beneficial manner. The upper limit of water distribution defined the boundary of the project for that volume of available water.

As it turned out, it was generally more beneficial to pass by the lower lands in favor of the more beneficial orchard areas. The total size of the system, then, became quite dynamic, with a fairly sensitive response to the total water supply available.

OPTDES proved to be valuable on the Mosida Project for quite different reasons than those given for the Sixth Water Project. Due to the above-mentioned factors, the Mosida System was subject to significant fluctuations in the total amount of water available for the project, hence significant changes in the overall project size. The ability to quickly and reliably determine total costs, benefits, feature sizes and system configuration for various water supplies became the real benefit of the optimization exercise. The difference in net benefits between the optimum water usage determined by OPTDES and the maximum development was over $730,000/year. Once again, however, it is difficult to determine how much of this savings would have been realized through continued design by traditional methods.

SUMMARY

The application of optimization software to these projects proved to be very useful from a planning perspective. Through use of the software, literally thousands of combinations of feature sizes were anlayzed. Also important were the trends that became evident during the optimization process. These trends furnished valuable information concerning the sensitivy of the objective function to individual, as well as combinations of, design parameters.

Possibly most important from a planning standpoint, however, was the ability to do the "what if's", to quickly explore a lot of alternative scenarios. What is the impact of a different interest rate on the annual benefits? Does a change in the demand pattern change the ideal feature sizes, or just require a modified operation? What happens if we try to maximize the benefit/cost ratio, or the rate of return, instead of net benefits? The software made it possible to quickly and accurately respond to these types of questions, something that would not have been possible to do by hand.

The author feels that the incorporation of computer aided optimization early in the planning process would be of significant benefit, and could result in considerable savings in both cost and time.

STUDY OF STOCHASTIC PLANNING AND DESIGN OF MULTIRESERVOIR SYSTEMS

by

M. C. Chaturvedi[1] and P. K. Bhatia[2]

Abstract

A new approach named Lumped to Discrete Programming (LDP) coupled
with constrained stochastic optimization and successive approximation
approach amongst reservoirs gives promise of subtantially reducing the
operation time and offers explicit consideration of multidimensional
multireservoir stochastic planning and design problem. The LDP starts
with all the periods of operation year lumped into two or three
intervals to be ultimately discretized in subsequent stages to actual
number of operation periods. Multireservoir problem is handled by
mutually adjusting releases / states among adjoining reservoirs.

The new approach was applied to the planning of a real life
complex system in India with four large reservoirs irrigating seven
planning zones. The year is divided into 10 day operating periods.
Study has been made for irrigation and power tradeoff with sensitivity
analysis to two cropping patterns, irrigation pattern and irrigation
level, and turbine capacity under stochastic inflows with varying
starting/ending storage states.

INTRODUCTION

Planning of multireservoirs under multiobjectives with stochastic
inflows is an important part of water resources development (1).
Linear programming and dynamic programming have generally been used in
this context (2, 3, 4). Although considerable advances have been made
both the techniques pose computational difficulties with increase in
dimensionality of the problem. Linear Programming has limitation in
its direct application to systems or constraints which are nonlinear
in nature. For nonlinear explicit stochastic optimization problems
it, therefore, requires excessivily high computational time. In such
cases, a linear decision rule has sometimes been resorted to. But the
rule reduces considerably the range of alternate feasible operating
policies and itself acts as a constraint (5).

---

1.   Professor, Indian Institute of Technology, (I.I.T.) New Delhi,
      70016.   India and Visiting Professor, University of Houston,
      University Park, Houston, TX 77004. U.S.A.

2.   Assistant Engineer. Irrigation Department. Government of Uttar
      Pradesh and Research Scholar, I.I.T. New Delhi, India.

Dynamic Programming, on the other hand, can handle nonlinear problems and is especially, suited for sequential-decision problems, but in conventional dynamic programming, the storage and computation time requirements increase exponentially with increase in state variables. To reduce dimensionality of dynamic programming, different approaches, viz. Incremental Dynamic Programming (IDP), Discrete Differential Dynamic Programming (DDDP), State Increment Dynamic Programming (SIDP), Multilevel Incremental Dynamic Programming (MIDP), Dynamic Programming Successive Approximation (DPSA), constrained Differential Dynamic Programming. (DDP) have been developed (3, 4, 6). Though the first four algorithms reduce computer storage requirement, they are not free from exponential increase in computer time and the core storage requirements. The latter two, however, have overcome the drawback of dimensionality, but computational difficulties continue for multireservoir problems, particularly with explicit consideration of hydrologic stochasticity.

A new method called Lumped to Discrete Programming (LDP) following Progressive Optimality algorithm (7) has been developed. Its computational efficiency is tested for a single reservoir for deterministic case. It is then extended to a multireservoir case and computational efficiency is tested for 4 and 10 reservoir multireservoir single objective case as studied in literature. Next stochastic planning is developed. Finally, applications are made to a large scale system under multiobjectives. Progressive optimality algorithm has also been used by Turgeon (8, 9, 10) but both the basic approach and scheme of decomposition of multireservoirs is different and further multiobjective analysis has also been carried out.

LUMPED TO DISCRETE PROGRAMMING (LDP).

Considering the case of a single reservoir, reduction in computation time has been achieved by starting optimizations with all the periods of operation horizon lumped, as the case permits, into two or three intervals. The discretization of lumped intervals is done in subsequent stages of optimization to ultimately arrive at the actual number of total discrete operation periods. At every stage of discretization, best trajectory is obtained by applying non-overlapping progressive optimality algorithm. The optimizations proceed over consecutive non-overlapping two intervals for deciding best level of intermediate storage with respect to ending storages of the two intervals. At the end of each trial, a locally improved trajectory is obtained which is used as an initial trajectory in the next trial of optimizations till the convergence criteria at full discretization stage are fulfilled. The optimization-runs through lumped to full discretization stage yield a trajectory quite close to the optimal trajectory using very small fraction of a total computation time.

During the process of optimization at each stage of discretization, the level of intermediate storage for two consecutive intervals is changed by a value delta (Δ). With the same value of Δ, trials are carried out till the convergence criteria are met. After this, the value of Δ is reduced and optimization is carried out for the next stage of discretization. The approach is diagrammatically shown in Fig. 1. The proposed LDP algorithm for single reservoir problems has been extended to solve problems of integrated operation of multireservoir systems by mutually adjusting releases/states, successively, among adjoining reservoirs (10). The flow chart for multireservoirs is shown in Fig. 2 and the details are given by Bhatia (4).

In order to test the validity of the proposed LDP approach, initially a single reservoir of about 2600 MCM live storage capacity with a 600 MW variable head power plant was considered as shown in Fig. 3(a). Using realistic data, its release policy for thirty six ten-day periods was formulated to maximize energy generation over an operation horizon of one year. This example was also solved using Incremental Dynamic Programming (IDP) algorithm. The results obtained by two algorithms programmed on ICL 2960 computer are shown in table 1. The LDP results are comparable to and on the better side than those obtained by IDP, thus validating the proposed approach.

The generalized algorithm for multireservoir analysis has been operationalized by taking a 4 reservoir and 10 reservoir problem shown in Fig. 3 (b) and (c) from literature. These examples have already been solved by other algorithms, viz. the first one by DPSA (12), DDDP (13), MIDP (14), DDP (15), and the second by DDP (15). The computational results are shown in Table I.

Table I. Comparative Computational Results

Algorithm	Returns	Execution (CPU) Time in Seconds	Computer Used
1. One Reservoir Problem			
IDP	3790.0	8.609	ICL 2960
LDP	3793.7	3.675	ICL 2960
2. Four Reservoir Problem			
DPSA (12)	401.3	30	B - 500
DDDP (13)	401.3	35.32/31.04	IBM 360/75
DDP (15)	401.2	9.63	CDC 6400
LDP	400.0	2.29	ICL 2960
3. Ten Reservoir Problem			
DDP (15)	1190.65	53.0	CDC Cyber 175
LDP	1185.37	5.89	ICL 2960

It will be seen that the proposed approach is relatively more efficient.

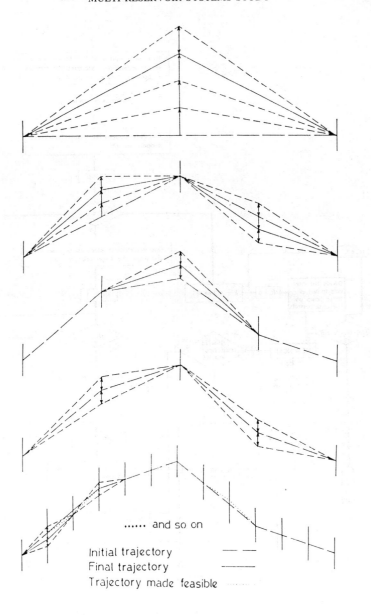

...... and so on

Initial trajectory   — — —
Final trajectory   ————
Trajectory made feasible   ....

FIG. I   PICTORIAL   REPRESENTATION   OF   THE   LUMPED   TO
DISCRETE   PROGRAMMING   (LDP)   APPROACH

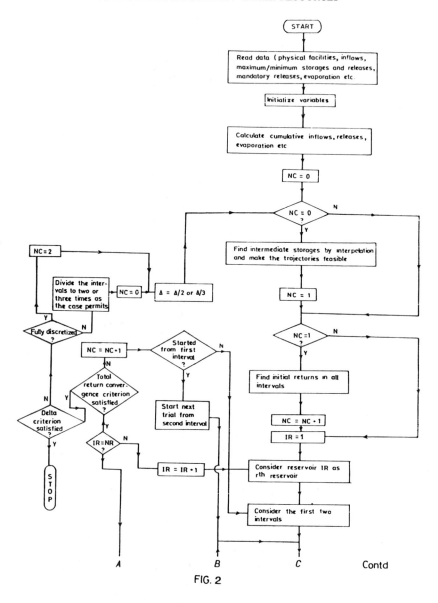

FIG. 2

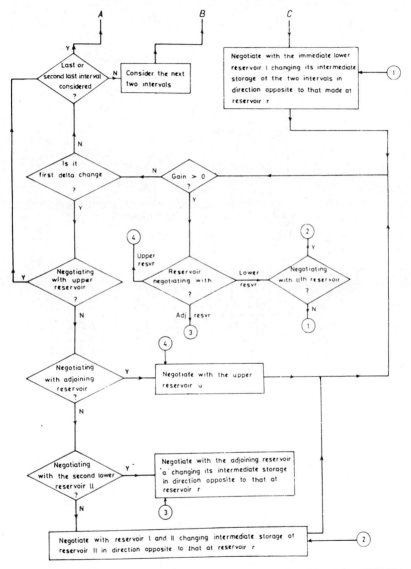

FIG. 2   BROAD FRAMEWORK OF THE LUMPED TO DISCRETE APPROACH
          FOR DETERMINISTIC ANALYSIS OF MULTIRESERVOIR OPERATION

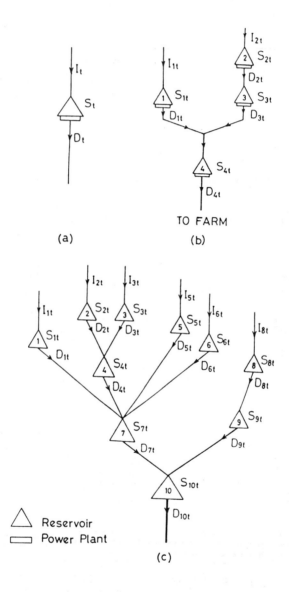

FIG. 3   SYSTEM CONFIGURATION OF ILLUSTRATIVE EXAMPLES

ALGORITHM FOR STOCHASTIC ANALYSIS

The stochasticity of natural streamflows, treating flows as lag-1 Markov process, has been considered through a constrained approach. The best trajectories obtained through deterministic analysis for certain percentage water availability levels are taken as initial trajectories corresponding to operation reliabilities, each equivalent to the respective water availability percentage. The algorithm starts at full discretization stage using this as initial trajectory. The basic approach of optimization is similar to deterministic case. It differs mainly in the evaluation of returns. For a particular reliability level of operating the system, three possible inflows corresponding to the availability levels of more than, equal to, and less than the reliability level have been taken. It leads to reduction in search, from considering all possible inflows and reservoir states simultaneously which otherwise introduces severe computational difficulties for stochastic analysis of multireservoirs operation. The flow chart is given by Bhatia (4).

The proposed approach has been applied to a four reservoir system in the Ganges basin in India serving multipurposes of energy generation, flood protection and the environmental enhancement. The deterministic as well as stochastic analyses have been carried out to obtain optimal ten day release policies to maximize annual energy generation meeting periodwise requirements of irrigation and other water requirements without letting the the reservoir storages to exceed the flood control level or violate the minimum required storage during each ten day period.

The irrigated area consists of seven agricultural zones served by the reservoir system through a complex network. Each has specific groundwater availability and conjunctive use of surface and ground waters has been used to (i) meet the irrigation requirements and (ii) maintain dynamic equilibrium of the system by avoiding groundwater mining or waterlogging. Multiobjective analysis has been carried out by studying tradeoff between agricultural and energy returns with sensitivity to two cropping patterns, level of irrigation and irrigation pattern, turbine capacity, under stochastic flows with varying starting/ ending storage states.

CONCLUSION

Following work in multireservoir multiobjective stochastic planning, an efficient method has been developed and applied in the context of a major complex real life system of four very large reservoirs serving seven command areas for irrigation in the Gangetic basin in India adopting realistic but hypothetical data.

APPENDIX 1 - REFERENCES

1. Chaturvedi, M.C., "Large Scale Water Resources Systems Planning - Approach and Case Study", ASCE Water Resources Planning and Management Division Specialty Conference, Computer Applications in Water Resources, Buffalo, NY, June 1985.

2. Chaturvedi, M.C., "Systems Approach to Water Resources Planning and Management", Tata - McGraw Hill, New Delhi, (due) 1985.

3. Yeh, W.W-G., "State of the Art Review: Theories and Applications of Systems Analysis Techniques to the Optimal Management and Operation of a Reservoir System", Water Resources Program, University of California, Los Angeles, 1982.

4. Bhatia, P.K., "Modeling Integration of Multipurpose Multireservoir Water Resources Systems", Ph.D. Thesis, Indian Institute of Technology, New Delhi, 1984.

5. Loucks, D.P., and P.J. Dorfman, "An Evaluation of Some Linear Decision Rules in Chance Constrained Models for Reservoir Planning and Operation", Water Resources Research, Vol. 11, No. 6, pp. 777-782, Dec. 1975.

6. Yakowitz, S., "Dynamic Programming Applications in Water Resources", Water Resources Research, 18(9), 673-696, 1982.

7. Howson, H.R., and N.G.F. Sancho, "A New Algorithm for the Solution of Multistate Dynamic Programming Problems", Math. Programming, Vol. 8, pp. 104-116, 1975.

8. Turgeon, A., "Optimal Operation of Multireservoir Power Systems with Stochastic Inflows, Water Resources Research, 16(2), 275-283, 1980.

9. Turgeon, A., "A Decomposition Method for the Long-Term Scheduling of Reservoirs in Series", Water Resources Research, 17(6), 1565-1570, 1981.

10. Turgeon, A., "Optimal Short-Term Hydro Scheduling from the Principles of Progressive Optimality", Water Resources Research, Vol. 17, No. 3, pp. 481-486, 1981.

11. Chara, A.M., "Optimal Sequencing and Operating Policies of Multipurpose Multireservoir River Basin Projects", Ph.D. Thesis, University of Roorkee, India, 1982.

12. Larson R.E., "State Increment Dynamic Programming", American Elsevir, New York, 1968.

13. Heidari, M., V.T. Chow, P.V. Kokotovic and D.D. Meredith, "Discrete Differential Dynamic Programming Approach to Water Resources Optimization", Water Resources Research, Vol. 7, No. 2, pp. 273-282, April 1971.

14. Nopmongocal, P., and A. Askew, "Multilevel Incremental Dynamic Programming", Water Resources Research, Vol. 12, No. 6, pp. 1291-1297, 1976.

15. Murray, D.M. and S.J. Yakowitz, "Constrained Differential Dynamic Programming and its Application to Multireservoir Control", Water Resources Research, Vol. 15, No. 5, pp. 1017-1027, Oct., 1979.

SOLVING A STATE ENVIRONMENTAL AGENCY COMPUTER MAZE

William A. Gast*

ABSTRACT

This discussion relates the experiences of a state
environmental agency in addressing a decade of inadequate attention
to the importance of computers and automated data processing to
the agency's planning, management and regulatory responsibilities.
When the problem received the attention of the agency head, a
special task force of user representatives was organized to
examine the direction of current and future computer systems
development, to establish policy and management direction for
computer operations and systems development, and to optimize the
agency's financial and staff investment.

The task force identified seven problems and recommended
remedial measures for each.

Fortunately, management was committed to solving the
computer maze and in fact implemented, to the extent practicable,
the recommendations of the task force; the results have been
quite favorable. Out of the task force process itself has grown
a greater cooperative spirit among those involved, namely the key
participants in the agency's daily EDP activities. That cooperative commitment at the user level combined with focused commitment
from management has resulted in significant progress toward
elimination of the EDP maze.

Background

In order to understand the nature of the EDP** problems
related in this discussion, it is helpful to first have a picture
of the Agency*** which encountered those problems and subsequently
took the actions necessary to erradicate them. Like the environmental agencies in many states, this Agency was formed at the
height of the environmental movement, in the late 1960's to early
1970's, in fact in 1970, through the merger of parts or all of
several existing agencies, including those concerned with both
management and regulation of the state's air, land and water
resources.

---

*Chief, State Water Plan Division, Pennsylvania Department of
Environmental Resources, P. O. Box 1467, Harrisburg, PA 17120
**EDP - Electronic Data Processing
***The author has been employed in the Pennsylvania Department of
Environmental Resources or its predecessor since 1969, and has
fifteen years experience in the development and use of EDP
systems in a water resources planning and management program.

This merger brought together an array of program organizations, many of which had related responsibilities. Generally,
the regulatory functions were organized into one Office within
the Agency and the management functions were organized into a
second Office. Those two offices, dwarfing the additional administrative and legal offices, comprised the majority of the Agency.
The Agency's early years were marked by autonomy on the part of
program directors and resistance to effective cooperation and
coordination toward furthering the Agency's overall EDP goals.
The effects upon EDP activities throughout the Agency were to be
felt for nearly ten years as individual program areas continued
to independently pursue their own EDP systems, many of which had
been initiated prior to the merger.

By 1980, a computer had been purchased and an EDP
Bureau had been given oversight responsibility for EDP actions
agency-wide. In fact, the EDP Bureau had absorbed all the EDP
staff from the other program areas of the agency. The move
toward centralization of EDP functions was seemingly solving no
problems, however.

A Charge to Identify the Problem

In 1980, the Agency's head took action to check the
proliferation of independent fragmented data base information
systems. He established a Computer Task Force, comprised of
program level EDP users from throughout the Agency, ten in all,
representing perhaps twice as many user program areas. The Task
Force was charged to establish the Agency's policy and management
direction for computer operations and systems development and to
optimize the Agency's financial and staff investment. The members
were to develop short and long range management plans for implementation of Agency information systems development policy.

Certain ground rules or limitations were established by
the Agency head. First, the Agency would remain committed to
retention and development of the main frame computer operation.
Remember that the Agency had only very recently purchased its own
main frame, the costs for which had not yet been fully paid by
the Agency. Those costs were in fact already escalating as the
development of unanticipated systems was necessitating the acceleration of planned hardware expansion. There was apprehension about
growing computer budgets infringing upon payroll funds as the
Agency faced annual budget tightening. This concern, in fact,
constituted the second ground rule--budget projections indicated
limited or nonexistent overall personnel and funding expansions
for the Agency. Third, the EDP industry was projecting shortages
of qualified programmers, which would limit or make prohibitively
expensive, the development of customized software systems at
least through the 1980's. This was significant, in that the
trend throughout the Agency had to date always been toward customized
software systems. The final ground rule was that the Agency
could not afford to continue to develop or operate numerous,
fragmented, massive data base information systems, and there
should be a reduction of independent program information systems.

In addition to ground rules and preconditions, the Task
Force was provided with a rather lengthy list of "perceived"
problems which it was to investigate. The emphasis is on perceived,
because as determined through subsequent Task Force investigations
and discussions, many were actually symptoms rather than ills.

The Agency head made quite clear his personal commitment
to the effort. The supervisors and managers of all Task Force
members were informed in writing that the effort was of top
priority in the Agency and that full time devotion by the Task
Force members was expected for three or four days per week for up
to six weeks and that total cooperation from all other Agency
staff was expected.

The Task Force, in its first few meetings developed an
extensive list of problems, including those which had been provided
with the charge. The list was scrutinized to determine those
which were real and those which were perceptual. Real problems
were reduced to those which were of Agency significance; many
applied to specific program areas and were not amenable to an
Agency solution. The Task Force agreed with unanimity on seven
problem areas which should be addressed in an Agency policy for
EDP development.

Upper Management Decision-Making And Commitment

Perhaps the most important problem identified was the
lack of upper management decision-making and commitment to information
systems. Largely as a result of the manner in which the Agency
was formed and the concomitant autonomy of individual program
directors, data processing decisions were frequently being made
by lower level management. Unfortunately, their decisions in
many cases exceeded their authority to commit resources. Deputies,
who oversaw Offices and answered directly to the Agency head, had
limited authority to commit money and manpower resources over
multi-year periods. Bureau directors and their subordinate
Division chiefs had no such authority, and yet it was at those
two lower levels that most data processing decisions were being
made, including decisions regarding development of major data
base systems which could span two, three or more years.

In other areas, where a program bureau or division had
no computer-knowledgeable staff of its own, the Agency's EDP
Bureau was forced to make critical data processing decisions by
default. The EDP Bureau, trying to please everyone, quickly
found itself over-committing its own staff resources. The resultant lack of timely response was cause for considerable dis-
gruntlement among the user program areas who relied upon them for
systems development and maintenance.

For the Task Force a solution was obvious. Vest the
decision-making process in top level management, who had the
authority to establish priorities among the various program
Bureaus and to then commit for necessary periods of time, both

the personnel and money resources required to effect EDP actions consistent with those priorities. The Task Force agreed that the Agency head would not want burdened with such a time-consuming responsibility. However, the Deputies also met the prerequisites: therefore, they should act jointly as an Agency Systems Steering Committee to prioritize and authorize data processing systems development and operations within the agency.

The Deputies could:

1. Commit both personnel and funds on a multi-year basis,
2. Establish program and system priorities between, within and throughout their own Offices, and
3. Approve long-range plans within their Office.

The Systems Steering Committee would review all proposals for new EDP systems. Based upon the findings of a preliminary study to be conducted jointly by the EDP Bureau and the user bureau, the Steering Committee would assign a priority and staff resources to conduct either a detailed system study if warranted and/or final design of the system. With full cognizance of the EDP Bureau's staff resources and commitments and the funding capabilities of the user bureau, the Committee would also decide which systems should be developed in-house and which should be contracted.

The Steering Committee should have available at all times the resources of the Director of the EDP Bureau; at the same time he should be removed from decisions of the Steering Committee, lest he become arbitrator in split decisions of the Steering Committee, thus returning to his bureau the burdens of making inappropriate decisions. The Task Force recommended that he act as executive director for the Steering Committee and not participate in any decisions of the Committee.

Program Level Management Commitment To EDP Systems

A second problem identified by the Task Force was the lack of management commitment to information systems at the program level. After the EDP Bureau absorbed the EDP-related personnel from throughout the Agency, most program bureaus were left with few or no computer-knowledgeable staff. They were suddenly totally dependent upon the EDP Bureau for their systems development and maintenance needs. This resulted in communications breakdowns between the program bureaus and the EDP Bureau and failure to define true systems needs. No person within the program bureau was available to provide liaison with the EDP Bureau; consequently the EDP Bureau was being forced to define program needs and develop systems recommendations for the program areas without the program areas having a clear understanding of what their program needs actually were.

To alleviate this problem, the Task Force recommended that within each program area, a program systems coordinator function be established to provide full-time liaison with the EDP Bureau. The function should have or be delegated the authority level of the Bureau director in order to assume the following responsibilities:

1. Control, define and establish real program needs (needs vs. wants)
2. Define and communicate program needs to the EDP Bureau
3. Perform the role of Liaison (communicator and translator) between the program and the EDP Bureau's project manager
4. Be the sole point of contact within the program area for all information systems development functions.

With the limited resources available, it was important that "needs" rather than "wants" be addressed. The program systems coordinator, being a staff member within the user bureau would be better able to make those determinations. He would then be the sole point of communication between the EDP and the user bureaus. The EDP staff would not be faced with conflicting positions from several user staff. A single liaison would also help insure that all EDP activity within the user bureau was coordinated.

Commitment to Systems Planning

Through the process envisioned by the Task Force, EDP needs would be identified within program areas. Then the Program Systems Coordinator would initiate discussions with the EDP Bureau to conduct a preliminary study of the needs and determine feasible EDP solutions and estimated costs. Anticipation of this planning process posed a third problem to the Task Force, a lack of commitment to systems planning. In order for the EDP Bureau to participate in the preliminary project phases there needed to be established within that Bureau a planning function, supported by the necessary staff resources, which would be responsible for 1) preliminary project studies, 2) preparation of five-year EDP plans for the Agency, 3) development of internal programming and systems standards and documentation, 4) preparation of an annual EDP Inventory for the Agency, and quite importantly 5) pro-active systems planning. Most of those responsibilities were being handled on an impromptu basis with little or no long-term commitment.

The preliminary project studies would be key to the envisioned process because it would be the results of those studies which would be presented to the Systems Steering Committee in order to secure their determination of priority and commitment of resources to complete the EDP project.

Pro-active planning was needed to address the unrecognized EDP needs of program areas which had no program systems coordinator sufficiently computer-knowledgeable to recognize potential applications of EDP processes to improve operations within the program area. This was a problem in many areas of the Agency.

Commitment To Systems Maintenance

At the time the Agency's EDP staff were all absorbed into the EDP Bureau, there was a subsequent negative reaction throughout the program areas from which they were drawn. While much of the reaction may have been "sour grapes" there was legitimacy for the concern that maintenance of existing operational systems faltered. The EDP Bureau was overwhelmed by requests to continue development of those systems which were already underway, to develop new systems for program areas who previously had no EDP staff of their own and now saw the EDP Bureau as a new vehicle to address their EDP needs, and to maintain existing systems. Offering greater appeal, systems development won out over maintenance. This was and always is unfortunate, because without a maintenance commitment most systems are doomed to partial if not total collapse and failure.

Of great importance is the recognition that probably no system can meet exactly the needs for which it was designed. This is true because the user seldom if ever fully understands his needs. His success in relating his needs to the EDP staff can never be perfect and the EDP Bureau's attempts to develop a solution to those needs can likewise never be perfect. Even if perfection could be achieved in all those respects, needs, particularly in an environmental agency with ever changing laws and regulations, are a "moving target" subject to gradual change.

It is important that the user feel confident, once his system is implemented and he begins to identify its shortcomings, that steady progress will be made toward rectifying those shortcomings. The speed with which those shortcomings may be corrected is not so important as the feeling on the part of the user that something is being done to correct them. It is important that he understand when his problems may be eliminated. This sense of progress can only be provided by the knowledge that resources, regardless of the amount, are committed to maintenance.

The Task Force recommended that maintenance of operational EDP systems should be established as the top priority for utilization of resources within the EDP Bureau. Little benefit would be derived from management effectiveness in pursuing the most efficient systems if those systems were to fail, after expenditures of valuable resources, due to the lack of commitment of sufficient resources to maintaining their usefulness and workability.

Uniformity Among EDP Systems

Historically, systems development responsibility in the
Agency was fragmented among various bureaus. This resulted in
incompatabilities between the many EDP systems which existed.
While total integration of all or some of those systems or even
of future systems into one common system showed little promise of
being either practical or achievable, partial integration of some
systems could be expected to provide worthwhile benefits to
management. It was recognized that even limited integration of
the existing systems could be achieved only at considerable cost.
In some cases the short term costs of revising data processing
procedures for the existing systems would be intolerable, even if
the long term benefits were expected to exceed the costs.
Integration of existing systems needed to be approached cautiously.

The Task Force recommended that upper management determine
their decision-making needs; whereupon the Steering Commiteee
should then approve common definitions, identifiers and data
processing procedures necessary to achieve those needs. Integration
of existing systems should be pursued only to the extent necessary
to satisfy management's most essential data needs.

Recognizing the long term benefits of systems integration,
the Task Force agreed that future systems should be integrated to
the maximum extent practical. Short term integration costs are
negligible if integration is designed into systems during their
early developmental stages rather than after implementation has
been completed. Management's needs as well as practicality
should be the determining factors in decisions regarding integration of future systems. The Task Force recommended that the
Agency pursue the integration of future information systems to
the maximum extent needed and practical.

Revisions To The EDP Project Management System

The Task Force considered three additional problems
which were in a sense not quite so general or broad in scope, but
rather were specific to the particular circumstances. One was a
problem which did not actually exist but rather would be created
by the implementation of the previous recommendations.

The Agency had in place at the time an EDP Project
Management System which was described in an EDP Project Management
Manual. Since the recommendations put forth by the Task Force
would revise many of the procedures in the Project Management
System, it would be necessary to revise as well the manual.

It was widely felt among the Task Force that the existing
system and its manual were arbitrarily conceived and flavored
with EDP Bureau biases, since the EDP Bureau had developed them
single-handedly. In order for the new manual to enjoy wider
acceptance among the user community, the Task Force recommended
that the Steering Committee appoint a committee of EDP Bureau

staff as well as representatives from the user bureaus to rewrite the Project Management Manual to conform to the recommended new procedures. The new manual was to address the new Steering Committee role in the project development process as well as better reflect user perspectives of the process.

It was a commonly held feeling among the user community that the EDP Bureau was forcing too many EDP decisions in their own behalf and giving greater consideration to their own concerns than to the users' needs. Removal of key decision-making functions from the EDP Bureau to the Steering Committee, where the user community was better represented, as recommended previously, was the key to solving this problem. Clear definition of that decision-making role in the Project Management System Manual was essential. A committee composed at least partially of users would ensure that the manual would better reflect user perspectives of the project development process.

Review of Existing Manpower Requirements

The Task Force members had identified what they felt were the key problems, which if properly remedied would significantly reduce the ineffectiveness and inefficiencies of the existing EDP efforts and activities in the Agency. One problem remained yet to be addressed, however, and the perception of this problem was probably the most significant driving force behind the creation of the Task Force. That problem was the lack of sufficient EDP manpower to handle all the Agency's needs. While nothing the Task Force could do would change the levels of manpower available, it was at least generally agreed that the recommendations provided so far would serve to direct the manpower toward efforts that would best serve the user community and thus quell temperaments among that community.

The best possible product which could result from the Task Force effort would be a clear move toward cooperation rather than competition between the EDP Bureau and the user community. A clear definition of manpower availability, manpower requirements, and allocation of manpower resources based upon a concensus of agreement among the users would achieve more positive results than all the administrative changes combined. The user community needed control of their own destinies and needed some control of EDP staff resources. The Steering Committee, representing the user community, would control decision-making and achieve that important goal.

The Task Force recommended that the Steering Committee conduct an immediate study of EDP needs Agency-wide and assign EDP staff resources to address those needs according to a clearly defined schedule.

Conclusions

The experiences related herein all revolve about a central theme--autonomy. We begin with decentralized autonomy and an agency in which EDP decisions and activities are occurring independently and to the long-term detriment of efficient Agency operations. An initial solution was centralization of manpower and the decision-making processes within an EDP Bureau. The unfortunate result of this solution was a widely-felt perception of centralized autonomy, which appeared to generate more conflict than cooperation. By pooling its resources in a specially assigned Task Force, the Agency was able to examine the roots of its EDP ills and solve a somewhat complex maze of problems to embark on a path of greater cooperation leading toward better achievement of overall Agency goals and objectives through the aid of powerful electronic data processing systems.

In this case the solution involved centralization of EDP staffing and EDP planning, systems development and maintenance functions, but decentralization of the decision-making process so that the entire user community in a more democratic forum could decide priorities for use of EDP resources.

THE ADP PROBLEMS OF A RIVER BASIN COMMISSION

by George J. Lazorchick

ABSTRACT

The Susquehanna River Basin Commission is an independent governmental agency that recently acquired its first in-house minicomputer system. The staff usage of this system has created two types of problems which are described in detail. Solutions to the problems have been found in some cases, but the elimination of the problems has yet to be achieved.

INTRODUCTION

The Susquehanna River Basin Commission is a four party, Federal-Interstate agency created through legislation by the States of New York, Maryland, and Pennsylvania, along with the Federal Government. This Commission was created in December 1970 and charged with overseeing the conservation, utilization, development, management, and control of the water resources of the 27500 sq mile (71225 sq kilometer) river basin. Figure No. 1 shows the general location and features of the Susquehanna Basin.

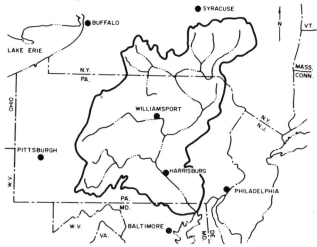

Figure No. 1 - The Susquehanna River Basin

1. Hydraulic Engineer, Susquehanna River Basin Commission, 1721 North Front Street, Harrisburg, PA 17102

The members of the Commission are the Secretaries of the New York Department of Environmental Conservation, the Pennsylvania Department of Environmental Resources, The Maryland Department of Natural Resources, and the U.S. Department of Interior. Each member of the Commission is represented by a designated alternate. Each member has an equal voice in the actions, decisions, and directions of the Commission.

The day to day operations of the Commission are carried out by a full time staff of approximately 27 people. This staff is made up of administrators, engineers, planners, water quality specialists, technicians, and clerical personnel spread throughout five different operating groups, namely the Executive Division, the Administrative Services Division, the Staff Services Division, the Planning and Operations Division, and the Resource Quality Management and Protection Division.

DESCRIPTION OF COMPUTER SYSTEM

In December of 1983 the Commission took delivery of an in-house minicomputer system valued at approximately $58000. The system hardware consists of five intelligent terminal workstations, a 20 megabyte Winchester hard disk, a high speed magnetic tape streamer, a six pen graphics plotter, a 150 cps dot matrix printer, a 55 cps letter quality printer, and a 300/1200 baud auto answer modem. The system is capable of reading from and writing to both 5.25 in (133.4 mm) and 8 in (203.2 mm) floppy disks. The major system software consists of a word processing package, an electronic spread sheet package, a screen editor, a data manager package, both FORTRAN and BASIC languages, a graphics package, and a telecommunications package. Figure No. 2 shows the layout of the system along with the amount of random access memory installed in each workstation.

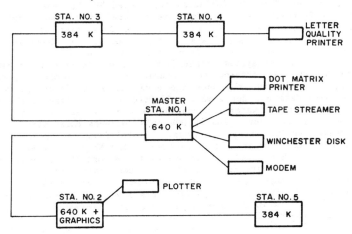

Figure No. 2 - The SRBC Minicomputer System

This equipment has greatly enhanced the Commissions automated data processing capabilities. It supplements a single IBM Displaywriter which was acquired in October 1982 and essentially replaces an HP 9830 programmable calculator which has been in use since May of 1975.

INSTITUTIONAL PROBLEMS CREATED BY COMPUTERIZATION

There are two types of problems that have surfaced as a result of the Commissions acquisition of a minicomputer system. The first type can be called "external institutional" problems and they arise as a result of the Commissions automated data processing interactions with other agencies. The second type are identified as "internal institutional" problems. These are the numerous problems that are created within the Commission as staff becomes more and more familiar with the inhouse computer system, resulting in steadily increasing usage. Each type of problem will be discussed in detail.

EXTERNAL PROBLEMS

The first example of an "external" problem concerns data gathering. Most of the Commissions ongoing programs use various types and amounts of data. This data includes streamflow records, groundwater levels, land uses, electrical generation records, precipitation and other climatic data, water use information, etc. In order to conduct basinwide analyses of water resource management problems, these types of information must be gathered for the entire basin. This is where the problems arise. For example, if an analysis required surface water usage data for the entire basin, several different sources would have to be tapped. Some water usage data in the State of New York are collected and stored by the Department of Health. In Pennsylvania, these data are gathered by the Department of Environmental Resources. In Maryland, the Department of Natural Resources and the Maryland State Geologic Survey are the agencies responsible. Generally, these data are stored on each individual agencies own computer system. Therefore, in order to access the data the Commission must attempt to communicate with several computer systems. In addition, the data are never in a consistent format. Also, the same data are not always collected by every agency. The PA DER collects surface water consumption data regardless of what the water is being used for. The NY DOH only collects consumption data for licensed public water suppliers. Industrial, commercial, and agriculture usage data are not considered in the NY DOH system. This may cause a fourth or even a fifth agency to be contacted in order to gather all the necessary information. In some cases even contacting all the proper agencies is not sufficient. For example, the Commission had to conduct its own water use inventory in the New York portion of the basin because this type of information was not available from any other source. This style of data gathering can easily snowball into a major time consuming operation. A similar situation exists with respect to geohydrologic data. The PA DER tries to maintain records on all water wells drilled in the state. This

information is submitted to DER by the company that actually drills
the well. However, this system is totally voluntary and many wells
are drilled with no report being filed, or, if a report is filed it is
often sketchy and incomplete. The situation is similar in Maryland
with one slight, but critical, difference. Every water well drilled
in the State is permitted by the Department of Health and Mental
Hygiene. One of the conditions of the permit is the mandatory
completion and submittal of a very detailed information form. This
information is then entered into the Departments computerized data
base. This presents problems for the Commission. Any basinwide
groundwater analysis has very detailed information for one part of the
basin and somewhat less detailed information for another portion.
Unfortunately, in most cases the more specific data generally suffers
when it is combined with the poorer data. In either case, when all
the data are retrieved, more time must be spent putting the
information into a consistent format for use in the Commissions basin
wide analyses. It is very easy to see how data gathering and
reformating can quickly become a very large part of any project.

The second example of an "external" problem concerns applications
programming. Commission staff interacts closely with personnel from
many different agencies while working on the various programs of the
Commission. During the course of these projects staff often finds
that other agencies have developed small, very specific computer
programs which would be useful in some portions of the Commissions
work. Since these programs are not copyrighted or protected in any
way, copies can be made and used by the Commission. Again, problems
generally arise. The program is usually developed on an operating
system that is not compatible with Commission equipment. Secondly,
the program may be written in a language that is not installed on the
Commissions system. Thirdly, even if the languages are the same the
program may not work because different "brands" of the same language
often perform differently. Therefore, there is generally some amount
of time spent in modifying programs in order to make them operational
on the Commission system. The time necessary could vary anywhere from
several hours to several months, depending on the complexity of the
problem. In general, "swapping" programs is not as easy as it sounds.

INTERNAL PROBLEMS

The Commissions acquisition of a minicomputer system has created
many "internal" problems as well. The first problem that cropped up
concerned staff training and prior computer experience. When the
Commission purchased the new equipment several training sessions were
included. It was intended to have almost every member of the staff go
through an initial "how to" course for both the word processing and
spreadsheet software. These lessons were supposed to ensure that
everyone would use the system in the proper manner. The problem was
that about half of the staff had some prior computer experience,
either on mainframe computers or on home personals. These people,
either consciously or unconsciously, felt that they did not need to be
instructed on the basics of some of the software packages. Instead,
some of these people immediately began to explore the full range of
all the software applications rather than paying attention to the

basic operations of the system. This resulted in their "going off" on their own tangents while the people with no prior experience were learning the proper techniques. Invariably, these people would develop problems and had to be assisted by the instructor, causing numerous disruptions to an otherwise well structured class. This left the majority of the class sitting until the problem was solved. Consequently, the instructional time that was purchased was not used to its greatest advantage.

Secondly, the decision was made that the management of all the Commissions computer resources would be placed in the hands of a four person committee with one person selected to chair the committee. In retrospect, a four person committee was too large. This committee has since been reduced to two people, which seems to be ideal. The committee established user guidelines so that the newly acquired equipment would be equally available to all staff desiring to use such. The committee is also responsible for the day to day operations of the system and the purchasing of supplies. The committee also coordinates advanced training and is charged with recommending the purchase of both software and hardware as it is needed. Management by committee is fine, but a single person still should be designated and recognized as a system administrator. This person would be mainly responsible for system software changes and operating system modifications. The administrator would also be responsible for the general "upkeep" of the system and should be the sole contact between the computer resources of the agency and all other parties, both inside and outside the agency. Currently, the committee chairman takes care of all the day to day operating chores and software modifications, but there still is not a designated system administrator who is involved in all aspects of computer system business. Many times members of the staff misrepresent, misinterpret, or underestimate exactly what the systems capabilities are. Having a system administrator who is included in all aspects of computer related business would eliminate many unnecessary problems and much confusion.

Finally, there is a problem with the "acceptance" of the computerization process that has taken place within the Commission. This ranges from some members of the staff totally ignoring the equipment and its capabilities, to other staff members occupying workstations for the entire day. Either situation is not desirable. The staff members who ignore the equipment spend more time than is necessary manually performing some work tasks that are ideal computer applications. Conversely, the staff members who are always on the system are generally professionals who are doing, in part, their own basic wordprocessing and report preparation. This leaves the clerical staff underutilized and prevents other staff members from accessing the system because workstations are not being used efficiently.

SUMMARY

The acquisition of a minicomputer by the Susquehanna River Basin Commission has greatly changed the day to day routines of the Commission staff. Even though the equipment has been in place for only a year and a half, almost every member of the staff is utilizing some aspect of the systems capabilities. During a normal workday, it is often difficult to find an unoccupied workstation. Several members of the staff have taken computer programming courses on their own time in order to better utilize the newly acquired equipment. Other members of the staff have spent time developing programs and procedures to computerize work tasks that were previously done by hand. All of these are positive signs that the "computerization" process of the Susquehanna River Basin Commission is underway. At the present time, serious consideration is being given to obtaining a more powerful central processor unit and expanding the number of workstations from five to seven. There have been problems in the past and there will continue to be problems in the future, but the benefits gained through the computerization process far outweigh the problems encountered. Also, I expect the benefits will continue to increase as more and more of the systems capabilities are explored. Hopefully, the problems that are encountered in the future, both "internal" and "external", will continue to be surmountable, even though the elimination of both types of problems is probably an unattainable goal.

THE WSSC INTEGRATED SYSTEM IMPLEMENTATION PROJECT

Stephen E. Robinson

INTRODUCTION

The software development effort conducted for the Washington Suburban Sanitary Commission began in October, 1981 and has been in process since that date. The goal of the effort is to produce an integrated software environment that coordinates the efforts of three primary groups within the commission. These groups are described in the paragraphs which follow.

The Permits Processing Section is responsible for issuing permits for attachment to water and sewer mainlines. This group is also responsible for the licensing of plumbers and sewer cleaners in the Washington Suburban Sanitary District.

The Assessments Section is responsible for assessing Front Foot Benefit charges against constructed mainlines. A second responsibility is the collection of costs for deferred payment house connections.

The Maintenance Department is responsible for mainline system maintenance. Two general forms of maintenance are employed. The first form is preventive in nature, while the second form involves emergency maintenance generally triggered by customer complaint.

This paper discusses the approach taken by L. DiGioia, Manager, Information Systems Division, in establishing the project direction taken in the development of the application systems targeted toward achieving an integrated environment for these operational groups. The paper describes the statement of the situation that existed at the WSSC in October, 1981, followed by the theoretical System Development Life Cycle (SDLC) approach that was employed throughout the project. Project staffing levels are then discussed. The reasons for the success of the project are identified in the section entitled CONCLUSIONS.

STATEMENT OF THE PROBLEM

The software support at the WSSC consisted of independent application systems supporting the various groups within the commission. Software support quality varied from organization to organization. Some groups were served by relatively new systems. Others were supported by software requiring rewrite. A few organizations employed

This paper was written by Stephen E. Robinson, Principal Consultant to the WSSC Project, DBD Systems, Inc., 1500 N. Beauregard Street, #108, Alexandria, Virginia 22311.

manual systems. To upgrade these environments, it was necessary to determine WSSC organizational interrelationships in the business sense. The central problem was, "If one system is upgraded, what must be done to other systems?" The advent of fourth generation system development tools permitted widely scattered system development to occur. The impact of independent system development could not be easily determined. The primary problem areas are described in the paragraphs which follow.

New construction was supported by a limited application system. At project start-up, it was unknown to what extent the process of contract issuing, construction permit procurement and contract monitoring affected the other business activities. A specification for a Consolidated Engineering System (CES) had been written before the commencement of the integration project, but the relationship between the two projects was unclear.

The Permits Processing Section was served by a new system that assisted in the issuing of permits for mainline water and sewer system connection. New requirements had evolved since the completion of the Permits system that forced its reexamination. It was felt that plumbing inspection and support for toxic substance tracking should be included. The implementation of the CES would probably affect the Permits environment, but the nature of the change was not clearly defined.

Customer Service was served by a system that permitted ready access to the current customer database. The Customer Service system became aware of new customers when certain types of permits received their final inspection. Other relationships between the Customer Service system, Maintenance and Assessment were known to exist, but the exact nature of those relationships was difficult to quantify.

The Assessments Section is responsible for cost recovery for Mainline and House Connection construction. The mechanism used for Mainline cost recovery is the Front Foot Benefit Charge. The Assessment Section had little automated support for its activities. The data for cost recovery was contained on thousands of index cards that spanned thirty (30) years. Providing support for the Assessments Section was a primary goal of the development effort. The Assessments process was heavily interconnected with the processes of the other areas of the commission but the exact nature of those connections was unclear.

Maintenance on existing water and sewer mainlines and house connections was supported by an aging system that was in need of replacement. A second primary goal of the development effort was to produce an upgraded Maintenance system. The Maintenance system received extensive upates from the Customer Service system. The relationships existing between Maintenance and other organizations were unclear at the outset of the project.

THE SYSTEM LIFE CYCLE APPROACH

The System Development Life Cycle (SDLC) is a tool by system developers for functionally decomposing a problem into smaller parts. The life cycle steps used by the WSSC effort are described in the following paragraphs. The typical life cycle approach is expanded because of the project Multi-System and Multi-Organization scope. The creation of the Information System Plan (ISP) permitted the identification of primary relationships existing between the WSSC business groups. The ISP identified PROPERTY as a primary central concept within the commission. The existence of a central unifying concept provided a strong focus for the life cycle steps which followed. The major steps of the life cycle are described in the paragraphs which follow.

The Information System Plan (INFOMAP*)

The Information System Planning phase creates the foundation to which the subsequent life cycle steps attach. Its completion permitted the identification of key development concepts requiring follow-up tracking. It also permitted the simultaneous implementation of the primary systems of interest. Parallel implementation of the interrelated systems is always dangerous. However, if the pattern of interrelationship is known in advance, simultaneous implementation presents significantly fewer problems. At its peak, five major and tightly integrated WSSC systems were under such development. With the concept of PROPERTY identified, integration across the system boundaries required only observing how the system interfaces dealt with PROPERTY. This knowledge permitted a far more focused management effort than would have otherwise been the case.

The Detailed Requirements

The list of key transactions performed by the WSSC business areas was a primary output of the ISP. The transactions list provided the focus for the Detailed Requirements phase of the life cycle. An ISP transaction is a business perspective of a task to be performed. The Detailed Requirements phase identifies the computer support appropriate for each of those transactions. This phase can be described in the following manner.

SOFTWARE REQUIREMENT identified needed software support.

HUMAN REQUIREMENT identified what the human operator requirement was.

INTERFACE DESCRIPTION identified the report layout, screen layout, and operational keys and forms permitting the operator access to the software. The interface description is the External Design specification and is a separate deliverable apart from the Requirements document.

---

*INFOMAP is a trademark of DBD Products, Inc., 53 North Park Avenue, Rockville Centre, New York 11570.

Conversion

Conversion produces test data during system and integration testing and loads the database from current sources during Cutover. The
earliest possible time to begin the conversion effort follows the
Requirements Analysis phase. Then information is available concerning
the types of data required to support the new systems. The Conversion
sub-phases are described in the paragraphs which follow.

The first conversion task identifies the data needed to load the
database in support of the system requirements. The External Specification document is a good source of information for determining the
required data elements. The elements referenced in the External
Specification document tie to current sources of information or to
sources that will come to exist as a result of the development effort.

With data sources identified, the means of recognizing correct
occurrences of the data must be determined. For each data element, a
specific Edit and Validation (E/V) rule is constructed. The forms of
typically used rules are EDIT MASK, VALUE RANGE and VALUE LIST.

Once the E/V rules are known, the process of identifying invalid
data is next. This step usually requires programming. The WSSC Conversion team used the Data Dictionary/Directory System, IDD, to record
E/V rules for each element. The team then wrote an interpreter to
query the dictionary on a source by source basis to identify elements
that did not pass the E/V tests.

After invalid data has been identified, the principal task of
conversion begins. It is typical for large percentages of the source
files to fail the new edit and validation rules. Sometimes the percentages are alarmingly high. The following approaches are used to
resolve the validation problem. Invalid data can sometimes be automatically corrected. In these cases, programs are written to convert
one set of codes into another that do pass the edit rule.

Where translation does not apply, the end user must make the data
corrections. Sufficient time must be allocated to permit the user to
make the needed corrections before cutover. It is reasonable to expect that a large percentage of invalid data will have to be manually
corrected.

After the clean-up phase, validated data may be loaded into the
database. Load programs are written to convert validated source data
into the format acceptable to the data base design. The load programs
must be thoroughly designed, tested and documented. These programs are
useful for data maintenance long after the systems are operational.

Designing The Systems

System Design translates the Requirements into a specification
describing software which is to be implemented. The principal components are the Data Base Design and the System Design. Data Base Design
is performed by the Data Base Administration function. System Design
is performed by the System Design Team.

Data Base Design translates the data requirements into successively refined Data Structure Diagrams. The diagrams depict relationships existing between record types. During the Data Base Design process at the WSSC, about 100 such record types were identified.

The HIPO chart is the primary System Design tool and end product of the System Design step. Each transaction is translated into a chart that identified inputs, outputs and logic. Since both input and output are products of Data Base Design, the two aspects of system design clearly intertwine. The schedules of both groups must be carefully coordinated.

Implementation

Implementation translates HIPO diagrams into operating programs that are coded and tested with programmer generated test data.

Data Structure Diagrams are translated into areas, records and set relationships of IDMS, the project DBMS. This phase of the Data Base Design is called the Logical Design phase.

Testing

Testing involves many levels of product examination before cutover can occur. Although testing is identified as a separate Life Cycle phase, several levels of testing occur throughout implementation. The levels of testing are described below.

Unit testing is performed by the programmer using programmer created test data. The program cannot be submitted to the project manager until successful unit testing certified by the team leader is complete.

Subsystem testing is performed by the application team leader. During subsystem testing, the team leader creates test data and operates the subsystem examining specifically for boundary conditions. Invalid data is used to assure that the programs properly respond to those conditions.

System testing verifies that all functions perform as intended between subsystems using live test data. The system is tested with databases containing approximately 10 to 15% of the production data base. Interfaces to other systems are simulated.

Integration testing assures that system interfaces work properly. Again, about 10 to 15% of the production data is used for this stage of testing. The project manager conducts integration testing.

Parallel testing involves the end user and 100% of the data complement is used. The end user performs the test in parallel with the normal production workload. Errors encountered are fixed and parallel testing continues.

Cutover

The final copy of the current conversion data is loaded into the database and current system activity stops.

STAFFING THE PROJECT

The WSSC project was broken into three phases to facilitate staffing. The steps of the life cycle were mapped across the three phases to be discussed in the paragraphs which follow.

The Information System Plan

The information system planning phase was staffed through most of the effort by four persons. The effort required about six months. The major efforts are described in the paragraphs which follow.

The personnel conducting the interviews consisted of a consultant from DBD Systems, Inc. and two members of the commission's Data Base Administration (DBA) staff. The fourth member was supplied by the commission Internal Auditing Staff. Thirty-five (35) interviews were conducted across all levels of WSSC management. Each interview required one day to complete on the average. A team of two people was assigned to each interview team.

A four member team performed the ISP analysis phase. During this 2 month period, the analysis team identified the WSSC Business Functions, Data Classes and the business function triggering transactions. On completion, the map of business activity provided an excellent overview of the principal activities occurring within the WSSC. Additionally, the analysis step provided a high level data structure chart detailing the WSSC information interrelationships. This view was helpful during the Data Base Design activity which was to occur during the design and implementation phases.

The third phase 1 step established the long range plan to guide the development teams for the remainder of the project. A Standards guide, Implementation guide, Training guide and Project Organization guide were produced during the final two month period of the phase. Four people were employed for this task during this two month period.

Requirements And Design

The Requirements and Design phase was completed in 11.5 months. Four teams were fielded during the Requirements step. Each team was responsible for one area. The four areas were Permits Processing, Assessments, Customer Service and Maintenance.

The project management staff consisted of the Project Manager and the Project Principal Consultant. These two individuals monitored project progress, completeness of deliverables and provided general guidance in matters of procedure and WSSC business area interface, and reported directly to the Manager, Information Systems Division.

The DBA function began its primary activities during the External
Design step of the phase. During this step, data elements were
identified and entered into the Dictionary. Each screen and report
produced by the project teams was evaluated for data elements. Careful
organizational control over Dictionary input reduced the defined number
of redundant elements substantially. As central names were assigned,
they were published for project team use. 1500 elements were added to
the Dictionary during the External Design step. Over 700 external document deliverables were examined for element content. Each deliverable
contained 20 element references on the average. The Data Base Administration team consisted of three persone, each responsible for processing the elements produced by his or her assigned project team.

Requirements documents were produced for the four areas mentioned
above. This step required three persone for each of the four systems
for four months. Upon completion, the Customer Service area was
dropped due to budgetary constraints.

External Design specification production required three persons
for six weeks for each of the three remaining projects. The specification produced report, form and screen layouts for an average of 100
programs per project. The programs split between online and batch
modes with about two thirds online.

Detailed System Design

The Detailed System Design step was completed in six months. Four
persons were assigned to each of the three project teams. HIPO diagrams and related descriptive information documenting the batch reports
and the online screens were produced. In many instances, the online
screens for updating and modification required both pre-display and
post-response diagrams. Each diagram was tracked through scheduled
start, scheduled finish, actual start, actual finish, subsystem start
and subsystem finish. Over 700 individual tasks were tracked during
this six month step.

The DBA was responsible for two functions during System Design.
The first function provided detailed central definitions for data
elements to the project teams. The second function produced the database design for the three projects before the start of the Implementation phase. These functions are described in the paragraphs
which follow.

The DBA group drove its schedule of activities on a two week cycle
in advance of the project teams. The intent was to assign central
names to the elements required by the programs to be designed during
the next two week period, and to update the dictionary with element
usage information. To accomplish this task, the project teams submitted in advance the programs that would be designed during each two
week period until the end of the design step. The schedule thus became the central link between the DBA and the project teams. Slip-
pages were submitted at the end of each two week cycle, and the
schedule was openly distributed. On receipt of the bi-weekly workload
from the project teams, the DBA group verified element usage and
resolved any differences. At the end of each reporting period, a new

copy of the Dictionary was produced for use by the project teams. During this phase, the 1500 defined elements were reduced to about 800.

Data Base Design bridged the end of System Design and Implementation start. During this three month period, individual project databases were created and integrated. The staffing for the design effort included the Data Base Design team member and members from the Project team. In several instances, the end user participated in final reviews. The Data Base Design was first proposed by the team Data Base Designer and then reviewed by the project team. The second review consisted of representatives from all teams.

Implementation

Project Management consisted of a single individual. This individual established a program production schedule, created a stable machine environment, and stabilized the Data Base Design. Throughout the initial months of the Implementation phase, these factors were in a state of flux, but were brought under control during the fourth month of the phase.

DBA consisted of two persons during Implementation. This group enhanced the Data Base Design as changes arose, provided a stable processing and test environment for the project teams, determined the space requirements for the data base load for parallel testing, and assisted the conversion team with the data base load for subsystem, system, integrated and parallel testing.

The Application Development teams remained staffed at four persons per team throughout the duration of the implementation phase. Each project team produced an average of 100 tested programs during the next 1.5 years of the phase.

Conversion

The Conversion team consisted of three people. The effort remained active for over two years.

CONCLUSIONS

Certain factors played significant roles in the WSSC project. The notable factors are identified below.

The Benefits Of ISP

The effects of the ISP throughout the project cannot be over-emphasized. The study provided a structure upon which the project was constructed. Literally thousands of ideas jelled into one working integrated system thanks to that initial effort.

The Need For Detailed Planning

The steps of the External Design Specification, Detailed System
Design, Data Base Design and Implementation phase made extensive use
of detailed task oriented charts produced from the Project Plan.   In
each case, tasks were identified that consisted of no more than two
person weeks. These tasks were plotted and monitored at the formal
bi-weekly status meeting where non-completed deliverables were examined a deliverable at a time. This examination produced a high
degree of project awareness on the part of the participants.

The Sleeper, Conversion

Although WSSC Management was well aware of the possible impact of
the Conversion on the successful and timely completion of the project
and took steps to start the Conversion effort at the earliest possible
time, Conversion is causing scheduling problems for the Assessment
System. The thirty years of manual cards and procedures is a significant problem. The entire compliment of data is required to produce an effective system, and little can be done to streamline the
Conversion process. The manual system appears to have more exceptions
than rules. Each of these exceptions must be incorporated into the
Conversion programming if a successful Conversion effort is to be
performed.

GROUNDWATER MODELLING

George F. Pinder*

Introduction

The numerical simulation of groundwater flow and transport has
evolved from a technical curiosity to a established method of hydrological analysis. In this brief review the progress that has been
made in this technological area over the past two decades will be
summarized. While groundwater modelling may appear to be a relatively
narrow topic, it has many dimensions. Consequently, this overview will,
unfortunately, be less than exhaustive and the references provided
are meant to be indicative rather than all encompassing.

Groundwater modelling can be subdivided into flow modelling and
transport modelling. Each of these topics will be considered
separately, because their physical and mathematical attributes are
distinctly different. Let us begin with the simplest problem formulation, saturated groundwater flow.

Groundwater flow in the *saturated zone* has been modelled using
many novel approaches. Drawing on the analogy between electrical
current and porous medium flow, very large arrays of resistors and
capacitors were construction to simulate flow in groundwater reservoirs.
Only with the advent of widely accessible digital computers did
numerical models displace electrical analog models.

The equations describing saturated groundwater flow are easily
approximated. Thus they are amenable to solution by even the most
primitive numerical procedures. Moreover, the resulting set of
algebraic equations are linear and the matrices well behaved. It is
not surprising therefore that saturated flow problems were among the
earliest to be considered numerically [1-6]. Because of their
mathematical robustness and the relative simplicity of their field
application, such models are now widely used by groundwater hydrologists.
While transient two dimensional models remain the mainstay of the
modelling community, very efficient three dimensional codes are now
available [7-8].

Simulation of the *unsaturated flow* is considerably more
challenging than simulation of saturated flow. Not only are the
governing equations non-linear and consequently more difficult to
solve, but also the constitutive relationships required for a complete
description of the problem are very difficult to determine. Neverthe-

*George F. Pinder, Dept. of Civil Engineering, Princeton University,
Princeton, New Jersey 08544.

less, at about the same time as groundwater hydrologists were
developing saturated flow models, soil physicists and hydrologists
were independently developing models for flow in the unsaturated zone
[9-14]. Although it is necessary to approximate the unsaturated flow
equations with great care because of the difficulties associated with
their non-linearity, nevertheless, finite difference, finite element
and even collocation algorithms have been developed. While these
models are less ubiqitous than their saturated counterparts, multidimensional unsaturated flow models are available [15].

While unsaturated flow is normally simulated assuming a static
air phase, models exist that accommodate a dynamic air phase. Such
two phase models are becoming of increasing importance with the
enhanced concern about transport of contaminants in the unsaturated
zone. Although two phase models are well known in the oil industry,
they have only recently been introduced into the groundwater literature
[16].

With the discovery of non-aqueous phase organic compounds in
both the unsaturated and saturated zones, there evolved the need for
a *three phase* fluid flow simulator. Such models are well known in the
oil industry [17-18] but only recently have appeared in the water
resources literature [19-20] and they are not widely disseminated.
Mathematically very complex, only models based upon finite-difference
formulations are currently available.

Contaminant transport, while conceptually and mathematically
relatively straight-forward, is quite difficult to model numerically.
Early groundwater transport models focused on the problem of salt-
water intrusion [21-23]. More recently the emphasis has shifted
to forecasting the movement of chlorinated hydrocarbons [24-30].
Many clever numerical strategies have been used in an attempt to
obtain a satisfactory solution to the transport equation. However,
a computationally efficient yet rigorous algorithm that has general
applicability eludes us. In addition, recent experiments have cast
some doubt on the validity of the transport equation itself in certain
field situations.

Whereas the inclusion of adsorption in the transport equation is
relatively straightforward, the rigorous accommodation of *chemical
and biological reactions* is generally difficult. To date only a few
such problems have been analyzed. The existing models are formulated
using finite element, finite difference and collocation approximations
[31-33]. An important aspect of simulating transport with chemical
reactions is the large system of coupled non-linear equations that
arise. Clever, computationally efficient algorithms must be formulated if cost effective and robust models are to become routinely
available.

Recently non-aqueous phase organic solvents have been observed
in the groundwater system at several field locations. These observations have precipitated a need for models capable of describing the
dynamics of three phase flow (water, air, non-aqueous phase liquids)
when the organic phase is slightly miscible. While the completely
immiscible problem is well known to the oil industry, the slightly

miscible case appears unique to groundwater flow. Models capable of
treating the immiscible case are beginning to appear in the groundwater
literature[19] but the more complex slightly miscible problem has only
recently been addressed [20].

A problem closely related to contaminant transport is that of
thermal energy transport. The single phase case with temperature
dependent density is computationally closely related to the problem of
salt-water intrusion wherein the fluid density depends upon the
chloride concentration. Both finite element and finite difference
formulations of this problem may be found in the literature [34-36].
A much more computationally challenging variant on this theme is the
simulation of steam water behavior such as encountered in geothermal
systems. The equations describing this system are highly nonlinear
and constitute a difficult computational problem. Nevertheless,
multiphase geothermal reservoirs have been modelled successfully,
principally using finite difference methods [37-38].

The simulation of *ice water systems* has received increased
attention in recent years. The porous flow physics and thermodynamics
attendant to this problem make it both theoretically and computationally challenging. Recent papers addressing this problem have
approximated the non-linear partial differential equations using
finite element theory [39].

The simulation of *flow through fractured media* remains one of the
most vexing problems in subsurface flow. Although fractured reservoirs
play an important role in oil production, geothermal energy production and the transport of contaminants in the subsurface, their
behavior is poorly represented by our current suite of models. The
problems in this case center around the formulation of the governing
equations and the field measurement of the resulting constitutive
parameters. There are two schools of thought regarding fractured
reservoir simulation [40-47]. One school maintains that it is
necessary to represent, at least in principal, the geometry and hydrodynamic properties of each fracture. The other believes that
fractured media should be viewed as continua and that the basic concepts of continuum mechanics provide the mathematical vehicle for the
formulation of the governing equations. The Achilles' heel of both
approaches is the determination of the constitutive parameters.

The *inverse problem* is the term generally used to describe the
determination of fluid flow and transport properties of a reservoir
based upon an observed distribution of hydraulic heads and concentrations [48-52]. Because the principal focus of this conference is this
topic, it will not be further dealt with herein.

The last problem to be considered is *simulation under uncertainty*.
The uncertainty in question derives from our inadequate knowledge of
the geohydrological system. Constitutive parameters such as hydraulic
conductivity can only be established approximately and at a limited
number of spatial locations. The uncertainty in these parameters

should be accommodated in the simulation. In such a simulator the uncertainty in the input data would result in an uncertain output or solution. The analyst would therefore be able to make the decision maker aware of the influence and importance of the modelling uncertainty. In spite of the potential significance of modelling with uncertainty, very few models are capable of its accommocation. Several mathematical approaches to the problem have been tested [53-57], but a computationally efficient, robust and generally applicable strategy has yet to be formulated.

REFERENCES

[1]   Remson, I., C. A. Appel, and R. A. Webster, "Groundwater Models
        Solved by Digital Computer", J. Hydraulic Div. Amer. Soc.
        Civil Eng., 91 (HY3), 133-147, 1965.

[2]   Bittenger, M. W., H. R. Duke, and R. A. Longenbaugh, "Mathe-
        matical Simulations for Better Aquifer Management", Pub. No.
        72 IASH, 509-519, 1967.

[3]   Freeze, R. A. and P. A. Witherspoon, "Theoretical Analysis of
        Regional Groundwater Flow; 1. Analytical and Numerical
        Solutions to the Mathematical Model", Water Resour. Res. 2, 641-
        656, 1966.

[4]   Pinder, G. F. and J. D. Bredehoeft, "Application of the Digital
        Computer for Aquifer Evaluation", Water Resour. Res. 4, 1069-
        1093, 1968.

[5]   Javandel, I. and P. A. Witherspoon, "Application of the Finite
        Element Method to Transient Flow in Porous Media", Soc. Pet.
        Eng. J., 8, 241-252, 1968.

[6]   Zienkiewicz, O. C., P. Meyer and Y. K. Cheung, "Solution of
        Anistropic Seepage Problems by Finite Elements", Proc. Am. Soc.
        Civ. Eng. 92 (EM1), 111-120, 1966.

[7]   Babu, D. K. and G. F. Pinder, "A Three-dimensional Hybrid Finite
        Element-Finite Difference Scheme for Groundwater Simulation",
        10th IMACS World Congress on System Simulation and Scientific
        Computation, Montreal, 292-294, 1982.

[8]   Huyakorn, P. S., "Techniques for Making Finite Elements Com-
        petitive in Modelling Three-Dimensional Flow and Transport"
        Proceedings of the 5th Intern. Conf. on Finite Elements in
        Water Resources, June 1984, 187-197, 1984.

[9]   Klute, A., "A Numerical Method for Solving the Flow Equation
        for Water in Unsaturated Materials", Soil Sci., 73, 105-116, 1952.

[10]   Day, P. R. and J. N. Luthin, "A Numerical Solution of the
        Differential Equation of Flow for a Vertical Drainage Problem",
        Soil Sci. Soc. Am. Proc., 20, 443-447, 1956.

[11]   Youngs, E. G., "Moisture Profiles During Vertical Infiltration",
        Soil Sci., 84, 283-290, 1957.

[12[Whisler, F. D. and A. Klute, "The Numerical Analysis of Infil-
        tration, Considering Hysteresis into a Vertical Soil Column
        at Equilibrium Under Gravity", Soil Sci. Soc. Am Proc. 29,
        489-494, 1965.

[13]   Rubin, J., "Theoretical Analysis of Two-Dimensional, Transient
        Flow of Water in Unsaturated and Partly Unsaturated Soils",
        Soil Sci. Soc. Am. Proc. 32, 607-615, 1968.

[14] Freeze, R. A., "Three-dimensional, Transient, Saturated-Unsaturated flow in a Groundwater Basin", Water Resources Res., 7, 347-366, 1971.

[15] Yeh, G.T. and R.H. Strand, "FECWATER: User Manual of a Finite Element Code for Simulating Water Flow through Saturated-Unsaturated Porous Media", ORNL Report TM-7316, pp. 237, 1982.

[16] Green, D. W., H. Dabiri, and C. F. Weinaug, "Numerical Modelling of Unsaturated Groundwater Flow and Comparison to a Field Experiment", Water Resources Res., 6, 862-874, 1970.

[17] Roebuck, I. F., G. E. Henderson, J. Douglas, Jr., and W. T. Ford, "The Compositional Reservoir Simulator: The Linear Model", Soc. Pet. Eng. J., 9, 115-130, 1969.

[18] Coats, K. H., "An Equation of State Compositional Model", Soc. Pet. Eng. J., 20, 363-376, 1980.

[19] Hochmuth, D. P., "Two-phase Flow of Immiscible Fluids in Groundwater Systems", M.S. thesis, Dept. of Civil Engineering, Colorado State University, Fort Collins, Colorado, pp. 100, 1981.

[20a] Abriola, L. M. and G. F. Pinder, "A Multiphase Approach to the Modeling of Porous Media Contamination by Organic Compounds - Part I: Equation Development", Water Resources Res., (in press).

[20b] Abriola, L. M. and G. F. Pinder, "A Multiphase Appraoch to the Modeling of Porous Media Contamination by Organic Compounds - Part II: Equation Development", Water Resources Res., (in press).

[21] Pinder, G.F. and H. H. Cooper, Jr., "A Numerical Technique for Calculating the Transient Position of The Saltwater Front", Water Resour. Res., 6, 875-882, 1970.

[22] Reddell, D. L. and D. K. Sunada, "Numerical Simulation of Dispersion in Groundwater Aquifers", Hydrol. paper 41, Colorado State University, Fort Collins, Colorado, 1970.

[23] Segol, G. and G. F. Pinder, "Transient Simulation of Saltwater Intrusion in Southeastern Florida", Water Resources Research, 12, 62-70, 1976.

[24] Pinder, G.F. and J. D. Bredehoeft, "Application of the Digital Computer for Aquifer Evaluation", Water Resources Presearch, 4, 1069-1093, 1968.

[25] Oster, C. A., J. C. Sonnichsen and P.T. Jaske, "Numerical Simulation of the Convective Diffusion Equation", Water Resour. Research, 6, 1746-1752, 1970.

[26] Pinder, G. F., "A Galerkin-Finite Element Simulation of Groundwater Contamination on Long Island, New York", Water Resources Research, 9, 1657-1669, 1973.

[27] Guymon, G., "A Finite Element Solution of the One-Dimensional Diffusion Convection Equation", Water Resources Res., 6, 204-210, 1970.

[28] Duguid, J. O. and M. Reeves, "Material Transport in Porous Media: A Finite Element Galerkin Model", Oak Ridge National Laboratory, ORNL-4928, pp. 198, 1976.

[29] Shamir, U. Y. and D. F. Harleman, "Dispersion in Layered Porous Media", J. Hydraul. Div. Amer. Soc. Civil Eng. 93, 237-260, 1967.

[30] Orlob, G.T. and P.C. Woods, "Water Quality Management in Irrigation Systems", ASCE J. Irrig. Drain. Div., 93, 49-66, 1967.

[31] Rubin, J. and R. V. James, "Dispersion-affected Transport of Reacting Solutes in Saturated Porous Media: Galerkin Method Applied to Equilibrium-controlled Exchange in Unidirectional Steady Water Flow", Water Resources Res., 9, 1332-1356, 1973.

[32] Nguyen, V.V., G.F. Pinder, W. G. Gray, and J. F. Botha, "Numerical Simulation of Uranium In-Situ Mining", Water Resour. Program Report 81-WR-10, Princeton University, Princeton, N.J., 1981.

[33] Sykes, J. F., S. Soyupak and G. F. Farquhar, "Modelling of Leachate Organic Migration and Attenuation in Groundwater Below Sanitary Landfills", Water Resources Res., 135-145, 1982.

[34] Aziz, K., P. H. Holst and P. S. Kanra, "Natural Convection in Porous Media", Pet. Soc. C.I.M. Paper 6813, presented at 19th Annual Technical Meeting, Calgary, Alberta, Canada, 1968.

[35] Mercer, J. and G. F. Pinder, "Galerkin Finite-element Simulation of a Geothermal Reservoir", Geothermics, 2, 81-89, 1973.

[36] Henry, H. R. and J. B. Hilleke, "Exploration of Multiphase Fluid Flow in a Saline Aquifer System Affected by Geothermal Heating", Final Report to U. S. Geological Survey by the Bureau of Engineering Research, University of Alabama, 1972.

[37] Faust, C.R. and J.W. Mercer, "Geothermal Reservoir Simulation, 1. Mathematical Models for Liquid-and Vapor-Dominated Hydrothermal Systems", Water Resour. Res., 15(1), 23-30, 1979.

[38] Faust, C.R. and J.W. Mercer, "Geothermal Reservoir Simulation 2. Numerical Solution Techniques for Liquid-and Vapor-Dominated Hydrothermal Systems", Water Resour.Res., 15(1), 31-46, 1979.

[39] O'Neill, K. O. and R. D. Miller, "Numerical Solutions for a Rigid-ice Model of Secondary Frost Heave", CRREL Report 82-13, pp. 11, 1982.

[40] Russell, D. G. and N. E. Truitt, "Transient Pressure Behavior in Vertically Fractured Reservoirs", Trans AIME, 231, 1159-1170, 1964.

[41] Kazemi, H., "Pressure Transient Analysis of Naturally Fractured Reservoirs with Uniform Fracture Distribution", Soc. Pet. Eng. J., 9, 451-462, 1969.

[42] Wilson, C.R. and P.A. Witherspoon, "An Investigation of Laminar Flow in Fractured Porous Rocks", Dept. of Civil Engineering Report No. 70-6, University of California at Berkeley, 1970.

[43] Castillo, E., R. J. Krizek and G. M. Kardi, "Comparison of Dispersion Characteristics in Fissured Rock", Proc. of the 2nd Symposium on Fundamentals of Transport Phenomena in Porous Media, University of Guelph, 778-797, 1972.

[44] Pinder, G. F., H.J. Ramey, A. Shapiro and L. Abriola, "Block Response to Reinjection in a Fractured Geothermal Reservoir", Proc. of the Fifth Stanford Geothermal Workshop, Stanford University, 189-196, 1979.

[45] Duguid, J. O. and P.C.Y. Lee, "Flow in Fractured Porous Media", Water Resour. Res., 13, 558-566, 1977.

[46] O'Neill, K., "The Transient Three-dimensional Transport of Liquid and Heat in Fractured Porous Media", a Ph.D. dissertation, Princeton University, 1977.

[47] Shapiro, A., "Fractured Porous Media: Equation Development and Parameter Identification", a Ph.D. dissertation, Princeton University, 1981.

[48] Yeh, W., W-G., "Aquifer Parameter Identification", J. Hydraul. Div. Am. Soc. Civ. Eng., 101(HY9), 1197-1209, 1975.

[49] Cooley, R. L., "A Method of Estimating Parameters and Assessing Reliability for Models of Steady State Groundwater Flow, 1, Theory and Numerical Properties", Water Resources Research, 13, 318-324, 1977.

[50] Nelson, R. W., "In Place Determintaion of Permeability Distribution for Heterogeneous Porous Media Through Analysis of Energy Dissipation, Soc. Pet. Eng. J., 8, 33-42, 1968.

[51] Tang, D. H. and G. F. Pinder, "A Direct Solution to the Inverse Problem in Groundwater Flow", Adv. in Water Resources, 2, 97-99, 1979.

[52] Tang, D. G. and G. F. Pinder, "Solution of an Inverse Problem in Groundwater Flow Using Uncertain Data", in Computational Methods and Experimental Measurements, Springer-Verlag, 53-63, 1982.

[53]   Tang, D. H. and G. F. Pinder, "Simulation of Groundwater Flow
       and Mass Transport Under Uncertainty", Adv. Water Resources,
       1, 25-30, 1977.

[54]   Freeze, R. A., "A Stochastic Conceptual Analysis of One-
       Dimensional Groundwater Flow in Nonuniform Homogeneous Media",
       Water Resources Res., 11, 725-741, 1975.

[55]   Dettinger, M. D. and J. L. Wilson, "First-Order Analysis of
       Uncertainty in Numerical Models of Groundwater Flow, 1. Mathe-
       matical Development", Water Resources Res., 17, 149-161, 1981.

[56]   Page, R. H., "Solving Differential and Numerical Models of
       Systems with Uncertain Material Parameters: Application to Con-
       vection-Dispersion Equations", Ph.D. dissertation, Princeton
       University, 1983.

[57]   Anderson, J. and A. M. Shapiro, "Stochastic Analysis of One-
       dimensional Steady State Unsaturated Flow: A Comparison of
       Monte Carlo and Perturbation Methods", Water Resources Res., 19,
       121-133, 1983.

NUMERICAL MODELING OF GROUNDWATER-LAKE SYSTEMS

Mary P. Anderson*

Groundwater has traditionally been neglected in limnological studies. However, several recent investigations have demonstrated that groundwater may constitute a significant portion of a lake's water budget. Furthermore, groundwater inflows can have important effects on the chemistry and biology of a lake ecosystem. For example, studies of lakes in Northern Wisconsin documented localization of ferromanganese nodules around high groundwater discharge zones (9) and demonstrated a relationship between groundwater inflows and macrophyte occurrences. It has also been suggested that groundwater inflows to Lake Michigan may, in part, control the location of historic trout spawning grounds (2). Furthermore, if contaminated by septic system discharge, groundwater may be an important source of nutrients to a lake. In this paper, examples of numerical modeling applications are discussed in order to illustrate the utility of models in lake studies.

Introduction

While a number of investigators have used numerical models to study hypothetical groundwater-lake systems (e.g., see reference 10), we have concentrated our efforts on the analysis of real world lake systems. A number of our applications will be reported here. These applications include simulations to estimate groundwater inflow and outflow rates, lag times for transport of contaminants to lakes, the effects of dredging of lake sediments on groundwater inflow rates, and the changes induced by construction of a cooling lake.

General Flow System Example

A simple hypothetical system is considered first as an example to illustrate the general methodology used in numerical modeling of groundwater flow systems. The form of the governing equation used in this example is:

$$\frac{\partial}{\partial x}(K_x \frac{\partial h}{\partial x}) + \frac{\partial}{\partial z}(K_z \frac{\partial h}{\partial z}) = 0 \tag{1}$$

where K_x is the hydraulic conductivity in the x direction; K_z is the hydraulic conductivity in the z direction. Use of this equation implies that the system may be heterogeneous and anisotropic but is at steady state. The boundary conditions are:

*Associate Professor, Department of Geology and Geophysics, University of Wisconsin-Madison, 1215 W. Dayton St., Madison, WI 53706.

$$\frac{\partial h}{\partial x} = 0 \quad \text{for} \quad x = 0 \quad \text{and} \quad x = X \quad \text{and all values of } z \qquad (2a)$$

$$h = H_1 \quad \text{for} \quad 0 \leq x \leq f(x,z) \quad \text{and} \quad 0 \leq z \leq f(x,z) \qquad (2b)$$

$$h(x,0) = \frac{H_2 - H_1}{L} x + H_1 \quad \text{for} \quad x > f(x,z) \qquad (2c)$$

$$\frac{\partial h}{\partial z} = 0 \quad \text{for} \quad z = Z \quad \text{and all values of } x \qquad (2d)$$

where H_1 and H_2 are the heads at $x = 0$ and $x = L$, respectively. Boundary condition 2(b) is used to simulate a lake at the left hand end of the flow system; L is the distance from the lake shore to the groundwater divide and X and Z are respectively, the length and depth of the flow system.

The general finite difference expression for equation (1) is:

$$\frac{1}{\Delta x}\left(KX_{i+1/2,j} \frac{h_{i+1,j} - h_{ij}}{\Delta x} - KX_{i-1/2,j} \frac{h_{ij} - h_{i-1,j}}{\Delta x}\right)$$

$$\frac{1}{\Delta z}\left(KZ_{i,j+1/2} \frac{h_{i,j+1} - h_{ij}}{\Delta z} - KZ_{i,j-1/2} \frac{h_{i,j} - h_{i,j-1}}{\Delta z}\right) = 0 \qquad (3)$$

where Δx and Δz are constants.

The system of algebraic equations generated when equation (3) is applied to a specified array of nodal points, can be solved using a simple iteration scheme based on equation (3):

$$h_{ij}^{n+1} = \frac{1}{KK}\left[\frac{\Delta z^2}{\Delta x^2}\left(KX_{i+1/2,j} \, h_{i+1,j}^{n} + KX_{i-1/2,j} \, h_{i-1,j}^{n+1}\right)\right.$$

$$\left. + KZ_{i,j+1/2} \, h_{i,j+1}^{n} + KZ_{i,j-1/2} \, h_{i,j-1}^{n+1}\right] \qquad (4)$$

where $\quad KK = \left(KX_{i-1/2,j} + KX_{i+1/2,j}\right) \frac{\Delta z^2}{\Delta x^2} + KZ_{i,j-1/2} + KZ_{i,j+1/2}$

A Fortran computer program using equation (4) to solve for heads within an 11 x 6 array of nodal points is shown in Fig. 1. The equivalent of equation (4) can be found within the "DO 40" do loop of the computer program. The boundary conditions given in equations (2) require the use of a 7th row of fictitious nodes to represent the no flow boundary at the bottom of the system, as well as two columns of fictitious nodes to represent the groundwater divides on either side of the problem domain. Details regarding the introduction of fictitious nodes into the iteration equation as well as details on the finite difference method are given in (13).

```
C   REGIONAL GROUNDWATER FLOW SYSTEM WITH LAKE
      REAL KX,KZ,KK,KXX,KZZ
      DIMENSION H(13,7),KX(13,7),KZ(13,7),QWT(13)
      READ(5,3) HO,H1,H2,EL
      READ(5,3) DX,DZ,KXX,KZZ
    3 FORMAT (4F10.2)
C    DEFINE THE KX AND KZ ARRAYS
      DO 4 J=1,7
      DO 4 I=1,13
      KX(I,J)=KXX
      KZ(I,J)=KZZ
    4 CONTINUE
      DO 44 I=8,13
      KX(I,4)=KXX/10.
   44 CONTINUE
C    INITIALIZE ALL HEADS TO HO
      DO 5 J=1,7
      DO 5 I=1,13
      H(I,J)=HO
    5 CONTINUE
C   SET WATER TABLE BOUNDARY
      DO 10 I=4,12
      H(I,1)=((H2-H1)/EL)*(DX*(I-4))+H1
   10 CONTINUE
C   SET HEADS IN THE LAKE
      DO 11 I=2,4
      DO 11 J=1,2
      H(I,J)=H1
   11 CONTINUE
      H(2,3)=H1
      H(3,3)=H1
C   BEGIN THE ITERATION LOOP AND KEEP TRACK OF
C   NUMBER OF ITERATIONS & LARGEST ERROR.
C   RESET NO-FLOW BOUNDARIES WITHIN EACH ITERATION LOOP
      NUMIT = 0
   35 AMAX = 0.
      NUMIT = NUMIT + 1
C   LEFT AND RIGHT NO-FLOW BOUNDARIES
      DO 20 J=1,7
      H(1,J) = H(3,J)
      H(13,J) = H(11,J)
   20 CONTINUE ·
C   BOTTOM NO-FLOW BOUNDARY
      DO 30 I=2,12
      H(I,7) = H(I,5)
   30 CONTINUE
```

Figure 1.

```
C  SWEEP INTERIOR POINTS WITH ITERATION EQN.
C  BUT SKIP OVER LAKE NODES
      SPACE=(DZ*DZ)/(DX*DX)
      DO 40 J=2,6
      DO 40 I=2,12
      IF (J.EQ.2.AND.I.EQ.2) GO TO 40
      IF (J.EQ.2.AND.I.EQ.3) GO TO 40
      IF (J.EQ.2.AND.I.EQ.4) GO TO 40
      IF (J.EQ.3.AND.I.EQ.2) GO TO 40
      IF (J.EQ.3.AND.I.EQ.3) GO TO 40
      OLDVAL = H(I,J)
      KK=(KX(I-1,J)+KX(I,J))*SPACE+KZ(I,J-1)+KZ(I,J)
      H(I,J)=(KX(I,J)*H(I+1,J)+KX(I-1,J)*H(I-1,J))*SPACE
     1+KZ(I,J)*H(I,J+1)+KZ(I,J-1)*H(I,J-1)
      H(I,J)=H(I,J)/KK
      ERR = ABS(H(I,J) - OLDVAL)
      IF(ERR.GT.AMAX) AMAX=ERR
40    CONTINUE
C  DO ANOTHER ITERATION IF LARGEST ERROR
C  AFFECTS 3RD DECIMAL PLACE
      IF(AMAX.GT.0.001) GO TO 35
C COMPUTE FLOW ACROSS THE WATER TABLE IN FT3/DAY/FT
C (-) MEANS DISCHARGE AND (+) MEANS RECHARGE
      DO 45 I=5,12
      QWT(I)=(H(I,1)-H(I,2))/DZ*KZ(I,1)*DX
45    CONTINUE
      QWT(12)=QWT(12)/2.
C COMPUTE FLOW INTO THE LAKE
      Q1=((H(5,1)-H(4,1))/DX*KXX*DZ)/2.
      Q2=(H(5,2)-H(4,2))/DX*KXX*DZ
      Q3=(H(4,3)-H(3,3))/DX*KXX*DZ
      Q4=(H(4,3)-H(4,2))/DZ*KZZ*DX
      Q5=(H(3,4)-H(3,3))/DZ*KZZ*DX
      Q6=((H(2,4)-H(2,3))/DZ*KZZ*DX)/2.
      QLAKE=Q1+Q2+Q3+Q4+Q5+Q6
      WRITE(9,50) NUMIT,((H(I,J),I=2,12),J=1,6)
50    FORMAT(1X,'NUMBER OF ITERATIONS IS ',I5,///6(11F7.2///))
      WRITE(9,53)
      WRITE(9,54) (QWT(I),I=5,12)
53    FORMAT(1X,'VOLUMETRIC FLOW RATE IN CUBIC FT/DAY/FT')
54    FORMAT(1X,8E9.3///)
C PRINT THE FLOW INTO THE LAKE IN CUBIC FT/DAY/FT
      WRITE(9,55)
      WRITE(9,56) Q1,Q2,Q3,Q4,Q5,Q6,QLAKE
55    FORMAT(1X,'FLOW INTO LAKE IN CUBIC FT/DAY/FT')
56    FORMAT(1X,6E9.3,15X,E9.3///)
      STOP
      END
```

Figure 1 (continued).

For this example, L was equal to 4000 ft (1220 m); the nodal
spacing in the x-direction was set to 500 ft (153 m) while the nodal
spacing in the z-direction was set to 50 ft (15 m). H1 was equal to
100 ft (31 m) and H2 was equal to 110 ft (34 m). The main aquifer was
assumed to have a horizontal hydraulic conductivity (K_x) equal to
30 ft/day (1.1×10^{-6} m/ sec) and an anisotropy ratio (K_x/K_z) of 100/1.
A lens of lower permeability was inserted into the fourth layer of the
model The lens was assumed to be isotropic with a hydraulic conductivity of 3 ft/day (1.1×10^{-7} m/sec).

The output for this problem is shown in Fig. 2. The outline of the
lake and equipotential lines were sketched in by hand. Note that the
program also computes flow in and out of the system. This mass balance
check not only provides useful information but also constitutes a check
on the numerical accuracy of the solution. A mass balance check should
be included in every numerical model. The flow into the lake equals
13.000 ft^3/day per ft of shoreline (1.3993×10^{-5} m^3/sec/m). The total
flow into the system is 14.327 ft^3/day/ft (1.5421×10^{-5} m^3/sec/m).
Note that discharge into a wetland area near the lake amounts to
0.255 ft^3/day/ft (1.7848×10^{-8} m^3/sec/m). Therefore, the total
discharge from the system is 13.255 ft^3/day/ft (1.4268×10^{-5} m^3/sec/m),
giving the model a mass balance error of around 8%. Much of the error
in the mass balance is probably due to the approximation of the head
gradient in the vicinity of the lake rather than to numerical errors in
the calculation of heads. Accuracy could be improved by use of smaller
nodal spacing in the vicinity of the lake. Introduction of irregular
grid spacing would require modifications in the code of Fig. 1.

Application to Groundwater-Lake Systems

Some useful information can be obtained from a study of
hypothetical lake systems such as the one considered in the previous
example. However, studies of hypothetical systems (10) skirt many of
the complexities present in the real world. Our work at UW-Madison
has emphasized the analysis of real world groundwater-lake systems.
Several of our lake sites are shown in Fig. 3.

Our modeling applications can be divided into two categories:
(1) those which deal with artificial lakes or lakes influenced by
dredging or other engineered actions and (2) those which deal with
natural lake systems.

Engineered Lake Systems

Artifical lakes are created for water supply, recreational use and
as cooling ponds. Construction of these lakes necessarily alters the
natural flow system; groundwater models are powerful tools in
predicting the probable nature and magnitude of changes in the flow
system. A two-dimensional profile model was used to analyze changes in
the flow system beneath a wetland area adjacent to the Wisconsin River,
in response to the construction of a cooling lake (site #5, Fig. 3) for
a coal-fired power plant (4). The model showed that construction of

NUMBER OF ITERATIONS IS   104

```
100.00 100.00 100.00 101.25 102.50 103.75 105.00 106.25 107.50 108.75 110.00
100.00 100.00 100.00 101.34 102.49 103.59 104.68 105.76 106.76 107.59 108.06
100.00 100.00 100.69 101.60 102.53 103.46 104.36 105.35 106.18 106.79 107.05
100.59 100.71 101.17 101.84 102.59 103.34 103.96 105.09 105.84 106.35 106.55
100.95 101.07 101.44 102.00 102.66 103.36 104.06 104.87 105.51 105.94 106.10
101.07 101.18 101.53 102.05 102.68 103.37 104.07 104.80 105.41 105.81 105.95
```

VOLUMETRIC FLOW RATE IN CUBIC FT/DAY/FT
-.255+000 .278-001 .469+000 .968+000 .148+001 .223+001 .348+001 .292+001

FLOW INTO LAKE IN CUBIC FT/DAY/FT
.187+001 .401+001 .208+001 .208+001 .212+001 .886+000 .130+002

Figure 2.

Figure 3.   Lake Sites.

(1)   Bass Lake (references 11-12)
(2)   Trout Lake (references 1,9)
(3)   Snake Lake (reference 3)
(4)   Nepco Lake (references 7,11)
(5)   cooling lake (references 4-5)
(6)   Lilly Lake (reference 6)

the lake had dramatically altered the natural flow system, causing
groundwater discharge rates into the marsh area between the cooling
lake and the Wisconsin River to be six times greater after filling of
the lake. Furthermore, the lake now provided the only source of water
to the wetland. A groundwater flow model was coupled to a heat flow
model (5) in order to study the impact on the thermal regime in the
wetland. This model, as well as field studies, showed that the thermal
alteration of groundwater was confined to within 300 ft (100 m) of the
cooling lake. However, within the thermally altered zone, temperature
fluctuations in the plant rooting zone were out of phase with normal
seasonal patterns contributing to changes in vegetation in this part of
the marsh.

Nepco Lake (site 4, Fig. 3) is a reservoir formed by an earthen dam
on a creek in central Wisconsin and used for water supply by Nekoosa
Papers. Although the amount of groundwater entering Nepco Lake is
relatively small, groundwater contributes almost all of the streamflow
entering the lake. A relatively short term field study indicated that
water seeps out of the lake into the groundwater system over much of
the lakebed (7). A modeling study was undertaken to identify the
factors responsible for these downward gradients in order to establish
whether such gradients are typical of this system or whether they are
transitory features. A two-dimensional steady state profile model
constructed along a flowline through Nepco Lake showed upward flow
into the lake under all reasonable scenarios (11). However, a three-
dimensional model of the system showed that the shape of the water
table immediately upgradient of the lake, the distribution and
thickness of fine-grained lake sediments and the transmissivity of an
inferred zone of high hydraulic conductivity under a portion of the
lake, were significant in causing downward vertical gradients. While
the downward gradients over part of the lakebed may in fact be transitory, downward gradients over the upstream portion of the lakebed are
probably steady state features of the flow system.

Shoreline property owners around Bass Lake (site #1, Fig. 3)
alleged that high water levels in Bass Lake during the early 1970's
were caused by regulation of water levels in a reservoir 1.5 miles
(2.4 km) south of the lake. Field studies (12) suggested that there
was no groundwater flow between the reservoir and the lake and furthermore, that groundwater flowing out of the reservoir was diverted away
from Bass Lake by a trough in the potentiometric surface probably
caused by the presence of a fault zone at depth. A two-dimensional,
areal-view, transient flow model was used to demonstrate that above
average precipitation during the early 1970's was sufficient to account
for the observed rise in water levels in the lake and that lowering or
raising the water level of the reservoir would have a negligible effect
on the lake. Additional modeling studies (11) provided insight into
the groundwater component of the water budget for Bass Lake. These
studies showed that the parameters which are most important in
governing the magnitude of the flow rate are the ratio of horizontal
to vertical hydraulic conductivity of the aquifer and the vertical
hydraulic conductivity of the littoral lakebed sediments.

Groundwater models can also be used to study the effects of dredging of lake sediments. Steady-state profile models of the groundwater system around Lilly Lake (site #6, Fig. 3) demonstrated that groundwater seepage into Lilly Lake could increase up to 89% after dredging of lake sediments (6).

Natural Lake Systems

We have also used models to study natural lake systems. Seasonal fluctuations in flow patterns around lakes have been documented at several lakes in Wisconsin (3,6,8) and were studied in detail at Snake Lake, with the aid of two-dimensional areal view and profile models (3). The modeling results illustrated the transient development of a stagnation point on the downgradient side of Snake Lake. Formation of the stagnation point caused a reversal in flow and drastically altered the distribution and quantity of groundwater seepage into the lake. Changes in the lake budget were quantified with the aid of a two-dimensional areal view model.

Models can also be useful in hypothesis testing. For example, a two-dimensional profile model was used to test the hypothesis that the presence of a lens of coarse-grained sediment was responsible for localization of groundwater discharge into Trout Lake (site #2, Fig. 3). Chemical evidence (9) suggested that formation of patches of ferromanganese nodules was due to a special chemical environment in high groundwater discharge zones. Modeling results (9) showed that the presence of a high permeability layer in the model reproduced what appeared to be anomalous field-measured downward head gradients in the near shore area and also reproduced field measured discharge rates, suggesting that the hypothesis regarding the formation of ferromanganese nodules is plausible.

In addition to the use of flow models in groundwater-lake studies, there is also the potential to use coupled models such as coupled water/heat flow models (5). Many additional applications can be imagined for the use of coupled flow/solute transport models. For example, we applied a flow model coupled to a solute transport model to a quasi-hypothetical lake systems based on parameters from a suite of lakes in Northern Wisconsin (site #2, Fig. 3) to illustrate that lag times in transport of acidity through the groundwater system to lakes can delay the onset of lake acidification for more than 100 years (1).

Summary and Conclusions

Provided sufficient field data are available, groundwater models can yield considerable insight into the probable effects of a variety of engineered actions including construction of cooling lakes and other reservoirs, dredging of lake sediments and manipulation of water levels in reservoirs. Models are also useful in studying natural lake systems. Applications range from the use of flow models in water budget studies to the application of solute transport models to study acid rain effects and other contamination problems.

APPENDIX.- REFERENCES

1. Anderson, M. P. and Bowser, C. J., "The Role of Groundwater in Delaying Lake Acidification", in preparation.
2. Anderson, M. P., Cherkauer, D. S., Taylor, R. W., "Geophysical Assessment of the Hydraulic Connection between Lake Michigan and the Aquifers along its Western Boundary", Final Report to Sea Grant, Sept. 1984, 32 p.
3. Anderson, M. P. and Munter, J. A., "Seasonal Reversals of Groundwater Flow Around Lakes and the Relevance to Stagnation Points and Lake Budgets", Water Resour. Res. 17(4), 1981, p. 1139-1150.
4. Andrews, C. B. and Anderson, M. P., "Impact of a Power Plant on the Groundwater System of a Wetland", Ground Water 16(2), 1978, p. 105-111.
5. Andrews, C. B. and Anderson, M. P., "Thermal Alteration of Groundwater caused by Seepage from a Cooling Lake", Water Resour. Res. 15(3), 1979, p. 595-602.
6. Beauheim, R. L., "The Effects of Dredging on Groundwater-Lake Interactions at Lilly Lake", Wisconsin, M.S. Thesis, Univ. of Wisc.-Madison, 1980, 178 p.
7. Karnauskas, R. J. and Anderson, M. P., "Ground-Water Lake Relationships and Ground-Water Quality in the Sand Plain Province of Wisconsin-Nepco Lake", Ground Water 16(4), 1978, p. 273-281.
8. Kenoyer, G., "A Hydrogeochemical Study of Crystal Lake, Vilas County, Wisc.", Ph.D. Thesis, Univ. of Wisc.-Madison, in preparation.
9. Krabbenhoft, D. P., "Hydrologic and Geochemical Controls of Freshwater Ferromanganese Deposit Formation at Trout Lake, Vilas County, Wisc.", M.S. Thesis, Univ. of Wisc.-Madison, 1984, 137 p.
10. McBride, M. S. and Pfannkuch, H. O., "The Distribution of Seepage within Lakebeds", Jour. Res. U.S. Geol. Survey 3(5), 1975, p. 505-512.
11. Munter, J. A. and Anderson, M. P., "The Use of Ground-Water Flow Models for Estimating Lake Seepage Rates", Ground Water 19(6), 1981, p. 608-616.
12. Rinaldo-Lee, M. B. and Anderson, M. P., "High Water Levels in Ground-Water Dominant Lakes-A Case Study from Northwestern Wisconsin", Ground Water 18(4), 1980, p. 334-339.
13. Wang, H. F. and Anderson, M. P, "Introduction to Groundwater Modeling: Finite Difference and Finite Element Methods", W.H. Freeman, 1982, 237 p.

Utilization of Numerical Models in Groundwater

Paul K.M. van der Heijde*

Abstract

For many years numerical models have been used in groundwater hydrology. In a recent assessment of the availability and use of models, a number of problem areas were identified. Some of these are discussed in this paper. A distinction is made between model research and code development on one side and code selection and application on the other. Special attention is given to such aspects of selection as availability, user-friendliness, documentation, code support and maintenance, and code credibility. Finally, some improvements in model use are suggested.

Introduction

According to Freeze and Back (4), the earliest application of numerical simulation to a subsurface flow problem was that of Shaw and Southwell in 1941 (7). In those days all calculations had to be done by hand. Stallman (8) is considered the first to have shown the feasibility of applying numerical methods in groundwater hydrology.

The advent of high-speed computers in the late 1950s and early 1960s facilitated a rapid expansion of capability to solve large sets of equations for complex problems encountered in field situations. Because of the resulting progress in the development and application of numerical models in groundwater management, in the early 1970s the Scientific Committee on Problems of the Environment (SCOPE/ICSU) initiated an assessment of groundwater models. This study, carried out at the Holcomb Research Institute in 1976–1977, presented the essential information on most of the available models capable of simulating groundwater flow and the transport and deformation processes in aqueous subsurface systems (1). In a recent update of this model inventory, the status, accessibility, and usability of groundwater models, and the transfer of groundwater modeling technology, were reassessed (2). A summary of the results of this recent review of 399 groundwater models was presented by van der Heijde (11). During this survey special attention was given to problems encountered in the transfer of models from the research stage to the application stage. This paper discusses the problems encountered in the application of numerical models to groundwater management. Areas needing improvement through research, development, technology transfer, and training, are identified.

*Director, International Ground Water Modeling Center, Holcomb Research Institute, Butler University, 4600 Sunset Ave., Indianapolis, IN 46408.

Groundwater Modeling

Development versus Use of Models

Groundwater modeling is a methodology for the analysis of the mechanisms and controls of groundwater systems and for the evaluation of policies, actions, and designs affecting those systems. Successful utilization of modeling can be assured only if the methodology is properly integrated with a variety of other techniques and approaches available for evaluation of hydrologic and other characteristics of the system.

Although a consensus may exist as to what groundwater modeling entails, this is much less the case with the word *model*. As a generalized definition, a model is a non-unique simplified version of a real system, describing its essential features, depending on the purpose for which the model has been developed, and including various constraints and assumptions. In groundwater technology, the word has been used in such contexts as conceptual model, mathematical model, analytic or numerical model, computer model, simulation model, and in a general sense, groundwater model. In this paper a groundwater model includes the mathematical framework, the computer coding, and the simulation of laboratory or field experiments, or the behavior of systems under field conditions, by assigning values to the parameters and variables utilized in the code.

The development and use of models encompasses a broad spectrum of technical expertise. At one end is management, and at the other end is scientific research. Between are two principal categories: model builders engaged in the development of models, and technical experts concerned with their operational use (1). The four categories are not rigidly separated. However, considering the categories as distinct helps elucidate the general framework of model development and use and of modeling-related problems.

Model Research and Code Development

The roots of model building lie in research. The fundamental understanding of a groundwater system is the product of research synthesized by theory in the form of conceptual models. The causal relationships among various components of the system and its environment are defined in mathematical terms, resulting in a mathematical model.

The solution of a mathematical model can take various forms. If the solution is complex, as with some analytic solutions, or when many repetitious calculations are necessary, as with numerical solutions, the use of computers is essential. This requires the coding of the solution in a programming language, resulting in a computer code.

The next step, code testing, takes place to remove programming errors, to test the algorithms, to evaluate the operational characteristics of the code, and to compare the computed results with the concepts originally formulated. Finally, data from field sites are used, if available, to validate the code. However, for many types of groundwater models, no such test data sets are currently available.

As a set of simplifying assumptions, equations, and boundary conditions cast in the form of a computer code, the model may hardly be operational. Accurate instructions are needed for the preparation of data sets which will form the input for the code. Therefore, the next stage in the development of an operational model, the preparation of documentation, is an important step in the establishment of the code's utility. With proper documentation, the code can be externally validated, a process which includes independent review and testing.

When all these steps have been taken, the code is operational and ready to apply to management problems. In the course of its use, the code gains confidence by proving its reliability and applicability. This can be further improved by provisions for continuing support and maintenance.

Not all simulation codes resulting from research into the physical and chemical processes of groundwater systems reach this final stage. This is partly due to the objectives of the research and development and in part to the way the project has been launched, or initialized. Basically, three possible courses of action are possible. One, codes can be developed primarily as research tools. Such codes frequently are considered experimental and are not prepared or released for external use. Two, other codes are intended to provide practical, descriptive, and predictive management tools for solving field problems. This type of code is often developed at the special request of planning, management, or enforcement agencies. The third category is formed by codes developed by consultants as an investment for future consultancy. Codes from the last two groups generally come with some form of documentation and have undergone at least limited testing.

Code Selection and Application

Model Application Process

The preparation of an operational model of a groundwater system can be divided into three distinct stages: initialization, calibration, and prediction. Each stage consists of various steps; often, results from a certain step are used as feedback in previous steps, resulting in a rather iterative process. The modeling process is initiated with the formulation of the modeling objectives and modeling scenarios derived from an analysis of the management problem under study. Within this context, compilation, inspection, and interpretation of available data result in a first conceptualization of the system under study.

Conceptualization of a groundwater system consists of four elements: identification of the state of the system, its controls both active and passive, and the level of uncertainty in the system (5). To identify the state of the system, its hydraulic, chemical, thermal, and hydrogeologic characteristics are defined, and conservation of mass, energy, and momentum are quantified. The active input refers to such system controls and constraints as pumpage schedules, artificial recharge, development of new well fields, and the construction of impermeable barriers, and clay caps and liners. If the studied system includes economic or decision-making policy aspects, active input may also include interest rates, pumping and waste generation or disposal taxes, and policies for conjunctive use. Passive or uncontrollable inputs include elements of the hydrologic cycle external to the system under study, such as natural recharge, evapotranspiration, subsidence, and natural water quality. They also refer to external management factors such as water demand resulting from population growth.

Based on the objectives of the study and the characteristics of the system, the need for and complexity level of the simulation model must be determined. Selection of a computer code takes place, followed by a period in which the technical staff become familiar with the code's operational characteristics.

The second stage, calibration, starts with the design or improvement of the model grid and the preparation of an input file by assigning nodal or elemental values and other data pertinent to the execution of the selected computer code. The actual computer simulation then takes place, followed by the interpretation of the computed results and comparison with observed data. The results of this first series of simulations are used to further improve the concepts of the system and the values of the parameters. Sensitivity runs are performed to assist in the calibration procedure. More data may be needed during the calibration process.

In some cases the code is used initially to design a data collection program. These newly collected data are then used both to improve the conceptualization of the system and to prepare for the predictive simulations.

After the calibration stage has been concluded satisfactorily, it is followed by the prediction stage, in which the computer code is used to obtain answers to such management problems as the impacts of proposed policies, engineering designs, and system alterations. The use of uncertainty analysis in this stage of the modeling process provides insight into the reliability of the computed predictions.

Code Selection

In the model application process, code selection is critical in ensuring an optimal tradeoff between effort and result. The result is generally expressed as the expected effectiveness of the modeling effort in terms of forecast accuracy. The effort is ultimately represented by the costs. Such costs should not be considered independently from those of field data acquisition. For a proper assessment of modeling cost, such measures as choice between the development of a new code or the acquisition of an existing code, the implementation, maintenance, and updating of the code, and the development and maintenance of data bases, need to be considered. Modeling costs consist of two elements: time costs for conceptualization, code selection, training, data preparation and entry, and postsimulation analysis; and computer costs for data entry, simulation, and post-processing.

In code selection, various project criteria are used, such as objectives and scale of modeling, budget constraints, available personnel and equipment, amount of available data, and sensitivity of the project for incorrect or imprecise answers or risk involved (5).

In selecting a code, its applicability and usability are important criteria. In evaluating a code's applicability to a problem, a good description of its operating characteristics should be accessible. For a large number of groundwater modeling codes, such information is obtainable from the International Ground Water Modeling Center (IGWMC) which operates a clearinghouse service for information and software pertinent to groundwater modeling. A code's usability is defined in terms of its availabilty, quality, and documentation; its transferability to other computers; its user-friendliness (ease of use); existence of test and field validation of the code; and support and maintenance (2). Other important selection criteria include the code's sensitivity to variation in system stresses and parameters, and its computation stability and efficiency. Because these assessments may be difficult for the potential user, well-established codes with histories of high confidence in their capabilities and usability are frequently preferred. Although documentation is important, a less well-documented, widely known code might be selected over a recently developed, less-known, but well-documented code.

Code Availability

An important aspect of code usability as previously defined is the code's availability. In this context a code is considered available if it can be obtained or accessed easily by users (3). Various types of availability can be distinguished, e.g., public domain; licensed use with limited distribution; lease either for a limited or open-ended period and including maintenance and update and support services; and finally, royalty-based use, wherein a royalty fee is due each time the code is accessed on the host computer (11). The establishment of the International Ground Water Modeling Center clearinghouse for groundwater models and modeling information has reduced greatly the effort normally required to acquire model information and modeling software (6). About fifty-five percent of the recently surveyed models are available to potential users free of charge or at nominal cost. Most of these have been developed at universities and by federal and state agencies (2).

Documentation

Adequate documentation is essential for efficient model use. It should include a description of the features of the code, its physical and mathematical framework, limitations in its use, the structure of the code, a discussion of computer system requirements, a user's manual, and sample data sets (3). Both a description of operational characteristics and a set of user's instructions are available for only 53 percent of the recently surveyed numerical groundwater models (2). However, in many such cases, information regarding computer system requirements and complete sample data sets including input and output, are lacking. Also, good and complete documentation facilitates efficient code modification by others than the original model developers. Where documentation exists, it is often incomplete and written inconsistently, partly as a collection of published papers. A user's manual generally contains a certain selection of the elements comprising a complete documentation set. Often, the user's manual is too condensed, resulting in a significant increase of the user's time spent on making the model operational.

A number of reasons have been put forward for the inadequacies of present documentation. One such is that documentation is the last step in the code development process and is in fact not necessary for the immediate solution of the problem for which the model was developed. Typically, most available funds are exhausted in the building of the model and little money may be left for the preparation of a user's manual. Furthermore, documentation is expensive and time-consuming and is not readily written by model builders, who may have little training or interest in detailed expository writing. Finally, modelers may have insufficient incentives to document; they may be reluctant to expose particular features, uncertainties, or assumptions which their model contains; or the time-consuming documentation process is not rewarded academically.

It is significant that the quality or extent of code documentation tends to vary with the type of institution in or for which model development takes place. At present, the most complete documentation of groundwater models is available from such federal agencies as the U.S. Geological Survey, the Nuclear Regulatory Commission, and the Office of Nuclear Waste Isolation of the U.S. Department of Energy. For private consulting firms, the marketability of their services is often an effective incentive to prepare adequate documentation and user-friendly software. The least extensive documentation is often written for codes developed in the university community, where much modeling is commonly undertaken in conjunction with doctoral programs or research grants. These projects generally do not require the preparation of an operational code that includes complete documentation.

The quality of documentation can often be improved by adopting the standards and quality control procedures established by some funding agencies.

Ease of Code Use

Various terms are used to describe the user-friendliness of a code. Codes which facilitate rapid understanding of their operational characteristics and which are easy to use are called user-friendly. In such codes special attention is given to error-free data preparation, program execution, and interpretation of results, thus increasing the efficiency of the modeling effort (10). Generally, this is achieved by the development of interactive textual and graphic pre- and postprocessing software. The code's user-friendliness is further enhanced by good documentation. As Table 1 shows, fifty-two percent of the 399 surveyed codes are available and have documentation. About half of these codes have some form of support (2).

TABLE 1.—State of Usability of Surveyed Models (After Bachmat et al. 1985)

Model Category	Total	Docu-mented[1]	Available[2]		Applied[3]	Usable[4]	
			Total	Public Domain		Total	Sup-ported[5]
Prediction							
Flow	203	120	172	117	155	118	44
Mass Transport	84	39	69	45	49	39	22
Heat Transport	22	15	18	15	13	15	9
Deformation	12	8	11	10	7	8	5
Multipurpose	16	8	14	5	8	8	8
Management	33	8	18	13	19	7	1
Identification	29	13	16	15	21	11	1
Total	399	211	318	220	272	206	92
Percentage	100	53	80	55	68	52	23

[1]including theoretical framework, user's instructions, and example problem
[2]available as public domain or proprietary model through sale, leasing, licensing, etc.
[3]applied at least once
[4]documented and available
[5]usable models for which active support by code-developing or -maintaining team is provided

Support and Maintenance

Various problems can be encountered when a simulation code is implemented on the user's computer system. Such difficulties may arise from compatibility problems between the computer system on which the code has been developed and the user's system. Other causes might be coding errors in the original code or user errors in data input or operation of the code. Although the first and third type of problem can be solved through available code support, such assistence does not replace the need for proper training in the use of the code. Support requested from model developers may assume such proportions that the developer becomes a consulting service. This potentiality is generally recognized by model developers, but not always by model users. The third type of problem may diminish as the user becomes more familiar with the code. Here, the user benefits from good documentation.

Code Credibility

One of the most cited factors hampering the utility of models in groundwater management is managerial lack of confidence in models as decision-making tools (2). This credibility gap may in some cases be more apparent than real. One major reason for a credibility gap may be that in recent years groundwater modeling has become an increasingly sophisticated science that has developed rapidly.

Lack of managerial understanding gives rise to what is known as the "black box" approach. While some managers are willing at the

outset to accept practically any model output uncritically, such
initial enthusiasm often leads to disappointments and consequent mis-
trust. Or, the fault may lie with the professionals who build and
apply the models; some modelers have oversold their product, claiming
that their models can represent more than is realistically possible,
or have otherwise misrepresented the capabilities of their code or
modeling approach. Such overzealousness has led to to disillusionment
on the part of the managers and to their consequent generalization
that models cannot produce efficient, reliable, and usable results for
decision-making purposes.

Training

The use of models is often inhibited by the technical expert's
limited understanding of available codes; by inability to determine
which of those codes are appropriate for a particular problem; and by
inability to determine how the codes, once identified, should be
applied or modified to fit particular needs. Because model builders
cannot be involved in all applications of their codes, training of
technical personnel for this task is necessary. The lack of technicians with adequate training in model application is due in part to
the rapid development of modeling in the last fifteen years, a development that has bypassed many groundwater professionals—and to the
significant increase in the number of problems which require analysis
by such sophisticated methods as modeling. As models become more
complex, a higher level of training is necessary to use them efficiently.

Improving the Use of Groundwater Models

Although the precise formulation of a management problem can be
quite thorny, it is prerequisite to the solution. The manner in which
a problem is defined bears heavily on how the professional approaches
a solution. Improved problem definition is likely to result from more
interactive participation of managers and technical personnel in model
design and application, both in a project's initial stage, as is
usually the case, and during the modeling effort itself. Code output
is often a barrier to more effective utilization of the code. Program
managers and decision makers need to have model results presented in a
way that is both meaningful and compatible with decisions that must be
made. The uncertainties contained in various decision alternatives
are especially important to assess.

In recent years, a great deal of energy and resources has been
directed to the development of groundwater models. Still, various
kinds of models, yet undeveloped or seriously deficient, are needed
urgently for the management of groundwater resources (2, 11). Therefore, improvements in certain existing models are warranted; and
development of new models, based on continuing research into the
fundamental physical concepts, deserves further attention. Codes that
are easy for others than the model-builder to understand and use
should be made available. Existing codes should be improved in their
structure, flexibility and readability, transferability to other
computers, adaptability to supporting software, and in their computational efficiency and accuracy.

Finally, modeling provides a framework to order and interpret data within the decision-making process. The effectiveness of any model is dependent on the accuracy of the data acquired. In many applications, the lack of data inflicts a severe constraint upon obtaining useful model results. Further attention is necessary for the integration, within each project, of data acquisition and modeling, and modeling activities themselves.

References

1. Bachmat, Y., Andrews, B., Holtz, D., and Sebastian, S. "Utilization of Numerical Groundwater Models for Water Resource Management," Rep. *600/8-78-012*, U.S. Environmental Protection Agency, Cincinnati, Ohio, 1978.
2. Bachmat, Y., Andrews, B., Holtz, D., and Sebastian, S., *Groundwater Management: The Use of Numerical Models*, 2nd Edition, edited by P.K.M. van der Heijde. Water Resources Monograph 5, Am. Geoph. Union, Washington, D.C., 1985.
3. El-Kadi, A. I., "Modeling Infiltration for Water Systems," HRI Paper *21*, Holcomb Research Institute, Butler University, Indianapolis, Indiana, 1983.
4. Freeze, R. A., and Back, W., *Physical Hydrogeology*. Hutchinson Ross Pub. Co., Stroudsburg, Pennsylvania, 1983.
5. Kisiel, C. C., and Duckstein, L., "Ground-Water Models," *Systems Approach to Water Management,* A.K. Biswas, ed., McGraw-Hill, New York, 1976, pp. 80–155.
6. OTA, "Use of Models for Water Resources Management, Planning, and Policy," OTA-O-159, Office of Technology Assessment, U.S. Congress, Washington, D.C., 1982.
7. Shaw, F. S., and Southwell, R. V., "Relaxation Methods Applied to Engineering Problems, VII: Problems Relating to the Percolation of Fluids through Porous Materials," *Proceedings of the Royal Society, London.* 178A, 1941, pp. 1–17.
8. Stallman, R. W., "Use of Numerical Methods for Analyzing Data on Ground Water Levels," International Association of Scientific Hydrology, Publication 41, 1956, pp. 227–231.
9. van der Heijde, P. K. M., "Availability and Applicability of Numerical Models for Ground Water Resources Management," *Proceedings NWWA/IGWMC Conference on Practical Application of Ground Water Models,* Columbus, Ohio, August 15–17, pp. 1–16, 1984.
10. van der Heijde, P. K. M., and Srinivasan, P., "Aspects of the Use of Graphic Techniques in Ground Water Modeling," *Proceedings Water Development to Management: The Universities' Role, UCOWR Annual Meeting,* July 24–27, 1983, Columbus, Ohio, pp. 78–90.
11. van der Heijde, P. K. M., "Modeling Contaminant Transport in Groundwater: Approaches, Current Status, and Needs for Further Research and Development," *Proceedings of the Engineering Foundation/UCOWR Conference on Groundwater Contamination,* Santa Barbara, Calif., Nov. 12–16, 1984, in press.

RISK ASSESSMENT FOR GROUNDWATER CONTAMINATION: I

Yacov Y. Haimes*, F. ASCE
Vira Chankong**
Chenggui Du***

ABSTRACT

This paper constitutes Part I of a two-part article. Both parts focus on the risk assessment and management process in terms of the ever-present problem of groundwater contamination and its prevention and correction. Part I provides a brief definition of terms and concepts in risk assessment and management, develops a brief taxonomy of risk assessment methodologies, and briefly discusses the imperativeness of multiple-objective optimization in risk assessment and management. Part II details the mathematical process of risk quantification (a nontrivial task that deserves much more attention in the literature than it has been given so far), illustrates the risk assessment and management process through a specific example problem concerned with groundwater contamination, focusing on its risk quantification aspects, uses the partitioned multiobjective risk method (PMRM) to demonstrate an effective methodology for handling extreme events, analyzes the computational results in terms of management policy options and multiobjective trade-offs, and relates the entire risk assessment and management process to multiobjective trade-off analysis and to decision support systems.

The division of the article into two parts, while semi-arbitrary and dictitated by rules governing paper length, reflects the fact that the two parts were presented at two separate, albeit related, sessions of the Conference.

1. Introduction

The prolific literature on the subject of the assessment and management of risk addresses such issues as the nature of risk; the perception and behavioral aspects of risk assessment; risk identification, quantification, evaluation, and characterization; and various approaches, tools, and methodologies for risk assessment and management, etc. Several publications that provide such a review of the extensive literature of the subject can be found elsewhere (e.g., [9], [12], [2], [21], [5], [16], [22], [6]).

*   Chairman of Systems Engineering Department, and Professor of Systems and Civil Engineering, Case Western Reserve University, (CWRU), Cleveland, Ohio 44106.

**   Visiting Associate Professor, Systems Engineering Department, CWRU, Cleveland, Ohio 44106.

*** Grad. Research Asst., Systems Engineering Department, CWRU, Cleveland, Ohio 44106.

This paper focuses on a specific collection of risk assessment and management methods useful for groundwater contamination problems. In the next section, we give a brief overview of risk assessment and management principles and philosophies in the context of groundwater contamination. Section 3 reviews and classifies selected risk analysis methods and proposes a framework for integrating them. Finally, Section 4 describes the need for an integrated decision aid in the form of a decision support system and suggests how such a system can be constructed.

2.   Risk Assessment and Management: An Overview

Risk is the possibility of suffering harm, loss, danger, failure, or some kind of adverse effects as a result of taking an action or a sequence of actions. There are thus two basic elements associated with risk: its magnitude and the likelihood it will cause harm or adverse effects. To describe a risky situation, we must therefore adequately describe these two basic elements.

To perform the complete process of risk assessment for a particular problem, the following tasks need to be carried out:

1) Risk identification, which involves identification of the nature, types, and sources of risks and uncertainties. In general, the major types of risks are financial, health-related, environmental, and technical (e.g., performance and supportability). The end products of this task are a complete description of risky events and elements of major concern along with their causative factor and mechanism.

2) Risk quantification, which entails formulating appropriate measures of risk and estimating the likelihood (probability) of occurrence of all consequences associated with risky events as well as the magnitude of such consequences.

3) Risk evaluation, which includes selection of an evaluation procedure (e.g., optimizing expected value, trade-off analysis) and analysis of various possible impacts of risky events.

4) Risk acceptance and aversion, which require decision making regarding both an acceptable level of risk and its equitable distribution. This phase of risk assessment also involves the development of risk control (i.e., measures to reduce or prevent risk).

5) Risk management, which involves the formulation of policies, the development of risk control options (i.e., methods to reduce or prevent risk), and execution of such policy options.

The last two stages of the risk assessment process--risk acceptance and aversion and risk management--overlap to a large extent and require the subjective judgment of the appropriate decision makers in trading-off the noncommensurate beneficial and adverse consequences resulting from the ultimate "acceptable risk" decision. The existence of these fundamental trade-offs among conflicting and noncommensurate multiple objectives and attributes demands the consideration of risk management as an integral part of the overall decision-making process--which is the imperative premise assumed in this paper [12].

The quality and quantity of information available are clearly an important determining factor of how we should assess and manage risks. It is often useful to distinguish among the following three risk-related situations reflecting the different levels of information available for risk assessment and management:

* risk situations--situations in which the potential outcome can be described by reasonably well-known probability distributions.
* imprecision situations--situations having potential outcomes that cannot be described in terms of objectively known probability distributions, but which can be estimated by subjective probabilities.
* uncertainty situations--situations in which potential outcomes cannot be described in terms of objectively or subjectively known probability distributions.

To convey to the reader the essence of the risk quantification process, groundwater contamination is used here as the vehicle for demonstrating the various components, steps, and phases of the risk quantification process. If planners and decision makers are to understand groundwater contamination from various sources with the intention of either its prevention or correction, it is essential that they be able to

* estimate the current load and predict the future load of potential contaminants based on existing and projected economic, industrial, and demographic outlooks
* understand the infiltration process to estimte the actual contamination of a groundwater system
* understand the movement of pollutants in the groundwater system
* understand how and to what extent people and the environment might be exposed to and affected by groundwater contamination
* perform necessary analyses and test various management options, and to do these with a quick turn-around time

The complete process by which groundwater can be contaminated by various causes (such as municipal and industrial waste disposal, industrial spills and agricultural activities) is depicted in Figure 1, which also shows the socioeconomic, health, and environmental impacts of the contamination.

The overall process is clearly complex and contains a multitude of uncertainties. To cope with such inherent complexity and uncertainties, a number of different risk assessment tools are needed to perform the myriad tasks in the overall risk assessment and management process. The next section reviews and classifies some of these methods with specific reference to groundwater contamination.

3. Risk Assessment Methods for Groundwater Contamination

We now need to identify and select potential useful analytical

tools for performing various tasks in assessing and managing risks
associated with groundwater contaminations. Along the way, we will
indicate how these tools can be grouped according to their specific
purposes and emphasis.

As already mentioned, the complete process of risk assessment and
management consists of a number of activities which can be grouped into
five major tasks--identification, quantification, evaluation,
acceptance, and management of risk.

For groundwater contamination, there are three major risk
categories--socioeconomic risks, health-related risks, and environmental
risks. Typical tasks in groundwater risk identification then involve
pinning down precisely the specific risk concerns within each category
(e.g., cost of clean-up, health effects, effects on aquatic and/or
terrestial life); identifing the particular sources of contaminations
and contaminants as well as their relevance and priorities at local,
regional, and national levels; identifying an appropriate set of
attributes to serve as measures of the risk level (e.g., expected value
of concentration, conditional expected values of concentrations,
probability of exceedance, cumulative concentration, cost); and
identifying the level of information and knowledge that is available or
can be expected to be accessible or obtainable.

Knowledge of data availability will enhance our insight and
understanding of the problem and will also be useful in the selection of
tools for subsequent tasks. Generally, risk identification is a
problem-specific task involving the articulation and organization of
ideas and issues related to the problem. Group-process techniques and
other collective inquiry aids may be useful for this task.

Once the nature, type, sources, and measures of risk are
identified, the next step is to quantify the risks. This involves
relating risk measures to various determining factors. Risks consist of
two primary components: the magnitude or severity of harm or adverse
effects, and the probability or likelihood of harm. To quantify risk
is, thus, to quantify these two components, at least as an initial step.

Since risk is induced by some form of uncertainty, the first step
in quantifying risk is to identify its sources and types. Risk may be
caused by a mixture of random and uncontrollable factors and lack of
knowledge of some specific part(s) of the system.

In tracking contaminants as they move from sources to water users,
we may identify several factors that affect their level of concentration
and the composition as they pass through the aquifer, as illustrated in
Table 1. Some of these factors are random in nature while others are
physical characteristics that are unknown but otherwise nonrandom.
Still other factors may represent quantities that can be manipulated or
controlled. For example, the rate of generation of leachate or effluent
from a particular dump site depends on many factors, including the type
and amount of waste dumped (controllable), local precipitation and
evapotranspiration characteristics (random), and composition of
contaminants in the waste (random). On the other hand, the flow and
transport of contaminants through an aquifer depends on transmissivity,

hydraulic   conductivity,   effective   porosity,   and   other   porosity
characteristics of the aquifer.   Although these parameters can be
adequately treated as some nonrandom quantities, their values are often
not completely known, thus becoming a source of uncertainty.

The basic difference between the two types of uncertainty is that
the "random" type is impossible to eliminate, while it might be possible
to remove uncertainty resulting from lack of knowledge given the right
kind of technology and an appropriate level of effort. For example, one
can never give a completely accurate forecast of a purely random event,
such as precipitation, no matter how many measurements are made or how
much research is done.   On the other hand, it is conceivable that the
uncertainty surrounding the AIDS disease, which uncertainty currently
exists due to our lack of knowledge of the disease, will sometime
disappear as more research is done to learn more about it.

In terms of risk quantification, different tools are usually needed
to deal with different types of uncertainty, as exemplified in Table 1.
Table 2 furnishes an expanded list of the quantification methods given
in Table 1, but these are reclassified according to type and level of
data availability.   To illustrate, consider the case where we need to
estimate   the   probability distribution of a particular type   of
contaminant generated at a dump site. If adequate samples are taken and
reasonably accurate measurements performed, this may correspond to the
"full" and "objective" information case, in which time-series and/or
statistical data analyses are very useful.   If, however, samples have
not and cannot be taken but some substantial expert knowledge about the
contaminant and its generation is available, and if such "soft"
information can be completely assessed by the experts, then such
techniques as the subjective probability assessment method [17,   28],
cross-impact analysis [10, 26], and event-tree analysis [1] may be
quite useful tools.   At the other extreme, if no information, whether
objective or subjective, can be expected, then one can use the the
Bayesian estimation procedure based on noninformative priors [4, 18],the
sensitivity risk index method (such as the USIM [15] and RDIM [24]
discussed in Part II of this paper), and/or the worst-case analysis.
Between the two extremes, where only partial "objective" information is
available initially, the empirical Bayes method (which uses part of the
information to generate priors and the other part to serve as sampling
information to be combined with priors to compute posteriors) has a
great potential.   If the partial information is subjective, maximum
entropy estimation [4, 18] or estimation based on an assumed functional
form [4] appears promising (e.g., assume log normal, gamma, beta, or
uniform family of distributions and then use partial information to
compute the parameters of the assumed distribution).

When the risk measures are well formulated and adequately
quantified, the next step is to evaluate various alternative options to
prevent, detect, and/or correct groundwater contamination. A number of
tools are available for this task.   For example, cost-benefit analysis
[25] and allied methods can be used to appraise various alternatives
(discrete or continuous) based on monetary measures.   To apply these
methods, substantial effort is devoted to valuation procedures,
especially if many of the involved goods and services do not have direct
market values.   Multiattribute utility theory [20] is another commonly

used class of evaluation method used in problems with multiple attributes. The main thrust of methods in this class is to explicitly quantify preference in the form of a multiattribute utility function as a means of collapsing multiple attributes into a simple function. The information is even further collapsed into a single index by computing expected utility. An alternative with maximum expected utility is thus considered the best. Although these methods may be appropriate risk evaluation tools for a class of problems with moderate-to-high frequency of risk and moderate-to-low damage, they fail to capture the possibly devastating effects of the low-frequency, high-damage characteristics typical of extreme events. Here, as a typical expected-value approach, extreme events with a low probability of occurrence are given the same proportional weight and importance (in the multiobjective commensuration process) regardless of their potential catastrophic and irreversible impact. Yet it is a commonly acknowledged fact that the outcome of a catastrophic accident that may cause 10,000 death with a low frequency of 10^{-5} is neither perceived nor accepted to be in the same category of more common accidents that occur with a much higher frequency of, say, 10^{-1}, but may cause the death of one person each time. The partitioned multiobjective method (PMRM) [2] used in conjunction with the surrogate worth trade-off (SWT) method [3, 14] furnishes a means of overcoming this and other shortcomings. The PMRM provides a means of explicitly formulating and quantifying risk measures to reflect extreme events. The SWT method, on the other hand, allows explicit trade-off analysis to be performed in a convenient and effective way. The overall approach will be discussed and illustrated in Part II of this paper. In addition to those already mentioned, the multistage, multiobjective impact assessment method [11], Bayesian decision analysis [4, 28], the decision tree [17], and event and fault tree analysis [1] are among the potentially useful tools for risk evaluation of groundwater contamination problems.

The remaining tasks of risk assessment--risk acceptance and risk management--contain some activities that overlap those used in risk evaluation--the generation and evaluation of new alternatives. For these activities, the evaluation tools mentioned above may be useful. The other part of risk acceptance and management is oriented more toward action and implementation. It involves the formulation of policies, the development of risk control and monitoring options, and the execution of such policy options. Clearly, to perform these tasks adequately, the art and techniques of policy analysis and policy making, Congressional hearings, public hearings, and law and regulation formulation will be extremely useful, since groundwater is mostly a public concern.

The above discussion points out that a number of tools have been developed to perform one or more tasks in the overall risk assessment and management process in general, and some of these can take care of tasks related to groundwater contamination problems in particular. These tools are indeed diverse in nature, emphasis, purpose, and degree of comprehensiveness and sophistication. Cursory inspection of the list of available methods in the literature reveals that no single tool can adequately support all the tasks that need to be done in the overall process of risk assessment and management. Nor can any one method claim to be a general-purpose procedure that can deal with all types of risk (socioeconomic, health, and environmental) in all types of risky situations.

Because of the diversity of the risk problems that may arise and of the tasks that need to be done, a general-purpose method, even if it can be developed, would be almost without content, and thus would most likely be useless. What is needed is therefore an ensemble of tools that collectively span the whole spectrum of risk assessment and management tasks for whatever problem is encountered. Figure 2 provides an example of such an ensemble as well as a procedural framework for integrating those techniques listed. To translate such a framework into a flexible working tool (to allow decision makers and/or program planners to make more-informed decisions in a timely and efficient manner), some form of a packaging device is needed. For this we propose the use of a decision support system (DSS), which we will now discuss.

4. A Decision Support System (DSS) and Its Roles in Groundwater Risk Assessment

The wide use of mathematical models for water resources management has been substantiated and documented by a recent study on the subject conducted by the Congressional Office of Technology Assessment [23]. The wide use of computers (mini-, micro-, personal-, etc.) has become integral to our lives in the eighties. What is not as widely appreciated (and is just now gaining more ground) is the more intimate integration of mathematical models and personal computers into an intelligent man-machine mode. This man-machine mode is often referred to as a decision support system (DSS). Thus, although mathematical models and numerical and optimization methods have been increasingly used in management decisions and risk assessment, the interactive man-machine mode of these management tools is becoming more and more dominant. The usefulness of DSS as a management tool is becoming more evident in terms of the effective and convenient access that DSSs have to multiple data bases, various simulation and analytical models, and advanced numerical and optimization techniques, especially their marked capabilities to make use of optimal design, trade-off and impact analysis, and risk assessment. DSSs offer great applications capabilities in water resources management.

DSSs consist essentially of three basic components. The first component is the data base, which contains primitive data in a form that is easily accessed, retrieved, and updated. The second component is the model base, which is often called the brain of the DSS. It comprises a collection of models that translate data into some form of intelligence by consolidating, transforming, and interpreting primitive data from the data base. Much of the power, flexibility, and usability of a DSS is derived from the third component--the dialogue system--which provides interactive capabilities between the system and the user. From the DSS user's point of view, the dialogue component is the system [27]. According to Bennett [3], the dialogue experience can be divided into three parts:

1. "The Action Language": what the user "can do" in communicating with system. It includes such options as the availability of a regular keyboard, function keys, touch panels, joy stick, voice command, and so on.

2. "The Display or Presentation Language": what the user "sees." The
    display language includes options such as the character or line
    printer, a display screen, graphics, color, plotter, audio output,
    and so on.

3. "The Knowledge Base": what the user "must know." The knowledge
    base consists of what the user needs to bring to a session with
    the system in order to use it effectively.

The DSS as a concept is well-suited for water resources systems in
general and for groundwater contamination risk assessment and management
in particular. Within the specific context of the latter, the inherent
complexity of the groundwater contamination process as depicted in
Figure 1 and the multitude of tasks to be accomplished (as discussed in
the preceding section) clearly indicate a great need for an integrated
decision support tool that is capable of doing the following.

   i)   Allow the user to define appropriate input configurations
         related to the pertinent economic, industrial, and demographic
         conditions of the study area.
   ii)   Allow the user to employ the model at different levels of
         resolution depending on the user's needs and the availability
         of data.
   iii) Incorporate into the DSS, if possible, the various types of
         infiltration, flow, and transport models based on the
         different types of soil and the geologic and hydrologic
         conditions of the study system in order to add yet another
         dimension of flexibility.
   iv)   Provide an option to perform multiobjective trade-off
         analysis, systematic sensitivity analysis, and risk assessment.
   v)   Provide a man-machine interactive mode option to allow
         planners and decision makers to interact with the model with a
         quick turn-around time.

A well-designed DSS can clearly afford such capabilities and can
improve the performance of managers and decision makers in a continuous
and sustained mode. For example, a DSS for the correction of groundwater contamination can (i) make use of an extensive hydrologic data
base (for groundwater recharge and for contaminant concentration) and a
technological data base (for cost and attributes of various clean-up
technologies such as air stripping, granular activated carbon, etc.),
(ii) have as its brain or model base several two- and three-dimensional
solute transport models (such as the Konikow-Bredehoeft model), (iii)
incorporate into its decision-making component several risk assessment
and management models (such as the partitioned multiobjective risk
methods (PMRM) and the surrogate worth trade-off (SWT) method), and (iv)
develop a dialogue or software system than is most suitable to the user.

Figure 3 is an example of such a DSS, which is built upon the
structure of the groundwater contamination process in Figure 1.

With a view toward furnishing such desirable features as economic
and technical data inputting, desired level of precision of output, and
flexibility and practicality of applications, the model exemplified in

Figure 3 consists of six modules, thus illustrating a modular approach to model building.

The data module converts field measurements or other existing raw data into specific parameters describing the characteristics of the soil, the aquifer, and the waste load. These parameters are necessary for calculations in subsequent modules. By isolating each data preparation task into a separate module, great flexibility in handling problems with different levels of data availability should be achieved.

The pollutant load module takes in the current and projected sanitary engineering practices and technology within the study area, the economic and demographic conditions, the rainfall statistics, and data about the composition of various wastes (from the data module), and it uses these to estimate or project the total volume and composition of pollutants loaded onto the system.

The infiltration module estimates the rate of infiltration and the percentage of the total pollutant load that reaches and contaminates the groundwater. Here, it is recognized that not all wastewater and/or leachates dumped into the system reach the groundwater system. Some will be attenuated or filtered by soil particles. Some may be converted to immobile compounds through reaction with microorganisms or other substances in the soil. Estimation processes included in the module may be as simple as an ad-hoc estimation of infiltration coefficients or as complex as a sophisticated model of unsaturated flow.

Essentially, the flow module models the flow of water in the aquifer to generate information concerning flow patterns that include head and pressure distribution, groundwater potentials, flow velocities, flow paths, flow rates, and travel times.

The transport module describes the movement of contaminants in the groundwater system through various transport mechanisms (e.g., convection and dispersion for conservative contaminants and ion exchange for some nonconservative contaminants such as radionuclides). The output of this module and hence of the groundwater-quality module (which combines flow and transport modules) is a plot of the areal distribution of the concentrations of each type of contaminant as well as the dynamics of these contaminants.

Finally, the risk assessment module is one that provides a means for accounting for the potential adverse impacts of groundwater contaminations. Sensitivity analysis, which is critical for a model of this size and complexity due to the usually questionable data quality, can also be performed. This module may, indeed, be structured to contain all the risk assessment and management tools that are indicated in Figure 2.

5. Concluding Remarks

What we have tried to do in this paper is to share with the reader our perception and experience on risk assessment and management. Although our discussion was made with specific reference to groundwater contamination, most of the ideas and concepts are applicable far beyond groundwater contamination and other water resources problems. Perhaps the single most important point we try to make in this paper is that groundwater contamination is indeed a complex process, laden by uncertainties of different forms and intensities, and that a comprehensive risk assessment and management system integrating various types of specific tools is not only appealing but necessary. The DSS is also identified as a device for packaging these tools into one powerful, workable unit. In the second part of this paper, some of the concepts already discussed in this paper will be illustrated, using specific examples.

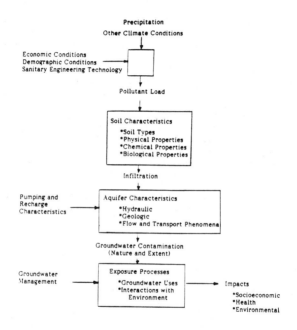

Figure 1   A System View of the Process and
Impact of Groundwater Contamination

Figure 2   A Procedural Framework for WSA Risk Assessment and Management
            of Groundwater Contamination

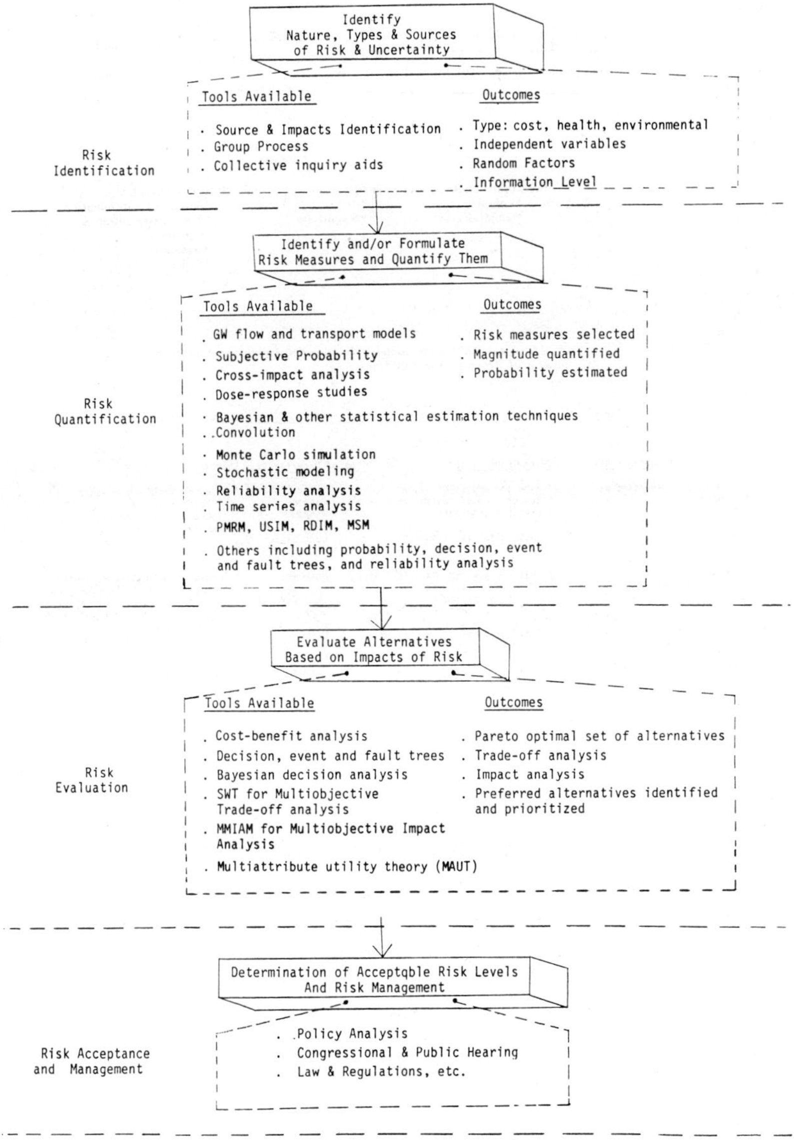

Identify
Nature, Types & Sources
of Risk & Uncertainty

Risk Identification

Tools Available   Outcomes

· Source & Impacts Identification   · Type: cost, health, environmental
· Group Process   · Independent variables
· Collective inquiry aids   · Random Factors
                                     · Information Level

Identify and/or Formulate
Risk Measures and Quantify Them

Risk Quantification

Tools Available   Outcomes

· GW flow and transport models   · Risk measures selected
· Subjective Probability   · Magnitude quantified
· Cross-impact analysis   · Probability estimated
· Dose-response studies
· Bayesian & other statistical estimation techniques
· Convolution
· Monte Carlo simulation
· Stochastic modeling
· Reliability analysis
· Time series analysis
· PMRM, USIM, RDIM, MSM
· Others including probability, decision, event
  and fault trees, and reliability analysis

Evaluate Alternatives
Based on Impacts of Risk

Risk Evaluation

Tools Available   Outcomes

· Cost-benefit analysis   · Pareto optimal set of alternatives
· Decision, event and fault trees   · Trade-off analysis
· Bayesian decision analysis   · Impact analysis
· SWT for Multiobjective   · Preferred alternatives identified
  Trade-off analysis   and prioritized
· MMIAM for Multiobjective Impact
  Analysis
· Multiattribute utility theory (MAUT)

Determination of Acceptqble Risk Levels
And Risk Management

Risk Acceptance and Management

· Policy Analysis
· Congressional & Public Hearing
· Law & Regulations, etc.

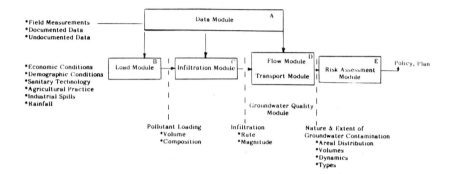

Figure 3   A Typical Integrated Decision Support Model for Studying and Assessing
the Impacts of Groundwater Pollutions.

Table 1. Uncertainty in Groundwater Problems: Sources, Types and Qualification Tools

Path of Contaminants	Determining Factor	Type of Uncertainty	Quantification Tools
Contaminant generated at sources	* Type and amount of waste * Composition of contaminants * Precipitation pattern * Waste disposal technology	Controllable Random Random Controllable	* Study of Sources and waste characteristics * Time-series and statistical analysis

Contaminants infiltrated and transported	* Soil and aquifer characteristics
	  . hydrologic
	  . geologic
	  . chemical
	  . biological
	* Flow and transport mechanism
		Unknown
		
		Random
			* Subjective probability, cross-impact analysis, Bayesian and other statistical estimation techniques and event and fault tree analysis
			* Groundwater models

Contaminant discharged and exposed	* Methods of discharge (e.g., wells, springs, rivers, lakes, wetland and ocean
	* Exposure process
	  . type of used of contaminated water
	  . pattern of use
	  . water treatment technology
		Random/ Unknown
		
		Random/ Unknown
		
		Controllable
			* Impulse-response and convolution
			* Monte-Carlo simulation/ Stochastic modeling
			* PMRM, USIM, RDIM
			* Study of utilization pattern and exposure process
			* Dose-response

Table 2   Classifying Risk Quantification Tools According to Type and Level of Information Available.

Knowledge Spectrum

Type of Information \ Level of Availability	No Information (or not assessable)	Partial Information (or partially assessable)	Full Information Available (or assessable)
Objective	* Worst-case analysis (mini-max or maximum) * Sensitivity analysis (e.g., USIM, RDIM)	* Empirical Bayes * Bayesian estimation techniques	* Time series analysis * Adaptive identification procedures
Subjective	* Noninformative prior	* Given functional form estimates * Bayesian estimation * Maximum entropy prior * Fuzzy set concepts	* Subjective assessment * Cross-impact analysis * Event and fault tree analysis

Appendix 1.--References

1. Ang, A. H. S., and Tang, W. H., Probability Concepts in Engineering
    Planning and Design, Vol. II., Wiley, New York, N.Y., 1984, pp.
    485-517.

2. Asbeck, E., and Haimes, Y. Y., "The Partitioned Multiobjective Risk
    Method (PMRM)," Large Scale Systems, Vol. 6, No. 1, Feb., 1984, pp.
    13-38.

3. Bennett, J., "User-Oriented Graphics: Systems for Decision Support
    in Unstructured Tasks," in User-Oriented Design of Interactive
    Graphics Systems, S. Treu, ed., Assoc. for Computing Machinery, New
    York, N.Y., 1977.

4. Berger, J. O., Statistical Decision Theory: Foundations, Concepts
    and Methods, Springer-Verlag, New York, N.Y., 1980.

5. Brott, C. M., "Integrated Risk and Uncertainty Assessment: A
    methodological Approach," M.S. Thesis, Systems Engineering
    Department, Case Western Reserve University, Cleveland, Ohio 1984.

6. Brott, C. M., and Haimes, Y. Y., "Integrated Risk and Uncertainty
    Assessment," Technical paper No. SEC-85-11, Systems Engineering
    Department, Case Western Reserve University, Cleveland, Ohio, 1985.

7. Chankong, V., and Haimes, Y. Y., "The Interactive Surrogate Worth
    Trade-off (ISWT) Method for Multiobjective Decision Making," in
    Multi-Criteria Problem Solving, Stanley Zionts, ed., Springer-
    Verlag, New York, N.Y., 1978.

8. Chankong, V., and Haimes, Y. Y., Multiobjective Decision Making:
    Theory and Methodology, Elsevier-North Holland, New York, N.Y.,
    1983.

9. Fischhoff, B., Lichtenstein, S., Slovic, P., Keeney, R., and Derby,
    S., Approaches to Acceptable Risk: A Critical Guide, Oak Ridge
    National Laboratory, Oak Ridge, Tennessee, NUREG/CR-1614 and
    ORNL/Sub-7656/1, Dec., 1980.

10. Gordon, T. J., and Hayward, H., "Initial Experiments with the
    Cross-Impact Matrix Method of Forecasting," Futures, Vol. 1, No. 2,
    Dec., 1968, pp. 100-116.

11. Gomide, F., and Haimes, Y. Y., "The Multiobjective, Multistage
    Impact Analysis Method: Theoretical Basis," IEEE Transactions on
    Systems, Man, and Cybernetics, Vol. SMC-14, No. 1, 1984, pp. 88-98.

12. Haimes, Y. Y., ed., Risk/Benefit Analysis in Water Resources
    Planning and Management, Plenum, New York, N.Y., 1981.

13. Haimes, Y. Y., and Hall, W. A., "Multiobjectives in Water Resources
    Systems Analysis: The Surrogate Worth Trade-off Method," Water
    Resources Research, Vol. 10, No. 4, Aug., 1974, pp. 615-624.

14. Haimes, Y. Y., Hall, W. A., and Freedman, H. T., Multiobjective Optimization in Water Resources Systems: The Surrogate Worth Trade-off Method, Elsevier Scientific Publ. Co., Amsterdam, The Netherlands, 1975.

15. Haimes, Y. Y., and Hall, W. A., "Sensitivity, Responsivity, Stability, and Irreversibility as Multiple Objectives in Civil Systems," Advances in Water Resources, Vol. 1, No. 2, 1977, pp. 71-81.

16. Haimes, Y. Y., and Leach, M. R., "Risk Assessment and Management in a Multiobjective Framework," in Decision Making with Multiple Objectives, Y. Y. Haimes and V. Chankong, eds., Springer-Verlag, N.Y., 1985 (in press).

17. Holloway, C. A., Decision Making Under Uncertainty: Models and Choices, Prentice-Hall, Englewood Cliffs, N.J., 1979.

18. Jaynes, E. T., "Prior Probabilities," IEEE Transactions on Systems, Man, and Cybernetics, Vol. SMC-4, 1968, pp. 227-241.

19. Jeffreys, H., Theory of Probability, 3rd ed., Oxford University Press, London, England, 1961.

20. Keeney, R. L., and Raiffa, H., Decisions with Multiple Objectives, Wiley, New York, N.Y., 1976.

21. Leach, M. R., "Risk and Impact Analysis in a Multiobjective Framework," M.S. thesis, Systems Engineering Department, Case Western Reserve University, Cleveland, Ohio, 1984.

22. Leach, M., and Haimes, Y. Y., "Multiobjective Risk-Impact Analysis Method," Technical Paper No. SED-101-85, Systems Engineering Department, Case Western Reserve University, Cleveland, Ohio, 1985.

23. Office of Technology Assessment, U.S. Congress, Use of Models for Water Resources Management, Planning and Policy, Government Printing Office, Washington, D.C., 1982.

24. Rarig, H., and Haimes, Y. Y., "Risk Dispersion Index Method in a Multiobjective Framework," IEEE Transactions on Systems, Man, and Cybernetics, Vol. SMC-13, 1983, pp. 317-328.

25. Riggs, J. L., Engineering Economics, 2nd ed., McGraw-Hill, New York, N.Y., 1982.

26. Sage, A. P., Methodology for Large Scale Systems, McGraw-Hill, New York, N.Y., 1977.

27. Sprague, R. H., Jr., and Carlson, E. D., Building Effective Decision Support Systems, Prentice-Hall, Englewood Cliffs, N.J., 1982.

28. Winkler, R. L., Introduction to Bayesian Inference and Decision, Holt, Rinehart and Winston, New York, N.Y.,, 1972.

RISK ASSESSMENT FOR GROUNDWATER CONTAMINATION: II

Vira Chankong*
Yacov Y. Haimes**, F. ASCE
Chenggui Du***

ABSTRACT

This paper constitutes Part II of a two-part article. Both parts focus on the risk assessment and management process in terms of the ever-present problem of groundwater contamination and its prevention and correction. Part I provides a brief definition of terms and concepts in risk assessment and management, develops a brief taxonomy of risk assessment methodologies, and briefly discusses the imperativeness of multiple-objective optimization in risk assessment and management. Part II details the mathematical process of risk quantification (a nontrivial task that deserves much more attention in the literature than it has been given so far), illustrates the risk assessment and management process through a specific example problem concerned with groundwater contamination, focusing on its risk quantification aspects, uses the partitioned multiobjective risk method (PMRM) to demonstrate an effective methodology for handling extreme events, analyzes the computational results in terms of management policy options and multiobjective trade-offs, and relates the entire risk assessment and management process to multiobjective trade-off analysis and to decision support systems.

The division of the article into two parts, while semi-arbitrary and dictated by rules governing paper length, reflects the fact that the two parts were presented at two separate, albeit related, sessions of the Conference.

1. Introduction

The concepts and ideas of risk assessment and management that were discussed in Part I of this two-part article have laid the foundation for this paper, in which we will see how these can be translated into a working device. To make the illustration concrete and specific, we will focus mainly on risk quantification (one of the five tasks that comprise risk assessment and management), and will offer a specific example problem. Other aspects of the problem (e.g., risk evaluation) will also be touched upon. As we go through this illustrative exercise, we shall

*   Visiting Associate Professor, Systems Engineering Department, Case
      Western Reserve University (CWRU), Cleveland, Ohio 44106
**   Chairman, Systems Engineering Department and Professor of Systems
      and Civil Engineering, CWRU, Cleveland, Ohio 44106.
***   Graduate Research Assistant, Systems Engineering Department, CWRU,
      Cleveland, Ohio 44106.

1081

see how several existing tools can be combined to serve a common goal. Most notable among these tools are numerical groundwater models, statistical estimation procedures, impulse-response and convolution concepts from linear systems theory, the partitioned multiobjective risk method (PMRM), and the surrogate worth trade-off (SWT) method.

2. The Problem: An Example

Consider an aquifer that has two potential sources of contaminants--two newly proposed industrial dump sites. Downstream from these are two water wells--one serving as an observation well and the other as a major source of water supply to the surrounding community. The water supply manager of the community wishes to know how the proposed dump sites will affect the quality of the community groundwater supply system.

This manager, in assessing the risks, will need several pieces of information, as suggested by Figure 1 in Part I of this two-part article. More specifically, let us assume that the volume and characteristics (physical, chemical, and biological) of the anticipated wastes are known. Then, answers to the following questions will provide important additional information for the manager's risk-assessment task:

1)   How much contamination is generated at the source? And what fraction of it reaches the groundwater table?

2)   How much of the contamination entering the aquifer reaches the two water wells? At what level of concentration? In what form? And in what time frame?

3)   What effects (health-related, environmental, financial, and socio-economic) will this have on the community and on industry?

To obtain information on 1) requires estimation of leachate or effluent production rate (L/EPR) at the sources based partly on known information concerning the volume and characteristics of the wastes and partly on relevant data such as precipitation and soil characteristics. Information on 2) requires knowledge of the flow pattern of the groundwater and the transport mechanism of each contaminant. Finally, information generated by the last group of questions involves the formulation and computation of various measures of risk and use of these measures to evaluate alternative options through trade-off analysis.

Each of the groups of information-generating questions above will require different analytical tools. In what follows, we describe a specific set of methods and procedures that may be used to serve the purposes of the manager. We believe that they together form a well-defined risk quantification and evaluation methodology that is useful not only for this specific example problem but also in many other problem settings relating to groundwater contamination.

3.   The Methodology

Our objective is to generate the various pieces of information described earlier and to synthesize them in the way illustrated in Figure 1.

3.1. Estimating contamination generated at sources

The first step is to estimate the magnitude and the probability of occurrence of the contamination generated at the sources in the form of leachate or effluent. These, of course, depend on many factors including the type, amount, and characteristics of the wastes (which are assumed known, here) and the hydrological and soil characteristics of the aquifer. Because of dependency on a multitude of factors, some of which are purely random (e.g., precipitation), the leachate or effluent production rate, to be denoted from here on by X, should also be treated as a random quantity (rather than a fixed estimate, as traditionally used). For a source with a leachate/effluent production rate that is highly correlated with precipitation and evapotranspiration conditions, an empirical distribution derived from such climatic conditions can be assumed, should sufficient data be available. In the absence of data, we may begin by assuming a functional form. Here, log-normal and gamma families of distributions are rich enough to cover any plausible distribution of an unbounded X (i.e., X lying between 0 and ∞). In the case where the X is known (or can be assumed) to lie in a finite interval, the modified beta family of distributions is also known to be sufficiently rich, covering any plausible distributions (including uniform distribution) of such X. Each of the three nonempirical distributions mentioned is a two-parameter distribution. Data is still needed to estimate such parameters even if a functional form is assumed. It is expected that site-specific data (e.g., total or daily volume of waste dumped, and precipitation and evapotranspiration records) will be available when the proposed methodology is applied to a particular site or region. Such data will be used to estimate moments (such as mean, variance) or fractiles (e.g., median, 25th percentiles, 75th percentiles), which will then be translated to parameter values through some least-square or other numerical procedure. Point estimates of X may be available for computation and can be used as estimates of the mean value. On the other hand, a range estimate can serve as an interval bounding a uniformly distributed X. Should objective data be unavailable in any specific application, subjective estimates of moments or fractiles should be sought and used in the same manner. Along with the distribution of the leachate/effluent production rate, the concentrations of each contaminant will also be computed. Point and range estimates, should they become available, should also be used to estimate distributions of concentration parameters.

For illustrative purposes, we shall assume in this paper that X lies between 0 and ∞ and is a log-normal variate with mean μ and variance σ^2, i.e.,

$$X \sim LN(\mu,\sigma^2) \tag{1a}$$

or

$$\ln X \sim N(\mu_\ell,\sigma_\ell^2) \tag{1b}$$

where $\mu_\ell = \ln[\, \mu/(\sigma^2 + \mu^2)^{\frac{1}{2}}\,]$ and $\sigma_\ell^2 = \ln[(\sigma^2 + \mu^2)/\,\mu^2]$. In general, due to possible time dependency of some factors affecting X, the mean μ and variance σ^2 of X may also be dependent on time. The generation of X by (1) with time-dependent μ and σ^2 then becomes a stochastic process, as depicted in Figure 2.

For simplicity, we shall assume a stationary process in this paper; i.e., both μ and σ^2 are time-invariant parameters.

The modeling of an infiltration process is also needed. Depending on availability of data, one may choose from a range of very simple models (e.g., assuming a fixed percentage of infiltration as used by Miller [14]) through intermediate models (see, for example, Oaks [15]) to sophisticated transport models, as usually included in most numerical groundwater models. We will use the last strategy in this paper.

3.2 Groundwater modeling and concentration at a production well

Understanding the movement of contaminants through porous media and their chemical and biological behavior is imperative for either the prevention or the correction of groundwater contamination. This paper selects and extends the two-dimensional advection-dispersion model for mass transport developed by Konikow and Bredehoeft [10] to incorporate sources of contamination that are random rather than deterministic. The basic Konikow-Bredehoeft (K-B) model is well documented, handles many types of aquifer and transport mechanisms, and runs efficiently on mainframe computers. The objective here is to use the K-B model as one module among many others within a decision support system (DSS) on a microcomputer.

The main function of the K-B model is to support the computation of the response of the groundwater-aquifer system to inputs such as that given in Figure 2(b). Like most other groundwater models, the K-B model can only take step inputs (i.e., a constant rate of concentration entering the system after some initial time t_0). Several simulation runs may be needed to generate responses to any general inputs such as that shown in Figure 2(b). This may take several hours on a microcomputer, which is too long for a DSS. To overcome this difficulty, we propose the use of impulse-response and convolution concepts from linear systems theory [16]. Such concepts have already been used extensively in water resource systems (see, for example, [12]; [13]; [4]; [9]). To use such an approach, we must assume that the groundwater system is linear (the response of a linear combination of concentration inputs is equal to the linear contribution of the responses to individual concentration inputs) and time invariant (the response to a concentration input sequence, shifted by time t_0, is equal to the response of the unshifted input sequence being shifted by t_0). These are reasonable assumptions since the flow and transport equations describing the groundwater models can adequately be treated as linear constant-coefficient partial differential or difference equations. Several experimental runs that we have made also confirm these assumptions.

The main steps in using this approach to groundwater risk quantification for discrete-time models can be summarized as follows:

1)   Use the K-B model to find the unit step response $s[k]$

(the concentration at a specific well under study) of the groundwater system by applying the unit step input sequence $u[k]$ (the entering concentration for a specific source) to a well-calibtated K-B model

2) Find the impulse response, $h[k]$, of the system by using the formula

$$h[k] = s[k] - s[k-1] \qquad (2)$$

3) Compute the response $c[k]$ (the concentration of contaminants at the observation or water supply well at discrete-time k) to any input $x[k]$ (the concentration entering the system at discrete-time k at a single source) by using the convolution between $x[k]$ and $h[k]$; i.e.,

$$c[k] = \sum_{i=-\infty}^{\infty} x[i]h[k-i] = \sum_{i=-\infty}^{\infty} x[k-i]h[i] \qquad (3)$$

Furthermore, if we assume a) there is no concentration at a well at any time before the concentration at sources entering the system (i.e., $c[k] = 0$ for $k < k_o$ whenever $x[k] = 0$ for $k < k_o$) and b) there is no concentration at sources entering the system before time $k = 0$ (i.e., $x[k] = 0$ for all $k < 0$), then (3) becomes

$$c[k] = \sum_{i=0}^{k} x[i]h[k-i] \qquad (4)$$

If we are dealing with multiple sources, we compute $h[k]$ and then $c[k]$ for each source. The overall output is simply equal to the sum of the contributions from each source; i.e.,

$$c[k] = \sum_{j=1}^{M} c_j[k] = \sum_{j=1}^{M} \sum_{i=0}^{k} x_j[i]h_j[k-i] \qquad (5)$$

where $x_j[k]$, $h_j[k]$, and $c_j[k]$ are input concentration, impulse response, and output concentration (at time k) due to source j, respectively. Typical input and output sequences of concentration for a two-source problem are shown in Figure 3.

Since the concentration of contaminants at the source X follows a stochastic process, so also is the output concentration of contaminants at a given well (or any other location) similarly random. If we generate a large number of input concentration sequences X using Eq. (1), and if, for each input sequence, an output sequence C is generated using Eq. (4) and/or (5), then we will have enough information to estimate the necessary statistics (e.g., the estimated mean μ and estimated variance σ^2 of C, including its probability distribution. The mean and variance can be easily estimated using the maximum likelihood estimators, whereas the distribution can be obtained empirically through standard curve fitting. An alternative approach for estimating the distribution is to assume a functional form and then estimate its parameters using the statistics of C generated above. For example, if it is assumed that the input X at a given time is a log-normal variate and that the groundwater system is linear and time-invariant, it follows that the output C at a specific time will also be log-normal with mean and variance computable using simulation as explained above.

The probability distribution of C along with its other necessary statistics just obtained will serve as prior information. Should sampling data at the observation or production well become available, it can be combined with the prior distribution to obtain the posterior distribution in the usual Bayesian manner (see Raiffa and Schlaifer [17]).

Assume that C is a stationary log-normal variate (i.e., the true mean μ_c and true variance σ_c^2 do not change with time). And suppose that n_s independent samples were taken at the production well using a log-normal sampling process (meaning that each sample is taken from an independent log-normal process $LN(\mu_c, \sigma_c^2)$). Let $\bar{c}$ and s_c^2 be the sample mean and variance, respectively. Suppose we further assume that the population variance σ_c^2 is known, with

$$\tilde{\sigma}_c^2 = \frac{\hat{n}}{\hat{n}+n_s} \sigma_c^2 + \frac{n_s}{\hat{n}+n_s} s_c^2 \qquad (6)$$

being a very accurate estimate of its value (where $\hat{n}$ = number of simulated input sequences used to generate $\hat{\mu}_c$ and $\hat{\sigma}_c^2$). Then the posterior density of lnC is clearly normal, with the posterior mean equal to

$$\tilde{\mu}_c = \frac{\hat{n}}{\hat{n}+n_s} \hat{\mu}_c + \frac{n_s}{\hat{n}+n_s} \bar{c} \qquad (7)$$

In other words,

$$\ln C \sim N(\tilde{\mu}_c, \tilde{\sigma}_c^2) \qquad (8)$$

Should the population variance σ_c^2 be assumed to have an inverse-gamma prior distribution (instead of being known), then the posterior density of lnC will follow a normal-inverse gamma model. (Raiffa and Schlaifer [17] and Lavalle [11] give more detail on the above as well as other possible sampling models.)

3.3 Risk functions: formulation and uses

Having obtained the probability density of the output concentration C, whether prior or posterior, the next step is to collapse the distributional information into some risk indices, each of which is scalar in nature. The probability of exceeding a given standard level of concentration, $P(C > C_o)$, and the expected value of concentration, $E(C)$, are two of the commonly used indices. When consideration of extreme events must be highlighted and made explicit, the partitioned multiobjective risk method (PMRM) [1] should be used . The idea is to divide the concentration-probability scales into three (or more) ranges representing the low-probability/high-concentration region, the intermediate-probability/moderate-concentration range, and the low-probability/low-concentration range. Three (or more) risk functions, each representing the conditional expected concentration in a region, can be formed. This is illustrated in Figure 4.

In Figure 4a, it is assumed that it is meaningful to partition the concentration scale into a low range (LCR: 0 to C_1), a moderate range (MCR: C_1 to C_2), and a high range (HCR: C_2 and higher). The corresponding risk function representing the conditional expected concentration at a specific time t in each range can be formulated as follows:

$$E_t(C|LCR) = \{\int_o^{C_1} c f_t(c)dc\}/\int_o^{C_1} f_t(c)dc \qquad (9)$$

$$E_t(C|MCR) = \{\int_{C_1}^{C_2} c f_t(c)dc\}/\int_{C_1}^{C_2} f_t(c)dc \qquad (10)$$

$$E_t(C|HCR) = \{\int_{C_2}^{\infty} c f_t(c)dc\}/\int_{C_2}^{\infty} f_t(c)dc \qquad (11)$$

where $f_t(c)$ is the probability density of C at time t.

It may be more meaningful and convenient for the manager to partition the probability scale (rather than the concentration scale) into low range (LPR: 0 to ϕ_2), medium range (MPR: ϕ_2 to ϕ_1), and high range (HPR: from ϕ_1 upward). From Figure 4b, it is clear that the partitioning in the probability scale can be converted into partitioning in the concentration scale by using

$$C_1 = F_t^{-1}(\phi_1) \quad \text{and} \quad C_2 = F_t^{-1}(\phi_2) \qquad (12)$$

where $F_t(C)$ is the cumulative distribution of C at time t and F_t^{-1} is the inverse function of F_t . Eqs. (9) - (11) can then be used to find the conditional expected concentration in each range, as before.

In addition to the above partitioned risk functions, the usual expected-value risk function, namely,

$$E(C) = \int_{0}^{\infty} cf(c)dc \qquad (13)$$

can also be added to the list for consideration in conjunction with the others already mentioned.

Having obtained a number of relevant risk functions, particularly one that reflects the effects of extreme events, we next incorporate these functions into other decision criteria (e.g., various types of cost) and use them to evaluate various alternative options. A number of risk-evaluation methods exist (see, for example, Figure 2 of Part I of this article). We propose that the surrogate worth trade-off (SWT) method and its variants [7], [8] be used since, with these methods, explicit trade-off analysis can be performed conveniently and nonlinear problems can be handled easily. Subsequent tasks of risk assessment and management can then be carried out.

Figure 5 summarizes the risk quantification and evaluation methodology explained in this section. The next section illustrates the method by applying it, using specific numerical values, to the example problem stated at the beginning of this paper.

4. Numerical Example

We now reconsider the water manager's problem, and assign the specific numerical values and arrangement as shown in Figure 6.

As the first step, the K-B model was used to find the step responses $s_{ij}[k]$ (at discrete-time k), of the unit step input concentration at source i (i = 1 or 2) at well j (j = A or B). Eq. (4) was then used to compute the corresponding impulse responses $h_{ij}[k]$. The time scale is automatically discretized by the model and this is based on some numerical convergence criteria built into the model. The time duration of the simulation was five years and the discrete-time interval used by the model was 0.1316 year. Table 1 and Figure 7 show typical results of this computation, with Table 1 depicting the first-year values of the unit step response and the unit impulse response at well A to input concentration at sources 1 and 2. Figure 7, on the other hand, displays in graphical form the full variations over the five-year simulated period of the unit step and impulse responses at well A to input concentration at source 1.

The oscillations exhibited in Figure 7 for both s[k] and h[k] are due mainly to the numerical procedure of the K-B model (particularly the convergence criteria that contribute to oscillations through their effects on the sampling time interval). Research on ways of correcting this computational problem is clearly needed. For this paper, we will use the "uncorrected" impulse responses, as illustrated in Figure 7(b).

Next, for each source, we generate a sufficient number (three, in our example) of input concentration sequences; each of these represents a particular waste-management scenario and was instituted either by industry or by the community. We assume that each waste-management scenario, when it is translated into action, can be completely characterized by the means and variances of input concentrations at sources 1 and 2.

The input concentration stochastic sequence $x_i[k]$ at source i (i = 1 or 2) for each management scenario was then randomly generated using the log-normal model with the mean and variance corresponding to that scenario. The output concentration sequence $c_j[k]$ (j = A or B) was next computed by convolving $x_i[k]$ with $h_i[k]$ for each source i and adding the results for all sources, as in Eq. (5). Selective results are shown in Table 2, which shows the means and standard deviations of the output concentration c_j at well j at three time instants for each scenario. Figure 8 shows the densities and cumulative distributions of output concentration at well A at time instant t_2 for each scenario.

With this information, the PMRM can now be applied. Suppose the water manager is interested in comparing low-probability events with medium-probability and high-probability events and he considers a probability between 0 and 0.2 to be low, between 0.2 and 0.8 to be medium, and between 0.8 and 1 to be high. The probability scale is then partitioned accordingly, and the corresponding partitions on the concentration scale for each scenario and at each well are computed using a cumulative distribution similar to those shown in Figure 8(b). This is further illustrated in Figure 9.

Let $\hat{c}_{j,t}(s_q)$ and $\tilde{c}_{j,t}(s_q)$ be the partition points on the concentration scale corresponding the "0.2" and "0.8" partition points on the probability scale, respectively. As can be seen, $\hat{c}$ and $\tilde{c}$ will depend on time-instant t and scenario s_q in addition to the particular output location j of interest.

The conditional expected concentration at each output location j and for each scenario s_q at time instant t can then be computed using Eqs. (9)-(11) with c_1 and c_2 replaced by the respective values of $\hat{c}$ and $\tilde{c}$. The results for well A at time t_2 are shown in Table 3.

Three appropriate risk measures representing conditional expected concentrations can then be formulated, one for each partition I_i in Table 3. Let these risk functions corresponding to the three partitions be f_1, f_2, and f_3, respectively. To illustrate, we assume that the combined effects of concentrations at the two sources for each scenario, $X_1(s_q)$ and $X_2(s_q)$, can be represented by the variable Y:

$$Y(s_q) = X_1(s_q) + X_2(s_q)$$

Although different weights for X_1 and X_2 can be used to reflect different scales of impacts of the two sources, for simplicity, we chose unit weight for both sources. There is thus a one-to-one correspondence between Y and s_q. An analytical relationship between f_i and Y can thus be determined through regression.

Carrying out the necessary computations, we found that a linear relationship between f_i and Y was quite adequate. Table 4 shows typical results, again at well A and at time t_2. Now suppose we want to evaluate various scenarios based on the above risk indices and the following cost functions:

$$f_o(y) = \begin{cases} (y^2 - 15{,}600y + 60{,}836{,}430)\ 10^{-6} \ M\$ & \text{if } y < 7{,}800 \\ 0 & \text{if } y > 7{,}800 \end{cases}$$

(i.e., it will cost industry and the community $f_o(y)$ M\$ to maintain the total entering concentration at y ppb.)

We can use the SWT method for this purpose and generate noninferior (Pareto optimal) scenarios by solving the following vector optimization problem (VOP):

$$\text{VOP: } \min_{0 \leqslant y \leqslant 7{,}800} \{f_o(y),\ f_1(y),\ f_2(y),\ f_3(y)\} \qquad (13)$$

where $f_o(y)$ is given above, $f_1(y) = .0246y - 15.08$ ppb, $f_2(y) = 0.0292y - 9.81$ ppb, and $f_3(y) = .0262y + .32$ ppb. Converting the VOP into a series of ε-constraint problems and solving them yields Pareto optimal frontiers, as shown in Figure 9. Each curve traces the Pareto optimal (noninferior) combination of cost $f_o(y)$ and each conditional expected concentration $f_i(y)$ as y changes. The slope of each curve at a particular point y_o thus represents the trade-off rate between $f_o(y_o)$ and $f_i(y_o)$ at the point y_o.

Scenarios S_1, S_2, and S_3 as used in Table 2 can also be located on Figure 9, as shown. The water manager can then use the information depicted (including trade-offs) in combination with any other information, as appropriate, to evaluate the pros and cons of existing waste-management scenarios or even to generate new ones.

5. Conclusion

What we have tried to illustrate in this paper are i) typical tasks that need to be done in quantifying and evaluating risks related to groundwater contamination, ii) the kind of tools that can be used to accomplish such tasks, and iii) the way in which these tools can be combined to form a unified package. In particular, we have demonstrated how the impulse-response and convolution concepts and certain statistical estimation techniques can be used in combination with existing groundwater models to estimate the probability distribution of output concentration at any output location. Also we have shown how the PMRM and the SWT method can be used to formulate and evaluate risk functions for problems highlighted by extreme events. Much work still needs to be done, particularly in the areas of the design and incorporation of sampling information in the estimation process, further improvement on the use of impulse-response, convolution, and other concepts of linear systems theory in the quantification of risk, and the development of DSSs for specific classes of groundwater contamination problems.

Well A					
Time		Due to Source 1		Due to Source 2	
k	year	(k)	h(k)	(k)	h(k)
0	0.0	0.0000	0.0000	0.0000	0.0000
1	0.1316	0.0000	0.0000	0.0000	0.0000
2	0.2632	0.0000	0.0000	0.0000	0.0000
3	0.3974	0.0002	0.0002	0.0000	0.0000
4	0.5263	0.0014	0.0012	0.0000	0.0000
5	0.6579	0.0050	0.0036	0.0001	0.0001
6	0.7895	0.0139	0.0089	0.0002	0.0001
7	0.9211	0.0222	0.0083	0.0004	0.0002
8	1.0526	0.0310	0.0088	0.0007	0.0003

Table 1. First year unit step and impulse response sequences at Well A due to source 1 and source 2

Concentration at		Scenario S_1		Scenario S_2		Scenario S_3	
		Mean	S.D.	Mean	S.D.	Mean	S.D.
Well A	t_1	170	10	56	7	28	4
	t_2	213	12	71	9	35	5
	t_3	215	14	72	10	35	6
Well B	t_1	19	2	7	1	3	5
	t_2	500	28	182	14	90	7
	t_3	554	36	199	18	98	9

where S_1 ≡ mean input at source 1 = 3000 ppb and S.D. = 500 ppb
mean input at source 2 = 5000 ppb and S.D. = 1500 ppb
S_2 ≡ mean input at source 1 = 1000 ppb and S.D. = 400 ppb
mean input at source 2 = 2000 ppb and S. D. = 500 ppb
S_3 ≡ mean input at source 1 = 500 ppb and S.D. = 200 ppb
mean input at source 2 = 1000 ppb and S.D.= 300 ppb
and t_1 = 1.579, t_2 = 3.158 and t_3 = 4.737 (year)

Table 2. Means and standard deviations of output concentrations at the two wells at different times for different scenarios.

Partition I_i Prob. Scale	S_1 Action A1	S_2 Action A2	S_3 Action A3
$I_1 = 0.0 - 0.2$	0.18328900E+03	0.51188710E+02	0.27540410E+02
$I_2 = 0.2 - 0.8$	0.22404390E+03	0.74914360E+02	0.36028700E+02
$I_3 = 0.8 - 1.0$	0.20961140E+03	0.79077500E+02	0.39379490E+02

Table 3. Conditional expected concentration at well A at
time t_2: $E(C_{A,t_2} | I_i : s_q)$

$f_i(y)$	Coefficient A	Coefficient B	Corelation
1	-15.07907000	0.02458043	0.99673410
2	-9.80503100	0.02915216	0.99968730
3	0.31991650	0.02616869	0.99999670

Table 4. Relationships between f_i and y: $f_i(y) = A + By$

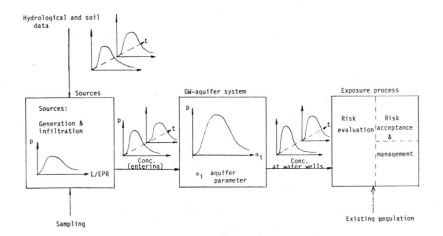

Figure 1. Groundwater contamination quantification process

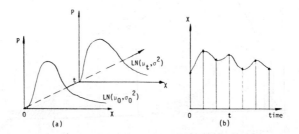

Figure 2. Time-dependent distribution and stochastic process of X

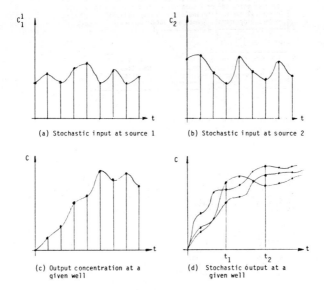

(a) Stochastic input at source 1

(b) Stochastic input at source 2

(c) Output concentration at a given well

(d) Stochastic output at a given well

Figure 3. Contaminant concentration at sources and output wells

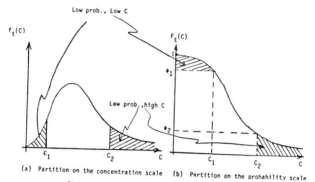

(a) Partition on the concentration scale   (b) Partition on the probability scale

Figure 4. Formulation of partitioned risk indices

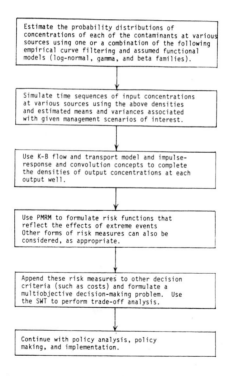

Estimate the probability distributions of concentrations of each of the contaminants at various sources using one or a combination of the following empirical curve filtering and assumed functional models (log-normal, gamma, and beta families).

Simulate time sequences of input concentrations at various sources using the above densities and estimated means and variances associated with given management scenarios of interest.

Use K-B flow and transport model and impulse-response and convolution concepts to complete the densities of output concentrations at each output well.

Use PMRM to formulate risk functions that reflect the effects of extreme events Other forms of risk measures can also be considered, as appropriate.

Append these risk measures to other decision criteria (such as costs) and formulate a multiobjective decision-making problem. Use the SWT to perform trade-off analysis.

Continue with policy analysis, policy making, and implementation.

Figure 5. An integrated risk quantification/evaluation methodology for a typical groundwater contamination problem

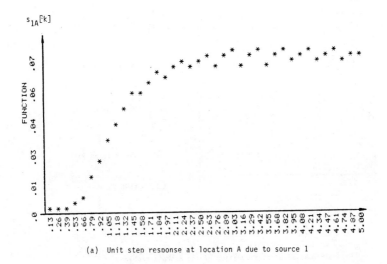

(a) Unit step response at location A due to source 1

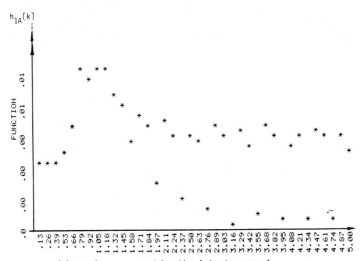

(b) Impulse response at Location A due to source 1

Figure 7. Example results of impulse response computations at location A

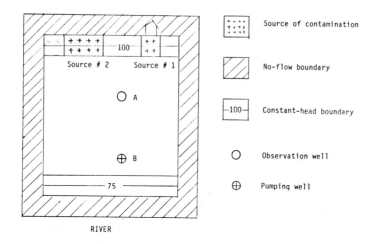

Figure 6. Physical configuration of the example problem

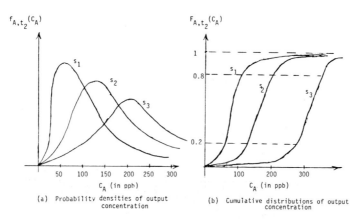

(a) Probability densities of output
concentration

(b) Cumulative distributions of output
concentration

Figure 8. Distributions of output concentration at well A at time t_2

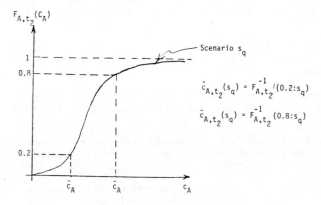

Figure 9. Converting probability partitions into concentration partitions

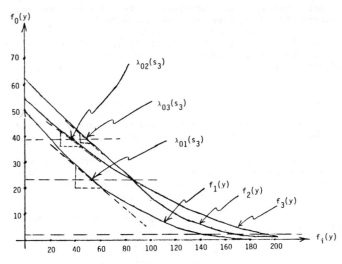

Figure 10. Cost-risk Pareto frontier

Note: $\lambda_{0i}(s_q)$ represents trade-off rate between f_0 and f_i at scenario s_q

APPENDIX 1.   REFERENCES

1. Asbeck, E. L., and Haimes,Y. Y.,"Partitioned Multiobjective Risk Method (PMRM) Large Scale Systems, Vol. 6, No. 1, Feb., 1984, pp. 13-38.

2. Bachmat, Y., Bredehoeft, J., Andrews, B., Holz D., and Sebastian, S., Groundwater Management: The Use of Numerical Models, AGU, Washington, D.C., 1985

3. Chankong, V., and Haimes, Y. Y., Multiobjective Decision Making: Theory and Methodology, Elsevier North Holland, New York, N.Y., 1983.

4. Driezin, Y. and Haimes, Y.Y., "A Hierarchy of Response Functions for Groundwater Management," Water Resources Research, Vol. 13, No. 1, 1977, pp. 78-86.

5. Haimes, Y. Y., Hierarchical Analyses of Water Resources Systems: Modeling and Optimization of Large Scale Systems, McGraw-Hill, New York, N.Y., 1977.

6. Haimes, Y. Y., ed., Risk/Benefit Analysis in Water Resources Planning and Management, Plenum Publishing Company, New York, N.Y., 1981.

7. Haimes, Y.Y., and Hall, W.A., "Multiobjectives in Water Resources Systems Analysis: The Surrogate Worth Trade-Off Method," Water Resources Research, Vol. 10, 1974, pp. 615-624.

8. Haimes, Y. Y., Hall, W. A., and Freedman, H. T.,Multiobjective Optimization in Water Resources Systems: The Surrogate Worth Trade-off Method, Elsevier Scientific Publishing Company, Amsterdam, The Netherlands, 1975.

9. Kaunas, J. R., and Haimes, Y. Y., Risk Analysis of Groundwater Contamination: Computational Results, Technical Report No. CLSSPA-1, Center for Large Scale Systems and Policy Analysis, Case Western Reserve University, Cleveland, Ohio 44106, 1985.

10. Konikow, L. F., and Bredehoeft, J. D., "Computer Model of Two-Dimensional Solute Transport and Dispersion in Groundwater," in Techniques of Water Resources Investigations, Book 7, Chapter 2, U.S. Geological Survey, Reston, Virginia, 1978.

11. LaValle, I. H., Fundamentals of Decision Analysis, Holt, Rinehart and Winston, New York, N.Y.,1978.

12. Maddock, T.,III, "Algebraic Technological Function from a Simulation Model," Water Resources Research, 8(1), 1972, pp. 129-134.

13. Maddock, T.,III, and Haimes, Y. Y., A Tax System for the Planning and Management of Groundwater, Water Resources Research, Vol. 11, No. 1, 1975, pp. 7-14.

14. Miller, D.W., ed., Waste Disposal Effects on Groundwater, Premier Press, Berkeley, CA, 1980.

15. Oaks, D.B., "Use of Idealized Models in Predicting the Pollution of Water Supplies Due to Leachate From Landfill Sites," in Groundwater Quality-Measurement, Prediciton and Protection Water Research Center, Medmonham, England,1977, pp. 611-624.

16. Oppenheim, A. V., Willsky, A. S., and Young, I. T., Signals and Systems, Prentice-Hall, Inc., Englewood Cliffs, N.J., 1983.

17. Raiffa H., and Schlaifer, R., Applied Statistical Decision Theory, Division of Research, Graduate School of Business Administration, Harvard University, Boston, MA, 1961.

Acknowledgements

Support for this study was provided, in part, by the U.S. Department of the Interior, Bureau of Reclamation, Contract No. 4-FG-93-00090, under the project title "Risk Assessment for the Protection From and the Prevention of Groundwater Contamination."

Special thanks are due to Mrs. Virginia Benade for her editorial assistance, and to Mrs. Mary Ann Pelot and Mrs. Toni Sowa for their extraordinary patience in typing and retyping this two-part article with professional skill.

DETERMINISTIC AND STATISTICAL
WATER QUALITY MODELING

Miguel A. Medina, Jr.[1], M.ASCE

ABSTRACT:

An integrated methodology is presented, based on a hierarchical
package of computer models ranging from simple micro-computer programs
to more complex mainframe simulation, to address the impact of water
quality fluctuations in determining instream flow strategies. The
models are applied to derive the frequency and duration of violations
of established stream standards according to State stream use
classifications. Both physically-based (deterministic) continuous
simulation models and statistically-based (derived distribution)
models are compared for the same study site (Salem Creek,
Winston-Salem, N.C.) and hydrologic time series (November 1980 to
August 1981). The predicted responses of the stream receiving
intermittent storm runoff were found to be equivalent for continuous
steady-state deterministic simulation and the simplified probabilistic
models--in terms of the frequency distribution of pollutant
concentrations. The more detailed approach of continuous
deterministic simulation of water quality transients provides the
frequency distribution of the duration of consecutive violations at
higher computational cost.

INTRODUCTION AND OVERVIEW

Rainfall and, therefore, surface runoff (streamflow) are both
inherently random events. It is appropriate to analyze water quality
effects for instream flow strategies within a probabilistic setting.
It does not follow, however, that the mathematical models themselves
should be exclusively statistical black boxes. Indeed, the response
of receiving waters to pollutant mass discharges may and has been
described by deterministic mass balance models. Continuous, long term
deterministic simulation allows representation of water quality
effects in terms of the probability of occurrence of events of various
magnitudes. Stochastic inputs to such a deterministic model will
result in random output. Probabilistic analysis attempts to calculate
the probability distribution of receiving water quality concentrations
given the probability distribution of model inputs: for example,
hydrology, pollutant loadings, stream temperature, etc. A framework

---

[1] Associate Professor of Civil Engineering, Duke University,
Durham, North Carolina 27706

is presented in which both statistical and deterministic models can be
integrated in the analysis to achieve: long-term characterization of
the rainfall-runoff process and derivation of both hydrologic and
water quality frequency distributions. If the level at which a
particular pollutant concentration impairs the use of the receiving
stream is known, then the concentration probability distribution
specifies the frequency (and duration in the case of simulation of
transients) with which that use (fisheries, waste allocation) will be
impaired. If the assumptions upon which the statistical models are
based are met, for a particular study site and hydrologic time series,
the calculations can be easily performed on a microcomputer and the
data requirements are relatively simple. These models are very useful
for preliminary water resource assessment. They can be followed by a
more refined approach if it is justified. Continuous deterministic
simulation (both steady-state and transient) accounts for the actual
sequencing of storm event loads. Much more complex statistical
procedures (often impractical) would be required to approximate this
phenomena. Deterministic models also produce a more complete time
history of system response to excitation, representing not only
individual storm properties but also cumulative effects of closely-
spaced events. These models can be relatively expensive to execute,
are data intensive and require large memory devices for data
manipulation and storage. Advances in microcomputer technology are
making it possible to load these large programs into memory but
execution times are still extremely long.

The relationship between probabilistic water quality analysis and
time variable deterministic simulation has been noted earlier
(e.g., 11,6). The probabilistic analysis begins with the simplest
deterministic model: a mass balance at the location where the
pollutant loads can be assumed to enter the stream. Then, probability
distributions are assumed or derived for each of the variables in the
mass balance equation (flows and concentrations for the source and the
stream). Analytical methods based on moments (mean and variance) have
been presented (14,6,7) as well as a semi-analytical (numerical
integration) method (6) and Monte Carlo simulations (14) of
"independent" random variables. In Monte Carlo simulation, a value is
drawn randomly from each of the distributions (river flow, discharge
flow, river water quality concentration, discharge water quality
concentration) and these values are subsequently used to calculate the
water quality concentration downstream from the discharge. The aim of
Monte Carlo simulation is to produce a set of equally-likely events
that are statistically indistinguishable from the historical data, for
the length of time required or appropriate to the task. Both Warn and
Brew (14) and DiToro (6,7) assumed lognormally-distributed flows and
concentrations. This characterization seems justified for many
streams and stormwater runoff data sets on the basis of published
results of the Nationwide Urban Runoff Program (NURP) (15). However,
each site-specific hydrologic time series must be checked accordingly.

Conceptually-based time variable "deterministic" model simulations
attempt to predict the system response time series for each variable
of interest at various locations--in the exact temporal sequence that
would occur from the input time series (historical or synthetically

derived). After sufficiently long simulation, the predicted time series can be evaluated, as noted above, in terms of frequency distributions of the magnitude of these events and their duration. The probabilistic models are highly-dependent on how well the distributions of the original variables can be hypothesized. The physically-based models are highly-dependent on the input variable time series. Because many of these model parameters are difficult to estimate (infiltration rates, pollutant accumulation and washoff coefficients, reaction rates, dispersion, etc.) the deterministic label is quite optimistic. Monte Carlo techniques have been combined with physically-based models to attempt to produce an output time series more representative of catchment characteristics and historical hydrologic time series. The central, unifying theme of this hierarchical modeling package is the derivation of the frequency with which pollutant concentrations are exceeded in a river reach, on the basis of established stream standards. Thus, the methodology lends itself to both fixed standards or standards based on probability.

METHODOLOGY

Rainfall Time Series Analysis

An integral part of the assessment of storm-derived pollutant loads on receiving water quality is the statistical evaluation of rainfall records. The purpose is to summarize the variables of interest (volume, duration, intensity and time between storm events) and satistically characterize the rainfall record to determine seasonal trends (4). The hourly rainfall data are summarized by storm events, each with an associated unit volume, duration, average intensity and time since the preceding storm (measured from the midpoint of the successive storms). Thus, a storm definition must be established to determine when in the hourly record a storm begins and ends. To avoid an arbitrary definition of independence, a minimum interevent time was derived on the basis of autocorrelation analysis of the hourly rainfall of a representative year in the time series. The representative year was selected after analysis of a 28-year record of hourly rainfall at a first-order station, and evaluation of yearly frequency histogram plots.

Deterministic Hydrologic and Water Quality Modeling

A distributed routing rainfall-runoff model was used which provides detailed simulation of storm-runoff periods with soil-moisture accounting between storms (3). A drainage basin is essentially represented as a set of overland-flow, channel and reservoir segments. Kinematic wave theory is used for routing flows over contributing overland-flow areas and through the channels. Routing through reservoirs is commonly accomplished by the modified Puls method.

Surface Runoff Quality

Perhaps the <u>least</u> deterministic aspect of water quality modeling is the procedure for computation of surface runoff quality, from assumptions made of pollutant accumulation and washoff processes. There are, generally, that: (1) the amount of pollutant which can be removed during a storm event is dependent on rainfall duration and initial quantity of pollutant <u>available</u> for removal; (2) no pollutants decay due to chemical changes or biological degradation during the runoff process, and (3) the amounts of pollutants percolating into the soil by infiltration are not significant. Most field data consist of measurements of stage (converted to discharge through a rating curve) and pollutant concentrations <u>at the subcatchment outlet</u>. These data represent the combined effects of accumulation, washoff, routing and contributions from rainfall: the pollutant loads may include contributions from different land-use types with different accumulation rates.

When a significant portion of the pollutants come from non-urban land uses, a daily pollutant accumulation method (8) can be used:

$$P_p = \sum_{i=1}^{L} (F_{pi} \cdot (A \cdot PT_i) \cdot N_D) + P_{po} \quad \dots \dots \dots \dots \quad (1)$$

where P_p = pollutant p at beginning of storm, total pounds (kg)

F_{pi} = accumulation of pollutant p on land use i, lbs/acre/day (kg/ha/day)

A = total area in basin, acres (ha)

PT_i = percent of basin in land use i

N_D = number of days without runoff since last storm

P_{po} = pollutant p remaining at end of the last storm, total pounds (kg), and

L = number of land use types.

Washoff, at each time step of simulation, is made proportional to runoff rate:

$$- P_t = \frac{dP}{dt} = - a \, r^b \, P_o \quad \dots \dots \dots \dots \dots \dots \quad (2)$$

where P_t = pollutant load washed off at time t, lb/sec (kg/sec)

P_o = load available for washoff at time t, lb(kg)

r = runoff rate, in/hr (mm/hr)

a = washoff coefficient, including conversion units, and

b = a power constant.

Sediment data from streams supports the rating curve in equation (2). Procedures for estimating accumulation and washoff parameters, including optimization methods are discussed by Alley (2) and Alley and Smith (1). The limitations and research needs are presented by Sonnen (13).

Pollutant Transport

Pollutant transport processes may be represented by the one-dimensional version of the classical advective-dispersive equation:

$$\frac{\partial C}{\partial t} = \frac{\partial}{\partial x} [E \frac{\partial C}{\partial x} - UC] \pm \Sigma S_i \quad \ldots \ldots \ldots \ldots \ldots \ldots \quad (3)$$

where C = concentration of water quality parameter (pollutant), M/L^3,

t = time, T,

$-E\frac{\partial C}{\partial x}$ = mass flux due to longitudinal dispersion along the flow axis, the x direction, $M/L^2 T$,

UC = mass flux due to advection by the fluid containing the mass of pollutant, $M/L^2 T$,

S_i = sources or sinks of   the substance C, $M/L^3 T$,

i = 1,2, . . ., n,

n = number of sources or sinks,

U = flow velocity, L/T, and

E = longitudinal dispersion coefficient, L^2/T.

Equation (3) can be applied to storage/treatment systems, pipe segments, streams, etc. For the biochemical oxygen demand (BOD)-dissolved oxygen (DO) coupled reaction for continuously discharging plane sources in the y-z plane for a non-tidal receiving stream are:

$$\frac{\partial L}{\partial t} + U \frac{\partial L}{\partial x} = E_x \frac{\partial^2 L}{\partial x^2} - K_{13}L \quad \ldots \ldots \ldots \ldots \ldots \quad (4)$$

$$\frac{\partial D}{\partial t} + U \frac{\partial D}{\partial x} = E_x \frac{\partial^2 D}{\partial x^2} + K_{13}L - K_2 D \quad \ldots \ldots \ldots \ldots \quad (5)$$

where L = BOD concentration, M/L^3

K_{13} = biochemical oxidation rate and sedimentation rate coefficient for carbonaceous BOD, $1/T$,

D = DO deficit $\equiv C_s - C, M/L^3$,

C_s = saturation concentration of DO at stream temperature, M/L^3 ,

C = concentration of DO in stream, M/L^3 , and

K_2 = reaeration rate coefficient , $1/T$.

For steady-state analysis, equations (4) and (5) become:

$$U \frac{\partial L}{\partial x} = E_x \frac{\partial^2 L}{\partial x^2} - K_{13}L \quad \ldots \ldots \ldots \ldots \ldots \ldots \ldots \quad (6)$$

$$U \frac{\partial D}{\partial x} = E_x \frac{\partial^2 D}{\partial x^2} + K_{13}L - K_2 D \quad \ldots \ldots \ldots \ldots \ldots \quad (7)$$

Solutions to these equations are presented in detail elsewhere (9, 10) for various components of the physical system and other pollutant combinations.

Statistical Water Quality Models.

In essence, the statistical models calculate the probability distribution of receiving water pollutant concentrations, given the probability distribution of the model inputs (e.g., flows, pollutant loadings, etc.). Whereas the deterministic models attempt to predict the time histories of the output variables and perform frequency analyses on the basis of the historical series, probabilistic water quality analysis attempts to calculate the frequency distributions without computation of the exact sequence of events. Instead, the probability distributions and correlation structure of the input variables are used to compute directly the frequency distribution of the output variables. These statistical models are conceptual simplifications, which require only the statistical properties of the input time series (e.g., medians, means, coefficients of variations, cross-correlations).

The simplest mass balance that can be used to calculate river quality downstream from a pollutant discharge is:

$$C_T = \frac{Q_s C_s + Q_p C_p}{Q_s + Q_p} \quad \dots\dots\dots\dots\dots\dots\dots\dots\dots \quad (8)$$

where C_T = mixed pollutant concentration in the river, downstream from the pollutant discharge location
   Q_s = upstream river flow
   C_s = upstream pollutant concentration
   Q_p = point pollutant source flow rate, and
   C_p = point pollutant source concentration.

Warn and Brew (14) proposed an analytical method based on the first two months (mean, variance) of a two-parameter log-normal distribution, assumed to represent adequately certain ratios of the variables in equation (8) above. For nonpoint source contributions, Q_R and C_R may replace Q_p and C_p :

$$C_T = \frac{Q_s}{Q_s + Q_R} C_s + \frac{Q_R}{Q_s + Q_R} C_R \quad \dots\dots\dots\dots\dots\dots \quad (9)$$

The probability model that follows assumes that Q_s, Q_R, C_s and C_R are jointly lognormally distributed.

Moments Approximation

As noted by Warn and Brew (14) and as modified by DiToro (6,7), the mass balance equation can be rewritten in the form:

$$C_T = C_R \phi + C_s (1 - \phi) \quad \dots\dots\dots\dots\dots\dots\dots \quad (10)$$

where

$$\phi = \frac{Q_R}{Q_R + Q_S} = \text{runoff flow fraction.}$$

If ϕ and $(1 - \phi)$ were lognormaly distributed, and since C_R and C_S are also assumed to be lognormal, the products $C_R \phi$ and $C_S(1 - \phi)$ would also be lognormal. This is an approximation based on the fact that sums of lognormal random variables have been reported to have tails which are also approximately lognormal (6). Assuming independence, and if C_T is assumed lognormal, the relationships between the arithmetic moments, $\mu(C_T)$ and $\sigma^2(C_T)$, and the log mean, μ_ℓ, and log standard deviation, σ_ℓ, are (6):

$$\mu_\ell(C_T) = \ell n \left[\frac{\mu(C_T)}{\sqrt{1 + v^2(C_T)}} \right] \quad \ldots \ldots \ldots \ldots \ldots \quad (11)$$

and

$$\sigma_\ell^2(C_T) = \ell n \ [1 + v^2(C_T)] \quad \ldots \ldots \ldots \ldots \ldots \ldots \quad (12)$$

where

$$v(C_T) = \frac{\sigma(C_T)}{\mu(C_T)} \quad \ldots \ldots \ldots \ldots \ldots \ldots \ldots \ldots \ldots \quad (13)$$

$$= \text{coefficient of variation of } C_T.$$

The quantiles of C_T are:

$$C_{T\alpha} = \exp \ [\mu_\ell(C_T) + z_\alpha \ \sigma_\ell(C_T)] \quad \ldots \ldots \ldots \ldots \ldots \quad (14)$$

which is the concentration that is exceeded with probability $(1 - \alpha)$, where z_α is the standard normal α quantile.

Warn and Brew (14) suggest a numerical integration to compute the moment of ϕ; however, DiToro (6,7) notes that, since the method is approximate, numerical techniques are best reserved for the evaluation of the exact distribution of C_T. He derived the following approximate expressions:

$$\mu_\ell(\phi) = \frac{1}{2} \ [\ell n(\phi_\alpha) + \ell n(\phi_{1-\alpha})] \quad \ldots \ldots \ldots \ldots \ldots \quad (15)$$

and

$$\sigma_\ell(\phi) = \frac{1}{2z_\alpha} \; [\ell n(\phi_\alpha) - \ell n(\phi_{1-\alpha})] \quad \ldots \ldots \ldots \ldots \quad (16)$$

He chose $z = 1.645$ to force agreement of this straight-line approximation of the 5% and 95% quantities. Once the log mean and standard deviation are computed from equations (15) and (16), then the arithmetic moments follow from the lognormal assumption:

$$\mu(\phi) = \exp \; [\mu_\ell(\phi) + \frac{1}{2} \sigma_\ell^2(\phi)] \quad \ldots \ldots \ldots \ldots \ldots \quad (17)$$

and

$$\nu^2(\phi) = \exp \; [\sigma_\ell^2(\phi)] - 1 \quad \ldots \ldots \ldots \ldots \ldots \ldots \quad (18)$$

where $\quad \sigma(\phi) = \mu(\phi)\nu(\phi)$.

These arithmetic moments of ϕ are subsequently used to compute the arithmetic moments of C_T from:

$$\mu(C_T) = \mu(C_R)\mu(\phi) + \mu(C_s)[1 - \mu(\phi)] \quad \ldots \ldots \ldots \ldots \quad (19)$$

and

$$\sigma^2(C_T) = \sigma^2(\phi)[\mu(C_R) - \mu(C_s)]^2$$

$$+ \; \sigma^2(C_R)[\sigma^2(\phi) + \mu^2(\phi)] \quad \ldots \ldots \ldots \ldots \quad (20)$$

$$+ \; \sigma^2(C_s)[\sigma^2(\phi) + (1 - \mu(\phi))^2]$$

where $\quad \mu(\;\;) = $ mean of $(\;\;)$

$\qquad \sigma^2(\;\;) = $ variance of $(\;\;)$.

An alternative numerical integration (Gaussian quadrature) method which is mathematically more exact is presented by DiToro (6). Both methods are easily programmed for use with microcomputers, and results are shown to be equivalent in the application section for the study site in North Carolina (10).

APPLICATION

Salem Creek drains much of the city of Winston-Salem (in the Piedmont region of North Carolina), and is a tributary to Muddy Creek which discharges into the Yadkin River. Wastes entering the Yadkin River from the Winston-Salem area, particularly during heavy rains, resulted in several major fish kills in the late 1960's and the early 1970's (5).

Accurate land use information was obtained from the computerized Land Resources Information Service (LRIS) of the State of North Carolina. Impervious cover percentages were obtained from published U.S. Geological Survey data (12). Predicted hydrographs were calibrated against measured flows and key deterministic hydrologic and water quality model parameters (e.g., velocity, depth, longitudinal dispersion, deoxygenation and reaeration rates) were adjusted to average values obtained from State stream intensive survey data for Salem Creek. A comparison of DO cumulative frequency curves during wet weather periods from November 1980 to August 1981 is presented in Figure 1, for both the steady-state and transient water quality models, at a selected distance downstream. The steady-state model is conservative up to a DO concentration of about 5.5 mg/l (slightly beyond the stream standard). The predicted cumulative DO frequency curves for both the continuous deterministic steady-state and the statistical (method of moments) models are very similar (see Figure 2). The frequency distribution of the duration of violations of a 5.0 mg/l DO standard is presented in Figure 3. For example, there were 8 occurrences of violation for 12 consecutive hours and one occurrence of violation for as many as 60 consecutive hours. These results could only be derived from analysis of water quality transients.

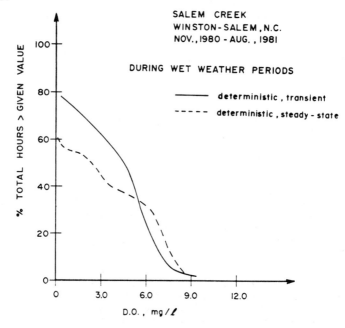

Figure 1.   Comparison of Deterministic Steady-State and Transient Simulation, Salem Creek

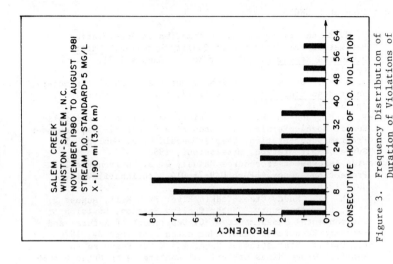

Figure 3. Frequency Distribution of Duration of Violations of the Stream DO Standard, Salem Creek

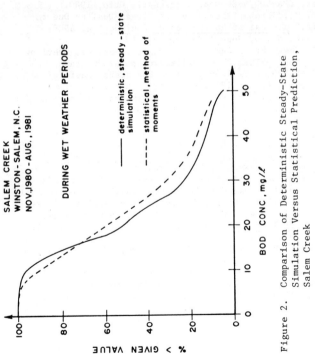

Figure 2. Comparison of Deterministic Steady-State Simulation Versus Statistical Prediction, Salem Creek

APPENDIX I. - REFERENCES

1. Alley, W. M. and P. E. Smith, "Estimation of Accumulation
    Parameters for Urban Runoff Quality Modeling," Water
    Resources Research, Vol. 17, No. 4, August 1981,
    pp. 1161-1166.
2. Alley, W. M., "Estimation of Impervious-Area Washoff Parameters,"
    Water Resources Research, Vol. 17, No. 6, December 1981,
    pp. 1657-1664.
3. Alley, W. M., and Smith, P. E., "Distributed Routing Rainfall-
    Runoff Model--Version II," Open File Report 82-344, Computer
    Program Documentation, User's Manual, U. S. Geological
    Survey, NSTL Station, Mississippi, 1982.
4. Areawide Assessment Procedures Manual, U. S. Environmental
    Protection Agency, EPA-600/9-76-014, Cincinnati, Ohio,
    July 1976.
5. Benton, L. P., "Muddy Creek-Yadkin River Fish Kill, August 8,
    1976, Forsyth County," Water Quality Section, Division of
    Environmental Management, N. C. Department of Natural and
    Economic Resources, Memorandum dated September 24, 1976.
6. DiToro, D. M., "Statistics of Receiving Water Response to
    Runoff," Proceedings of National Conference on Urban Storm-
    water and Combined Sewer Overflow Impact on Receiving Water
    Bodies, EPA-600/9-80-056, Cincinnati, Ohio, 1980.
7. DiToro, D. M., "Probability Model of Stream Quality Due to
    Runoff," Journal of Environmental Engineering, ASCE,
    Vol. 110, No. 3, June 1984, pp. 607-628.
8. Hydrologic Engineering Center, "Storage, Treatment, Overflow,
    Runoff Model-STORM," Generalized Computer Program
    723-S8-L7520, U.S. Army Corps of Engineers, Davis,
    California, August 1977.
9. Medina, M. A., Jr., "Hydrologic and Water Quality Modeling for
    Instream Flow Strategies," WRRI Report No. 183,
    Raleigh, N.C., 1982.
10. Medina, M. A., Jr., "An Integrated Methodology for Instream
    Flow Strategies," WRRI Report No. 210, Raleigh, N.C., 1983.
11. Papoulis, A., Probability, Random Variables and Stochastic
    Processes, McGraw-Hill, N.Y., 1965.
12. Putnam, Arthur L., "Effect of Urban Development on Floods In
    The Piedmont Province of North Carolina," U.S. Geological
    Survey Open-File Report, Raleigh, North Carolina, 1972.
13. Sonnen, M. B., "Urban Runoff Quality: Information Needs,"
    Journal of Technical Councils, ASCE, Vol. 106, No. TC1,
    August 1980, pp. 29-40.
14. Warn, A. E., and J. S. Brew, "Mass Balance," Water Research,
    Vol. 14, 1980, pp. 1427-1434.
15. Water Planning Division, "Results of Nationwide Urban Runoff
    Program," WH-554, U. S. Environmental Protection Agency,
    Vol. I, II and III, Washington, D. C., December 1983.

Water Quality Modeling Of Key Largo Coral Reef

Raymond Walton[1], M. ASCE, Larry A. Roesner[2], M. ASCE,
Ming P. Wang[3], A. M. ASCE, and W. Martin Williams[4], A.M. ASCE

ABSTRACT: A numerical model called CORALSIM has been developed for the Key Largo Coral Reef National Marine Sanctuary in the Florida Keys. The model was developed as a management tool to study the potential impacts on the coral reef due to man's activities. Since we are concerned with the health of the reef ecosystem, we selected model state variables that best represent measures of this health. For coral reefs, this may be represented by carbon exchanges between the reef system and its surrounding environment. These exchanges are expressed as community gross photosynthesis, community gross respiration, and the community gain in fixed inorganic carbonates. Consequently, the model was developed in terms of carbon dioxide and dissolved oxygen budgets, and includes other constituents such as suspended solids, the nutrient cycle, chlorophyll-a, phosphates, and a toxic constituent. The model was calibrated and verified to current meter, water quality, and primary productivity data collected during the study. The development of the model is significant because it will enable NOAA to postulate activities, investigate their consequence, and avoid harm to the reef through anticipatory management practices. The model is in an early stage of evolution. As more is learned about the ecosystem response, through experience with the model, we can better refine the simulation tool and provide more reliable management information.

Introduction

The Key Largo Coral Reef National Marine Sanctuary (NMS) is part of the only coral reef system within the continental United States (Figure 1). It lies between $25°$ and $25°30'$ north, which is towards the northern limits of latitude within which coral reefs can grow. The NMS is an area in which the corals rise to within a few feet of

---

[1]Senior Water Resources Engineer, Camp Dresser & McKee, Annandale, VA 22003

[2]Vice President, Camp Dresser & McKee, Annandale, VA 22003

[3]Senior Engineer, formerly Camp Dresser & McKee, now with Mitre Corporation, McLean, VA 22102

[4]Water Resources Engineer, Camp Dresser & McKee, Annandale, VA 22003

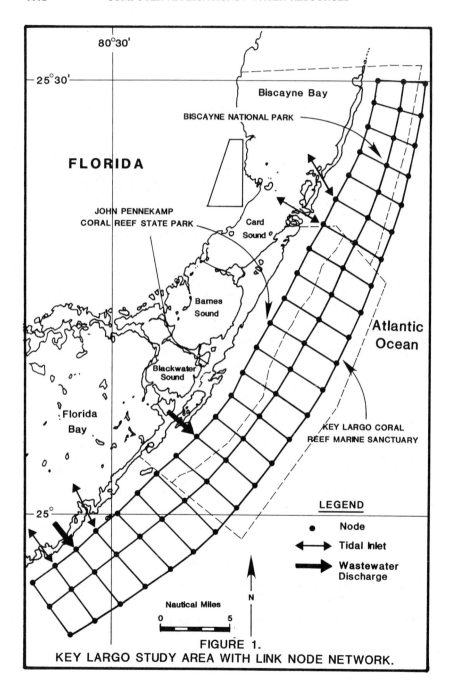

FIGURE 1.
KEY LARGO STUDY AREA WITH LINK NODE NETWORK.

the surface; and consequently, being so close to shore, they attract many recreational scuba divers and snorklers wishing to view the reef's abundant corals and fish.

Since they are on the fringe of their natural growth areas, the coral reefs of the NMS live in a precarious balance with nature. Physically, we know that spin off eddies from the nearby Florida Current can wash colder bottom waters over the reefs. Storm systems and hurricanes can churn up bottom materials, increasing turbidity and decreasing light penetration. In spite of these factors, corals continue to grow in the northern Florida Keys.

These areas are now facing a new assault--from man. He undeniably has the ability to do the greatest long term damage, but also the ability to understand his actions and manage them. Potential impacts on the coral reefs are damage from anchor and boat groundings, diving, fishing, dredge and fill activities, channelization, and waste pollution (waste water treatment plants, etc.).

The ultimate objective of the Sanctuary Program Office of NOAA is to be able to manage activities in the NMS. To do this they embarked on a four-year study which included field measurements, numerical modeling, and management strategies. The scope of this paper is to describe the development and testing of the numerical models developed for the study area.

Approach

The aim of the numerical model development was to produce a computer model that would simulate the major physio-biochemical processes that would provide indications of reef health. It was felt that the health of the coral reef ecosystem may be detected by the changes in carbon and oxygen fluxes which the reef system exchanges with its surrounding environment (2).

As a basis for numerical model development, the models SIM3D and ECOSIM were selected. SIM3D is a three-dimensional current processor that interpolates a velocity vector field onto a numerical grid based on field observations (9). The program interprets the velocity distribution, and uses an "out-of-kilter" algorithm (3, 4) to satisfy continuity, while optimizing flow adjustments using "least-cost" principles. ECOSIM is a compatable three-dimensional ecosystem model (7). This model was modified for this study to simulate carbon dioxide and oxygen balances, and is called CORALISM (10). Both models are based on a link-node representation of the study area (Figure 1).

On the basis of physical and ecological oceanographic observations, the NMS and adjacent areas were divided into four flow areas (Figure 2):

1. Hawk Channel

2. Reef Flats

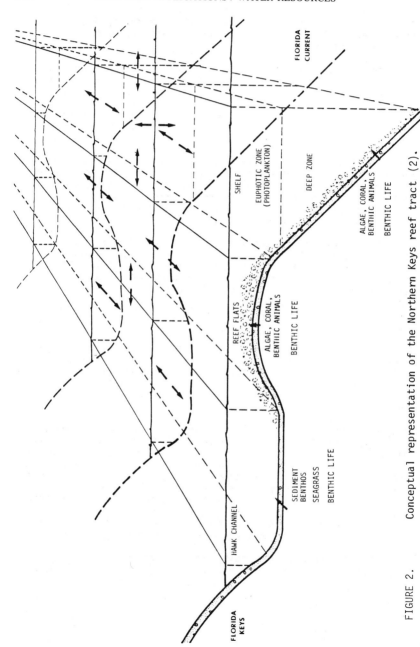

FIGURE 2.   Conceptual representation of the Northern Keys reef tract (2).

3. Upper Florida Current (Euphotic Zone)

4. Lower Florida Current

Hawk Channel is shallow, relatively turbid, and has some sediment
bottom which exerts an oxygen demand on the overlying water. In this
region, turtle grass is abundantly present and therefore is likely the
major primary producer. Anaerobic decomposition within the sediment
layer probably acts as a nutrient source. Photosynthetic activity
here may be hindered, however, due to turbidity in the waste produced
by meteorologic conditions and barge traffic.

Over the reef flats the water is shallow and very clear. The
predominant ecologic features are benthic algae, coral, and benthic
animals. In the coral reefs, the major primary producer is the coral
symbiont zooxanthellae.

In the shelf area, the water is deep and consists of the edge of the
Florida Current. Here are found benthic algae, deeper corals, and
associated benthic animal communities, but less dense than on the reef
flats. In this region, phytoplankton may have more of a significant
effect on dissolved oxygen and carbon dioxide concentrations in the
water than they do on the reef flats.

Data Collection

From July 1982 until November 1983, a comprehensive data collection
program was performed by General Oceanics (current meter study),
Biscayne National Park, and John Pennekamp Coral Reef State Park
(water quality study) and Applied Biology, Inc. (productivity study).
Twelve current meters were deployed during the period. The meters
were serviced every 3-4 months and the raw data filtered to produce
2-week and seasonal averages. Through the reef tract and adjacent
bays (Florida Bay and Biscayne Bay), 21 water quality stations were
sampled at an interval of one month for the following constituents:
conductivity, temperature, dissolved oxygen, pH, wind speed and
direction, turbidity, Nitrate, Nitrite, Ammonia, and Phosphate.
Finally, two primary productivity measurements were made in July and
November 1983.

Circulation Patterns

The flow fields developed by SIM3D are nonuniform, and steady state.
The approach used for this study of Key Largo was to divide the
current meter records into seasonal flow patterns, which when run
consecutively would form a reasonable approximation to year-round
hydrodynamic conditions in the reef tract.

For the purposes of this study, the current meter records were divided
into seasonal average flows--this being done by Dr. T.N. Lee of the
University of Miami. From the current meter records, four seasons
flows were defined - fall, winter, spring and summer.

Using the seasonal-averaged current meter data, seasonal circulation patterns were developed using the three-dimensional current processor, SIM3D. For each season, the available current meter data was interpolated to all the nodes of the system (Figure 1) and the model was run to develop a circulation pattern that (a) satisfies mass continuity, and (b) minimizes changes in the initially prescribed flow field. Weighting factors were supplied to the model that allow greatest deviation from initial values far from current meter locations, and the least adjustment near observed values.

Water Quality Model

Kinsey (6) suggests that carbon fluxes are a useful indication of coral reef health. They may be expressed in terms of the following:

1.   Community gross photosynthesis (P) - all CO_2 fixed by all photosynthetic organisms in the reef community,

2.   Community gross respiration (R) - all CO_2 released by all decomposition and respiration processes with the community, including the respiration of the autotrophs themselves,

3.   Community gain in fixed inorganic carbonate (G) - an estimate of net-precipitation of carbonates.

Therefore, the biochemical model development for this study, CORALSIM, is based on carbon dioxide and oxygen mass balances (Figure 3).

Other modeled variables include phytoplankton, chorophyll a, BOD, ammonia, nitrite, nitrate, phosphate, a user specified toxic substance with a first order decay, suspended solids, and light. The mass balance equation for a passively transported constituent in the water states that the change in concentration with time is the cumulative result of the changes due to transport processes (advection and diffusion), the transformation processes, and external input. CORALISM solves the governing mass transport equations at each new time level by the following steps:

o   Horizontal mass transfers,
o   Vertical mass transfer (including settling velocity),
o   Mass inflows, outflows and decays, and
o   Reaction rates.

Model Calibration

The ecosystem was divided into seagrass and five coral reef community categories to represent variations in respiration and productivity that occurs between benthic communities inhabiting the study area. The distribution was based on maps: "Florida Reef Tract - Marina Habitats and Ecosystems" by Donald S. Marszalek of the University of Miami and a document on the ecology of South Florida Coral Reefs (5).

CORALSIM was calibrated to water quality measurements of the Fall 1982 season. The Florida current nodes are presently being modeled as

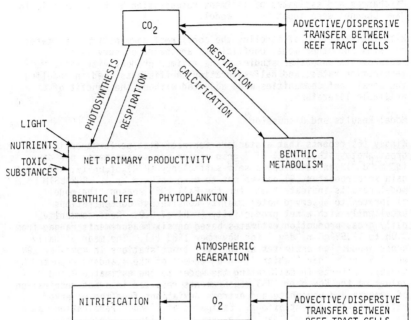

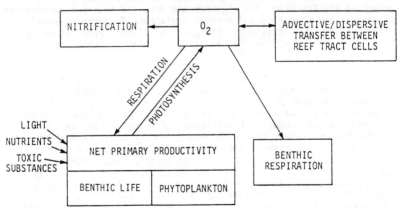

FIGURE 3.   Schematic representation of carbon dioxide and oxygen balance
for the Northern Keys Reef Tract (2).

fixed node boundaries. Other boundaries include tidal exchanges at inlets along the Keys in Hawk Channel. Observed water quality observations were averaged for the season and became the basis for initial conditions and boundary conditions. Existing wastewater discharges and estimates of sediment resuspension by barge traffic in Hawk Channel were input to the model.

With the exception of modeling the coral reef communities, estimates of rates and other model coefficients are based on surveys of measurements and other studies. The maximum productivity rate, respiration rates, and half-saturation coefficients used in modeling the coral reef communities were adjusted without the benefit of available literature.

Model Results and Discussion

Kinsey (6) reports that a standard for reef flat performance is a gross photosynthesis (P) of 7 gram carbon per square meter per day ($gC\ m^{-2}d^{-1}$), an autotrophic self-sufficiency (P/R) of unity, and a net gain in carbonates (G) equivalent to 4 kg $CaCO_3\ m^{-2}y^{-1}$. CORALSIM model results indicate that, for the Fall 1982 season, the model calibrates to observed water quality consitutent concentrations excellently with a net productivity (P-R) of 0.0. Reef community daily gross production estimates based on six measurements ranged from 3.08 to 12.98 $gC\ m^{-2}day^{-1}$ for November 1983 (1). The mean of daily gross production estimates at the reef tract stations in November 1983 was 7.57 $gC\ m^{-2}day^{-1}$ which is in agreement of the standard reported by Kinsey. Efforts in calibrating the model to the estimated P and R values of the November 1983 measurements resulted in a net respiration of ammonia and phosphate and extreme deviations from the observed water quality concentrations. Estimates of 24-hour respiration had a mean value of 13 g $mC^{-2}day^{-1}$, however indicating a heterotrophic community.

Based on the analyses of the Fall 1982 season, the following statements can be made. First, the reef tract may indeed have a seasonal or annual P/R ratio of unity and the productity estimates of November 1983 cannot be extrapolated to 1982. Second, the limited data used in the productivity estimates of November 1983 may be insufficient to assess the metabolism of the system. Third, the model may be overly sensitive to net differences in productivity and respiration. While it is realized that benthic communities generally have a higher carbon to nitrogen and phosphorous ratios then, say, phytoplankton (8), the nutrient exchange during respiration may be orders of magnitude lower than anticipated. A need exists to obtain additional data on productivity and respiration of different benthic coral communities as a basis for estimating the existing metabolism of the sanctuary and growth and respiration rates and half-saturation coefficients for modeling.

From this point the model needs to be verified against other seasons to determine if the model is biased towards the Fall 1982 season. The model can then be used to analyze the impacts of hypothetical scenarios as a tool to managing the Key Largo Coral Reef Marine Sanctuary.

Acknowledgements

The Key Largo National Marine Sanctuary Water Quality Assessment and Modeling Program, NA81-GA-C-00047, was funded by the National Oceanic and Atmospheric Administration, Office of Coastal Zone Management, Sanctuary Program Office. Additional support has been provided by the National Park Service and the John Pennekamp Coral Reef State Park (CRSP), for a multi-agency program involving current measurements and water quality studies. Camp Dresser & McKee is working under contract to Applied Biology, Inc. on this study. The authors wish to express thanks to the people in these agencies for their support during the development of this project, and for administrative and technical assistance which was so generously provided throughout the initial planning phases of this water quality modeling effort. We wish to express our thanks to Messrs. John Hamilton and Robert Comegys of Applied Biology, Inc., Dr. Nancy Foster and Ms. Carroll Curtis of the NOAA Sanctuary Program Office; Ms. Linda Dye, Mr. Richard Curry, and Dr. Jim Tilmont of the National Park Service; Mr. Walter Jaap of the Florida Department of Natural Resources; and Dr. Donald Kinsey, University of Georgia Marine Institute. Finally, under a parallel project, General Oceanics of Miami, Florida (Chris Casagrande, President) conducted an 18-month bottom moored current meter survey. These data were reviewed by Dr. T. N. Lee of the Universtiy of Miami to develop seasonal current averages.

Appendix A - References

1. Applied Biology, Inc., "Key Largo Water Quality Assessment and Modeling Program Chemical and Biological Data Report," Contract No. NA81-GA-C-00047, Decatur, Georgia, January 1985.

2. Applied Biology, Inc. and Camp Dresser & McKee Inc., "Key Largo National Marine Sanctuary Water Quality Assessment and Modeling Program: Phase I," Contract No. NA81-GA-C-00047, Atlanta, Georgia, June 1982.

3. Durbin, E.P. and D.M. Kroenke, "The Out-of-Kilter Algorithm: A Primer," Memorandum RM-5472-PR, The Rand Corporation Santa Monica, California, December 1967.

4. Ford, L.R., Jr. and D.R. Fulkerson, Flows in Networks, Princeton University Press, Princeton, New Jersey, 1962.

5. Jaap, Walter C., "Ecology of the South Florida Coral Reefs: A Community Profile," Florida Department of Natural Resources Marine Research Laboratory, St. Petersburg, Florida, April 1983.

6. Kinsey, D.W., "Carbon Turnover and Accumulation by Coral Reefs," dissertation presented to the University of Hawaii in 1979 in partial fulfillment of the requirements for the degree of Doctor of Philosophy in Oceanography.

7. Nichandros, H.M. and L.A. Roesner, "Ecosystem Response of Monterey Bay to Alternative Wastewater Management Plans," ASCE National Meeting on Water Resources Engineering, Los Angeles, California, January 1974.

8. Smith, S.V., "Net Production of Coral Reef Ecosystems," The Ecology of Deep and Shallow Coral Reefs," results of a workshop on Coral Reef Ecology by the American Society of Zoologists held in Philadelphia, Pennsylvania, NOAA's: Undersea Research Program, Vol. 1, No. 1, 1983.

9. Walton, Raymond, Ming P. Wang, W. Martin Williams, L.A. Roesner, "Documentation for the Three-Dimensional Coral Reef Simulation Model CORALSIM," Camp Dresser & McKee Inc., Annandale, Virginia, November 1984.

10. Walton, Raymond, W. Martin Williams, and L.A. Roesner, "Documentation for the Three-Dimensional Current Processor Model SIM3D," Camp Dresser & McKee Inc., Annandale, Virginia, February 1984.

ESTIMATING DELAYS AT NAVIGATION LOCKS

Michael S. Bronzini,* M. ASCE

Abstract

Tow delay is an important component of cost at navigation locks, and delay reduction is a major benefit of lock improvement. Computer simulation is a valuable method of estimating lock delay under a variety of existing and future or proposed conditions. However, a single simulation run, which can be quite costly in terms of both computer and analyst time, produces a delay estimate for only one traffic level under one set of conditions. This paper describes methods which can be used to estimate an entire delay vs. traffic curve from a limited amount of simulation data. Estimation techniques appropriate for various amounts of data are derived, and factors affecting the accuracy of the delay estimates are discussed. Applications of these methods to inland waterway planning projects are given.

Economic Analysis of Navigation Projects

Recent studies of the inland waterway system in the United States, including the National Waterways Study (13) and the Upper Mississippi River Master Plan (14), conclude that many navigation structures are near the end of their physical or economic lives and will require either replacement or major rehabilitation. Decisions are also imminent on several major projects such as replacement of Gallipolis Lock on the Ohio River and the Inner Harbor Lock in New Orleans, and provision of a second chamber at the new Lock 26 on the Mississippi River. Since these programs involve the investment of user fee revenues and other public funds, there is a continuing need to develop sound methods for economic analysis of navigation projects.

The basics of economic analysis as applied to inland waterways have been stated by numerous authors; a concise treatment is given in (11). Figure 1 is a simple diagram of some of the important relationships involved at locks or other system constraint points. Curve D is the typical downward sloping demand curve, which shows the amount of use the facility will receive at different levels of user cost. Curve AC is the average cost curve, which shows how the cost incurred by each user varies with the traffic level. This primarily shows the effect of traffic congestion and waiting time, since most

*Director, Transportation Center, The University of Tennessee, Knoxville, TN 37996-0700.

Note.--A substantially similar paper appears in Proceedings--Transportation Research Forum, Vol. 25, No. 1, 1984, pp. 420-428.

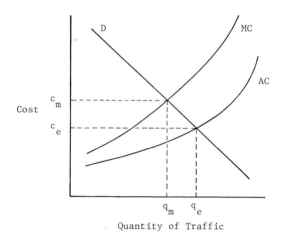

Figure 1. Cost-Flow Relationships at Navigation Locks

other user costs do not vary significantly with the number of vessels transiting the lock. The marginal cost imposed on all users by each additional traffic unit is shown by curve MC. Under normal conditions the traffic at the lock will be q_e, where the user cost, c_e, is exactly equal to the willingness to pay of the marginal user. In congestion pricing theory, the socially optimal traffic level is defined to be q_m, where marginal cost and marginal willingness to pay are both c_m.

Figure 1 illustrates the importance of having accurate estimates of lock delays. The relationship between average tow delay and lock traffic level, commonly referred to as the lock delay curve, is the primary determinant of the AC curve. Under current planning regulations, project benefits are measured as the reduction in average cost which the project produces. Consequently, changes in the lock delay curve which occur in response to system improvements show up directly in the benefit/cost analysis. In addition, current regulations call for consideration of a congestion toll as one means of avoiding or delaying investment in new facilities. The vertical distance between the MC and AC curves defines the theoretically optimum schedule of congestion tolls. However, there is no convenient way to directly observe the marginal cost curve, so it must be derived from the average cost curve. As already noted, this curve depends heavily on the lock delay curve.

Computer Simulation of Waterway Locks

It is virtually impossible to observe lock operations over a sufficiently large range of traffic levels to develop a totally empirical delay curve. Consequently, computer simulation is routinely used to generate estimates of lock delays. This has the added advantages of putting the analyst firmly in control of the conditions under which each delay estimate is made, and allowing relatively quick and convenient investigation of a variety of alternative lock improvements. The simulation approach also insures that the alternatives will be compared under a common set of assumptions about commodity flows, barge loadings, empty barge traffic, tow sizes, lock operating rules, etc.

Navigation lock simulation models are currently at a rather advanced stage of development. Much of the work in this field is reviewed in (3) and (7). Some of the earliest work was by Carroll, who developed models of both single locks (6) and systems of locks (8, 11). Carroll's work was seminal, in that many of his concepts have been carried through to succeeding models. These include: the locking routines in the waterway system simulator developed for the Corps of Engineers Inland Navigation Systems Analysis project (3); Hayward's (10) multiple chamber single lock model, LOKSIM; and a more detailed single lock model, LOKSIM2 (1), developed for the Upper Mississippi study (14). A deterministic model called LOKCAP (4, 5), which is based on a combination of simulation concepts and data and queueing theory, is also in widespread use (13, 14).

A simulation model replicates the operation of a lock for a short period of time, typically 30 days, with a constant average vessel arrival rate. The model output indicates the average delay per tow during the simulated time interval. Thus each simulation run provides a single estimate of average delay at a single traffic level. Producing an entire delay curve requires additional model runs at different traffic levels, and replications of each run, so that the relationship between delay and traffic can be captured. Unfortunately, simulation runs often require considerable time and effort, so generating each lock delay curve can be rather costly. The next section introduces a mathematical lock delay function which can be estimated with only a limited amount of simulation data, and gives methods for estimating the function's parameters.

Lock Delay Function

The delay curve for any lock may be represented as the following hyperbolic function:

$$d = \frac{Dq}{Q - q} \ , \qquad 0 \leq q < Q \tag{1}$$

where:

q = lock traffic level
d = average delay per tow at traffic level q
Q = lock capacity
D = lock delay parameter.

The lock flow and capacity, q and Q, are expressed in units of traffic flow per time period, such as tows per month or tons per year. This congestion function was first proposed, in a slightly different form, by Mosher (12); it can also be derived from queueing theory (9).

The delay curve parameters, Q and D, both have useful physical interpretations. Equation 1 shows that as q approaches Q, delay becomes infinite. Thus Q is the theoretical capacity of the lock, and has the same meaning as the maximum service capacity defined in queueing theory. Looking again at equation 1, it is seen that D is a scaling factor with units of delay. Setting d = D and solving for q yields q = Q/2. In other words, D is the average delay when the flow is 50 percent of capacity. The function also has the desirable feature that d = 0 at q = 0. Taken together, these properties allow the function to be easily visualized and, in fact, sketched rather accurately.

Estimating the Delay Curve

If either parameter Q or D is known with certainty and one data point (q, d) is available, then equation 1 can be used to solve for the missing parameter. In the usual situation neither parameter is fixed, so at least two data points are needed. Given two points, (q_1, d_1) and (q_2, d_2), equation 1 can be solved for Q and D to yield:

$$Q = \frac{1 - (d_1/d_2)}{1 \ (d_1 q_2)/(d_2 q_1)} \ q_2 \tag{2}$$

and

$$D = \frac{d_2(Q - q_2)}{q_2} = \frac{d_1(Q - q_1)}{q_1}. \tag{3}$$

This method is referred to later on as the two-point method. If the two data points are selected judiciously, the delay curve estimated in this fashion is quite accurate. This estimation method offers the obvious advantage that only two simulation runs (plus replications) are required.

In the most general case, a number of data points (q_i, d_i), are obtained. The problem is to find values for Q and D which best fit the data. Although a general nonlinear estimation procedure could be used, a simple search technique is also available. Given an independent estimate of Q, the least squares estimate of D is (5):

$$D = \frac{\sum_i (d_i \ q_i)/(Q - q_i)}{\sum_i q_i^2/(Q - q_i)^2}, \qquad q_i < Q. \tag{4}$$

Thus, the estimation problem can be reduced to a one dimensional search over various values of Q.

The following procedure can be used to estimate the delay function parameters.

1. Arrange the n data points in the order $q_1 < q_2 < \ldots < q_n$. Select the first and last data points, (q_1, d_1) and (q_n, d_n), and compute a trial value Q^* using equation 2.

2. Select the following values of Q_k as the search set: $(0.90Q^*, 0.95Q^*, Q^*, 1.05Q^*, 1.10Q^*)$, subject to $Q_1 > q_n$. In cases where this condition does not hold, use $Q_1 = 1.02 q_n$.

3. For each Q_k in the search set:

   (a) Compute D_k with equation 4

   (b) Compute estimated delays, $\hat{d}_i$, for each data point, using Q_k, D_k, and equation 1

   (c) Given values $(d_i, \hat{d}_i)$, compute their squared linear correlation coefficient, $R_k^2(\hat{d}_i, d_i)$.

4. Plot the R_k^2 values from step 3 against the corresponding values of Q_k. Draw a smooth curve through these points, and select as the best estimate of Q that value at which the R^2 curve reaches its maximum. Compute D from equation (4) and compute R^2 for these final estimates of Q and D.

This procedure was developed in (2) to estimate delay curves based on simulation data for railroad lines, where it was observed to produce highly satisfactory results. For small amounts of data, it is readily implemented on a small manual or programmable calculator, and it is easily programmed on a microcomputer.

The data points used to estimate the parameters of the hyperbolic delay function, whether obtained from direct observation or computer simulation, are subject to random error. The question then arises as to what effect this error has on the parameter values and subsequent delay estimates. Normally, the traffic levels, q_i, are known without error (in a statistical sense). Thus, attention can be focused on the delay observations, d_i.

Equation 4 shows that parameter D is linearly dependent on the delay values. In fact, the last one or two data points, at the higher values of q and d, contribute the most to the estimate of D. This is the very region of the flow regime where average delay can fluctuate widely, due to the instability of the queueing system. Consequently, it is a good idea to have replications of the high delay data points, to avoid propagating random error to the D estimate. Obviously (equation 1), the delay estimates calculated with the function are linearly dependent on D, so errors in D are propagated to the final function values and to any further economic analyses based on the delay curve.

The situation is a little less clear for the capacity parameter. Using the search technique suggested above, the estimate of Q which provides the best fit of the delay curve to the data points is selected, so there will normally be little estimation error. This can also be argued by considering equation 2 for the two-point method. Using the first and last data points (q_1, d_1), and (q_n, d_n), the expression for Q is dominated by the ratio d_1/d_n, which appears in both the numerator and the denominator. Thus, capacity estimates are very robust with respect to random error in the delay data.

Estimation of a Lock Delay Curve

Table 1 gives the results of simulating four traffic levels at Peoria Lock on the Illinois Waterway. The lock chamber is 600 feet (183 m) long and 110 feet (33.6 m) wide, so it will accommodate a maximum of nine jumbo barges. The simulations were conducted in 1981 using commodity mix and tow size data for the year 1976, when the lock was passing approximately 32 million tons (29 Gg) per year. At each traffic level a separate simulation was conducted for each season, and the data were annualized. Thus, each data point is a composite of four simulation runs, which provides the replications needed to accommodate random error.

Table 1. Simulation Data for Peoria Lock on the Illinois Waterway

i Run No.	q_i Annual Traffic (net kilotons)	d_i Average Delay per Tow (min.)
1	15,980	28
2	32,065	123
3	36,864	253
4	42,457	701

Does not include effect of navigable pass conditions.

Note: 1 ton = 907 kg.

Table 2 gives the results of applying the search technique to estimate the delay curve parameters. In step 1, the trial value Q^* was computed to be 45,600 kilotons (41.4 Gg), and the other trial values (step 2) are shown in column 2 of the table. For each trial value, Q_k, the remaining columns give the items computed at step 3. The delay estimates in each row can be compared with the data in Table 1 to assess the representativeness of each of these potential delay curves. Panel (a) in Figure 2 shows the R^2 plot obtained at step 4. Based on this plot, the best estimate of Q is 46,200 kilotons (41.9 Gg). The sixth row of Table 2 gives the corresponding D

Table 2. Estimation of Delay Curve Parameters for Peoria Lock

Trial k	Capacity (kilotons) Q_k	Delay (min.) D_k	$\hat{d}_1$	$\hat{d}_2$	$\hat{d}_3$	$\hat{d}_4$	R_k^2
	Parameters		Estimated Delays, $\hat{d}_i$ (min.)				
1	43,300	14.40	8.4	41.1	82.5	725	.9498
2	43,320	14.75	8.6	42.0	84.2	726	.9504
3	45,600	52.6	28.4	125	222	711	.997
4	47,880	85.8	43	174	287	672	.994
5	50,160	116	54	206	322	639	.976
Opt.#	46,200	61.8	33	140	244	701	.9988
2-point*	45,610	52.0	28	123	219	700	.9968

#Optimum estimate of Q; see Figure 2.

*Parameters estimated by passing delay curve through second and fourth data points (i = 2 and 4 in Table 1).

Note: 1 ton = 907 kg.

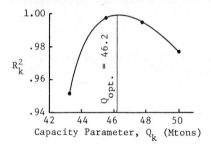

(a) Plot of R^2 vs. Q for Peoria Lock

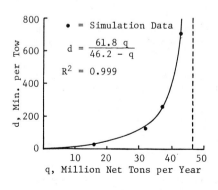

(b) Peoria Lock Delay Curve

Figure 2. Estimation of Delay Curve for Peoria Lock

estimate (from equation 4) and the resulting delay estimates at each of the flow levels, q_i. For this function a nearly perfect linear correlation between the data points and the fitted curve is obtained ($R^2 = 0.9988$). Panel (b) of Figure 2 shows the data points and the delay curve.

Although only four data points are used, the curves in Figure 2 are representative of the results which are obtained when using this method to fit a hyperbolic function to simulation data, even when more data is available. The R^2 values are typically very high, and the R^2 plot normally has a rather flat portion near its peak. This means that small variations in the capacity estimate will not have much effect on the goodness of fit.

The last row of Table 2 gives the parameter estimates obtained using the two-point method. The two points used are at flows which are 69 percent and 92 percent of capacity. The parameter estimates are very close to those determined with the search procedure using all of the data, and the statistical fit of this curve to the data is excellent ($R^2 = 0.9968$). This result is typical. For judicious selection of the data points, the two-point method will normally produce a highly satisfactory delay curve. For this result to hold, the two data points should be at flow values which produce lock utilizations in the neighborhood of 50 percent and 75 percent of capacity.

Analysis of Lock Improvements

LOKSIM2 was used to simulate the effects on lock capacity and delay of various potential nonstructural improvements. Some of these measures were designed to expedite the handling of large tows and reduce the marginal delays caused by double lockages (where the tow is too large to be locked through the chamber in one pass). Three of these measures are:

1. Bowboats--extra power units placed at the head of a tow to assist in maneuvering and in entering and exiting locks;

2. Helper Boats--low horsepower towboats stationed at locks and used to remove unpowered cuts from the lock chamber; and

3. Switchboats--towboats somewhat larger than helper boats which remove unpowered cuts from the chamber and move them to remote mooring facilities, which allows the remake of the double lockage tow to occur without tying up the lock approach/exit area.

Detailed descriptions of these measures and how they were simulated are given in (14).

Delay curves for the base condition and each improvement were estimated from the simulation data, using the two-point method. The

results are given in Table 3. It appears that bowboats and switch-
boats provide benefits of the same order of magnitude. Both alternatives would increase capacity by 9 to 10 percent and reduce average
delays by 20 to 25 percent. The helper boat alternative, in contrast, has negligible benefits.

Table 3. Delay Curves for Nonstructural Improvements
at Peoria Lock

Lock Improvement Alternative	Parameters	
	Capacity Q ktons/yr.	Delay D min./tow
Base Condition	44,090	40.1
Bowboats	47,910	30.9
Helper Boats	45,120	41.1
Switchboats	48,400	32.6

Note: 1 ton = 907 kg.

Conclusions

The hyperbolic delay curve is a flexible and accurate means of
representing the flow and delay characteristics of inland waterway
locks. The simple methods described in this paper can be used to
estimate the parameters of the delay curve which best fits the delay
data generated by computer simulation. It is possible to determine
acceptable delay curves from as few as two simulation runs at different traffic levels, though accuracy will be increased if more points
and replications of individual runs (especially at high flow and
delay levels) are utilized. The delay curves obtained by this method
have been successfully used as the basis for average cost curves in a
number of navigation studies.

References

1. Bronzini, M. S., and Margiotta, R. A., "Analysis of Lock Capac-
    ity by Simulation," Transportation Research Record, No. 880,
    1982, pp. 7-13.

2. Bronzini, M. S., and Sherman, D., "Railroad Routing and Cost-
    ing," Electric Power Research Institute, Palo Alto, Calif.
    (forthcoming).

3. CACI, Inc., "Inland Navigation Systems Analysis; Vol. V--Water-
    way Analysis," Office of the Chief of Engineers, Corps of Engi-
    neers, Washington, D.C., July, 1976.

4. CACI, Inc., "Waterway and Rail Capacity Analysis," Transporta-
    tion Systems Center, U.S. Department of Transportation, Cam-
    bridge, Mass., Sept., 1976.

5. CACI, Inc., "Improvement of the LOKCAP Model to Handle Double Chamber Queueing," Office of the Chief of Engineers, Corps of Engineers, Washington, D.C., Sept., 1979.

6. Carroll, J. L., "Waterway Lock Simulation Model," Papers-- Sixth Annual Meeting, Transportation Research Forum, 1965, pp. 217-238.

7. Carroll, J. L., and Bronzini, M. S., "Simulation of Waterway Transport Systems," Transportation Engineering Journal of ASCE, Vol. 97, No. TE3, Proc. Paper 8311, Aug., 1971, pp. 527-539.

8. Carroll, J. L., and Bronzini, M. S., "Waterway Systems Simula- tion; Vol. I--Summary Report," TTSC 7108, Pennsylvania Trans- portation Institute, Pennsylvania State University, University Park, Penna., Aug., 1971.

9. Davidson, K. B., "A Flow Travel Time Relationship for Use in Transportation Planning," Proceedings, Australian Road Research Board, Vol. 3, No. 1, 1966, pp. 183-194.

10. Hayward, J. C., "Simulation Analysis of a Multiple Chamber Lock on the Inland Waterways," TTSC 7211, Pennsylvania Transportation Institute, Pennsylvania State University, University Park, Penna., Aug. 1972.

11. Howe, C. W., et al., Inland Waterway Transportation; Studies in Public and Private Management and Investment Decisions, Resour- ces for the Future, Inc., The Johns Hopkins Press, Baltimore, Md., 1969.

12. Mosher, W. E., Jr., "A Capacity Restraint Algorithm for Assign- ing Flow to a Transportation Network," Highway Research Record, No. 6, 1963, pp. 258-289.

13. "National Waterways Study--Final Report," U.S. Army Engineer Water Resources Support Center, Institute for Water Resources, Ft. Belvoir, Va., 1982.

14. Upper Mississippi River Basin Commission, "Comprehensive Master Plan for the Management of the Upper Mississippi River System," Oct. 1981.

Micro-Computer Water Development Screening Models

By

Noel R. Gollehon, Daryoush Razavian,
Raymond J. Supalla and Ann S. Bleed[*]

Abstract

A micro-computer screening model was developed to analyze the physical and economic efficiencies of a large number of alternative options associated with a given water development project. The screening model simulated water losses and uses of different diversion quantities for each option, and calculated the associated system costs and potential benefits. The model was designed to operate at a low cost over a wide range of economic and physical evaluation criteria. This paper presents the overall methodology and an example of its application to the Platte River in Nebraska

Introduction

With the increased cost of feasibility studies for water projects, the need to focus on the most attractive water development options has never been more critical. Policy needs to screen "the best alternatives" from a wide range of potential water diversion quantities over a multitude of project alternatives was the problem that prompted this research effort. The basic purpose of the water project screening model was to identify clearly inferior alternatives so that further efforts could concentrate on the more viable options. However, the identification of inferior alternatives depends upon the evaluation criteria employed. Potential evaluation criteria included in this effort were economic efficiency, project irrigation efficiency, total costs and the portion of the costs that can be charged to the private sector. It was the issue of what evaluation criteria to use in the elimination of inferior alternatives that prompted the development of the simulation (not optimization) based screening models discussed below. The sheer volume of potential alternatives necessitated flexible, low-cost models to permit screening inferior alternatives under several criteria.

---

[*]Authors are respectively, Research Technologist, Department of Agricultural Economics; Water Scientist, Water Resources Center; Professor, Department of Agricultural Economics; and Assistant Professor, Water Resources Center. All are associated with the University of Nebraska-Lincoln and may be contacted in care of the Department of Agricultural Economics, 306 H.C. Filley Hall--East Campus, Lincoln, Nebraska, 68583-0922.

Model Structure

The basic design of the screening models was a micro-computer based simulation model. The model sequentially simulates water "flow" in a project from a specified diversion point to final utilization. This was done by considering a proposed diversion as an aggregation of components. For example, a proposed water project could consist of diversion from a surface water source, to an off-stream reservoir that provided surface water for irrigation to a specified area. The screening model's view of this alternative would be a sequence of a diversion dam, supply canal, dam and associated reservoir, service canal, and an area specific distribution system of canals and laterals. This disaggregated project would then be evaluated by the screening model in a sequential manner, based upon an initial diversion quantity with the outflow from one component comprising the inflow to the next. The model sequentially evaluated each component of the disaggregated project for losses, benefits and costs.

For the purpose of this study every equation developed for and included in the screening models was translated into the total quantity of water (cubic meters) by basing the volume on an annual diversion schedule. The general equation form of the water simulation model for each component was:

$$I_{i,j} + G_{i,j} - L_{i,j} - U_{i,j} = O_{i,j} = I_{i+1,j} \tag{1}.$$

Where:

i = component of the project (supply canal, dam and reservoir, service canal, or distribution system);

j = project under consideration;

$I_{i,j}$ = inflow to component i in project j

$G_{i,j}$ = total gains (surface water runoff and precipitation) in component i of project j;

$L_{i,j}$ = losses (seepage and evaporation) in component i of project j;

$U_{i,j}$ = planned water use (surface water at field headgate) in component i of project j; and

$O_{i,j}$ = outflow from component i in project j.

The remainder of this paper is dedicated to the methods and procedures that were necessary to make the simulation screening model operational and to the models use. A description of the engineering section, which includes component design and estimation of losses, will be followed by a description of the economic section which includes costs and benefits. The last section of the paper will be a brief description of the model's application to the Platte River in Nebraska, including the computer implementation and output of the model. The reader should again be aware that this model was designed at the prefeasibility level. As more or improved data becomes available some elements of the model will change, perhaps significantly.

Engineering Elements

The design characteristics and the water losses of each component were the key elements in the sequential water simulation procedure.

Component Design

In order to achieve the flexibility necessary to evaluate the range of alternative projects, it was necessary to predetermine the specifications and limitations of each component's design. There specifications and limitations included canal shape and hydraulic properties, basic dam section and reservoir storage, and average lateral density per hectare of lands served. However, component design was determined on a site specific basis within the given specifications. This enabled consideration of local soil types, geology, topography, etc. Where possible, existing pre-feasibility level studies were utilized as the basis for this information (1, 4, and 10). Specifications of the Bureau of Reclamation, U.S. Army Corps of Engineers and other secondary data sources were used as guidelines in the design of project components.

Much of the design effort was concentrated on the dams. Dams were designed to provide multi-purpose reservoirs that could also meet peak irrigation requirements. Potential dam sites considered in this study were based on existing pre-feasibility level studies or on a Nebraska dam site survey conducted by Kuzelka (6). All dams in the study were zoned earth structures, having Bureau of Reclamation specifications (11). Spillway design was based on U.S. Army Corps of Engineers design standards, using the designed PMP storm (12). The dams were designed to capture part of the designed SPF volume in a flood surcharge storage with adequate freeboard to prevent overtopping of the dam by wave action. The outlet works were positioned to provide a permanent recreation pool, and to provide adequate head for irrigation. In addition, the outlet works and distribution system were designed to release and deliver 25 percent of the active conservation storage in a 10-day period. Every attempt was made to be as accurate as possible using the secondary data sources available.

Losses

Seepage and evaporation were the water losses accounted for in each component of each project. Seepage was determined for each component for a wide range of potential water inflows, independent of the screening model. Least squares regression was then used to estimate seepage loss coefficients as a function of inflow. These coefficients were then used in the water flow simulation model. The seepage loss equations took the following general form:

$$SL_{i,j} = a + b * (I_{i,j})^c \qquad (2).$$

Where:

$SL_{i,j}$ = seepage loss in component i of project j;

$I_{i,j}$ = water inflow to component i of project j; and

a, b, c = regression coefficients.

Data used to estimate canal seepage losses were based on the Bureau of Reclamation experience with Nebraska projects (Personal communications with the Bureau of Reclamation, Nebraska-Kansas Projects Office, 1983). Factors considered in the development of regression coefficients were canal length, canal dimensions, canal lining (unlined, earth lined, concrete or membrane) and the average time a canal would be in use. Reservoir seepage losses were estimated from existing prefeasibility studies (1, 4, and 10). Reservoir seepage coefficients considered the inundated area, static head and geology of the reservoir site. Seepage losses from the distribution laterals were estimated from Davis and Sorensen (2).

Evaporation losses for each project component were estimated based on Missouri River Basin studies (7) and Class A pan evaporations at National Weather Service stations in and near the project sites (3). As in the case of seepage losses, evaporation losses were estimated as a function of inflow before, and then included in the screening model. These equations had the same form as the seepage loss equations.

Economic Elements

Costs and benefits were calculated on a piecemeal basis as water "flowed" through each component. The projects costs and benefits were the sum of the components costs and benefits.

Costs

Project component costs were determined in much the same manner as seepage losses. First, costs for each component were determined for a wide range of alternative inflows, outside the simulation model. Then, regression analysis was used to estimate component cost coefficients which were then entered into the simulation model. The general form of the cost equations were:

$$C_{i,j} = a + b * (I_{i,j})^c \qquad (3).$$

Where:

$C_{i,j}$ = cost of component i in project j;

$I_{i,j}$ = water inflow to component i of project j; and

a,b,c = regression coefficients.

The data used to estimate the regression coefficients for costs of canals and laterals were based on the Bureau of Reclamation experience with Nebraska projects (Personal communications with the Bureau of Reclamation, Nebraska-Kansas Projects Office, 1983). Factors considered in the regression equations were canal length, design capacity, topography and canal lining (unlined, earth lined, concrete or membrane). Reservoir costs were based on the costs of the embankment, spillway, outlet works, right-of-way, relocations and pumping plants, using U.S. Army Corps of Engineers (12) data.

Benefits
       All benefits for each project alternative were computed in terms
of annual benefits to the state of Nebraska. Benefits were compared
to costs as a measure of economic efficiency, after discounting the
benefits to a base year (the year construction was completed). The
present value of future annual benefits were determined using a social
discount rate of five percent.

       Surface Water Irrigation Benefits. The approach used to compute
surface water irrigation benefits was to calculate the net returns to
land and management per hectare, for both surface water irrigation and
the present land uses. Net returns were computed for two present land
uses: ground water irrigated crop production and dryland crop production. Annual net benefits per hectare to surface water irrigation
represents the difference between the two net returns to land and
management. Net returns per hectare were computed utilizing a cost
and returns approach for four selected years in the projects estimated
fifty year life. Net returns for the years not directly calculated
were computed as a linear interpolation of the computed years.
Returns were averaged across crops by adjusting for both present and
estimated future cropping patterns. The calculation of future net
returns relied heavily on local adjustments of the projections made by
and for the Ogallala High Plains Study (5). Projections made for the
Ogallala High Plains Study included future crop prices, crop yields,
crop water requirements, pumping lifts and production costs.

       The general equation form of annual surface water irrigation
benefits may be represented as:

$$BSW_{i,j,k} = ((SWR_{i,j,k} - GWR_{i,j,k}) * GWA_{i,j,k}) + ((SWR_{i,j,k} - DLR_{i,j,k}) * DLA_{i,j,k}) \qquad (4).$$

Where:

$BSW_{i,j,k}$ = annual surface water irrigation benefits from
      component i of project j in year k;
$SWR_{i,j,k}$ = average surface irrigation net returns per hectare
      on component i of project j in year k;
$GWR_{i,j,k}$ = average groundwater irrigated net returns per
      hectare on component if of project j in year k;
$GWA_{i,j,k}$ = area groundwater irrigated expressed in hectares;
$DLR_{i,j,k}$ = average dryland net returns per hectare; and
$DLA_{i,j,k}$ = area dry farmed expressed in hectares.

       Ground Water Recharge Benefits. Another major agricultural
benefit was that associated with recharging the existing ground water
aquifer. Economic benefits from ground water recharge for irrigation
purposes are only realized when water is withdrawn from the aquifer.
Benefits occur due to reduced pumping costs, and because the aquifer
life is extended. In terms of pumping costs, if recharge is able to
stop or slow the rate of aquifer decline, then the pumping cost
benefit is equal to the difference in the amount spent on pumping with
the project versus what would have been spent without it. In terms of
aquifer extension, recharge of a declining aquifer would make it
possible to irrigate for additional years. The economic value of this

aquifer extension effect is equal to what an irrigator could afford to pay for the water that enabled continued irrigation and be at least as well off as he could be without it.

The annual value of recharge benefits may be represented by:

$$BRC_{i,j,k} = P_k * L_{i,j} * W_{i,j,k} + V_k (Z_{i,j,k} - W_{i,j,k}) \qquad (5).$$

Where:

$BRC_{i,j,k}$ = annual recharge benefits in component i on project j in year k;

P_k = Pumping cost per cubic meter pumped, per meter of lift in year k;

$L_{i,j}$ = annual change in lift in meters per year (equation 6);

$W_{i,j,k}$ = amount of ground water pumped in the area affected by recharge on component i of project j without recharge (without project j being built);

V_k = value of aquifer supplied irrigation water in year k; and

$Z_{i,j,k}$ = gross aquifer pumpage in cubic meters in the area affected by recharge on component i of project j over time with recharge (with project j being built).

Since lift is directly affected by the quantity of water that enters the underlying aquifer through seepage and deep percolation losses, annual changes in lift are an important part of the benefit equation. The annual change in lift may be represented by:

$$L_{i,j} = S_{i,j} / (C * H_{i,j}) \qquad (6).$$

Where:

C = long term storage coefficient;

$L_{i,j}$ = annual change in lift in meters per year;

$S_{i,j}$ = seepage in cubic meters per year; and

$H_{i,j}$ = hectares of affected land.

As was the case with surface water irrigation benefits much of the estimation of future conditions was taken from local adaptation of the Nebraska Ogallala High Plains Study (8). The methodology for recharge benefits was based on work completed by Supalla and Comer (9).

Recreation Benefits. Surface water recreation benefits were estimated on a visitor-day basis. Visitor-days for existing Nebraska reservoirs were estimated by regression techniques as a function of surface water area and population within a 97 kilometer (60 mile) radius. For each potential reservoir site, surface area was estimated as a function of inflow to each site. Annual recreation benefits were estimated using the following relationship:

$$BR_{i,j} = (a + b * SA + c * (SA_{ij})^d + e * POP_{i,j}) * V \qquad (7).$$

Where:

$BR_{i,j}$ = annual surface water recreation benefits with reservoir i associated with project j;

a,b,c,d,e = estimated regression coefficients;

$SA_{i,j}$ = surface area of reservoir i with project j;

$POP_{i,j}$ = 1980 population within a 97 kilometer radius; and

V = value per visitor day.

Flood Control Benefits. The estimated flood control benefits used in the analyses were based on previous studies, and were indexed to current dollars (1, 4 and 10).

Applications

The previously described simulation screening model was utilized to eliminate clearly inferior options for three water diversion projects in Nebraska. The projects evaluated in this study included those in the Little Blue, Big Blue and Central Platte Natural Resources Districts. The screening models (one for each area) were operated on an IBM-PC with 256K RAM. Each model was written in IBM BASIC and compiled using Microsoft's basic compiler. The data required for the models were stored in sequential files and moved into the program when needed.

A schematic diagram of a proposed project in the Big Blue Natural Resources District is presented in Figure 1. The components labeled 1,000 to 1,999 are supply canals, (1011 includes the diversion dam). Components labeled 2,000 to 2,999 represent dams and associated reservoirs. Labels from 4,000 to 4,999 represent service canals (with the pumping plant included in 4212). Surface irrigation water and distribution areas are labeled 3,000 to 3,999. This proposed project sequentially moves water through 3 supply canal components (1011, 1012 and 1313) into reservoir 2304 before releasing water into service canal 4317 to serve lands in component 3306. For each component, costs and benefits were computed and the amount of water lost or utilized was subtracted before sending the water to the next component. This process continues until either the reservoir reaches design capacity, or the potential irrigated land area is fully served. When either of these conditions are met, the quantity of water not required in this "branch" of the project is diverted into the next specified supply canal component (1214). Water then flows through the supply canals 1214 and 1215, into reservoir 2202, through service canal component 4212 and to the irrigation service area 3202. As was the case in the previous "branch", all appropriate calculations are made as the water moves from one component to the next.

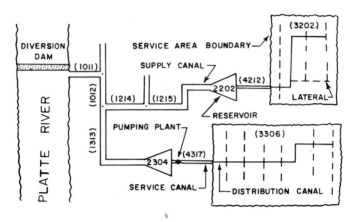

Figure 1. Schematic Diagram of a Diversion Project.

The proposed diversion project was evaluated by the screening
model over a range of initial water diversions. The water diversion
range considered was from a low of 25 million cubic meters to the
level where the last reservoir was full or all lands served.

The results, assuming a diversion of 184.5 million cubic meters,
are presented in Table 1. The first part of Table 1 contains descriptive statistics: quantity diverted, time when the project comes online, identification of project components, lining types used,
seepage and water applied. In the second section three comparative
project evaluation criteria are presented: irrigation efficiency,
costs that can be charged to the private sector and B/C ratio.
Section three of the results indicate the areas irrigated and
impacted by ground water recharge. The recharge impacted area is
adjusted for the hectares that would receive ground water recharge
from more than one component. This adjustment is illustrated under
the label "overlap". The final section of Table 1 presents
information on benefits and costs. Costs are allocated to the
benefit categories on a separable costs remaining benefits basis and
presented under cost allocation.

Summary

This paper presents both a methodology and a representative
solution for a simulation based water project screening model. The
model relies on a sequential water flow process that disaggregates a
large water diversion project into a series of components, and
simulates water flow from one component to the next. Each component
was evaluated on the basis of water losses, costs and benefits. The
screening model has been adapted to three Natural Resources Districts
in Nebraska. The model has proven to be a flexible, relatively
low-cost method of selecting projects for further consideration.

Table 1. Example of Screening Model Output.

Summary for Diverson = 184,500,000 M^3
Project comes on line in the year 2000
Project is comprised of the following components: 1011, 1012, 1313,
    2304, 4317, 3306, 1214, 1215, 2202, 4212, 3202
Laterals are unlined: Canals are unlined.
Total Seepage = 76,130,000 M^3
Total Surface water applied = 90,121,000 M^3

Irrigation Efficiency = 48.85%
Agriculture's costs are 86.50% of total costs.
B/C Ratio = 1.34

Lands Impacted

Surface Irrigated			Recharge Impacted	
Component	Percent	Hectares	Component	Hectares
			2304	37,320
3306	100.0	9,620	3306	27,990
			2202	72,310
3202	78.0	14,140	3202	66,180
			Overlap	− 52,230
TOTAL		23,760		151,570

Item	Present Value	Annualized Value	Annualized value per 1,000 M^3 diverted
	$1,000	$1,000	dollars
Benefits			
Agriculture	222,238	12,173	65.98
Irrigation	154,032	8,437	45.73
Recharge	68,206	3,736	20.25
Recreation	39,870	2,184	11.84
Flood	6,728	369	2.00
TOTAL	268,836	14,726	79.82
O & M	47,393	2,599	14.09
Net Benefits	221,393	12,127	65,73
Costs			
Supply Canal	32,429	1,776	9.63
Reservoirs	62,845	3,442	18.66
Service Canal	55,600	3,046	16.51
Distribution	14,764	809	4.38
TOTAL	165,638	9,073	49.18
Cost Allocation			
Agriculture	143,269	7,848	42.54
Recreation	19,139	1,048	5.68
Flood	3,230	177	0.96

APPENDIX 1.--REFERENCES

1. Boyle Engineering Corporation, "Little Blue Water Resources
    Project Summary of Prefeasibility Engineering and Economic Report
    on Proposed Plan of Irrigation Development." Sponsored by Little
    Blue Natural Resources District, Newport Beach, California, Sept.
    1976.
2. Davis, C.V., and Sorensen, K.E. Handbook of Applied Hydraulics,
    Third Edition, McGraw-Hill Book Company, Inc., New York, 1969,
    Sec. 33, pp. 31-36.
3. Fransworth, R.K., and Thompson, E.S. "Mean Monthly, Seasonal,
    and Annual Pan Evaporation for the United States", NOAA Technical
    Report NWS 34, U.S. Dept. of Commerce, NOAA, National Weather
    Service, Washington, D.C., Dec. 1982, pp. 38-39.
4. Gilbert, D.P., et al., "Development of Quantative Planning
    Technology", Working Draft Sponsored by the Upper Big Blue
    Natural Resources District, Nebraska Water Resources Center,
    University of Nebraska-Lincoln, Lincoln, Nebraska, Mar. 1981.
5. High Plains Associates, "Summary--Six-State High Plains Ogallala
    Aquifer Regional Resources Study". Report to the U.S. Department
    of Commerce and High Plains Study Council, High Plains
    Associates, Austin, Texas, July 1982.
6. Kuzelka, R.D., "Proposed Sites and Existing Facilities for
    Storage of 1,000 Acre-Feet or More in Nebraska," Map,
    Conservation and Survey Division, Institute of Agriculture and
    Natural Resources, University of Nebraska-Lincoln, Lincoln,
    Nebraska, no date.
7. Missouri River Basin Commission, "Platte River Basin, Nebraska
    Level B Study". Hydrology and Hydraulics Technical Paper,
    Missouri River Basin Commission, Nov. 1975, pp. 22-24.
8. Nebraska Natural Resources Commission, "Summary of the Nebraska
    Research for the Six-State High Plains Ogallala Aquifer Study,"
    Nebraska Natural Resources Commission, Lincoln, Nebraska, Dec.,
    1981.
9. Supalla, R.J. and Comer, D.A., "The Economic Value of Ground
    Water Recharge for Irrigation Use," Water Resources Bulletin,
    Volume 18, Number 4, Aug. 1982, pp. 679-686.
10. U.S. Bureau of Reclamation, Nebraska-Kansas Projects Office,
    "Prairie Bend Unit, Backup Data," Unpublished Report, Bureau of
    Reclamation, Grand Island, Nebraska, Dec. 1979.
11. U.S. Bureau of Reclamation, Design of Small Dams, second
    edition, U.S. Government Printing Office, Washington D.C., 1977.
12. U.S. Corps of Engineers, Southwestern Division, "Cost and Design
    Manual: for the Water Transfer Elements of the High Plains
    Ogallala Aquifer Study," Sponsored by the High Plains Associates,
    Unpublished Report, High Plains Associates, Austin, Texas, Aug.
    1980.

LARGE SCALE WATER RESOURCES SYSTEMS PLANNING -

APPROACH AND CASE STUDY

M. C. Chaturvedi[1]

Abstract

Planning approach for large scale water resource systems planning
backed by models has been developed. Four hierarchial stages are
identified and multilevel multiobjective models have been developed.
Planning has been carried out in the context of the State of Uttar
Pradesh, in the Ganges Basin, India.

INTRODUCTION

Water resources development of a river basin involves multilevel
decision making, phased planning and multiobjective development.
Computer based modelling helps in performing thought experiments and
several approaches have been adopted appropriate to objectives of
planning. However, these do not address to the real life problems faced
in developments of very large basins with multiple state agencies and
long periods of time involving phased planning-development. Planning of
a large region, in a very large river basin was undertaken in this
context. A set of Physical System Studies, Socio-Economic Studies and
Water Resources Developmental System Studies were undertaken. The planning morphology, issues, models and some policy and modelling results of
the water resources developmental studies are briefly described,
preceded by a brief description of the system. Further details are
given elsewhere.

THE SYSTEM

The Ganges system, which includes its tail end tributaries, the
river Brahamputra and the river Barak (or Meghna), is one of the worlds
most richly endowed land-water system. The river Ganges and Brahmaputra
are the fifth and fourth largest rivers of the world and together the
system is the second largest, second only to the Amazon (Leeden, 1976).
The total population of the basin was about 326 million in the year
1971. It is growing rapidly and is expected to almost triple by about
2050 AD at medium projection which shall be about eight times the
population of the region at the beginning of this century. Once a
prosperous region it is now one of the poorest areas of the world with a

[1] Professor, Indian Institute of Technology, New Delhi, 110016, India;
and Visiting Professor, University of Houston, University Park,
Houston, TX 77004.

very high population density of about 280 per square kilometre. The
system is shown schematically in Figure 1.

The region covers three countries, Nepal at the upstream in the
Himalyas, India and Bangladesh as the delta. In India the major states
are Uttar Pradesh, Bihar and W. Bengal from upstream to downstream in R.
Ganges. Uttar Pradesh is the largest state in India, with a population
of about 100 million, more than the population of Nepal and Bangladesh
combined. Its surface water potential is 130,000 m. cu. m (105.4 m. ac.
ft.) and groundwater potential is 104.890 m. cu. m (85 m. ac. ft.).
Although a complex network of canal systems and groundwater has been
developed, about 50 percent of the potential with several of worlds
highest dams has yet to be developed.

ISSUES AND APPROACH

In view of scale, administrative jurisdiction by states, phased
development, and multiobjectives, a hierarchial multilevel approach is
adopted. Four levels of planning can be identified. Issues and models
used are summarized in Fig. 2. Verbal description of the approach is
given in Fig. 3.

1. River Basin - Regional Coordination/Screening - Coordination Model

First at the national level or river basin level, the issue is
allocation of resources to the states in the basin and screening of the
technological options and their impacts in the totality. Several developmental objectives are possible depending upon economic-political
policy. For instance, one may be river basin economic efficiency with
equity amongst states. We have adopted the objective of river basin
efficiency in terms of physical targets of power and irrigation, as
currently adopted in India. Flood mitigation is not considered an
objective in this study which is methodological. Other objectives such
as minimum flows from environmental considerations and international
committments are considered as constraints. Allocation amongst tributaries or states is based on efficiency of contribution at the tributary
or state level. Tradeoff study amongst irrigation in two seasons and
power are part of policy.

For convenience of planning, five technological sets can be
identified (i) storage reservoirs, (ii) diversion canals to utilize the
unutilized flows, (iii) groundwater development, (iv) watershed development, and (v) modernization of distribution and use system. Diversion
canals have been largely constructed to utilize the low period (non-
monsoon) flows but there is need to develop the monsoon period flows
(Kharif channels). In groundwater development, besides conjunctive
development, and issue of private and public development there is the
problem of state owned augmentation tubewells to enhance low flows of
canals. Watershed development also includes a new proposal of induced
groundwater recharge and land management for flood mitigation and water
resources enhancement. Modernization of distribution system embraces
lining of canals and field level distribution system.

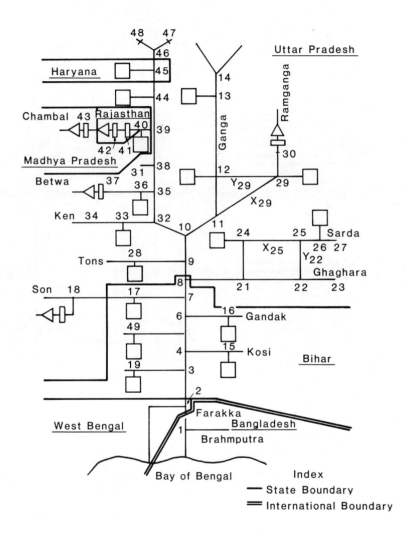

Fig. 1 Network Diagram Of Ganga Basin With Political Units

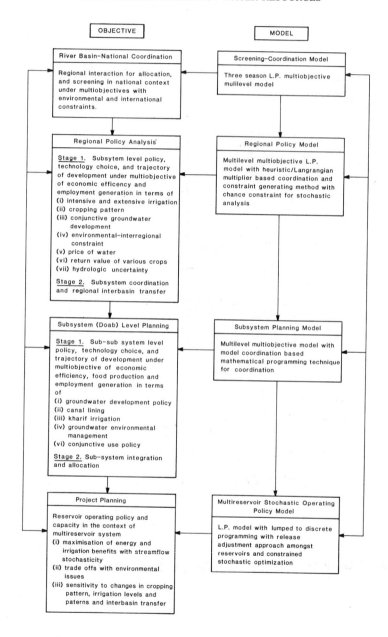

Fig. 2 System Studies Planning – Modeling Scheme

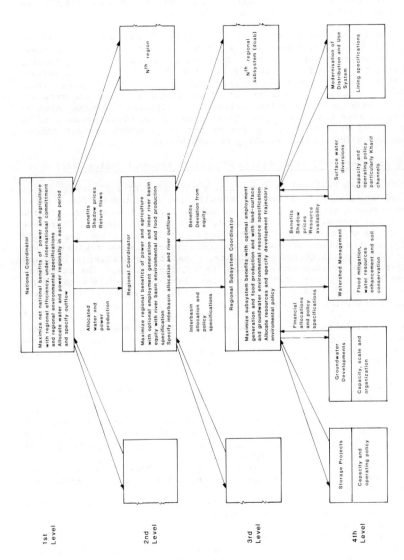

Fig. 3 Hierarchial Multilevel Multiobjective Systems Planning For Large Scale Water Resouces Systems

There is a progression from policy to projects from level 1 to level 4. The technological aspects are considered in a simplified manner at level I and are detailed in level 4.

The system is visualized as a network and a L.P. model is constructed. Objective function is maximization of irrigated area under two seasons and power, with usual hydrologic, agricultural, and capacity constraints. Low flows from environmental considerations at various locations and international committments are set as constraints. Tradeoff between two seasons of irrigation and power are studied. Tradeoff between technological option of development and management by lining is also studied. Allocation of water and power production by tributaries or states is carried by two level model through shadow prices based incremental marching process heuristically.

2. State (Regional) Level Policy Analysis / Regional Policy Model

The state (region) is the primary unit of policy planning. With the information allocation and constraints from the national level reconnaissance study, more detailed policy study follows. Each region (state) has several large rivers as tributaries to R. Ganges. There are two levels of policy study. First level, called the subsystem policy study, is the study of several policy issues in each subsystem and identification of technology choice, capacity, operating policy and trajectory of development according to multiobjectives. The subsystem is the region between two tributaries, known as doab in vernacular. Second regional policy study, is the issue of regional interbasin transfer according to multiobjectives.

The multiobjectives are returns and employment generation with the constraint of appropriate cropping pattern from nutritional considerations. At the subsystem stage of analysis some policy issues for which sensitivity analysis is required are as follows.

1. Cropping pattern in the context of multiobjectives.
2. Choice of irrigation policy viz full irrigation or differential irrigation. The latter refers to less than full irrigation to give maximum production. The question arises because (i) irrigation from surface and part of groundwater is in public sector and is highly subsidized and (ii) water availability is not adequate for irrigating all the cultivated area.
3. Limits of monthly groundwater development. There is a capital and recurring cost and for planning purposes it is convenient to have the sensitivity analysis.
4. Implication of minimum downstream releases from environmental, administrative or other considerations.
5. Price of water
6. Return value of various crops.
7. Effect of variability of surface flows and policy of conjunctive surface and groundwater development in that context.

For the level I, the subsystem policy study, a L.P. model maximizing returns from irrigation in terms of various technologies was constructed. Multiobjectives were economic returns and employment generation with constraint of appropriate cropping pattern from nutritional considerations. Multiobjective analysis was carried out through constraint generating method. The second level model maximizes returns and minimizes per capita income deviation of the regions. Coordination was carried out through shadow priced based incremental marching process heuristically as well as by Langrangian multiplier technique.

3. Subsystem (Doab) Level Planning / Subsystem Planning Model

The doabs are large areas of high populations served by vast canals and extensive groundwater development, as shown in Fig. 4. Further, large scale technological activities are being planned. Doabs are adopted as the basis of systems planning-design and we move from policy analysis to planning.

The doab canal systems are large and again two levels of planning are identified. First, again is technology choice, scale and operating policy under multiobjectives but with details in the context of technological planning. The multiobjectives were taken to be economic efficiency, employment generation with appropriate food production. Second level refers to subsystem coordination and allocation.

Several more detailed policy studies with sensitivity analysis are carried out for the following:

1. Analysis of crop activities in context of multiobjectives.
2. Analysis of groundwater development in terms of policy issues of public sector and private sector development, change in energy prices and financial charges.
3. Groundwater augmentation by lining of field channels, distributaries and main canals.
4. Utilization of monsoon flows through Kharif channels.
5. Groundwater environmental management.
6. Conjunctive use policy.

For the level I, the sub-subsystem planning, a L.P. model similar to regional policy model but more detailed to take account of water losses in distribution system and various options of groundwater development is developed. Model coordination method is used for coordination through iterative process in terms of the three multiobjectives in various combinations to investigate the tradeoffs between them using Benders partitioning procedure.

4. Project Planning / Multireservoir Stochastic Operating Policy Model

After the policy and planning studies, the last stage of project planning in the context of financial allocations and policy specifications follows. Detailed capacities, operating policies and scheduling specifications of the five different technological options have to be integrally worked out, each competing for the financial allocations under policy specifications in terms of benefits, shadow prices and resource availability. The issue of groundwater development, surface water diversions and modernization of distribution systems were embedded in regional subsystem planning model but are shown specifically in Fig. 2 to complete the technology set.

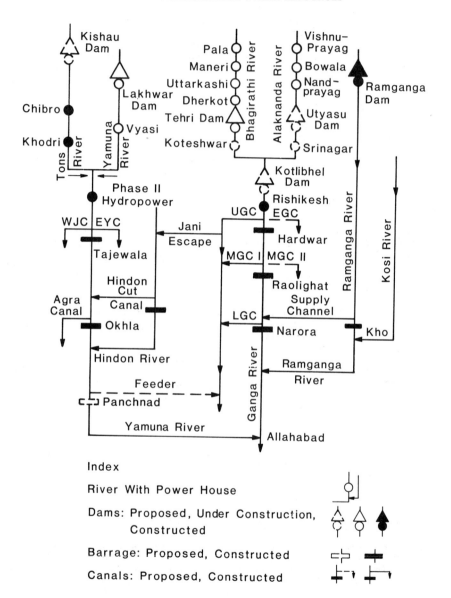

Fig. 4 Line Diagram Of Yamuna – Ganga System

Storage projects are also included in the planning models in terms of water availability at different time periods being exogenously specified on basis of power generation considerations in view of its dominance in power and irrigation as brought out in the River Basin - Regional Coordination and Regional Policy Analysis studies. However, detailed analysis is needed in view of the magnitude of the individual projects, large number of them and the stochastic nature of hydrologic inputs. The policy issues are as follows.

1. Maximization of agriculture and energy benefits under conditions of streamflow stochasticity
2. Tradeoffs with environmental issues, and
3. Sensitivity analysis to changes in cropping patterns, irrigation levels and patterns, and interbasin transfer.

A new approach of explicit stochastic optimization using constrained stochastic optimization (CSO) with lumped to discrete programming algorithm (LPD) was developed. This reduces the search in terms of states and stages through state decomposition and the lumping of stages to be ultimately discretized to the actual operation periods. CSO reduces number of states by taking account of the fact that almost 80 percent of the precipitation is in monsoons. Thus for a percentage water availability it appears less significant to probe all states of the live storage. Lumped to Discrete Programming (LPD), somewhat similar to Dynamic Programming but more efficient, starts with all the stages of operation horizon lumped into two or three stages and proceeds with further discretizations in subsequent iterations ultimately leading to the actual number of operation periods.

In view of the aforesaid characteristic the system's integrated operation, is carried out, using LDP algorithm, for certain percentage of water availabilies to know the possible range of reservoir states to be probed further stochastically corresponding to wetness of the operation year. While optimizing each reservoirs operation, its mutual adjustment of releases with neighbouring reservoirs is carried out for joint operation, besides considering joint probabilities of flows between different reservoir sites. Multireservoir interaction is accounted through planning each one independently and planning joint operation through release adjustments amongst the reservoirs.

RESULTS

It is not possible to give the results due to limitations of space except to emphasize that many current approaches are found to be wrong.

CONCLUSION

For large scale systems planning, hierarchial multilevel multiobjective planning is required leading integrally from policy to project planning. For a very large river basin with a number of major tributaries and states/administrative regions four levels of planning are identified. These are River Basin - Regional Coordination, State Level Policy Analysis, Subsystem Level Planning and Project Planning.

Hierarchial two-level multiobjective linear programming models coordinated heuristically through incremental marching process or through mathematical programming methods on basis of shadow prices have been developed for each of the first three levels. They give valuable insight about the interaction amongst system components, behavior of the system regarding interrelated policy issues and tradeoffs amongst the multiobjectives leading to creative engineering of the projects. Finally at the project level, a new approach of modelling integrated operation of multipurpose - multireservoir system has been developed for stochastic optimization which is appreciably efficient than currently available methods.

ACKNOWLEDGEMENT

The study was sponsored by the Ford Foundation and the Government of Uttar Pradesh who also deputed officers to carry out the studies with the author. The four component studies were carried out by U.C. Chaube, B.N. Asthana, D.K. Gupta and P.K. Bhatia respectively as part of their doctoral work. The support of the agencies and the work of the scholars is gratefully acknowledged.

APPENDIX 1 - REFERENCES

1. Chaturvedi, M.C., Regional Water Resources Systems Planning - A Case Study, Specialty Conference, ASCE Water Resources Planning and Management Division, Baltimore, MD, May 28-31, 1984.

2. Chaturvedi, M.C., Scientific Development of Environmental Resources A Case Study, due 1985.

3. Chaube, U.C., Two Level Multi-Objective Reconnaisance System Study of a Large Water Resource System, Ph.D. Thesis, Indian Institute of Technology, Delhi, 1982.

4. Asthana, B.N., System Studies for Regional Environmental Resources Planning in a Developing Economy, Ph.D. Thesis, Indian Institute of Technology, New Delhi, 1984.

5. Gupta, D.K., System Studies for Large Scale Multiobjective Integrated Irrigation Management, Ph.D. Thesis, Indian Institute of Technology, Delhi, 1984.

6. Bhatia, P.K., Modelling Integrated Operation of Multipurpose, Multi-reservoir Water Resources Systems, Ph.D. Thesis, Indian Institute of Technology, Delhi, 1984.

THE WATER RESOURCES MODELS OF THE
INSTREAM FLOW GROUP

Robert T. Milhous, M ASCE*

ABSTRACT

The Instream Flow Group of the U.S. Fish and Wildlife Service has five analytical systems designed to assist in the development of instream flow criteria for water resources projects. These five systems are:

1. The physical habitat simulation system (PHABSIM), used to develop a physical habitat versus streamflow relationship;

2. A system used to determine steady state stream temperatures in a stream network;

3. A collection of programs used to investigate the relationship between reservoir operations and instream flows;

4. A steady state water quality model; and,

5. A collection of programs to do time series analyses of physical habitat and streamflows.

Of the five, the PHABSIM system has the largest use and currently is being used in all regions of the United States and in Canada, Australia, and New Zealand.

INTRODUCTION

One of the purposes of the Instream Flow Group is to develop analytical "tools" that can be used in the development of instream flow criteria for the operation of water control projects and in the allocation of water through the water rights systems of the various states.

A number of these "tools" are water resources-related models, available to users as computer programs. These tools can be grouped into five systems:

---

*Hydraulic Engineer, Instream Flow Group,Western Energy and Land Use Team, U.S. Fish and Wildlife Service, 2627 Redwing Road, Ft. Collins, CO 80526-2899.

1. A physical habitat simulation system;

2. A time series analysis system;

3. A water temperature system;

4. A water quality analysis system; and

5. A reservoir analysis system.

The physical habitat simulation system (PHABSIM) is used to develop a relationship between streamflow and the physical habitat for an aquatic animal or determine the space available for recreational use.

The time series analysis system is used to analyze the time stream of physical habitat and streamflows. The system contains programs used to generate time series of habitat, given the results from PHABSIM and a time series of streamflows; programs used to display time series graphically; and programs used to simulate the operation of relatively simple water management systems. The time series-related programs are organized into a system called TSLIB.

The water temperature system is used to simulate the water temperature in rivers so that the interaction of streamflows and water temperatures can be included in the development of instream flow criteria. The system has three principal components: a regression model for smoothing data at locations of recorded water temperatures; a group of physical process models for heat flux simulation; and a model for heat transport. The system is called SNTMP.

The water quality analysis system is a steady state network used to calculate various water quality parameters throughout the network. The system has the name SSAMIV.

The reservoir operation system consists of a simulation model of a network of channels and reservoirs, along with a set of programs that link PHABSIM and the temperature model. The reservoir simulation model is called HYDROSS.

The general configuration of the various systems is illustrated in Figure 1. There are overlaps and linkages between these five systems. For instance, the water resource system can be analyzed using elements of TSLIB, and the linkage programs associated with HYDROSS can do some of the same tasks as TSLIB.

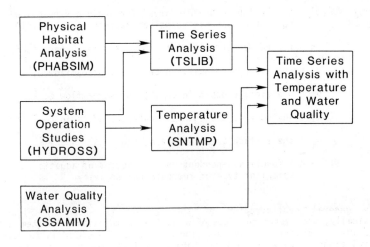

Figure 1. General configuration of the various analytical systems of the Instream Flow Group.

Two computer-based information systems of the Instream Flow Group must be mentioned before discussing the various systems further. These are:

1. IFIS STUDIES - A data base that contains information about instream flow studies; and

2. IFIS STRATEGIES - A data base that contains information about water law and water politics, as related to instream flows.

These two systems provide information that improves the quality of instream flow studies and associated management decisions.

PHABSIM

The critical element of the Physical Habitat Simulation System (PHABSIM) is the equation:

$$WUA(Q) = \sum_{i=1}^{n} CF(v_i, d_i, CI_i) * a_i$$

where WUA(Q) = the "weighted useable area" for a given streamflow (Q) for an aquatic animal or recreational activity;

n = the number of cells into which a stream reach is divided;

v_i = the average velocity in cell i at streamflow Q;

d_i = the average depth in cell i for streamflow Q;

CI_i = an index to the channel characteristics in cell i;

a_i = the surface area of cell i; and

CF( ) = a function dependent on the species of aquatic animal or type of recreational activity.

The general configuration of the system is shown in Figure 2. Basically, the system consists of a habitat simulation subsystem and a hydraulic simulation subsystem. The major use of PHABSIM is to develop a relationship between physical habitat and streamflow for a specific species of aquatic animal or type of recreational activity. An example of the type of relationship obtained with PHABSIM is given in Figure 3.

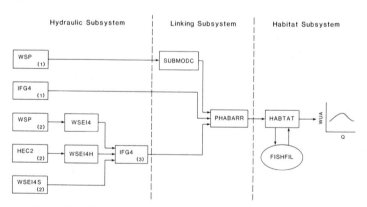

1. Calculates both velocities and water surface elevations
2. Calculates water surface elevations only
3. Calculates velocities only

Figure 2. The PHABSIM system.

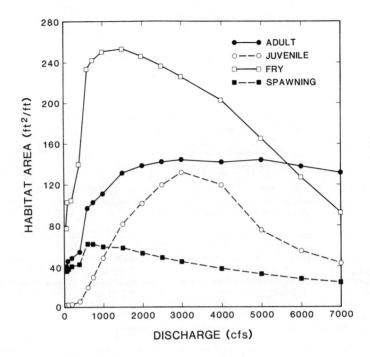

Figure 3. Physical habitat vs. streamflow relationships for
Lower Big Blue River, Kansas.

The PHABSIM system is described in Milhous (2, 4), the user's
guide is Milhous, Wagner, and Waddle (5), and the logic behind the use
of species preferenda is given in Stalnaker (6).

SNTMP

The instream flow temperature model (SNTMP) can be used to calculate average daily temperatures and diurnal fluctuations in water
temperature through a stream network with steady streamflows. The
system uses readily available meteorological and hydrological data.

The system consists of three general parts: (1) development of
input needed by the other two parts; (2) heat flux calculation; and
(3) heat transport calculation. The models within the system are:

1. Regression models used to smooth and fill in missing water
    temperature data at the headwater and internal locations;

2. Models used to predict changes in air temperature, relative humidity, and atmospheric pressure as a flucation of elevation;

3. A shade model used to determine the solar radiation and weighted shading resulting from both topography and riparian vegetation;

4. A solar model used to calculate the solar radiation penetrating the water as a function of latitude, time of year, and meteorological conditions;

5. A heat flux model used to predict the energy balance between the water and the surrounding environment; and

6. A heat transport model used to calculate the average daily water temperature and diurnal fluctuations in water temperature as functions of stream distance.

An example application of the SNTMP system is the development of relationships between riparian vegetation, water temperature, and salmonid habitats. The system was used to determine the water temperature responses of the Tucannon River in Washington State to different riparian vegetation conditions. The salmonid population was related to the aquatic habitat, as affected by water temperature. The results are illustrated in Figure 4. This example is discussed in Theurer, Lines, and Nelson (8). The alternatives are related to the location of climax riparian vegetation and the nature of the channel.

An example of the application of the system to an endangered species problem is given in Theurer, Voos, and Prewitt (7). The SNTMP system is described in detail in Theurer, Voos, and Miller (9).

WATER RESOURCES SYSTEMS MODELS

The major water resources system model used by the Instream Flow Group is the HYDROSS model. This model was developed by the Upper Missouri Region of the U.S. Bureau of Reclamation (10). The model has been adopted by the Instream Flow Group for use with results from the use of PHABSIM and SNTMP. The model uses a monthly time step. The model is of the same class of models as HEC3 of the Hydrologic Engineering Center, U.S. Army Corps of Engineers with one unique aspect: water of different "ownerships" can be tracked by the HYDROSS model.

Another model used is the RESYLD program, significantly modified from a program of the same name developed by the Hydrology Engineering Center. The program includes only one reservoir and is used as a test base for application of operations criteria to instream flow studies that can be used in the HYDROSS, HEC3, or other monthly time step models.

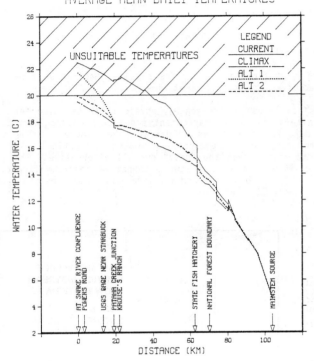

Figure 4. Example of the use of SNTMP model.

The third model is a model of a typical run-of-the-river project of a type common for small hydro projects. This model uses daily streamflows.

TSLIB

The time series library of programs allows the results of PHABSIM to be linked to the results from water resources system studies. The concept that a physical habitat versus streamflow function can be used as a surrogate for an economic production function has been discussed by Milhous (3). In treating the physical habitat versus streamflow function as a surrogate production function, the assumption is made that the value of the instream flows is proportional to the habitat produced by the flows. Consequently, as with other economic benefits, it is desirable to know the time series of benefits produced.

The equation for the habitat versus streamflow function can be written as:

$$HA = f_i(Q)$$

where HA is the physical habitat, Q is the streamflow, and $f_i(\ )$ is the functional relationship illustrated in Figure 3. The subscript i refers to the specific life stage, such as adult or spawning. If a time series of flows is known, the physical habitat at time t can be calculated given the streamflow at time t.

A principle use of the monthly physical habitat time series is to compare alternative water management schemes. One such approach is to compare duration curves, as illustrated in Figure 5. The duration curves for alternative projects or water allocation rules can be compared to help select the "best" overall alternative. The specific comparison in Figure 5 is of two alternative instream flow criteria, one proposed by the U.S. Fish and Wildlife Service and the other proposed by the U.S. Army Corps of Engineers.

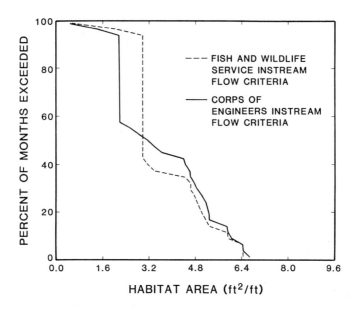

Figure 5. Comparison of physical habitat in June for adult channel catfish in the Marais des Cygnes River below Melvern Reservoir, with alternative instream flow criteria and 30 cfs diversion (1 ft²/ft = 0.305 m²/m).

An element of TSLIB can be used to develop a basin-wide physical habitat time series, using a number of specific sites and streamflow time series.

SSAMIV

The Stream Simulation and Assessment Models: Version IV (SSAMIV) is a steady state model used to simulate water quality in a network. The system can be used to simulate 12 water quality constituents. Two of these constituents are defined by the user; the other 10 are: (1) total coliform bacteria; (2) fecal coliform bacteria; (3) ultimate biochemical oxygen demand; (4) planktonic algae; (5) onthophosphate; (6) ammonia; (7) nitrate; (8) benthic algae; (9) dissolved oxygen; and (10) temperature.

The SSAMIV model consists of two major components: a steady state hydraulic model of the network and a water quality model that uses the results of the hydraulic model to simulate water quality. Details of the model are given in Grenney and Kraszewski (1).

SUMMARY

Models that simulate the physical habitat in a stream, the water resources system, water temperature, and water quality have been developed or modified by the Instream Flow Group. Other models are used to link these models.

APPENDIX.-REFERENCES

1. Grenney, W. J., and A. K. Kraszewski. 1981. Description and Application of the Stream Simulation and Assessment Model: Version IV (SSAMIV). Instream Flow Information Paper 17. U.S. Fish Wildl. Serv. FWS/OBS-81/46.

2. Milhous, Robert T. 1979. "The PHABSIM System for Instream Flow Studies" in Proceedings: 1979 Summer Computer Simulation Conference, Toronto, Ontario, July 19, 1979. pp. 440-446. Society for Computer Simulation.

3. Milhous, Robert T. (In Press). "Instream Flow Values as a Factor in Water Management." Proceedings: Regional and State Water Resources Planning, American Water Resources Association.

4. Milhous, Robert T. 1984. "The Physical Habitat Simulation System for Instream Flow Studies." Proceedings: Third Conference on Computing in Civil Engineering, ASCE.

5. Milhous, R. T., D. L. Wagner, T. J. Waddle. 1984. User's Guide to the Physical Habitat Simulation System (PHABSIM). Instream Flow Information Paper 11. U.S. Fish Wildl. Serv. FWS/OBS-81/43.

6. Stalnaker, Clair B. 1979. "The Use of Habitat Structure Preferenda for Establishing Flow Regimes Necessary for Maintenance of Fish Habitat in Streams with Regulated Discharges." First International Symposium on Regulated Streams, Erie, PA, April 18-20, 1979. Plenum Press.

7. Theurer, F. D., K. V. Voos, and C. G. Prewitt. 1983. "Application of IFG's Instream Water Temperature Model in the Upper Colorado River" in Proceedings: International Symposium on Hydrometeorology, A. I. Johnson and R. A. Clark editors, American Water Resources Association.

8. Theurer, F. D., I. Lines, and T. Nelson. (In Press). Interaction between riparian vegetation, water temperature, and salmonid habitat. American Water Resources Association.

9. Theurer, F. D., K. A. Voos, and W. J. Miller. (In Press). Instream Water Temperature Model. Instream Flow Information Paper 16. U.S. Fish Wildl. Serv.

10. U.S. Bureau of Reclamation. 1983. HYDROSS-Hydrologic River Operation Study System. User's Guide.

COMPUTER MODEL FOR WASTEWATER RECLAMATION

By Robert W. Hinks[1], M. ASCE and Mario B. Saldamando[2], M. ASCE

ABSTRACT

This paper describes how an efficient computer model can be constructed and used to evaluate planning options for wastewater reclamation. The situation in the City of Scottsdale, Arizona, is described. A rapidly-growing community in a semi-arid desert, Scottsdale foresees reclaimed effluent as a major 'new' source of water for greenbelt irrigation purposes. Under consideration by the City is a network of small (i.e., under 3 mgd capacity) wastewater reclamation plants that will be located adjacent to trunk sewer lines, and provide effluent for irrigation of nearby floodways, parks, golf courses and other landscaped areas. Output from the computer model includes a ranking of preferred development alternatives; it also provides information on the economics of effluent recycling, and enables estimates to be made as to the magnitude of possible savings (e.g., in groundwater pumping) by using reclaimed effluent. This paper describes 1) the mathematical model used to represent the situation in Scottsdale, and 2) the input data to the model. Subsequent papers will describe model results.

INTRODUCTION

In those communities that use advanced processes for the treatment of wastewater, reclaimed effluent is a potentially large new source of water for agricultural and 'greenbelt' irrigation purposes. The use of reclaimed wastewater to meet these demands will allow groundwater and surface water supplies to be extended to meet projected potable water needs.

Confronted with rapidly-expanding populations, many communities—especially those in 'sun-belt' states—face growing pressure to utilize their effluent resources. For example, cities in the Phoenix metropolitan area face phenomenal population increases: the population of the City of Scottsdale, Arizona, is projected to increase from 100,000 persons in 1982 to over 150,000 in 2000, while the City of Chandler is projected to grow from 37,000 persons in 1982 to 200,000 persons by the turn of the century. Other communities in the area are also projecting large increases in population. Currently, the water being consumed is largely groundwater which—because of low rainfall—

---

[1]Asst. Prof., Dept. of Civil Engrg., Arizona State Univ., Tempe, AZ 85287

[2]Water Res. Director, City of Scottsdale, Scottsdale, AZ 85251

is not being significantly replenished by natural recharge. Moreover, one of the strictest groundwater codes in the country, which mandates safe yield by 2025, imposes a mandatory decrease in groundwater use. How do we supplement groundwater? Clearly one of the most stable sources is sewage effluent.

HOW should communities develop their effluent resources? This is the major question that needs to be addressed. In the Phoenix metropolitan area most cities currently send wastewater flows to a large regional treatment plant (the 120 million gallon per day (mgd) 91st Avenue Treatment Plant), which--for some of the cities--is located up to 30 miles from local agricultural and greenbelt areas (the potential effluent 'demand locations'). The regional plant is currently committed to furnishing effluent for cooling purposes at the Palo Verde Nuclear Power Plant, which will begin operation at the end of 1985. Effluent reuse studies--such as this one--must compare the benefits of local reuse with the benefits and obligations of regional reuse such as the power plant cooling.

There are numerous aspects to the problem of effluent recycling that now confront water resources planners and political decisionmakers. For example, how will the development of new 'satellite' wastewater reclamation plants in close proximity to demand locations affect cities' existing treatment capacity? Another major factor is the expected rate of urban growth. Residences and commercial and industrial enterprises are the primary sources of wastewater and the rate of increase in sewer flows is directly proportional to growth in these sectors of urban activity. The implications to development plans of different growth scenarios must be investigated.

Which feasible treatment plant sites should be developed? What is the relationship between treatment plant economy of scale and system flexibility? (The former tends to favor fewer, larger plants while the latter is served best by a network of smaller plants). What will be the optimal rate of plant construction over time? What will be the impact of seasonal sewer flows and seasonal user demand on the optimal network of treatment plants? The last question is very important to those southwestern cities, such as Scottsdale, that have a large influx of winter visitors. Scottsdale has recorded winter average sewer flows up to 140% of summer average flows. The importance of this fact is apparent when one realizes that, for irrigation, the potential maximum effluent demand is in summer, or about six months 'out-of-phase' with the time of maximum effluent availability. Should plants be developed to handle maximum waste flows (winter), maximum demand (summer) or some average of these two extremes?

The City of Scottsdale has started to implement a wastewater reclamation system in partnership with private developers. One plant, at the planned community of Gainey Ranch, is now in operation. It was built by developers Markland Properties, Inc., to assure water supply for a golf course, city park and other landscaped areas in the development. This plant is also operated by the private sector-- Envirotech Operating Services. Two other similarly financed reclamation plants are being developed to the north of the study area.

This study focuses on the intensively developed greenbelt in the Indian Bend Wash floodway, an internationally renowned urban flood control/reclamation area. To demonstrate the model, six possible sites for wastewater reclamation plants have been identified (Fig. 1). These sites are located adjacent or close to trunk sewer lines that serve the

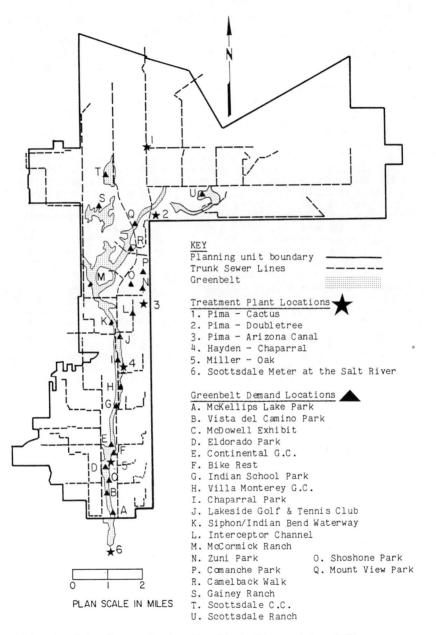

KEY

Planning unit boundary ————
Trunk Sewer Lines — — — —
Greenbelt

Treatment Plant Locations ★
1. Pima - Cactus
2. Pima - Doubletree
3. Pima - Arizona Canal
4. Hayden - Chaparral
5. Miller - Oak
6. Scottsdale Meter at the Salt River

Greenbelt Demand Locations ▲
A. McKellips Lake Park
B. Vista del Camino Park
C. McDowell Exhibit
D. Eldorado Park
E. Continental G.C.
F. Bike Rest
G. Indian School Park
H. Villa Monterey G.C.
I. Chaparral Park
J. Lakeside Golf & Tennis Club
K. Siphon/Indian Bend Waterway
L. Interceptor Channel
M. McCormick Ranch
N. Zuni Park   O. Shoshone Park
P. Comanche Park   Q. Mount View Park
R. Camelback Walk
S. Gainey Ranch
T. Scottsdale C.C.
U. Scottsdale Ranch

PLAN SCALE IN MILES

Fig. 1 - Major Sewers, Reclamation Plant Sites and Greenbelt
Demand Locations
City of Scottsdale, Arizona. Planning Units 1-4.

southern half of the city and parts of north-east Phoenix and Paradise Valley. In the same general area is approximately 1100 acres of green-belt (predominantly parks and golf courses in Indian Bend Wash floodway and the planned communities of McCormick Ranch, Gainey Ranch and Scottsdale Ranch). Irrigation water demand in this greenbelt ranges from 3 mgd in winter (December-January-February) to 11 mgd in July. This water demand is currently satisfied by groundwater pumping.

Projected average day trunk sewer flows in 1995 at the treatment plant sites range from a low of 1.0 mgd (summer day, 1995, site #1) to a high value of 19.0 mgd (winter day, 1995, site #6). (5)

OBJECTIVES

A mathematical model has been developed to assist decisionmakers in the evaluation and comparison of the options available for utilizing reclaimed effluent in Scottsdale. The model is used to help determine which treatment plant locations should be developed, how large each developed facility should be, and how each facility should be expanded over time. The model examines the economics a) of plant construction, operation and maintenance and, b) of delivering effluent from treatment plants to greenbelt facilities. By indicating the preferred alternatives, the model can also provide information on associated questions, such as the economic impact of a network of local reclamation plants on the City's existing and proposed capacity in the regional treatment plant, the impact of effluent recycling on sewer user fees (how is reclamation to be paid for if current production costs exceed the sale price of the reclaimed wastewater?), and how the economics of effluent recycling compare with the use of other sources--such as groundwater pumping--for greenbelt irrigation.

Mathematical Model. The mathematical model examines and evaluates feasible treatment plant--greenbelt demand locations based on a minimum overall cost criterion. Treatment plant construction and operating costs, pipeline construction and effluent pumping costs have been determined, together with projected inflation factors for capital and operating (e.g., pumping energy) costs. This economic analysis serves as a basis upon which other socio-economic criteria and planning, management and environmental factors can be superimposed.

The objective function and constraints of the model are presented as equations (1) through (4):

Objective Function:

$$\underset{x,u}{\text{minimize}} \sum_{i=1}^{m} \sum_{j=1}^{n} \left[c_{ij}(x_{ij}) + c_i(u_i) \right] \tag{1}$$

Constraints:

$$\sum_{j=1}^{n} x_{ij} = u_i \qquad i = 1,2,\ldots,m \tag{2}$$

$$\sum_{i=1}^{m} x_{ij} = b_j \qquad j = 1,2,\ldots,n \tag{3}$$

$$0 \le x_{ij} \le \min\left(a_i, b_j\right) \qquad \begin{aligned} i &= 1,2,\ldots,m \\ j &= 1,2,\ldots,n \end{aligned} \tag{4}$$

Definition of terms:

i = effluent source location (max. number = m)

j = effluent demand location (max. number = n)

x_{ij} = 'transportation' of reclaimed effluent between source i and demand location j

$c_{ij}(x_{ij})$ = (non-linear) transportation cost function between source i and demand location j

u_i = total quantity of reclaimed effluent from source i

$c_i^i(u_i)$ = (non-linear) treatment and/or pumping cost function at source i

a_i = (prespecified) upper limit on effluent abstraction from source i

b_j = level of irrigation demand at demand location j

The model described above assumes that the effluent sources (i.e., the treatment plants) are independent. However, in the case of Scottsdale, the effluent sources are not independent. Wastewater flow removed from the sewer by upstream plants is not available to plants further downstream the sewer network. This dependence of sources is expressed mathematically as:

Dependence constraint:

$$a_i' = a_i - \sum_{j=1}^{i-1} u_j \qquad i = 2,3,\ldots,m \qquad (5)$$

Thus, (4) becomes:

$$0 \le x_{ij} \le \min\left(a_i', b_j\right) \qquad \begin{array}{l} i = 1,2,\ldots,m \\ j = 1,2,\ldots,n \end{array} \qquad (4a)$$

Algorithm:

Define:

$$f_n(u_1,u_2) = \underset{x_{1j},x_{2j}}{\text{minimize}} \left[\sum_{j=1}^{n} [c_{1j}(x_{1j})+c_{2j}(x_{2j})+c_{3j}(b_j-x_{1j}-x_{2j})]\right\} \qquad (6)$$

define:

$$r_j(x_{1j},x_{2j}) = c_{1j}(x_{1j}) + c_{2j}(x_{2j}) + c_{3j}(b_j-x_{1j}-x_{2j}) \qquad (7)$$

and define:

$$b = \sum_{j=1}^{n} b_j \qquad (8)$$

which implies:

$$x_{3j} = b_j - x_{1j} - x_{2j} \qquad (9)$$

$$u_3 = b - u_1 - u_2 \qquad (10)$$

The dynamic programming recursive equations for a 3-source (m = 3) problem are (1,2):

$$f_1(u_1,u_2) = \min \quad \{r_1(x_{11},x_{21})\} \tag{11}$$

$$0 \leq x_{11} + x_{21} \leq b_1$$
$$0 \leq x_{11} \leq \min (u_1,b_1)$$
$$0 \leq x_{21} \leq \min (u_2,b_1)$$

$$f_2(u_1,u_2) = \min \quad \{r_2(x_{12},x_{22}) + f_1(u_1-x_{12}, u_2-x_{22})\}$$

$$0 \leq x_{12} + x_{22} \leq b_2 \tag{12}$$
$$0 \leq x_{12} \leq \min (u_1,b_2)$$
$$0 \leq x_{22} \leq \min (u_2,b_2)$$

$$f_n(u_1,u_2) = \min \quad \{r_n(x_{1_n},x_{2_n}) + f_{n-1}(u_1-x_{1_n},u_2-x_{2_n})\}$$

$$0 \leq x_{1_n} + x_{2_n} \leq b_n \tag{13}$$
$$0 \leq x_{1_n} \leq \min (u_1,b_n)$$
$$0 \leq x_{2_n} \leq \min (u_2,b_n)$$

The overall objective of the model, represented by equation (1), adds the source costs $C_i(u_i)$:

$$\min_{\substack{\alpha_1 \leq u_1 \leq a_1' \\ \alpha_2 \leq u_2 \leq a_2'}} \{f_n(u_1,u_2) + C_1(u_1) + C_2(u_2) + C_3(u_3)\} \tag{14}$$

where:

$$\alpha_1 = \max (0, b-a_2'-a_3') \tag{15}$$

$$\alpha_2 = \max (0, b-a_1-a_3') \tag{16}$$

The dynamic programming algorithm represented by (11)-(13), together with the final level of optimization (equation (14)), yields the optimal allocations of effluent from sources i=1 and i=2:

$$\begin{array}{lll} x_{11}^0 & x_{21}^0 & \Rightarrow \quad x_{31}^0 = b_1 - x_{11}^0 - x_{21}^0 \\ x_{12}^0 & x_{22}^0 & \Rightarrow \quad x_{32}^0 = b_2 - x_{12}^0 - x_{22}^0 \\ \cdot & \cdot & \cdot \\ \cdot & \cdot & \cdot \\ \cdot & \cdot & \cdot \\ x_{1n}^0 & x_{2n}^0 & \Rightarrow \quad x_{3n}^0 = b_n - x_{1n}^0 - x_{2n}^0 \end{array} \tag{17}$$

with

$$\sum_{j=1}^{n} x_{1j}^0 = u_1^0 \quad ; \quad \sum_{j=1}^{n} x_{2j}^0 = u_2^0 \quad ; \quad u_3^0 = b-u_1^0-u_2^0 \tag{18}$$

INPUT DATA FOR THE MATHEMATICAL MODEL

The data required for this analysis includes: 1) the amount of wastewater available at each feasible treatment plant site (the variable

variable a_i), 2) the effluent demand at each demand location in the greenbelt (b_j), 3) the costs of transporting treated wastewater from the plants to the demand points (functions $c_{ij}(x_{ij})$), and 4) the costs associated with development, operation and maintenance of the treatment plants $(C_i(u_i))$. This data has been obtained through an extensive review of existing reports on wastewater flows and treatment plant design, studies by the City of Scottsdale on greenbelt water demand, and analysis of consultants' general design guidelines for small wastewater reclamation plants in the City.

Wastewater Availability: Recent projections (5) estimate that future residential and resort average day per capita wastewater production in Scottsdale will be of the order of 90 gallons per capita-day by 2000. Effluent production in the commercial and industrial sectors will be approximately 15 gallons per employee-day. Winter/summer sewer flow variations are projected to be ± 15% of average day production. Another important factor is that not all of the sewer flow is available for reclamation--some wastewater will have to remain in the sewer to transport primary and waste-activated sludge for disposal in the regional treatment plant. In the absence of more substantial data, this study assumes that 80% of the sewer flow is available for reclamation and reuse.

The wastewater production, variability and sewer retention estimates outlined above, together with estimates of population growth, provide information for Table 1, which shows projected winter/summer average day wastewater availability at each of the six treatment plant sites for the years 1995, 2015 and 2035.

Effluent Demand: Since wastewater flows are analyzed for winter and summer conditions, the winter and summer demand for reclaimed effluent is required. The greenbelt irrigation demands are estimated to range from 3.0 inches per month in winter to 10.4 inches per month in summer. These demands are assumed to remain constant throughout the period of study.

As previously described, the reclaimed effluent will irrigate golf courses, parks and other landscaped areas in south and central Scottsdale. To reduce computational effort, the twenty-one greenbelt demand locations shown in Figure 1 are grouped into public parks, public golf courses and private property categories. (It is possible that the effluent distribution system will be constructed with such category considerations in mind). Table 2 shows the acreage of each greenbelt area, the grouping scheme (denoted by demand numbers), and the winter and summer effluent requirements of each demand group. The appropriate formula used to compute water requirements is:

water required (mgd) = inches/acre-month * acres * 0.000892

Wastewater Reclamation Plant Development Costs: The capital and annual O&M costs of different size wastewater treatment plants have been estimated (4) to be:

mgd	Capital Cost (1984) ($)	Annual O&M ($)
0.05	844,000	62,700
0.80	4,580,000	211,000
3.00	11,070,000	558,000

Capital costs include land acquisition at $45,000/acre, a 10% contingency on construction and land costs, and engineering,

Treatment Plant Location	1995		2015		2035	
	winter	summer	winter	summer	winter	summer
1. Pima/Cactus	1.37	1.01	1.90	1.39	1.90	1.39
2. Pima/Double-tree Rd.	2.73	1.97	4.34	3.03	5.45	3.87
3. Pima/Arizona canal	11.74	9.18	14.98	12.63	18.07	14.68
4. Hayden/Chaparral*	13.31	10.38	17.02	13.54	19.74	15.99
5. Miller/Oak*	16.74	12.89	20.37	15.94	23.10	18.36
6. Scotts. Meyer/Salt River	18.96	14.47	22.74	17.67	25.32	19.97

*
includes projected 8.00 mgd from NE Phoenix (1995)
includes projected 10.00 mgd from NE Phoenix (2015)
includes projected 12.00 mgd from NE Phoenix (2035)

Table 1 - Projected Winter/Summer Average Day
Wastewater Availability at Treatment
Plant Sites (mgd)

Wastewater Effluent User Location	Area (ac)	Demand* No.	Total Area (ac)	Water Requirements (mgd)	
				winter	summer
McKellips Lake Pk.	24				
Vista Del Camino Pk.	49	1	135	0.37	1.24
McDowell Exhibit	8				
El Dorado Pk.	54				
Continental G.C.	144	2	145.5	0.40	1.34
Bike Rest	1.5				
Indian School Pk.	60	3	60	0.16	0.55
Villa Monterey G.C.	35	4	35	0.10	0.32
Chaparral Pk.	70	5	70	0.19	0.64
Lakeside Golf & Tennis Club	25	6	84	0.23	0.77
Siphon Ind. Bend Water-way	59				
Interceptor Channel	12				
Zuni Pk.	3.4	7	30.4	0.08	0.28
Shoshone Pk.	3				
Comanche Pk.	12				
McCormick Ranch	365	8	365	0.99	3.35
Mt. View Pk.	20	9	40	0.11	0.37
Camelback Walk	20				
Scottsdale C.C.	103	10	103	0.28	0.95
Scottsdale Ranch	120	11	120	0.33	1.10
TOTALS			1187.9	3.24	10.91

*Utilized in the Dynamic Programming Algorithm (n=11)

Table 2 - Projected Effluent User Demands

administration and legal costs of 25% of construction and land costs. The annual O&M costs assume electricity costs of $0.07/Kilowatt-hour, and include personnel, materials, supplies and general services. Amortizing capital costs over 20 years at an interest rate of 8.125% total annual costs can be estimated as:

mgd	Amortized Annual Capital Cost ($)	Total Annual Costs ($)
0.05	86,800	150,000
0.80	471,000	682,000
3.00	1,138,000	1,696,000

By plotting the annual costs and drawing the line of best fit through the data points, the annual costs of a wastewater plant can be expressed as a function of plant size as:

$$C_i(u_i) = 200,000 + 513,333\, u_i, \quad c_i(u_i=0)=0 \qquad (19)$$

where: $C_i(u_i)$ = annual cost ($) of developing treatment plant i to produce u_i (mgd) units of reclaimed wastewater.

u_i = size of treatment plant i (mgd)

Equation (19) is based on data for only three sizes of wastewater reclamation plants. Future studies may warrant a more detailed investigation of treatment plant size vs. cost.

Effluent Distribution Costs. Research of various sources (e.g., 3) yields a breakdown of pipe installation costs for ductile iron pipe as:

Pipe Size (in.)	Installed Cost ($) per Linear Foot
4	16
6	23
8	29
10	39
12	48
16	64
20	80

For the purposes of illustrating the mathematical model described in this paper, a pipe size of 12 inches (diameter) has been assumed for the entire effluent distribution network. Future studies should include economic analyses to determine the optimal pipe size for each part of the distribution network.

Obtaining distances from a scaled map (the shortest routes along major streets were chosen as pipeline routes for this analysis), approximate capital costs of installing 12 inch pipe from each source to a central point at each demand location may be determined. Annual costs of the effluent distribution system (construction and development costs) are shown in Table 3.

The electrical costs of pumping water can be expressed as:

SOURCE DEMAND	1	2	3	4	5	6
1	268.7	223.2	157.1	90.0	11.4	64.9
2	238.0	192.4	126.4	59.2	13.7	85.4
3	199.3	153.7	87.7	20.5	55.8	111.6
4	187.9	142.3	76.3	9.1	67.2	123.0
5	171.9	126.4	60.4	9.1	85.4	142.3
6	156.0	110.5	44.4	22.8	101.3	157.1
7	123.0	75.2	26.2	61.5	137.8	193.6
8	161.7	110.5	60.4	77.4	153.7	209.5
9	70.6	22.8	56.9	95.7	171.9	227.7
10	51.2	68.3	134.4	154.9	231.2	287.0
11	80.9	56.9	118.4	202.7	279.0	334.8

i = 8.125%, costs amortized over 20 years.

Table 3 - Total Annual Costs for the Effluent Distribution Network

$$(\$ \times 10^{-3})$$

$$\text{electrical cost } (\text{¢/hr}) = \frac{x_{ij} \times \frac{1550}{2.23} \times H_{ij} \times 0.746 \times \text{KWH cost}}{3960 \times \eta} \qquad (20)$$

where: x_{ij} = amount of water pumped from source i to demand j (mgd).

$1550/2.23$ = factor to convert mgd to gpm
H_{ij} = total dynamic head between source i and demand j (ft).

H_{ij} is equal to the elevation and pressure heads beyond the pump discharge against which pumpage occurs, plus the head due to friction and turbulence of flow.
 0.746 = factor to convert brake horsepower to KW.
 KWH cost = cost of electricity (¢/KWH).
 3690 = constant for conversion of units.
 η = overall pump efficiency
 For application of the model to the situation in Scottsdale, an electricity cost of 7¢/KWH and an overall pump efficiency of 0.65 were assumed. Also, in determining total dynamic head, the head due to friction and turbulence was assumed to be 5 feet loss per 1000 feet of pipe. It is also assumed that water will be pumped into storage facilities at the various demand sites, which assumes that the pressure head against which pumpage occurs is zero. Using various maps, distances, elevation differences, and the total dynamic head for every combination of source and demand may be determined.
 Using the above procedure, the costs $C_{ij}(X_{ij})$, of distributing water from the reclamation plants to the greenbelt features may be determined.

SUMMARY

Aspects of the use of reclaimed wastewater effluent for greenbelt irrigation have been described in this paper. An efficient computer model for optimizing the development of a network of small wastewater reclamation plants has been formulated, and typical input data described. The computer model uses an IBM 3083 mainframe computer. A microcomputer version is currently under development. A subsequent paper will describe model output, using the City of Scottsdale, Arizona, as a case study.

APPENDIX - References

1. Bellman, R. E., Dynamic Programming, Princeton University Press, Princeton, N.J., 1957.
2. Dreyfus, S. E., Law, A. M., The Art and Theory of Dynamic Programming, Academic Press, 1977.
3. Engineering News Record, 213:10, Sept. 6, 1984.
4. Greeley & Hansen (Consulting Engineers), "Master Design Guidelines - Water Reclamation Plants," Report to the City of Scottsdale, Sept. 1984.
5. Hinks, R. W., von Allworden, B., "Investigation into the Optimal Development of Wastewater Reclamation Facilities in the City of Scottsdale," Report to the City of Scottsdale, Aug. 1984.

PERSONNEL POLICIES FOR OPERATIONS MANAGEMENT IN THE COMPUTER AGE

Gordon G. Green, F. ASCE *

ABSTRACT

The human factor is an essential ingredient and the key element in successful computer applications for water resources or any other field. Engineers in general, and engineering managers in particular, need to understand not only the physical laws of nature but also the human, non-physical forces affecting their work, their lives and those around them. This paper introduces the subject of personnel policies in the computer age to be discussed by a panel especially as it relates to operations management in the field of water resources.

REVOLUTIONARY TRENDS

Three of ten trends in John Naisbitt's best selling book Mega-trends are of particular interest in illustrating important points that we want to examine that are changing the nature of the engineer's work today. History has established the third quarter of the 18th century as the beginning of the Industrial Revolution. For several interesting reasons Naisbitt claims the years 1956 and 1957 were a historical turning point when we became predominantly an information society. It is estimated that over 60% of Americans work in information occupations today as engineers, programmers, secretaries, managers, accountants, bankers, etc, while less than 15% of our labor force is engaged in manufacturing operations and less than 5% in agricultural production.

INFORMATION ERA

From a historical perspective, we have literally just crossed the threshold of a new age, the Information Era, and revolutionary changes are taking place. This is the first megatrend. We, as engineers, are used to working with physical laws, but how perceptive are we of the social forces, the human, non-physical forces that are at work today changing our world? Do we care? Before we dismiss them, we had better know what they are. We'd best learn at least how to live with them so we don't become overwhelmed and if possible we should learn how to manage or control them.

*Chief, Reservoir Control Center, North Pacific Division, U. S. Army Corps of Engineers, P.O. Box 2870, Portland, Oregon 97208-2870

ORGANIZATIONAL STRUCTURES

The second megatrend identified by Naisbitt that is of particular interest to us today, is how the Information Era is affecting organizational structures. There is a trend away from hierarchies toward networks. Advances in computers, communications and the human potential movement are the driving forces behind this trend. The traditional pyramid structure of large organizations is giving way in many places to a more efficient and satisfying network structure where more people talk directly to each other, share ideas, information and resources without going through a manager or a controller of information. Naisbitt claims that the computer is smashing the pyramid. This new network is egalitarian, forcing significant changes in elitist groups that sometimes protect the self-interest of a limited few. We are being affected by this trend, whether we realize it or not.

MULTIPLE OPTIONS

The third megatrend of Naisbitt's that we are considering today relates to the broad trend in society away from limited choices toward numerous options. For our purposes this is epitomized by the computer and the multiplicity of options available to the engineer today. With the computer, the engineer can examine a whole array of scenarios. With so many options, the importance of making a decision, or in other works choosing the right option, was never more important. The computer can rapidly manipulate data and convert it into information, but in the last analysis, it is a human that makes the decision to accept or act upon the computer output, or even to allow the computer to take some action.

PERSONNEL ASPECTS

These megatrends serve to illustrate the important accumulative impact of small, gradual changes going on around the engineer on a day-to-day basis, but often unseen. These trends relate to the human, social aspect of engineering.

HARDWARE + SOFTWARE + PERSONNEL = COMPUTER APPLICATIONS

For computer applications to be successful in the field of water resources, there must be three factors in balance: hardware, software and personnel. Most of the discussions at this ASCE Water Resources Planning and Management Division Specialty Conference have dealt with hardware and softfware aspects, while the human aspect is often taken for granted or forgotten. The purpose of this session is to provide a specific opportunity to focus on the human portion of this triad.

PANEL MEMBERS AND TOPICS

Civil engineering is a people-serving profession conducted by engineers and their organizations. That is our ultimate objective and we must not lose sight of it. Large numbers of civil engineers use hardware and software as a means to accomplish this objective. They do it by being problem solvers and quality-of-life improvers. There are over 92,000 members of ASCE and in order to better focus our attention on the theme of this conference, "Computer Applications in Water Resources", and to bring our subject to a more manageable size, a panel of knowledgeable and experienced civil engineers, with a diversity of viewpoints and from different geographical areas, have been selected to discuss personnel policies for operations management of water resource projects in the computer age. The panel members and the main viewpoint from which they will be speaking are:

The Academia Viewpoint and Findings
    Dr. John W. Labadie
    Professor, Department of Civil Engineering
    Colorado State University
    Fort Collins, Colorado

The Central Headquarters Viewpoint and the Federal Agency Experience
    Mr. Earl E. Eiker
    Chief, Water Control/Quality Branch
    Army Corps of Engineers
    Washington, D.C.

The Engineer Programmer Viewpoint
    Ms. Esther M. Grossman
    Energy Modelling Engineer
    B.C. Hydro and Power Authority
    Vancouver, British Columbia

The Municipal and State Operating Agency Viewpoint
    Mr. Richard F. Lanyon
    Assistant Director for Research and Development
    Metropolitan Sanitary District of Greater Chicago
    Chicago, Illinois

The Field Office Experience Controlling a Large Reservoir System
    Mr. Gordon G. Green
    Chief, Reservoir Control Center
    Army Corps of Engineers
    Portland, Oregon

OUTPUT VS DECISION

Managers of water resource projects have to live in the real world of striving to achieve a balanced performance among competing and sometimes conflicting interests. The number of factors to be considered are too numerous to be completely and accurately modeled by computer. These factors can range from economic or budgetary considerations to environmental or political issues, with the need to provide optimum water supply, power generation, flood control, etc in the middle. The operations manager must know how the parts relate to the whole. In the final analysis a human decision must be made regardless of how good or how poor are the results or recommendations of a computerized system. The decisions of an organization's personnel are the critical factor. Some of the personnel related questions and items concerning computer applications on which the panel members have been asked to share their experiences and insights are discussed in following paragraphs.

ATTRACTING TALENT

What can be done to recruit and retain some of the best and brightest engineers into the field of operations management of water resource projects? The "brain drain" into electronics, aerospace or other more publicized and what to the public seem to be more glamorous fields, can be stiff competition. A recent survey by the "Wall Street Journal" found that many engineers that had left basic industry did so because they felt stifled by their old work environment and an unwillingness of the industries to adapt new technologies or to be receptive to innovation, and because of limited opportunities for career advancement. The survey concluded that the loss of some of the best engineering and scientific talent away from these so-called "smoke-stack" industries created a partial vacuum that ultimately contributed to their decline.

TEAM COMMUNICATION

What is the best organizational structure for operations management personnel? What are the best combinations of specialists and support staff in an organization? Organizations of engineering firms and agencies tend to grow first horizontally, with added departments or divisions, and then secondly they grow vertically as new positions are added. It has been suggested that with a computer terminal at every desk, including even the head of the agency or the president of the firm, that the middle manager's job may be in jeopardy; or, maybe it's the support staff or even the upper echelon management that is in jeopardy. Close observers tell us there is a trend for the number of managment levels in large organizations to be reduced, probably as a result of computer applications and a need to stay competitive, but most of all it's because of personnel satisfaction. An alternative approach to the traditional organization that has been successfully used, is to place personnel into small but relatively self-sufficient groups or teams. This greatly improves communication between team members and communications have been found to be a key to successful organizations.

PRODUCTIVITY REQUIRES BALANCE

How can the computer help improve productivity in operations management? What are the dangers? Productivity is defined, not as squeezing more work out of people, but rather producing more and better results from the water resources being managed. It has been said that the biggest obstacle to automation is not organized labor, but rather, unorganized management. In operations management, computer applications can greatly reduce the number of pieces of paper being handled or filed. Computerized systems are used to monitor resource conditions, maintain data bases, make forecasts, serve as process controllers, etc. For the best productivity an organization's personnel and computers need to be mutually supportive and in balance. Computers can give erroneous output and they can fail completely at a critical time. Top management could be tempted to rely too much on computers and reduce the human staff to a critical level.

SOFTWARE VS JUDGEMENT

How do we know that the answer from the computer is correct? How reliable is it? How much confidence should we put in it? Computers tend to become accepted as instant experts, and while they certainly have an important place, we must not let software replace sound engineering judgment. Engineers should check computer answers intuitively and not merely rationalize the answers. Claims of artificial intelligence for computers are still exaggerated. As an analogy, compare computer programs for the games of checkers and chess. The computer can be programmed to never lose at checkers. It will either win or draw, because checkers is a game of tactics, and not strategy. But a chess master can often beat the most sophisticated computer because computers still are unable to "out-think" the chess master at all the levels necessary to develop an effective winning strategy.

PERSONNEL AND COMPUTER PRIORITIES

Are people still the key asset in a water resources management organization or is this being eroded by computers? The Dale Carnegie personnel training courses are famous for saying "An organization is only as good as its people". Has the time arrived when it can be said that an organization is only as good as its computers? You would think so by listening to some managers talk. If a management decision had to be made between either people or computers, but not both, then the clear choice would be people. But that is not the usual question. It is usually a matter of degrees and priorities.

INCREASING IMPORTANCE OF OPERATIONS MANAGEMENT

How has the role of the engineer working in the water resources operations field changed with the computer age? The nature of the work, the number of projects being managed, and how it is done have greatly changed. For one thing, operations management of water resources has increased in importance as more projects have been constructed. In contrast, the number of new projects in the design and construction phases has been declining in recent years, so that construction in the U.S. as a percentage of gross national product has declined from over 11% in the last 20 years to below 6% today. Ironically, personnel classification standards in some large organizations, including the U.S. government, still do not adequately recognize operations management of water resource projects as compared to other specialties in engineering.

SUPPORT STAFF IMPORTANT

Has the role of the non-engineer working in a water resources management organization changed? Computer programmers, secretaries, technicians, specialists of a wide variety are employed in the water resources field, along with engineers. Office automation and word processors have already resulted in many changes and more can be expected in the future. Paper and telephone communications are being replaced in some degree by computer communications. In some cases, the computers upgrade the office work situation and present interesting challenges. In other cases they are said to degrade work, even though they increase efficiency.

Some predict an expansion in the number of supporting jobs for engineering organizations in the future, while others think that when everyone in an organization has their own keyboard and a computer terminal with word processing capabilities, it will reduce the number of phone calls, paperwork and clerical jobs. The consensus seems to be however that the nature of the supporting jobs will change and actually increase in number. The U.S. Department of Commerce estimates that for every high-tech job, there are 6 or 7 low-tech jobs created. The comparable worth issue seems likely to upgrade many jobs in the future and bring more fairness among the supporting staff.

TRAINING

What about computer training? What can be done to overcome the reluctance of some to fully embrace the use of computers today? It is said that today the half-life of an engineer's education is only 5 years. Studies show that the yearly supply of scientific information grows at 13% and it is estimated this could increase to 30% per year by the year 2000. There is an explosion in the number of computers, especially microcomputers. According to a recent survey, the number of micrcomputers in large U.S. school districts has doubled during the last school year. The National Technological University (NTU), the nation's first electronic university devoted to advanced engineering studies, began initial operations at 13 sites across the country in the fall of 1984. The Federal Emergency Management Agency (FEMA) provides an example of using computers for innovative training of its staff and others for disaster response.

MORALE

What about morale, job satisfaction or burnout, ergonomics, etc in the engineering office today? There are a lot of subjective opinions on these with little factual information as yet, except that they are important. These and other questions concerning the human factor in the "Hardware plus Software plus Personnel equals Computer Applications" equation should be examined.

CONCLUSION

Our country has made much progress, but with demands on water resources increasing, water problems are not about to disappear. There are many changes taking place, but one thing remains constant. People are still the key asset in operations management and they now have a tremendous opportunity to use the new computer tools to improve productivity and job satisfaction at the same time. To paraphrase the last line in John Naisbitt's book <u>Megatrends</u>:

"My God, what a fantastic time to be an engineer."

Basalt System Characterization: Inverse Technique

A. H. Lu*

William W. G. Yeh†
Member ASCE

ABSTRACT

The Basalt Waste Isolation Project (BWIP) has been established to assess the feasibility of the Columbia River Basalt Group as a host medium for a high-level radioactive waste repository. Representative hydraulic parameter values are needed to predict site performance. Thus, a series of multiple-well large-scale, hydraulic stress (LHS) tests of selected hydrogeologic units in deep basalts are planned. An automatic parameter estimation technique has been incorporated into the quasi-three-dimensional model[7] as one of the tools to be used for interpretation of the LHS tests. This paper presents test cases that incorporate important geological and hydrological features character- istic of Pasco Basin basalts. Results of preliminary studies are promising in terms of identifying critical parameters in one- and two-layer applications.

Introduction

The BWIP has been established to assess the feasibility of the Columbia River Basalt Group as a repository for high-level radioactive wastes. The BWIP is administered by Rockwell Hanford Operations for the U.S. Department of Energy.

The BWIP reference repository location is on the Hanford Site within the Pasco Basin in south-central Washington State, a structural basin formed by a series of anticlinal ridges (fig. 1). The candidate repository horizons and the preferred repository horizon are contained within the Grande Ronde Basalt Formation, which is ~2,500 ft (760 m) below the land surface at the reference repository location. Represen- tative hydraulic parameter values of these and adjacent horizons are necessary for repository performance assessment. Thus, a series of multiple-well LHS tests of selected hydrogeologic units of the Grande Ronde Basalt are planned. An automatic parameter estimation technique has been incorporated into a quasi-three-dimensional model[7] as one of tools to be used for interpretation of LHS tests. The inverse computer program is called TRESCOTT-INVERT.

*Staff Hydrologist, Basalt Waste Isolation Project, Rockwell Hanford Operations, Richland, Washington 99352
†Professor, Civil Engineering Department, University of California, Los Angeles, California 90024

Though the optimization procedure for parameter identification has been applied to groundwater management and characterization problems by some researchers[2,5], the applicability of the technique to a deep basalt flow system has been questioned because of limited availability of observation points and the heterogeneous nature of the flow system.

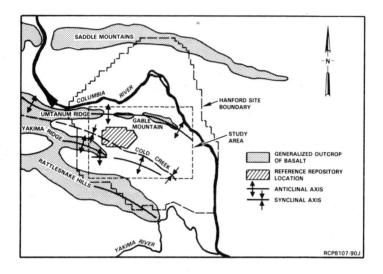

Figure 1. Structural Setting of the Reference Repository Location Within the Pasco Basin.

Inverse techniques are being developed to support the planning and design, as well as interpretation, of LHS tests. This paper presents four test cases that incorporate important geological and hydrological features characteristic of Pasco Basin basalts. Monitoring well configuration, typical of those that will be employed during the tests, also are used.

Hydrogeology

The reference repository location lies within the Cold Creek syncline in the Pasco Basin. The Pasco Basin extends to the Saddle Mountains on the north and to the Rattlesnake Hills on the south, both of which are anticlinal ridges of the Yakima fold belt. The reference repository location area is bounded by the Umtanum Ridge-Gable Mountain anticline on the north, the Yakima Ridge on the southwest, and an apparent hydraulic "barrier" known as the Cold Creek barrier in the Cold Creek syncline to the west of the reference repository location. The existence of such a barrier is supported by the evidence that the seasonal water-level variations due to irrigation, which are observed in the boreholes on the west side of the barrier, do not appear in the boreholes on the east side of the barrier.

The bedrock in the Pasco Basin is comprised of basalt flows of the Columbia River Basalt Group. Within the reference repository location, the basalt flows are grouped into three formations in the order of oldest to youngest: (1) Grande Ronde, (2) Wanapum, and (3) Saddle Mountains Basalts. Four horizons within the Grande Ronde Basalt Formation (Umtanum, McCoy Canyon, Cohassett, and Rocky Coulee flows) have been identified as candidates for the reference repository horizon.

Groundwater in the layered basalt sequence in the reference repository location and vicinity is under confined conditions. The measured values of hydraulic conductivity from small-scale single borehole tests range primarily between 10^{-5} to 10^2 ft/d (3.5×10^{-11} to 3.5×10^{-4} m/s) for the flow top zones in the Grande Ronde Basalt. For the dense flow interior zones, the measured, hydraulic conductivity ranges from about 10^{-7} to 10^{-5} ft/d (3.5×10^{-13} to 3.5×10^{-11} m/s)[5]. The hydraulic heads in the confined system are estimated to range from 395 to 420 ft (120 to 128 m) above mean sea level.

Initial Test Plan

The first LHS tests will use well RRL-2B as a pumping well. The site for this well is centrally located within the reference repository location (fig. 2). Pumping well RRL-2B will be constructed so that a hydraulic stress can be imposed on selected hydrogeologic units within the Grande Ronde Basalt using a drill-test staged approach. The first test at the RRL-2B site will be in the Rocky Coulee flow top. Near-field facilities will include a pumping well (RRL-2B) and two observation wells (RRL-2A, RRL-2C) that are ~250 and 500 ft (76 to 152 m) from the RRL-2B site, respectively. Additional observation points range from 1.4 mi (2.3 km) to >10 mi (16 km) from the RRL-2B site. Principle among these are observation wells DC-16, RRL-6, DC-20, DC-19, and DC-22 (see fig. 2). These wells will be used as multiple-level observation wells, each capable of monitoring several selected hydrogeologic units. Other wells will be monitored but are not likely to be influenced by the induced stress.

Numerical Code Description

A parameter identification subroutine has been developed in such a way that it can be operated in conjunction with the Trescott[7] quasi-three-dimensional, finite-difference model. The Trescott model utilizes a block-centered, finite-difference grid in which variable spacing is permitted. The iterative numerical technique uses the strongly implicit procedure. Three dimensions are simulated by a series of two-dimensional models, with an interaquifer transfer coefficient (TCF) determining the flow between the layers based on a simple Darcy flow. The TCF is a quantity that, when multiplied by vertical head differences, yields the flow quantity being transferred between the layers. The TFC values for each confining bed are

$$TCF = K_v/b \qquad\qquad (1)$$

where K_v is the vertical hydraulic conductivity, and b is the thickness of the dense interior.

The governing equation for each layer is

$$\frac{\partial}{\partial x}(T\frac{\partial h}{\partial x}) + \frac{\partial}{\partial y}(T\frac{\partial h}{\partial y}) + (TCF)\Delta h_z = S\frac{\partial h}{\partial t} + Q \qquad (2)$$

where T is the transmissivity, S is the storage coefficient, Δh_z is hydraulic head difference between two layers, and Q is the source function.

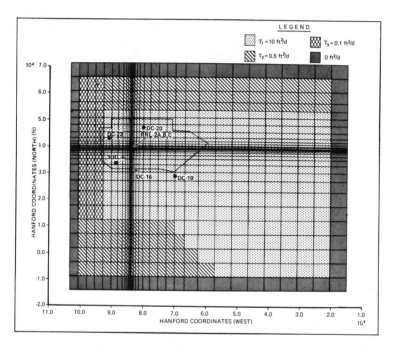

Figure 2. Grid plot, well Locations, and Assumed Transmissivity for One of the Flow Tops in Grande Ronde Basalt.

Two types of boundaries that can be treated by the model are constant head and constant flux. A constant flux may be zero (impermeable boundaries) or have finite values.

The computer program TRESCOTT-INVERT is capable of handling multilayer, transient flow problems. It provides estimates of parameters T, S, and TCF. The areal heterogeneity of the flow system is estimated by dividing the flow region into a number of zones in which the transmissivities can be considered as constant. The program estimates the value of the parameters by minimizing an objective function of the form:

$$\min_{\underline{\theta}} J = \sum_{i=1}^{N} (h_i - h_i^*)^2$$

where $\overline{\theta}$ is the parameter vector (T, TCF, S); N is the total number of observations, which is a product of the number of observation wells and number of time steps; h_i represents the model solutions that are commensurate with observations, and h_i^* represents the observations.

Equation 3 is subject to the following constraints

$$\overline{\theta}^{\ell} \leq \overline{\theta} \leq \overline{\theta}^{u} \tag{4}$$

where superscripts ℓ and u represent lower and upper bounds of the parameter, which may be obtained from prior geologic information. Uniform weights have been assumed in the objective function.

Using vector notation, we can rewrite equation 3 as

$$\min_{\overline{\theta}} J = \overline{e}^{T} \cdot \overline{e} \tag{5}$$

where $\overline{e}(\overline{\theta})$ is $\overline{h} - \overline{h}^*$ and superscript "_" represents a vector quantity.

Expanding equation 5 about an initial estimate $\overline{\theta}^0$ by a first order Taylor series yields

$$\min_{\overline{\theta}^1} J^1 = \left[\overline{e}(\overline{\theta}^0) + J_\theta^{T}(\overline{\theta}^1 - \overline{\theta}^0) \right]^T$$

$$* \left[\overline{e}(\overline{\theta}^0) + J_\theta^{T}(\overline{\theta}^1 - \overline{\theta}^0) \right] . \tag{6}$$

where J_θ is the Jacobian matrix whose entries are defined by

$$J_{\ell,i} = \frac{\partial e_i}{\partial \theta_\ell}, \qquad i = 1,\ldots,N \qquad \ell = 1,\ldots,L$$

where e_i is given as an implicit function, numerical value of J_θ can only be approximated by a finite-difference method. The discrete version of J_θ, called the influence coefficient matrix by Becker and Yeh[1], can be written as

$$J_{\ell,i} = \frac{\Delta e_i}{\Delta \theta_\ell}, \qquad i = 1,\ldots,N \qquad \ell = 1,\ldots,L \tag{7}$$

where $\Delta\theta_\ell$ is a small increment of θ_ℓ and Δe_i is the consequent change in error.

Optimization Procedures

Equation 6 subject to constraint (eq. 4) can be solved by the following procedures.

● Step 1:
  Select an initial estimate of the parameter vector $\overline{\theta}^0$.

● Step 2:
  Approximate the Jacobian matrix by the influence coefficient method (eq. 7) of Becker and Yeh[1]. The Jacobian matrix is approximated by sequentially operating the Trescott three-dimensional model for each of the L changes, θ_1, θ_2, ..., θ_L, and in each case obtain the incremental change Δe_i, i = 1, ..., N. Thus, this step will involve (L+1) operations of the Trescott three-dimensional model over the stipulated time period.

● Step 3:
  Solve equation 6 subject to constraint (eq. 4) by a modified Gausian-Newton method to obtain θ^1.

● Step 4:
  Check stopping criteria and repeat, if necessary.

Covariance Analysis

A subroutine has also been incorporated into the model to calculate the covariance matrix of the estimated parameters. The approach is essentially based on the work of Yeh and Yoon[8,9]. The parameter uncertainty error can be characterized by the diagonal terms of the covariance matrix of the estimated parameters. Yeh and Yoon have shown that the covariance matrix of the estimated parameters for the proposed nonlinear least-squares type minimization is

$$\text{Cov } (\overline{\theta}^*) = \frac{J(\theta^*)}{N-L}(J_\theta{}^T J_\theta)^{-1} \tag{8}$$

where $\overline{\theta}^*$ is the optimized $\overline{\theta}$, $J(\theta^*)$ is the minimized least-square error, N is the total number of observations as defined in equation 3, L is the parameter dimension, and J_θ is the Jacobian matrix evaluated at $\overline{\theta}^*$.

Model Setup

The model has been set up to perform a pretest analysis to provide a conceptual basis for planning and designing of LHS tests. The model area includes the reference repository location, which lies within the central portion of the Cold Creek syncline, apparent geological structures, and an apparent hydrogeologic barrier on the north, west, and southwest. On the east, the finite-different grid is extended far enough from the project area so that the boundary will have a negligible effect in the area of interest during the simulation period. An impermeable boundary was assigned along the outmost nodes automatically by the computer code. The model grid consisted of 32 rows and 34 columns, varying from 183 ft (50 m) to 1 mi (1.6 km), representing a 16- by 17-mi^2 (26- by 27-km^2) simulation area.

One of the objectives of the LHS tests is to assess how the geologic structures behave hydrologically to influence groundwater flow across the reference repository location. Because the role of the structures in the flow system is uncertain[3,4], a conceptual model was chosen in which low transmissivities were assigned to the structural areas. Figure 2 shows the transmissivity distribution used to represent the true properties for one flow top in the Grande Ronde basalts.

Another objective of the LHS tests is to estimate the degree of leakage through a dense basalt flow interiors. A second flow top is added to demonstrate that the parameters that characterize the vertical flow in the dense basalt interior can be identified. The hydraulic stress is exerted only on the first flow top.

Test Cases and Discussions

Several test cases are used to demonstrate the applicability of the TRESCOTT-INVERT computer program. The first three cases considered one layer and Case 4 considered two layers. A brief discussion of each case follows.

Case 1. The flow top is initially at a steady-state condition with the hydraulic head equal to 400 ft throughout the flow top. A hydraulic stress is exerted on well RRL-2B with a pumping rate of 30 gal/min (1.9 x 10^{-3} m^3/s). The duration of the pumping test is 30 d. The assumed true parameters are: T_1 = 10 ft^2/d (1.08 x 10^{-5} m^2/s); T_2 = 0.5 ft^2/d (5.4 x 10^{-7} m^2/s; T_3 = 0.1 ft^2/d (1.08 x 10^{-7} m^2/s; and S = 8 x 10^{-6}. The contour plot of drawdown after 30 d of pumping is shown in figure 3 to provide a perspective view of how the system is stressed. The cone of depression has reached the tight zone on the west and north and barely reached the south. The generated hydraulic heads obtained for Δt = 1 d are recorded at seven observation wells and are used for parameter identification.

Initially the flow top is assumed to be homogeneous and optimization is carried out. The lower and upper constraints of transmissivity are set to be 0.001 ft^2/d (1.1 x 10^{-9} m^2/s) to 100 ft^2/d (1.1 x 10^{-4} m^2/s) throughout this study. Table 1 shows the initial estimate of the parameter, its sequence of convergence, and the least-square error (J) at each iteration. The corresponding variance of the optimized parameters is also indicated. Note that even though the optimized T^* is very close to the true value of T_1, the least square error was almost steady after four iterations and remains high. Further comparisons of the calculated hydraulic heads with the true heads (not presented) show greatest error at wells DC-22, a significant

error at well RRL-6, and small errors at other wells, except DC-19, in
which the error is negligible. These observations provide an
indication that the cone of depression has reached into a flow region
with different characteristics. This information is then used to aid
further zoning to reoptimize the system.

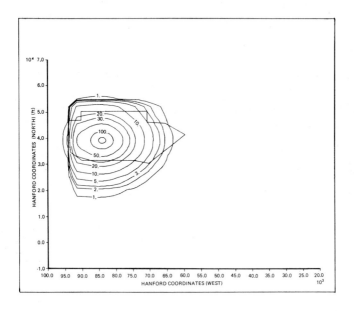

Figure 3. Drawdown (feet) After 30 d Pumping: s = 8 x 10⁻⁶;
Q = 30 gal/min (1.9 x 10⁻³ m³/s); and T = See Distribution
Map.

Case 2. The flow top is then subdivided into three subregions
that are the same, as it is used to generate the true hydraulic heads.
The generated true heads remain the same as in Case 1. The system is
reoptimized. The least square error is reduced drastically and the
true T's are completely recovered. It should be noted that actual test
interpretation might require a number of trials of zoning based on the
prior geological information and scrutinized analysis of the previous
results.

Case 3. This run shows the effect of the measurement error of
hydraulic heads. The generated heads are corrupted with Gaussian noise
of standard deviation σ = 0.7 ft, and are used as observations for
parameter identification. The least square error is increased drastically for this case. Though the T_1 and T_3 are almost completely
recovered, the optimized T_2^* is only 40% of the true one. The
corresponding variance of $\hat{T}_2^*$ is high because less information is
gathered in this subregion. However, a better estimate could be

Table 1. Results of Successive Iterations.

Test case	Parameter	Units	True value	Initial estimate	Error % in initial estimate	Iter 1	Iter 2	Iter 3	Iter 4	Iter 5	Iter 6	Iter 7	Iter 8	Iter 9	Variance (σ_θ^2)
Case 1, $\sigma=0$	T_1	ft²/d	10	5[b]	100	8.83	10.31	9.81	10.05	9.94	9.99	9.97	9.98	9.97	5.4×10^{-3}
	T_2	ft²/d	0.5												
	T_3		0.1												
	J		0	3.1×10^6		6.1×10^4	5.8×10^3	3.0×10^3	2.1×10^3	2.0×10^3	2.0×10^3	1.9×10^3	1.9×10^3	1.9×10^3	
Case 2, $\sigma=0$	T_1	ft²/d	10	5	100	8.84	9.15	10.29	9.86	10.06	9.97	10.01	10.00	10.00	3.1×10^{-5}
	T_2	ft²/d	0.5	1.0	100	7.16	0.001	0.334	0.594	0.415	0.512	0.484	0.507	0.497	
	T_3		0.1	0.2	100	0.164	0.138	0.578	0.117	0.091	0.104	0.098	0.108	0.100	
	J		0	3.1×10^6		6.0×10^4	3.0×10^4	2.8×10^3	7.3×10^2	1.3×10^2	2.9×10^1	5.8×10^0	1.2×10^0	2.5×10^{-1}	
Case 3, $\sigma=0.7$	T_1	ft²/d	10	5	100	8.84	9.28	10.26	9.88	10.06	9.98	10.01	10.00	10.00	3.1×10^{-5}
	T_2	ft²/d	0.5	1.0	100	2.79	0.001	0.175	0.270	0.142	0.207	0.183	0.195	0.190	2.0
	T_3		0.1	0.2	100	0.160	0.125	0.063	0.115	0.092	0.103	0.098	0.100	0.100	1.2×10^{-3}
	J		0	3.1×10^6		6.0×10^4	2.1×10^4	2.3×10^3	6.7×10^2	2.1×10^2	1.3×10^2	1.1×10^2	1.1×10^2	1.1×10^2	
Case 4, $\sigma=0.3$	T_1	ft²/d	10	5	100	8.84	9.32	10.25	9.88	10.06	9.96	10.01	10.00	10.00	6.9×10^{-6}
	T_2	ft²/d	0.5	0.4	20	4.46	0.010	0.504	0.646	0.591	0.625	0.611	0.618	0.615	8.7×10^{-2}
	T_3		0.1	0.2	100	0.186	0.139	0.071	0.118	0.098	0.108	0.103	0.105	0.104	8.2×10^{-5}
	TCF	$\times 10^7$/d	0.2	0.3	50	0.235	0.223	0.198	0.199	0.199	0.199	0.199	0.199	0.199	6.7×10^{-6}
	J		0	4.4×10^6		8.4×10^4	2.6×10^4	3.1×10^3	8.4×10^2	2.0×10^2	8.9×10^1	6.3×10^1	5.7×10^1	5.6×10^1	

a TCF = transfer coefficient.
b Homogeneity assumed.

P85-2067

obtained by stressing the system longer, so that more responses from
subregion 2 would be registered in the near by monitoring wells.

Case 4. Two layers are set up for study. The parameters in the
first layer are the same as described in cases above while adding TCF =
2×10^{-8}/d (2.3×10^{-13}/s) to account for hydraulic properties of the
basalt dense interior between two layers. The TCF was obtained by
assuming $K_v = 10^{-6}$ ft/d (3.5×10^{-12} m/s) and b = 50 ft (15 m),
respectively. The lower and upper constraints of TCF are set to 1 x
10^{-9}/d (3.5×10^{-15}/s) and 1 x 10^{-5}/d (3.5×10^{-11}/s). The
transmissivity distribution of the second flow top is similar to that
of the first flow top but the values are doubled (i.e., $T_4 = 2T_1$; $T_5 =$
$2T_2$; and $T_6 = 2T_3$). Four parameters are to be identified: T_1, T_2, T_3,
and TCF. The generated heads are corrupted with Gaussian noise of
standard deviation $\sigma = 0.3$, which is the best estimate of the
measurement error. Initially the pumping duration was set up for 30 d
for parameter identification. For the 30-d pumping period, the
calculated heads are insensitive to the change of T_2 and instability
resulted because the cone of depression barely reached subregion 2.
This was due to additional water supply through leakage. The pumping
duration was then increased to 40 d. For the 40-d pumping period, the
parameters T_1, T_3, and TCF are almost completely recovered; however,
the optimized T_2^* is only 80% of the true value. The corresponding
variance of T_2^* remains high due to less recorded responses from
subregion 2.

The robustness of the method will be examined further to apply the
inverse method to the synthetic data that will be generated by another
party to determine how much prior information would be needed to
recover the parameter values.

Conclusion

Planning and design, as well as interpretation of a pumping test
in deep Hanford Site basalt flow systems is a challenging task.
Transmissivities measured from small-scale single borehole tests range
over several orders of magnitude. Though LHS tests are expected to
integrate highly localized heterogeneity of the flow system to obtain
an average value, the existence of areal heterogeneities due to
geological features (e.g., faults, tectonic breccias, structures) would
complicate the analyses of the tests. The assumptions on which most
analytical solutions are based may be seriously violated. Thus,
numerical modeling, coupled with a parameter identification program, is
used to provide an additional tool to perform analyses. One clear
advantage of using an inverse procedure at the planning stage as
demonstrated by numerical experiments is that it allows the planner to
determine locations where data should be collected. The results of
this study are promising in terms of identifying critical parameters in
one- and two-layer applications. Nonunique solutions might occur in
some applications; thus, additional tests would be conducted to reduce
ambiguities in interpretation of test results. A strategic series of
tests, with clear goals in mind for each test, will enhance the
conceptual understanding of the Hanford Site basalt groundwater flow
system.

Appendix 1--References

1. Becker, L., and Yeh, W. W-G., "Identification of Parameters in Unsteady Open Channel Flow," Water Resources Research, 8(4), 1972, pp. 956-965.

2. Carrera, J., Walter, G. R., Kuhn, M. W., and Bentley, H. W., "Three-Dimensional Modeling of Saline Pond Leakage Calibrated by INVERT-3, A Quasi-Three-Dimensional, Transient, Parameter-Estimation Program," presented at the August 15-17, 1984, NWWA Symposium on Practical Applications of Groundwater Models, held at Columbus, Ohio.

3. Gephart, R. E., Arnett, R. C., Baca, R. G., Leonhart, L. S., and Spane, F. A., Jr., Hydrologic Studies Within the Columbia Plateau, Washington: An Integration of Current Knowledge, RHO-BWI-ST-5, Rockwell Hanford Operations, Richland, Washington, 1979.

4. Lu, A. H., "Opportunistic Use of Drilling-Stress Data to Estimate Aquifer Parameters," presented at the August 15-17, 1984, NWWA Symposium on Practical Applications of Groundwater Models, held at Columbus, Ohio.

5. Neuman, S., Fogg, G. E., and Jacobson, E. A., "A Statistical Approach to the Inverse Problem of Aquifer Hydrology: 2. Case Study," Water Resources Research, 16(1), 1980, pp. 33-58.

6. Strait, S. R., Spane, F. A., Jr., Jackson, R. L., and Pidcoe, W. W., Hydrologic Testing Methodology and Results from Deep Basalt Boreholes, RHO-BW-SA-189 P, Rockwell Hanford Operations, Richland, Washington, 1982.

7. Trescott, P. C., "Documentation of Finite-Difference Method for Simulation of Three-Dimensional Groundwater Flow," Open File Report 75-438, U.S. Geological Survey, Washington, D.C., 1975.

8. Yeh, W. W-G., and Yoon, Y. S., "A Systematic Procedure for the Identification of Inhomogeneous Aquifer Parameters," Advances in Groundwater Hydrology, American Water Resources Association, Minneapolis, Minnesota, 1976, pp. 72-82.

9. Yeh, W. W-G., and Yoon, Y. S., "Aquifer Parameter Identification with Optimum Dimension in Parameterization," Water Resources Research, 17(3), 1981, pp. 664-672.

Parameter Identification in Water System Models

Wen-sen Chu, A.M.* and Eric W. Strecker

Abstract

Parameter identification (PI) is an automatic model calibration technique with which the unknown physical parameters in a mathematical model are determined from a constrained optimization formulation. A number of PI techniques have been proposed in modeling both surface and subsurface water systems to date. In this paper, the application of a generalized PI algorithm is presented. The PI algorithm was applied to a two-dimensional estuarine hydrodynamics model and a two-dimensional groundwater contaminant transport model. Both applications deal with realistic problems where only limited data are available. The implementation procedures of the algorithm and computational experience are presented.

Introduction

 With the increased use of simulation models for design and planning problems, water resources engineers spend a large portion of their time in model calibration. Model calibration is normally accomplished by fitting model predictions to limited observation data through careful adjustment of selected model parameters. This process normally involves a trial and error approach, which can be very time consuming and often leads to results which are not entirely satisfactory.

An alternative to trial and error calibration is parameter identification (PI). PI is a procedure with which the unknown parameters in a mathematical model are estimated from a constrained optimization problem. PI has been applied in various scientific disciplines, including water resources systems modeling (1, 2, 3, 6, 7, 8, 12, 14).

This paper introduces the development and implementation of a generic PI algorithm which can be incorporated into any existing numerical model with only minor modifications. The algorithm has been applied to an estuarine hydrodynamics model and a groundwater contaminant transport model. The experience learned from the applications of the proposed method are presented.

*Respectively, Assistant Professor and Graduate Student, Department of Civil Engineering, FX-10, University of Washington, Seattle, WA 98195

The Mathematical Formulation

Let $\vec{x}$ be the model solutions of some water system variables at selected locations and times where observations of the variables $\vec{x}*$ are available, and let $\vec{p}$ be the vector containing all the model parameters that are chosen to be adjusted to match $\vec{x}$ with $\vec{x}*$. We may define an error measure $\vec{e}$, which is:

$$\vec{e} = \vec{x} - \vec{x}* \qquad (1)$$

If we assume that the errors (discrepancies) are due only to the incorrect parameter values $\vec{p}$, then Eq. (1) can be written as:

$$\vec{e}(\vec{p}) = \vec{x} - \vec{x}* \qquad (2)$$

To obtain an explicit relation between $\vec{e}$ and $\vec{p}$, we expand Eq. (2) by a first order Taylor series around some known (given) conditions, $\vec{p}^o$ (and therefore $\vec{e}^o$) yielding:

$$\vec{e}(\vec{p}) = \vec{e}^o(\vec{p}^o) + J^{-1} \cdot (\vec{p} - \vec{p}^o) \qquad (3)$$

where J is the Jacobian matrix containing the derivative of each error measure with respect to each parameter variation.

The basic formulation of the proposed PI method is to minimize the error measures with the definition of $\vec{e}$ (Eq. 3) and the physical constraints of the parameters. The optimization can be written as:

$$\underset{\vec{p}}{\text{minimize}} \ ||\vec{e}|| \qquad (4)$$

$$\text{subject to:} \ \vec{e}(\vec{p}) = \vec{e}^o(\vec{p}^o) + J^{-1} \cdot (\vec{p} - \vec{p}^o) \qquad (5)$$

$$\vec{p}^l \leq \vec{p} \leq \vec{p}^u \qquad (6)$$

where $\vec{p}^l$ and $\vec{p}^u$ are the lower and upper bounds for the parameter $\vec{p}$, and $||\cdot||$ can be a particular norm (measure) of our choice. For example, using the least-square criterion, the formulation can be written as:

$$\underset{\vec{p}}{\text{minimize}} \ \vec{e}^T W \vec{e} \qquad (7)$$

$$\text{subject to} \ \vec{e}(\vec{p}) = \vec{e}(\vec{e}^o) + J^{-1}(\vec{p} - \vec{p}^o) \qquad (8)$$

$$\vec{p}^l \leq \vec{p} \leq \vec{p}^u \qquad (9)$$

where W is the weighting matrix.

Substituting the expansion term into the objective function, the least-square optimization problem can be written as:

minimize $[\vec{e}^{o}(\vec{p}^{o}) + J \cdot (\vec{p}-\vec{p}^{o})]^{T}$ W $[\vec{e}^{o}(\vec{p}^{o}) + J^{-1} \cdot (\vec{p}-\vec{p}^{o})]$ (10)
$\vec{p}$

subject to: $\vec{p}^{l} \leq \vec{p} \leq \vec{p}^{u}$ (11)

which because of the quadratic objective function and linear
constraints, is known as a quadratic programming problem. The
quadratic programming problem (Eqs. (10) and (11)) is solved by an
efficient Wolfe's algorithm (13).

The unknown variables in Eq. (10) are the paramters p that need to
be adjusted and the estimated error $\vec{e}$. The proposed quadratic programming problem has a small dimension with a convex constraint set. The
introduction of the error measure $\vec{e}$ allows the optimization formulation
to be independent from the solution algorithm of any particular model.
The necessary mathematical relationship which bridge Eqs. (10) and (11)
with any model is embedded in the Jacobian matrix, J, whose entries are
the changes in error estimates due to small perturbations in every
model parameter value being estimated. Because of the linear
approximation of $\vec{e}(\vec{p})$, the parameter values must be determined by
iterative solution of Eqs. (10) and (11) from an initial estimate of
$\vec{p}^{o}$.

Algorithm

The PI formulation (Eqs. (10) and (11)) is coded in FORTRAN 77 with
a specific feature which allows easy merging with any existing model
that is written in FORTRAN. To implement it, users will have to define
particular error measures in a subroutine, and in certain cases, may
need to rearrange the orders of execution of the model slightly. The
flow diagram showing the merging of the PI algorithm with a water
system model is shown in Figure 1.

Applications

1. In Estuarine Hydrodynamics Modeling

In the first application, the PI algorithm was applied to an
estuarine hydrodynamics modeling study (4). In the study, the bottom
roughness coefficient used in a two-dimensional depth-averaged
hydrodynamics model was estimated from synoptic tidal elevation data
collected from four land-based stations.

Using the discrepancies between model predicted tides and observed
tides as the error function (Eq. (1)), and assuming that the prediction
errors are due only to incorrect bottom roughness coefficient and
observation noise, the algorithm can find the optimal spatially varying
bottom roughness coefficients within a short time period. Specifically, the efficiency of the PI approach was compared to that of an
earlier trial-and-error calibration attempt. It was found that the PI
approach can save several man-months of calibration work (4).

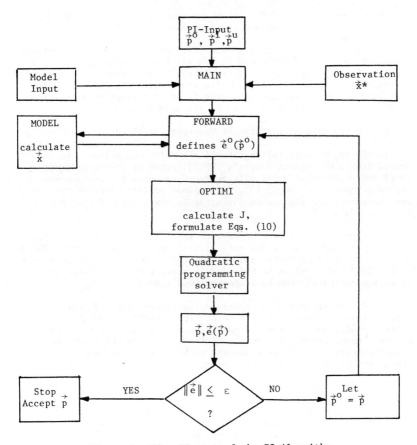

Figure 1. Flow Diagram of the PI Algorithm

   A number of limiting factors in the present application are briefly reported here. First of all, the differences between model solutions and observations are due not just to incorrect parameter values and observation noise. Other systematic errors from model derivation, numerical computation, and boundary conditions also contribute to the discrepancies between model solutions and obervations. Incorporating all of the errors in the PI formulation is difficult, but certainly not impossible. Work of this nature is still being investigated.

   Secondly, the present application did not use any velocity data (because none were available) in the PI calibration. Model parameters that are determined from tide elevations alone may produce velocities that are far from the observed. Collecting synoptic and accurate depth-averaged velocity data in estuaries and coastal seas is very expensive, but badly needed. Using scattered or highly corrupted velocity data will only worsen the parameter estimation.

Finally, it should be recognized that the optimal bottom roughness parameter values are influenced by the discrete resolution used in the model. The parameter estimates are likely to vary when the estuary is approximated by a different grid size resolution. Incorporating the grid size and other systematic errors in the optimization formulation will be a significant improvement to the methodology.

2. In Groundwater Contaminant Transport Modeling

In the second application, the PI algorithm was attached to the United States Geological Survey's (USGS) Method of Characteristics (MOC) two dimensional vertically averaged, groundwater contaminant transport model (USGS-MOC) (5). Only minor modifications of the code were necessary and the combined program is now called PI USGS-MOC or simply PI-MOC.

The PI-MOC code allows the user to specify which parameters (transmissivity(s) and dispersivity cofficients) are to be estimated. Particularly, the current PI-MOC code allows the contaminant transport part of the USGS-MOC model to be bypassed in cases when only transmissivities are estimated from head observations alone.

The PI-MOC algorithm was tested using limited unsteady-state observations from a synthetic heterogeneous, isotropic aquifer. Initial conditions of head and concentration, boundary conditions, source concentration, storage coefficient, porosity and the pattern of transmissivity zonation were assumed to be known. The aquifer was characterized by nine distinct transmissivity zones.

With two years of monthly head and concentration data generated by USGS-MOC at 23 observation wells, PI-MOC was able to recover all nine transmissivity values, as well as the dispersivity coefficients (longitudinal and transverse), very accurately and efficiently. In a separate test in which PI-MOC assumed that the aquifer was homogeneous (but still using the same data generated from nine zones of transmissivities), it was found that PI-MOC was able to identify parameters which will enable the model to predict fairly accurate piezometric head and contaminant plume shape within a short simulation time period. The actual values of concentration at various locations were not accurate when simpler characterization (zoning) of the aquifer was assumed. Details of the testing of PI-MOC are given in Strecker and Ref. (11).

Again, in this application, the formulation of the PI-MOC algorithm assumes that the differences between model predictions and observations (errors) are due to incorrect parameter values only. Other important factors in the error terms include those from simplifying assumptions made in the USGS-MOC model formulation, numerical computations, assumed initial and boundary conditions, estimates of parameters not identified by PI-MOC, and the modelers choice of zonation pattern for transmissivity values.

In field applications, it is suggested that the modelers should first determine whether the aquifer being studied can be adequately described by the formulation of the USGS MOC model. Then, they should estimate as accurately as possible, the initial and boundary conditions, aquifer thickness, storage coefficient, porosity, and transmissivity (including proper zonation for the heterogeneous case) from available geological information. With these basic data, PI-MOC could then be used to identify the chosen model parameters from the given data and information. Prior information about an aquifer, even though limited, is very important to the success of the PI application. PI-MOC is a tool designed to speed up the calibration process. As for any other method of calibration, good engineering judgement should always be used in its application.

Concluding Remarks

An automatic model calibration technique is presented in this paper. The generic algorithm is applied to calibrations of an estuarine hydrodynamics model and a groundwater contaminant transport model. The algorithm is shown to be an effective and efficient calibration tool for both water system modeling applications. The algorithm is developed such that an extension of the method to any other water system model can be easily done.

The proposed algorithm is based on the assumption that the model prediction error is a function of the unknown parameters. Further development in the PI method should incorporate the other types of errors (errors in the numerical solution of the governing equations, and estimation of boundary conditions, etc.) into the optimization formulation.

As in any other means of model calibration, the proposed method is more effective when there are more useful data. Despite the continuous efforts in data gathering from surface as well as ground water systems, very little data are actually useful for calibration of the more physically based models. Very few data bases (regarding surface and groundwater systems) are synoptic (concurrent), and they are normally collected in too small an area over too long a sampling interval (frequency). The proposed PI method can also be extended to study the data requirement and sampling network design problems in water systems modeling.

Acknowledgements

The work reported here is supported by a grant from the Graduate School Research Fund at the University of Washington, and by the Office of Water Research, Bureau of Reclamation, U.S. Department of the Interior, under grant No. 4-FG-93-00010. A portion of computing support was provided by the College of Engineering, the University of Washington. The contributions by William Yeh, Dennis Lettenmaier, James Mock, and Lori Nagle are appreciated.

References

1. Bard, Y., _Nonlinear Parameter Estimation_, Academic Press, New York, 1974, 341 pp.

2. Becker, L. and Yeh, W. W-G., "Identification of Parameters in Unsteady Open-Channel Flows", _Water Resources Research_, Vol. 8, No. 4, 1972, pp. 956-965.

3. Chu, W-S., and Yeh, W. W-G., "Parameter Identification in Estuarine Modeling", _Proc. of the 17th Int. Conf. on Coastal Engineering_, at Sydney, Australia, ASCE, New York, 1980, pp. 2433-2449.

4. Chu, W-S., "Calibration of a Two-Dimensional Hydrodynamics Model", paper submitted to _Coastal Engineering_, 1985.

5. Konikow, L.F. and Bredehoeft, J.D., "Computer Model of Two Dimensional Solute Transport and Dispersion in Ground Water," Chapter C2, _Tech. of Water Resources Investigation of the United States Geological Survey, Book 7_, Reston, Virginia, 1978, 90 pp.

6. Kubrusly, C.S., "Distributed Parameter System Identification, A Survey", _Int. J. of Control_, Vol. 26, No. 4, 1977, pp. 509-535.

7. Neuman, S.P., "Calibration of Distributed Parameter Groundwater Flow Models Viewed as a Multiple Objective Decision Process Under Uncertainty", _Water Resources Research_, Vol. 9, No. 7, 1984, pp. 1006-1021.

8. Sadeghipour, J. and Yeh, W. W-G., "Parameter Identification of Groundwater Aquifer Models: A Generalized Least Squares Approach", _Water Resources Research_, Vol. 20, No. 7, 1984, pp. 971-979.

9. Seinfeld, J.H., "Identification of Parameters in Partial Differential Equations", _Chemical Engineering Science_, Vol. 24, 1969, pp. 65-74.

10. Sorooshian, S., "Comparison of Two Direct Search Algorithms Used in Calibration of Rainfall-Runoff Models", in _Water and Related Land Resources Systems_, ed. by Y.Y. Haimes and J. Kindler, Pergamon, N.Y., 1981, pp. 477-485.

11. Strecker, E.W. and Chu, W-S., "Parameter Identification of a Groundwater Contaminant Transport Model", paper submitted to _Ground Water_, 1985.

12. Wormleaton, P.R. and Karmegan,M. "Parameter Optimization in Flood Routing", _J. of Hydraulic Engineering_, ASCE, Vol. 110, No. 12, 1984, pp. 1799-1814.

13. Wolfe, P., "The Simplex Method for Quadratic Programming", _Econometrica_, Vol. 27, 1959, pp. 382-398.

14. Yeh, W.W-G., "Aquifer Parameter Identification", J. of the
    Hydraulics Div., ASCE, Vol. 101, No. HY9, 1975, pp. 1197-1209.

DIGITAL SIMULATION OF FLOWS IN HAWAIIAN SOILS

by Edmond D.H. Cheng,[*] M. ASCE

ABSTRACT: In attempting to numerically solve the non-linear equation for flows in porous media, the Galerkin process, which bears a great similarity to direct methods of the calculus of variations, is being investigated. In the finite element formulation of the groundwater flow equation, systems of nonlinear algebraic equations are developed on the basis of linear two-dimensional triangular elements. These nonlinear algebraic equations are solved simultaneously, at each time step, by a programmed logic of iterations.

The second and third degrees of polynomial interpretations of moisture diffusivity, $D(\theta)$, and hydraulic conductivity $K(\theta)$, of the media are also conducted. Our preliminary results indicate that the third degrees of polynomial can accurately describe both the $D(\theta)$ and $K(\theta)$ functions of most Hawaiian soils. Solution of unsteady flow in Molokai soil on the island of Oahu, Hawaii is demonstrated.

INTRODUCTION

The recent increased demand in urban development, irrigation systems design, and water resources management, etc., have reemphasized the need for better analysis and predictive methods of flows in porous media. The nonlinear partial differential equations delineating soil-moisture relations are obtained by using dynamic equations, which interrelated the energy dissipated in the system with the velocity, i.e., Darcy's law, induced in a conservation of mass statement yielding the desired basic equations for flows in porous media.

Earlier, numerical integration methods were applied to solve the nonlinear partial differential equations (5,12). Later, among numerous approaches, the finite difference and finite element methods were developed for numerical solutions of the flow equations (1,2,3,4,6,7,9,10,11,13). In this paper, the Galerkin process of approximation of solving an unsteady flow equation for Hawaiian soils is studied and reported herein.

---

[*]Associate Professor, Dept. of Civil Engineering, University of Hawaii at Manoa, Honolulu, Hawaii, 96822

GALERKIN PROCESS

The governing equation for water rising from a groundwater table or for water infiltration into porous media may be expressed in the following nonlinear one-dimensional form (8):

$$\frac{\partial \theta}{\partial t} = \frac{\partial}{\partial z} [D(\theta)\frac{\partial \theta}{\partial z}] - \frac{\partial K(\theta)}{\partial z} \tag{1}$$

where θ = volumetric moisture content; D = moisture diffusivity of the medium; K = hydraulic conductivity of the medium; z = the vertical ordinate with positive sign downward; and t = time.
    In an attempt to solve Eq. 1, let

$$g(z,t) = \frac{\partial \theta(z,t)}{\partial t} \tag{2}$$

and

$$A[\theta] = \frac{\partial}{\partial z} [D(\theta)\frac{\partial \theta}{\partial z}] - \frac{\partial K(\theta)}{\partial z} \tag{3}$$

where A is a differential operator.
    Thus, Eq. 1 may be expressed as

$$g(z,t) = A[\theta] \tag{4}$$

Equation 4 is valid in a solution region E. An approximate solution to Eq. 4 can be expressed in a linear trial-function (14):

$$\theta(z,t) = \sum_{i=1}^{n} C_i(z,t) \, \theta_i(z,t) \tag{5}$$

Then a residual $R(z,t)$ may be defined as:

$$R(z,t) = A(\sum_{i=1}^{n} C_i \theta_i) - g \neq 0 \tag{6}$$

The n parameters C_i in Eq. 6 are determined by the n integral equations:

$$\int_E W_r R(z,t) \, dE = 0 \tag{7}$$

or,

$$\int_E W_r [A(\sum_{i=1}^{n} C_i \theta_i) - g] \, dE = 0 \tag{8}$$

or,

$$\int_E N_i [A(\sum_{i=1}^{n} C_i \theta_i) - g] \, dE = 0 \tag{9}$$

for $r=1,2,\ldots,n$. Where W_r = weighing functions, N_i = a shape function for linear triangular elements, and dE = a subregion of E. If E is divided into finite number of elements, then dE will be one of the elements. Equation 9 is the Galerkin process, which leads, in general, to the best approximation (15,17).

It is evident that the differential operator $A[\theta]$ in Eq. 9 will result in a higher order of differential terms which may impose some difficulties in the process of solution. Equation 9 may be expressed as

$$\int_E [N_i \frac{\partial D(\theta)}{\partial z} \frac{\partial \theta}{\partial z} + N_i D(\theta)\frac{\partial^2 \theta}{\partial z^2} - N_i \frac{\partial K(\theta)}{\partial z} - N_i \frac{\partial \theta}{\partial t}]dzdt = 0 \qquad (10)$$

The appearance of the second term in Eq. 10 will severely limit the choice of shape functions. To overcome this situation, the second term of Eq. 10 may be transformed by means of integration by parts (17). That is:

$$\int_E N_i D(\theta)\frac{\partial^2 \theta}{\partial z^2} dzdt = \int_S N_i D(\theta)\frac{\partial \theta}{\partial z} dt - \int_E [N_i\frac{\partial \theta}{\partial z} \frac{\partial D(\theta)}{\partial z}$$
$$+ D(\theta)\frac{\partial \theta}{\partial z} \frac{\partial N_i}{\partial z}]dzdt = 0 \qquad (11)$$

Therefore, Eq. 10 becomes:

$$\int_E [D(\theta)\frac{\partial \theta}{\partial z} \frac{\partial N_i}{\partial z} + N_i \frac{\partial K(\theta)}{\partial z} + N_i\frac{\partial \theta}{\partial t}]dzdt - \int_S N_i D(\theta)\frac{\partial \theta}{\partial z} dt = 0 \qquad (12)$$

where S = external surface area of solution region E.

An approximate solution to Eq. 12 was chosen in a trial-function form so that the solution would be valid from neighboring nodal points of adjacent elements, and extends to the entire solution region. Consider the following linear trial-function for triangular elements:

$$\theta(z,t) = \sum_{i=1}^{n} \sum_{j=1}^{3} N_{ij}\theta_{ij} \qquad (13)$$

Therefore, Eq. 12 becomes:

$$F(I) = \int_E [D(\theta)\frac{\partial}{\partial z} (\sum_{i=1}^{n} \sum_{j=1}^{3} N_{ij}\theta_{ij} \frac{\partial N_i}{\partial z} + N_i \frac{\partial K(\theta)}{\partial z}$$
$$+ N_i \frac{\partial}{\partial t} (\sum_{i=1}^{n} \sum_{j=1}^{3} N_{ij}\theta_{ij})]dzdt$$
$$- \int_S N_i D(\theta)\frac{\partial}{\partial z} (\sum_{i=1}^{n} \sum_{j=1}^{3} N_{ij}\theta_{ij})dt = 0 \qquad (14)$$

Equation 14 is the Galerkin representation of the one dimensional flow equation using triangular elements.

FINITE ELEMENT SOLUTION

Triangular elements are adopted in this study. The shape functions, N_i, N_j and N_k, of a typical triangular element, Δ_{ijk}, in Fig. 1 may be defined as

$$N_i = \frac{a_i + b_i z + c_i t}{2\Delta}, \qquad N_j = \frac{a_j + b_j z + c_j t}{2\Delta}, \qquad N_k = \frac{a_k + b_k z + c_k t}{2\Delta} \qquad (15)$$

where Δ = area of Δ_{ijk}

$$a_i = z_j t_k - z_k t_j \qquad a_j = z_k t_i - z_i t_k \qquad a_k = z_i t_j - z_j t_i$$

$$b_i = t_j - t_k \qquad b_j = t_k - t_j \qquad b_k = t_i - t_j$$

$$c_i = z_k - z_j \qquad c_j = z_i - z_k \qquad c_k = z_j - z_i$$

Relationship between the natural coordinate system and the Cartesian coordinate system may be expressed as (Fig. 1):

$$z = N_i z_i + N_j z_j + N_k z_k, \quad t = N_i t_i + N_j t_j + N_k t_k, \quad N_i + N_j + N_k = 1 \qquad (16)$$

The basic computer programming strategy in solving Eq. 14 is to consider a group of three adjacent elements at a time (Fig. 2). As indicated in Fig. 2, moisture contents along the z and t coordinates were established, as initial and boundary conditions, respectively. A nonlinear algebraic equation containing the five nodal points (with θ_{11}, t_1 and θ_{33}, t_1 as unknowns) of the three considered elements can be obtained. Similarly, a set of nonlinear algebraic equations pertaining to the first time step can thus be established by considering the second, third, ..., groups of triangular elements (3). Solutions for the unknowns at each time step are provided by a programmed logic of iterations (16).

In this study, third degrees of polynomial interpretations of the moisture diffusivity, D, and hydraulic conductivity, K, of the media were conducted. Their respective system of nonlinear algebraic equations may be expressed as follows:

For $\qquad D(\theta) = D_0 + D_1\theta + D_2\theta^2 + D_3\theta^3, \quad K(\theta) = K_0 + K_1\theta + K_2\theta^2 + K_3\theta^3 \qquad (17)$

Then $\qquad F(I) = \sum_{i=1}^{3} (T1_i \cdot T2_i + T3_i + T4_i + T5_i + T6_i + T7_i + T8_i) = 0 \qquad (18)$

where $\qquad T1_i = \frac{1}{4\Delta_i} [b_{i1}^2(I)\theta_{i1}(I)b_{i1}(I)b_{i2}(I)\theta_{i2}(I) + b_{i1}(I)b_{i3}(I)\theta_{i3}(I)];$

$$T2_i = [D_0 + \frac{1}{2}D_1 \sum_{j=1}^{3} \theta_{ij}(I)];$$

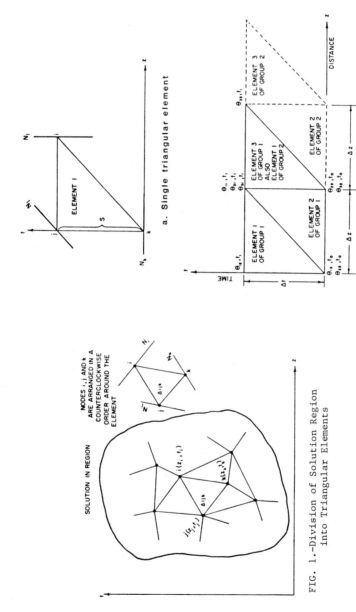

FIG. 1.—Division of Solution Region into Triangular Elements

a. Single triangular element

b. Triangular elements in first time step

FIG. 2.—Natural Coordinate System for Triangular Elements

$$T_{3i} = \frac{1}{6} D_2 \left[\sum_{j=1}^{3} \theta_{ij}^2(I) + \theta_{i1}(I)\theta_{i2}(I) + \theta_{i1}(I)\theta_{i3}(I) \right. $$

$$\left. + \theta_{i2}(I)\theta_{i3}(I) \right];$$

$$T_{4i} = \frac{1}{6} K_1 \left[\sum_{j=1}^{3} b_{ij}(I)\theta_{ij}(I) \right];$$

$$T_{5i} = \frac{1}{6} K_2 \left\{ b_{i1}(I)\theta_{i1}^2(I) + \frac{1}{2} b_{i2}(I)\theta_{i2}^2(I) + \frac{1}{2} b_{i3}(I)\theta_{i3}^2(I) \right.$$

$$+ \left[\frac{1}{2} b_{i1}(I) + b_{i2}(I)\right]\theta_{i1}(I)\theta_{i2}(I) + \left[\frac{1}{2} b_{i1}(I)\right.$$

$$\left. + b_{i3}(I)\right]\theta_{i1}(I)\theta_{i3}(I) + \frac{1}{2}\left[b_{i2}(I) + b_{i3}(I)\right]\theta_{i2}(I)\theta_{i3}(I) \right\};$$

$$T_{6i} = \frac{1}{6} \sum_{j=1}^{3} c_{ij}(I)\theta_{ij}(I);$$

$$T_{7i} = \frac{1}{10} D_3 \left\{ \sum_{j=1}^{3} \theta_{ij}^3(I) + \theta_{i1}(I)\left[\theta_{i2}^2(I) + \theta_{i3}^2(I)\right] + \theta_{i2}(I)\left[\theta_{i1}^2(I) \right.\right.$$

$$\left.\left. + \theta_{i3}^2(I)\right] + \theta_{i3}(I)\left[\theta_{i1}^2(I) + \theta_{i2}^2(I) + \theta_{i1}(I)\theta_{i2}(I)\right]\right\}; \quad \text{and}$$

$$T_{8i} = \frac{1}{20} K_3 \left\{ 2b_{i1}(I)\theta_{i1}^3(I) + \sum_{j=1}^{3} b_{ij}(I)\theta_{ij}^3(I) \right.$$

$$+ \theta_{i1}(I)\theta_{i2}^2(I)\left[2b_{i2}(I) + b_{i1}(I)\right] + \theta_{i1}(I)\theta_{i3}^2(I)\left[2b_{i3}(I)\right.$$

$$\left. + b_{i1}(I)\right] + \theta_{i1}^2(I)\theta_{i2}(I)\left[2b_{i1}(I) + 3b_{i2}(I)\right]$$

$$+ \theta_{i1}^2(I)\theta_{i3}(I)\left[2b_{i1}(I) + 3b_{i3}(I)\right]$$

$$+ \left[b_{i2}(I) + b_{i3}(I)\right]\left[\theta_{i2}(I)\theta_{i3}^2(I) + \theta_{i2}^2(I)\theta_{i3}(I)\right]$$

$$\left. + \theta_{i1}(I)\theta_{i2}(I)\theta_{i3}(I)\left[b_{i1}(I) + 2b_{i2}(I) + 2b_{i3}(I)\right]\right\}.$$

APPLICATION

The observed and interpreted diffusivity, as well as hydraulic conductivity of Molokai soil are presented in Figs. 3 and 4, respectively. Computer solution of vertical moisture profiles for 10, 20, and 40 minutes after water infiltration took place are shown in Fig. 5. In examining the validity of the results presented in Fig. 5, Boltzmann's transformation function was applied (8). That is

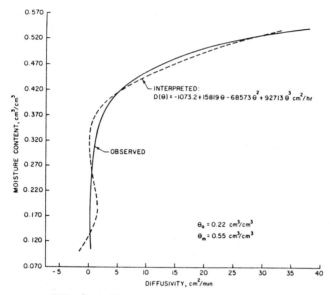

FIG. 3.-Soil Water Diffusivity for Molokai Soils

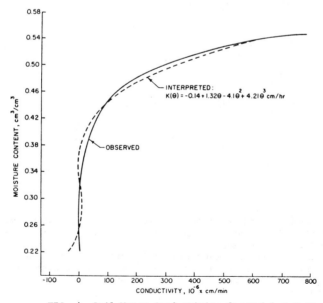

FIG. 4.-Soil Water Conductivity for Molokai Soils

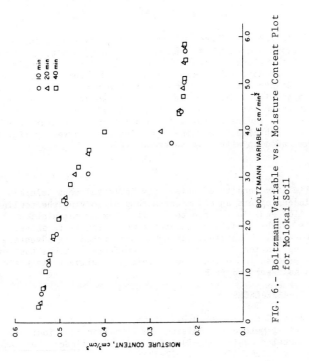

FIG. 6.– Boltzmann Variable vs. Moisture Content Plot for Molokai Soil

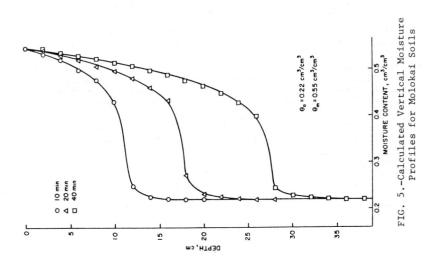

FIG. 5.–Calculated Vertical Moisture Profiles for Molokai Soils

$$\lambda(\theta) = zt^{-1/2} \qquad (19)$$

where $\lambda(\theta)$ is the well-known Boltzmann variable. Let t in the Boltzmann transformation equal a constant, such as $t=t_1$, a curve of λ vs. θ at various depths, z can thus be obtained. Similarly, curves for various t values can also be found. For the problem on hand, data points for $t_1 = 10$ min, $t_2 = 20$ min and $t_3 = 40$ min are calculated and identified in Fig. 6. It is apparent in Fig. 6 that all of the three sets of points follow a similar pattern. The result seems to indicate that a valid solution of moisture profiles may have been obtained. For invalid solutions, curves in Fig. 6 would have ended up with diverse trends (8).

CONCLUSION

Preliminary results of this study indicated that Galerkin process indeed offers an efficient method of solving the nonlinear moisture flow equation. Once the finite element formulation of the problem is established, the computer programming is relatively straightforward. This study further demonstrated the advantage of computer application in achieving the seemingly cumbrous task of iterative process in solving the systems of nonlinear algebraic equations as described in Eq. 18.

APPENDIX I.—REFERENCES

1. Ashcroft, G.C., Marsh, D.D., Evans, D.D., Boersman, L., "Numerical Method for Solving the Diffusion Equation: 1. Horizontal Flow in Semi-Infinite Media," Soil Sci. Soc. Amer. Proc., Vol. 26, 1962, pp. 522-525.
2. Batu, V., "A Finite Element Dual Mesh Method to Calculate Nodal Darcy Velocities in Nonhomogeneous and Anisotropic Aquifers," Water Resources Research, Vol. 20, No. 11, Nov., 1984, pp. 1705-1717.
3. Bruch, J.C., "Nonlinear Equation of Unsteady Ground-Water Flow," Journal of Hydraulic Division, ASCE, Vol. 99, No. HY3, 1973, pp. 395-403.
4. Freeze, R.A., "The Mechanism of Natural Groundwater Recharge and Discharge. 1. One-Dimensional Vertical, Unsteady Unsaturated Flow Above a Recharging or Discharging Groundwater Flow System," Water Resources Research, Vol. 5, No. 1, 1969, pp. 153-171.
5. Gardner, W.R., and Mayhugh, M.S., "Solutions and Tests of the Diffusion Equation for the Movement of Water in Soil," Soil Sci. Amer. Proc., Vol. 22, 1958, pp. 197-201.
6. Gupta, S.K., Cole, C.R., and Pinder, G.F., "Finite-Element Three-Dimensional Groundwater (FE3DGW) Model for a Multiaquifer System," Water Resources Research, Vol. 20, No. 5, May 1984, pp. 553-563.
7. Hanks, R.J., Klute, A., and Bresler, E., "A Numeric Method for Estimating Infiltration, Redistribution, Drainage, and Evaporation of Water from Soil," Water Resources Research, Vol. 5, 1969, pp. 1064-1069.

8. Kirkham, D., and Powers, W.L., " Advanced Soil Physics, New
    York, N.Y., 1972, Wiley-Interscience.
9. Narasimhan, T.N., Neuman, S.P., and Witherspoon, P.A., "Finite
    Element Method for Subsurface Hydrology Using a Mixed
    Explicit-Implicit Scheme," Water Resoures Research, Vol. 14,
    No. 5, October 1978, pp. 863-877.
10. Neuman, S.P., "Finite Element Computer Programs for Flow in
    Saturated-Unsaturated Porous Media," Volcani Institute of
    Agriculture, Israel Institute of Technology, Haifa, Israel,
    1972.
11. Neuman, S.P., and Witherspoon, P.A., "Analysis of Nonsteady
    Flow with a Free Surface Using the Finite Element Method,"
    Water Resources Research, Vol. 7, No. 3, 1971, pp. 611-623.
12. Philip, J.R., "Theory of Infiltration," Advances in Hydro-
    science, Vol. 5, Edited by V.T. Chow, Academic Press, New
    York, N.Y., 1969, pp. 215-296.
13. Pickens, J.F., and Gillham, R.W., "Finite Element Analysis of
    Solute Transport Under Hysteretic Unsaturated Flow Condi-
    tions," Water Resources Research, Vol. 16, No. 6, Dec., 1980,
    pp. 1071-1078.
14. Pinder, G.F., and Frind, E.O., "Application of Galerkin's Pro-
    cedure to Aquifer Analysis," Water Resources Research, Vol. 8,
    No. 1, Feb., 1972, pp. 108-120.
15. Pinder, G.F., and Gray, W.G., Finite Element Simulation in
    Surface and Subsurface Hydrology, Academic Press, New York,
    N.Y., 1977.
16. Powell, M.J.D., "A Fortran Subroutine for Solving Systems of
    Nonlinear Algebraic Equations," Numerical Methods for Non-
    linear Algebraic Equations, Edited by P. Rabinowitz, Gordon
    and Breach Science, New York, N.Y., 1970, pp. 115-161.
17. Zienkiewicz, O.C., The Finite Element in Engineering Science,
    McGraw-Hill, New York, N.Y., 1971.

Risk-Cost Analysis and Spillway Design

Jery Stedinger, A.M., and Jan Grygier[*]

ABSTRACT

The NRC's recent report on dam safety proposes risk cost analysis to help select among alternative spillway modifications for existing dams. This paper examines the sensitivity of conclusions drawn from such procedures to the probability assigned to the probable maximum flood (PMF) and to the flood frequency model employed. Uncertainty as to the return period of the PMF can easily change the relative attractiveness of alternative designs. The distribution chosen to extend the frequency curve to the PMF can also influence the results. Likely errors in estimated damage functions and their shape seem relatively less important.

Introduction

Since many large dams were built, additional meteorological and hydrologic data and corresponding gains in scientific knowledge have resulted in revisions to the probable maximum floods and safety evaluation floods used to determine the adequacy of emergency spillways. As a result, the U.S. Bureau of Reclamation and the Army Corps of Engineers must decide what structural and operating policy modifications are appropriate, if any, when a large dam's emergency spillway does not satisfy current spillway design criteria.

The concerns of these two agencies led them to consult the National Research Council, which recently issued a committee report (7). The NRC committee felt that it was inappropriate to arbitrarily apply current spillway design criteria to an existing structure, if its failure during an extraordinary flood would not significantly increase the likely loss of life. Rather, they suggested that the economic damages due to dam failure should be balanced against the cost of structural and operating policy changes using risk-cost analysis. Similar recommendations have been made by the NRC (6), the Bureau of Reclamation (8) and researchers at MIT (2,10) and Stanford (5).

A question that remains is whether risk-cost analysis can provide reasonable reliable economic rankings of retrofit alternatives, given the uncertainties in flood frequency distributions and damage estimates from floods larger than any yet experienced at a particular site. An initial appraisal of the reliability of risk-cost analyses is provided in the appendices of the NRC committee report (7). This paper provides a more complete investigation of the issue.

[*] Dept of Environmental Engineering, Cornell University, Ithaca, N.Y. 14853.

Description of the Model

To illustrate the effects of the selected flood frequency distribution and damage function on the ranking of design alternatives, we consider a generalization of the example in NRC (7). In this example an existing dam has been found to have a spillway which is capable of passing only a fraction of the PMF. The spillway can safely pass only 40,000 cfs (1100 m³/s), while the current estimate of the PMF is 150,000 cfs (4200 m³/s). The 100-yr flood is 20,000 cfs (550 m³/s).

Four alternative plans will be considered: (1) do nothing, (2) modify the existing spillway to pass 60,000 cfs (1700 m³/s), (3) rebuild the spillway and raise the dam so that the spillway can pass 120,000 cfs (3400 m³/s), or (4) lower the spillway crest and lengthen it so as to pass the full PMF. Table 1 summarizes these options and their amortized annual costs. In all cases, overtopping of the dam would result in its structural failure and release of the impounded water.

Flood Damage Function. - If one is to weigh the costs and benefits of the alternatives, the expected flood damages to property downstream (and possibly upstream) of the dam must be computed. Following the NRC example, consider a case in which no loss of life is anticipated even in the event of dam failure, because of adequate time for warning and evacuation as well as a low population density in the area. Also, property damage is negligible for flows below 10,000 cfs (280 m³/s), the 10-yr flood. Above that value, property damage increases towards an upper bound of M as long as the dam holds, according to the relationship

$$D(q) = M \left[\frac{(q/s)^r}{1 + (q/s)^r} \right] = \frac{M}{1 + (q/s)^{-r}} \qquad (1)$$

for q > 10,000 cfs (r, s > 0). Thus for large flows (q > > s) damages approach M asymptotically; for small flows (10,000 cfs < q < < s) damages vary approximately as $(q/s)^r$. Here r is a shape parameter and s, the "half-damage flood", determines the flow at which damages equal M/2. Note that option 4 would increase downstream flows from small

Table 1. Design options and cost

Option	Design flow in cfs (m³/s)	Amortized construction cost in $/year
1. Do nothing	40,000 (1100)	0
2. Modify spillway	60,000 (1700)	50,000
3. Rebuild spillway and raise dam	120,000 (3400)	120,000
4. Rebuild spillway with lower crest	150,000 (4200)	80,000

floods, which we simulated by reducing the value of s by 5,000 cfs (140 m³/s).

If the dam fails, the flood wave will cause massive destruction resulting in downstream damages of M. One should also consider the loss resulting from interruption of services until the dam or some other facility can be built, if in fact the services are ever again provided. The loss of service and replacement cost is denoted L. The complete damage function is then

$$D(q) = \begin{cases} 0 & q < 10,000 \text{ cfs} \\ M/[1 + (q/s)^{-r}] & 10,000 \text{ cfs} < q < q_c \\ M + L & q_c < q \end{cases} \qquad (2)$$

where q_c is the critical flow above which the dam fails for a given design.

With this particular function one can obtain damage functions with different characteristic shapes by varying the parameters s and r, as shown in Figures 1, 2 and 3.

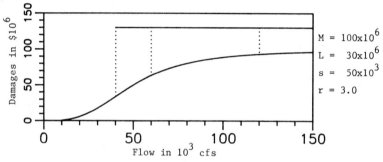

Figure 1: Damage function in $ 10^6 for s = 50,000 cfs, r = 3

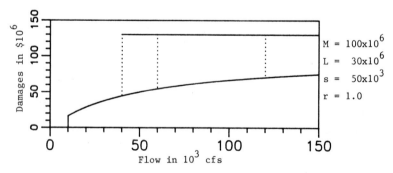

Figure 2: Damage function in $ 10^6 for s = 50,000 cfs, r = 1

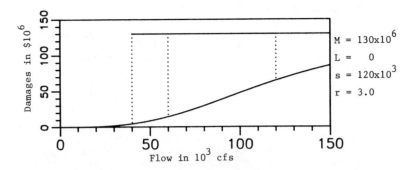

Figure 3: Damage function in $ 10^6 for s = 120,000 cfs, r = 3

Flood Frequency Distributions. - To compute the expected annual flood damages that would occur with each design option one must know the damages associated with the flows of interest and also the likelihood of such flows occurring. In this example the annual flood flows follow a log-normal distribution from the maximum no-damage flood of 10,000 cfs (280 m^3/s) to the hundred year flood of 20,000 cfs (550 m^3/s). To interpolate between the 100-yr flood and the PMF, the PMF is considered to have a return period of T years (T = 10^4 to 10^7). Then, given the magnitude and return period (or exceedence probability) of both the 100-yr flood and the PMF, one can obtain an analytical frequency distribution which interpolates between them. In our example we employed the Gumbel, log-normal, log-Gumbel and Pareto distributions. This can also be viewed as interpolating linearly between the 100-yr flood and the PMF using the appropriate probability paper (Gumbel, log-normal, log-Gumbel, or log flow versus log exceedence probability).

Expected Annual Cost. - The total annual cost considered here is the sum of the annualized construction cost and the expected annual damages. We consider only damages from floods smaller than the current probable maximum flood. Any flows larger than the PMF would overwhelm all of the proposed dam/spillway designs. Thus the resulting damages would not depend on the design selected and they can be neglected in this design comparison.

The expected annual damage costs were computed by numerical integration of f(q)·D(q), the product of the probability density function of annual floods f(q) and the damage function D(q) in equation (2). Since the damage function is discontinuous at the critical flow q_c and the probability density function is discontinuous at the 100-yr flood, we broke the interval of integration at those points. We used Romberg extrapolation though one could also use other high order methods such as Simpson's rule. However, Gould (4) has found that the first-order mid-point method often used to compute expected damages can yield very inaccurate estimates with the interval sizes often employed.

Results of Sensitivity Analysis

A risk cost analysis of flood-control works depends on estimates of the damages caused by a range of floods and the probabilities that they occur. Both types of information may be quite uncertain. We looked at a number of models for the damage function and flood frequency distribution, and investigated the sensitivity of the relative costs of alternative options to the damage function and frequency distribution parameters employed.

The results are presented in the form of "regret matrices" as in Table 2. Let C_{ij} be the cost of design option i in row i for the assumed value of T in column j. The bottom row of each matrix lists for each column j, the minimum expected annual cost C_j^* over the four options, in thousands of dollars per year. The other elements in column j are the "regrets," equal to $C_{ij} - C_j^*$, associated with choosing design i when T has the value associated with column j. The original C_{ij} can be reconstructed by adding C_j^* to the other entries in the j'th column. Regrets are a good measure for the ranking of options because they indicate how much more expensive (in expectation) each option is relative to the least expensive option, for a particular choice of model parameters. The least expensive option for each parameter choice has zero regret.

Variations in Flood Likelihood. - The return period of the PMF is extremely difficult to determine. The NRC's Committee on Safety Criteria of Dams suggests using return periods of 10^4 and 10^6 years (7). Buehler (3) recommends using the 10^6 value and the ANSI standard (1) suggests that the return period may be greater than 10^7 years. We examined the ranking of the different design options with PMF return periods ranging from 10^4 to 10^7 years. Table 2 indicates that the return period assigned to the PMF can have a considerable influence on the relative costs of our design options. In particular, if the PMF is assigned a return period of 10^7 the "do nothing" option (option 1) yields the lowest expected annual cost; if the return period is 10^4 years then that option has the highest expected annual cost. The regrets associated with the more expensive modifications also change significantly over this range. This example corresponds to the damage function shown in Figure 1, using a log-normal distribution to extrapolate between the 100-yr flood and the PMF of 150,000 cfs (4200 m^3/s).

For our model, the return period assigned to the PMF was even more critical when damages increased rapidly at the higher flows. This is illustrated in Table 3, which corresponds to the damage function shown in Figure 3.

Surprisingly, the type of distribution used to interpolate between the 100-yr flood and the PMF can have a comparable effect. We considered four possible distributions, listed here in order of decreasing tail thickness: Pareto, Log-Gumbel, log-normal and Gumbel. All four have been used as flood frequency distributions. The log-normal distribution is a common special case of the log-Pearson type III distribution recommended by the U.S. Water Resources Council (9). Use of the Pareto distribution is equivalent to a straight line interpolation of log flow versus log exceedence probability. The tail of the

Table 2. Dependence of relative costs on return period of PMF
with damage function of Figure 1

T =	10^7	10^6	10^5	10^4
40K	0	15	50	95
60K	10	0	0	0
120K	75	60	50	20
150K	85	75	65	35
Min. Cost	230	260	300	390

PDF=Log-Nor   PMF=150×10^3 M=100×10^6 L=30×10^6 s=60×10^3 r=3

Table 3. Relative costs versus PMF return period with damage
function of Figure 3

T =	10^7	10^6	10^5	10^4
40K	0	30	75	185
60K	0	0	0	50
120K	65	55	35	35
150K	30	20	1	0
Min. Cost	90	100	135	160

PDF=Log-Nor   PMF=150×10^3 M=130×10^6 L=0×10^6 s=120×10^3 r=3

Pareto distribution is similar to that of log-Gumbel. The Gumbel distribution has a thinner tail than the others; its popularity in the U.S. has declined but it is still widely used as a flood frequency distribution in Europe.

The shapes of flood frequency distributions for return periods less than 100 years are generally thought to be between those of the Pareto and Gumbel distributions. These distributions were therefore taken as the limits of reasonable distributions for extending our flood frequency curves up to the PMF in Table 4.

Table 4. Relative costs with various flood frequency distributions

PDF =	Pareto	Log-Gumbel	Log-Normal	Gumbel
40K	0	0	15	130
60K	15	15	0	0
120K	80	80	60	30
150K	90	90	75	55
Min. Cost	220	220	260	360

T=10^6 PMF=150×10^3 M=100×10^6 L=30×10^6 s=60×10^3 r=3

Table 4 shows that the cost rankings of the alternatives are fairly similar for the Pareto, log-Gumbel and log-normal distributions. However, they are very different for the Gumbel distribution. Thin-tailed distributions such as Gumbel tend to favor more conservative options (i.e., modifying the spillway to pass a larger fraction of the PMF), while the other thicker-tailed distributions favor less conservative options.

Variation in PMF Magnitude. - The magnitude of the PMF is much easier to estimate than the corresponding return period. The procedure for computing probable maximum precipitation (PMP) is well established (7); the PMF is then obtained by routing PMP storms through the watershed assuming reasonable antecedent conditions. However, PMP estimates in the Eastern U.S. have generally increased by 10-30% since 1947, while some estimates in the Tennessee Valley have dropped (7). Given this history of change in estimates of the probable maximum precipitation and other issues associated with the choice of initial conditions and routing parameters, we decided to examine the effects of changing the modelled PMF by up to a third.

In our example, such a variation in the PMF's magnitude seems less critical than reasonable variations in its return period or in the frequency distribution used to interpolate between the 100-yr flood and the PMF. As shown in Table 5, these modest changes in the PMF had a relatively small effect on regret values, although they did affect the ranking of options 1 and 2.

Variations in Estimated Damages. - The damage function cost parameters M and L and shape parameters s and r can define different economic settings for dam retrofit decisions. In this final section, these four parameters were varied to see how the least-cost decision would change from one economic setting to another. Our analysis also shows the sensitivity of the least-cost decision to errors in the estimation of these parameters.

As Table 6 indicates, variations in the maximum damage cost M affect the relative annual cost of options much less than they affect the cost of the least expensive option. However, with our model a factor of three difference in the value of M can change the regrets considerably, and switch the relative ranking of several options (1 and 2, and 3 and 4). Similar variations in the loss of service and replacement cost L have similar effects, as shown in Table 7. However, the minimum annual cost is much less sensitive to variations in L because damages from small floods depend upon M but not L.

Reasonable variations in the half-damage flood s or shape parameter r make little difference to regret values. As Table 8 shows, the value of s affects significantly only the relative cost of option 4. This is because option 4 lowers the lip of the spillway which increases damages from small floods. We simulated this by reducing the value of s for option 4 by 5000 cfs (140 m^3/s) in each case. If the damages from small floods are significant (small s) option 4 has substantially higher annual damages than the other options.

Table 5. Relative costs versus magnitude of the PMF

PMF =	100×10^3	125×10^3	150×10^3	175×10^3	200×10^3
40K	0	0	15	25	35
60K	15	0	0	0	0
120K	85	65	60	60	55
150K	95	75	75	70	70
Min. Cost	215	245	260	270	285

$T=10^6$ PDF=Log-Nor $M=100 \times 10^6$ $L=30 \times 10^6$ $s=60 \times 10^3$ $r=3$

Table 6. Relative costs versus maximum flood damages M

M =	10×10^6	30×10^6	100×10^6	300×10^6
40K	0	0	15	100
60K	25	15	0	0
120K	90	80	60	50
150K	55	60	75	170
Min. Cost	50	100	260	670

$T=10^6$ PDF=Log-Nor $PMF=150 \times 10^3$ $L=30 \times 10^6$ $s=60 \times 10^3$ $r=3$

Table 7. Relative costs versus loss of service and replacement cost L

L =	10×10^6	30×10^6	100×10^6	300×10^6
40K	1	15	60˙	190
60K	0	0	0	0
120K	65	60	50	25
150K	75	75	65	40
Min. Cost	255	260	270	295

$T=10^6$ PDF=Log-Nor $PMF=150 \times 10^3$ $M=100 \times 10^6$ $s=60 \times 10^3$ $r=3$

Table 8. Relative costs versus half-damage flood s

s=	40×10^3	50×10^3	60×10^3	80×10^3	100×10^3
40K	0	5	15	25	30
60K	5	0	0	0	0
120K	70	65	60	60	55
150K	250	125	75	35	25
Min. Cost	625	380	260	155	110

$T=10^6$ PDF=Log-Nor $PMF=150 \times 10^3$ $M=100 \times 10^6$ $L=30 \times 10^6$ $r=3$

The shape parameter r controls how smoothly damages increase close to the half-damage flood s. With $r \leq 1$ the slope of the damage function is greatest for small floods, as in Figure 2. With $r > 1$ the maximum slope occurs at the half-damage flood, and as r increases that slope increases (see Figure 1). In our model the shape parameter r has little effect on relative costs but a large effect on the minimum annual costs, as shown in Table 9.

Table 9. Relative costs versus shape parameter r

r =	0.5	1.0	2.0	3.0	4.0
40K	5	5	10	15	15
60K	0	0	0	0	0
120K	60	60	60	60	60
150K	115	155	120	75	50
Min. Cost	3300	1970	650	260	145

$T=10^6$ PDF=Log-Nor $PMF=150 \times 10^3$ $M=100 \times 10^6$ $L=30 \times 10^6$ $s=60 \times 10^3$

A smaller r implies significant damages from small (and relatively likely) floods, increasing the expected annual damages significantly and worsening the relative position of option 4. However, even over a wide range of r values, the regrets of the other options were almost constant. This is because r affects primarily the annual damages associated with floods smaller than the current spillway capacity.

Conclusions

Risk-cost analysis can provide a systematic basis for ranking alternative retrofit decisions for large dams. However, the sensitivity analyses presented here indicate that our inability to specify the return period of the PMF and perhaps the flood distribution between the 100-yr flood and the PMF impairs our ability to estimate the risk-cost associated with alternative designs. As a result, risk-cost analyses can fail to provide the definitive and objective guidance one would like. However, careful study of the frequency and severity of large storms in different regions of the country may provide more reliable estimates of these parameters than are currently available.

Appendix 1. - References

1. American Nuclear Society, "American National Standard for Determining Design Basis Flooding at Power Reactor Sites," Report ANSI/ANS-2.8-1981, American Nuclear Society, La Grange Park, Ill., 1981.
2. Bohnenblust, H., and Vanmarcke, E.H., "Decision Analysis for Prioritizing Dams for Remedial Measures: A Case Study," Research Report R82-12, Department of Civil Engineering, Massachusetts Institute of Technology, Cambridge, Mass., June, 1982.
3. Buehler, B., discussion of "Realistic Assessment of Maximum Flood Potentials" by D. W. Newton, Journal of Hydraulic Engineering, Vol. 110, No. 8, Aug., 1984, pp. 1166-1168.

4. Gould, B.W., discussion of "Bias in Computed Flood Risk" by C.H. Hardison and M.E. Jennings, Journal of Hydraulics Division, ASCE, Vol. 99, No. HY1, Jan., 1973, pp. 270-273.
5. McCann, M.W., Jr., Franzini, J.B., Kavazanjian, E., Jr., and Shah, H.C., "Preliminary Safety Evaluation of Existing Dams," Draft Report prepared for Federal Emergency Management Agency, Contract EMW-C-0458, Department of Civil Engineering, Stanford University, Stanford, Calif., Nov., 1984.
6. U.S. National Research Council, Committee on the Safety of Existing Dams, Safety of Existing Dams - Evaluation and Improvement, National Academy Press, Washington, D.C., 1983.
7. U.S. National Research Council, Committee on Safety Criteria of Dams, Safety of Dams - Flood and Earthquake Criteria, National Academy Press, Washington, D.C., 1985.
8. U.S. Department of the Interior, Bureau of Reclamation, "Criteria for Selecting and Accommodating Inflow Design Floods for Storage Dams, And Guidelines for Applying Criteria to Existing Storage Dams," Technical Memorandum No. 1, Bureau of Reclamation, Denver, Colo., Nov., 1981.
9. U.S. Water Resources Council, "Guidelines for Determining Flood Flow Frequency", Bulletin 17B, Revised edition, U.S. Water Resources Council, Washington, D.C., Sept., 1981.
10. Vanmarcke, E.H., and Bohnenblust, H., "Risk-Based Decision Analysis for Dam Safety," Research Report R82-11, Department of Civil Engineering, Massachusetts Institute of Technology, Cambridge, Mass., June, 1982.

RELIABILITY AND RISK ASSESSMENT FOR WATER SUPPLY SYSTEMS

Uri Shamir[1], M.ASCE and Charles D.D. Howard[2], M.ASCE

ABSTRACT.-Analytical methods for computing the reliability of water supply systems are described and demonstrated. A case study serves to show how risk, which is the economic loss due to shortfalls, can be assessed and incorporated into the decision making on capacity expansion to aimed at improving supply reliability.

Introduction

A water supply system is designed and operated to take water from sources, treat, store, convey, and distribute it to customers who are spread over an area, and whose demands change over time. The supply system may fail to supply all of the water which is expected by the customers; that expected amount is called the demand. The actual consumption is the intersection of the demands and the system's supply capability. Shortfalls are the difference between demand and consumption.

Reliability of the supply system is a measure defined upon the frequency, duration and magnitude of the shortfalls. The measures which are used to define a system's reliability must consider the consequences of the shortfalls, which, in turn, depend on the uses of the water.

In this paper we shall examine how reliability of water supply systems is defined, how it may be computed, and how reliability can be used as one of the performance criteria in making decisions about expanding the capacity of the system to meet future demands. This entails assessment of the economic risks (losses) associated with shortfalls in water supply in the future, which are not easy to evaluate.

1 Professor, Faculty of Civil Engineering, Technion - Israel Institute of Technology, and Visiting Professor, Department of Civil Engineering, M.I.T, Cambridge, MA 02139.
2 President, Charles Howard & Associates, Ltd., 300-1144 Fort Street, Victoria, B.C., Canada V8V 3K8.

Measures of Reliability

An individual domestic consumer may be only slightly
annoyed by brief interruptions in water supply, provided
that they are not too frequent. A single longer
interruption may, on the other hand, be considered quite
unacceptable, even though the economic consequenses of such
an event may not be significant. An industry which uses
water in its production process may suffer considerable
economic loss by any interruption of supply longer than
some critical duration. Its losses may well be
quantifiable. A farmer who uses the water for irrigation
will place a very different value on water availability at
different stages of the growing season; if water is not
available at some critical time for the crop, then no
amount of water at some other time will compensate, since
the crop is lost.

For a system which supplies a number of consumers, the
reliability measure(s) must somehow integrate over all of
them, simply because we cannot cope with too many measures
of reliability as parameters in the planning, design and
operation decisions. It is therefore necessary to integrate
over all consumers and over all times, to obtain a
manageable number of reliability measures.

In summary, for each particular water system one must
examine the forecasted consequences of supply shortfalls,
and define appropriate measures of reliability.

Any reliability measure is a random variable. The
actual value that the measure will take on at some future
time cannot be predicted with certainty, because it is a
function of the random factors mentioned above. In certain
cases it is possible to compute the entire probability
distribution of the reliability, as was done by Shamir and
Howard (10) and demonstrated in later sections. In other
cases it is possible to compute by analytical means only
some moments of the the reliability's probability
distribution, usually the mean and possibly also the
variance. In more complex cases the only possible way to
compute the reliability is by stochastic simulation.

Causes for Less-Than-Perfect Reliability

Several random factors may affect the supply system's
reliability. These include:
- Deviations of the actual demands from those which were
  used in designing the system and its operation.
- Fluctuations of the amount of water in the sources.
- Fluctuations in the quality of water in the sources.
- Failure of major facilities: treatment plants,
  conveyance pipelines, pumping stations.
- Failure of components in the distribution system: pipes,

booster pumps, valves.
- Failure of the operators to store enough water in the
reservoirs to meet peak demands.

The important factor for decision making is not whether
supply falls short of the amounts which had been "promised"
in advance, those which we earlier called the demands, but
rather what are the negative consequences of these
shortfalls. It is well known that consumers adapt to
situations of shortage by modifying their demands. This is
done by curtailing unessential uses for the duration of the
failure event. Experience has shown that urban consumers
can indeed reduce their consumption quite considerably, for
time periods extending up to several months, while a
drought occurs. Appeal to the public is effective at such
times, and there seems to be no appreciable economic loss
due to the curtailment. This does not necessarily hold true
for other types of consumers in the urban area, primarily
industry.

Risk is a measure of the consequences - especially
economic, but possibly others as well - of supply
shortfalls. The appropriate measures of reliability to be
used in any particular situation should depend on the risk
associated with the shortfalls.

Analytical Computation of Reliability Probability Functions

Consider the system shown in Figure 1. Water is to be
supplied to an urban area from two sources: a reservoir of
capacity V with a random inflow I, and an aquifer which may
be considered of infinite capacity. The reservoir contains
S0 at the beginning of the year. We investigate the
system's reliability in supplying the annual demands.

The cost of supplying from the reservoir is lower and
therefore the first preference is to supply from it. Water
from both sources has to be treated and conveyed over some
distance, in two separate systems, to the consumption area.
These two links have each a known annual carrying capacity
- Q1 and Q2 - and a given probability of failure during any
year: p1 for the link from the reservoir and p2 for the
ink from the aquifer. The demand itself is a random
variable, which can be explained by its dependence on the
weather.

The probability distributions of the inflow to the
reservoir, I, and the demand, D, are shown in Figure 2.

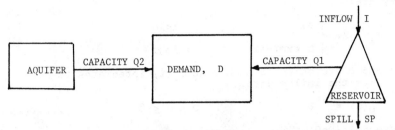

Figure 1. A Water Supply System

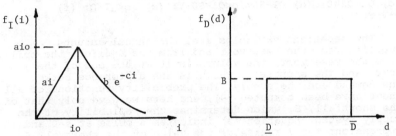

Figure 2. Probability Distributions for Inflow (I) and Demand (D)

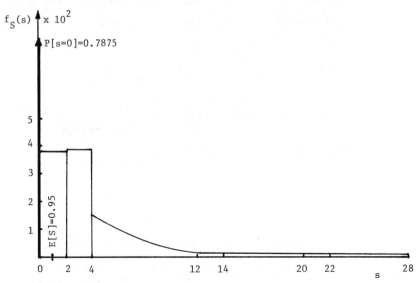

Figure 3. Probability Distribution of Shrotfalls - Eq. (4)

They are:

$$f_I(i) = \begin{cases} ai & i \leq io \\ b\exp(-ci) & io \leq i \end{cases} \qquad \ldots(1)$$

a,b and c are selected such that $f_I(i)$ integrates to 1.0, and fits the inflow data.

$$f_D(d) = B \qquad \underline{D} \leq d \leq \overline{D} \qquad \ldots(2)$$

where $B=1/(\overline{D}-\underline{D})$.

The following assumptions are made: (a) $Q2<V<Q1$; (b) $\underline{D}<S0$; (c) $Q1+Q2<\overline{D}$; (d) $Q1-S0<io<Q1-S0+V$; (e) $io<Q1-\underline{D}$; (f) $\underline{D}+V-S0<io$.

The dependent variables are: the annual amounts supplied from the reservoir and from the aquifer, the spill from the reservoir, the volume in it at the end of the year, and the shortfall, which is the difference between the demand and the supply. The probability functions of all these have been computed (9), and here we give only that of the shortfall, S, which determines the reliability of the supply system. Equation (3) indicates a pulse at s=0 and expressions for 7 ranges of the value of the shortfall S.

$$f_S(s) = \begin{cases} (1-p1)B[Q1-\underline{D}-a(Q1-S0)^3/6+(1-p2)B(Q2-p1\underline{D}) & \text{for} \quad s=0 \\ (1-p1p2)B & \text{for} \quad 0<s\leq\underline{D} \\ B & \text{for} \quad \underline{D}<s\leq\overline{D}-Q1-Q2 \\ B[(p1+p2-p1p2)+(1-p1)(1-p2)a(\overline{D}-Q2-S0-s)^2]/2 & \text{for } \overline{D}-Q1-Q2<s\leq\overline{D}-Q1 \\ B[p1+(1-p1)(1-p2)a(\overline{D}-Q2-S0-s)^2/2+ \\ \quad +(1-p1)p2a(\overline{D}-S0-s)^2/2] & \text{for} \quad \overline{D}-Q1<s\leq\overline{D}-S0-Q2 \\ B[p1+(1-p1)p2a(\overline{D}-S0-s)^2/2] & \text{for} \quad \overline{D}-S0-Q2<s\leq\overline{D}-Q2 \\ B[p1p2+(1-p1)p2a(\overline{D}-S0-s)^2/2] & \text{for} \quad \overline{D}-Q2<s\leq\overline{D}-S0 \\ p1p2B & \text{for} \quad \overline{D}-S0<s\leq\overline{D} \end{cases} \qquad \ldots(3)$$

Equation (4) and Figure 3 give the specific form of this probability distribution for the following data (all physical variables are in a common unit of volume or volume/year): $\underline{D}=2$; $\overline{D}=28$; $Q1=16$; $Q2=8$; $V=12$; $S0=6$; $io=12$; $p1=p2=0.02$.

$$f_S(s) = \begin{cases} 0.7875 & \text{for} \quad s=0 \\ 0.0384 & \text{for} \quad 0<s\leq2 \\ 0.0385 & \text{for} \quad 2<s\leq4 \\ 0.0001s^2-0.0033s+0.0255 & \text{for} \quad 4<s\leq12 \\ 0.0001s^2-0.0034s+0.0282 & \text{for} \quad 12<s\leq14 \\ 0.000002s^2-0.00001s+0.0013 & \text{for} \quad 14<s\leq20 \\ 0.000002s^2-0.00001s+0.0012 & \text{for} \quad 20<s\leq22 \\ 0.00001 & \text{for} \quad 22<s\leq28 \end{cases} \quad \dots(4)$$

A general equation has be developed for the expected value of the shortfall, which will not be given here for lack of space. For the data above it yields $E[S]=0.95$. Similarly, expressions for other moments or quantiles of the probability distribution can be developed, or, much more easily, can be computed for the specific form of the distribution after the values of the parameters have been inserted, as in Equation (4).

The analytical integration which leads to results such as (3) above can become quite complicated, and error prone. Still, if it can be carried out then the results are extremely useful, because they allow insight into the role of the various variables. The analytical expression can also be used for sensitivity analysis, as well as in an economic optimization of the system.

When the system is more complicated, and it is no longer possible to compute the probability distributions, it may still be possible to obtain analytical expressions for reliability measures, after making certain assumptions. Consider the system shown in Figure 4. Water is supplied from two sources, through separate systems. The facilities in the system are each subject to random failures, and the repair duration is also a random variable. If it is assumed that times between failures as well as repair durations of facilities are exponentially distributed independent random variables, then it is possible to compute reliability measures for the supply at the demand area.

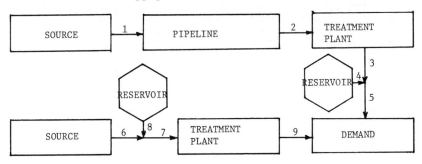

Figure 4. A Water Supply System with Two Sources

For times to failures, t_w:

$$\Pr[t_w \geq t] = \exp\{-t/T\} \qquad \dots\dots (5)$$

with

$$T = E[t_w] = MTBF \qquad \dots\dots (6)$$

and for the repair durations, t_f:

$$\Pr[t_f \geq t] = \exp\{-t/M\} \qquad \dots\dots (7)$$

with:

$$M = E[t_f] = MTTR \qquad \dots\dots (8)$$

The availability (7,8) of the component is defined as the average portion of time during which it is operational:

$$A = T/(T+M) \qquad \dots\dots (9)$$

For components in series, the availability is:

$$A_S = \prod A_i = T_S/(T_S+M_S) \qquad \dots\dots (10)$$

where:

$$T_S = [\, \sum (1/T_i)\,]^{-1} \qquad \dots\dots (11)$$

and

$$M_S = T_S[\, \prod (1+M_i/T_i)-1] \qquad \dots\dots (12)$$

For components in parallel:

$$A_p = 1 - \prod (1-A_i) = T_p/(T_p+M_p) \qquad \dots\dots (13)$$

where:

$$M_p = [\, \sum (1/M_i)\,]^{-1} \qquad \dots\dots (14)$$

and

$$T_p = M_p[\, \prod (1+T_i/M_i)-1] \qquad \dots\dots (15)$$

For a system which contains a storage reservoir the failure of components between that point and the source causes a shortfall only if the reservoir does not contain enough water to supply the demand while these components are being repaired. Denote by t_R the time to deplete the reservoir in supplying the demand, t_R = (volume in storage)/(demand rate), and by the subscript u that part of the system leading into the point where the reservoir is located, then the probability that the reservoir will be emptied before the failed components are repaired is:

$$(1-A_u)\exp\{-t_R/M_u\} \qquad \dots\dots (16)$$

and the resultant availability of the system with the reservoir is:

$$A_R = 1-(1-A_u)\exp\{-t_R/M_u\} \qquad \dots\dots (17)$$

The expected value of the time to failure is:

$$E[t_R] = T_R = (T_u+M_u)\exp\{t_R/M_u\}-M_u \qquad \dots\dots (18)$$

For $T_u >> M_u$, which normally holds in practice:

$$E[t_R] = T_u \exp\{t_R/M_u\} \qquad \qquad \ldots (19)$$

The MTBF increases exponentially with the size of the volume which is in storage when the failure occurs.

Fault Tree Analysis

The fault tree method (7,8,11) uses the topology of the network and the probabilities of failures and repair durations of the individual components, and computes the availability at demand nodes. Availability is defined as the existence of a continuous link connecting the demand node to a source. This does not consider, therefore, the capacity of the remaining network (after a failure) to deliver water with adequate quantity and pressure.

To determine the availability, the minimal cut-sets of the network are identified. A cut-set = if all components in a cut-set fail then no water can reach the demand done. It is termed "minimal" if the number of failed components is minimal. In Figure 4 , such minimal cut-sets are (5,9) and (1,4,8). For the supply from Source 1 alone, the following are minimal cut-sets: (5), (1,4). The second of these includes the case of Reservoir 1 emptying before Source 1 comes back on line. The availability of the system is closely approximated by:

$$A = 1 - \sum (1-A_i) + \sum (1-A_i)(1-A_j) \qquad \ldots (20)$$

where the second term contains all pairs of i and j, and higher order terms have been neglected.The capacities of different supply paths can be used, together with their availabilities, to compute the shortfalls in meeting the demands.

The fault tree method is workable only as long as the system is not too complex, because identifying all the cut-sets becomes complicated and carrying out the computations is expensive.

A Case Study

Figure 5 shows demand projections to the year 2030 for Seattle, Washington(3). The mean was computed by projecting the population and per capita consumption. The distribution over the range, between E_1 and E_2, was developed on the basis of the variability observed in the historical demands - 48 years, from 1929 to 1976. It was assumed that the demand probabilities over this range are of the same shape as in the historical record, just scaled up to the projected demand level.

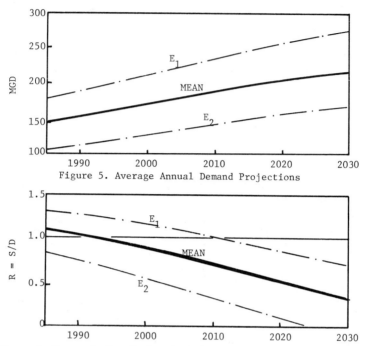

Figure 5. Average Annual Demand Projections

Figure 6. Seasonal (Oct-Dec) Reliability with no Source Developmet

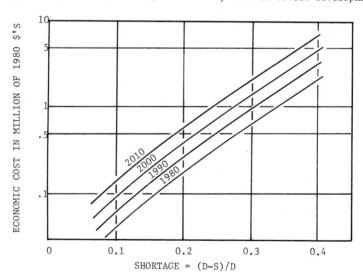

Figure 7. Economic Cost of Shortages, Wet Months (Oct-Dec)

The histogram of the available annual supply in the 48 year record was used as the probability distribution for future supplies, if no additional sources or facilities are developed.reliability is defined as the ratio of supply, S, to demand, D, i.e., R = S/D. For every future year it is possible to compute the histogram of reliability, R, from: $Pr[r_1 \leq R \leq r_2] = Pr[r_1 \leq S/D \leq r_2]$ simply by counting the (relative) number of times that (S/D) falls in the considered range.

Costs due to water shortages were found to be greatest in the wet winter months (October to December), because in the summer, when demands are higher, consumers have more flexibility to reduce their consumption. Shortfalls will therefore occur in October and November, after the reservoirs have been depleted and many of the discretionary uses of water have been terminated. Thus the reliability and risk analysis was carried out for the winter months.

The projected mean reliability for the winter months, and its range, are shown in Figure 6 for the case where no additional sources or other facilities are developed.

An economic analysis of the region used historicasl marginal cost data for water supply and the concepts of consumer surplus to develop estimates for the costs of shortages at various levels of demand. Figure 7 shows this cost function, which is now used to assess future economic costs (losses) due to shortfalls.

Several proposed alternatives of capacity expansion were examined. For each, future reliability distribution was developed, and converted into economic costs. These were added to the capital costs of the plan, all expressed in present values, so that the different alternatives can be compared. Figures 8 and 9 show the reliability and costs of shortfalls for one of these alternatives.

Appendix I.- References

1. Allan, R.N., Billinton, R. and Lee, S.H., "Bibliography On the Application of Probability Mehtods in Power System Reliability Evaluation", IEEE Tansactions on Power Apparatus and Systems,PAS-103(2), February 1984, pp. 275-282.
2. Billinton, R., Wee, C.L. and Hamoud, G., "Digital Computer Algorithms for the Calculation of Generating Capacity Reliability Indices", IEEE Transactions on Power Apparartus and Systems, PAS-101(1), January 1982, pp. 203-211.
3. Charles Howard & Associates, "Water Supply Reliability and Risk", Study for the City of Seattle, May 1984.
4. Damelin, E., Shamir, U. and Arad, N., "Engineering and Economic Evaluation of the Reliability of Water Supply" Water Resources Research, 8(4), 1972, pp.861-881.

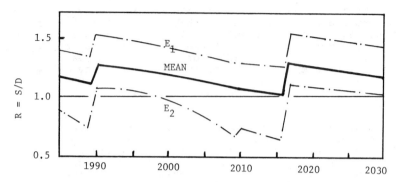

Figure 8. Seasonal Reliability (Oct-Dec), Alternative I

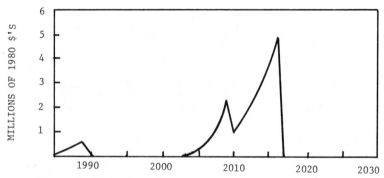

Figure 9. Risk of Seasonal Shortage (Oct-Dec), Alternative I

5. Haimes, Y.Y. (ed.), "Risk/Benefit Analysis in Water Resources Planning and Management", Plenum, 1981.
6. Hashimoto,T., Stedinger, J. and Loucks, D.P., "Reliability, Resiliency and Vulnerability Criteria for Water Resources Systems Performance Evaluation", Water Resources Research, 18(1), 1982, pp. 14-20.
7. Henley, E.J. and Kumamoto, H., "Reliability Engineering and Risk Assessment", Prentice-Hall, 1981.
8. Lie, C.H., Hwang, C.L. and Tillman, F.A., "Availability of Maintained Systems: A State-of-the-Art Survey", AIIE Transactions, 9(3), September 1977, pp. 247-257.
9. Lvovsky, M., "Statistical-Analytical Models for Analysis of Water Resources Systems", M.Sc. Thesis, Faculty of Civil Engineering, Technion, February 1984.
10. Shamir, U. and Howard, C.D.D.,"Water Supply Reliability Theory", Journal of the AWWA, July 1981, pp. 379-384.
11. Tangena, B.H. and Koster,P.K., "Reliability of Drinking Water Supply Systems", in: Proceedings of the IWSA Specialty Conference on Security in Water Supply, Brussels 1983.

Reliability Analysis of Urban Water Supply

Benjamin F. Hobbs[1], Aff. ASCE

Abstract: The high economic and environmental costs of large water supply projects are forcing engineers to consider not only alternative means of increasing system reliability, such as interconnections, water reuse, and demand management, but also the option of accepting a lower standard of reliability. There is a need for improved computer-based methods for estimating and optimizing the reliability of bulk water supply and transmission for public water systems while considering all significant sources of supply unreliability. The purpose of this paper is to survey the application of reliability models to bulk water supply systems and to highlight some promising new approaches.

Introduction

Traditionally, planners of municipal water supply systems have viewed their responsibility as consisting of efficiently meeting water demands when and where they occur with the highest level of reliability achievable [29]. The standard response to demand growth was to expand supply, often in the form of large storage and interbasin diversion projects. But social and economic changes over the last two decades have made traditional solutions so expensive and politically controversial that they often become infeasible. As a result, many municipal water supply systems cannot meet all demands during severe droughts.

Water supply planners now recognize that large expansions of supply are difficult and that they must therefore better manage what resources they have. New strategies are being adopted, many of them less costly and environmentally damaging than large projects and, surprisingly, some of them more effective than traditional approaches. The most celebrated example is the recent discovery that interconnection and coordination of the supply systems of the Washington D.C. metropolitan area could increase the yield of existing supplies by 50% [28]. In general, such interconnections can increase the reliability of all systems involved by taking advantage of supply and demand diversity and opportunities for coordination [8].

Other possibilities for increasing the reliability of urban water supply include conjunctive surface-groundwater management and installation of spare pump and transmission capacity. Conservation is yet another option. "Conservation" is defined here as water management practices that reduce water use or losses and yield a net increase in social welfare [2]. Like the electric power industry in the 1970's, urban water supply systems today are just awakening to the possibility of demand management for preventing shortages and avoiding costly system expansion. The ideas of peak load pricing and utility sponsorship of conservation programs are starting to prove just as effective

[1] Assistant Professor, Department of Systems Engineering, Case Western Reserve University, Cleveland, OH 44106.

in water systems as in power systems.

But inexpensive supply and conservation options for increasing system reliability are not available to all municipal water systems. For some, it may be that more frequent shortages, sometimes accompanied by stringent demand reduction measures, will be more acceptable than the high political and financial costs of new supplies. In the past, planners have rarely given explicit consideration to tradeoffs between reliability and cost. But now, these tradeoffs are more important, and planners will be forced to weigh them in the future [6,29].

To accurately assess these tradeoffs, recognition must be made not only of the randomness of stream flows, the focus of most reliability studies in the past, but also of other important sources of unreliability. These include 1) failures of pipelines, pumps, and other equipment; 2) water supply contamination; and 3) demand uncertainty. Pipeline breaks made news recently by interrupting the water supplies of hundreds of thousands of people in New Jersey and Illinois. New York City's recognition of its vulnerability should one of its aqueducts fail is motivating the construction of a third extremely expensive aqueduct under the Hudson. Well failure because of sand pumpage and other problems is a constant worry for many smaller western communities. Giardia contamination episodes are increasing in frequency. Groundwater contamination is a threat to water supply systems throughout the nation. Finally, excessive demands brought on by unusual weather or faster than anticipated growth also stress many systems. To overemphasize provision of storage to counteract unreliable stream flows and to underemphasize management of other sources of unreliability can result in a waste of resources -- i.e., higher costs and worse reliability than is necessary.

The wider range of alternatives for increasing water supply system reliability, the increasing importance of failures caused by contamination and equipment problems, and the greater need to consider tradeoffs between reliability and cost imply a need for better methods of estimating reliability. Presently, no methods have been developed for estimating the overall reliability of a urban water supply system, while considering supply sources, bulk water transmission, pumping, storage, and demand. Satisfactory means for modeling the reliability of each of the individual elements have not been developed. Better methods would provide 1) more accurate estimates of system reliability and 2) improved means of quantifying the benefits and costs of supply and demand management alternatives, while simultaneously being 3) understandable and inexpensive to use. The purpose of this paper is survey the range of approaches available for evaluating the reliability of bulk water supply, with an emphasis on potentially applicable methods used by electric utilities to assess bulk power reliability. Methods for evaluating distribution system reliability are disregarded here; the reader can refer to reviews of that topic by Mays [25] and Tung [34].

Reliability: Indices and Approaches

Reliability studies have three elements: 1) an engineering model of the system; 2) an index of reliability; and 3) parameter estimates. The traditional engineering definition of reliability refers to the ability of a system to meet demand at any given time. Several specific indices of reliability that have been defined include:

    1. The ability of a system to meet demand under a defined set of

contingencies. In water supply studies, a system might be judged reliable if it can meet demand under the drought of record.

2. Loss of load probabilities, equaling the chance that demand will exceed available supply or capacity. Probabilities of system failure are frequently used in water supply studies [22].

3. Severity indices, which describe how large supply shortfalls are. In several water supply studies, 'reliability' has been defined as the ratio of available supply to demand [10,26,30].

4. Frequency and duration indices, which indicate how frequently shortfalls of a given severity occur and how long they last. Such indices underlie many electric utility planning studies [4] and hydrologic investigations [22], and are beginning to be applied to aspects of water supply other than stream flow [32].

5. Economic consequences of shortages. In water supply studies, this has been called 'vulnerability' [14] and 'risk' [10,26].

The earliest reliability studies of engineering systems were 'contingency' analyses. The problem with that index of reliability is its inconsistency: different utilities using the the same nominal criterion for reliability (e.g., meet demand during the drought of record) can have very different probabilities of failure, since the contingency is often a random or arbitrarily defined variable. For that reason, engineers have moved towards probability-based indices of reliability. For example, systems are often designed to meet a predefined probability-based level of reliability. An example would be a water system designed to fail, on average, only once every 50 years. Although probability-based analyses of system reliability are generally more comprehensive and consistent than contingency analyses, the choice of reliability level itself has often been arbitrary or based on engineering 'rules-of-thumb'. Recently, reliability studies in the power and water industries have attempted to correct this problem by optimizing the level of reliability [e.g., 10]. This is done by balancing the economic effects of shortages with the costs of providing reliable service.

Reliability Studies of Water Systems: General Considerations

Most municipal water supply systems have the following elements: a source of water; bulk water pumping and transmission; finished water storage; and a distribution network. Shortfalls of water can result from a failure by any of the elements to provide sufficient capacity (the ability to provide the instantaneous rate of flow demanded, in units of $L^{**}3/T$) or stored water (stored water, in units of $L^{**}3$). When there are no changes in storage, decisions concerning operation of capacity at one time do not affect available capacity at others. In contrast, decisions concerning water storage at one time can affect the amount of supply available later. An inability to meet demand can result from either a decrease in capacity or water supply, and/or an increase in the quantity demanded. A comprehensive assessment of a system's reliability and means for improving it would have to consider all elements and their interactions.

Capacity failures are distinguished from storage failures because timing and rate of delivery is as important as total quantity supplied over a year and because different methods are used to model failures in each. Fire flow needs are an obvious example of the importance of capacity. The Chicago water supply system provides another example. Its greatest challenge is to encourage its new suburban customers to

use water during off-peak times to conserve scarce capacity [37].
Methods that can be used to calculate the reliability of elements
of water supply systems can be classified as follows:
1. Methods for calculating reliability of capacity vs. methods for
   calculating reliability of systems with storage.
2. Methods based on contingency analysis, vs. methods which calculate probability of failure ('loss of load expectation methods'),
   vs. methods which also calculate frequency, durations, and sever-
   ities of outages ('frequency-duration methods').
3. Methods which calculate reliability indices using only data on
   probabilities of component outages and demand levels vs. methods
   which also consider uncertainty regarding parameters of probability distributions [e.g., 3,33].
4. Methods which only calculate reliability statistics vs. those
   which also calculate total operating costs, vs. those which also
   calculate marginal operating costs.
5. Analytical probabilistic methods, which can be flexible and
   inexpensive, while giving approximate estimates of reliability
   and/or cost, vs. Monte Carlo simulation, which can be more realistic but whose estimates for low frequency events are unstable.
In the remainder of this paper, methods that have been used or
proposed for modeling the reliability of the various elements of bulk
water supply systems are reviewed.

Water Source

For surface water sources, the most important source of variability
is that of streamflow. If there is no surface water storage, then a
change in stream flow can be considered to be a change in capacity, as
its use in one period will not affect its availability in another. The
reliability of capacity at time t can then be expressed as probability
distribution which is not conditioned on water use at any other time.
Such reliability models will be referred to here as static models.
But in most cases, there is surface water storage. Calculation of
the distribution of water supply available to users becomes more complicated since, in general, use of the source in time t will decrease
the amount of water available in later periods. A model of the source's reliability must, therefore, be a dynamic one, explicitly considering the sequence of withdrawal and storage operating decisions.
Such models have long been used by water planners [22]. The most
common method is to simulate the operation of a set of reservoirs using
predetermined operating policies and the historical inflows. Synthetic
inflows generated by stochastic hydrologic methods are also used.
Water source availabilities, equipment outages, and demands in
different systems are often imperfectly correlated. A purpose of water
supply system interconnection is to take advantage of these imperfect
correlations to increase the reliability of one or both systems. The
cases of independence (zero correlation) and perfect correlation are
relatively easy to model. But non-zero imperfect correlations pose
analytical problems. There exist methods for generating imperfectly
correlated synthetic streamflows at different locations [22], but because data limitations cause estimates of intercorrelations to be
unstable, historic streamflows are usually used instead in simulations
(e.g., as in [28]).
Contamination by pathogens and toxics, in general, is not as much a

threat to source capacity as drought, but can still be significant, especially for systems relying on groundwater. Well failure because of screen clogging and other problems also causes losses of capacity. In addition, overpumpage and drought can lead to well failure; such problems would have to be modeled as a dynamic system because of storage in aquifers. At least one model has been developed for including contamination in calculations of water system reliability [19].

Static models of power system reliability can be applied to water supply capacity outages. For example, a system consisting of a N wells with insignificant storage can be easily simulated using such models. If well outages are independent events, then available well capacity is multinomially distributed with 2**N possible supply availability states. If, in addition, 1) each well's marginal operating cost is approximately constant from zero output to its capacity and 2) demand variations are described by a 'load duration curve' (basically, the cumulative probability distribution of demand), then a loss of load expectation method, 'probabilistic simulation' [7,36], can be used to calculate several useful indices. These include: 1) probability (both average over a given period, and conditioned on level of demand) of capacity falling short of demand; 2) expected amount of water demanded but not supplied in a given period; 3) operating costs, assuming that a well does not operate unless every well with a cheaper marginal cost is also operating. Probabilistic simulation and its variants are efficient means of calculating the probability distribution of capacity levels, comparing it with the cumulative probability distribution of demand, and calculating the various reliability and cost indices. Because of the way the calculations are made, it is easy to examine the effect upon cost and reliability of adding or subtracting a well, changing its reliability or cost, or altering the demand distribution.

The original version of probabilistic simulation is used to model systems whose components are subject to independent outages. Extensions of the method can approximate more complicated cases, including: 1) dependent or partial equipment outages; 2) the calculation of marginal system cost; 3) storage that is filled during hours of slack demand and drawn upon during system peaks; and 4) nonconstant component marginal costs (e.g., [5,9,36]; see also [1]).

Frequency-duration models, which calculate mean duration and frequency for capacity shortage states, have recently found application in the power industry [4]. Such models represent capacity outage and demand states as Markov processes. In addition to the outage probabilities needed by probabilistic simulation, they require departure rates for the various capacity and demand states. For wells and other equipment, these rates could be calculated from mean times between failures and mean repair times. For water demanded, departure rates could be calculated, for example, using a simplified model of the daily cycle of water use (see [4]). Shamir and Howard [32] also propose an approximate method for calculating frequencies and durations of capacity outages in a water system. Applications of both the Billinton [4] method and a loss of load expectation model to a hypothetical water supply system are contained in [16].

Frequency-duration methods can be interfaced with probability distributions of storage levels in a finished water reservoir to estimate the reliability of a system with some storage. This would be accomplished by comparing the probability distribution of duration for each capacity outage state with the probability distribution of storage to calculate statistics regarding how much stored water is drawn upon and how much water demand is unmet [21,32]. But the many simplifying assumptions made by these methods may imply that the resulting reliability estimates are suspect. Hence, comparisons of their results with those of detailed system simulations [e.g., 11] are needed.

One problem that often arises in water system planning is that of comparing water sources having different reliabilities. One approach is to describe the 'firm yield' of each source, which is the yield under either the drought of record or one with a prespecified expected frequency [e.g., 15,31]. A generalization of this idea is 'effective load carrying capability' (LCC) [12]. The LCC of a new water source is defined as the increase in total water demanded that can be supported by the source while maintaining the present level of system reliability. The advantages of the LCC concept are: 1) it permits use of a wider range of reliability indices and is not tied to the low flow of record; 2) it allows comparison of different supply and conservation measures whose failures may be very different in nature (e.g., droughts vs. aqueduct failure); and 3) it considers how a proposed water source would interact with the sources and usage patterns of a specific system, which firm yield methods fail to do. Another advantage is the quick method Garver [12] describes for approximating the LCC of small additions to capacity.

Bulk Water Transmission, Pumpage, and Treatment

These elements are considered together because failure of any of them would represent a capacity rather than storage failure. Vandalism, earthquakes, and facility deterioration are the major threats to transmission. Mechanical problems, flooding, weather, fire, earthquakes, and blackouts can all cause pump failures [35]. Analysis of treatment plant outages is more complex, because treatment usually involves several different processes.

Little analysis has been made of the reliability of these systems. Damelin et al. [11] used Monte Carlo simulation to estimate the reliability of a pump system feeding into storage. Their analysis illustrated some of the problems of Monte Carlo simulation. These include: 1) stable estimates of reliability require very lengthy simulations, as outages occur infrequently; 2) sensitivity analyses require that the model be rerun from scratch; and 3) the cost of computer runs and absence of marginal cost information makes optimization awkward. No doubt these problems were at least in part the motivation for Shamir and Howard's [32] analytical model of pump system reliability. Analytical models, such as probabilistic simulation, provide inexpensive and stable (though perhaps inaccurate) reliability estimates, and ease sensitivity analysis and optimization. Lvovsky [23] presents a analytical water supply model which includes a transmission line subject to random outages (see also Tangena and Koster [18]).

Koenig [20] provides a model for minimizing cost of water treatment subject to the constraint that the system be able to meet demand even if its largest unit fails. This constraint can only be considered to be a rule of thumb, as reliability in terms of probability of failure is not quantified. Novak [27] and others recommend a similar 'contingency analysis' approach. They suggest that expected system capacity after hypothesized natural disasters be estimated and that contingency plans be made to maintain system integrity.

Because transmission, pump, and treatment plant outages represent capacity failures, loss of load expectation and frequency-duration methods can be applied, as can the concept of load carrying capability [12]. 'Multiarea' versions of these models have been developed which simulate the operation of interconnected subsystems whose demands and equipment outages are imperfectly correlated between subsystems and whose transmission links are subject to random outages [1,4].

Finished Water Storage

Finished water storage is provided to minimize pumping costs, to enable peak demands to be met, and to furnish water for fire flow and during capacity failures. But tradeoffs between cost and reliability are rarely considered in system design. Storage for meeting peaks is usually calculated using a variant of the Rippl diagram; the benefits and costs of different levels of reliability are not considered. Fire flow requirements are usually taken from industry standards, and tradeoffs are rarely analyzed. This is sensible for small systems, since the benefit of analysis is probably far outweighed by its cost. But for large systems, this might not be so. Because fire protection costs can amount to a large proportion of water system costs in cities, analysis might yield large cost savings. Several of the methods summarized above which consider storage are applicable to these problems.

Water Users

Water demands must be considered in reliability analyses, as capacity or storage failures in and of themselves mean nothing unless the amount of water demanded exceeds that available. Models of water system reliability generally assume that the future demands are known. But demand levels are actually random because they depend on weather, consumer preferences, income, and level of economic development, none of which can be predicted exactly. Ideally, reliability assessments should explicitly consider this randomness.

Efforts in this direction are being made. Stochastic models which generate synthetic time series of water demands have been developed for several water supply systems [e.g.,24]. Boland et al. [6] used such a model to determine the reliability of the Washington, D.C. water supply system under alternative system designs. They simulated the system using actual streamflows and synthetic sequences of demands based on weather records. Another tack was taken in a planning study for Seattle [10,26]. A simulation model was developed which compared water supplies based on historic streamflows with probability distributions of demand based on historic variability.

But stochastic models of demands have rarely been used in analytical models of water supply systems (exceptions include theses by Lvovsky [23] and Norrie [26]). Nevertheless, this could be easily done. Loss of load expectation models consider demand randomness through load duration curves. Frequency-duration models used by the power industry also consider the random nature of demand, and could be adapted for application to water systems. An advantage of frequency-duration methods is that the implementation of emergency supply and conservation measures can depend on the supply and demand state of the system [4].

Models which include stochastic representations of demand could be used to assess the reliability and cost consequences of different

<u>supply</u> system designs and operation policies.   But alternative <u>demand</u> management measures present problems in that their effects on probability distributions of demand are in dispute.   For example, will voluntary conservation programs lower demand peaks to the same extent they lower average demands?   Uncertainties due to lack of knowledge about the effectiveness of alternative conservation policies or forecasting errors might be handled in reliability models by sensitivity analysis. Alternatively, if one was willing to specify a subjective a priori distribution over the set of possible load duration curves, Bayesian analysis could be used to derive a single curve that includes the uncertainty [4].   Methods for quantifying the effect of uncertainty in demands and equipment outages and translating those uncertainties into an estimate of the variance of reliability indices have also been developed [3] and could be applied to water supply systems.

Another important problem on the demand side is the assessment of the costs of customer outages.   As Shamir and Howard [32] note, these depend on a number of factors, many of which are poorly quantified. Estimates of some, but not all of the costs of shortages have been made [e.g., 17].   As long as knowledge about the benefits of reliability is scanty, reliability optimization will remain a multiobjective problem and choice of reliability level will be somewhat arbitrary.

The different types of costs shortages impose and their nonlinear relationship to shortage length and severity mean that, absent a widely accepted economic metric of the impact of shortages, no simple indicator of shortage impact will be completely satisfactory.   Besides the loss of load expectation and frequency-duration indices, other types of indicators have been proposed.   Shamir and Howard [32] suggest an index that is a nonlinear combination of the magnitude and length of shortage. Several risk analysts have proposed multidimensional representations of risk (e.g., [13]).   But the problem with many of these more complex indices is that decision makers lack intuitive feeling for their meaning and would have a difficult time trading them off against cost and other objectives.   Research on the economic impact of shortages would help in the creation of better shortage indices.

Conclusion

Traditionally, analysts have considered water supply reliability to be synonymous with stream flow reliability.   Computerized methods have been developed recently that are capable of analyzing other sources of system unreliability, including equipment failure, contamination, and demand variation.   These models are capable of evaluating not only the effect of additional supplies upon system reliability, but also the impact of, e.g., system interconnection, spare pump capacity, and demand management.   In many cases, these methods need further development so that they can be applied to water systems; all methods require more applications to demonstrate their usefulness.

Acknowledgment

The author would like to thank U. Shamir, J.J. Boland, and G.K. Beim for their helpful comments on an earlier version of this paper.   But the author bears sole responsibility for any opinions or misconceptions expressed.

Appendix.--References

1. Allan, R.N., Billinton, R., and Lee, S.H., "Bibliography on the Application of Probability Methods in Power System Reliability Evaluation," IEEE Transactions, Power Apparatus and Systems, Vol. PAS-103, No. 2, 1984.

2. Baumann, D.D., Boland, J.J., and Sims, J.H., "Water Conservation: The Struggle over Definition," Water Resources Research, Vol. 20, No. 4, 1984, pp. 428-434.

3. Billinton, R., and Hamoud, G., "An Approximate and Practical Approach to Including Uncertainty Concepts in Generating Capacity Reliability Evaluation," IEEE Transactions, Power Apparatus and Systems, Vol. PAS-100, 1981.

4. Billinton, R., and Allan, R.N. Evaluation of Power System Reliability, Plenum Press, New York, N.Y., 1984.

5. Bloom, J., and Charny, L.M., "Long Range Generation Planning with Limited Energy and Storage Plants, Part I: Production Costing," IEEE Transactions Power Apparatus and Systems, Vol. PAS-102, No. 9, 1983, pp. 2861-2870.

6. Boland, J.J., Carver, P.H., and Flynn, C.R., "How Much Water Supply Capacity is Enough?", Journal American Water Works Association, Vol. 72, No. 7, 1980, pp. 368-374.

7. Booth, R.R., "Power System Simulation Model Based on Probability Analysis," IEEE Transactions, Power Apparatus and Systems, Vol. PAS-91, 1972, pp. 62-69.

8. Boyle, D.B., "Interagency Connections: Insurance Against Interruptions in Supply," Journal American Water Works Association, Vol. 72, No. 4, 1980, pp. 192-194.

9. Caramanis, M.C., Tabors, R.D., Nochur, K.S., and Schweppe, F.C., "The Introduction of Nondispatchable Technologies as Decision Variables in Long-Term Generation Expansion Models," IEEE Transactions, Power Apparatus and Systems, Vol. PAS-101, No. 8, 1982.

10. Chas. Howard and Associates, Inc., "Water Supply Reliability and Risk", Reported Prepared for City of Seattle, Victoria, B.C., 1984.

11. Damelin, E., Shamir, U., and Arad, N., "Engineering and Economic Evaluation of the Reliability of Water Supply," Water Resources Research, Vol. 8, No. 4, 1972, pp. 861-881.

12. Garver, L.L., "Effective Load-Carrying Capability of Generating Units," IEEE Transactions, Power Apparatus and Systems, Vol. PAS-85, 1966, pp. 910-919.

13. Haimes, Y.Y., ed., Risk/Benefit Analysis in Water Resources Planning and Management, Plenum, New York, N.Y., 1981.

14. Hashimoto, T., Stedinger, J.R., and Loucks, D.P., "Reliability, Resiliency, and Vulnerability Criteria for Water Resource System Performance Evaluation," Water Resources Research, Vol. 18, 1982.

15. Hobbs, B.F., "Water for Power in the Texas-Gulf Region," Journal of Water Resources Planning and Management, Vol. 110, No. 4, 1984.

16. Hobbs, B.F., "Reliability Analysis of Urban Water Supply System Capacity," Hydraulics and Hydrology in the Small Computer Age, W.R. Waldrop, ed., ASCE, Aug., 1985.

17. Hoffmann, M.R., Glickstein, and Liroff, S., "Urban Drought in the San Francisco Bay Area: A Study of Institutional and Social Resiliency," Journal American Water Works Association, Vol. 71, No. 7, 1979, pp. 356-363.

18. International Water Supply Association, Proceedings, Symposium on

Reliability of Water Supply, Brussels, Sept. 1983, London, 1984.
19. Johnson, R.C., and Dendrou, S.A., "Evaluation of the Potential Water Supply Impacts Posed by the Transgulf Pipeline, Broward County, Florida," presented at the May, 1984, ASCE Urban Water '84 Conference, held at Baltimore, Md.
20. Koenig, L., "Optimal Fail-Safe Process Design," Journal Water Pollution Control Federation, Vol. 65, No. 4, 1973, pp. 647-654.
21. Kuliasha, M.A., "Procedure for the Determination of Dependable Capacity Gains in Hydroplants Due to Headwaters Improvements," Report, Oak Ridge Natl. Laboratory, Oak Ridge, Tenn., Sept., 1983.
22. Loucks, D.P., Stedinger, J.R., and Haith, D.A., Water Resource Systems Planning and Analysis, Prentice-Hall, Englewood Cliffs, N.J., 1981.
23. Lvovsky, M., "Statistical-Analytical Models for Water Resources Systems," M.Sc. Thesis, Technion Institute, Israel (in Hebrew).
24. Maidment, D.R., and Parzen, E., "Cascade Model of Monthly Municipal Water Use," Water Resources Research, Vol. 20, 1984, pp. 15-23.
25. Mays, L.W., "Review of the State-of-the-Art Methods for Reliability Analysis of Water Distribution Systems," Hydraulics and Hydrology in the Small Computer Age, W.R. Waldrop, ed., ASCE, Aug., 1985.
26. Norrie, D.J.W., "Optimal Reliability in Water Supply Planning: Risk versus Cost of Supply Tradeoffs," M.Sc. Thesis, Department of Civil Engineering, Massachusetts Institute of Technology, 1983.
27. Novak, J.T., "Planning for Emergencies at Water Utilities," Journal American Water Works Association, Vol. 67, No. 4, 1975.
28. Palmer, R.N., Smith, J.A., Cohon, J.L., and ReVelle, C.S., "Reservoir Management in the Potomac Basin," Journal of the Water Resources Planning and Management Division (ASCE), Vol. 108, No. WR1, 1982, pp. 47-66.
29. Prasifka, D.W., "Water Supply Management Enters a New Era," Civil Engineering, Vol. 54, No. 3, 1984, pp. 45-47.
30. Randall, D., Houck, M.H., and Wright, J.R., "Building a Water Supply Optimization Model for Indianapolis," Proceedings, 1984 International Symposium on Urban Hydrology, Hydraulics, and Sediment Control, 1984.
31. Rubenstein, J., and Ortolano, L., "Water Conservation and Capacity Expansion," Journal of Water Resources Planning and Management, Vol. 110, No. 2, 1984, pp. 220-237.
32. Shamir, U., and Howard, C.D.D., "Water Supply Reliability Theory," Journal American Water Works Association, Vol. 73, 1981, 379-384.
33. Stedinger, J.R., and Taylor, M.R., "Synthetic Streamflow Generation 2. Effect of Parameter Uncertainty," Water Resources Research, Vol. 18, No. 4, 1982, pp. 919-924.
34. Tung, Y.K., "Evaluation of Water Distribution Network Reliability," Hydraulics and Hydrology in the Small Computer Age, W.R. Waldrop, ed., ASCE, 1985.
35. Valcour, H.C., "Pumping Station Reliability: How and How Much," Journal American Water Works Association, Vol. 72, No. 4, 1980.
36. Vardi, J., and Avi-Itzhak, B., Electric Energy Generation: Economics, Reliability, and Rates, MIT Press, Cambridge, Mass., 1981.
37. Zullo, J.A., "Chicago's Water Commissioner Describes His City's System," Journal American Water Works Association, Vol. 76, No. 6, 1984, p. 20 et seq.

A POST-AUDIT OF THE POTOMAC EUTROPHICATION MODEL

by Stuart A. Freudberg[1]

Abstract

An unusual, unexpected, and unpredicted event -- "the Potomac Algae Bloom of 1983" -- prompted a "post-audit" examination of the primary tool being used for guiding the continuing development of the nutrient control strategy for the Potomac River Estuary near Washington, D.C., a water body historically plagued with massive blue-green algae blooms. The Potomac Eutrophication Model (PEM), had been thoroughly and successfully calibrated and verified to seven years of historical data covering the late 1960's and 1970's and was subsequently used to evaluate alternative control strategies for the major estuary discharger, a 310 mgd facility. At the time that recommendations were being formulated for revision of the effluent limits for the facility, coincident with achievement of its its best performance ever, an unusually large outbreak of blue-green algae took place for the first time in six years. The PEM, in a "post-audit" evaluation of the bloom, was able to successfully capture the onset of the bloom up to 100 ug/l chlorophyll-a, but did not predict its intensification to 250 ug/l, due to a calculated phosphorus limitation. Hypothesis-testing with the model in conjunction with field studies and other analyses by an Expert Panel convened to investigate this event attributed the unpredicted intensification to several complex mechanisms beyond the present model formulation, including pH-mediated sediment release, estuarine circulation, and algal species dynamics. Thus it is concluded that since conventional eutrophication modeling was inadequate to explain this event, a revised version of the model framework should include more complex hydrodynamics, sediment-layer and water column chemistry, and multiple algal species. It is suggested that the existing nutrient control program be maintained until an improved formulation is developed which fully explains this event.

An unusual, unexpected, and unpredicted event -- "the Potomac Algae Bloom of '83" -- has prompted a second look at the primary tool being used for guiding the continuing development of the nutrient control strategy for protection of the Potomac River Estuary near Washington, D.C. (see location in Figure 1). The particular problem setting and consequent modeling experience is likely to be somewhat unique to the Potomac ecosystem. However, the experience conveys important lessons concerning the development and application of any water quality modeling tool, especially one which has been created specifically to assist the public policy decision-making process. In the sections that follow, the water quality history and problems of the Potomac are summarized, the modeling tool is explained, and the results and implications of what happened when the model was given a hard second look are explored.

Potomac Estuary Water Quality Problems and Solutions -- A Synopsis

The Potomac River estuary near Washington, D.C. has been plagued with periodic water quality problems for over a century. The primary source of the problems can be attributed to the impact of urbanization:

[1]Principal Environmental Engineer, Metropolitan Washington Council of Governments, 1875 Eye St., N.W., Washington, D.C. 20006

increased loadings of organic matter and nutrients from untreated and treated sewage and the effects of urban runoff. Probably the most chronic of the water quality problems has been the repeated occurrence of massive, noxious, blue-green algae blooms which have been frequently observed since the 1960's during low flow summer periods in the tidal fresh portion of the estuary. Extensive surface matting up to a foot in thickness has been reported (11). Algal densities, as represented by measurements of the pigment chlorophyll-a, have exceeded 250 µg/l throughout the water column.

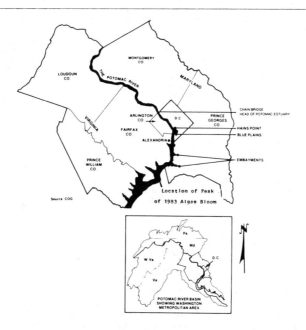

Figure 1.   Washington Metropolitan Area and Potomac River Basin

In 1969, in response to the frequent outbreaks of algal bloom conditions, and also due to the observance of extremely low oxygen levels in the tidal fresh estuary (as low as 1 mg/l), an ambitious sewage treatment plant control program was initiated to help restore the "nation's river." (Sewage treatment plants consititute the predominant point source dischargers to the Potomac.) This program consisted of upgrading certain primary and secondary facilities with a combined discharge in 1969 of 370 million gallons per day (mgd), or 16.2 m³/s, to advanced treatment levels which included BOD reduction to 5 mg/l, phophorus removal to 0.2 mg/l or less, and nitrification/denitrification to 2.4 mg N/l. The intended goal of the program was elimination of nuisance algal blooms (a chlorophyll-a goal of 25 µg/l was set to accomplish this) and restoration of dissolved oxygen levels to a 5 mg/l standard (4).

During the 1970's, a capital investment totalling $1 billion (6) was made in area sewage treatment facilities intended to implement these limits. By 1980, it appeared that substantial improvement in water quality had taken place even though the advanced treatment program had yet to be completed. Further, with the exception of 1977, no significant algae blooms had occurred since 1971, and the main blue-green algal culprit, Microcystis aeruginosa, had seemingly disappeared.

Buoyed by the belief that the treatment plant control program had significantly improved estuary water quality far short of implementation of the 1969 requirements, and cognizant of the major investment still needed for full achievement, local officials and state/federal regulatory agencies questioned further completion of the original program. Such assessments were tempered with the recognition that during one of the few extended low flow summers of the decade of the 1970's, a major blue-green bloom did occur, albeit not of the most undesirable surface variety but nevertheless still a warning sign that all was not well.

In view of these considerations, coupled with the legitimate suggestion that some degree of nonpoint source control might be traded-off or used to supplement the point source control effort, a local/state/EPA/consultant team was assembled to develop a new water quality modeling tool to address these concerns. The Potomac Eutrophication Model (PEM) was born.

The PEM Described

The PEM was designed to capture the principal features of the eutrophication process in the upper 35-50 miles (56-80 km) of the Potomac Estuary (the tidal fresh zone). It was developed as a one-dimensional, tidally-averaged model which contained 76 model segments (23 main channel segments, 15 embayments, and a sediment segment underlying each water column segment). A series of linked differential equations which described the transport and kinetic interactions among the variables were solved by the finite-difference method to produce concentrations estimates in space and time for algal biomass (chlorophyll-a), four phosphorus forms (dissolved and particulate, inorganic and organic), three nitrogen forms (organic nitrogen, ammonia, and nitrite plus nitrate), chlorides, biochemical oxygen demand, and dissolved oxygen. Because of the nature of the modeling framework and parameter estimates, the time-scale of the model output was considered on a seasonal basis, although daily comparisons of the model predictions and observed data were made. The model is considered to represent the conventional state-of-the-art in eutrophication modeling. It has been fully described in (1) and (10).

Compromises in Formulating the PEM

As with any model development effort, a balance must be struck among available resources and time, level of scientific understanding and supporting data, and the perceived nature of the problem. Such considerations led to a number of compromises in formulation of the PEM, the consequences of which as seen later, were only partially anticipated.

A major advance in the model framework was the inclusion of a mass balance in the sediment layer to capture the dynamic nature of the sediment release process, particularly for phosphorus. This was in contrast to previous models of the estuary which treated sediment fluxes as just another loading source. It was included because it was believed that the sediment nutrient source was a major contributor to the 1977 bloom and the ability to predict the long-term sediment nutrient interaction was the key to evaluating control efforts (9). Some had maintained that control of point source phosphorus could never be effective in limiting algal growth because of this sediment source (2), while others believed that the sediment release rates would decrease as the point source removal program remained in place for a number of years (7), and thus the problem would diminish.

Compromises were made here, however. First, only an active surface sediment layer was included, because it was thought that simulation at this level was sufficient to reproduce observed flux rates and that most of the sediment flux changes were due to surface phenomena. Second, a true sediment transport model was not attempted because it was viewed as too costly, the database was insufficient, and development time was an important factor. It was also recognized that just including the underlying sediment layer was doubling the computational cost.

The sediment chemistry was also crude, particularly for phosphorus. Rather than compute the actual kinetics of the sediment reactions including time-variable changes in the phase (adsorbed or desorbed) of phosphate in the bottom sediments, the partitioning of phosphorus between particulate and dissolved phases was fixed in each sediment segment based on observed data, and the flux to the overlying water column was dependent only on the dissolved concentration gradient between sediment layer and water column. Such an approach was believed adequate to address the long-term sediment behavior, at least assuming that the present chemistry would remain unchanged and only the total mass would shift.

Other potentially significant compromises in the model formulation included the decision not to compute "real-time" hydrodynamics, to keep the model one-dimensional (laterally and vertically averaged) and to simulate only one algal species. Of somewhat lesser apparent importance to the algal issues was the decision to model nitrification with just one first-order rate parameter, rather than including nitrifying bacteria kinetics.

Calibration and Verification of the PEM

The PEM was calibrated over a four year period in the late 1960's and verified to a three year period in the late 1970's. (The material summarized in this section is drawn from (10).) Both the calibration and verification periods spanned a wide range of hydrology and eutrophication status of the estuary. Also, phosphorus removal and BOD reduction were partially implemented by the verification period.

The observed data was reproduced well over the seven year period using a consistent set of parameters. Calibration and verification of

the PEM was primarily evaluated based on visual and statistical comparisons between computed and observed data, and was focused on summer averages. Model transport was calibrated using observed chlorides (salinity) data, with the tidal-averaged dispersion coefficient used as a
calibration parameter.

In the quality calibration, over all variables and years, for the
summer period, the PEM had a median relative error of 21%. For the
most important variable, chlorophyll-a, the PEM achieved a 20% median
relative error. Further, 77% of the segments examined across all years
and all variables had no statistically significant difference between
computed and observed summer averages. Typical visual comparisons of
the summer-average predictions and observations for the tidal fresh
estuary for chlorophyll-a and total phosphorus are shown in Figure 2.
The comparisons are seen to be quite good.

On an individual survey basis, as one might expect, there was somewhat more divergence between model prediction and observation, although the patterns in the data were generally reproduced. This is
illustrated in Figure 3 (a-c) for chlorophyll-a, total phosphorus, and
dissolved inorganic nitrogen. A notable underprediction is seen for
chlorophyll-a in August, 1977, wherein the PEM does not completely capture the peak chlorophyll-a concentrations (Figure 3a). It was decided
to accept this underprediction as an understandable consequence of using a consistent set of parameters over seven years, rather than trying
to specifically "tune" the model to a particular dataset. In retrospect, a closer look at this event may have provided an early clue to
what lay ahead in 1983, because as seen in Figure 3b, total phosphorus
was underpredicted in the bloom area in 1977.

The basic conclusion of the calibration and verification effort was
that the PEM represented a useful planning tool and a firm basis for
evaluating the effectiveness of various control scenarios.

Model Applications

The PEM was applied extensively for projection purposes in a detailed sensitivity analysis (5). The primary conclusions from the sensitivity analysis relevant here were that (i) the chlorophyll-a goal of
25 µg/l could not be achieved in the estuary, even with full implementation of the 1969 control program; 50-70 µg/l was about the best
achievable; (ii) the phosphorus removal program would only be effective in the upper 30-35 miles (48 to 56 km) of the estuary and beyond
that sediment phosphorus release would offset the control program;
(iii) nitrogen removal, while likely limiting some algal species, had
the potential to encourage undesirable, nitrogen-fixing blue-green algae; (iv) there was some potential for nonpoint source control
tradeoffs if sewage treatment plant controls were at or beyond advanced
secondary levels. Such results were important information milestones
in the control program reexamination effort.

Using varying hydrologies, the PEM was also employed to examine over
30 alternatives for the expansion from 310 mgd (13.6 m³/s) to 370 mgd
(16.2 m³/s) at the region's largest sewage treatment facility,

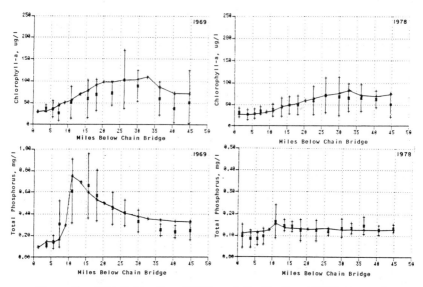

Figure 2. PEM Calibration (1969) and Verification (1978) Comparisons for Chlorophyll-a (top) and Total Phosphorus (bottom) - Summer Avgs.

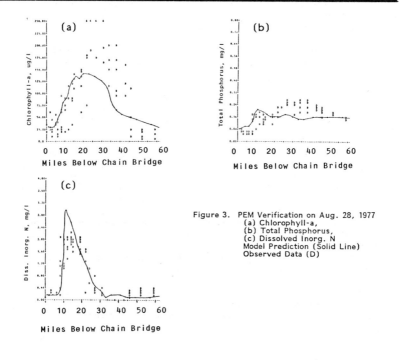

Figure 3. PEM Verification on Aug. 28, 1977
(a) Chlorophyll-a,
(b) Total Phosphorus,
(c) Dissolved Inorg. N
Model Prediction (Solid Line)
Observed Data (D)

the District of Columbia's Blue Plains plant. Six alternatives were deemed acceptable based upon their simulated water quality response. All represented improvement over historical conditions, and all were believed to minimize the likelihood of future algal blooms. The recommended alternative, which had the lowest overall cost, represented a relaxation from the 1969 recommendations by about a factor of 2 in phosphorus removal levels (0.35 vs. 0.18 mg P/l), no wintertime limit for phosphorus, and continued deferral of nitrogen removal other than that obtained via nitrification. It was expected to yield compliance with water quality standards and to keep summer-average chlorphyll-a below 100 µg/l. With the exception of wintertime relaxation of phosphorus removal requirements, the recommendation represented maintenance of the status quo. Even so, the cost for implementation of the recommendation was estimated at $330 million (3). As of this writing, the study has not been acted upon by the regulatory bodies because its release coincided with the 1983 algae bloom.

The 1983 Potomac Estuary Algae Bloom

An estuary is an extremely complex water body, and even the best efforts at understanding and mathematically describing its interactions may be incomplete. The Potomac in the summer of 1983 was a noteworthy example of such a situation. With the highest levels of treatment in place since the control program was initiated (ironically roughly equivalent to the alternative recommended in the Blue Plains study), a major outbreak of the nuisance blue-green algal species, Microcystis aeruginosa, took place from late July into early November in a 25-mile stretch (40km) of the tidal fresh Potomac estuary. The bloom conditions were very reminiscent of those occurring during the late 1960's before any nutrient reduction program had begun. Chlorophyll-a concentrations in the 250 µg/l to 300 µg/l range again were commonplace. The bloom represented a major disappointment to those who believed that the existing control program was sufficient to eliminate this problem, and the effectiveness of the $1 billion control effort was thereby called into question.

While the bloom was viewed environmentally and politically as a negative event, from the PEM perspective it represented an important opportunity to test the model subsequent to verification after implementation of advanced treatment levels. Such an analysis has been termed a "post-audit" of a model (11). The post-audit analysis of the PEM was carried out in conjunction with an EPA-convened "expert panel" investigation into the causes of the 1983 bloom. That process and conclusions are fully discussed in (11). The following discussion is narrowly focused on the PEM post-audit analysis.

PEM Post-Audit Simulation

The 1983 PEM post-audit run was initially conducted without any changes in model parameters but with the meteorology, hydrology, and nutrient input loads as observed for 1983. The model inputs were varied on a daily basis. Examination of the model output revealed immediately that while the model captured the early phase of the bloom up to 100 µg/l at the end of July, it was unable to reproduce the intensification to 250 µg/l during August and September. This is seen clearly in Figure 4, a time-series plot of chlorophyll-a for a station about 20 miles (32 km) downstream of Washington, D.C., near the center of the bloom area. The model phosphorus calculation indicated that the model's inability to capture the bloom after late July was due to a computed phosphorus limitation not evident in the observed data. Total phosphorus concentration at the peak of the bloom was underpredicted by a factor of 2 to 5. The model was therefore indicating that something quite unusual had taken place in 1983, at considerable odds with the understanding developed and embodied in the seven-year calibration and verification effort. Such a conclusion was important, for had the model predicted the bloom, it would have meant that the bloom was "expected," and the model framework deemed sufficient. Thus, although PEM didn't fully reproduce the 1983 Potomac algae bloom, it did give a critical clue concerning the cause: an unknown phosphorus source must have been operative in 1983. A search for its source was the EPA Panel's main preoccupation. The PEM was used to help confirm its existence.

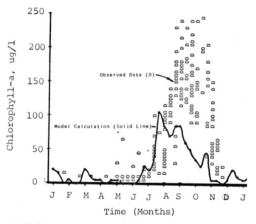

Figure 4.   PEM Post-Audit Simulation of 1983 Bloom at Indian Head, Md. (River Mile 30, Kilometer 48)

Two parallel tracks were followed in an attempt to "adjust" the PEM to better reproduce the bloom and quantify the phosphorus source. The first track was simply to add phosphorus load, in the form of dissolved inorganic phosphorus, in the "right" location to see if the computation could be improved. While certainly crude, this approach had the appeal of yielding a quick answer to the location, magnitude and duration of the unknown source. After some trial and error, the best estimate of this source was 4,000 lbs. P/day (8,800 kg/day) from July 15 to October 15, in a 10 mile (16 km) reach centered about 30 miles (48km) below head of tide. Such a magnitude was nearly 3 times the combined daily loadings of all treatment plants and an order of magnitude greater than the known aerobic sediment phosphate flux rates. A comparison of the resulting model predictions using this input are shown in Figure 5. A significant improvement over the initial post-audit run is evident. Such a run confirmed that the algal kinetics in PEM were still fundamentally sound: given the "correct" nutrient inputs, the model reproduced the bloom.

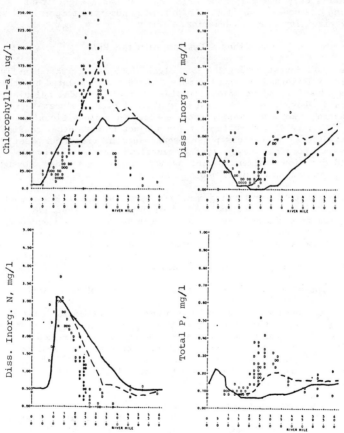

Figure 5.   PEM Post-Audit Simulation of 1983 Bloom (Aug. 28, 1983)
-- Base Case and Additional Phosphorus Load Runs
Base Case (Solid Line ——), Addl. P load (Dashed Line --), Observed Data (D)

The alternative approach to trying to improve the 1983 simulation was to change model parameters. This approach argued that there were factors in 1983 which were different than other years (low suspended solids in the estuary, a sometimes buoyant, surface-dwelling algal species, and apparent toxicity to chlorides were cited), and thus by various attempts at revising model parameters the bloom could be "explained" more simply as an abberant year but still falling within the existing model framework. After considerable testing, a parameter set was obtained which yielded an improvement over the original post-audit calculation but still fell short of properly reproducing the phosphorus profile. The analysis also demonstrated that the constraint of simulating only one composite algal species was a significant factor limiting the model's ability to capture the observed temporal and spatial variability in algal dynamics.

Hypothesis Testing With the PEM

The Panel investigating the 1983 algae bloom came to rely heavily on the PEM as it sorted through the mass of data and formulated hypotheses on the cause(s) and remedies for this event. The model calculations discussed above indicated that a sustained event, almost certainly originating from a sediment source, enabled the intensification of the bloom. This permitted ruling out (in conjuction with other confirming investigations) short-term pulse events such as treatment plant malfunctions, combined sewer system overflows and runoff events, and limited duration sediment pulses such as might be induced through a brief period of anoxia or from bioturbation.

Further hypothesis-testing with the PEM also was able to confirm that climatic conditions were of major importance, that 1983's high spring runoff could not have been the sole source of the unknown phosphorus, that suspended solids reductions at the treatment plants may have reduced water column adsorption of phosphorus permitting downstream transport of this nutrient to the bloom area, and that the processes in a small side embayment could not have caused the bloom.

Hypotheses Requiring a Change in the Model Framework

Two hypotheses were advanced which were beyond examination with the existing model framework. The first of these was that the two-dimensional estuarine circulation in the transition zone was responsible for transporting and retaining nutrients in the bloom area. Such a circulation of course, was always present in the Potomac estuary. It was argued, however, that the effect was masked until low effluent levels were achieved in 1983.

Supporting evidence for the hypothesis is presented in (11), in which it was demonstrated that the concentration of a distributed sediment source at the upstream tail of the salinity intrusion would be five times greater had a vertical two-dimensional model been employed rather than the one-dimensional formulation.

The other hypothesis advanced to explain the cause of the 1983 bloom beyond the current model formulation was termed the "pH-mediated" sediment release theory. This hypothesis held that algal uptake of carbon dioxide raised the pH in the water column to a point where the high pH water diffused in the surface sediment layer, followed by phosphate desorption and flux into the overlying water column. The evidence for this hypothesis is substantial, and includes special laboratory studies (8). A critical element of the hypothesis was that the alkalinity or buffering capacity of the estuary was unusually low in 1983, thereby permitting the pH to rise to nearly 11 in the bloom region and enabling the high sediment phosphorus release. To analytically demonstrate this theory, the interaction between phytoplankton growth dynamics and the pH, carbon dioxide, and alkalinity balance would have to be included in the model framework, along with some relationship between pH and sediment release.

Implications for the PEM as a Management Tool

The calibration, verification, application, and post-audit analysis of the Potomac Eutrophication Model has helped advance the understanding of a complicated natural system, and guide the decision-making process in pursuit of an effective eutrophication control program for the tidal-fresh Potomac estuary. The modeling effort has reached an important cross-roads, however, wherein continuation of the effort will require important modifications to the existing tool. These modifications include the two-dimensional hydrodynamic calculation, inclusion of the pH-alkalinity chemistry, possible addition of more algal species, and modeling of sediment transport. Such changes would appear to be needed to simulate a worst-case eutrophication event not predicted using the present, conventional modeling approach.

Regulators are thus faced with a dilemma. Maintenance of the existing level of nutrient control would almost certainly result in a repeat of the 1983 bloom sometime in the future. Yet to go beyond the present level of control, for example to implement unproven nitrogen-removal technology, brings with it even greater uncertainty concerning the estuary's response, yet the certainty of much higher costs. It would seem more prudent to hold the line at the present limits (including nonpoint inputs) until an updated technical tool is available that can reproduce and explain the unusual events of 1983.

The lesson of the Potomac estuary is that even after 20 years of research, a simple solution to reversing its eutrophication remains elusive. It is therefore suggested that the existing nutrient control program be maintained until an improved model formulation is developed that fully explains the bloom of 1983. To confidently support modifications to the existing control effort will require a major improvement in the modeling state-of-the-art. Fortunately, the groundwork has been laid to accomplish this process through the rigorous post-audit of the Potomac Eutrophication Model.

References

1. Fitzpatrick, J.J., Freudberg, S.A., Mountford, K., Sullivan, M.,
    and Thomann, R.V. "Calibration/Verification of the Potomac Estu-
    ary Eutrophication Model," Presented at the ASCE Environmental
    Specialty Conference, Boulder, CO, July, 1983.

2. Flaherty, T.P., and Harris, R.H. "Impact of Nutrients on the Poto-
    mac Estuary," Environmental Defense Fund, Washington, D.C., Dec.
    1979.

3. Greeley and Hansen, Inc. "Blue Plains Feasibility Study," Final
    Report to D.C. Dept. of Public Works, August, 1984.

4. Jaworski, N.A., Clark, L.J., and Feigner, K.D. "A Water
    Resources-Water Supply Study of the Potomac Estuary," Technical
    Report No. 35, EPA Water Quality Office, Middle Atlantic Region,
    April, 1971.

5. Metropolitan Washington Council of Govts. "Potomac Estuary Water
    Quality Sensitivity Analysis," report to Water Resources Planning
    Board and Blue Plains Chief Administrative Officers, Oct. 6, 1982.

6. _____. "Potomac River Water Quality, 1982:
    Conditions and Trends in Metropolitan Washington," August, 1983.

7. Pendergast, J.F. "Significance of Phosphorus Release in PEM Pro-
    jections," Memorandum for Blue Plains Feasibility Study, LTI, Lim-
    noTech, Inc., Ann Arbor, MI, November 17, 1982.

8. Seitzinger, S.P. "The Effect of Oxygen Concentration and pH on Sed-
    iment-Water Nutrient Fluxes in the Potomac River," The Academy of
    Natural Sciences of Philadelphia, Phila., PA, January 28, 1985.

9. Thomann, R.V., and Fitzpatrick, J.J. "Overview of Potomac Estuary
    Modeling, Tasks I and II -- Dissolved Oxygen and Eutrophication,"
    HydroQual, Inc., Mahwah, N.J., August, 1980.

10. Thomann, R.V. and Fitzpatrick, J.J. "Calibration and Verification
    of a Mathematical Model of the Eutrophication of the Potomac Estu-
    ary," HydroQual, Inc., Mahwah, NJ, August, 1982.

11. Thomann, R.V., Jaworski, N.J., Nixon, S.W., Paerl, H.W., and Taft,
    J. "The 1983 Algal Bloom in the Potomac Estuary," Expert Panel Re-
    port to the Potomac Strategy State/EPA Management Committee,
    March, 1985 (in press).

APPLICATION OF PHOSPHORUS MODELS
TO NEW MEXICO RESERVOIRS

Susan Bolton Bolin, Timothy J. Ward, M. ASCE, and Richard A. Cole*

ABSTRACT: Many empirical, mass-balance phosphorus models have been developed and tested on northern, temperate lakes and previously published. Fourteen of those published models were tested on New Mexico reservoirs to determine their usefulness in simulating reservoir behavior in the Rio Grande basin. Models were applied to seasonal data. All of the models overpredicted measured phosphorus concentrations in the reservoirs. Model predictions were improved by establishing a relationship between removal rates of phosphorus and certain hydrologic variables. The relationship between settling velocity of phosphorus and reservoir flushing rate was the most significant. Using settling velocity as a function of flushing rate, the Pearson's r between the natural log values of measured and predicted phosphorus is 0.89. Flushing rate also was significantly correlated (r = 0.86) with the loading rate of suspended solids. This helps explain the high removal rates observed in the reservoirs. High flushing rates bring in high loads of suspended solids which may combine with the phosphorus and remove it from the water column as the solids settle.

INTRODUCTION

During the last fifteen years, several models have been developed for predicting phosphorus concentrations in lakes (e.g. 4, 20). Many of these models are derived from a mass-balance approach in which phosphorus concentration in lake water is a function of incoming phosphorus minus outflowing phosphorus and lake-water losses of phosphorus. Reckhow (18) presented three major forms of steady-state solutions to the mass-balance equations as:

$$P = \frac{L}{z(\sigma+\rho)} \dots\dots\dots\dots\dots\dots\dots\dots\dots\dots\dots\dots\dots\dots\dots\dots\dots\dots\dots (1)$$

$$P = \frac{L}{v_s + q_s} \dots\dots\dots\dots\dots\dots\dots\dots\dots\dots\dots\dots\dots\dots\dots\dots\dots\dots\dots\dots (2)$$

$$P = \frac{L\tau}{z}(1-R) \dots\dots\dots\dots\dots\dots\dots\dots\dots\dots\dots\dots\dots\dots\dots\dots\dots\dots (3)$$

in which P = lake phosphorus concentration in mg/l; L=areal mass loading rate of phosphorus in $g/m^2/yr$; ρ = flushing rate of the lake, per year; σ = phosphorus sedimentation coefficient, per year; v_s =apparent settling velocity of phosphorus in m/yr; q_s = areal water loading in m/yr,($q_s = z/\tau$); τ=hydraulic retention time in years, ($\tau=1/\rho$); R = phosphorus retention coefficient.

*The authors are, respectively, Research Assistant, Dept. of Civil Engineering; Associate Professor, Dept. of Civil Engineering; and Associate Professor, Dept. of Fisheries and Wildlife Science, New Mexico State University, Las Cruces, New Mexico.

Equation 1 has a depth-dependent settling velocity (σz). Equation 2 implies a constant settling velocity (v_s) and equation 3 is based on how much phosphorus is retained in the lake.

Calibration and verification of these models have been restricted mostly to north-temperate natural lakes in the United States, Canada and Europe. Therefore, the empirical constants derived from these tests may not be suitable for reservoirs in general or specifically for lakes or reservoirs in areas with geologic and climatic features different from those areas tested (10).

PREVIOUS MODEL COMPARISONS

Tests of models on other water bodies in areas different from those where the models were first developed have been limited by insufficient data. Since the release of the National Eutrophication Survey (NES) by the U.S. Environmental Protection Agency (e.g. 7). Several workers (1,9,16,17,21) have tested various empirical, mass-balance models on the new data sets. The NES data include lakes and reservoirs from every state in the United States. Results of these applications range from finding the lake-calibrated parameters invalid for Western reservoirs (17) to the development of new parameters that yield good estimates of phosphorus concentrations over a wide range of conditions (1).

Few workers (12,17) have contrasted reservoirs with lakes specifically and those that did used NES data. The NES data for New Mexican reservoirs are limited. Only annual information is listed, and that is insufficient for models that require realistic estimates of seasonal phosphorus levels, as was needed for a Rio Grande Basin model being developed for the New Mexico Department of Game and Fish (23). Also, morphologic and hydrologic data reported in the NES are for reservoirs at maximum capacity, an unrealistic assumption for most New Mexico conditions. This led to further data collection in New Mexico to verify existing models.

DATA SET

Four reservoirs , Abiquiu, Cochiti, Caballo, and Sumner, (Fig. 1) were sampled from early September to mid-November, 1983, and in May and June, 1984. Water samples from inflows, outflows, and from three to eight in-lake locations were analyzed for total phosphorus using a persulfate digestion following EPA (8) procedure 365.1. In addition to phosphorus, other analyses were performed, including total nitrogen and total suspended solids, on surface samples and bottom samples.

Because of fluctuations in reservoir storage, it is difficult to fulfill the assumption of steady-state water levels over an annual cycle, as is made for most empirical models. In New Mexico reservoirs a steady-state condition is more likely to be achieved over a shorter time period, such as a three-month season. Therefore, seasonal data for the New Mexico reservoirs were used in

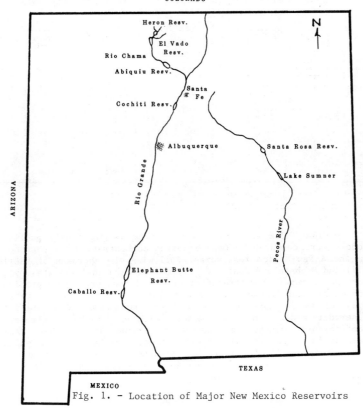

Fig. 1. – Location of Major New Mexico Reservoirs

the models. Even though these models usually are applied to annual data, Dillon (4) indicates that any time period can be used. Seasons are defined as follows:

    Winter = January through March;
    Spring = April through June;
    Summer = July through September;
    Fall   = October through December.

Except for the sampling of Lake Sumner in September, 1983, all sampling was done in the fall and spring.

Morphometric and hydrologic data for the four reservoirs are summarized in Table 1. Seasonal flows and volumes were calculated with data for water year, 1984, collected and provided by the Bureau of Reclamation, the Army Corps of Engineers, and the U.S. Geological Survey. Different flow conditions occur during fall and spring. In the fall, inflows are low and reservoir volumes change slowly. During spring run off, inflows are higher and volumes can change rapidly.

TABLE 1 - Morphologic and Hydrologic Data for the Sampled New Mexico Reservoirs

Reservoir	Season	Volume, in 10^6 cubic meters	Area, in hectares	Inflow, in cubic meters per second	Outflow, in cubic meters per second	Retention time, in days	Mean depth, in meters	Areal water loading, in meters per day	Settling velocity, in meters per day	Sedimentation coefficient, in per day
Abiquiu	Fall	127.2	1154.7	6.5	7.1	209	11.1	0.05	0.15	0.013
	Spring	219.7	1581.1	55.1	50.6	50	13.9	0.28	0.40	0.029
Cochiti	Fall	56.8	471.8	20.3	17.3	38	11.2	0.29	0.42	0.035
	Spring	67.6	548.8	136.9	130.7	6	12.4	2.07	9.59	0.78
Caballo	Fall	52.2	1350.3	2.3	0.3	2457	3.9	0.002	0.02	0.006
	Spring	125.6	2450.7	56.5	42.6	34	5.2	0.15	0.28	0.06
Lake Sumner	Summer	10.0	315.5	14.2	15.8	7	3.2	0.46	1.12	0.35
	Spring	18.1	453.6	5.7	7.9	27	4.0	0.15	1.12	0.28

Note: 1 m^3=8.13 x 10^{-4} acre-ft; 1 ha=2.47 acres; 1 cms=35.3 cfs; 1 m=3.28 ft.

ORGINAL MODELS. - Publications from 14 previously published models were compared to mean measured concentrations of phosphorus in the 4 New Mexico reservoirs. Following the approach of Mueller (17) and Bachman and Canfield (1), correlation analysis was applied to the natural log transformations of measured and predicted concentrations (Table 2). The correlation coefficients range from 0.34 for a TVA model (10) to 0.85 for Bachman and Canfield's (1) reservoir model. The four models with the highest correlation coefficients overpredict measured phosphorus in New Mexico reservoirs (Fig. 2). This result differs from Mahamah and Bhagat's (16) study of NES data which indicated that previously published lake models tended to underestimate phosphorus concentration in Western lakes and reservoirs.

The discrepancy between the published-model predictions and measured values in the New Mexico reservoirs may be due to several factors. Certainly, for some of the models, the limitations described by Reckhow (18) are violated by the reservoir data. In

Table 2. - Model References and Correlation Coefficients for Natural-log Tranformations of Measured and Predicted Phosphorus.

Model	Reference	Pearson's r*
Bachman and Canfield	1 (reservoirs)	0.85
Chapra	2	0.40
Chapra and Reckhow	3	0.83
Dillon and Rigler	6	0.71
Higgins and Kim	10 (v_s = 92m/yr)	0.34
Higgins and Kim	10 (v_s = 61m/yr)	0.35
Jones and Bachman	11	0.67
Kircher and Dillon	13	0.50
Larsen and Mercier	14 (R = $\frac{11.73}{11.73+q_s}$)	0.43
Larsen and Mercier	14 (eqn.5)	0.82 (n=7)
Reckhow	18 (general model)	0.79
Reckhow	18 (q_s <50m/yr)	0.57
Reckhow	19	0.45
Vollenweider	22	0.44
Walker	20	0.85

*Values greater than 0.70 are significant at the p = 0.05 level.

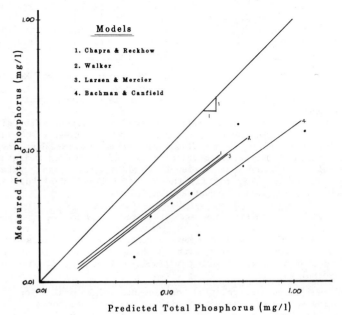

Fig. 2. - Best Fit Lines for the Four Best Literature Models (Plotted points are for Bachman and Canfield's Model Only)

some cases, the loadings are too high and the retention times are short. Compared to lakes, reservoirs often have higher settling rates (12) which are not reflected in the lake-calibrated models.

To further assess the validity of the models, regression slopes were checked to see if they differed significantly from one. Also, Leggett and William's (15) reliability index for models, K_g, was calculated. The K_g value can be looked at as the factor within which the models are predicting the measured values. The "fits" of the four models with the highest correlation coefficients are summarized in Table 3.

Table 3. - Measures of "Fit" for the Published Models

Model	Is the slope statistically different from 1? (p = 0.05 level)	Kg**	Pearson's r *
Bachman and Canfield	No	4.04	0.85
Chapra and Reckhow	No	2.49	0.83
Larsen and Mercier	No	2.36	0.82 (N=7)
Walker	No	2.67	0.85

*Values above 0.70 are significant at the p = 0.05 level.
**Kg values are ≥ 1. Values of 1 indicate a perfect fit between measured and predicted values.

The Bachman and Canfield (1) model is in the form of equation 1. The Walker (20) model has a depth- and time-dependent settling velocity and the other two models (3,14) are in the form of equation 3.

MODEL ADJUSTMENT. -- To calibrate the models to New Mexico reservoirs, the techniques used by Bachman and Canfield (1) and Reckhow (19) were followed. Bachman and Canfield solved equation 1 for the sedimentation coefficient, and established a procedure for estimating the sedimentation rate from morphologic and hydrologic data. For reservoirs, their best relationship was between σ and the volumetric loading rate (L/z) of phosphorus. Reckhow (19) solved equation 2 for settling velocity, v_s, and then used weighted least-squares to find v_s as a function of q_s, the areal water loading. His model does not fit the New Mexico data well but his approach is analogous to Bachman and Canfield's.

Correlation coefficients are presented in Table 4 for the sedimentation coefficient, σ, and settling velocity, v_s, versus several other variables in New Mexico reservoirs. The values of σ and v_s are highly correlated with flushing rate, ρ, areal water load, q_s, and with the loading variables, including loading of suspended solids.

Table 4. - Pearson's Correlation Coefficients for Natural - log Transformed Values of Reservoir Variables and the Phosphorus Sedimentation Coefficient, σ and the Settling Velocity, v_s *

Flushing rate,	Mean depth, z	Areal Loading Rate Of Phosphorus, L	Volumetric Loading Rate Of Phosphorus, L/z	Areal Water Loading, (z/τ)	Areal Loading of Suspended Solids
σ 0.90	-0.12	0.80	0.88	0.80	0.73
v_s 0.93	0.24	0.89	0.85	0.92	0.86
*Values above 0.70 are significant at the p=0.05 level					

Values for the sedimentation coefficient, σ, were calculated from equation 1. Regression of these values for σ with flushing rate and volumetric loading rate yielded the following relationships for New Mexico reservoirs:

$\sigma = 3.66 \, \rho^{0.807}$ based on flushing rate   r=0.818.........(4)
$\sigma = 12.8 \, (L/z)^{0.856}$ based on volumetric loading   r=0.779.........(5)

The same procedure was used for equation 2 to get an estimate of settling velocity, v_s. The following relationships were found for settling velocity in New Mexico reservoirs:

$v_s = 25.1 \, \rho^{0.845}$ based on flushing rate   r=0.860 ......(6)
$v_s = 5.79 \, q_s^{0.775}$ based on areal water load   r=0.853.......(7)

The power relationship for v_s fit New Mexico reservoir data much better than did the linear relationship used by Reckhow (19).

The calculated relationships for sedimentation coefficient and settling velocity were put into equation 1 and 2, respectively.

Using these removal rates in the models improves model prediction
(Fig. 3). The models no longer categorically overpredict. Of the
four adjusted models, the two using equations 6 and 7 for v_s
in equation 2 are better than those using equations 4 and 5 for σ
in equation 1. For equation 1, the sedimentation coefficient, σ as
a function of flushing rate gives better results than σ as a function
of volumetric loading rate of phosphorus.

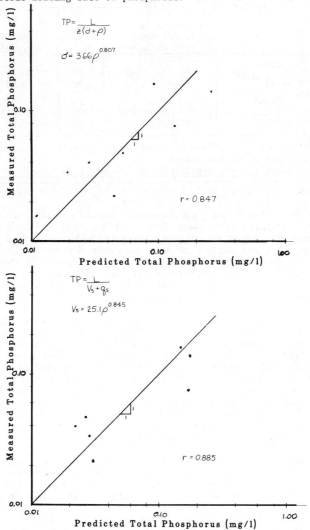

Fig. 3. - Plots of the Best Models for Equation 1 and 2 with
Adjusted Phosphorus Removal Rates

For the adjusted models, slopes of the regression of predicted values on measured values are not statistically different from 1 and the intercepts are not significantly different from zero ($p=0.05$ level). The "fits" of the adjusted models are summarized in Table 5.

Table 5. Measure of "Fit" for the Models with Adjusted Phosphorus Removal Rates.

Model	Is the slope statistically different from 1? ($p=0.05$ level)	Kg*	Pearson's r**
Eqn.1 with			
$\sigma = 3.66 \ \rho^{0.807}$	No	1.68	0.85
$\sigma = 12.8 \ (L/z)^{0.856}$	No	1.79	0.68
Eqn.2 with			
$v_s = 25.1 \ \rho^{0.845}$	No	1.55	0.88
$v_s = 5.79 \ q_s^{0.775}$	No	1.60	0.87

* Kg values are ≥ 1. Values of 1 indicate a perfect fit between measured and predicted values.
** Values above 0.7 are significant at the $p = 0.05$ level.

DISCUSSION

Overprediction by the lake-calibrated models probably reflects some basic differences between lakes and New Mexico reservoirs. Except when dam gates are closed, hydraulic retention times are relatively short and imply high flushing rates. The reservoirs all have bottom-draw outflows which counteract development of thermal stratification. Higher flushing rates in the models decrease phosphorus predictions but that alone is not sufficient to bring the predictions into line with measured values.

Jones and Bachman (12) found that reservoirs have higher average sedimentation rates than lakes. Accordingly, model predictions of phosphorus concentrations in New Mexico reservoirs were improved by adjusting the removal rates to reflect conditions in the reservoirs. Bachman and Canfield (1) suggested that one reason sedimentation rates are highly correlated with flushing rates is that large amounts of water moving through the lake contain something that increases phosphorus sedimentation—more specifically they proposed suspended solids. Particulate material entering the reservoir may combine with the phosphorus and carry it out of the water column as the particles settle.

A reasonable estimate of sedimentation rate or apparent settling velocity is a key to good model performance for reservoirs. All other model variables are fairly easy to measure. For New Mexico, flushing rate, ρ, is the variable most highly correlated with the areal loading of suspended solids. This result supports Jones and Bachman's (1) idea that phosphorus is more quickly removed from the water column in conjunction with higher loads of sediment.

As shown by the fitted models, providing a good estimate of the term representing water-column losses of phosphorus was the key to having the previously published literature models predict accurately. Flushing rate appears to be the key variable that indirectly regulates settling velocity and sedimentation rates as well as the sediment loads which may directly control the high rate of phosphorus removal from the water-column in reservoirs.

Several studies (1,10,12,17) have indicated that reservoirs have unique characteristics that limit the applicability of the lake calibrated models. More work needs to be done on reservoirs to clarify the water-column phosphorus removal processes. Assuming the hydrologic and morphologic variables can be adequately measured, mass-balance model performance depends on accurate estimates of water-column phosphorus removal rates. This paper demonstrates that a seasonal approach is appropriate in order to limit violation of the steady-state assumption and that estimates of removal rates specific to reservoirs improves model prediction.

ACKNOWLEDGMENT. The authors wish to thank the New Mexico Department of Game and Fish, the New Mexico Water Resources Research Institute, and the New Mexic Interstate Stream Commission for funding research upon which this paper is based.

APPENDIX I.-REFERENCES

1. Bachman, R.W. and Canfield, Jr., D.E., "Role of Sedimentation in the Phosphorus Budget of Natural and Artificial Iowa Lakes, Completion Report No. 97, Iowa State Water Resources Research Institute, Ames, Iowa, 1979.

2. Chapra, S.C., "Comment on 'An Empirical Method of Estimating Retention of Phosphorus in Lakes' by W.B. Kirchner and P.J. Dillon," Water Resources Research, Vol. 11, No. 6, Dec., 1975, pp. 1033-1034.

3. Chapra, S.C. and Reckhow, K.H., "Expressing the Phosphorus Loading Concept in Probabilistic Terms," Journal of the Fisheries Research Board of Canada, Vol. 36, No. 2, Feb., 1979, pp. 225-229.

4. Dillon, P.J., "A Critical Review of Vollenweider's Nutrient Budget Model and Other Related Models," Water Resources Bulletin, Vol. 10, No. 5, Oct., 1974, pp. 969-989.

5. Dillon, P.J. and Kirchner, W.B., "Reply," Water Resources Research, Vol. 11, No. 6, Dec., 1975, pp. 1035-1036.

6. Dillon, P.J. and Rigler, F.H., "A Test of a Simple Nutrient Budget Model Predicting the Phosphorus Concentration in Lake Water," Journal of the Fisheries Research Board of Canada, Vol. 31, No.11, 1974, pp. 1771-1778.

7. Environmental Protection Agency, "A Compendium of Lake and Reservoir Data Collected by the National Eutrophication Survey in the Western United States," Working Paper No. 477, United States Environmental Protection Agency, National Eutrophication Survey, Corvallis, Oregon, Sept. 1978

8. Environmental Protection Agency, "Methods for Chemical Analysis of Water and Waste," EPA-600/4-79-020, Environmental Monitoring and Support Laboratory, Cincinnati, Ohio, 1979.

9. Hern, S.C. Lambou, V.W. and Williams, L.R., "Comparisons of Models Predicting Ambient Lake Phosphorus Concentrations," EPA-600/3-79-012, Environmental Protection Agency, Las Vegas, Nev., Feb., 1979, pp.2-10.

10. Higgins, J.M. and Kim, B.R., "Phosphorus Retention Models for Tennessee Valley Authority Reservoirs," Water Resources Research, Vol. 17, No. 3, June, 1981, pp. 571-576.

11. Jones, J.R. and Bachman, R.W., "Prediction of Phosphorus and Chlorophyll Levels in Lakes," Journal of the Water Pollution Control Federation, Vol. 48, No. 9, Sept., 1976, pp. 2176-2182.

12. Jones, J.R. and Bachman, R.W., "Phosphorus Removal by Sedimentation in some Iowa Reservoirs," Verhandlungen Internationale Vereinigung fur Theoretische und Angewandte Limnologie, Stuttgart, Germany, Vol. 20, Nov., 1978, pp. 1576-1580.

13. Kirchner, W.B. and Dillon, P.J., "An Empirical Method of Estimating the Retention of Phosphorus in Lakes," Water Resources Research, Vol. 11, No. 1, Jan., 1975, pp. 182-183.

14. Larsen, D.P. and Mercier, H.T., "Phosphorus Retention Capacity of Lakes," Journal of the Fisheries Research Board of Canada, Vol. 33, No. 8, Aug., 1976, pp. 1742-1750.

15. Leggett, R.W. and Williams, L.R., "A Reliability Index for Models," Ecological Modelling, Vol. 13, No. 4, Sept., 1981, pp. 303-312.

16. Mahamah, D.S. and Bhagat, S.K., "Performance of some Empirical Phosphorus Models," Journal of the Environmental Engineering Division, ASCE, Vol. 108, No. EE4, 1982, pp. 722-729.

17. Mueller, D.K., "Mass Balance Model Estimations of Phosphorus Concentration in Reservoirs," Aquatic Resources Management of the Colorado River Ecosystem, V.D. Adams and V.A. Lamarra, eds., 1st ed. Ann Arbor Science Publishers, Inc., Ann Arbor, Mich., 1983, pp. 71-90.

18. Reckhow, K.H., "Empirical Lake Models for Phosphorus: Development, Applications, Limitation, and Uncertainty," Perspectives on Lake Ecosystem Modeling, D. Scavia and A. Robertson, eds., 1st ed., Ann Arbor Science Publishers, Inc., Ann Arbor, Mich., 1979, pp. 193-222.

19. Reckhow, K.H., "Uncertainty Analysis Applied to Vollenweider's Phosphorus Loading Criteria," Journal of the Water Pollution Control Federation, Vol 51, No. 8, Aug., 1979, pp. 2123-2127.

20. Reckhow, K.H. and Chapra, S.C., Engineering Approaches for Lake Management, 1st ed., Vol. 1, Butterworth Publishers, Woburn, Mass., 1983.

21. Tapp, J.S., "Eutrophication Analysis with Simple and Complex Models," Journal of the Water Pollution Control Federation, Vol. 50, No. 3, March, 1978, pp. 484-493.

22. Vollenweider, R.A., "Input-Output Models with Special Reference to the Phosphorus Loading Concept in Limnology," Schweizerische Zeitschrift fur Hydrologie, Switzerland, Vol. 37, No. 1, Jan., 1975, pp. 53-84.

23. Ward, T.J., Cole, R.A., Ward, F.A., Turner, P.R., and Sabol, G.V., "Modeling the Rio Grande River System in New Mexico for Economic and Social Trade-offs: An Overview of a Current Study," Analysis of Ecological Systems: State-of-the-Art in Ecological Modeling, W. K. Laueroth, G.V. New York, N.Y., 1983, pp. 781-786.

A Riverine Toxic Spill Model

Roland C. Steiner, M.ASCE, Brian A. Spielmann
and Daniel P. Sheer, M.ASCE[1]

Abstract

In the event of a spill of toxic material reaching the main stem of the Potomac River, predictive information regarding its location and concentration would aid in the minimization of its effects on water utilities, industry and the environment. Useful tools for providing that information are developed as a time of travel and dispersion model and a wave travel model. The models may be applied to actual or practice situations, and may be used to provide information for other purposes.

Introduction

The Potomac river provides an increasing proportion of the water supply for the Washington, D.C. metropolitan area (WMA). The drainage area upstream of the intakes for the water supply utilities in the WMA is moderately large: 11,000 sq miles (28,490 km^2). Ample opportunities exist for accidental spills of toxic material to quickly reach the river or one of its tributaries. The risk of an accident is real -- at least one potentially dangerous spill has reached the river in recent years (2). In the event of a toxic spill, some means of estimating the fate of that material in the river is vital to industrial and water utility managers who use the river as a source of supply. The Interstate Commission on the Potomac River Basin has developed a response plan for emergency use in such cases. This plan establishes of a riverine toxic spill management center. Estimated times of travel and concentrations would be produced for the spill at critical points along the river, e.g. water utility and industrial intakes. A large release can be made from an upstream reservoir in order to move the pollutant more quickly past an intake. Mathematical models of travel time and dispersion have been developed for both particle and wave motion.

[1] Respectively: Systems Planning Engineer, Intern, and Director of CO-OP Section, Interstate Commission on the Potomac River Basin, 6110 Executive Boulevard, Suite 300, Rockville, Maryland 20852

Spill Management Response Outline

A procedure for managing the aftermath of a toxic spill has been developed. It provides a conceptual framework for alerting all concerned agencies and minimizing the potential harmful effects. It includes provisions for employing both the spill model and the wave model as discussed below. The spill should be tagged with a substance which can be easily tracked, and clean-up or neutralizing procedures should be implemented. In addition, the cause and management of a spill incident should be documented in a report which includes conclusions and recommendations.

Outline

1. Receive notification of spill into water course:
   Date, time, location, duration and amount of spill, and river flow.

2. Set up Spill Management Information Center.

3. Run Spill Model:
   Is spill a problem to water utilities?
   Consult reference material on toxicity limits and remedial action.

4. Notify concerned agencies:
   Water utilities, industrial abstractors, state emergency management and civil defense agencies, state Depts of Health and Natural Resources, state police, USEPA, National Spill Alert Center, U.S. Geological Survey, state geological surveys.

5. Tag the spill with a readily identifiable tracer.

6. Initiate clean-up and/or neutralization.

7. Run Wave Model:
   If appropriate, schedule a release.

8. Monitor the river in order to track the spill and wave:
   Update the model runs.

9. Provide continuing coordination and advice to agencies.

10. Determine and notify when danger has passed.

11. Determine cause of spill.

12. Produce documentation:
    Cause and behavior of spill, response efforts, resulting effects, conclusions and recommendations.

Spill Model

A mathematical model has been developed to simulate the behavior of a slug of soluble material as it travels down the Potomac river system. The model is based on dye studies conducted by the U.S. Geological Survey. It is calibrated for the main stem of the river and several of its major tributaries.

Two dye studies were conducted on the main stem at flows with exceedence probabilities of 60 percent and 90 percent respectively (2). These studies covered the lower end of the flow spectrum and produced data which are useful in determining the time of travel and dispersion characteristics of a soluble substance moving down the river. Those data provide the basis for developing the functional relationships to be reflected in the spill simulation model.

For the purpose of the dye studies, the river was divided into a small number of sub-reaches between Cumberland, Maryland and Washington, D.C.. Rhodamine dye was introduced to the river at the top of each of the sub-reaches. It was subsequently monitored by fluorometer analysis at several cross-sections. The time of travel and the dispersive effect of the river motion is evident in the data from the studies. The peak concentration of the dye cloud was reduced and its duration was increased as it moved downstream. The degree of these transport effects varies from place to place along the river and depends on the magnitude of flow. The model is based on routing unit peak concentrations through each of the sub-reaches. Thus, by proportional transformation, any concentration of a pollutant can be represented.

The time, date and location of a spill are the principal data required by the model. In order to estimate the resulting concentrations at up to three destination points downstream, their location, the rate of flow in the river, and the duration and amount of spilled material must be known or estimated. The model is written in Fortran and operates in an interactive mode where a screen display prompts the user for values of the required parameters.

As results, the model provides the velocity of the peak concentration in the pollutant cloud. Additionally, the travel time of the leading edge and trailing edge, and hourly concentrations of pollutant are given for the specified destination points. All the results are annotated and provided in a format which is easy to read and understand. They are preserved in a magnetic disk file which can be viewed on a monitor screen or directed to a line printer for hard copy.

Wave Model

One of the effects of a pollutant traveling down a river is the reluctance by industrial and utility managers to withdraw the affected water. One possible way of reducing the inconvenience of closing an intake would be to arrange for a release to increase the velocity of flow when the pollutant is in the vicinity. Such a release could be made from an upstream reservoir. A wave moves down a river channel faster than the water molecules which compose it. That is, water enters the wave at its leading edge, rises in the wave and passes out the trailing edge to be part of the flow after the wave has passed. The velocity in the river at any point along its length increases during the passage of the wave.

A mathematical model has been developed to simulate the hydraulic behavior of a release from an upstream reservoir. The duration of a cloud of pollutant at a downstream intake is inversely proportional to the velocity in the river, which in turn is directly proportional to the depth of flow. Therefore, if a wave can be produced to pass a critical intake when a pollutant cloud is causing a shut-down, the period of that shut-down may be reduced. The reduction factor for the time it takes a pollutant to pass a point is equal to the ratio of velocities of the lower and higher flows respectively.

The model requires stage-discharge relations, sub-reach lengths and channel widths at gage sites. From present stage data the model computes the underlying velocity of the river at each of several gage sites. The celerity of the wave is directly proportional to this underlying velocity [1].

$$c = 1.5v_1$$

where: c = celerity (velocity) of wave
v_1 = underlying velocity in the river

Thus, the timing of the wave can be readily computed. However, it is the velocity of the water which reduces the duration of the pollutant cloud. Computation of the velocity of water in the wave requires values for width of channel and stage at the point of interest. The rate of flow is determined from stage-discharge rating tables.

$$v_2 = \frac{q_2}{wh_2}$$

where: v_2 = velocity of water particles in the wave
q_2 = discharge at stage h_2
w = width of channel
h_2 = river stage of wave

Data derived from wave travel studies are used to route stage in preference to theoretical methods. The wave model operates in a manner similar to the spill model in that it interactively prompts the user for input data and provides annotated results. Those results include wave celerity, time of travel and the reduction factor for the time it would take a pollutant cloud to pass. Trombley (3) developed a model based on mean flow and other parameters.

Fortunately, the Potomac River intakes of the water utilities in the WMA are concentrated in an eight mile stretch of the channel. The reservoirs which might provide a release wave are located on a small tributary just a few miles upstream of the intakes, and at 200 miles (320 km) upstream.

Applications

This response plan has obvious applications in the event of an accidental spill or act of sabotage. The models can provide information useful to the operation and temporary shut-down of water supply intakes or for other purposes. In addition, the plan could be a valuable tool for use in conducting spill readiness practice exercises. The methodology developed in the Potomac River basin is transferable to other river basins.

APPENDIX I. -- References

1. Linsley, R.K., Kohler, M.A., and Paulhus J.L.H., Hydrology for Engineers, McGraw-Hill Book Co., New York, 1958, pp. 216-219.

2. Taylor, K.R., James, R.W.Jr., and Helinsky, B.M., "Traveltime and Dispersion in the Potomac River, Cumberland, Maryland, to Washington, D.C.", Open-File Report 83-861, U.S. Geological Survey, Towson, Maryland, 1984.

3. Trombley, Thomas J., "Downstream Effects of Reservoir Releases to the Potomac River from Luke, Maryland to Washington, D.C.", Water-Resources Investigations Report 82-4062, U.S. Geological Survey, Towson, Maryland, 1982.

APPENDIX II. -- Notation

The following symbols are used in this paper:
  c = celerity (velocity) of wave;
  h_2 = river stage (height) of wave;
  q_2 = discharge at stage h_2;
  v_1 = underlying water particle velocity in the river;
  v_2 = water particle velocity in the wave;
  w = width of channel (assumed constant)

Use of a Two-Dimensional Flow Model to Quantify Aquatic Habitat
by
D. Michael Gee[1] and Daniel B. Wilcox[2]

Introduction

This paper describes the use of a numerical two-dimensional flow
model to evaluate the impacts of potential hydropower retrofits on
downstream flow distributions at Lock and Dam No. 8 (Fig. 1) on the
upper Mississippi River. The model used (RMA-2 (6)) solves the
complete Reynolds equations for two-dimensional free-surface flow in
the horizontal plane using a finite element solution scheme. RMA-2
has been in continuing use and development at the Hydrologic
Engineering Center and elsewhere for the past decade (2,3,4,5).
Although designed primarily for the simulation of hydraulic
conditions, RMA-2 may be used in conjunction with related numerical
models to simulate sediment transport and water quality (5,7). In
this study, velocity distributions were evaluated with regard to
environmental, navigational and small-boat safety considerations.
Aquatic habitat was defined by depth, substrate type and current
velocity. Habitat types were quantified by measuring the areas
between calculated contours of velocity magnitude (isotachs) for
existing and project conditions. The capability for computing and
displaying isotachs for the depth-average velocity, velocity one
foot from the bottom and near the water surface was developed for
this study. The product of this study effort is an application of
the RMA-2 model that allows prediction of structural aquatic habitat
in hydraulically complex locations. Elements of the instream flow
group methodology (1) could be incorporated to provide detailed
predictions of impacts to habitat quality.

Calibration of the numerical model to field measurements of
velocity magnitude and direction is also described.

Project Description:

Lock and Dam No. 8 is located on the upper Mississippi River
679.2 river miles (1094 km) above the mouth of the Ohio River, 23.3
miles (37.5km) below Lock and Dam No. 7, and 31.3 river miles

---

[1] Chief, Computer Support Center
The Hydrologic Engineering Center
U.S. Army Corps of Engineers
609 Second Street
Davis, California

[2] Fisheries Biologist
St. Paul District, U.S. Army Corps of Engineers
St. Paul, Minnesota

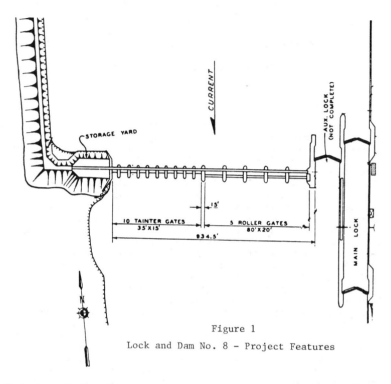

Figure 1

Lock and Dam No. 8 - Project Features

(50.4km) above Lock and Dam No. 9. The lock is on the left bank, or Wisconsin side of the river 0.3 miles (0.5 km) below the village of Genoa, Wisconsin, which is on State Highway No. 35, 17 miles (27 km) south of the City of La Crosse, Wisconsin.

The main lock is 110 feet (33.6 m) wide and 600 feet (182 m) long, and the upper gate bay of an auxiliary lock is provided in the event it becomes necessary to add another lock in the future. From the river wall of the auxiliary lock, a movable dam section consisting of five roller gates, 20 feet (6.1 m) x 80 feet (24.4 m), and 10 tainter gates, 15 feet (4.6 m) x 35 feet (10.7 m), extends across the main channel to the right bank of the river.

Hydropower installations were being considered by the Corps of Engineers for the storage yard at the west abutment or in the auxiliary lock location. In addition to the Corps plans, privately funded installation of floating powerplants, "hydrobarges", is being considered for some of the roller gate bays.

Network Development:

A key component of the successful application of RMA-2 is the development of a well designed finite element network that accurately

represents flow boundaries, bottom topography, inflow and outflow
locations, and contains enough detail to resolve flow patterns of
interest. A study area was selected extending from the downstream
face of the dam downstream approximately 2.2 miles (3.5 km). The
downstream boundary was set at approximately river mile 677 (km
1090). This location was judged to be sufficiently far downstream
from the dam that differing flow distributions at the structure,
representing the different project configurations, would not affect
the water surface elevation (assumed horizontal) at the boundary.

Bathymetry for the study reach was provided at 1:2400 map scale
with a 5 ft. (1.5 m) contour interval. A finite element network was
constructed to define the study area with adequate detail at the dam
face to distinguish releases from individual spillway bays. Several
wing dams and training structures within the study reach are
reflected in the network as well as a large island in the lower half
of the reach (Fig. 2). Curved-sided elements were used along lateral
flow boundaries to allow for smooth tangential flows at the sides
(slip flow boundary conditions). The network was revised somewhat
during calibration. The final network consisted of 375 elements and
1,189 nodes. Both triangular and quadrilateral elements were used.

Boundary Conditions:

Boundary condition selection was straightforward for this study.
Releases from the spillway bays and/or powerplants were described as
flows. The downstream boundary condition was a specified water
surface elevation, assumed horizontal across the river. That
elevation was varied, depending upon the flow magnitude, based upon
information provided by the St. Paul District. Lateral boundaries
were generally "slip" conditions which allow flow parallel to the
boundary. In some cases where sharp corners exist on the boundary a
zero velocity was specified (stagnation point boundary condition).
All simulations assumed steady flow, although RMA-2 can readily be
used to simulate unsteady flow problems as well.

Calibration:

An essential ingredient to any modeling effort, be it physical
or numerical, is calibration of various model parameters or
coefficients such that model results acceptably reproduce prototype
observations. The parameters available for calibration of RMA-2 are
bottom roughness and turbulent exchange coefficients. Calibration
strategy typically consists of estimation of bottom roughness values
(based upon knowledge of bed material) followed by adjustment to
reproduce prototype head loss within the study reach. Turbulent
exchange coefficients are then adjusted to reproduce details of
prototype velocity distributions. Thus, it is desirable to have
prototype measurements of velocity (magnitude and direction).

Velocity measurements were obtained at ten transects in the
study reach. Coverage was very good consisting of up to five point
measurements at each of up to ten locations across each transect.
This calibration data set was obtained during the period 15-16
August 1984 at a river flow of 25,400 cfs (711 m³/sec) using a

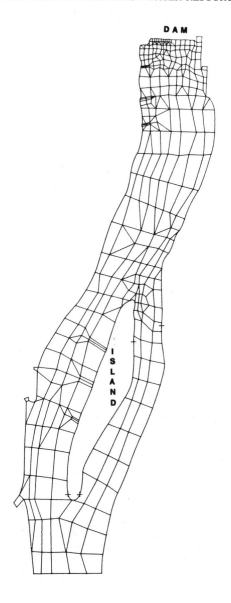

Figure 2
Finite Element Network - Flow is from Top to Bottom

Price Meter. Although the Price meter only yields directional
information for near-surface measurements, these directions were
assumed to apply to the entire water column at each point.

Based upon these velocity measurements, roughness coefficients
were adjusted to match the flow distribution around the island
indicated by the data; approximately 65% to the west, 35% to the
east. Additionally, the transverse velocity distributions at
certain transects were not symmetric, with lower velocities on the
right (west) side than on the left. This did not appear to be
entirely due to the presence of the right bank wing dams, therefore,
the bottom roughness was increased along the right side of the
channel from the wing dams to about the head of the island to
reproduce the skewed velocity distributions (see Figure 3).
Roughness used, in terms of Manning n-values, varied from 0.030 to
0.060.

The turbulent exchange coefficients were set at 25 pound-second/
feet² (120 kg-sec/m²) for small elements and 50 pound-second/
feet² (240 kg-sec/m²) for all others. This set of coefficients
and network yielded well-behaved numerical solutions that generally
converged in four iterations. Internal continuity checks, an
indicator of network adequacy, were generally within ± 5%.

Calibration of a numerical two-dimensional flow model such as
RMA-2 is a judgmental process. That is, no objective, or statistical, measures of error between measured and simulated velocities or
water surface elevations are used. In this study, plots of velocity
vectors (observed and simulated) were examined visually.
Coefficients were then adjusted until, in the judgment of the
modeler, an acceptable balance was achieved between reproduction of
the measurements and physically realistic coefficient values. Some
network modifications were made. Additional detail was added in some
areas to better reproduce observed velocity gradients. A portion of
the simulated and measured flow fields is shown in Figure 3.

Production Simulations:

All project (i.e., hydropower) simulations were made in
conjunction with a corresponding existing (i.e., no hydropower)
condition simulation. Thus, project impacts are defined as
differences between project and existing conditions. Approximately
25 different conditions were analyzed.

Results of the numerical simulations were presented in the
following formats for further analysis:

1. Plots of velocity vectors approximately one foot (0.3 m)
    above the bottom.

2. Plots of velocity vectors near the water surface.

3. Plots of velocity vectors of vertically averaged velocity
    (the model output).

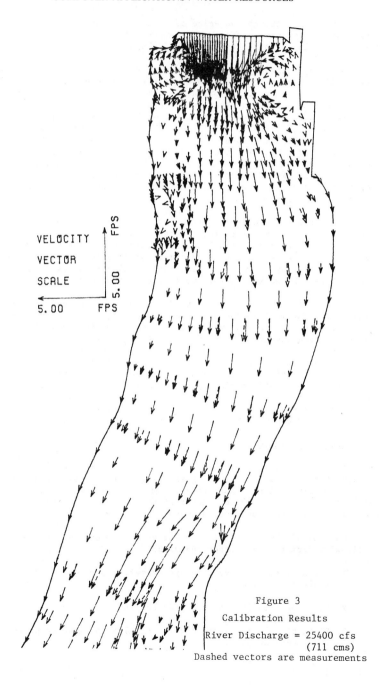

Figure 3

Calibration Results

River Discharge = 25400 cfs
(711 cms)
Dashed vectors are measurements

4. Isotachs (i.e., contours of equal velocity magnitude) one
   foot (0.3 m) above the bottom.

5. Isotachs near the surface.

6. Pathline plots depicting paths taken by particles traveling at
   the vertically-averaged velocity released at various points.

These plots are not reproduced herein in their entirety due to
space limitations; examples of the above graphical displays are
shown in Figures 4-6.

The velocities near the bottom and surface were estimated from
the computed vertically-averaged velocity by fitting a classic
logarithmic velocity profile at each point.

Interpretation of Results

Riverine habitat types, defined by substrate type, depth, and
current velocity, vary in areal extent and distribution with river
discharge. The location and extent of habitats in the tailwater of
lock and dam 8 were quantified using the model simulations of current
velocity at one foot above the bottom. Model results indicate that
hydropower operation would affect the pattern of habitat types only
within 2,000 feet (610 m) of the dam. The greatest net change in
aquatic habitat between existing and with-project conditions would
occur at the lowest river discharges. Model results indicate that
hydropower operation would cause little disruption of habitat types
and fish distribution during the high discharge period in spring
when saugers, walleyes, and anglers congregate below the dam.

An analysis similar to that used to quantify aquatic habitat at
lock and dam 8 could be used to evaluate effects of hydropower
operation on navigation, by employing simulations of surface
currents.

Conclusions

The application of RMA-2 described herein represents a new use
of the model that had previously been used for hydraulic, water
quality, and sediment transport studies. The importance of graphics
post processors for interpretation of the results of two-dimensional
flow simulations is highlighted in this study. The methods of
extracting meaningful information from simulated flow fields
illustrated herein should prove valuable for habitat evaluation in
general.

Acknowledgements

This study was performed for and sponsored by the U.S. Army
Corps of Engineer District, St. Paul. We wish to thank Tom McAloon
of the St. Paul District for much of the data preparation and
assistance with the numerical simulations. The opinions expressed
herein are those of the authors and not necessarily those of the
U.S. Army Corps of Engineers.

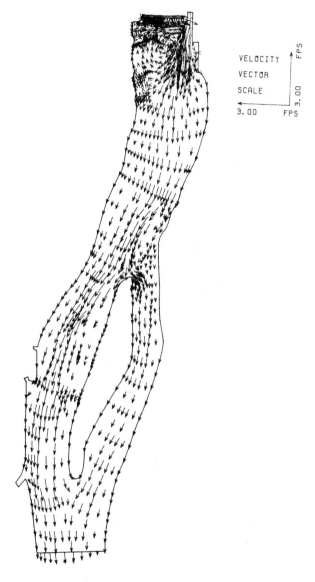

VELOCITY
VECTOR
SCALE

3.00   FPS

Figure 4   Example Vector Plot

Spillway Discharge = 3000 cfs (84 cms)
Powerplant Discharge = 7000 cfs (196 cms)
(located in auxiliary lock)

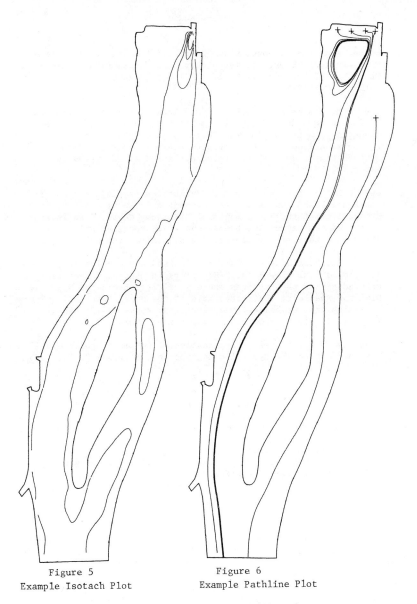

Figure 5
Example Isotach Plot

Figure 6
Example Pathline Plot

Spillway Discharge = 3000 cfs (84 cms)
Powerplant Discharge = 7000 cfs (196 cms)
(located in auxiliary lock)

References

1. Bovee, K.D. and Milhous, R.T.,"Hydraulic Simulation in Instream
    Flow Studies: Theory and Techniques." Instream Flow Information
    Paper No. 5, Cooperative Instream Flow Service Group, Ft.
    Collins, CO, 1978.

2. Gee, D.M. and MacArthur, R.C., "Development of Generalized Free
    Surface Flow Models Using Finite Element Techniques," Finite
    Elements in Water Resources; Proceedings of the Second
    International Conference on Finite Elements in Water Resources,
    Pentech Press, July 1978. (Also published as HEC Technical
    Paper No. 53.)

3. Gee, D.M. and MacArthur, R.C., "Evaluation and Application of
    the Generalized Finite Element Hydrodynamic Model RMA-2,"
    Proceedings of the First National U.S. Army Corps of Engineers-
    Sponsored Seminar on Two-Dimensional Flow Modeling held at The
    Hydrologic Engineering Center, Davis, California, July 7-9, 1981.

4. Gee, D.M., "Calibration, Verification and Application of a
    Two-Dimensional Flow Model," Frontiers in Hydraulic Engineering,
    Proceedings of the American Society of Civil Engineers Hydraulics
    Division Specialty Conference held at the Massachusetts Institute
    of Technology, Cambridge, Massachusetts, August 9-12, 1983.
    (Also published as HEC Technical Paper No. 90)

5. McAnally, W.H., et. al., "Application of Columbia Hybrid Modeling
    System," Journal of Hydraulic Engineering, American Society of
    Civil Engineers, Vol. 110, No. 5, May 1984, pp. 627-642.

6. Norton, W.R. and King, I.P., "User's Guide and Operating
    Instructions for The Computer Program RMA-2," report to The
    Sacramento District, U.S. Army Corps of Engineers, Resource
    Management Associates, December 1976.

7. U.S. Army Engineer District, San Francisco, "Numerical Simulation
    of the Circulation and Water Quality within Fisherman's Wharf
    Harbor," August 1984, at press.

HYDRAULIC PROFILE COMPUTATION USING CADD

Stanley E. Johnson, P.E.*
Member ASCE

ABSTRACT
The data preparation to perform hydraulic profile calculations using a computer program, such as the Corps of Engineers' HEC-2 step-backwater computer program, has traditionally been done by hand. Aerial surveyed cross section ground points and field survey data are plotted as cross sections and then combined with field reconnaissance Manning "n" values. This data is ordered into the necessary coding format on computer input forms and then entered into a computer file ready to be run with the computer program.

The data preparation can also be performed by directly recording onto a computer tape the aerial survey cross section ground points and the field survey work. A computer program can then check the data for errors, reduce the field notes, and transfer all information to the computer-aided design and drafting (CADD) system. The CADD system can combine the appropriate cross section ground points and soundings, enlarge parts of cross sections, superimpose cross sections, and calculate bridge opening areas. A hard copy can be obtained of any of the items viewed on the screen and reviewed by an engineer for modifications or simplification of the data. The marked-up copy can then be used to modify the CADD computer file. The modified file is then processed into a computer file ready to be run with the hydraulic profile computer program.

This method of utilizing the computer and CADD system results in significant savings in time and money.

INTRODUCTION
The ability to determine water surface profiles along natural channels has been of interest to hydraulicians for a long time. Since the eighteenth century, hydraulicians have worked on developing the theory of gradually varied flow to make this determination (Reference 1). By making several basic assumptions, the main one being that the head loss at a section is the same as for a uniform flow having the velocity and hydraulic radius of that section, a differential equation for gradually varied flow was developed. The computation of the gradually varied flow basically involves the solution of the differential equation for gradually varied flow.

*Chief Engineer, Burgess & Niple, Limited, 5085 Reed Road, Columbus, Ohio 43220

Broadly classified, there are three methods of computation: the graphical-integration method, the direct-integration method, and the standard step method. Each method has advantages and disadvantages, but the standard step method is best suited for natural channels. It is generally necessary to conduct a field survey to collect data at all sections considered in the computation. With the distance between sections given, the computation is carried out by a set of mathematical steps from section to section where the hydraulic characteristics have been determined. This procedure results in a determination of the depth of flow at each section by trial and error.

The effort in obtaining a solution by trial and error through hand calculation was significantly reduced with the advance of calculators and is now further expedited by the use of computers. The Corps of Engineers (COE) has developed the computer program 723-X6-2202A HEC-2 Water Surface Profiles (Reference 2) which is widely accepted and currently used to calculate water surface profiles. The data entered into the program is usually done by hand. However, with the aid of a CADD system, the data can be processed with a minimum of hand transfer of data, resulting in an efficient and cost-effective method of obtaining water surface profile results.

WATER SURFACE PROFILE INPUT

The present trend in obtaining cross section data for determining water surface profiles is to collect the data by photogrammetric methods in conjunction with field survey methods. The photogrammetric service can provide computer tapes of the cross section data or actual plots of the cross section.

Figure 1 shows the typical steps used in preparing data for the HEC-2 computer program to calculate water surface profiles. In preparing the data for the program, it is necessary to determine the area to be studied; layout the cross sections; obtain aerial and field data of the cross sections, roadway profiles, and bridge openings; assign roughness coefficients; determine the distances between sections; and order all the preceding into the computer program via computer input forms.

As shown in the figure, the following steps require hand manipulation of the data as it is ordered into the necessary coding format onto computer forms and then entered into a computer file ready to be run with the computer program.

1. Assign Manning's "n" value
2. Determine flow length between cross sections
3. Combine and plot field and aerial roadway/bridge data
4. Combine and plot field and aerial cross section data
5. Eliminate ineffective flow areas on the cross section plot
6. Identify ground points where roughness changes on the cross section plot
7. Identify bank stations on the cross section plot
8. Reduce the number of points on the cross section plot
9. Determine equivalent geometry for the bridge opening plot
10. Align the roadway/bridge opening plot with adjacent sections and identify common station points

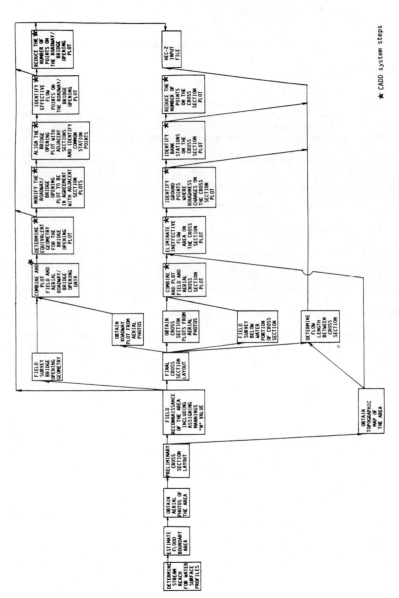

Figure 1 - Steps in Preparing HEC-2 Computer Data

★ CADD system steps

11. Modify the roadway/bridge opening plot to be in agreement with adjacent section plots

12. Identify effective flow points on the roadway/bridge opening plot

13. Reduce the number of points on the roadway/bridge opening plot

CADD DEVELOPMENT

The CADD system provides an alternative method of preparing some of the data traditionally done by hand for the HEC-2 computer program. The steps using the CADD system are indicated in Figure 1 with an asterisk. The CADD system requires as input the aerial data, consisting of cross sections and roadway profiles, and the field survey of the below water portion of the cross section and the bridge opening geometry.

Four computer programs were developed to eliminate hand manipulation of the data (References 3, 4, 5, and 6). The programs designed to check, reduce, and process the aerial and field data into the CADD system are Ground and Bridge Points Check (GRBTCHK), Field Note Reduction (FNOTE), and Final Section Plot (FSEC). These programs are written in Fortran IV computer language. The program developed to transfer final aerial and field data from the CADD system to a HEC-2 input format is the Flood Insurance Study Version 10 (FIS10.XBA). This program is written in BASIC language.

The programs were designed for a system consisting of a Prime 550 mainframe with 2 megabytes main memory and 460 megabytes of disk storage and a Tektronix 4114 graphic terminal with tablet digitizer and tablet controller using McAuto's Graphic Design System.

The GRBTCHK program checks and displays the aerial data. The section or roadway profile data, consisting of geometry points identified as station and elevation, is displayed for each section or roadway profile on the CRT for a visual check for any obvious errors. If a station value does not increase, the computer displays an error message. The number of geometry points for each section or roadway profile is also displayed. By this visual inspection of the data, the aerial data is quickly verified for reasonableness.

The FNOTE program allows unreduced field survey data of below water portions of the cross section and bridge opening geometry to be coded directly from the field book to a data file. The data identification is the same as used for the aerial data. The data is entered for each section assuming only one field survey setup of the level and with individual ground points entered as distances and rod readings. An output file is generated that contains the reduced field survey data which is then used as input to the FSEC program.

The FSEC program is used in conjunction with the CADD system to plot the aerial and field data. The FSEC program takes aerial data and data from the FNOTE program and creates a file which contains instructions allowing the CADD system to draft the plots. The plots are used as a basis for all further CADD work.

A CADD operator can then display on the screen all the aerial and field data and combine the appropriate aerial and field sections requested by the hydrologist to be combined. Once the data is combined, an 8 1/2" x 11" copy can be made from the Tektronix copier for marking any changes or call-outs. A copy can be made of a whole section; an enlarged part of a section, such as the channel or bridge opening geometry; or any superimposed adjacent sections, such as at bridges. The copies of whole sections may not be scalable with an engineer's scale. The enlarged copies can be made to be scalable with an engineer's scale and are all at the same scale. Each data point is visibly marked. The area of a bridge opening is given by the computer. Figure 2 shows an aerial cross section combined with the appropriate below water field section.

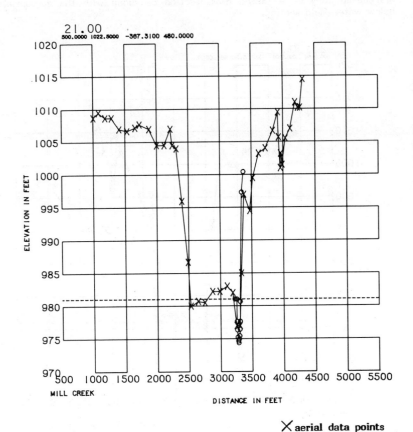

X aerial data points
o field data points

Figure 2 - Initial Cross Section

The hard copies are given to a hydrologist for review. By using a topographic map along with the copies, ineffective flow areas can be eliminated. The correct representation can be designated on the copy. The cross section can be marked to indicate where roughness changes and to show locations of the bank stations. Any unnecessary points can then be eliminated. The marked-up copy thus shows the final points from the aerial and field data and the additional points marked by the hydrologist for roughness changes, bank stations, or ineffective flow areas. For roadway crossings, the hydrologist can see that the roadway profile points coincide with the adjacent cross section, identify the points to define artificial levees for the effective flow option at bridges, and eliminate any unnecessary points. Figure 3 shows a final marked-up copy of an aerial cross section combined with the appropriate below water field section.

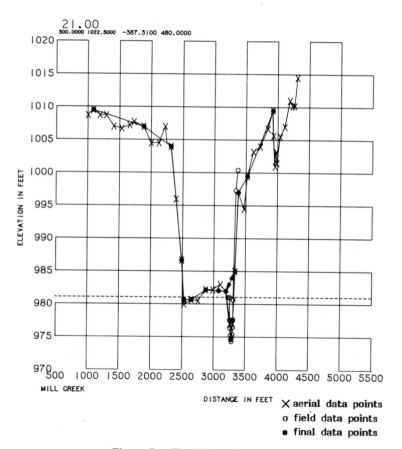

X aerial data points
o field data points
● final data points

Figure 3 - Final Cross Section

The marked-up copies are then returned to the CADD operator so that changes can be made to the data in the CADD system. This can be done visually by the operator. The original points are not destroyed, but the final points use a different recognizable symbol. Once the changes are completed, a new hard copy is made. This provides the hydrologist with a final check of the data.

Upon the hydrologist's approval of the plots, the FIS10.XBA program extracts the final data and puts it in the computer file format for the HEC-2 program. The file indicates by using HEC-2 terminology what other data needs to be included, such as flow length between sections, roughness values, discharges, starting slope, starting elevation, and additional information required at bridges. Once this data has been added to the file, the HEC-2 computer program can calculate the water surface profiles. Figure 4 shows a sample of the data in the computer file format. All the numeric data in this file was created directly by CADD processing.

```
T1      MARYSVILLE, OHIO - FLOOD INSURANCE STUDY
T2      ANALYSIS OF MILL CREEK
T3      MILL CREEK                      10 YEAR FLOOD FREQUENCY
J1      2.                      STRT                            WSEL
J2 1.           -1.
J3 38.  42.     1.      43.     50.     51.     4.      8.      10.     40.
J3 46.  13.     15.     0.      38.     39.     42.     1.      41.     40.
J3 53.  54.     4.      3.      26.     25.     0.      201.
QT 4.   Q10     Q50     Q100    Q500
NCXNL   XNR     XNCH    0.1     0.3
X118.00 19.     3599.   3787.5  XLOBL   XLOBR   XLCH
GR1003.72485.   1001.   2900.   999.    3061.   979.5   3152.   979.    3416.6
GR978.7 3599.   976.2   3678.   973.2   3691.6  973.2   3711.6  976.2   3753.
GR978.7 3787.5  981.2   3822.   981.2   4210.8  985.7   4314.   989.    4518.
GR994.7 4642.   997.    4968.   1000.   5249.6  1007.7  5292.
NCXNL   XNR     XNCH    0.1     0.3
X119.00 21.     3320.2  3402.   XLOBL   XLOBR   XLCH
GR1003.71172.   1000.   1392.   999.    2141.   998.    2196.   993.2   2223.3
GR993.2 2630.   980.5   2693.   980.2   3046.   980.2   3290.2  978.    3320.2
GR976.5 3333.   972.6   3342.5  972.8   3382.5  976.5   3393.   978.    3402.
GR980.7 3422.   981.2   3516.   991.    3934.   997.5   4095.   1000.5  4284.
GR1004. 4330.
NCXNL   XNR     XNCH    0.1     0.3
X120.00 20.     2797.5  2913.   XLOBL   XLOBR   XLCH
GR1002.21534.   1002.   2212.   1001.   2314.   998.2   2469.   982.5   2599.7
GR982.5 2789.   980.    2797.5  974.5   2815.5  974.5   2857.3  980.7   2913.
GR983.2 2979.   985.    3068.   982.7   3089.6  982.7   3274.   990.    3435.
GR990.  3579.4  995.5   3678.   996.    3788.   996.    4004.9  1003.   4123.
NCXNL   XNR     XNCH    0.1     0.3
X121.00 16.     3253.5  3304.5  XLOBL   XLOBR   XLCH
GR1009.51084.   1007.   1878.   1004.   2308.   986.7   2486.   980.7   2522.7
GR980.7 2642.   982.2   2870.   982.1   3074.5  982.    3191.   977.6   3253.5
GR974.6 3273.5  974.9   3285.5  977.6   3304.5  997.    3378.   999.5   3520.
GR1009.53919.
NCXNL   XNR     XNCH    0.1     0.3
X122.00 14.     3190.   3277.2  XLOBL   XLOBR   XLCH
GR1015.51545.   1010.7  1941.   1007.   2083.   997.5   2259.   991.    2456.
GR984.2 2815.   984.2   3184.   982.5   3190.   977.5   3210.   977.5   3261.
GR982.5 3277.2  988.2   3312.   1008.5  3532.   1011.7  3599.
NCXNL   XNR     XNCH    0.1     0.3
X123.00 15.     3561.   3644.1  XLOBL   XLOBR   XLCH
GR1014.21658.   1008.5  1921.   1002.   2139.   993.7   2364.   984.7   2871.
GR984.7 3500.   981.5   3561.   976.5   3581.7  976.5   3626.7  981.5   3644.1
GR984.2 3647.7  984.5   3769.   997.5   3814.   1006.5  3875.   1012.2  3992.
```

Figure 4 - Computer File Format

```
NCXNL    XNR      XNCH     0.1      0.3
X124.00 16.       3234.7   3372.    XLOBL    XLOBR    XLCH
GR1012.21377.     1010.    1477.    1009.7   1675.    1005.2   2056.    998.2    2236.
GR987.2 2331.     987.     2900.    986.     2963.    985.2    3223.    982.7    3234.7
GR977.5 3250.7    977.5    3359.7   982.7    3372.    994.     3414.    1006.7   3678.
GR1009. 3822.
NCXNL    XNR      XNCH     0.1      0.3
X124.10 16.       3425.    3497.6   XLOBL    XLOBR    XLCH
GR1003. 1111.     1000.7   1516.    1000.2   1920.    997.2    2117.    989.7    2548.3
GR988.6 3000.     987.8    3373.1   983.7    3390.    982.5    3425.    978.     3477.7
GR982.5 3497.6    998.7    3536.    1003.2   3594.    1006.    3756.    1006.    3964.
GR1009.54170.
NCXNL    XNR      XNCH     0.3      0.5
X1SECNO                             XLOBL    XLOBR    XLCH              PSXECE
X310.0                                                        994.7    1006.5
SBXK     XKOR     COFQ     RDLEN    BWC      BWP      BAREA    SS       ELCHU    ELCHD
X1SECNO                             XLOBL    XLOBR    XLCH              PSXECE
X2                1.0      ELLC     ELTRD
X310.0                                                        994.7    1006.5
BT6.     1063.    1007.    0.       2065.    1002.2   0.       2710.    994.7    0.
BT2961.  995.     0.       3541.    1006.5   0.       3696.    1013.2   0.
NCXNL    XNR      XNCH     0.3      0.5
X124.40 17.       3265.    3376.4   XLOBL    XLOBR    XLCH
GR1011.71730.     1006.9   1948.5   1002.5   2152.    996.7    2299.    988.7    2538.
GR987.5 2783.     987.2    3210.    984.7    3265.    978.2    3292.3   978.2    3364.9
GR985.  3376.4    987.5    3844.3   992.5    3987.    997.7    4088.    1001.5   4128.
GR1001.54432.4    1008.2   4445.
EJ
T1       MARYSVILLE, OHIO - FLOOD INSURANCE STUDY
T2       ANALYSIS OF MILL CREEK
T3       MILL CREEK              50 YEAR FLOOD FREQUENCY
J1       3.                     STRT                           WSEL
J2 2.             -1.
T1       MARYSVILLE, OHIO - FLOOD INSURANCE STUDY
T2       ANALYSIS OF MILL CREEK
T3       MILL CREEK             100 YEAR FLOOD FREQUENCY
J1       4.                     STRT                           WSEL
J2 3.             -1.
T1       MARYSVILLE, OHIO - FLOOD INSURANCE STUDY
T2       ANALYSIS OF MILL CREEK
T3       MILL CREEK             500 YEAR FLOOD FREQUENCY
J1       5.                     STRT                           WSEL
J2 15.            -1.


ER
```

Figure 4 (Continued)

CONCLUSION

By using the computer model as described, several benefits are realized. From the initial gathering, the aerial and field data is stored in the computer and then reviewed, modified, and transferred within the computer to the final HEC-2 input format. Because the computer is utilized in handling the data, there is less likelihood of error in reducing field notes, plotting cross sections, and keypunching the data into the computer. Each task could cause an error if hand done, resulting in the need to discover and correct the mistake.

The CADD system allows for easier record keeping as the hard copies are on 8 1/2" x 11" sheets, allowing for ease in filing, storing, and tracking of data. The CADD system annotates all initial points and final points using different symbols so identification of the points is easily done.

The CADD system provides a fast method of preparing data for input into the HEC-2 computer program. Due to the inherent speed of the computer, the time required to plot data and code forms is shortened. In recent Flood Insurance Studies (References 7, 8, and 9) using the CADD system, it is estimated that data preparation time has been reduced by 10 percent.

The CADD system is a cost-effective way of preparing input for the HEC-2 computer program. In recent Flood Insurance Studies (References 7, 8, and 9) using the CADD system, a reduction of about 5 percent of the cost of doing the water surface profiles has been realized over doing the work by hand. Part of the savings is due to the reduction of the number of points needed in the cross sections or roadway profiles. A 50 percent reduction in the number of points results in about a 20 percent reduction in computer costs.

This method of data preparation also allows maximum utilization of support people to ready the computer files. By facilitating the plotting, coding, and keypunching operation, the time that drafters, keypunch operators, and hydrologists spend on a project has been reduced.

Use of the CADD system will likely be extended in the future. Topographic maps from digitized data provided by the photogrammetrist can be developed. The flood area can then be transferred to such maps using a CADD system. Programs can be developed to calculate other bridge variables, thus reducing hand computation and keypunching of data.

The GRBTCHK, FNOTE, and FSEC programs are finding application in other areas. Since the programs allow cross sections to be plotted, they are applicable for highway construction work and land development work where cross sections need to be developed.

REFERENCES

1. Ven Te Chow, "Theory and Analysis, and Methods of Computation", Open-Channel Hydraulics, McGraw-Hill, New York, 1959, pp. 217 to 296.

2. U.S. Army Corps of Engineers, Hydrologic Engineering Center, Computer Program 723-X6-L202A, HEC-2, Water Surface Profiles, Davis, California, (updated) March 1982.

3. Greg Barden, "GRBTCHK User's Manual", Burgess & Niple, Limited, Columbus, Ohio, 1984. Unpublished.

4. Greg Barden, "FNOTE User's Manual", Burgess & Niple, Limited, Columbus, Ohio, 1984. Unpublished.

5. Greg Barden, "FSEC User's Manual", Burgess & Niple, Limited, Columbus, Ohio, 1984. Unpublished.

6. Greg Barden, "FIS10.XBA User's Manual", Burgess & Niple, Limited, Columbus, Ohio, 1984. Unpublished.

7. U.S. Department of Housing and Urban Development, Federal Insurance Administration, Flood Insurance Study, Village of Killbuck, Ohio.

8. U.S. Department of Housing and Urban Development, Federal Insurance Administration, Flood Insurance Study, Village of Chauncey, Ohio, Unpublished.

9. U.S. Department of Housing and Urban Development, Federal Insurance Administration, Flood Insurance Study, City of Marysville, Ohio, Unpublished.

ACKNOWLEDGMENTS
The author gratefully acknowledges the support provided by Burgess & Niple, Limited. Thanks are also due to Daniel Hill and Greg Barden for review of this manuscript and to the Word Processing Section of Burgess & Niple, Limited for typing and proofreading.

BAKWATR (3)

Computation of Gradually Varied Flow

Richard L. Schaefer, P.E.   *

Abstract

The BAKWATR computer program computes profiles of gradually
varied flow in open channels of irregular shape using a microcomputer.
Channel cross sections are defined by a series of points outlining the
channel boundaries, each having a horizontal and vertical coordinate.
The program generates tables of area, hydraulic radius and surface
width as functions of flow depth. These tables are then used to
determine the depth of flow at each defined cross section by a
standard step method. Results are printed in tabular form and include
water surface elevation, depth of flow, cross-sectional area,
hydraulic radius, velocity and velocity head at each section, and
friction and eddy losses in the reach of channel downstream of each
section. Application of the BAKWATR program is limited to steady
gradually varied flow behavior in subcritical flow regimes. Options
are provided for establishing the depth of flow at the control
section, as BAKWATR can compute the steady flow depth through
rectangular weirs and submerged or unsubmerged circular culverts, or
the user may input a known depth at the control section for the given
flow rate.

Introduction

The BAKWATR computer program was developed to compute profiles of
gradually varied flow in open channels of irregular shape using a
microcomputer. Prior to this, microcomputer software was commercially
available only for solutions of regularly shaped channels, such as
circular and trapezoidal sections. Profiles of natural channels could
be generated only by larger frame computers capable of supporting
complex software such as HEC-2 (U.S. Army Corps of Engineers) and
WSP2 (U.S. Department of Agriculture, Soil Conservation Service).

*URS Engineers, 2615 Fourth Avenue, Seattle, Washington 98121, USA

The BAKWATR program, written in the BASIC language, makes available to smaller microcomputer users some of the capabilities heretofore found only in the realm of mainframe and larger-capacity microcomputer software. BAKWATR can also be applied to simpler man-made channel shapes. BAKWATR offers cost savings when used in the analysis of channel problems where the simplifying assumptions used by the program can be tolerated. In those projects where such assumptions cannot be allowed, BAKWATR may still be usable as a screening tool in preliminary design or study phases.

Model Description - Input

The BAKWATR program utilizes a standard-step method of solution, as described by Chow (1). The input data required to operate the program are described below:

Flow rate

Manning's roughness coefficients

Velocity distribution coefficient

Eddy loss coefficient

Cross section geometry

Type of control section:

   1) Known water surface elevation for the given flow,

   2) Circular culvert (number of pipes, diameter, invert elevation, coefficient of discharge), or

   3) Weir (number of gates, total length, crest elevation, height of weir face, weir coefficient).

The cross section geometry at each described section along the channel is defined by a series of points outlining the channel bottom. Each describing point has a horizontal coordinate and an elevation, as shown in Figure 1. The program has been written to prompt the user for each piece of data and, once stored, the data can be recalled using a menu format for editing or running simulations.

Control Section

As noted above, three types of control sections are available to the user. The known water surface option requires the user to simply input the water surface elevation at the control section for the given flow rate.

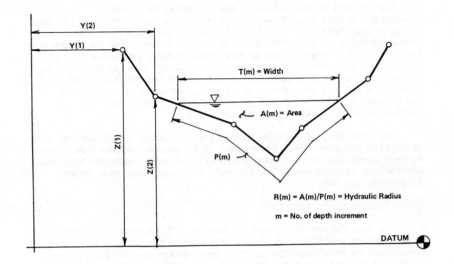

FIGURE 1

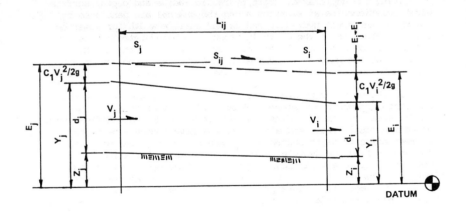

FIGURE 2

The culvert option computes the headwater required to discharge the specified flow through any number of culverts. All the culverts must have the same diameter and invert elevation. The headwater depth is computed using an algorithm developed by Malcom & New (2). The culvert(s) may be submerged or only partially full; however, it is assumed by the model that culvert discharge is inlet controlled, and this assumption should be checked for its validity. Should the culvert be hydraulically long, independent computation of the resulting headwater could be made and this result input to the program as a known water surface elevation.

The weir control section allows for the use of any number of weir gates with the same crest elevation. The program computes the water surface elevation using common sharp-crested weir discharge formulae. Contraction effects are accounted for, although minor weir nappe influences are not.

Cross Section Characteristics

The methodology which enables the BAKWATR program to compute water surface profiles for irregularly shaped channels is the generation of relationships between depth and cross-sectional area, depth and hydraulic radius, and depth and surface width, referred to as the cross-section characteristics. In a circular, triangular, trapezoidal or other man-made channel, these characteristics usually can be described by equations. For the irregularly shaped channel, approximating these relationships using equations is unsatisfactory due to the variety of possible shapes. Instead, segmented curves describing the depth/area, depth/hydraulic radius and depth/ surface width relationships at sections along the channel are generated by computing the area, hydraulic radius and surface width for numerous depths. The size of the depth increment can be adjusted and is established as a percentage of the overall cross section depth. Accuracy of the curves improves with an increase in the number of increments and a corresponding decrease in the size of each increment.

In the computer program, the relationships between the characteristics and depth are stored not as curves but as arrays. The depth, area, hydraulic radius and surface width are each defined by a one-dimensional array, and all the arrays have common subscripts corresponding to depth increments. (See Figure 1.) During calculations to find the depth at a station, the characteristics corresponding to any particular depth are found by interpolating between values in the arrays. From this it becomes apparent that use of smaller depth increments provides for improved accuracy in the resulting water surface profile.

Computing the Profile

The standard-step method is employed by BAKWATR to compute the
water surface profile of the channel. Because the program is limited
to subcritical flow regimes, the control section is at the
downstream end of the channel, and the calculation procedure moves
upstream to the next described cross section. Once the control
section depth is determined, an estimate is made of the depth of flow
at the immediate upstream section and the corresponding cross-
sectional area, hydraulic radius and surface width are interpolated
from the characteristics arrays. The velocity, velocity head and
total energy corresponding to the estimated depth at the section are
then calculated, and Manning's equation is used to find the friction
slope.

$$Ej = Yj + CvVj^2/2g$$

$$Sj = \left[\frac{VjN}{1.49\ AjRj^{2/3}}\right]^2 \quad \text{or} \quad Sj = \left[\frac{VjN}{AjRj^{2/3}}\right]^2 \quad \text{(SI units)}$$

where

      Ej = total energy at the upstream section
      Yj = water surface elevation at the upstream section
      Cv = velocity distribution coefficient
      Vj = velocity of flow at the upstream section
      Sj = friction slope at the upstream section
      Aj = cross sectional area at the upstream section
      Rj = hydraulic radius at the upstream section

To determine the accuracy of the depth estimate, a second
calculation of the total energy at the upstream station is made using
the following equation:

$$Ej = Ei + Lij(Si + Sj)/2 + CeCv\left|Vj^2 - Vi^2\right|/2g$$

where

      Ei = total energy at the downstream section
      Lij= length of channel between upstream and downstream sections
      Si = friction slope at the downstream section
      Ce = eddy loss coefficient
      Vi = velocity of flow at the downstream section

The two methods of calculating the total energy at the upstream
section are illustrated in Figure 2. If the two computed values agree
within the required tolerance, the depth estimate is confirmed as the

actual depth at the section and computation proceeds upstream to
the next section described. If the values do not agree, the depth
estimate is adjusted and the energy recomputed until agreement
results.

Validation

The BAKWATR program was first validated using a trapezoidal
channel problem from Chow. This problem was solved using both
BAKWATR and HEC-2. The results of the computations are compared in
Table 1 and indicate that the BAKWATR profile agrees closely with both
Chow and the HEC-2 program, the differences amounting to less than 0.07
feet over a channel length of 2,375 feet. The HEC-2 program was
operated using the alternate average friction slope algorithm, as this
algorithm is utilized by BAKWATR. Further, the HEC-2 documentation
notes that the average friction slope is most suitable for simulating M1
profiles (4).

TABLE 1
Comparison of Computed Profiles

(Trapezoidal channel, side slope 2H:1V, Q=400 cfs, n=.025,
S=.0016, velocity distribution coefficient = 1.10, eddy
loss coefficient = 0.0)

Station Upstream (ft)	Water Surface Elevation (ft)		
	Chow	BAKWATR	HEC-2 *
0	605.00	605.00	605.00
155	605.048	605.046	605.05
318	605.109	605.101	605.11
491	605.186	605.173	605.19
679	605.286	605.272	605.29
891	605.426	605.413	605.43
1,146	605.633	605.626	605.65
1,304	605.786	605.769	605.80
1,500	605.999	605.980	606.01
1,623	606.146	606.112	606.16
1,777	606.343	606.304	606.36
1,898	606.507	606.453	606.52
2,050	606.720	606.667	606.73
2,187	606.919	606.862	606.93
2,375	607.201	607.152	607.21

* HEC-2 program run using average friction slope algorithm.
Note: 1 ft. = 0.305 m.

The above results indicate that BAKWATR accurately processes the
cross-section data into the depth/area, depth/hydraulic radius and

depth/surface width relationships. The results further show that the program successfully replicates Chow's standard–step methodology and produces results similar to those of the highly regarded HEC–2 model.

Conclusions

The BAKWATR program provides an economical means of computing gradually varied flow profiles of irregularly shaped channels using a microcomputer. The programs's application is limited to steady flow in subcritical flow regimes.

BAKWATR reliably implements the standard–step method of Chow and processes cross section data of irregularly shaped channels. Use of BAKWATR is recommended for analysis of natural or irregularly shaped channels where average friction slope is the accepted solution algorithm and where the application can tolerate the simplifying assumptions used by the program. In those situations where more complex channel geometry exists, requiring the use of more sophisticated software such as HEC–2 or WSP2, the BAKWATR program can be used as an economical means of screening design alternatives during the project's study phase.

Appendix

1 Chow, Ven Te, Open–Channel Hydraulics, McGraw–Hill, 1959.

2 Malcom, H.R. and New, V.E., "Design Approaches for Stormwater Management in Urban Areas", North Carolina State University, Raleigh, NC, May 1975.

3 Copyright 1983, Richard L. Schaefer.

4 U.S. Army Corps of Engineers, "HEC–2 Water Surface Profiles Users Manual", September 1982.

Optimal Muskingum River Routing

German Gavilan[1] and Mark H. Houck[2], Member, ASCE

The Muskingum method of river routing is well established and frequently used. An attempt is made to improve the method by optimal
selection of the model parameters. The common linear Muskingum and the
less common, nonlinear Muskingum models are considered. For a test
case, the Muskingum model parameters are estimated using the conventional approach, using procedures suggested by other researchers, and
using the new constrained optimization approach. The performance of
each of these fitted models is compared to the others.

INTRODUCTION

The Muskingum method is one of the standard and commonly used techniques to route water through an open channel. Its linear form consists
of a continuity equation and a linear relationship between storage in a
channel reach and the inflow and outflow rates for the reach. In general, these two equations may be written as:

$$\frac{dS}{dt} = I - 0 \tag{1}$$

$$S = k[xI + (1-x)0] \tag{2}$$

The notation is defined as:

    I = rate of inflow to the channel reach (cfs)
    0 = rate of outflow from the channel reach (cfs)
    S = storage volume in the channel (cu ft)
    t = time (s)
    x = a parameter of the Muskingum routing model
    k = a parameter of the Muskingum routing model; for
        a translatory wave (x=0.5), k generally equals
        the time lag between inflow and outflow hydro-
        graphs

---

1 Graduate Student, School of Civil Engineering, Purdue University,
West Lafayette, IN 47907.

2 Associate Professor, School of Civil Engineering, Purdue University,
West Lafayette, IN 41907.

The linear Muskingum model may be inappropriate for representing channel routing through some reaches. It is possible that the storage vs weighted flow relationship is not always linear as implied in Equation 2. In this case, it is necessary to find a suitable non-linear relationship which may be used for routing instead of Equation 2. A common, non-linear routing equation found in text books (6), and (1) is:

$$S = \frac{b}{a}[xI^{m/l} + (1-x)0^{m/l}] \tag{3}$$

where

a , l = parameters of the routing model associated with the depth-discharge characteristics of the reach

b , m = parameters of the routing model associated with the mean depth-storage characteristics of the reach

By lumping some parameters together (k = b/a; n = m/l), it is possible to rewrite Equation 3 as:

$$S = k[xI^{n} + (1-x)0^{n}] \tag{4}$$

The selection of parameter values for either Equation 2 or Equation 4 is a complex problem. Numerous procedures for parameter selection have been proposed in the past (3), (4), (7); most of these have used standard linear regression techniques and have focused on minimizing the sum of the squared deviations of actual storages during some historical period from model-predicted storages. An extension of these procedures with added restrictions on x (0 < x < 1), k (k > 0) and n (n > 0) is presented here. Another parameter selection procedure incorporating these restrictions but using an objective of minimizing the maximum deviation of actual storage from model-predicted storage is also presented.

In the next section, two of the standard parameter selection procedures are described. Two new selection procedures are presented in the following section and a comparison of the four procedures using the Wabash River as an example completes the paper.

STANDARD PARAMETER ESTIMATION TECHNIQUES

Through an analysis of streamflow records at the top and bottom of a river reach, it is possible to construct a set of data comprising the inflow rates at the top of the reach, the outflow rates at the bottom of the reach and the storage volumes in the reach at selected times over some historical period. These data may be denoted by:

S_t = actual or measured storage in the reach at

time t (cu ft)

I_t = actual or measured inflow rate at the
top of the reach at time (cfs)

0_t = actual or measured outflow rate at the
bottom of the reach at time t (cfs)

The standard, linear Muskingum model for channel routing assumes a relationship between storage, inflow and outflow defined by Equation 2. A standard selection procedure for parameters of the model is to minimize the sum of the squared deviations of model-predicted storage and actual storage (3). One way to define this procedure for the standard linear (SL) model is with the mathematical program in Equations 5 and 6.

$$\text{Minimize} \qquad L = \sum_t (S_t - PS_t)^2 \tag{5}$$

subject to:

$$PS_t = k[xI_t + (1-x)0_t] \qquad t=1,2,\ldots,T \tag{6}$$

In this model, the values of the parameters--x and k--are unrestricted in value and sign. The model-predicted storage value is denoted by PS_t and it is also unrestricted in value and sign. The mathematical program is solved by substituting the constraints into the objective, thereby eliminating all variables but k and x; the solution is then obtained by traditional calculus methods -- setting all partial derivatives equal to zero and solving for the optimal values of k and x.

Parameter selection for the standard nonlinear (SN) Muskingum model is also often based on minimizing the sum of squared deviations of model-predicted storage and actual storage (4). The mathematical program in Equations 7 and 8 defines this procedure.

$$\text{Minimize} \qquad N = \sum_t (S_t - PS_t)^2 \tag{7}$$

subject to:

$$PS_t = k[xI_t^n + (1-x)0_t^n] \qquad t=1,2,\ldots,T \tag{8}$$

(4) describes one solution method for the mathematical program: (1) select a group of values for n (e.g. n=0.05, 0.10, ...); for each value of n, solve the resulting mathematical program using traditional calculus methods as described for the standard linear Muskingum model; (3) choose that value of n and the associated values of k and x that produced the minimum value of the objective function, N.

The standard nonlinear (SN) Muskingum model is a more general model and should perform better in terms of the objective to minimize the sum of the squared deviations of actual storage from model-predicted storage -- than the standard linear model. However it suffers from the same problem as the standard linear model: the parameters k and x are unrestricted in value and sign.

CONSTRAINED PARAMETER ESTIMATION TECHNIQUES

The first constrained parameter estimation technique is an extension of the standard, linear Muskingum parameter estimation methods. It involves the addition of two constraints to the mathematical program of Equations 5 and 6. The constraints restrict the parameter values to be not less than zero and the value of x to be not greater than 0.5. This upper limit on the value of x is to ensure the stability of the model (2). The entire constrained, linear (CL) model includes Equations 5,6,9, and 10.

$$x \leqslant 0.5 \qquad\qquad\qquad (9)$$

$$k,x \geqslant 0 \qquad\qquad\qquad (10)$$

The constrained, nonlinear (CN) Muskingum model is an extension of the standard nonlinear model (SN). Two constraints restricting the values of the parameters are added to the mathematical program of Equations 7 and 8. The parameters x,n and k are all restricted to be nonnegative and x is restricted to not exceed one to prevent the coefficinet multiplying the outflow in Equation 8 from being negative. These constraints may be written as:

$$x,k,n \geqslant 0 \qquad\qquad\qquad (11)$$

$$x \leqslant 1 \qquad\qquad\qquad (12)$$

The complete constrained, nonlinear (CN) Muskingum model is defined by the mathematical program in Equations 7,8,11 and 12.

Solving the constrained, nonlinear (CN) model (Equations 7,8,11,12) or the constrained linear (CL) model (Equations 5,6,9,10) is more difficult than the unconstrained or standard models. Consider the constrained nonlinear model. It is no longer possible to eliminate all of the constraints (Equations 8,11,12) by substitutions in the objective function; therefore, classical calculus techniques are not useful. However, the mathematical program may still be solved in a three step procedure: (1) select a group of values for n (e.g. 0.05, 0.10,...); (2) for each value of n, solve the resulting mathematical program; and (3) choose the values of n and the associated values of k and x that produced the smallest value of the objective, N.

The mathematical program solved in step 2 contains several nonlinearities and may appear to be difficult to solve. It is not. The nonlinearity in Equation 8 due to the exponent n on the inflows and outflows is removed in step 1; n is not a variable in the mathematical program solved in step 2. The other nonlinearity in Equation 8 is due to the multiplication of k and x. A simple substitution of a new variable p for the product of k and x eliminates this nonlinearity. The restrictions in Equations 11 and 12 can be replaced by constraints requiring x and p to be non-negative and requiring p not to exceed k (p-k $\leqslant$ 0). This second constraint is equivalent to Equation 12. The mathematical program is now solvable as a quadratic program or as a linear program with an approximated, piece-wise linear objective function (9).

Another constrained parameter estimation technique called constrained maximum deviation (CMD) employs an objective of minimizing the maximum deviation of model-predicted storage from actual storage. The entire mathematical program may be written as:

$$\text{Minimize} \quad Z = \text{MAX} \tag{13}$$

subject to:

$$\text{MAX} \geqslant S_t - k[x\, I_t^n + (1-x)\, O_t^n] \quad t=1,2,\ldots,T \tag{14}$$

$$\text{MAX} \geqslant k[x I_t^n + (1-x)\, O_t^n] - S_t \quad t=1,2,\ldots,T \tag{15}$$

$$x \leqslant 1 \tag{16}$$

$$x,k,n,\ \text{MAX} \geqslant 0 \tag{17}$$

In Equations 14 and 15, the variable MAX is restricted to exceed the absolute value of the difference between the model-predicted storage and actual storage at each time increment. The objective (Equation 13) is to minimize MAX or to minimize the maximum deviation between model-predicted and actual storages. Equations 16 and 17 contain the restrictions on the model parameters. As with the other nonlinear parameter estimation techniques, a three step procedure is used to solve the mathematical program. The same substitution of p for the product of k and x described above is used here. If the value of n is fixed, the entire problem (Equations 13-17) is solvable as a linear program. Therefore, the solution procedure is: (1) select a set of values for n (e.g. n=0.05,0.10,...); (2) for each value of n, solve the resulting linear program; and (3) choose the value of n and the associated values of k and x that produced the smallest value of the objective Z.

EXAMPLE

To illustrate the use of these four parameter estimation techniques, streamflow data for the San Francisco River between Alma and Glenwood USGS stations in New Mexico were analyzed. The results presented here are intended solely as a single numerical example and should not be used to draw general conclusions about the merits of any of the techniques.

Streamflow data for the period March 6-25, 1966, were used in each of the parameter estimation techniques. The optimal values of the parameters are listed in Table 1 and the resulting outflows as well as the actual outflows from the reach for the 20 day period are listed in Table 2. Also listed in Table 1 are several key statistics. These include the maximum deviations of model-predicted storages and outflows from actual storages outflows, the storage prediction standard error (SPSE), and an outflow prediction standard error (OPSE).

$$ SPSE = \sqrt{\frac{\sum_t (S-\hat{S}_t)^2}{N-2}} \tag{18} $$

$$ OPSE = \sqrt{\frac{\sum_t (O_t - \hat{O}_t)^2}{N-2}} \tag{19} $$

The objective of each parameter estimation technique is related to channel storage. Therefore, consider the storage related statistics from Table 1 first. The SN model is a more general version of the SL model and should produce a better value of their objective function or the standard error of storage prediction (SPSE). The CN model is equivalent to the SN model except that it contains two additional constraints. Therefore, the CN objective value (or its SPSE) cannot exceed the SN objective value (or its SPSE) and may be less than the SN value. Although the constraints on the parameters of the CMD and CN models are the same, the objective of the CMD model is not the same as the objectives for the SL, SN, and CN models. Therefore, the SPSE value for the CMD model cannot be less than the SPSE model for the CN model.

Next consider the parameter values. In the SL and SN models, the parameters k and x are not limited to non-negative values and there is no upper limit on the value of x. It is not unusual to obtain negative values or unrealistically large values of x when using these models. However, in this case, the values of k and x do satisfy the usual limits (e.g. Equations 11 and 12). The CN and CMD models explicitly restrict the parameter values to realistic ranges.

The outflows from the channel reach are not explicitly considered in the objective function of the parameter estimation techniques. Therefore, it is impossible to predict which technique will reduce or control best the deviations of model-predicted outflow from actual outflow. If outflow prediction is the primary goal of calibrating a Muskingum model, then using a technique that includes outflows explicitly in the objective may be appropriate (8, 9).

TABLE 1. PARAMETERS AND KEY STATISTICS FOR STANDARD AND
CONSTRAINED ESTIMATION TECHNIQUES FOR LINEAR AND
NONLINEAR MUSKINGUM RIVER ROUTING MODELS (STORAGES
ARE 10^3 cu ft , OUTFLOWS ARE cfs).

Model	Parameters	Maximum Storage Deviation	SPSE	Maximum Outflow Deviation	OPSE
SL	X=0.22 k=0.65 n=1.00	570.	328.	10.2	4.5
SN	x=0.21 k=0.75 n=0.75	371.	268.	9.1	4.3
CN	x=0.08 k=0.63 n=1.11	777.	268.	9.8	4.4
CMD	x=0.24 k=0.70 n=1.16	285.	35.	11.0	0.5

Note: 1 cu ft = 0.028 m^3 ; 1 cfs = 0.028 m^3/s

SUMMARY

     Selecting parameters for a Muskingum river routing model may be
done in a variety of ways. The satandard tecniques use an objective of
minimizing the sum of squared deviations of model-predicted channel
storages from actual storages; and they do not explicitly restrict the
values of the model parameters to reasonable ranges. It is possible to
add the constraints that restrict the parameter values. Further, it is
possible to use other objectives such as minimizing the maximum deviation of model-predicted outflow from actual outflow to estimate the
model parameters.

TABLE 2. ACTUAL AND PREDICTED OUTFLOWS

DISCHARGES (cfs)				
Days	Actual	SL	SN	CN	CMD
1	6.0	6.0	6.0	6.0	6.0
2	7.1	6.4	6.2	6.5	6.5
3	10.9	8.4	7.7	8.9	8.7
4	21.5	14.6	12.8	15.6	15.0
5	50.4	31.7	28.4	33.6	31.4
6	67.2	56.3	55.2	55.9	54.9
7	78.0	71.0	71.3	70.4	69.6
8	96.0	84.3	85.2	84.3	82.4
9	120.0	104.4	106.3	103.9	101.3
10	127.0	122.4	124.0	120.6	119.9
11	126.0	126.6	126.8	125.8	125.9
12	126.0	126.6	125.9	126.0	126.0
13	120.0	123.9	123.5	123.7	124.4
14	100.0	112.4	111.4	112.8	115.2
15	92.8	97.5	96.3	98.8	99.7
16	80.1	88.3	87.6	88.6	89.4
17	67.2	75.6	74.9	76.0	77.3
18	49.2	60.9	60.5	60.9	62.6
19	41.4	46.5	46.7	47.1	47.5
20	38.4	40.4	40.6	40.6	40.7

Note: 1 cu ft = 0.028 m^3 ; 1 cfs = $0.028 \text{ m}^3/\text{s}$

References

1. Chow, V.T. , Open Channel Hydraulics, Mc Graw-Hill, New York, N.Y.

2. Cunge, J.A., "On the Subject of a Flood Propagation Computation Method (Muskingum Method)," Journal of Hydraulic Research, Vol 7, No. 2, 1969, pp. 205-230.

3. Gill, M.A., "Gill, M.A.," Flood Routing by the Muskingum Method," Journal of Hydrology, Vol. 36, Feb., 1978, pp. 353-363.

4. Gill, M.A., and Mustafa, S., "Technical Note on the Muskingum Method of Flood Routing," Advances in Water Resources, Vol. 2, No. 1, March, 1979.

5. Katz, P.G., and Toebes, G.H., "Green River Basin Flow Forcasting Models," Technical Report No. 136, Purdue University Water Resources Research Center, Oct. 1980.

6. Lisley, R.K., Kohler, M.A., and Paulhus, J.L.H., Hydrology for Engineers, 2nd edition, Mc Graw-Hill, New York, N.Y. 1975.

7. Singh, V.P., and McCann, R.C., "Some Notes on Muskingum Method of Flood Routing," Journal of Hydrology, Vol. 48, April, 1980, pp. 343-361.

8. Todini, E., and Wallis, J.K., "Using CLS for Daily or Longer Rainfall Modeling," In: Mathematical Models for Surface Hydrology, Wiley, New York, N.Y., 1977, pp. 149-168.

9. Wagner, H.M., Principles of Operational Research, 2nd ed., Prentice-Hall, Inc., Englewood Cliffs, New Jersey, 1975.

SETUP AND USAGE OF MULTITASKING MICROCOMPUTERS
FOR WATER MANAGEMENT PROBLEM SOLVING

Soronadi Nnaji*

Abstract

Software and hardware that were developed in the evolution of the
microcomputer from the Altair to today's state of the art multitasking
systems are discussed. The rationale and setup of possible
configurations for multitasking applications are examined. A listing
of water management and control applications that are amenable to
multitasking is given.

Eight-Bit Processors Without Software-The First Generation

This section includes a brief review of the evolution of the
personal (micro-) computer and a description of the basic elements of
a computer system. For in-depth exposition on the former the reader
is referred to Augarten (1), Ditlea (2) and Levy (3). The paper by
Parker (4) provides such history starting with Ed. Robert's Altair
8800 which was built in 1975. It is generally accepted that the Altair was the first micro-computer to be marketed. The machine was
designed for the hobbyist in the form of a kit. Several machines such
as DEC's LINC and IBM's SCAMP, which predate the Altair, were never
marketed due to high unit production costs.

The evolution may be considered in terms of the hardware and the
software which make up the computer system. Hardware is here defined
as the electrical and mechanical parts of the system and the software
is a program (set of instructions) used to solve problems with the
computer. There are three classes of software the **Operating System,**
software used to direct the operation of the hardware, and the Applications software used to compute solutions or perform manipulations
with the computer and the Language Translator (compiler) software
which is used to translate the application software into a machine
understandable program. A schematic of the basic components of the
typical hardware subsystem is given in Figure 1. The broken lines in
this figure indicate flow of instructions, the solid lines indicate
flow of data or processed information and the dotted lines indicate
flow of control. The **Central Processing Unit** (CPU) is made up of the
control unit and the arithmetic - logic unit. The CPU and the Memory
Unit constitute the Computer. Specifically, the control unit
coordinates and directs the operations of the computer while the
Arithmetic Logic unit performs the calculations and decision making
operations. The primary memory unit stores computer instructions and
data as long as the operating system is resident in memory. It is
referred to as the **Random - Access - Memory (RAM)** to distinguish it

*Associate Professor of Civil Engineering, FAMU/FSU College
of Engineering, Tallahassee, Florida 32307-0807

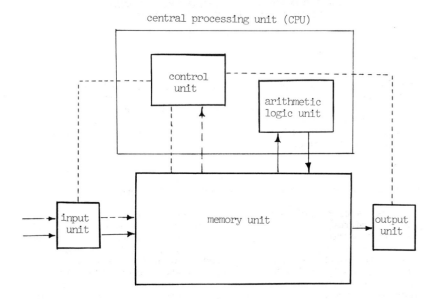

Figure 1. Basic Components of the Microcomputer Hardware

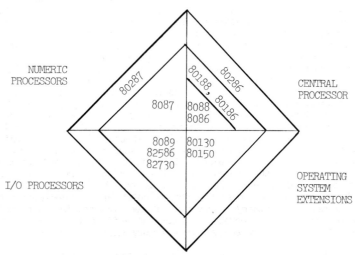

Figure 2. Progression of INTEL's General Purpose and Dedicated Processors

from the **Read - Only - Memory** (ROM) which stores instructions on a permanent basis. Any storage units that are housed outside the computer are usually referred to as an auxiliary memory units and are typically flexible ('floppy') or hard sectored disks. These units are also connected to the CPU and store instructions and data that are not currently being used by the CPU.

The Altair did not have a keyboard, monitor nor auxiliary memory. It had a primary memory of 256 bytes of RAM and was equipped with an INTEL 8080 CPU. A byte is a measure of storage space consisting of a packet of binary digits (bits). A bit takes on one of two possible values - 0 or 1 in mathematics and low or high voltage in electronics. A byte is generally considered to have a packet size of 8 bits. A computer that uses 8 bits to represent a character is said to have an 8-bit processor. Thus, the Altair was an 8-bit processor computer. Since it did not have a keyboard of any sort, job execution was through direct interfacing with the machine usually by flipping switches on (positive voltage) and off (zero voltage). The Altair and other subsequent computers which had similar features did not, therefore, operate with software. They are considered in this paper as the first generation micro computers.

Eight-Bit Processors With Software-The Second Generation

Software development for the micro-computers actually started with the second generation machines with the most popular applications programming language being BASIC, acronym for Beginner's All-purpose Symbolic Instruction Code. This generation included the features which the first generation machines lacked i.e. keyboard, monitor, increased RAM and some auxiliary memory. They were targeted to a different market-the home user for entertainment and to a lesser extent, initially at least, for education. The most noted machines among this generation are Apple's Apple II, Radio Shack's TRS-80 and Commodore's PET. These were also 8-bit machines. With the advent of the first business application software-Peachtree's text processor developed for the Wang Computer, micro-computers became a serious tool for addressing business functions. The above machines and others that followed were also used to perform scientific and engineering tasks such as modeling simple systems, hydrologic flow routing, pipe network analysis. The capacity to handle large pipe networks, for example, was only limited by the speed of the processor and the availability of primary memory.

Sixteen-Bit Processors-The Third Generation

The third generation of micro computers was motivated by the need to provide increased processing speed and larger primary as well as auxiliary memory. These machines used one CPU that was typically 16-bit. The popular 16-bit processors include INTEL 8086, Zilog's Z8000 and Motorola's MC68000. Since these processors represent characters with 16-bits they are much faster and more accurate than their 8-bit counterparts, particularly for numerical calculations.

The INTEL 8088 which was adopted by IBM in its standard setting IBM-PC is also characterized as a 16-bit processor. It however represents each character with 8 bits and so operates on two characters at a time. Computers of this generation also came with primary memory of between 64 kilobytes and 256 kilobytes (KB) which is a vast improvement over the 16 KB to 64 KB of the second generation computers.

Many micro computers, compatible with the IBM-PC to varying degree, have since been introduced by different manufactures. One only needs to skim through the various computer related magazines to appreciate the variety of machines in the market today. Montague et. al. (5) and Luhn (6) have discussed the technical aspects of the compatibility issue at length. The latter paper included a table of specifications on the type of processor supported, the minimum RAM, and the maximum memory expansion possibility. Maxima of 640 KB or more are, in practice, usually not attainable due to limitations in the operating systems driving the computer. The most popular operating systems are microsoft's disk operating system (MS DOS), IBM's disk operating system (IBM DOS) also developed by Microsoft and Digital Research's CP/M-86.

At this stage micro-computers with the above attributes have found popular usage in practical water resources engineering, analysis and management and in other disciplines of Civil Engineering. The section on the 'Engineering Marketplace' in the Civil Engineering magazine attests to the availability of engineering problem solving softwares and their popularity in engineering practice. Since most of these machines can be expanded to 256 KB without difficulty, they can run the FORTRAN compiler and, with it, a large array of programs written in that language. The IBM-PC and other members of its family now come with 256 KB of memory. Unfortunately, the size of problems that can be handled using the third generation microcomputers continue to be limited by both available CPU's and Operating Systems.

Multi-Tasking Systems-The Fourth Generation

New developments in software technology such as screen splitting (window concept), virtual memory; continuous saving to disk storage to maximize RAM space, mouse and light pen support for Computer Aided Design, Instruction and Manufacture and print spooling add to the need to develop new ways of more efficient use of existing processors and operating systems.

To this end, micro computer innovations now center on the concept of multitasking of central processor operations burrowing from methods that have been applied in mainframe and minicomputer systems. Multitasking means the ability to perform multiple tasks concurrently i.e. within a small interval of time. Depending on the system configuration and the tasks to be performed the interval may be reduced to an instant in which case the multiple execution of tasks is simultaneous. Multitasking may be attained through design of the operating system or in the hardware configuration. The basic idea is to get more tasks accomplished in a given time span or, conversely, to do the tasks at a shorter time span. The fourth generation micro computers have been designed variously to meet the needs for concurrency.

Multitasking Through Software Design

The objective is to design the software such that it can direct a single processor to do multiple tasks concurrently. Practical methods to date have precluded simultaneous multitasking.

Tasks may included the processing of programs, operating input/output (I/O) peripherals, data communications, text processing, graphics, decision support systems and monitoring activities at several stations. When the tasks only involve programs, the process is referred to as Multiprogramming-the concurrent processing of two or more programs in memory. Operation shifts back and forth between the programs which may also be shuttled between primary and auxiliary memory.

Most microcomputer operating systems now have batch processing features in which a batch of jobs is fed in and processed sequentially under multiprogramming. Implementing the edit and compile programs on the IBM-PC by using the batch routine, EDFOR is a typical example of interactive sequential multiprogramming. The FORCLG.BAT file, found in the Library diskette of the FORTRAN compiler packet contains an IBM-PC batch program for compiling, linking and running a FORTRAN source program. Thus, multiprogramming saves time, in the above examples, by eliminating the need for the user to load the next program – a relatively slow process. Certain tasks such as I/O are also very slow relative to the speed of the processor. Since I/O are routed through the CPU, they tie up the system thus precluding meaningful multitasking. Several approaches have been attempted for improving system performance when diverse tasks are involved. The approach of primary memory partitioning has been shown to work well and is discussed next.

Memory Partitioning: In this software technology, the operating system enables the user to accommodate multiple tasks by dividing the primary memory into a number of partitions which may be of varying sizes. The maximum number of partitions depends on the size of the available memory as well as the operating system's design. Each task is operated upon, by the single CPU, in a separate partition. Control is given to the tasks on a round-robin basis i.e. tasks are switched whenever the current tasks needs to wait for I/O or when its allotted time slice expires. To be credible, the Operating System must contain a mechanism to prevent interaction, by accident or otherwise, between tasks running within the different partitions. The basic assumption is, of course, that each partition has enough memory to support the assigned task.

Several software houses have developed operating systems that have such multitasking capabilities. Digital Research Corporation is marketing concurrent versions (CCP/M - 86 and CCP/M - 86 with windows) of its 16-bit operating system, CP/M - 86. The window concept allows the user to view, as windows on the screen, the status or results of several tasks simultaneously. The IBM-DOS does not yet have a multitasking version. Most of the other multitasking programs are not operating systems but have rather been designed to add multitasking capabilities to the IBM-DOS. Such programs include Software Link's MULTILINK and B & L Computer Consultants' MULTI-JOB as examples. During the fall of 1984 Digital Research introduced a new operating system - Concurrent PC DOS or C/PC-DOS designed to operate CP/M, MS DOS or IBM-DOS based application programs in an multitasking mode. The C/PC - DOS can create, format or be loaded into a CCP/M - 86 or IBM DOS disk partition. A limitation is that it does not support some features of IBM DOS versions 2.0 and above such that there is a significantly high IBM DOS software as well as some hardware incompatibility. Given these serious problems it is doubtful that the advent of C/PC DOS will make multitasking add-ons, such as MULTILINK, obsolete. The MULTILINK and the C/PC DOS have been reviewed by Roskos (7) and Awalt (8) respectively.

Additional features available variously in the operating systems/programs that support multitasking include password protection, simultaneous printing from several windows, print spooling, foreground and background partitioning, communications, certain screen handling features such as cursor positioning and MULTI-USER capabilities among others. The multi-user capability requires hardware considerations in addition to support from the operating system to be implementable and is discussed next.

It should be noted that several operating systems that have been specifically designed to handle multitasking, multiuser systems are presently available. In addition to the C/PC-DOS already discussed, others include AT&T's UNIX operating system and its commercial adaptations XENIX, Idris, Cromix, Coherent, PC/IX. Others are the several levels and versions of PolyFORTH by FORTH, Inc.

Multitasking Through Hardware Configuration

Ideally, multitasking should be simultaneous and as observed concurrent multitasking cannot attain the above goal using only one processor. Hardware configuration based multitasking strives to be simultaneous through parallelism of operations. The basic attributes of such a system are: two or more processors working in parallel and sharing primary and auxiliary memory and, in some cases, also sharing I/O peripherals.

Figure 2 shows the INTEL Corporation product line of processors and their sequence of development. The family of central processors perform general purpose functions while the other families perform dedicated functions. As observed earlier, the 8088 and the 8087 are INTEL's initial 16 bit processors. The 80188 and 80186 are upgraded versions of the above corresponding processors while the 80286 is the multiuser, multitasking version of the 80186. The 8087 and its multiuser, multitasking version, the 80287 were designed for numeric intensive applications. Correspondingly the 8089, 82586 and 82730 are for I/O intensive applications while the 80130 and 80150 are operating system extension processors.

The IBM-PC and many of the micro computers that are compatible
with it have a slot for the 8087 co-processor. The processor handles
floating point arithmetic and other numeric functions thus freeing up
the central processors for other tasks.

Hardware Configurations: Guttman (9) has reviewed hardware
configurations that have been set up for multiuser multitasking and
also included a listing of vendors for such systems. Depending on
needs the configuration selected may be user oriented or task
oriented. The operating system is chosen correspondingly. In user
oriented configurations a user performs tasks independent of other
users and only shares common peripherals. The simplest configuration
would be one in which users, performing single tasks, connect to a
central multiprocessor such as the INTEL 80286. Common peripherals
can then be accessed by the users through the processors. The response time for this setup deteriorates fast with increasing number of
users. From the vantage point of the processors, the configuration is
multitasking. For no more than a four user system say, a natural extension would for each user to do multitasking. Task oriented configurations allow both sharing of resources and between user communication. The operating system may interrupt or switch a user on or off.
The user is simply viewed as a workstation through which one or more
tasks are effected.

In most setups more than one processor is used and this
significantly increases the number of possible configurations. A
couple of these are illustrated below:

(1) A multiprocessor CPU supporting dedicated coprocessors such
as the 8087 processor and concurrently processing tasks from
several non-in-teracting users who share hard disk and output
peripherals represents a user oriented multitasking configuration
which may be depicted as in figure 3.

(2) A task oriented setup exists if each user/station is served
by a local general purpose processor and the central multiprocessor acting as a server by routing tasks to and from I/0 and dedicated processors. This configuration is depicted in Figure 4.

A listing of water management and control applications that are
amenable to multitasking as discussed in this paper is given below:

1) Evaluation of time streams of benefits and costs of interrelated
    water projects;

2) Modular design of programs for water system modeling;

3) Expansion modeling of water supply system with multple components
    e.g. reservoirs, aqueducts, treatment plants;

4) Multistage water allocation systems;

5) Flood forecasting at multiple sites along a river;

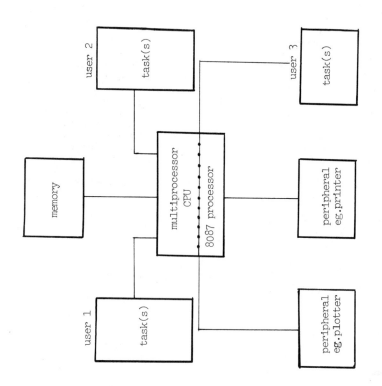

Figure 3.   User – Oriented System – No interaction between users

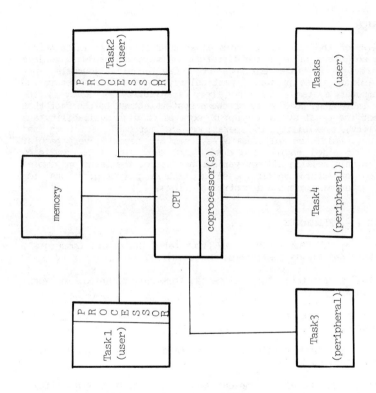

Figure 4. Task – Oriented System – Users can interact

6)   Cost allocation among several projects;

7)   Model choice and decision support systems;

8)   Data base updating and interactive data analysis.

CONCLUSION

A lot of the material of this paper currently exist in technical manuals and users guide of the different software and hardware vendors and as reviews in trade magazines and a few technical journals. Further, bulk of these products, particularly in the fourth generation microcomputer systems, have not been standardized. However, the rapidly increasing popularity of these systems attest to the fact that they meet the usual system design objectives of high availability and reliability, flexibility in operations and improved efficiency and throughput. Multiuser multitasking systems are becoming very popular in computer aided engineering design and analysis. The remaining papers in this session address various aspects of the setup and implementation of microcomputer based multitasking configurations for solving water management and control problems.

APPENDIX I - REFERENCES

1. Augarten, S., "Bit by Bit: An Illustrated History of Computers", Ticknor and Fields Publishers, New York, NY, 1984.

2. Ditlea, S. (editor), "Digital Deli", Workman Publishing, New York, NY, 1984.

3. Levy, S., "Hackers: Heroes of the Computer Revolution", Anchor Press/Doubleday, Garden City, NY, 1984.

4. Parker, W., "From Altair to AT", PC World Magazine, Vol. 3, No. 3, March 1985, pp 78-88.

5. Montague C. et. al, "Technical Aspects of IBM PC Compatibility", BYTE Magazine, Vol. 8, No.11, November 1983, pp 247-251.

6. Luhn, R., "The Compatibles Line Up", PC World Magazine, Vol. 3 No. 4, April 1984 pp 102-125.

7. Roskos, J.R., "Multilink", PC Tech Journal, Vol. 2, No. 4, October 1984 pp 65-74.

8. Awalt, D., "Concurrent PC-DOS", PC Tech Journal, Vol. 3, No. 3, March 1985.

9. Guttman, M.K., "Multi-User Micros", Computers and Electronics, Vol. 23, No.2, February 1985, pp 70-75.

HYDROLOGIC WORK GROUP SYSTEM
USING DISTRIBUTED TASK PROCESSING

William James, M. ASCE and Ali Unal*

Abstract

The notion behind work group systems is that a collection of co-workers, numbering from a few to a few tens of people, is the logical unit around which to build a centralized microcomputer system. The users of these computers share both information and computer resources within the group. The three primary technologies for achieving this are (a) local area networks, (b) multi-user microcomputers, and (c) data base management systems. Typical activities of a hydrologic/hydraulic work group are listed. Continuous modelling is shown to be an important emerging technique, and concomitant centralized time series management is briefly described. Typical sizes of the central time-series store are given. A minimum hardware configuration that is mainframe compatible is described, and typical costs are indicated. The performance of the system is described.

Introduction

The old computing environment (a single computer serving the whole organization's computational needs) is rapidly being replaced by a new environment, wherein a large number of separate but interconnected computers complete the tasks. These systems are called "computer networks". Distinct from "distributed systems", the term "computer networks" is used here to mean a collection of interconnected autonomous computers. Two computers are said to be interconnected if they are capable of exchanging information. The connection need not be a copper wire; lasers, microwaves, and earth satelites can also be used. If one computer can externally start, stop or control another, these computers are not autonomous.

Computer networks which are distributed within a perimeter of a few kilometers are usually called "local area networks" (LAN's). LAN's generally have two other distinctive characteristics: (a) a total data rate exceeding 1 Mbps and (b) they are owned by a single organization. High-band width cable(s) can be used instead of public telephone networks because of the short distance between the processors. This is highly advantageous.

---

*Computational Hydraulics Group, McMaster University, Hamilton, Ontario Canada L8S 4L7 Telephone: 416/526-6944

The most reliable personal computer networks are designed to use centralized network control, where a data-management computer becomes the network's logical hub. A centralized network manager, called the Boss, is responsible for managing data files and hardware resources, maintaining data security, and handling intercomputer communication and synchronization. This approach gives added control and reduces processing time, compared with a decentralized network (1).

As an alternative, a multi-user dedicated boss computer with intelligent communications can be used. In particular, microcomputers may tap directly into mainframes, giving users more timely and flexible access to central databases. These links range from programs that let the microcomputer act like a terminal, to complex packages that integrate mainframe links with micro-based spread sheets. Terminal-emulation packages enable a microcomputer to duplicate the protocols used by a terminal when it communicates with another computer. The boss computer thinks it is talking to a standard terminal; the microcomputer typically displays what a terminal would display.

Integrated software links, recently introduced, reside partly in the boss computer and partly in the microcomputer nodes. Users accessing the links can select information from mainframe databases and load it directly into spreadsheets or other programs without having to wrestle with intimidating data base languages (2).

A centralized configuration of personal microcomputers in a 2-level hierarchial form, can be used for distributed parallel processing of centralized data as indicated in Figure 1. This is the network adopted by our Computational Hydraulics Group (CHG).

Parallel processing, when done in multi-user single processors, is called multi-tasking. In our distributed parallel processing network, the independent blocks of a large program are assigned to the nodes in the lower level of the hierarchy. The nodes usually require input time series data or provide output time series data as a result of the processing. The boss computer at the top level of the hierarchy holds an intelligent time series manager (TSM) which supplies data when nodes so request, or store data when supplied by the nodes. The nodes are protected from the details of storage. Although the output from one node may be the required input to the next, the data flow is done through the boss computer and TSM. The term "distributed processing of centralized data" refers to the system which distributes the centralized database to the various computers. Generally the nodes are all executing an independent portion of a large package concurrently. This, if synchronized properly, is a more efficient computing environment than any sequential processing scheme in which a single processor is utilized.

During a distributed data processing application it may be important to synchronize the processing at each node of the local area network. The boss computer distributes the data from the time series

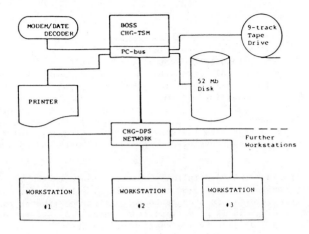

Figure 1

store (TSS) on a hard disk to the satellites. The objective is to reach an efficient computing environment. It will never be possible to optimize the computing such that each node is actively computing all the time, never waiting for data to arrive. On the other hand, if the nodes end up waiting for data for an unreasonable span of time the whole distributed processing approach will be meaningless, since a single processor can do the whole job with comparable efficiency.

Consequently it is important to estimate the time a node will take to finish computing once the data is downloaded from the DBMS. Program measurement techniques make it possible to obtain timing relations. Program measurement forms part of the boss computer software together with the TSM, (4).

Integrated Hydrologic Software

The typical activities of a hydrologic/hydraulic work group may include:

(a) Field instrumentation,
(b) Data capture and management,
(c) Atmospheric fallout, pollution build-up and wash-off modelling,
(d) Storm dynamics modelling,
(e) Large scale continuous modelling,
(f) Modelling unsteady flow in complex networks,
(g) Receiving water modelling,
(h) Statistical post-processing and modelling, and

(i)   Real-time control.

There is a critical need for measuring rainfall intensity and stormwater discharge accurately in urban areas. This requires high spatial and time resolution, typically at one-minute intervals. To meet this need, rainfall intensity monitoring equipment was developed by CHG, based on single-chip microcomputers utilizing reusable cassette tape as a recording medium. The equipment is currently in use in Hamilton (14 gauges), in Ontario as part of the acid precipitation network (6 gauges), in the Arctic (3 gauges), the Ottawa area (6 gauges), the Halifax area (20 gauges), Oslo (6 gauges) and Kentucky. Software (DASUTIL) was developed to process the data and to archive it on tape.

An important interdisciplinary research topic is the relation of atmospheric pollution to stormwater modelling. Fallout from industry and vehicular traffic is thought to be a major contributor to surface pollutant loadings in large metropolitan areas. An attempt was made by our group to identify the sources of pollutants available for washoff, and the mechanisms of build-up and washoff. The computer program is known as ATMDST.

The development of appropriate software to determine the movement of stormwater pollutants through a city-wide network of combined sewers is a closely related problem. This software processes information on the dates of street cleaning activities and incorporates algorithms for processes such as traffic, interception by the leaf canopy, and so on. The program is called CHGQUAL.

A computer program package, RAINPAK, has been developed for simulating storm dynamics. Variations in storm speed and direction were found to produce storm flows and pollutant concentrations significantly different from the conventional assumptions of stationary storm distributions. The model accounts for temporal and spatial variations in storms, such as ageing, merging, splitting of storm cells, and so on. Analysis of data from rain sensors is performed by the programs STOVEL, THOR3D, THOR4D, and THOR4DPT, in RAINPAK.

A computer model, OVRFLO3, was developed for modelling sideweir diversion structures. This was motivated by the need to accurately model the first flush loadings from urban areas which will reach the treatment facility, or be diverted to the outfalls.

A computer model, TOTSED, was developed to predict bed sediment and suspended sediment load as a function of time and distance along a one-dimensional quasi-steady-state receiving area near a combined sewer outfall. The model was calibrated using data obtained through a sampling program carried out in the Chedoke Creek outfall channel in Coote's Paradise in Hamilton. TOTSED provides an interface between an urban drainage network and a receiving water body.

In order to facilitate the use of these models in a teaching environment, a series of pre-processing programs has been developed. These programs, FASTSWMM3, FASTHEC2 and FASTHYMO, prompt the user for input data in the appropriate sequence, to which he responds by providing data in free-format and/or optional commands which direct the job path along various routes. The pre-processors take care of all system job control language, design file manipulation, and sequentially execute the programs. In this way the user can focus on the hydrologic problems without having to be concerned about the computer system, thereby reducing time expended on learning and/or carrying out calibration, validation or sensitivity analyses. The system has been adapted to IBM-PC compatibles and is known as PCSWMM3, depicted in Figure 2. The models ATMDST, CHGQUAL, RAINPAK, OVRFLO AND TOTSED were designed to be incorporated as additional "blocks" of SWMM3. Each will be incorporated in PCSWMM3.

Using observed event rainfall intensity, discharge and pollutant concentration data, obtained from the field program, a discrete event model of the Hamilton urban drainage system was constructed, calibrated and validated.

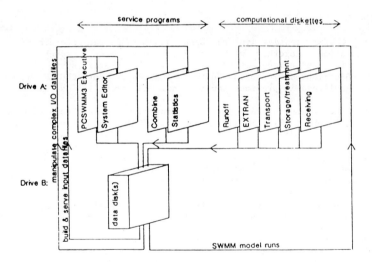

Figure 2

The RUNOFF Block of SWMM3 was used for this purpose. The basic time-step for the general model is five minutes. A coarse model of the system (time-step of one hour) was also developed; all diversion structures were assumed to be operating such that flow was directed to the receiving waters.

The coarse model of the drainage system was run continuously for a period of nine years (May to October inclusive) at a time-step of one hour using rainfall data from the Environmental Canada Archives, in order to develop long-term loadings of pollutants to the Hamilton receiving waters. Special routines (DATANAL) were written to interface with these data tapes. The results of the continuous modelling were subjected to statistical analyses, in order to develop "easy-to-evaluate" equations for predicting stormwater pollutant loadings for interfacing with a model of the Hamilton Harbour.

To lessen the impact of pollutant loadings in the receiving waters, due to sewer overlfows, real-time control by microcomputers located in diversion structures and in storage tanks should be considered. A detailed study of the design of a microprocessor circuit for installation in a specific, existing overflow structure was conducted. The software is called RTCONTROL (part of DASUTIL). This instrumentation integrates with the rainfall and discharge monitoring equipment mentioned earlier to control overflows and make maximum use of in-system storage.

CHGTSM

CHGTSM resides in the boss computer of the hierarchial configuration together with program measurement, synchronization, security and communication protocols. The overall system is called CHG-Distributed Processing Software (CHGDPS). Both CHGTSM and CHGDPS are explained in previous papers (Unal and James, 1984 a,b).

The Computational Hydraulics Group Time Series Store (CHGTSS) is prepared by the Time Series Manager (CHGTSM). CHGTSM is a custom-made applications-oriented pseudo-relational data base management system which provides easy access to Time Series Data, independent of details of storage. CHGTSM prepares, manages and distributes the CHGTSS, like any other DBMS and imposes security restrictions by which unprivileged users are not allowed to write information into the data base (3).

One important feature of CHGTSM is the capability of compressing redundant data through the access method. Savings in memory space using CHGTSM is displayed in Table 1. The first line in Table 1 gives the size for a fictious time series data file in Kbytes. The file represents one year of rain data collected at a one minute time step. Compression takes place in two stages: externally (i.e. when the data file is read by CHGTSM) and internally (i.e. when data is structured in the database). The significance of internal compression increases with the increase in the number of rainy days. The bottom line in Table 1 gives the estimated sizes of the same data if CHGTSM was written in a programming language which allows variable-size records in a file. Note that the performance displayed in Table 1 is under ideal conditions. Although it is possible to obtain even better results with CHGTSM, storage conditions may result in less efficient use of space. The need for a file with variable record sizes increases under these circumstances.

TABLE 1: STORAGE SAVINGS

# OF RAINY DAYS	50	100	150	200
Size before (Kbytes) CHGTSM	2102.4 (0%)	2102.4 (0%)	2102.4 (0%)	2102.4 (0%)
Size After External Compression by CHGTSM	393.9 (81.2%)	692.9 (67%)	991.9 (52.8%)	1290.9 (38.6%)
Size After Internal Compression by CHGTSM	185.9 (91.2%)	282.2 (86.6%)	367.9 (82.5%)	458.9 (78.2%)
If written in a Superior Language	104.0 (95.1%)	213.3 (89.9%)	312.0 (85.2%)	416.0 (80.2%)

% savings are displayed in brackets

Hardware System

The hardware installed by our group is as follows:

(a) Boss:

8088-based portable PC-compatible, 512kbytes memory, 2 floppy disk drives, 8087 co-processor;

9-track tape drive, interface card, TIP software;

52 Mbyte hard disk (43 formatted), interface card, software;

Modem: 1200 BAUD, dial-up;

Printer: High resolution, dot matrix.

(b) 5 Nodes: same as boss CPU

(c) Software: MS-DOS 2.1, MS-FORTRAN 3.2, Network.

The approximate cost per station is $5000.

The PC-compatibles were selected on the basis of a large power supply and a large fan. The speed of computation with the 8087 math co-processor has been found to be as fast as one-fifth that of a CDC CYBER 172, for typical computations, obtained by programming measurement techniques (3).

Regarding large disk storage, the primary constraints are imposed by MS-DOS, which restricts logical disk volumes to 32 Mbytes. Because of this the data base may need to be segmented.

The 9-track drive unit includes an intelligent interface that utilizes a Z-80 microprocessor and proprietary firmware to provide data transfer between a Personal Computer, and an IBM mainframe-compatible 9-track tape drive with an embedded formatter. Supplied by the manufacturer of the hardware is a software interface package, TIP (Tape Interchange Program). Utilizing TIP the user may freely transfer data between Personal Computers and the 9-track tape drive. The interface occupies a single slot in the PC Bus, and is interfaced directly to the 9-track tape drive via two 50-pin data cables.

The tape subsystem is both self-loading and self-threading for ease of use. The subsystem provides disk-to-tape transfer at rates of 0.7 megabytes per minute, with up to 42 megabytes of data storage per tape. The tape unit supports 1600 BPI tapes, with user-specified recording formats from 2 bytes to 16 kilobytes per block. The tape drive will accept all standard 9-track tape drive reel sizes up to 10-1/2 inches in diameter.

Each tape subsystem includes a single density 5-1/4 inch diskette containing three comprehensive programs and two utilities that allow the user to read, write, or inspect a 9-track tape:

1. TREAD - A tape-to-disk-copy/conversion program which will read ANSI compatible data records from the 9-track tape and convert them to DOS compatible ASCII format, record segmentation of user's choice, and user-specified file name and disk selection.

2. TWRITE - The counterpart of TREAD, TWRITE is a disk-to-copy/conversion program. TWRITE copies DOS compatible disk files to tape in ANSI compatible format. This program allows for ASCII to EBCDIC format, and a user-specified tape record structure.

3. TDUMP - This program allows the user to dump the contents of a 9-track tape to either the user's console or to the system printer. This utility is extremely useful to determine the format in which a tape has been written.

4. TUTIL - This file contains the primary assembly language subroutines that are used in TIP. These subroutines may

easily be linked into other 'High Level Language' programs
to create user-customized tape control programs.

5. TLINK - A tape control utility module designed to be linked
   into Basic programs to allow the user to create simple, yet
   powerful, customized tape control programs.

References

1. Dahmke, M. 1982. "Local Networks Save Money, Increase Re-
   liablility". Popular Computing. April, 1982, pp. 138-140.

2. Freedman, D.H. 1984. "Tapping the Corporate Database". Business
   Terminology. April, 1984, pp. 27-29.

3. Unal, A. and James, W. 1984(a). "SWMM3 Program Measurement for
   Optimal Use on a Personal Microcomputer Network". Proceedings of
   the Stormwater and Water Quality Modelling Conference, USEPA,
   Burlington, Ontario, September 6-7, 1984, pp. 101-110.

4. Unal, A. and James, W. 1984(b). "Centralized Time Series Management Programs for Continuous SWMM3 on Personal Microcomputers",
   Proceedings of the Stormwater and Water Quality Modelling Conference, USEPA, Burlington, Ontario, September 6-7, 1984, pp. 91-
   100.

Ground-Water Flow Model of Soda-Ash Waste Beds

Marjory B. Rinaldo-Lee*

Abstract

A recent application by a steel manufacturing plant to obtain a permit for an industrial landfill located on top of abandoned soda-ash waste beds in the City of Syracuse, New York, resulted in an extensive hydrogeologic investigation. The investigation included developing a three-dimensional ground-water flow model of the soda-ash waste beds.

The extensive hydrogeologic investigation performed at this site was due to 1) previous disposal of hazardous waste by the metal manufacturer at the site, and 2) the unique location of the landfill on top of pre-existing waste beds on the shores of a large lake (Onondaga Lake). The purpose of this study was to investigate site hydrogeology and predict the fate of leachate released by the metals manufacturing waste using a ground-water flow model. Using data gathered from the field program a three-dimensional ground-water flow model was developed for the area using the USGS Model (2),(3) to simulate three-dimensional water flow. Seven layers were used in the ground-water flow model. Good correlation between observed ground-water flow patterns and simulated ground-water flow was obtained using field and laboratory measurements for hydraulic conductivity of the different geologic units. Results from the investigation indicated leachate from the waste will flow predominantly vertically downward through 65 feet (20 m) of soda-ash waste before discharging into Onondaga Lake and an adjacent stream.

Introduction

Permitting an existing landfill is a situation currently confronting many industries due to recent State and Federal Solid Waste regulations. Facilities which had been used for many years to dispose of a variety of wastes, including some now classified as hazardous under Federal regulations, are being upgraded to meet the new regulations. This investigation was initiated to obtain a permit for an existing disposal site for a specialty steel mill located outside of Syracuse, New York.

Although only non-hazardous wastes are currently disposed of in the landfill, previous disposal of materials classified as hazardous wastes at the landfill and the unique location of the landfill on top of pre-existing soda-ash waste beds on the shores of a large lake resulted in an extensive hydrogeologic investigation. The

*Senior Hydrogeologist, Empire-Thomsen, 105 Corona Avenue, Groton, NY 13073.

investigation was more extensive than for a similar waste type in another setting. The purpose of this paper is to present the results of the hydrogeologic investigation at the site.

Procedure

Seventy-six monitoring points were installed in the vicinity of the steel mill landfill including 41 monitoring wells, 25 piezometers, 5 lysimeters, and 5 seepage galleries. Water level readings were taken at the wells over a 16 month period to define the groundwater flow regime. Hydraulic conductivity of the underlying deposits was examined using slug tests on 16 wells following the methodology of Bouwer and Rice (1) and performing 5 laboratory permeability tests on undisturbed samples (4). Physical characteristics of the unconsolidated deposits were determined by grain size analyses on 15 soil samples and 1 soda-ash waste sample in accordance with ASTM Particle-Size Analysis of Soils (D 422-63). A three-dimensional ground-water flow model was used to corroborate field data and estimated flow patterns, and investigate the route of leachate migration generated by the steel mill wastes (2),(3).

Results and Discussion

Site Setting

The landfill is located on the southwestern shore of Onondaga Lake, a large lake near Syracuse, New York. A large area along the eastern shore of the lake is covered with up to 65 feet (20 m) of soda-ash process wastes. The steel mill wastes have been placed as a thin cap on only a small portion of the soda-ash waste beds. The landfill occupies about 17 acres (69,000 m^2) of the 370 acres (1.5 m^2) covered by the soda-ash waste beds. The steel mill wastes are only 2 feet (0.5 m) to 6 feet (2.0 m) in depth on top of 65 feet (20 m) of soda-ash wastes.

The soda-ash wastes were hydraulically deposited between the 1880's and 1950's in large impoundments along the lake shore. The impoundments were filled with the slurried waste, then allowed to dewater. To allow for expansion of the waste beds during the early part of the century, Ninemile Creek was diverted to its present location at the base of the soda-ash waste beds. The former creek bed is buried beneath the waste beds directly below the steel mill landfill (Figure 1).

Geology

The borings for the monitoring wells provided information on the unconsolidated deposits beneath the steel mill wastes. The landfill is underlain by at least 140 feet (42 m) of unconsolidated deposits, consisting of five geologic units: soda-ash waste, swamp and lacustrine deposits, alluvial deposits, glacio-lacustrine deposits and ablation till. The interrelationship of these units is shown on cross section A-A' perpendicular to the lake shore and roughly parallel to the old creek channel (Figure 2).

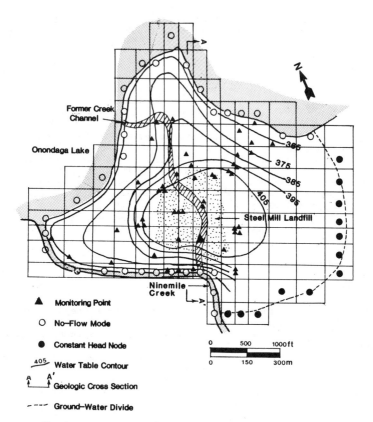

Fig. 1. GROUND-WATER OF AREA AROUND STEEL MILL LANDFILL

The uppermost unit is soda-ash waste. The soda-ash wastes are 65 feet (20 m) thick beneath the steel mill landfill and consist primarily of silt-size particles of insoluble residues, hydroxides and various salts. Hydraulic placement has resulted in interbedded and interfingered layers of waste ranging from thin to massive layers, 8 inches (20 cm) or more in thickness. Frequent partings and laminae, as well as thin layers of gray waste consisting of mixed flyash and soda-ash waste are found throughout the beds.

Although secondary permeability and channelization flow within the waste was an area of concern due to evidence of vertical jointing, laboratory and field testing indicated that the joints do not cross individual stratigraphic boundaries. Laboratory permeability tests on undisturbed soda-ash waste samples were used to estimate vertical hydraulic conductivity of the waste. Field slug tests were used to estimate horizontal hydraulic conductivity of the waste beds. The mean horizontal hydraulic conductivity was 2×10^{-6} ft/sec

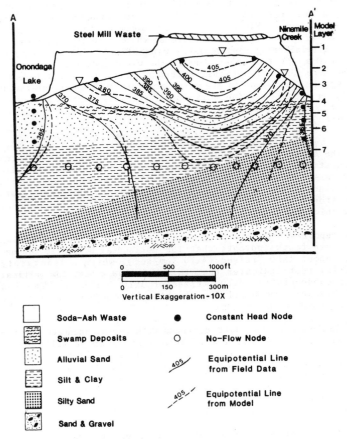

Fig. 2. GEOLOGIC CROSS SECTION A-A

(6x10^{-5} cm/sec) as compared to the mean vertical hydraulic conductivity of 3x10^{-7} ft/sec (8x10^{-6} cm/sec). Thus, the horizontal hydraulic conductivity is about seven times the vertical hydraulic conductivity. Since the waste was deposited in layers, the horizontal hydraulic conductivity would be expected to be higher than the vertical hydraulic conductivity.

Beneath the waste beds are swamp and lacustrine deposits which are 8 feet (2.5 m) to 16 feet (5.0 m) thick. These deposits consist of peat, marl, silt, fine sand and clay. The vertical hydraulic conductivity of this layer was measured in the laboratory as 2x10^{-8} ft/sec (7x10^{-7} cm/sec). Due to the low vertical hydraulic conductivity of these deposits, this layer will retard the downward flow of groundwater.

Beneath the swamp deposits is either alluvial silty sands in the area of the old creek channel or glaciolacustrine deposits. The cross section shown in Figure 2 is roughly parallel to the old creek channel, so alluvial silty sands are shown beneath the swamp deposits. The alluvial silty sand deposits range from 8 feet (2.5 m) to 20 feet (6.0 m) in thickness beneath the waste beds and increase in thickness where the post glacial stream channel entered the lake. The stream channel deposits are more permeable than either overlying or underlying deposits. The horizontal hydraulic conductivity of this layer measured by a field test was 3×10^{-3} ft/sec (9×10^{-4} cm/sec).

Below the alluvial sands in the Ninemile Creek channel or directly below the swamp deposits outside the stream channel is a thick glaciolacustrine unit. The upper portion of the glaciolacustrine deposit consists of alternating layers of silt, clay and sandy silt. The glaciolacustrine silts and clays increase in thickness toward the lake trough and ranges from about 26 feet (8 m) to 42 feet (13 m) in thickness beneath the site.

These deposits are less permeable than the overlying alluvial sands. Field tests indicate that the horizontal hydraulic conductivity is about 1×10^{-6} ft/sec (4×10^{-5} cm/sec), while a laboratory permeability test indicates that this unit has a very low vertical hydraulic conductivity (2×10^{-7} ft/sec or 5×10^{-8} cm/sec). The low vertical hydraulic conductivity of this unit further restricts the downward movement of groundwater.

The glaciolacustrine unit coarsens with depth. Beneath the upper silt and clay layers is a more permeable layer of silty sand. This sequence of thick silt and clay deposits overlying more granular silty sand is found throughout the area. The top of the silty sands is 108 feet (33 m) to 150 feet (46 m) below the steel mill wastes. The sandy silt ranges from 49 feet (15 m) to 69 feet (21 m) in thickness beneath the site. The horizontal hydraulic conductivity of this unit is estimated at 1×10^{-5} ft/sec (4×10^{-4} cm/sec).

Beneath the thick sequence of glaciolacustrine deposits is a thin deposit of ablation till. This unit consists of sand and gravel, 13 feet (4 m) to 16 feet (5 m) in thickness. The hydraulic conductivity of the ablation till measured in field test was 1×10^{-4} ft/sec (4×10^{-3} cm/sec). Shale bedrock underlies the ablation till.

Ground-Water Flow

Ground-water levels were measured over a 16 month period to define the ground-water flow regime. The water table contours are shown on Figure 1. A large ground-water mound is found in the soda-ash waste beds beneath the steel mill wastes. Ground water from the mound flows toward Onondaga Lake and Ninemile Creek. A ground-water divide exists south of the site, and all water from the site ultimately discharges into Onondaga Lake. The ground-water mound beneath the landfill is the result of 1) greater infiltration through the steel mill wastes than in adjacent areas of soda-ash

waste 2) low permeability of the soda-ash waste. Ground-water flow
beneath the site is complex due to the subsurface deposits. The
direction of ground-water flow in the subsurface deposits can be
seen in Cross Section A-A', Figure 2. Although some ground water
from the site discharges into Ninemile Creek directly from the
soda-ash waste, the majority of ground-water flow from the site
moves through the swamp and lacustrine deposits and underlying silt
and sand deposits before discharge into surface waters.

Ground-Water Model

    In order to further examine the ground-water flow regime in the
vicinity of the steel mill waste landfill, a three-dimensional
ground-water flow model was developed for the area. The purpose of
the model was to 1) investigate the ultimate fate of leachate generated by the steel mill wastes and 2) provide a means of checking our
field data and estimated ground-water flow patterns. The groundwater flow model used was developed by the United States Geological
Survey (2), (3). The model uses a finite-difference approximation
to solve the partial differential equations of ground-water flow. A
steady-state simulation was used to examine ground-water flow
patterns.

    The area around the steel mill landfill was divided into a
series of blocks for the model (Figure 1). A variable grid spacing
was used to concentrate nodes in the area of the steel mill waste.
The boundary of the area used in the model was Onondaga Lake on the
north, east and northwest; Ninemile Creek on the southwest; and a
ground-water divide on the south. Ninemile Creek and Onondaga Lake
were assumed to be constant-head boundaries and the ground-water
divide was assumed to be a no-flow boundary.

    To simulate three-dimensional flow, the unconsolidated deposits
were divided into seven layers. The seven layers were based on the
geologic units underlying the steel mill wastes. Due to model constraints on allowable changes in thickness between adjacent layers,
the top 3 layers of the model were soda-ash waste. The swamp and
lacustrine deposits below the soda-ash waste constitute the fourth
layer. The fifth layer was predominantly alluvial silty sand, while
the bottom two layers of the model were the glaciolacustrine deposits. Layer six was predominantly the upper glaciolacustrine deposit
of silt and clay and the bottom layer was the lower glaciolacustrine
deposit of silty sand. Because the subsurface deposits do not consist of uniform, flat layers, extending to the edges of the area
modelled, adjustments were made in the imput data to compensate for
actual geologic conditions of the site.

    The top four layers are relatively flat so that model layer
boundaries coincide with the subsurface deposits. However, the geologic units beneath the swamp/lacustrine deposits dip and increase
in thickness toward the lake. Transmissivity values were adjusted
in the lower three layers because these units include different
deposits in different areas of the layer due to the dipping and increasing thickness of the deposits.

The lateral boundaries of the upper two layers of the model also had to be adjusted because the soda-ash waste forms a truncated pyramid. Thus, the upper two layers of the model are smaller than the lower layers and do not extend to the lake or stream which from the boundaries for the lower layers of the model. Constant head boundaries were placed around the edges of these upper two layers.

Initial values for the parameters needed for the model were obtained from field and laboratory data. Water levels from monitoring wells on the site were used to construct equipotential lines along two model cross sections. Initial head values for nodes in each layer were estimated from these cross sections. Original transmissivity values for each layer were estimated from field and laboratory data. Initial values for infiltration were obtained using a model developed by the Environmental Protection Agency (EPA) to estimate infiltration into the landfills (5). Infiltration values were computed for both areas covered by steel mill waste and areas where soda-ash waste was at the surface. The model was calibrated by changing transmissivity and infiltration values by trail and error until the head distribution generated by the model matched the initial head distribution.

Table 1 shows a comparison between the estimated values for hydraulic conductivity based on field data and final values used to calibrate the model.

TABLE 1 – Comparison of Hydraulic Conductivity Estimated From Field and Laboratory Data and Hydraulic Conductivity Values Used in Ground-Water Flow Model.

Model Layer	Predominant Geologic Unit	K (cm/sec)		K_H/K_V	
		Field	Model	Field/Lab	Model
1	Soda Ash Waste	2×10^{-6}	2×10^{-6}	7	6
2	Soda Ash Waste	2×10^{-6}	2×10^{-6}	7	6
3	Soda Ash Waste	2×10^{-6}	2×10^{-6}	7	6
4	Swamp/Lacustrine	7×10^{-7}	7×10^{-7}	30	15
5	Alluvial Silty Sand	3×10^{-5}	7×10^{-5}	50	50
6	Silt, Clay & Sandy Silt (Upper Glaciolacustrine Deposits	1×10^{-6}	3×10^{-6}	800	100
7	Silty Sand (Lower Glaciolacustrine Deposits)	1×10^{-5}	3×10^{-6}	100	100

Note: 1 ft/sec = 30 cm/sec

The final values used for hydraulic conductivity were very close to the original estimates obtained from field data. Since estimated values for hydraulic conductivity for the upper layers were based on a large number of samples, while very few hydraulic conductivity tests were run on samples from the lower deposits, the final values used for the model show closer agreement for the upper layers. However, the hydraulic conductivity values used for the model for even the lower layers show very good agreement with the estimated values.

Infiltration values were also changed by trial and error during model calibration. Using the amount of infiltration estimated by the EPA model (5) through the soda-ash waste (8.7 in./year or 22 cm/year) provided a good calibration of the model in areas outside the steel mill landfill. However, a much higher infiltration value was needed than predicted by the EPA model (5) for the area of the steel mill landfill and a parking lot adjacent to the landfill to produce the observed ground-water elevations beneath the landfill. The EPA model predicted 13 inches/year (33 cm/year) of infiltration in these areas whereas 23 inches/year (58 cm/year) were needed in the ground-water model to match ground-water contours beneath the steel mill wastes. The discrepancy is probably due to the fact that 1) the model was calibrated to water-table elevations measured during the spring when recharge is high and 2) the EPA model assumed 13 inches (33 cm) of water could runoff, whereas the landfill is flat so runoff from the landfill is negligible.

The results of the model agree very well with the estimated equipotential lines drawn from measured water levels as shown on the geologic cross section (Figure 2). These results corroborate conclusions from field data that 1) the majority of water infiltrating through the steel mill wastes flows vertically downward through the underlying soda-ash waste and swamp and lacustrine deposits before moving laterally toward the lake and 2) a small percentage of water passing through the steel mill wastes moves vertically downward through the soda-ash wastes before discharging into the creek.

In addition to corroborating estimated hydraulic conductivity of the various subsurface deposits and ground-water flow patterns based on field data, the model provided estimates of ground-water discharge from the various layers to both the lake and stream. This information was helpful in assessing the impact of leachate on surface water by providing estimates of both leachate dilution by ground water before discharge into the lake or stream, and the relative amounts of ground-water discharge into the lake and stream. The calculated discharge from the base of the soda-ash waste, swamp, and lacustrine deposits into Ninemile Creek was 925,000 gallons/year (3.3×10^{-6} L/year) while the calculated amount of ground-water discharge into Onondaga Lake from the alluvial sand and glaciolacustrine deposits was 3.9×10^{7} gallons/year (1.4×10^{8} L/year). The calculated discharge into Ninemile Creek was only 2% of the ground-water discharge into Onondaga Lake.

Conclusions

Results from the study indicate that the majority of water infiltrating through the steel mill wastes flows vertically downward through the underlying soda-ash waste and swamp and lacustrine deposits before moving laterally toward the lake. However, a small percentage of water passing through the steel mill wastes moves vertically downward through the soda-ash wastes before discharging into the creek. The three-dimensional ground-water flow model developed for the site corroborated field data and estimated ground-water flow patterns.

Developing a ground-water flow model to investigate the ultimate fate of leachate generated by the steel mill wastes, was an important factor in enabling the industry to obtain a permit for continued disposal of waste at the site.

Appendix 1 - References

1. Bouwer, H. and Rice, R. C., "A Slug Test for Determining Hydraulic Conductivity of Unconfined Aquifers With Completely or Partially Penetrating Wells," Water Resources Research, Vol. 12, No. 3, 1976, pp. 423-428.

2. Trescott, P. C., "Documentation of Finite-Difference Model for Simulation of Three-Dimensional Ground-Water Flow", USGS Open File Report 75-438, 1976.

3. Trescott, P. C. and S. P. Larson, "Supplement to Open File Report 75-438", USGS Open File Report 76-591, 1976.

4. United States Army Corps of Engineers, "Laboratory Soils Testing", Engineering Manual EM 1110-2-1906, Appendix 7, Section 7, 1970.

5. United States Environmental Protection Agency, "Hydrologic Simulation on Solid Waste Disposal Sites", SW-868, 1980.

GROUNDWATER MODELS IN CHOOSING

WATER TREATMENT METHODS

PAUL W. GROSSER, Ph.D., P.E., ASSOCIATE MEMBER ASCE*

ABSTRACT

The choice of water treatment techniques for the removal of volatile halogenated organic chemicals from
groundwater is dependent on the expected period that the
well will be contaminated. The length of time that the
well is expected to be contaminated dictates the design
life and therefore the annual cost of a given alternative.
Groundwater modeling can provide insight into the source
of contamination and then determine the length of time
required to remove the contamination.

This paper presents an example of the use of groundwater models to identify the source of contamination and
then design a treatment scheme. Included is a discussion
of several different methods of organics treatment (air
stripping, spray aeration and granular activated carbon),
their costs and which is most appropriate based upon the
results of the groundwater modeling effort.

Conclusions to be drawn from the paper are that
groundwater models can be a major part of the water resource management decision process. Their use provides
not only physical information about the response of an
aquifer system, but information of importance for an economic evaluation as well.

INTRODUCTION

The choice of an optimum method for treatment of contaminated groundwater, whether for public water supply or
aquifer restoration, is based, in part, on the design life
of the project. The design life can be defined as the
period of time that the raw water quality will exceed some
predefined standard, such as drinking water standards.
This is particularly important in choosing water treatment
methods for the reduction of volatile organic compounds.
Viable alternatives for the reduction of volatile organic
compounds include granular activated carbon, specialized
adsorption resins, air stripping towers, spray irrigation
with aquifer recharge and spray irrigation into a storage

*Project Manager - Holzmacher, McLendon & Murrell, P.C.,
125 Baylis Road, Melville, N.Y. 11747

tank. Each of these alternatives have widely varying capital and operations and maintenance costs with none of them
clearly more economical in all cases.

Insight into the necessary design life can be gained
through the use of groundwater flow models utilizing microcomputers. The flow model is used to simulate groundwater
conditions (levels) in the vicinity of a contaminated well
while it is pumping. This can be relatively simply converted to contaminant travel times to the well in an area
identified in which contaminant sources must be located.
Possible contaminant sources can be identified and their
discharge history investigated to determine period of discharge, contaminants in the discharge and quantity of discharge. This information is then compared with the
characteristics of the well contamination to implicate a
contaminant source with the well contamination. This
methodology was used to identify possible contaminant
sources of a drinking water supply well in the Hicksville
Water District, Long Island, New York.

APPLICATION

Plant No. 8 of the Hicksville Water District was
first developed in 1957 when Wells 8-1 and 8-2 were constructed on the site. Well 8-1 is 637 feet deep and has a
capacity of 1,400 GPM. For the last four years, Well 8-1
has been the lag well at this plant behind Well 8-3.

Well 8-2 is 477 feet deep and has a capacity of 1,190
GPM. As a result of elevated levels of nitrates in this
well, it has not been used in the last four years except
for testing.

In 1977, Well 8-3 was constructed 75 feet north of
Well 8-1. The well is 635 feet deep and has a capacity of
1,400 GPM. For the last four years, Well 8-3 has been the
lead well at the plant pumping approximately 90 percent of
the water pumped at the plant in 1983.

Annual chemical analyses have been taken at each of
the three wells on the site since they were constructed.
Over the years, these reports have indicated that the
water quality in each of the three wells has deteriorated,
particularly with regard to nitrates. Well No. 8-2 has
been impacted the most, since its water currently exceeds
the USEPA standard for nitrate concentration in drinking
water (10 mg/l). The source of most nitrate contamination
in shallow wells on Long Island is the cumulative effects
of increasing densities of on-site sewage disposal (septic
systems). This should improve in the future as sewering
substantially reduces these groundwater discharges.

Wells 8-1 and 8-3 maintained minimal concentrations of nitrate over the years, although very recent trends may indicate that the nitrates in these wells may also be on the rise. Since these are recent trends, it is very difficult to distinguish if they are legitimate at this time. Of greater concern than the nitrate contamination is the sudden rise in the concentration of volatile halogenated organics in Wells 8-1 and 8-3. Table 1 indicates these chemicals and their concentrations found in Wells 8-1 and 8-3. The primary contaminants of concern are tetrachloroethylene and trichloroethylene.

TABLE 1

	Well 8-1	Well 8-3
1,2-dichloroethylene	1 ppb	
trichloroethylene	3 ppb	1 ppb
tetrachloroethylene	29 ppb	11 ppb

Tetrachloroethylene, also known as perchloroethylene, is commonly used in the dry cleaning industry (dry cleaning fluid), for degreasing metals and as a solvent. Trichloroethylene is used as a solvent for fats, waxes, resins, oils, rubber, paints and varnishes and also as a dry cleaning agent. The source of these contaminants is most likely related to a dry cleaner or a metal working shop of some kind. The possibility does exist that the trichloroethylene and 1,2-dichloroethylene originated as tetrachloroethylene, since they are decomposition products of tetrachloroethylene. If this is the case, the most likely source of the contamination is related to the dry cleaning industry, since it utilizes a much larger portion of tetrachloroethylene than any other industry in the area.

A groundwater model was utilized to identify the source of contamination and evaluate various remediation alternatives. The groundwater model used was the Prickett-Lonnquist Aquifer Simulation Model (PLASM) run on an Apple IIE microcomputer. This model is in common usage and can be readily found compatible with a number of computer hardware systems from micros to main frames. The model is relatively simple to use, requiring only aquifer transmissivities, storage coefficients, initial heads and confining layer characteristics and stresses to calculate aquifer heads with time. Due to its ease of use, it can be run many times so that sensitivity analyses can be performed on the system under study. It is these sensitivity studies that provide the investigator with the insight to evaluate the system.

The model utilized a variable grid spacing to simulate the impact of various pumping schemes on piezometric heads within the portion of the Magothy aquifer screened by Wells 8-1 and 8-3. The model was calibrated by reproducing a field test where Well 8-3 was pumped and the drawdowns measured in both 8-1 and 8-3. Based on this calibration of the model to pump test results, a transmissivity of 33,400 gpd/ft, storage coefficient of .003, aquifer thickness of 80 feet and vertical conductivity of overlying beds of .00144 gpd/cf were used for all scenarios. Using the above values, the model results straddle the actual drawdowns with reasonable closeness, although additional accuracy can be obtained but was limited by the project budget.

Three different pumping scenarios were modeled to represent the most typical pumping pattern and two other more extreme pumping patterns. The three scenarios were as follows:

(1)   Well No. 8-3 pumping at a rate of 2.016 MGD. This is the actual condition which exists at Plant No. 8 slightly over 50 percent of the time.

(2)   Well No. 8-3 pumping at a rate of 2.016 MGD and Well No. 8-2 pumping at a rate of 2.13 MGD. This condition exists at Plant No. 8 less than 6 percent of the time.

(3)   Plant No. 8 pumping at a rate of 4.15 MGD and Plant No. 9 (upstream) pumping at a rate of 4.0 MGD. This is a worst case situation used to evaluate the interaction of Plants No. 8 and 9.

From the scenarios, it can be seen that there must be considerable latitude in interpreting the model results, since the three scenarios indicate conditions only less than 60 percent of the time. The results of scenarios 1 and 3 are shown in Figures 1 and 2, respectively. Groundwater levels in Figure 1 have been converted to contaminant travel times within the aquifer.

A review of the land use within this area showed that it is predominantly residential with scattered commercial strips along the main roads. The closest probable source of contamination was a former dry cleaning shop located on Jerusalem Avenue approximately 1,000 feet due west of Plant No. 8. Based upon the analysis of travel times, this was approximately two years horizontally away from

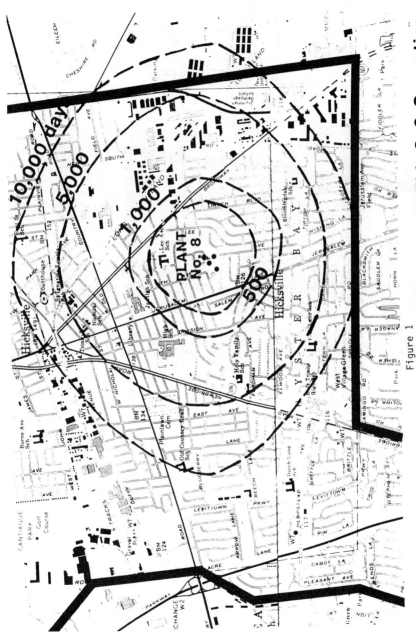

Figure 1

Travel Times to WELL 8-3 – WELL 8-3 Operating

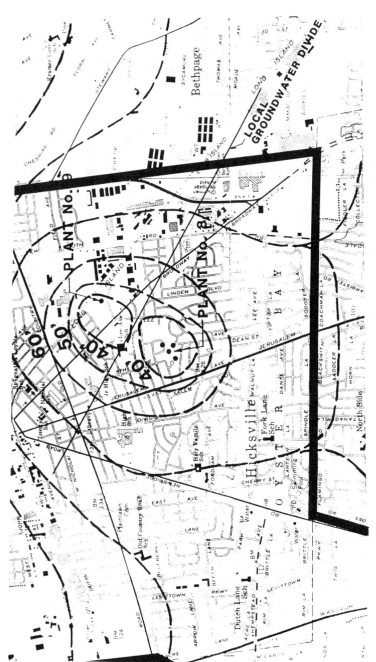

Piezometric Levels Plants No.8 & 9 Operating

Figure 2

Plant No. 8. Based on the calculated drawdowns at this distance and a 40:1 ratio between horizontal and vertical conductivities, it was estimated that it will take 12 years for the contaminant to reach the screen depths of Wells 8-1 and 8-3. This then yields an overall travel time of approximately 14 years under best conditions. It was expected that this travel time may actually range from 14 to 20 years. This corresponded well with the period of time in which this dry cleaner was operating (1960-1974).

The next closest probable source of contamination was a dry cleaning shop located on Broadway approximately 2,000 feet due east of Plant No. 8. Based on the analysis of travel times, this was approximately 6 years horizontally away from Plant No. 8. It was estimated that it will take over 15 years for the contaminant to reach the screen depths of Wells 8-1 and 8-3. This then yields an overall travel time of approximately 21 years under best conditions. It was expected that this travel time may actually range from 25 to 30 years. This also corresponded to the period of time in which this dry cleaner has been operating (1955 to present). This possible source of contamination must be considered less likely than the previous one discussed due to possible influences of Plant No. 9. The travel times from these two contaminant sources are illustrated in Figure 3.

Based on the above analysis, four possible treatment alternatives were identified, based on the premise that the contamination is the result of both possible sources over a period of years. Period of discharge ended with the construction of sewers within the last five years. The alternatives are as follows:

1. Rest Wells 8-1 and 8-3 for prolonged periods and use them only for peaking periods. Since the wells are not in the natural path of the organic contamination, if the wells are rested, the contamination should flow away from the wells at the natural groundwater velocity. The wells can then be pumped for short periods before the contamination returns. As a rough estimate, if the wells are rested for eleven months of the year, they could possibly be operated for one month of the year on a nearly continuous basis. For this approach to be satisfactory, the base pumpage currently supplied by Well 8-3 must be shifted to another well or wells within the District.

2. Construct air stripping towers at the site (similar to Plant No. 1) to remove the volatile halogenated organics from the well water. This is cost effective at this site, since there already is storage capacity, low head pumps on the wells and a booster pump system. The total capital cost was estimated to be $500,000.

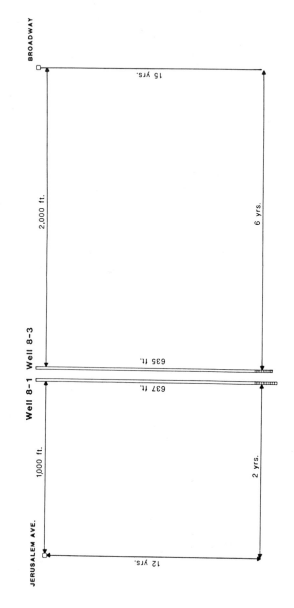

CONTAMINANT TRANSPORT TIMES FROM SOURCES TO WELLS

Figure 3

3. Construct a spray aeration system within the existing ground storage tank. Although the spray aeration technology has been used before, it has never been applied
within a ground storage tank with its limited or static
air exposure. Research would be required on this project
to determine optimal spray angles and heights for maximum
removal and quantity of air needed to pass through the
tank air spaces. In addition, it must be determined if
the existing well pumps can supply adequate discharge pressures so that satisfactory pressure can be maintained at
the spray nozzles. This may be done at Well 8-1 by over-
speeding the diesel engine. The total capital cost, including ground storage tank repair, was estimated to be
$105,000. If adequate pressures cannot be obtained, the
existing pumps and motors will have to be replaced at an
additional construction cost of approximately $90,000.

Each of the previous three alternatives require little
additional operations and maintenance costs above those
which are currently incurred at the plant.

4. Install granular activated carbon filters on the
pump discharge. For the purpose of evaluating an activated carbon system, the capital and operating cost data
were estimated. Design was based on only one well with a
maximum pumpage of 1400 GPM.

Based on the normally accepted design requirements for
activated carbon treatment of 7.5 minutes retention time
in the carbon bed and an application rate of 1 gpm/cf of
carbon bed volume, 1400 cubic feet of granular activated
carbon would be required. This offers a contact time of a
little over 8.0 minutes. Two carbon treatment units, each
10 feet in diameter and 14 feet high (with carbon bed
height of 10 feet) containing 20,000 pounds or 750 cf of
granular activated carbon are required. Each unit would
be capable of handling approximately 700 GPM of water.
The units can be connected (without major piping and pumping modifications) into the well discharge prior to the
ground storage tank. Since the pressure drop across each
unit was anticipated to be about 5-7 psi, the existing
well pumps are adequate, with only a small capacity reduction, to pass the water through the carbon bed and then
into the system. The units can be installed on the existing site and operated without a superstructure enclosure,
providing adequate screening is available and the units
are either drained or used extensively during cold weather
to avoid freezing. The capital cost for implementing the
two unit carbon treatment system was estimated at $200,000.
The primary component of the operating costs for the carbon system is the cost of replacing the spent carbon (once
its adsorption capacity has been depleted). The cost of
replacing activated carbon was estimated at $1.00/pound.

This includes removal and disposal of spent carbon, and refilling the carbon units with fresh granular activated carbon. It was estimated that the activated carbon must be replaced between 1 and 2 times a year, depending on well pumpage. This translates to an estimated yearly operations and maintenance cost between $40,000. and $80,000.

Based upon the model results which indicated that the wells will probably be contaminated for a fairly long period of time (i.e., 10 to 20 years), a most cost-effective alternative was chosen. Further consideration of the granular activated carbon filter was eliminated due to the high operations and maintenance cost over the design lifetime. The air stripping tower alternative was also eliminated due to its high capital cost. Since the Water District did not want to restrict the use of its wells, it was decided to follow the spray aeration system in the existing ground storage tank alternative. This system is currently under design.

CONCLUSIONS

It can be seen that the use of groundwater flow models utilizing microcomputers can be helpful in identifying sources of groundwater contamination. Based on the history of the contaminant source and the groundwater flow characteristics, reasonable projections can be made as to contaminant trends in the future. From these projections, water treatment alternatives can be evaluated with regard to both capital and annual costs.

Simultaneous Withdrawal of Saline/Fresh Waters in a Stratified Aquifer

Eiji Fukumori[1], Emett M. Laursen[2], and Akio Wake[3]

Introduction

The objective of this study is to develop computational tools for simulating the flow behavior of an aquifer in response to simultaneous pumping of two stratified fluids from both sides of the interface. A typical application can be found in coastal aquifers where supply wells are often contaminated by salinity intrusion resulting from the uncontrolled upconing of the interface. Conceptually, it can be envisioned that a simultaneous withdrawal of the underlying saline water by an additional well placed in the saline region would result in an equal tendency for downconing, with a net effect on the interface not being displaced. Despite its practical applicability and intriguing theoretical concepts, little literature [Underhill and Atherton (1964), Fader (1957), Long (1965), Wickersham (1977), Abed (1982), and Souissi (1984)] can be found on this subject and no mathematical modeling effort has been made prior to the present study.

One of the major simplifications applied to this study is the assumption of the 'sharp' interface between the two fluids: fresh water and the underlying saline water. Except for the cases of petroleum-water interface, there is always a transition zone between the fluids whose thickness is a function of various local aquifer characteristics and the rates of pumpage themselves. However, the assumption of 'sharp' interface is a widely accepted practice for the various mathematical analyses of coastal aquifers and is known to provide reasonable results.

Even with this simplifying assumption, the mathematical formulation for the problem is highly nonlinear and solutions can be obtained only by a numerical approximation technique. Two well-known numerical methods, the finite element method and the boundary element method, have been applied in the present study. Solutions were compared to bench-scale experimental results using a Hele-Shaw model and a sandbox model.

Formulation of the Problem

The simplest two-well system can be represented by a two-dimensional system in which two fully penetrating pipes (infinitely

[1,3]Department of Civil Engineering, State University of New York at Buffalo, Buffalo, NY 14260.
[2]Department of Civil Engineering, The University of Arizona, Tucson, AZ 85721.

extended) are installed horizontally near the interface, as shown in Figure 1. The system may be considered to emulate a part of a double horizontal well system such as two Ranny wells (Ranny,1981) placed in both sides of the interface.

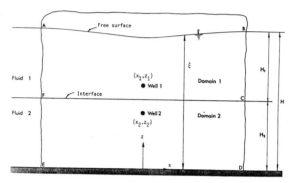

Figure 1. Two-Well System

The system shown in Figure 1 has not only the interface but also the free surface. This combination creates a strong nonlinear behavior for the mathematical model. For the steady state, the hydraulic pressure in Domain 1 must be equal to the pressure in Domain 2 on the interface, i.e.,

$$\gamma_1(h_1 - z) = \gamma_2(h_2 - z) \tag{1}$$

in which z is the elevation of the interface; γ_1, γ_2, and h_1, h_2 are the specific weight and the piezometric head of Domains 1 and 2, respectively. Along the free surface, the pressure is atmospheric; therefore, the piezometric head is equal to the elevation of the free surface, i.e., $h_1 = z$. It is assumed here that the Darcy's law is valid throughout the domain.

Under further assumptions of steady state, an immiscible sharp interface, and isotropy for each of the two domains, the entire system as shown in Figure 1 can be expressed in the integral form as,

$$\iint [\nabla^2 h_1 - \frac{Qp_1}{bK_1} \delta (r_1 - r)] \, dA = 0 \qquad \text{within Domain 1,}$$

$$\iint [\nabla^2 h_2 - \frac{Qp_2}{bK_2} \delta (r_2 - r)] \, dA = 0 \qquad \text{within Domain 2,}$$

$$h_1 = \xi \quad \text{and} \quad \frac{\partial h_1}{\partial n} = 0 \qquad \text{along A - B,}$$

$$h_1 = H \quad \text{along B - C and A - F,}$$

$$\gamma_1 (h_1 - z) = \gamma_2 (h_2 - z) \quad \text{along F - C,}$$

$$\frac{\partial h_2}{\partial z} = 0 \quad \text{along } E - D,$$

and $\qquad h_2 = H^* \quad \text{along } F - E \text{ and } C - D$ $\qquad\qquad$ (2)

where the vector, r_i indicates the location of the wells for Domains 1 and 2, whose discharges are $Qp_i = bq_{pi}$; δ is the delta function; and b is the aquifer width; and K_i is the hydraulic conductivity. Other notations are given in Figure 1.

The piezometric head H^* must be uniquely determined so that the pressures in Domains 1 and 2 are the same at Point C where the interface line begins. At any point along the segment C-D the pressure is given by

$$P_2 = \gamma_1 H_1 + \gamma_2 (H_2 - z) \qquad\qquad (3)$$

and the piezometric head is expressed as

$$H^* = \frac{P_2}{\gamma_2} + z = \frac{\gamma_1}{\gamma_2} H_1 + H_2 = H - \frac{\Delta\gamma}{\gamma_2} H_1 \qquad (4)$$

where $\qquad \Delta\gamma = \gamma_2 - \gamma_1$ and $H = H_1 + H_2$.

If the porous matrix in Domain 1 is assumed to be the same as that in Domain 2, the hydraulic conductivities are governed only by the properties of the two fluids. The specific viscosity of standard sea water at 20°C is about 1.07 while the specific density is 1.025. If these conditions are held in the entire domain, the specific hydraulic conductivity, defined as K_2/K_1, becomes 0.96, indicating that the saline water domain is less conductive than the fresh water domain.

Numerical Domain

For the problem investigated herein, it is assumed that the flow behavior around the two-dimensional (horizontal) wells is symmetrical left to right. The location of wells is assumed to be halfway between the constant heads. The aquifer is, thus, symmetric about the vertical line on which the two wells are located and the numerical domain is defined as shown in Figure 2. In the figure, the horizontal component of the specific discharge at the line of symmetry is zero so that the line can be treated as an impervious wall. The wells are then located on the

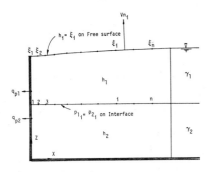

Figure 2. Half Domain

wall and the pumpage becomes the flow across the boundary, i.e., Neumann-type boundary condition. This system, thus, reduces the governing equation to the Laplace equation, and the number of required solutions becomes almost half of the case for the entire domain.

Numerical Methods

Two popular methods, the finite element method and the boundary element method, have been applied to the present study.

Finite Element Method

The Galerkin's form of the finite element equation for each of the two aquifer systems can be written in a general form as

$$\iint_\omega [B]^T [K][B] \, dA\{h\} = \int_\gamma [M]^T [M] \, dS\{q_n\} - \iint_\omega [N]^T [N] \, dA\{s\} \qquad (5)$$

where $[B]$ is the gradient matrix; $[K]$ is the conductivity tensor; $\{h\}$ is the piezometric head vector; $[M]$ is the shape function on the boundary; $\{q_n\}$ is the boundary flux vector; $[N]$ is the shape function; and $\{s\}$ is the source vector. Equation (5) is applied to the domains consisting of linear triangular elements. Details of the finite element derivations can be found in, for example, Huebner (1975).

Boundary Element Method

The general form of the boundary element equation for each of the aquifer domains may be expressed as

$$\oint_\gamma \left[\frac{\partial h(x)}{\partial n} G(x,\xi) - h(x) \frac{\partial G(x,\xi)}{\partial n} \right] dS(x) = c(\xi) \, h(\xi) \qquad (6)$$

where $h(x)$ is the piezometric head on the boundary; $G(x,\xi) =$ is the fundamental solution for the system, i.e., $G(x,\xi) = 1/2\,\pi \cdot \log_e (1/r)$; and $c(\xi)$ is given by $c(\xi) = -\oint \partial G(x,\xi)/\partial n \, dS$. Equation (6) is applied to the aquifer domains consisting of linear boundary elements as shown in Figure 2. Since the boundary is no longer smooth for the discretized boundary, Equation (6) is rewritten for linear elements as

$$c_i h_i + \sum_{j=1}^{n} \int_{\partial D_j} h \frac{\partial G}{\partial n} \, dS_j = \sum_{j=1}^{n} \int_{\partial D_j} G \, q_n dS_j \qquad (7)$$

where n is the number of nodes, $c_i \neq 1/2$, and $q_n = \partial h/\partial n$. A more detailed treatment of the boundary element derivations can be found in Brebbia (1978), and are summarized in Fukumori (1982).

Numerical Treatment of Free Surface and Interface

Regardless of the numerical method chosen, the conditions for the free surface are $V_n = 0$ (without infiltration), and $h = \xi$ where ξ indicates the location of free surface, and V_n is the specific discharge normal to the free surface. The requirements for the interface are $\gamma_1(h_1 - z) - \gamma_2(h_2 - z) = 0$ as given in Equations (2). In order to satisfy these nonlinear relationships, ξ and h_i must be determined iteratively, beginning from good initial guess values. The standard Jacobian form of the Newton-Raphson method, i.e., $[J]\{\Delta z\} = -\{f\}$ has been adopted for the present study. The elements of the Jacobian $[J]$, $\partial f_i/\partial z_i$ must be numerically determined for each of the discretized node locations.

It has been found by numerical experiments that for the interface location, the Newton-Raphson method does not converge as rapidly as it does for the free surface location. As expected from the physical consideration, the method is very slow to converge or is often divergent for small values of $\Delta\gamma$ or large pumpage of Q_{p1} and Q_{p2}. In order to assure the convergence, a relaxation procedure has been devised and successfully applied, i.e., $\{\Delta z\} = -\alpha[J]^{-1}\{f\}$. The parameter, α, which is less than or equal to unity and its optimum value, has been empirically determined as $\alpha = \Delta\gamma/(\Delta\gamma + \varepsilon/\beta)$ where ε is the maximum absolute error in $\{\Delta z\}$ and β is a constant unique to a given system. The optimum value of α is automatically computed and applied to each iteration step as ε decreases towards the exact solution. Fukumori (1982) has shown that this procedure not only stabilizes the computation but also dramatically accelerates the rate of convergence.

Presentation of Results

Single Fluid-Single Well Case

The model behavior was first examined for a single fluid flow with a single well bounded by the free surface and an impervious layer as shown in Figure 3. The model equation for this case was evaluated by the two numerical methods as described above and the results were compared with the Dupuit assumptions and the experimental results, using the Hele-Shaw model (Abed, 1982). The following dimensional parameters were used for comparison and calibration with the Hele-Shaw physical model (Figure 3).

Horizontal length,	$L = 228$ cm
Height,	$H_1 = 60$ cm
Width,	$b = 1$ cm
Well location,	$a = 15$ cm for $q = 1$ to 4 cm^2/min
''	$= 10$ cm for $q = 5$ cm^2/min

After successful verification by the Hele-Shaw physical model with the equivalent hydraulic conductivity, $K = b^2\gamma/12\mu$ (Bear 1972), a more realistic value, $K = 0.678$ cm/min, was used for comparison with the Dupuit assumptions (Harr, 1962). The Dupuit approximating theory for single fluid - single well case is given by

$$h = \sqrt{h_1^2 - (h_1^2 - h_2^2)\frac{x}{L}} \quad \text{and} \quad q = K\,\frac{h_1^2 - h_2^2}{2L} \tag{8}$$

where h_1 and h_2 are the upstream and the downstream depths, and L is the horizontal length of the unconfined aquifer. Figure 3 shows a comparison of the free surface profiles for a pumping rate of 4cm^2/min between the numerical solutions and the Dupuit theory. Although the Dupuit theory is based on a fully penetrating vertical well, it has been concluded that the approximating theory gives reasonable values of h if q is small or the aquifer is deep. Close to the well, the Dupuit theory is not as good as it is far from the well. There is only a slight difference in the free surface profiles between the two numerical methods as seen in Figure 3.

Two Fluids - Single Well Case

The two numerical methods were next applied to two stratified fluids with a single well located in the fresh water domain as shown in Figure 4. The difference between the single and the two fluids cases is the additional iterative computation for the interface. As mentioned earlier, a special numerical treatment is required for the interface prediction.

The upconing phenomenon resulting from the pumpage for q = 0.012 cm²/min, K = 0.678 cm/min and $\Delta\gamma/\gamma_1$=0.025 is shown in Figure 5. It can be seen that the Dupuit approximating theory is in excellent agreement with the finite element solution. At an increased pumping rate of q = 0.036 cm²/min, both the Dupuit theory and the numerical solution showed that the interface height exceeds the well location, giving a maximum limit of fresh water pumpage rate for this aquifer system.

Imaged Wells

The model behavior for the two-well case was first examined for the same aquifer by placing an additional saline water well symmetrically imaged about the interface. The dimensions and the other quantities are shown in Figure 6. Figure 7a shows the formation of the interface line at the steady state with q_{p1} = q_{p2} = 0.06 cm²/min and a_1 = a_2 = 10 cm. Due to the small pumpage rate, the free surface dropped only 0.3 cm for this case. Figure 7b shows that

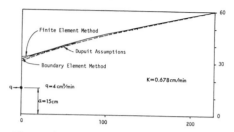

Figure 3. Single Well - Single Fluid Downconing of Free Surface

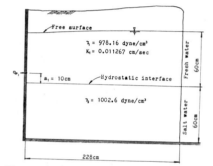

Figure 4. Single Well-Two Fluids Case

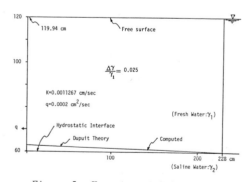

Figure 5. Upconing of Interface

the computed interface profile is identical to the hydrostatic line for the case of fresh water pumpage at 0.06138 cm^2/min, i.e., $q_{p1} = q_{p2} \times 1.023$ at $q_{p2} = 0.06$ cm^2/min indicating q_{p2} approaches $(\gamma_1/\gamma_2) \times q_{p1}$ as $q_{p1} \rightarrow 0$.

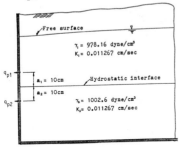

Figure 6. Two-Well Case

Figure 7. Interface Formed by a) $q_{p1}=q_{p2}$, b) $q_{p1}=1.023q_{p2}$

A series of cases was examined for various values of q_{p1} and q_{p2} with $K_1=K_2 = 0.676$ cm/min and $a_1 = a_2 = 10$ cm for which the interface remains horizontal. The results are given in Table 1.

Table 1. Computed q_{p1}, D_2, and h

$q_{p2} \times 10^2$ (cm^2/min)	$q_{p1} \times 10^2$ (cm^2/min)	D_2 (cm)	h_1 (cm)
6	6.138	59.999	59.846
12	12.258	60.029	59.677
18	18.348	59.969	59.552
24	24.426	59.935	59.428
30	30.492	59.993	59.228
36	36.540	59.818	59.158
42	42.582	60.522	58.651
45	45.624	unstable	

As seen in the table, the fresh water yield for the two-well system can be increased more than tenfold without net motion of the interface compared to the maxim yield of $q_{p1} = 0.036$ cm^2/min for the single well case. Further increase in pumpage, however, resulted in uncontrollable instability in computation. This instability was also physically observable in the Hele-Shaw model at greater pumpage rates, suggesting its physical origin rather than the numerical stability. The physical model studies of the two-well stratified aquifer system by a sandbox model (Souissi, 1984) and a Hele-Shaw model (Abed, 1982) have also shown that the maximum fresh water yield for the imaged well system is approximately ten times the yield for the single well system.

To generalize, the parameters were nondimensionalized as $q_r = q_{p2}/q_{p1}$, $X = q_{p1}/(h_1 K_1)$, and $Y = q_r(K_1 h_1 \gamma_2)/(K_2 D_2 \gamma_1)$.

The nondimensional equivalent of Table 1 is plotted in Figure 8 with comparison to the Dupuit approximating theory. It is seen that the Dupuit assumptions give reasonable agreement with the numerical solutions for the symmetrically imaged well system.

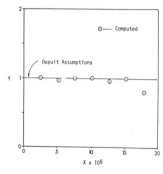

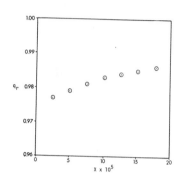

Figure 8a. Dupuit Theory vs. Computed Values for $a_1=a_2$

Figure 8b. q_r vs. X for $a_1=a_2$

Wells Nonsymmetrically Imaged About the Interface

Since the location of the wells in natural aquifers cannot always be imaged about the hydrostatic interface, a nonsymmetrically imaged case was considered, in which the distance between the interface and the lower well is doubled, i.e., $a_2 = 2a_1 = 20$ cm. Figures 9a and 9b show the computed interface profiles for such a case

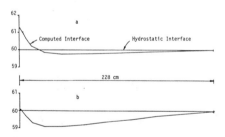

Figure 9. Interface Formed for $a_2=2a_1$ a)$q_{p1}=q_{p2}$, b)$q_{p2}=1.025q_{p1}$

for $q_{p1} = q_{p2} = 0.06$ cm^2/min and $q_{p2} = 1.025$ x $q_{p1} = 0.0615$ cm^2/min. It can be seen that, unlike the cases of symmetrically imaged wells, the interface profiles are no longer horizontal because of the asymmetry of equipotential lines about the interface.

A series of cases for various values of q_{p1} and q_{p2} for the nonsymmetrically imaged case are plotted in the nondimensional form in Figure 10. It can be seen that, the numerical solutions differ significantly from the Dupuit approximation theory. There is the tendency that, as a_2 becomes greater than a_1, the required value of specific pumpage (q_{p2}/q_{p1}) also increases in order to suppress the upconing. This tendency has also been evidenced by the physical model studies by Abed (1982) and Souissi (1984). For field applications of the two-well system it is, therefore, desirable to avoid highly nonsymmetrical well arrangement in order to minimize the saline water pumpage for a given amount of fresh water withdrawal.

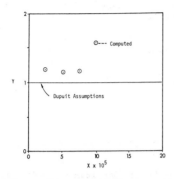

Figure 10a. Dupuit Theory vs.
Computed Values for $a_2=2a_1$

Figure 10b. q_r vs. X
for $a_2=2a_1$

The trends of the computed results in Figures 8b and 10b suggest the existence of a certain combination of a_1 and a_2 that gives a constant specific pumpage for any given value of X. Fukumori (1982) suggests that the following type of empirical expression may be developed as an analytical tool for the two-well systems:

$$\frac{dq_r}{dX} = \lambda \ (\frac{a_2}{a_1} - r)^\sigma \ (q_r - q_{r\infty})$$

in which r is a value of a_2/a_1 for which the specific pumpage is constant; σ and λ are constants which may be a function of K_i, γ_i, etc.; and $q_{r\infty}$ is the specific pumpage to which q_r approaches assymptotically. Determination of the constants, however, will require a large number of systematic numerical experiments.

Summary and Conclusions

Although the notion of the two-well system for coastal aquifers seems to have achieved some recognition, no mathematical modeling effort has been made prior to the present study. Governing equations for the two-well system can be derived by the concept of mass conservation provided that the Darcy's law is valid throughout the flow domain. Since the model equations are nonlinear, involving moving boundaries of the free surface as well as the interface, they cannot be solved in closed form. The finite element and the boundary element methods have been used to obtain two-dimensional solutions, in conjunction with an effective iterative technique devised for this study. With the two numerical methods, results were only slightly different. In terms of the computation time, the linear finite element method is more efficient than the linear boundary element method. However, the former method requires a substantially larger amount of data input than the latter. The accuracy of the linear boundary element method depends on the number of Gaussian integration points. For most applications, four integration points have been found to be sufficient.

The Dupuit theory, an often-used simplification for aquifer analyses, has been found to be a good approximation for the two-well system symmetrically imaged about the hydrostatic interface for the region far from the well. For nonsymmetrically imaged well system, the Dupuit approximation is no longer applicable.

As evidenced by the physical model studies, the results of the computational experiments suggest, the two-well system could increase the fresh water yield up to ten times the maximum yield for the single-well system. The feasibility of practical field applications seems quite promising.

References

Abed, Sami A. A., 'Wells Imaged About an Interface: Hele-Shaw Model,' M.S. thesis, the University of Arizona, 1982.

Bear, Jacob, Dynamics of Fluids in Porous-Media, American Elsevier Pub. Co., New York, NY, 1972.

Brebbia, C. A., The Boundary Element Method for Engineers, John Wiley and Sons, New York, NY 1978.

Fader, S. W., 'An analysis of Contour Map of 1955 Water Levels, with a Discussion of Salt-Water Problems in Southwestern Louisiana,' Dept. of Conservation, Louisiana Geological Survey and Louisiana Dept. of Public Works, Water Resources Pamphlet No. 4, 1957, pp. 16-21.

Fukumori, E., 'Wells Imaged About an Interface: a Mathematical Model,' M.S. thesis, the University of Arizona, 1982.

Harr, H. E., Groundwater and Seepage, McGraw-Hill Book Co., New York, NY 1962.

Huebner, K. H., The Finite Element Method for Engineers, John Wiley and Sons, New York, NY 1975.

Ranney Method Western Corporation, 'Supply Water,' Kennewick, Wash. 1981.

Long, R. A., 'Feasibility of a Scavenger Well System as a Solution of the Problem of Vertical Salt-Water Encroachment,' Dept. of Conservation, Louisiana Geological Survey and Louisiana Dept. of Public Works, Water Resources Pamphlet No. 15, 1965, pp. 1-22.

Souissi, A., 'Wells Imaged About an Interface: a Sand Model,' M.S. thesis, the University of Arizona, 1984.

Underhill, H. W. and M. J. Atherton, 'A Coastal Ground Study in Lybia and a Discussion of a Double Pumping Technique,' J. Hydrology, Vol 2, pp. 52-64.

Wickersham, G., 'Review of C. E. Jacob's Doublet Well,' J. Ground Water Vol. 15, No. 5, pp. 344-347.

The National Water Well Association's
Ground Water Software Centre

Barbara J. Graves[1], Phil Hall[2] and John Achilles[3]

The National Water Well Association (NWWA) offers a new service
to the members of the ground water industry. NWWA's Ground Water Software Centre markets computer programs and ground water models that are
of value to professionals in the industry. NWWA has developed a catalog of programs that will be of immediate value to well drilling contractors, ground water technologists and hydrogeologists. The bulk of
the present catalog of programs has been developed for NWWA by Model
Management Limited, Alberta, Canada. All of the programs that are
offered through the Ground Water Software Centre are designed for IBM
personal computers. Many of the programs are also offered for Apple
computers. The programs may be utilized for tasks involving; water
well inventory, well log data retrieval, well construction details,
geologic cross-sections, pumping test analysis, ground water quality
investigations, aquifer simulations and contaminant transport. This
paper provides a listing and brief description of the available programs.

Introduction

The use of the microcomputer in ground water investigations has
become advantageous over the past few years due to its portability, low
operating costs, ease of operation and ability to process large amounts
of data rapidly. Microcomputers are now considered valuable tools for
compiling, storing and processing data that are utilized in a wide variety of hydrogeologic investigations. Ground water supply studies,
ground water quality studies, geologic and hydrogeologic setting evaluations and ground water contamination studies are a few of the investigations that benefit from the utilization of ground water computer programs. NWWA created the Ground Water Software Centre to promote the
use of computer programs, to provide economical software and to advance
education on the use of computers in the ground water industry.

Equipment and Program Support

NWWA programs are designed to run on the computer equipment that is
specified in Table 1. Many programs are also available for Apple computers and some of the programs may be customized to run on additional
types of computer equipment.

[1]Co-Director of Research and Education, National Water Well Association,
500 West Wilson Bridge Road, Worthington, Ohio 43085
[2]Hydrogeologist, Model Management Limited, P.O. Box 189, St. Albert,
Alberts T8N 1N3
[3]Computer Specialist, Model Management Limited, P.O. Box 189, St. Albert,
Alberta T8N 1N3

TABLE 1 EQUIPMENT REQUIREMENTS FOR IBM-PC PROGRAMS

Equipment	Type	Minimum Requirements
1. computer	IBM-PC	128 K RAM 2 disk drives color graphic board and compatible monitor
2. printer	One of the following: EPSON (MX or FX series) OKIDATA IBM	dot matrix with parallel port
3. plotter	One of the following: HOUSTON INSTRUMENTS DMP29; DMP40; PC695 HEWLETT -PACKARD HP-7470; HP-7475A	serial port

All of the programs from the Ground Water Software Centre are menu-driven and written in "Basic". Some of the models are also written in "C", a language that is comparable to "Lotus". The menu-driven format provides ease in operation and use of the software. NWWA has a complete computer support staff that provides assistance and information to software users.

Programs

Two sets of programs have been developed; a non-plotter series (Table 2) that illustrates graphics on the monitor screen; and a plotter series (Table 3) that utilizes any of the plotters listed in Table 1 to create high-resolution graphics.

TABLE 2 IBM-PC PROGRAMS - NON-PLOTTER SERIES (NP) WITH SCREEN GRAPHICS

PUMPING TEST PROGRAMS

NP (1)	Semi-log drawdown graph
NP (2)	Semi-log recovery graph
NP (3)	Semi-log distance-drawdown graph

These programs utilize time and depth to water table data to calculate elapsed time and drawdown. Aquifer coefficients may be calculated from a straight line or least-squares fit between specified points. OUTPUT: Tables of values; semi-log graph; aquifer coefficients.

CHEMISTRY PROGRAMS

NP (4)	Piper diagram
NP (5)	Stiff diagram
NP (6)	Pie diagram

Input chemical analyses in parts per million (ppm) or miligrams per liter (mg/l). Program converts to equivalents per million (epm) and per cent epm and checks anion/cation balance.

WELLFIELD SIMULATION

NP (7)   Combination of Analytical and Finite Difference Models

Analytical Models
* Confined
* Unconfined
* Leaky

These programs use a 20x20 grid, and can take up to 10 wells (real and image). Wells may be located on or off the grid and do not have to be located at node points. Boundary conditions are simulated by image wells.

Finite Difference Models (Modified after Prickett and Lonnquist, 1971)
* Basic Aquifer Simulation Model
* Leaky Artesian Simulation Model
* Water Table Simulation Model
* Induced Infiltration Simulation Model
* Storage Coefficient Conversion Model

Grids may be uniform or irregular and are displayed on the screen, data is entered in menu-driven node cards in hydrogeologists' units..transmissivity, storage co-efficient, leakage factors, etc. The program calculates the storage factor.

These programs produce tables of drawdown which can be stored on disk and printed. The stored results can be used in the screen graphics program or the plotter programs.

GRAPHICS ENHANCEMENTS TO MODELS

NP (8)	Contours
NP (9)	3-D Surface

NP (10)	Time-Drawdown Curves-for up to 5 node points
NP (11)	Datamap Plot of Data-transmissivity, storage Coefficient

These are displayed in high-resolution on the screen, and may be printed on a dot matrix printer.

COMPATIBLE MODELS BASED ON THE USGS TRESCOTT-PINDER-LARSON FINITE DIFFERENCE MODEL (1976) WILL SHORTLY BE AVAILABLE.

NP (12)   Pumpsim

This program generates pumping test data from specified aquifer conditions and pumping rates for CONFINED, LEAKY OR WATER TABLE CONDITIONS. Data is generated for an observation well at user-specified X-Y coordinates. Multiple pumping wells may be used. Data is plotted by programs NP (1) or P (2).

NP (13)   Dran

Calculates flow to and drawdown around a drain using the Glover (1977) equations.

NP (14)   Sink

Uses the Theis (1935) line-sink solution to predict drawdown around multiple rows of line sinks. Each row may have wells or wellpoints spaced on different centers and each well may have different pumping rates.

NP (15)   Mound

Uses equations by Hantush (1967) to determine the rise of the water table beneath circular or rectangular recharge areas - e.g. lagoons, drainfields, recharge pits.

NP (16)   Random Walk

Calculates contaminant movement due to a variety of aquifer conditions. (Modified after Prickett, Naymik and Lonnquist, 1981)

NP (17)   Sieve Graph

Calculates cumulative sum weights of sieves and cumulative percentages and shows plot of data.

NP (18)   Convert

Will convert pumping test data from English to Metric units or vice versa.

BIT GRAPHICS EPSON PRINTER PROGRAMS

These programs directly address each dot on the print head of the Epson MX or FX printers producing a higher graphics resolution than screen dumps. These programs will not work on other printers.

BG (1)	Semi-log drawdown graph
BG (2)	Semi-log recovery graph
BG (3)	Slugtest data plot
BG (4)	Sieve analysis graph
BG (5)	Piper diagram

TABLE 3 IBM-PC PROGRAMS - PLOTTER SERIES (P)

Numerical data is printed on a dot matrix printer connected to a parallel port. Diagrams are printed on 8½" x 11" or 11" x 17" paper on the following plotters - Houston Instruments DMP-29 (8 pen), DMP-40 (single pen), Hewlett Packard HP 7475A (six pen), HP 7470 (single pen). Plotters should be connected to a serial port. Plots may be single or multi-colored, and multiple copies may be plotted.

PUMPING TEST PROGRAMS

P (1)	Step-drawdown plot
P (2)	Semi-log drawdown plot
P (3)	Log-log drawdown plot
P (4)	Semi-log recovery plot
P (5)	Distance drawdown semi-log plot
P (6)	Type curve plots

* Boulton (1954)
* Theis (1935)
* Walton (1962)

Semi-log plots may be analyzed

* manually
* straight line between specified points
* least square fit

CHEMISTRY PROGRAMS

Convert parts per million (ppm) to equivalents per million (epm), balance anions/cations, calculate Sodium Adsorption Ratio (SAR).

P (7)	Stiff - Plot up to 5 stiff diagrams/page.
P (8)	Pie - Plot up to 5 pie diagrams/page, the sizes of the pies are proportional to the total dissolved solids (tds).
P (9)	Piper 1 - Plot up to 5 analyses on one Piper trilinear diagram. Circle sizes are proportional to the t.d.s.
P (10)	Chemplot 2 - Plot up to 99 samples on one Piper trilinear diagram.
P (11)	Chemplot 3 - Plot up a single diagram of one chemical analysis showing Piper, Stiff and Pie diagrams on one page.

WELLFIELD DRAWDOWN PREDICTION PROGRAMS

Analytical Solutions

P (12)	Dranplot - Calculate flow to and drawdown around a drain. Plot up time - drawdown curves in profile through the drain.
P (13)	Sinkplot - Calculate drawdown due to a line sink (representing a row of wells or well points). Up to 5 rows may be super-imposed. Each row may have a different well spacing and different pumping rates.

WELL SIMULATION - Analytical solutions. Grid size 20x20, assumes infinite conditions. Up to 30 production wells may be used on or off the grid. Wells do not have to be on node points. Boundary conditions may be simulated by image wells. Models - Require package NP (7) for calculations.

P (14)	Gridplot - Plot of grid with location of wells.
P (15)	Contplot - Contour plots for specific times.
P (16)	Timeplot - Time-drawdown curves for up to 5 node points on individual or composite graphs.
P (17)	3-Dplot - 3-D surface of specific times.

FINITE DIFFERENCE MODELS ONLY:

P (18)	Finigrid - Plot of grid with location of wells and summary of data on 8½" x 11" size paper.
P (19)	Finidata - Plot of input data eg. storage coefficients, transmissivity values. The program carries out a frequency analysis of data and allows user to specify plotted ranges.

P (20)   Finiplot - Contour map of drawdown, regular and irregular grids.

P (21)   Fini 3D - 3-D surface of specified times.

P (22)   Finitime - Time-drawdown curves of up to 5 node points.

WELL PROGRAMS

P (23)   Willlith

Draws borehole lithology on 8½" x 11", 20 Symbols may be user-defined. Scale may be feet or meters. Plots single or multi-colored borehole log.

P (24)   Wellcons

Draws well construction details to same scale as above. Multiple casings, screens or slotted pipe, packers, wash-down valve, submersible pump, static and pumping water level. Menu-driven and figures are drawn at specified depths.

P (25)   Lithcon

Combination of Wellith and Wellcons on 11" x 17" or 8½" x 11" paper.

P (26)   Gsec

Draws geological cross sections. Well logs are drawn up at correct locations and elevations, join specific horizons. Drawings are 8½" x 11" or 11" x 17".

P (27)   Gscshade

Infills delineated areas on geologic sections, the angle of dip may be specified for the fill.

P (28)   Testplot

Draws simplified lithologs and well details-3 per page (8½" x 11").

P (29)   Lithgsec or Gseclith

Lithology data stored in P (23), and P (25) may be transferred to program P (26).

Gseclith data stored for program P (26) may be transferred to programs P (23) or P (25).

MISCELLANEOUS

P (30)	Dewater - Analytical solutions for designing a dewatering system.
P (31)	Pumpcost
	Analyzes cost of pumping water using discount - cashflow method. Compares higher capital costs vs. lower operating costs.
P (32)	Sieveplot - Analyzes and plots up to 5 sieve analyses.
P (33)	Slugplot - Analyzes and plots slug test data.
p (34)	Moundplot
	Uses Hantush's (1967) method to calculate the rise of water table beneath a circular or rectangular recharge area. Estimates water-table rise beneath holding ponds, tailings ponds, disposal fields, etc.
P (35)	Chartplot 1
	Plots pumpage rate or water usage for up to 6 wells and plots as bar or line graphs. A seventh variable will automatically total the first six wells. Graphs may be plotted on a daily, weekly, monthly, or yearly basis.
P (36)	Chartplot 2
	Plots 7 variables such as hydrographs, chemistry and bar charts of pumping rates or precipitation. Variables are user-defineable and up to 3 different scales may be used and labelled on the Y axis. Data may be plotted up on a daily, weekly, monthly basis, or for every 2-5 months, 6-12 months, 2-30 years.
P (37)	Drawsim
	Analytical solution to simulate pumping test data. Aquifer parameters may be varied, boundaries moved. Data is plotted up by PUMPTEST programs. May also read PUMPTEST times from data disk or original pumping test or enter own times.
P (38)	Random Walk
	Mass transport model, aquifer parameters may be varied, interceptor wells or sinks may be simulated. (modified after Prickett, Naymik and Lonnquist, 1981)

P (38) Cont.   Plots grid, contours, 3-D

P (39)   Coneplot

                Finite difference model after Rushton, (1979) in the
                vertical plane around a single well. Cone of depres-
                sion is/plotted for various times.

Currently, many of the data files that are used as input for a program or are generated as output from a program may be used as input data
in other programs. The interactive nature of the programs will continue
to be enhanced, culminating with the integration of all programs into a
water well records management system. Ultimately, a variety of computer
models will be able to interact with several data bases and then be
utilized for a number of hydrogeologic investigations.

NWWA's Ground Water Software Centre has been established to provide
useful investigative tools for the ground water industry. The use of
microcomputers and ground water software will increase the ease and
efficiency with which data are processed, whether it involves a simple
geologic investigation with well lithology data or a full hydrogeologic
study utilizing model data to deliniate contaminant flow.

Appendix 1 -- References

1. Boulton, N.S., "The Drawdown of the Water Table Under Non-Steady
   Conditions Near a Pumped Well in an Unconfined Formation", Proceedings of the Institute of Civil Engineers, Vol. 3, 1954, pp. 564-579.
2. Glover, R.E., Transient Ground Water Hydraulics, Water Resources
   Publications, Fort Collins, CO, 1977.
3. Hantush, M.S., "Growth and Decay of Groundwater - Mounds in Response
   to Uniform Percolation", Water Resources Research, Vol. 3, No. 1,
   Jan. 1967, pp. 227-234.
4. Prickett, T.A. and Lonnquist, C.G., "Selected Digital Computer Techniques for Groundwater Resource Evaluation", Bulletin 55, Illinois
   State Water Survey, Champaign, IL, 1971, pp. 1-62.
5. Prickett, T.A., Naymik, T.G., and Lonnquist, C.G., "A Random-Walk
   Solute Transport Model for Selected Groundwater Quality Evaluations",
   Bulletin 65, Illinois State Water Survey, Champaign, IL, 1981,
   pp. 1-103.
6. Rushton, R.R. and Redshaw, S.C., Seepage and Groundwater Flow, John
   Wiley & Sons, New York, NY, 1979.
7. Theis, C.V., "The Relation Between the Lowering of the Piezometric
   Surface and the Rate and Duration of Discharge of a Well Using
   Groundwater Storage", Transactions of the American Geophysical
   Union, Vol. 2, 1935, pp. 519-524.
8. Trescott, P.C., Pinder, G.F., and Larson, S.P., "Finite-Difference
   Model for Aquifer Simulation in Two Dimensions with Results of
   Numerical Experiments", Techniques of Water-Resources Investigations
   of the United States Geological Survey, Book 7, Ch. C1, United States
   Government Printing Office, Washington, DC, 1976.

9. Walton, W.C., "Selected Analytical Methods for Well and Aquifer Evaluation", Bulletin 49, Illinois State Water Survey, Champaign, IL, 1962, pp. 1-81.

Microcomputer Application in Predicting
Upland Erosion

Reza M. Khanbilvardi and Andrew S. Rogowski[*]

Abstract

An erosion-deposition model, originally developed for a mainframe
computer, was adapted for an Apple IIe. With minimal adjustment it can
also be used on other personal microcomputers. The model is user
oriented and utilizes readily available data. It predicts distribution
of erosion and deposition on a watershed and provides information for
selecting optimal management practices. Its application is illustrated
using rainfall, topography, and soil data from a mined and reclaimed
watershed in Pennsylvania. The model satisfactorily predicted sediment
load at the outlet of the watershed and at the holding ponds. The simulation package can be used to plan location of detention basins, in
channel design studies, and in land use planning.

Introduction

Surface mining for coal, sand, or other minerals often results in
environmental pollution. Among the foremost problems is the increased
erosion potential of freshly reclaimed land. During the mining and
reclamation operations soil structure at the surface is generally
destroyed, decreasing infiltration and increasing runoff. Easily
erodible topsoil carried from these areas by runoff accounts for much
of the nonpoint sediment load in heavily mined parts of United States.
Rill erosion on long slopes, concentrating into narrow channels, may
lead to substantial gullying before adequate vegetative cover becomes
established. The problems remain serious in the absence of erosion
control planning. Consequently, erosion control practices are becoming
an integral part of successful reclamation. Runoff control and soil
entrapment are the two practices normally used on freshly reclaimed
areas. Runoff control is basic to any effective nonpoint source pollution control system, and involves a variety of structures to divert or
slow down surface runoff and enhance infiltration. Diversion of runoff
will generally cause a reduction in offsite load as well as onsite soil
loss by reducing the velocity and sediment carrying capacity of surface
flows and by entrapping sediment in diversions. Onsite control
structures may thus reduce or altogether eliminate the need for offsite
sediment ponds.

[*]Assistant Professor, Department of Civil Engineering, The City College
of The City University of New York, Convent Avenue at 138th Street, New
York, NY 10031; Soil Scientist, Northeast Watershed Research Center,
U.S. Department of Agriculture, ARS, 110 Research Building A, University
Park, PA 16802.

Action agencies continue to emphasize entrapment capability of structural measures such as sediment ponds as a safeguard against possible offsite damages by a rare large storm following reclamation. To clear the runoff water of suspended soil particles before it leaves a mining site is the goal of most soil entrapment strategies. Thus sediment basins must be large enough to handle runoff for a characteristic critical design storm in a given area.

Entrapment is mandated by law. The Surface Mining Control and Reclamation Act of 1977 (Public Law 95-87) requires that all surface runoff from a disturbed area be collected and diverted to a suitable facility for removal of sediment (10). The act also specifies that all surface runoff from a mined area pass through a sedimentation pond before leaving the site and that sedimentation ponds have a 7000 cubic feet capacity for each disturbed acre in a reclaimed area. The regulations impose further constraints on effluent discharge. The discharge of storm water from areas disturbed by surface coal mining activities is prohibited unless runoff can meet EPA's effluent standards of 70 milligrams per litre of total suspended solids, with a daily average of 35 milligrams per litre based on 30 days of consecutive discharge.

Compared to simulation modeling data collection in the field can be time consuming and expensive. Here therefore, we will briefly describe principal features and illustrate an application of an Erosion-Deposition Model (EDM). In an example the model will be used to evaluate an effect of alternate holding pond placement to comply with the federal effluent standards on a freshly reclaimed minesite.

Methods and Materials

Effective planning to control onsite erosion and offsite sediment yield from a reclaimed area may depend on scientific tools and on the abilities of the conservation planner. In general, modeling approaches capable of simulating erosion and the efficiency of control structures, are not widely used by planners and operators at a local level. Erosion models can be classified either as lumped parameter or distributed parameter models. Lumped parameter models attempt to condense the parameters associated with sediment yield, watershed characteristics and climatic influences into a single expression (11, 12). In contrast, distributed parameter models (also known as parametric, or physically based) are derived from theory of erosion mechanics (1, 4, 9) and can provide information on possible distribution of erosion and sediment yield in space and time. Since these models are usually run for individual storm events they have a potential for greater accuracy and more diversified output than the lumped parameter models, provided data are available to estimate the necessary parameters.

Erosion-Deposition Model (EDM) developed recently (2) is a hybrid lumped parameter-distributed parameter model. It is based on theoretical relationships associated with sediment transport, on Philip's (5) approach to infiltration, and on USLE (12). EDM predicts patterns of sediment and runoff flow, total sediment yield, and areal distribution of erosion and deposition for individual storm events. It can also be used for simulating nonpoint source pollution (assuming pollutants are attached to soil particles) and for planning control measures on agricultural as well as on stripmined areas.

Application of the model requires that a site be represented by a square grid of equal size elements (subareas). The size of an element should be small enough so that USLE and infiltration parameters within it can be considered uniform. Therefore, size of elements depends on the degree of homogeneity as well as on the intended use of the model. On stripmined areas, we have used elements of 10 m by 10 m (0.01 ha) (3). However, elements up to 100 m by 100 m (1 ha) can also be used (8). To make the model compatible with remotely sensed data a 30 m by 30 m grid is recommended.

The model structure is based on availability of runoff, computed from rainfall parameters and Philip's (5) infiltration equation, availability of sediment, computed from USLE, and mass balance calculations involving sediment transport capacity of rill, or channel flow. Subject to the hydrologic and physiographic parameters, the output from one grid element becomes the input to the adjacent one.

The input parameters include precipitation and temperature data, infiltration potential, ground surface elevations, soil type, texture and aggregate size distribution. The rainfall excess constitutes the critical overland flow component in the form of sheet flow. The model computes rainfall excess (R) for each grid element,

$$R = P-I \qquad [1]$$

where P = precipitation (cm), and
       I = cumulative infiltration (cm)

Cumulative infiltration (I) is approximated using Philip's (5) infiltration equation,

$$I = ST^{1/2} + At \qquad [2]$$

where S = sorptivity (cm/sec$^{1/2}$)
       t = time (sec), and
       A = a parameter related to hydraulic conductivity (cm/sec)

The S and A-values in equation [2] are determined experimentally (7). On large watersheds where data are lacking these values can be approximated from Soil Conservation Service estimates of hydraulic conductivity and moisture characteristic (6).

To route runoff and sediment load properly it is necessary to estimate runoff velocity, V,

$$V = \frac{R}{t_c} \qquad [3]$$

where R = rainfall excess (cm)
       t_c = time of concentration (sec) for each grid element

Utilizing runoff velocity value from equation [3] soil erodibility and slope steepness, rill patterns and contributing interrill areas are generated by a computer. Subsequently, using USLE, the model computes amounts of detached soil for each contributing subarea. The detached soil is added to the amounts contributed by rill flow from the adjacent upslope elements and to the rill scour component between nodes of the two elements. The total amount now becomes available for transport out of an element. This amount is compared to the rill flow transport capacity, which accounts for the distribution of sediment between transport and deposition components and determines the actual rate of soil movement to the next grid element. From a practical point of view EDM can be used to estimate how much the sediment yield of each subarea will be reduced by the use of conservation practices during reclamation, and thus can predict the amount of soil that needs to be trapped in sediment ponds to prevent excessive soil movement offsite.

Although EDM is a relatively comprehensive model, it was developed originally to be user-oriented. The original computer program (available on request from the authors) contains 12 subroutines and 1150 FORTRAN statements. The model requires 250 K memory; computer time and cost for each run are minimal about 3 sec at $0.06/sec on an IBM 3081 mainframe computer[1].

The program was written in Standard FORTRAN since FORTRAN is especially suitable for work in engineering and the sciences. In 1966 the American National Standards Institute (ANSI) issued a standard for FORTRAN that helped to clarify the language. This is sometimes referred to as a Standard FORTRAN or ANSI FORTRAN 66 and the EDM model was originally written in this language. In 1977 continued development of FORTRAN resulted in a new and improved version of Standard FORTRAN called ANSI FORTRAN 77.

Because of popularity and availability of microcomputers, decision was made to reprogram the model for use on Apple IIe. To develop a new software package, two options were available: (1) to rewrite the whole program in BASIC, or (2) to use available software to recompile the program written for mainframe computer on a microcomputer. Second option was chosen since the Apple FORTRAN software package was commercially available. To use this package the program first had to be rewritten in ANSI FORTRAN 77 and compiled using Apple FORTRAN on Apple IIe. The new package is presently operational on an Apple IIe with 128 K extended memory card, and preferably two disk drives.

Results and Discussion

The site selected as an example of model application was a 6.8 ha (17 acres) area on which reclamation planning started in 1980. Figure 1 shows the pertinent features of the site, topography, and the measuring grid of square 7.6 x 7.6 m elements. The dominant soil type is Gilpin silt loam, and a 1 yr-24 hr design storm (5.84 cm) is used to demonstrate model performance and selected outputs.

[1]The mention of trade names does not constitute an endorsement of the product by the U.S. Department of Agriculture over other products not mentioned.

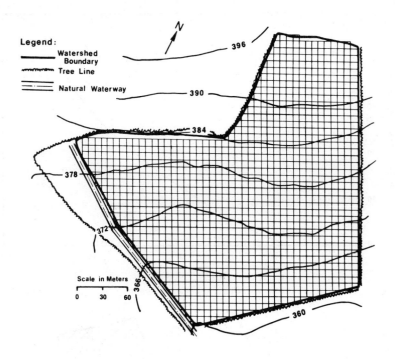

Figure 1. Square Grid Superimposed on the Topography of the
           Experimental Site.

Sediment size plays an important role in soil detachment and
transport. To model properly the influence of particle size on erosion
the soil particle size distribution at the site is needed. This information is critical because reclaimed minesoils in Appalachia contain
many coarse stone fragments. Figure 2 shows the particle size distribution at the site; d_{90} (90 percent of soil particles are finer by
weight), one of the model input parameters, is seen to be about 30 mm.

The model was first executed for a situation when erosion control
measures were applied to the site. Figure 3 shows generated rill patterns and their outlet points. When reclamation started at the site in
1980, three diversions and a sedimentation pond were installed. To
investigate effectiveness of this conservation plan, EDM model was
executed using the above constraints. Figure 4 shows changes in the
rill pattern and outlet location while the summary of computer output in
Table 1 indicates that although initial control measures can reduce
total offsite sediment yield by 40 to 50% for d_{90} = 1 to 10 mm soil effluent would not meet the suspended solids standard of 70 mg/L. An
alternate procedure was therefore recommended.

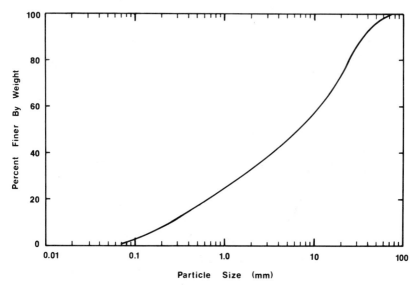

Figure 2.   Distribution of Soil Particle Sizes at the Experimental Site.

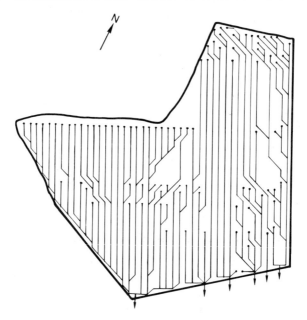

Figure 3.   Rill Patterns and Flow Outlets Predicted by the Model
            for Condition with no Control Structures.

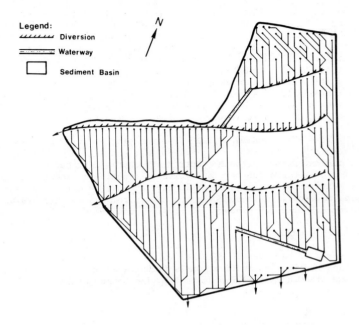

Figure 4.   Rill Patterns and Flow Outlets Predicted by the Model
for a Site with Three Diversions and a Sedimentation
Pond.

Table 1.   Summary of Computer Output

Option[1]	Particle size (d_{90})	Sediment yield	Reduction	Effluent concentration
	(mm)	(metric tons)	%	mg/L
1	1	74.5	–	>1000
	10	17.14	–	>1000
	30	0.40	–	420
2	1	44.4	40	> 700
	10	8.3	51	> 700
	30	0.43	–	452
3	1	14.6	80	> 600
	10	3.8	78	> 600
	30	0.03	92	40

[1]Option 1: no control structures (Figure 3); Option 2 = 3 diversions
and 1 pond (old system, Figure 4); Option 3 = 3 diversions and new
pond (optimal system, Figure 5).

Analysis of the EDM output suggested a new location for the sediment pond. Figure 5 shows a new rill pattern as the result of these changes. The analysis of the new situation showed a significant reduction (80% for d_{90} = 1 mm soil and 92% for d_{90} = 30 mm) in the total sediment yield as well as a compliance (for d_{90} = 30 mm soil) with the effluent standards. Model output indicated that a 220 cubic meter (7760 cu ft) sedimentation pond would be sufficiently large to accommodate potential runoff from a 1 yr-24 hr storm. The new pond holding capacity at a rate of 33 cu m/ha (460 cu ft/acre) is substantially less than the 7000 cu ft/acre required by law.

Figure 6 shows sediment yield from the site at different times after runoff has started for d_{90} = 1 mm (a), and d_{90} = 30 mm (b). The figure indicated that although control structures introduced at the beginning of reclamation were effective in reducing sediment yield for a fine textured minesoil, they could have an adverse effect on coarse textured minesoil. This suggests that a control system which is not optimized may actually enhance the erosion problem.

Summary and Conclusions

A software package was compiled for a recently developed Erosion-Deposition Model. Its application is illustrated on a stripmined and reclaimed area in central Pennsylvania. The output includes

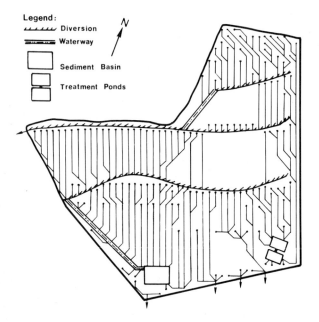

Figure 5.   Rill Patterns and Flow Outlets Predicted by the Model for Optimally Placed Control Structures.

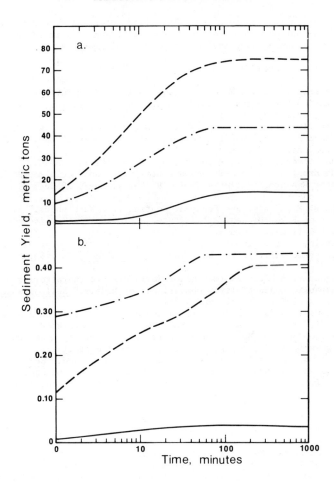

Figure 6. Sediment Yield Predicted by the EDM Model for (a)
d_{90} = 1 mm, and (b) d_{90} = 30 mm at different times
after the runoff has started; – – – no control
structures, —·—· three diversions and a sediment
pond (Figure 4), —— three diversions and an
optimally placed pond (Figure 5).

recommendations for reducing the total sediment yield and for optimal
location of the sediment pond. The results appear to reflect well the
observed field conditions.

This model has given reasonable results under a variety of surface,
soil, hydrology, and management conditions when used to quantify soil
losses from agricultural watersheds as well as stripmined areas. It can

provide information on total sediment yield, overland flow patterns and
areal distribution of erosion and deposition, and thus it appears well
suited for planning nonpoint pollution control programs.

Appendix 1.--References

1. Foster, G. R., and Meyer, L. D., "A Closed-Form Soil Erosion
   Equation for Upland Areas," Sedimentation (Einstein), H. W.
   Shen, ed., 1972, pp. 1-19.
2. Khanbilvardi, R. M., Rogowski, A. S., and Miller, A. C., "Modeling
   Upland Erosion," Water Resources Bulletin, Vol. 19, No. 1, Feb.,
   1983a, pp. 29-35.
3. Khanbilvardi, R. M., Rogowski, A. S., and Miller, A. C., "Predicting Erosion and Deposition on a Stripmined and Reclaimed Area,"
   Water Resources Bulletin, Vol. 19, No. 4, Aug., 1983b,
   pp. 585-593.
4. Li, R. M., "Water and Sediment Routing from Watersheds," Proceedings of River Mechanics Institute, Colorado State University,
   Fort Collins, Colorado.
5. Philip, J. R., "The Theory of Infiltration: 4. Sorptivity and
   Algebraic Infiltration Equation," Soil Science, Vol. 84, No. 3,
   1957, pp. 257-264.
6. Rogowski, A. S., "Estimation of Soil Moisture Characteristic and
   Hydraulic Conductivity: Comparisons of Models," Soil Science,
   Vol. 114, No. 6, 1972, pp. 423-429.
7. Rogowski, A. S., "Hydrologic Parameter Distribution on a Mine
   Spoil," Proceedings of the ASCE Symposium on Watershed
   Management '80, Boise, Idaho, July 21-23, 1980, pp. 764-780.
8. Rogowski, A. S., Khanbilvardi, R. M., and DeAngelis, R. J.,
   "Estimating Erosion on a Plot, Field and Watershed," Soil
   Erosion and Conservation, S. A. El-Swaify, W. C. Moldenhauer,
   and A. Lo, eds., Soil Conservation Society of America, Ankeny,
   Iowa, USA, 1985, pp. 149-166.
9. Rose, C. W., Williams, J. R., Sander, G. C., and Barry, D. A., "A
   Mathematical Model of Soil Erosion and Deposition Processes: I.
   Theory for a Plane Land Element," Soil Science Society of America
   Journal, Vol. 47, 1983, pp. 991-1000.
10. United States Congress, Surface Mining Control and Reclamation
    Act of 1977, 95th Congress, Washington, D.C., 1977.
11. Williams, J. R., "Predicting Sediment Yield Frequency for Rural
    Basins to Determine Man's Effect on Long-Term Sedimentation,"
    Effects of Man on the Interface of the Hydrological Cycle with
    the Physical Environment, International Association of
    Hydrological Sciences, Publication No. 113, 1974, pp. 105-108.
12. Wischmeier, W. H., and Smith, D. D., Predicting Rainfall Erosion
    Losses - A Guide to Conservation Planning, Agriculture Handbook
    No. 537, U.S. Department of Agriculture, Washington, D.C.,
    1978, 58 pp.

HYDROGRAPH DECOMPOSITION: USING A TECHNCIAL DATABASE

Charles R. Bristol[1]
Larry A. Roesner[2]
Sue Ann Hanson[3]

Trouble shooting for infiltration/inflow (I/I) problems in a sewer
system is made much easier with the aid of a computerized hydrograph
decomposition methodology. A methodology has been developed which
combines the technical algorithm of separating the three components of
total wet weather flow (baseflow, groundwater infiltration (GWI), and
rainfall-related infiltration/inflow (I/I) with the efficiency of a
database. This methodology is divided into three sequential analyses:
rainfall data analysis, determination of baseflow and GWI, and calculation of the I/I components. The entire procedure consists of
several interactive and batch (or background) report programs interfacing with a database containing rain and flow data. The purpose of
this paper is to present these procedures.

The rain and flow data are collected from 14 rain gages and 91 flow
meters and stored in the database in half-hourly increments. Using
interactive software written within the database, the engineer/hydro-
logist can selectively and quickly retrieve rain data and/or flow data
for a specific gage and/or meter. The software is menu driven with
screens designed to help the user through the analysis. Figure 1
presents a process flowchart showing the interaction between the
screens, menus, and reports.

The hydrograph decomposition software processes raw rain and sewage
flow data from the database to prepare several database records and to
conduct an annual and partial series analysis on the rainfall data. A
frequency analysis is also conducted on the dry hours found in the
rainfall record and the wet hours (rainfall) to assist the user in
defining periods of primarily baseflow and wet-weather flows. The
programs are used to calculate base wastewater flows, minimum and
maximum GWI,and I/I levels for each mini-basin. Figure 2 presents an
example of the rainfall hyetograph and the components of the total

---

[1]Senior Engineer, Camp Dresser & McKee, Annandale, Virginia

2Vice-President, Camp Dresser & McKee, Annandale, Virginia

3Senior Engineer, James M. Montgomery, Consulting Engineers, Reston,
  Virginia

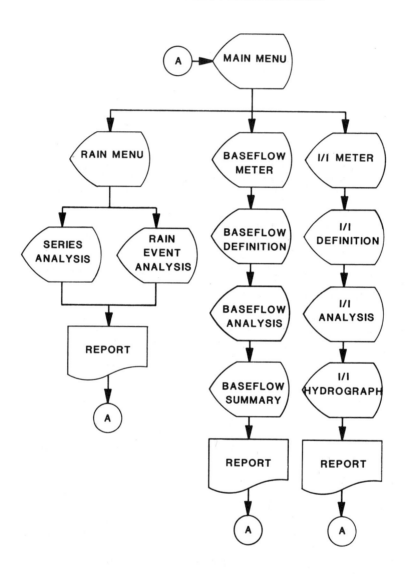

FIGURE-1 HDP PROCESS FLOWCHART

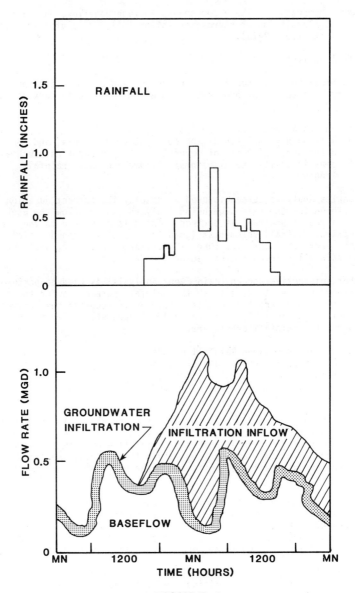

FIGURE-2

HYDROGRAPH DECOMPOSITION

measured hydrograph. These components include baseflow, GWI, and
total I/I (consisting of stormwater inflow (SI) and rainfall-respon-
sive infiltration (RRI)).

Rainfall Analysis

The rainfall analysis section of the hydrograph decomposition program
consists of a series of programs which allow the user to conduct the
following:

    o an annual and partial series analysis,
    o a frequency analysis of the consecutive dry hours, and
    o a frequency analysis of several rainfall parameters, such as
       peak intensity, total rainfall volume and total rainfall
       length.

The Series Analysis screen is used to display the current duration
data stored for the rain gage being analyzed and to allow the user to
submit a report program, if desired. The data displayed to the user
are maximum rainfall volumes assigned to each of fifteen duration
lengths (1hr, 2hr, 3hr,.... 10hr, 12hr, 14hr, 18hr, 20hr, and 24hr).
These rainfall volumes are stored on the database.

Another interactive screen (Rain Event Analysis) is used to perform
two procedures -- (1) to display the rainfall parameters for the total
period of record, and (2) to allow the user to redefine the parameters
for their specific analysis. The rainfall parameters used to define
and shape the rainfall events are:

    o Dry-Hours Between Rainfall Events,
    o Dry-Hours Preceding Rainfall Events,
    o Rainfall Event Duration (hours),
    o Peak Intensity (inches/hour), and
    o Total Volume (inches).

Initially the program accesses the database and reads all the records
stored under the particular gage in question. The screen is then
displayed showing the total number of rainfall events in the period of
record and the minimum and maximum values found during the search.
The user can examine these limits and enter new limits for any or all
parameters.

By redefining the parameter limits the user can combine single rainfall events into an aggregate event, meeting the user's specific
requirements. For example, if the user redefines the minimum number
of dry hours between rainfall events from 1 to 10, then all events
with 2, 3 or 4 ... 10 hours between them would be combined.

This re-definition procedure can be repeated as long as the user
wishes. The purpose of redefining the limits is to segregate rainfall
events into classes such as:

    o high intensity/short duration,
    o low intensity/long duration,
    o high intensity/long duration, and

o low intensity/short duration.

Once completed, the user can submit a program to generate the frequency report specific to the user-defined events.

Baseflow Analysis

The four screens in the Baseflow Analysis permit the user to examine
unique days of measured flow data to determine the average baseflow
conditions for a meter. The first interactive screen (Baseflow Meter)
provides the avenue into the series of programs which develop base
wastewater flows for each subbasin within a metered area. Keying on a
meter number supplied by the user, this program retrieves the meter
information from the database for display. This meter information
consists of the following:

o Basin and mini-basin numbers,
o Basin name,
o Meter identification,
o Data available for meter,
o Metered area,
o Parallel meter numbers,
o Upstream meter number,
o Base wastewater flow (mgd),
o Groundwater infiltration (gpd),
o Number of contributing subbasins, and
o The date the baseflows were last analyzed.

The next interactive screen (Baseflow Definition) allows the user to
select periods of minimum flows (i.e., base wastewater) from the period of record. The user enters the start and end dates for the period
of expected baseflow. The start day of the week is also required.

After the user enters the three required input parameters (start date,
end date, day of the week), the program reads the database to retrieve
the flow data for the period of data selected. The average daily flow
(ADF) is retrieved and displayed to the user. The user is then required to select the start day of flow data and the end day of flow
data as a further refinement of the baseflow period.

Several other calculations are made to help the user select the days
of flow data to be included in the baseflow analysis. The program
calculates the percent return and estimated GWI for each day of flow
data selected, and displays these calculated parameters on the screen.
The percent return is calculated by dividing the average daily water
consumption recorded for the metered area by the average daily sewage
flow measured.

The estimated GWI is calculated if the percent return is calculated to
be greater than 100 percent. By reviewing the percent return in conjunction with the GWI the user can select only the days within the
displayed baseflow period which have no GWI or a very low percent
return.

After the days are selected from the list of displayed flow days
another interactive screen (Baseflow Analysis) is called to display
the total number of baseflow periods selected. The program presents
the user with a summary listing of the baseflow periods selected
during this analysis. The user can add more baseflow periods, delete
selected baseflow periods, or modify a baseflow period. For each
baseflow period selected the user is presented with the following:

o   the Start Date,
o   the End Date,
o   the estimated groundwater infiltration (GWI) for both weekdays
    and weekends,
o   the calculated percent return for weekdays and weekends, and
o   the average base wastewater flow for weekdays and weekends.

As more and more baseflow periods are added to the list, the average
of the average baseflow, the minimum average baseflow, and the maximum
average baseflow retrieved and presented, are listed on the screen.
Also the minimum GWI and maximum GWI found in the analysis are presented.

The next interactive screen (Baseflow Summary) is called when all the
desired baseflow periods have been selected, reviewed and refined.
The user is presented with the newly calculated average hourly hydrograph and the old average hourly hydrograph retrieved from the database. If the results are acceptable, the user can store the new
average hourly hydrograph values, the minimum GWI, the maximum GWI, or
the average daily flow in the database.

I/I Analysis

The I/I Analysis section includes four programs which allow the user
to examine wet weather flow periods; to develop a relationship between
the rainfall volume and the measured flow volume; and to refine the
I/I parameters for use in generating synthetic wastewater inflows.
The analysis is conducted for a specific meter and assigned rain gage
and results are stored in the database for the meter and all subbasins
draining to the meter.

The first interactive screen (I/I Meter) is used to select the meter
where the I/I analysis is to be completed. After the meter information is displayed, the user is sent to the I/I Definition screen.
This screen is used to select periods (in hours) of expected I/I. The
user enters the start date, the end date, the day of the week and a
level of GWI. After the user enters the four input parameters, the
program reads the database to retrieve the measured flow and rain data
for the days selected. The following parameters are displayed for
every hour of the I/I flow period selected:

o   the observed total wastewater flow,
o   the total rainfall, and
o   the calculated I/I volume.

The I/I volume is calculated by subtracting the baseflow hydrograph and the GWI constant flow from the total measured wastewater flow. The relationship between baseflow, GWI, and I/I was shown earlier in Figure 2.

After examining the calculated I/I volume using this screen, the user selects the hours to be transferred to the next screen for summarization and for calculation of the R, T and K parameters. Figure 3 presents a graphic definition of the I/I parameters R, T and K. R is the ratio of measured rainfall volume over the measured I/I volume. T and K define the shape of the response hydrograph.

The next screen (I/I Analysis) presents the following:

- o the start date and hour,
- o the end date and hour,
- o the total rainfall for that time period,
- o the estimated groundwater infiltration (GWI),
- o the R value for each time period,
- o the maximum (T+TK) for each time period,
- o the calculated I/I flow,
- o the observed average flow, and
- o the total residual sum of the squares between calculated and observed values.

As more and more I/I flow periods are added to the list, the average of the I/I hydrograph parameters--R, T and K--for three unit hydrograph curves defining the total hydrograph, are listed on the screen.

The next screen (I/I Hydrograph) provides an interactive iterative process by which the user can refine the three I/I parameters used in calculating the hourly I/I hydrograph. The program presents a first cut of the parameters and the relationship between the measured flow data and the calculated flows. The user can modify the prediction parameters to refine the calculated I/I flows so the best match between observed and calculated can be made.

For each hour of metered flow data, the average baseflow and the GWI (a constant) is subtracted from the hour of total metered flow. The resultant (I/I) flow for this hour represents the I/I response to the rainfall event under analysis. The hourly rainfall data are also presented for the current I/I flow event.

For each I/I flow event being analyzed, the R parameter is calculated. This ratio is calculated from the equation:

$$R = V/PA$$

where;

R = Ratio of I/I volume to rainfall volume,
V = Volume of I/I in event response, cubic inches,
P = Volume of rainfall in event, inch, and
A = Drainage area, square inches.

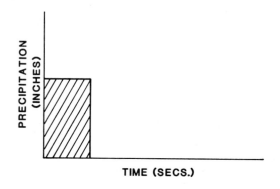

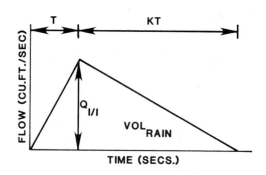

FIGURE 3
HOURLY SYNTHETIC I/I HYDROGRAPH SCHEMATIC

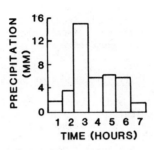

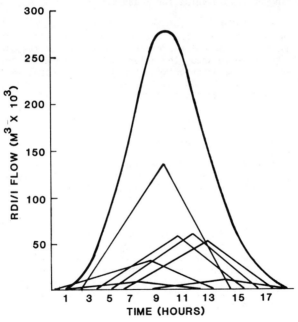

FIGURE-4
TOTAL FLOW INFLOW HYDROGRAPH

V is calculated from the area under the flow hydrograph.

Using the above equation the volume of I/I is calculated for each hour of recorded rainfall. The hourly I/I volume is then inserted into the following equation to calculate the peak I/I flow for that hour:

$$Q = 2V/(T + TK)$$

where;

Q = Peak I/I flow for hour, cubic inches/sec,
V = Volume of I/I for hour, cubic inches,
T = Time of concentration, sec, and
K = Recession constant.

Values of T and K are initially retrieved from the database.

Using the initial values of T and K found in the database, the synthetic I/I hydrograph is calculated every hour for the entire event. Each hourly synthetic I/I hydrograph value is offset by one hour and summed for each hour of the event's duration. Figure 4 presents a schematic of the I/I hydrograph built from each hour's calculated hydrograph using a defined value for T and K.

The total synthetic hydrograph for the I/I flow event under analysis is displayed along with the actual metered flow. The total residual sum of the squares is also calculated and presented. If the user decides that the match is good, the values of R, T and K for this event are saved. If the match between synthetic and actual is not good, the user will be prompted again to enter new values for R, T and K, to recalculate the synthetic hydrograph, and to compare the new values to the actual values. This procedure is repeated until a good match between actual and predicted hydrographs is achieved.

After all the I/I flow events have been analyzed the next process is to average the final R, T and K values for all events. These average values will be stored in the database along with the hourly flow response to each hour of input rainfall. The SI and RRI responses will have their own unique sets of T and K.

Summary

With the data stored in the database consisting of average baseflow, GWI and I/I parameters, the user can proceed to more detailed analysis of their sewer system. Design storms, predicted developments and "trouble-shooting" within existing system networks are only a few of the possible applications. Without this data, stored on an inter-active database at a subbasin level, detailed analysis would be difficult, if not impossible.

The "SRI" Technique For
Flood Frequency Analysis

Brent A. McCarthy, Member, ASCE[1]
Guillermo J. Vicens, Ph.D, Assoc. M. ASCE[2]
Roy R. Evans, Member, ASCE[3]

ABSTRACT

This paper presents a technique for flood flow frequency analysis
called the Storm Response Index (SRI), and a case study using the
technique. The SRI method is based on the development of a long term
synthetic rainfall record and detailed simulation of selected events
from this record with a rainfall-runoff model. It is useful when basin
response has been affected by urbanization, when runoff records are not
available, and when potential benefits from an accurate flood frequency
determination are high. The case study presents results from a study of
the highly urbanized Mystic River Basin near Boston, Massachusetts,
where the SRI method was applied.

INTRODUCTION

Water resources engineers are often faced with the task of
determining flood-frequency relationships. Of particular concern is
determining the characteristics of rare events. Sometimes, the solution
is straight forward. The engineer performs a statistical analysis on
streamflow records from a nearby stream gauge with a long-term record
which is unaffected by physical changes to the basin. More often, the
problem is more complex. Many times, there are no stream gauges located
in or near the area of interest. Assuming gauges exist, the record may
be too short to accurately predict rare events. Finally, where there is
a long-term record, the basin may have undergone physical changes which
affect how accurately the historical record reflects current or future
basin conditions. Another common problem in engineering planning and
design is the assessment of the impact of a proposed project on flood-
frequency relationships. For the solution of this problem, an
intricate knowledge of the rainfall-runoff process is necessary to be
able to predict what the frequency relationship will be after the
proposed project is on line.

The "Storm Response Index" (SRI) method was developed to solve these
common engineering problems. It is well suited to determine flood flow

[1]Water Resources Engineer, Camp Dresser & McKee, Inc., One Center Plaza,
Boston, Massachusetts, 02108

[2]Vice President, Camp Dresser & McKee, Inc., One Center Plaza, Boston,
Massachusetts, 02108

[3]Water Resources Engineer, Camp Dresser & McKee, Inc., 2300 15th Street,
Denver, Colorado, 80202

or stage-frequency relationships. Since rainfall-runoff modeling is an integral component of the method, it is also well suited for determining changes to the flood-frequency relationship attributable to proposed projects. It is particularly useful in cases where urbanization has significantly affected basin response and the potential benefits from an accurate flood frequency determination are high.

The SRI method is based on the development of a long-term synthetic rainfall record and the detailed simulation of selected events from this record with a rainfall-runoff model. The SRI method has the following inherent advantages:

o   The ability to analyze flood-frequency relationships at locations with limited streamflow records. Generally, rainfall records are more extensive, both in number of gauge locations and length of record, then are streamflow records.

o   Greater confidence in flood-frequency results. Barring climatic change, rainfall records remain statistically unchanged over time; they are not subject to changes due to urbanization or regulation that often affect streamflow records.

o   The ability to develop flood-frequency information for a wide variety of proposed scenarios thereby aiding in the selection of "optimal" projects.

THEORETICAL BACKGROUND OF THE SRI METHOD

The SRI method is based on the concept of derived distributions. If a process of a random, unpredictable nature excites a deterministic system, the resulting output has a probabilistic distribution dependent on the input process properties and on the deterministic transfer function. In a hydrologic context, rainfall (the input) occurs randomly in time and space. If a given rainfall event produces a known runoff event, then information on the variability of runoff may be derived. In determining runoff, the deterministic transfer function (the rainfall-runoff process) is itself complicated, but relative to the other uncertainties can be considered known.

In a simple but formal statement, this approach can be stated as follows. If the ultimate goal is the determination of the probability description of the output variable, i.e., discharge or stage, then the following steps are required:

1.   Obtain a probabilistic description of the input or rainfall process, e.g., probability density function of rainfall intensities, $f_I(i)$.

2.   Define a deterministic relation between input and output, or rainfall and discharge, $q=g(i)$.

3.   Derive the probabilistic description of the output variable (discharge) through integration over the range of input variable possibilities, i.e.,

$$F_Q(q) = P\left[Q \leqslant q\right] \tag{1}$$

$$= P\left[\text{I takes on any value i such that}\atop g(i) \leqslant \bar{q}\right] \tag{2}$$

$$= \int_{R_y} f_I(i)di \tag{3}$$

where: R_y = region where $(g)i \leqslant q$

Because of the complexity of the rainfall-runoff process, and the fact that several input variables affect the output, a direct analytical approach is difficult to obtain. Eagleson (3) has pursued this approach.

Alternatively, a Monte Carlo simulation approach can be taken to the solution of Equation (3). Such a general approach has been described by Fleming and Franz (4) using long-term rainfall and catchment simulation, and LeClerc and Schaake (7) who described event generation applied to hypothetical catchments.

The output, a probability description of the flood discharges, is determined by the method of Monte Carlo simulation. The steps involved in the Monte Carlo technique are as follows:

1. Quantitatively define the probabilistic nature of the rainfall process.

2. Generate sequences of storms exhibiting the same statistical characteristics as those observed in the historical rainfall record.

3. Use the generated storms as input to a deterministic rainfall-runoff model.

4. Statistically analyze the series of resulting outflows to develop flood-frequencies at points of interest in the basin.

This paper describes a short cut in the simulation effort by use of a screening procedure to select key events, or the "SRI method," and an application to a case study.

DETAILS OF THE SRI METHOD

The SRI method involves four specific steps:

1. Rainfall Generation,
2. Screening and SRI Generation,
3. Rainfall-Runoff modeling, and
4. Determination of discharge or flood stage frequency relationships.

The Rainfall Generation Computer Model (RANG) is used to accomplish the first two steps. A rainfall-runoff computer simulation model (such as HEC-1 or MITCAT) (Hydrologic Engineering

Center, 6, Harley et.al., 5), is used to accomplish the third step, and
the fourth step is accomplished by plotting the information on frequency
paper.

Rainfall Generation

The purpose of rainfall generation is to synthetically extend the
existing rainfall record. Then it is possible to generate infinitely
more scenarios of the rainfall and the state of the basin (i.e.,
antecedent conditions) then are available from the historical streamflow
or rainfall records. These scenarios involve the relative sequence of
both the events and the hydrologic conditions of the basin. The
extended rainfall record is generated by determining statistical
parameters for the historical rainfall record and randomly creating new
rainfall sequences that have the same statistical parameters. The
resulting rainfall record provides an extended data base suitable for
use in frequency analysis of hydrologic variables.

For the purposes of this paper, we will assume that a long-term
(e.g., 200-500 years) synthetic rainfall record has been generated, and
that it consists of discrete events which are described by variables
such as time between events, total storm depth, and total storm
duration. Although the details of the rainfall generation model have
not been formally published (Resource Analysis, Inc., 8), a similar and
more general model is discussed in Bras, et. al., (1).

SCREENING AND SRI GENERATION

The purposes of frequency analysis is to provide data on rare
events. When several hundred years of synthetic records are developed,
tens of thousands of individual storms are computed. Only a small
number of these storms are of interest when considering flood potential.
Most of the storms are not severe enough to have an impact on the flood
frequency relationship. The SRI method serves the purpose of screening
out smaller storms in order to provide a more manageable data base.
The screening is based on criteria specified by the engineer. First, a
minimum storm duration is set. All storms with shorter durations than
specified are excluded from further consideration. A minimum storm
depth is also selected. Finally, for the storms that both exceed the
minimum duration and exceed the minimum depth, the user selects a
minimum average storm intensity. By this screening method, more than
three quarters of the storm events can usually be eliminated from
further analysis.

The second step in the screening process is to perform simplified
rainfall-runoff computations to establish a "storm ranking" of the
remaining storms. This procedure is designed to rank storms by their
runoff characteristics rather than their rainfall properties. The
quantitative measure of the storm ranking is the "storm response index"
(SRI).

Thus far, no consideration has been given to the hydrologic
condition of the basin. It is at this second or screening step where
such consideration is first given. In some methods of frequency
analysis, it is necessary to assume that the T-year rainstorm falling

on a basin under otherwise average hydrologic conditions will cause the
T-year discharge. This simplifying assumption is not required when
using the SRI method.

The general steps involved in the computation of the SRI are:

1. Based on the antecedent precipitation, convert total rainfall
   depth to total runoff depth over the basin by deducting
   infiltration and other losses.

2. Develop a triangular storm hyetograph that preserves the
   exterior storm characteristics.

3. Using the unit hydrograph response of a set of linear
   reservoirs, compute an output or SRI response to the given
   storm for all locations of interest.

Infiltration losses can be estimated by SCS techniques. The SCS
assigns curve numbers (CN) to particular soils that represent their
infiltration capabilities. These curve numbers differ according to the
amount of time since the last rainfall. Using this method, a curve
number is assigned to the basin for individual storm events.

The unit hydrograph for a set of linear reservoirs and the basin
response or output can be computed analytically with ease. Therefore,
a measure of the "severity" of each of the thousands of synthetic
storms can be easily computed.

RAINFALL-RUNOFF MODELING

At this point in the analysis, an initial frequency determination of
the runoff response can be made by ranking the SRI's, computing the
plotting position, and plotting the information on frequency paper.
However, the purpose of computing the SRI is not to establish final
flood frequency information; the simplified analysis technique is not
adequate for such a definitive determination. Rather, the purpose is
to aid in the selection of storms that merit closer attention. The
basin response using detailed rainfall-runoff modeling techniques and
detailed hyetographs of the synthetic storms developed from the
rainfall model, will then form the basis for determining the flood-
frequency relationship. To obtain good definition of the frequency
relationship, several storms selected from different portions of the
frequency vs. SRI curve are selected for detailed rainfall-runoff
modeling. Rainfall-runoff models such as MITCAT or HEC-I can be used
for this step in the analysis.

DETERMINATION OF FREQUENCY-DISCHARGE RELATIONSHIPS

Based on the results from the detailed simulations of the basin, a
plot of frequency vs. discharge (or frequency vs. elevation) can be
produced at desired locations that accurately reflect conditions in the
basin. The frequency relations are determined by the following steps:

1. Rank and plot storm SRI's versus return period (Figure 1.a).

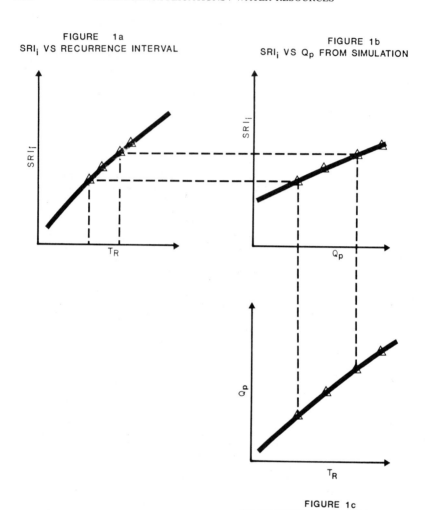

FIGURE 1a
SRI$_i$ VS RECURRENCE INTERVAL

FIGURE 1b
SRI$_i$ VS Q$_p$ FROM SIMULATION

FIGURE 1c
QP VS RECURRENCE INTERVAL

FIGURE 1
FREQUENCY ANALYSIS PROCEDURE
(all plots are on log scales)

2. Select 5 to 20 events which cover the range of interest in both return period and storm characteristics.

3. Perform detailed simulations of the selected storms.

4. Plot simulation results (Q_i or H_i) versus SRI_i for all storms, i (Figure 1.b).

5. Perform graphical transformations to determine a discharge (or elevation) for return period of interest (Figure 1.c).

CASE STUDY: MYSTIC RIVER BASIN, BOSTON, MA

As an example of the application of this procedure the analysis performed for the Mystic River Basin is discussed here (CDM, 2). The Mystic River Basin is a highly urbanized basin located in Boston's northern suburbs. The basin has a total drainage area of 61.9 square miles and consists of land use ranging from older very dense urban development in the southern portion to more recent and moderate urban and suburban development in its northern fringes. There is significant storage in lakes and ponds separating the upper portions from the lower portions of the basin. The only USGS streamflow gauge (#01102500) located in the basin is on the Aberjona River, a tributary to the Mystic, which drains through the northern portion of the basin and has a drainage area of 24.2 square miles. The flood of record on the Mystic River was caused by Hurricane Diane in 1955. Since that time, several changes have taken place in the basin to affect its response during flood events. First, urbanization has accelerated, especially in the northern portions of the basin. The communities located in or abutting the northern portion of the basin have grown between thirty and six hundred percent since 1950. A hydraulic structure which caused severe flow restrictions, the Cradock Locks, was removed in 1981. Finally, the Amelia Earhart Dam was built at the mouth in the early 1970's. It prevents tidal influences from being felt upstream and was built for recreation and flood control. Pumps at the Dam can discharge 4000 cubic feet per second (113 cubic meters per second) against a high tide. These and other factors have combined to make the present or future flood potential of the Mystic River highly uncertain.

The purpose of studying the Mystic River was to better establish the flood potential of the basin and recommend flood prevention measures. It was evident that conventional methods would not adequately describe this flood potential because:

o   Due to the storage in the lakes below the gauge, it was difficult to transpose results from the gauge to the lower portion of the basin, the main area of interest.

o   Even if the results could have been transposed, streamflow characteristics due to urbanization above the gauge made statistical analysis of the gauge record difficult. Depending on the assumptions regarding record length, log-Pearson analysis showed results for 100-year discharges ranging from 1470 cfs (42 cms) to 2160 cfs (61 cms).

o   The AmeliaEarhart Dam changed flow characteristics by
    preventing tidal flooding in the basin and by assuring outflow
    from the basin even during adverse tidal conditions.

o   Removal of the Cradock Locks changed the hydraulics of river
    flow.

It was especially important to establish accurate frequency data
along the Mystic River because small differences in flood elevations
could have had large differences in the cost of recommended
improvements. Estimated annual damages were computed based on the
derived elevation-frequency relationships. Small differences in
predicted frequency relationships would have caused large differences in
expected annual damages and could have significantly affected final
recommendations.

To demonstrate the procedure, an example of an elevation-frequency
determination at the confluence of the Mystic River and one of its
tributaries, Alewife Brook, will be shown. The specific steps followed
were:

o   Plots of SRI vs. Recurrence Interval for various assumed lag
    times for the set of linear reservoirs were generated. The
    graph with the best fit represented the probable actual basin
    lag and was selected (Figure 2.a).

o   Seven of the storms from various locations on the SRI vs.
    Recurrence Interval plot were chosen for closer simulation
    using more detailed rainfall-runoff models of the Mystic
    Basin. SRI vs. Water Surface Elevation was plotted
    (Figure 2.b).

o   Both the SRI vs. Recurrence Interval plot and SRI vs. Water
    Surface Elevation Plot have SRI in common. The next step was
    then to establish the Recurrence Interval vs. Water Surface
    Elevation relationship, as shown in Figure 2.c.

The impacts of each potential flood prevention measure was
determined by adjusting the detailed rainfall-runoff model of the basin
to include the measure, then re-simulating the rainfall-runoff response
of each of the seven storms. The result was a Recurrence Interval vs.
Water Surface Elevation relationship for each flood prevention measure.

SUMMARY

The SRI method was introduced as a means to develop accurate flood-
frequency relationships. The method is based on developing a long-term
synthetic rainfall record and a detailed simulation of selected events
with a rainfall-runoff model. The method which is based on the concept
of derived distributions involves four specific steps; (1) rainfall
generation, (2) Screening and SRI generation, (3) Rainfall-Runoff
Modeling, and (4) determination of the flood-frequency relationships.

A case study showing results from a study of the Mystic River Basin
in Boston, Massachusetts was presented. The SRI method was used in the

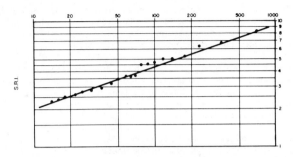

RECURRENCE INTERVAL

FIGURE 2.a
SRI VS RECURRENCE INTERVAL FOR 9-HOUR LAG TIME

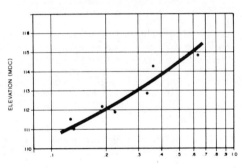

S.R.I.

FIGURE 2.b

WATER SURFACE ELEVATION VS SRI FOR 9-HOUR LAG

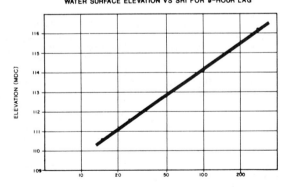

RECURRENCE INTERVAL

FIGURE 2.c

**WATER SURFACE ELEVATION VS RECURRENCE
INTERVAL-CONFLUENCE OF MYSTIC RIVER AND ALEWIFE BROOK**

Mystic River Basin because of the need to determine accurate flood-frequency relationships in a basin where frequency characteristics have changed due to urbanization, the removal of a hydraulic constr1ction, and the addition of a tidal barrier dam.

The chief advantages of the method are that it can be used at locations with limited streamflow records, at locations where urbanization or regulation have affected streamflow reocrds, and where it is necessary to assess the impact of proposed projects on the flood-frequency relationships.

The SRI method requires extensive computational effort. Thus, its use should be limited to those cases where accurate flood-frequency relationships are essential either because of the magnitude of potential flood damages or if potential flood prevention solutions are sensitive to the flood-frequency relationship.

APPENDIX 1 - REFERENCES

1. Bras, R.L., D.R. Gaboury, D.S. Grossman, and G.J. Vicens, "Analysis of Flood Risk Using a Rainfall Model with Spatial Variation," submitted to Journal of Water Resources Planning and Management, ASCE, 1984.

2. Camp Dresser & McKee Inc., "Mystic River Comprehensive Hydrology Study Final Report," Metropolitan District Commission, Auburndale, Massachusetts, September, 1981.

3. Eagleson, P.S., "Dynamics of Flood Frequency," Water Resources Research, American Geophysical Union, Vol. 8, No. 4, August, 1972, pp. 878.

4. Fleming, G., and D.D. Franz, "Flood Frequency Estimating Techniques For Small Watersheds," ASCE-HY9, September, 1971.

5. Harley, B.M., F.E. Perkins, and P.S. Eagleson, "A Modular Distributed Model of Catchment Dynamics," Report No. 133, Ralph M. Parsons Laboratory, Massachusetts Institute of Technology, December, 1970.

6. Hydrologic Engineering Center, U.S. Army Corps of Engineers, HEC-1 Flood Hydrograph Package, Users Manual, Davis, California, 1981.

7. LeClerc, G., and J.C. Schaake, "Methedology for Assessing the Potential Impact of Urban Runoff," Report No. 167, Ralph M. Parsons Laboratory, Massachusetts Institute of Technology, 1973.

8. Resource Analysis, Inc., Rainfall Analysis and Generation Model, Internal Report, 1974.

CONJUNCTIVE USE/SUSTAINED GROUNDWATER YIELD DESIGN

Richard C. Peralta, A.M. ASCE[1]

ABSTRACT

Assuring the sustained availability of groundwater from all parts of an aquifer system is analagous to assuring that the potentiometric surface does not change over the long term. Such a steady-state surface is maintained by a specific spatially distributed pattern of groundwater withdrawal. The finite difference form of the linearized Boussinesq equation for steady two-dimensional flow through porous media is used in models that design optimal regional potentiometric surfaces and the conjunctive water use/sustained yield strategies that maintain them. Presented objectives of such models include minimization of unmet water needs, minimization of the regional cost of attempting to satisfy water needs and bi-objective optimization.

INTRODUCTION

"Seventy percent of the 1.8 billion people requiring new supplies of water during the International Water Decade should be provided with supplies from groundwater" (15). Assuring the sustained availability of groundwater is important for many regions of the world. In some cases, satisfying real or desirable water demand in a sustained yield scenario necessitates the coordinated (conjunctive) use of groundwater and surface water.

Assuring a sustained yield requires insuring that, on the long-term, as much water enters each part of an aquifer as leaves it. This is analagous to achieving steady-state conditions. An infinite number of sustained yield strategies are possible for any aquifer system. Assuming that diverted surface water can also be used in many "cells" of a system, the question arises as to how much groundwater and diverted river water should be used in each. Since an infinite number of sustained yield strategies are possible for any aquifer system, an infinite number of conjunctive water use/sustained groundwater withdrawal strategies also exist. Depending on regional objectives, some strategies may be more desirable than others. The purpose of this paper is to compare the results of including several different objectives in models that develop optimal regional strategies.

[1]
Agricultural Engineering Department, University of Arkansas, Fayetteville, Arkansas, U.S.A.

THEORY AND MODEL FORMULATIONS

Governing Equations

Development of a regional steady-state set of target groundwater levels requires the use of a steady-state equation for each cell. The following has been developed for two-dimensional steady flow in a heterogeneous isotropic aquifer from both the linearized Boussinesq equation (7,14) and the Darcy equation (11):

$$q_{i,j} = - t_{i-1/2,j} s_{i-1,j} - t_{i+1/2,j} s_{i+1,j}$$

$$+ [t_{i-1/2,j} + t_{i+1/2,j} + t_{i,j-1/2} + t_{i,j+1/2}] s_{i,j}$$

$$- t_{i,j-1/2} s_{i,j-1} - t_{i,j+1/2} s_{i,j+1} \qquad (1)$$

where $q_{i,j}$ is the net volume flux rate of groundwater moving moving into or out of the aquifer in cell (i,j). It is positive when flow is out of the aquifer, negative when flow is into the aquifer, (L^3/T).

$s_{i,j}$ is the vertical distance between a horizontal datum located above the ground surface, and the potentiometric surface. In this paper it is a steady state drawdown, (L).

$t_{i-1/2,j}$ is the geometric average of the transmissivities of cells (i,j) and $(i-1,j)$, (L^2/T).

To express this equation in matrix form for a groundwater system, the row-column notation is replaced with single integer identification of each cell. Thus for a groundwater flow system of n cells:

$$(Q) = [T](S) \qquad (2)$$

where (Q) is an n x 1 column vector of net steady-state volume flux values, (L^3/T).

$[T]$ is an n x n symmetric diagonal matrix of finite difference transmissivities, (L^2/T).

(S) is a column vector of steady-state drawdowns, (L).

The following equation describes the range of acceptable flux values that are in harmony with a regional aquifer volume balance.

$$(L_q) \leq (Q) = [T](S) \leq (U_q) \qquad (3)$$

where (L_q) and (U_q) are n x 1 column vectors whose elements respectively are the lower and upper bounds on volume flux in all cells in the system, (L^3/T).

The appropriate range of potentiometric surface values is described by:

$$(L_s) \leq (S_*) \leq (U_s) \tag{4}$$

where (L_s) and (U_s) are m x 1 column vectors of the lower and upper bounds, respectively, on the optimal steady-state drawdowns in the m internal cells, (L).
(S_*) is an m x 1 vector of optimal drawdowns, (L).

Both Equations 3 and 4 are used as constraints within the three models (strategies) discussed below. Optimization within the models was accomplished using the QPTHOR subroutine (9).

Minimizing Unsatisfied Demand or Maximizing Groundwater Withdrawal (Strategy A)

It is assumed that diverted river water is available only in certain cells within the study area and that adequate diverted water is available to completely satisfy water needs in those cells. In cells in which no diverted surface water is available, only groundwater is used. Minimizing unsatisfied water needs for such cells is accomplished by maximizing groundwater usage in those cells. The linear objective function used to maximize groundwater pumping, p, for a group of mm cells (8) is similar to formulations used by other researchers for small systems (1,2,3):

$$\max z = \sum_{i=1}^{mm} p(i) \tag{5}$$

subject to Equations 3 and 4,

where z is the total volume of groundwater annually pumped from mm cells.

In this formulation, surface water is available in mc of the internal cells. Therefore, the number of cells without the alternative source, mm, equals m-mc.

Minimizing Regional Cost of Conjunctive Water Supply (Strategy B)

In this paper, we make use of a quadratic optimization model (10) that minimizes the total cost of attempting to satisfy regional demand from conjunctive water resources. The model uses the costs of groundwater and diverted surface water in cells in which diverted water is available. It uses the cost of groundwater and the opportunity cost of unsatisfied water needs in cells in which diverted water is unavailable. A simple statement of the model is:

$$\min y = \sum_{i=1}^{n} c_e(i) \, p(i) \, f(s(i)) + c_m(i) \, p(i) + c_a(i) \, p_a(i) \qquad (6)$$

subject to Equations 3 and 4,

where:

y	=	the total annual cost of the water supply and the opportunity costs of inadequate supply, ($/yr).
$c_e(i)$	=	the pumping plant energy, repair and lubrication costs associated with raising a volume of groundwater one unit distance, ($/L^4).
$f(s(i))$	=	a linear function of steady state drawdown which describes the total dynamic head at cell i, (L).
$c_m(i)$	=	the pump maintenance cost of pumping a unit volume of groundwater, ($/L^3).
$c_a(i)$	=	either the cost per unit volume of river water used in cell i to which water can be diverted, or, the opportunity cost associated with each unit volume of unmet needs in that cell, ($/L^3).
$p_a(i)$	=	either the annual volume of diverted water or the annual volume of unsatisfied demand in cell i, (L^3/yr).

Biobjective Optimization between Minimizing Cost and Minimizing Unsatisfied Water Needs (Strategy C)

The constraint method of multiobjective optimization is commonly used to develop the pareto optimum for the simultaneous consideration of multiple objectives (5). An application of this method, described by Killian and Peralta (unpublished manuscript) was used in this paper to simultaneously consider minimizing cost while minimizing unsatisfied water demand. To avoid having nonlinear constraints in the optimization formulation, the linear maximum pumping function (Equation 5) is used as the constrained objective and the quadratic least-cost objective function (Equation 6) is the primary function.

SAMPLE APPLICATION AND RESULTS

The physical and legal feasibility of utilizing a regional strategy of spatially distributed groundwater withdrawals to maintain a steady-state potentiometric surface has been demonstrated for Arkansas (10). Within the state water plan (11), it is proposed that such a strategy is implementable only in

regions with a critical groundwater problem and where adequate
divertable river water is available to satisfy existing demand
that cannot be met by groundwater. The Grand Prairie of Arkansas
(Figure 1), an important agricultural and aquacultural production
region that has relied heavily on groundwater, is potentially
such a region.

Groundwater levels in the Grand Prairie have been declining
and Peralta et al (13) project further declines. Water users and
managers are interested in the possibility of assuring the
sustained availability of groundwater in the region. Dixon and
Peralta (unpublished manuscript) have estimated that there is
adequate divertable water in nearby rivers to significantly
reduce reliance on groundwater. Since groundwater simulation
models have been validated for the Grand Prairie (4,13), and
aquifer parameters are known with reasonable confidence, the
Grand Prairie is an appropriate region for demonstration of the
techniques presented in this paper.

Assumptions and Constraints

The following assumptions are used in applying the models to
the Arkansas Grand Prairie. Since recharge is negative in sign
and there is insignificant deep percolation (recharge) to the
aquifer in internal cells in the Grand Prairie, the lower bound
on volume flux shown in Equation 3 is zero for those cells. For
constant-head cells, the lower bound is the maximum annual
recharge rate estimated using the Boussinesq equation and the
springtime hydraulic gradients of 1972–83.

For constant-head cells the upper bound on volume flux is a
large positive number––the models need the freedom to discharge
from a boundary if it will enhance regional objective attainment.
For internal cells the upper bound on flux (pumping) is a demand
assumed from historic acreages of aquaculture, rice and irrigated
soybeans. In developing a strategy, each of the models is limited
so that total water use in each cell cannot exceed that cell's
assumed maximum demand. Demand not satisfied by a combination of
groundwater and surface water is considered "unmet demand".

Satisfactory groundwater table elevations and saturated
thicknesses are assured to result from all optimizations by
appropriately bounding the steady state drawdowns via Equation 4.
In each cell, the optimal water level is constrained such that it
never exceeds the ground surface elevation. In addition, the
optimal saturated thickness for each cell is constrained to be at
least 20 feet (6 m).

In order to develop a strategy to minimize regional cost,
the c_e, c_m and c_a values used in Equation 6 must first be estimated. Values of 0.18 \$/ac-ft-ft (0.48 \$/dam^3/m) and 1.65 \$/ac-ft
(1.34 \$/dam^3) were used for c_e and c_m respectively. Values of
c_a, shown in Figure 2, were assumed as follows.

The value of c_a for cells in which diverted river water is

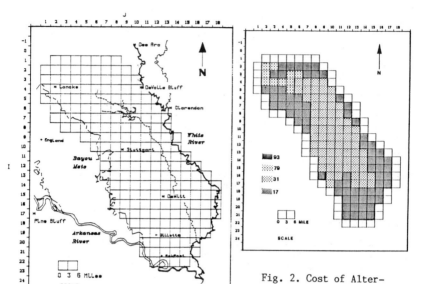

Fig. 1. The Grand Prairie Study Area

Fig. 2. Cost of Alternative Water and Opportunity Cost ($/ac-ft)

potentially available is the cost of delivering that water to fields in those cells. Reconnaissance level studies by the U. S. Army Corps of Engineers estimate costs of 14 $/ac-ft (11.3 $/dam³) for diverting Arkansas River water through the Bayou Meto (16) and 28 $/ac-ft (22.7 $/dam³) for distributing White River water through a canal system to cells within the area (personal communication Dwight Smith). For this paper we assume an additional 3 $/ac-ft (2.4 $/dam³) expense to move the water from a waterway to the field. Figure 2 shows the resulting costs of 17 $/ac-ft and 31 $/ac-ft (13.8 and 25.1 $/dam³) in those cells to which Arkansas River water and White River water may be diverted.

For cells at which no diverted surface water is available, it is possible, as a result of constraint Equations 3 and 4, that not all demand can be satisfied. If there is insufficient groundwater to satisfy the maximum demand in those cells, there is less net economic return than there would be if all demand were met. Thus an opportunity cost results from having to grow unirrigated soybeans instead of fish or an irrigated crop.

Aquaculture accounts for most of the maximum water demand in certain cells in the northwestern portion of the region. Rice predominates in other parts of the region. Figure 2 shows opportunity costs of 79 and 93 $/ac-ft (64.1 and 75.4 $/dam³) for those cells in which unsatisfied maximum demand will result in unirrigated soybean production instead of aquaculture or rice respectively.

Results of Strategy Implementation

Table I contains a summary of the three conjunctive water use/sustained groundwater yield strategies that are developed using Equations 5 and 6 and multiobjective optimization. Strategy A, using Equation 5, tries to minimize unsatisfied maximum demand in cells in which no diverted water is available. There is no unsatisfied demand in cells where surface water is available, therefore this strategy has the smallest volume of unsatisfied demand, 31,000 ac-ft (38,200 dam^3).

Strategy B differs from Strategy A in that its objective is to minimize the regional expense of attempting to satisfy maximum water demand. It requires the use of significantly more groundwater and less diverted water than Strategy A. The net economic return for the aquacultural, irrigated and unirrigated acreages appropriate for Strategy B is $6,238,000. Strategy A has $271,000 less net return and 2,000 ac-ft fewer unsatisfied demand, a 135.50 $/ac-ft (109.90 $/dam^3) trade-off.

Table 1: Annual consequences of strategy implementation

	STRATEGIES		
	A	B	C
WATER NEEDS (1000 AC-FT)	259	259	259
GROUNDWATER USE (1000 AC-FT)	63	92	86
SURFACE WATER USE (1000 AC-FT)	165	134	141
UNMET WATER NEEDS (1000 AC-FT)	31	33	32
DIFFERENCE IN NET ECONOMIC RETURN FROM THAT OF STRATEGY B # (1000 DOLLARS)	-271	NA	-41

\# Based on published crop budgets and including only specified costs.

These two strategies represent objectives that conflict over part of the range of feasible regional strategies. Choosing one of the strategies may not be as satisfactory as selecting a compromise strategy between them. Use of the constraint method of multiobjective optimization mentioned previously results in the pareto optimum shown in Figure 3. A compromise strategy lying on the pareto optimum was selected arbitrarily for purposes of this paper. Notice that the compromise strategy, Strategy C, has values lying between those of Strategies A and B for the last four rows of Table I.

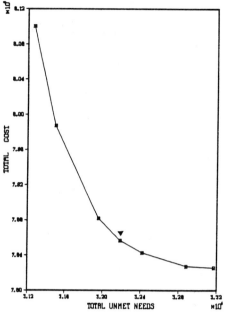

Fig. 3. Pareto Optimum of Minimizing Cost and Minimizing Unmet Needs ($/ac-ft)

SUMMARY

The formulation of finite difference optimization models for the design of alternative conjunctive water use/sustained groundwater withdrawal strategies is demonstrated. Three alternative strategies are presented for the Arkansas Grand Prairie, the aquifer of which is assumed to be bounded on all sides by constant-head cells. In the development of the strategies the sustained withdrawal of groundwater is limited to be less than the sum of the assumed sustainable recharges to the aquifer at all constant-head cells. It is assumed that historical recharge to the region will continue and that the water table elevations of the peripheral cells will be maintained. In addition, an upper limit exists for the combined volume of diverted river water and groundwater that can be used in each cell. This upper limit represents the water demand that each model attempts to satisfy and represents specific acreages of different crops in each cell.

Peralta and Killian (10) have demonstrated the gradual evolution of groundwater levels into an optimal "target" potentiometric surface once a sustained yield strategy is implemented. The steady-state potentiometric surface that will evolve from implementation of any of the strategies presented in the current paper is such that at least 20 (6 m) feet of saturated thickness is assured in each cell.

Total feasible recharge to the area is less than maximum demand, resulting in unsatisfied demand. Since the volume of unsatisfied demand is different for each strategy, the acreages supplied with water differ for each strategy also. Strategy A, which minimizes unsatisfied demand, uses more total water than Strategy B, which minimizes the cost of attempting to satisfy demand. The model developing Strategy B considers the cost of supplying water as well as the opportunity cost of missed production from not filling demand. Strategy B has the greatest annual net economic return, $6,238,000. Strategy C is a compromise between the different regional objectives of Strategies A and B.

There are an infinite number of possible sustained yield strategies for the region. Certainly, the "best" conjunctive use of groundwater and surface water depends on the specific objectives of the water users and decision makers. Datta and Peralta (unpublished manuscript) describe application of the Surrogate Worth Trade-off Method (6) to assist a group of decision makers in selecting a compromise strategy. Peralta and Killian (10) and Killian and Peralta (unpublished manuscript) present procedures for refining a compromise regional strategy to better satisfy local (cell) objectives. Thus, the capability exists to tailor-make a regional conjunctive water use/sustained groundwater yield strategy.

APPENDIX I.-REFERENCES

1. Aguado, E., Remson, I., Pikul, M. F. and Thomas, W. A., "Optimal Pumping in Aquifer Dewatering", Journal of the Hydraulics Division, ASCE, Vol. 100, No. HY7, 1974, pp. 860-877.

2. Alley, W. M., Aguado, E. and Remson, I., "Aquifer Management under Transient and Steady-State Conditions", Water Resources Bulletin, Vol. 12, No. 5, 1976, pp. 963-972.

3. Elango, K., and Rouve, G. "Aquifers: Finite-Element Linear Programming Model", Journal of the Hydraulics Division, ASCE, Vol. 106, No. HY10, 1980, pp. 1641-1658.

4. Griffis, C. L., "Modelling a Groundwater Aquifer in the Grand Prairie of Arkansas", Transactions, American Society of Agricultural Engineers, Vol. 15, No. 2., 1972, pp. 261-263.

5. Haimes, Y. Y., "Integrated System Identification and Optimization", Advances in Control Systems Theory and Applications, C. T. Leondes, Ed., Vol. 10, Academic Press, New York, 1973, pp. 435-518.

6. Haimes, Y. Y., and Hall, W. A., "Multiobjectives in Water Resources Systems Analysis: the Surrogate Worth Trade-off Method", Water Resources Research, Vol. 10., No.4, 1974, pp. 615-624.

7. Illangasekare, T., Morel-Seytoux, H. J., and Verdin, K., "A Technique of Reinitialization for Efficient Simulation of Large Aquifers Using the Discrete Kernel Approach", Water Resources Research, Vol. 20, No., 11, 1984, pp. 1733-1742.

8. Killian, P. J., "Optimization of Sustained Yield Groundwater Withdrawal", thesis presented to the University of Arkansas, at Fayetteville, in 1985, in partial fulfillment of the requirements for the degree of Master of Science in Agricultural Engineering.

9. Lieffson, T., Morel-Seytoux, H. J., and Jonch-Clausen, T., "User's Manual for QPTHOR: A FORTRAN IV Quadratic Programming Routine", HYDROWAR Program, Colorado State University, Fort Colins, Colorado, 1981.

10. Peralta, R. C. and Killian, P. J., "Optimal Regional Potentiometric Surface Design: Least-Cost Conjunctive Use/Sustained Groundwater Yield", In review for publication in Transactions, American Society of Agricultural Engineers.

11. Peralta, R. C. and Peralta, A. W., "Arkansas Groundwater Management Via Target Levels", Transactions, American Society of Agricultural Engineers, Vol. 27, No. 6, 1984a, pp. 1696-1703.

12. Peralta, R. C. and Peralta, A. W., "Using Target Levels to Develop a Sustained Yield Pumping Strategy in Arkansas, a Riparian Rights State", Arkansas State Water Plan Special Report, Arkansas Soil and Water Conservation Commission, Little Rock, Arkansas, 1984b.

13. Peralta, R. C., Yazdanian, A., Killian, P. and Shulstad, R. N., "Future Quaternary Groundwater Accessibility in the Arkansas Grand Prairie 1993", Bulletin No. 877, Agricultural Experiment Station, University of Arkansas, Fayetteville, Arkansas, 1985.

14. Pinder, G. F. and Bredehoeft, J. D., "Application of the Digital Computer for Aquifer Evaluation", Water Resources Research, Vol. 4, No. 5, 1968, pp. 1069-1093.

15. Troise, F., ed.,The Groundwater Newsletter, Water Information Center, Inc., Vol. 11, No. 7, 16 April 1982, pp. 1.

16. U. S. Army Corps of Engineers, Little Rock District, "Reconnaissance Report, Interbasin Transfer Arkansas River to Bayou Meto and Lower White Basin", Arkansas State Water Plan Special Report, Arkansas Soil and Water Conservation Commission, Little Rock, Arkansas, 1984.

REGIONAL TARGET LEVEL MODIFICATION
FOR GROUNDWATER QUALITY

Bithin Datta* and Richard C. Peralta*, A.M. ASCE

A procedure for modifying an optimal regional potentiometric surface designed solely on the basis of quantitative considerations, is
described. These modifications are based on quality considerations in
a sub-system of the regional system. The affected changes in the water
levels are shown to satisfy optimality criteria under specific conditions. An illustrative example is also provided.

Introduction

Inclusion of groundwater quality considerations in the development
of optimal regional strategies is a complex undertaking because of the
dependency of contaminant transport on hydraulic stresses and gradients. Louie et. al. (1984) solved this problem by using influence coefficients which describe the effect of regional quantitative groundwater use on regional groundwater quality. Other researchers have
demonstrated combined quantitative/qualitative optimization approaches
for small hydrologic systems. An excellent review of some of these
approaches is found in Gorelick (1983). Several researchers have proposed the use of hydraulic gradient control as a means of preventing
contaminant spread by convection (Remson and Gorelick, 1980; Peralta
and Peralta, 1984). Zero or reverse gradients can easily be imposed
as constraints in groundwater management models. There are many cases,
however, in which some contaminant concentration is acceptable in parts
of an aquifer. In such situations, the prevention of all convective
contaminant movement by rigid gradient control may be overly conservative.

The first purpose of this paper is to describe a procedure for
modifying an optimal regional potentiometric surface developed solely
with quantitative considerations, in order to satisfy groundwater
quality constraints. Although hydraulic gradient control is used
within the procedure, it is a flexible control, which permits groundwater quality to approach, without exceeding, specified limits.

An overview of the procedure is as follows:
1) An optimal regional potentiometric surface and the conjunctive
water use sustained yield strategy that will maintain that surface is
developed using the approach of Peralta and Killian (1985).

*Department of Agricultural Engineering, University of Arkansas, Fay-
etteville, AR 72701

2) A portion of the region where groundwater quality should be considered is identified as the study subsystem. The steady state hydraulic stresses that will maintain the groundwater levels within the subsystem in compliance with the optimal regional strategy are determined.

3) The steady state groundwater concentrations resulting from the strategy are determined for the selected subsystem, using a modified form of the two-dimensional solute transport model (Konikow and Bredehoeft, 1978).

4) The computed concentrations are compared with acceptable water use limits.

5) If groundwater quality is unsatisfactory, the change in concentration that will result from any small change in hydraulic head in the selected subsystem is determined. The result is a vector of cell by cell influence coefficients.

6) These influence coefficients are used to develop new hydraulic head constraints to be added to the initially used groundwater quantity management model.

7) The modified optimization model can be derived by using the constrained derivatives for a quadratic optimization model. The modified optimum decision variables include new values of sustained yield groundwater withdrawal which maintain quality criteria imposed within the critical subsystem.

8) Because the influence coefficients used in developing the water quality constraints are not exact, the steady state concentrations resulting from the revised strategy are calculated to verify acceptability. If the water quality results are satisfactory in all cells, the procedure is complete. If not, influence coefficients are calculated for the strategy developed in step 7, and steps 5 to 8 are repeated.

The second purpose of this paper is to demonstrate the application of the technique to a region in Arkansas. Although the region is one for which several optimal regional sustained yield strategies have been developed, the groundwater quality problem that is posed is hypothetical. A plausible situation for the hypothetical illustrative example is a contaminated canal running along the eastern boundary of the subsystem. The sub-system consists of a township with a potential groundwater contamination problem. The goal is to modify a given optimal steady state groundwater pumping strategy so that the contaminant concentration of the groundwater in this particular area is below a specified municipal (or any other) standard.

The main advantage of the proposed procedure for computing the influence coefficients is, that these coefficients are derived directly from the solute transport equation. This method eliminates the necessity of repeated simulations through a solute transport model.

Finite Difference Approximation Of The Two-Dimensional Solute Transport Equation

A finite difference approximation of the two-dimensional groundwater solute transport model for steady state conditions was developed. Finite difference grids, each 5 km (3 miles) square were assumed. Each individual cell was considered affected by four neighboring cells and relevant boundary conditions. Co-ordinates (node) i, j were assumed to be coincident with the center of a given cell (i,j). A detailed discussion of this equation and its finite difference approximation is given in Peralta and Datta (1985).

We have used a modified version of Konikow and Bredehoeft's (1978) simulation model to approximately simulate steady state concentrations. While it may require thousands of years to acheive a steady state, it is appropriate to look at a limited time horizon (such as 200 years in our case), so that the change in concentrations with respect to a single time step is insignificant (close to zero). In our study the time step is one year, and at the end of 200 years of simulation the yearly changes in concentrations were small. Other methods of solving for the steady state concentrations may require the solution of a set of linear equations and are more appropriate by some considerations. However, in such a case one may commit the mistake of trying to rectify a situation which can arise only after thousands of years. This may not be a desirable approach from a planning perspective.

The assumptions used in developing the influence coefficients are as follows. In our study the hydraulic conductivity is assumed homogeneous and isotropic. It was assumed that a small change in the piezometric head in a particular cell (5 km x 5 km) would not significantly change that portion of the steady state concentration contributed by dispersion. Even assuming the dispersion part of the solute transport equation to remain significantly unchanged, the terms describing transport and boundry conditions must still be re-evaluated, in order to compute the resulting steady state concentrations affected by a small (1.0% to 5%) change in the hydraulic head ($h_{i,j}$).

The steady state finite difference form of the solute transport equation can be stated in an expanded form as:

$$C_1 + K_1 C_{i,j} h_{i,j} + K_2 h_{i,j} + K_3 + K_4 - \frac{C_{i,j}^1 W_{i,j}}{\epsilon (b)_{i,j}} = 0 \qquad (1)$$

$$K_1 = -(2 K/ \epsilon \Delta x^2) \qquad (2)$$

C_1 = sum of all the terms   containing the coefficients of dispersion

$$K_2 = -(C_{i+1,j} + C_{i-1,j} + C_{i,j+1} + C_{i,j-1}) \cdot (K/2\epsilon \Delta x)^2 \qquad (3)$$

$$K_3 = (K/2\epsilon \Delta x^2) \cdot (C_{i+1,j} h_{i+1,j} + C_{i-1,j} h_{i-1,j}^+ + C_{i,j+1} h_{i,j+1}$$

$$+ C_{i,j-1} h_{i,j-1}) \qquad (4)$$

$$K_4 = \frac{K}{2\epsilon \Delta x^2} C_{i,j} (h_{i+1,j} + h_{i-1,j} + h_{i,j+1} + h_{i,j-1}) \qquad (5)$$

Following notation is used.

$(W^* = W \cdot b)$

t = time variable

W = volume flux per unit area (positive for inflow negative for outflow)

K = vertical hydraulic conductivity

C　=　concentration of the solute (ML^{-3})
ϵ　=　effective porosity (dimensionless)
C^1 =　concentration of solute in source or sink fluid (ML^{-3})
$W*$ =　volume flux per unit volume through a source or sink (negative for inflow) (T^{-1})
b　=　saturated thickness of the aquifer (L)
D　=　coefficient of dispersion (L^2T^{-1})

Therefore, for a known steady state concentration computed through any aquifer solute transport model, the assumed constant term C_1 can be computed as:

$$C_1 = \frac{C^1_{i,j} \, W_{i,j}}{\epsilon \, (b)_{i,j}} - K_1 \, C_{i,j} \, h_{i,j} - K_2 \, h_{i,j} - K_3 - K_4 \qquad (6)$$

To find the change in concentration in cell (i,j) due to a unit change in $h_{i,j}$ (= influence coefficient at cell (i,j)). Equation (6) can be differentiated with respect to $h_{i,j}$, so that both the concentrations and the volume flux $(W_{i,j})$ are considered as functions of $h_{i,j}$. The hydraulic heads at other cells are assumed to remain constant. Change in $W_{i,j}$, due to small change in $h_{i,j}$, can be computed by using the finite difference form of the groundwater flow equation. Therefore:

$$\partial C_{i,j}/\partial h_{i,j} = - (C^1_{i,j} \, W_{i,j}/\epsilon \, b_{i,j})/K_1 \cdot h^2_{i,j} + (C^1_{i,j}/\epsilon \, b_{i,j} \cdot h_{i,j}) \cdot$$

$$(\partial W_{i,j}/\partial h_{i,j})/K_1 + 1/K_1(C_1 + K_3 + K_4)/h^2_{i,j} - (\partial K_3/\partial h_{i,j})/(K_1 \, h_{i,j})$$

$$- (\partial K_2/\partial h_{i,j})/K_1 - \partial K_4/\partial h_{i,j} (^1/h_{i,j})/K_1 \qquad (7)$$

Simulation Of An Equivalent System

The procedure presented in this paper is based on the premise that only a subsystem of the entire region is potentially critical in terms of solute concentrations. Therefore, is is appropriate to identify those cells with potential for exceeding the desirable concentration limits, and group these cells into a small subsystem of the regional system. If the hydraulic stresses and boundary conditions are simulated, so that this subsystem can be treated independently for the purpose of developing the concentration influence coefficients, then the solute transport model is to be applied to only a small subsystem rather than the entire region. Note that the assumptions made in the finite difference approximations implicitly discount the influence of hydraulic stresses at far away cells, on a particular cell.

A modified version of the AQUISIM model (Verdin et. al., 1981) is used to simulate the equivalent hydraulic stresses (withdrawal and recharge) in a subsystem, that will maintain initially obtained steady state hydraulic heads at all cells of the sub-system. The initial heads were the optimal values obtained from a regional groundwater management model, which was solved without any contamination constraints. Subsequently, these equivalent stresses for the subsystem are used to compute the influence coefficients that reflect the impact of a unit change in the hydraulic head at a given cell in the subsystem on the resulting steady state concentration at that cell. These influence coefficients are used to formulate new constraints for the previously used optimiza-

tion model, in order to develop a modified optimal steady state groundwater withdrawal strategy with groundwater quality constraints.

Incorporation Of Influence Coefficients In An Optimization Model

The following additional constraints are introduced in an optimization model to incorporate quality (concentration) criteria in a regional conjunctive surface water and groundwater management strategy. These
constraints are based on concentration influence coefficients defined
as: $(\partial C_{i,j} / \partial h_{i,j})$. The new constraints may be stated as:

1. $C_{i,j} \leq C_{i,j}^{*}$ (8)

2. $\bar{C}_{i,j} + \Delta h_{i,j} \cdot \left(\dfrac{\partial C_{i,j}}{\partial h_{i,j}}\right) \leq C_{i,j}^{*}$ (9)

3. $h_{i,j} \leq \bar{h}_{i,j} + \Delta h_{i,j}^{max}$ (10)

4. $h_{i,j} \leq \bar{h}_{i,j} - \Delta h_{i,j}^{max}$ (11)

5. $h_{i,j} - \bar{h}_{i,j} = \Delta h_{i,j}$ (12)

$\bar{h}_{i,j}$ = initial head (or drawdown measured from a datum) obtained
from the solution of the optimization without any water
quality constraints.

$\bar{C}_{i,j}$ = concentration simulated from initial optimal strategy

$C_{i,j}^{*}$ = upper limit on concentration in cell i,j

$\Delta h_{i,j}^{max}$ is determined by the valid range of linear approximations involved in computing the influence coefficients.

The constrained derivatives (V_j) which represent the change in the
objective function Y for a given change in the decision variable d_j is
defined as: $V_j = (\partial Y / \partial d_j)$ (13)

It can be shown that, a quadratic programming model must calculate
V_j only at the first iteration of a particular partition between state
and decision variables. V_j is calculated using the coefficients of the
objective function and the constraints. Changes in these constrained
derivatives at successive iterations can be easily computed once the optimal allowable changes in the decision variable values have been determined. A detailed description of the constrained derivatives and their
application to constraining groundwater contaminant movement are given
in Peralta and Datta (1985).

It is possible to separate the regional groundwater management
model, including the concentration constraints for a sub-system, into
two models to be solved sequentially: i) the original groundwater withdrawal model including all physical constraints, and excluding any quality (or concentration); and ii) the following optimization model which
uses the optimal $\bar{h}_{pq}$ output from the quantative model and the resulting
simulated $\bar{C}_{pq}$; for i,j≠p,q.

Minimize: $\left| h_{pq} - \bar{h}_{pq} \right|$ subject to the constraints 8 to 12 and the additional constraint: $[h_{ij}] = \overline{h}_{ij}$ For i,j $\neq$ p,q   (14)

In general an optimal solution to this modified model based on the output from the original management model without any concentration constraints will be an optimal solution to a model including the original constraints and the concentration constraints. The exception is the unlikely case in which the drawdowns at cells i,j = p,q: and the related pumping values are all state variables at the optimality of the original model. A necessary criterion for the modified strategy to be an optimal strategy is that the original bounds on the variables (such as hydraulic heads and pumping) are not violated. If in order to satisfy the new constraints these bounds are needed to be violated, then the partitioning between the state and decision variables will have to change, and the entire optimization model with concentration constraints will need to be solved again. However, because the influence coefficients are determined external to the optimization model for specific optimal hydraulic heads, an iterative procedure to recalculate the influence coefficients, is to be initiated in such a situation. A numerical example is presented in the next section to illustrate the methodology discussed so far.

Illustrative Example

The regional groundwater management model was applied to an aquifer in the Grand Prairie Region of south east Arkansas. The major portion of the groundwater withdrawal is for agricultural usage. The objectives of the model (Peralta and Killian, 1985) is the minimization of the total cost of conjunctive surface water and groundwater use, subject to the availability of surface water, and the opportunity cost of not producing crops due to the unavailibility of water required for irrigation. The objective function of minimizing the total cost of conjunctive ground and surface water use is quadratic, because both the groundwater levels and groundwater withdrawals are decision variables and their product is used to estimate the cost of groundwater in the objective function. Therefore, the model is solved through a non-linear quadratic programming algorithm, as detailed in Peralta and Killian (1985).

The model constraints include:

1. The finite difference relationship defining steady state groundwater withdrawal or recharge in a particular cell as a function of average groundwater level in that cell and the neighboring cells.
2. Total water supply deficit in a particular cell equals the difference between the supply and demand. The deficit values are used to compute the opportunity cost of deficits in the objective function.

Other constraints include: upper and lower bound on pumping in each cell; upper bound on recharge at constant head cells; upper bound on water levels for all internal cells; and non-negativity constraint on total water supply deficit in all the internal cells.

The finite difference equation defining the pumping in cell k (co-ordinate i,j) as a function of the drawdown in that particular cell and four neighboring cells is given by Illangasekare and Morel-Seytoux (1980); and Peralta and Killian (1985).

A subsystem of 49 cells, which belong to a regional system of 204 cells, is considered critical in terms of groundwater quality criteria. The outermost layer of cells are assumed to constitute a no-flow boundary in the model used for simulating an equivalent hydraulic stresses, that maintain a given steady state piezometric head distribution. These head distributions are obtained from an initial solution of the optimization model without any water quality constraints. The next layer of cells are considered constant head cells without any constraints on the amount of recharge.

The hydraulic heads obtained as optimal values from the optimization model are input to a modified two-dimensional groundwater flow simulation model (AQUISIM; Verdin et. al., 1981), to simulate equivalent excitations in the subsystem.

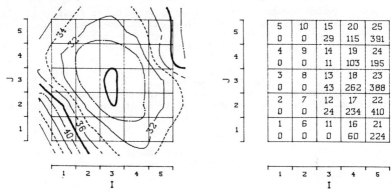

Figure 1. Contour of piezometric   Figure 2. Cell numbering system
           heads in the sub-system   and simulated concen-
                                                      trations resulting from
                                                      implementation of unmod-
                                                      ified regional strategy

The simulated distributed excitations (pumping in each cell), initial concentration of a single non-reactive contaminant in the aquifer, concentration in recharge or injection (if any), and the aquifer properties are then input to a groundwater solute transport model (a modified version of the model developed by Konikow and Bredehoeft, 1978). Figure 1 shows the cell sub-system with the piezometric heads obtained from the initial optimization model. The steady state concentrations resulting from the steady state pumping strategy are shown in Figure 2. This model is now used to simulate the steady state concentrations at each cell resulting from the given optimal drawdowns or piezometric heads. This modified model is capable of computing the influence coefficients that show the expected change in the steady state concentration in any particular cell due to a unit change in the water level at that cell. These coefficients are now introduced into the modified optimization model incorporating quality constraints. However, as discussed before, except for some special cases, it is sufficient to compute the change in the original objective function and the changes in the cell variables caused by the required change in the hydraulic head in a particular cell, which has been identified as a critical one. This procedure will guarantee an optimal solution to the original optimization model, with the second optimization model for the subsystem embedded as a secondary model, so long the partitioning between the state and decision variables of the original model are not forced to change due to the additional criteria set by the secondary model.

For the purpose of illustration it is assumed that cell 18 (i,j = 4,3) is a critical cell with a concentration of 262ppm. It is required to limit the concentration resulting from a steady state pumping strategy to 235ppm. The influence coefficient in this cell is 85.5ppm per m, with allowable range of change in drawdown (about 2.0% of the saturated thickness) equal to 0.50 m. Therefore, for the secondary model, the inputs are: $\Delta h_{4,3}^{max} = 0.5$ m; $C_{4,3}^* = 235$ppm; $\overline{C}_{4,3} = 262$ppm.

The required change in the drawdown in cell number 18 (i,j=4,3) is 0.3 m. Because the influence coefficient is positive, the hydraulic head must be decreased in this cell, in order to decrease the concentration. The initial optimal value of the cost is $9.1 million.

The required change in water level in this cell affects the pumping and recharge values in cell numbers 13, 17, 18, 19, and 23. The new value of water level in cell number 18 will be 62.5 m (62.2 + 0.3) from a datum 91.4 m above sea level. It is found that at the original optimality the decision variables at that stage of iteration consist of the pumping values at cell numbers 13, 18, and 19. All water level values and pumping or recharges in all other cells are state variables. The constrained derivatives with respect to these decision variables are given as: change in total cost due to unit change in pumping in cells 13, 18, and 19 are, - 2058.6; 596.7; and $983.7 $/10^6 m^3 respectively.

The resulting changes in pumping (affected decision variables) due to change in water level in cell 18 are:
1. Cell number 13, -0.18 million m^3/year (decrease)
2. Cell number 18,   0.48 million m^3/year (increase)
3. Cell number 19, -0.22 million m^3/year (decrease)

The total change in cost due to this revised optimal policy is (-2058.6) * -0.18 + 596.8* 0.48 + 983.7 * (-0.22) = 3800.0 $/year. Therefore, the total minimum cost for the entire system (204) cells is 9.1038 million $/year compared to 9.1 million $/year cost when no water quality criterion was included. Thus, to meet the new quality constraint in a single cell the modified optimal strategy will cost an additional $3800.0 annually. It must be noted here that the maximum change in the decision variables (Δd_p)$_s$ allowable without violating the condition that any of the affected decision variables change into state variable is also computed. The required changes in the decision variables do not violate this condition. Hence these results are optimal. If any of these limits were violated it would be necessary to resolve the original optimization model with the new constraints, using any standard quadratic programming routine.

lm=3.28 ft; 1 cubic m = 35.3 cubic ft.

Validation of Results

     To check the validity of the results, the concentrations in the
aquifer were again simulated using the solute transport model. For
this purpose, the equivalent excitations in the sub-system with modified water level in cell number 18 was again simulated using the modified AQUISIM model. It should be noted here that the new excitation
(pumping) value for cell number 18 was computed by a finite difference
equation defining the pumping in a cell as a function of the water levels in the four neighboring cells (for computing influence coefficients).

     The new simulated concentration at cell number 18 resulting from a
change in head of 0.3 m at this particular cell is 232.5ppm. Therefore,
the imposed limit of concentration equal to 235ppm is not violated, and
the solution for decreasing the water level by 0.3 m in this cell is
acceptable with some safety margin. The simulation result also shows
that the expected change (obtained from the influence coefficient) in
concentration (85.5), is fairly close to the value of 98.5, obtained
by simulation. Other cases have also been tested for validation.

Summary And Conclusions

     The methodology discussed here, is useful for: 1) simulating the
concentration of any single conservative solute contaminant at the nodes
of a finite difference grid system which is a subsystem of a larger regional system; 2) determining the influence of a change in an optimal
steady state pumping strategy on steady state concentrations; 3) modifying a steady state optimal pumping strategy with various quantity and
quality constraints, to accomodate quality considerations. An added
advantage of the procedure presented here, is that the influence coefficients are derived directly from a set of specified optimal drawdown
values. This eliminates the necessity of computing these coefficients
through subsequent simulations with changed hydraulic conditions.

     The influence coefficients, when incorporated in an optimization
model, permit the development of an optimal conjunctive surface water
and groundwater management strategy that ensures: 1) sustained (steady
state) groundwater yields from an aquifer; 2) compliance of water quality constraints at critical cells of an aquifer (which are identified
by a solute transport model); 3) the most economic conjunctive management of surface and groundwater.

     This procedure relies on the validity of the approximation involv-
ed in computing the influence coefficients, and the assumption that hydraulic heads and concentrations are linearly related through these coefficients for a small range of change in these heads. This procedure,
in its present state of development is not capable of computing the influences of simultaneous changes in the piezometric heads at all the
cells of a subsystem, on the concentration at one or more cells. We
are in the process of developing a method to overcome this limitation.
However, given the complexities involved in the simultaneous modeling
of groundwater flow and solute transport in an aquifer, to develop an
optimal regional pumping strategy, this method can be an acceptable approximation.

Appendix 1 - References

1. Gorelick, S. M., 1983. A review of distributed parameter ground-
    water management model methods. Water Resources Research, 19(2),
    305-319.

2. Illangasekare, T. and Morel-Seytoux, H. J., 1980 . A technique
    of re-initialization for efficient simulation of large aquifers
    using the discrete kernel approach. Unpublished, Hydrowar Pro-
    gram, Colorado State University, Fort Collins.

3. Konikow, L. F., and Bredehoeft, J. D. 1978. Computer Model for
    two-dimensional solute transport and dispersion in ground water,
    U.S. Geological Survey, Techniques of Water Resources Investiga-
    tions, 7.

4. Louie, W. F., Yeh, W. W. G., and Hsu, N. S., 1984. Multiobjective
    Water Resources Management Planning, Journal of Water Resources
    Planning and Management, A.S.C.E., 110(1), 39-56.

5. Peralta, R. C. and Killian, P., 1985. Optimal regional potentio-
    metric surface design, least-cost conjunctive water use/sustained
    groundwater yield. In review, for publication in the Transactions
    of the American Society of Agricultural Engineers.

6. Peralta, R. C. and Peralta, A. W., 1984. Arkansas Groundwater
    management via target level. Transactions of the American Society
    of Agricultural Engineers, vol. 27, No. 6.

7. Remson, I., and Gorelick, S. M., 1980. Management models incorpor-
    ating groundwater variables, in Operations Research in Agricultural
    and Water Resources, edited by D. Yaron, and C. S. Tapiero, North
    Holland Amsterdam.

8. Peralta, R. C., and Datta, B., 1985. Optimal modification of re-
    gional potentiometric surface design for groundwater contaminant
    containment, submitted for publication in: Transactions of the
    American Society of Agricultural Engineers.

9. Verdin, K. L., Morel-Seytoux, H. J. and Illangasekare, T., 1981.
    User's Mannual for AQUISIM, HYDROWAR program, Colorado State Uni-
    versity, Fort Collins.

EVALUATING WATER POLICY OPTIONS BY SIMULATION

Ann W. Peralta, Richard C. Peralta, A.M., and Keyvan Asghari*

ABSTRACT

Computer simulation models are used to predict the effects of three sample water policy decisions on selected conjunctive water use/sustained groundwater yield strategies for the Arkansas Grand Prairie. The three applications illustrate the facility of the target objective approach in providing an interface for legal, economic and engineering analysis. The approach is used to evaluate potential water management decisions at the judicial, legislative and water management district levels.

INTRODUCTION

Water resources management requires consideration of physical, legal and economic realities. Too often, attempts by legislators, judges and administrtors to manage the physical environment result in laws that are physically impossible (or nearly impossible) to implement. A Colorado Act illustrates this problem.

The Water Right Determination and Administration Act of 1969 defined the water policy of Colorado as the integration of "the appropriation, use and administration of underground water tributary to a stream with the use of surface water in such a way as to maximize the beneficial use of all the waters of this state." As Hubert Morel-Seytoux, et al (7) point out
"...the lawmaker may not have fully realized the meaning of the 'zeroth law' of Operations Research. It is not possible to maximize the beneficial use of surface water and to maximize the beneficial use of groundwater at the same time. It is possible, however, to maximize the beneficial use of surface water while maintaining a given level of beneficial use of groundwater, or vice versa. Or, more significantly, it is possible to maximize an overall beneficial use of groundwater and surface water. What this overall objective function should be is not precisely spelled out by the Act."

* Research Associate, Arkansas Water Resources Research Center; Assistant Professor and Graduate Research Assistant, Agricultural Engineering Department, respectively, University of Arkansas, Fayetteville, Arkansas, U.S.A.

Furthermore, if the Colorado legislature really intended to "integrate" groundwater and surface water "appropriations, use and administration", then the creation of separate institutional entities to govern groundwater, as provided for in the Act, is not a logical move (5). Tension, competition and conflict accompany interagency efforts to coordinate management (16). For this reason, achieving conjunctive use of ground and surface water is more likely when both are managed by one agency (8,9). Numerous other deficiencies of the Act (which will not be discussed here) have been enumerated from the perspectives of a political scientist (5) and of an engineer (7).

As the preceeding indicates, formulating adequate water laws and rules is not easy. Besides the uncertainties of nature, the legislator, judge, or administrator must also consider social and political realities. Unfortunately, true interdisciplinary analyses of potential effects of water laws are rarely made until after legislation is passed or court decisions are rendered. Those responsible for determining public water policy are often unaware of available technological tools or are uncertain about how such tools can be used. Perhaps because of groundwater's hidden nature, this lack of awareness is nowhere more apparent than in efforts to provide a legal framework for groundwater management. The development of laws governing groundwater use has usually preceeded an understanding of an aquifer's characteristics. As a result, perfected legal rights may bear scant resemblance to an aquifer's actual ability to sustain the legally permissible rate of pumping (12).

One major difficulty in utilizing the best existing technology to analyze proposed policy changes lies in defining an interface between legal, economic and physical systems (15). Operationalizing terms, for example, translating legal terms into constraints suitable for inclusion in a computer groundwater simulation model, requires either a working knowledge of both law and engineering or cooperation and communication between practitioners of both disciplines (4). Even choosing units of measure can be a source of misunderstanding. Gallons were selected as the units of measure for water use in a draft version of a proposed Arkansas water code. One water resources engineer spent considerable time explaining to a legislative subcommittee why gallons would not be a feasible unit in application. (Another engineer observed in 1909 that "measuring water to irrigators in gallons would be like selling coal to railroads by the ounce" <6>.) Considering the general lack of familiarity with basic engineering principles in our society, it is not surprising that highly technical methodologies require some elucidation. The water resources engineer is obligated to make his work accessible and understandable if he hopes to facilitate the systematic design of water laws (7).

This paper describes efforts to accomplish this goal for the Arkansas Grand Prairie, a major rice, soybean, and aquacultural production area. A shallow Quaternary aquifer supplies more than half of the Grand Prairie's irrigation and other water needs.

Average annual withdrawals from the aquifer have long exceeded
recharge and a number of wells have become unusable (13). In
recent years, concern over (i) the 1980 drought and (ii) dropping
water levels has provided impetus for the formation of an
irrigation district in the Grand Prairie and for efforts by the
State legislature to reformulate and codify Arkansas water law
(9). Computer simulation models are utilized to predetermine the
effects of three sample policy decision scenarios on Grand
Prairie Quaternary water users.

TARGET LEVEL AND TARGET OBJECTIVE APPROACHES

Quantitative groundwater models have traditionally been used
to predict water levels that result from given pumping rates.
They are not designed to calculate the annual spatial
distribution of pumping which will maintain groundwater at
desired, or target, elevations. A different modeling approach
has been developed to determine groundwater pumping that will
maintain preselected target levels (12,13). The utility of the
target level approach for maintaining 1982 Grand Prairie
Quaternary water levels (as the chosen target levels) and the
legal feasibility of using the approach with only minor
modifications to Arkansas water law has been demonstrated
(12,13).

A refinement of the target level approach allows the
investigator to choose a policy objective (10,11) rather than a
specified potentiometric surface, such as the 1982 water levels
previously reported. This target objective approach allows the
simultaneous determination of (i) the optimal steady state
potentiometric surface that best achieves the chosen objective
and (ii) the conjunctive use/sustained yield strategy that will
create and maintain that surface. Models with this capability are
valuable tools in the a priori analysis of water policy decisions
before implementation. This paper illustrates the ramifications
of three alternative policy decisions using the target objective
approach.

TESTED POLICIES AND RESULTS

The Court-Imposed Correlative Rights Scenario

As is true in most humid eastern states, water rights in
Arkansas are based on the old English Common Law (a,b,c,d,f,i,j)
and are delineated on a case by case basis (9). Under the common
law, the right to use surface water is contingent upon ownership
of riparian lands—lands directly adjacent to surface water—and
is an actual part and parcel of the soil (h,k). Similarly, the
right to use groundwater is incident to ownership of land
overlying a groundwater basin (f,g).

The "reasonable use" rule is the standard for both surface
and groundwater use in Arkansas (d,f). Riparian or overlying

owners share a co-equal right to make reasonable use of the water supply as long as such use does not unreasonably interfere with the rights of similarly situated users (d). No user "has priority in use of water in derogation of another's rights" (k).

An owner of land overlying groundwater in Arkansas has the legal right to use the water "to the full extent of his needs if the common supply is sufficient, and to the extent of a reasonable share thereof, if the supply is so scant that the use by one will affect the supply of other overlying users" (f). In times of scarcity, the California correlative rights doctrine governs, allowing each overlying landowner a proportionate or prorated share of the available supply (e,f). In a number of California cases, the correlative rights doctrine has been interpreted by the courts to require: (i) adjudication of a groundwater basin, (ii) determination of a safe yield, and (iii) assignment of rights to a share of the available supply based on extraction prior to adjudication (1,7).

Current pumping from the Quaternary aquifer underlying the Grand Prairie is such that the use by one does "affect the supply of other overlying users". The fact that a growing number of wells are becoming unusable due to falling water levels and inadequate saturated thicknesses is ample proof of this (14). In the absence of effective water management, it is probably only a matter of time before an injured water user initiates litigation that will result in a court-ordered prorated reduction of pumping to achieve a (safe) sustained yield. The question is, then, what across-the-board percentage reduction of current extraction is necessary in order to attain a sustained yield from the aquifer?

Utilizing the target objective approach, as described by Peralta, et al (11), the consequences of a strict application of the correlative rights doctrine can be predicted. Under a court ordered proportionate reduction, only 14% of 1982 pumping would be allowed in each cell. This 86% reduction in Quaternary groundwater use would result in a short term net economic reduction of over $8,000,000 per year for rice, irrigated soybeans and aquaculture. Being able to predict the result of delaying groundwater management decisions (and by default turning the courts into water management agencies) makes the need for active management measures obvious. It has been demonstrated that, over the long term, Quaternary groundwater can supply less than half of the demands currently being placed on the aquifer (11). This inability makes the need for conjunctive use of ground and surface water evident.

Two Least-Cost Conjunctive Use/Sustained Yield Policy Scenarios

Two versions of a water code have been introduced in the 1985 Arkansas legislative session. One measure, House Bill 85 and Senate Bill 131, is a slight modification of the comprehensive water code proposed to (and rejected by) the 1983 legislature. The second, Senate Bill 33 and House Bill 126, is a slightly more modified version of the 1983 proposal. There are a number of differences between the two measures currently under consideration , but one common feature is the definition of legal water use as "reasonable beneficial use". Reasonable beneficial use is defined as "the use of water in such quantity as is necessary for economic and efficient utilization for a purpose and in a manner which is both reasonable and consistent with the public interest."

Operationalizing this definition for inclusion in a water resources simulation model requires agreement on certain assumptions. First, as discussed above, the reasonable use rule allows only those uses which are not "in derogation of another's rights" (k). Neither groundwater (f) nor surface water (d) users may unreasonably interfere with the rights of others. As a logical extension of this interpretation, uses which result in saturated thicknesses so thin that wells become unusable, may well be ruled "unreasonable". For an agricultural economy dependent on Quaternary groundwater, the economic results of exhausting the aquifer's usefulness would be catastrophic. Finally, mining which leads to excessive declines in the groundwater level may permanently damage the aquifer through compaction, lessening its future utility. Therefore, implementing a pumping strategy which guarantees a sustained yield "is both reasonable and consistent with the public interest."

Since Quaternary groundwater alone can meet less than half of the long term demand, conjunctive use of ground and surface water is a necessity (11). "Economic and efficient utilization for a purpose and in a manner which is both reasonable and consistent with the public interest", then, may be translated as a "least-cost conjunctive use/sustained yield strategy" for testing policy alternatives.

For these alternatives, the target objective approach (10) is used to minimize the cost of attempting to satisfy the pre-existing water needs for aquaculture, rice, and irrigated soybeans with ground water and supplemental diverted surface water. In performing the minimization, the model considers: (i) the cost per unit volume of Quaternary groundwater (based on the total dynamic head of a representative well in the center of each three mile by three mile cell in the study area); (ii) the cost per unit volume of diverted river water (in all cells to which diversion is feasible); and (iii) the opportunity cost—reduction in net economic return—per unit volume of unsatisfied water demand (in cells to which diversion of river water is not feasible). The model assumes that divertable surface water resources are adequate to completely satisfy demand not met by Quaternary groundwater in the cells to which surface water may be diverted.

The model output is a regional strategy consisting of the specified annual volumes of Quaternary groundwater and supplemental diverted surface water to be used in each cell. In

the least-cost conjunctive use/sustained yield strategy, there
are some demands (water needs currently being supplied by mining
the Quaternary aquifer) that cannot be met over the long term by
Quaternary groundwater or diverted surface water) in the
northern part of the Grand Prairie. Each of the following
scenarios represents a policy designed to balance actual
groundwater withdrawals in each cell with those specified in the
optimal least cost strategy.

The alternate crop switch scenario.
    The alternate crop switch scenario outlines a mechanism for
reducing water demand in cells where water needs cannot be
conjunctively met over the long term. To reduce demand, acreages
are switched on a crop by crop basis from aquaculture, rice or
irrigated soybeans to nonirrigated soybeans. The question is how
to prioritize the crop switch. Aquaculture provides the highest
net economic return per acre, but the lowest net economic return
per acre-foot of water. Irrigated soybeans provide the lowest
net economic return on a per acre basis, but the highest net
economic return per acre-foot of water used. If crops are
switched on the basis of the least loss in return per acre,
irrigated soybean acreages are switched first to dryland
soybeans, followed by rice, and aquacultural acreages are
switched last. If, on the other hand, one wishes to minimize the
reduction in net economic return per acre-foot of unsatisfied
demand, then aquacultural acreages are switched to dryland
soybeans first, followed by rice, and finally by irrigated
soybeans. Table 1 shows a comparison of the two alternatives.

TABLE 1.—Impact of changing acreages to dryland soybeans.		
	Minimizing loss in return per acre	Minimizing loss in return per acre-foot
Change from current acres Aquaculture	-2,980	-3,338
Change from current acres Rice	-7,643	-6,806
Change from current acres Irri. Soybeans	-4,555	-3,265
Change in net economic return ($s)	-2,778,000	-2,705,000

    Most regional economic analyses are performed on a per acre
basis. That approach implicity assumes that land is the limiting
criteria. It is interesting to note in Table 1 that the
reduction in net economic return is slightly less when the crop

switch is implemented on a per acre-foot basis. This suggests
that in a sustained yield setting, water may be the limiting
criteria and rules for strategy implementation may be at least as
appropriately formulated on a per acre-foot basis.

The economic incentive/disincentive scenario.
        Under the economic incentive/disincentive scenario, rebates
and surcharges are utilized. The following example merely
illustrates the utility of the target objective approach, and is
not a policy recommendation. Assuming that economic
considerations are the driving forces behind a water user's
decision to use groundwater or surface water or to voluntarily
switch to nonirrigated soybeans, the incentive (rebate) and the
disincentive (surcharge) must be sufficient to motivate
compliance with the conjunctive use/sustained yield strategy.
Water has traditionally been unvalued or undervalued (2,7).
Disincentives have, as a reflection of the societal devaluation
of water, often been too small to have any significant effect
upon water use patterns.

        Orange County (California) Water District has successfully
balanced the charge for overusing groundwater with the cost of
importing supplemental surface water (3,9). The Orange County
Water District Act authorizes the district to (i) determine
whether an overdraft exists; and, if so, to (ii) "levy and assess
a charge or replenishment assessment". The assessment varies
according to the price of supplemental water, to insure that no
water user has an economic incentive to overpump groundwater.
The set of incentives and disincentives for the Arkansas Grand
Prairie is necessarily different from the Orange County model.
In Orange County, all needs are met through groundwater and
purchased supplemental surface water. Unfortunately, it is not
feasible to supply supplemental surface water to some cells in
the Grand Prairie, so surcharges are calculated based on
opportunity costs as well as the cost of diverted river water.

        The cost of groundwater is a function of the total dynamic
head at the center of each cell and corresponding maintenance and
energy costs. The cost of not using groundwater in a cell is
either the cost of delivering diverted river water to the field
or the opportunity cost of converting from a current crop to dryland soybeans. If the unit cost of an alternative to groundwater
is less than the cost of groundwater, then a rebate is offered,
as needed, to encourage adequate pumping to maintain regionally
desirable hydraulic gradients. In the sample simulation, rebates
are never required in cells not receiving supplemental surface
water. If the unit cost of alternatives is greater than the unit
cost of groundwater, then a surcharge is levied for any pumping
that exceeds desired annual volumes. Costs are calculated on an
acre-foot basis and generally vary from cell to cell. The
opportunity costs and surcharges are also different for each
crop, since the net economic return per unit volume of consumed
water varies from crop to crop.

It should be noted that after implementation of a sustained yield strategy, groundwater levels gradually evolve from current levels to the target objective surface. During this process, the cost of groundwater changes from year to year (as do rebates and surcharges) until the target surface is reached (10). The discussion in this paper is limited to determining rebate and surcharge rates for the first year of management, based on current data.

Rebates range up to $9.80 per acre-foot in cells where diverted surface water is more costly than groundwater. Since there is no unsatisfied demand in these cells, rebates are the same for each crop. The purpose of the rebates is to insure than water users are not penalized for pumping more expensive groundwater to help maintain the regional optimal strategy, when less expensive diverted surface water is available.

Surcharges exist for all cells that do not qualify for rebates. Again, assuming current costs, surcharges in cells with available diverted surface water range up to $17.89/acre-foot, although for most cells it is less than $10/acre-foot. For cells without access to diverted surface water, the greatest surcharges are $71.50/acre-foot for aquacultural use, $96.50/acre-foot for rice irrigation, and $122.60/acre-foot for soybean irrigation. Table 2 shows the maximum possible surcharges for 1985 water use.

Table 2.--Maximum Calculated Seasonal Surcharges

	Maximum Surcharge ($/ac-ft)	Seasonal Water Use (ac-ft/ac)	Maximum Seasonal Surcharge ($/ac)
Aquaculture	71.50	7	500.50
Rice	96.50	2	193.00
Irrigated Soybeans	122.60	0.4	49.00

The surcharges are of such magnitude that the profit of production would be eliminated, making it unlikely that producers would overpump groundwater. If dramatic increases in crop values occur after surcharge rates are fixed for the year, water users might wish to continue pumping at current rates. In such a case, some $2,234,000 in total surcharge revenues would be generated.

CONCLUSIONS

Formulating appropriate water laws and rules is not easy. Besides the vagaries of nature, water policy decision makers must also consider the social and political ramifications of their actions. Too often, judges, legislators and administrators are unaware of availble techniical tools for water management or are uncertain about how these tools can be used. Water resource engineers have the obligation not only to develop such tools, but to also make them accessible and understandable.

The paper presents applications of the target objective approach to regional water management. The approach is readily adapted to interdisciplinary analysis and provides an interface between legal, economic and engineering systems. It allows the simultaneous determination of (i) the optimal steady state potentiometric surface that best achieves the chosen regional objective and (ii) the conjunctive use/sustained yield strategy that will create and maintain that surface.

The applications represent possible policy choices made on the judicial, legislative and water management district levels. The potential for future use is not limited to research initiated within a single discipline, but to investigations in law, economics, political science and sociology as well as in engineering.

APPENDIX I. REFERENCES CITED

1. Anderson, T. L., Burt, O. R. and Fractor, D. T., "Privatizing Groundwater Basins", in Water Rights, Pacific Institute for Public Policy Research, San Francisco, Calif., 1983, pp.223–248.

2. Church, A. M., Conflicts Over Resource Ownership, D. C. Heath and Co., Lexington, Mass., 1982.

3. Dunbar, R.G., Forging New Rights in Western Waters, University of Nebraska Press, Lincoln, Nebraska, 1983, p.161

4. Flack, J. E., ed., Proceeding of the Conference on Interdisciplinary Analysis of Water Resource Systems, American Society of Civil Engineers, New York, N.Y., June, 1973.

5. Foss, P. "Institutional Arrangements for Effective Water Management in Colorado", Completion Report No. 88, Colorado Water Resources Research Institute, Fort Collins, Colo., 1978, p. 189.

6. Mead, E. Irrigation Institutions, The MacMillan Co., New York, N.Y., 1909, p. 101.

7. Morel-Seytoux, H. J., Young, R. A., Radosevich, G. E., "Systematic Design of Legal Regulations for Optimal Surface-Groundwater Usage—Phase I", Completion Report No. 53, Colorado Water Resources Research Institute, Fort Collins, Colo., 1973.

8. National Water Commission, Water Policies for the Fututre, U. S. Government Printing Office, Washington, D. C., 1973, p.235.

9. Peralta, A. "Alternative Institutional Arrangements for Water Management in Arkansas", The Winthrop Rockefeller Foundation, Inc., Little Rock, Arkansas, 1982.

10. Peralta, R. C. and Killian, P. J., "Optimal Regional Potentiometric Surface Design: Least-Cost Conjunctive Use/Sustained Groundwater Yield", In review for publication in Transactions, American Society of Agricultural Engineers.
11. Peralta, R. C., Killian, P. J., and Asghari, K., "Optimizing Sustained Groundwater Yields for Multiple Water Policy Options", In review for publication in Water Resources Bulletin, American Water Resources Association.
12. Peralta, R. C. and Peralta, A. W., "Arkansas Groundwater Management Via Target Levels", Transactions, American Society of Agricultural Engineers, Vol. 27, No. 6, 1984a, pp. 1696–1703.
13. Peralta, R. C. and Peralta, A. W., "Using Target Levels to Develop a Sustained Yield Pumping Strategy in Arkansas, a Riparian Rights State", Arkansas State Water Plan Special Report, Arkansas Soil and Water Conservation Commission, Little Rock, Arkansas, 1984b.
14. Peralta, R. C., Yazdanian, A., Killian, P. J., and Shulstad, R. N., "Future Quaternary Groundwater Accessibility in the Arkansas Grand Prairie--1993", Bulletin No. 877, Agricultural Experiment Station, University of Arkansas, Fayetteville, Arkansas, 1985.
15. Poister, T. H., Public Program Analysis--Applied Research Methods, University Park Press, Baltimore, MD, 1978, pp.59–85.
16. Wright, D. S., Understanding Intergovernmental Relations, Duxbury Press, North Scituate, Mass., 1978.

APPENDIX II. LEGAL CASES AND STATUTES CITED

a. Ark. Stat. Ann. 1-101.
b. Boone v. Wilson, 125 Ark. 364, 188 S.W. 1160 (1916).
c. Harrell v. City of Conway, 224 Ark. 100, 271 S.W. 2d 924 (1954).
d. Harris v. Brooks, 225 Ark. 436, 283 S.W. 2d 129 (1955).
e. Hudson v. Dailey, 156 Cal. 617, 105 (1909).
f. Jones v.OZ-ARK-VAL Poultry Co.,228 Ark.76,306 S.W. 2d 111 (1957).
g. Lingo v. City of Jacksonville, 258 Ark. 63, 522 S.W. 2d 403 (1975).
h. Meriwether Sand and Gravel Co. v. State, 181 Ark. 216, 26 S.W. 2d 57 (1930).
i. Scott v. Slaughter, 237 Ark. 394, 373 S.W. 2d 577 (1963).
j. Taylor v. Rudy, 99 Ark. 128, 137 S.W. 574.
k. Thomas v. LaCotts, 222 Ark. 171, 257 S.W. 2d 936 (1953).

SUBJECT INDEX

Page number refers to first page of paper.

AUTHOR INDEX

Page number refers to first page of paper.

BIBL. UNIV. LAUR. UNIV. LIB.

3 0007 00105755 2